Microsoft®

KU-007-555

LIVERPOOL JMU LIBRARY

3 1111 01385 9234

WITHDRAWN

Programming
Microsoft® ASP.NET 4

Dino Esposito

PUBLISHED BY
Microsoft Press
A Division of Microsoft Corporation
One Microsoft Way
Redmond, Washington 98052-6399

Copyright © 2011 by Dino Esposito

All rights reserved. No part of the contents of this book may be reproduced or transmitted in any form or by any means without the written permission of the publisher.

Library of Congress Control Number: 2011920853
ISBN: 978-0-7356-4338-3

Printed and bound in Canada.

Microsoft Press books are available through booksellers and distributors worldwide. For further information about international editions, contact your local Microsoft Corporation office or contact Microsoft Press International directly at fax (425) 936-7329. If you need support related to this book, e-mail Microsoft Press Book Support at *mspinput@microsoft.com*. Please tell us what you think of this book at *http://www.microsoft.com/learning/booksurvey*.

Microsoft and the trademarks listed at http://www.microsoft.com/about/legal/en/us/IntellectualProperty/Trademarks/EN-US.aspx are trademarks of the Microsoft group of companies. All other marks are property of their respective owners.

The example companies, organizations, products, domain names, e-mail addresses, logos, people, places, and events depicted herein are fictitious. No association with any real company, organization, product, domain name, e-mail address, logo, person, place, or event is intended or should be inferred.

This book expresses the author's views and opinions. The information contained in this book is provided without any express, statutory, or implied warranties. Neither the authors, Microsoft Corporation, nor its resellers, or distributors will be held liable for any damages caused or alleged to be caused either directly or indirectly by this book.

Acquisitions Editor: Devon Musgrave
Developmental Editor: Devon Musgrave
Project Editor: Roger LeBlanc
Editorial Production: Waypoint Press
Technical Reviewer: Scott Galloway
Cover: Tom Draper Design

Body Part No. X17-45994

To Silvia, with love

Contents at a Glance

Table of Contents

Part I   The ASP.NET Runtime Environment

What do you think of this book? We want to hear from you!

Microsoft is interested in hearing your feedback so we can continually improve our books and learning resources for you. To participate in a brief online survey, please visit:

www.microsoft.com/learning/booksurvey/

Part III Design of the Application

Part IV **Infrastructure of the Application**

What do you think of this book? We want to hear from you!

Microsoft is interested in hearing your feedback so we can continually improve our books and learning resources for you. To participate in a brief online survey, please visit:

www.microsoft.com/learning/booksurvey/

Acknowledgments

As is usual for a book, the cover of this book shows only the name of the author, but in no way can an author produce a book all alone. In fact, a large ensemble of people made this book happen. First, I want to thank **Devon Musgrave** for developing the idea and scheduling new books for me to author at an amazingly quick pace for the next two years!

Next comes **Roger LeBlanc**, whom I've had the pleasure to have as a copy editor on previous books of mine—including the first edition of this *Programming ASP.NET* book (Microsoft Press, 2003). This time, Roger assisted me almost every day—not just as the copy editor, but also as the development manager. I dare to say that as my English gets a little bit better every year, the amount of copy editing required does not amount to much for a diligent editor like Roger. So he decided to take on extra tasks.

In the middle of this project, I had to take a short break to have back surgery. The surgery increased the number of lengths I could swim and improved my tennis game, especially the penetration of my first serve and my top-spin backhand, but it put a temporary stop to my progress on the book. As a result, Roger and I had to work very hard to get the book completed on a very tight schedule.

Steve Sagman handled the production end of the book—things like layout, art, indexing, proofreading, prepping files for printing, as well as the overall project management. Here, too, the tight schedule required a greater effort than usual. Steve put in long days as well as weekends to keep everything on track and to ensure this edition equals or exceeds the high standards of previous editions.

Scott Galloway took the responsibility of ensuring that this book contains no huge technical mistakes or silly statements. As a technical reviewer, Scott provided me with valuable insights, especially about the rationale of some design decisions in ASP.NET. Likewise, he helped me understand the growing importance JavaScript (and unobtrusive JavaScript) has today for Web developers. Finally, Scott woke me up to the benefits of Twitter, as tweeting was often the quickest way to get advice or reply to him.

To all of you, I owe a monumental "Thank you" for being so kind, patient, and accurate. Working with you is a privilege and a pleasure, and it makes me a better author each time. And I still have a long line of books to author.

My final words are for Silvia, Francesco, and Michela, who wait for me and keep me busy. But I'm happy only when I'm busy.

—*Dino*

Introduction

In the fall of 2004, at a popular software conference I realized how all major component vendors were advertising their ASP.NET products using a new word—Ajax. Only a few weeks later, a brand new module in my popular ASP.NET master class made its debut—using Ajax to improve the user experience. At its core, Ajax is a little thing and fairly old too—as I presented the engine of it (*XmlHttpRequest*) to a C++ audience at TechEd 2000, only four weeks before the public announcement of the .NET platform.

As emphatic as it may sound, that crazy little thing called Ajax changed the way we approach Web development. Ajax triggered a chain reaction in the world of the Web. Ajax truly represents paradigm shift for Web applications. And, as the history of science proves, a paradigm shift always has a deep impact, especially in scenarios that were previously stable and consolidated. We are now really close to the day we will be able to say "the Web" without feeling the need to specify whether it contains Ajax or not. Just the Web—which has a rich client component, a made-to-measure layer of HTTP endpoints to call, and interchangeable styles.

Like it or not, the more we take the Ajax route, the more we move away from ASP.NET Web Forms. In the end, it's just like getting older. Until recently, Web Forms was a fantastic platform for Web development. The Web, however, is now going in a direction that Web Forms can't serve in the same stellar manner.

No, you didn't pick up the wrong book, and you also did not pick up the wrong technology for your project.

It's not yet time to cease ASP.NET Web Forms development. However, it's already time for you to pay a lot more attention to aspects of Web development that Web Forms specifically and deliberately shielded you from for a decade—CSS, JavaScript, and HTML markup.

In my ASP.NET master class, I have a lab in which I first show how to display a data-bound grid of records with cells that trigger an Ajax call if clicked. I do that in exactly the way one would do it—as an ASP.NET developer. Next, I challenge attendees to rewrite it without inline script and style settings. And yes—a bit perversely—I also tell anyone who knows jQuery not to use it. The result is usually a thoughtful and insightful experience, and the code I come up with gets better every time. ASP.NET Web Forms is not dead, no matter what ASP.NET MVC—the twin technology—can become. But it's showing signs of age. As a developer, you need to recognize that and revive it through robust injections of patterns, JavaScript and jQuery code, and Ajax features.

In this book, I left out some of the classic topics you found in earlier versions, such as ADO.NET and even LINQ-to-SQL. I also reduced the number of pages devoted to controls. I brought in more coverage of ASP.NET underpinnings, ASP.NET configuration, jQuery, and patterns and design principles. Frankly, not a lot has changed in ASP.NET since version 2.0.

Because of space constraints, I didn't cover some rather advanced aspects of ASP.NET customization, such as expression builders, custom providers, and page parsers. For coverage of those items, my older book *Programming Microsoft ASP.NET 2.0 Applications: Advanced Topics* (Microsoft Press, 2006) is still a valid reference in spite of the name, which targets the 2.0 platform. The new part of this book on principles of software design is a compendium of another pretty successful book of mine (actually coauthored with Andrea Saltarello)— *Microsoft .NET: Architecting Applications for the Enterprise* (Microsoft Press, 2008).

Who Should Read This Book?

This is not a book for novice developers and doesn't provide a step-by-step guide on how to design and code Web pages. So the book is not appropriate if you have only a faint idea about ASP.NET and expect the book to get you started with it quickly and effectively. Once you have grabbed hold of ASP.NET basic tasks and features and need to consolidate them, you enter the realm of this book.

You won't find screen shots here illustrating Microsoft Visual Studio wizards, nor any mention of options to select or unselect to get a certain behavior from your code. Of course, this doesn't mean that I hate Visual Studio or that I'm not recommending Visual Studio for developing ASP.NET applications. Visual Studio is a great tool to use to write ASP.NET applications but, judged from an ASP.NET perspective, it is only a tool. This book, instead, is all about the ASP.NET core technology.

I do recommend this book to developers who have knowledge of the basic steps required to build simple ASP.NET pages and easily manage the fundamentals of Web development. This book is not a collection of recipes for cooking good (or just functional) ASP.NET code. This book begins where recipes end. It explains to you the how-it-works, what-you-can-do, and why-you-should-or-should-not aspects of ASP.NET. Beginners need not apply, even though this book is a useful and persistent reference to keep on the desk.

System Requirements

You'll need the following hardware and software to build and run the code samples for this book:

- Microsoft Windows 7, Microsoft Windows Vista, Microsoft Windows XP with Service Pack 2, Microsoft Windows Server 2003 with Service Pack 1, or Microsoft Windows 2000 with Service Pack 4.

- Any version of Microsoft Visual Studio 2010.

- Internet Information Services (IIS) is not strictly required, but it is helpful for testing sample applications in a realistic runtime environment.

- Microsoft SQL Server 2005 Express (included with Visual Studio 2008) or Microsoft SQL Server 2005, as well as any newer versions.

- The Northwind database of Microsoft SQL Server 2000 is used in most examples in this book to demonstrate data-access techniques throughout the book.

- 766-MHz Pentium or compatible processor (1.5-GHz Pentium recommended).

- 256 MB RAM (512 MB or more recommended).

- Video (800 x 600 or higher resolution) monitor with at least 256 colors (1024 x 768 High Color 16-bit recommended).

- CD-ROM or DVD-ROM drive.

- Microsoft Mouse or compatible pointing device.

Code Samples

All of the code samples discussed in this book can be downloaded from the book's Companion Content page accessible via following address:

http://go.microsoft.com/fwlink/?Linkid=209772

Errata & Book Support

We've made every effort to ensure the accuracy of this book and its companion content. If you do find an error, please report it on our Microsoft Press site at oreilly.com:

1. Go to *http://microsoftpress.oreilly.com.*

2. In the Search box, enter the book's ISBN or title.

3. Select your book from the search results.

4. On the book's catalog page, under the cover image, you'll see a list of links.

5. Click View/Submit Errata.

You'll find additional information and services for your book on its catalog page. If you need additional support, please e-mail Microsoft Press Book Support at *mspinput@microsoft.com.*

Please note that product support for Microsoft software is not offered through the addresses above.

We Want to Hear from You

At Microsoft Press, your satisfaction is our top priority, and your feedback our most valuable asset. Please tell us what you think of this book at:

http://www.microsoft.com/learning/booksurvey.

The survey is short, and we read every one of your comments and ideas. Thanks in advance for your input!

Stay in Touch

Let's keep the conversation going! We're on Twitter: *http://twitter.com/MicrosoftPress.*

Part I
The ASP.NET Runtime Environment

Chapter 1
ASP.NET Web Forms Today

Inspiration is wonderful when it happens, but the writer must develop an approach for the rest of the time. The wait is simply too long.

—Leonard Bernstein

In its early years, the Web pushed an unusual programming model and a set of programming tools and languages that were unknown or unfamiliar to the majority of programmers. Anybody who tried to build even a trivial Web site in the 1990s had to come to grips with the HTML syntax and at least the simplest JavaScript commands and objects. That required developing a brand new skill set, which forced people to neglect other, perhaps more productive, activities.

The code and user interface of Web pages—sometimes referred to as the *markup mix*—had to be written manually in the past decade. And this created a sort of trench separating die-hard C/C++/Java programmers from freaky Web developers. And a growing number of developers using Microsoft Visual Basic were left sitting in the middle and, in some way, were kept from taking a decisive step in either direction—whether it was toward C++ server programming or client Web programming.

Microsoft scored a remarkable victory in the Web industry with the introduction of the ASP.NET platform back in 2001. ASP.NET opened the doors of Web development to a huge number of professionals and contributed to changing the development model of Web applications. ASP.NET wasn't alone in producing this effort. ASP.NET followed up the progress made by at least a couple of earlier technologies: classic Active Server Pages (ASP) and Java Server Pages (JSP).

So ASP.NET was a success and, more importantly, it has been adopted for nearly any new Web project that has been started in the past decade when targeting the Microsoft platform. Today, ASP.NET is unanimously considered a stable, mature, and highly productive platform for Web development.

Microsoft significantly improved and refined ASP.NET along the way. Today ASP.NET includes a number of extensibility points that weren't part of it in the beginning. It also offers a rich platform for AJAX development, and built-in controls have been adapted to better support cascading style sheet (CSS) and XHTML requirements.

For a long time, "ASP.NET" just referred to applications written using the Web Forms programming model. More specifically, we could say that ASP.NET refers to the underlying platform and runtime environment whereas "Web Forms" refers to how you create your pages and applications. For about a decade, the two terms mostly were used interchangeably.

3

A decade is a lot of time, however, especially in the software world. An alternative framework for Web development—ASP.NET MVC—is available these days, and it's growing and maturing quickly. Is ASP.NET Web Forms still an excellent option for companies developing Web applications? Is the Web Forms model the best model possible? Should we look around for an alternative approach?

While the present book is all about architecting Web applications for the ASP.NET 4 platform and using the Web Forms model, this first chapter offers an annotated overview of the Web Forms model and attempts to outline future developments of Web frameworks for the Microsoft platform.

Note In this book (and other works of mine), you might sometimes find the term "classic ASP.NET" used to refer to ASP.NET applications written according to the Web Forms programming model. The term is analogous to "classic ASP," which is often used to distinguish the Active Server Pages technology from ASP.NET Web Forms.

The Age of Reason of ASP.NET Web Forms

ASP.NET was devised in the late 1990s as a way to improve on the current best practices defined by ASP developers. Many of these practices were engineered and baked into a new framework. Even better, the framework was perfectly integrated with the emerging Rapid Application Development (RAD) model that was largely responsible for the success of Visual Basic.

At the time, RAD was coming out as a lightweight, and often more effective, alternative to object-oriented programming (OOP). With a RAD approach supported by visual designers and editors, nearly everybody could quickly and easily prototype, demonstrate, and test an application in a matter of minutes. There was no need for the extra complexity and analysis work required by more theoretical (and bothersome?) approaches like object-oriented design and programming. "You don't need object-orientation and software principles to write good and effective software on time"—that was the payoff offered by the advertising campaign promoting RAD about a decade ago.

The Original Strengths

The ASP.NET Web Forms model was originally devised to bring the power of RAD to the world of the Web. Hence, the quest for productivity was the primary driving force behind most of the features that still represent the major characteristics and pillars of ASP.NET.

There are three pillars to the Web Forms model: *page postbacks*, *view state*, and *server controls*. They work together according to the model depicted in Figure 1-1.

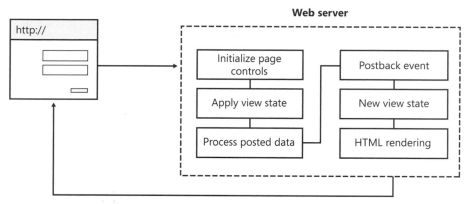

FIGURE 1-1 The Web Forms model in action.

Each HTTP request that hits the Web server and is mapped to the ASP.NET runtime goes through a number of stages centered on the processing of the postback event. The postback event is the main action that the user expects out of her request.

First, the request is processed to extract preparatory information for the successive postback action. Information includes the state of controls that altogether will produce the final HTML for the page. Following the postback, the HTML response is arranged for the browser, including the new state of controls to be used upon the next request.

All of the server-side steps are wrapped up together according to the definition of the Page Controller pattern. In light of this, each request is seen as processed by a controller entity ultimately responsible for outputting an HTML page. The page controller entity is implemented as a class that fires a few events in the developer's code, thus giving the developer a way to interact with the request and influence the final output.

To better understand the sense of the Web Forms model and the reasons for its success, look at the following code snippet:

```
void Button1_Click(Object sender, EventArgs args)
{
    Label1.Text = TextBox1.Text;
}
```

Defined in a Web Forms class, the *Button1_Click* function represents the handler of a postback event. When the user clicks the HTML element with a matching ID (in this case, Button1), a request occurs that is resolved by running the code just shown. If it weren't for the stateless nature of the Web protocols, this would be like the standard event-driven programming model that many of us used (and enjoyed) in the early Visual Basic days of the late 1990s.

In the body of the handler method, you can access in a direct manner any other page elements and set its state accordingly as if you were just touching on the user interface.

Interestingly enough, though, the preceding code runs on the Web server and needs a bit of extra work to mediate between the client HTML and the server environment. But it works, and it is easy—extraordinarily easy—to understand and apply.

Page Postbacks

An ASP.NET page is based on a single form component that contains all of the input elements the user can interact with. The form can also contain submission elements such as buttons or links.

A form submission sends the content of the current form to a server URL—by default, the same URL of the current page. The action of posting content back to the same page is known as the *postback* action. In ASP.NET, the page submits any content of its unique form to itself. In other words, the page is a constituent block of the application and contains both a visual interface and some logic to process user gestures.

The click on a submit button or a link instructs the browser to request a new instance of the same page from the Web server. In doing so, the browser also uploads any content available in the (single) page's form. On the server, the ASP.NET runtime engine processes the request and ends up executing some code. The following code shows the link between the button component and the handler code to run:

```
<asp:Button runat="server" ID="Button1" OnClick="Button1_Click" />
```

The running code is the server-side handler of the original client-side event. From within the handler, the developer can update the user interface by modifying the state of the server controls, as already shown and as reiterated here:

```
public void Button1_Click(object sender, EventArgs args)
{
    // Sets the label to display the content of the text box
    Label1.Text = "The textbox contains: " + TextBox1.Text;
}
```

At the time the handler code runs, any server controls on the page have been updated to hold exactly the state they had during the last request to the page, plus any modifications resulting from posted data. Such stateful behavior is largely expected in a desktop scenario; in ASP.NET, however, it requires the magic of page postbacks.

The View State

The view state is a dictionary that ASP.NET pages use to persist the state of their child controls across postbacks. The view state plays an essential role in the implementation of the postback model. No statefulness would be possible in ASP.NET without the view state.

Before ASP.NET, in classic, VBScript-based ASP, developers frequently used hidden fields to track critical values across two successive requests. This approach was necessary when multiple HTML forms were used in the page. Posting from one would, in fact, reset any values in the fields within the other. To make up for this behavior, the values to track were stored in a hidden field and employed to programmatically initialize fields during the rendering of the page.

The view state is just an engineered and extended version of this common trick. The view state is a unique (and encoded) hidden field that stores a dictionary of values for all controls in the (unique) form of an ASP.NET page.

By default, each page control saves its entire state—all of its property values—to the view state. In an average-sized page, the view state takes up a few dozen KBs of extra data. This data is downloaded to the client and uploaded to the server with every request for the page. However, it is never used (and should not be used) on the client. The size of the view state has been significantly reduced over the years, but today the view state is still perceived as something that has a heavy impact on bandwidth.

It is definitely possible to write pages that minimize the use of the view state for a shorter download, but the view state remains a fundamental piece of the ASP.NET Web Forms architecture. To eliminate the view state from ASP.NET, a significant redesign of the platform would be required.

ASP.NET 4 introduces new features that deliver to developers more control over the size of the view state without compromising any page functionality.

Server Controls

Server controls are central to the ASP.NET Web Forms model. The output of an ASP.NET page is defined using a mix of HTML literals and markup for ASP.NET server controls. A server control is a component with a public interface that can be configured using markup tags, child tags, and attributes. Each server control is characterized by a unique ID and is fully identified by that.

In the ASP.NET page markup, the difference between a server control and a plain HTML literal string is the presence of the *runat* attribute. Anything in the source devoid of the *runat* attribute is treated as literal HTML and is emitted to the output response stream as is. Anything flagged with the *runat* attribute is identified as a server control.

Server controls shield developers from the actual generation of HTML and JavaScript code. Programming a server control is as easy as setting properties on a reusable component. When processed, though, the server control emits HTML. In the end, programming server controls is a way of writing HTML markup without knowing much about its unique syntax and feature set.

Server controls consume view state information and implement postback events. In addition, server controls are responsible for producing markup and do that without strictly requiring strong HTML skills on your end.

Today's Perceived Weaknesses

In the beginning of ASP.NET Web Forms, requiring very limited exposure to HTML and JavaScript was definitely a plus. However, the bold advent of AJAX in the middle of the past decade modified the perspective of Web applications and, more importantly, significantly changed user expectations of them. As a result, much more interaction and responsiveness are required.

To increase the degree of responsiveness of Web applications, you can increase the amount of script code that runs within the browser only when a given page is being displayed. This simple fact raised the need for developers to gain much more control over the actual markup being sent out.

More Control over HTML

To code AJAX features, developers need to make clear and reliable assumptions about the structure of the Document Object Model (DOM) displayed within the browser. It turns out that smart black boxes, which are what ASP.NET server controls were initially conceived as, are no longer ideal tools to build Web pages.

Developers need to be sure about the layout of the HTML being output; likewise, developers need to control the ID of some internal elements being inserted into the resulting DOM. The adoption of the Web model in a large area of the industry and the public sector has resulted in the creation of applications with a potential audience of a few million people—not necessarily power users, perhaps users with disabilities, and not necessarily users equipped with the latest version of a given browser. And still developers are tasked with ensuring that all of this heterogeneous audience has the best experience and a common interface.

As you can see, the advent of AJAX brought about the complete turnaround of one of the ASP.NET pillars. Originally designed to favor independence from HTML, ASP.NET is now asked to favor a programming model that heralds total control over HTML. As you'll see in the rest of the book, although this is far from being a mission-impossible task, it requires you to pay much more attention to how you configure controls and design pages. It also requires you, on your own, to attain a lot more awareness of the capabilities of the platform.

Separation Between Processing and Rendering

ASP.NET made the Web really simple to work with and made every developer a lot more productive. To achieve this result, ASP.NET was designed to be UI focused. All you do as a page developer is author pages and the code that runs behind the page.

The page gets input; the page posts back; the page determines the output for the browser. The underlying model leads you to perceive any requests simply as a way to generate HTML through a page. The page entity dwarfs anything else; you don't really see any correspondence between a request and a subsequent server action. All you see is an incoming HTTP request and a server page object that takes care of it and returns HTML.

In this model, there's no clear separation between the phase of processing the request to grab raw data to be incorporated in the response (for example, a list of records to be displayed in a grid) and the phase of formatting the raw data into an eye-catching, nice-looking layout.

Again, you'll see in the rest of the book that achieving separation between processing and rendering is definitely possible in ASP.NET Web Forms and is not at all a mission-impossible task. However, it requires that you pay a lot more attention and have more discipline when it comes to writing pages and the code behind pages. Figure 1-2 extends the schema of Figure 1-1 and provides a more detailed view of the page-based pattern used to process requests in ASP.NET Web Forms. (I'll return in a moment to the Page Controller pattern.)

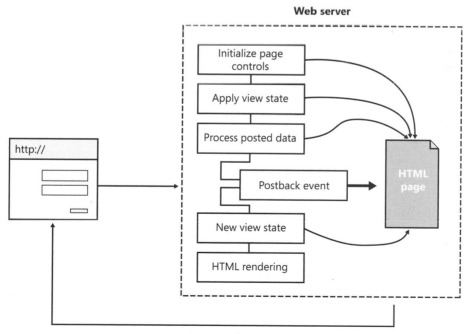

FIGURE 1-2 ASP.NET request processing and HTML rendering.

The entire processing of an HTTP request is done by progressively updating the state of the server controls the page is made of. At the end of the cycle, the current state of controls is flushed to the response output stream and carried to the browser. The entire cycle is based on the idea of building a page, not performing an action and showing its results.

For years, this aspect of Web Forms was just accepted for what it was, with no special complaints and some praises. Today, the growing complexity of the business logic of applications built on top of the ASP.NET platform raises the need for unit tests and static analysis that are harder to set up in a runtime environment strongly focused on the plain UI.

Again what was a huge winning point in the beginning is now slowly turning into a significant weakness.

Lightweight Pages

The view state is a fundamental element of the ASP.NET puzzle because it allows for the simulated statefulness of the Web Forms model. Many developers who recently embraced ASP.NET MVC—the alternate framework for ASP.NET development fully integrated in Visual Studio 2010—still find it hard to understand that each view can have shared data that must be refilled even though nothing in the request processing happened to modify it. More simply, it is the lack of view state that keeps any UI element (grids, drop-down lists, and text boxes) empty until explicitly filled on each and every request.

The view state has always been a controversial feature of ASP.NET. Starting with ASP.NET 2.0 (some five years ago), however, Microsoft introduced significant changes to the internal implementation of the view state and reduced the average size of the view state hidden field by a good 40 percent.

The view state is functional only to an application model extensively based on server controls and using server controls extensively to generate HTML. At a time when architects question the applicability of the classic ASP.NET model to their applications and look for more client-side interaction, separation of concerns (SoC), and control over the markup, the view state feature—a pillar of ASP.NET—is not that significant. Hence, it is now, more than ever, perceived as deadweight to get rid of.

Important More and more applications require pages rich with client code that limit the number of postbacks and replace many postbacks with AJAX calls. In this context, Web Forms can be adapted—maybe even to a great degree—but the approach has some architectural limitations that must be known and taken into account. These limitations are not necessarily something that would make you lean toward an alternate framework such as ASP.NET MVC, but they also are not something a good architect can blissfully ignore.

How Much Is the Framework and How Much Is It You?

Introduced a decade ago, ASP.NET Web Forms has evolved and has been improved over the years. Its flexible design allowed for a lot of changes and improvements to be made, and the framework is still effective and productive. Although the design of the ASP.NET framework was inspired by a totally different set of principles and priorities than the ones you would apply today, most of the alleged limitations of ASP.NET that I've outlined so far (heavyweight pages, limited control over markup, lack of testability) can still be largely worked out, smoothed over, and integrated to serve up an effective solution. This is to say that the advent of a new framework such as ASP.NET MVC doesn't necessarily mean that ASP.NET Web Forms (and, with it, your existing skills) are out of place. There's always a strong reason for new things (frameworks in this regard) to be developed, but understanding needs, features, and capabilities is still the only proven way of dealing with hard decisions and architecture.

ASP.NET Web Forms is designed around the Page Controller pattern. Let's find out a bit more about the pattern and what you can do to limit some of its current downsides.

The Page Controller Pattern

The ASP.NET Web Forms model resolves an incoming request by dispatching the request to an HTTP handler component. (An HTTP handler component is simply a class that implements the *IHttpHandler* interface.) According to the ASP.NET Web Forms model, the HTTP handler is expected to return HTML for the browser. (You'll find out more about HTTP handlers in Chapter 4, "HTTP Handlers, Modules, and Routing.") The way in which the HTML for the browser is prepared is strongly oriented to the creation of a Web page. The pattern behind this approach is the Page Controller pattern.

The pattern envisions the processing of a request as a task that goes through a number of steps, such as instantiating the page, initializing the page, restoring the page's state, updating the page, rendering the page, and unloading the page. Some of these steps have been rendered in Figure 1-2, and all of them will be discussed in detail in Chapter 2, "ASP.NET and IIS," and in Chapter 3.

In the implementation of the pattern, you start from a base page class and define a strategy to process the request—the page life cycle. In the implementation of the page life cycle, you come up with an interface of virtual methods and events that derived pages will have to override and handle. (See Figure 1-3.)

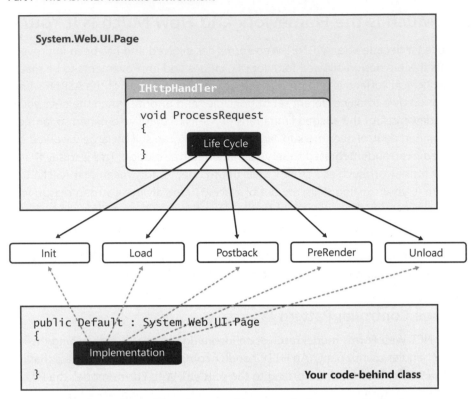

FIGURE 1-3 The internal page life cycle exposed to user code via page controller classes.

Derived page classes are known as *code-behind* classes in ASP.NET jargon. Writing an ASP.NET page ultimately means writing a code-behind class plus adding a description of the user interface you expect for it. The code-behind class is the repository of any logic you need to serve any possible requests that can be originated by the input elements in the page. A code-behind class derives from a system class—the *System.Web.UI.Page* class.

Taken individually, a code-behind class is simply the "controller" object responsible for processing a given request. In the context of an application, on the other hand, it can lead you to building a small hierarchy of classes, as shown in Figure 1-4.

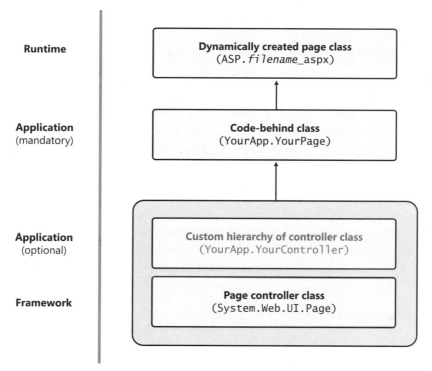

FIGURE 1-4 A sample hierarchy of classes.

Your code-behind class can inherit from the system base class or from intermediate classes with a richer behavior. Developers can extend the hierarchy shown in the figure at will. Especially in large applications, you might find it useful to create intermediate page classes to model complex views and to fulfill sophisticated navigation rules. Building a custom hierarchy of page classes means placing custom classes in between the page controller and the actual code-behind class.

The ultimate reason for having a custom hierarchy of pages is to customize the page controller, with the purpose of exposing a tailor-made life cycle to developers. An intermediate class, in fact, will incorporate portions of common application behavior and expose specific new events and overridable methods to developers.

Revisiting the Page Controller Pattern

Today the main focus of Web architectures is more oriented toward the action rather than the concrete result. This is essentially because of a paradigm shift that generalized the use of the Web tool—it's no longer just a way to get HTML pages but is a lower level producer of data with its own (variable) representation.

To serve the needs of the new Web, you probably don't need all the thick abstraction layer that purposely was added on top of the Web Forms model ten years ago with the precise goal of simplifying the production of the sole conceivable output—the HTML page.

A framework like ASP.NET MVC—even though it is built on the same runtime environment as ASP.NET Web Forms—will always adhere more closely than ASP.NET Web Forms to the new paradigm. It's a matter of structure, skeleton, and posture; it's not a matter of gesture or behavior. However, there's some room for teams of developers to revisit the Web Forms model and change its posture to achieve benefits in terms of both testability and separation of concerns.

Revisiting the Page Controller pattern today means essentially taking into account design patterns that privilege separation of concerns between involved parts of the system. This probably doesn't mean that you can rearrange the entire page life cycle—you need a new framework for that similar to ASP.NET MVC—but you can restructure some portions of the page life cycle to isolate portions of code as distinct components that are testable and writable in isolation.

For example, revisiting the Page Controller pattern means applying the Model View Presenter (MVP) pattern to decouple the implementation of the postback mechanism with the subsequent rendering of the view. We'll get back to this topic in Chapter 15, "The Model-View-Presenter Pattern."

In the end, in the second decade of the 2000s ASP.NET Web Forms is approaching an architectural dead end. On one hand, it is recommended that you do not unconsciously ignore newer frameworks (for example, ASP.NET MVC); on the other hand, however, Web Forms is still highly effective, mature, and functional and certainly doesn't prevent you from achieving great results.

Whether you're considering shifting to ASP.NET MVC or sticking to Web Forms, it is essential that you reconsider the design and architecture of your views and pages. The classic Page Controller pattern is getting obsolete and needs solutions to make it more testable and layered. An effective Web Forms application today needs separation of concerns, interface-based programming, and cohesive components. No framework will give you that free of charge, but with Web Forms you need a great deal of awareness and commitment.

The AJAX Revolution

Like it or not, the Web is changing, and this time it is changing for developers and architects. In the evolution of software, we first observe a spark of genius triggering an innovative process and the teaching of new tricks and new ways of doing things. In this case, it was the spark of AJAX and the need to build effective and rich user experiences. Next, developers start generalizing and abstracting things to make them reusable and easy to replicate repeatedly in a variety of scenarios. When this happens, we have a *paradigm shift*.

Today we are moving away from many of the ideas and pillars of Web Forms. It's not a process that has a well-known and defined completion date yet, but nobody doubts that such a day is in our near future.

The spark of AJAX was just the realization that we can place out-of-band requests, bypass the classic browser machinery, and gain total control of the request and subsequent response. Is this just a little, geeky detail? Maybe, but this little detail triggered a huge transformational process—an entire paradigm shift—whose results will be clear and definitive only in a few years. That's my guess, at least. Let's briefly consider what paradigm shifts are and what they mean (and have meant) to humans throughout history.

Moving Away from Classic ASP.NET

As drastic as it might sound, the Web revolutionized the concept of an application. Now AJAX is revolutionizing the concept of a Web application. The Web will always remain separate from the desktop, but Web applications are going to enter a new age.

What's a Paradigm Shift?

According to Wikipedia, a *paradigm shift* describes a change in most of the basic assumptions within the ruling theory of a science. The shift creates a break and clearly contrasts with the current ideas and approaches. A paradigm shift is a long process that begins naturally when enough significant limitations and anomalies have been found within the current state of the art in a discipline.

At this point, new ideas are tried—often ideas that were considered years before and then discarded. The community proceeds by trial and error, experimenting and trying to come to general conclusions. Inevitably, a paradigm shift puts the discipline into a *state of crisis*. (This is the term used by Thomas Kuhn, who coined the term *paradigm shift* and formalized these concepts.) The state of crisis manifests itself through a number of attempts to change, each presented as possibly definitive but that hardly work for everybody, at least in the original form.

The impact of a paradigm shift is particularly deep in areas that appear to be stable and mature. A great example of a paradigm shift is the changes in physics at the beginning of the twentieth century. Before the advent of Einstein's theory of relativity, physics was unanimously considered to be a largely worked-out system. The theory of relativity he formulated in 1905 changed everything in the field, but it was only about three decades later that the process of redefining the fundamentals of physics was completed. For more information, pay a visit to *http://en.wikipedia.org/wiki/Paradigm_shift*. It's definitely illuminating reading.

So now, how does this apply to ASP.NET and AJAX?

The AJAX Paradigm Shift

Even though we tend to date the advent of AJAX around the 2004, one of the core tools of AJAX—the *XmlHttpRequest* object—is much older. In the late 1990s, we already had all the technologies we are using today to set up AJAX solutions. For a number of reasons, the idea of using JavaScript, the HTML DOM, and the *XmlHttpRequest* object to update pages asynchronously was discarded for most applications, even though Outlook Web Access and a number of niche applications continued using it.

It was tried again in the early 2000s, and this time it really stuck.

Like physics in the early twentieth century, ASP.NET Web Forms was a stable and mature platform when AJAX experiments started. In the beginning, it was simply a matter of spicing up some pages with a piece of JavaScript code and downloading raw data from an HTTP endpoint. However, it is one thing to download a number or a string and refresh the small portion of the user interface that contains it, but it's quite another to download a collection of data objects to repopulate a grid. And what if you intend to post the content of a form and then update a large section of the current view?

The underlying machinery and tools remain the same, but the way in which they are organized, exposed to developers, and consumed requires a lot of thinking and perhaps a brand new application model.

In particular, the advent of AJAX raised the need for developers to embed more JavaScript code in HTML pages. The JavaScript code, however, has to deal with HTML DOM elements, each of which is commonly identified with a unique ID. In an ASP.NET Web Forms application, it's the set of server controls defined in a page that ultimately determines the structure of the HTML DOM and the ID of the constituent elements.

To support AJAX deeply and effectively, Web Forms developers have to dig out some of the internal details of the server control black boxes. In doing so, developers attack one of the pillars of the Web Forms model. The more AJAX you want, the more control you need over HTML; the more control over HTML you want, the more you are mining the foundation of ASP.NET Web Forms.

But there's more than just this.

The Data-for-Data Model

For years, the Web worked around a *Pages-for-Forms* model. It was just fine in the beginning of the Web age when pages contained little more than formatted text, hyperlinks, and maybe some images. The success of the Web has prompted users to ask for increasingly more powerful features, and it has led developers and designers to create more sophisticated services and graphics. As a result, today's pages are heavy and cumbersome. (See Figure 1-5.)

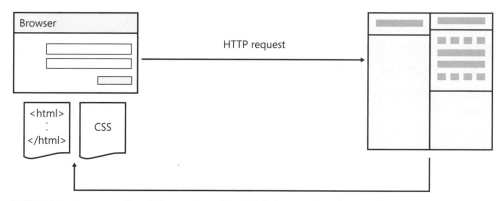

FIGURE 1-5 A page sends out the content of an HTML form and receives an HTML page.

Given the current architecture of Web applications, each user action requires a complete redraw of the page. Subsequently, heavier pages render out slowly and produce a good deal of flickering. Projected to the whole set of pages in a large, portal-like application, this mechanism is perfect for causing great frustration to the poor end user.

AJAX just broke this model up. A request might or might not post a form and request an entire page. More often, an HTTP request might just pass raw data and request raw data—an overall simplification of the interaction model. (See Figure 1-6.)

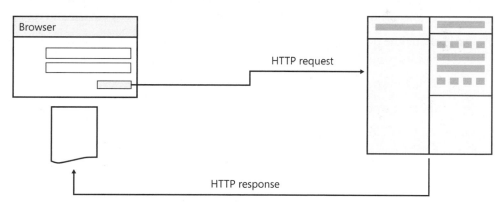

FIGURE 1-6 HTML elements fire out-of-band calls passing raw data and getting raw data, not necessarily HTML pages.

ASP.NET Web Forms was created to receive forms and return pages. It is difficult to turn it into a model that fully supports the Data-for-Data model of AJAX. Web Forms hides a lot of its machinery and offers a higher level view of the Web operation than many demand today.

This fact can't be ignored when making architectural decisions about which platform to use for a given Web project.

It's not relevant whether Web Forms was designed in the wrong or right way. It was right for the time it was designed. The advent of AJAX created different business conditions; in these conditions, Web Forms is not necessarily the ideal framework.

But is there any ideal ASP.NET framework out there?

What Web Do We Want for Developers?

A decade ago, we just wanted applications deployed through the Web. And Web Forms worked just fine to satisfy us. Later on, we wanted richer applications that were quicker and smoother to use and more responsive. And a good set of AJAX capabilities added to Web applications made us happier as end users.

What about developers?

We probably completed the step of understanding what kind of Web applications we want to serve to our users. We don't yet have an effective set of developer tools to make the creation of modern Web applications quick, easy, and productive—in one word, *effective*. So we're in search of the perfect framework. Developers need to build user interfaces to be served and consumed over the Web and within a Web browser. Such a framework must simplify a number of common tasks. Here's a list of the capabilities we expect:

- The user interface must be dynamic and adjust itself as the user interacts. This means, for example, hiding or showing panels and buttons as the user makes a choice.

- The user interface must be responsive and perform quick cross-checks on data displayed, and it must perform remote validation whenever possible and required.

- It should be possible to start a remote operation and update the current view even with a new user interface if necessary.

- It should be possible to display dialog boxes on top of the existing pages.

- It should be possible to request data for remote application-specific endpoints.

In terms of technologies, we definitely need a rich client infrastructure, a simple controller component to parse HTTP requests and dispatch commands to the back end, and we need a layered architecture to keep business tasks separate from presentation and data access.

The development team is directly responsible for the architecture and for adding as many layers as they think are necessary. The framework, on the other hand, should simplify the other aspects and provide smooth integration between client and server code and naturally and effectively process the incoming requests. We don't yet have the perfect framework. It will probably take a couple more years for this to materialize. But we see all around signs of libraries and tools being consolidated.

The family of jQuery libraries (including the jQuery UI library and various plug-ins) seems to be the catalyst for dynamic user interfaces; ASP.NET MVC seems to be the simpler framework to start with and to build new made-to-measure abstractions. Abstraction is still important because it's only via abstraction that you build productivity.

Whatever emerges as the ideal ASP.NET framework for the next decade, my guess is that it will build on jQuery and most of the principles and solutions in ASP.NET MVC. ASP.NET Web Forms today is in the middle of a transition. It is neither the future nor the past. It can be adapted and still be effective. It requires an awareness of the changes, in business and subsequently architecture, we are experiencing.

AJAX as a Built-in Feature of the Web

The biggest challenge of ASP.NET development today is unifying the programming model, which is currently split in two: ASP.NET Web Forms on one side and ASP.NET MVC on the other side. The biggest challenge of Web development in general, though, is removing the label "AJAX" from the term "Web."

Because it started such a huge paradigm shift, AJAX can't simply be considered an umbrella term to refer to a specific set of software capabilities. AJAX today is a constituent part of the Web. We would like to be able to write the next generation of Web applications using a framework in which AJAX is just part of the deal. You might be asked to configure it once, and then enjoy it free of charge and without any additional cost of writing specific code.

As a built-in feature of a Web framework, AJAX requires you to have an API to code against that just does AJAX without needing developers to think about it. ASP.NET offered a common and familiar programming model for writing Web applications, and this was one of the keys to its rapid adoption. Before ASP.NET, there were various ways of writing Web applications and different tools. You had to choose the tool beforehand and adapt to its vision of the Web. Today with AJAX, we are experiencing something similar. You have an AJAX API in ASP.NET Web Forms based on a technology known as partial rendering; you have the possibility of defining ASP.NET endpoints and exposing them as Web services; you have similar technologies in ASP.NET MVC; you have direct scripting via jQuery and a bunch of other JavaScript libraries. We don't have yet a unique (and updated) model for doing Web development with AJAX in it. AJAX changed the Web; now we want a framework for writing Web applications with AJAX built inside.

Selective Updates

Basically, there are two ways in which you can incorporate AJAX into a Web framework. I like to refer to them as *selective updates* and *direct scripting*.

You perform a selective update when you execute a server action and then return a chunk of HTML to selectively update the current view. This approach descends from the *HTML Message* AJAX pattern as summarized at *http://ajaxpatterns.org*. The trick is all in bypassing the browser when a request—form post or hyperlink—has to be submitted. You place a script interceptor at the DOM level (for example, a handler for the Form DOM object *submit* event), capture the ongoing request, cancel the operation, and replace it with your own asynchronous implementation. When a response is received, it is assumed to be HTML and integrated into the current DOM at a given location.

An ASP.NET framework that fully supports the Selective Update model will specify details for how the script interceptor has to be defined and for how the current view has to be modified. In ASP.NET Web Forms, the Selective Update model is implemented via *partial rendering*. In ASP.NET MVC, it comes through the services of the *AJAX* HTML helper.

Direct Scripting

Direct scripting is plain JavaScript code through which you connect to a remote endpoint to send and receive data. You likely rely on a rich JavaScript framework (for example, jQuery) and use the JSON format to move complex data around.

In my opinion, the Direct Scripting model is good for little things that can improve a feature of the user interface. I don't see the Direct Scripting model growing to become the reference pattern for AJAX applications. To be effective, direct scripting requires an ad hoc architecture and a new set of standards. Rich Internet Application (RIA) services and open protocols such as Open Data (oData) and Open Authorization (oAuth) are coming out, but direct scripting remains an option for a subset of sites and applications.

I wouldn't pick up direct scripting as the solution for a unified programming model that accommodates the server-side Web and the client-side Web. Why not? With direct scripting, you are indissolubly bound to JavaScript and HTML. This is certainly great for some applications, but not for all.

To achieve direct scripting capabilities, today you have to look in the direction of the jQuery library and its plug-ins. I'll cover jQuery in Chapter 21, "jQuery."

ASP.NET of the Future

ASP.NET 4 is the latest release of the ASP.NET framework that has seen the light in the same timeframe as Visual Studio 2010. As expected, ASP.NET 4 comes with a number of improvements mostly in the area of controlling the markup served by controls. You also find in ASP.NET 4 a richer caching API, routing support, further extensions of the provider model, and a few new server controls.

If you try to weigh out the new features in the framework, you probably find enough to justify a new release, but not necessarily a fundamental release in the history of the product. Why is this so?

As mentioned, ASP.NET as we've known it for a decade is really approaching an architectural dead end. There's not much else that can be added to the Web Forms model; likewise, there are a few aspects of it that sound a bit obsolete today, but changing them would require a significant redesign of the system. From here, the following question arises: What will be the ASP.NET of the future?

Will it be just a further improved version of ASP.NET MVC? Will it be Web Forms with some built-in infrastructure that makes it easier to write testable and layered code? If I look into the future of ASP.NET, I see big two challenges:

- Having AJAX on board without calling for it
- One ASP.NET platform that offers testability, simplicity, layering, control, styling, AJAX, and productivity

Nothing is in sight yet at the moment that handles both challenges. So we're left with using ASP.NET Web Forms the best we can and exploring alternatives. The entire book is devoted to examining ways to write smarter and better ASP.NET Web Forms code. For now, let's briefly explore two alternatives.

ASP.NET MVC

With version 2 released at the same time as ASP.NET 4 (and version 3 released by the time you read this book), ASP.NET MVC is a good candidate to find a place in the sun in the ASP.NET arena. As clearly stated by Microsoft, ASP.NET MVC is not the successor to Web Forms. It is rather a fully fledged, and fully qualified, alternative to Web Forms. Each framework has its own set of peculiarities. At the end of the day, it is difficult, and also kind of pointless, to try to decide objectively which one is better.

Choosing between ASP.NET Web Forms and ASP.NET MVC is essentially a matter of personal preference, skills, and of course, customer requirements. As an architect or developer, however, it is essential that you understand the structural differences between the frameworks so that you can make a thoughtful decision.

ASP.NET MVC Highlights

ASP.NET MVC is a completely new framework for building ASP.NET applications, designed from the ground up with SoC and testability in mind. With ASP.NET MVC you rediscover the good old taste of the Web—stateless behavior, full control over every single bit of HTML, and total script and CSS freedom.

Processing the request and generating the HTML for the browser are distinct steps and involve distinct components—the *controller* and the *view*. The controller gets the request and decides about the action to take. The controller grabs the raw response and communicates it to the view engine for the actual writing onto the browser's output stream.

In ASP.NET MVC, there's no dependency on ASPX physical server files. ASPX files might still be part of your project, but they now serve as plain HTML templates that the default view engine uses as a template for creating the HTML response for the browser. When you author an ASP.NET MVC application, you reason in terms of controllers and actions. Each request must be mapped to a pair made by a controller and an action. Executing the action produces data; the view engine gets raw data and a template and produces the final markup (or whatever else it is expected to produce, such as JSON or JavaScript). Figure 1-7 shows the sequence of steps that characterize a typical ASP.NET MVC request.

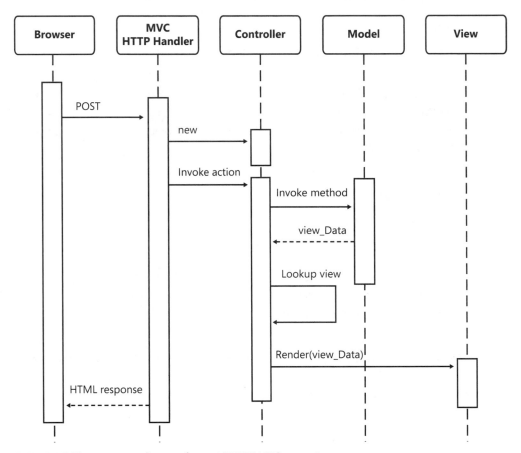

FIGURE 1-7 The sequence diagram for an ASP.NET MVC request.

A Runtime for Two

The runtime environment that supports an ASP.NET MVC application is largely the same as in ASP.NET Web Forms, but the request cycle is simpler and more direct. An essential part of the Web Forms model, the page life cycle, is now just an optional implementation detail in ASP.NET MVC. Figure 1-8 compares the run time stack for Web Forms and ASP.NET MVC.

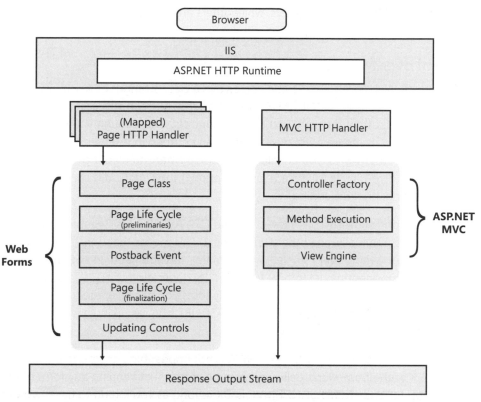

FIGURE 1-8 The run-time stack of ASP.NET MVC and Web Forms.

As you can see, the run-time stack of ASP.NET MVC is simpler and the difference is due to the lack of a page life cycle. As mentioned earlier, the page life cycle and the entire thick abstraction layer built by Web Forms saves the developer a lot of work.

ASP.NET MVC is closer to the metal, and this has its own side effects. If you need to maintain state, that is up to you. For example, you can store it into *Session* or *Cache*, or you can even create, guess what, your own tailor-made, view state–like infrastructure. In the end, the simplicity of ASP.NET MVC is due to different architectural choices rather than to some overhead in the design of the Web Forms model.

So ASP.NET MVC brings to the table a clean design with a neat separation of concerns, a leaner run-time stack, full control over HTML, an unparalleled level of extensibility, and a working environment that enables, not penalizes, test-driven development (TDD).

ASP.NET Web Forms and ASP.NET MVC applications can go hand in hand and live side by side in the same process space. The runtime environment must be configured to host an ASP.NET MVC application. This means installing a routing module that intercepts requests at the gate and decides how they are to be processed. An ASP.NET MVC application lists one or more URL patterns it will accept. Requests whose URL matches any defined patterns are processed as ASP.NET MVC requests, while others are left to the standard processing engine of Web Forms.

Control over Markup

Just like with Web Forms, what some perceive as a clear strength of ASP.NET MVC, others may see as a weakness. ASP.NET MVC doesn't offer server controls of its own and also severely limits the use of classic ASP.NET server controls. Even though you describe the view of an ASP.NET MVC page via ASPX markup, you can't embed in it server controls that handle postbacks. In other words, you are allowed to use a *DataGrid* if your goal is creating a table of records, but your code will receive an exception if the *DataGrid* is configured to allow paging, sorting, or inline editing.

To gain full control over HTML, JavaScript, and CSS, ASP.NET MVC requires that you write Web elements manually, one byte after the next. This means that, for the most part, you are responsible for writing every single *<li>* or *<table>* tag you need. In ASP.NET MVC, there's no sort of component model to help you with the generation of HTML. As of today, HTML helpers and perhaps user controls are the only tools you can leverage to write HTML more quickly. Overall, some developers might see ASP.NET MVC as taking a whole step backward in terms of usability and productivity.

Adding visual components to ASP.NET MVC is not impossible per se; it is just arguably what most users of the framework really want. My opinion is that keeping any form of markup abstraction far away from ASP.NET MVC is OK as long as you intend to have two distinct frameworks for ASP.NET development. But I do hope that we move soon to a new framework that unifies the Web Forms and ASP.NET MVC models. In this new framework, if it ever arrives, I do expect some markup abstraction as the only way to increase productivity and have people move to it.

ASP.NET MVC and Simplicity

Simplicity is a characteristic that is often associated with ASP.NET MVC. If you look at Figure 1-8, you can hardly contest the point—ASP.NET MVC is architecturally simpler than Web Forms because the sequence of steps to process a request follows closely the rules of the underlying protocols, with no abstractions created by the framework.

This is a correct statement, but it is a bit incomplete. ASP.NET MVC processes a request through an action and passes return values to a view engine. In doing so, though, ASP.NET MVC offers a number of free services that you might or might not need. For example, when a form posts its content, the framework attempts to bind posted data to the formal parameters of the action method in charge of serving the request. There's a lot of reflection involved in this approach, and some work is done that might not strictly be needed. Can you opt out of this model binding, and how easy is it to do so?

This is the point that shows why ASP.NET MVC targets simplicity in a much more effective way than Web Forms.

In ASP.NET MVC, opting out of a built-in feature simply requires that you use a different coding convention. There's nothing to disable and no closure to crack open to get a different behavior. Any complexity in ASP.NET MVC is built in a bottom-up manner, by composing layers of code one on top of the other. At any time, you can step back and remove the topmost layer to replace it or simply do without it.

In Web Forms, opting out of any built-in feature is much harder because the framework was deliberately built around them in a top-down manner. You can still create HTML-based pages in Web Forms, but it will be significantly hard and counterintuitive. To alter the default behavior of Web Forms, you have to resort to tricks or override methods. In ASP.NET MVC, you just change your programming style or simply replace the component.

ASP.NET Web Pages

ASP.NET Web Forms was relatively easy to embrace for developers and software professionals. ASP.NET MVC requires a bit of extra work and doesn't really lend itself to being learned and discovered on a trial-and-error basis. So how high is the barrier to get into the world of ASP.NET?

ASP.NET Web Pages offers a new approach. ASP.NET Web Pages is not a framework aimed at professional developers, but still it is part of the ASP.NET platform and will be updated in the future. Let's find out more.

Small, Simple, and Seamless

ASP.NET Web Pages targets an audience of Web developers who are involved in very simple projects either because they're not software specialists or because the site to create is extremely simple indeed. This audience would benefit from even further simplicity such as a single page model and a simplified way of writing code and the view. ASP.NET Web Pages comes with a new IDE called WebMatrix and a simplified version of IIS, aptly named IIS Express. WebMatrix, in particular, wraps up server code, markup, and database tables in a new designer environment that makes it a snap to write pages and publish them to a site.

Code and View Together

With ASP.NET Web Pages, you write pages using a mixed syntax that incorporates both markup and code, but in a way that is a bit cleaner than today with either Web Forms or ASP.NET MVC code blocks. By using the @*xxx* syntax, where *xxx* is a built-in object, you can insert in the markup some dynamically calculated value and also use those components to emit ad hoc markup. Here's an example:

```
<body>
   Today is @DateTime.Now
</body>
```

Such objects are more similar to ASP.NET MVC HTML helpers than to Web Forms controls, and they represent dynamic code you can interact with in a single environment while building the output you expect.

 Note The syntax supported by ASP.NET Web Pages (formerly codenamed Razor) is the new default language for defining views in ASP.NET MVC 3.

Summary

ASP.NET Web Forms is the Microsoft premier platform for Web applications. It was originally designed a decade ago to fit as closely as possible the skills and needs of the average developer of the time. Ten years ago, the typical developer was either a former C/C++/ Java developer or an early adopter of HTML willing to do fancier things that JavaScript could just not support. In the middle, there was the Visual Basic developer, accustomed to RAD programming and slowly absorbing the basic concepts of object-oriented programming. ASP.NET Web Forms was designed for these developers. And it worked great for several years. Now, however, it is showing some clear signs of age.

The advent of AJAX revolutionized the perception of a Web application and sparked a paradigm shift—a long process that we have probably gone through for no more than 70 percent of its natural length. Web Forms is really close to its architectural end. If you lead a team of developers, and if your business is based on ASP.NET and Web applications, you should make sure that the framework of choice will take you just where you want and do it comfortably enough.

In the past years, the number of Web applications (including simple sites) has grown beyond imagination. As a developer, you might be asked to design and build anything from a simple site with just a small collection of data-driven pages up to the Web front end of an enterprise-class application, where scalability, extensibility, and customization are high on the priority list.

Is Web Forms up to the task? Sure it is, but you should consider that the conventional way of working of Web Forms doesn't lend itself very well to creating testable code, mockable views, and layers. Web Forms is essentially UI focused and highly optimized for the RAD paradigm. I recommend that you seriously consider alternatives such as ASP.NET MVC or a new set of patterns and practices to make the most of the Web Forms framework.

To learn about ASP.NET MVC, I recommend an earlier book of mine, *Programming Microsoft ASP.NET MVC* (Microsoft Press, 2010). The rest of this book focuses instead on how to make the most of Web Forms today.

Chapter 2
ASP.NET and IIS

As a general rule, the most successful man in life is the man who has the best information.

—*Benjamin Disraeli*

Any Web application is hosted within a Web server; for ASP.NET applications, the Web server uses typically Microsoft Internet Information Services (IIS). A Web server is primarily a server application that can be contacted using a bunch of Internet protocols, such as HTTP, File Transfer Protocol (FTP), and Simple Mail Transfer Protocol (SMTP). IIS—the Web server included with the Microsoft Windows operating system—is no exception.

A Web server such as IIS spends most of its time listening to a variety of ports, including port 80, which is where HTTP packets are usually forwarded. The Web server captures incoming requests and processes them in some way. The details of how that happens depend on both the programming interface of the Web server and the functionalities of the additional components installed on the server.

These components altogether form the *runtime environment* of ASP.NET and are collectively responsible for processing an incoming HTTP request to produce some response for the client browser. Note that this ASP.NET runtime machinery is the same for both ASP.NET Web Forms and ASP.NET MVC. Among other things, this means that classic ASP.NET pages and ASP.NET MVC resources can be hosted side by side in the same application.

In this chapter, I'll first review the architecture and application model of the ASP.NET runtime environment and then explain the work it does to serve a request. In the second part of the chapter, I'll discuss tools and techniques to publish and administer ASP.NET applications hosted on an IIS Web server.

> **Note** Any Web framework needs a Web server for applications to stay online, and ASP.NET is no exception. ASP.NET works very well with IIS—the Microsoft Web server—and very few attempts have been made to run ASP.NET applications outside the Microsoft stack of server products. Furthermore, many of these attempts are just experiments, if not just toy projects. Overall, because IIS is so tightly integrated with ASP.NET, it does not make much sense to look around for an alternate Web server.
>
> With this said, however, note that with the proper set of add-on modules you can also make ASP.NET run on other Web servers, such as Apache. In particular, for Apache the *mod_mono* module is used to run ASP.NET applications. The *mod_mono* module runs within an Apache process and forwards all ASP.NET requests to an external Mono process that actually hosts your ASP.NET application. For more information, pay a visit to *http://www.mono-project.com/ Mod_mono*.

The Web Server Environment

At the dawn of ASP.NET planning, IIS and the ASP.NET framework were supposed to be a tightly integrated environment sharing the same logic for processing incoming requests. In this regard, ASP.NET was expected to be the specialist capable of handling page requests through port 80, whereas IIS was envisioned as the general-purpose Web server capable of serving any other type of requests on a number of predefined ports.

This is more or less what we have today with the latest IIS 7.5 and Microsoft Windows Server 2008 R2; it took a while to get there though.

A Brief History of ASP.NET and IIS

Back in 2002, ASP.NET 1.0 was a self-contained, brand new runtime environment bolted onto IIS 5.0. With the simultaneous release of ASP.NET 1.1 and IIS 6.0, the Web development and server platforms have gotten closer and started sharing some services, such as process re-cycling and output caching. The advent of ASP.NET 2.0 and newer versions hasn't changed anything, but the release of IIS 7.0 with Windows Server 2008 signaled the definitive fusion of the ASP.NET and IIS programming models.

Let's step back and review the key changes in the IIS architecture and the architecture's interaction with ASP.NET applications.

The Standalone ASP.NET Worker Process

Originally, the ASP.NET and IIS teams started together, but at some point the respective deadlines and needs created a fork in the road. So ASP.NET 1.0 couldn't rely on the planned support from IIS and had to ship its own worker process. Figure 2-1 shows the runtime architecture as of Windows 2000 and IIS 5.0.

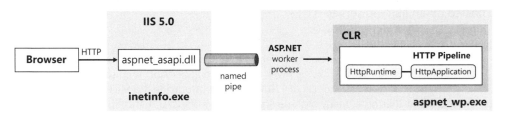

FIGURE 2-1 ASP.NET requests processed by a separate worker process outside IIS.

Captured by the IIS executable listening on port 80, an HTTP request was mapped to an IIS extension (named *aspnet_isapi.dll*) and then forwarded by this component to the ASP.NET worker process via a named pipe. As a result, the request had to go through a double-stage pipeline: the IIS pipeline first and the ASP.NET runtime pipeline next. The ASP.NET developer had little control over preliminary steps (including authentication) performed at the IIS gate and could gain control over the request only after the request had been assigned to the ASP.NET worker process. The ASP.NET worker process was responsible for loading an instance of the Common Language Runtime (CLR) in process and triggering the familiar request life cycle, including application startup, forms authentication, state management, output caching, page compilation, and so forth.

The IIS Native Worker Process

With Windows Server 2003 and IIS 6.0, Microsoft redesigned the architecture of the Web server to achieve more isolation between applications. IIS 6.0 comes with a predefined executable that serves as the worker process for a bunch of installed applications sharing the same application pool. Application pools are an abstraction you use to group multiple Web applications under the same instance of an IIS native worker process, named *w3wp.exe*.

IIS 6.0 incorporates a new HTTP protocol stack (*http.sys*) running in kernel mode that captures HTTP requests and forwards them to the worker process. The worker processes use the protocol stack to receive requests and send responses. (See Figure 2-2.)

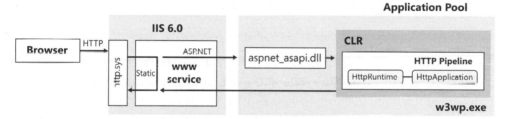

FIGURE 2-2 The worker process isolation mode of IIS 6.0.

An ad hoc service—the WWW publishing service—connects client requests with hosted sites and applications. The WWW service knows how to deal with static requests (for example, images and HTML pages), as well as ASP and ASP.NET requests. For ASP.NET requests, the WWW service forwards the request to the worker process handling the application pool where the target application is hosted.

The IIS worker process loads the aspnet_isapi.dll—a classic IIS extension module—and lets it deal with the CLR and the default ASP.NET request life cycle.

A Shared Pipeline of Components

Before IIS 7, you had essentially two distinct runtime environments: one within the IIS process and one within the application pool of any hosted ASP.NET application. The two runtime environments had different capabilities and programming models. Only resources mapped to the ASP.NET ISAPI extension were subjected to the ASP.NET runtime environment; all the others were processed within the simpler IIS machinery.

With IIS 7, instead, you get a new IIS runtime environment nearly identical to that of ASP.NET. When this runtime environment is enabled, ASP.NET requests are authenticated and preprocessed at the IIS level and use the classic managed ASP.NET runtime environment (the environment centered on the managed *HttpRuntime* object) only to produce the response. Figure 2-3 shows the model that basically takes the ASP.NET pipeline out of the CLR closed environment and expands it at the IIS level.

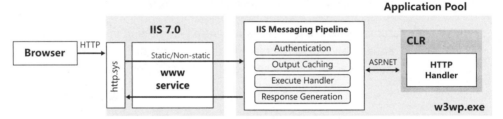

FIGURE 2-3 The unified architecture of IIS 7 that offers an integrated pipeline for processing HTTP requests.

An incoming request is still captured by the kernel-level HTTP stack and queued to the target application pool via the WWW service. The difference now is that whatever request hits IIS is forwarded run through the unified pipeline within the application pool. Application services such as authentication, output caching, state management, and logging are centralized and no longer limited to requests mapped to ASP.NET. In this way, you can, for example, also subject HTML pages or JPEG images to forms authentication without having to first map them to an ASP.NET-specific extension.

Note that in IIS 7, the unified architecture is optional and can be disabled through the IIS Manager tool, as shown in Figure 2-4. The Integrated Pipeline mode, however, is the default working mode for new application pools. In the rest of the chapter, I'll assume application pools are configured in Integrated Pipeline mode unless otherwise specified.

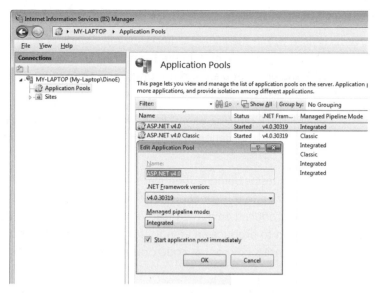

FIGURE 2-4 Configuring the application pool Integrated Pipeline mode in IIS 7.

The Journey of an HTTP Request in IIS

To make sense of the IIS architecture, let's go through the steps of the typical journey of HTTP requests that hit an ASP.NET application.

Any HTTP request that knocks at the IIS door is queued to the application pool that the target application belongs to. The worker process picks up the request and forwards it to the application. The details of what happens next depend on the IIS 7 pipeline mode—Classic or Integrated Pipeline. (IIS 7 configured to work in Classic mode behaves according to the model of its predecessor, IIS 6.)

In IIS 7.0 running in Integrated Pipeline mode, no explicit handoff of the request from IIS to ASP.NET ever occurs. The runtime environment is unified and each request goes through only one chain of events.

Events in the Request Life Cycle

The following list of events is fired within the IIS messaging pipeline. Handlers for these events can be written through managed code both in the form of HTTP modules (as discussed in Chapter 4, "HTTP Handlers, Modules, and Routing") and code snippets in *global.asax*. Events are fired in the following sequence:

1. *BeginRequest* The ASP.NET HTTP pipeline begins to work on the request. For the first request ever in the lifetime of the application instance, this event reaches the application after *Application_Start*.

2. *AuthenticateRequest* The request is being authenticated. ASP.NET and IIS integrated authentication modules subscribe to this event and attempt to produce an identity. If no authentication module produced an authenticated user, an internal default authentication module is invoked to produce an identity for the unauthenticated user. This is done for the sake of consistency so that code doesn't need to worry about null identities.

3. *PostAuthenticateRequest* The request has been authenticated. All the information available is stored in the *HttpContext*'s *User* property at this time.

4. *AuthorizeRequest* The request authorization is about to occur. This event is commonly handled by application code to perform custom authorization based on business logic or other application requirements.

5. *PostAuthorizeRequest* The request has been authorized.

6. *ResolveRequestCache* The runtime environment verifies whether returning a previously cached page can resolve the request. If a valid cached representation is found, the request is served from the cache and the request is short-circuited, calling only any registered *EndRequest* handlers. ASP.NET Output Cache and the new IIS 7.0 Output Cache both feature "execute now" capabilities.

7. *PostResolveRequestCache* The request can't be served from the cache, and the procedure continues. An HTTP handler corresponding to the requested URL is created at this point. If the requested resource is an *.aspx* page, an instance of a page class is created.

8. *MapRequestHandler* The event is fired to determine the request handler.

9. *PostMapRequestHandler* The event fires when the HTTP handler corresponding to the requested URL has been successfully created.

10. *AcquireRequestState* The module that hooks up this event is willing to retrieve any state information for the request. A number of factors are relevant here: the handler must support session state in some form, and there must be a valid session ID.

11. *PostAcquireRequestState*   The state information (such as *Application* or *Session*) has been acquired. The state information is stored in the *HttpContext*'s related properties at this time.

12. *PreRequestHandlerExecute*   This event is fired immediately prior to executing the handler for a given request.

13. *ExecuteRequestHandler*   At this point, the handler does its job and generates the output for the client.

14. *PostRequestHandlerExecute*   When this event fires, the selected HTTP handler has completed and generated the response text.

15. *ReleaseRequestState*   This event is raised when the handler releases its state information and prepares to shut down. This event is used by the session state module to update the dirty session state if necessary.

16. *PostReleaseRequestState*   The state, as modified by the page execution, has been persisted.

17. *UpdateRequestCache*   The runtime environment determines whether the generated output, now also properly filtered by registered modules, should be cached to be reused with upcoming identical requests.

18. *PostUpdateRequestCache*   The page has been saved to the output cache if it was configured to do so.

19. *LogRequest*   The event indicates that the runtime is ready to log the results of the request. Logging is guaranteed to execute even if errors occur.

20. *PostLogRequest*   The request has been logged.

21. *EndRequest*   This event fires as the final step of the pipeline. At this point, the response is known and made available to other modules that might add compression or encryption, or perform any other manipulation.

Another pair of events can occur during the request, but in a nondeterministic order. They are *PreSendRequestHeaders* and *PreSendRequestContent*. The *PreSendRequestHeaders* event informs the *HttpApplication* object in charge of the request that HTTP headers are about to be sent. The *PreSendRequestContent* event tells the *HttpApplication* object in charge of the request that the response body is about to be sent. Both these events normally fire after *EndRequest*, but not always. For example, if buffering is turned off, the event gets fired as soon as some content is going to be sent to the client.

Speaking of nondeterministic application events, it must be said that a third nondeterministic event is, of course, *Error*.

Let's delve deeper into the mechanics of ASP.NET request processing.

> **Note** Technically, most of the IIS pipeline events are exposed as events of the ASP.NET
> *HttpApplication* class. A significant exception is *ExecuteRequestHandler*. You find this event in the
> IIS messaging pipeline, but you won't find an easy way to subscribe to it from within ASP.NET
> code. Internally, the ASP.NET runtime subscribes to this event to receive notification of when an
> ASP.NET request needs to produce its output. This happens when using unmanaged code that is
> not publicly available to developers. If you want to control how an incoming request is executed
> by IIS, you have to resort to Win32 ISAPI filters. If you want to control how an ASP.NET request is
> executed, you don't need the IIS *ExecuteRequestHandler* event, because a simpler HTTP handler
> will do the job.

ASP.NET Request Processing in Integrated Pipeline Mode

In an integrated pipeline, an ASP.NET request is like any other request except that, at some
point, it yields to a sort of simplified ASP.NET runtime environment that now just prepares
the HTTP context, maps the HTTP handler, and generates the response.

When the application pool that contains an ASP.NET application running in Integrated
Pipeline mode is initialized, it hosts ASP.NET in the worker process and gives ASP.NET a
chance to register a set of built-in HTTP modules and handlers for the IIS pipeline events.
This guarantees, for example, that Forms authentication, session state, and output caching
work as expected in ASP.NET. At the same time, the ASP.NET runtime also subscribes to receive notification of when an ASP.NET request needs processing.

In between the *PreRequestHandlerExecute* and *PostRequestHandlerExecute* events, IIS hands
an ASP.NET request to some code in the ASP.NET runtime environment for actual processing.
Hosted in the IIS worker process, the ASP.NET environment is governed by a new class—the
ApplicationManager class. This class is responsible for creating and managing any needed
AppDomains to run the various ASP.NET applications located in the same pool. During the
initialization, the *ApplicationManager* class invokes a specific *PipelineRuntime* object, which
ultimately registers a handler for the *ExecuteRequestHandler*.

This ASP.NET internal handler is called back by IIS whenever an ASP.NET request needs to be
processed. The handler invokes a new static method on the *HttpRuntime* object that kicks in
to take care of the request notification. The method retrieves the HTTP handler in charge of
the request, prepares the HTTP context for the request, and invokes the HTTP handler's public interface. Figure 2-5 offers a graphical view of the steps involved.

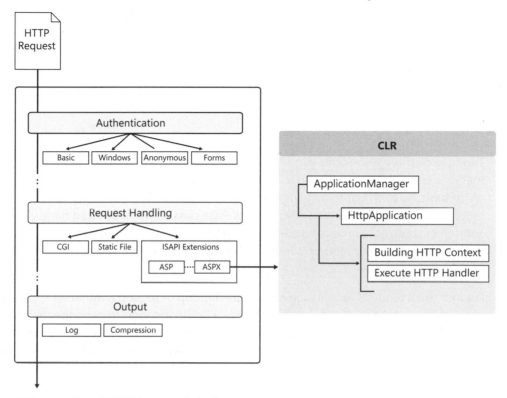

FIGURE 2-5 How the IIS 7 integrated pipeline processes an ASP.NET request.

Building a Response for the Request

Each ASP.NET request is mapped to a special component known as the *HTTP handler*. The ASP.NET runtime uses a built-in algorithm to figure out the HTTP handler in charge of a given ASP.NET request.

In Web Forms, this algorithm is based on the URL of the requested page. You have a different HTTP handler for each page requested. If you requested, say, *page.aspx*, the HTTP handler is a class named *ASP.page_aspx* that inherits from the code-behind class you specified in your source code. The first time the request is made this class doesn't exist in the AppDomain. If the class does not exist, the source code for the class is obtained by parsing the ASPX markup and then it's compiled in memory and loaded directly into the AppDomain. Successive requests then can be served by the existing instance.

An HTTP handler is a managed class that implements the *IHttpHandler* interface, as shown in the following code snippet. The body of the *ProcessRequest* method ultimately determines the response for the request.

```
public interface IHttpHandler
{
    void ProcessRequest(HttpContext context);
    bool IsReusable { get; }
}
```

The base class for Web Forms pages—the *System.Web.UI.Page* class—is simply a class that provides an extremely sophisticated implementation of the *IHttpHandler* interface, which basically turns out to be a full implementation of the Page Controller pattern. The *ProcessRequest* method of the *System.Web.UI.Page* class consumes posted data, view state, and server controls to produce the resulting HTML for the client. Needless to say, the *Page* class assumes that your request is for an HTML page as described by the content available in a server ASPX file.

For individual requests, or for a logically defined group of requests, within an application you can define an alternate handler class that employs different logic to generate the response. This alternate HTTP handler can be mapped to a particular URL, and it doesn't have to point necessarily to an existing server resource. Ultimately, this is just what ASP.NET MVC does.

> **Note** As you'll see in Chapter 4, ASP.NET Web Forms supports URL routing, which essentially allows you to map an incoming URL to a specific ASPX page. The standard algorithm for mapping URLs to HTTP handler classes as described here only works if you're not using Web Forms URL routing.

Adding Your Own Code to the Pipeline

As mentioned, you can write your own handlers for many of the request life-cycle events listed earlier in the chapter. You can do that by writing a managed HTTP module or by adding code to the *global.asax* file of your ASP.NET application. Let's briefly consider what it takes to extend the *global.asax* file. Here's a piece of code that shows what you end up with:

```
protected void Application_PostAuthenticateRequest()
{
    // Your code here
}
```

You use the *Application_Xxx* notation to define a handler for the *Xxx* event fired at the application level. For example, the code snippet gives you a chance to run some custom code after the request has been authenticated. These handlers affect your application only.

As you'll see in much more detail in Chapter 4, a managed HTTP module is a class that implements a specific interface—the *IHttpModule* interface. In its startup code, the HTTP module programmatically registers as the handler for one or more of the request events. Next, you register the module with the application and just wait for it to kick in for each and every application request.

Note that the HTTP module can be registered in two ways: via the configuration file of the application (*web.config*) or administratively through the IIS Manager tool. Mappings set directly within IIS Manager are stored in the *applicationHost.config* file.

In IIS Manager, you select the Modules applet and then bring up the dialog box shown in Figure 2-6 to add a new module by specifying its unique name and, of course, the type.

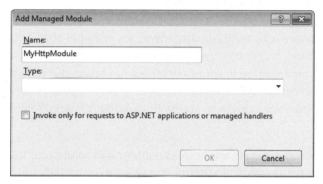

FIGURE 2-6 Adding a new HTTP module in IIS Manager.

An HTTP module can operate on both ASP.NET managed and native requests. A native request is intended as a request that doesn't strictly require the ASP.NET runtime machinery to be served successfully. The canonical example of a native request is a JPEG image or a static HTML page.

Some New Features in IIS 7.5

Recently, IIS 7 has been further refined to better serve the needs of Web developers and site administrators. Here's a quick list of new features you might want to take advantage of to improve the performance and effectiveness of ASP.NET applications.

Note that the list is not exhaustive and is mostly meant to serve the needs of members of an ASP.NET development team rather than site administrators. For example, IIS 7.5 incorporates a number of administrator-level extensions that have been released along the way as add-ons to IIS 7, such as the Application Request Routing and the URL Rewrite Module. The former is a routing module that forwards HTTP requests to content servers based on predefined settings to ensure proper balancing of traffic. The latter is a highly configurable module to block, redirect, and rewrite incoming requests.

For developers, features like application warm-up and hardened security are perhaps more attractive.

Autostarting Web Applications

It comes as no surprise that some Web applications might take a while to get up and running and ready to serve the first request. Application restarts happen for a number of reasons, and sometimes they're beyond the explicit control of the site administrators. (I'll get back to application restarts in a moment.)

If the application needs to perform expensive initialization tasks before serving the first request, every restart is a performance hit. The user all of a sudden experiences significant delays and can't easily figure out why. There are no fancy ways to solve the issue; in the end, all you need to do is keep your application awake and "distribute" the time it takes to initialize your application across its entire uptime. This might mean, for example, that if your application requires lengthy database processing, you ensure that data is cached in a location that's faster to access than the database itself. Some effective solutions in this regard have been arranged using an always running Windows service. All the service does is periodically refresh a cache of data for the Web application to access from within the *Application_Start* event handler in *global.asax*.

ASP.NET 4 and IIS 7.5 on Windows Server 2008 R2 offer an integrated solution to this relatively frequent issue. A new feature named *autostart* provides a controlled approach for starting up an application pool and initializing the ASP.NET application before the application can accept HTTP requests.

You edit the configuration file of IIS to inform IIS of your intentions and then provide your own component that performs the warm up and accomplishes whatever tasks are required for your application to be as responsive as expected. The feature is a joint venture between IIS 7.5 and ASP.NET 4. ASP.NET ensures the preloader component is invoked in a timely manner; IIS 7.5, on the other hand, prevents the ASP.NET application from receiving any HTTP traffic until it is ready. As you can see, the warm-up is not really magic and does not squeeze extra computing power out of nowhere; it stems from the fact that users perceive the application is down until it is ready to accept and promptly serve requests.

I'll demonstrate concretely how to set up the IIS 7.5 autostart feature later in the chapter in the section about the configuration of IIS.

Application Pool Custom Identities

For years, worker processes under both IIS 6.0 and IIS 7.0 have run under the aegis of the NETWORKSERVICE account—a relatively low-privileged, built-in identity in Windows. Originally welcomed as an excellent security measure, in the end the use of a single account for a potentially high number of concurrently running services created more problems than it helped to solve. In a nutshell, services running under the same account could tamper with each other.

In IIS 7.5, worker processes by default run under unique identities automatically and transparently created for each newly created application pool. (The underlying technology is known as Virtual Accounts and is currently supported by Windows Server 2008 R2 and Windows 7. For more information, have a look at *http://technet.microsoft.com/en-us/library/ dd548356(WS.10).aspx*.)

You can still change the identity of the application pool using the IIS Manager dialog box shown in Figure 2-7.

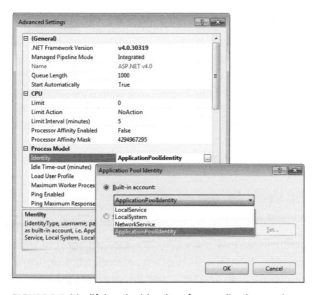

FIGURE 2-7 Modifying the identity of an application pool.

Deploying ASP.NET Applications

An ASP.NET application must be installed on an IIS machine for it to be usable by its end users. Installing a Web application means moving files and configuration from the development server to a staging server first or directly to the production environment. In general, deployment of a Web application entails a number of steps that relate to moving settings and data around a few server machines. This process can obviously be accomplished manually but does offer a high degree of automation. Automation is always useful and welcome; it becomes a necessity, though, when you need to install on a hosted server instead of an enterprise server that you might have direct access to.

In the beginning of the Web development era, deployment was not an exact science and everybody developed their own set of practices and tools to simplify and speed up necessary tasks. Today, Web deployment is part of the job, and effective tools are integrated into the development environment and are taken care of as part of the development cycle.

Not all scenarios are the same for the deployment of Web applications. You still can recognize simple and less simple scenarios and pick appropriate tools for each. Let's start with plain XCopy deployment for Web site projects and then move on to consider more enterprise-level tools, such as the IIS 7 integrated Web Deployment Tool, that are better suited for Web application projects.

Note In Microsoft Visual Studio, you can choose between two main types of Web projects—Web Site Project (WSP) and Web Application Project (WAP). The biggest difference between the two is the deployment of the source code. In a WSP, you deploy markup and source code; in a WAP, you deploy markup and compiled code. There are, of course, pros and cons in both situations. Having source code deployed to the Web server enables you to apply quick fixes and updates even via FTP. If you need to control the rollup of updates, or you are subject to strict rules for deployment, a WAP is preferable as you build a single package and run it through the server.

A comprehensive comparison of WSP and WAP can be found in the whitepaper available at *http://msdn.microsoft.com/en-us/library/aa730880(VS.80).aspx#wapp_topic5*. An interesting post that helps you make the choice through a series of questions is found at *http://vishaljoshi. blogspot.com/2009/08/web-application-project-vs-web-site.html.*

XCopy Deployment for Web Sites

In simple scenarios, installing an ASP.NET application is simply a matter of performing a recursive copy of all the files (assemblies, scripts, pages, style sheets, images) to the target folder on the target server machine. This process is often referred to as performing an XCopy. Performing an XCopy doesn't preclude applying additional configuration settings to the IIS machine, but you keep XCopy and configuration on two distinct levels and run them as distinct operations.

The Copy Web Site Function of Visual Studio 2010

Visual Studio 2010 offers XCopy capabilities only for Web site projects through the *Copy Web Site* function on the Website menu. The typical user interface is shown in Figure 2-8.

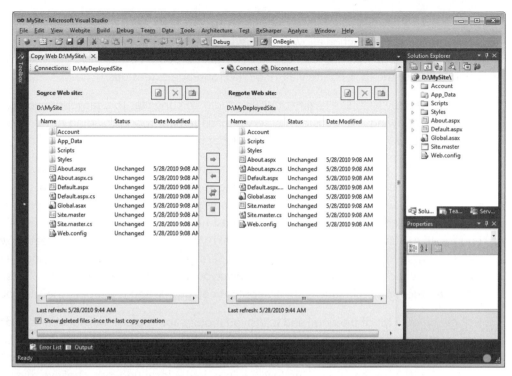

FIGURE 2-8 The Copy Web Site function of Visual Studio 2010.

Visual Studio offers you two list boxes representing the source and remote Web sites. All you do is copy files from the source to the target and synchronize content if needed.

This approach works very well if you just want to have the source on the server machine in a native format that can be edited live to apply updates and fixes. In a WSP, Visual Studio does not really compile your source code and doesn't deploy assemblies. It is limited to validating the correctness of the code by running the ASP.NET compiler in the background and spotting possible failures.

The actual compilation occurs only when the page is requested by some end users. This ensures that any applied change is promptly detected without the need of an extra step of compilation and deployment.

> **Note** As mentioned, the Copy Web Site function is enabled only for Web site projects. There are no technical reasons, however, that prevent the feature from also being implemented for Web application projects. It was merely a matter of opportunity and a design choice. The assumption is that if you opt for a WAP, you primarily intend to deploy compiled assemblies and markup files. This means that editing a code-behind class on the fly and live on the production server (for example, to apply a sensitive update) is not a priority of yours. Therefore, you are probably more interested in an automated deployment experience.

Copying Files

The Copy Web Site function allows you to sync up your project files directly with the target directory on the IIS machine (as illustrated in Figure 2-8) or in other ways. For example, you can connect to the IIS Web site via FTP or via FrontPage extensions.

Beyond the Copy Web Site facility of Visual Studio, to copy files to a target site you can use any of the following: FTP transfer, any server management tools providing forms of smart replication on a remote site, or an MSI installer application.

Each option has pros and cons, and the best fit can be found only after you know exactly the runtime host scenario and if the purpose of the application is clearly delineated. Be aware that if you're going to deploy the application on an ISP host, you might be forced to play by the rules (read, "use the tools") that your host has set. If you're going to deliver a front end for an existing system to a variety of servers, you might find it easier to create a setup project. On the other hand, FTP is great for general maintenance and for applying quick fixes. Ad hoc tools, on the other hand, can give you automatic sync-up features. Guess what? Choosing the right technique is strictly application-specific and is ultimately left to you.

FTP gives you a lot of freedom, and it lets you modify and replace individual files. It doesn't represent a solution that is automatic, however—whatever you need to do must be accomplished manually. Assuming that you have gained full access to the remote site, using FTP is not much different than using Windows Explorer in the local network. I believe that with the Copy Web Site functionality the need for raw FTP access is going to lessen. If nothing else, the new Copy Web Site function operates as an integrated FTP-like tool to access remote locations.

The new copy function also provides synchronization capabilities too. It is not like the set of features that a specifically designed server management tool would supply, but it can certainly work well in a number of realistic situations. At the end of the day, a site replication tool doesn't do much more than merely transfer files from end to end. Its plusses are the user interface and the intelligence that are built around and atop this basic capability. So a replication tool maintains a database of files with timestamps, attributes, and properties, and it can sync up versions of the site in a rather automated way, minimizing the work on your end.

Building a Setup Project

Another common scenario involves using an out-of-the-box installer file. Deploying in this way is a two-step operation. First, create and configure the virtual directory; next, copy the needed files. Visual Studio makes creating a Web setup application a snap. You just create a new type of project—a Web Setup Project—select the files to copy, and build the project.

Ideally, you proceed by adding a Web Setup Project to the solution that contains the Web application. In this way, you can automatically instruct the tool to copy the project output in the *Bin* folder and copy the content files directly in the root of the Web application folder. The benefit is that you don't have to deal with specific file names but can work at a higher level of abstraction.

You create a Web application folder to represent the virtual directory of the new application on the target machine. The Properties dialog box lets you configure the settings of the new virtual directory. For example, the *AllowDirectoryBrowsing* property lets you assign browsing permission to the IIS virtual folder you will create. You can also control the virtual directory name, application execute permissions, the level of isolation, and the default page. The *Bin* subfolder is automatically created, but you can have the setup process create and populate as many subfolders as you need. (See Figure 2-9.)

FIGURE 2-9 Configuring the Web application folder in a Web setup project.

When you build the project, you obtain a Windows Installer *.msi* file that constitutes the setup to ship to your clients. The default installer supports repairing and uninstalling the application. The setup you obtain in this way—which is the simplest you can get—does not contain the Microsoft .NET Framework, which must be installed on the target machine or explicitly included in the setup project itself.

Packaging Files and Settings

The XCopy strategy is well suited for relatively simple scenarios where you don't need to do much more than copy files. All in all, the Web setup project is a solution that works well for implementing an XCopy strategy in a context (for example, hosted servers) where you don't have direct access to the IIS machine.

LIVERPOOL JOHN MOORES UNIVERSITY
LEARNING SERVICES

In general, installing an ASP.NET Web application is not simply a matter of copying a bunch of files and assemblies. It is likely that you will have to perform additional tasks, including adapting configuration settings to the destination environment, creating databases, configuring the Web server environment, and installing security certificates. In the first place, you must be able to express the detailed deployment logic you need (that is, what has to be done, and where and how it must be done). Second, you need tools that allow you to push content to one server (or more) in an automated way so that manual steps are eliminated, which decreases the possibility of making mistakes.

For WAP projects only, Visual Studio 2010 offers a powerful set of tools centered on the Web Deployment Tool.

The Web Deployment Tool

The Web Deployment Tool (WDT, or Web Deploy) is an IIS tool that recognizes ad hoc deploy packages and runs them in the server environment. A deploy package contains setup instructions for a Web application, including the list of files to copy, assemblies to install, database scripts to run, certificates, and IIS and registry configuration.

You don't even need administrative privileges to deploy these packages to IIS—delegated access to IIS is enough to run Web Deploy packages. You can get Web Deploy for IIS 6 and IIS 7 from *http://www.iis.net/download/webdeploy*. As shown in Figure 2-10, you can install the tool on an IIS machine via the latest version of Web Platform Installer.

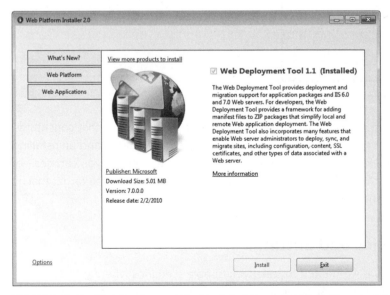

FIGURE 2-10 The Web Deployment Tool installed through Web Platform Installer.

After you have WDT on board, all you need to do is prepare a deployment script and push it to the tool installed on the IIS machine.

Notice that you can use WDT for clean installations as well as for updating existing applications. In other words, the tool gives you an API to synchronize files over HTTP, the ability to execute setup and configuration commands remotely; more importantly, it works in both enterprise and hosted environments.

The strict requirement, of course, is that WDT must be installed on the server machine.

> **Note** To successfully operate with WDT, you need compatible versions of WDT installed on the server and the client machine. However, note that WDT is automatically installed if you have Visual Studio 2010. In addition, you must have appropriate permissions on the target computer to perform the tasks you require.

Building a WDT Package

A deployment package is a zipped file with a manifest. The package includes all the information required to set up the IIS application and the files to copy. In a package, in addition to the application's source files and binaries, you find IIS and application pool settings, changes required to the *web.config* file in the production environment, database scripts, security certificates, registry settings, and assemblies to place in the global assembly cache (GAC).

You can create a WDT package either from Visual Studio 2010 or using Windows PowerShell or the command-line version of the tool. From Visual Studio 2010, you have a highly automated user interface you control through the Package/Publish Web tab. (See Figure 2-11.)

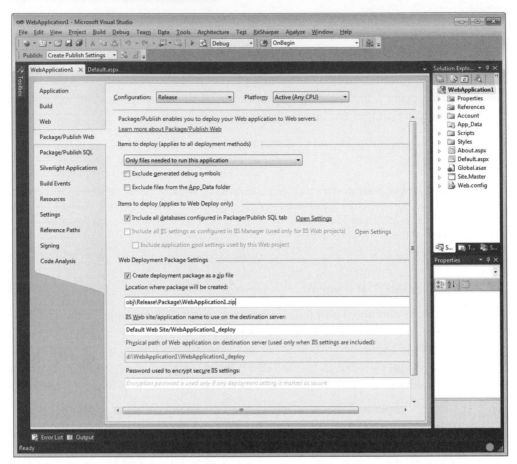

FIGURE 2-11 The Package/Publish Web tab, which is used to configure default settings for WDT.

You access the tab from the Project menu and use it to set your default settings for the projects. Interestingly, the tab goes hand in hand with the Package/Publish SQL tab, where you can list the databases you intend to configure and script on the server. The tool also offers to load some database information from your *web.config* file.

In Visual Studio 2010, you can choose to publish the application directly or you can build a WDT package and deploy it later. To build a package, you select the Build Deployment Package item from the Project menu. You obtain a ZIP file in the specified location that, among other things, contains a Windows PowerShell script to be used on a server machine. Figure 2-12 shows the content of such a package.

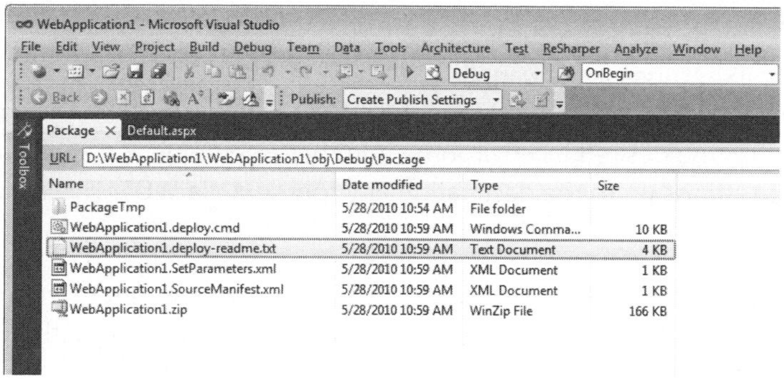

FIGURE 2-12 The content of a sample WDT package.

You can also publish the application in single step by choosing the Publish item on the Build menu. You are then shown the dialog box seen in Figure 2-13 where you indicate the full name of the target site or application and whether you want it to be a new application or simply a virtual directory. To turn the newly installed package into a new application, you select the Mark As IIS Application On Destination check box. For the entire operation to work, you need to run Visual Studio 2010 in administrative mode.

FIGURE 2-13 Publishing a Web application via Web Deploy.

If you choose to deploy a new IIS application, it will be placed in the default application pool. Obviously, if the application pool is configured for, say, the .NET Framework 2.0, it can't be used to host an ASP.NET 4 application.

Propagating IIS Settings

How would you specify IIS settings for the application? The first option is importing a package that will be installed in the application pool of choice, configured as appropriate. Another option is creating the desired IIS environment in the development machine and then just propagating those settings up to the destination environment via WDT. There are some snags, though.

The Visual Studio Publish Wizard doesn't let you determine the target application pool unless the source Web project is an IIS Web project. So what's an IIS Web project, exactly?

An IIS Web project is a project that relies on the local IIS Web server instead of the ASP.NET Development Server that comes with Visual Studio. (Note that this internal Web server is also referred to as the *Visual Studio Development Server* or, more familiarly, *Cassini*.) For a WAP, you switch to the local IIS Web server by selecting the Web tab in the application properties dialog box, as shown in Figure 2-14.

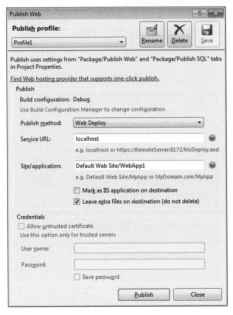

FIGURE 2-14 Switching to an IIS Web project.

At this point, when you open the Publish Settings tab you find a couple of check boxes selected that allow you to propagate current IIS settings down to the destination. (See Figure 2-15.) To configure the local IIS for the current project, you just click the Open Settings link. Any application pool or configuration scenario you define will be reported in the deployment script.

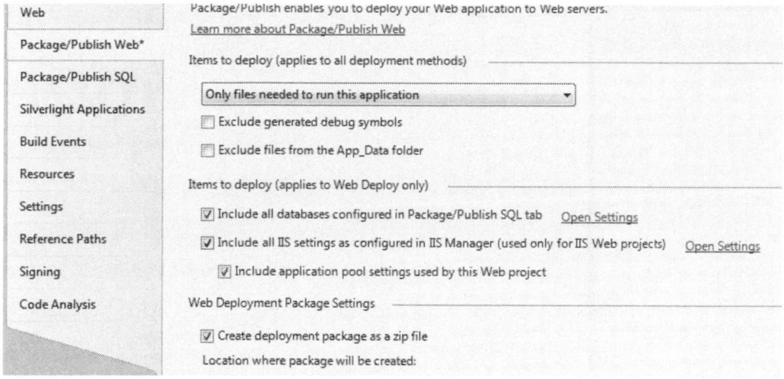

FIGURE 2-15 Propagating IIS settings.

Web.config Transformations

During the development of a Web site, you rely on a bunch of settings stored in the *web.config* file that refer to the current environment. So, for example, the data access layer targets a development database and the security settings are different from those required by the production environment. When it comes to deploying the site to the real host, you need to tweak the *web.config* appropriately. This is usually a manual process. You open the development version of the *web.config* in Visual Studio and then proceed with any required changes.

To make the whole matter even more complicated, sometimes you need to go through a battery of integration tests. An integration test is typically a situation in which you test the behavior of your site (or part of it) in an environment that simulates the production environment and in which multiple elements are being tested together. You might need yet another *web.config* file for this scenario. In the end, you likely need about three different versions of the *web.config* file: debug, release, and test. How do you deal with that?

The simplest, but not necessarily most effective, solution is managing distinct files and keeping them in sync by manual intervention. However, if you made the switch to Visual Studio 2010, you can rely on a new IDE feature that automatically maintains a single copy of the *web.config* file—the skeleton—and then transforms it into as many versions as you need when you publish the solution using WDT. This feature is supported by Web application projects and is not available for simple Web site projects.

The *web.config* file of a Visual Studio 2010 WAP looks like the one shown in Figure 2-16. It shows up as a subtree in Solution Explorer. If you expand the node, you see two child files— *web.debug.config* and *web.release.config*. The debug version of *web.config* looks like a regular configuration file except for a little detail.

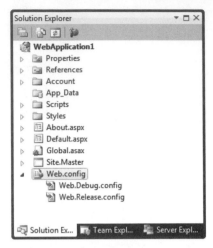

FIGURE 2-16 Predefined transformations of the *web.config* file.

Here's how the root *<configuration>* element appears for transformation files:

```
<configuration xmlns:xdt="http://schemas.microsoft.com/XML-Document-Transform">
```

The element includes the definition of a new namespace whose suffix is *xdt*. The namespace refers to a specific XML schema used to express transformations required on the content of the file. You use *xdt* elements to insert commands in the configuration file to be processed during the publish process to apply transformations to the actual *web.config* file being deployed for a given configuration (debug, release, or any other one you want to support).

Suppose, for example, that the *web.config* file you use for development purposes contains a *<connectionString>* node that needs be updated for a production install to target a real database. You edit the *web.release.config* file to contain the following:

```
<connectionStrings>
    <add name="YourDatabase"
        xdt:Locator="Match(name)"
        xdt:Transform="Replace"
        connectionString="..." />
</connectionStrings>
```

The *Transform* attribute indicates the operation to perform on the current element. In this case, you intend to perform a Replace. The *Locator* attribute, on the other hand, refers to the attribute to process. In the example, the target of the replacement is any attribute that matches the value of the *name* attribute. In other words, when processing the development *web.config* file, the Publish Wizard will try to locate any connection string entry there that matches the *YourDatabase* name. If any is found, the entire *<add>* subtree is replaced with the one provided in the transformation file.

If you open up the Release transformation file that comes with the default Visual Studio ASP.NET template, you find the following:

```
<configuration xmlns:xdt="http://schemas.microsoft.com/XML-Document-Transform">
  <system.web>
    <compilation xdt:Transform="RemoveAttributes(debug)" />
  </system.web>
</configuration>
```

The *<compilation>* element is definitely one that needs to be updated when you move to a production environment. The *Transform* element indicates that a given attribute—the *debug* attribute—must be removed. As a result, when the *web.release.config* file is transformed, the *debug* attribute is removed from the *<compilation>* element.

The overall idea is that you write a base *web.config* file for the development environment and then express the delta between it and any other one you might need through transformations. At a minimum, you need a transformation for the release version for the configuration file. The delta results from the transformation applied via the XDT transform. The XDT processor is incorporated in the Web Deployment Tool.

You can have a distinct transformation of the *web.config* for each build configuration you handle in your solution. Figure 2-17 shows how to define a custom build configuration. After you successfully add a new custom build configuration, you right-click the *web.config* file and select the Add Config Transform menu item. This will add a new *web.Xxx.config* file, where *Xxx* is the name of the new configuration. At this point, you can edit the file at will and add as many XDT tags as needed. The file transformation occurs only when you generate a deployment package from the Project menu.

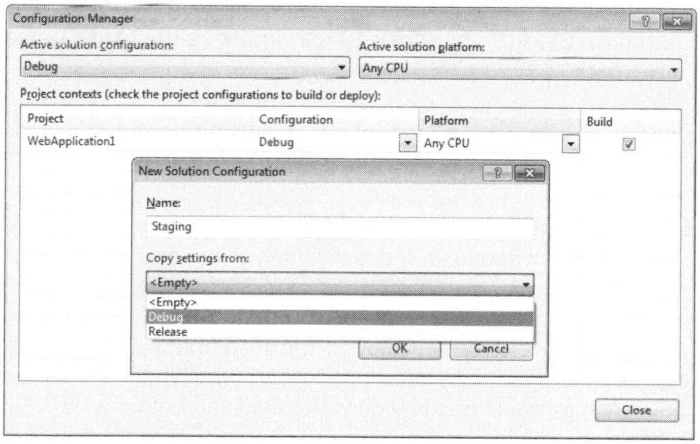

FIGURE 2-17 Adding a new build configuration.

Site Precompilation

Another aspect related to deploying an ASP.NET application is the site precompilation. Every ASP.NET page needs an extra step of runtime compilation to serve its markup. As you'll see in the upcoming chapters, when you author an ASP.NET page you write a markup file (ASPX) plus a code-behind class using C#, Visual Basic, or any other supported .NET language.

In a WSP scenario, you deploy markup and code-behind classes as is and wait for the users to make requests to have them compiled. In a WAP scenario, you deploy markup files and one or more assemblies containing the compiled code-behind classes. In both cases, the dynamic compilation step for each available page is still required at least the first time a given page is served. The WAP project type simply saves you from deploying the source code of your classes.

In Visual Studio, when you attempt to publish a WSP project you are shown a different user interface than for a WAP project where a new term is introduced: *site precompilation*. In spite of this, site precompilation is a general ASP.NET feature and is not limited to WSP projects. It's the Visual Studio 2010 user interface that seems to limit it to Web site projects.

Is site precompilation really useful?

Site precompilation consists of programmatically invoking all pages so that the ASP.NET runtime can process them as if a user had already invoked each. The benefit is that users won't experience any extra delay after the first request. In addition, you catch any compile-time errors that slipped into pages after the previous tests.

Precompilation doesn't necessarily deliver a huge performance improvement; most of the time, it is a small-scale optimization instead. However, if you have pages that cache a lot of data and take a while to initialize, this little bit of speed can improve the user's perception of your application.

Precompilation can take two forms: in-place precompilation and deployment precompilation.

Note Site precompilation is sometimes sold as a feature that saves you from having to deploy your source code to the production environment. This is definitely the wrong way to approach things. ASP.NET allows you to deploy pages with their source code-behind classes, but it doesn't mandate it. It's ultimately your choice, and the option has both pros and cons. If you don't want to deploy source code, just opt for a Web application project instead of a Web site project. Site precompilation can be applied to any ASP.NET project regardless of the type and in spite of the Visual Studio tooling support that for some reason is only offered if you opt for a WSP.

In-Place Precompilation

In-place precompilation consists of running a tool over the entire set of project files to request each page as if it were being used by end users. As a result, each page is compiled as if it's for ordinary use. The site is fully compiled before entering production, and no user will experience a first-hit compilation delay.

In-place precompilation usually takes place after the site is deployed but before it goes public. To precompile a site in-place, you use the following command, where */yourApp* indicates the virtual folder of the application:

```
aspnet_compiler –v /yourApp
```

Note that with the previous syntax, *YourApp* is assumed to be deployed within the default Web site. If that is not your case, you might want to indicate the site explicitly, as shown here:

```
aspnet_compiler –v /W3SVC/2/Root/YourApp
```

In this case, you are addressing *YourApp* within the Web site characterized by an ID of 2.

If you precompile the site again, the compiler skips pages that are up to date and only new or changed files are processed and those with dependencies on new or changed files. Because of this compiler optimization, it is practical to compile the site after even minor updates.

Precompilation is essentially a batch compilation that generates all needed assemblies in the fixed ASP.NET directory on the server machine. If any file fails compilation, precompilation will fail on the application. The ASP.NET compiler tool also supports a target directory. If you choose this option, the tool will generate all of its output in a distinct directory. Next, you can zip all of the content and deploy it manually to the IIS machine. I'll discuss the command line of the ASP.NET compiler tool in a moment.

Precompilation for Deployment

Precompilation for deployment generates a representation of the site made of assemblies, static files, and configuration files—a sort of manifest. This representation is generated on a target machine and also can be packaged as MSI and then copied to and installed on a production machine. This form of precompilation doesn't require source code to be left on the target machine.

Precompilation for deployment is also achieved through the *aspnet_compiler* command-line tool. Here's a common way to use the tool:

```
aspnet_compiler –m metabasePath
                -c virtualPath
                -p physicalPath
                targetPath
```

The role of each supported parameter is explained in Table 2-1.

TABLE 2-1 Parameters of the *aspnet_compiler* Tool

Switch	Description
−aptca	If this switch is specified, compiled assemblies will allow partially trusted callers.
−c	If this switch is specified, the precompiled application is fully rebuilt.
−d	If this switch is specified, the debug information is emitted during compilation.
−delaysign	If this switch is specified, compiled assemblies are not fully signed when created.
−errorstack	Shows extra debugging information.
−m	Indicates the full IIS metabase path of the application.
−f	Indicates that the target directory will be overwritten if it already exists and existing contents will be lost.
−fixednames	If this switch is specified, the compiled assemblies will be given fixed names.
−keycontainer	Indicates the name of the key container for strong names.
−keyfile	Indicates the physical path to the key file for strong names.
−p	Indicates the physical path of the application to be compiled. If this switch is missing, the IIS metabase is used to locate the application. This switch must be combined with −v.
−u	If this switch is specified, it indicates that the precompiled application is updatable.
−v	Indicates the virtual path of the application to be compiled. If no virtual path is specified, the application is assumed to be in the default site: W3SVC/1/Root.

If no target path is specified, the precompilation takes place in the virtual path of the application, and source files are therefore preserved. If a different target is specified, only assemblies are copied, and the new application runs with no source file in the production environment. The following command line precompiles *YourApp* to the specified disk path:

```
aspnet_compiler −v /YourApp c:\DeployedSite
```

Static files such as images, *web.config*, and HTML pages are not compiled—they are just copied to the target destination.

Precompilation for deployment comes in two slightly different forms—with or without support for updates. Sites packaged for deployment only are not sensitive to file changes. When a change is required, you modify the original files, recompile the whole site, and redeploy the new layout. The only exception is the site configuration; you can update *web.config* on the production server without having to recompile the site.

Sites precompiled for deployment and update are made of assemblies obtained from all files that normally produce assemblies, such as class and resource files. The compiler, though, doesn't touch *.aspx* page files and simply copies them as part of the final layout. In this way, you are allowed to make limited changes to the ASP.NET pages after compiling them. For example, you can change the position of controls or settings regarding colors, fonts, and other visual parameters. You can also add new controls to existing pages, as long as they do not require event handlers or other code.

In no case can new pages be added to a precompiled site without recompiling it from scratch.

The *fixednames* parameter in Table 2-1 plays an important role in update scenarios for sites that need to release updates to specific portions without redeploying the entire set of assemblies. In this case, you must be able to just replace some of the dynamically created assemblies and subsequently require that their names be fixed.

> **Note** In Visual Studio 2010, you have a graphical user interface for site precompilation only if you create a Web site project. If this is the case, and you get to publish the site, you are offered a nice dialog box with options to select to make the precompiled site updatable and to enable strong naming on precompiled assemblies.

Configuring IIS for ASP.NET Applications

Because an ASP.NET application lives within the context of the IIS Web server, the settings you apply to IIS might have an impact on the application itself. Let's review some of the aspects of IIS you want to consider for achieving good performance and stability.

Recycling Policies

The application pool that hosts your ASP.NET application is subject to process recycling. Process recycling is a configurable setting by means of which you determine when the application pool (and subsequently all of its contained applications) is to be restarted. Recycling is not necessarily a bad thing and doesn't necessarily indicate a problem. However, if it happens too often and without a clear reason, well, it's not really a good sign.

Process recycling is an IIS feature introduced as a sort of insurance against programming errors that can cause the application to leak memory, hang, or just slow down. By recycling the worker process behind the application pool regularly, the Web server tries to ensure an acceptable average quality of service.

In light of this, process recycling is expected to happen naturally but occasionally, and in a way that doesn't affect the perceived performance. What if, instead, you detect that the application is restarted too often?

There are many reasons for a recycle of the worker process to be triggered. Natural reasons are those configured through the wizard shown in Figure 2-18.

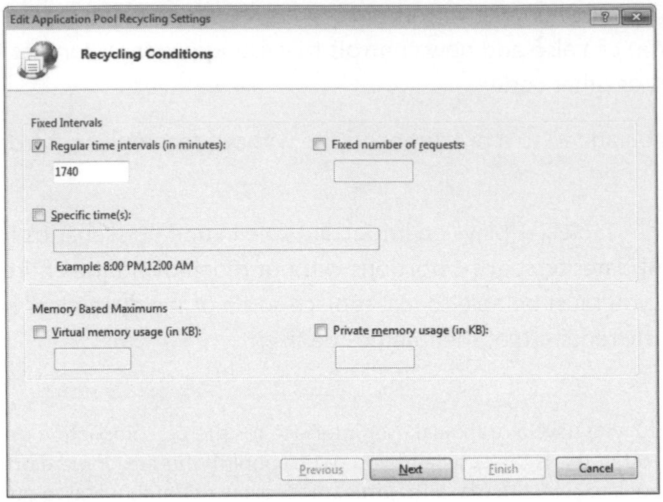

FIGURE 2-18 Application pool recycling settings.

The application pool can be recycled at regular intervals (which is the default choice, as shown in Figure 2-18), after serving a fixed number of requests, at specific times, or when enough memory is consumed. Beyond this, the pool is recycled when you apply changes to the deployed site and modify configuration files or the *Bin* folder. If you frequently update bits and pieces of the site (for example, you published it as a Web site), an application restart also happens when a given number of assemblies is loaded in memory.

In the .NET Framework, you can't unload a given assembly. Therefore, when an ASP.NET page is modified, it is recompiled upon the next access, resulting in a new assembly being loaded in the AppDomain. The number of recompiles allowed is not unlimited and is controlled by the *numRecompilesBeforeAppRestart* attribute in the *<compilation>* section of the configuration file. When the maximum number of recompiles is exceeded, the application just restarts.

Unexpected Restarts

Aside from all these reasons, an application pool can recycle because of unhandled exceptions, timeouts, low memory, or threads or connection pool issues. In general, the worker process recycling is a defensive measure aimed at keeping the application in shape and preventing any worse troubles. An application restart is not free of issues because it causes the user's session to disappear, for example; however, that is probably the lesser evil compared to having a site that hangs or crashes.

An application restart is not something you can spot easily. It manifests through diminished and periodical responsiveness of the site. Diagnosing the cause is usually hard. When you suspect undue process recycling, the first place to look is in the event viewer to see whether some interesting information is being tracked. Memory usage is another good successive area to investigate.

In IIS 7.x, you can use the settings shown in Figure 2-19 to determine which event log entries you want to be generated in the case of process recycling events.

FIGURE 2-19 Setting up event log entries for process recycling.

To make sure you track effective termination of the application, or to handle that in a customized way, you can resort to using the following code, adapted from an old but very nice post by Scott Guthrie:

```
public static class HttpApplicationExtensions
{
    public static void TrackAppShutdown(this HttpApplication theApp)
    {
        // Use reflection to grab the current instance of the HttpRuntime object
        var runtime = typeof(HttpRuntime).InvokeMember("_theRuntime",
                BindingFlags.NonPublic | BindingFlags.Static | BindingFlags.GetField,
                null, null, null);
        if (runtime == null) return;

        // Use reflection to grab the current value of an internal property explaining the
        // reason for the application shutdown
        var messageShutdown = runtime.GetType().InvokeMember("_shutDownMessage",
                BindingFlags.NonPublic | BindingFlags.Instance | BindingFlags.GetField,
                null, runtime, null);

        // Log an entry in the event viewer (or elsewhere ...)
        if (!EventLog.SourceExists("YourApp"))
            EventLog.CreateEventSource("YourApp", "Application");
        var log = new EventLog { Source = "YourApp" };
        log.WriteEntry(messageShutdown, EventLogEntryType.Error);
    }
}
```

Written as an extension method for the *HttpApplication* object, the method can be invoked easily from the *Application_End* handler in *global.asax*, as shown here:

```
void Application_End(object sender, EventArgs e)
{
    this.TrackAppShutdown();
}
```

The result is an entry written in the application log for each restart. It's not a magic wand, but it's a nice extension you can incorporate into all applications or just in case of problems.

Output Caching Settings

Devised in the context of earlier versions of ASP.NET, output caching in IIS 7 is a fully fledged feature of the Web server. Output caching refers to caching for performance reasons some of the semi-dynamic content served by the Web server. Semi-dynamic content is any content that partially changes from request to request. It is the opposite of static content, such as JPEG images or HTML pages, and also different from classic ASP.NET pages that need to be entirely regenerated for every request.

The whole point of output caching is skipping the processing of a given ASP.NET page for a number of seconds. For each interval, the first request is served as usual; however, its response is cached at the IIS level so that successive requests for the same resource that could be placed in the interval are served as if they were for some static content. When the interval expires, the first incoming request will be served by processing the page as usual but caching the response, and so forth. I'll say a lot more about output caching in Chapter 17, "ASP.NET State Management."

When it comes to configuring output caching in IIS, you proceed by first defining the extensions (for example, *aspx*) you intend to cache, and then you have to choose between user-mode and kernel-mode caching. What's the difference?

It all depends on where IIS ends up storing your cached data. If you opt for user-mode caching, any content will be stored in the memory of the IIS worker process. If you go for kernel-mode caching, it is then the *http.sys* driver that holds the cache.

Using the kernel cache gives you a throughput of over ten times the throughput you would get with a user-mode cache. Additionally, the latency of responses is dramatically better. There are some drawbacks too.

Kernel caching is available only for pages requested through a GET verb. This means that no kernel caching is possible on ASP.NET postbacks. Furthermore, pages with semi-dynamic content that needs to be cached based on form values or query string parameters are not stored in the kernel cache. Kernel caching only supports multiple copies of responses based on HTTP headers. Finally, note that ASP.NET Request/Cache performance counters will not be updated for pages served by the kernel cache.

Application Warm-up and Preloading

As mentioned, an ASP.NET application is hosted in an IIS application pool and run by an instance of the IIS worker process. An application pool is started on demand when the first request for the first of the hosted applications arrives. The first request, therefore, sums up different types of delay. There's the delay for the application pool startup; there's the delay for the ASP.NET first-hit dynamic compilation; and finally, the request might experience the time costs of its own initialization. This delay sums up any time the application pool is recycled, or perhaps the entire IIS machine is rebooted.

In IIS 7.5, with the IIS Application Warm-up module (also available as an extension to IIS 7), any initialization of the application pool is performed behind the scenes so that it doesn't add delays for the user. The net effect of the warm-up module is simply to improve the user experience; the same number of system operations is performed with and without warm-up.

Behavior of a Warmed-up Application Pool

You apply the warm-up feature to an application pool. An application pool configured in this way has a slightly different behavior when the whole IIS publishing service is restarted and in the case of process recycling.

In the case of an IIS service restart, any application pools configured for warm-up are started immediately without waiting for the first request to come in, as would the case without warm-up.

When warm-up is enabled, IIS also handles the recycling of the worker process differently. Normally, recycling consists of killing the current instance of the worker process and starting a new one. For the time the whole process takes, however, IIS keeps getting requests; of course, these requests experience some delay. With warm-up enabled, instead, the two operations occur in the reverse order. First a new worker process is started up, and next the old one is killed.

When the new process is up and running, it notifies IIS that it is ready to receive requests. At this point, IIS shuts down the old worker process and completes the recycle in a way that doesn't add hassle for the user.

Setting Up the Application Pool

To configure an application pool for warm-up, you need to edit the *applicationHost.config* file under the IIS directory. The folder is *\inetsrv\config* and is found under the Windows System32 folder. You need to change the value of the *startMode* attribute of the application pool entry from *OnDemand* to *AlwaysRunning*. Here's the final snippet you need to have:

```
<applicationPools>
    <add name="MyAppWorkerProcess"
         managedRuntimeVersion="v4.0"
         startMode="AlwaysRunning" />
</applicationPools>
```

You can achieve the same effect in a much more comfortable way via the IIS Manager user interface, as shown in Figure 2-20.

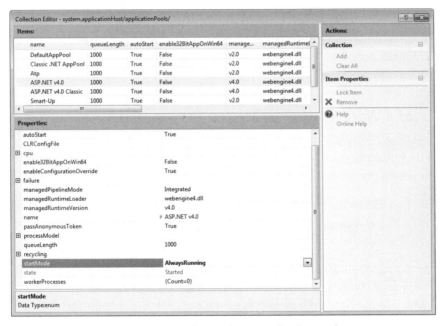

FIGURE 2-20 Activating the warm-up feature for an application pool.

Because an application pool can host multiple ASP.NET applications, you also need to specify which applications the warm-up applies to. You can do that either by entering the following script into the *applicationHost.config* file or by using the IIS Manager interface:

```
<sites>
    <site name="YourApp" serverAutoStart="true" ...>
    ...
</sites>
```

From within IIS Manager, you just navigate to the application and select the Warm-up applet for it.

Note Warm-up is configured at the host level, not the application level. As mentioned, changes are saved to the *applicationHost.config* file, not the *web.config* file. This means that the hoster (including a hosting company) or the administrator decides about the policy and whether or not warm-up is allowed. (In a hosting scenario, that could cause a lot of extra data to be hanging around and, subsequently, a loss of performance.)

Specifying the Warm-up Code

So far, we've configured the application pool for warming up, but we haven't discussed yet the actions to take to actually warm up an application. At the IIS level, all you need to indicate is a URL to your application that runs the warm-up code.

.The Warm-up applet in IIS Manager gives you a dialog box where you enter the URL to the page on your site that will execute the preloading code. You also indicate a range of acceptable HTTP status codes that indicate the success of the operation.

This approach works with both IIS 7 and IIS 7.5.

With IIS 7.5, however, you can define an autostart service provider—namely, a managed component that runs any required preloading code for a given application. Such providers are registered in the IIS configuration using the following new section:

```
<serviceAutoStartProviders>
    <add name="MyPreloader" type="Samples.MyPreloader, MyWebApp" />
    . . .
</serviceAutoStartProviders>
```

There's no visual interface to configure this aspect. You either edit the configuration file manually or resort to the generic configuration editor of IIS Manager. After you have registered a bunch of autostart providers, you can pick up one for a particular application, as shown here:

```
<sites>
    <site name="YourApp" serverAutoStart="true">
        <application serviceAutoStartProvider ="MyPreloader" ... />
    . . .
</sites>
```

An autostart provider is a class designed to execute any initialization or cache-loading logic you want to run before requests are received and processed. Here's an example:

```
using System.Web.Hosting;

public class MyPreloader : IProcessHostPreloadClient
{
    public void Preload(String[] parameters)
    {
        // Perform initialization here...
    }
}
```

When the *Preload* method on the autostart provider returns, IIS sets up the application to receive incoming requests. If the *Preload* method throws an unhandled exception, the worker process is shut down and the whole warm-up feature fails. The result is that the worker process will be activated on demand by the next Web request as in the default scenario.

However, if the preload continues to fail, at some point IIS will mark the application as broken and put it in a stopped state for awhile. (All these parameters are configurable. For more information, refer to *http://www.iis.net/ConfigReference*.)

 Note The warm-up feature is an IIS feature. Autostart providers are an ASP.NET 4 extension that works for any type of ASP.NET applications, including Web Forms applications and ASP.NET MVC applications. Furthermore, warm-up also works for Windows Communication Foundation (WCF) services running under IIS.

Summary

With the release of IIS 7 just a couple of years ago, the ASP.NET platform and the Microsoft Web server platform are finally aligned to the same vision of HTTP request processing. A request that hits the IIS Web server goes through a number of steps—nearly the same set of steps that for years have characterized the ASP.NET runtime environment.

Today, you need to understand the internal mechanics of IIS to optimize deployment and configuration of ASP.NET applications. The great news is that if you know ASP.NET and its runtime machinery, you're more than halfway to understanding and leveraging IIS capabilities.

Put another way, the integration between ASP.NET 4 and IIS 7.x couldn't be tighter and more rewarding for Web application developers. In this chapter, I reviewed the key facts of the internal workings of IIS and ASP.NET when they process a request and discussed some of the features you want to dig out to deploy an application and optimize its behavior in a production environment.

In the next chapter, I'll take a look at some details of the configuration of ASP.NET applications and discuss the schema of configuration files.

Chapter 3
ASP.NET Configuration

Computers are useless. They can only give you answers.

—Pablo Picasso

The .NET Framework defines a tailor-made, XML-based API to access configuration files and, in doing so, forces developers to adopt a common, rich, and predefined schema for storing application settings. In the more general context of the .NET configuration scheme, ASP.NET applications enjoy specific features such as a hierarchical configuration scheme that allows settings inheritance and overriding at various levels: machine, application, or specific directories.

Configuration files are typically created offline or during the development of the application. They are deployed with the application and can be changed at any time by administrators. Changes to such critical files are promptly detected by the ASP.NET runtime, Internet Information Services (IIS), or both, and they typically cause a restart of the worker process. ASP.NET pages can use the classes in the *System.Configuration* namespace to read from, and to write to, configuration files.

In this chapter, I'll specifically delve into the ASP.NET configuration machinery. You'll see how to fine-tune the ASP.NET runtime and review the whole collection of parameters you can set for an individual application.

The ASP.NET Configuration Hierarchy

Configuration files are standard XML files that rigorously follow a given schema. The schema defines all possible settings for machine and application files. Configuration in ASP.NET is hierarchical by nature and is based on a unique, machine-specific file known as the *machine.config* file plus a number of *web.config* files. The syntax of *machine.config* and *web.config* files is identical.

Note ASP.NET protects its configuration files from direct Web access by instructing IIS to block browser access to configuration files. An HTTP access error 403 (forbidden) is returned to all browsers that attempt to request a *.config* resource as a URL. At least, this was considered to be true for a few years. In September 2010, an ASP.NET vulnerability was discovered and fixed by Microsoft via a security patch. You can read about it at *http://weblogs.asp.net/scottgu/ archive/2010/09/18/important-asp-net-security-vulnerability.aspx*. The article includes a link to the patch, which is also available through standard Windows Update channels. Why is that important here? One of the effects of the vulnerability was that it fooled a system HTTP handler to return the content of any file being requested, including *web.config*.

Configuration Files

The ASP.NET runtime processes configuration information hierarchically, proceeding from a root common to all applications on the machine—*machine.config*—down to all the *web.config* files found in the various folders of the particular application.

Note The *machine.config* file is located in the CONFIG directory under the ASP.NET installation folder. The installation folder is located under the Windows directory at the following path: \Microsoft.NET\Framework\[version]\. For the .NET Framework 4, the version folder is *v4.0.30319*. If you take a look at the contents of the CONFIG directory, you'll find three similar files: *machine. config*, *machine.config.default*, and *machine.config.comments*. Provided for educational purposes, the latter two files provide the description and default values of each configuration section. To gain a bit of performance, and a lot of readability, the contents of the *machine.config* file contain only the settings that differ from their defaults.

The Tree of Configuration Files

When an ASP.NET application starts, all configurable parameters are set to the default values defined in *machine.config*. These values can be overridden in the first place by a *web.config* file placed in the root folder of the application. The *web.config* file can also add new application-specific settings. In theory, a root *web.config* file can also clear all the settings in the original machine configuration and replace them altogether. However, in practice it is rare that you would reconfigure ASP.NET for your application to this extreme.

You can also define additional *web.config* files in child folders to apply other settings to all the resources contained in the subtree rooted in the folder. Also in this case, the innermost *web.config* can overwrite, restrict, or extend the settings defined at upper levels. Figure 3-1 illustrates how ASP.NET processes system and application settings for each page in the Web site.

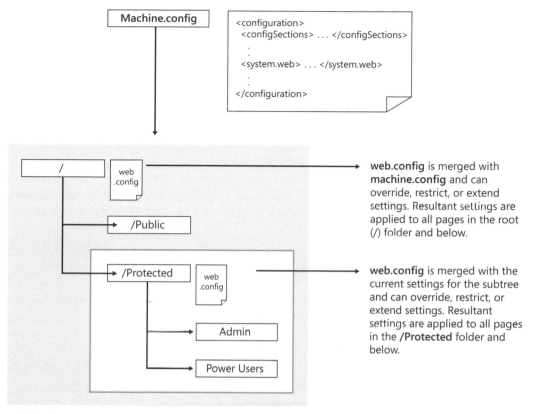

FIGURE 3-1 The hierarchical nature of ASP.NET configuration.

Configuring the machine file is an administrative task and should be performed with the server offline when the application is deployed or during periodical maintenance. Application settings can be changed on the fly administratively or even programmatically. Usually, changes to the application's configuration file result in a process recycling. However, in IIS 7 application pools can be configured to make recycling after a configuration change optional.

Important Only in very special cases should the application write to its *web.config* file. If you need to persist some data on the server (for example, user profile data), you should take advantage of cookies or, better yet, the user profile API or some custom form of storage. The need for writing to a configuration file should be taken as an alarm bell that warns you against possible bad design choices. ASP.NET comes with a set of tailor-made classes, maps all the feasible sections and nodes in the configuration schema, and exposes methods to read and write. The primary role of configuration files is just the overall configuration of the system, namely a set of options that can be changed offline without recompiling the system.

The Configuration Schema

All configuration files have their root in the *<configuration>* element. Table 3-1 lists the main first-level children of the *<configuration>* element. Each node has a specified number of child elements that provide a full description of the setting. For example, the *<system.web>* element optionally contains the *<authorization>* tag, in which you can store information about the users who can safely access the ASP.NET application.

TABLE 3-1 Main Children of the *<configuration>* Element

Element	Description
<appSettings>	Contains custom application settings.
<configSections>	Describes the configuration sections for custom settings. If this element is present, it must be the first child of the *<configuration>* node.
<connectionStrings>	Lists predefined connection strings that are useful to the application.
<configProtectedData>	Contains ciphered data for sections that have been encrypted.
<runtime>	Run-time settings schema; describes the elements that configure assembly binding and run-time behavior such as probing and assembly redirect.
<startup>	Startup settings schema; contains the elements that specify which version of the common language runtime (CLR) must be used.
<system.diagnostics>	Describes the elements that specify trace switches and listeners that collect, store, and route messages.
<system.net>	Network schema; specifies elements to indicate how the .NET Framework connects to the Internet, including the default proxy, authentication modules, and connection parameters.
<system.runtime.remoting>	Settings schema; configures the client and server applications that exploit the .NET Remoting.
<system.serviceModel>	Contains configuration settings for Windows Communication Foundation (WCF) services being used by the ASP.NET application.
<system.web>	The ASP.NET-specific configuration section; it contains the elements that control all aspects of the behavior of an ASP.NET application.
<system.web.extensions>	Contains elements that configure ASP.NET AJAX capabilities and services and control their behavior.
<system.webServer>	Specifies settings for the IIS 7 Web server (and newer versions) that configure the host environment for the ASP.NET application.

Because we're discussing ASP.NET applications, in this chapter I'll focus primarily on the *<system.web>* section, with a look at *<system.webServer>*. I'll cover *<system.web.extensions>* later on in Chapter 20, which is dedicated to AJAX programming. Other sections for which you'll find significant coverage here are *<connectionStrings>* and *<configProtectedData>*. However, this doesn't mean that, as an ASP.NET developer, you'll never be using other sections—most certainly not!

For example, the *<configSections>* element defines the sections that will be used to group information in the rest of the document. The *<appSettings>* element contains user-defined nodes whose structure has been previously defined in the *<configSections>* node. You might need to interact with the *<system.diagnostics>* section if you want to use a custom trace listener that logs its results to an application-defined file.

Another section that is often found in the configuration of ASP.NET applications is *<system.serviceModel>*. The section is used to store settings about WCF services your ASP.NET application is going to use. Settings typically include binding information (transportation, security, credentials) and endpoint details (URL, contract, operations).

Sections and Section Groups

All sections used in a configuration file must be declared in the initial *<configSections>* section. The following code snippet demonstrates how the *<system.web>* section is declared in *machine.config*:

```
<configSections>
    <sectionGroup name="system.web"
            type="System.Web.Configuration.SystemWebSectionGroup, ...">
        <section name="authentication"
            type="System.Web.Configuration.AuthenticationSection, ..."
            allowDefinition="MachineToApplication" />
        ...
    </sectionGroup>
</configSections>
```

The *<sectionGroup>* element has no other role than marking and grouping a few child sections, thus creating a sort of namespace for them. In this way, you can have sections with the same name living under different groups. The *<section>* element takes two attributes: *name* and *type*. The *name* attribute denotes the name of the section being declared. The *type* attribute indicates the name of the managed class that reads and parses the contents of the section from the configuration file. The value of the *type* attribute is a comma-separated string that includes the class and full name of the assembly that contains it.

The *<section>* element also has two optional attributes: *allowDefinition* and *allowLocation*. The *allowDefinition* attribute specifies which configuration files the section can be used in. Feasible values for the *allowDefinition* attribute are listed in Table 3-2.

TABLE 3-2 Values for the *allowDefinition* Attribute

Value	Description
Everywhere	The section can be used in any configuration file. (Default.)
MachineOnly	The section can be used only in the *machine.config* file.
MachineToApplication	The section can be used in the *machine.config* file and in the application's *web.config* file. You cannot use the section in *web.config* files located in subdirectories of the virtual folder.

The *allowLocation* attribute determines whether the section can be used within the *<location>* section. The *<location>* section in a *machine.config* file allows you to apply the specified machine-wide settings only to the resources below a given path. (I'll say more about the *<location>* section shortly.)

Many sections in the configuration files support three special elements, named *<add>*, *<remove>*, and *<clear>*. The *<add>* element adds a new setting to the specified section, while *<remove>* removes the specified one. The *<clear>* element clears all the settings that have previously been defined in the section. The *<remove>* and *<clear>* elements are particularly useful in ASP.NET configuration files in which a hierarchy of files can be created. For example, you can use the *<remove>* element in a child *web.config* file to remove settings that were defined at a higher level in the configuration file hierarchy.

The *<remove>* and *<clear>* elements don't affect the actual data stored in the configuration file. Removing a section doesn't erase the related data from the file, it simply removes the data from the in-memory tree of settings that ASP.NET builds and maintains for an application.

> **Note** Sections are a necessary syntax element in configuration files. However, you don't need to declare sections in all application-specific *web.config* files. When processing a *web.config* file, in fact, ASP.NET builds a configuration tree starting from the root *machine.config* file. Because all standard sections are already declared in the *machine.config* file that ships with the .NET Framework, your application needs to declare only custom sections you plan to use. Finally, bear in mind that an exception is thrown if a configuration section lacks a corresponding entry in the *<configSections>* section and when the layout of the data does not match the declaration.

Let's start our tour of the configuration schema with a closer look at the *<location>* section.

The *<location>* Section

The *<location>* section serves one main purpose in two distinct scenarios. The section provides an alternative technique to apply different settings to various parts of an application. You typically employ the *<location>* section to apply different settings to subdirectories of the same application and to configure distinct applications installed on the same machine.

When defined inside an application's root *web.config* file, it allows you to apply different settings to different subdirectories. Instead of defining child *web.config* files, you can create a single *web.config* file in the root folder and specify settings on a per-directory basis. Basically, the *<location>* element lets you create embedded configuration sections associated with a particular directory. From a functional point of view, this is equivalent to having a *web.config* file in each directory.

When defined inside the *machine.config* file, or in a site's root *web.config* file, the *<location>* section enables you to specify different machine-wide settings for various Web applications. Used in this way, the section turns out to be an extremely powerful tool to let multiple applications apply individual machine-wide settings in an ISP scenario.

> **Important** Note the difference between the application's root *web.config* file and the site's root *web.config* file. The application's root configuration file is the *web.config* file you find in the application's root folder. You use this file to adapt ASP.NET settings to the needs of the particular application and its subdirectories. In contrast, the site's root *web.config* file is located in the same folder as *machine.config*, and therefore is well outside the Web space of any deployed applications. This file is a sort of appendix of *machine.config* and should be used as an additional level of settings personalization. A *<location>* element defined in this file can be scoped to any applications on the machine. A *<location>* element without the path attribute will affect all applications in the machine.

Centralized Configuration

The *<location>* section has two attributes: *Path* and *allowOverride*. The *Path* attribute represents the virtual path to which the embedded settings apply. The following snippet shows how it works. The code shown is taken from a *web.config* file. Note that the name of the folder must be relative and should not begin with slashes, backslashes, or dots.

```
<configuration>
    <system.web>
        <!-- Settings for the application go here -->
    </system.web>

    <location path="Reserved">
        <system.web>
            <!-- Settings for the /Reserved folder go here -->
        </system.web>
    </location>
</configuration>
```

The defining characteristic of this approach is that you have a single, centralized *web.config* file to maintain and can still configure subdirectories individually and independently. This feature saves you from the burden of maintaining several *web.config* files, but it also introduces some unpleasant side effects that in the long run can turn out to be quite harsh. For example, any change to the file results in a new compilation for all the pages in the application. If you maintain distinct *web.config* files, the compilation occurs only for the pages really affected by the change.

> **Note** If the path attribute is omitted in the *<location>* element, the embedded settings will apply to all subfolders of the application in the case of an application's root *web.config*. Settings will affect all installed applications on the server machine if the *<location>* element that is missing the path attribute is found in the site's root *web.config* or *machine.config*.

Machinewide Settings

Used within the *machine.config* file or the site's root *web.config* file, the *<location>* element lets you specify different machinewide settings for all the Web applications hosted on the server machine. Note that in this case, though, you must indicate the name of the application you're configuring prefixed by the IIS name of the Web site. The Web site name is read in the IIS Manager. The following script applies to the *YourApp* application in the default Web site:

```
<location path="Default Web Site/YourApp">
    <system.web>
        <!-- Settings for the Web site go here -->
    </system.web>
</location>
```

When you develop the ASP.NET code, you typically test it on a development machine with its own copies of *machine.config* and site *web.config* files. When you deploy the application on a production box, especially in an ISP scenario, you might not be able to restore the same settings. One possible reason is that the administrator does not want you to modify the current settings because they work well for all other applications or because of security concerns.

You can work around the issue by simply replicating any needed global settings into the application's root *web.config*. If you are deploying your code to a service provider, you might find that many configuration elements have been locked down and cannot be overridden. (I'll say more about this aspect in a moment.) In this case, a new application-specific *<location>* section created in *machine.config* or the site's *web.config* can contain all the machine settings needed for your application without breaking others.

Whenever possible, though, you should try to replicate needed changes into the application's *web.config*. This should always be the first option considered because it makes the entire application self-contained.

Unmodifiable Settings

The second *<location>* attribute you can specify—*allowOverride*—allows you to lock some settings at either the machine or application level. By grouping settings in a *<location>* element with the *allowOverride* attribute set to *false*, you tell the ASP.NET configuration system to raise an exception whenever a protected setting is overridden in a lower-level configuration file.

```
<location path="Default Web Site/YourApp" allowOverride="false">
    <system.web>
        <!-- These settings cannot be overridden -->
    </system.web>
</location>
```

The ultimate goal of this feature is to enable administrators to control the settings of a server that provides ASP.NET hosting. When a new application is installed in production, changes might be required on the target machine to reflect the native environment of the application. Updating the *machine.config* file on the production machine is not an issue as long as yours is the only application running or if you can directly control and configure all the applications hosted on that machine. However, in an application-hosting scenario, the administrator might decide to lock some machine settings to prevent installed applications from modifying them. In this way, the administrator can preserve, to the extent possible, the integrity of the hosting environment and guarantee that all applications run under the same conditions.

> **Note** By default, nearly all predefined sections can appear within a *<location>* section. In general, sections can be disallowed from appearing in *<location>* by using the *allowLocation* attribute. The *allowLocation* attribute of the *<section>* element determines the section's capability of being customized for a particular path. Set it to *false*, and the section is not allowed to be used within a *<location>* section.

The *<system.web>* Section

The *<system.web>* section contains all the configuration elements that set up the ASP.NET runtime environment and controls how ASP.NET applications behave. Table 3-3 lists the entire sequence of first-level elements and their override level.

TABLE 3-3 **The Full List of Important Sections Allowed Within *<system.web>***

Section	Overridable	Description
<anonymousIdentification>	Machine, application	Configures identification for users that are not authenticated.
<authentication>	Machine, application	Sets the authentication mechanism.
<authorization>	Everywhere	Indicates authorized users.
<browserCaps>	Everywhere	Lists known browser capabilities.
<clientTarget>	Everywhere	Lists predefined client targets.
<compilation>	Everywhere	Settings for batch compilation.
<customErrors>	Machine, application	Settings for custom error pages.
<deployment>	Machine only	Indicates how the application is deployed.

Section	Overridable	Description
<deviceFilters>	Everywhere	Lists known mobile device capabilities.
<fullTrustAssemblies>	Machine, application	Lists full-trust assemblies for the application.
<globalization>	Everywhere	Settings for application localization.
<healthMonitoring>	Machine, application	Settings to monitor the status of the application.
<hostingEnvironment>	Machine, application	Defines configuration settings that control the behavior of the application hosting environment.
<httpCookies>	Everywhere	Configures properties for cookies used by an ASP.NET application.
<httpHandlers>	Everywhere	Lists registered HTTP handlers.
<httpModules>	Everywhere	Lists registered HTTP modules.
<httpRuntime>	Everywhere	Lists HTTP runtime settings.
<identity>	Everywhere	Sets impersonation.
<machineKey>	Machine, application	Encryption key for sensitive data.
<mobileControls>	Everywhere	Configures the behavior of mobile controls. *In ASP.NET 4.0, mobile controls are deprecated.*
<membership>	Machine, application	Defines settings for user authentication via ASP.NET membership.
<pages>	Everywhere	Controls features of ASP.NET pages.
<partialTrustVisibleAssemblies>	Machine, application	Lists partial-trust visible assemblies for the application
<processModel>	MachineOnly	Configures the process model.
<profile>	Machine, application	Defines settings for user profile's data model.
<roleManager>	Machine, application	Defines settings for role management.
<securityPolicy>	Machine, application	Defines allowed trust levels.
<sessionPageState>	Everywhere	Defines page view-state settings for mobile controls.
<sessionState>	Machine, application	Configures the *Session* object.
<siteMap>	Machine, application	Defines settings used to support the navigation infrastructure.
<trace>	Everywhere	Configures the tracing system.
<trust>	Machine, application	Defines the default trust level.

Section	Overridable	Description
<urlMappings>	Machine, application	Defines routes mapping a requested URL to a real page.
<webControls>	Everywhere	Locates client scripts.
<webParts>	Everywhere	Managed Web Parts.
<webServices>	Everywhere	Configures Web services. The Web Services technology is considered obsolete, as is this section.
<xhtmlConformance>	Everywhere	Defines settings for XHTML conformance.

Each of the elements listed in Table 3-3 features its own schema and provides attributes and enumerations to pick values from.

In addition to the sections listed in Table 3-3, the *<system.web>* group contains a subgroup named *<Caching>*. Table 3-4 lists the child elements.

TABLE 3-4 Sections Allowed Within *<Caching>*

Section	Overridable	Description
<cache>	Machine, application	Configures the global cache settings for an ASP.NET application.
<outputCache>	Machine, application	Configures the output cache for a Web application.
<outputCacheSettings>	Machine, application	Defines caching profiles.
<sqlCacheDependency>	Machine, application	Configures the SQL cache dependencies for an ASP.NET application.

Let's examine some of the aforementioned sections in a bit more detail. For a complete reference, though, you might want to check out the excellent MSDN online documentation starting at *http://msdn.microsoft.com/en-us/library/b5ysx397.aspx.*

The *<anonymousIdentification>* Section

Anonymous identification is a feature that assigns a predefined identity to users who connect anonymously to an application. Anonymous identification has nothing to do with the anonymous user you can set at the IIS level, nor does it affect the authentication mechanism of ASP.NET. The feature is designed to work with the user profile API to simplify the way you write code in scenarios where both authenticated and unauthenticated users can use the site.

The *<anonymousIdentification>* section allows you to configure how it works. Here's the overall schema of the section:

```
<anonymousIdentification
    enabled="[true | false]"
    cookieless="[UseUri | UseCookies | AutoDetect | UseDeviceProfile]"
    cookieName=""
    cookiePath=""
    cookieProtection="[None | Validation | Encryption | All]"
    cookieRequireSSL="[true | false]"
    cookieSlidingExpiration="[true | false]"
    cookieTimeout="[DD.HH:MM:SS]"
    domain="cookie domain"
/>
```

Basically, anonymous identification creates a cookied or cookieless ticket and associates it with the ongoing request. The enabled attribute turns the feature on and off; the *cookieless* attribute instructs the ASP.NET runtime about cookie usage. Table 3-5 illustrates the options for the *cookieless* attribute.

TABLE 3-5 **Options for the *cookieless* Attribute**

Value	Description
AutoDetect	Uses cookies if the browser has cookie support currently enabled. It uses the cookieless mechanism otherwise.
UseCookie	Always uses cookies, regardless of the browser capabilities.
UseDeviceProfile	Uses cookies if the browser supports them, and uses the cookieless mechanism otherwise. When this option is used, no attempt is made to check whether cookie support is really enabled for the requesting device. This is the default option.
UseUri	Never uses cookies, regardless of the browser capabilities.

All other attributes relate to the cookie, if one gets created. You can set its name—the default name is .ASPXANONYMOUS—as well as its path, domain, protection, expiration, and timeout. You can also indicate whether Secure Sockets Layer (SSL) should be used to transmit the cookie.

The *<authentication>* Section

The *<authentication>* section allows you to configure a Web site for various types of user authentication, including Forms authentication as well as Passport and IIS-driven authentication. This section has two mutually exclusive subsections—*<forms>* and *<passport>*—and the *mode* attribute to control the authentication mode requested by an application. Allowable values for the *mode* attribute are shown in Table 3-6.

TABLE 3-6 Supported Authentication Modes

Value	Description
Forms	Makes use of a custom form to collect logon information.
Passport	Exploits the authentication services of Microsoft Passport (now LiveID). *In ASP.NET 4, classes dealing with Passport authentication are marked obsolete.*
None	Indicates ASP.NET should not enforce any type of authentication, which means only anonymous users can connect or the application itself provides a built-in mechanism.
Windows	Exploits any authentication services of IIS—basic, digest, NTLM\Kerberos, or certificates. This is the default mode.

When using Forms authentication, you are allowed to specify a few additional parameters, such as name, *loginURL*, *protection*, and *cookieless*. Table 3-7 lists the attributes of the *<forms>* element.

TABLE 3-7 Attributes of the <forms> Element

Attribute	Description
cookieless	Defines whether and how cookies are used for authentication tickets. Feasible values are the same as those listed in Table 3-5.
defaultUrl	Defines the URL to redirect after authentication. The default is *default. aspx*.
domain	Specifies a domain name to be set on outgoing authentication cookies.
enableCrossAppRedirects	Indicates whether users can be authenticated by external applications when authentication is cookieless. The setting is ignored if cookies are enabled. When cookies are enabled, cross-application authentication is always possible.
loginUrl	Specifies the URL to which the request is redirected for login if no valid authentication cookie is found.
name	Specifies the name of the HTTP cookie to use for authentication. The default name is .ASPXAUTH.
path	Specifies the path for the authentication cookies issued by the application. The default value is a slash (/). Note that some browsers are case-sensitive and will not send cookies back if there is a path case mismatch.
protection	Indicates how the application intends to protect the authentication cookie. Feasible values are *All*, *Encryption*, *Validation*, and *None*. The default is *All*.
requireSSL	Indicates whether an SSL connection is required to transmit the authentication cookie. The default is *false*. If *true*, ASP.NET sets the *Secure* property on the authentication cookie object so that a compliant browser does not return the cookie unless the connection is using SSL.
slidingExpiration	Indicates whether sliding expiration is enabled. The default is *false*, meaning that the cookie expires at a set interval from the time it was originally issued. The interval is determined by the timeout attribute.
timeout	Specifies the amount of time, in minutes, after which the authentication cookie expires. The default value is 30.

Note that the description of cookie-related attributes in Table 3-7 works also for similar attributes in the *<anonymousIdentification>* section.

I'll return to authentication and security in Chapter 19, "ASP.NET Security." In particular, in that chapter you'll discover various flavors of Forms authentication that, although described as custom types of Forms authentication, are gaining wide acceptance in real-world applications. Two examples are OpenID and claims-based Windows Identity Foundation (WIF).

Overall, when it comes to providing authentication for an ASP.NET application, the primary choice is Forms authentication, including when it's in the form of OpenID implementations such as dotnetOpenAuth. Windows authentication and Passport are seldom used today even though both, especially Windows authentication, still serve the needs of a particular segment of applications. An emerging approach is based on Windows Identity Foundation (WIF). With a WIF integrated with Web Forms, the user navigates to inside the application and then, when authentication is required, the user is redirected to the configured Security Token Service (STS), logs in there, and is then redirected back to the application with his own set of claims. (I'll return to WIF in Chapter 19.)

The *<authorization>* Section

The *<authorization>* section is used to define a declarative filter to control access to the resources of the application. The *<authorization>* section contains two subsections, named *<allow>* and *<deny>*, that can be used to allow and deny access to users. Both elements feature three attributes—*users*, *roles*, and *verbs*—filled with a comma-separated list of names, as the following code demonstrates:

```
<authorization>
    <allow users="comma-separated list of users"
           roles="comma-separated list of roles"
           verbs="comma-separated list of verbs" />
    <deny users="comma-separated list of users"
          roles="comma-separated list of roles"
          verbs="comma-separated list of verbs" />
</authorization>
```

The *<allow>* element authorizes access to any user whose name appears in the list—that is, to all users with any of the specified roles. Authorized users can execute only the HTTP verbs (for example, POST and GET) indicated by the *verbs* attribute.

Conversely, the *<deny>* element prohibits listed users from executing the specified actions. The default setting allows all users free access to the resources of the application. When specifying the user name, a couple of shortcuts are allowed. The asterisk (*) means "all users," whereas the question mark (?) stands for the "anonymous user."

> **Important** The *<authorization>* section is all about declarative authorization. It uses a fixed syntax to feed authorization modules (*UrlAuthorization* and *FileAuthorizationModule*) and have them block unauthorized users as they try to access a URL or a file. Most applications, instead, prefer to incorporate authorization within their business layer in a fluent way. In doing so, applications associate users with roles and check roles before proceeding with any critical operations. For this approach, you don't need the *<authorization>* section. The section, however, remains quite useful for relatively simple scenarios when you just want to limit access to a specific subset of users or protect the entire content of pages in a given area of the application. (See Chapter 19.)

The *<browserCaps>* Section

The *<browserCaps>* section enumerates the characteristics and capabilities of the supported browsers, including mobile devices. The *<browserCaps>* section is tightly coupled with the *HttpBrowserCapabilities* class and *MobileCapabilities*, which allows the ASP.NET runtime to gather technical information about the browser that is running on the client.

So ASP.NET supports the concept of browser capabilities and gives you a chance to check them and build your applications accordingly. You use any browser information available through the *Browser* property of the intrinsic *Request* object. The point is, where would ASP.NET find information to feed the *Browser* property?

Internally, the *Request* object first looks at the user-agent information that comes with the HTTP request and then matches this information to some sort of provider. The internal structure of the browser provider has evolved quite significantly lately and especially in ASP.NET 4.

In the beginning, the *<browserCaps>* section was the only repository for browser information. Under the *<browserCaps>* section, you find a number of commercial browsers described in terms of their run-time capabilities, such as cookies, tables and frames support, accepted script languages, XML DOM, and operating system. The element can be declared at any level in the application, thus making it possible for you to enable certain levels of browser support for certain applications. The list of available browsers can be updated as required to detect future browsers and browser capabilities. The use of the *<browserCaps>* element to define browsers was deprecated already in ASP.NET 2.0. It is, however, fully supported still today.

An alternate approach to using *<browserCaps>* is reading browser information from matching files with a *.browser* extension located in the folder *Microsoft.NET\framework\ [version]\config\browsers*. Figure 3-2 shows the default content of the folder for a site equipped with ASP.NET 4.

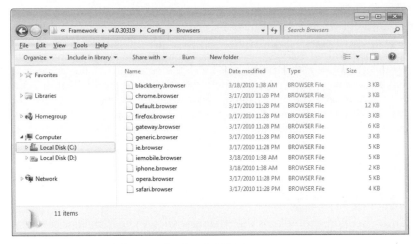

FIGURE 3-2 The list of *.browser* files in ASP.NET 4.

In ASP.NET 4, yet another approach is supported to provide browser capabilities—browser providers. In a nutshell, a *browser provider* is a class you register with the application using the classic provider model, as shown in the following code snippet, or using a line of code in *global.asax*:

```
<system.web>
  <browserCaps provider="Samples.CustomProvider, Samples" />
</system.web>
```

The browser provider usually derives from the system-provided base class *HttpCapabilitiesProvider* and extends it by overriding some methods.

The *<caching>* Section

The *<caching>* section configures the cache settings for an ASP.NET application. It consists of four child sections: *cache*, *outputCache*, *outputCacheSettings*, and *sqlCacheDependency*.

The *<cache>* section defines a few application-wide settings that relate to caching. For example, the *percentagePhysicalMemoryUsedLimit* and *privateBytesLimit* attributes indicate the maximum size of memory (percentage and bytes) that can be occupied before the cache starts flushing expired items and attempting to reclaim memory. Here's the schema of the section with default values:

```
<cache disableMemoryCollection = "false"
    disableExpiration = "false"
    privateBytesLimit = "0"
    percentagePhysicalMemoryUsedLimit = "89"
    privateBytesPollTime = "00:02:00" />
```

The default time interval between polling for the memory usage is 2 minutes. Note that by setting the *disableExpiration* attribute you can disable the automatic scavenging of expired cache items—the most defining trait of ASP.NET cache.

The *<outputCache>* section takes care of output caching. Here is the schema of the section with default values:

```
<outputCache defaultProvider="AspNetInternalProvider"
    enableOutputCache = "true"
    enableKernelCacheForVaryByStar = "false"
    enableFragmentCache = "true"
    sendCacheControlHeader = "true"
    omitVaryStar = "false">
</outputCache>
```

If output or fragment caching is disabled in the configuration file, no pages or user controls are cached regardless of the programmatic settings. The *sendCacheControlHeader* attribute indicates whether the *cache-control:private* header is sent by the output cache module by default. Similarly, the *omitVaryStar* attribute enables or disables sending an *HTTP Vary: ** header in the response. The *enableKernelCacheForVaryByStar* attribute controls whether kernel caching is enabled or not. You should note that kernel caching is supported only for compressed responses. This means that regardless of the attribute's value, kernel caching won't work any time the client requests an uncompressed response.

The *defaultProvider* attribute indicates the component that takes care of storing and serving the cached output. The default provider is based on the same code that powered output caching in earlier versions of ASP.NET. The store is the in-memory cache. By writing your own provider, you can change the storage of the output cache. Note that the *AspNetInternalProvider* provider name doesn't really match any class in the *system.web* assembly. It is simply a moniker that instructs the system to go with the built-in logic that worked for any previous versions of ASP.NET. The framework offers a new abstract class—*OutputCacheProvider*—that represents your starting point on the way to building custom output cache providers.

The *<outputCacheSettings>* section contains groups of cache settings that can be applied to pages through the *@OutputCache* directive. The section contains only one child section, named *<outputCacheProfiles>*. An output cache profile is simply a way of referencing multiple settings with a single name. Here's an example:

```
<outputCacheSettings>
  <outputCacheProfiles>
    <add name="ServerOnly"
      duration="60"
      varyByCustom="browser" />
  </outputCacheProfiles>
</outputCacheSettings>
```

In the example, the *ServerOnly* profile defines a cache duration of 60 seconds and stores different versions of the page based on browser type. Here is the schema of *<outputCacheProfiles>*:

```
<outputCacheProfiles>
    <add name = ""
        enabled = "true"
        duration = "-1"
        location = ""
        sqlDependency = ""
        varyByCustom = ""
        varyByControl = ""
        varyByHeader = ""
        varyByParam = ""
        noStore = "false"/>
</outputCacheProfiles>
```

A database dependency is a special case of custom dependency that consists of the automatic invalidation of some cached data when the contents of the source database table changes. In ASP.NET, this feature is implemented through the *SqlCacheDependency* class. The *<sqlCacheDependency>* section defines the settings used by the *SqlCacheDependency* class when using database caching and table-based polling against versions of Microsoft SQL Server equal or newer than version 7.

```
<sqlCacheDependency enabled="true" pollTime="1000">
    <databases>
        <add name="Northwind" connectionStringName="LocalNWind" />
    </databases>
</sqlCacheDependency>
```

The *pollTime* attribute indicates (in milliseconds) the interval of the polling. In the preceding sample, any monitored table will be checked every second. Under the *<databases>* node, you find a reference to monitored databases. The name attribute is used only to name the dependency. The *connectionStringName* attribute points to an entry in the *<connectionStrings>* section of the *web.config* file and denotes the connection string to access the database. Which tables in the listed databases will really be monitored depends on the effects produced by another tool—*aspnet_regsql.exe*. I'll return to this form of caching in Chapter 18, "ASP.NET Caching."

Any values stored in the *<sqlCacheDependency>* section have no effect when using *SqlCacheDependency* in conjunction with query notifications on SQL Server 2005 and newer versions.

The *<customErrors>* Section

The *<customErrors>* section specifies the error-handling policy for an ASP.NET application. By default, when an error occurs on a page, the local host sees the detailed ASP.NET error page, while remote clients are shown a custom error page or a generic page if no custom page is specified. This policy is controlled through the *Mode* attribute.

The *Mode* attribute can be set to *On*, *Off*, or *RemoteOnly*, which is the default. If it's set to *On*, custom error pages are displayed both locally and remotely; if it's set to *Off*, no special error-handling mechanism is active and all users receive the typical ASP.NET (yellow) error page with the original runtime's or compiler's error message and the stack trace.

Custom error pages can be specified in two ways. You can provide a generic error page as well as error-specific pages. A custom error page that is not error-specific can be set through the *defaultRedirect* attribute of the *<customErrors>* element. This setting is ignored if the mode is *Off*.

```
<customErrors defaultRedirect="Errors/appGenericError.aspx" mode="On">
    <error statusCode="404" redirect="Errors/notfound.aspx" />
    <error statusCode="500" redirect="Errors/internal.aspx" />
</customErrors>
```

The *<customErrors>* section supports a repeatable child *<error>* tag that is used to associate a custom page with a particular error code. You should note that only certain status codes are supported. Some error codes, such as 403, might come directly from IIS and never get to ASP.NET.

The *<error>* tag has two optional attributes, *redirect* and *statusCode*. The *redirect* attribute points to the URL of the page, whereas the *statusCode* specifies the HTTP status code that will result in an error. If the custom mode is enabled, but no error-specific page is known, the default redirect is used. If the custom mode is enabled, but no custom page is specified, the ASP.NET generic error page is used.

> **Important** The aforementioned ASP.NET vulnerability discovered in September 2010 brought about a best practice as far ASP.NET security is concerned. You are now discouraged from using any *<error>* element to return an error-specific page. By examining the error code, in fact, the attacker could learn enough to compromise your system. The recommended approach is setting the *Mode* attribute to *On* and to have all errors handled by the same error page, which is set through the *defaultRedirect* attribute. The content of the default error page is not relevant; what matters is that you don't provide means to potential attackers to distinguish between types of responses.

The *<deployment>* Section

The *<deployment>* section indicates the deployment mode of the application and has only one Boolean attribute, named *retail*. The attribute indicates whether the application is intended to be deployed for production (*retail* equals *true*) or test (*retail* equals *false*).

```
<deployment retail="true" />
```

When *retail* is set to *true*, ASP.NET automatically disables certain configuration settings, such as trace output, custom errors, and debug capabilities. When the default value of *retail* is *false*, each application is automatically deployed for testing.

The *<globalization>* Section

The *<globalization>* section configures the globalization settings of ASP.NET applications so that requests and responses take into account encoding and culture information. The attributes of the *<globalization>* section are shown in Table 3-8.

TABLE 3-8 Globalization Attributes

Attribute	Description
culture	Specifies the culture to be used to process requests.
fileEncoding	Specifies the encoding for ASP.NET resource files (.aspx, .asmx, and .asax). Unicode and UTF-8 files saved with the byte order mark prefix are recognized regardless of the value of the attribute.
requestEncoding	Specifies the assumed encoding of each request, including posted data and the query string. The default is UTF-8.
responseEncoding	Specifies the content encoding of responses. The default is UTF-8.
uiCulture	Specifies the culture name to be used to look up locale-dependent resources at run time.

Note that, if specified, the *Accept-Charset* attribute in the request overrides the default *requestEncoding* setting. If you remove any encoding setting from the configuration files, ASP.NET defaults to the server's locale. In the majority of cases, *requestEncoding* and *responseEncoding* have the same value.

Valid names for the *culture* and *uiCulture* attributes are non-neutral culture names such as *en-US*, *en-AU*, and *it-IT*. A culture name is made of two elements—the language and country/region—and both are to be specified in this context.

The *<httpHandlers>* Section

The section allows you to register application-specific HTTP handlers that take care of ad hoc URLs invoked over given HTTP verbs. I'll dissect the syntax and usage of the *<httpHandlers>* section in the next chapter.

The *<httpModules>* Section

The *<httpModules>* section allows you to register application-specific HTTP modules that take care of hooking up specific stages during the processing of an ASP.NET request. I'll dissect the syntax and usage of the *<httpModules>* section in the next chapter.

The *<healthMonitoring>* Section

Health monitoring is a system feature that allows the production staff to monitor the status of a deployed application and track significant events related to performance, failures, and anomalies. The ASP.NET health monitoring system works by firing events to providers. The event contains actual information about what happened; the provider processes the information. Here is the overall schema:

```
<healthMonitoring
    enabled="true|false"
    heartbeatInterval="HH:MM:SS">
    <bufferModes>...</bufferModes>
    <providers>...</providers>
    <eventMappings>...</eventMappings>
    <profiles>...</profiles>
    <rules>...</rules>
</healthMonitoring>
```

The *enabled* attribute specifies whether health monitoring is enabled. It is *true* by default. The *heartbeatInterval* attribute indicates how often the heartbeat event is raised. The heartbeat event serves as a timer for the whole subsystem and is raised at regular intervals to capture useful runtime state information. The heartbeat is just one of the events that the health monitoring system can detect. Other events track unhandled exceptions, request processing, application lifetime, and the success and failure audits. Child sections, listed in Table 3-9, let you configure the whole subsystem.

TABLE 3-9 Elements for Health Monitoring

Element	Description
bufferModes	Used with Microsoft SQL Server and Web event providers (with built-in e-mail capability) to determine how often to flush the various events to the provider and the size of the intermediate buffer.
eventMappings	Maps friendly event names to the event classes. You use this element to register custom event types.
profiles	Defines parameter sets to use when configuring events.
providers	Defines the health monitoring providers that process events. Predefined providers write to a SQL Server table and the Event Log, and they send e-mail. You use this element to register custom Web event providers.
rules	Maps events to providers.

The interval for the heartbeat event is set to 0 by default, meaning that no heartbeat event is raised by default.

The *<hostingEnvironment>* Section

The *<hostingEnvironment>* section defines configuration settings that control the behavior of the application-hosting environment. As you can see in the following code segment, the section has three attributes: *idleTimeout*, *shadowCopyBinAssemblies*, and *shutdownTimeout*:

```
<hostingEnvironment idleTimeout="HH:MM:SS"
                    shadowCopyBinAssemblies="true|false"
                    shutdownTimeout="number"
                    urlMetadataSlidingExpiration="HH:MM:SS" />
```

The *idleTimeout* attribute sets the amount of time to wait before unloading an inactive application. It is set to *Infinite* by default, meaning that inactive applications are not automatically unloaded. Note also that "inactive" doesn't mean nonresponsive; an application is inactive if no user is working with it, and this is normally not by itself a good reason to kill it. The *shadowCopyBinAssemblies* attribute indicates whether the assemblies of an application in the *Bin* directory are shadow-copied to the application's ASP.NET temporary files directory. It is *true* by default. Finally, the *shutdownTimeout* attribute sets the number of seconds (30 by default) it should take to shut down the application. Finally, the *urlMetadataSlidingExpiration* attribute indicates for how long the URL metadata will be cached by ASP.NET. The default is 1 minute. Both *idleTimeout* and *urlMetadataSlidingExpiration* attributes can be set to any time span, ranging from seconds to minutes and hours.

> **Note** Shadow-copy is a feature of the .NET Framework that ASP.NET uses extensively. When shadow-copy is enabled on an AppDomain, assemblies loaded in that AppDomain will be copied to an internal cache directory and used from there. In this way, the original file is not locked and can be changed at will. In ASP.NET, you can control the feature through the *shadowCopyBinAssemblies* attribute.

The *<httpCookies>* Section

The *<httpCookies>* section is used to configure properties for cookies used by ASP.NET applications. Here is the overall schema:

```
<httpCookies domain="string"
             httpOnlyCookies="true|false"
             requireSSL="true|false" />
```

The *domain* attribute indicates the default Internet domain of the cookie and is set to the empty string by default. The *requireSSL* attribute is *false* by default. If it's *true*, SSL is required for all cookies. The *httpOnlyCookies* attribute enables ASP.NET to output an extra *HttpOnly* cookie attribute that can help mitigate cross-site scripting threats that result in stolen cookies. When a cookie that has the *HttpOnly* attribute set to *true* is received by a compliant browser such as Internet Explorer 6 SP1 (and superior), it is inaccessible to client-side script.

Adding the *HttpOnly* attribute is as easy as appending the *HttpOnly* string to the path of all response cookies.

> **Caution** The *HttpOnly* attribute is helpful when it comes to raising the security bar, but it is not a silver bullet. Any network monitoring tool, in fact, can easily detect it, thus giving malicious users an important bit of help.

Finally, note that any settings defined in the *<httpCookies>* section can be overridden by classes that actually create cookies in ASP.NET pages.

The *<httpRuntime>* Section

The *<httpRuntime>* section configures some run-time parameters for the ASP.NET pipeline. Interestingly enough, the section can be declared at any level, including subdirectory levels. This fact accounts for the great flexibility that allows you to set up the run-time environment with the finest granularity. Configurable attributes are listed in Table 3-10.

TABLE 3-10 ASP.NET Runtime Attributes

Attribute	Description
apartmentThreading	Enables apartment threading for classic ASP compatibility. The default is *false*.
appRequestQueueLimit	Specifies the maximum number of requests the application is allowed to queue before returning error 503—Server too busy. The default is 5000.
delayNotificationTimeout	Specifies the timeout for delaying notifications. The default is 5 seconds.
Enable	Specifies whether the AppDomain is enabled to accept incoming requests. This is *true* by default.
enableHeaderChecking	Specifies whether ASP.NET should check the request header for potential injection attacks. If an attack is detected, ASP.NET responds with an error. This is *true* by default.
enableKernelOutputCache	Enables the *http.sys* kernel-level cache on IIS 6 and higher. The default is *true*.
enableVersionHeader	Outputs a header with the ASP.NET version with each request. The default is *true*. You can disable it for production sites.
encoderType	Indicates the class to be used for any encoding and decoding tasks in ASP.NET, such as those performed by *HttpServerUtility*.
executionTimeout	Specifies the maximum number of seconds a request is allowed to execute before ASP.NET automatically times it out. The default is 110 seconds.
maxQueryStringLength	Indicates the maximum accepted size of the query string. The default is 260.

Attribute	Description
maxRequestLength	Indicates the maximum accepted size (in KB) of a Web request. No request is accepted if its overall length exceeds the threshold of 4 MB.
maxUrlLength	Indicates the maximum accepted size of the URL. The default is 260.
minLocalRequestFreeThreads	Indicates the minimum number of free threads needed to allow the execution of new local requests. The default threshold value is set to 4.
minFreeThreads	Indicates the minimum number of free threads needed to allow the execution of new Web requests. The default threshold value is set to 8.
requestLengthDiskThreshold	Specifies the input stream buffering threshold limit in number of bytes. Its value should not exceed the *maxRequestLength*. The default is 256 bytes.
requireRootedSaveAsPath	Specifies whether the file name parameter in a *Request*'s *SaveAs* method must be an absolute path.
requestValidationMode	Indicates whether HTTP request validation can be customized (only in ASP.NET 4) or whether it should happen through a system-provided layer (as in earlier versions). The default value is "4.0". Anything else is considered as "do as ASP.NET 2.0 does."
requestValidationType	Indicates the name of a type that is used to validate HTTP requests.
sendCacheControlHeader	Specifies whether to send a cache control header.
shutDownTimeout	Number of seconds that are allowed for the worker process to shut down. When the timeout expires, ASP.NET shuts down the worker process. The default is 90 seconds.
useFullyQualifiedRedirectUrl	Indicates whether client redirects must be automatically converted to fully qualified URLs (*true*) or used as specified in the page source code (*false*). The default is *false*.
waitChangeNotification, max-WaitChangeNotification	Indicates the minimum and maximum number of seconds to wait (0 by default) before restarting the AppDomain after a file change notification. This is actually pretty important for XCopy deployment, especially with named assemblies in precompiled sites.

Notice that ASP.NET won't process a request if not enough free threads are available in the thread pool. When this happens, the request is queued to the application until the threshold set by the *appRequestQueueLimit* is exceeded. But why, in the default case, does ASP.NET need at least eight free threads to execute a request? These free threads are at the disposal of ongoing requests (for example, the request for a download of linked images, style sheets, or user controls) if they issue child requests to complete processing.

Another small number of threads (four by default) is kept reserved for child requests coming through the local host. If the request has been generated locally—that is, the client IP is 127.0.0.1 or matches the server IP—it is scheduled on one of the threads in the pool reserved for local calls. Often local requests originate as child requests—for example, when an

ASP.NET page invokes a Web service on the same server. There's no need in this case to consume two threads from the pool to serve two related requests, one of which is waiting for the other to terminate. By using an additional thread pool, you actually assign local requests a slightly higher priority and reduce the risk of deadlocks.

The *<identity>* Section

The *<identity>* section controls the identity of the ASP.NET application. It supports three attributes: *impersonate*, *userName*, and *password*. The key attribute is *impersonate*. It is set to *false* by default, which means that the application does not impersonate any client user.

```
<identity impersonate="true" />
```

When impersonate is set to *true*, each request is served by ASP.NET impersonating either the Windows user currently logged on or the user specified through the *userName* and *password* attributes.

Note that user name and password are stored in clear text in the configuration file. Although IIS never serves requests for configuration files, a *web.config* file can be read by other means. You should consider forms of protection for the contents of the section. In ASP.NET, you can encrypt the *<identity>* section using XML Encryption.

The *<machineKey>* Section

Valid at the machine and application levels, the *<machineKey>* section configures the keys to encrypt and decrypt forms authentication tickets and view-state data. Here's the schema:

```
<machineKey
  validationKey="AutoGenerate,IsolateApps"
  decryptionKey="AutoGenerate,IsolateApps"
  validation="HMACSHA256"
  decryption="Auto" />
```

The *validationKey* and *decryptionKey* attributes are strings and specify the encryption and decryption keys, respectively. An encryption key is a sequence of characters whose length ranges from a minimum of 40 characters to a maximum of 128.

The *validation* attribute, on the other hand, indicates the type of encryption used to validate data. Allowable values are SHA1, MD5, 3DES, AES, HMACSHA256 (the default), HMACSHA384, and HMACSHA512.

Finally, the *decryption* attribute indicates the type of hashing algorithm that is used for decrypting data. Feasible values are DES, AES, and 3DES. The default is *Auto*, meaning that ASP.NET determines which decryption algorithm to use based on the configuration default settings.

The default value of both the *validationKey* and *decryptionKey* attributes is *AutoGenerate,IsolateApps*. This means that keys are autogenerated at setup time and stored in the Local Security Authority (LSA). LSA is a protected subsystem of Windows NT–based operating systems that maintains information about all aspects of local security on a system. The *IsolateApps* modifier instructs ASP.NET to generate a key that is unique for each application.

Settings in the *<machineKey>* section are a critical element of applications hosted on multiple machines, such as in a Web farm or a failover cluster. All machines across a network must share the same *<machineKey>* settings. For this reason, you might want to set *validationKey* and *decryptionKey* attributes manually to ensure consistent configuration in a multiserver environment.

The *<membership>* Section

The *<membership>* section defines parameters for managing and authenticating user accounts through the ASP.NET membership API. Here's the schema of the section:

```
<membership
    defaultProvider="provider name"
    userIsOnlineTimeWindow="number of minutes"
    hashAlgorithmType="SHA1">
    <providers>
      ...
    </providers>
</membership>
```

The *defaultProvider* attribute indicates the name of the default membership provider—it is *SqlMembershipProvider* by default. The attribute named *userIsOnlineTimeWindow* specifies how long a user can be idle and still be considered online. The interval is set to 15 minutes by default. The *hashAlgorithmType* refers to the name of the encryption algorithm that is used to hash password values. (The default is SHA1.)

The *<providers>* child section lists all registered membership providers. Here's the schema:

```
<membership>
   <providers>
     <add name="MyProvider"
         type="Samples.MyMembershipProvider"
         connectionStringName="MyConnString"
         enablePasswordRetrieval="false"
         enablePasswordReset="true"
         requiresQuestionAndAnswer="true"
         passwordFormat="Hashed" />
     ...
   </providers>
</membership>
```

You use the *<providers>* section to add custom membership providers. Each provider has its own set of attributes, as shown in the upcoming sections.

The *<pages>* Section

The *<pages>* section sets default values for many of the *@Page* directive attributes and declaratively configures the run-time environment for a Web page. Table 3-11 enumerates the supported attributes.

TABLE 3-11 **Attributes to Configure ASP.NET Pages**

Attribute	Description
asyncTimeout	Number of seconds to wait for an asynchronous handler to complete during asynchronous processing. The default is 45 seconds.
autoEventWireup	Indicates whether page events are automatically assigned to event handlers with a particular name (for example, *Page_Load*). It's set to *true* by default.
buffer	Indicates whether or not response buffering is enabled. It's set to *true* by default.
clientIDMode	Specifies the algorithm to use to generate the client ID for server controls. Feasible values are *AutoID*, *Static*, *Predictable*, and *Inherit*.
compilationMode	Indicates whether an ASP.NET page or control should be compiled at run time. Allowable values are *Never*, *Auto*, and *Always*—the default. *Auto* means that ASP.NET will not compile the page, if possible.
controlRenderingCompatibilityVersion	Indicates how controls are expected to render out their markup. The default value is 4.0, meaning that the markup is updated to the latest version. By setting it to 3.5 (no other values are supported), you fall back to the behavior of earlier versions of ASP.NET.
enableEventValidation	Specifies whether pages and controls validate postback and callback events. The default is *true*.
enableSessionState	Indicates whether session state is enabled. It's set to *true* by default; it also accepts as values *false* and *ReadOnly*. The session state is disabled altogether if the attribute is set to *false*; it is accessible only for reading if set to *ReadOnly*.
enableViewState	Specifies whether view state is enabled. It's set to *true* by default.
enableViewStateMac	Specifies whether the view state of a page should be checked for tampering on each page postback. It's set to *true* by default.
maintainScrollPositionOnPostBack	If this is set to *true*, the page maintains the same scroll position after a postback.

Attribute	Description
masterPageFile	Specifies the master page for the pages in the scope of the configuration file.
maxPageStateFieldLength	Indicates the maximum length of the view-state field. A negative value indicates that no upper limit exists. If the size of the view state exceeds the maximum, the contents will be sent in chunks.
pageBaseType	Indicates the base code-behind class that *.aspx* pages inherit by default—unless a code-behind class is explicitly provided. The default class is *System.Web.UI.Page*. The new class name must include assembly information.
pageParserFilterType	Specifies the type of filter class that is used by the ASP.NET parser to determine whether an item is allowed in the page at parse time.
smartNavigation	Specifies whether smart navigation is enabled. This is set to *false* by default. It's deprecated in favor of the *maintainScrollPositionOnPostBack* attribute.
styleSheetTheme	Name of the style-sheet theme used for the pages in the scope of the configuration file.
theme	Name of the theme used for the pages in the scope of the configuration file.
userControlBaseType	Indicates the code-behind class that *.ascx* user controls inherit by default. The default class is *System.Web.UI.UserControl*. The new class name must include assembly information.
validateRequest	Indicates that ASP.NET examines all input from the browser for potentially dangerous data. It's set to *true* by default.
viewStateEncryptionMode	Indicates the encryption mode of the view state. Feasible values are *Always*, *Never*, or *Auto*. *Auto* means that the view state is encrypted only if a control requests it.

In particular, the *pageBaseType* attribute is an extremely powerful setting you might want to leverage when all your application pages inherit from a common code-behind class. In this case, instead of modifying all the pages, you centralize the setting in the *web.config* file at the level (machine, application, or subdirectory) you want.

An interesting attribute is *maxPageStateFieldLength*. One of the problems developers might experience with a too-large view state is that some legacy firewalls and proxy servers might not be capable of carrying all those bytes back and forth for a single input field. As a result, the content of the view state is truncated and the application fails. This is particularly likely to happen on pretty simple Web browsers, such as those you find in palmtops and smartphones. If the real size of the view state exceeds the upper limit set through the *maxPageStateFieldLength* attribute, ASP.NET automatically cuts the view state into chunks and sends it down using multiple hidden fields. For example, if you set *maxPageStateFieldLength* to 5, here's what the page contains:

```
<input type="hidden" id="__VIEWSTATEFIELDCOUNT" value="..." />
<input type="hidden" id="__VIEWSTATE" value="/wEPD" />
<input type="hidden" id="__VIEWSTATE1" value="wUKLT" />
<input type="hidden" id="__VIEWSTATE2" value="I2MjI" />
...
```

The final byte count of the client page is even a bit higher than in the default case, but at least your page won't fail because of a truncated view state on simple and not too powerful Web browsers.

A sign of the evolution of the Web platform is the *clientIDMode* attribute introduced in ASP.NET 4. Earlier versions of ASP.NET use a built-in algorithm to generate the client ID values for HTML elements output by server controls. The algorithm guarantees uniqueness but do not necessarily result in predictable IDs. Until the advent of AJAX, that has never been a problem. AJAX brought developers to write more client-side code and subsequently raised the need for accessing in a reliable and easy way any DOM element added by ASP.NET controls. The *clientIDMode* attribute offers two main options: using static IDs (and thus accepting the potential risk of having duplicates) and using predictable IDs. A predictable ID is essentially an ID generated by ASP.NET but through a much simpler algorithm that doesn't walk through the entire list of naming containers like the default algorithm we used for years.

The *<pages>* section contains a bunch of child sections, as shown here:

```
<pages>
    <controls>...</controls>
    <namespaces>...</namespaces>
    <tagMapping>...</tagMapping>
    <ignoreDeviceFilters>...</ignoreDeviceFilters>
</pages>
```

The *<controls>* and *<namespaces>* sections define a collection of *@Register* and *@Import* directives to be implicitly added to any page. The *<tagMapping>* section, instead, plays the role of remapping an existing control type to another type specified in the markup:

```
<pages>
    <tagMapping>
       <add
          tagType=
             "System.Web.UI.WebControls.TextBox"
          mappedTagType=
             "Samples.MyTextBox" />
    </tagMapping>
</pages>
```

As an example, you can use this tag to automatically invoke a *TextBox* of yours wherever the source code invokes, instead, the standard *TextBox* control out of the *<asp:TextBox>* markup.

Finally, *<ignoreDeviceFilters>* defines a collection of elements that identify the device-specific content that ASP.NET should ignore when it displays a page. Device-specific content is listed through a *<filter>* child element. The usefulness of this feature is illustrated by the following example. Suppose you have the following markup in an ASP.NET page:

```
<asp:Text moz:Text="Hello Mozilla" ie:Text="Hello IE">
```

In this instance, *moz* and *ie* are device filters, meaning that the property they attribute should be used only if the user agent matches the filter. So where's the problem? The problem arises with some AJAX functionality and microformats that extended the schema to allow additions. An example is when some JavaScript libraries add their own expando attributes prefixed with a string, as shown here:

```
<asp:Text sys:Text="Hello from Ajax">
```

Without countermeasures, the *sys* prefix would be mistaken for a device filter and the whole attribute would be stripped off in absence of a matching filter. In fact, *sys* is not likely to be the nickname of any browser.

```
<pages>
   <ignoreDeviceFilters>
     <filter add="sys" />
   </ignoreDeviceFilters>
</pages>
```

In ASP.NET 4, by adding the previous script to the configuration file you instruct ASP.NET to ignore some of the names that appear to be device filters.

The *<processModel>* Section

This section configures the ASP.NET process model—that is, the procedure that brings a request to be processed in the HTTP pipeline. The attributes of the *<processModel>* section are actually read by unmanaged code—the *aspnet_isapi.dll* ISAPI extension. For this reason, you need to restart IIS to have any changes applied. For the same reason, you can never override any attributes in the *<processModel>* section in a *web.config* file. The *<processModel>* section can exist only within a *machine.config* file, and it affects all ASP.NET applications that are running on the server. The following code snippet illustrates the schema of the section:

```
<processModel
   enable="true|false"
   timeout="hrs:mins:secs|Infinite"
   idleTimeout="hrs:mins:secs|Infinite"
   shutdownTimeout="hrs:mins:secs|Infinite"
   requestLimit="num|Infinite"
   requestQueueLimit="num|Infinite"
   restartQueueLimit="num|Infinite"
   memoryLimit="percent"
   webGarden="true|false"
```

```
cpuMask="num"
userName="username"
password="password"
logLevel="All|None|Errors"
clientConnectedCheck="hrs:mins:secs|Infinite"
comAuthenticationLevel="Default|None|Connect|Call|
            Pkt|PktIntegrity|PktPrivacy"
comImpersonationLevel="Default|Anonymous|Identify|
            Impersonate|Delegate"
responseDeadlockInterval="hrs:mins:secs|Infinite"
responseRestartDeadlockInterval="hrs:mins:secs|Infinite"
autoConfig="true|false"
maxWorkerThreads="num"
maxIoThreads="num"
minWorkerThreads="num"
minIoThreads="num"
serverErrorMessageFile=""
pingFrequency="Infinite"
pingTimeout="Infinite"
maxAppDomains="2000" />
```

As mentioned, the *machine.config* file remains the root of the configuration hierarchy also in IIS 7 and newer versions. The second level in the hierarchy is given by the root *web.config* file located in the same folder as *machine.config*.

Under IIS 7, or newer, an additional level in the hierarchy is represented by the *applicationHost.config* file located in the *system32\inetsrv\config* folder. To edit the content of this file, and thus configure most of the settings of the process model, you can use the visual editors in the IIS Manager tool. Figure 3-3 shows how to configure some parameters of the process model for a given application pool in the server.

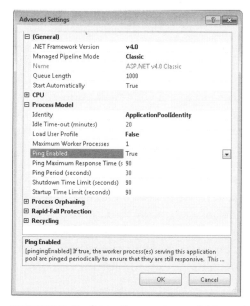

FIGURE 3-3 Configure the process model for a given application pools in IIS 7.5.

By default, the *machine.config* file contains the following:

```
<system.web>
    <processModel autoConfig="true"/>
    ...
</system.web>
```

This means that ASP.NET automatically configures some critical attributes to achieve optimal performance. You might want to tweak some of these attributes to tailor a configuration for your specific application. Table 3-12 describes these attributes.

TABLE 3-12 Optimizing the ASP.NET Process Model

Attribute	Description
maxIoThreads	Indicates the maximum number of IO threads per CPU in the thread pool. The default is 20 (indicating a total of 20x*N* threads on a machine with *N* CPUs).
maxWorkerThreads	Indicates the maximum number of worker threads per CPU in the thread pool. The default is 20 (meaning a total of 20x*N* threads on a machine with *N* CPUs).
memoryLimit	Indicates the percentage of memory that the worker process can consume before being recycled by IIS. The number indicates the percentage of the total system memory. The default value is 60.
minIoThreads	Configures the minimum number of I/O threads to use for the process on a per-CPU basis. The default is 1.
minWorkerThreads	Configures the minimum amount of worker threads to use for the process on a per-CPU basis. The default is 1.
requestQueueLimit	Indicates the number of requests the ASP.NET process can queue before returning error 503 (Server too busy.) The default is 5000.
responseDeadlockInterval	Indicates the time after which a process with queued requests that has not returned a response is considered deadlocked and is shut down. The default is three minutes.

Let's consider some alternatives, starting with memory limits. The default value of 60 has been determined by looking at an average scenario where your application is likely not to be the only one on the server. However, if you're lucky enough to be the only server process that consumes memory, the number can set to a higher threshold such as 75 without raising significant issues.

I/O threads are threads used to perform asynchronous operations that tend to take a while to complete. The typical example is reading a file or calling into a Web service. I/O threads are implicitly set up by high-level code you call usually through *BeginXxx* methods. Worker threads are, instead, threads used for plain operations. You might want to increase the number of I/O threads or worker threads based on the characteristics of your application. As you might have noticed, two minimum settings exist for threads: *minIoThreads* and *minWorkerThreads*. These values determine the lower bound that, when reached, cause ASP.NET to queue successive requests. A new request for a worker process is queued when fewer than the *minWorkerThreads* free threads are counted. The same happens for I/O threads.

Process Model and IIS 7.x Integrated Mode

ASP.NET uses threads differently when an application is hosted in an application pool running under IIS 7 in integrated mode. The biggest difference is that by default ASP. NET counts and keeps under control the number of concurrent requests instead of the number of concurrent threads. Is this really different? The two quantities are the same except when asynchronous requests are present. Asynchronous requests, in fact, might be pending without blocking an ASP.NET thread. As a result, you can have far more requests than threads.

You can still use the settings for threads exposed by the *<processModel>* section, but they are just ignored in integrated mode. How can you configure the maximum number of concurrent requests per CPU? A new configuration file has been added that supports an extra section named *<applicationPool>*. The new configuration file is *aspnet.config* and is available in the .NET Framework folder. For ASP.NET 4, it is *\microsoft.net\framework\v4.0.30319* under the Windows folder. You can add the following section:

```
<system.web>
    <applicationPool
        maxConcurrentRequestsPerCPU="5000"
        maxConcurrentThreadsPerCPU="0"
        requestQueueLimit="5000" />
</system.web>
```

The *requestQueueLimit* value specified in *aspnet.config* is the same as in *<processModel>* and will override any value you assign at the *machine.config* level.

Note that in integrated mode any requests are handed to ASP.NET by IIS for mere execution. When this happens, a thread switch occurs—from the IIS thread to a CLR thread. If you set *maxConcurrencyRequestPerCPU* to 0, the request will execute on the IIS I/O thread, without switching to a CLR thread. This is not a recommended approach because it could slow down the application when it comes to serving static resources. If you have IIS threads engaged in dynamic (and likely lengthier) requests, there are more chances that at peak times no threads are left to serve simpler requests.

In integrated mode, ASP.NET defaults to counting requests instead of threads. You can change this behavior by tweaking the values of *maxConcurrencyRequestsPerCPU* and *maxConcurrencyThreadsPerCPU*. You can also set both to nonzero values, in which case ASP.NET will manage to honor both of your settings.

The *<profile>* Section

The *<profile>* section is used to configure storage and layout of the user-profiling feature. Basically, each user can be assigned a set of properties whose values are loaded and persisted automatically by the system when the request begins and ends. A profile provider takes care of any I/O activity using a particular data store. The default profile provider, for example, uses the *AspNetDb.mdf* file and SQL Server Express.

The *<profile>* section has the following schema:

```
<profile
    enabled="true|false"
    inherits="fully qualified type reference"
    automaticSaveEnabled="true|false"
    defaultProvider="provider name">
    <properties>...</properties>
    <providers>...</providers>
</profile>
```

The *enabled* attribute indicates whether user profiles are enabled. The default value is *true*. The set of properties that is associated with each authenticated user is defined in the *<properties>* child element:

```
<profile>
    <properties>
        <add name="BackColor" type="string" />
        <add name="ForeColor" type="string" />
    </properties>
</profile>
```

Table 3-13 lists the attributes allowed on the *Profile* property.

TABLE 3-13 Attributes of the *Profile* Property

Attribute	Description
allowAnonymous	Allows storing values for anonymous users. It's *false* by default.
customProviderData	Contains data for a custom profile provider.
defaultValue	Indicates the default value of the property.
name	Name of the property.
provider	Name of the provider to use to read and write the property.
readOnly	Specifies whether the property value is read-only. It's *false* by default.
serializeAs	Indicates how to serialize the value of the property. Possible values are *Xml*, *Binary*, *String*, and *ProviderSpecific*.
type	The .NET Framework type of property. It is a string object by default.

All properties are packaged in a dynamically created class that is exposed to user code through the *Profile* property on the *HttpContext* object. The *Inherits* attribute allows you to define the base class of this dynamically created profile class. The *automaticSaveEnabled* attribute specifies whether the user profile should be automatically saved at the end of the execution of an ASP.NET page. (The default is *true*.) Note that the profile is saved only if the HTTP module in charge of it detects that the profile has been modified.

The *<providers>* element lists all available profile providers. You use this section to register custom providers. The *defaultProvider* attribute indicates the currently selected provider that pages will use.

The *<roleManager>* Section

The *<roleManager>* section configures role management for an ASP.NET application. Role management is carried out by two components: an HTTP module that intercepts incoming requests, and a role provider that retrieves and sets role information for the authenticated user. The provider acts as a proxy for the data store where the role information is stored. All available providers are listed in the *<providers>* child section. A new provider should be added here. The default provider is specified in the *defaultProvider* attribute. The overall schema of the section is shown here:

```
<roleManager
    cacheRolesInCookie="true|false"
    cookieName="name"
    cookiePath="/"
    cookieProtection="All|Encryption|Validation|None"
    cookieRequireSSL="true|false "
    cookieSlidingExpiration="true|false "
    cookieTimeout="number of minutes"
    createPersistentCookie="true|false"
    defaultProvider="provider name"
    domain="cookie domain">
    enabled="true|false"
    maxCachedResults="maximum number of role names cached"
    <providers>...</providers>
</roleManager>
```

After the HTTP module receives the role information from the currently selected provider, it usually creates a cookie to cache the information for future requests. All cookie-related attributes you see in the schema configure a different aspect of the cookie. The default name is .ASPXROLES.

The *<securityPolicy>* Section

In the *<securityPolicy>* section, you define mappings between security levels and policy files. The section can be configured at the application level but not in subdirectories. The section contains one or more *<trustLevel>* elements with *name* and *policyFile* attributes. You also can use the section to extend the security system by providing your own named trust levels mapped to a custom security policy file.

Here's an excerpt from the site's root *web.config* file that ASP.NET installs:

```
<securityPolicy>
    <trustLevel name="Full" policyFile="internal" />
    <trustLevel name="High" policyFile="web_hightrust.config" />
    <trustLevel name="Medium" policyFile="web_mediumtrust.config" />
    <trustLevel name="Low"  policyFile="web_lowtrust.config" />
    <trustLevel name="Minimal" policyFile="web_minimaltrust.config" />
</securityPolicy>
```

The *name* attribute can be set to Full, High, or Low in all versions of the .NET Framework. Each trust level identifies a particular security level that you map to a policy file. Security policy files are XML files located in the same folder as *machine.config*.

Notice that in ASP.NET the Full level of trust doesn't need to have an associated policy file full of permission sets and code-group definitions. The reason is that ASP.NET doesn't add extra security settings in the case of Full trust, so in such cases the content of the *policyFile* attribute is ignored.

The *<sessionState>* Section

The *<sessionState>* section stores session-state settings for the current application. The section determines the behavior and implementation details of the ASP.NET *Session* object. The *Session* object can work in different modes to accommodate the application's requirements for performance, robustness, and data reliability. In Table 3-14, you can see the list of acceptable attributes for the element. The *mode* attribute is the only mandatory attribute. Some attributes are mutually exclusive.

TABLE 3-14 Session-State Attributes

Attribute	Description
allowCustomSqlDatabase	If this is set to *true*, it enables you to specify a custom SQL Server database to store session data instead of using the default ASPState database.
compressionEnabled	Specifies whether compression is applied to the session-state data.
cookieless	Specifies how to communicate the session ID to clients. Feasible values are those listed in Table 3-5.
cookieName	Name of the cookie, if cookies are used for session IDs.
customProvider	Name of the custom session-state store provider to use for storing and retrieving session-state data.

Attribute	Description
mode	Specifies the implementation mode of the session state. Acceptable values are *Off*, *InProc*, *Custom*, *StateServer*, and *SQLServer*. When it's set to *Off*, session-state management is disabled and the *Session* object is not available to the application. *InProc* is the default working mode, and it stores session data locally in the Web server's memory. Alternatively, the session state can be stored on a remote server (*StateServer*) or in a SQL Server database (*SQLServer*). The *Custom* option indicates that the application is using a custom data store.
partitionResolverType	Indicates the type and assembly of the partition resolver component to be loaded to provide connection information when session state is working in *SQLServer* or *StateServer* mode. If a partition resolver can be correctly loaded, the *sqlConnectionString* and *stateConnectionString* attributes are ignored.
regenerateExpiredSessionId	When a request is made with a session ID that has expired, if this attribute is *true*, a new session ID is generated; otherwise, the expired one is revived. The default is *false*.
sessionIDManagerType	Null by default. If this attribute is set, it indicates the component to use as the generator of session IDs.
sqlCommandTimeout	Specifies the number of seconds a SQL command can be idle before it is canceled. The default is 30.
sqlConnectionRetryInterval	Specifies the time interval, in seconds, between attempts to connect to the database. The default is 0.
sqlConnectionString	Used when the mode is set to *SQLServer*; specifies the connection string for the SQL Server database to use for storing session data.
stateConnectionString	Used when the mode is set to *StateServer*; specifies the server name and port where session state should be stored.
stateNetworkTimeout	Specifies the number of seconds the TCP/IP network connection between the Web server and the state server can be idle before the request is canceled. The default is 10.
timeout	Specifies the number of minutes a session can be idle before it is abandoned. The default is 20.
useHostingIdentity	Indicates that the ASP.NET process identity is impersonated to access a custom state provider or the *SQLServer* provider configured for integrated security. It's *true* by default.

In addition, the child *<providers>* section lists custom session-state store providers. ASP.NET session state is designed to enable you to easily store user session data in different sources, such as a Web server's memory or SQL Server. A store provider is a component that manages the storage of session-state information and stores it in alternative media (for example, an Oracle database) and with an alternative layout.

The default connection string for the *SQLServer* mode is set to the following:

```
data source=127.0.0.1;Integrated Security=SSPI
```

As you can see, it doesn't contain the database name, which defaults to *AspState*. You create this database before the application is released using either T-SQL scripts or the *aspnet_regsql* command-line utility.

The default connection string for the *StateServer* mode is set to

```
tcpip=127.0.0.1:42424
```

You can change the TCP/IP address and the port used at will. Note, though, that to change the port you must edit the Port entry under the registry key:

```
HKEY_LOCAL_MACHINE\
    SYSTEM\CurrentControlSet\Services\aspnet_state\Parameters
```

In other words, just writing the new port number in the configuration file is not enough.

The *<siteMap>* Section

The *<siteMap>* section configures settings and providers for the ASP.NET site navigation system. The schema of the section is quite simple:

```
<sitemap
  enabled="true|false"
  defaultProvider="provider name">
  <providers>...</providers>
</siteMap>
```

The feature relies on site-map providers—that is, made-to-measure components that return information representing the structure of the site. ASP.NET comes with one predefined provider: the *AspNetXmlSiteMapProvider* class. The default site-map provider is specified through the *defaultProvider* attribute. All available providers, including custom providers, are listed in the *<providers>* section.

The *<trace>* Section

Tracing refers to the program's ability to send informative messages about the status of the execution. In general, tracing is a way to monitor the behavior of an application in a production environment, and debugging is used for development time testing. The *<trace>* section defines attributes that can modify the behavior of application-level tracing. The attributes are listed in Table 3-15.

TABLE 3-15 Application-Level ASP.NET Tracing Attributes

Attribute	Description
enabled	Specifies whether tracing is enabled for an application. The default is *false*. Tracing must be enabled in order to use the trace viewer (*trace.axd*) and other tracing facilities.
localOnly	If this attribute is set to *true*, the trace viewer is available only on the local host; if it's set to *false*, the trace viewer is also available remotely. The default is *true*. Note that *trace.axd* is one of the default HTTP handlers registered at installation time.
pageOutput	Specifies whether trace output is rendered at the end of each page. If this attribute is set to *false*, trace output is accessible through the trace viewer only. The default is *false*. Regardless of this global setting, individual pages can enable tracing using the *Trace* attribute of the *@Page* directive.
requestLimit	Indicates the maximum number of trace results to store on the server that are subsequently available through *trace.axd*. The default value is 10. The maximum is 10,000.
traceMode	Indicates the criteria by which trace records are to be sorted and displayed. Acceptable values are *SortByTime* (the default) or *SortByCategory*. Sorting by time means that records are displayed in the order in which they are generated. A category, on the other hand, is a user-defined name that can be optionally specified in the trace text.
writeToDiagnosticsTrace	This is *false* by default. It specifies whether trace messages should be forwarded to the diagnostics tracing infrastructure, for any registered listeners.

In the .NET Framework, tracing is provided through a unified, abstract API that uses ad hoc drivers to physically output the messages. These drivers are called *listeners* and redirect the tracing output to the specified target—typically a log file or an output stream. Listeners are defined in the *<system.diagnostics>* section. When *writeToDiagnosticsTrace* is *true*, any ASP.NET-generated trace message is also forwarded to all registered listeners.

The *<trust>* Section

The *<trust>* section configures the trust level under which the application will be run and determines the code-access security (CAS) restrictions applied to the application. By default, all ASP.NET applications run on the Web server as fully trusted applications and are allowed to do whatever their account is allowed to do. The CLR doesn't sandbox the code. Hence, any security restrictions applied to an application (for example, the inability to write files or write to the registry) are not the sign of partial trust but simply the effect of the underprivileged account under which ASP.NET applications normally run. Here's the schema for the section:

```
<trust
    hostSecurityPolicyResolverType ="security policy resolution type"
    legacyCasModel = "[True|False]"
    level="[Full|High|Medium|Low|Minimal]"
    originUrl="URL"
    permissionSetName = "name of the permission set"
    processRequestInApplicationTrust = "[True|False]"
/>
```

You act on the *<trust>* section if you want to run a Web application with less than full trust. The following code snippet shows the default *<trust>* setting in the site root *web.config*:

```
<trust level="Full" originUrl="" />
```

Allowable values for the level attribute are all the *<trustLevel>* entries defined in the *<securityPolicy>* section.

The *originUrl* attribute is a sort of misnomer. If you set it, what really happens is quite simple: the application is granted the permission of accessing the specified URL over HTTP using either a *Socket* or *WebRequest* class. Of course, the Web permission is granted only if the specified *<trust>* level supports that. Medium and higher trust levels do.

The *<trust>* section supports a Boolean attribute named *processRequestInApplicationTrust*. If *true* (the default), the attribute dictates that page requests are automatically restricted to the permissions in the trust policy file applied to the application. If it's *false*, there's the possibility that a page request runs with higher privileges than set in the trust policy.

> **Note** The *<trust>* section is allowed only at the machine level and application level because of technical reasons, not because of security concerns. An ASP.NET application runs in its own AppDomain, and the trust level for that application is set by applying the appropriate security policy to the AppDomain. Although policy statements can target specific pieces of code, the AppDomain is the lowest level at which a security policy can be applied. If the CLR has a policy level more granular than the AppDomain, you can define different trust levels for various portions of the ASP.NET application.

The following script shows how to specify Medium trust-level settings for all applications on a server. The script is excerpted from a site's root *web.config* file. With *allowOverride* set to *false*, the trust level is locked and cannot be modified by the application's root *web.config* file.

```
<location allowOverride="false">
  <system.web>
    <trust level="Medium" originUrl="" />
  </system.web>
</location>
```

By adding the following script, instead, you release the lock for a particular application on the machine:

```
<location allowOverride="true" path="Default Web Site/MySite40">
  <system.web>
    <trust level="Medium" originUrl="" />
  </system.web>
</location>
```

With the .NET Framework 4, Microsoft made some significant changes to the CAS model for managed applications. These changes might actually cause some ASP.NET applications to fail. At risk are partial-trust ASP.NET applications that either rely on trusted code running in the global assembly cache (GAC) or require extensive modifications to machine CAS policy files. For this reason, the *legacyCasModel* attribute has been added to revert partial-trust ASP.NET 4 applications to the behavior of earlier versions of ASP.NET built for earlier versions of the CLR. All you do is set *legacyCasModel* to *true* if you want to include a legacy CAS-related behavior from your ASP.NET 4 application.

In ASP.NET 4, there are various ways of associating a permission set with any assemblies required by the application. As in earlier versions, you can shape up the permission set by editing the partial-trust policy file for an individual trust level (for example, *web_mediumtrust.config*). In addition, you can specify a permission set explicitly through the *PermissionSetName* attribute. In ASP.NET 4, there are three possible permission sets: *FullTrust*, *ASP.Net*, and *Nothing*.

The *FullTrust* permission set makes any code run as fully trusted. The *ASP.Net* permission set is typically used for partial-trust applications and is the default name assigned to the *PermissionSetName* attribute. *Nothing* is not really an alternate permission set; rather, it is simply the empty permission set. The CLR throws a security exception for any assembly associated with the empty permission set. When you change the name of the permission set, ASP.NET 4 will search the partial-trust policy file with the same name.

> **Note** Changing the name of the default partial trust permission set is not an action you want to take without a valid reason. The feature exists mostly for when you need a SharePoint application to define its own set of permissions distinct from those of typical ASP.NET applications. Keep in mind that with the new CAS model of the .NET Framework 4, you are no longer allowed to have multiple named permission sets to define partial-trust permissions. So you can change the name from ASP.Net to something else, but that won't give you multiple partial trust permission sets for each application.

Finally, you can also opt for a programmatic approach to the task of choosing the permission set for an assembly. The CLR queries a *HostSecurityManager* object every time an assembly is loaded. One of the tasks associated with the *HostSecurityManager* type is returning the permission set for the assembly being loaded. In ASP.NET 4, you can gain control over this process by defining your own resolver type. A resolver type is registered through the *hostSecurityPolicyResolverType* attribute and consists of a type derived from the system's *HostSecurityPolicyResolver* type. I'll return to CAS for ASP.NET 4 applications in Chapter 19. You can find some good literature about this topic at *http://msdn.microsoft.com/en-us/library/dd984947%28VS.100%29.aspx.*

The *<urlMappings>* Section

The *<urlMappings>* section contains a list of mappings between fake URLs and real endpoints in the application. Here's a quick example that is worth a thousand words:

```
<urlMappings enabled="true">
    <add url="~/main.aspx" mappedUrl="~/default.aspx?tab=main" />
</urlMappings>
```

The *url* attribute indicates the URL that users request from their browser. The *mappedUrl* attribute indicates the corresponding URL that is passed on to the application. Both URLs are application-relative. In addition to the *<add>* node, the *<urlMappings>* section also supports the *<remove>* and *<clear>* nodes.

> **Note** The *<urlMappings>* section was introduced as the declarative counterpart of the *RewritePath* method defined on the *HttpContext* class. In ASP.NET 4, the URL-rewriting API has been further improved with the introduction of routing. You might want to choose the new routing API as your first option in an ASP.NET 4 application. (I'll cover routing in the next chapter.)

The *<webControls>* Section

The *<webControls>* section contains only the *clientScriptsLocation* attribute that specifies the default path to ASP.NET client script files. These files are included in the HTML code generated for *.aspx* pages when these pages require client-side functionalities such as smart navigation and client-side control validation.

```
<webControls clientScriptsLocation="/aspnet_client/{0}/{1}/" />
```

The preceding code snippet represents the default contents of the *<webControls>* section. The content of *clientScriptsLocation*, properly expanded, is the URL used for searching scripts to be included. The *aspnet_client* directory is automatically created under the Web server's root when you install ASP.NET. The two placeholders in the string represent subdirectories whose name might change in future versions of ASP.NET. The first placeholder is always set to *system_web*. The second placeholder expands to a subdirectory name based on the version of the .NET Framework.

ASP.NET 4 doesn't use this folder to store client script files. Client script files are, in fact, embedded as resources in the *system.web* assembly and are injected in pages through the *webresource.axd* HTTP handler.

You can use the client script folder to store script files employed by any custom ASP.NET controls you might write.

The *<xhtmlConformance>* Section

The *<xhtmlConformance>* section designates the XHTML rendering mode for an application. The default rendering for pages and controls is XHTML 1.0 Transitional. This is also the default for new pages created in Microsoft Visual Studio 2010. You can configure the preferred rendering by setting options in the *<xhtmlConformance>* section, which enables you to select XHTML 1.0 Transitional, XHTML1.0 Strict, and legacy rendering.

```
<xhtmlConformance mode="Transitional|Legacy|Strict"/>
```

If you opt for Legacy, pages and controls will render as in ASP.NET 1.x.

Other Top-Level Sections

The sections under the *<system.web>* element don't exhaust the list of configuration elements that are useful to ASP.NET developers. At least three other sections should be known and mastered.

The *<appSettings>* Section

The *<appSettings>* section stores custom application configuration data such as file paths, URLs of interest, or any other application-wide information:

```
<configuration>
    <appSettings>
        <add key="DefaultCacheDurationForData" value="..." />
    </appSettings>
</configuration>
```

The syntax of the *<appSettings>* section is defined as follows:

```
<appSettings>
    <add key="..." value="..." />
    <remove key="..." />
    <clear />
</appSettings>
```

The *<add>* element adds a new setting to the internal collection. This new setting has a value and is identified by a unique key. The *<remove>* element removes the specified setting from the collection. The setting is identified using the key. Finally, the *<clear>* element clears all settings that have previously been defined in the section.

As the name of the section implies, you should store in the section application-specific settings and avoid storing user-specific information. For user-specific information, you can use the user profile API. (See Chapter 8, "Page Composition and Usability.")

Any contents you design for storage in the *<appSettings>* section can be saved to an external XML file that is linked to the section through the *file* attribute:

```
<appSettings file="myfile.config" />
```

The content of the file pointed to by the *file* attribute is read as if it is an *<appSettings>* section in the *web.config* file. Note that the root element of the file must match *<appSettings>*.

> **Note** Changes to the external file are not detected until the application is restarted. If you incorporate *<appSettings>* in the *web.config* file, any changes are instead detected in real time.

The *<connectionStrings>* Section

The section is specifically designed to contain connection strings and is laid out as follows:

```
<connectionStrings>
    <add name="NWind"
        connectionString="SERVER=...;DATABASE=...;UID=...;PWD=...;"
        providerName="System.Data.SqlClient"  />
</connectionStrings>
```

You can manipulate the contents of the section by using *<add>*, *<remove>*, and *<clear>* nodes. Each stored connection is identified with a name you set through the *name* attribute. The connection parameters are set in the *connectionString* attribute. Finally, the *providerName* attribute indicates the ADO.NET data provider to use.

Connection names are also used within the configuration file to link a connection string to other sections, typically the *<providers>* section of *<membership>* and *<profile>* nodes.

> **Note** You are not really forced to place all of your connection strings in the *<connectionStrings>* section. You can place your strings in *<appSettings>* as well as in a custom section. Look at this section as a system facility for a common task you would accomplish anyway.

The *<configProtectedData>* Section

ASP.NET lets you encrypt specific sections of configuration files that might contain sensitive data. It does that through industry-standard XML encryption. XML encryption (which you can learn more about at *http://www.w3.org/TR/xmlenc-core*) is a way to encrypt data and represent the result in XML.

Encryption of configuration sections is optional, and you can enable it for any configuration sections you want by running a command-line tool, as you'll see later in this chapter in the section "Managing Configuration Data."

You can specify the type of encryption you want by selecting the appropriate provider from the list of available encryption providers. The .NET Framework 4.0 comes with two predefined providers: *DPAPIProtectedConfigurationProvider* and *RSAProtectedConfigurationProvider*. The former uses the Windows Data Protection API (DPAPI) to encrypt and decrypt data; the latter (the default provider) uses the RSA encryption algorithm to encrypt and decrypt data.

Most configuration sections that are processed by the managed configuration system are eligible for protection. The *<configProtectedData>* section itself, though, can't be protected. In this case, clear text is necessary to describe the behavior of the system. Similarly, sections consumed by the CLR from Win32 code or from ad hoc managed XML parsers can't be protected by this system because they don't employ section handlers to consume their configuration. This includes at least the following sections: *<processModel>*, *<runtime>*, *<mscorlib>*, *<startup>*, and *<system.runtime.remoting>*.

The *<system.web.extensions>* Section

This section contains elements that configure AJAX-related services and control their behavior. The section is laid out as shown here:

```
<system.web.extensions>
   <scripting>
     <scriptResourceHandler
          enableCompression="true|false"
          enableCaching="true|false" />
   </scripting>
   <webServices>
     <jsonSerialization ... />
     <authenticationService ... />
     <roleService ... />
     <profileService ... />
   </webServices>
</system.web.extensions>
```

The *scriptResourceHandler* element allows you to specify whether script files embedded as resources in a given application assembly are to be cached or compressed. Both options are *false* by default.

The content of the *<webServices>* element is related to Web or WCF services used by AJAX-enabled applications. The *<jsonSerialization>* element configures JSON serialization and is made of two attributes: *maxJsonLength* and *recursionLimit*. The former indicates the maximum length of a JSON string; the latter sets the maximum level of nesting allowed in the type being serialized.

The *<authenticationService>* element configures the ASP.NET authentication API exposed as a Web service to ASP.NET AJAX applications. The section has only two Boolean attributes: *enabled* and *requireSSL*. Both are *false* by default.

The *<roleService>* element configures the ASP.NET role management API exposed as a Web service to ASP.NET AJAX applications. The section has only Boolean attribute—*enabled*— which is *false* by default.

The *<profileService>* element configures the ASP.NET profile API exposed as a Web service to ASP.NET AJAX applications. The section has three attributes—*enabled*, *readAccessProperties*, and *writeAccessProperties*. The latter two properties consist of a list of comma-separated names of properties to be read and written as part of the user's profile.

The *<system.webServer>* Section

In general, the *<system.webServer>* section contains site-level settings for IIS 7.x. Defined within the *applicationHost.config* file and edited via the user interface of IIS Manager, the section specifies any settings used by the Web server engine and modules. Full documentation is available at *http://www.iis.net/ConfigReference/system.webServer.*

The section can also be used within the application's *web.config* file to make some of the settings specific to a given application. There's a specific situation, though, that requires you to have a *<system.webServer>* section in the application's *web.config* file—an ASP.NET application that employs HTTP modules, HTTP handlers, or both and runs under IIS 7.x in integrated mode.

Before IIS 7 came along, any ASP.NET request had to go through two distinct pipelines: one right at the IIS gate, and one mapped to the ASP.NET runtime environment. Subsequently, an ASP.NET application in need of supporting special HTTP modules or handlers simply registered them in the *web.config* file and waited for them to be invoked. In IIS 7 integrated mode, instead, the request pipeline is unified at the IIS level. As a result, any HTTP handlers and HTTP modules you might have registered in the *<httpHandlers>* and *<httpModules>* sections of the *web.config* file will be blissfully ignored.

For an IIS 7–integrated ASP.NET application to properly deal with HTTP modules and handlers, you have to move the *<httpHandlers>* and *<httpModules>* sections to a new *<system.webServer>* section in the same application's *web.config* file. There are some snags though.

> **Important** When developing HTTP handlers and modules, you should be aware of a key point. The ASP.NET Development Server (also known as Cassini) doesn't honor the content of the *<webServer>* section. This means that, *for development purposes only*, you should copy the registration of your handlers and modules also in the *<httpHandlers>* and *<httpModules>* section, regardless of whether your application will actually be deployed on IIS 7. The ASP.NET Development Server that comes with Visual Studio is designed to capture and process all requests within its own pipeline; in this regard, its overall behavior is more similar to IIS 6 than IIS 7.

Under *<system.webServer>*, sections have been renamed *<modules>* and *<handlers>* and have a slightly different set of attributes. In particular, each handler must have a *name* attribute and support additional attributes, namely *precondition* and *allowpolicy*. The *precondition* attribute lists what's required for the handler to work: type of pipeline (*classicMode* or *integratedMode*), bitness (32 or 64), and runtime version of ASP.NET (v2 or v4). The *allowPolicy* attribute sets the permissions granted to the handler: read, write, execute, or script.

The *<modules>* section counts a couple of Boolean attributes, such as *runAllManagedModulesForAllRequests* and *runManagedModulesForWebDavRequests*. Both properties default to *false*. This is the typical content for *<system.webServer>* in a new ASP.NET 4 application in Visual Studio 2010.

```
<modules runAllManagedModulesForAllRequests="true">
</modules>
```

The attribute *runAllManagedModulesForAllRequests* indicates that all managed modules can process all requests, even if the request was not for managed content. Instead, the attribute *runManagedModulesForWebDavRequests* specifies whether managed modules can process WebDAV requests.

These differences between classic and integrated mode lead you toward using different *web.config* files to set up handlers and modules for the same application deployed in different scenarios. By using the *<validation>* element, however, you can have a single *web.config* file with settings for both classic and integrated IIS 7 working modes:

```
<system.webServer>
    <validation validateIntegratedModeConfiguration="false" />
    ...
    </system.webServer>
```

The *<validation>* element tells IIS not to validate the schema of the *web.config* file against the known configuration schema of integrated mode. In this way, when you are working in integrated mode, *<httpHandlers>* and *<httpModules>* are ignored; and when you are in classic mode, the entire *<system.webServer>* section is ignored.

Note If you're having trouble while hosting an ASP.NET application under IIS 7.x in integrated mode, you might want to read the following article for more information and a very good background of the whole topic: *http://learn.iis.net/page.aspx/381/aspnet-20-breaking-changes-on-iis-70.*

Managing Configuration Data

Configuration data can be managed by developers and administrators in two main ways: programmatically through an ad hoc API, and manually through command-line utilities, XML editors, or perhaps the Web Site Administration Tool (WSAT). Let's take a closer look at these options.

Using the Configuration API

ASP.NET includes a full configuration management API that enables you to navigate, read, and write an application's configuration files. Configuration settings are exposed as a set of strongly typed objects that you can easily program against. These classes—one for each section in the overall schema—are all defined in the *System.Configuration* namespace.

The configuration API is smart enough to provide a merged view of all the settings that apply to that level. When settings are modified, the API automatically writes changes to the correct node in the correct configuration file. The management API can be used to read and write configuration settings of local and remote applications. Custom configuration sections are automatically manageable through the API.

Retrieving Web Configuration Settings

You use the *WebConfigurationManager* class to get access to the ASP.NET configuration files. The class is the preferred way to work with configuration files related to Web applications. The following code snippet illustrates how to retrieve the HTTP handlers in use in the current application:

```
void Button1_Click(object sender, EventArgs e)
{
    var name = @"system.web/httpHandlers";
    var cfg = WebConfigurationManager.OpenWebConfiguration("/");
    var handlers = (HttpHandlersSection) cfg.GetSection(name);
    EnumerateHandlers(handlers);
}

void EnumerateHandlers(HttpHandlersSection section)
{
    foreach (var handler in section.Handlers)
    {
        ...
    }
}
```

You open the configuration file using the *OpenWebConfiguration* method. The parameter you pass to the method indicates the level at which you want to retrieve information. If you specify *null* or /, you intend to capture configuration data at the site's root level. If you want information at the machine level, you resort to the *OpenMachineConfiguration* method.

The *OpenWebConfiguration* method returns a *Configuration* object on which you can call *GetSection* to retrieve the contents of a particular section. For HTTP handlers, you do as follows:

```
HttpHandlersSection section;
section = (HttpHandlersSection) cfg.GetSection(@"system.web/httpHandlers");
```

Each section class has a programming interface that closely reflects the attributes and child sections on the element.

To access configuration data at the application level, you pass the application's URL to the *OpenWebConfiguration* method:

```
var path = Request.CurrentExecutionFilePath;
Configuration cfg = WebConfigurationManager.OpenWebConfiguration(path);
```

To retrieve information about other sections, you use the same pattern illustrated earlier by changing section names and section classes.

> **Note** The .NET Framework offers two similar classes to achieve the same goals: the aforementioned *WebConfigurationManager* and *ConfigurationManager*. Their functionalities overlap to a good extent, but they are not the same thing. In particular, they do the same thing if all you need to do is read data from mapped sections such as *AppSettings* and *ConnectionStrings* If you need to access a specific section, remember that *WebConfigurationManager* can be configured to open a Web configuration file, whereas *ConfigurationManager* is designed for other types of applications.

Retrieving Application Settings

As mentioned, most ASP.NET applications need to access data in sections outside the *<system.web>* element. Canonical examples are *<appSettings>* and *<connectionString>*. For sections not included in the *<system.web>* element, you normally use the *ConfigurationManager* class. However, *WebConfigurationManager* contains a couple of helper public properties to access *AppSettings* and *ConnectionStrings* collections. The following code snippet shows the implementation of these properties in *WebConfigurationManager*:

```
public static NameValueCollection AppSettings
{
    get {return ConfigurationManager.AppSettings;}
}
```

```
public static NameValueCollection ConnectionStrings
{
    get {return ConfigurationManager.ConnectionStrings;}
}
```

As you can see, to access application settings and connection strings you can interchangeably use the *AppSettings* and *ConnectionStrings* collections on both *WebConfigurationManager* and *ConfigurationManager*. Here's how to obtain a registered connection string named *Northwind*:

```
WebConfigurationManager.ConnectionStrings["Northwind"].ConnectionString
```

For a value stored in the *<appSettings>* section, you need the following:

```
WebConfigurationManager.AppSettings["CacheDurationForData"]
```

In case you need to access other sections outside *<system.web>*, the *ConfigurationManager* class supplies the *OpenMachineConfiguration* method to access the tree of configuration data. Here's the code to retrieve the supported protocol prefixes for Web requests (https, http, ftp, and the like):

```
var name = @"system.net/webRequestModules";
Configuration cfg = ConfigurationManager.OpenMachineConfiguration();
var section = (WebRequestModulesSection) cfg.GetSection(name);
foreach (WebRequestModuleElement m in section.WebRequestModules)
{
    ...
}
```

To explore the content of a section, you need to cast the return value of the *GetSection* method to a specific type. A section type is defined for each system-provided supported section in the *system.configuration* assembly. Note, though, that you won't find any such section classes for elements under the *<system.webServer>* section. If you need to programmatically read or write within the *<system.webServer>* section, you must reference the *Microsoft.Web.Administration* assembly where such classes are defined. You find the assembly in the IIS folder, specifically under *System32\inetsrv*.

Updating Application Settings

The entire content of the configuration tree is exposed to applications through a sort of Document Object Model (DOM). This DOM is modifiable in memory. After you're done, you can persist changes by calling the *Save* method on the corresponding *Configuration* class. The following code snippet shows how to programmatically add a new HTTP handler to the current application:

```
var name = @"system.web/httpHandlers";
var path = "/myapp";

var config = WebConfigurationManager.OpenWebConfiguration(path);
var section = (HttpHandlersSection) config.GetSection(name);

var newHandler = new HttpHandlerAction("*.xyz", "System.Web.HttpForbiddenHandler", "*");
section.Handlers.Add(newHandler);
config.Save();
```

The newly added handler configures the system so that requests for *.xyz* files are blocked. The application's *web.config* file is modified as follows:

```
<httpHandlers>
    ...
    <add path="*.xyz"
         verb="*"
         type="System.Web.HttpForbiddenHandler" />
</httpHandlers>
```

To re-enable *.xyz* resources, you need to remove the handler that was just added. The following code shows how to proceed programmatically:

```
var name = @"system.web/httpHandlers";
var path = "/myapp";

var config = WebConfigurationManager.OpenWebConfiguration(path);
var section = (HttpHandlersSection) config.GetSection(name);

section.Handlers.Remove("*", "*.xyz");
config.Save();
```

After this, any request for an *.xyz* resource is likely to produce the, perhaps more familiar, "resource not found" message.

Encrypting a Section

With the exceptions listed earlier while discussing the *<protectedData>* section, all sections in a configuration file can be encrypted both programmatically using the configuration API and in offline mode using a command-line tool. Let's tackle this latter option first.

Using a Command-Line Tool

You use the newest version of a popular system tool: *aspnet_regiis.exe*. Here's a sample usage of the utility to encrypt connection strings for the */MyApp* application. Note that the section names are case-sensitive.

```
aspnet_regiis.exe –pe connectionStrings –app /MyApp
```

After running this command, the *web.config* looks different. The *<connectionStrings>* section now incorporates a child *<EncryptedData>* section, which is where the ciphered content has been stored. If you open the *web.config* file after encryption, you see something like the following:

```
<configuration>
  <connectionStrings
     configProtectionProvider="RsaProtectedConfigurationProvider">
    <EncryptedData ...>
      ...
      <CipherData>
        <CipherValue>cQyofWFQ ... =</CipherValue>
      </CipherData>
    </EncryptedData>
  </connectionStrings>
</configuration>
```

To restore the *web.config* file to its original clear state, you use the –pd switch in lieu of –pe in the aforementioned command line. The nice part of the story is that this form of encryption is completely transparent to applications, which continue working as before.

Using a Programmatic Approach

To encrypt and decrypt sections programmatically, you use the *ProtectSection* and *UnprotectSection* methods defined on the *SectionInformation* object. Here's how to proceed:

```
var name = "connectionStrings";
var path = "/myApp";
var provider = "RsaProtectedConfigurationProvider";

var config = WebConfigurationManager.OpenWebConfiguration(path);
var section = (ConnectionStringsSection) cfg.GetSection(name);

section.SectionInformation.ProtectSection(provider);
config.Save();
```

To unprotect, you change the call to *ProtectSection* with the following:

```
section.SectionInformation.UnprotectSection();
config.Save();
```

Note that to persist changes it is still essential to place a call to the *Save* method on the *Configuration* object.

Choosing the Encryption Provider

Any page that uses protected sections works like a champ as long as you run it inside the local Web server embedded in Visual Studio. You might get an RSA provider configuration error if you access the same page from within a canonical (and much more realistic) IIS virtual folder. What's up with that?

The RSA-based provider—the default protection provider, if you use the command-line tool—needs a key container to work. A default key container is created upon installation and is named *NetFrameWorkConfigurationKey*. The *aspnet_regiis.exe* utility provides a lot of command-line switches for you to add, remove, and edit key containers. The essential point is that you have a key container created before you dump the RSA-protected configuration provider. The container must not only exist, but it also needs to be associated with the user account attempting to call it. The system account (running the local Web server) is listed with the container; the ASP.NET account on your Web server might not be. Note that granting access to the key container is necessary only if you use the RSA provider.

Assuming you run ASP.NET under the NETWORK SERVICE account (the default on Windows Server 2003 machines), you need the following code to add access to the container for the user:

```
aspnet_regiis.exe -pa "NetFrameworkConfigurationKey"
        "NT AUTHORITY\NETWORK SERVICE"
```

It is important that you specify a complete account name, as in the preceding code. In IIS 7.5 where *ApplicationPoolIdentity* is used by default in lieu of NETWORK SERVICE, how would you identify the account exactly? Here's how:

```
aspnet_regiis.exe -pa "NetFrameworkConfigurationKey"
        "IIS APPPOOL\YourAppPool"
```

You use IIS APPPOOL followed by the name of the IIS application pool whose identity you want to retrieve.

Both the RSA and DPAPI providers are great options for encrypting sensitive data. The DPAPI provider dramatically simplifies the process of key management—keys are generated based on machine credentials and can be accessed by all processes running on the machine. For the same reason, the DPAPI provider is not ideal to protect sections in a Web-farm scenario, where the same encrypted *web.config* file will be deployed to several servers. In this case, either you manually encrypt all *web.config* files on each machine or you copy the same container key to all servers. To accomplish this, you create a key container for the application, export it to an XML file, and import it on each server that will need to decrypt the encrypted *web.config* file. To create a key container, you do as follows. Using the command-line utility is mandatory here.

```
aspnet_regiis.exe -pc YourContainerName -exp
```

Next, you export the key container to an XML file:

```
aspnet_regiis.exe -px YourContainerName YourXmlFile.xml
```

Next, you move the XML file to each server and import it as follows:

```
aspnet_regiis.exe -pi YourContainerName YourXmlFile.xml
```

As a final step, grant the ASP.NET account permission to access the container.

> **Note** For more information about the *aspnet:_regiis* tool and its command line, refer to the
> following URL: *http://msdn.microsoft.com/en-us/library/k6h9cz8h(VS.80).aspx*.

Creating Custom Configuration Sections

The predefined XML schema for configuration files fits the bill in most cases, but when you
have complex and structured information to persist, none of the existing schemas appear
to be powerful enough. At this point, you have two possible workarounds. You can simply
avoid using a standard configuration file and instead use a plain XML file written according to the schema you feel is appropriate for the data. Alternatively, you can embed your
XML configuration data in the standard application configuration file but provide a tailor-
made configuration section handler to read it.

Creating a new section (plus an optional new section group) requires editing the *web.config*
file to register the section (or section group). While registering the new section, you need to
specify the section handler component—that is, the piece of software in charge of parsing
the contents of the section to processable data. Depending on what kind of data you're
going to store in the section, you can use one of the existing handlers or, more likely, create
your own section handler.

In ASP.NET, the configuration section handler is a class that ultimately inherits from the
ConfigurationSection class. The section handler class defines public properties and maps
them to attributes in the XML element. In addition, these class properties are decorated with
a special attribute named *ConfigurationProperty*. The following example shows how to create
the handler for a new *<MyPages>* section with just one attribute—*pageBackColor*:

```
public class MyPagesSection : ConfigurationSection
{
    private static readonly ConfigurationProperty propPageBackColor = null;

    static MyPagesSection()
    {
        MyPagesSection.propPageBackColor = new ConfigurationProperty(
            "PageBackColor", typeof(string), "yellow",
            ConfigurationPropertyOptions.IsRequired);
    }
```

```
[ConfigurationProperty("pageBackColor")]
public string PageBackColor
{
    get { return (string) base[MyPagesSection.propPageBackColor]; }
    set { base[MyPagesSection.propPageBackColor] = value; }
}
}
```

The mapping between a property and a section attribute is established through the *ConfigurationProperty* attribute. The parameter of the attribute constructor indicates the name of the section attribute used to feed the decorated property.

A custom section must be registered to work properly. Here's how to do it:

```
<configuration>
  <configSections>
    <section name="myPages"
             type="Samples.MyPagesSection, Samples" />
  </configSections>
  ...
<configuration>
```

The *type* property in the *<section>* tag indicates the class being used to read and write the contents of the section. For the sample *<myPages>* section, the system will use the *MyPagesSection* class in the specified assembly. If the assembly is strongly typed and located in the GAC, you should indicate its full name.

Summary

ASP.NET applications have many configurable settings. The various settings can all be controlled at different levels and overridden, extended, or restricted as appropriate. ASP.NET configuration is hierarchical by nature and lets you apply different configuration schemes at various levels of granularity—the machine, the Web site, the application, and even the folder.

Configuration files are probably the most critical aspect to consider when preparing the deployment of ASP.NET applications. Arranging a setup program has never been as easy as it is with Visual Studio (not considering third-party products), but deciding how to replicate the settings of the native environment might not be trivial. ASP.NET applications, in fact, can be deployed on a Web farm or in an ISP scenario, which requires particular care of the *machine.config* and *web.config* files.

Tweaking the content of the myriad sections you can have in a configuration file is a delicate art that requires awareness of the IIS runtime environment, the ASP.NET process model, and the endless list of settings and default values that this chapter attempted to cover in detail.

Chapter 4
HTTP Handlers, Modules, and Routing

Advice is what we ask for when we already know the answer but wish we didn't.

—Erica Jong

HTTP handlers and modules are truly the building blocks of the ASP.NET platform. Any requests for a resource managed by ASP.NET are always resolved by an HTTP handler and pass through a pipeline of HTTP modules. After the handler has processed the request, the request flows back through the pipeline of HTTP modules and is finally transformed into markup for the caller.

The *Page* class—the base class for all ASP.NET runtime pages—is ultimately an HTTP handler that implements internally the page life cycle that fires the well-known set of page events, including postbacks, *Init*, *Load*, *PreRender*, and the like. An HTTP handler is designed to process one or more URL extensions. Handlers can be given an application or machine scope, which means they can process the assigned extensions within the context of the current application or all applications installed on the machine. Of course, this is accomplished by making changes to either the site's *web.config* file or a local *web.config* file, depending on the scope you desire.

HTTP modules are classes that handle runtime events. There are two types of public events that a module can deal with. They are the events raised by *HttpApplication* (including asynchronous events) and events raised by other HTTP modules. For example, *SessionStateModule* is one of the built-in modules provided by ASP.NET to supply session-state services to an application. It fires the *End* and *Start* events that other modules can handle through the familiar *Session_End* and *Session_Start* signatures.

In Internet Information Services (IIS) 7 integrated mode, modules and handlers are resolved at the IIS level; they operate, instead, inside the ASP.NET worker process in different runtime configurations, such as IIS 7 classic mode or IIS 6.

HTTP modules and handlers are related to the theme of request routing. Originally developed for ASP.NET MVC, the URL routing engine has been incorporated into the overall ASP.NET platform with the .NET Framework 3.5 Service Pack 1. The URL routing engine is a system-provided HTTP module that hooks up any incoming requests and attempts to match the requested URL to one of the user-defined rewriting rules (known as *routes*). If a match exists, the module locates the HTTP handler that is due to serve the route and goes with it. If no match is found, the request is processed as usual in Web Forms, as if no URL routing engine was ever in the middle. What makes the URL routing engine so beneficial to applications? It actually enables you to use free-hand and easy-to-remember URLs that are not necessarily bound to physical files in the Web server.

In this chapter, we'll explore the syntax and semantics of HTTP handlers, HTTP modules, and the URL routing engine.

The ISAPI Extensibility Model of IIS

A Web server generally provides an application programming interface (API) for enhancing and customizing the server's capabilities. Historically speaking, the first of these extension APIs was the Common Gateway Interface (CGI). A CGI module is a new application that is spawned from the Web server to service a request. Nowadays, CGI applications are almost never used because they require a new process for each HTTP request, and this approach poses severe scalability issues and is rather inadequate for high-volume Web sites.

More recent versions of Web servers supply an alternate and more efficient model to extend the capabilities of the server. In IIS, this alternative model takes the form of the ISAPI interface. When the ISAPI model is used, instead of starting a new process for each request, the Web server loads a made-to-measure component—namely, a Win32 dynamic-link library (DLL)—into its own process. Next, it calls a well-known entry point on the DLL to serve the request. The ISAPI component stays loaded until IIS is shut down and can service requests without any further impact on Web server activity. The downside to such a model is that because components are loaded within the Web server process, a single faulty component can tear down the whole server and all installed applications. Some effective countermeasures have been taken over the years to smooth out this problem. Today, IIS installed applications are assigned to application pools and each application pool is served by a distinct instance of a worker process.

From an extensibility standpoint, however, the ISAPI model is less than optimal because it requires developers to create Win32 unmanaged DLLs to endow the Web server with the capability of serving specific requests, such as those for ASPX resources. Until IIS 7 (and still in IIS 7 when the classic mode is configured), requests are processed by IIS and then mapped to some ISAPI (unmanaged) component. This is exactly what happens with plain ASPX requests, and the ASP.NET ISAPI component is *aspnet_isapi.dll*. In IIS 7.x integrated mode, you can add managed components (HTTP handlers and HTTP modules) directly at the IIS level. More precisely, the IIS 7 integrated mode merges the ASP.NET internal runtime pipeline with the IIS pipeline and enables you to write Web server extensions using managed code. This is the way to go.

Today, if you learn how to write HTTP handlers and HTTP modules, you can use such skills to customize how any requests that hit IIS are served, and not just requests that would be mapped to ASP.NET. You'll see a few examples in the rest of the chapter.

Writing HTTP Handlers

As the name suggests, an HTTP handler is a component that handles and processes a request. ASP.NET comes with a set of built-in handlers to accommodate a number of system tasks. The model, however, is highly extensible. You can write a custom HTTP handler whenever you need ASP.NET to process certain types of requests in a nonstandard way. The list of useful things you can do with HTTP handlers is limited only by your imagination.

Through a well-written handler, you can have your users invoke any sort of functionality via the Web. For example, you could implement click counters and any sort of image manipulation, including dynamic generation of images, server-side caching, or obstructing undesired linking to your images. More in general, an HTTP handler is a way for the user to send a command to the Web application instead of just requesting a particular page.

In software terms, an HTTP handler is a relatively simple class that implements the *IHttpHandler* interface. An HTTP handler can either work synchronously or operate in an asynchronous way. When working synchronously, a handler doesn't return until it's done with the HTTP request. An asynchronous handler, on the other hand, launches a potentially lengthy process and returns immediately after. A typical implementation of asynchronous handlers is asynchronous pages. An asynchronous HTTP handler is a class that implements a different interface—the *IHttpAsyncHandler* interface.

HTTP handlers need be registered with the application. You do that in the application's *web. config* file in the *<httpHandlers>* section of *<system.web>*, in the *<handlers>* section of *<system.webServer>* as explained in Chapter 3, "ASP.NET Configuration," or in both places. If your application runs under IIS 7.x in integrated mode, you can also configure HTTP handlers via the Handler Mappings panel of the IIS Manager.

The *IHttpHandler* Interface

Want to take the splash and dive into HTTP handler programming? Well, your first step is getting the hang of the *IHttpHandler* interface. An HTTP handler is just a managed class that implements that interface. As mentioned, a synchronous HTTP handler implements the *IHttpHandler* interface; an asynchronous HTTP handler, on the other hand, implements the *IHttpAsyncHandler* interface. Let's tackle synchronous handlers first.

The contract of the *IHttpHandler* interface defines the actions that a handler needs to take to process an HTTP request synchronously.

Members of the *IHttpHandler* Interface

The *IHttpHandler* interface defines only two members: *ProcessRequest* and *IsReusable*, as shown in Table 4-1. *ProcessRequest* is a method, whereas *IsReusable* is a Boolean property.

TABLE 4-1 Members of the *IHttpHandler* Interface

Member	Description
IsReusable	This property provides a Boolean value indicating whether the HTTP runtime can reuse the current instance of the HTTP handler while serving another request.
ProcessRequest	This method processes the HTTP request from start to finish and is responsible for processing any input and producing any output.

The *IsReusable* property on the *System.Web.UI.Page* class—the most common HTTP handler in ASP.NET—returns *false*, meaning that a new instance of the HTTP request is needed to serve each new page request. You typically make *IsReusable* return *false* in all situations where some significant processing is required that depends on the request payload. Handlers used as simple barriers to filter special requests can set *IsReusable* to *true* to save some CPU cycles. I'll return to this subject with a concrete example in a moment.

The *ProcessRequest* method has the following signature:

```
void ProcessRequest(HttpContext context);
```

It takes the context of the request as the input and ensures that the request is serviced. In the case of synchronous handlers, when *ProcessRequest* returns, the output is ready for forwarding to the client.

A Very Simple HTTP Handler

The output for the request is built within the *ProcessRequest* method, as shown in the following code:

```
using System.Web;
namespace AspNetGallery.Extensions.Handlers
{
    public class SimpleHandler : IHttpHandler
    {
        public void ProcessRequest(HttpContext context)
        {
            const String htmlTemplate = "<html><head><title>{0}</title></head><body>" +
                                        "<h1>Hello I'm: " +
                                        "<span style='color:blue'>{1}</span></h1>" +
                                        "</body></html>";

            var response = String.Format(htmlTemplate,
                    "HTTP Handlers", context.Request.Path);
            context.Response.Write(response);
        }
        public Boolean IsReusable
        {
            get { return false; }
        }
    }
}
```

You need an entry point to be able to call the handler. In this context, an entry point into the handler's code is nothing more than an HTTP endpoint—that is, a public URL. The URL must be a unique name that IIS and the ASP.NET runtime can map to this code. When registered, the mapping between an HTTP handler and a Web server resource is established through the *web.config* file:

```
<configuration>
    <system.web>
        <httpHandlers>
            <add verb="*"
                path="hello.axd"
                type="Samples.Components.SimpleHandler" />
        </httpHandlers>
    </system.web>
    <system.webServer>
        <validation validateIntegratedModeConfiguration="false" />
        <handlers>
            <add name="Hello"
                preCondition="integratedMode"
                verb="*"
                path="hello.axd"
                type="Samples.Components.SimpleHandler" />
        </handlers>
    </system.webServer>
</configuration>
```

The *<httpHandlers>* section lists the handlers available for the current application. These settings indicate that *SimpleHandler* is in charge of handling any incoming requests for an endpoint named *hello.axd*. Note that the URL *hello.axd* doesn't have to be a physical resource on the server; it's simply a public resource identifier. The *type* attribute references the class and assembly that contain the handler. Its canonical format is *type[,assembly]*. You omit the assembly information if the component is defined in the *App_Code* or other reserved folders.

> **Important** As noted in Chapter 3, you usually don't need both forms of an HTTP handler declaration in *<system.web>* and *<system.webServer>*. You need the former only if your application runs under IIS 6 (Windows Server 2003) or if it runs under IIS 7.x but is configured in classic mode. You need the latter only if your application runs under IIS 7.x in integrated mode. If you have both sections, you enable yourself to use a single *web.config* file for two distinct deployment scenarios. In this case, the *<validation>* element is key because it prevents IIS 7.x from strictly parsing the content of the configuration file. Furthermore, as discussed in Chapter 3, the *<httpHandlers>* and *<httpModules>* sections help in testing handlers and modules within Visual Studio if you're using the embedded ASP.NET Development Server (also known as, Cassini).

If you invoke the *hello.axd* URL, you obtain the results shown in Figure 4-1.

FIGURE 4-1 A sample HTTP handler that answers requests for *hello.axd*.

The technique discussed here is the quickest and simplest way of putting an HTTP handler to work, but there is more to know about the registration of HTTP handlers and there are many more options to take advantage of.

> **Note** It's more common to use the ASHX extension for a handler mapping. The AXD extension is generally reserved for resource handlers that inject embedded content such as images, scripts, and so forth.

Registering the Handler

An HTTP handler is a class and must be compiled to an assembly before you can use it. The assembly must be deployed to the *Bin* directory of the application. If you plan to make this handler available to all applications, you can copy it to the global assembly cache (GAC). The next step is registering the handler with an individual application or with all the applications running on the Web server.

You already saw the script you need to register an HTTP handler. Table 4-2 expands a bit more on the attributes you can set up.

TABLE 4-2 Attributes Required to Register an HTTP Handler in *<system.web>*

Attribute	Description
path	A wildcard string, or a single URL, that indicates the resources the handler will work on—for example, **.aspx*.
type	Specifies a comma-separated class/assembly combination. ASP.NET searches for the assembly DLL first in the application's private *Bin* directory and then in the system global assembly cache.
validate	If this attribute is set to *false*, ASP.NET loads the assembly with the handler on demand. The default value is *true*.
verb	Indicates the list of the supported HTTP verbs—for example, GET, PUT, and POST. The wildcard character (*) is an acceptable value and denotes all verbs.

All attributes except for *validate* are mandatory. When *validate* is set to *false*, ASP.NET delays as much as possible loading the assembly with the HTTP handler. In other words, the assembly will be loaded only when a request for it arrives. ASP.NET will not try to preload the assembly, thus catching earlier any errors or problems with it.

Additional attributes are available if you register the handler in *<system.webServer>*. They are listed in Table 4-3.

TABLE 4-3 Attributes Required to Register an HTTP Handler in *<system.webServer>*

Attribute	Description
allowPathInfo	If this attribute is set to *true*, the handler processes full path information in the URL or just the last section. It is set to *false* by default.
modules	Indicates the list of HTTP modules (comma-separated list of names) that are enabled to intercept requests for the current handler. The standard list contains only the *ManagedPipelineHandler* module.
name	Unique name of the handler.
path	A wildcard string, or a single URL, that indicates the resources the handler will work on—for example, **.aspx*.
preCondition	Specifies conditions under which the handler will run. (More information appears later in this section.)
requireAccess	Indicates the type of access that a handler requires to the resource, either read, write, script, execute, or none. The default is script.
resourceType	Indicates the type of resource to which the handler mapping applies: file, directory, or both. The default option, however, is *Unspecified*, meaning that the handler can handle requests for resources that map to physical entries in the file system as well as to plain commands.
responseBufferLimit	Specifies the maximum size, in bytes, of the response buffer. The default value is 4 MB.
scriptProcessor	Specifies the physical path of the ISAPI extension or CGI executable that processes the request. It is not requested for managed handlers.
type	Specifies a comma-separated class/assembly combination. ASP.NET searches for the assembly DLL first in the application's private *Bin* directory and then in the system global assembly cache.
verb	Indicates the list of the supported HTTP verbs—for example, GET, PUT, and POST. The wildcard character (*) is an acceptable value and denotes all verbs.

The reason why the configuration of an HTTP handler might span a larger number of attributes in IIS is that the *<handlers>* section serves for both managed and unmanaged handlers. If you configure a managed handler written using the ASP.NET API, you need only *preCondition* and *name* in addition to the attributes you would specify in the *<httpHandlers>* section.

Preconditions for Managed Handlers

The *preCondition* attribute sets prerequisites for the handler to run. Prerequisites touch on three distinct areas: bitness, ASP.NET runtime version, and type of requests to respond. Table 4-4 lists and explains the various options:

TABLE 4-4 Preconditions for an IIS 7.x HTTP Handler

Precondition	Description
bitness32	The handler is 32-bit code and should be loaded only in 64-bit worker processes running in 32-bit emulation.
bitness64	The handler is 64-bit and should be loaded only in native 64-bit worker processes.
integratedMode	The handler should respond only to requests in application pools configured in integrated mode.
ISAPIMode	The handler should respond only to requests in application pools configured in classic mode.
runtimeVersionv1.1	The handler should respond only to requests in application pools configured for version 1.1 of the ASP.NET runtime.
runtimeVersionv2.0	The handler should respond only to requests in application pools configured for version 2.0 of the ASP.NET runtime.

Most of the time you use the *integratedMode* value only to set preconditions on a managed HTTP handler.

Handlers Serving New Types of Resources

In ASP.NET applications, a common scenario when you want to use custom HTTP handlers is that you want to loosen yourself from the ties of ASPX files. Sometimes you want to place a request for a nonstandard ASP.NET resource (for example, a custom XML file) and expect the handler to process the content and return some markup.

More in general, you use HTTP handlers in two main situations: when you want to customize how known resources are processed and when you want to introduce new resources. In the latter case, you probably need to let IIS know about the new resource. Again, how you achieve this depends on the configuration of the application pool that hosts your ASP.NET applications.

Suppose you want your application to respond to requests for *.report* requests. For example, you expect your application to be able to respond to a URL like */monthly.report?year=2010*. Let's say that *monthly.report* is a server file that contains a description of the report your handler will then create using any input parameters you provide.

In integrated mode, you need to do nothing special for this request to go successfully. Moreover, you don't even need to add a *.report* or any other analogous extension. You can specify any custom URL (much like you do in ASP.NET MVC) and as long as you have a handler properly configured, it will work.

In classic mode, instead, two distinct pipelines exist in IIS and ASP.NET. The extension, in this case, is mandatory to instruct IIS to recognize that request and map it to ASP.NET, where the HTTP handler actually lives. As an example, consider that when you deploy ASP.NET MVC in classic mode you have to tweak URLs so that each controller name has an *.mvc* suffix. To force IIS to recognize a new resource, you must add a new script map via the IIS Manager, as shown in Figure 4-2.

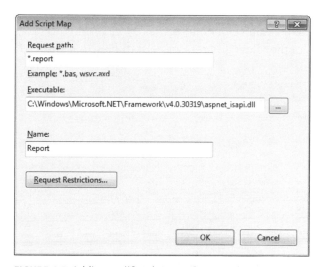

FIGURE 4-2 Adding an IIS script map for *.report* requests.

The executable is the ISAPI extension that will be bridging the request from the IIS world to the ASP.NET space. You choose the *aspnet_isapi* DLL from the folder that points to the version of the .NET Framework you intend to target. In Figure 4-2, you see the path for ASP.NET 4.

Note In Microsoft Visual Studio, if you test a sample *.report* resource using the local embedded Web server, nothing happens that forces you to register the *.report* resource with IIS. This is just the point, though. You're not using IIS! In other words, if you use the local Web server, you have no need to touch IIS; you do need to register any custom resource you plan to use with IIS before you get to production.

Why didn't we have to do anything special for our first example, *hello.axd*? Because AXD is a system extension that ASP.NET registers on its own and that sometimes also can be used for registering custom HTTP handlers. (AXD is not the recommended extension for custom handlers, however.)

Now let's consider a more complex example of an HTTP handler.

The Picture Viewer Handler

To speed up processing, IIS claims the right to personally serve some typical Web resources without going down to any particular ISAPI extensions. The list of resources served directly by IIS includes static files such as images and HTML files.

What if you request a GIF or a JPG file directly from the address bar of the browser? IIS retrieves the specified resource, sets the proper content type on the response buffer, and writes out the bytes of the file. As a result, you'll see the image in the browser's page. So far so good.

What if you point your browser to a virtual folder that contains images? In this case, IIS doesn't distinguish the contents of the folder and returns a list of files, as shown in Figure 4-3.

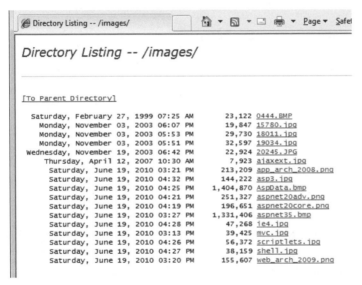

FIGURE 4-3 The standard IIS-provided view of a folder.

Wouldn't it be nice if you could get a preview of the contained pictures instead?

Designing the HTTP Handler

To start out, you need to decide how to let IIS know about your wishes. You can use a particular endpoint that, when appended to a folder's name, convinces IIS to yield to ASP.NET and provide a preview of contained images. Put another way, the idea is to bind your picture viewer handler to a particular endpoint—say, *folder.axd*. As mentioned earlier in the chapter, a fixed endpoint for handlers doesn't have to be an existing, deployed resource. You make the *folder.axd* endpoint follow the folder name, as shown here:

```
http://www.contoso.com/images/folder.axd
```

The handler processes the URL, extracts the folder name, and selects all the contained pictures.

> **Note** In ASP.NET, the *.axd* extension is commonly used for endpoints referencing a special service. *Trace.axd* for tracing and *WebResource.axd* for script and resources injection are examples of two popular uses of the extension. In particular, the *Trace.axd* handler implements the same logic described here. If you append its name to the URL, it will trace all requests for pages in that application.

Implementing the HTTP Handler

The picture viewer handler returns a page composed of a multirow table showing as many images as there are in the folder. Here's the skeleton of the class:

```
class PictureViewerInfo
{
    public PictureViewerInfo() {
        DisplayWidth = 200;
        ColumnCount = 3;
    }
    public int DisplayWidth;
    public int ColumnCount;
    public string FolderName;
}

public class PictureViewerHandler : IHttpHandler
{
    // Override the ProcessRequest method
    public void ProcessRequest(HttpContext context)
    {
        PictureViewerInfo info = GetFolderInfo(context);
        string html = CreateOutput(info);

        // Output the data
        context.Response.Write("<html><head><title>");
        context.Response.Write("Picture Web Viewer");
        context.Response.Write("</title></head><body>");
        context.Response.Write(html);
        context.Response.Write("</body></html>");
    }

    // Override the IsReusable property
    public bool IsReusable
    {
        get { return true; }
    }
    ...
}
```

Retrieving the actual path of the folder is as easy as stripping off the *folder.axd* string from the URL and trimming any trailing slashes or backslashes. Next, the URL of the folder is mapped to a server path and processed using the .NET Framework API for files and folders to retrieve all image files:

```
private static IList<FileInfo> GetAllImages(DirectoryInfo di)
{
    String[] fileTypes = { "*.bmp", "*.gif", "*.jpg", "*.png" };
    var images = new List<FileInfo>();
    foreach (var files in fileTypes.Select(di.GetFiles).Where(files => files.Length > 0))
    {
        images.AddRange(files);
    }
    return images;
}
```

The *DirectoryInfo* class provides some helper functions on the specified directory; for example, the *GetFiles* method selects all the files that match the given pattern. Each file is wrapped by a *FileInfo* object. The method *GetFiles* doesn't support multiple search patterns; to search for various file types, you need to iterate for each type and accumulate results in an array list or equivalent data structure.

After you get all the images in the folder, you move on to building the output for the request. The output is a table with a fixed number of cells and a variable number of rows to accommodate all selected images. For each image file, a new *<img>* tag is created through the *Image* control. The *width* attribute of this file is set to a fixed value (say, 200 pixels), causing browsers to automatically resize the image. Furthermore, the image is wrapped by an anchor that links to the same image URL. As a result, when the user clicks on an image, the page refreshes and shows the same image at its natural size.

```
private static String CreateOutputForFolder(PictureViewerInfo info, DirectoryInfo di)
{
    var images = GetAllImages(di);

    var t = new Table();
    var index = 0;
    var moreImages = true;

    while (moreImages)
    {
        var row = new TableRow();
        t.Rows.Add(row);

        for (var i = 0; i < info.ColumnCount; i++)
        {
            var cell = new TableCell();
            row.Cells.Add(cell);
```

```
            var img = new Image();
            var fi = images[index];
            img.ImageUrl = fi.Name;
            img.Width = Unit.Pixel(info.DisplayWidth);

            var a = new HtmlAnchor {HRef = fi.Name};
            a.Controls.Add(img);
            cell.Controls.Add(a);

            index++;
            moreImages = (index < images.Count);
            if (!moreImages)
                break;
        }
    }
}
```

You might want to make the handler accept some optional query string parameters, such as the width of images and the column count. These values are packed in an instance of the helper class *PictureViewerInfo* along with the name of the folder to view. Here's the code to process the query string of the URL to extract parameters if any are present:

```
var info = new PictureViewerInfo();
var p1 = context.Request.Params["Width"];
var p2 = context.Request.Params["Cols"];
if (p1 != null)
    info.DisplayWidth = p1.ToInt32();
if (p2 != null)
    info.ColumnCount = p2.ToInt32();
```

ToInt32 is a helper extension method that attempts to convert a numeric string to the corresponding integer. I find this method quite useful and a great enhancer of code readability. Here's the code:

```
public static Int32 ToInt32(this String helper, Int32 defaultValue = Int32.MinValue)
{
    Int32 number;
    var result = Int32.TryParse(helper, out number);
    return result ? number : defaultValue;
}
```

Figure 4-4 shows the handler in action.

FIGURE 4-4 The picture viewer handler in action with a given number of columns and a specified width.

Registering the handler is easy too. You just add the following script to the *<httpHandlers>* section of the *web.config* file:

```
<add verb="*"
    path="folder.axd"
    type="PictureViewerHandler, AspNetGallery.Extensions" />
```

You place the assembly in the GAC and move the configuration script to the global *web.config* to extend the settings to all applications on the machine. If you're targeting IIS 7 integrated mode, you also need the following:

```
<system.webServer>
  <handlers>
    <add name="PictureFolder"
        preCondition="integratedMode"
        verb="*"
```

```
        path="folder.axd"
        type="PictureViewerHandler, AspNetGallery.Extensions" />
   </handlers>
</system.webServer>
```

Serving Images More Effectively

Any page you get from the Web these days is topped with so many images and is so well conceived and designed that often the overall page looks more like a magazine advertisement than an HTML page. Looking at the current pages displayed by portals, it's rather hard to imagine there ever was a time—and it was only a decade ago—when one could create a Web site by using only a text editor and some assistance from a friend who had a bit of familiarity with Adobe PhotoShop.

In spite of the wide use of images on the Web, there is just one way in which a Web page can reference an image—by using the HTML *<img>* tag. By design, this tag points to a URL. As a result, to be displayable within a Web page, an image must be identifiable through a URL and its bits should be contained in the output stream returned by the Web server for that URL.

In many cases, the URL points to a static resource such as a GIF or JPEG file. In this case, the Web server takes the request upon itself and serves it without invoking external components. However, the fact that many *<img>* tags on the Web are bound to a static file does not mean there's no other way to include images in Web pages.

Where else can you turn to get images aside from picking them up from the server file system? One way to do it is to load images from a database, or you can generate or modify images on the fly just before serving the bits to the browser.

Loading Images from Databases

The use of a database as the storage medium for images is controversial. Some people have good reasons to push it as a solution; others tell you bluntly they would never do it and that you shouldn't either. Some people can tell you wonderful stories of how storing images in a properly equipped database was the best experience of their professional life. With no fear that facts could perhaps prove them wrong, other people will confess that they would never use a database again for such a task.

The facts say that all database management systems (DBMS) of a certain reputation and volume have supported binary large objects (BLOB) for quite some time. Sure, a BLOB field doesn't necessarily contain an image—it can contain a multimedia file or a long text file— but overall there must be a good reason for having this BLOB supported in Microsoft SQL Server, Oracle, and similar popular DBMS systems!

To read an image from a BLOB field with ADO.NET, you execute a SELECT statement on the column and use the *ExecuteScalar* method to catch the result and save it in an array of bytes. Next, you send this array down to the client through a binary write to the response stream. Let's write an HTTP handler to serve a database-stored image:

```csharp
public class DbImageHandler : IHttpHandler
{
    public void ProcessRequest(HttpContext ctx)
    {
        // Ensure the URL contains an ID argument that is a number
        var id = -1;
        var p1 = context.Request.Params["id"];
        if (p1 != null)
            id = p1.ToInt32(-1);
        if (id < 0)
        {
            context.Response.End();
            return;
        }

        var connString = "...";
        const String cmdText = "SELECT photo FROM employees WHERE employeeid=@id";

        // Get an array of bytes from the BLOB field
        byte[] img = null;
        var conn = new SqlConnection(connString);
        using (conn)
        {
            var cmd = new SqlCommand(cmdText, conn);
            cmd.Parameters.AddWithValue("@id", id);
            conn.Open();
            img = (byte[])cmd.ExecuteScalar();
        }

        // Prepare the response for the browser
        if (img != null)
        {
            ctx.Response.ContentType = "image/jpeg";
            ctx.Response.BinaryWrite(img);
        }
    }

    public bool IsReusable
    {
        get { return true; }
    }
}
```

There are quite a few assumptions made in this code. First, we assume that the field named *photo* contains image bits and that the format of the image is JPEG. Second, we assume that images are to be retrieved from a fixed table of a given database through a predefined connection string. Finally, we assume that the URL to invoke this handler includes a query string parameter named *id*.

Notice the attempt to convert the value of the *id* query parameter to an integer before proceeding. This simple check significantly reduces the surface attack area for malicious users by verifying that what is going to be used as a numeric ID is really a numeric ID. Especially when you're inoculating user input into SQL query commands, filtering out extra characters and wrong data types is a fundamental measure for preventing attacks.

The *BinaryWrite* method of the *HttpResponse* object writes an array of bytes to the output stream.

> **Note** If the database you're using is Northwind, an extra step might be required to ensure that the images are correctly managed. For some reason, the SQL Server version of the Northwind database stores the images in the *photo* column of the Employees table as OLE objects. This is probably because of the conversion that occurred when the database was upgraded from the Microsoft Access version. As a matter fact, the array of bytes you receive contains a 78-byte prefix that has nothing to do with the image. Those bytes are just the header created when the image was added as an OLE object to the first version of Access.
>
> Although the preceding code works like a champ with regular BLOB fields, it must undergo the following modification to work with the *photo* field of the Northwind.Employees database:
>
> ```
> Response.OutputStream.Write(img, 78, img.Length-78);
> ```
>
> Instead of using the *BinaryWrite* call, which doesn't let you specify the starting position, use the code shown here.

A sample page to test BLOB field access is shown in Figure 4-5. The page lets users select an employee ID and post back. When the page renders, the ID is used to complete the URL for the ASP.NET *Image* control.

```
var url = String.Format("photo.axd?id={0}", DropDownList1.SelectedValue);
Image1.ImageUrl = url;
```

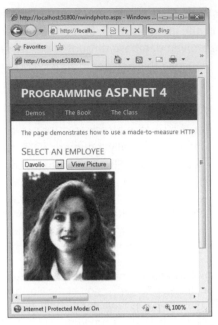

FIGURE 4-5 Downloading images stored within the BLOB field of a database.

An HTTP handler must be registered in the *web.config* file and bound to a public endpoint. In this case, the endpoint is *photo.axd* and the script to enter in the configuration file is shown next (in addition to a similar script in *<system.webServer>*:

```
<httpHandlers>
    <add verb="*"
         path="photo.axd"
         type=" NorthwindPhotoImageHandler, AspNetGallery.Extensions" />
</httpHandlers>
```

> **Note** The preceding handler clearly has a weak point: it hard-codes a SQL command and the related connection string. This means that you might need a different handler for each different command or database to access. A more realistic handler would probably use an external and configurable database-specific provider. Such a provider can be as simple as a class that implements an agreed-upon interface. At a minimum, the interface will supply a method to retrieve and return an array of bytes.
>
> Alternatively, if you want to keep the ADO.NET code in the handler itself, the interface will just supply members that specify the command text and connection string. The handler will figure out its default provider from a given entry in the *web.config* file.

Serving Dynamically Generated Images

Isn't it true that an image is worth thousands of words? Many financial Web sites offer charts and, more often than not, these charts are dynamically generated on the server. Next, they are served to the browser as a stream of bytes and travel over the classic response output stream. But can you create and manipulate server-side images? For these tasks, Web applications normally rely on ad hoc libraries or the graphic engine of other applications (for example, Microsoft Office applications). ASP.NET applications are different and, to some extent, luckier. ASP.NET applications, in fact, can rely on a powerful and integrated graphic engine integrated in the .NET Framework.

In ASP.NET, writing images to disk might require some security adjustments. Normally, the ASP.NET runtime runs under the aegis of the NETWORK SERVICE user account. In the case of anonymous access with impersonation disabled—which are the default settings in ASP.NET—the worker process lends its own identity and security token to the thread that executes the user request of creating the file. With regard to the default scenario, an access-denied exception might be thrown if NETWORK SERVICE (or the selected application pool identity) lacks writing permissions on virtual directories—a pretty common situation.

ASP.NET provides an interesting alternative to writing files on disk without changing security settings: in-memory generation of images. In other words, the dynamically generated image is saved directly to the output stream in the needed image format or in a memory stream.

Writing Copyright Notes on Images

The .NET Framework graphic engine supports quite a few image formats, including JPEG, GIF, BMP, and PNG. The whole collection of image formats is in the *ImageFormat* structure of the *System.Drawing* namespace. You can save a memory-resident *Bitmap* object to any of the supported formats by using one of the overloads of the *Save* method:

```
Bitmap bmp = new Bitmap(file);
...
bmp.Save(outputStream, ImageFormat.Gif);
```

When you attempt to save an image to a stream or disk file, the system attempts to locate an encoder for the requested format. The encoder is a module that converts from the native format to the specified format. Note that the encoder is a piece of unmanaged code that lives in the underlying Win32 platform. For each save format, the *Save* method looks up the right encoder and proceeds.

The next example wraps up all the points we've touched on. This example shows how to load an existing image, add some copyright notes, and serve the modified version to the user. In doing so, we'll load an image into a *Bitmap* object, obtain a *Graphics* for that bitmap, and use graphics primitives to write. When finished, we'll save the result to the page's output stream and indicate a particular MIME type.

The sample page that triggers the example is easily created, as shown in the following listing:

```html
<html>
<body>
    <img id="picture" src="dynimage.axd?url=images/pic1.jpg" />
</body>
</html>
```

The page contains no ASP.NET code and displays an image through a static HTML *<img>*
tag. The source of the image, though, is an HTTP handler that loads the image passed
through the query string and then manipulates and displays it. Here's the source code for the
ProcessRequest method of the HTTP handler:

```csharp
public void ProcessRequest (HttpContext context)
{
    var o = context.Request["url"];
    if (o == null)
    {
        context.Response.Write("No image found.");
        context.Response.End();
        return;
    }

    var file = context.Server.MapPath(o);
    var msg = ConfigurationManager.AppSettings["CopyrightNote"];
    if (File.Exists(file))
    {
        Bitmap bmp = AddCopyright(file, msg);
        context.Response.ContentType = "image/jpeg";
        bmp.Save(context.Response.OutputStream, ImageFormat.Jpeg);
        bmp.Dispose();
    }
    else
    {
        context.Response.Write("No image found.");
        context.Response.End();
    }
}
```

Note that the server-side page performs two different tasks indeed. First, it writes copyright
text on the image canvas; next, it converts whatever the original format was to JPEG:

```csharp
Bitmap AddCopyright(String file, String msg)
{
    // Load the file and create the graphics
    var bmp = new Bitmap(file);
    var g = Graphics.FromImage(bmp);

    // Define text alignment
    var strFmt = new StringFormat();
    strFmt.Alignment = StringAlignment.Center;

    // Create brushes for the bottom writing
    // (green text on black background)
    var btmForeColor = new SolidBrush(Color.PaleGreen);
    var btmBackColor = new SolidBrush(Color.Black);
```

```
    // To calculate writing coordinates, obtain the size of the
    // text given the font typeface and size
    var btmFont = new Font("Verdana", 7);
    var textSize = g.MeasureString(msg, btmFont);

    // Calculate the output rectangle and fill
    float x = (bmp.Width-textSize.Width-3);
    float y = (bmp.Height-textSize.Height-3);
    float w = (x + textSize.Width);
    float h = (y + textSize.Height);
    var textArea = new RectangleF(x, y, w, h);
    g.FillRectangle(btmBackColor, textArea);

    // Draw the text and free resources
    g.DrawString(msg, btmFont, btmForeColor, textArea);
    btmForeColor.Dispose();
    btmBackColor.Dispose();
    btmFont.Dispose();
    g.Dispose();

    return bmp;
}
```

Figure 4-6 shows the results.

FIGURE 4-6 A server-resident image has been modified before being displayed.

Note that the additional text is part of the image the user downloads on her client browser. If the user saves the picture by using the Save Picture As menu from the browser, the text (in this case, the copyright note) is saved along with the image.

> **Important** All examples demonstrating programmatic manipulation of images take advantage of the classes in the *System.Drawing* assembly. The use of this assembly is not recommended in ASP.NET and is explicitly not supported in ASP.NET Web services. (See *http://msdn.microsoft.com/ en-us/library/system.drawing.aspx*.) This fact simply means that you are advised not to use classes in *System.Drawing* because Microsoft can't guarantee it is always safe to use them in all possible scenarios. If your code is currently using *System.Drawing*—the GDI+ subsystem—and it works just fine, you're probably OK. In any case, if you use GDI+ classes and encounter a malfunction, Microsoft will not assist you. Forewarned is forearmed.
>
> You might be better off using an alternative to GDI+, especially for new applications. Which one? For both speed and reliability, you can consider the WPF Imaging API. Here's an interesting post that shows how to use Windows Presentation Foundation (WPF) for resizing images: *http:// weblogs.asp.net/bleroy/archive/2010/01/21/server-side-resizing-with-wpf-now-with-jpg.aspx*.

Controlling Images via an HTTP Handler

What if the user requests the JPG file directly from the address bar? And what if the image is linked by another Web site or referenced in a blog post? By default, the original image is served without any further modification. Why is this so?

For performance reasons, IIS serves static files, such as JPG images, directly without involving any external module, including the ASP.NET runtime. In this way, the HTTP handler that does the trick of adding a copyright note is therefore blissfully ignored when the request is made via the address bar or a hyperlink. What can you do about it?

In IIS 6, you must register the JPG extension as an ASP.NET extension for a particular application using IIS Manager. In this case, each request for JPG resources is forwarded to your application and resolved through the HTTP handler.

In IIS 7, things are even simpler for developers. All you have to do is add the following lines to the application's *web.config* file:

```
<system.webServer>
    <handlers>
        <add name="Jpeg"
             preCondition="integratedMode"
             verb="*"
             path="*.jpg"
             type="DynImageHandler, AspNetGallery.Extensions" />
    </handlers>
</system.webServer>
```

You might want to add the same setting also under *<httpHandlers>*, which will be read in cases where IIS 7.x is configured in classic mode:

```
<httpHandlers>
    <add verb="*" path="*.jpg" type="DynImageHandler, AspNetGallery.Extensions"/>
</httpHandlers>
```

This is yet another benefit of the unified runtime pipeline we experience when the ASP.NET application runs under IIS 7 integrated mode.

> **Note** An HTTP handler that needs to access session-state values must implement the *IRequiresSessionState* interface. Like *INamingContainer*, it's a marker interface and requires no method implementation. Note that the *IRequiresSessionState* interface indicates that the HTTP handler requires read and write access to the session state. If read-only access is needed, use the *IReadOnlySessionState* interface instead.

Advanced HTTP Handler Programming

HTTP handlers are not a tool for everybody. They serve a very neat purpose: changing the way a particular resource, or set of resources, is served to the user. You can use handlers to filter out resources based on runtime conditions or to apply any form of additional logic to the retrieval of traditional resources such as pages and images. Finally, you can use HTTP handlers to serve certain pages or resources in an asynchronous manner.

For HTTP handlers, the registration step is key. Registration enables ASP.NET to know about your handler and its purpose. Registration is required for two practical reasons. First, it serves to ensure that IIS forwards the call to the correct ASP.NET application. Second, it serves to instruct your ASP.NET application on the class to load to handle the request. As mentioned, you can use handlers to override the processing of existing resources (for example, *hello.aspx*) or to introduce new functionalities (for example, *folder.axd*). In both cases, you're invoking a resource whose extension is already known to IIS—the *.axd* extension is registered in the IIS metabase when you install ASP.NET. In both cases, though, you need to modify the *web.config* file of the application to let the application know about the handler.

By using the ASHX extension and programming model for handlers, you can also save yourself the *web.config* update and deploy a new HTTP handler by simply copying a new file in a new or existing application's folder.

Deploying Handlers as ASHX Resources

An alternative way to define an HTTP handler is through an *.ashx* file. The file contains a special directive, named *@WebHandler*, that expresses the association between the HTTP handler endpoint and the class used to implement the functionality. All *.ashx* files must begin with a directive like the following one:

```
<%@ WebHandler Language="C#" Class="AspNetGallery.Handlers.MyHandler" %>
```

When an *.ashx* endpoint is invoked, ASP.NET parses the source code of the file and figures out the HTTP handler class to use from the *@WebHandler* directive. This automation removes the need of updating the *web.config* file. Here's a sample *.ashx* file. As you can see, it is the plain class file plus the special *@WebHandler* directive:

```
<%@ WebHandler Language="C#" Class="MyHandler" %>

using System.Web;

public class MyHandler : IHttpHandler {

    public void ProcessRequest (HttpContext context) {
        context.Response.ContentType = "text/plain";
        context.Response.Write("Hello World");
    }

    public bool IsReusable {
        get {
            return false;
        }
    }
}
```

Note that the source code of the class can either be specified inline or loaded from any of the assemblies referenced by the application. When *.ashx* resources are used to implement an HTTP handler, you just deploy the source file and you're done. Just as for XML Web services, the source file is loaded and compiled only on demand. Because ASP.NET adds a special entry to the IIS metabase for *.ashx* resources, you don't even need to enter changes to the Web server configuration.

Resources with an *.ashx* extension are handled by an HTTP handler class named *SimpleHandleFactory*. Note that *SimpleHandleFactory* is actually an HTTP handler factory class, not a simple HTTP handler class. We'll discuss handler factories in a moment.

The *SimpleHandleFactory* class looks for the *@WebHandler* directive at the beginning of the file. The *@WebHandler* directive tells the handler factory the name of the HTTP handler class to instantiate when the source code has been compiled.

Important You can build HTTP handlers both as regular class files compiled to an assembly and via *.ashx* resources. There's no significant difference between the two approaches except that *.ashx* resources, like ordinary ASP.NET pages, will be compiled on the fly upon the first request.

Prevent Access to Forbidden Resources

If your Web application manages resources of a type that you don't want to make publicly available over the Web, you must instruct IIS not to display those files. A possible way to accomplish this consists of forwarding the request to *aspnet_isapi* and then binding the extension to one of the built-in handlers—the *HttpForbiddenHandler* class:

```
<add verb="*" path="*.xyz" type="System.Web.HttpForbiddenHandler" />
```

Any attempt to access an *.xyz* resource results in an error message being displayed. The same trick can also be applied for individual resources served by your application. If you need to deploy, say, a text file but do not want to take the risk that somebody can get to it, add the following:

```
<add verb="*" path="yourFile.txt" type="System.Web.HttpForbiddenHandler" />
```

Should It Be Reusable or Not?

In a conventional HTTP handler, the *ProcessRequest* method takes the lion's share of the overall set of functionality. The second member of the *IHttpHandler* interface—the *IsReusable* property—is used only in particular circumstances. If you set the *IsReusable* property to return *true*, the handler is not unloaded from memory after use and is repeatedly used. Put another way, the Boolean value returned by *IsReusable* indicates whether the handler object can be pooled.

Frankly, most of the time it doesn't really matter what you return—be it *true* or *false*. If you set the property to return *false*, you require that a new object be allocated for each request. The simple allocation of an object is not a particularly expensive operation. However, the initialization of the handler might be costly. In this case, by making the handler reusable, you save much of the overhead. If the handler doesn't hold any state, there's no reason for not making it reusable.

In summary, I'd say that *IsReusable* should be always set to *true*, except when you have instance properties to deal with or properties that might cause trouble if used in a concurrent environment. If you have no initialization tasks, it doesn't really matter whether it returns *true* or *false*. As a margin note, the *System.Web.UI.Page* class—the most popular HTTP handler ever—sets its *IsReusable* property to *false*.

The key point to determine is the following: Who's really using *IsReusable* and, subsequently, who really cares about its value?

Once the HTTP runtime knows the HTTP handler class to serve a given request, it simply instantiates it—no matter what. So when is the *IsReusable* property of a given handler taken into account? Only if you use an HTTP handler factory—that is, a piece of code that dynamically decides which handler should be used for a given request. An HTTP handler factory can query a handler to determine whether the same instance can be used to service multiple requests and thus optionally create and maintain a pool of handlers.

ASP.NET pages and ASHX resources are served through factories. However, none of these factories ever checks *IsReusable*. Of all the built-in handler factories in the whole ASP.NET platform, very few check the *IsReusable* property of related handlers. So what's the bottom line?

As long as you're creating HTTP handlers for AXD, ASHX, or perhaps ASPX resources, be aware that the *IsReusable* property is blissfully ignored. Do not waste your time trying to figure out the optimal configuration. Instead, if you're creating an HTTP handler factory to serve a set of resources, whether or not to implement a pool of handlers is up to you and *IsReusable* is the perfect tool for the job.

But when should you employ an HTTP handler factory? You should do it in all situations in which the HTTP handler class for a request is not uniquely identified. For example, for ASPX pages, you don't know in advance which HTTP handler type you have to use. The type might not even exist (in which case, you compile it on the fly). The HTTP handler factory is used whenever you need to apply some logic to decide which handler is the right one to use. In other words, you need an HTTP handler factory when declarative binding between endpoints and classes is not enough.

HTTP Handler Factories

An HTTP request can be directly associated with an HTTP handler or with an HTTP handler factory object. An HTTP handler factory is a class that implements the *IHttpHandlerFactory* interface and is in charge of returning the actual HTTP handler to use to serve the request. The *SimpleHandlerFactory* class provides a good example of how a factory works. The factory is mapped to requests directed at *.ashx* resources. When such a request comes in, the factory determines the actual handler to use by looking at the *@WebHandler* directive in the source file.

In the .NET Framework, HTTP handler factories are used to perform some preliminary tasks on the requested resource prior to passing it on to the handler. Another good example of a handler factory object is an internal class named *PageHandlerFactory*, which is in charge of serving *.aspx* pages. In this case, the factory handler figures out the name of the handler to use and, if possible, loads it up from an existing assembly.

HTTP handler factories are classes that implement a couple of methods on the *IHttpHandlerFactory* interface—*GetHandler* and *ReleaseHandler*, as shown in Table 4-5.

TABLE 4-5 Members of the *IHttpHandlerFactory* Interface

Method	Description
GetHandler	Returns an instance of an HTTP handler to serve the request.
ReleaseHandler	Takes an existing HTTP handler instance and frees it up or pools it.

The *GetHandler* method has the following signature:

```
public virtual IHttpHandler GetHandler(
                HttpContext context,
                String requestType,
                String url,
                String pathTranslated);
```

The *requestType* argument is a string that evaluates to GET or POST—the HTTP verb of the request. The last two arguments represent the raw URL of the request and the physical path behind it. The *ReleaseHandler* method is a mandatory override for any class that implements *IHttpHandlerFactory*; in most cases, it will just have an empty body.

The following listing shows a sample HTTP handler factory that returns different handlers based on the HTTP verb (GET or POST) used for the request:

```
class MyHandlerFactory : IHttpHandlerFactory
{
    public IHttpHandler GetHandler(HttpContext context,
        String requestType, String url, String pathTranslated)
    {
        // Feel free to create a pool of HTTP handlers here
        if(context.Request.RequestType.ToLower() == "get")
            return (IHttpHandler) new MyGetHandler();
        else if(context.Request.RequestType.ToLower() == "post")
            return (IHttpHandler) new MyPostHandler();
        return null;
    }

    public void ReleaseHandler(IHttpHandler handler)
    {
        // Nothing to do
    }
}
```

When you use an HTTP handler factory, it's the factory (not the handler) that you want to register in the ASP.NET configuration file. If you register the handler, it will always be used to serve requests. If you opt for a factory, you have a chance to decide dynamically and based on runtime conditions which handler is more appropriate for a certain request. In doing so, you can use the *IsReusable* property of handlers to implement a pool.

Asynchronous Handlers

An asynchronous HTTP handler is a class that implements the *IHttpAsyncHandler* interface. The system initiates the call by invoking the *BeginProcessRequest* method. Next, when the method ends, a callback function is automatically invoked to terminate the call. In the .NET Framework, the sole *HttpApplication* class implements the asynchronous interface. The members of the *IHttpAsyncHandler* interface are shown in Table 4-6.

TABLE 4-6 Members of the *IHttpAsyncHandler* Interface

Method	Description
BeginProcessRequest	Initiates an asynchronous call to the specified HTTP handler
EndProcessRequest	Terminates the asynchronous call

The signature of the *BeginProcessRequest* method is as follows:

```
IAsyncResult BeginProcessRequest(
            HttpContext context,
            AsyncCallback cb,
            Object extraData);
```

The *context* argument provides references to intrinsic server objects used to service HTTP requests. The second parameter is the *AsyncCallback* object to invoke when the asynchronous method call is complete. The third parameter is a generic cargo variable that contains any data you might want to pass to the handler.

> **Note** An *AsyncCallback* object is a delegate that defines the logic needed to finish processing the asynchronous operation. A delegate is a class that holds a reference to a method. A delegate class has a fixed signature, and it can hold references only to methods that match that signature. A delegate is equivalent to a type-safe function pointer or a callback. As a result, an *AsyncCallback* object is just the code that executes when the asynchronous handler has completed its job.

The *AsyncCallback* delegate has the following signature:

```
public delegate void AsyncCallback(IAsyncResult ar);
```

It uses the *IAsyncResult* interface to obtain the status of the asynchronous operation. To illustrate the plumbing of asynchronous handlers, I'll show you what the HTTP runtime does when it deals with asynchronous handlers. The HTTP runtime invokes the *BeginProcessRequest* method as illustrated here:

```
// Sets an internal member of the HttpContext class with
// the current instance of the asynchronous handler
context.AsyncAppHandler = asyncHandler;

// Invokes the BeginProcessRequest method on the asynchronous HTTP handler
asyncHandler.BeginProcessRequest(context, OnCompletionCallback, context);
```

The *context* argument is the current instance of the *HttpContext* class and represents the context of the request. A reference to the HTTP context is also passed as the custom data sent to the handler to process the request. The *extraData* parameter in the *BeginProcessRequest* signature is used to represent the status of the asynchronous operation. The *BeginProcessRequest* method returns an object of type *HttpAsyncResult*—a class that implements the *IAsyncResult* interface. The *IAsyncResult* interface contains a property named *AsyncState* that is set with the *extraData* value—in this case, the HTTP context.

The *OnCompletionCallback* method is an internal method. It gets automatically triggered when the asynchronous processing of the request terminates. The following listing illustrates the pseudocode of the *HttpRuntime* private method:

```
// The method must have the signature of an AsyncCallback delegate
private void OnHandlerCompletion(IAsyncResult ar)
{
    // The ar parameter is an instance of HttpAsyncResult
    HttpContext context = (HttpContext) ar.AsyncState;

    // Retrieves the instance of the asynchronous HTTP handler
    // and completes the request
    IHttpAsyncHandler asyncHandler = context.AsyncAppHandler;
    asyncHandler.EndProcessRequest(ar);

    // Finalizes the request as usual
    ...
}
```

The completion handler retrieves the HTTP context of the request through the *AsyncState* property of the *IAsyncResult* object it gets from the system. As mentioned, the actual object passed is an instance of the *HttpAsyncResult* class—in any case, it is the return value of the *BeginProcessRequest* method. The completion routine extracts the reference to the asynchronous handler from the context and issues a call to the *EndProcessRequest* method:

```
void EndProcessRequest(IAsyncResult result);
```

The *EndProcessRequest* method takes the *IAsyncResult* object returned by the call to *BeginProcessRequest*. As implemented in the *HttpApplication* class, the *EndProcessRequest* method does nothing special and is limited to throwing an exception if an error occurred.

Implementing Asynchronous Handlers

Asynchronous handlers essentially serve one particular scenario—a scenario in which the generation of the markup is subject to lengthy operations, such as time-consuming database stored procedures or calls to Web services. In these situations, the ASP.NET thread in charge of the request is stuck waiting for the operation to complete. Because threads are valuable resources, lengthy tasks that keep threads occupied for too long are potentially the perfect scalability killer. However, asynchronous handlers are here to help.

The idea is that the request begins on a thread-pool thread, but that thread is released as soon as the operation begins. In *BeginProcessRequest*, you typically create your own thread and start the lengthy operation. *BeginProcessRequest* doesn't wait for the operation to complete; therefore, the thread is returned to the pool immediately.

There are a lot of tricky details that this bird's-eye description just omitted. In the first place, you should strive to avoid a proliferation of threads. Ideally, you should use a custom thread pool. Furthermore, you must figure out a way to signal when the lengthy operation has terminated. This typically entails creating a custom class that implements *IAsyncResult* and returning it from *BeginProcessRequest*. This class embeds a synchronization object—typically a *ManualResetEvent* object—that the custom thread carrying the work will signal upon completion.

In the end, building asynchronous handlers is definitely tricky and not for novice developers. Very likely, you are more interested in having asynchronous pages than in generic asynchronous HTTP handlers. With asynchronous pages, the "lengthy task" is merely the *ProcessRequest* method of the *Page* class. (Obviously, you configure the page to execute asynchronously only if the page contains code that starts I/O-bound and potentially lengthy operations.)

ASP.NET offers ad hoc support for building asynchronous pages more easily and more comfortably than through HTTP handlers.

Caution I've seen several ASP.NET developers use an *.aspx* page to serve markup other than HTML markup. This is not a good idea. An *.aspx* resource is served by quite a rich and sophisticated HTTP handler—the *System.Web.UI.Page* class. The *ProcessRequest* method of this class entirely provides for the page life cycle as we know it—*Init*, *Load*, and *PreRender* events, as well as rendering stage, view state, and postback management. Nothing of the kind is really required if you only need to retrieve and return, say, the bytes of an image. HTTP handlers are an excellent way to speed up particular requests. HTTP handlers are also a quick way to serve AJAX requests without writing (and spinning up) the whole machinery of Windows Communication Foundation (WCF) services. At the very end of the day, an HTTP handler is an endpoint and can be used to serve data to AJAX requests. In this regard, the difference between an HTTP handler and a WCF service is that the HTTP handler doesn't have a free serialization engine for input and output values.

Writing HTTP Modules

So you've learned that any incoming requests for ASP.NET resources are handed over to the worker process for the actual processing. The worker process is distinct from the Web server executable so that even if one ASP.NET application crashes, it doesn't bring down the whole server.

On the way to the final HTTP handler, the request passes through a pipeline of special runtime modules—HTTP modules. An HTTP module is a .NET Framework class that implements the *IHttpModule* interface. The HTTP modules that filter the raw data within the request are configured on a per-application basis within the *web.config* file. All ASP.NET applications, though, inherit a bunch of system HTTP modules configured in the global *web.config* file. Applications hosted under IIS 7.x integrated mode can configure HTTP modules that run at the IIS level for any requests that comes in, not just for ASP.NET-related resources.

An HTTP module can pre-process and post-process a request, and it intercepts and handles system events as well as events raised by other modules.

The *IHttpModule* Interface

The *IHttpModule* interface defines only two methods: *Init* and *Dispose*. The *Init* method initializes a module and prepares it to handle requests. At this time, you subscribe to receive notifications for the events of interest. The *Dispose* method disposes of the resources (all but memory!) used by the module. Typical tasks you perform within the *Dispose* method are closing database connections or file handles.

The *IHttpModule* methods have the following signatures:

```
void Init(HttpApplication app);
void Dispose();
```

The *Init* method receives a reference to the *HttpApplication* object that is serving the request. You can use this reference to wire up to system events. The *HttpApplication* object also features a property named *Context* that provides access to the intrinsic properties of the ASP.NET application. In this way, you gain access to *Response*, *Request*, *Session*, and the like.

Table 4-7 lists the events that HTTP modules can listen to and handle.

TABLE 4-7 *HttpApplication* **Events in Order of Appearance**

Event	Description
BeginRequest	Occurs as soon as the HTTP pipeline begins to process the request.
AuthenticateRequest, PostAuthenticateRequest	Occurs when a security module has established the identity of the user.
AuthorizeRequest, PostAuthorizeRequest	Occurs when a security module has verified user authorization.
ResolveRequestCache, PostResolveRequestCache	Occurs when the ASP.NET runtime resolves the request through the output cache.
MapRequestHandler, PostMapRequestHandler	Occurs when the HTTP handler to serve the request has been found. *It is fired only to applications running in classic mode or under IIS 6.*
AcquireRequestState, PostAcquireRequestState	Occurs when the handler that will actually serve the request acquires the state information associated with the request.
PreRequestHandlerExecute	Occurs just before the HTTP handler of choice begins to work.
PostRequestHandlerExecute	Occurs when the HTTP handler of choice finishes execution. The response text has been generated at this point.
ReleaseRequestState, PostReleaseRequestState	Occurs when the handler releases the state information associated with the current request.
UpdateRequestCache, PostUpdateRequestCache	Occurs when the ASP.NET runtime stores the response of the current request in the output cache to be used to serve subsequent requests.
LogRequest, PostLogRequest	Occurs when the ASP.NET runtime is ready to log the results of the request. Logging is guaranteed to execute even if errors occur. *It is fired only to applications running under IIS 7 integrated mode.*
EndRequest	Occurs as the last event in the HTTP pipeline chain of execution.

Another pair of events can occur during the request, but in a nondeterministic order. They are *PreSendRequestHeaders* and *PreSendRequestContent*.

The *PreSendRequestHeaders* event informs the *HttpApplication* object in charge of the request that HTTP headers are about to be sent. The *PreSendRequestContent* event tells the *HttpApplication* object in charge of the request that the response body is about to be sent. Both these events normally fire after *EndRequest*, but not always. For example, if buffering is turned off, the event gets fired as soon as some content is going to be sent to the client. Speaking of nondeterministic application events, it must be said that a third nondeterministic event is, of course, *Error*.

All these events are exposed by the *HttpApplication* object that an HTTP module receives as an argument to the *Init* method. You can write handlers for such events in the *global.asax* file of the application. You can also catch these events from within a custom HTTP module.

A Custom HTTP Module

Let's come to grips with HTTP modules by writing a relatively simple custom module named *Marker* that adds a signature at the beginning and end of each page served by the application. The following code outlines the class we need to write:

```
using System;
using System.Web;

namespace AspNetGallery.Extensions.Modules
{
    public class MarkerModule : IHttpModule
    {
        public void Init(IHttpApplication app)
        {
            // Register for pipeline events
        }

        public void Dispose()
        {
            // Nothing to do here
        }
    }
}
```

The *Init* method is invoked by the *HttpApplication* class to load the module. In the *Init* method, you normally don't need to do more than simply register your own event handlers. The *Dispose* method is, more often than not, empty. The heart of the HTTP module is really in the event handlers you define.

Wiring Up Events

The sample *Marker* module registers a couple of pipeline events. They are *BeginRequest* and *EndRequest*. *BeginRequest* is the first event that hits the HTTP application object when the request begins processing. *EndRequest* is the event that signals the request is going to be terminated, and it's your last chance to intervene. By handling these two events, you can write custom text to the output stream before and after the regular HTTP handler—the *Page*-derived class.

The following listing shows the implementation of the *Init* and *Dispose* methods for the sample module:

```
public void Init(HttpApplication app)
{
    // Register for pipeline events
    app.BeginRequest += OnBeginRequest;
    app.EndRequest += EndRequest;
}

public void Dispose()
{
}
```

The *BeginRequest* and *EndRequest* event handlers have a similar structure. They obtain a reference to the current *HttpApplication* object from the sender and get the HTTP context from there. Next, they work with the *Response* object to append text or a custom header:

```csharp
public void OnBeginRequest(Object sender, EventArgs e)
{
    var app = (HttpApplication) sender;
    var ctx = app.Context;

    // More code here
    ...

    // Add custom header to the HTTP response
    ctx.Response.AppendHeader("Author", "DinoE");

    // PageHeaderText is a constant string defined elsewhere
    ctx.Response.Write(PageHeaderText);
}

public void OnEndRequest(Object sender, EventArgs e)
{
    // Get access to the HTTP context
    var app = (HttpApplication) sender;
    var ctx = app.Context;

    // More code here
    ...

    // Append some custom text
    // PageFooterText is a constant string defined elsewhere
    ctx.Response.Write(PageFooterText);
}
```

OnBeginRequest writes standard page header text and also adds a custom HTTP header. *OnEndRequest* simply appends the page footer. The effect of this HTTP module is visible in Figure 4-7.

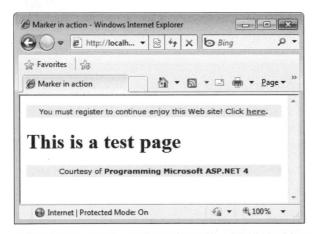

FIGURE 4-7 The *Marker* HTTP module adds a header and footer to each page within the application.

Registering with the Configuration File

You register a new HTTP module by adding an entry to the *<httpModules>* section of the configuration file. The overall syntax of the *<httpModules>* section closely resembles that of HTTP handlers. To add a new module, you use the *<add>* node and specify the *name* and *type* attributes. The *name* attribute contains the public name of the module. This name is used to select the module within the *HttpApplication*'s *Modules* collection. If the module fires custom events, this name is also used as the prefix for building automatic event handlers in the *global.asax* file:

```
<system.web>
  <httpModules>
    <add name="Marker"
        type="MarkerModule, AspNetGallery.Extensions" />
  </httpModules>
</system.web>
```

The order in which modules are applied depends on the physical order of the modules in the configuration list. You can remove a system module and replace it with your own that provides a similar functionality. In this case, in the application's *web.config* file you use the *<remove>* node to drop the default module and then use *<add>* to insert your own. If you want to completely redefine the order of HTTP modules for your application, you can clear all the default modules by using the *<clear>* node and then re-register them all in the order you prefer.

Note HTTP modules are loaded and initialized only once, at the startup of the application. Unlike HTTP handlers, they apply to any requests. So when you plan to create a new HTTP module, you should first wonder whether its functionality should span all possible requests in the application. Is it possible to choose which requests an HTTP module should process? The *Init* method is called only once in the application's lifetime, but the handlers you register are called once for each request. So to operate only on certain pages, you can do as follows:

```
public void OnBeginRequest(object sender, EventArgs e)
{
    HttpApplication app = (HttpApplication) sender;
    HttpContext ctx = app.Context;
    if (!ShouldHook(ctx))
        return;
    ...
}
```

OnBeginRequest is your handler for the *BeginRequest* event. The *ShouldHook* helper function returns a Boolean value. It is passed the context of the request—that is, any information that is available on the request. You can code it to check the URL as well as any HTTP content type and headers.

Accessing Other HTTP Modules

The sample just discussed demonstrates how to wire up pipeline events—that is, events fired by the *HttpApplication* object. But what about events fired by other modules? The *HttpApplication* object provides a property named *Modules* that gets the collection of modules for the current application.

The *Modules* property is of type *HttpModuleCollection* and contains the names of the modules for the application. The collection class inherits from the abstract class *NameObjectCollectionBase*, which is a collection of pairs made of a string and an object. The string indicates the public name of the module; the object is the actual instance of the module. To access the module that handles the session state, you need code like this:

```
var sessionModule = app.Modules["Session"];
sessionModule.Start += OnSessionStart;
```

As mentioned, you can also handle events raised by HTTP modules within the *global.asax* file and use the *ModuleName_EventName* convention to name the event handlers. The name of the module is just one of the settings you need to define when registering an HTTP module.

Examining a Real-World HTTP Module

The previous example gave us the gist of an HTTP module component. It was a simple (and kind of pointless) example, but it was useful to demonstrate what you can do with HTTP modules in a real application. First and foremost, not all applications need custom HTTP modules. ASP.NET comes with a bunch of built-in modules, which are listed in Table 4-8.

TABLE 4-8 Native HTTP Modules

Event	Description
AnonymousIdentificationModule	Manages anonymous identifiers for the ASP.NET application
DefaultAuthenticationModule	Ensures that the *User* object is always bound to some identity
FileAuthorizationModule	Verifies that the user has permission to access the given file.
FormsAuthenticationModule	Manages Forms authentication
OutputCacheModule	Implements output page caching
ProfileModule	Implements the data retrieval for profile data
RoleManagerModule	Manages the retrieval of role information
ScriptModule	Manages script requests placed through ASP.NET AJAX
SessionStateModule	Manages session state
UrlAuthorizationModule	Verifies that the user has permission to access the given URL
UrlRoutingModule	Implements URL routing
WindowsAuthenticationModule	Manages Windows authentication

All these HTTP modules perform a particular system-level operation and can be customized by application-specific code. Because an HTTP module works on any incoming request, it usually doesn't perform application-specific tasks. From an application perspective, an HTTP module is helpful when you need to apply filters on all requests for profiling, debugging, or functional reasons.

Let's dissect one of the system-provided HTTP modules, which will also slowly move us toward the next topic of this chapter. Enter the URL-routing HTTP module.

The *UrlRoutingModule* Class

In ASP.NET 3.5 Service Pack 1, Microsoft introduced a new and more effective API for URL rewriting. Because of its capabilities, the new API got a better name—*URL routing*. URL routing is built on top of the URL rewriting API, but it offers a richer and higher level programming model. (I'll get to URL rewriting and URL routing in a moment.)

The URL routing engine is a system-provided HTTP module that wires up the *PostResolveRequestCache* event. In a nutshell, the HTTP module matches the requested URL to one of the user-defined rewriting rules (known as *routes*) and finds the HTTP handler that is due to serve that route. If any HTTP handler is found, it becomes the actual handler for the current request. Here's the signature of the module class:

```
public class UrlRoutingModule : IHttpModule
{
    public virtual void PostResolveRequestCache(HttpContextBase context)
    {
        ...
    }

    void IHttpModule.Dispose()
    {
        ...
    }

    void IHttpModule.Init(HttpApplication application)
    {
        ...
    }
}
```

The class implements the *IHttpModule* interface implicitly, and in its initialization phase it registers a handler for the system's *PostResolveRequestCache* event.

The *PostResolveRequestCache* Event

The *PostResolveRequestCache* event fires right after the runtime environment (IIS or ASP. NET, depending on the IIS working mode) has determined whether the response for the current request can be served from the output cache or not. If the response is already cached, there's no need to process the request and, subsequently, no need to analyze the content of the URL. Any system events that follow *PostResolveRequestCache* are part of the request processing cycle; therefore, hooking up *PostResolveRequestCache* is the optimal moment for taking control of requests that require some work on the server.

The first task accomplished by the HTTP module consists of grabbing any route data contained in the URL of the current request. The module matches the URL to one of the registered routes and figures out the handler for the route.

The route handler is not the HTTP handler yet. It is simply the object responsible for handling the route. The primary task of a route handler, however, is returning the HTTP handler to serve the request.

In the end, HTTP modules are extremely powerful tools that give you control over every little step taken by the system to process a request. For the same reason, however, HTTP modules are delicate tools—every time you write one, it will be invoked for each and every request. An HTTP module is hardly a tool for a specific application (with due exceptions), but it is often a formidable tool for implementing cross-cutting, system-level features.

URL Routing

The whole ASP.NET platform originally developed around the idea of serving requests for physical pages. Look at the following URL:

```
http://northwind.com/news.aspx?id=1234
```

It turns out that most URLs used within an ASP.NET application are made of two parts: the path to the physical Web page that contains the logic to apply, and some data stuffed in the query string to provide parameters. In the URL just shown, the *news.aspx* page incorporates the logic required to retrieve and display the data; the ID for the specific news to retrieve is provided, instead, via a parameter on the query string.

This is the essence of the Page Controller pattern for Web applications. The request targets a page whose logic and graphical layout are saved to disk. This approach has worked for a few years and still works today. The content of the news is displayed correctly, and everybody is generally happy. In addition, you have just one page to maintain, and you still have a way to identify a particular piece of news via the URL.

A possible drawback of this approach is that the real intent of the page might not be clear to users. And, more importantly, search engines usually assign higher ranks to terms contained in the URL. Therefore, an expressive URL provides search engines with an effective set of keywords that describe the page. To fix this, you need to make the entire URL friendlier and more readable. But you don't want to add new Web pages to the application or a bunch of made-to-measure HTTP handlers. Ideally, you should try to transform the request in a command sent to the server rather than having it be simply the virtual file path name of the page to display.

> **Note** The advent of Content Management Systems (CMS) raised the need to have friendlier URLs. A CMS is an application not necessarily written for a single user and that likely manages several pages created using semi-automatic algorithms. For these tools, resorting to pages with an algorithmically editable URL was a great help. But, alas, it was not a great help for users and search engines. This is where the need arises to expose user-friendly URLs while managing cryptic URLs internally. A URL rewriter API attempts to bridge precisely this gap.

The URL Routing Engine

To provide the ability to always expose friendly URLs to users, ASP.NET has supported a feature called *URL rewriting* since its inception. At its core, URL rewriting consists of an HTTP module (or a *global.asax* event handler) that hooks up a given request, parses its original URL, and instructs the HTTP runtime environment to serve a "possibly related but different" URL.

URL rewriting is a powerful feature; however, it's not free of issues. For this reason, Microsoft more recently introduced a new API in ASP.NET. Although it's based on the same underlying URL rewriting, the API offers a higher level of programmability and more features overall—and the URL routing engine in particular.

Originally devised for ASP.NET MVC, URL routing gives you total freedom to organize the layout of the URL recognized by your application. In a way, the URL becomes a command for the Web application; the application is the only entity put in charge of parsing and validating the syntax of the command. The URL engine is the system-provided component that validates the URL. The URL routing engine is general enough to be usable in both ASP.NET MVC and ASP.NET Web Forms; in fact, it was taken out of the ASP.NET MVC framework and incorporated in the general ASP.NET *system.web* assembly a while ago.

URL routing differs in ASP.NET MVC and ASP.NET Web Forms only with regard to how you express the final destination of the request. You use a controller-action pair in ASP.NET MVC; you use an ASPX path in ASP.NET Web Forms.

Original URL Rewriting API

URL rewriting helps you in two ways. It makes it possible for you to use a generic front-end page such as *news.aspx* and then redirect to a specific page whose actual URL is read from a database or any other container. In addition, it also enables you to request user-friendly URLs to be programmatically mapped to less intuitive, but easier to manage, URLs.

Here's a quick example of how you can rewrite the requested URL as another one:

```
protected void Application_BeginRequest(object sender, EventArgs e)
{
    // Get the current request context
    var context = HttpContext.Current;

    // Get the URL to the handler that will physically handle the request
    var newURL = ParseOriginalUrl(context);

    // Overwrite the target URL of the current request
    context.RewritePath(newURL);
}
```

The *RewritePath* method of *HttpContext* lets you change the URL of the current request on the fly, thus performing a sort of internal redirect. As a result, the user is provided the content generated for the URL you set through *RewritePath*. At the same time, the URL shown in the address bar remains as the originally requested one.

In a nutshell, URL rewriting exists to let you decouple the URL from the physical Web form that serves the requests.

> **Note** The change of the final URL takes place on the server and, more importantly, within the context of the same call. *RewritePath* should be used carefully and mainly from within the *global.asax* file. In Web Forms, for example, if you use *RewritePath* in the context of a postback event, you can experience some view-state problems.

One drawback of the URL rewriting API is that as the API changes the target URL of the request, any postbacks are directed to the rewritten URL. For example, if you rewrite *news.aspx?id=1234* to *1234.aspx*, any postbacks from *1234.aspx* are targeted to the same *1234.aspx* instead of to the original URL.

This might or might not be a problem for you and, for sure, it doesn't break any page behavior. However, the original URL has just been fully replaced while you likely want to use the same, original URL as the front end. If this is the case (and most of the time, this is exactly the case), URL rewriting just created a new problem.

In addition, the URL rewriting logic is intrinsically monodirectional because it doesn't offer any built-in mechanism to go from the original URL to the rewritten URL and then back.

URL Patterns and Routes

The URL routing module is a system component that intercepts any request and attempts to match the URL to a predefined pattern. All requested URLs that match a given pattern are processed in a distinct way; typically, they are rewritten to other URLs.

The URL patterns that you define are known as *routes*.

A route contains placeholders that can be filled up with values extracted from the URL. Often referred to as a *route parameter*, a placeholder is a name enclosed in curly brackets { }. You can have multiple placeholders in a route as long as they are separated by a constant or delimiter. The forward slash (/) character acts as a delimiter between the various parts of the route. Here's a sample route:

```
Category/{action}/{categoryName}
```

URLs that match the preceding route begin with the word "Category" followed by two segments. The first segment will be mapped to the *action* route parameter; the second segment will be mapped to the *categoryName* route parameter. As you might have guessed, *action* and *categoryName* are just arbitrary names for parameters. A URL that matches the preceding route is the following:

```
/Category/Edit/Beverages
```

The route is nothing more than a pattern and is not associated with any logic of its own. Invoked by the routing module, the component that ultimately decides *how* to rewrite the matching URL is another one entirely. Precisely, it is the *route handler*.

Technically speaking, a route handler is a class that implements the *IRouteHandler* interface. The interface is defined as shown here:

```
public interface IRouteHandler
{
    IHttpHandler GetHttpHandler(RequestContext requestContext);
}
```

In its *GetHttpHandler* method, a route handler typically looks at route parameters to figure out if any of the information available needs to be passed down to the HTTP handler (for example, an ASP.NET page) that will handle the request. If this is the case, the route handler adds this information to the *Items* collection of the HTTP context. Finally, the route handler obtains an instance of a class that implements the *IHttpHandler* interface and returns that.

For Web Forms requests, the route handler—an instance of the *PageRouteHandler* class—resorts to the ASP.NET build manager to identify the dynamic class for the requested page resource and creates the handler on the fly.

Important The big difference between plain URL rewriting and ASP.NET routing is that with ASP.NET routing, the URL is not changed when the system begins processing the request. Instead, it's changed later in the life cycle. In this way, the runtime environment can perform most of its usual tasks on the original URL, which is an approach that maintains a consistent and robust solution. In addition, a late intervention on the URL also gives developers a big chance to extract values from the URL and the request context. In this way, the routing mechanism can be driven by a set of rewriting rules or patterns. If the original URL matches a particular pattern, you rewrite it to the associated URL. URL patterns are an external resource and are kept in one place, which makes the solution more maintainable overall.

Routing in Web Forms

To introduce URL routing in your Web Forms application, you start by defining routes. Routes go in the *global.asax* file to be processed at the very beginning of the application. To define a route, you create an instance of the *Route* class by specifying the URL pattern, the handler, and optionally a name for the route. However, you typically use helper methods that save you a lot of details and never expose you directly to the API of the *Route* class. The next section shows some code that registers routes.

> **Note** The vast majority of examples that illustrate routing in both ASP.NET MVC and Web Forms explicitly register routes from within *global.asax*. Loading route information from an external file is not be a bad idea, though, and will make your application a bit more resilient to changes.

Defining Routes for Specific Pages

In *Application_Start*, you invoke a helper method inside of which new routes are created and added to a static route collection object. Here's a sample *global.asax* class:

```
public class Global : System.Web.HttpApplication
{
    void Application_Start(object sender, EventArgs e)
    {
        RegisterRoutes(RouteTable.Routes);
    }

    public static void RegisterRoutes(RouteCollection routes)
    {
        routes.MapPageRoute("Category",
            "Category/{action}/{categoryName}",
            "~/categories.aspx",
            true,
            new RouteValueDictionary
                {
                    { "categoryName", "beverages" },
                    { "action", "edit" }
                });
    }
}
```

All routes for the application are stored in a global container: the static *Routes* property of the *RouteTable* class. A reference to this property is passed to the helper *RegisterRoutes* method invoked upon application start.

The structure of the code you just saw is optimized for testability; nothing prevents you from stuffing all the code in the body of *Application_Start*.

The *MapPageRoute* method is a helper method that creates a *Route* object and adds it to the *Routes* collection. Here's a glimpse of its internal implementation:

```
public Route MapPageRoute(String routeName,
                          String routeUrl,
                          String physicalFile,
                          Boolean checkPhysicalUrlAccess,
                          RouteValueDictionary defaults,
                          RouteValueDictionary constraints,
                          RouteValueDictionary dataTokens)
{
    if (routeUrl == null)
    {
        throw new ArgumentNullException("routeUrl");
    }

    // Create the new route
    var route = new Route(routeUrl,
        defaults, constraints, dataTokens,
        new PageRouteHandler(physicalFile, checkPhysicalUrlAccess));

    // Add the new route to the global collection
    this.Add(routeName, route);
    return route;
}
```

The *MapPageRoute* method offers a simplified interface for creating a *Route* object. In particular, it requires you to specify the name of the route, the URL pattern for the route, and the physical ASP.NET Web Forms page the URL will map to. In addition, you can specify a Boolean flag to enforce the application of current authorization rules for the actual page. For example, imagine that the user requests a URL such as *customers/edit/alfki*. Imagine also that such a URL is mapped to *customers.aspx* and that this page is restricted to the admin role only. If the aforementioned Boolean argument is *false*, all users are allowed to view the page behind the URL. If the Boolean value is *true*, only admins will be allowed.

Finally, the *MapPageRoute* method can accept three dictionaries: the default values for URL parameters, additional constraints on the URL parameters, plus custom data values to pass on to the route handler.

In the previous example, we aren't using constraints and data tokens. Instead, we are specifying default values for the *categoryName* and *action* parameters. As a result, an incoming URL such as */category* will be automatically resolved as if it were */category/edit/beverages*.

Programmatic Access to Route Values

The *MapPageRoute* method just configures routes recognized by the application. Its job ends with the startup of the application. The URL routing HTTP module then kicks in for each request and attempts to match the request URL to any of the defined routes.

Routes are processed in the order in which they have been added to the *Routes* collection, and the search stops at the first match. For this reason, it is extremely important that you list your routes in decreasing order of importance—stricter rules must go first.

Beyond the order of appearance, other factors affect the process of matching URLs to routes. One is the set of default values that you might have provided for a route. Default values are simply values that are automatically assigned to defined placeholders in case the URL doesn't provide specific values. Consider the following two routes:

```
{Orders}/{Year}/{Month}
{Orders}/{Year}
```

If you assign the first route's default values for both *{Year}* and *{Month}*, the second route will never be evaluated because, thanks to the default values, the first route is always a match regardless of whether the URL specifies a year and a month.

The URL-routing HTTP module also uses constraints (which I'll say more about in a moment) to determine whether a URL matches a given route. If a match is finally found, the routing module gets the HTTP handler from the route handler and maps it to the HTTP context of the request.

Given the previously defined route, any matching requests are mapped to the *categories.aspx* page. How can this page know about the route parameters? How can this page know about the action requested or the category name? There's no need for the page to parse (again) the URL. Route parameters are available through a new property on the *Page* class—the *RouteData* property.

RouteData is a property of type *RouteData* and features the members listed in Table 4-9.

TABLE 4-9 Members of the *RouteData* Class

Member	Description
DataTokens	List of additional custom values that are passed to the route handler
GetRequiredString	Method that takes the name of a route parameter and returns its value
Route	Returns the current *Route* object
RouteHandler	Returns the handler for the current route
Values	Returns the dictionary of route parameter values

The following code snippet shows how you retrieve parameters in *Page_Load*:

```
protected void Page_Load(object sender, EventArgs e)
{
    var action = RouteData.GetRequiredString("action");
    ...
}
```

The only difference between using *GetRequiredString* and accessing the *Values* dictionary is that *GetRequiredString* throws if the requested value is not found. In addition, *GetRequiredString* uses protected access to the collection via *TryGetValue* instead of a direct reading.

Structure of Routes

A route is characterized by the five properties listed in Table 4-10.

TABLE 4-10 Properties of the *Route* Class

Property	Description
Constraints	List of additional constraints the URL should fulfill to match the route.
DataTokens	List of additional custom values that are passed to the route handler. These values, however, are not used to determine whether the route matches a URL pattern.
Defaults	List of default values to be used for route parameters.
RouteHandler	The object responsible for retrieving the HTTP handler to serve the request.
Url	The URL pattern for the route.

Constraints, *DataTokens*, and *Defaults* are all properties of type *RouteValueDictionary*. In spite of the fancy name, the *RouteValueDictionary* type is a plain *<String, Object>* dictionary.

Most of the time, the pattern defined by the route is sufficient to decide whether a given URL matches or not. However, this is not always the case. Consider, for example, the situation in which you are defining a route for recognizing requests for product details. You want to make sure of the following two aspects.

First, make sure the incoming URL is of the type *http://server/{category}/{productId}*, where *{category}* identifies the category of the product and *{productId}* indicates the ID of the product to retrieve.

Second, you also want to be sure that no invalid product ID is processed. You probably don't want to trigger a database call right from the URL routing module, but at the very least, you want to rule out as early as possible any requests that propose a product ID in an incompatible format. For example, if product IDs are numeric, you want to rule out anything passed in as a product ID that is alphanumeric.

Regular expressions are a simple way to filter requests to see if any segment of the URL is acceptable. Here's a sample route that keeps URLs with a string product ID off the application:

```
routes.MapPageRoute(
    "ProductInfo",
    "Category/{category}/{productId}/{locale}",
    "~/categories.aspx",
    true,
    new { category = "Beverages", locale="en-us" },
    new { productId = @"\d{8}",
          locale = ""[a-z]{2}-[a-z]{2}" }
);
```

The sixth parameter to the *MapPageRoute* method is a dictionary object that sets regular expressions for *productId* and *locale*. In particular, the product ID must be a numeric sequence of exactly eight digits, whereas the locale must be a pair of two-letter strings separated by a dash. The filter doesn't ensure that all invalid product IDs and locale codes are stopped at the gate, but at least it cuts off a good deal of work. An invalid URL is presented as an HTTP 404 failure and is subject to application-specific handling of HTTP errors.

More in general, a route constraint is a condition that a given URL parameter must fulfill to make the URL match the route. A constraint is defined via either regular expressions or objects that implement the *IRouteConstraint* interface.

Preventing Routing for Defined URLs

The ASP.NET URL routing module gives you maximum freedom to keep certain URLs off the routing mechanism. You can prevent the routing system from handling certain URLs in two steps. First, you define a pattern for those URLs and save it to a route. Second, you link that route to a special route handler—the *StopRoutingHandler* class.

Any request that belongs to a route managed by a *StopRoutingHandler* object is processed as a plain ASP.NET Web Forms endpoint. The following code instructs the routing system to ignore any *.axd* requests:

```
// In global.asax.cs
protected void Application_Start(Object sender, EventArgs e)
{
    RegisterRoutes(RouteTable.Routes);
}

public static void RegisterRoutes(RouteCollection routes)
{
  routes.IgnoreRoute("{resource}.axd/{*pathInfo}");
    ...
}
```

All that *IgnoreRoute* does is associate a *StopRoutingHandler* route handler to the route built around the specified URL pattern, thus preventing all matching URLs from being processed.

A little explanation is required for the *{*pathInfo}* placeholder in the URL. The token *pathInfo* simply represents a placeholder for any content following the *.axd* URL. The asterisk (*), though, indicates that the last parameter should match the rest of the URL. In other words, anything that follows the *.axd* extension goes into the *pathInfo* parameter. Such parameters are referred to as *catch-all parameters*.

> **Note** Earlier in this chapter, I presented HTTP handlers as a way to define your own commands for the application through customized URLs. So what's the difference between HTTP handlers and URL routing? In ASP.NET, HTTP handlers remain the only way to process requests; URL routing is an intermediate layer that pre-processes requests and determines the HTTP handler for them. In doing so, the routing module decides whether the URL meets the expectations of the application or not. In a nutshell, URL routing offers a more flexible and extensible API; if you just need one specially formatted URL, though, a direct HTTP handler is probably a simpler choice.

Summary

HTTP handlers and HTTP modules are the building blocks of the ASP.NET platform. ASP.NET includes several predefined handlers and HTTP modules, but developers can write handlers and modules of their own to perform a variety of tasks. HTTP handlers, in particular, are faster than ordinary Web pages and can be used in all circumstances in which you don't need state maintenance and postback events. To generate images dynamically on the server, for example, an HTTP handler is more efficient than a page.

Everything that occurs under the hood of the ASP.NET runtime environment occurs because of HTTP handlers. When you invoke a Web page or an ASP.NET Web service method, an appropriate HTTP handler gets into the game and serves your request.

HTTP modules are good at performing a number of low-level tasks for which tight interaction and integration with the request/response mechanism is a critical factor. Modules are sort of interceptors that you can place along an HTTP packet's path, from the Web server to the ASP.NET runtime and back. Modules have read and write capabilities, and they can filter and modify the contents of both inbound and outbound requests.

In ASP.NET 4, a special HTTP module has been introduced to simplify the management of application URLs and make the whole process more powerful. The URL routing HTTP module offers a programmer-friendly API to define URL patterns, and it automatically blocks calls for nonmatching URLs and redirects matching URLs to specific pages. It's not much different from old-fashioned URL rewriting, but it offers a greater level of control to the programmer.

With this chapter, our exploration of the ASP.NET and IIS runtime environment terminates. With the next chapter, we'll begin a tour of the ASP.NET page-related features.

Part II

ASP.NET Pages and Server Controls

Chapter 5
Anatomy of an ASP.NET Page

The wise are instructed by reason; ordinary minds by experience; the stupid, by necessity; and brutes by instinct.

—Cicero

ASP.NET pages are dynamically compiled on demand when first requested in the context of a Web application. Dynamic compilation is not specific to ASP.NET pages alone (.aspx files); it also occurs with services (.svc and asmx files), Web user controls (.ascx files), HTTP handlers (.ashx files), and a few more ASP.NET application files such as the *global.asax* file. A pipeline of run-time modules takes care of the incoming HTTP packet and makes it evolve from a simple protocol-specific payload up to the rank of a server-side ASP.NET object—whether it's an instance of a class derived from the system's *Page* class or something else.

The ASP.NET HTTP runtime processes the page object and causes it to generate the markup to insert in the response. The generation of the response is marked by several events handled by user code and collectively known as the *page life cycle*.

In this chapter, we'll review how an HTTP request for an *.aspx* resource is mapped to a page object, the programming interface of the *Page* class, and how to control the generation of the markup by handling events of the page life cycle.

 Note By default in release mode, application pages are compiled in batch mode, meaning that ASP.NET attempts to stuff as many uncompiled pages as possible into a single assembly. The attributes *maxBatchSize* and *maxBatchGeneratedFileSize* in the *<compilation>* section let you limit the number of pages packaged in a single assembly and the overall size of the assembly. By default, you will have no more than 1000 pages per batched compilation and no assembly larger than 1 MB. In general, you don't want users to wait too long when a large number of pages are compiled the first time. At the same time, you don't want to load a huge assembly in memory to serve only a small page, or to start compilation for each and every page. The *maxBatchSize* and *maxBatchGeneratedFileSize* attributes help you find a good balance between first-hit delay and memory usage.

Invoking a Page

Let's start by examining in detail how the *.aspx* page is converted into a class and then compiled into an assembly. Generating an assembly for a particular *.aspx* resource is a two-step process. First, the source code of the resource file is parsed and a corresponding class is created that inherits either from *Page* or another class that, in turn, inherits from *Page*. Second, the dynamically generated class is compiled into an assembly and cached in an ASP.NET-specific temporary directory.

The compiled page remains in use as long as no changes occur to the linked *.aspx* source file or the whole application is restarted. Any changes to the linked *.aspx* file invalidate the current page-specific assembly and force the HTTP runtime to create a new assembly on the next request for the page.

 Note Editing files such as *web.config* and *global.asax* causes the whole application to restart. In this case, all the pages will be recompiled as soon as each page is requested. The same happens if a new assembly is copied or replaced in the application's *Bin* folder.

The Runtime Machinery

Most of the requests that hit Internet Information Services (IIS) are forwarded to a particular run-time module for actual processing. The only exception to this model is made for static resources (for example, images) that IIS can quickly serve on its own. A module that can handle Web resources within IIS is known as an ISAPI extension and can be made of managed or unmanaged code. The worker process that serves the Web application in charge of the request loads the pinpointed module and commands it through a contracted programming interface.

For example, old-fashioned ASP pages are processed by an ISAPI extension named *asp.dll* whereas files with an *.aspx* extension—classic Web Forms pages—are assigned to an ISAPI extension named *aspnet_isapi.dll*, as shown in Figure 5-1. Extension-less requests like those managed by an ASP.NET MVC application are intercepted at the gate and redirected to completely distinct runtime machinery. (At least this is what happens under IIS 7 in integrated mode. In older configurations, you still need to register a specific extension for the requests to be correctly handled by IIS.)

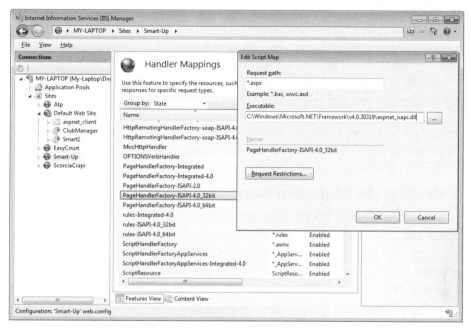

FIGURE 5-1 Setting the handler for resources with an *.aspx* extension.

Resource Mappings

IIS stores the list of recognized resources in the IIS metabase. Depending on the version of IIS you are using, the metabase might be a hidden component or a plain configuration file that an administrator can freely edit by hand. Regardless of the internal implementation, the IIS manager tool provides a user interface to edit the content of the metabase.

Upon installation, ASP.NET modifies the IIS metabase to make sure that *aspnet_isapi.dll* can handle some typical ASP.NET resources. Table 5-1 lists some of these resources.

TABLE 5-1 IIS Application Mappings for *aspnet_isapi.dll*

Extension	Resource Type
.asax	ASP.NET application files. Note, though, that any .asax file other than global.asax is ignored. The mapping is there only to ensure that global.asax can't be requested directly.
.ascx	ASP.NET user control files.
.ashx	HTTP handlers—namely, managed modules that interact with the low-level request and response services of IIS.
.asmx	Files that represent the endpoint of old-fashioned .NET Web services.
.aspx	Files that represent ASP.NET pages.
.axd	Extension that identifies internal HTTP handlers used to implement system features such as application-level tracing (*trace.axd*) or script injection (*webresource.axd*).
.svc	Files that represent the endpoint of a Windows Communication Foundation (WCF) service.

In addition, the *aspnet_isapi.dll* extension handles other typical Microsoft Visual Studio extensions such as *.cs*, *.csproj*, *.vb*, *.vbproj*, *.config*, and *.resx*.

As mentioned in Chapter 2, "ASP.NET and IIS," the exact behavior of the ASP.NET ISAPI extension depends on the process model selected for the application—integrated pipeline (the default in IIS 7 and superior) or classic pipeline. Regardless of the model, at the end of the processing pipeline the originally requested URL that refers to an *.aspx* resource is mapped to, and served through, an instance of a class that represents an ASP.NET Web Forms page. The base class is the *System.Web.UI.Page* class.

Representing the Requested Page

The aforementioned *Page* class is only the base class. The actual class being used by the IIS worker process is a dynamically created derived class. So the ASP.NET HTTP runtime environment first determines the name of the class that will be used to serve the request. A particular naming convention links the URL of the page to the name of the class. If the requested page is, say, *default.aspx*, the associated class turns out to be *ASP.default_aspx*. The transformation rule applies a fixed ASP namespace and replaces any dot (.) with an underscore (_). If the URL contains a directory name, any slashes are also replaced with an underscore.

If no class exists with the specified name in any of the assemblies currently loaded in the AppDomain, the HTTP runtime orders that the class be created and compiled on the fly. This step is often referred to as the *dynamic compilation* of ASP.NET pages.

The source code for the new class is created by parsing the source code of the *.aspx* resource, and it's temporarily saved in the ASP.NET temporary folder. The parser attempts to create a class with an initializer method able to create instances of any referenced server controls found in the ASPX markup. A referenced server control results from tags explicitly decorated with the *runat=server* attribute and from contiguous literals, including blanks and carriage returns. For example, consider the following short piece of markup:

```
<html>
<body>
<asp:button runat="server" ID="Button1" text="Click" />
</body>
</html>
```

When parsed, it sparks three distinct server control instances: two literal controls and a *Button* control. The first literal comprehends the text "<html><body>" plus any blanks and carriage returns the editor has put in. The second literal includes "</body></html>".

Next, the *Page*-derived class is compiled and loaded in memory to serve the request. When a new request for the same page arrives, the class is ready and no compile step will ever take place. (The class will be re-created and recompiled only if the source code of the *.aspx* source changes at some point.)

The *ASP.default_aspx* class inherits from *Page* or, more likely, from a class that in turn inherits from *Page*. More precisely, the base class for *ASP.default_aspx* will be a combination of the code-behind, partial class you created through Visual Studio and a second partial class dynamically arranged by the ASP.NET HTTP runtime. The second, implicit partial class contains the declaration of protected properties for any explicitly referenced server controls. This second partial class is the key that allows you to write the following code successfully:

```
// No member named Button1 has ever been explicitly declared in any code-behind
// class. It is silently added at compile time through a partial class.
Button1.Text = ...;
```

Partial classes are a hot feature of .NET compilers. When partially declared, a class has its source code split over multiple source files, each of which appears to contain an ordinary class definition from beginning to end. The keyword *partial*, though, informs the compiler that the class declaration being processed is incomplete. To get full and complete source code, the compiler must look into other files specified on the command line.

Partial Classes in ASP.NET Projects

Partial classes are a compiler feature originally designed to overcome the brittleness of tool-generated code back in Visual Studio 2003 projects. Ideal for team development, partial classes simplify coding and avoid manual file synchronization in all situations in which many authors work on distinct segments of the class logical class.

Generally, partial classes are a source-level, assembly-limited, non-object-oriented way to extend the behavior of a class. A number of advantages are derived from intensive use of partial classes. As mentioned, you can have multiple teams at work on the same component at the same time. In addition, you have a neat and elegant way to add functionality to a class incrementally. In the end, this is just what the ASP.NET runtime does.

The ASPX markup defines server controls that will be handled by the code in the code-behind class. For this model to work, the code-behind class needs to incorporate references to these server controls as internal members—typically, protected members. In Visual Studio, the code-behind class is a partial class that just lacks members' declaration. Missing declarations are incrementally added at run time via a second partial class created by the ASP.NET HTTP runtime. The compiler of choice (C#, Microsoft Visual Basic .NET, or whatever) will then merge the two partial classes to create the real parent of the dynamically created page class.

Processing the Request

So to serve a request for a page named *default.aspx*, the ASP.NET runtime gets or creates a reference to a class named *ASP.default_aspx*. Next, the HTTP runtime environment invokes the class through the methods of a well-known interface—*IHttpHandler*. The root *Page* class implements this interface, which includes a couple of members: the *ProcessRequest* method and the Boolean *IsReusable* property. After the HTTP runtime has obtained an instance of the class that represents the requested resource, invoking the *ProcessRequest* method—a public method—gives birth to the process that culminates in the generation of the final response for the browser. As mentioned, the steps and events that execute and trigger out of the call to *ProcessRequest* are collectively known as the page life cycle.

Although serving pages is the ultimate goal of the ASP.NET runtime, the way in which the resultant markup code is generated is much more sophisticated than in other platforms and involves many objects. The IIS worker process passes any incoming HTTP requests to the so-called HTTP pipeline. The HTTP pipeline is a fully extensible chain of managed objects that works according to the classic concept of a pipeline. All these objects form what is often referred to as the *ASP.NET HTTP runtime environment*.

This ASP.NET-specific pipeline is integrated with the IIS pipeline in place for any requests when the Web application is configured to work in IIS 7 Integrated mode. Otherwise, IIS and ASP.NET use distinct pipelines—an unmanaged pipeline for IIS and a managed pipeline for ASP.NET.

A page request passes through a pipeline of objects that process the original HTTP payload and, at the end of the chain, produce some markup code for the browser. The entry point in this pipeline is the *HttpRuntime* class.

The *HttpRuntime* Class

The ASP.NET worker process activates the HTTP pipeline in the beginning by creating a new instance of the *HttpRuntime* class and then calling its *ProcessRequest* method for each incoming request. For the sake of clarity, note that despite the name, *HttpRuntime.ProcessRequest* has nothing to do with the *IHttpHandler* interface.

The *HttpRuntime* class contains a lot of private and internal methods and only three public static methods: *Close*, *ProcessRequest*, and *UnloadAppDomain*, as detailed in Table 5-2.

TABLE 5-2 Public Methods in the *HttpRuntime* Class

Method	Description
Close	Removes all items from the ASP.NET cache, and terminates the Web application. This method should be used only when your code implements its own hosting environment. There is no need to call this method in the course of normal ASP.NET request processing.
ProcessRequest	Drives all ASP.NET Web processing execution.
UnloadAppDomain	Terminates the current ASP.NET application. The application restarts the next time a request is received for it.

Note that all the methods shown in Table 5-2 have limited applicability in user applications. In particular, you're not supposed to use *ProcessRequest* in your own code, whereas *Close* is useful only if you're hosting ASP.NET in a custom application. Of the three methods in Table 5-2, only *UnloadAppDomain* can be considered for use if, under certain run-time conditions, you realize you need to restart the application. (See the sidebar "What Causes Application Restarts?" later in this chapter.)

Upon creation, the *HttpRuntime* object initializes a number of internal objects that will help carry out the page request. Helper objects include the cache manager and the file system monitor used to detect changes in the files that form the application. When the *ProcessRequest* method is called, the *HttpRuntime* object starts working to serve a page to the browser. It creates a new empty context for the request and initializes a specialized text writer object in which the markup code will be accumulated. A context is given by an instance of the *HttpContext* class, which encapsulates all HTTP specific information about the request.

After that, the *HttpRuntime* object uses the context information to either locate or create a Web application object capable of handling the request. A Web application is searched using the virtual directory information contained in the URL. The object used to find or create a new Web application is *HttpApplicationFactory*—an internal-use object responsible for returning a valid object capable of handling the request.

Before we get to discover more about the various components of the HTTP pipeline, a look at Figure 5-2 is in order.

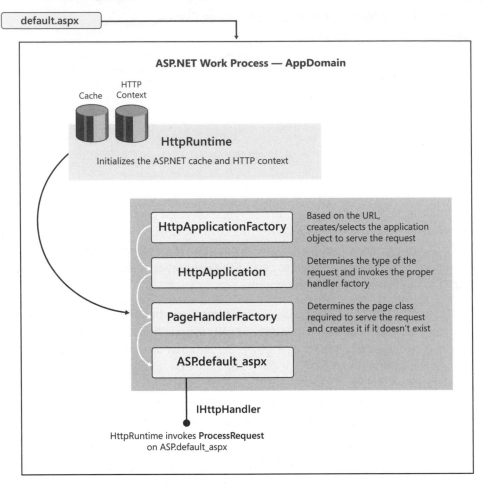

FIGURE 5-2 The HTTP pipeline processing for a page.

The Application Factory

During the lifetime of the application, the *HttpApplicationFactory* object maintains a pool of *HttpApplication* objects to serve incoming HTTP requests. When invoked, the application factory object verifies that an AppDomain exists for the virtual folder the request targets. If the application is already running, the factory picks an *HttpApplication* out of the pool of available objects and passes it the request. A new *HttpApplication* object is created if an existing object is not available.

If the virtual folder has not yet been called for the first time, a new *HttpApplication* object for the virtual folder is created in a new AppDomain. In this case, the creation of an *HttpApplication* object entails the compilation of the *global.asax* application file, if one is present, and the creation of the assembly that represents the actual page requested. This event is actually equivalent to the start of the application. An *HttpApplication* object is used to process a single page request at a time; multiple objects are used to serve simultaneous requests.

The *HttpApplication* Object

HttpApplication is the base class that represents a running ASP.NET application. A derived HTTP application class is dynamically generated by parsing the contents of the *global.asax* file, if any is present. If *global.asax* is available, the application class is built and named after it: *ASP.global_asax*. Otherwise, the base *HttpApplication* class is used.

An instance of an *HttpApplication*-derived class is responsible for managing the entire lifetime of the request it is assigned to. The same instance can be reused only after the request has been completed. The *HttpApplication* maintains a list of HTTP module objects that can filter and even modify the content of the request. Registered modules are called during various moments of the elaboration as the request passes through the pipeline.

The *HttpApplication* object determines the type of object that represents the resource being requested—typically, an ASP.NET page, a Web service, or perhaps a user control. *HttpApplication* then uses the proper handler factory to get an object that represents the requested resource. The factory either instantiates the class for the requested resource from an existing assembly or dynamically creates the assembly and then an instance of the class. A handler factory object is a class that implements the *IHttpHandlerFactory* interface and is responsible for returning an instance of a managed class that can handle the HTTP request— an HTTP handler. An ASP.NET page is simply a handler object—that is, an instance of a class that implements the *IHttpHandler* interface.

Let's see what happens when the resource requested is a page.

The Page Factory

When the *HttpApplication* object in charge of the request has figured out the proper handler, it creates an instance of the handler factory object. For a request that targets a page, the factory is a class named *PageHandlerFactory*. To find the appropriate handler, *HttpApplication* uses the information in the *<httpHandlers>* section of the configuration file as a complement to the information stored in the IIS handler mappings list, as shown in Figure 5-3.

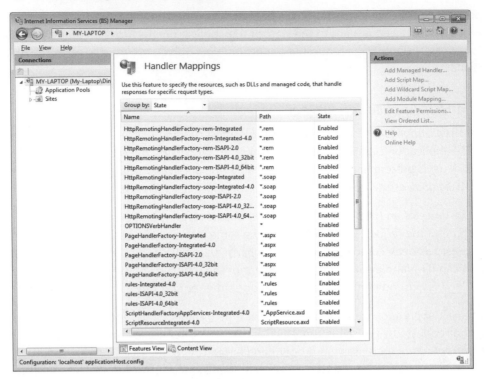

FIGURE 5-3 The HTTP pipeline processing for a page.

Bear in mind that handler factory objects do not compile the requested resource each time it is invoked. The compiled code is stored in an ASP.NET temporary directory on the Web server and used until the corresponding resource file is modified.

So the page handler factory creates an instance of an object that represents the particular page requested. As mentioned, the actual object inherits from the *System.Web.UI.Page* class, which in turn implements the *IHttpHandler* interface. The page object is returned to the application factory, which passes that back to the *HttpRuntime* object. The final step accomplished by the ASP.NET runtime is calling the *IHttpHandler*'s *ProcessRequest* method on the page object. This call causes the page to execute the user-defined code and generate the markup for the browser.

In Chapter 17, "ASP.NET State Management," we'll return to the initialization of an ASP.NET application, the contents of *global.asax*, and the information stuffed into the HTTP context—a container object, created by the *HttpRuntime* class, that is populated, passed along the pipeline, and finally bound to the page handler.

What Causes Application Restarts?

There are a few reasons why an ASP.NET application can be restarted. For the most part, an application is restarted to ensure that latent bugs or memory leaks don't affect the overall behavior of the application in the long run. Another reason is that too many changes dynamically made to deployed ASPX pages might have caused too large a number of assemblies (typically, one per page) to be loaded in memory.

Note that any applications that consume more than a certain share of virtual memory are automatically killed and restarted by IIS. In IIS 7, you can even configure a periodic recycle to ensure that your application is always lean, mean, and in good shape.

Furthermore, the hosting environment (IIS or ASP.NET, depending on the configuration) implements a good deal of checks and automatically restarts an application if any the following scenarios occur:

- The maximum limit of dynamic page compilations is reached. This limit is configurable through the *web.config* file.

- The physical path of the Web application has changed, or any directory under the Web application folder is renamed.

- Changes occurred in *global.asax*, *machine.config*, or *web.config* in the application root, or in the *Bin* directory or any of its subdirectories.

- Changes occurred in the code-access security policy file, if one exists.

- Too many files are changed in one of the content directories. (Typically, this happens if files are generated on the fly when requested.)

- You modified some of the properties for the application pool hosting the Web application.

In addition to all this, in ASP.NET an application can be restarted programmatically by calling *HttpRuntime.UnloadAppDomain*.

The Processing Directives of a Page

Processing directives configure the run-time environment that will execute the page. In ASP.NET, directives can be located anywhere in the page, although it's a good and common practice to place them at the beginning of the file. In addition, the name of a directive is case insensitive and the values of directive attributes don't need to be quoted. The most important and most frequently used directive in ASP.NET is *@Page*. The complete list of ASP.NET directives is shown in Table 5-3.

TABLE 5-3 Directives Supported by ASP.NET Pages

Directive	Description
@ Assembly	Links an assembly to the current page or user control.
@ Control	Defines control-specific attributes that guide the behavior of the control compiler.
@ Implements	Indicates that the page, or the user control, implements a specified .NET Framework interface.
@ Import	Indicates a namespace to import into a page or user control.
@ Master	Identifies an ASP.NET master page. (See Chapter 8, "Page Composition and Usability.")
@ MasterType	Provides a way to create a strongly typed reference to the ASP.NET master page when the master page is accessed from the *Master* property. (See Chapter 8.)
@ OutputCache	Controls the output caching policies of a page or user control. (See Chapter 18, "ASP.NET Caching.")
@ Page	Defines page-specific attributes that guide the behavior of the page compiler and the language parser that will preprocess the page.
@ PreviousPageType	Provides a way to get strong typing against the previous page, as accessed through the *PreviousPage* property.
@ Reference	Links a page or user control to the current page or user control.
@ Register	Creates a custom tag in the page or the control. The new tag (prefix and name) is associated with the namespace and the code of a user-defined control.

With the exception of *@Page*, *@PreviousPageType*, *@Master*, *@MasterType*, and *@Control*, all directives can be used both within a page and a control declaration. *@Page* and *@Control* are mutually exclusive. *@Page* can be used only in *.aspx* files, while the *@Control* directive can be used only in user control *.ascx* files. *@Master*, in turn, is used to define a very special type of page—the master page.

The syntax of a processing directive is unique and common to all supported types of directives. Multiple attributes must be separated with blanks, and no blank can be placed around the equal sign (=) that assigns a value to an attribute, as the following line of code demonstrates:

```
<%@ Directive_Name attribute="value" [attribute="value"...] %>
```

Each directive has its own closed set of typed attributes. Assigning a value of the wrong type to an attribute, or using a wrong attribute with a directive, results in a compilation error.

> **Important** The content of directive attributes is always rendered as plain text. However, attributes are expected to contain values that can be rendered to a particular .NET Framework type, specific to the attribute. When the ASP.NET page is parsed, all the directive attributes are extracted and stored in a dictionary. The names and number of attributes must match the expected schema for the directive. The string that expresses the value of an attribute is valid as long as it can be converted into the expected type. For example, if the attribute is designed to take a Boolean value, *true* and *false* are its only feasible values.

The *@Page* Directive

The *@Page* directive can be used only in *.aspx* pages and generates a compile error if used with other types of ASP.NET files such as controls and Web services. Each *.aspx* file is allowed to include at most one *@Page* directive. Although not strictly necessary from the syntax point of view, the directive is realistically required by all pages of some complexity.

@Page features over 40 attributes that can be logically grouped in three categories: compilation (defined in Table 5-4), overall page behavior (defined in Table 5-5), and page output (defined in Table 5-6). Each ASP.NET page is compiled upon first request, and the HTML actually served to the browser is generated by the methods of the dynamically generated class. The attributes listed in Table 5-4 let you fine-tune parameters for the compiler and choose the language to use.

TABLE 5-4 *@Page* Attributes for Page Compilation

Attribute	Description
ClassName	Specifies the name of the class that will be dynamically compiled when the page is requested. It must be a class name without namespace information.
CodeFile	Indicates the path to the code-behind class for the current page. The source class file must be deployed to the Web server.
CodeBehind	Attribute consumed by Visual Studio, indicates the path to the code-behind class for the current page. The source class file will be compiled to a deployable assembly.
CodeFileBaseClass	Specifies the type name of a base class for a page and its associated code-behind class. The attribute is optional, but when it is used the *CodeFile* attribute must also be present.
CompilationMode	Indicates whether the page should be compiled at run time.
CompilerOptions	A sequence of compiler command-line switches used to compile the page.
Debug	A Boolean value that indicates whether the page should be compiled with debug symbols.
Explicit	A Boolean value that determines whether the page is compiled with the Visual Basic *Option Explicit* mode set to *On*. *Option Explicit* forces the programmer to explicitly declare all variables. The attribute is ignored if the page language is not Visual Basic .NET.

Attribute	Description
Inherits	Defines the base class for the page to inherit. It can be any class derived from the *Page* class.
Language	Indicates the language to use when compiling inline code blocks (<% ... %>) and all the code that appears in the page <script> section. Supported languages include Visual Basic .NET, C#, JScript .NET, and J#. If not otherwise specified, the language defaults to Visual Basic .NET.
LinePragmas	Indicates whether the run time should generate line pragmas in the source code to mark specific locations in the file for the sake of debugging tools.
MasterPageFile	Indicates the master page for the current page.
Src	Indicates the source file that contains the implementation of the base class specified with *Inherits*. The attribute is not used by Visual Studio and other Rapid Application Development (RAD) designers.
Strict	A Boolean value that determines whether the page is compiled with the Visual Basic *Option Strict* mode set to *On*. When this attribute is enabled, *Option Strict* permits only type-safe conversions and prohibits implicit conversions in which loss of data is possible. (In this case, the behavior is identical to that of C#.) The attribute is ignored if the page language is not Visual Basic .NET.
Trace	A Boolean value that indicates whether tracing is enabled. If tracing is enabled, extra information is appended to the page's output. The default is *false*.
TraceMode	Indicates how trace messages are to be displayed for the page when tracing is enabled. Feasible values are *SortByTime* and *SortByCategory*. The default, when tracing is enabled, is *SortByTime*.
WarningLevel	Indicates the compiler warning level at which you want the compiler to abort compilation for the page. Possible values are *0* through *4*.

Attributes listed in Table 5-5 allow you to control to some extent the overall behavior of the page and the supported range of features. For example, you can set a custom error page, disable session state, and control the transactional behavior of the page.

Note The schema of attributes supported by *@Page* is not as strict as for other directives. In particular, any public properties defined on the page class can be listed as an attribute, and initialized, in a *@Page* directive.

TABLE 5-5 *@Page* **Attributes for Page Behavior**

Attribute	Description
AspCompat	A Boolean attribute that, when set to *true*, allows the page to be executed on a single-threaded apartment (STA) thread. The setting allows the page to call COM+ 1.0 components and components developed with Microsoft Visual Basic 6.0 that require access to the unmanaged ASP built-in objects. (I'll return to this topic in Chapter 16, "The HTTP Request Context.")
Async	If this attribute is set to *true*, the generated page class derives from *IHttpAsyncHandler* rather than having *IHttpHandler* add some built-in asynchronous capabilities to the page.

Attribute	Description
AsyncTimeOut	Defines the timeout in seconds used when processing asynchronous tasks. The default is 45 seconds.
AutoEventWireup	A Boolean attribute that indicates whether page events are automatically enabled. It's set to *true* by default. Pages developed with Visual Studio .NET have this attribute set to *false*, and page events for these pages are individually tied to handlers.
Buffer	A Boolean attribute that determines whether HTTP response buffering is enabled. It's set to *true* by default.
Description	Provides a text description of the page. The ASP.NET page parser ignores the attribute, which subsequently has only a documentation purpose.
EnableEventValidation	A Boolean value that indicates whether the page will emit a hidden field to cache available values for input fields that support event data validation. It's set to *true* by default.
EnableSessionState	Defines how the page should treat session data. If this attribute is set to *true*, the session state can be read and written to. If it's set to *false*, session data is not available to the application. Finally, if this attribute is set to *ReadOnly*, the session state can be read but not changed.
EnableViewState	A Boolean value that indicates whether the page *view state* is maintained across page requests. The view state is the page call context—a collection of values that retain the state of the page and are carried back and forth. View state is enabled by default. (I'll cover this topic in Chapter 17. "ASP.NET State Management.")
EnableTheming	A Boolean value that indicates whether the page will support themes for embedded controls. It's set to *true* by default.
EnableViewStateMac	A Boolean value that indicates ASP.NET should calculate a machine-specific authentication code and append it to the view state of the page (in addition to Base64 encoding). The *Mac* in the attribute name stands for *machine authentication check*. When the attribute is *true*, upon postbacks ASP.NET will check the authentication code of the view state to make sure that it hasn't been tampered with on the client.
ErrorPage	Defines the target URL to which users will be automatically redirected in case of unhandled page exceptions.
MaintainScrollPositionOnPostback	A Boolean value that indicates whether to return the user to the same position in the client browser after postback.
SmartNavigation	A Boolean value that indicates whether the page supports the Microsoft Internet Explorer 5 or later smart navigation feature. Smart navigation allows a page to be refreshed without losing scroll position and element focus.
Theme, StylesheetTheme	Indicates the name of the theme (or style-sheet theme) selected for the page.

Attribute	Description
Transaction	Indicates whether the page supports or requires transactions. Feasible values are *Disabled*, *NotSupported*, *Supported*, *Required*, and *RequiresNew*. Transaction support is disabled by default.
ValidateRequest	A Boolean value that indicates whether request validation should occur. If this attribute is set to *true*, ASP.NET checks all input data against a hard-coded list of potentially dangerous values. This functionality helps reduce the risk of cross-site scripting attacks for pages. The value is *true* by default.

Attributes listed in Table 5-6 allow you to control the format of the output being generated for the page. For example, you can set the content type of the page or localize the output to the extent possible.

TABLE 5-6 *@Page* Directives for Page Output

Attribute	Description
ClientTarget	Indicates the target browser for which ASP.NET server controls should render content.
ClientIDMode	Specifies the algorithm to use to generate client ID values for server controls. *This attribute requires ASP.NET 4.*
CodePage	Indicates the code page value for the response. Set this attribute only if you created the page using a code page other than the default code page of the Web server on which the page will run. In this case, set the attribute to the code page of your development machine. A code page is a character set that includes numbers, punctuation marks, and other glyphs. Code pages differ on a per-language basis.
ContentType	Defines the content type of the response as a standard MIME type. Supports any valid HTTP content type string.
Culture	Indicates the culture setting for the page. Culture information includes the writing and sorting system, calendar, and date and currency formats. The attribute must be set to a non-neutral culture name, which means it must contain both language and country/region information. For example, *en-US* is a valid value, unlike *en* alone, which is considered country/region neutral.
LCID	A 32-bit value that defines the locale identifier for the page. By default, ASP.NET uses the locale of the Web server.
MetaDescription	Sets the "description" meta element for the page. The value set through the *@Page* directive overrides any similar values you might have specified as literal text in the markup. *This attribute requires ASP.NET 4.*
MetaKeywords	Sets the "keywords" meta element for the page. The value set through the *@Page* directive overrides any similar values you might have specified as literal text in the markup. *This attribute requires ASP.NET 4.*
ResponseEncoding	Indicates the character encoding of the page. The value is used to set the *CharSet* attribute on the content type HTTP header. Internally, ASP.NET handles all strings as Unicode.

Attribute	Description
UICulture	Specifies the default culture name used by Resource Manager to look up culture-specific resources at run time.
ViewStateEncryptionMode	Determines how and if the *view state* is encrypted. Feasible values are *Auto*, *Always*, or *Never*. The default is *Auto*, meaning that view state will be encrypted only if an individual control requests that.
ViewStateMode	Determines the value for the page's *ViewStateMode* property that influences the way in which the page treats the view state of child controls. (More details are available in Chapter 17.) *This attribute requires ASP.NET 4.*

As you can see, many attributes discussed in Table 5-6 are concern with page localization. Building multilanguage and international applications is a task that ASP.NET, and the .NET Framework in general, greatly simplify.

The *@Assembly* Directive

The *@Assembly* directive adds an assembly to a collection of assembly names that are used during the compilation of the ASP.NET page so that classes and interfaces in the assembly are available for early binding to the code. You use the *@Assembly* directive when you want to reference a given assembly only from a specific page.

Some assemblies are linked by default for any ASP.NET application. The complete list can be found in the root *web.config* file of the Web server machine. The list is pretty long in ASP.NET 4, but it no longer includes the *System.Web.Mobile* assembly that was there for older versions of ASP.NET. The mobile assembly is now deprecated, but if you're trying to upgrade an existing application to ASP.NET 4 that uses the assembly, you are required to add the assembly explicitly via an *@Assembly* directive or via a custom *<compilation>* section in the application.

Table 5-7 lists some of the assemblies that are automatically provided to the compiler for an ASP.NET 4 application.

TABLE 5-7 Assemblies Linked by Default in ASP.NET 4

Assembly File Name	Description
mscorlib	Provides the core functionality of the .NET Framework, including types, AppDomains, and run-time services
System.dll	Provides another bunch of system services, including regular expressions, compilation, native methods, file I/O, and networking
System.Configuration.dll	Defines classes to read and write configuration data.
System.Core.dll	Provides some other core functionality of the .NET Framework, including LINQ-to-Objects, the time-zone API, and some security and diagnostic classes

System.Data.dll	Defines data container and data access classes, including the whole ADO.NET framework
System.Data.DataSetExtensions.dll	Defines additional functions built over the ADO.NET *DataSet* object
System.Drawing.dll	Implements the GDI+ features
System.EnterpriseServices.dll	Provides the classes that allow for serviced components and COM+ interaction
System.Web.dll	Indicates the assembly implements the core ASP.NET services, controls, and classes
System.Web.ApplicationServices.dll	Provides classes that enable you to access ASP.NET authentication, roles, and profile functions via a bunch of built-in WCF services
System.Web.DynamicData.dll	Provides classes behind the ASP.NET Dynamic Data framework
System.Web.Entity.dll	Contains the code for the *EntityDataSource* component that supports Entity Framework
System.Web.Extensions.dll	Contains the code for AJAX extensions to ASP.NET
System.Web.Services.dll	Contains the core code that makes Web services run
System.Xml.dll	Implements the .NET Framework XML features
System.Xml.Linq.dll	Contains the code for the LINQ-to-XML parser

Note that you can modify, extend, or restrict the list of default assemblies by editing the global settings in the root *web.config* file under

```
%Windows%\Microsoft.NET\Framework\v4.0.30319\Config
```

If you do so, changes will apply to all ASP.NET applications run on that Web server. Alternatively, you can modify the assembly list on a per-application basis by editing the *<assemblies>* section under *<compilation>* in the application's specific *web.config* file. Note also that the *<compilation>* section should be used only for global assembly cache (GAC) resident assemblies, not for the private assemblies that you deploy to the *Bin* folder.

By default, the *<compilation>* section in the root *web.config* file contains the following entry:

```
<add assembly="*" />
```

It means that any assembly found in the binary path of the application should be treated as if it were registered through the *@Assembly* directive. To prevent all assemblies found in the *Bin* directory from being linked to the page, remove the entry from the root configuration file. To link a needed assembly to the page, use the following syntax:

```
<%@ Assembly Name="AssemblyName" %>
<%@ Assembly Src="assembly_code.cs" %>
```

The *@Assembly* directive supports two mutually exclusive attributes: *Name* and *Src*. *Name* indicates the name of the assembly to link to the page. The name cannot include the path or the extension. *Src* indicates the path to a source file to dynamically compile and link against the page. The *@Assembly* directive can appear multiple times in the body of the page. In fact, you need a new directive for each assembly to link. *Name* and *Src* cannot be used in the same *@Assembly* directive, but multiple directives defined in the same page can use either.

> **Note** In terms of performance, the difference between *Name* and *Src* is minimal, although *Name* points to an existing and ready-to-load assembly. The source file referenced by *Src* is compiled only the first time it is requested. The ASP.NET runtime maps a source file with a dynamically compiled assembly and keeps using the compiled code until the original file undergoes changes. This means that after the first application-level call, the impact on the page performance is identical whether you use *Name* or *Src*.

Any assemblies you register through the *@Assembly* directive are used by the compiler at compile time, which allows for early binding. After the compilation of the requested ASP.NET file is complete, the assembly is loaded into the application domain, thus allowing late binding. In the end, any assemblies listed through the directive (implicitly through the root configuration or explicitly through the application configuration) is loaded into the AppDomain and referenced on demand.

> **Important** Removing an assembly from the Visual Studio project doesn't help much to keep the AppDomain lean and mean. To ensure you load all the assemblies you want and only the ones you want, you should insert the following code in your configuration file:
>
> ```
> <assemblies>
>   <add assembly="..." />
>   ...
>   <add assembly="*" />
> </assemblies>
> ```
>
> The ** tag removes all default configurations; the subsequent tags add just the assemblies your application needs. As you can verify for yourself, the default list will likely load assemblies you don't need.
>
> In debug mode, you can track the list of assemblies actually loaded in the AppDomain for the site using the following code:
>
> ```
> var assemblies1 = Assembly.GetExecutingAssembly().GetReferencedAssemblies();
> var assemblies2 = AppDomain.CurrentDomain.GetAssemblies();
> ```
>
> The size of the two arrays can vary quite a bit. The former counts just the dynamically referenced assemblies at the current stage of execution. The latter counts the number of assemblies physically loaded in the AppDomain (which can't be unloaded unless you recycle the application).

The *@Import* Directive

The *@Import* directive links the specified namespace to the page so that all the types defined can be accessed from the page without specifying the fully qualified name. For example, to create a new instance of the ADO.NET *DataSet* class, you either import the *System.Data* namespace or specify the fully qualified class name whenever you need it, as in the following code:

```
System.Data.DataSet ds = new System.Data.DataSet();
```

After you've imported the *System.Data* namespace into the page, you can use more natural coding, as shown here:

```
DataSet ds = new DataSet();
```

The syntax of the *@Import* directive is rather self-explanatory:

```
<%@ Import namespace="value" %>
```

@Import can be used as many times as needed in the body of the page. The *@Import* directive is the ASP.NET counterpart of the C# *using* statement and the Visual Basic .NET *Imports* statement. Looking back at unmanaged C/C++, we could say the directive plays a role nearly identical to the *#include* directive. For example, to be able to connect to a Microsoft SQL Server database and grab some disconnected data, you need to import the following two namespaces:

```
<%@ Import namespace="System.Data" %>
<%@ Import namespace="System.Data.SqlClient" %>
```

You need the *System.Data* namespace to work with the *DataSet* and *DataTable* classes, and you need the *System.Data.SqlClient* namespace to prepare and issue the command. In this case, you don't need to link against additional assemblies because the *System.Data.dll* assembly is linked by default.

> **Note** *@Import* helps the compiler only to resolve class names; it doesn't automatically link required assemblies. Using the *@Import* directive allows you to use shorter class names, but as long as the assembly that contains the class code is not properly referenced, the compiler will generate a type error. In this case, using the fully qualified class name is of no help because the compiler lacks the type definition. You might have noticed that, more often than not, assembly and namespace names coincide. The latest version of Visual Studio (as well as some commercial products such as JetBrains ReSharper) is able to detect when you lack a reference and offers to import the namespace and reference the assembly with a single click. This is pure tooling activity—namespaces and assemblies are totally different beasts.

The @*Implements* Directive

The directive indicates that the current page implements the specified .NET Framework interface. An interface is a set of signatures for a logically related group of functions. An interface is a sort of contract that shows the component's commitment to expose that group of functions. Unlike abstract classes, an interface doesn't provide code or executable functionality. When you implement an interface in an ASP.NET page, you declare any required methods and properties within the *<script>* section. The syntax of the @*Implements* directive is as follows:

```
<%@ Implements interface="InterfaceName" %>
```

The @*Implements* directive can appear multiple times in the page if the page has to implement multiple interfaces. Note that if you decide to put all the page logic in a separate class file, you can't use the directive to implement interfaces. Instead, you implement the interface in the code-behind class.

The @*Reference* Directive

The @*Reference* directive is used to establish a dynamic link between the current page and the specified page or user control. This feature has significant implications for the way you set up cross-page communication. It also lets you create strongly typed instances of user controls. Let's review the syntax.

The directive can appear multiple times in the page. The directive features two mutually exclusive attributes: *Page* and *Control*. Both attributes are expected to contain a path to a source file:

```
<%@ Reference page="source_page" %>
<%@ Reference control="source_user_control" %>
```

The *Page* attribute points to an *.aspx* source file, whereas the *Control* attribute contains the path of an *.ascx* user control. In both cases, the referenced source file will be dynamically compiled into an assembly, thus making the classes defined in the source programmatically available to the referencing page. When running, an ASP.NET page is an instance of a .NET Framework class with a specific interface made of methods and properties. When the referencing page executes, a referenced page becomes a class that represents the *.aspx* source file and can be instantiated and programmed at will. For the directive to work, the referenced page must belong to the same domain as the calling page. Cross-site calls are not allowed, and both the *Page* and *Control* attributes expect to receive a relative virtual path.

Note Cross-page posting can be considered as an alternate approach to using the *@Reference* directive. Cross-page posting is an ASP.NET feature through which you force an ASP.NET button control to post the content of its parent form to a given target page. I'll demonstrate cross-page posting in Chapter 9, "Input Forms."

The *Page* Class

In the .NET Framework, the *Page* class provides the basic behavior for all objects that an ASP.NET application builds by starting from *.aspx* files. Defined in the *System.Web.UI* namespace, the class derives from *TemplateControl* and implements the *IHttpHandler* interface:

```
public class Page : TemplateControl, IHttpHandler
{
    ...
}
```

In particular, *TemplateControl* is the abstract class that provides both ASP.NET pages and user controls with a base set of functionality. At the upper level of the hierarchy, you find the *Control* class. It defines the properties, methods, and events shared by all ASP.NET server-side elements—pages, controls, and user controls.

Derived from a class—*TemplateControl*—that implements *INamingContainer*, the *Page* class also serves as the naming container for all its constituent controls. In the .NET Framework, the naming container for a control is the first parent control that implements the *INamingContainer* interface. For any class that implements the naming container interface, ASP.NET creates a new virtual namespace in which all child controls are guaranteed to have unique names in the overall tree of controls. (This is a very important feature for iterative data-bound controls, such as *DataGrid*, and for user controls.)

The *Page* class also implements the methods of the *IHttpHandler* interface, thus qualifying it as the handler of a particular type of HTTP requests—those for *.aspx* files. The key element of the *IHttpHandler* interface is the *ProcessRequest* method, which is the method the ASP.NET runtime calls to start the page processing that will actually serve the request.

Note *INamingContainer* is a marker interface that has no methods. Its presence alone, though, forces the ASP.NET runtime to create an additional namespace for naming the child controls of the page (or the control) that implements it. The *Page* class is the naming container of all the page's controls, with the clear exception of those controls that implement the *INamingContainer* interface themselves or are children of controls that implement the interface.

Properties of the *Page* Class

The properties of the *Page* class can be classified in three distinct groups: intrinsic objects, worker properties, and page-specific properties. The tables in the following sections enumerate and describe them.

Intrinsic Objects

Table 5-8 lists all properties that return a helper object that is intrinsic to the page. In other words, objects listed here are all essential parts of the infrastructure that allows for the page execution.

TABLE 5-8 ASP.NET Intrinsic Objects in the *Page* Class

Property	Description
Application	Instance of the *HttpApplicationState* class; represents the state of the application. It is functionally equivalent to the ASP intrinsic *Application* object.
Cache	Instance of the *Cache* class; implements the cache for an ASP.NET application. More efficient and powerful than *Application*, it supports item priority and expiration.
Profile	Instance of the *ProfileCommon* class; represents the user-specific set of data associated with the request.
Request	Instance of the *HttpRequest* class; represents the current HTTP request.
Response	Instance of the *HttpResponse* class; sends HTTP response data to the client.
RouteData	Instance of the *RouteData* class; groups information about the selected route (if any) and its values and tokens. (Routing in Web Forms is covered in Chapter 4, "xxx.") *The object is supported only in ASP.NET 4.*
Server	Instance of the *HttpServerUtility* class; provides helper methods for processing Web requests.
Session	Instance of the *HttpSessionState* class; manages user-specific data.
Trace	Instance of the *TraceContext* class; performs tracing on the page.
User	An *IPrincipal* object that represents the user making the request.

I'll cover *Request*, *Response*, and *Server* in Chapter 16; *Application* and *Session* are covered in Chapter 17; *Cache* will be the subject of Chapter 19. Finally, *User* and security will be the subject of Chapter 19, "ASP.NET Security."

Worker Properties

Table 5-9 details page properties that are both informative and provide the foundation for functional capabilities. You can hardly write code in the page without most of these properties.

TABLE 5-9 Worker Properties of the *Page* Class

Property	Description
AutoPostBackControl	Gets a reference to the control within the page that caused the postback event.
ClientScript	Gets a *ClientScriptManager* object that contains the client script used on the page.
Controls	Returns the collection of all the child controls contained in the current page.
ErrorPage	Gets or sets the error page to which the requesting browser is redirected in case of an unhandled page exception.
Form	Returns the current *HtmlForm* object for the page.
Header	Returns a reference to the object that represents the page's header. The object implements *IPageHeader*.
IsAsync	Indicates whether the page is being invoked through an asynchronous handler.
IsCallback	Indicates whether the page is being loaded in response to a client script callback.
IsCrossPagePostBack	Indicates whether the page is being loaded in response to a postback made from within another page.
IsPostBack	Indicates whether the page is being loaded in response to a client postback or whether it is being loaded for the first time.
IsValid	Indicates whether page validation succeeded.
Master	Instance of the *MasterPage* class; represents the master page that determines the appearance of the current page.
MasterPageFile	Gets and sets the master file for the current page.
NamingContainer	Returns *null*.
Page	Returns the current *Page* object.
PageAdapter	Returns the adapter object for the current *Page* object.
Parent	Returns *null*.
PreviousPage	Returns the reference to the caller page in case of a cross-page postback.
TemplateSourceDirectory	Gets the virtual directory of the page.
Validators	Returns the collection of all validation controls contained in the page.
ViewStateUserKey	String property that represents a user-specific identifier used to hash the view-state contents. This trick is a line of defense against one-click attacks.

In the context of an ASP.NET application, the *Page* object is the root of the hierarchy. For this reason, inherited properties such as *NamingContainer* and *Parent* always return *null*. The *Page* property, on the other hand, returns an instance of the same object (*this* in C# and *Me* in Visual Basic .NET).

The *ViewStateUserKey* property deserves a special mention. A common use for the user key is to stuff user-specific information that is then used to hash the contents of the view state along with other information. A typical value for the *ViewStateUserKey* property is the name of the authenticated user or the user's session ID. This contrivance reinforces the security level for the view state information and further lowers the likelihood of attacks. If you employ a user-specific key, an attacker can't construct a valid view state for your user account unless the attacker can also authenticate as you. With this configuration, you have another barrier against one-click attacks. This technique, though, might not be effective for Web sites that allow anonymous access, unless you have some other unique tracking device running.

Note that if you plan to set the *ViewStateUserKey* property, you must do that during the *Page_Init* event. If you attempt to do it later (for example, when *Page_Load* fires), an exception will be thrown.

Context Properties

Table 5-10 lists properties that represent visual and nonvisual attributes of the page, such as the URL's query string, the client target, the title, and the applied style sheet.

TABLE 5-10 Page-Specific Properties of the *Page* Class

Property	Description
ClientID	Always returns the empty string.
ClientIDMode	Determines the algorithm to use to generate the ID of HTML elements being output as part of a control's markup. *This property requires ASP.NET 4.*
ClientQueryString	Gets the query string portion of the requested URL.
ClientTarget	Set to the empty string by default; allows you to specify the type of browser the HTML should comply with. Setting this property disables automatic detection of browser capabilities.
EnableViewState	Indicates whether the page has to manage view-state data. You can also enable or disable the view-state feature through the *EnableViewState* attribute of the *@Page* directive.
EnableViewStateMac	Indicates whether ASP.NET should calculate a machine-specific authentication code and append it to the page view state.
EnableTheming	Indicates whether the page supports themes.
ID	Always returns the empty string.
MetaDescription	Gets and sets the content of the *description* meta tag. *This property requires ASP.NET 4.*
MetaKeywords	Gets and sets the content of the *keywords* meta tag. *This property requires ASP.NET 4.*
MaintainScrollPositionOnPostback	Indicates whether to return the user to the same position in the client browser after postback.
SmartNavigation	Indicates whether smart navigation is enabled. Smart navigation exploits a bunch of browser-specific capabilities to enhance the user's experience with the page.

Property	Description
StyleSheetTheme	Gets or sets the name of the style sheet applied to this page.
Theme	Gets and sets the theme for the page. Note that themes can be programmatically set only in the *PreInit* event.
Title	Gets or sets the title for the page.
TraceEnabled	Toggles page tracing on and off.
TraceModeValue	Gets or sets the trace mode.
UniqueID	Always returns the empty string.
ViewStateEncryptionMode	Indicates if and how the view state should be encrypted.
ViewStateMode	Enables the view state for an individual control even if the view state is disabled for the page. *This property requires ASP.NET 4.*
Visible	Indicates whether ASP.NET has to render the page. If you set *Visible* to *false*, ASP.NET doesn't generate any HTML code for the page. When *Visible* is *false*, only the text explicitly written using *Response.Write* hits the client.

The three ID properties (*ID*, *ClientID*, and *UniqueID*) always return the empty string from a *Page* object. They make sense only for server controls.

Methods of the *Page* Class

The whole range of *Page* methods can be classified in a few categories based on the tasks each method accomplishes. A few methods are involved with the generation of the markup for the page; others are helper methods to build the page and manage the constituent controls. Finally, a third group collects all the methods related to client-side scripting.

Rendering Methods

Table 5-11 details the methods that are directly or indirectly involved with the generation of the markup code.

TABLE 5-11 Methods for Markup Generation

Method	Description
DataBind	Binds all the data-bound controls contained in the page to their data sources. The *DataBind* method doesn't generate code itself but prepares the ground for the forthcoming rendering.
RenderControl	Outputs the HTML text for the page, including tracing information if tracing is enabled.
VerifyRenderingInServerForm	Controls call this method when they render to ensure that they are included in the body of a server form. The method does not return a value, but it throws an exception in case of error.

In an ASP.NET page, no control can be placed outside a *<form>* tag with the *runat* attribute set to *server*. The *VerifyRenderingInServerForm* method is used by Web and HTML controls to ensure that they are rendered correctly. In theory, custom controls should call this method during the rendering phase. In many situations, the custom control embeds or derives an existing Web or HTML control that will make the check itself.

Not directly exposed by the *Page* class, but strictly related to it, is the *GetWebResourceUrl* method on the *ClientScriptManager* class. (You get a reference to the current client script manager through the *ClientScript* property on *Page*.) When you develop a custom control, you often need to embed static resources such as images or client script files. You can make these files be separate downloads; however, even though it's effective, the solution looks poor and inelegant. Visual Studio allows you to embed resources in the control assembly, but how would you retrieve these resources programmatically and bind them to the control? For example, to bind an assembly-stored image to an <IMG> tag, you need a URL for the image. The *GetWebResourceUrl* method returns a URL for the specified resource. The URL refers to a new Web Resource service (*webresource.axd*) that retrieves and returns the requested resource from an assembly.

```
// Bind the <IMG> tag to the given GIF image in the control's assembly
img.ImageUrl = Page.GetWebResourceUrl(typeof(TheControl), GifName));
```

GetWebResourceUrl requires a *Type* object, which will be used to locate the assembly that contains the resource. The assembly is identified with the assembly that contains the definition of the specified type in the current AppDomain. If you're writing a custom control, the type will likely be the control's type. As its second argument, the *GetWebResourceUrl* method requires the name of the embedded resource. The returned URL takes the following form:

```
WebResource.axd?a=assembly&r=resourceName&t=timestamp
```

The timestamp value is the current timestamp of the assembly, and it is added to make the browser download resources again if the assembly is modified.

Controls-Related Methods

Table 5-12 details a bunch of helper methods on the *Page* class architected to let you manage and validate child controls and resolve URLs.

TABLE 5-12 Helper Methods of the *Page* Object

Method	Description
DesignerInitialize	Initializes the instance of the *Page* class at design time, when the page is being hosted by RAD designers such as Visual Studio.
FindControl	Takes a control's ID and searches for it in the page's naming container. The search doesn't dig out child controls that are naming containers themselves.

Method	Description
GetTypeHashCode	Retrieves the hash code generated by *ASP.xxx_aspx* page objects at run time. In the base *Page* class, the method implementation simply returns *0*; significant numbers are returned by classes used for actual pages.
GetValidators	Returns a collection of control validators for a specified validation group.
HasControls	Determines whether the page contains any child controls.
LoadControl	Compiles and loads a user control from an *.ascx* file, and returns a *Control* object. If the user control supports caching, the object returned is *PartialCachingControl*.
LoadTemplate	Compiles and loads a user control from an *.ascx* file, and returns it wrapped in an instance of an internal class that implements the *ITemplate* interface. The internal class is named *SimpleTemplate*.
MapPath	Retrieves the physical, fully qualified path that an absolute or relative virtual path maps to.
ParseControl	Parses a well-formed input string, and returns an instance of the control that corresponds to the specified markup text. If the string contains more controls, only the first is taken into account. The *runat* attribute can be omitted. The method returns an object of type *Control* and must be cast to a more specific type.
RegisterRequiresControlState	Registers a control as one that requires control state.
RegisterRequiresPostBack	Registers the specified control to receive a postback handling notice, even if its ID doesn't match any ID in the collection of posted data. The control must implement the *IPostBackDataHandler* interface.
RegisterRequiresRaiseEvent	Registers the specified control to handle an incoming postback event. The control must implement the *IPostBackEventHandler* interface.
RegisterViewStateHandler	Mostly for internal use, the method sets an internal flag that causes the page view state to be persisted. If this method is not called in the prerendering phase, no view state will ever be written. Typically, only the *HtmlForm* server control for the page calls this method. There's no need to call it from within user applications.
ResolveUrl	Resolves a relative URL into an absolute URL based on the value of the *TemplateSourceDirectory* property.
Validate	Instructs any validation controls included in the page to validate their assigned information. If defined in the page, the method honors ASP.NET validation groups.

The methods *LoadControl* and *LoadTemplate* share a common code infrastructure but return different objects, as the following pseudocode shows:

```
public Control LoadControl(string virtualPath)
{
    Control ascx = GetCompiledUserControlType(virtualPath);
    ascx.InitializeAsUserControl();
    return ascx;
}
public ITemplate LoadTemplate(string virtualPath)
{
    Control ascx = GetCompiledUserControlType(virtualPath);
    return new SimpleTemplate(ascx);
}
```

Both methods differ from the *ParseControl* method in that the latter never causes compilation but simply parses the string and infers control information. The information is then used to create and initialize a new instance of the control class. As mentioned, the *runat* attribute is unnecessary in this context. In ASP.NET, the *runat* attribute is key, but in practice, it has no other role than marking the surrounding markup text for parsing and instantiation. It does not contain information useful to instantiate a control, and for this reason it can be omitted from the strings you pass directly to *ParseControl*.

Script-Related Methods

Table 5-13 enumerates all the methods in the *Page* class related to HTML and script code to be inserted in the client page.

TABLE 5-13 Script-Related Methods

Method	Description
GetCallbackEventReference	Obtains a reference to a client-side function that, when invoked, initiates a client callback to server-side events.
GetPostBackClientEvent	Calls into *GetCallbackEventReference*.
GetPostBackClientHyperlink	Appends *javascript:* to the beginning of the return string received from *GetPostBackEventReference*. For example: *javascript:__doPostBack('CtlID','')*
GetPostBackEventReference	Returns the prototype of the client-side script function that causes, when invoked, a postback. It takes a *Control* and an argument, and it returns a string like this: *__doPostBack('CtlID','')*
IsClientScriptBlockRegistered	Determines whether the specified client script is registered with the page. *It's marked as obsolete.*
IsStartupScriptRegistered	Determines whether the specified client startup script is registered with the page. *It's marked as obsolete.*

Method	Description
RegisterArrayDeclaration	Use this method to add an *ECMAScript* array to the client page. This method accepts the name of the array and a string that will be used verbatim as the body of the array. For example, if you call the method with arguments such as *theArray* and *"'a', 'b'"*, you get the following JavaScript code: *var theArray = new Array('a', 'b');* *It's marked as obsolete.*
RegisterClientScriptBlock	An ASP.NET page uses this method to emit client-side script blocks in the client page just after the opening tag of the HTML *<form>* element. *It's marked as obsolete.*
RegisterHiddenField	Use this method to automatically register a hidden field on the page. *It's marked as obsolete.*
RegisterOnSubmitStatement	Use this method to emit client script code that handles the client *OnSubmit* event. The script should be a JavaScript function call to client code registered elsewhere. *It's marked as obsolete.*
RegisterStartupScript	An ASP.NET page uses this method to emit client-side script blocks in the client page just before closing the HTML *<form>* element. *It's marked as obsolete.*
SetFocus	Sets the browser focus to the specified control.

As you can see, some methods in Table 5-13, which are defined and usable in ASP.NET 1.x, are marked as obsolete. In ASP.NET 4 applications, you should avoid calling them and resort to methods with the same name exposed out of the *ClientScript* property.

```
// Avoid this in ASP.NET 4
Page.RegisterArrayDeclaration(...);

// Use this in ASP.NET 4
Page.ClientScript.RegisterArrayDeclaration(...);
```

The *ClientScript* property returns an instance of the *ClientScriptManager* class and represents the central console for registering script code to be programmatically emitted within the page.

Methods listed in Table 5-13 let you emit JavaScript code in the client page. When you use any of these methods, you actually tell the page to insert that script code when the page is rendered. So when any of these methods execute, the script-related information is simply cached in internal structures and used later when the page object generates its HTML text.

Events of the *Page* Class

The *Page* class fires a few events that are notified during the page life cycle. As Table 5-14 shows, some events are orthogonal to the typical life cycle of a page (initialization, postback, and rendering phases) and are fired as extra-page situations evolve. Let's briefly review the events and then attack the topic with an in-depth discussion of the page life cycle.

TABLE 5-14 Events a Page Can Fire

Event	Description
AbortTransaction	Occurs for ASP.NET pages marked to participate in an automatic transaction when a transaction aborts
CommitTransaction	Occurs for ASP.NET pages marked to participate in an automatic transaction when a transaction commits
DataBinding	Occurs when the *DataBind* method is called on the page to bind all the child controls to their respective data sources
Disposed	Occurs when the page is released from memory, which is the last stage of the page life cycle
Error	Occurs when an unhandled exception is thrown.
Init	Occurs when the page is initialized, which is the first step in the page life cycle
InitComplete	Occurs when all child controls and the page have been initialized
Load	Occurs when the page loads up, after being initialized
LoadComplete	Occurs when the loading of the page is completed and server events have been raised
PreInit	Occurs just before the initialization phase of the page begins
PreLoad	Occurs just before the loading phase of the page begins
PreRender	Occurs when the page is about to render
PreRenderComplete	Occurs just before the pre-rendering phase begins
SaveStateComplete	Occurs when the view state of the page has been saved to the persistence medium
Unload	Occurs when the page is unloaded from memory but not yet disposed of

The Eventing Model

When a page is requested, its class and the server controls it contains are responsible for executing the request and rendering HTML back to the client. The communication between the client and the server is stateless and disconnected because it's based on the HTTP protocol. Real-world applications, though, need some state to be maintained between successive calls made to the same page. With ASP, and with other server-side development platforms such as Java Server Pages and PHP, the programmer is entirely responsible for persisting the state. In contrast, ASP.NET provides a built-in infrastructure that saves and restores the state of a page in a transparent manner. In this way, and in spite of the underlying stateless protocol, the client experience appears to be that of a continuously executing process. It's just an illusion, though.

Introducing the View State

The illusion of continuity is created by the view state feature of ASP.NET pages and is based on some assumptions about how the page is designed and works. Also, server-side Web controls play a remarkable role. In brief, before rendering its contents to HTML, the page encodes and stuffs into a persistence medium (typically, a hidden field) all the state information that the page itself and its constituent controls want to save. When the page posts back, the state information is deserialized from the hidden field and used to initialize instances of the server controls declared in the page layout.

The view state is specific to each instance of the page because it is embedded in the HTML. The net effect of this is that controls are initialized with the same values they had the last time the view state was created—that is, the last time the page was rendered to the client. Furthermore, an additional step in the page life cycle merges the persisted state with any updates introduced by client-side actions. When the page executes after a postback, it finds a stateful and up-to-date context just as it is working over a continuous point-to-point connection.

Two basic assumptions are made. The first assumption is that the page always posts to itself and carries its state back and forth. The second assumption is that the server-side controls have to be declared with the *runat=server* attribute to spring to life when the page posts back.

The Single Form Model

ASP.NET pages are built to support exactly one server-side *<form>* tag. The form must include all the controls you want to interact with on the server. Both the form and the controls must be marked with the *runat* attribute; otherwise, they will be considered plain text to be output verbatim.

A server-side form is an instance of the *HtmlForm* class. The *HtmlForm* class does not expose any property equivalent to the *Action* property of the HTML *<form>* tag. The reason is that an ASP.NET page always posts to itself. Unlike the *Action* property, other common form properties such as *Method* and *Target* are fully supported.

Valid ASP.NET pages are also those that have no server-side forms and those that run HTML forms—a *<form>* tag without the *runat* attribute. In an ASP.NET page, you can also have both HTML and server forms. In no case, though, can you have more than one *<form>* tag with the *runat* attribute set to *server*. HTML forms work as usual and let you post to any page in the application. The drawback is that in this case no state will be automatically restored. In other words, the ASP.NET Web Forms model works only if you use exactly one server *<form>* element. We'll return to this topic in Chapter 9.

Asynchronous Pages

ASP.NET pages are served by an HTTP handler like an instance of the *Page* class. Each request takes up a thread in the ASP.NET thread pool and releases it only when the request completes. What if a frequently requested page starts an external and particularly lengthy task? The risk is that the ASP.NET process is idle but has no free threads in the pool to serve incoming requests for other pages. This happens mostly because HTTP handlers, including page classes, work synchronously. To alleviate this issue, ASP.NET has supported asynchronous handlers since version 1.0 through the *IHTTPAsyncHandler* interface. Starting with ASP.NET 2.0, creating asynchronous pages was made easier thanks to specific support from the framework.

Two aspects characterize an asynchronous ASP.NET page: a tailor-made attribute on the *@Page* directive, and one or more tasks registered for asynchronous execution. The asynchronous task can be registered in either of two ways. You can define a *Begin/End* pair of asynchronous handlers for the *PreRenderComplete* event or create a *PageAsyncTask* object to represent an asynchronous task. This is generally done in the *Page_Load* event, but any time is fine provided that it happens before the *PreRender* event fires.

In both cases, the asynchronous task is started automatically when the page has progressed to a well-known point. Let's dig out more details.

> **Note** An ASP.NET asynchronous page is still a class that derives from *Page*. There are no special base classes to inherit for building asynchronous pages.

The *Async* Attribute

The new *Async* attribute on the *@Page* directive accepts a Boolean value to enable or disable asynchronous processing. The default value is *false*.

```
<%@ Page Async="true" ... %>
```

The *Async* attribute is merely a message for the page parser. When used, the page parser implements the *IHttpAsyncHandler* interface in the dynamically generated class for the *.aspx* resource. The *Async* attribute enables the page to register asynchronous handlers for the *PreRenderComplete* event. No additional code is executed at run time as a result of the attribute.

Let's consider a request for a *TestAsync.aspx* page marked with the *Async* directive attribute. The dynamically created class, named *ASP.TestAsync_aspx*, is declared as follows:

```
public class TestAsync_aspx : TestAsync, IHttpHandler, IHttpAsyncHandler
{
    ...
}
```

TestAsync is the code file class and inherits from *Page* or a class that in turn inherits from *Page*. *IHttpAsyncHandler* is the canonical interface that has been used for serving resources asynchronously since ASP.NET 1.0.

The *AddOnPreRenderCompleteAsync* Method

The *AddOnPreRenderCompleteAsync* method adds an asynchronous event handler for the page's *PreRenderComplete* event. An asynchronous event handler consists of a *Begin/End* pair of event handler methods, as shown here:

```
AddOnPreRenderCompleteAsync (
    new BeginEventHandler(BeginTask),
    new EndEventHandler(EndTask)
);
```

The call can be simplified as follows:

```
AddOnPreRenderCompleteAsync(BeginTask, EndTask);
```

BeginEventHandler and *EndEventHandler* are delegates defined as follows:

```
IAsyncResult BeginEventHandler(
    object sender,
    EventArgs e,
    AsyncCallback cb,
    object state)
void EndEventHandler(
    IAsyncResult ar)
```

In the code file, you place a call to *AddOnPreRenderCompleteAsync* as soon as you can, and always earlier than the *PreRender* event can occur. A good place is usually the *Page_Load* event. Next, you define the two asynchronous event handlers.

The *Begin* handler is responsible for starting any operation you fear can block the underlying thread for too long. The handler is expected to return an *IAsyncResult* object to describe the state of the asynchronous task. When the lengthy task has completed, the *End* handler finalizes the original request and updates the page's user interface and controls. Note that you don't necessarily have to create your own object that implements the *IAsyncResult* interface. In most cases, in fact, to start lengthy operations you just use built-in classes that already implement the asynchronous pattern and provide *IAsyncResult* ready-made objects.

The page progresses up to entering the *PreRenderComplete* stage. You have a pair of asynchronous event handlers defined here. The page executes the *Begin* event, starts the lengthy operation, and is then suspended until the operation terminates. When the work has been completed, the HTTP runtime processes the request again. This time, though, the request processing begins at a later stage than usual. In particular, it begins exactly where it left off—that is, from the *PreRenderComplete* stage. The *End* event executes, and the page finally completes the rest of its life cycle, including view-state storage, markup generation, and unloading.

> **Important** The *Begin* and *End* event handlers are called at different times and generally on different pooled threads. In between the two methods calls, the lengthy operation takes place. From the ASP.NET runtime perspective, the *Begin* and *End* events are similar to serving distinct requests for the same page. It's as if an asynchronous request is split in two distinct steps: a *Begin* step and *End* step. Each request is always served by a pooled thread. Typically, the *Begin* and *End* steps are served by threads picked up from the ASP.NET thread pool. The lengthy operation, instead, is not managed by ASP.NET directly and doesn't involve any of the pooled threads. The lengthy operation is typically served by a thread selected from the operating system completion thread pool.

The Significance of *PreRenderComplete*

So an asynchronous page executes up until the *PreRenderComplete* stage is reached and then blocks while waiting for the requested operation to complete asynchronously. When the operation is finally accomplished, the page execution resumes from the *PreRenderComplete* stage. A good question to ask would be the following: "Why *PreRenderComplete*?" What makes *PreRenderComplete* such a special event?

By design, in ASP.NET there's a single unwind point for asynchronous operations (also familiarly known as the *async point*). This point is located between the *PreRender* and *PreRenderComplete* events. When the page receives the *PreRender* event, the async point hasn't been reached yet. When the page receives *PreRenderComplete*, the async point has passed.

Building a Sample Asynchronous Page

Let's roll a first asynchronous test page to download and process some RSS feeds. The page markup is quite simple indeed:

```
<%@ Page Async="true" Language="C#" AutoEventWireup="true"
        CodeFile="TestAsync.aspx.cs" Inherits="TestAsync" %>
<html>
<body>
    <form id="form1" runat="server">
        <% = RssData %>
    </form>
</body>
</html>
```

The code file is shown next, and it attempts to download the RSS feed from my personal blog:

```
public partial class TestAsync : System.Web.UI.Page
{
    const String RSSFEED = "http://weblogs.asp.net/despos/rss.aspx";
    private WebRequest req;

    public String RssData { get; set; }

    void Page_Load (Object sender, EventArgs e)
    {
        AddOnPreRenderCompleteAsync(BeginTask, EndTask);
    }

    IAsyncResult BeginTask(Object sender,
                           EventArgs e, AsyncCallback cb, Object state)
    {
        // Trace
        Trace.Warn("Begin async: Thread=" +
                   Thread.CurrentThread.ManagedThreadId.ToString());

        // Prepare to make a Web request for the RSS feed
        req = WebRequest.Create(RSSFEED);

        // Begin the operation and return an IAsyncResult object
        return req.BeginGetResponse(cb, state);
    }

    void EndTask(IAsyncResult ar)
    {
        // This code will be called on a(nother) pooled thread

        using (var response = req.EndGetResponse(ar))
        {
            String text;
            using (var reader = new StreamReader(response.GetResponseStream()))
            {
                text = reader.ReadToEnd();
            }

            // Process the RSS data
            rssData = ProcessFeed(text);
        }

        // Trace
        Trace.Warn("End async: Thread=" +
                   Thread.CurrentThread.ManagedThreadId.ToString());

        // The page is updated using an ASP-style code block in the ASPX
        // source that displays the contents of the rssData variable
    }
```

```
    String ProcessFeed(String feed)
    {
        // Build the page output from the XML input
        ...
    }
}
```

As you can see, such an asynchronous page differs from a standard one only for the aforementioned elements—the *Async* directive attribute and the pair of asynchronous event handlers. Figure 5-4 shows the sample page in action.

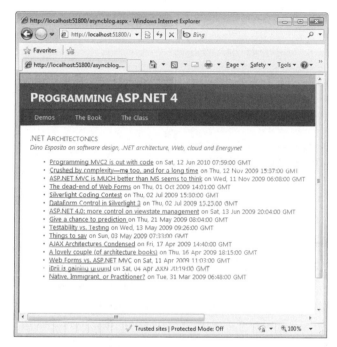

FIGURE 5-4 A sample asynchronous page downloading links from a blog.

It would also be interesting to take a look at the messages traced by the page. Figure 5-5 provides visual clues of it. The *Begin* and *End* stages are served by different threads and take place at different times.

Note the time elapsed between the *Exit BeginTask* and *Enter EndTask* stages. It is much longer than intervals between any other two consecutive operations. It's in that interval that the lengthy operation—in this case, downloading and processing the RSS feed—took place. The interval also includes the time spent to pick up another thread from the pool to serve the second part of the original request.

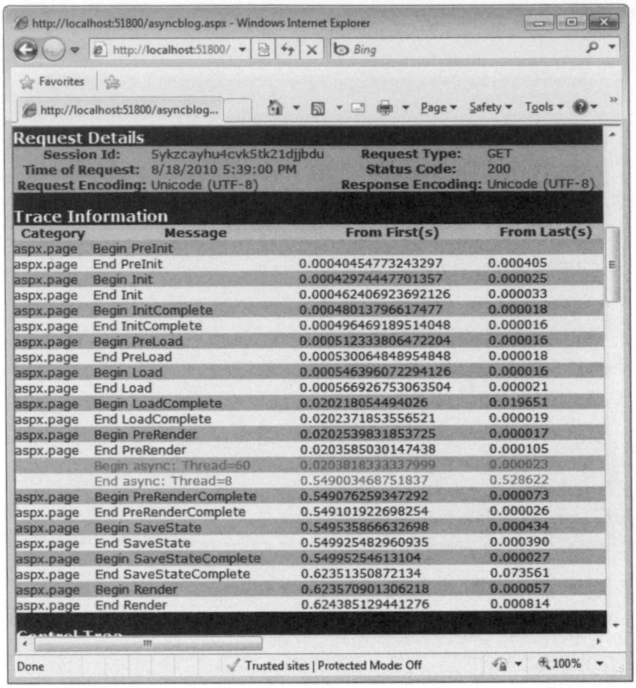

FIGURE 5-5 The traced request details clearly show the two steps needed to process a request asynchronously.

The *RegisterAsyncTask* Method

The *AddOnPreRenderCompleteAsync* method is not the only tool you have to register an asynchronous task. The *RegisterAsyncTask* method is, in most cases, an even better solution. *RegisterAsyncTask* is a *void* method and accepts a *PageAsyncTask* object. As the name suggests, the *PageAsyncTask* class represents a task to execute asynchronously.

The following code shows how to rework the sample page that reads some RSS feed and make it use the *RegisterAsyncTask* method:

```
void Page_Load (object sender, EventArgs e)
{
    PageAsyncTask task = new PageAsyncTask(
        new BeginEventHandler(BeginTask),
        new EndEventHandler(EndTask),
        null,
        null);
    RegisterAsyncTask(task);
}
```

The constructor accepts up to five parameters, as shown in the following code:

```
public PageAsyncTask(
    BeginEventHandler beginHandler,
    EndEventHandler endHandler,
    EndEventHandler timeoutHandler,
    object state,
    bool executeInParallel)
```

The *beginHandler* and *endHandler* parameters have the same prototype as the corresponding handlers you use for the *AddOnPreRenderCompleteAsync* method. Compared to the *AddOnPreRenderCompleteAsync* method, *PageAsyncTask* lets you specify a timeout function and an optional flag to enable multiple registered tasks to execute in parallel.

The timeout delegate indicates the method that will get called if the task is not completed within the asynchronous timeout interval. By default, an asynchronous task times out if it's not completed within 45 seconds. You can indicate a different timeout in either the configuration file or the *@Page* directive. Here's what you need if you opt for the *web.config* file:

```
<system.web>
    <pages asyncTimeout="30" />
</system.web>
```

The *@Page* directive contains an integer *AsyncTimeout* attribute that you set to the desired number of seconds.

Just as with the *AddOnPreRenderCompleteAsync* method, you can pass some state to the delegates performing the task. The *state* parameter can be any object.

The execution of all tasks registered is automatically started by the *Page* class code just before the async point is reached. However, by placing a call to the *ExecuteRegisteredAsyncTasks* method on the *Page* class, you can take control of this aspect.

Choosing the Right Approach

When should you use *AddOnPreRenderCompleteAsync*, and when is *RegisterAsyncTask* a better option? Functionally speaking, the two approaches are nearly identical. In both cases, the execution of the request is split in two parts: before and after the async point. So where's the difference?

The first difference is logical. *RegisterAsyncTask* is an API designed to run tasks asynchronously from within a page—and not just asynchronous pages with *Async=true*. *AddOnPreRenderCompleteAsync* is an API specifically designed for asynchronous pages. That said, a couple of further differences exist.

One is that *RegisterAsyncTask* executes the *End* handler on a thread with a richer context than *AddOnPreRenderCompleteAsync*. The thread context includes impersonation and

HTTP context information that is missing in the thread serving the *End* handler of a classic asynchronous page. In addition, *RegisterAsyncTask* allows you to set a timeout to ensure that any task doesn't run for more than a given number of seconds.

The other difference is that *RegisterAsyncTask* makes the implementation of multiple calls to remote sources significantly easier. You can have parallel execution by simply setting a Boolean flag, and you don't need to create and manage your own *IAsyncResult* object.

The bottom line is that you can use either approach for a single task, but you should opt for *RegisterAsyncTask* when you have multiple tasks to execute simultaneously.

Async-Compliant Operations

Which required operations force, or at least strongly suggest, the adoption of an asynchronous page? Any operation can be roughly labeled in either of two ways: CPU bound or I/O bound. *CPU bound* indicates an operation whose completion time is mostly determined by the speed of the processor and amount of available memory. *I/O bound* indicates the opposite situation, where the CPU mostly waits for other devices to terminate.

The need for asynchronous processing arises when an excessive amount of time is spent getting data in and out of the computer in relation to the time spent processing it. In such situations, the CPU is idle or underused and spends most of its time waiting for something to happen. In particular, I/O-bound operations in the context of ASP.NET applications are even more harmful because serving threads are blocked too, and the pool of serving threads is a finite and critical resource. You get real performance advantages if you use the asynchronous model on I/O-bound operations.

Typical examples of I/O-bound operations are all operations that require access to some sort of remote resource or interaction with external hardware devices. Operations on non-local databases and non-local Web service calls are the most common I/O-bound operations for which you should seriously consider building asynchronous pages.

Important Asynchronous operations exist to speed up lengthy operations, but the benefits they provide are entirely enjoyed on the server side. There's no benefit for the end user in adopting asynchronous solutions. The "time to first byte" doesn't change for the user in a synchronous or asynchronous scenario. Using AJAX solutions would give you at least the means to (easily) display temporary messages to provide information about the progress. However, if it's not coded asynchronously on the server, any lengthy operation that goes via AJAX is more harmful for the system than a *slow-but-asynchronous* classic Web Forms page.

The Page Life Cycle

A page instance is created on every request from the client, and its execution causes itself and its contained controls to iterate through their life-cycle stages. Page execution begins when the HTTP runtime invokes *ProcessRequest*, which kicks off the page and control life cycles. The life cycle consists of a sequence of stages and steps. Some of these stages can be controlled through user-code events; some require a method override. Some other stages— or more exactly, substages—are just not public, are out of the developer's control, and are mentioned here mostly for completeness.

The page life cycle is articulated in three main stages: setup, postback, and finalization. Each stage might have one or more substages and is composed of one or more steps and points where events are raised. The life cycle as described here includes all possible paths. Note that there are modifications to the process depending upon cross-page posts, script callbacks, and postbacks.

Page Setup

When the HTTP runtime instantiates the page class to serve the current request, the page constructor builds a tree of controls. The tree of controls ties into the actual class that the page parser created after looking at the ASPX source. Note that when the request processing begins, all child controls and page intrinsics—such as HTTP context, request objects, and response objects—are set.

The very first step in the page lifetime is determining why the run time is processing the page request. There are various possible reasons: a normal request, postback, cross-page postback, or callback. The page object configures its internal state based on the actual reason, and it prepares the collection of posted values (if any) based on the method of the request— either *GET* or *POST*. After this first step, the page is ready to fire events to the user code.

The *PreInit* Event

This event is the entry point in the page life cycle. When the event fires, no master page or theme has been associated with the page as yet. Furthermore, the page scroll position has been restored, posted data is available, and all page controls have been instantiated and default to the properties values defined in the ASPX source. (Note that at this time controls have no ID, unless it is explicitly set in the *.aspx* source.) Changing the master page or the theme programmatically is possible only at this time. This event is available only on the page. *IsCallback*, *IsCrossPagePostback*, and *IsPostback* are set at this time.

The *Init* Event

The master page, if one exists, and the theme have been set and can't be changed anymore. The page processor—that is, the *ProcessRequest* method on the *Page* class—proceeds and iterates over all child controls to give them a chance to initialize their state in a context-sensitive way. All child controls have their *OnInit* method invoked recursively. For each control in the control collection, the naming container and a specific ID are set, if not assigned in the source.

The *Init* event reaches child controls first and the page later. At this stage, the page and controls typically begin loading some parts of their state. At this time, the view state is not restored yet.

The *InitComplete* Event

Introduced with ASP.NET 2.0, this page-only event signals the end of the initialization substage. For a page, only one operation takes place in between the *Init* and *InitComplete* events: tracking of view-state changes is turned on. Tracking view state is the operation that ultimately enables controls to *really* persist in the storage medium any values that are programmatically added to the *ViewState* collection. Simply put, for controls not tracking their view state, any values added to their *ViewState* are lost across postbacks.

All controls turn on view-state tracking immediately after raising their *Init* event, and the page is no exception. (After all, isn't the page just a control?)

> **Important** In light of the previous statement, note that any value written to the *ViewState* collection before *InitComplete* won't be available on the next postback.

View-State Restoration

If the page is being processed because of a postback—that is, if the *IsPostBack* property is *true*—the contents of the __VIEWSTATE hidden field is restored. The __VIEWSTATE hidden field is where the view state of all controls is persisted at the end of a request. The overall view state of the page is a sort of call context and contains the state of each constituent control the last time the page was served to the browser.

At this stage, each control is given a chance to update its current state to make it identical to what it was on last request. There's no event to wire up to handle the view-state restoration. If something needs be customized here, you have to resort to overriding the *LoadViewState* method, defined as protected and virtual on the *Control* class.

Processing Posted Data

All the client data packed in the HTTP request—that is, the contents of all input fields defined with the *<form>* tag—are processed at this time. Posted data usually takes the following form:

```
TextBox1=text&DropDownList1=selectedItem&Button1=Submit
```

It's an &-separated string of name/value pairs. These values are loaded into an internal-use collection. The page processor attempts to find a match between names in the posted collection and ID of controls in the page. Whenever a match is found, the processor checks whether the server control implements the *IPostBackDataHandler* interface. If it does, the methods of the interface are invoked to give the control a chance to refresh its state in light of the posted data. In particular, the page processor invokes the *LoadPostData* method on the interface. If the method returns *true*—that is, the state has been updated—the control is added to a separate collection to receive further attention later.

If a posted name doesn't match any server controls, it is left over and temporarily parked in a separate collection, ready for a second try later.

> **Note** As mentioned, during the processing of posted data, posted names are matched against the ID of controls in the page. Which ID? Is it the *ClientID* property, or rather, is it the *UniqueID* property? Posted names are matched against the unique ID of page controls. Client IDs are irrelevant in this instance because they are not posted back to the server.

The *PreLoad* Event

The *PreLoad* event merely indicates that the page has terminated the system-level initialization phase and is going to enter the phase that gives user code in the page a chance to further configure the page for execution and rendering. This event is raised only for pages.

The *Load* Event

The *Load* event is raised for the page first and then recursively for all child controls. At this time, controls in the page tree are created and their state fully reflects both the previous state and any data posted from the client. The page is ready to execute any initialization code related to the logic and behavior of the page. At this time, access to control properties and view state is absolutely safe.

Handling Dynamically Created Controls

When all controls in the page have been given a chance to complete their initialization before display, the page processor makes a second try on posted values that haven't been matched to existing controls. The behavior described earlier in the "Processing Posted Data" section is repeated on the name/value pairs that were left over previously. This apparently weird approach addresses a specific scenario—the use of dynamically created controls.

Imagine adding a control to the page tree dynamically—for example, in response to a certain user action. As mentioned, the page is rebuilt from scratch after each postback, so any information about the dynamically created control is lost. On the other hand, when the page's form is submitted, the dynamic control there is filled with legal and valid information that is regularly posted. By design, there can't be any server control to match the ID of the dynamic control the first time posted data is processed. However, the ASP.NET framework recognizes that some controls could be created in the *Load* event. For this reason, it makes sense to give it a second try to see whether a match is possible after the user code has run for a while.

If the dynamic control has been re-created in the *Load* event, a match is now possible and the control can refresh its state with posted data.

Handling the Postback

The postback mechanism is the heart of ASP.NET programming. It consists of posting form data to the same page using the view state to restore the call context—that is, the same state of controls existing when the posting page was last generated on the server.

After the page has been initialized and posted values have been taken into account, it's about time that some server-side events occur. There are two main types of events. The first type of event signals that certain controls had the state changed over the postback. The second type of event executes server code in response to the client action that caused the post.

Detecting Control State Changes

The whole ASP.NET machinery works around an implicit assumption: there must be a one-to-one correspondence between some HTML input tags that operate in the browser and some other ASP.NET controls that live and thrive in the Web server. The canonical example of this correspondence is between *<input type="text">* and *TextBox* controls. To be more technically precise, the link is given by a common ID name. When the user types some new text into an input element and then posts it, the corresponding *TextBox* control—that is, a server control with the same ID as the input tag—is called to handle the posted value. I described this step in the "Processing Posted Data" section earlier in the chapter.

For all controls that had the *LoadPostData* method return *true*, it's now time to execute the second method of the *IPostBackDataHandler* interface: the *RaisePostDataChangedEvent* method. The method signals the control to notify the ASP.NET application that the state of the control has changed. The implementation of the method is up to each control. However, most controls do the same thing: raise a server event and give page authors a way to kick in and execute code to handle the situation. For example, if the *Text* property of a *TextBox* changes over a postback, the *TextBox* raises the *TextChanged* event to the host page.

Executing the Server-Side Postback Event

Any page postback starts with some client action that intends to trigger a server-side action. For example, clicking a client button posts the current contents of the displayed form to the server, thus requiring some action and a new, refreshed page output. The client button control—typically, a hyperlink or a submit button—is associated with a server control that implements the *IPostBackEventHandler* interface.

The page processor looks at the posted data and determines the control that caused the postback. If this control implements the *IPostBackEventHandler* interface, the processor invokes the *RaisePostBackEvent* method. The implementation of this method is left to the control and can vary quite a bit, at least in theory. In practice, though, any posting control raises a server event letting page authors write code in response to the postback. For example, the *Button* control raises the *onclick* event.

There are two ways a page can post back to the server—by using a submit button (that is, *<input type="submit">*) or through script. A submit HTML button is generated through the *Button* server control. The *LinkButton* control, along with a few other postback controls, inserts some script code in the client page to bind an HTML event (for example, *onclick*) to the form's *submit* method in the browser's HTML object model. We'll return to this topic in the next chapter.

> **Note** The *UseSubmitBehavior* property exists on the *Button* class to let page developers control the client behavior of the corresponding HTML element as far as form submission is concerned. By default, a *Button* control behaves like a submit button. By setting *UseSubmitBehavior* to *false*, you change the output to *<input type="button">*, but at the same time the *onclick* property of the client element is bound to predefined script code that just posts back. In the end, the output of a *Button* control remains a piece of markup that ultimately posts back; through *UseSubmitBehavior*, you can gain some more control over that.

The *LoadComplete* Event

The page-only *LoadComplete* event signals the end of the page-preparation phase. Note that no child controls will ever receive this event. After firing *LoadComplete*, the page enters its rendering stage.

Page Finalization

After handling the postback event, the page is ready for generating the output for the browser. The rendering stage is divided in two parts: pre-rendering and markup generation. The pre-rendering substage is in turn characterized by two events for pre-processing and post-processing.

The *PreRender* Event

By handling this event, pages and controls can perform any updates before the output is rendered. The *PreRender* event fires for the page first and then recursively for all controls. Note that at this time the page ensures that all child controls are created. This step is important, especially for composite controls.

The *PreRenderComplete* Event

Because the *PreRender* event is recursively fired for all child controls, there's no way for the page author to know when the pre-rendering phase has been completed. For this reason, ASP.NET supports an extra event raised only for the page. This event is *PreRenderComplete*.

The *SaveStateComplete* Event

The next step before each control is rendered out to generate the markup for the page is saving the current state of the page to the view-state storage medium. Note that every action taken after this point that modifies the state could affect the rendering, but it is not persisted and won't be retrieved on the next postback. Saving the page state is a recursive process in which the page processor walks its way through the whole page tree, calling the *SaveViewState* method on constituent controls and the page itself. *SaveViewState* is a protected and virtual (that is, overridable) method that is responsible for persisting the content of the *ViewState* dictionary for the current control. (We'll come back to the *ViewState* dictionary in Chapter 19.)

ASP.NET server controls can provide a second type of state, known as a "control state." A control state is a sort of private view state that is not subject to the application's control. In other words, the *control state* of a control can't be programmatically disabled, as is the case with the view state. The control state is persisted at this time, too. Control state is another state storage mechanism whose contents are maintained across page postbacks much like the view state, but the purpose of the control state is to maintain necessary information for a control to function properly. That is, state behavior property data for a control should be kept in the control state, while user interface property data (such as the control's contents) should be kept in the view state.

The *SaveStateComplete* event occurs when the state of controls on the page have been completely saved to the persistence medium.

Note The view state of the page and all individual controls is accumulated in a unique memory structure and then persisted to storage medium. By default, the persistence medium is a hidden field named __VIEWSTATE. Serialization to, and deserialization from, the persistence medium is handled through a couple of overridable methods on the *Page* class: *SavePageStateToPersistenceMedium* and *LoadPageStateFromPersistenceMedium*. For example, by overriding these two methods you can persist the page state in a server-side database or in the session state, dramatically reducing the size of the page served to the user. Hold on, though. This option is not free of issues, and we'll talk more about it in Chapter 19.

Generating the Markup

The generation of the markup for the browser is obtained by calling each constituent control to render its own markup, which will be accumulated in a buffer. Several overridable methods allow control developers to intervene in various steps during the markup generation—begin tag, body, and end tag. No user event is associated with the rendering phase.

The *Unload* Event

The rendering phase is followed by a recursive call that raises the *Unload* event for each control, and finally for the page itself. The *Unload* event exists to perform any final cleanup before the page object is released. Typical operations are closing files and database connections.

Note that the unload notification arrives when the page or the control is being unloaded but has not been disposed of yet. Overriding the *Dispose* method of the *Page* class—or more simply, handling the page's *Disposed* event—provides the last possibility for the actual page to perform final clean up before it is released from memory. The page processor frees the page object by calling the method *Dispose*. This occurs immediately after the recursive call to the handlers of the *Unload* event has completed.

Summary

ASP.NET is a complex technology built on top of a substantially thick—and, fortunately, solid and stable—Web infrastructure. To provide highly improved performance and a richer programming toolset, ASP.NET builds a desktop-like abstraction model, but it still has to rely on HTTP and HTML to hit the target and meet end-user expectations.

It is exactly this thick abstraction layer that has been responsible for the success of Web Forms for years, but it's being questioned these days as ASP.NET MVC gains acceptance and prime-time use. A thick abstraction layer makes programming quicker and easier, but it necessarily takes some control away from developers. This is not necessarily a problem, but its impact depends on the particular scenario you are considering.

There are two relevant aspects in the ASP.NET Web Forms model: the process model and the page object model. Each request of a URL that ends with *.aspx* is assigned to an application object working within the CLR hosted by the worker process. The request results in a dynamically compiled class that is then instantiated and put to work. The *Page* class is the base class for all ASP.NET pages. An instance of this class runs behind any URL that ends with *.aspx*. In most cases, you won't just build your ASP.NET pages from the *Page* class directly, but you'll rely on derived classes that contain event handlers and helper methods, at the very minimum. These classes are known as code-behind classes.

The class that represents the page in action implements the ASP.NET eventing model based on two pillars: the single form model (page reentrancy) and server controls. The page life cycle, fully described in this chapter, details the various stages (and related substages) a page passes through on the way to generate the markup for the browser. A deep understanding of the page life cycle and eventing model is key to diagnosing possible problems and implementing advanced features quickly and efficiently.

In this chapter, I mentioned controls several times. Server controls are components that get input from the user, process the input, and output a response as HTML. In the next chapter, we'll explore the internal architecture of server controls and other working aspects of Web Forms pages.

Chapter 6
ASP.NET Core Server Controls

"Everything happens to everybody sooner or later if there is time enough."

—*George Bernard Shaw*

ASP.NET Web Forms pages are typically made of a markup template—the ASPX file—and a back-end class—the code-behind class. In the ASPX template, you find literal text mixed with special markup tags (featuring the *runat* attribute) that identify server controls. In the code-behind class, you insert some request-processing logic—mostly presentation logic. So what's the role of server controls?

Server controls are components with a declarative and programming interface used to generate a specific piece of HTML markup based on the request and associated presentation logic. As you saw in Chapter 5, "Anatomy of an ASP.NET Page," anything you place in the ASPX template is mapped to a server control. The ASP.NET runtime then combines the output of all controls and serves the client an HTML response to display in a browser. The programming richness of ASP.NET springs from the wide library of server controls that covers the basic tasks of HTML interaction—for example, collecting text through input tags—as well as more advanced functionalities such as calendaring, menus, tree views, and grid-based data display.

There are two main families of server controls: HTML server controls and Web server controls. HTML server controls are implemented through server-side classes whose programming interface faithfully represents the standard set of attributes for the corresponding HTML tag. Web controls, in turn, are a more abstract library of controls in which adherence of the proposed API to HTML syntax is much less strict. As a result, Web and HTML controls share a large common subset of functionalities and, in spite of a few exceptions, we could say that Web controls, functionally speaking, are a superset of HTML controls. Web controls also feature a richer development environment with a larger set of methods, properties, and events, and they participate more actively in the page life cycle.

Let's start looking at the generalities of ASP.NET server controls.

Generalities of ASP.NET Server Controls

All ASP.NET server controls, including HTML and Web controls plus any custom controls you create or download, descend from the *Control* class. Defined in the *System.Web.UI* namespace, the class is also the foundation for all ASP.NET pages. The *Control* class is declared as follows:

```
public class Control : IComponent, IDisposable, IParserAccessor,
    IUrlResolutionService, IDataBindingsAccessor,
    IControlBuilderAccessor, IControlDesignerAccessor,
    IExpressionsAccessor
```

The *IComponent* interface defines the way in which the control interacts with the other components running in the common language runtime (CLR), whereas *IDisposable* implements the common pattern for releasing managed objects deterministically. Table 6-1 explains the role of the other interfaces that the *Control* class implements.

TABLE 6-1 **Interfaces Implemented by the *Control* Class**

Interface	Goal
IControlBuilderAccessor	Internal-use interface; provides members to support the page parser in building a control and the child controls it contains
IControlDesignerAccessor	Internal-use interface; provides members to make the control interact with the designer
IDataBindingsAccessor	Makes the control capable of supporting data-binding expressions at design time
IExpressionsAccessor	Internal use interface; defines the properties a class must implement to support collections of expressions
IParserAccessor	Enables the control to work as the container of child controls and to be notified when a block of child markup is parsed
IUrlResolutionService	Provides members to resolve relative URLs both at run time and design time

The *IDataBindingsAccessor* interface defines a read-only collection—the *DataBindings* property—that contains all the data bindings for the controls available to Rapid Application Development (RAD) designers such as Microsoft Visual Studio. Note that the collection of data bindings exists only at design time and, as such, is useful only if you write a RAD designer for the control.

Properties of the *Control* Class

The properties of the *Control* class have no user interface–specific features. The class, in fact, represents the minimum set of functionalities expected from a server control. The list of properties for the *Control* class is shown in Table 6-2.

TABLE 6-2 **Properties Common to All Server Controls**

Property	Description
AppRelativeTemplateSourceDirectory	Gets or sets the application-relative virtual directory of the page (or user control) that contains the control.
BindingContainer	Gets the control that represents the logical parent of the current control as far as data binding is concerned.
ClientID	Gets the ID assigned to the control in the HTML page. In ASP.NET 4, the composition of the string can be very different depending on the value of the ClientIDMode property.
ClientIDMode	Indicates the algorithm being used to determine the ID of HTML elements being created for the output of the control. This property requires ASP.NET 4.
Controls	Gets a collection filled with references to all the child controls.
DataItemContainer	Gets a reference to the naming container if the naming container implements the IDataItemContainer interface. This property requires ASP.NET 4.
DataKeysContainer	Gets a reference to the naming container if the naming container implements the IDataKeysControl interface. This property requires ASP.NET 4.
EnableTheming	Indicates whether themes apply to the control.
EnableViewState	Gets or sets whether the control should persist its view state—and the view state of any child controls across multiple requests—to the configured medium (for example, HTML hidden field, session state, and server-side databases or files).
ID	Gets or sets the name that will be used to programmatically identify the control in the page.
NamingContainer	Gets a reference to the control's naming container. The naming container for a given control is the parent control above it in the hierarchy that implements the INamingContainer interface. If no such control exists, the naming container is the host page.
Page	Gets a reference to the Page instance that contains the control.
Parent	Gets a reference to the parent of the control in the page hierarchy.
RenderingCompatibility	Indicates the version of ASP.NET that the rendered HTML of the control will be compatible with. This property requires ASP.NET 4.
Site	Gets information about the container that hosts the current control when rendered on a design surface. For example, you use this property to access the Visual Studio designer when the control is being composed in a Web form.
SkinID	Gets or sets the name of the skin to apply to the control. A skin is a particular subset of attributes in a theme.

Property	Description
TemplateControl	Gets a reference to the template that contains the current control.
TemplateSourceDirectory	Gets the virtual directory of the host page.
UniqueID	Gets a hierarchically qualified ID for the control.
ViewStateMode	Indicates how to treat the view state for the control regardless of the settings defined at the page level. *This property requires ASP.NET 4.*
Visible	Gets or sets whether ASP.NET has to render the control.

The *Control* class is the ideal base class for new controls that have no user interface and don't require ASP.NET-based style information.

> **Important** As you can see in the preceding table, ASP.NET 4 still supports themes and skins. These are features through which you can style server controls using a fluent, .NET-based API. All in all, an ASP.NET theme is a superset of a cascading style sheet (CSS) and ultimately works by applying CSS styles to HTML elements being output by controls. Introduced with great pomp and ceremony, ASP.NET themes are today commonly deprecated in favor of plain HTML-level CSS styles.

Identifying a Server Control

A server control usually generates a piece of HTML markup. The root HTML element in the markup is always given a unique client-side ID. In ASP.NET 4, the client ID of a control can be generated in a number of different ways that I'll cover in a moment.

In older versions, the client ID is always generated from the value of the *UniqueID* property—the truly server-side identifier that ASP.NET generates for each control. In versions of ASP.NET prior to version 4, the content of the *ClientID* property differs from *UniqueID* simply in that all occurrences of the dollar symbol ($), if any, are replaced with the underscore (_). Note that dollar symbols in the *UniqueID* string are possible only if the control belongs to a naming container different from the page.

In turn, ASP.NET generates the value for the *UniqueID* property based on the value of the *ID* property that the programmer indicates. If no *ID* has been specified, ASP.NET autogenerates a name such as _ctlX, where *X* is a progressive 0-based index. If the control's naming container is the host page, *UniqueID* simply takes the value of *ID*. Otherwise, the value of *ID* is prefixed with the string representing the naming container and the result is assigned to *UniqueID*.

What if the returned markup contains multiple elements that need a client ID? The author of the control is responsible for ensuring that any required ID is available and unique. The need for multiple IDs arises when multiple individual controls are aggregated in a hierarchy. Since its first version, ASP.NET has implemented a built-in algorithm that prevents name conflicts on hierarchies of controls. As an example, think of a *DataGrid* control where the first cell of each column contains a text box. In your server template for the grid, you put a *TextBox* control with a given ID. However, that ID is going to be repeated for each row added to the grid.

An ASP.NET control that can contain child controls and is at risk of having conflicting IDs should be created as a naming container—that is, it should implement the *INamingContainer* (marker) interface. A naming container has an effect on the default algorithm used for ID generation.

> **Note** A naming container is primarily a control that acts as a container for other controls. In doing so, the naming container generates a sort of virtual namespace so that ASP.NET roots the actual ID of contained controls in the ID of the naming container.
>
> To fully understand the role and importance of naming containers, consider the following example. Imagine you have a composite control, such as a user control, that includes a child control like a button. Entirely wrapped by the user control, the button is not directly accessible by the page code and can't be given a distinct and per-instance ID. In the end, the ID of the button is hard-coded in the outermost control that creates it.
>
> What happens when two or more instances of the composite control are placed on a page? Are you going to have two button child controls with the same ID? This is exactly what will happen unless you configure the composite control to be a naming container. A naming container is taken seriously by ASP.NET when it generates IDs automatically to avoid conflicts.

To see the ASP.NET ID autogeneration mechanism in action, consider the following code fragment. It features an ASP.NET *Repeater* control—a data-bound control whose content consists of repeating the item template for each object in a bound collection. (Data binding is the topic of Chapter 10, "Data Binding.")

```
<ul>
<asp:Repeater runat="server" ID="Repeater1">
    <ItemTemplate>
        <li><span id="Element">
        <%# DataBinder.Eval(Container.DataItem, "CustomerID") %>
        </span></li>
    </ItemTemplate>
</asp:Repeater>
</ul>
```

You populate the *Repeater* control using the following sample code:

```
protected void Page_Load(object sender, EventArgs e)
{
    // Load some data into the Repeater
    var customerIds = new Object[] {
            new { CustomerID = "ALFKI" },
            new { CustomerID = "ANATR" },
            new { CustomerID = "BOTTM" }
    };
```

```
    Repeater1.DataSource = customerIds;
    Repeater1.DataBind();
}
```

The *Repeater* then produces the HTML markup shown here:

```
<ul>
   <li><span id="Element">ALFKI</span></li>
   <li><span id="Element">ANATR</span></li>
   <li><span id="Element">BOTTM</span></li>
</ul>
```

The *<span>*'s ID is simply emitted as is for each data bound item. As a result, the page DOM will contain multiple elements with the same ID. This conflict violates the HTML standard but doesn't prevent a successful page display. However, it will make it hard to script *<span>* elements if you need to.

In this example, though, the *Repeater* control doesn't embed any other ASP.NET control. As a further step, let's try adding some server controls, instead, in the repeatable template:

```
<ul>
<asp:Repeater runat="server" ID="Repeater2">
    <ItemTemplate>
        <li><asp:Label runat="server" ID="Element">
        <%# DataBinder.Eval(Container.DataItem, "CustomerID") %>
        </asp:Label></li>
    </ItemTemplate>
</asp:Repeater>
</ul>
```

Bound to the same data source as in the previous example, the *Repeater* control for any version of ASP.NET older than version 4 produces a slightly different markup:

```
<ul>
   <li><span id="Repeater2_ct100_Element">ALFKI</span></li>
   <li><span id="Repeater2_ct101_Element">ANATR</span></li>
   <li><span id="Repeater2_ct102_Element">BOTTM</span></li>
</ul>
```

Note that if the ASPX markup is hosted by the content placeholder of a master page, the composed ID will be longer because it will be prefixed by the ID of the placeholder too:

*ct100_MainContentPlaceholder*_Repeater2_ct100_Element

In the client page, each *<span>* tag now has its own unique ID, and client scripting is much easier. Now if you want to, say, render in blue and bold the *<span>* element that contains ALFKI, you can add the following script. (The script assumes the jQuery library is being used. I'll cover the jQuery library in Chapter 21, "jQuery.")

```
<script type="text/javascript">
    $(document).ready(function () {
        var alfki = $("#ctl00_MainContentPlaceholder_Repeater2_ctl00_Element");
        alfki.css("color", "blue").css("font-weight", "bold");
    });
</script>
```

This wouldn't be too bad except that you need to figure out yourself what the actual ID of a bound element is going to be. The autogenerated ID ensures that each ID is unique, but the actual name is not always predictable.

Until ASP.NET 4, you had no way to change the naming algorithm. In ASP.NET 4, you can choose from a few options.

Client ID Modes

The default algorithm entails that the name of each repeated element be scoped into the naming container. This explains the first token of *Repeater1*. Note also that controls that are not assigned an explicit ID are given a system-provided progressive *ctlXX* string. In the previous example, each bound element is wrapped in an implicitly created *RepeaterItem* control with a *ctlXX* ID. This explains the progressive *ctlXX* token. Finally, the common name of the element is appended. Note that what makes two IDs unique is just the presence of implicitly named controls such as the *RepeaterItem*. In ASP.NET, any data-bound, template-based control follows a similar schema.

As mentioned, in ASP.NET 4 the base *Control* class features the *ClientIDMode* property. The property is declared to be of type *ClientIDMode*—an enumerated type. Table 6-3 lists the feasible values for the property.

TABLE 6-3 Values in the *ClientIDMode* Enumeration

Value	Description
AutoID	The control generates its child IDs using the legacy algorithm used by previous versions of ASP.NET.
Inherit	The control doesn't define its own policy for ID generation. The control inherits any policy valid on its parent. *This is the default option for individual controls.*
Predictable	Any ID is generated by simply concatenating the IDs of parent elements. *This is the default option for pages* and automatically propagates to controls unless you make some changes to the code.
Static	No mangled ID is generated; the assigned ID is emitted in the markup *as is*.

The value for the *ClientIDMode* property can be set at various levels: for individual controls, or for all controls in the page via the *@Page* directive. Finally, you can even set your preference for all pages in the application by storing the setting in the *<pages>* section of the *web.config* file:

```
<pages ClientIDMode="Predictable">
    ...
</pages>
```

When the *Static* option is selected, ASP.NET doesn't apply any name mangling to the original ID. The ID is emitted without concatenating the IDs of parent naming containers. In the case of repeated templates, however, you end up having multiple IDs in the client page. As mentioned, this violates the HTML standard, but it won't generate any run-time error in most browsers. The *Static* option is not a good one to use with iterative, data-bound controls such as *GridView*, *ListView*, and list controls.

On the other hand, the *Static* option is useful when you write user controls devoid of data-bound child controls. Because a user control can be located on different pages and in different container controls, the default algorithm for IDs will generate different IDs each time. Clearly, this makes it quite difficult for you to write client script for embedded elements. Although you can work out some tricks and solve the issue, the *Static* client ID mode makes it more direct and simpler to do so.

A more interesting scenario is when you set the *ClientIDMode* property to *Predictable*. In this case, ASP.NET still guarantees that unique IDs are generated but it uses a different algorithm. How is this new algorithm different from the legacy one that was the only option up to ASP.NET 3.5?

The legacy algorithm that generates the client ID of a control is generated by concatenating the ID values of *each* parent naming container with the ID of the control. Each segment is separated by an underscore character (_). With the *Predictable* option, the client ID of a control is generated by concatenating the value of the *ClientID* property of the parent naming container with the ID of the control. Because only the innermost parent naming container is considered, the algorithm won't ensure uniqueness in the case of data-bound controls that generate multiple rows. If the control also features the *ClientIDRowSuffix* property, that value is added at the end; otherwise, a progressive number is appended. The *ClientIDRowSuffix* property is part of the new interface *IDataKeysControl*.

When *Predictable* is used, the markup you get for the *Repeater* shown earlier takes the following form:

```
<ul>
    <li><span id="Repeater2_Element_0">ALFKI</span></li>
    <li><span id="Repeater2_Element_1">ANATR</span></li>
    <li><span id="Repeater2_Element_2">BOTTM</span></li>
</ul>
```

If the *Repeater* control is being used within a master page, the ID of the content placeholder will prefix the ID—something like this:

```
MainContentPlaceholder_Repeater2_Element_0
```

The key difference between the two algorithms is all in the trailing token, which is now easy to guess and script and still guarantees uniqueness. The *Predictable* mode represents the default behavior you get for ASP.NET 4 applications. This is a potentially breaking change. If you have an ASP.NET 3.5 piece of code written to take advantage of the old-fashioned syntax of autogenerated IDs (mostly client script code), well, that code might fail after the application is recompiled to ASP.NET 4.

> **Important** Many of the posts and articles you can find list *AutoID* as the default setting for pages. This is not the case with the released version of ASP.NET 4, as you can read here: *http://msdn.microsoft.com/en-us/library/950xf363(v=VS.100).aspx*. You can also verify that on your own, going step by step through the *Repeater* example presented earlier.

The *Predictable* algorithm allows you some degree of further control over the generated ID, at least for controls that implement *IDataKeysControl*:

```
public interface IDataKeysControl
{
    String[] ClientIDRowSuffix { get; }
    DataKeyArray ClientIDRowSuffixDataKeys { get; }
}
```

In ASP.NET 4, only two controls natively implement this interface: *GridView* and *ListView*. Similar view controls, such as *FormView* and *DetailsView* controls, do not support the *ClientIDRowSuffix* property because they are not expected to display multiple rows.

Let's consider a *GridView* control with a templated column:

```
<asp:GridView runat="server" ID="GridView1" AutoGenerateColumns="false">
    <Columns>
        <asp:TemplateField>
            <ItemTemplate>
                <asp:Label runat="server" ID="Element" Text='<%# Eval("CustomerID") %>' />
            </ItemTemplate>
        </asp:TemplateField>
    </Columns>
</asp:GridView>
```

With the default settings, the *Predictable* algorithm produces the following IDs for the elements via the *Label* control:

```
GridView1_Element_0
```

Try setting the *ClientIDRowSuffix* to a property name like the one shown here.

```
<asp:GridView runat="server" ID="GridView1" ClientIDRowSuffix="customerID">
```

The *GridView* will emit the following markup:

```
<table id="MainContent_GridView2">
  <tr>
    <th scope="col"> </th>
  </tr><tr>
    <td>
      <span id="GridView1_Element_ALFKI">ALFKI</span>
    </td>
  </tr><tr>
    <td>
      <span id="GridView1_Element_ANATR">ANATR</span>
    </td>
  </tr><tr>
    <td>
      <span id="GridView1_Element_BOTTM">BOTTM</span>
    </td>
  </tr>
</table>
```

The property is an array of strings; if it's set declaratively, you use a comma-separated string to list multiple properties whose values you want to retrieve in the ID. Note also that setting a parent to *Static* and then setting child elements to *Predictable* will start the naming container at the parent level, which is handy for always giving sections of pages unique IDs.

> **Note** The *ClientIDRowSuffix* property is not supported by the *Repeater* and *DataList* controls even though the control might output multiple rows. For any list controls, you have only the progressive number to distinguish between repeated templates. This was done essentially to discourage use of these controls, because they are considered deprecated in ASP.NET 4.

ASP.NET Control Containers

Naming containers are not the only type of container object available in ASP.NET. Another one is the binding container exposed through the *BindingContainer* property.

The binding container indicates which control in the page hierarchy represents the parent of a control as far as data binding is concerned. In other words, the binding container is the control that receives bound data from the host (typically, the page) and that passes it down to child controls.

As you can easily imagine, binding and naming containers often coincide. The only exception is when the control is part of a template. In that case, the *NamingContainer* property is generally set to the physical parent of the control, namely a control in the template. *BindingContainer*, instead, will point to the control that defines the template.

ASP.NET 4 introduced two additional special containers: data item and data keys containers. These containers are exposed through the *DataItemContainer* and *DataKeysContainer* properties. These containers don't introduce a new point in the ASP.NET control architecture. They simply identify some capabilities in an existing naming container. The capabilities are summarized by the *IDataItemContainer* and *IDataKeysControl* interfaces.

View State of Controls

The view state has been one of the most controversial features of ASP.NET since the advent of the platform. Too many developers are still convinced that the view state is a waste of bandwidth and an unacceptable burden for each and every ASP.NET page. Nearly the same set of developers eagerly welcomed ASP.NET MVC because of its complete absence of view state.

The view state is strictly functional for the Web Forms model because it caches some of the content for the controls in the page. Next, the ASP.NET infrastructure takes care of reading that information to restore the last known good state for each control within the page.

Since the beginning, the view state was designed with a hierarchical structure—if it is enabled for the parent, it is enabled also for the children. To keep the size of the view state under control, you might decide to disable the view state only on certain controls. The property *EnableViewState* seems to be just the perfect tool for the job.

Unfortunately, the capabilities of the *EnableViewState* property have been exaggerated in the past years. The strictly hierarchical nature of the view state requires that if the view state is enabled on the parent control, it *won't* be disabled on any of its child controls—regardless of the value assigned to *EnableViewState* on child controls. This issue has been fixed with ASP.NET 4, but for the sake of thousands of existing applications the fix comes through a new, dangerously similar property: the *ViewStateMode* property.

In summary, if the view state is enabled on the page (which is the default setting), you have no means to keep the state of individual controls off the storage. To gain some control over it in ASP.NET 3.5, you need to disable the view state at the page level and then re-enable it where needed. However, you should be aware that any container control that has the view state enabled will inevitably push its setting down to the list of its children.

Imagine you have a page with three hundred controls and need view state disabled only on three of them. Until ASP.NET 4, you had to disable the view state on the page first and then re-enable it for the 297 controls where you want to keep it. That's too much work, isn't it?

The *ViewStateMode* property allows for the enabling and disabling of the view state on any controls in the direct way that always seemed natural. The property accepts values from the following enumeration:

```
public enum ViewStateMode
{
    Inherit,
    Enabled,
    Disabled
}
```

Enabled and *Disabled* mean the view state is enabled or disabled for the specific control—no matter what. *Inherit* means the control inherits any settings defined on its parent. This is the default setting.

> **Note** To better understand the intricacy of the view state issue in earlier versions of ASP.NET, consider the following fact. Any ASP.NET control has a protected Boolean property named *IsViewStateEnabled*. As you can figure out, this property indicates whether view state is working or not for the control. Because of the weird behavior of *EnableViewState*, it might paradoxically occur that for the same control to have the property *IsViewStateEnabled* set to *true* and the property *EnableViewState* set to *false*! Specifically, this happens when you try to programmatically disable the view state for a control whose parent (for example, the page) has the view state enabled.

Visibility of a Server Control

If you set *Visible* to *false*, ASP.NET doesn't generate any markup code for the control. However, having *Visible* set to *false* doesn't really mean that no path in the control's code can output text. The control is still an active object that exposes methods and handles events. If a method, or an event handler, sends text directly to the output console through *Response. Write*, this text will be displayed to the user anyway. A control with the *Visible* attribute set to *false* is still part of the page and maintains its position in the control tree.

Methods of the *Control* Class

The methods of the *Control* class are listed and described in Table 6-4.

TABLE 6-4 Public Methods of a Server Control

Method	Description
ApplyStyleSheetSkin	Applies the properties defined in the page style sheet to the control. The skin properties used depend on the *SkinID* property.
DataBind	Fires the *OnDataBinding* event and then invokes the *DataBind* method on all child controls.

Method	Description
Dispose	Gives the control a chance to perform clean-up tasks before it gets released from memory.
Focus	Sets the input focus to the control.
FindControl	Looks for the specified control in the collection of child controls. Child controls not in the *Controls* collection of the current controls—that is, not direct children—are not retrieved.
GetRouteUrl	Gets the URL that corresponds to a set of route parameters. *This method requires ASP.NET 4.*
GetUniqueIDRelativeTo	Returns the prefixed portion of the *UniqueID* property of the specified control.
HasControls	Indicates whether the control contains any child controls.
RenderControl	Generates the HTML output for the control.
ResolveClientUrl	Use this method to return a URL suitable for use by the client to access resources on the Web server, such as image files, links to additional pages, and so on. It can return a relative path. The method is sealed and can't be overridden in derived classes.
ResolveUrl	Resolves a relative URL to an absolute URL based on the value passed to the *TemplateSourceDirectory* property.
SetRenderMethodDelegate	Internal use method, assigns a delegate to render the control and its content into the parent control.

Each control can have child controls. All children are stored in the *Controls* collection, an object of type *ControlCollection*. This collection class has a few peculiarities. In particular, it post-processes controls that are added to, and removed from, the collection. When a control is added, its view state is restored if needed and view state tracking is turned on. When a control is removed, the *Unload* event is fired.

Events of the *Control* Class

The *Control* class also defines a set of base events that all server controls in the .NET Framework support.

TABLE 6-5 Events of a Server Control

Event	Description
DataBinding	Occurs when the *DataBind* method is called on a control and the control is binding to a data source
Disposed	Occurs when a control is released from memory—the last stage in the control life cycle
Init	Occurs when the control is initialized—the first step in the life cycle
Load	Occurs when the control is loaded into the page; occurs after *Init*
PreRender	Occurs when the control is about to render its content
Unload	Occurs when the control is unloaded from memory

All server controls are rendered to HTML using the *RenderControl* method and, when this happens, the *PreRender* event is fired.

Other Features

Server controls also support some features that are especially related to the returned markup. In the beginning of the ASP.NET era, the focus was primarily on building pages quickly. Nobody really cared much about the emitted markup and its compliance with standards. The relevance of this aspect changed significantly over the years—by the way, ASP.NET is now 10 years old. Semantic markup, control over HTML, XHTML compliance, and browser-sensitive rendering are hot topics today. Let's see how ASP.NET controls address them.

Adaptive Rendering

ASP.NET controls are like HTML factories that accept external parameters and produce chunks of markup. As a developer, you can select and filter any parameters being assigned to control properties. As a developer, though, you can hardly control what the component does to generate the markup. The bad effect is that you end up with an HTML markup that might work differently on different browsers and different browser configurations. When this happens, though, the worst thing is that you have no way to fix it—the HTML is out of your reach. Before ASP.NET 4, *adaptive rendering* was the common way to address this problem.

Adaptive rendering is the process that enables controls to generate different markup for individual browsers. This result is obtained by delegating the generation of the markup to an external component—the adapter. When each control is about to render, it figures out its current adapter and hands the request over to that adapter. Nicely enough, a control adapter is a configurable component that you can declaratively unplug in any application to roll your own.

The selected adapter depends on the current browser. The adapter for a control is resolved by looking at the browser capabilities as configured in the ASP.NET browser database. If the browser record includes an adapter class for a given control, the class is instantiated and used. Otherwise, the default adapter for the control is used, which is an instance of the *ControlAdapter* class. The *ControlAdapter* class is a generic adapter and simply generates the markup for a control by calling the rendering methods on the control itself.

Note The ASP.NET database used for storing browser information is not a real database. It is, instead, a list of text files with a *.browser* extension located under the ASP.NET installation folder on the Web server. The exact path is the following:

```
%WINDOWS%\Microsoft.NET\Framework\[version]\CONFIG\Browsers
```

The data located in this folder is used to return browser capabilities.

A control holds a reference to the mapped adapter instance through the (protected) *Adapter* property. Each control has an associated adapter unless it is a composite control that defers to its child controls for rendering.

All ASP.NET controls have an entry point into the rendering engine in the *Render* method. Here's the method's signature:

```
protected virtual void Render(HtmlTextWriter writer)
{
    ...
}
```

The *Render* method ends up calling into an internal method whose implementation is nearly identical to the following pseudocode:

```
void RenderControlInternal(HtmlTextWriter writer, ControlAdapter adapter)
{
    if (adapter != null)
    {
        adapter.BeginRender(writer);
        adapter.Render(writer);
        adapter.EndRender(writer);
    }
    else
    {
        this.Render(writer);
    }
}
```

As you can see, if defined, a control adapter is used to generate the markup for the control. The adapter can be declaratively specified and is an external component that can be made to measure for your needs. Using an adapter to alter the markup of a given class of controls is an unobtrusive option that doesn't require any changes to existing pages using the control. It only requires you to add a browser definition file.

Browser definition files have a *.browser* extension and contain definitions that apply to a specific browser. At run time, ASP.NET determines the browser being used, uses the configuration file to determine the capabilities of the browser, and based on that figures out how to render markup to that browser. Here's a snippet that illustrates how to register a control adapter for the *Menu* for whatever browsers the user will employ:

```
<browsers>
  <browser refID="Default">
    <controlAdapters>
      <adapter controlType="System.Web.UI.WebControls.Menu"
               adapterType="Core35.MenuAdapter" />
      ...
    <controlAdapters>
  </browser>
</browsers>
```

Saved to a *.browser* file, the preceding snippet is deployed to the *App_Browsers* folder of an ASP.NET application.

An adapter class looks like the following class:

```
public class MenuAdapter :
            System.Web.UI.WebControls.Adapters.MenuAdapter
{
    ...
}
```

The class commonly overrides methods such as *Init*, *RenderBeginTag*, *RenderEndTag*, and *RenderContents*.

To write an adapter effectively, though, you must reasonably know a lot of details about the internal workings of the control you're hooking up. For more information on the architecture of control adapters, you might want to take a look at *http://msdn2.microsoft.com/en-us/library/67276kc5.aspx*.

This is only half the problem, however.

Getting CSS-Friendly HTML

The markup that too many ASP.NET server controls return makes excessive use of *<table>* tags (often nested) and inline style properties. Subsequently, ASP.NET controls make limited use of CSS styling. It might be easier and quicker, sure, but it's probably a shortsighted approach.

Based on community feedback, the ASP.NET team first released a free toolkit to enable a few built-in controls to output CSS-friendly markup where the *<table>* tag is not used or used less and in accordance with XHTML rules. The CSS Control Adapter Toolkit (CSSCAT) can be downloaded from *http://www.asp.net/cssadapters*. It comes with full source code and a permissions license that allows for unlimited further customization of the code. CSSCAT is built atop the control adapter architecture of ASP.NET.

CSSCAT defines CSS-friendly adapters for the following controls: *Menu*, *TreeView*, *DetailsView*, *FormView*, *DataList*, *GridView*, *PasswordRecovery*, *ChangePassword*, *Login*, *LoginStatus*, and *CreateUserWizard*. By using the source code of CSSCAT as a starting point, you can develop new adapters for other controls. For more information on the CSSCAT logic and internal architecture, pay a visit to *http://www.asp.net/cssadapters/whitepaper.aspx*.

ASP.NET 4 supports two rendering mechanisms: legacy and CSS-friendly. You control the rendering mechanism for all pages in the application using the *controlRenderingCompatibilityVersion* attribute added to the *<pages>* section in the configuration schema. You can set the attribute with one of the following two strings: "3.5" or "4.0".

```
<pages controlRenderingCompatibilityVersion="3.5" ...>
   ...
</pages>
```

If you set it to "3.5", rendering will occur as in older versions of ASP.NET. If you set it to "4.0", a number of controls (*Menu*, *GridView*, *Image*) will automatically render out cleaner and much more CSS-friendly HTML. It's still not perfect, but it's definitely a much better option, especially if you consider that all you need to do is add a line to the configuration file.

In ASP.NET 4, the *Control* class (and subsequently the *Page* class) features a new property, *RenderingCompatibility*, that informs you about the selected rendering machinery. It's key to notice that although the *RenderingCompatibility* property has a setter method, that is reserved for ASP.NET and using it programmatically doesn't necessarily result in visible effects. In other words, the following code compiles but doesn't produce any results:

```
// Default is 4.0
this.RenderingCompatibility = new Version(3, 5);
```

So for your own purposes, you should consider *RenderingCompatibility* to be a read-only property and resort to the *<pages>* section to change the rendering algorithm for all controls in all application pages. The default rendering version is 4.0 if you choose to create an ASP.NET 4 application.

Let's see the most relevant example of CSS friendliness enforced in ASP.NET 4. Here's the *Menu* control as it is being used in the sample ASP.NET project template:

```
<asp:Menu ID="NavigationMenu" runat="server"
        CssClass="menu"
        EnableViewState="false"
        IncludeStyleBlock="false"
        Orientation="Horizontal">
    <Items>
        <asp:MenuItem NavigateUrl="~/Default.aspx" Text="Home"/>
        <asp:MenuItem NavigateUrl="~/About.aspx" Text="About"/>
    </Items>
</asp:Menu>
```

This code in version 3.5 will produce the following markup:

```
<table id="NavigationMenu" class="menu NavigationMenu_2">
    <tr>
        <td onmouseover="Menu_HoverStatic(this)" onmouseout="Menu_Unhover(this)"
            onkeyup="Menu_Key(this)" id="NavigationMenun0">
            <table>
                <tr>
                    <td style="white-space:nowrap;">
                        <a class="NavigationMenu_1" href="Default.aspx">Home</a></td>
                </tr>
            </table>
        </td>
        <td style="width:3px;"></td>
```

```
<td onmouseover="Menu_HoverStatic(this)" onmouseout="Menu_Unhover(this)"
    onkeyup="Menu_Key(this)" id="NavigationMenun1">
    <table>
        <tr>
          <td style="white-space:nowrap;">
            <a class="NavigationMenu_1" href="About.aspx">About</a></td>
        </tr>
    </table>
  </td>
</tr>
```

```
</table>
```

As you can see, it is table-based output where most inline style information has been stripped off thanks to the *IncludeStyleBlock* property being set to *false*. Here's the markup you get according to the 4.0 rendering procedure:

```
<ul class="level1">
    <li><a class="level1" href="Default.aspx">Home</a></li>
    <li><a class="level1" href="About.aspx">About</a></li>
</ul>
```

The visual output is not the same as shown in Figure 6-1. To achieve a given visual result with the 3.5 rendering approach, you must add style information to the control declaration; in 4.0, you just edit at the CSS level.

FIGURE 6-1 Menu rendering according to version 3.5 (left) and 4.0 (right).

In ASP.NET 4, a bunch of other controls feature additional properties to let developers gain more control over the structure of the returned markup. For example, some view controls (for example, *FormView* and *Login*) stop rendering inside of a table if you set the property *RenderOuterTable* to *false*. Likewise, validation controls and the *Image* control stop rendering inline style blocks. Finally, list controls such as the *CheckBoxList* control have additional options for the repeat layout to emit plain ordered or unordered HTML lists.

Browser-Sensitive Rendering

In ASP.NET 4, as well as in older versions, you can declaratively assign a browser-specific value to a given control property. Here's a quick example:

```
<asp:Button ID="Button1" runat="server" Text="I'm a Button"
    ie:Text="IE Button"
    mozilla:Text="Firefox Button" />
```

The *Text* property of the button will contain "IE button" if the page is viewed through Internet Explorer and "Firefox button" if the page goes through Firefox. If another browser is used, the value of the unprefixed *Text* attribute is used. All properties you can insert in a tag declaration can be flagged with a browser ID. Each supported browser has a unique ID. As in the preceding code, *ie* is for Internet Explorer and *mozilla* is for Firefox. Unique IDs exist for various versions of Netscape browsers and mobile devices. Browser IDs are interspersed in *.browser* files, which you can find at this path:

```
%windows%\Microsoft.NET\Framework\[version]\CONFIG\Browsers
```

Themeable Controls

In ASP.NET jargon, a *theme* is a named collection of property settings that can be applied to controls to make them look consistent across pages. You can apply theme settings to an entire Web site, to a page and its controls, or to an individual control. A theme is identified by name and consists of CSS files, images, and control skins. A *control skin* is a text file that contains predefined values for some control properties. Applied together, these settings contribute to change the look and feel of the control and give the whole site a consistent (and, you hope, appealing) user interface. In addition, because themes are a sort of monolithic attribute, you can easily export that look from one application to the next. With themes enabled, if the developer adds, say, a *DataGrid* control to a page, the control is rendered with the default appearance defined in the currently selected theme.

Server controls can dynamically accept or deny theming through a Boolean property named *EnableTheming*, which is set to *true* by default. As a general rule, themes affect only properties that relate to the control's appearance. Properties that explicitly specify a behavior or imply an action should not be made themeable. Each control has the power to state which properties are themeable and which are not. This happens at compile time through attributes—in particular, the *Themeable* attribute. I'll return to themes in Chapter 8, "Page Composition and Usability."

Important Although fully supported and functional, themes are kind of deprecated in today's ASP.NET development, superseded by plain CSS classes and CSS-friendly development.

HTML Controls

HTML server controls look like plain HTML tags, only with an extra *runat=server* attribute. The additional *runat* attribute makes a huge difference, however. In ASP.NET, by simply adding the *runat* attribute, you can bring to life otherwise dead HTML text and transform it into a living instance of a server-side component. After it's transformed into a server object, the original HTML tag can be configured programmatically using an object-oriented approach.

By design, HTML controls expose a set of methods and properties that carefully reflect the HTML syntax. For example, to set the default text of an input form field, you use a property named *Value* instead of the more expressive *Text*. The name of the server control is determined by the value of the *ID* attribute. The following code snippet shows how to define a server-side input tag named *lastName*:

```
<input runat="server" id="lastName" type="text" />
```

In the example, the tag declaration does not include an explicit value for the *Value* attribute. You can also set it programmatically as follows:

```
void Page_Load(object sender, EventArgs e)
{
    lastName.Value = "Esposito";
}
```

After being processed by the ASP.NET runtime, the preceding declaration generates the following HTML code, which is forwarded to the browser:

```
<input name="myName" id="myName" type="text" value="Esposito" />
```

Notice that a server-side *ID* attribute expands to a pair of HTML attributes: *Name* and *ID*. The W3C HTML specification says that the attribute *name* is used for posting forms to the server; the *id* attribute is used, instead, for client-side purposes. In no way does this mean that on the server *Name* and *ID* can be interchangeably used to name the server instance of the control. The name of the server control instance is given by *ID*. If you specify both *Name* and *ID* on a server-side tag, the value assigned to *Name* will be silently overridden.

Generalities of HTML Controls

The .NET Framework provides predefined server controls for commonly used HTML elements such as *<form>*, *<input>*, and *<select>*, as well as for tables, images, and hyperlinks. All the predefined HTML server controls inherit from the same base class—the *HtmlControl* class. In addition, each control then provides its own set of specific properties and its own events.

Controls typically supply properties that allow you to manipulate the HTML attributes programmatically from within server code. HTML controls integrate well with data binding and the ASP.NET state maintenance, and they also provide full support for postback events and client scripting. For example, for a button that gets clicked, you can have some JavaScript code running on the client responding to the *onclick* event as well as some code that handles the event on the server if the page posts back as the result of that event.

HTML controls are defined in the *System.Web.UI.HtmlControls* namespace. Most, but not all, HTML tags have a direct control counterpart in the ASP.NET framework. HTML elements that don't map to a made-to-measure server control are rendered through the *HtmlGenericControl* class and have attributes set using generic collections rather than direct properties. Generic controls include *<iframe>*, *<hr>*, *<font>*, and *<body>*. In general, you should bear in mind that every element that can appear in an HTML page can be marked as *runat="server"* and programmed and styled on the server.

The *HtmlControl* Base Class

The *HtmlControl* class inherits from *Control* and defines the methods, properties, and events common to all HTML controls. Actually, many properties and all methods and events are simply inherited from the base class. Table 6-6 shows the list of properties specific to HTML controls.

TABLE 6-6 Specific Properties of an HTML Control

Property	Description
Attributes	Gets a collection object representing all the attributes set on the control with the corresponding value
Disabled	Gets or sets a Boolean value, which indicates whether the HTML control is disabled
Style	Gets a collection object representing all CSS properties applied to the control
TagName	Gets the name of the HTML tag behind the control

A disabled HTML server control is visible and always gets generated as HTML code. If the *Disabled* property is set to *true*, the *disabled* HTML attribute is inserted in the HTML output for the control. As mentioned earlier, if the *Visible* property is set to *false*, HTML is not generated for the control.

Working with HTML Attributes

Individual HTML controls feature more properties than just those listed in Table 6-6. Properties of HTML server controls map to HTML attributes, and the values assigned to the properties are replicated in the HTML output. For controls that don't have an HTML direct counterpart, the *Attributes* collection is used to set attributes on the resulting HTML tag. This collection can also be used to set properties not mapped by the control's interface and, if needed, to define custom HTML attributes. Any content of the *Attributes* collection is managed as a string.

Given the following HTML code snippet, let's see how to programmatically set some attributes on the *<body>* tag:

```
<script type="text/javascript">
function Init() {
    alert("Hello world");
}
</script>

<script runat=server language="C#">
void Page_Load(object sender, EventArgs e) {
   theBody.Attributes["onload"] = "Init()";
}
</script>

<html>
<body runat="server" id="theBody">
</body>
</html>
```

You bind a JavaScript script to the *onload* attribute of the *<body>* tag. The resulting HTML code that the browser displays is as follows:

```
<script type="text/javascript">
function Init() {
    alert("Hello");
}
</script>

<html>
<body id="theBody" onload="Init()">
</body>
</html>
```

The *Attributes* property is rendered through a special type of class named *AttributeCollection*. In spite of the name, the content of the class is not directly enumerable using the *for...each* statement because the *IEnumerable* interface is not supported. The *AttributeCollection* class provides ad hoc methods to render attributes of a text writer object and to add and remove elements. Interestingly, if you add an attribute named *Style*, the class is smart enough to reroute the assigned content to the *Style* collection.

> **Note** In the previous example, the server-side code used to add the *onload* attribute to the body element has been written through a server *<script>* tag for simplicity. You achieve the same results by moving the content of the server *<script>* tag to the code-behind class of the page.

Hierarchy of HTML Controls

Most HTML controls can be grouped into two main categories: container and input controls. A few controls, though, cannot be easily catalogued in either of the two groups. They are *HtmlImage*, *HtmlLink*, *HtmlMeta*, and *HtmlTitle*, and they are the ASP.NET counterpart of the *<img>*, *<link>*, *<meta>*, and *<title>* tags. Figure 6-2 shows the tree of HTML controls.

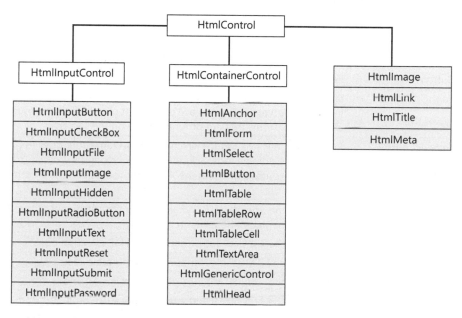

FIGURE 6-2 Grouping HTML controls by category.

The input controls category includes all possible variations of the *<input>* tag, from submit buttons to check boxes and from text fields to radio buttons. The container controls category lists anchors, tables, forms, and in general, all HTML tags that might contain child elements.

HTML Container Controls

The base class for container controls is the *HtmlContainerControl* class, which descends directly from *HtmlControl*. The HTML elements addressed by this tag are elements that must have a closing tag—that is, forms, selection boxes, and tables, as well as anchors and text areas. Compared to the *HtmlControl* class, a container control features a couple of additional string properties: *InnerHtml* and *InnerText*.

Both properties manipulate the reading and writing of literal content found between the opening and closing tags of the element. Note that you cannot get the inner content of a control if the content includes server controls. *InnerHtml* and *InnerText* work only in the presence of all literal content. The tag itself is not considered for the output. Unlike *InnerText*, though, *InnerHtml* lets you work with HTML rich text and doesn't automatically encode and decode text. In other words, *InnerText* retrieves and sets the content of the tag as plain text, whereas *InnerHtml* retrieves and sets the same content but in HTML format.

Table 6-7 lists the HTML container controls defined in ASP.NET.

TABLE 6-7 HTML Container Controls

Class	Description
HtmlAnchor	Represents an HTML anchor—specifically, the *<a>* tag.
HtmlButton	Represents the HTML *<button>* tag.
HtmlForm	Represents the *<form>* tag, but can be used only as a container of interactive server controls on a Web page. It cannot really be used to create HTML forms that are programmable on the server.
HtmlGenericControl	Represents an HTML tag for which the .NET Framework does not provide a direct class. Sample tags include *<font>*, *<hr>*, and *<iframe>*. You program these controls by using the *Attributes* collection and set attributes indirectly.
HtmlHead	Represents the *<head>* tag, and allows you to control meta tags, the style sheet, and the page title programmatically.
HtmlSelect	Represents the *<select>* tag—that is, an HTML selection box.
HtmlTable	Represents an HTML table—specifically, the *<table>* tag.
HtmlTableCell	Represents the *<td>* HTML tag—that is, a cell in a table.
HtmlTableRow	Represents the *<tr>* HTML tag—that is, a row in a table.
HtmlTextArea	Represents a multiline text box, and maps the *<textarea>* HTML tag.

Note that the *HtmlButton* control is different than *HtmlInputButton*, which represents the button variation of the *<input>* tag. The *HtmlButton* control represents the HTML 4.0–specific *<button>* tag. I'll say more about buttons in the next section while discussing the Web controls.

Server-side forms play a key role in the economy of ASP.NET applications because they are the means for implementing postbacks and guaranteeing state maintenance. For this reason, the *HtmlForm* control is not simply a form element you can program on the server. In particular, the *HtmlForm* hides the *Action* property and cannot be used to post content to a page different than the content that generated the HTML for the browser. I'll cover HTML forms in great detail in Chapter 9, "Input Forms."

Managing Header Information

An instance of the *HtmlHead* control is automatically created if the page contains a *<head>* tag marked with the attribute *runat=server*. Note that this setting is the default when you add a new page to a Visual Studio ASP.NET project, as shown in the following snippet:

```
<head runat="server">
    <title> </title>
    ...
</head>
```

The header of the page is returned through the new *Header* property of the *Page* class. The property returns *null* if the *<head>* tag is missing, or if it is present but lacks the *runat* attribute.

The *HtmlHead* control exposes three string properties: *Description*, *Keywords*, and *Title*. *Description* and *Keywords* contain meta information about the page. These properties are the actual storage for the content of the *Page* properties *MetaDescription* and *MetaKeywords* that have just been added in ASP.NET 4 to help the rank of your pages in search engine listings.

The *Title* property is used to retrieve and set the title of the page:

```
Header.Title = "This is the title";
```

Note that this property returns the correct page title only if the *<title>* tag is correctly placed within the *<head>* tag. Some browsers, in fact, are quite forgiving on this point and allow developers to define the title outside the header. To manipulate the *<title>* tag independently from the header, use the *HtmlTitle* control and mark the *<title>* tag with the *runat* attribute.

Finally, *HtmlHead* features a *StyleSheet* property of type *IStyleSheet*. The actual class that implements the interface is internal and named *StyleSheetInternal*. All this class does is let you create CSS style information programmatically. Note that the *StyleSheet* property is not a programmatic way to link a URL to an external CSS file. It is, instead, an API for you to create an ASP.NET–specific *Style* object that is then translated into a CSS block within the page. Here's an example:

```
protected void Page_Load(object sender, EventArgs e)
{
    var myAreaStyle = new Style {ForeColor = Color.Blue, BackColor = Color.LightGray};

    // Add the style to the header of the current page
    Page.Header.StyleSheet.CreateStyleRule(myAreaStyle, null, "DIV#MyArea");
}
```

The resulting page header looks like this:

```
<head>
  <title></title>
  <style type="text/css">
    DIV#MyArea { color:Blue;background-color:LightGrey; }
  </style>
</head>
```

The *RegisterStyle* method allows registered page-wide *Style* objects to be merged programmatically with the style object of individual server controls. You register a new control-focused style as shown here:

```
var labelStyle = new Style { ... };
...
Page.Header.StyleSheet.RegisterStyle(labelStyle, null);

// Right after registering the style, you apply it to or merge it with multiple controls
Label1.ApplyStyle(labelStyle);
Label2.MergeStyle(labelStyle);
```

Suppose now your page includes the following controls:

```
<asp:Label runat="server" ID="Label1" Text="Hello, world" />
<br />
<asp:Label runat="server" ID="Label2" CssClass="bold" Text="Hello, world (merged)" />
```

Here's the markup generated for the two *Label* controls:

```
<span id="MainContent_Label1" class="aspnet_s0">Hello, world</span>
<br />
<span id="MainContent_Label2" class="bold aspnet_s0">Hello, world</span>
```

The *class* attribute of the first control is set to an autogenerated CSS class; the *class* attribute of the second control is the result of merging the current style with the new one.

Linking External CSS Files

To link an external style sheet file, you use the following code:

```
var link = new HtmlLink {Href = "~/StyleSheet.css"};
link.Attributes.Add("rel", "stylesheet");
link.Attributes.Add("type", "text/css");
Page.Header.Controls.Add(link);
```

The *HtmlLink* control represents an individual *<link>* element. The *<link>* tag can appear only in the *<head>* section of a document, although it can appear any number of times.

Managing Meta Information

The *HtmlMeta* control is a helper object to allow programmatic control over the HTML *<meta>* element. Located within the *<head>* section, a *<meta>* tag contains some meta information about the rendered page. A *<meta>* element is characterized by a name and an associated value. You use *Name* property to specify the metadata property name, and the *Content* property to specify the associated value:

```
// Meta information providing some clue to search engines
var meta1 = new HtmlMeta
            {
                Name = "keywords",
                Content = "Key terms that describe your page"
            };
Page.Header.Controls.Add(meta1);
```

You can use the *Scheme* property to define some content for the *scheme* attribute of the HTML *<meta>* tag to provide additional information to user agents on how to interpret the meta information.

Finally, you use the *HttpEquiv* property instead of *Name* when you need to assign a value to the *http-equiv* attribute of the resulting HTML *<meta>* element.

> **Important** If your *<head>* section contains code blocks, you are not allowed to enter changes to its structure, such as adding new controls for *<meta>* and *<link>* tags. If you do so, you'll get a run-time exception. A common reason to have code blocks in a server-side *<head>* tag is to resolve script URLs. Here's a common example:
>
> ```
> <head runat="server">
>     <script src="<%= ResolveUrl("~/Scripts/jquery-1.4.2.min.js") %>"
>             type="text/javascript"></script>
> </head>
> ```
>
> This code just prevents you from programmatically adding new controls to the *Header* object. The workaround simply consists of moving the script tag away from the *<head>* block. A good place to move it could be the bottom of the page, which also would deliver better rendering performance for the page. The browser usually stops rendering when it encounters a *<script>* tag and resumes after the script is downloaded. By placing all the *<script>* tags at the bottom of the body, your page starts doing some graphic work sooner (at least if it is linked to large script files).

Navigating to a URL

The *HtmlAnchor* class is the programmatic way of accessing and configuring the *<a>* tag. With respect to the other container controls, the *HtmlAnchor* class provides a few extra properties, such as *HRef*, *Name*, *Target*, and *Title*. The *HRef* property sets the target of the hyperlink and can be used to navigate to the specified location. The *Name* property names a

LIVERPOOL JOHN MOORES UNIVERSITY
LEARNING SERVICES

section in the ASP.NET page that can be reached from anywhere on the same page through #-prefixed *HRef*s. The following code demonstrates a bookmarked anchor named *MoreInfo*:

```
<a name="MoreInfo" />
```

This anchor can be reached using the following hyperlink:

```
<a href="#MoreInfo">Get More Info</a>
```

The *Target* property identifies the target window or the frame where the linked URL will be loaded. Common values for *Target* are *_self*, *_top*, *_blank*, and *_parent*, as well as any other name that refers to a page-specific frame. Although the feature is mostly browser dependent, you should always consider these special names as lowercase. Finally, the *Title* property contains the text that virtually all browsers display as a ToolTip when the mouse hovers over the anchor's area.

Handling Events on the Server

In addition to being used for navigating to a different page, the anchor control—as well as the *HtmlButton* control—can be used to post back the page. Key to this behavior is the *ServerClick* event, which lets you define the name of the method that will handle, on the server, the event generated when the user clicks the control. The following code demonstrates an anchor in which the click event is handled on both the client and server:

```
<a runat=server onclick="Run()" onserverclick="DoSomething">
Click
</a>
```

The *onclick* attribute defines the client-side event handler written using JavaScript; the *onserverclick* attribute refers to the server-side code that will run after the page posts back. Of course, if both event handlers are specified, the client-side handler executes first before the postback occurs.

The *HtmlSelect* Control

The *HtmlSelect* control represents a list of options from which you choose one or more. You control the appearance and behavior of the control by setting the *Size* and *Multiple* properties. The *Size* property specifies the number of rows to be displayed by the control, whereas the *Multiple* property indicates whether more than one item can be selected in the control. Internal items are grouped in the *Items* collection, and each element is represented by a *ListItem* object. Interestingly, the *ListItem* class is not defined in the *HtmlControls* namespace but lives instead in the *WebControls* namespace. To specify the text for each selectable item, you can either set the *Text* property of the *ListItem* or simply define a series of *<option>* tags within the opening and closing tags of the *<select>* element.

By default, the *HtmlSelect* control shows up as a drop-down list. However, if multiple selections are allowed or the height is set to more than one row, the control is displayed as a list box. The index of the selected item in a single-selection control is returned through the *SelectedIndex* property. If the multiple selection is enabled, you just loop through the *Items* collection and check the *Selected* property on individual list items.

The *HtmlSelect* control supports data binding through additional properties. The *DataSource* property lets you set the data source, which can be any .NET object that implements the *IEnumerable* interface. If the data source contains multiple bindable tables (for example, a *DataSet* object), by using the *DataMember* property you can choose a particular one. Finally, the *DataTextField* and *DataValueField* properties are used to bind the list item's *Text* and *Value* properties to columns in the data source. (I'll cover data binding in Chapter 10.)

The *HtmlTextArea* Control

The *HtmlTextArea* control corresponds to the *<textarea>* HTML element and allows you to programmatically create and configure a multiline text box. The *HtmlTextArea* class provides the *Rows* and *Cols* properties to control the number of rows and columns of the text box. The *Value* property can be used to assign some text to display in the control area.

The *HtmlTextArea* class also provides a *ServerChange* event that fires during a postback and allows you to validate on the server the data contained in the control. Note that the *HtmlTextArea* control does not fire the event itself and does not directly cause the page to post back. Rather, when the page posts back in response to a click on a link or submit button, the *HtmlTextArea* control intervenes in the server side chain of events and gives the programmer a chance to run some code if the internal content of the control is changed between two successive postbacks.

All ASP.NET controls that, like *HtmlTextArea*, implement the *IPostBackDataHandler* interface can invoke user-defined code when the control's internal state changes. As discussed in Chapter 5, controls can fire custom events by overriding the *RaisePostDataChangedEvent* method on the aforementioned interface. The following pseudocode shows what happens in the method's implementation of *HtmlTextArea*:

```
void System.Web.UI.IPostBackDataHandler.RaisePostDataChangedEvent()
{
    this.OnServerChange(EventArgs.Empty);
}
```

Finally, note that the control raises the event only if the state has changed between two successive posts. To determine whether that has happened, the control needs to track the content it had the time before. This value can be stored only in the view state. Of course, the *ServerChange* even won't fire if you disable the view state for the host page or the control.

HTML Input Controls

In HTML, the *<input>* element has several variations and can be used to provide a submit button as well as a check box or text box. In ASP.NET, each possible instance of the *<input>* element is mapped to a specific class. All input classes derive from the *HtmlInputControl* class. *HtmlInputControl* is the abstract class that defines the common programming interface for all input controls. The class inherits from *HtmlControl* and simply adds three custom properties—*Name*, *Type*, and *Value*—to the inherited interface.

The *Name* property returns the name assigned to the control. In ASP.NET, this property is peculiar because, although it's marked as read/write, it actually works as a read-only property. The *get* accessor returns the control's *UniqueID* property, while the *set* accessor is just void. As a result, whatever value you assign to the property, either programmatically or declaratively, is just ignored and no exception or compile error is ever thrown.

The *Type* property mirrors the *type* attribute of the HTML input elements. The property is read-only. Finally, the *Value* property is read/write and represents the content of the input field.

Table 6-8 lists the HTML input controls defined in ASP.NET.

TABLE 6-8 HTML Input Controls

Class	Description
HtmlInputButton	Represents the various flavors of a command button supported by HTML. Feasible values for the *Type* attribute are *button*, *submit*, and *reset*.
HtmlInputCheckBox	Represents an HTML check box—that is, the *<input>* tag with a type equal to *checkbox*.
HtmlInputFile	Represents the file uploader—that is, the *<input>* tag with a type equal to *file*.
HtmlInputHidden	Represents a hidden buffer of text data—that is, the *<input>* tag with a type equal to *hidden*.
HtmlInputImage	Represents a graphic button—that is, the *<input>* tag with a type equal to *image*. Note that this tag is supported by all browsers.
HtmlInputPassword	Represents a protected text field—that is, the *<input>* tag with a type of *password*.
HtmlInputRadioButton	Represents a radio button—that is, the *<input>* tag with a type equal to *radio*.
HtmlInputReset	Represents a reset command button.
HtmlInputSubmit	Represents a submit command button.
HtmlInputText	Represents a text field—that is, the *<input>* tag with a type of either *password* or *text*.

The hidden and text input controls are nearly identical, and the contents of both are posted back. Essentially, they differ only in that hidden fields are not displayed and, subsequently, they don't provide some UI-related properties such as *MaxLength* and *Size*.

Command Buttons

The *HtmlInputButton* class is the most flexible button class in the .NET Framework. It differs from the *HtmlButton* class in that it renders through the *<input>* tag rather than the Internet Explorer–specific *<button>* tag. This fact ensures for the control much wider support from browsers.

The HTML input button controls support the *ServerClick* event, which allows you to set the code to run on the server after the button is clicked. Note that if you set the button type to *Button* and the *ServerClick* event handler is specified, the control automatically adds the postback script code to the *onclick* HTML attribute. In this way, any click causes the page to post back and the code to execute. Let's consider the following ASP.NET code:

```
<input runat="server" type="button" id="btn" value="Click"
    onserverclick="buttonClicked" />
```

The corresponding HTML code is as follows:

```
<input language="javascript" onclick="__doPostBack('btn','')"
    name="btn"
    type="button"
    value="Click" />
```

The client-side *__doPostBack* script function is the standard piece of code generated by ASP.NET to implement the postback. If the button type is set to *Submit*—that is, a value that would always cause a postback—no client-side script code is generated and the *onclick* attribute is not set.

In ASP.NET 2.0 and newer versions, more specific controls have been added to render submit and reset buttons. The controls are *HtmlInputSubmit* and *HtmlInputReset*.

> **Note** The *HtmlInputImage* control supports a nearly identical pattern for handling server-side events and validation. The *HtmlInputImage* control features a few more properties specific to the image it shows. In particular, you can set the alternate text for the image, the border, and the alignment with respect to the rest of the page. The *ServerClick* event handler has a slightly different form and looks like the following:
>
> ```
> void ImageClickEventHandler(object sender, ImageClickEventArgs e);
> ```
>
> When an image button is clicked, the coordinates of the click are determined by using the *X* and *Y* properties of the *ImageClickEventArgs* data structure.

Controlling Validation

The *HtmlInputButton* class, as well as the *HtmlButton* class, support a Boolean property named *CausesValidation*. The property indicates whether the content of the input fields should be validated when the button is clicked. By default, the property is set to *true*, meaning the validation always takes place. We'll examine data validation in Chapter 9. For now, it suffices to say, you can programmatically enable or disable the validation step by using the *CausesValidation* property.

Typically, you might want to disable validation if the button that has been clicked doesn't perform a concrete operation but simply clears the user interface or cancels an ongoing operation. By design, in fact, server-side page validation takes place just before the *ServerClick* event handler is executed. Setting the *CausesValidation* property to *false* is the only means you have to prevent an unnecessary validation.

Detecting State Changes of Controls

Earlier in this chapter, while discussing the features of the *HtmlTextArea* control, we ran into the *ServerChange* event and described it as the mechanism to detect and validate changes in the control's state between two successive postbacks. The *ServerChange* event is not an exclusive feature of the *HtmlTextArea* control; it's also supported by other input controls, such as *HtmlInputCheckBox*, *HtmlInputRadioButton*, *HtmlInputHidden*, and *HtmlInputText*. Let's look at an example in which you use the *ServerChange* event to detect which elements have been checked since the last time the control was processed on the server.

You build a page with a list of check boxes and a button to let the user post back to the server when finished. Notice, in fact, that neither the *HtmlInputCheckBox* control, nor any other input control except buttons, post back to the server when clicked. For this reason, you must provide another control on the Web page that supports posting to the server—for example, an *HtmlButton* or *HtmlInputButton* control. The following code implements the page shown in Figure 6-3:

```
<%@ Page Language="C#" %>
<html>
<script runat="server">
public void DetectChange(object sender, EventArgs e) {
    var cb = (HtmlInputCheckBox) sender;
    Label1.Text += "Control <b>" + cb.UniqueID + "</b> changed<br />";
}
</script>

<body>
<form runat="server">
    ...
    <input runat="server" type="checkbox" id="one"
        OnServerChange="DetectChange" />One<br />
    <input runat="server" type="checkbox" id="two"
        OnServerChange="DetectChange" />Two<br />
    <input runat="server" type="checkbox" id="three"
        OnServerChange="DetectChange" />Three<br />
```

```
        <input runat="server" type="submit" value="Submit" />
        <hr />
        <asp:Label runat="server" ID="Label1" />
    </form>
    </body>
    </html>
```

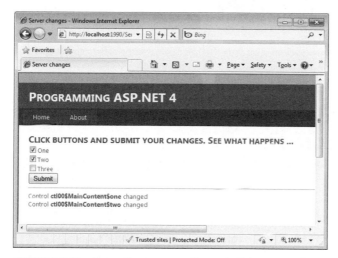

FIGURE 6-3 The *ServerChange* event fires only if the status of the control has changed since the last time the control was processed on the server.

The *ServerChange* event is fired only if the state of the control results changed after two postbacks. To get the first screen shot, you select the element and then submit. Next, if you submit again without selecting or deselecting anything, you get the second screen shot.

As mentioned in Chapter 5, when you implement the *IPostBackDataHandler* interface, each server control gets a chance to update its current state with data posted by the client.

Uploading Files

The *HtmlInputFile* control is the HTML tool for uploading files from a browser to the Web server. To take advantage of the *HtmlInputFile* control, you should first ensure that the server form's *Enctype* property is set to *multipart/form-data*. However, starting with ASP.NET 2.0, the proper *EncType* is automatically set, care of the *HtmlInputFile* control, before the control's markup is rendered. The *enctype* attribute in the code shown next is therefore unnecessary:

```
<form runat="server" enctype="multipart/form-data">
    <input runat="server" type="file" id="upLoader" >
    <input runat="server" type="submit" value="Upload..." />
</form>
```

The way in which the *HtmlInputFile* control is rendered to HTML is browser-specific, but it normally consists of a text box and a Browse button. The user selects a file from the local machine and then clicks the button to submit the page to the server. When this occurs, the browser uploads the selected file to the server, as shown in Figure 6-4.

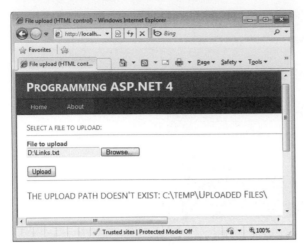

FIGURE 6-4 A new file has been uploaded to the Web server and copied to the destination folder.

> **Note** Prior to ASP.NET, a server-side process—the posting acceptor—was required to run in the background to handle multipart/form-data submissions. In ASP.NET, the role of the posting acceptor is no longer necessary because it is carried out by the ASP.NET runtime itself.

On the server, the file is parked into an object of type *HttpPostedFile* and stays there until explicitly processed—for example, saved to disk or to a database. The *HttpPostedFile* object provides properties and methods to get information on an individual file and to read and save the file. The following code shows how to save a posted file to a particular folder to disk:

```
<%@ Page language="C#" %>
<%@ Import Namespace="System.IO" %>

<script runat="server">
    void UploadButton_Click(object sender, EventArgs e)
    {
        // *** ASSUME THE PATH EXISTS ***
        string savePath = @"c:\temp\uploaded files\";
        if (!Directory.Exists(savePath)) {
            const String msg = "<h1>The upload path doesn't exist: {0}</h1>";
            UploadStatusLabel.InnerHtml = String.Format(msg, savePath);
            return;
        }

        // Verify that a file has been posted
        if (FileUpload1.PostedFile != null)
        {
            // Save the uploaded file to the specified path
            var fileName = Path.GetFileName(FileUpload1.Value);
            savePath += fileName;
            FileUpload1.PostedFile.SaveAs(savePath);
```

```
            // Notify the user of the name the file was saved under.
            UploadStatusLabel.InnerText = "File saved as: " + savePath;
        }
        else
        {
            // Notify the user that a file was not uploaded.
            UploadStatusLabel.InnerText = "No file specified.";
        }
    }
</script>

<html>
<head runat="server">
    <title>File Upload</title>
</head>
<body>
    <form runat="server">
      <h3>Select a file to upload:</h3>
        <hr />
        <b>File to upload</b><br />
        <input type="file" id="FileUpload1" runat="server" />
        <br><br>
        <input runat="server" id="UploadButton" type="submit"
            value="Upload" onserverclick="UploadButton_Click" />
        <hr />
        <span runat="server" id="UploadStatusLabel" />
    </form>
</body>
</html>
```

You can also use the *InputStream* property of the *HttpPostedFile* object to read the posted data before persisting or processing. The *HttpInputFile* control also allows you to restrict the file types that can be uploaded to the server. You do this by setting the *Accept* property with a comma-separated list of MIME types.

Caution When you use the *SaveAs* method, you should pay attention to specify the full path to the output file. If a relative path is provided, ASP.NET attempts to place the file in the system directory. This practice can result in an "access denied" error. Furthermore, make sure to provide write permission for the account used by ASP.NET for the directory where you want to store the file.

ASP.NET exercises some control of the amount of data being uploaded. The *maxRequestLength* attribute in the *<httpRuntime>* section of the configuration file sets the maximum allowable file size. An error is generated in the browser when the file exceeds the specified size—4 MB by default. Uploading large files might also generate another run-time error as a result of an excessive consumption of system memory. Finally, in a hosting scenario if you still experience problems regardless of the settings in your configuration, check out the maximum upload size on your Web server.

The *HtmlImage* Control

The *HtmlImage* class is the ASP.NET counterpart of the *<img>* tag. You can use it to configure on the server the display of an image. Possible parameters you can set are the size of the image, the border, and the alternate text. An instance of *HtmlImage* is created only when the *runat* attribute is added to the *<img>* tag. If you simply need to display an image within a page, and the image is not dynamically determined or configured, there is no need to resort to the *HtmlImage* control, which would add unnecessary overhead to the page.

The following code snippet shows how to configure a server-side *<img>* tag called to display an image whose name is determined based on run-time conditions:

```
theImg.Width = 100;
theImg.Height = 100;
theImg.Src = GetImageUrl(Request); // assume GetImageUrl is a method of yours
```

The *HtmlImage* control should be used to programmatically manipulate the image to change the source file, the width and height, or the alignment of the image relative to other page elements. The majority of properties of the *HtmlImage* control are implemented as strings, including *Src*—the URL of the image—and *Align*. Feasible values of *Align* are only a small set of words such as *left*, *right*, *top*, and so forth. These words would have been more appropriately grouped in a custom enumerated type, thus providing for a strongly typed programming model. If you think so, too, you just got the gist of the difference between HTML and Web server controls! HTML controls just mirror HTML tags; Web controls attempt to provide a more consistent and effective programming interface by exploiting the characteristics of the .NET Framework.

Literal Controls

Literal controls are a special type of server control that ASP.NET creates and uses whenever it encounters plain text that doesn't require server-side processing. In general, everything that appears in the context of an ASP.NET page is treated like a control. If a tag includes the *runat="server"* attribute, ASP.NET creates an instance of a specific class; otherwise, if no *runat* attribute has been specified, the text is compiled into a *LiteralControl* object. Literal controls are simple text holders that are added to and removed from pages using the same programming interface defined for other server controls.

Note that a literal control is created for each sequence of characters placed between two successive server controls, including carriage returns. Using a new line to separate distinct server controls and increase code readability actually affects the number of server controls being created to serve the page. Writing the page as a single string without carriage returns produces the smallest number of server controls.

Web Controls

Web controls are defined in the *System.Web.UI.WebControls* namespace and represent an alternative approach to HTML server controls. Like HTML controls, Web controls are server-side components that spring to life thanks to the *runat="server"* attribute. Unlike HTML controls, Web controls provide a programming interface that refactors the classic set of HTML attributes and events. For this reason, Web controls sometimes appear to be more consistent and abstract in the API design and richer in functionality, but they still generate valid markup. When hosted in *.aspx* pages, Web controls are characterized by the *asp* namespace prefix.

To a large degree, Web controls and HTML controls overlap and generate almost the same markup, although they do it through different programming interfaces. For example, the Web controls namespace defines the *TextBox* control and makes it available through the *<asp:textbox>* tag; similarly, the HTML controls namespace provides the *HtmlInputText* control and declares it using the *<input>* tag. Using either is mostly a matter of preference; only in a few cases will you run into slight functionality differences.

Generalities of Web Controls

The *WebControl* class is the base class from which all Web controls inherit. *WebControl* inherits from *Control*. The class defines several properties and methods that are shared, but not necessarily implemented, by derived controls. Most properties and methods are related to the look and feel of the controls (font, style, colors, CSS) and are subject to browser and HTML versions. For example, although all Web controls provide the ability to define a border, not all underlying HTML tags actually support a border.

Properties of Web Controls

Table 6-9 lists the properties available on the *WebControl* class.

TABLE 6-9 Specific Properties of Web Controls

Property	Description
AccessKey	Gets or sets the letter to press (together with Alt) to quickly set focus to the control in a Web form. It's supported on Internet Explorer 4.0 and newer.
Attributes	Gets the collection of attributes that do not correspond to properties on the control. Attributes set in this way will be rendered as HTML attributes in the resulting page.
BackColor	Gets or sets the background color of the Web control.
BorderColor	Gets or sets the border color of the Web control.
BorderStyle	Gets or sets the border style of the Web control.
BorderWidth	Gets or sets the border width of the Web control.

Property	Description
ControlStyle	Gets the style of the Web server control. The style is an object of type *Style*.
ControlStyleCreated	Gets a value that indicates whether a *Style* object has been created for the *ControlStyle* property.
CssClass	Get or sets the name of the cascading style sheet (CSS) class to be associated with the control.
DisabledCssClass	Get or sets the name of the cascading style sheet (CSS) class to be associated with the control when in a disabled state.
Enabled	Gets or sets whether the control is enabled.
Font	Gets the font properties associated with the Web control.
ForeColor	Gets or sets the foreground color of the Web control mostly used to draw text.
Height	Gets or sets the height of the control. The height is expressed as a member of type *Unit*.
Style	Gets a *CssStyleCollection* collection object made of all the attributes assigned to the outer tag of the Web control.
SupportDisabledAttribute	Returns *true* for the *WebControl* base class.
TabIndex	Gets or sets the tab index of the control.
ToolTip	Gets or sets the text displayed when the mouse pointer hovers over the control.
Width	Gets or sets the width of the control. The width is expressed as a member of type *Unit*.

The *ControlStyle* and *ControlStyleCreated* properties are used primarily by control developers, while the *Style* property is what application developers typically use to set CSS attributes on the outer tag of the control. The *Style* property is implemented using an instance of the class *CssStyleCollection*. The *CssStyleCollection* class is a simple collection of strings like those you assign to the HTML *style* attribute.

Styling Web Controls

The *ControlStyle* property evaluates to an object of type *Style*—a class that encapsulates the appearance properties of the control. The *Style* class groups together some of the properties that were shown in Table 6-9, and it works as the repository of the graphical and cosmetic attributes that characterize all Web controls. The grouped properties are *BackColor*, *BorderColor*, *BorderStyle*, *BorderWidth*, *CssClass*, *Font*, *ForeColor*, *Height*, and *Width*. All properties of the *Style* class are strongly typed. The properties just mentioned are not persisted to the view state individually, but they benefit from the serialization machinery supported by the *Style* object.

It should be clear by now that the *Style* class is quite different from the *Style* property, whose type is *CssStyleCollection*. Note that style values set through the *Style* property are not automatically reflected by the (strongly typed) values in the *Style* object. For example, you can set the CSS *border-style* through the *Style* property, but that value won't be reflected by the value of the *BorderStyle* property.

```
// Set the border color through a CSS attribute
MyControl.Style["border"] = "solid 1px black";

// Set the border color through an ASP.NET style property
MyControl.BorderColor = Color.Red;
```

So what happens if you run the preceding code snippet? Which setting would win? When a control is going to render, the contents of both the *ControlStyle* and *Style* properties are rendered to HTML *style* attributes. The *ControlStyle* property is processed first, so in the case of overlapping settings the value stuffed in *Style*, which is processed later, ultimately wins.

Managing the Style of Web Controls

The style properties of a Web control can be programmatically manipulated to some extent. For example, in the *Style* class, you can count on a *CopyFrom* method to duplicate the object and on the *MergeWith* method to combine two style objects.

```
currentStyle.MergeStyle(newStyle);
```

The *MergeWith* method joins the properties of both objects. In doing so, it does not replace any property that is already set in the base object but limits itself to defining uninitialized properties. Finally, the *Reset* method clears all current attributes in the various properties of the style object.

> **Note** I already mentioned this point a few times, but the best practice today is having ASP.NET controls emit style-ignorant markup. The emitted markup then will be decorated at will and made as colorful and attractive as it needs to be by using external CSS classes. In light of this, all of the control style features of ASP.NET lose much of their original appeal.

Methods of Web Controls

The *WebControl* class supports a few additional methods that are not part of the base *Control* class. These methods are listed in Table 6-10.

TABLE 6-10 Specific Methods of Web Controls

Method	Description
ApplyStyle	Copies any nonempty elements of the specified style object to the control. Existing style properties are overwritten.
CopyBaseAttributes	Imports from the specified Web control the properties *AccessKey*, *Enabled*, *ToolTip*, *TabIndex*, and *Attributes*. Basically, it copies all the properties not encapsulated in the *Style* object.
MergeStyle	Like *ApplyStyle*, copies any nonempty elements of the specified style to the control. Existing style properties are *not* overwritten, though.
RenderBeginTag	Renders the HTML opening tag of the control into the specified writer. The method is called right before the control's *RenderControl* method.
RenderEndTag	Renders the HTML closing tag of the control into the specified writer. The method is called right after the control's *RenderControl* method.

All these methods are rarely of interest to application developers. They are mostly designed to support control developers.

Core Web Controls

The set of Web controls can be divided into various categories according to the provided functionality—input and button controls, validators, data-bound controls, security-related controls, grid and view controls, plus a few miscellaneous controls that provide ad hoc functions and are as common on the Web as they are hard to catalogue (for example, calendar, ad rotator, and so forth).

In this chapter, we're focused on covering the most common and essential Web controls, such as the controls for capturing the user's input and posting data to the server. Table 6-11 details the core server controls of ASP.NET. (Other more advanced controls will be covered later when discussing input forms and data binding.)

TABLE 6-11 Core Web Controls

Control	Description
Button	Implements a push button through the *<input>* tag.
CheckBox	Implements a check box through the *<input>* tag.
FileUpload	Allows users to select a file to upload to the server.
HiddenField	Implements a hidden field.
HyperLink	Implements an anchor *<a>* tag, and lets you specify either the location to jump to or the script code to execute.
Image	Implements a picture box through the *<img>* tag.
ImageButton	Displays an image and responds to mouse clicks on the image like a real button.
ImageMap	Displays an image and optionally defines clickable hot spots on it.

Control	Description
Label	Represents a static, nonclickable piece of text. It's implemented through the *<span>* tag.
LinkButton	Implements an anchor *<a>* tag that uses only the ASP.NET postback mechanism to post back. It is a special type of hyperlink where the programmer can't directly set the target URL.
Localize	Reserves a location on a Web page for you to display localized text.
MultiView	Represents a control that acts as a container for a group of child *View* controls.
Panel	Implements an HTML container using the *<div>* block element. In ASP.NET 2.0, the container supports scrolling. Note that in down-level browsers the control renders out as a *<table>*.
RadioButton	Implements a single radio button through the *<input>* tag.
Table	Implements the outer table container. It's equivalent to the HTML *<table>* element.
TableCell	A table cell; it's equivalent to the HTML *<td>* element.
TableRow	A table row; it's equivalent to the HTML *<tr>* element.
TextBox	Implements a text box using the *<input>* or *<textarea>* tag as appropriate and according to the requested text mode. It can work in single-line, multiline, or password mode.
View	Acts as a container for a group of controls. A *View* control must always be contained within a *MultiView* control.

Most controls in Table 6-11 look like HTML controls. Compared to HTML controls, their programming model is certainly richer and more abstract, but in the end it still generates valid markup. If a given feature can't be obtained with raw HTML, there's no way a custom Web control can provide it. No matter how complex the programming model is, all Web controls must produce valid HTML for both up-level and down-level browsers.

Button Controls

In ASP.NET, controls that provide button functions are characterized by the *IButtonControl* interface. Core controls that implement the interface are *Button*, *ImageButton*, and *LinkButton*. In general, by implementing *IButtonControl* any custom control can act like a button on a form. Table 6-12 details the *IButtonControl* interface.

TABLE 6-12 The *IButtonControl* Interface

Name	Description
CausesValidation	Boolean value, indicates whether validation is performed when the control is clicked.
CommandArgument	Gets or sets an optional parameter passed to the button's *Command* event along with the associated *CommandName*.
CommandName	Gets or sets the command name associated with the button that is passed to the *Command* event.

Name	Description
PostBackUrl	Indicates the URL that will handle the postback triggered through the button control. This feature is known as cross-page postback.
Text	Gets or sets the caption of the button.
ValidationGroup	Gets or sets the name of the validation group that the button belongs to.

In addition to the properties defined by the *IButtonControl* interface, the *Button* class features two properties for handling the steps following the user's clicking. The properties are *OnClientClick* and *UseSubmitBehavior*. The former lets you define the name of the JavaScript function to run when the client-side *onclick* event is fired. The following two statements are perfectly legal and equivalent:

```
Button1.OnClientClick = "ShowMessage()";
Button1.Attributes["onclick"] = "ShowMessage()";
```

The *OnClientClick* property is also available on *LinkButton* and *ImageButton* controls.

By default, the *Button* class is rendered through an *<input type=submit>* tag. In this way, it takes advantage of the browser's submit mechanism to post back. The *UseSubmitBehavior* property allows you to change the default behavior. Set the *UseSubmitBehavior* property to *false* and the control will render out through an *<input type=button>* tag. Also in this case, though, the *Button* control remains a postback button. When *UseSubmitBehavior* is *false*, the control's *onclick* client event handler is bound to a piece of JavaScript code (the *__doPostBack* function) that provides the ASP.NET postback mechanism just like for *LinkButton* or *ImageButton* controls.

> **Important** Buttons are not the only controls that can trigger a postback. Text boxes and check boxes (plus a few more data-bound list controls, which you'll see in Chapter 10) also can start a postback if their *AutoPostBack* property is set to *true*. (Note that the default setting is *false*.) When this happens, the control wires up to a client-side event—*onchange* for text boxes, and *onclick* for check boxes—and initiates a postback operation via script. In light of this, virtually any control can be modified to post back.

HyperLinks

The *HyperLink* control creates a link to another Web page and is typically displayed through the text stored in the *Text* property. Alternatively, the hyperlink can be displayed as an image; in this case, the URL of the image is stored in the *ImageUrl* property. Note that if both the *Text* and *ImageUrl* properties are set, the *ImageUrl* property takes precedence. In this case, the content of the *Text* property is displayed as a ToolTip when the mouse hovers over the control's area.

The *NavigateUrl* property indicates the URL the hyperlink is pointing to. The *Target* property is the name of the window or frame that will contain the output of the target URL.

Images and Image Buttons

The *Image* control displays an image on the Web page. The path to the image is set through the *ImageUrl* property. Image URLs can be either relative or absolute, with most programmers showing a clear preference for relative URLs because they make a Web site inherently easier to move. You can also specify alternate text to display when the image is not available or when the browser doesn't render the image for some reason. The property to use in this case is *AlternateText*. The image alignment with respect to other elements on the page is set by using the *ImageAlign* property. Feasible values are taken from the homonymous *enum* type (for example: *ImageAlign.Left*, *ImageAlign.Middle*, and so forth).

The *Image* control is not a clickable component and is simply limited to displaying an image. If you need to capture mouse clicks on the image, use the *ImageButton* control instead. The *ImageButton* class descends from *Image* and extends it with a couple of events—*Click* and *Command*—that are raised when the control is clicked. The *OnClick* event handler provides you with an *ImageClickEventArgs* data structure that contains information about the coordinates for the location at which the image is clicked.

The *OnCommand* event handler makes the *ImageButton* control behave like a command button. A command button has an associated name that you can control through the *CommandName* property. If you have multiple *ImageButton* controls on the same page, the command name allows you to specify which one is actually clicked. The *CommandArgument* property can be used to pass additional information about the command and the control.

Finally, the *ImageMap* control deserves a few words. In its simplest and most commonly used form, the control displays an image on a page. However, when a hot-spot region defined within the control is clicked, the control either generates a postback to the server or navigates to a specified URL. The hot spot is a clickable region within the displayed image. The hot spot is implemented with a class that inherits from the *HotSpot* class. There are three predefined types of hot spots: polygons, circles, and rectangles.

Check Boxes and Radio Buttons

Check boxes and radio buttons are implemented through the *<input>* tag and with the *type* attribute set to *checkbox* or *radio*. Unlike the HTML control versions, the Web control versions of check boxes and radio buttons let you specify the associated text as a property. The HTML elements and corresponding HTML controls lack an attribute whose content becomes the text near the check box or radio button. In HTML, to make the text near the check box or radio button clickable, you have to resort to the *<label>* tag with the *for* attribute:

```
<input type="checkbox" id="ctl" />
<label for="ctl">Check me</label>
```

Neither the *HtmlInputCheckBox* nor the *HtmlInputRadioButton* control adds a label, which leaves you responsible for doing that. The counterparts to these Web controls, on the other hand, are not bound to the HTML syntax and do precisely that—they automatically add a *Text* property, which results in an appropriate *<label>* tag. For example, consider the following ASP.NET code:

```
<asp:checkbox runat="server" id="ctl" text="Check me" />
```

It results in the following HTML code:

```
<input type="checkbox" id="ctl" />
<label for="ctl">Check me</label>
```

Text Controls

The fastest way to insert text in a Web page is through literals—that is, static text inserted directly in the ASPX source. This text will still be compiled to a control but, at least, the number of dynamically created literal controls is the minimum possible because any sequence of consecutive characters are grouped into a single literal. If you need to identify and manipulate particular strings of text programmatically, you can resort to a *Literal* control or, better yet, to the richer *Label* control. Modifiable text requires a *TextBox*.

Over the years, ASP.NET text controls went through a number of minor changes but preserved core functionalities. In particular, I want to mention that the *TextBox* class implements two interfaces as a way to logically group its capabilities. Frankly, this aspect is not that relevant for the ASP.NET developer seeking coding tips and tricks. It makes a good statement, however, about the design of the control and, all in all, represents a good example of programming to learn from and reuse in our own classes. (This is related to one of the core design principle I'll cover in Chapter 13, "Principles of Software Design"—the *Interface Segregation Principle*.)

The two interfaces implemented by *TextBox* classes are *ITextControl* and *IEditableTextControl*. The former includes the sole *Text* property and is implemented by *Literal, Label, TextBox*, and list controls. The latter interface defines the *TextChanged* event and is specific to *TextBox* and list controls.

Speaking of text controls, it is also worth mentioning an accessibility feature of the *Label* control—the *AssociatedControlID* property. The property takes the ID of a control in the page—typically, an input control such as a *TextBox*—that you want to associate with the label. *AssociatedControlID* changes the way the *Label* control renders out. It is a *<span>* tag if no associated control is specified; it is a *<label>* tag otherwise. Let's consider the following example:

```
<asp:Label ID="Label1" runat="server" Text="Sample text" />
<asp:TextBox ID="TextBox1" runat="server" />
```

As is, it generates the following markup:

```
<span id="Label1">Sample text</span>
<input name="TextBox1" type="text" id="TextBox1" />
```

If you set the label's *AssociatedControlID* property to *TextBox1*, the markup changes as shown here:

```
<label for="TextBox1" id="Label1">Sample text</label>
<input name="TextBox1" type="text" id="TextBox1" />
```

The run-time behavior changes a bit because now any click on the label text will be extended to the associated control. For example, clicking on the label will move the input focus to a text box, or it will select or deselect a check box.

Hidden Fields and File Upload

If you're looking for a more comfortable programming interface to create hidden fields and upload files, two Web controls might help. The *HiddenField* and *FileUpload* controls add no new functionality to the ASP.NET programmer's bag, but they have been added to the toolbox for completeness. A hidden field can be created in two other ways that work with ASP.NET 1.x too. For example, you can use the *RegisterHiddenField* method on the *Page* class:

```
// Works in ASP.NET 1.x but is obsolete starting with 2.0
RegisterHiddenField("HiddenField1", "Great book!");
```

Note that the *RegisterHiddenField* method has been flagged as obsolete as of ASP.NET 4. The recommended code analogous to the previous snippet is shown next:

```
// Recommended code
ClientScriptManager.RegisterHiddenField("HiddenField1", "Great book!");
```

In addition, to create a hidden field you can resort to the HTML markup, adding a *runat* attribute if you need to set the value programmatically:

```
<input runat="server" id="HiddenField1" type="hidden" value="..." />
```

Analogous considerations can be made for the *FileUpload* control, which provides the same capabilities as the *HtmlInputFile* control that we discussed earlier. In this case, though, the programming interface is slightly different and perhaps more intuitive. The *HasFile* property and *SaveAs* method hide any reference to the object that represents the posted file. Likewise, the *FileName* property provides a more immediate name for the name of the posted file. The code to upload a file can be rewritten as follows:

```
if (FileUpload1.HasFile)
{
    // Get the name of the file to upload.
    var fileName = FileUpload1.FileName;
    var targetPath = GetSavePath(fileName);      // a function of yours...
    FileUpload1.SaveAs(targetPath);
}
```

Whether you use *FileUpload* or *HtmlInputFile* is mostly a matter of preference.

Miscellaneous Web Controls

The *WebControls* namespace also includes a few controls that provide useful functionality that is common in Web applications. In particular, we'll examine the *AdRotator* control, which works like an advertisement banner, and the *Calendar* control, which is a flexible and highly interactive control used to specify a date.

The *AdRotator* Control

Abstractly speaking, the *AdRotator* control displays an automatically sized image button and updates both the image and the URL each time the page refreshes. The image to display and other information is read from an XML file written according to a specific schema. More concretely, you use the *AdRotator* control to create an advertisement banner on a Web Forms page. The control actually inserts an image and hyperlink in the page and makes them point to the advertisement page selected. The image is sized by the browser to the dimensions of the *AdRotator* control, regardless of its actual size. The following code shows a typical XML advertisement file:

```
<Advertisements>
<Ad>
    <ImageUrl>6235.gif</ImageUrl>
    <NavigateUrl>www.microsoft.com/MSPress/books/6235.asp</NavigateUrl>
    <AlternateText>Introducing ASP.NET AJAX</AlternateText>
    <Impressions>50</Impressions>
</Ad>
<Ad>
    <ImageUrl>5727.gif</ImageUrl>
    <NavigateUrl>www.microsoft.com/MSPress/books/5727.asp</NavigateUrl>
    <AlternateText>Programming ASP.NET Applications</AlternateText>
    <Impressions>50</Impressions>
</Ad>
</Advertisements>
```

The *<Advertisement>* root node contains multiple *<Ad>* elements, one for each image to show. The advertisement file must reside in the same application as the *AdRotator* control. The syntax of the *AdRotator* control is as follows:

```
<%@ Page Language="C#" %>
<html>
<head><title>Ad Rotators</title></head>
<body>
    <form runat="server">
        <h1>Dino Esposito's Books</h1>
        <asp:AdRotator runat="server" id="bookRotator"
            AdvertisementFile="MyBooks.xml" />
    </form>
</body>
</html>
```

In the XML advertisement file, you use the *<ImageUrl>* node to indicate the image to load and the *<NavigateUrl>* node to specify where to go in case of a click. The *<AlternateText>* node indicates the alternate text to use if the image is unavailable, whereas *<Impressions>* indicates how often an image should be displayed in relation to other images in the advertisement file. Finally, each image can also be associated with a keyword through the *<Keyword>* node. Of all the elements, only *<ImageUrl>* is required.

Once per roundtrip, the *AdRotator* control fires the server-side *AdCreated* event. The event occurs before the page is rendered. The event handler receives an argument of type *AdCreatedEventArgs*, which contains information about the image, a navigation URL, alternate text, and any custom properties associated with the advertisement. The *AdCreated* event can be used to programmatically select the image to show. The XML schema of the advertisement is not fixed and can be extended with custom elements. All nonstandard elements associated with the selected advertisement will be passed to the *AdCreated* event handler stuffed in the *AdProperties* dictionary member of the *AdCreatedEventArgs* class.

> **Note** The *AdRotator* control can also get its advertisement feed through an XML or relational data source. Image and navigation URLs, as well as the alternate text, can be read from fields belonging to the data source. The control cannot be bound to more than one data source at a time. If more than one property—*AdvertisementFile*, *DataSourceID*, or *DataSource*—is set, an exception will be thrown.

The *Calendar* Control

The *Calendar* control (shown in Figure 6-5) displays a one-month calendar and allows you to choose dates and navigate backward and forward through the months of the year. The control is highly customizable both for appearance and functionality. For example, by setting the *SelectionMode* property, you can decide what the user can select—that is, whether a single date, week, or month can be selected.

```
<asp:calendar runat="server" id="hireDate"
    SelectedDate="2010-08-21" VisibleDate="2010-08-21" />
```

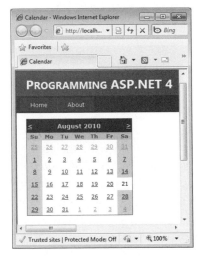

FIGURE 6-5 The *Calendar* control in action.

The *VisibleDate* property sets a date that must be visible in the calendar, while *SelectedDate* sets with a different style the date that is rendered as selected. The control also fires three ad hoc events: *DayRender*, *SelectionChanged*, and *VisibleMonthChanged*. The *DayRender* event signals that the control has just created a new day cell. You can hook the event if you think you need to customize the cell output. The *SelectionChanged* event fires when the selected date changes, while *VisibleMonthChanged* is raised whenever the user moves to another month using the control's selector buttons.

The *Calendar* control originates a roundtrip for each selection you make. Although it is cool and powerful on its own, for better performance you might also want to provide a plain text box for manually typing dates.

The *Xml* Control

The *Xml* control, defined by the *<asp:Xml>* tag, is used to inject the content of an XML document directly into an ASP.NET page. The control can display the source XML as-is or as the results of an XSL transformation (XSLT). The *Xml* control is a sort of declarative counterpart for the *XslTransform* class, and it can make use of the .NET Framework XSLT transform class internally.

You use the *Xml* control when you need to embed XML documents in a Web page. For example, the control is extremely handy when you need to create XML data islands for the client to consume. The control lets you specify a document to work with and, optionally, a transformation to apply. The XML document can be specified in a variety of formats—an XML document object model, string, or file name. The XSLT transformation can be defined through either an already configured instance of the .NET Framework *XslTransform* class or a file name.

```
<asp:xml runat="server"
    documentsource="document.xml"
    transformsource="transform.xsl" />
```

If you're going to apply some transformation to the XML data, you can also embed it inline between the opening and closing tags of the control. The control also makes it easier to accomplish a common task: apply browser-dependent transformations to portions of the page expressed in an XML meta language. In this case, you exploit the programming interface of the control as follows:

```
<asp:xml runat="server" id="theXml" documentsource="document.xml" />
```

In the *Page_Load* event, you just check the browser capabilities and decide which transformation should be applied:

```
void Page_Load(object sender, EventArgs e)
{
    if (IsInternetExplorer(Request.Browser))
        theXml.TransformSource = "ie5.xsl";
    else
        theXml.TransformSource = "downlevel.xsl";
}
```

The *PlaceHolder* Control

The *PlaceHolder* control is one of the few controls in the *WebControls* namespace that isn't derived from the *WebControl* class. It inherits from *Control* and is used only as a container for other controls in the page. The *PlaceHolder* control does not produce visible output of its own and is limited to containing child controls dynamically added through the *Controls* collection. The following code shows how to embed a placeholder control in a Web page:

```
<asp:placeholder runat="server" id="theToolbar" />
```

After you have a placeholder, you can add controls to it. As mentioned, the placeholder does not add extra functionality, but it provides for grouping and easy and direct identification of a group of related controls. The following code demonstrates how to create a new button and add it to an existing placeholder:

```
Button btn = new Button();
btn.Text = "Click me";
theToolbar.Controls.Add(btn);
```

The *PlaceHolder* control reserves a location in the control tree and can be extremely helpful in identifying specific areas of the page to customize and extend by adding controls programmatically.

> **Important** Note that each control dynamically added to the *Controls* collection of a parent control is not restored on postback. If the control generates some input elements on the client, the client data is regularly posted but there will be no server-side control to handle that. To avoid this, you must "remember" that you created a certain control dynamically and re-create it while the page loads on postbacks. To remember that a certain control was added to a parent, you can create a custom entry in the view state or use a hidden field.

View Controls

ASP.NET provides two related controls to create a group of interchangeable panels of child controls. The *MultiView* control defines a group of views, each represented with an instance of the *View* class. Only one view is active at a time and rendered to the client. The *View* control can't be used as a standalone component and can be placed only inside a *MultiView* control. Here's an example:

```
<asp:MultiView runat="server" id="Tables">
    <asp:View runat="server" id="Employees">
        ...
    </asp:View>
    <asp:View runat="server" id="Products">
        ...
    </asp:View>
    <asp:View runat="server" id="Customers">
        ...
    </asp:View>
</asp:MultiView>
```

You change the active view through postback events when the user clicks buttons or links embedded in the current view. To indicate the new view, you can either set the *ActiveViewIndex* property or pass the view object to the *SetActiveView* method.

Figure 6-6 shows a sample page in action. You select the page from the drop-down list and refresh the view:

```
void Page_Load(object sender, EventArgs e)
{
    // Views is an auto-postback drop-down list
    Tables.ActiveViewIndex = AvailableViews.SelectedIndex;
}
```

The combination of *View* and *MultiView* controls lends itself very well to implementing wizards. In fact, the new ASP.NET *Wizard* control uses a *MultiView* control internally. We'll cover the *Wizard* control in Chapter 8.

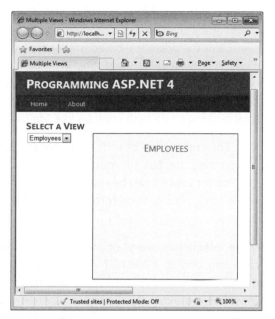

FIGURE 6-6 A multiview control in action.

ASP.NET Miscellaneous Controls and the AJAX Revolution

This book is designed to be a reference for ASP.NET developers. The book is designed to stay mostly idle on the desk and be used when you get in trouble and can't move further without a clear and deep understanding of a given ASP.NET feature. So this book puts more effort into explaining the underpinnings and architecture of ASP.NET components rather than trying to solve common problems by illustrating relatively common techniques. On the other hand, with Google you can navigate through zillions of blogs and can address your technical urgency effectively in a relatively quick time. With specialized sites such as *StackOverflow* (*http://www.stackoverflow.com*), you can likely just type in your question and find exactly the answer you were looking for.

So how does this relate to miscellaneous ASP.NET controls?

While planning this ASP.NET 4 programming book, I debated for long time whether to include this chapter. Why? Because I was supposed to discuss relevant things about most of the Web and HTML controls. But most of these controls are losing importance in modern Web applications.

The *Calendar* control you find in ASP.NET is fairly useless at this stage of Web development. If you need to let the user pick a date, you use a script-based, date-picker extension for a text box. If you need a real calendar to lock dates, either you resort to richer script-based solutions or you derive your own calendar from the base one. Most of the same things can be said for the *View* and *MultiView* controls. The underlying idea they represent is more valid than ever, but the postback-based implementation is not. You want to use AJAX scripts to switch between views and tabs. Wrapping a *MultiView* control in an updatable panel can do the trick of refreshing views with limited impact on the user. But the direction seems to be another—using script libraries such as jQuery UI. And such libraries have nothing to do with controls like *MultiView*.

Finally, let's discuss the *AdRotator* control. The importance of such a component is a no-brainer. Everybody wants to have ads on their site. But ads must not be bound to postbacks in AJAX-intensive sites. The *AdRotator* control can be revamped with partial rendering and updatable panels, but more often than not you resort to richer forms of display based on Silverlight or Flash.

In summary, more than five years after the "official discovery" of the AJAX paradigm, we realize that Web programming is changing, and so is ASP.NET. ASP.NET Web Forms is still valid and can still help in writing a lot of successful code. But some of its core components and ideas are becoming obsolete every day. Be aware of this when you pick up a book or, more importantly, when you write your code. ASP.NET MVC is a new paradigm that seems closer to the current needs of developers. For more information, check out my book *Programming ASP.NET MVC* (Microsoft Press, 2010).

Summary

In ASP.NET pages, server controls are vital components and transform the programming model of ASP.NET from a mere factory of HTML strings to a more modern and effective component-based model. ASP.NET features a long list of control classes. Looking at the namespaces involved, you should conclude that only two families of controls exist: HTML and Web controls. Controls in the former group simply mirror the set of elements in the HTML syntax. Each constituent control has as many properties as there are attributes in the corresponding HTML tag. Names and behavior have been kept as faithful to the originals as possible. The ultimate goal of the designers of HTML controls is to make the transition from ASP to ASP.NET as seamless as possible—just add *runat="server"* and refresh the page.

The overall design of Web controls is more abstract and much less tied to HTML. In general, Web controls do not promote a strict one-to-one correspondence between controls and HTML tags. However, the capabilities of Web and HTML controls overlap. All ASP.NET server controls render in HTML, but Web controls render to a more complex HTML representation than HTML controls.

In the next chapter, we'll touch on programming issues that relate to authoring an ASP.NET page—error handling, localization, and personalization.

Chapter 7
Working with the Page

"Divide and rule, a sound motto. Unite and lead, a better one."

—Wolfgang Goethe

Authoring an ASP.NET page is not simply a matter of putting together a well-organized hierarchy of server controls, literals, and JavaScript script blocks. That's definitely a fundamental step, but it's only the first step. First and foremost, a Web page is part of the presentation layer of a Web application. This means that the page is responsible for coordinating some user interface tasks aimed at providing end users with key information regarding bad requests and run-time anomalies, localized messages, and preferences.

Momentarily leaving aside any discussion on possible best practices for layering an ASP.NET Web Forms application, let's examine some aspects related to ancillary page development tasks. Tasks covered in this chapter relate to error handling, error pages, tracing, localization, and personalization, as well as effective techniques to add script files and style the content of ages.

I'll return to layers and design principles in Chapter 13, "Principles of Software Design."

Dealing with Errors in ASP.NET Pages

Any ASP.NET application can incur various types of errors. There are configuration errors caused by some invalid syntax or structure in one of the application's *web.config* files and parser errors that occur when the syntax on a page is malformed. In addition, you can run into run-time errors that show up during the page's execution. Finally, there are errors detected by the ASP.NET runtime infrastructure that have to do with bad requests or incorrect parameters.

Parser errors (both in configuration and markup) show up as soon as you start a debugging session, and their fix is immediate and part of the development process. What about other types of errors?

To prevent critical parts of your code from throwing exceptions at run time, you can resort to plain exception-handling practices as recommended by the Microsoft .NET Framework guidelines. To trap errors resulting from bad requests, invalid routing, or HTTP failures, you can take advantage of some of ASP.NET-specific facilities for page error handling.

Let's attack the topic with a quick overview of exception handling as it happens in .NET.

Basics of Exception Handling

Just like other .NET applications, ASP.NET applications can take advantage of common language runtime (CLR) exceptions to catch and handle run-time errors that occur in the code. As a reminder, it's worth mentioning here that in .NET development CLR exceptions are the recommended way of handling errors—they are the rule, not the exception!

Exceptions, though, should be taken just for what the name suggests—that is, events in the life of the application raised when something happens that violates an assumption.

Exceptions *should not* be used to control the normal flow of the program. If there is a way to detect possible inconsistent situations, by all means use that other method (mostly, conditional statements), and use exceptions as the last resort. The latest version of Microsoft Visual Studio 2010 (as well as many commercial products that assist you in development, such as JetBrains ReSharper and Telerik JustCode, to name a couple) offers coding tips and reminds you to check for possible null reference exceptions. That's a huge help, isn't it?

Although exceptions are the official tool to handle errors in .NET applications, they're not free and should not be overused. Running any piece of code in a *try/catch* block will cost you at least a little in terms of performance. Protection against possible run-time failure is a sort of insurance, and you have to pay for that no matter what happens.

Exceptions in Action

To execute a piece of code with the certainty that any (or just some) exceptions it might raise will be caught, you use the following code:

```
try
{
    // Your regular code here
    ...
}
catch
{
    // Your recovery code for all exceptions
    ...
}
```

The sample code snippet can have a number of variations and extensions. You can add a *finally* block, which will finalize the operation and run regardless of whether the execution flow went through the *try* or the *catch* block. The snippet shown will catch any exceptions. Because of its extreme generality, you might need to lose some valuable information about what has happened. A better approach consists of listing one or more *catch* blocks, each trying to cache a specific exception:

```
try
{
    // Your regular code here
    ...
}
catch(NullReferenceException nullReferenceException)
{
    // Your recovery code for the exception
    ...
}
catch(ArgumentException argumentException)
{
    // Your recovery code for the exception
    ...
}
finally
{
    // Finalize here but DON'T throw exceptions from here
    ...
}
```

Exceptions will be listed from the most specific to the least specific. From a *catch* block, you are allowed to swallow the exception so that other topmost modules will never know about it. Alternatively, you can handle the situation gracefully and recover. Finally, you can do some work and then re-throw the same exception or arrange a new one with some extra or modified information in it.

The *catch* block is fairly expensive if your code gets into it. Therefore, you should use the *catch* block judiciously—only when really needed and without overcatching.

Guidelines for Exception Handling

When writing a module (including ASP.NET pages), you should never throw an exception as an instance of the *System.Exception* class. It is strictly recommended that you try to use built-in exception types such as *InvalidOperationException*, *NullReferenceException*, and *ArgumentNullException* whenever these types apply. You should resist the temptation of having your very own exceptions all the way through, although for program errors you should consider defining your own exceptions.

In general, you should be very specific with exceptions. *ArgumentNullException* is more specific than *ArgumentException*. An exception comes with a message, and the message must be targeted to developers and, ideally, localized.

Swallowing an exception is possible and supported, but you should consider that in this case some modules might never know what went wrong. This approach might not be acceptable in some cases, so use it with extreme care. In general, don't be afraid to let exceptions propagate up the call stack.

When using exceptions, pay a lot of attention to cleanup code. The *finally* block serves exactly the purpose of ensuring that any cleanup code is always executed. Alternatively, when the cleanup code sees an object that implements *IDisposable*, you can resort to the *using* statement:

```
using(var someObject = new SomeDisposableObject())
{
    // Code at risk of exceptions
    ...
}
```

If placed in a *finally* block, the cleanup code is always executed. This is an important guarantee because if an unexpected exception is thrown, you might lose your cleanup code.

Finally, here are a few recommendations for situation in which you get to write your own exception classes. For a long time, Microsoft said you should derive your exception classes from *System.ApplicationException*. More recently, there's been a complete turnaround on this point: the new directive says the opposite. You should ignore *ApplicationException* and derive your exception classes from *Exception* or other more specific built-in classes. And don't forget to make your exception classes serializable.

Basics of Page Error Handling

When an exception occurs in an ASP.NET application, the CLR tries to find a block of code willing to catch it. Exceptions walk their way up the stack until the root of the current application is reached. If no proper handler shows up along the way, the exception gains the rank of unhandled exception and causes the CLR to throw a system-level exception.

At this point, ASP.NET users are shown a standard error page that some developers familiarly call the *YSOD* (yellow screen of death), which is a spinoff of the just as illustrious BSOD (blue screen of death) that we all have come to know after years of experience with the Microsoft Windows operating system. An unhandled exception originates an error and stops the application.

As a developer, how should you deal with unhandled exceptions in ASP.NET applications?

Default Error Pages

When an unrecoverable error occurs in an ASP.NET page, users always receive a page that, more or less nicely, informs them that something went wrong at a certain point. ASP.NET catches any unhandled exception and transforms it into a page for the user, as shown in Figure 7-1.

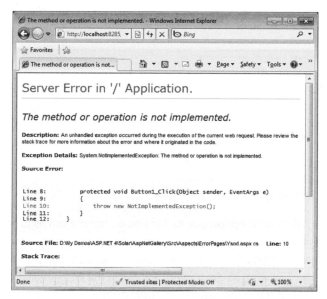

FIGURE 7-1 The error page generated by an unhandled exception (for the local user).

As you can guess from looking at the screen shot, the sample page contains a button whose click handler is bound to the following code:

```
protected void Button1_Click(Object sender, EventArgs e)
{
    throw new NotImplementedException();
}
```

More than the code itself, which is fairly trivial, the most interesting part of the story is how ASP.NET handles the exception and the machinery that ultimately produces the markup of Figure 7-1.

First and foremost, the typical error page differs for local and remote users.

By default, local users—namely, any user accessing the application through the local host—receive the page shown in Figure 7-1. The page includes the call stack—the chain of method calls leading up to the exception—and a brief description of the error. Additional source code information is added if the page runs in debug mode. For security reasons, remote users receive a less detailed page, like the one shown in Figure 7-2.

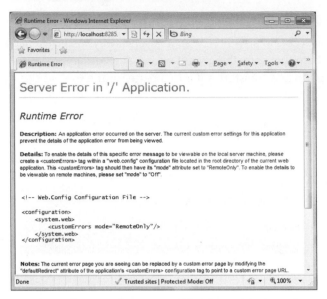

FIGURE 7-2 The page does not provide information about the error.

ASP.NET provides a couple of global interception points for you to handle errors program-matically, at either the page level or the application level. The *Page* base class exposes an *Error* event, which you can override in your pages to catch any unhandled exceptions raised during the execution of the page. Likewise, an *Error* event exists on the *HttpApplication* class, too, to catch any unhandled exception thrown within the application.

Page-Level Error Handling

To catch any unhandled exceptions wandering around a particular page, you define a handler for the *Error* event. Here's an example:

```
protected void Page_Error(Object sender, EventArgs e)
{
    // Capture the error
    var exception = Server.GetLastError();

    // Resolve the error page based on the exception that occurred
    // and redirect to the appropriate page
    if (exception is NotImplementedException)
        Server.Transfer("/ErrorPages/NotImplErrorPage.aspx");
    else
        Server.Transfer("/ErrorPages/GenericErrorPage.aspx");

    // Clear the error
    Server.ClearError();
}
```

You know about the raised exception through the *GetLastError* method of the *Server* object. In the *Error* handler, you can transfer control to a particular page and show a personalized and exception-specific message to the user. The control is transferred to the error page, and the URL in the address bar of the browser doesn't change. If you use *Server.Transfer* to pass control, the exception information is maintained and the error page itself can call into *GetLastError* and display more detailed information. Finally, after the exception is fully handled, you clear the error by calling *ClearError*.

Using *Server.Transfer* instead of *Response.Redirect* is also relevant from a Search-Engine Optimization (SEO) perspective because it performs a server-side redirect that is "invisible" to client applications, including Web browsers and, more importantly, Web spiders.

Important When displaying error messages, pay attention not to hand out sensitive information that a malicious user might use against your system. Sensitive data includes user names, file system paths, connection strings, and password-related information. You can make error pages smart enough to determine whether the user is local or whether a custom header is defined, and to display more details that can be helpful to diagnose errors:

```
if (Request.UserHostAddress == "127.0.0.1") {
    ...
}
```

You can also use the *Request.Headers* collection to check for custom headers added only by a particular Web server machine. To add a custom header, you open the Properties dialog box of the application's Internet Information Services (IIS) virtual folder and click the HTTP Headers tab.

Global Error Handling

A page *Error* handler catches only errors that occur within a particular page. This means that each page that requires error handling must point to a common piece of code or define its own handler. Such a fine-grained approach is not desirable when you want to share the same generic error handler for all the pages that make up the application. In this case, you can create a global error handler at the application level that catches all unhandled exceptions and routes them to the specified error page.

The implementation is nearly identical to page-level error handlers except that you will be handling the *Error* event on the *HttpApplication* object that represents your application. To do that, you write code in the predefined *Application_Error* stub of the application's *global.asax* file:

```
void Application_Error(Object sender, EventArgs e)
{
    ...
}
```

You could do something useful in this event handler, such as sending an e-mail to the site administrator or writing to the Windows event log to say that the page failed to execute properly. ASP.NET provides a set of classes in the *System.Net.Mail* namespace for just this purpose.

```
void Application_Error(Object sender, EventArgs e)
{
    // Code that runs when an unhandled error occurs
    var exception = Server.GetLastError();
    if (exception == null)
        return;

    var mail = new MailMessage { From = new MailAddress("automated@contoso.com") };
    mail.To.Add(new MailAddress("administrator@contoso.com"));
    mail.Subject = "Site Error at " + DateTime.Now;
    mail.Body = "Error Description: " + exception.Message;
    var server = new SmtpClient {Host = "your.smtp.server"};
    server.Send(mail);

    // Clear the error
    Server.ClearError();
}
```

If the SMTP server requires authentication, you need to provide your credentials through the *Credentials* property of the *SmtpClient* class. Figure 7-3 shows the e-mail message being sent.

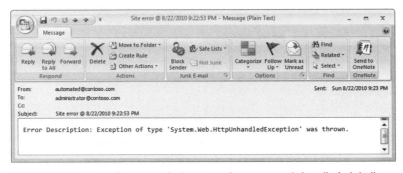

FIGURE 7-3 The e-mail message being sent when an error is handled globally.

As Figure 7-3 shows, the exception reported mentions a generic HTTP unhandled exception. Note that *GetLastError* returns the real exception in the context of *Page_Error*, but not later in the context of *Application_Error*. In the application context, the exception caught is a generic HTTP exception that wraps the original exception internally. To retrieve the real exception, you must go through the *InnerException* property, as shown here:

```
void Application_Error(Object sender, EventArgs e)
{
    // This is a generic HTTP failure exception
    var exception = Server.GetLastError();
    if (exception == null)
        return;

    // Put your hands on the original exception
    var originalException = exception.InnerException;
    ...
}
```

Essentially, when ASP.NET detects an internal application error—like it is an exception being thrown by one of the pages—it configures itself for an HTTP 500 response. The ASP.NET error-handling mechanism captures HTTP 500 errors but not other HTTP errors, such as 404. Errors other than HTTP 500 are handled by the Web server, and all that you can do is configure the ASP.NET error-handling machinery (and to some extent the routing mechanism too) to redirect automatically where you like. No full control over 404 and other HTTP errors is possible in ASP.NET Web Forms.

> **Note** What takes precedence if you have an application-level error handler and a page-level handler? The page handler runs first, followed by the application handler. For this reason, if you have both handlers, you should avoid calling *Server.ClearError* in the page handler so that you do not compromise any of the following steps.

Logging Exceptions

In addition or in alternative to sending an e-mail message, you can decide to write an entry to the Windows event log when an exception is caught. Here's the code:

```
void Application_Error(Object sender, EventArgs e)
{
    // Obtain the URL of the request
    var url = Request.Path;

    // Obtain the Exception object describing the error
    var exception = Server.GetLastError();

    // Build the message --> [Error occurred. XXX at url]
    var text = new StringBuilder("Error occurred. ");
    text.Append(error.Message);
    text.Append(" at ");
    text.Append(url);

    // Write to the Event Log
    var log = new EventLog();
    log.Source = "Your Log";
    log.WriteEntry(text.ToString(), EventLogEntryType.Error);
}
```

The Event Log *Source* must exist prior to its use in an ASP.NET application—in this case, in the *Application_Error* method in *global.asax*. Typical ASP.NET account credentials are established such that the ASP.NET account does not have Event Log source creation rights. You'll need to make sure the log is created first on each Web server your code will execute within prior to actually running your Web application.

Robust Error Handling

A good strategy for robust and effective ASP.NET error handling is based on the following three guidelines:

- Anticipate problems by wrapping all blocks of code that might fail in *try/catch/finally* blocks. This alone doesn't guarantee that no exceptions will ever show up, but at least you'll correctly handle the most common ones.

- Don't leave any exceptions unhandled. By following this guideline, even if you did not anticipate a problem, at least users won't see an exception page. You can do this both at the page and application levels. Needless to say, an application-level error handler takes precedence over page-level handlers. At the least, exceptions that are handled at the application level should be logged to feed reports and help the team to understand what went wrong and whether some bugs exist that need to be fixed.

- Make sure that error pages don't give away any sensitive information. If necessary, distinguish between local and remote users and show detailed messages only to the former. A local user is defined as the user that accesses the application from the Web server machine.

Outlined in this way, error handling is mostly a matter of writing the right code in the right place. However, ASP.NET provides developers with a built-in mechanism to automatically redirect users to error-specific pages. This mechanism is entirely declarative and can be controlled through the *web.config* file.

Mapping Errors to Pages

ASP.NET developers can also benefit from a declarative API to gain some control over the page being served to users after an unhandled exception. Such a declarative API relies on the information stored in the *<customErrors>* section of the application's *web.config* file.

The *<customErrors>* Section

You turn on custom error messages for an ASP.NET application by acting on the *<customErrors>* section. Here's an example:

```
<configuration>
    <system.web>
        ...
        <customErrors mode="RemoteOnly" />
    </system.web>
</configuration>
```

The *mode* attribute specifies whether custom error pages are enabled, disabled, or shown only to remote clients. The attribute is required. When the *mode* attribute is set to

RemoteOnly (the default setting), remote users receive a generic error page that informs them that something went wrong on the server. (See Figure 7-2.) Local users, on the other hand, receive pages that show lots of details about the ASP.NET error. (See Figure 7-1.)

The error-handling policy can be changed at will. In particular, ASP.NET can be instructed to display detailed pages to both local *and* remote users. To activate this functionality, you change the value of the *mode* attribute to *Off*. For obvious security reasons, *Off* should not be used in production environments—it might reveal critical information to potential attackers.

Using Custom Error Pages

Overall, whatever your choice is for the *mode* attribute, all users have a good chance to be served a rather inexpressive and uninformative error page. To display a more professional, friendly, and apologetic page that has a look and feel consistent with the site, you set *web.config* as follows. Figure 7-4 gives an idea of the results you can get.

```
<configuration>
    <system.web>
        <customErrors mode="On"
            defaultRedirect="/GenericErrorPage.aspx" />
    </system.web>
</configuration>
```

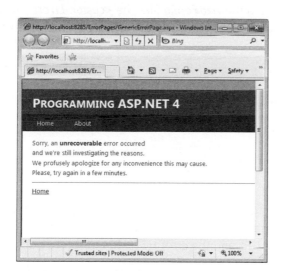

FIGURE 7-4 A more friendly error page.

Whatever the error is, ASP.NET now redirects the user to the *GenericErrorPage.aspx* page, whose contents and layout are completely under your control. This look is obtained by adding an optional attribute such as *defaultRedirect*, which indicates the error page to use to notify users. If *mode* is set to *On*, the default redirect takes on the standard error pages for all local and remote users. If *mode* is set to *RemoteOnly*, remote users will receive the custom error page while local users (typically, the developers) still receive the default page with the ASP.NET error information.

In most cases, the custom error page is made of plain HTML so that no error can recursively be raised. However, should the error page, in turn, originate another error, the default generic page of ASP.NET will be shown.

> **Note** When a default redirect is used, the browser receives an HTTP 302 status code and is invited to issue a new request to the specified error page. This fact has a key consequence: any information about the original exception is lost and *GetLastError*, which is called from within the custom error page, returns *null*.

Handling Common HTTP Errors

A generic error page invoked for each unhandled exception can hardly be context-sensitive—especially if you consider that there's no immediate way for the page author to access the original exception. We'll return to this point in a moment.

In addition to redirecting users to a common page for all errors, ASP.NET enables you to customize pages to show when certain HTTP errors occur. The mapping between error pages and specific HTTP status codes is defined in the *web.config* file. The *<customErrors>* section supports an inner *<error>* tag, which you can use to associate HTTP status codes with custom error pages.

```
<configuration>
  <system.web>
    <customErrors mode="On" defaultRedirect="/GenericErrorPage.aspx">
        <error statusCode="404" redirect="/ErrorPages/Error404.aspx" />
        <error statusCode="401" redirect="/ErrorPages/Error401.aspx" />
        ...
    </customErrors>
  </system.web>
</configuration>
```

The *<error>* element indicates the page to redirect the user to when the specified HTTP error occurs. The attribute *statusCode* denotes the HTTP error. Figure 7-5 shows what happens when the user mistypes the name of the URL and the error HTTP 404 (resource not found) is generated.

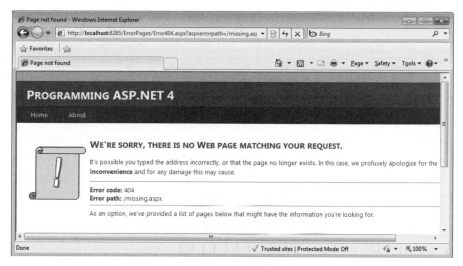

FIGURE 7-5 A custom page for the popular HTTP 404 error.

When invoked by the ASP.NET infrastructure, pages are passed the URL that caused the error on the query string. The following code shows the code-behind of a sample HTTP 404 error page:

```
public partial class Error404 : System.Web.UI.Page
{
    protected void Page_Load(object sender, EventArgs e)
    {
        var errPath = "<i>No error path information is available.</i>";
        var o = Request.QueryString["AspxErrorPath"];
        if (o != null)
            errPath = o;

        // Update the UI
        ErrorPath.InnerHtml = errPath;
    }
}
```

If you have custom error handling and a global application handler in place, you should not clear server errors. The sequence in which handlers are invoked is this: page, application, ASP.NET runtime with configured redirects.

Important In light of some security vulnerabilities discovered recently, returning a different output for different HTTP errors might help attackers to find out valuable information about the system. For this reason, it is recommended that you set a default redirect page and avoid adding error-specific pages.

Getting Information About the Exception

As mentioned, when you configure ASP.NET to redirect to a particular set of error pages, you lose any information about the internal exception that might have caused the error. Needless to say, no internal exception is involved in an HTTP 404 or HTTP 302 error. Unhandled exceptions are the typical cause of HTTP 500 internal errors. How do you make the page show context-sensitive information, at least to local users?

You get access to the exception in the *Error* event both at the page and application levels. One thing you can do is this: write a page-level error handler, capture the exception, and store the exception (or only the properties you're interested in) to the session state. The default redirect will then retrieve any context information from the session state.

```
protected void Page_Error(object sender, EventArgs e)
{
    // Captures the error and stores exception data
    var exception = Server.GetLastError();

    // Distinguish local and remote users
    if (Request.UserHostAddress == "127.0.0.1")
        Session["LastErrorMessage"] = exception.Message;
    else
        Session["LastErrorMessage"] = "Internal error.";

    // Clear the error (if required)
    Server.ClearError();
}
```

The preceding code checks the host address and stores exception-related information (limited to the message for simplicity) only for local users. The following code should be added to the *Page_Load* method of the page that handles the HTTP 500 error:

```
var msg = "No additional information available.";
var extraInfo = Session["LastErrorMessage"];
if (extraInfo != null)
    msg = (string) extraInfo;
Session["LastErrorMessage"] = null;

// Update the UI here
ExtraInfo.InnerHtml = msg;
...
```

Writing context-sensitive error pages requires a page-level *Error* handler to cache the original exception. This means that you should write the same handler for every page that requires context-sensitive errors. You can either resort to a global error handler or write a new *Page*-derived class that incorporates the default *Error* handler. All the pages that require that functionality will derive their code file from this class instead of *Page*.

Error Reporting

Let's put it down this way: fatal exceptions in software applications just happen. What do you do when such exceptions happen? Having some good exception-handling code is essential, but how would you collect any information related to the exception to study the case thoroughly?

Trapping and recovering from exceptions is only the first step, and it is largely insufficient in most cases. You need to figure out the section of the site that the user was visiting. You need to grab state information and the values currently stored in critical variables. Furthermore, you need to measure the frequency of the error to arrange a plan for bug fixing and maintenance. In a way, error reporting is the dark side of exception handling.

Features of an Error Reporting System

An effective error reporting system grabs error information and offers to report that in a variety of ways and stores. As you've seen, exceptions handled at the application level (that would otherwise go unhandled) should be logged and administrators should be notified.

What kind of information should be added to the log? At a minimum, the list includes values of local variables, the current call stack, and perhaps a screen shot of the failure. Is it sufficient to notify the webmaster of the failure? Although a notification is not a bad thing, an effective error reporting system reports exceptions to a centralized repository that is remotely accessible and groups them in some way—for example, by type.

Error Reporting Tools

Is such an error reporting system something you build from scratch once and adapt to any applications you write? Or is it an external framework you just plug into your solution?

In ASP.NET, there's just one way to capture fatal exceptions—writing a handler for the *Application_Error* event. This can be done in two ways, however.

You can write code directly in the application's *global.asax* file, or you can plug a made-to-measure HTTP module into the *web.config* file. The HTTP module would register its own handler for the *Error* application event. The two solutions are functionally equivalent, but the one based on the HTTP module can be enabled, disabled, and modified without recompiling the application. It is, in a way, less obtrusive. In the handler, you can log the exception the way you want—for example, by writing to the system's Event Log or by adding a record to some database. Information stored in a database requires that you have some infrastructure on your end, but it provides great flexibility because the content can be extracted and manipulated to create reports and statistics. Obviously, processing the uploaded logs is up to you.

A tool that is popular among ASP.NET developers is Error Logging Modules And Handlers (ELMAH). ELMAH is essentially made of an HTTP module that, once configured, intercepts the *Error* event at the application level and logs it according to the configuration to a number of back-end repositories. ELMAH comes out of an open-source project (*http://code.google.com/p/elmah*) and includes a number of extensions, mostly in the area of repositories. ELMAH offers some nice facilities, such as a Web page to view all recorded exceptions and drill down into each of them. Any error reporting system specifically designed for ASP.NET can't be, architecturally speaking, much different from ELMAH.

Note You might want to take a look at some commercial products that offer a reporting mechanism for ASP.NET applications. One of these products is Red Gate's SmartAssembly (*http://www.red-gate.com/products/smartassembly/error_reporting.htm*). Although it's not specifically designed for ASP.NET, the tool can be easily adapted to add reporting capabilities to ASP.NET applications. Essentially, it takes an existing assembly and parses its compiled code adding *try/catch* blocks that log any possible exceptions and upload the complete information to a given Web site. The tool also has a desktop front end to help you navigate through logged exceptions.

Self-Logging Exceptions

Another handmade solution consists of employing custom exception classes that derive from a user-defined class endowed with the ability to log automatically. In this way, at the cost of using custom exceptions everywhere, you can log any exceptions you're interested in regardless of whether the exception is fatal or not.

Debugging Options

Debugging an ASP.NET page is possible only if the page is compiled in debug mode. An assembly compiled in debug mode incorporates additional information for a debugger tool to step through the code. You can enable debug mode on individual pages as well as for all the pages in a given application. The *<compilation>* section in the *web.config* file controls this setting. In particular, you set the *Debug* attribute to *true* to enable debug activity for all pages in the application. The default is *false*. Note that Visual Studio, however, does this automatically if you just try to debug the application. To enable debugging for a single page, you add the *Debug* attribute to the *@Page* directive:

```
<% @Page Debug="true" %>
```

ASP.NET compiles the contents of any *.aspx* resource before execution. The contents of the *.aspx* resource is parsed to obtain a C# (or Microsoft Visual Basic .NET) class file, which is then handed out to the language compiler. When a page is flagged with the *Debug* attribute, ASP.NET doesn't delete the temporary class file used to generate the page assembly. This file is available on the Web server for you to peruse and investigate. The file is located under the Windows folder at the following path: *Microsoft.NET\Framework\[version]\Temporary ASP.NET Files*.

Debug mode is important for testing applications and diagnosing their problems. Note, though, that running applications in debug mode has a significant performance overhead. You should make sure that an application has debugging disabled before deploying it on a production server. In ASP.NET 4 and Visual Studio 2010, *web.config* transformations make these and other changes quite easy to achieve. In Chapter 2, "ASP.NET and IIS," you saw how to remove the *Debug* attribute with a *web.config* transformation.

Page Personalization

ASP.NET pages do not necessarily require a rich set of personalization features. However, if you can build an effective personalization layer into your Web application, final pages will be friendlier, more functional, and more appealing to use. For some applications (such as portals and shopping centers), though, personalization is crucial. For others, it is mostly a way to improve visual appearance. In ASP.NET, personalization is offered through the user profile API.

ASP.NET personalization is designed for persistent storage of structured data using a friendly and type safe API. Loading and saving personalized data is completely transparent to end users and doesn't even require the page author to know much about the internal plumbing.

Creating the User Profile

A user profile is a plain .NET class that exposes a bunch of properties. The class can be defined in two possible ways depending on the model of Web application you are building within Visual Studio.

If your project is a Web site project, you define the user profile model declaratively through attributes in the *web.config* file. At run time, the ASP.NET build machinery will group these properties into a dynamically generated class. When the application runs and a page is displayed, ASP.NET dynamically creates a profile object that contains, properly typed, the properties you have defined in the data model. The object is then added to the current *HttpContext* object and is available to pages through the *Profile* property.

For a Web Application Project (WAP), instead, a bit more work is required on your part, and type-safety comes at the cost of writing the user profile class manually. You don't use the *Profile* property directly from the *HttpContext* object but, at the end of the day, the work being done underneath is not different. The only difference is in who actually writes the code—you in a WAP scenario, or the ASP.NET runtime in a Web site project.

Any profile data is persisted on a per-user basis and is permanently stored until someone with administrative privileges deletes it. The data storage is far away from the user and, to some extent, also hidden from the programmers. The user doesn't need to know how and where the data is stored; the programmer simply needs to indicate what type of profile provider she wants to use. The profile provider determines the database to use—typically, a Microsoft SQL Server database, but custom providers and custom data storage models can also be used.

> **Note** In ASP.NET, the default profile provider is based on SQL Express, a lightweight version of SQL Server. The default physical storage medium is a local file named *aspnetdb.mdf*, which is commonly located in the *App_Data* folder of the Web application. You can rename and move the file as you wish. If you change its schema, though, you have to employ an ad hoc provider that understands the new schema. Because it is an MDF file, you can also host the database in a full edition of SQL Server on the host machine.

Definition of the Data Model in a Web Site Project

Let's begin our exploration of the profile API focusing on the tasks required in a Web site project. The profile API was originally introduced in ASP.NET 2.0 along with the Web site model at a time in which the popularity of the WAP model was in a downturn and everybody seemed to want to get rid of it. That sentiment was only a flash in the pan, however. The WAP model soon regained its prominent position in the minds of developers, and today Visual Studio 2010 offers two models to choose from. The choice is not painless when it comes to the profile API. I'll present the profile API from the perspective of a Web site application first—because it's likely you might have heard of it already. Next, I'll point out differences related to WAP projects.

To use the ASP.NET profile API, you first decide on the structure of the data model you want to use. Then you attach the data model to the page through the configuration file. The layout of the user profile is defined in the *web.config* file and consists of a list of properties that can take any of the .NET CLR types. The data model is a block of XML data that describes properties and related .NET Framework types.

The simplest way to add properties to the profile storage medium is through name/value pairs. You define each pair by adding a new property tag to the *<properties>* section of the configuration file. The *<properties>* section is itself part of the larger *<profile>* section, which also includes provider information. The *<profile>* section is located under *<system.web>*. Here's an example of a user profile section:

```
<profile>
  <properties>
    <add name="UseEuroMetricSystem" type="Boolean" />
    <add name="TemperatureSystem" type="String" />
  </properties>
  ...

</properties>
```

All the properties defined through an *<add>* tag become members of the dynamically created class and are then exposed as part of the HTTP context of each page. The *type* attribute indicates the type of the property. If no type information is set, the type defaults to *System.String*. Any valid CLR type is acceptable.

So in the preceding code snippet, we're defining a profile class made of two properties. The profile pseudoclass we have in mind looks like the one shown here:

```
class PseudoProfile
{
    public Boolean UseEuroMetricSystem {get; set;}
    public String TemperatureSystem {get; set;}
}
```

Table 7-1 lists the valid attributes for the *<add>* element. Only *name* is mandatory.

TABLE 7-1 Attributes of the *<add>* Element

Attribute	Description
allowAnonymous	Allows storing values for anonymous users. It is *false* by default.
customProviderData	Contains specific data to feed a custom profile provider, if any.
defaultValue	Indicates the default value of the property.
name	Name of the property.
provider	Name of the provider to use to read and write the property.
readOnly	Specifies whether the property value is read-only. It is *false* by default.
serializeAs	Indicates how to serialize the value of the property. Possible values are *Xml*, *Binary*, *String*, and *ProviderSpecific*.
type	The .NET Framework type of the property. It is a string object by default.

The User Profile Class Representation

There's no class like *PseudoProfile* anywhere in the application's AppDomain; yet the declared data model is dynamically compiled to a class for strongly typed programmatic access. The following code snippet gives you a much clearer idea of the class being generated by ASP.NET out of the profile's data model:

```
using System;
using System.Web;
using System.Web.Profile;

public class ProfileCommon : System.Web.Profile.ProfileBase
{
    public virtual bool UseEuroMetricSystem {
        get {
            return ((bool)(this.GetPropertyValue("UseEuroMetricSystem")));
        }
        set {
            this.SetPropertyValue("UseEuroMetricSystem", value);
        }
    }

    public virtual string TempSystem {
        get {
            return ((string)(this.GetPropertyValue("TempSystem")));
        }
        set {
            this.SetPropertyValue("TempSystem", value);
        }
    }

    public virtual ProfileCommon GetProfile(string username) {
        return ((ProfileCommon)(ProfileBase.Create(username)));
    }
}
```

This code is an excerpt from the real source code created by ASP.NET while compiling the content of the *web.config* file's *<profile>* section.

An instance of this class is associated with the *Profile* property of the HTTP context class and is accessed programmatically as follows:

```
// Use the UseEuroMetricSystem property to determine how to render the page
if (HttpContext.Profile.UseEuroMetricSystem)
{
    ...
}
```

There's a tight relationship between user accounts and profile information. We'll investigate this in a moment—for now, you need to take note of this because anonymous users are supported as well.

Note You can retrieve the hidden source code of the profile class (and other internal files) in the *Temporary ASP.NET Files* folder. The profile class in particular is located in a file named according to the pattern *App_Code.xxx.N.cs*, where *xxx* is a system-generated hash code and *N* is a 0-based index. Note that the path of the *Temporary ASP.NET Files* folder is different if you're using IIS or the embedded Visual Studio Web server. If you're using IIS, the path is

```
%Windows%\Microsoft.NET\Framework\v4.0.30319\Temporary ASP.NET Files
```

Otherwise, the path is

```
C:\Users\...\AppData\Local\Temp\Temporary ASP.NET Files
```

You can programmatically find out the real path being used by reading the value of the following expression:

```
HttpRuntime.CodegenDir
```

You can do that by placing a breakpoint somewhere in the page startup code and evaluating the expression in a Visual Studio QuickWatch window.

Using Collection Types

In the previous example, we worked with single, scalar values. However, the personalization engine fully supports more advanced scenarios, such as using collections or custom types. Let's tackle collections first. The following code demonstrates a *Locations* property that is a collection of strings:

```
<properties>
    <add name="Locations"
        type="System.Collections.Specialized.StringCollection" />
</properties>
```

Nonscalar values such as collections and arrays must be serialized to fit in a data storage medium. The *serializeAs* attribute simply specifies how. As mentioned, acceptable values are *String*, *Xml*, *Binary*, and *ProviderSpecific*. If the *serializeAs* attribute is not present in the *<properties>* definition, the *String* type is assumed. A collection is normally serialized as XML or in a binary format.

Using Custom Types

You can use a custom type with the ASP.NET personalization layer as long as you mark it as a serializable type. You simply author a class and compile it down to an assembly. The name of the assembly is added to the type information for the profile property:

```
<properties>
    <add name="ShoppingCart"
        type="My.Namespace.DataContainer, MyAssembly"
        serializeAs="Binary" />
</properties>
```

The assembly that contains the custom type must be available to the ASP.NET application. You obtain this custom type by placing the assembly in the application's *Bin* directory or by registering it within the global assembly cache (GAC).

Grouping Properties

The *<properties>* section can also accept the *<group>* element. The *<group>* element allows you to group a few related properties as if they are properties of an intermediate object. The following code snippet shows an example of grouping:

```
<properties>
    ...
    <group name="Metrics">
        <add name="Speed" type="string" defaultValue="mph" />
        <add name="Temperature" type="string" defaultValue="F" />
    </group>
</properties>
```

Two properties have been declared children of the *Metrics* group. This means that from now on any access to *Speed* or *Temperature* passes through the *Metrics* name, as shown here:

```
var windSpeedDisplayText = String.Format("{0} {1}",
        windSpeed, Profile.Metrics.Speed);
```

The *System.Web.UI.Page* class doesn't feature any *Profile* property. However, in a Web site project, the build machinery of ASP.NET generates an extra partial class where the *Profile* property is defined to just return *HttpContext.Current.Profile*.

> **Note** Default values are not saved to the persistence layer. Properties declared with a default value make their debut in the storage medium only when the application assigns them a value different from the default one.

Definition of the Data Model in a WAP Project

In a WAP project, you can choose between a weakly typed and strongly typed approach. The simplest approach (but most effective as well?) is the weak typing approach. In this case, you do exactly the same as you would do in a Web site project. The only difference is that you have no *Profile* property on the *Page* class and no dynamically built profile class.

As you saw earlier, however, a profile class is not a plain old CLR class—it is expected, instead, to inherit from *System.Web.Profile.ProfileBase*. The parent class features two generic methods to read and write properties: *GetPropertyValue* and *SetPropertyValue*. This is the real code that ultimately retrieves and stores the values from and to storage. The following code works like a champ in a WAP project:

```
HttpContext.Current.Profile.GetPropertyValue("UseEuroMetricSystem");
```

The drawback is that *GetPropertyValue* is designed to return an *Object* type. To get a Boolean or a String, you need to cast. The autogenerated profile class you would get in a Web site project just saves you from manually writing a few cast instructions. Here are the steps to take to define a strongly typed profile data model in a WAP project.

The idea is that you define your own strongly typed class and then attach its reference to the *<profile>* section of the *web.config* file. In this way, the profile built-in machinery will still be able to do its load-and-save work into the underlying base profile class—the *ProfileBase* class—and your wrapper will deliver you the pleasure of strongly typed programming.

```
<profile inherits="YourApp.UserProfile">
    ...
</profile>
```

Here's a possible implementation for the handmade *YourApp.UserProfile* wrapper class:

```
namespace YourApp {

public class UserProfile : ProfileBase
{
    public static UserProfile GetUserProfile()
    {
        var user = Membership.GetUser();

        // Anonymous user?
        if (user == null)
            return GetUserProfile("");   // throw if anonymous access is not permitted
        return GetUserProfile(user.UserName);
    }

    public static UserProfile GetUserProfile(String username)
    {
        var profileFromStorage = Create(username);
        return profileFromStorage as UserProfile;
    }

    [SettingsAllowAnonymous(true)]
    public Boolean UseEuroMetricSystem
    {
        get { return (Boolean)
                HttpContext.Current.Profile.GetPropertyValue("UseEuroMetricSystem"); }
        set { HttpContext.Current.Profile.SetPropertyValue("UseEuroMetricSystem", value); }
    }

    [SettingsAllowAnonymous(true)]
    public String TempSystem
    {
        get
        {
            var current = (String)
                HttpContext.Current.Profile.GetPropertyValue("TempSystem");
```

```
        if (String.IsNullOrEmpty(current))
            return "F";
        return (String) current;
    }
    set { HttpContext.Current.Profile.SetPropertyValue("TempSystem", value); }
  }
}
}
```

The *UserProfile* class you see is configured to support both authenticated and anonymous access. If you want to enable it only for authenticated users, throw an exception if no user is found and remove the turn to make the argument of the *SettingsAllowAnonymous* attribute false. (Or remove the attribute altogether.)

To access properties from within the code, you proceed as follows:

```
var profile = Your.UserProfile.GetUserProfile();
if (profile.UseEuroMetricSystem)
    speedFormat = "{0} kmh";
```

You invoke the static *GetUserProfile* method on your wrapper class and get an instance of your own profile class fed by the underlying ASP.NET profile API. The *Create* method that *GetUserProfile* uses internally is part of the profile API, and specifically it is the part that communicates with the storage layer.

Interacting with the Page

To enable or disable profile support, you set the *enabled* attribute of the *<profile>* element in the *web.config* file. If the property is *true* (the default), personalization features are enabled for all pages. If personalization is disabled, the *Profile* property on the HTTP context object isn't available to pages.

Creating the Profile Database

As mentioned earlier, profile support works strictly on a per-user basis and is permanently stored in a configured repository. Enabling the feature simply turns any functionality on, but it doesn't create the needed infrastructure for user membership and data storage. If you intend to use made-to-measure storage (for example, a non–SQL Server database or a SQL Server database with a custom schema of tables), creating any infrastructure is entirely up to you. If you're OK with the default table and structure, you resort to a free tool integrated in Visual Studio.

ASP.NET 4 (as well as earlier versions) comes with an administrative tool—the ASP.NET Web Site Administration Tool (WSAT)—that is fully integrated in Visual Studio. You invoke the tool by choosing the ASP.NET Configuration item from the Build menu. (See Figure 7-6.)

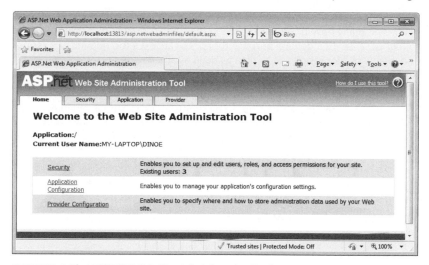

FIGURE 7-6 The ASP.NET Web Site Administration Tool.

You can use this tool to create a default database to store profile data. The default database is a SQL Server file named *aspnetdb.mdf,* which is located in the *App_Data* special folder of the ASP.NET application. A proper connection string is added to the configuration file to be consumed by various ASP.NET provider-based frameworks. By default, the application will use it as a plain file through SQL Server Express. However, if you decide to host it in a full installation of SQL Server, all you need to do is update the connection string in the *web.config* file of your application.

The tables and schema of the database are fixed. Note that the same database— the *aspnetdb.mdf* file—contains tables to hold user profiles and also membership and role information. The use of a membership database with users and roles is important because personalization is designed to be user-specific and because a user ID—either a local Windows account or an application-specific logon—is necessary to index data.

Profile data has no predefined duration and is permanently stored. It is up to the Web site administrator to delete the information when convenient.

As mentioned, WSAT is not necessarily the way to go; it's just one option for setting up the profile infrastructure. For example, if you're using a custom provider, the setup of your application is responsible for preparing any required storage infrastructure—be it a SQL Server table, an Oracle database, or whatever else. We'll cover the setup of profile providers in the next section.

> **Note** At this point, many developers start thinking that they probably don't want to be bound to *aspnetdb.mdf* because it's a general purpose tool or because it's too generic of a repository for their data. So, many developers decide to plan to build a tailor-made custom provider and run their own solution.
>
> Building custom providers is doable and fully supported by the framework. However, make sure that building such a provider doesn't turn out to be simply an extra (and avoidable) pain in the proverbial neck. The *aspnetdb.mdf* solution is effective and free, and it provides zero cost of ownership. After you have hosted it in a SQL Server installation, you have the full power of management tools at your disposal. And, by the way, although you can reasonably consider renaming the database on a per-application basis, the database (and the related ASP.NET API) is designed to support multiple applications. In other words, you can even have a single instance of *aspnetdb* also in a hosting scenario.
>
> Personally, I don't mind using *aspnetdb* when I need profile support. Membership and role management, though, might be a different story.

Working with Anonymous Users

Although user profiles are designed primarily for authenticated users, anonymous users can also store profile data. In this case, though, a few extra requirements must be fulfilled. In particular, you have to turn on the *anonymousIdentification* feature, which is disabled by default:

```
<anonymousIdentification enabled="true" />
```

The purpose of anonymous user identification is to assign a unique identity to users who are not authenticated and recognize and treat all of them as an additional registered user.

> **Note** Anonymous identification in no way affects the identity of the account that is processing the request. Nor does it affect any other aspects of security and user authentication. Anonymous identification is simply a way to give a "regular" ID to unauthenticated users so that they can be tracked as authenticated, "regular" users.

In addition, to support anonymous identification you must mark properties in the data model with the special Boolean attribute named *allowAnonymous*. Properties not marked with the attribute are not made available to anonymous users.

```
<anonymousIdentification enabled="true" />
<profile enabled="true">
    <properties>
        <add name="UseEuroMetricSystem" type="Boolean"
            defaultValue="false" allowAnonymous="true" />
        <add name="TempSystem" type="String"
            defaultValue="F" />
        <add name="Locations"
          type="System.Collections.Specialized.StringCollection" />
    </properties>
</profile>
```

In the preceding code snippet, anonymous users can pick up the European metrics but cannot modify the way in which temperatures are displayed nor add their favorite locations.

Accessing Profile Properties

In a Web site project, the *Page* object features an extra *Profile* property added by the system via a partial class during the dynamic compilation step. Before the request begins its processing cycle, the *Profile* property of the page is set with an instance of the profile class created out of the content in the *web.config* file.

When the page first loads, profile properties are set to their default values (if any) or they are empty objects. They are never null. When custom or collection types are used to define properties, assigning default values might be hard. The code just shown defines a string collection object—the property *Locations*—but giving that a default value expressed as a string is not supported. At run time, though, the *Locations* property won't be null—it will equal an empty collection. So how can you manage default values for these properties?

Properties that don't have a default value can be initialized in the *Page_Load* event when the page is not posting back. Here's how you can do that:

```
if (!IsPostBack)
{
    // Add some cities to the Locations property
    if (Profile.Locations.Count == 0) {
        Profile.Locations.Add("London");
        Profile.Locations.Add("Amsterdam");
    }
}
```

In a Web site project, the personalization data of a page is all set when the *Page_Init* event fires. However, when the *Page_PreInit* event arrives, no operation has been accomplished yet on the page, not even the loading of personalization data.

In a WAP project, if you opt for a strongly typed approach, you have no way to assign a default value to properties. The only workaround, obviously, is dealing with defaults right in the *getter* method of each property. Here's an example:

```
[SettingsAllowAnonymous(true)]
public String TempSystem
{
    get
    {
        var current = (String) HttpContext.Current.Profile.GetPropertyValue("TempSystem");
        if (String.IsNullOrEmpty(current))
            return "F";
        return (String) current;
    }
    set { HttpContext.Current.Profile.SetPropertyValue("TempSystem", value); }
}
```

In a Web site project, the personalization data of a page is available only on demand— precisely, the first time you access the profile object.

Let's consider some sample code that illustrates the power of the user profile API.

> **Note** The personalization data of a page is all set when the *Page_Init* event fires. However, when the *Page_PreInit* event arrives, no operation has been accomplished yet on the page, not even the loading of personalization data.

User Profiles in Action

Suppose you have a page that displays information according to user preferences. You should use the user profile API only to store preferences, not to store sensitive data. Losing the profile information should never cause the user any loss of money or serious inconvenience. Here's the code you might have at the startup of the page request. The page first grabs in some way some weather-related information and then displays it as configured by the user:

```
protected void Page_Load(Object sender, EventArgs e)
{
    if (!IsPostBack)
    {
        var info = GrabWeatherInfo();
        DisplayData(info);
    }
}

private static WeatherInfo GrabWeatherInfo()
{
    ...
}

private void DisplayData(WeatherInfo info)
{
    // Type-safe solution for Web Application projects
    // (reusing the YourApp.UserProfile wrapper class discussed earlier)

    // Get profile information from the underlying repository
    var profile = YourApp.UserProfile.GetUserProfile();

    // Metric system
    var speedFormat = "{0} mph";
    if (profile.UseEuroMetricSystem)
        speedFormat = "{0} kmh";
    var speedText = String.Format(speedFormat, info.WindSpeed);
```

```
    // Temperature
    var tempText = String.Format("{0} {1}", info.Temperature, profile.TempSystem);
    lblWindSpeed.Text = speedText;
    lblTemperature.Text = tempText;

    // The sample page also displays a panel for users to change settings.
    // Display current settings through the edit panel as well.
    chkEuroMetric.Checked = profile.UseEuroMetricSystem;
    rdlTempSystem.SelectedIndex = (profile.TempSystem == "F" ? 0 : 1);
}
```

The output of the page can change depending on the settings entered by individual users. Figure 7-7 shows what the same page might look like for distinct users.

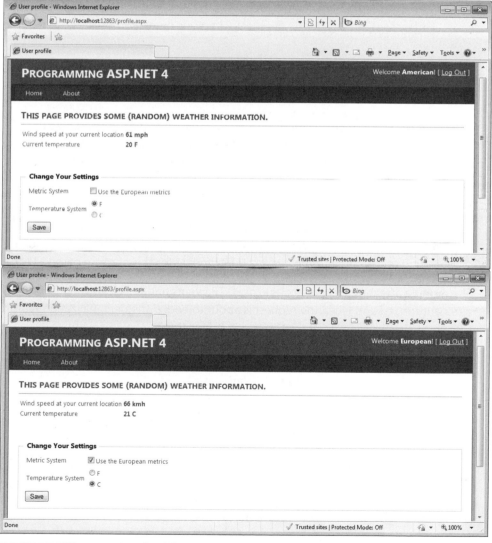

FIGURE 7-7 Different settings for different users.

If anonymous access is permitted, any unauthenticated user is treated as the same one—meaning that all anonymous users share the same settings and any can change in the settings of one user affects all the others. (Most of the time, though, sites where profiles are fundamental just don't allow anonymous access.)

How do you change settings? Here's the code you can associate with the *Save* button you see in Figure 7-7:

```
protected void Button1_Click(Object sender, EventArgs e)
{
    // Retrieve and update the profile for the current user
    var profile = YourApp.UserProfile.GetUserProfile();
    profile.UseEuroMetricSystem = chkEuroMetric.Checked;
    profile.TempSystem = rdlTempSystem.SelectedItem.Value;

    // Persist settings for the current user
    profile.Save();

    // Refresh the page to ensure changes are immediately visible
    Response.Redirect("/profile.aspx");
}
```

The *Redirect* call is not strictly required; however, if it's omitted, it won't give the user an immediate experience based on the changes entered. If you omit the redirect, the changes (which are stored in the repository, anyway) will be visible only upon the next request.

Personalization Events

As mentioned, the personalization data is added to the HTTP context of a request before the request begins its processing route. But which system component is in charge of loading personalization data? ASP.NET employs an HTTP module for this purpose named *ProfileModule*.

The module attaches itself to a couple of HTTP events and gets involved after a request has been authorized and when the request is about to end. If the personalization feature is off, the module returns immediately. Otherwise, it fires the *Personalize* event to the application and then loads personalization data from the current user profile. When the *Personalize* event fires, the personalization data hasn't been loaded yet. Handlers for events fired by an HTTP module must be written to the *global.asax* file.

```
void Profile_Personalize(object sender, ProfileEventArgs e)
{
    ProfileCommon profile = null;

    // Exit if it is the anonymous user
    if (User == null) return;

    // Determine the profile based on the role. The profile database
    // contains a specific entry for a given role.
```

```
    if (User.IsInRole("Administrators"))
        profile = (ProfileCommon) ProfileBase.Create("Administrator");
    else if (User.IsInRole("Users"))
        profile = (ProfileCommon) ProfileBase.Create("User");
    else if (User.IsInRole("Guests"))
        profile = (ProfileCommon) ProfileBase.Create("Guest");

    // Make the HTTP profile module use THIS profile object
    if (profile != null)
        e.Profile = profile;
    }
}
```

The personalization layer is not necessarily there for the end user's amusement. You should look at it as a general-purpose tool to carry user-specific information. User-specific information, though, indicates information that applies to the user, not necessarily information entered by the user.

The personalization layer employs the identity of the current user as an index to retrieve the proper set of data, but what about roles? What if you have hundreds of users with different names but who share the same set of profile data (such as menu items, links, and UI settings)? Maintaining hundreds of nearly identical database entries is out of the question. But the standard profile engine doesn't know how to handle roles. That's why you sometimes need to handle the *Personalize* event or perhaps roll your own profile provider.

The code shown previously overrides the process that creates the user profile object and ensures that the returned object is filled with user-specific information accessed through the user role. The static method *Create* on the *ProfileBase* class takes the user name and creates an instance of the profile object specific to that user. *ProfileCommon* is the common name of the dynamically created class that contains the user profile.

The handler of the *Personalize* event receives data through the *ProfileEventArgs* class. The class has a read-write member named *Profile*. When the event handler returns, the profile HTTP module checks this member. If it is null, the module proceeds as usual and creates a profile object based on the user's identity. If not, it simply binds the current value of the *Profile* member as the profile object of the page.

Migrating Anonymous Data

As mentioned, anonymous users can store and retrieve settings that are persisted using an anonymous unique ID. However, if at a certain point a hitherto anonymous user decides to create an account with the Web site, you might need to migrate to her account all the settings that she made as an anonymous user. This migration doesn't occur automatically.

When a user who has been using your application anonymously logs in, the personalization module fires an event—*MigrateAnonymous*. Properly handled, this global event allows you to import anonymous settings into the profile of an authenticated user. The following pseudocode demonstrates how to handle the migration of an anonymous profile:

```
void Profile_MigrateAnonymous(object sender, ProfileMigrateEventArgs e)
{
    // Load the profile of the anonymous user
    ProfileCommon anonProfile;
    anonProfile = Profile.GetProfile(e.AnonymousId);

    // Migrate the properties to the new profile
    Profile.UseEuroMetricSystem = anonProfile.UseEuroMetricSystem;
    ...
}
```

You get the profile for the anonymous user and extract the value of any property you want to import. Next you copy the value to the profile of the currently logged-on user.

Profile Providers

In ASP.NET, the profile API is composed of two distinct elements: the access layer and the storage layer.

The access layer provides a strongly typed model to get and set property values and also manages user identities. It guarantees that the data is retrieved and stored on behalf of the currently logged-on user.

The second element of the profile system is data storage. The system uses ad hoc providers to perform any tasks involved with the storage and retrieval of values. ASP.NET comes with a profile provider that uses SQL Server Express as the data engine. If necessary, you can also write custom providers. The profile provider writes profile data into the storage medium of choice and is responsible for the final schema of the data.

Important In ASP.NET, a provider is defined as a pluggable component that extends or replaces some system functionality. The profile provider is just one implementation of the ASP.NET provider model. Other examples of providers are the membership provider and role manager provider, both of which will be discussed later in the book. At its core, the provider infrastructure allows customers to change the underlying implementation of some out-of-the-box system functionalities while keeping the top-level interface intact. Providers are relatively simple components with as few methods and properties as possible. Only one instance of the provider exists per application domain.

Configuring Profile Providers

All features, such as user profiling, that have providers should have a default provider. Normally, the default provider is indicated via a *defaultProvider* attribute in the section of the configuration file that describes the specific feature. By default, if a preferred provider is not specified, the first item in the collection is considered the default.

The default profile provider is named *AspNetSqlProfileProvider* and uses SQL Server Express for data storage. Providers are registered in the *<providers>* section of the configuration file under the main node *<profile>*, as shown here:

```
<profile>
    <providers>
        <add name="AspNetSqlProfileProvider"
            connectionStringName="LocalSqlServer" applicationName="/"
            type="System.Web.Profile.SqlProfileProvider" />
    </providers>
</profile>
```

The *<add>* nodes within the *<providers>* section list all the currently registered providers. The previous code is an excerpt from the *machine.config* file. Attributes such as *name* and *type* are common to all types of providers. Other properties are part of the provider's specific configuration mechanism. Tightly connected with this custom interface is the set of extra properties—in this case, *connectionStringName* and *description*. The *description* attribute is simply text that describes what the provider does.

The *connectionStringName* attribute defines the information needed to set up a connection with the underlying database engine of choice. However, instead of being a plain connection string, the attribute contains the name of a previously registered connection string. For example, *LocalSqlServer* is certainly not the connection string to use for a local or remote connection to an instance of SQL Server. Instead, it is the name of an entry in the new *<connectionStrings>* section of the configuration file. That entry contains any concrete information needed to connect to the database.

The *LocalSqlServer* connection string placeholder is defined in *machine.config* as follows:

```
<connectionStrings>
    <add name="LocalSqlServer"
        connectionString="data source=.\SQLEXPRESS;
                        Integrated Security=SSPI;
                        AttachDBFilename=|DataDirectory|aspnetdb.mdf;
                        User Instance=true"
        providerName="System.Data.SqlClient" />
</connectionStrings>
```

As you can see, the connection string refers to an instance of SQL Server named SQLEXPRESS and attaches to the aspnetdb.mdf database located in the application's data directory—the *App_Data* folder.

Structure of AspNetDb.mdf

As a developer, you don't need to know much about the layout of the table and the logic that governs it; instead, you're responsible for ensuring that any needed infrastructure is created. To do so, you use the Build|ASP.NET Configuration menu item in Visual Studio to start the ASP.NET site administration tool. A view of the tables in the database is shown in Figure 7-8.

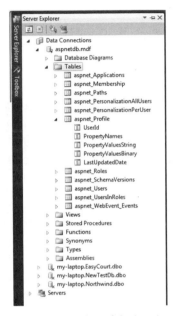

FIGURE 7-8 A view of the interior of the AspNetDb database and the profile table.

Note that the AspNetDb database isn't specific to the personalization infrastructure. As you can see in the figure, it groups all provider-related tables, including those for membership, roles, and users. The internal structure of each database is specific to the mission of the underlying provider.

Custom Profile Providers

The SQL Server profile provider is good at building new applications and is useful for profile data that is inherently tabular. In many cases, though, you won't start an ASP.NET application from scratch, but you will instead migrate an existing application. You often already have data to integrate with the ASP.NET profile layer. If this data doesn't get along with the relational model, or if it is already stored in a storage medium other than SQL Server, you can write a custom profile provider. An old but still helpful link is the following: *http://msdn. microsoft.com/msdnmag/issues/07/03/ASPNET2/default.aspx*.

Profile providers push the idea that existing data stores can be integrated with the personalization engine using a thin layer of code. This layer of code abstracts the physical characteristics of the data store and exposes its content through a common set of methods and properties. A custom personalization provider is a class that inherits *ProfileProvider*.

Finally, note that a custom provider doesn't necessarily have to be bound to all profile properties. You can also use the default provider for some properties and a custom provider for others. Here's how you specify the provider for a property using the declarative approach:

```
<properties>
    <add name="BackColor" type="string" provider="MyProvider" />
    ...
</properties>
```

In the preceding code, the *BackColor* property is read and written through the *MyProvider* provider. If you are in WAP, instead, and wrote your profile wrapper class, you resort to the *ProfileProvider* attribute:

```
[ProfileProvider("MyProvider")]
public String BackColor
{
    get { ... }
    set { ... }
}
```

Obviously, the provider name must correspond to one of the entries in the *<providers>* section.

Page Localization

The whole theme of localization is nothing new in the .NET Framework, and ASP.NET is no exception. You have had tools to write culture-specific pages since the very first version of ASP.NET. In addition, these tools didn't change significantly with the stream of versions, and today they form a rather stable API.

Localization is not a hard feature to build and doesn't touch any staggering peaks of technical difficulty. A successfully localizable application just requires planning, development care, and constant small-scale refactoring. Frankly, localization is not for just any (Web) application either. In this regard, I consider localization as an *all-or-nothing* feature of a Web project: either localization is a requirement or it is not. If it is a requirement, every little piece of UI (text, layout, CSS, script, and images) must be architected and implemented to be easily replaceable and configurable. Otherwise, I just don't care about localization and stuff literals in the page layouts.

Considering localization from the perspective of an entire application with a not-so-short expectation of life, there are three aspects of it that need to be addressed: how to make resources localizable, how to add support for a new culture, and how to use (or whether to use) databases as a storage place for localized information. Let's review the techniques that allow you to keep resources easily localizable.

Making Resources Localizable

A localizable ASP.NET Web Form uses resources instead of hard-coded text to flesh out the user interface. In this context, a *resource* is meant to be an item of stored text associated with a public name and typically compiled into its own assembly. A resource assembly is a standard class library that contains one or more RESX files. A RESX file is an XML document that contains resource names and content. Visual Studio provides a typical dialog box to add such a new item to the project. (See Figure 7-9.)

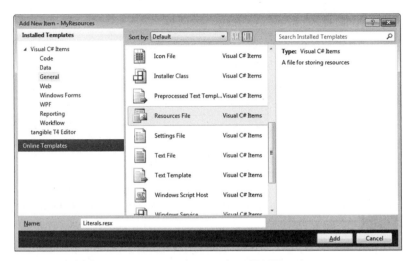

FIGURE 7-9 Adding a new resource item to the ASP.NET project.

You always use the resource name to refer to its content from within application pages. After a resource assembly is linked to the application, the ASP.NET runtime selects the correct value at run time according to the user's language and culture.

> **Note** Instead of creating and maintaining a resource assembly, you can simply create an *App_GlobalResources* folder under the site root and place there any resource RESX files you might need. Such files are compiled into resource assemblies on demand care of the ASP.NET runtime. A possible drawback is that the RESX files are deployed as source code to the site.

Global and Local Resources

The ASP.NET documentation distinguishes between global and local resources. Global resources are available to any pages in the application; local resources, instead, are specific to a single page or the pages located in a given directory hierarchy. In terms of syntax, global and local resources are the same thing—a RESX file. Local resources must be deployed to an App_LocalResources folder. You can have only one global resource folder in a site; instead, you can have multiple local resource folders, one for each section of the site you want to restrict resources to. In Figure 7-10, you can see a local resource folder under the Private folder that affects only the pages defined inside the Private folder and its child folders.

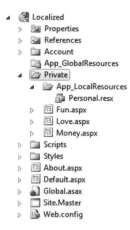

FIGURE 7-10 Global and local resource folders.

In a local resource folder, you can have resource files with folder-level visibility (such as *personal.resx* in Figure 7-10) as well as page-specific resource files. In this case, a simple naming convention binds the file to the page. If the page is named *sample.aspx*, its corresponding resource file will be *sample.aspx.resx*.

Global and local resource files can happily coexist in the same application. Finding the right balance between what's global and what's local is ultimately up to you. Overall, the best approach seems to be having multiple resource files—either local or global. You might start with a local resource file for each page, and then merge strings and other resources into a global resource file as you find them referenced from multiple pages.

Important From what I have learned on the battlefield, having a single global file to hold all localizable resources turns into a not-so-pleasant experience, even for a moderately complex Web application. One issue is the size of the file, which grows significantly; another issue, which is even more painful, is the possible concurrent editing that multiple developers might be doing on the same file with the subsequent need for a continuous merge. However, I encourage you not to overlook the naming issue.

When you have hundreds of strings that cover the entire application scope, how do you name them? Many strings look the same or differ only in subtle points. Many strings are not entire strings with some sensible meaning; they often are bits and pieces of some text to be completed with dynamically generated content. And the concatenation might be different for various languages.

Trust me: naming a few of them in the restricted context of only some pages is doable; handling hundreds of them for the entire application is really painful.

Using Resources: Declarative vs. Programmatic

In ASP.NET Web Forms, a key decision to be made early is whether you want to insert localizable text declaratively, programmatically, or both. Inserting localized text programmatically means writing a method on each *Page* class that assigns ad hoc text before display. This approach offers the maximum flexibility and allows you to retrieve localized text using the API that best suits you. Here's some code to read the value of the resource item named *Welcome* from a resource file named *literals.resx*:

```
MyResources.Literals.Welcome
```

MyResources is the default namespace of the assembly that contains the resource file. *Literals* is the name of the file and the class name that ultimately exposes text items as public static properties. Finally, *Welcome* is the name of the resource item. For this code to work, you must ensure you create an assembly with a *Literals.resx* file whose access modifier in Visual Studio is set to Public. Note that the default value is Internal, which will not make resource items publicly available. (See Figure 7-11.)

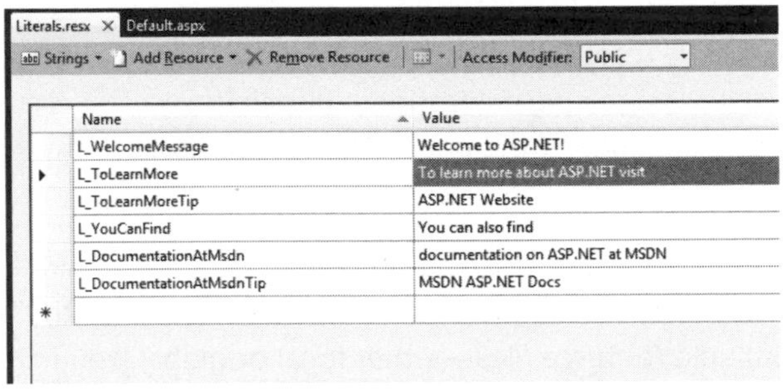

FIGURE 7-11 Editing a RESX document.

The preceding syntax is general enough to work with any RESX file, regardless of its local or global status. This is also the natural way of localizing applications in ASP.NET MVC. However, it doesn't get along very well with the ASP.NET server controls that populate Web Forms pages. The point is that you can't use the preceding expression in a <%= ... %> code block in all possible locations within a Web Forms page.

The following markup compiles just fine:

```
<h1><%= MyResources.Literals.BookTitle %> </h1>
```

Unfortunately, you can't embed the code block as the attribute of a server control. (This is where the key difference between Web Forms and ASP.NET MVC arises.) The following code won't even compile:

```
<asp:MenuItem NavigateUrl="~/Default.aspx" Text="<%= MyResources.Literals.Home %>"/>
```

The reason has to be found in the way in which a server control produces its own output.

In the end, for a Web Forms page the most convenient approach results from any of the following:

- Design your own localization layer that each page passes through to have its text localized. This layer is a sort of transformer that reads from localization storage and replaces placeholder text. Your localization storage can be RESX file or, why not, your own database table.

- Go with any shortcuts that Visual Studio and ASP.NET machinery might have released. This includes a tailor-made syntax for local resources and a specific expression builder for declaratively binding control attributes to localized text. However, the declarative syntax for global resources requires the App_GlobalResources folder and direct deployment of any RESX files.

Let's find out more about what's required to deal with globally defined resources.

Dealing with Global Resources

Using global resources programmatically entails writing for each page some code as shown next. The code will be invoked just before display:

```
protected void LocalizeTextInPage()
{
    // For each control you expect in the page, retrieve the localized text
    Label1.Text = MyResources.Literals.Welcome;
    ...
    Label2.Text = HttpContext.GetGlobalResourceObject("globals.resx", "Description");;
    ...
}
```

If your global resources are stored through plain RESX files, you can retrieve it using either of the two expressions just shown. In addition to using the object expression that navigates into the class hierarchy of the resource assembly, you can also employ the *GetGlobalResourceObject* method of the *HttpContext* object. If the localized text resides elsewhere, the API for retrieving it is up to you.

Alternatively, if you prefer to take the declarative route, use the object expression within plain page markup and resort to the ASP.NET-specific *$Resources* expression builder for control attributes. Here's an example:

```
<asp:Literal runat="server" Text="<% $Resources:Globals, WelcomeMessage %>" />
```

$Resources refers to an ASP.NET built-in expression builder. It accepts a parameter that is a comma-separated string trailing the colon (:) symbol. The first token indicates the name of the RESX file that is the source of the localized text. The second token indicates the name of the resource item to read. There are no facilities to bind declaratively localized text stored outside of RESX files.

Dealing with Local Resources

Local resources are strictly page-specific in the sense that if it's properly named after the ASPX source file, the content of a resource file can be referenced using direct syntax from the markup, as shown here:

```
<asp:Label runat="server" ID="Label1"
        meta:resourcekey="Label1_ResourceID" />
```

The *resourcekey* meta attribute indicates that property values for the *Label1* control are to be taken from a page-specific resource file. If the resource file for the page contains an entry such as *Label1_ResourceID.Text*, the *Text* property of *Label1* will be set to the stored value. The same can be done for any other properties of the control.

Resources and Cultures

A RESX file is a plain XML document. How can you distinguish a RESX file that represents French localized text from the RESX of German localized text? A RESX file name that doesn't include culture information is assumed to contain language-neutral text with no culture defined.

To create a resource assembly for a specific culture—say, French—you need to name the resource file as follows: *sample.aspx.fr.resx*. The *fr* string should be replaced with any other equivalent string that identifies a culture, such as *de* for German or *en* for English.

When resources from multiple cultures are available in the AppDomain, the ASP.NET runtime machinery detects the underlying culture and picks up the matching resource file. I'll return in a moment at how to set and change the culture programmatically.

Setting the Current Culture in .NET Applications

In the .NET Framework, the culture is set on the current thread through the *CurrentCulture* and *CurrentUICulture* properties. In general, both properties are necessary when you want to support multiple languages in a page or view. In fact, the two properties refer to distinct capabilities and have an impact on different areas of the user interface.

The *CurrentCulture* property affects the results of functions, such as the date, the number, and currency formatting. The *CurrentUICulture* property, on the other hand, determines the localized resource file from which page resources are loaded. The following code snippet shows a possible way to arrange a unit test aimed at testing whether culture-specific items are correctly retrieved. If you intend to test only whether resource files are being used as expected, you can comment out the setting of *CurrentCulture*.

```
const String culture = "it-IT";
var cultureInfo = CultureInfo.CreateSpecificCulture(culture);
Thread.CurrentThread.CurrentCulture = cultureInfo;
Thread.CurrentThread.CurrentUICulture = cultureInfo;
```

Note that the two culture properties might or might not have the same value. For example, you can switch the language of text and messages according to the browser's configuration while leaving globalization settings (such as dates and currency) constant.

> **Note** Culture names are a combination of two pieces of information: the language and the country/region that you intend to refer to. The two strings are combined with a dash symbol (-). Often, but not necessarily, the two strings coincide. For example, *it-IT* means the Italian culture for the country of Italy, whereas *en-US* indicates the English culture for the United States, which is expected to be different from *en-GB* or *en-SA*.

Setting the Current Culture in ASP.NET Pages

If you're writing an ASP.NET Web Forms application, you don't need to deal with the *Thread* class. In ASP.NET, you have culture properties ready-made on the *Page* class. They are string properties named *Culture* and *UICulture*.

The default value being assigned to both properties is *auto*, meaning that ASP.NET automatically detects the browser's language for the thread in charge of the request. The *getter* method of both properties is defined as shown here:

```
public String UICulture
{
    get { return Thread.CurrentThread.CurrentUICulture.DisplayName; }
    set { ... }
}
```

When the auto mode is on for the page culture, the end user is ultimately responsible for determining the language of the pages. All the developers need to do is ensure that proper resource files are available. If no suitable resource file is found for the detected culture, ASP.NET will fall back to the neutral (default) culture.

Obviously, a specific culture can be enforced programmatically or declaratively. You can employ a global setting for the culture by using the *<globalization>* section of the *web.config* file:

```
<globalization uiculture="it-IT" culture="it-IT" / >
```

A global and fixed setting for culture, however, is hardly what you want most of the time. Most of the time, instead, you want the ability to set the culture programmatically and the ability to change it on the fly as the user clicks an icon or requests a culture-specific URL.

Changing Culture on the Fly

To change the culture programmatically, you need to satisfy two key requirements. First, define how you'll be retrieving the culture to set. The culture can be a value you read from some database table or perhaps from the ASP.NET cache. It can also be a value you retrieve from the URL. Finally, it can even be a parameter you get via geo-location—that is, by looking at the IP address the user is using for connecting.

After you have the culture ID to set, you have to set it by acting on the current thread, as mentioned earlier. Note that the culture must be set for each request because each request runs on its own thread.

If you intend to read and set the culture as part of the page initialization work, note that the following code, which might appear obvious at first, just won't work:

```
void Page_Load(Object sender, EventArgs e)
{
    Culture = "IT";
    UICulture = "it-IT";
}
```

The *Page_Load* handler is fired too late to be effective. The recommended approach consists of overriding the *InitializeCulture* method on the *Page* class:

```
protected override void InitializeCulture()
{
    base.InitializeCulture();
    Culture = "IT";
    UICulture = "it-IT";
}
```

The *setter* method of both culture properties will then take care of setting culture information on the current thread. Setting the thread directly does work, but it's unnecessary to do so.

Changing the language on the fly as the user clicks on a link is a bit trickier. The idea is that you override the *InitializeCulture* method so that the page reads the language to use from global storage—for example, the ASP.NET *Cache* or *Session*.

```
protected override void InitializeCulture()
{
    base.InitializeCulture();
    UICulture = DetermineLocaleToEnforce();
}
```

```
private String DetermineLocaleToEnforce()
{
    var language = Cache["Language"] as String;
    if (String.IsNullOrEmpty(language))
        language = "en-US";
    return language;
}
```

When the user interacts with the user interface in the postback, you simply read the newly selected language, update the storage, and then redirect to the same page for a refresh:

```
protected void Button1_Click(Object sender, EventArgs e)
{
    var languageInfo = GetCurrentLocale();
    Cache["Language"] = languageInfo;
    Response.Redirect("/private/moneyintl.aspx");
}
private String GetCurrentLocale()
{
    return Languages.SelectedValue;
}
```

This is good enough if your user interface is limited to listing a few image buttons with flags. If you want a drop-down list of languages to choose from, you also must take care of re-indexing the list of items. This translates into some extra code in *Page_Load*.

```
protected void Page_Load(Object sender, EventArgs e)
{
    if (!IsPostBack)
    {
        var languageCode = DetermineLocaleToEnforce();
        var item = Languages.Items.FindByValue(languageCode);
        Languages.SelectedIndex = Languages.Items.IndexOf(item);
    }
}
```

Nicely enough, implementing the same feature is much simpler in ASP.NET MVC, even though ASP.NET MVC shares exactly the same run-time environment as ASP.NET Web Forms. The postback model, which is great at many things, makes some other things a bit harder than expected. In ASP.NET MVC, you can simply create your own action invoker and then, for each and every controller method, you retrieve the language and set it to the current thread. The action invoker is a way to intercept the execution of action methods in a rather unobtrusive way. In Web Forms, you can achieve the same result by using an HTTP module that kicks in for every request, reads the currently set language, and sets the culture on the current thread.

Note More and more Web sites check the location from where a user is connected and suggest a language and a culture. This feature requires an API that looks up the IP address and maps that to a country/region and then a culture. Some browsers (for example, Firefox 3.5, Safari, iPhone, and Opera) have built-in geo-location capabilities that work according to the W3C API. (See *http://www.mozilla.com/firefox/geolocation*.)

To support other browsers (including Internet Explorer), you can resort to third-party services such as Google Gears. Google Gears is a plug-in that extends your browser in various ways, including adding a geo-location API that returns the country/region of the user from the current geographical location. Note that Google returns the ISO 3166 code of the country/region (for example, *GB* for the United Kingdom) and its full name. From here, you have to determine the language to use. The country/region code doesn't always match the language. For the United Kingdom, the language is *en*. To install Google Gears, pay a visit to *http://gears.google.com*.

Adding Resources to Pages

An ASP.NET page is usually made of a bunch of auxiliary resources including script files, cascading style sheets (CSS), and images. When the browser downloads a page, it usually places a number of independent requests to the Web server and tracks when the document is ready. The display of the document, however, might begin before the entire document (and related links) has been downloaded. Developers of heavy pages made of several resources (a few dozens is not unusual) resort to a number of techniques to optimize the download experience of their pages. Let's review a few interesting techniques that simplify the management of scripts, images, and other resources.

Using Script Files

The only HTML-supported way of linking script files to a page is via the *<script>* tag and its *src* attribute. When a page has several scripts, the degree of parallelism at which the browser can operate is dramatically lowered, as is the load time of the page. Typically, in fact, browsers are idle while downloading a script code, regardless of the host name.

It turns out that managing scripts effectively, and sometimes refactoring the page to maximize its download and rendering time, is a critical topic. Let's see the most common techniques to deal with script files.

Scripts at the Bottom of the Page

Because of the way in which browsers operate, moving all *<script>* tags at the bottom of the page just before the *</body>* tag improves the download of the page. Unfortunately, this is not always possible.

Why do browsers stop any activity while downloading script code?

In general, the script being downloaded might contain some instructions, such as *document.write*, that could modify the status of the current Document Object Model (DOM). To avoid nasty situations that might derive from here, browsers download a script synchronously and run it right after downloading. A script that contains *document.write* calls can hardly be moved elsewhere without causing some damage.

Back with Internet Explorer 4, Microsoft introduced a little-known attribute for the *<script>* tag—the *defer* attribute. Later incorporated in the HTML 4 specification, the *defer* attribute was just meant to tell the browser whether or not loading the script can be deferred to the end of the page processing. A script that specifies the *defer* attribute implicitly states it is not doing any direct document writing. Using the *defer* attribute is not a standard technique because of the non-uniform way in which browsers support it. For this reason, moving script tags manually at the end is the most common trick to speed up pages. For more information on the *defer* attribute, have a read of *http://hacks.mozilla.org/2009/06/defer.*

> **Note** Two libraries are extremely popular as far as improving the script downloading is concerned. One is LABjs (available at *http://www.labjs.com*), and the other is RequireJS (available at *http://www.requirejs.org*). Both allow loading scripts (and other resources) in parallel, which maintains possible (declared) dependencies between files.

Using a Content Delivery Network

Among other things, the download time also depends on the physical distance between the client browser and the server expected to serve a given resource. For high-volume, international sites, this can be a significant problem.

A content delivery network (CDN) is a third-party, geographically distributed server that serves commonly accessed files from the nearest possible location. By using a CDN, you guarantee the best service without the costs for your organization of setting up such a wide network of servers.

For your code, the change is minimal—you just replace your local server URL with the CDN URL and get the script from there. Here's how to link the ASP.NET AJAX library from the Microsoft CDN:

```
<script type="text/javascript"
        src="http://ajax.microsoft.com/ajax/4.0/MicrosoftAjax.js" />
```

Popular libraries such as jQuery and Microsoft ASP.NET AJAX are being offered through Google and Microsoft CDN.

Using a CDN is also beneficial because it increases the likelihood that the browser cache already contains a resource that might have been referenced using the same URL by other sites using the same CDN. The perfect example of a file that would greatly benefit users when put on a CDN is the one mentioned a moment ago—the jQuery library. You won't benefit much, on the other hand, from placing on a CDN files that only one application uses.

Reasons for Minifying a Script File

A golden rule of Web site performance optimization says that once you have minimized the impact of static files (scripts, style sheets, and images), you're pretty much done. In addition to the time and distance of the download, the size also matters—the smaller, the better.

You can use Gzip compression on the Web server to serve any resources quickly. Regular pages, including ASP.NET pages, are often returned gzipped, but the same doesn't always happen for other static resources such as scripts and style sheets. Images on the other side are often already compressed (PNG, JPG, GIF), and any attempt to further compress them results in waste of time rather than an improvement.

Beyond this, consider that script files are rich with white spaces and blanks. Simply removing these characters can cut a significant percentage of software fat out of the file. This is just what *minifiers* are for.

A minifier is a tool that parses a given script file and rewrites it in a way that is functionally equivalent to the original but devoid of any unnecessary characters. The jQuery library is commonly served in its minified form. A minified script file is nearly impossible to read or understand for a human, so I don't recommend using minified files during development.

Microsoft released a minifier tool; you can get it at *http://aspnet.codeplex.com/releases/ view/40584*. This tool can work on script and CSS files. Also, in addition to removing white spaces and blanks, it safely attempts to reduce curly brackets and to make variable names shorter.

> **Note** You might want to look at build-time minifier tools such as Chirpy because having to manually minify several files can be a bit of a pain. See *http://chirpy.codeplex.com*.

Localized Scripts

Like other Web resources, scripts can be subject to localization. At the very end of the day, a script is a relatively long string of text, so there's really nothing that prevents you from embedding a script into the application resources along with a plain RESX file.

The method *GetWebResourceUrl* on the *ClientScript* property of the *Page* class can be used to return the URL to any resource stored in a satellite (localized) assembly. In this way, you link your scripts from the assembly, deploy the localized assembly, and you're done.

The only other alternative you have is maintaining different copies of the script and resolve the name programmatically. In ASP.NET 4, the *ScriptManager* control can streamline this task quite a bit. Here's how to use the script manager component:

```
<asp:ScriptManager ID="ScriptManager1" runat="server" EnableScriptLocalization="true">
    <Scripts>
        <asp:ScriptReference Path="Person.js" ResourceUICultures="it-IT, de-DE" />
    </Scripts>
</asp:ScriptManager>
```

When the property *EnableScriptLocalization* is *true*, the *<Scripts>* section lists all script files to be downloaded that might be subject to localization. Localization consists of mangling the provided name of the script in a way that incorporates culture information. For example, the preceding code will emit the following markup if the UI culture is set to Italian:

```
<script ... src="person.it-IT.js" />
```

The value of the page property *UICulture* determines the culture code being used to mangle the file name. When configuring the *ScriptManager* control, you indicate the supported cultures through the *ResourceUICultures* property on individual script references. If a related file is missing, you'll get a 404 error for the request. Otherwise, the markup will be emitted to target the language-neutral script file.

Using Cascading Style Sheets and Images

Cascading style sheets and images are the remaining two-thirds of the auxiliary static resources around most Web pages. Some consolidated techniques also exist to minimize the impact of these resources on your pages.

The first consideration to make is that the more requests you make, the more your users are likely to wait to see the page. Aggregating multiple scripts in a single (but larger) file is relatively easy and effective. It is doable for CSS files too; but with images? How can you combine multiple images to be used in distinct areas of the page and then reference just the section you need and where you need it?

Grouping Images into Sprites

To reduce the number of HTTP requests that a page requires in order to fetch all the images it needs, you use *sprites*.

A sprite is a single image that results from the composition of multiple images that are stored side by side, forming a grid of any size you like. You then link the image URL to any *<img>* tag where you need a section of it and use CSS styles to specify exactly which portion you want in a given place. Here's an example:

```
<img src="sprite.png" class="image1" />
<img src="sprite.png" class="image2" />
<img src="sprite.png" class="image3" />
```

You can even embed the reference to the image into the CSS as shown here:

```
<div class="UserInformation" />
```

The CSS class is defined as follows:

```
.UserInformation {
    width:123px;
    height:115px;
    background-image:url(sprite.png);
    background-position:-0px 0;
}
```

In other words, you pinpoint the fragment of the sprite you like using CSS attributes such as *background-position*, *background-image* and, of course, *width* and *height*.

Microsoft is currently working on an extension to ASP.NET 4 that supports sprites. For more information, check out *http://aspnet.codeplex.com/releases/view/50140*.

> **Note** *Image inlining* is another potentially useful technique for dealing with images and static resources more comfortably. Image inlining consists of streamlining a Base64-encoded version of the image file into a CSS file or an HTML page. As of today, very few browsers support this technique and, in addition, the Base64 encoding increases the size of individual images, making for a large download.

External References vs. Inline Content

This is one of those evergreen questions that are revamped periodically in geek talks. Is it better to embed script and style sheets (and to some extent images) into a page, or is it preferable to keep several distinct references that the browser can deal with?

External references increase the number of HTTP requests being made, but they keep the page size smaller (often significantly smaller) and, more importantly, can be cached by the browser. Frankly, inline content is a great thing at development time where, instead, the effects of browser caching can be quite annoying. For deployed sites, browser caching saves you HTTP requests and is a feature that you can fine-tune when preparing the response for a given page or resource.

As mentioned, just reducing the number of HTTP requests might not ensure optimal performance. You should work in two directions and try to produce a magical mix of fewer HTTP requests for not-so-large resources.

> **Note** To measure the performance and quality of Web pages, you can use YSlow—a Firefox add-on integrated with the Firebug Web development tool. (See *http://developer.yahoo.com/yslow*.) Based on a set of commonly accepted best practices, the tool analyzes a Web page and provides recommendations for improving the overall performance. As far as Internet Explorer is concerned, Internet Explorer 9 comes with the IE9 Developer toolbar, which provides similar capabilities.

Summary

In this chapter, we examined a few issues you might face when building pages and interacting with them—errors, personalization, and resource handling.

Often, good programs do bad things and raise errors. In the Web world, handling errors is a task architecturally left to the run-time environment that is running the application. The ASP.NET runtime is capable of providing two types of error pages, both of which are not very practical for serious and professional applications, although for different reasons. When a user who is locally connected to the application does something that originates an error, by default ASP.NET returns a "geek" page with the stack trace and the full transcript of the exception that occurred. The remote user, on the other hand, receives a less compromising page, but certainly not a user-friendly one. Fortunately, though, the ASP.NET framework is flexible enough to let you change the error pages, even to the point of distinguishing between HTTP errors.

Personalization allows you to write pages that persist user preferences and parametric data from a permanent medium in a totally automated way. As a programmer, you're in charge of setting up the personalization infrastructure, but you need not know anything about the internal details of storage. All you do is call a provider component using the methods of a well-known interface.

Finally, modern Web pages are much more than just HTML markup. Script files, images, CSSs, and literals need to be localized and effectively loaded. We examined a number of consolidated and effective techniques to localize pages, optimize page rendering, and download and minimize the impact of large and numerous scripts, style sheets and images.

In the next chapter, we'll take page authoring to the next level by exploring master pages and wizards.

Chapter 8
Page Composition and Usability

There is nothing like dream to create the future.

—Victor Hugo

It was only in the very early days of the Web that a Web site could be assembled by simply grouping distinct pages under the same host. Today, it is necessary for all pages in a Web site to define a common structure and share a common set of interface elements such as header, footer, navigation bar, ad rotators, and search and login box.

Beyond having a similar-looking and consistent layout, Web pages in a site must be easy to retrieve, understand, and navigate for users. In one word, Web pages must be enjoyable by their target audience. Most Web sites exist for strong business reasons; failing on the composition or usability aspects of site planning and development is a mistake that can cost your company much more than you might expect.

The challenge for a Web development platform is providing a technology that makes composing rich and usable pages effective in the first place, but also quick and at least relatively easy. This chapter is split into two parts, each providing a sort of checklist for the two aspects I've emphasized so far: composition and usability.

In the composition section, I'll discuss master pages, cascading style sheets (CSS), and ASP.NET themes. In the usability section, I'll touch on cross-browser rendering, site navigation, and search-engine optimization.

Page Composition Checklist

A successful Web site results from the combined effect of well-organized content and HTML appeal. You can't do without a strong *visual idea* of the site that contributes to spreading the brand and making the site recognizable and, in some way, giving the site its own character. Elaborating on a successful visual idea for a site is (fortunately?) beyond the reach of most developers and definitely is a different job that requires a different set of skills.

Some point of contact between the design and development teams, however, has to be found. When the underlying platform is going to be ASP.NET Web Forms, this point of contact comes in the form of a master page template and one or more cascading style sheets. Sometimes, the style of the site is represented through one or more ASP.NET *themes*. A theme is a superset of a CSS and includes multiple cascading style sheets plus additional files.

Let's begin our exploration of site composition with an in-depth look at master pages.

Working with Master Pages

In ASP.NET, *master pages* provide the ability to define a common layout and have it reused and shared across as many pages as you want throughout the site. Master pages improve the maintainability of the site while reducing code duplication. ASP.NET master pages basically benefits from the ASP.NET framework's ability to merge a super-template with user-defined content replacements.

A *master page* is a distinct file referenced at the application level, as well as at the page level, that contains the static layout of the page. The page layout consists of regions that each "derived" page can customize. Such regions are referenced in the master page with a special placeholder control. A derived page, also known as a *content page*, is simply a collection of blocks the run time will use to fill the regions in the master.

The contents of a master page are merged into the content page, and they dynamically produce a new page class that is served to the user upon request. The merge process takes place at compile time and only once.

It might seem that the idea of master and content pages revolves around some sort of visual inheritance such as the form inheritance feature you might experience in Windows Forms. Abstractly speaking, the content page really looks like an inherited page that overrides some virtual regions in the master. Although this is a possible high-level way of looking at things, it is not how master and content pages work in practice.

> **Note** In ASP.NET, a master page is not necessary for any page you add to the project. You can certainly create plain Web pages that don't import any layout information from the outside. In Microsoft Visual Studio, you are in fact given two options when you choose to add a new Web page to the project—you can add it with or without a master page. In the economy of a real-world site, though, using a master page (or even multiple master pages) is a necessity.

What's a Master Page, Anyway?

A master page is similar to an ordinary ASP.NET page except for the top *@Master* directive and the presence of one or more *ContentPlaceHolder* server controls. In addition, a master page doesn't derive from *Page* but has *UserControl* as its parent class. A *ContentPlaceHolder* control defines a region in the master page that can be customized in a derived page.

A master page without content placeholders is technically correct and will be processed correctly by the ASP.NET runtime. However, a placeholder-less master fails in its primary goal—to be the super-template of multiple pages that look alike. A master page devoid of placeholders works like an ordinary Web page but with the extra burden required to process master pages.

Here is a simple master page adapted from the master page of the Visual Studio 2010 sample ASP.NET project:

```
<%@ Master Codebehind=.Site.master.cs. Inherits=.YourApp.SiteMaster. %>
<html>
<head runat="server">
    <title></title>
    <link href="~/Styles/Site.css" rel="stylesheet" type="text/css" />
    <asp:ContentPlaceHolder ID="HeadContent" runat="server">
    </asp:ContentPlaceHolder>
</head>
<body>
    <form runat="server">
       <div class="page">
          <div class="header">
             <div class="title"><h1> Programming ASP.NET 4 </h1></div>
             <div class="loginDisplay">
                ...
             </div>
             <div class="clear menu">
                ...
             </div>
          </div>
          <div class="main">
            <asp:ContentPlaceHolder ID="MainContent" runat="server"/>
          </div>
          <div class="clear"></div>
       </div>
       <div class="footer">
          ...
       </div>
    </form>
</body>
</html>
```

As you can see, the master page looks like a standard ASP.NET page. Aside from the identifying *@Master* directive, the only key differences are *ContentPlaceHolder* controls. A page bound to this master automatically picks up the layout and contents of the master and can attach custom markup and server controls to each defined placeholder. The content placeholder element is fully identified by its *ID* property and normally doesn't require other attributes.

This is important to note because a content page is not allowed to include any content other than the markup strictly required to fill up a specific content placeholder. I'll return to this point in a moment.

The *@Master* Directive

The *@Master* directive distinguishes master pages from content pages and allows the ASP.NET runtime to properly handle each. A master page file is compiled to a class that derives from the *MasterPage* class. The *MasterPage* class, in turn, inherits *UserControl*. So, at the end of the day, a master page is treated as a special kind of ASP.NET user control.

The *@Master* directive supports quite a few attributes. For the most part, though, they are the same attributes that we reviewed in Chapter 5, "Anatomy of an ASP.NET Page," for the *@Page* directive. Table 8-1 details the attributes that have a special meaning to master pages.

TABLE 8-1 **Attributes of the *@Master* Directive**

Attribute	Description
ClassName	Specifies the name for the class that will be created to render the master page. This value can be any valid class name but should not include a namespace. By default, the class name for a simple.master is *ASP.simple_master*.
CodeBehind	Indicates the file that contains any source code associated with the master page, and is used for a Web Application Project (WAP).
	Note that the *CodeBehind* attribute is ignored by ASP.NET and simply exists to help Visual Studio edit the file. You can remove it in production without losing functionality.
CodeFile	Indicates the file that contains any source code associated with the master page, and is used for a Web site project.
Inherits	Specifies a code-behind class for the master page to inherit. This can be any class derived from *MasterPage*.
MasterPageFile	Specifies the name of the master page file that this master refers to. A master can refer to another master through the same mechanisms a page uses to attach to a master. If this attribute is set, you will have nested masters.

The master page is associated with a code file that looks like the following:

```
public partial class SiteMaster: System.Web.UI.MasterPage
{
    protected void Page_Load(Object sender, EventArgs e)
    {
        ...
    }
    ...
}
```

The *@Master* directive doesn't override attributes set at the *@Page* directive level. For example, you can have the master set the language to Visual Basic and one of the content pages can instead use C#. The language set at the master page level never influences the choice of the language at the content page level.

Likewise, you can use other ASP.NET directives in a master page—for example, *@Import*. However, the scope of these directives is limited to the master file and does not extend to child pages generated from the master.

The *ContentPlaceHolder* Container Control

The *ContentPlaceHolder* control acts as a container placed in a master page. It marks places in the master where related pages can insert custom content. A content placeholder is uniquely identified by an ID. Here's an example:

```
<asp:ContentPlaceHolder runat="server" ID="MainContent" />
```

A content page is an ASP.NET page that contains only *<asp:Content>* server tags. This element corresponds to an instance of the *Content* class that provides the actual content for a particular placeholder in the master. The link between placeholders and content is established through the ID of the placeholder. The content of a particular instance of the *Content* server control is written to the placeholder whose ID matches the value of the *ContentPlaceHolderID* property, as shown here:

```
<asp:Content runat="server" contentplaceholderID="MainContent">
   ...
</asp:Content>
```

In a master page, you define as many content placeholders as there are customizable regions in the page. A content page doesn't have to fill all the placeholders defined in the bound master. However, a content page can't do more than just fill placeholders defined in the master.

> **Note** A placeholder can't be bound to more than one content region in a single content page. If you have multiple *<asp:Content>* server tags in a content page, each must point to a distinct placeholder in the master.

Specifying Default Content

A content placeholder can be assigned default content that will show up if the content page fails to provide a replacement. Each *ContentPlaceHolder* control in the master page can contain default content. If a content page does not reference a given placeholder in the master, the default content will be used. The following code snippet shows how to define default content:

```
<asp:ContentPlaceHolder runat="server" ID="MainContent">
    <!-- Use the following markup if no custom
        content is provided by the content page -->
    ...
</asp:ContentPlaceHolder>
```

The default content is completely ignored if the content page populates the placeholder. The default content is never merged with the custom markup provided by the content page.

> **Note** A *ContentPlaceHolder* control can be used only in a master page. Content placeholders are not valid on regular ASP.NET pages. If such a control is found in an ordinary Web page, a parser error occurs.

Writing a Content Page

Once you have a master page, you think of your actual site pages in terms of a delta from the master. The master defines the common parts of a certain group of pages and leaves placeholders for customizable regions. Each *content page*, in turn, defines what the content of each region has to be for a particular ASP.NET page. Figure 8-1 shows the first step you take on the way to adding a content page to a Visual Studio project.

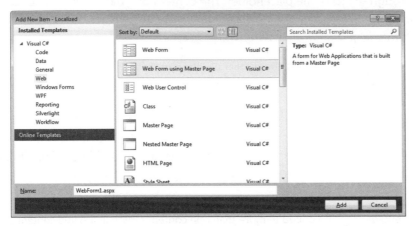

FIGURE 8-1 Adding a content page to a Visual Studio project.

The next step entails choosing a particular master page from within the folders of the current project. Normally, master pages are located in the root folder that defines their scope. If you have only one master page, it is usually located in the root of the site.

The *Content* Control

The key part of a content page is the *Content* control—a mere container for other controls. The *Content* control is used only in conjunction with a corresponding *ContentPlaceHolder* and is not a standalone control. The master file that we considered earlier defines a single placeholder named *PageBody*. This placeholder represents the body of the page and is placed right below an HTML table that provides the page's header. Figure 8-2 shows a sample content page based on the aforementioned master page.

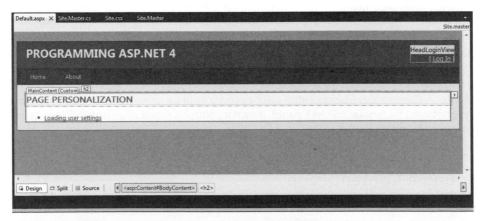

FIGURE 8-2 A preview of the content page in Visual Studio 2010.

Let's take a look at the source code of the content page:

```
<%@ Page Title="Home Page"
        Language="C#"
        AutoEventWireup="true"
        MasterPageFile="~/Site.master"
        CodeBehind="Default.aspx.cs"
        Inherits="UserProfileDemo._Default" %>

<asp:Content ID="HeaderContent" runat="server" ContentPlaceHolderID="HeadContent">
</asp:Content>

<asp:Content ID="BodyContent" runat="server" ContentPlaceHolderID="MainContent">
    <h2>
        Page personalization
    </h2>
    <div>
        <ul>
            <li><a href="/profile.aspx">Loading user settings</a></li>
        </ul>
    </div>
</asp:Content>
```

The content page is the resource that users invoke through the browser. When the user points her or his browser to this page, the output in Figure 8-3 is shown.

The replaceable part of the master is filled with the corresponding content section defined in the derived pages.

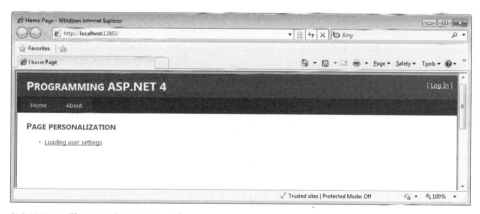

FIGURE 8-3 The sample page in action.

Content Pages and Auxiliary Content

A content page—that is, a page bound to a master—is a special breed of page in that it can *only* contain *<asp:Content>* controls. A content page is not permitted to host server controls outside of an *<asp:Content>* tag.

As a collection of *<asp:Content>* tags, a content page is not even allowed to include any markup that specifies general information such as the title of the page, inline styles, and even scripts.

You can declaratively set the title of a content page using the *Title* attribute of the *@Page* directive as shown here:

```
<@Page MasterPageFile="site.master" Title="Hello, world" %>
```

However, there's not much you can do to add styles and scripts in a content page unless the master page provides for specific placeholders. You can add styles and scripts to a placeholder if the placeholder's position in the layout allows you to include them. Most of the time, you create a placeholder within the *<head>* section and perhaps another at the bottom of the page to allow for styles and scripts. The default master you get in sample Visual Studio 2010 projects has the following:

```
<html>
<head runat="server">
    <title></title>
    <link href="~/Styles/Site.css" rel="stylesheet" type="text/css" />
    <asp:ContentPlaceHolder ID="HeadContent" runat="server">
    </asp:ContentPlaceHolder>
</head>
<body>
    ...
</body>
</html>
```

The *HeadContent* placeholder just exists so that content pages can fill it with any page head–specific content such as script or styles. Likewise, you can create a script-only placeholder and place it at the bottom of the page to improve the page's rendering speed, as discussed in Chapter 7, "Working with the Page."

Note, though, that a placeholder is just a container you can fill with whatever ends up producing valid HTML markup. You have no way to restrict a placeholder to contain only certain controls or certain fragments of HTML markup. Later in the chapter, I'll return to this point, contrasting placeholders with master page properties.

For now let's explore in a bit more detail the techniques to attach pages to masters.

Attaching Pages to a Master

So far, we have bound any content page to its master by using the *MasterPageFile* attribute in the *@Page* directive. The *MasterPageFile* attribute indicates the path to the master page. Page-level binding, however, is just one possibility—although it is the most common one.

You can also set the binding between the master and the content at the application or folder level. Application-level binding means that you link all the pages of an application to the same master. You configure this behavior by setting the *Master* attribute in the *<pages>* element of the principal *web.config* file:

```
<configuration>
    <system.web>
        <pages master="Site.master" />
    </system.web>
</configuration>
```

If the same setting is expressed in a child *web.config* file—a *web.config* file stored in a site subdirectory—all ASP.NET pages in the folder are bound to a specified master page.

Note that if you define binding at the application or folder level, all the Web pages in the application (or the folder) must have *Content* controls mapped to one or more placeholders in the master page. In other words, application-level binding prevents you from having (or later adding) a page to the site that is not configured as a content page. Any classic ASP.NET page in the application (or folder) that contains server controls will throw an exception.

Device-Specific Masters

Like all ASP.NET pages and controls, master pages can detect the capabilities of the underlying browser and adapt their output to the specific device in use. ASP.NET makes choosing a device-specific master easier than ever. If you want to control how certain pages of your site appear on a particular browser, you can build them from a common master and design the master to address the specific features of the browser. In other words, you can create multiple versions of the same master, each targeting a different type of browser.

How do you associate a particular version of the master and a particular browser? In the content page, you define multiple bindings using the same *MasterPageFile* attribute, but you prefix it with the identifier of the device. For example, suppose you want to provide ad hoc support for Microsoft Internet Explorer and Firefox browsers and use a generic master for any other browsers that users employ to visit the site. You use the following syntax:

```
<%@ Page masterpagefile="Site.master"
    ie:masterpagefile="ieSite.master"
    firefox:masterpagefile="ffSite.master" %>
```

The *ieSite.master* file will be used for Internet Explorer; the *ffSite.master*, on the other hand, will be used if the browser is Firefox. In any other case, a device-independent master (*site. master*) will be used. When the page runs, the ASP.NET runtime automatically determines which browser or device the user is using and selects the corresponding master page, as shown in Figure 8-4.

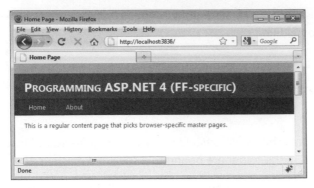

FIGURE 8-4 Browser-specific master pages.

The prefixes you can use to indicate a particular type of browser are those defined in the ASP.NET configuration files for browsers. Table 8-2 lists the most commonly used IDs.

TABLE 8-2 ID of Most Common Browsers

Browser ID	Browser Name
IE	Any version of Internet Explorer
Netscape3	Netscape Navigator 3.x
Netscape4	Netscape Communicator 4.x
Netscape6to9	Any version of Netscape higher than 6.0
Firefox	Firefox
Opera	Opera
Up	Openwave-powered devices
Blackberry	BlackBerry browser
iPhone	iPhone browser
Chrome	Google Chrome
ieMobile	Internet Explorer for mobile devices

Obviously, you can distinguish not just between up-level and down-level browsers, but you can also distinguish between browsers and other devices, such as cellular phones and personal digital assistants (PDAs). If you use device-specific masters, you must also indicate a device-independent master.

> **Note** Browser information is stored in text files with a *.browser* extension located in the *Browsers* folder under the ASP.NET installation path on the Web server. It's the same folder that contains *machine.config* and *WINDOWS%\Microsoft.NET\Framework\[version]\Config\Browsers*.

Processing Master and Content Pages

The use of master pages slightly changes how pages are processed and compiled. For one thing, a page based on a master has a double dependency—on the *.aspx* source file (the content page) and on the *.master* file (the master page). If either of these pages changes, the dynamic page assembly will be re-created. Although the URL that users need is the URL of the content page, the page served to the browser results from the master page being fleshed out with any replacement information provided by the content page.

Compiling Master Pages

When the user requests an *.aspx* resource mapped to a content page—that is, a page that references a master—the ASP.NET runtime begins its job by tracking the dependency between the source *.aspx* file and its master. This information is persisted in a local file created in the ASP.NET temporary files folder. Next, the runtime parses the master page source code and creates a Visual Basic or C# class, depending on the language set in the master page. The class inherits *MasterPage*, or the master's code file, and is then compiled to an assembly.

If multiple *.master* files are found in the same directory, they are all processed at the same time. Thus a dynamic assembly is generated for any master files found, even if only one of them is used by the ASP.NET page whose request triggered the compilation process. Therefore, don't leave unused master files in your Web space—they will be compiled anyway. Also note that the compilation tax is paid only the first time a content page is accessed within the application. When a user accesses another page that requires the second master, the response is faster because the previously compiled master is cached.

Serving the Page to Users

As mentioned, any ASP.NET page bound to a master page must have a certain structure— no server controls or literal text are allowed outside the *<asp:Content>* tag. As a result, the layout of the page looks like a plain collection of content elements, each bound to a particular placeholder in the master. The connection is established through the ID property. The *<asp:Content>* element works like a control container, much like the *Panel* control of ASP.NET or the HTML *<div>* tag. All the markup text is compiled to a template and associated with the corresponding placeholder property on the master class.

The master page is a special kind of user control with some templated regions. It's not coincidental, in fact, that the *MasterPage* class inherits from the *UserControl* class. After it is instantiated as a user control, the master page is completed with templates generated from the markup defined in the content page. Next, the resulting control is added to the control tree of the current page. No other controls are present in the final page except those brought in by the master. Figure 8-5 shows the skeleton of the final page served to the user.

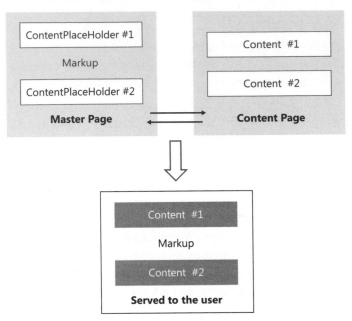

FIGURE 8-5 The structure of the final page in which the master page and the content page are merged.

Nested Master Pages

So far, we've seen a pretty simple relationship between a master page and a collection of content pages. However, the topology of the relationship can be made as complex and sophisticated as needed. A master can, in fact, be associated with another master and form a hierarchical, nested structure. When nested masters are used, any child master is seen and implemented as a plain content page in which extra *ContentPlaceHolder* controls are defined for an extra level of content pages. Put another way, a child master is a kind of content page that contains a combination of *<asp:Content>* and *<asp:ContentPlaceHolder>* elements. Like any other content page, a child master points to a master page and provides content blocks for its parent's placeholders. At the same time, it makes available new placeholders for its child pages.

Note There's no architectural limitation on the number of nesting levels you can implement in your Web sites. Performance-wise, the depth of the nesting has a negligible impact on the overall functionality and scalability of the solution. The final page served to the user is always compiled on demand and never modified as long as dependent files are not touched.

Let's expand on the previous example to add an intermediate master page. The root master page is the *Site.master* file we met earlier. The root master defines the header, the footer, and replaceable regions for the head and main content. Let's add an intermediate master page to further structure the main content. The intermediate master page is named *MainContent.master*.

```
<%@ Master Language="C#"
          AutoEventWireup="true"
          MasterPageFile="~/Site.Master"
          CodeBehind="MainContent.Master.cs"
          Inherits="Masters.MainContentMaster" %>

<asp:Content ID="Content1" ContentPlaceHolderID="HeadContent" runat="server">
    <!-- Won't be accessible from the final content page, anyway -->
</asp:Content>

<asp:Content ID="Content2" ContentPlaceHolderID="MainContent" runat="server">
  <fieldset>
    <legend>How <b>MainContent.Master</b> replaces MainContent</legend>
    <h2>
         <asp:Label runat="server" ID="MainContentTitle_Label">
            What is this page for?
         </asp:Label>
    </h2>

    <asp:ContentPlaceHolder ID="PageBody" runat="server" />
    <asp:ContentPlaceHolder ID="ScriptContentBottom" runat="server" />
  </fieldset>
</asp:Content>
```

As you can see, the master contains both a collection of *<asp:Content>* and *<asp:ContentPlaceHolder>* tags. The top directive is that of a master, but it contains the *MasterPageFile* attribute, which typically characterizes a content page.

An intermediate master page is essentially a content page and must fulfill the rules of content pages such as not having markup outside *<asp:Content>* controls. At the same time, it is allowed to specify the *@Master* directive and host some additional (well, nested) content placeholders.

Note that the final content page has access only to the placeholders of its immediate master. The *HeadContent* placeholder defined on the root master can be filled up by the intermediate master, but not by the final content page.

The following code illustrates *nesteddemo.aspx*—a content page that builds on two masters:

```
<%@ Page Title="Nested master pages"
        Language="C#"
        AutoEventWireup="true"
        CodeBehind="NestedDemo.aspx.cs"
        MasterPageFile="~/MainContent.Master"
        Inherits="Masters.NestedDemo" %>

<asp:Content ID="Content1" ContentPlaceHolderID="PageBody" runat="server">
  <fieldset>
    <legend>How <b>NestedDemo.aspx</b> replaces PageBody</legend>
    <h2>[Your custom markup here]</h2>
  </fieldset>
</asp:Content>
```

Figure 8-6 shows the results.

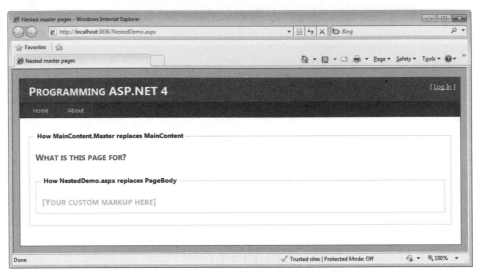

FIGURE 8-6 The page results from the combination of two master pages.

At this point, if you create a new page from *MainContent.Master* you'll be able to add custom content only below the label that says "What is this page for?". Everything else is fixed and can't be changed from the content page. Nested masters are fully supported by Visual Studio 2010, which provides you with a visual experience, as shown in Figure 8-7.

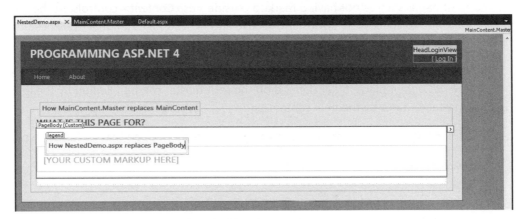

FIGURE 8-7 Nested masters in Visual Studio 2010.

What's the purpose of having nested master pages?

Whereas a master page helps share a common layout through multiple pages, nested master pages simply give you more control over the structure of the final pages. Especially in sites with hundreds of pages, a single layout is not realistic. More likely, you need a super-template in which different areas are filled in a way for a bunch of pages and in another way for another bunch of pages. Each group of pages might be derived from an intermediate master.

When you create a content placeholder in a master page, you are leaving to the content page author full freedom to put in the placeholder wherever she wishes. Sometimes, instead, you want pages to customize the content of certain areas but without altering the layout. In Figure 8-6, the *MainContent* placeholder defined on the root master has been filled up as follows. (I omitted the *fieldset* you see in Figure 8-6 for clarity.)

```
<asp:Content ID="Content2" ContentPlaceHolderID="MainContent" runat="server">
    <h2>
        <asp:Label runat="server" ID="MainContentTitle_Label">
            What is this page for?
        </asp:Label>
    </h2>

    <asp:ContentPlaceHolder ID="PageBody" runat="server" />
    <asp:ContentPlaceHolder ID="ScriptContentBottom" runat="server" />
</asp:Content>
```

The markup consists of an H2 element plus a couple of placeholders. This means that as the author of the master page, you always want a title string followed by the real content. However, the title string (the *Label* control in the code) is static. How can you make it dynamically settable from content pages? Here's where master page properties fit in.

Programming the Master Page

You can use code in content pages to reference properties, methods, and controls in the master page, with some restrictions. The rule for properties and methods is that you can reference them if they are declared as public members of the master page. This includes public page-scope variables, public properties, and public methods.

Exposing Master Properties

To give an identity to a control in the master, you simply set the *runat* attribute and give the control an ID. Can you then access the control from within a content page? Not directly. The only way to access the master page object model is through the *Master* property. Note, though, that the *Master* property of the *Page* class references the master page object for the content page. This means that only public properties and methods defined on the master page class are accessible.

The following code enhances the previous master page to make it expose the text of the label as a public property:

```
public partial class MainContentMaster : MasterPage
{
    protected void Page_Load(object sender, EventArgs e)
```

```
    {
    }

    public String MainContentTitle
    {
        get { return MainContentTitle_Label.Text; }
        set { MainContentTitle_Label.Text = value; }
    }
}
```

The control's protection level makes it inaccessible from the outside world, but the public property *MainContentTitle* defined in the preceding code represents a public wrapper around the *Label*'s *Text* property. In the end, the master page has an extra public property through which programmers can set the page description.

Invoking Properties on the Master

The *Master* property is the only point of contact between the content page and its master. The bad news is that the *Master* property is defined to be of type *MasterPage*; as such, it doesn't know anything about any property or method definition specific to the master you're really working with. In other words, the following code wouldn't compile because no *MainContentTitle* property is defined on the *MasterPage* class:

```
public partial class NestedDemo : System.Web.UI.Page
{
    protected void Page_Load(object sender, EventArgs e)
    {
        Master.MainContentTitle = "Nested demo";
    }
}
```

What's the real type behind the *Master* property?

The *Master* property represents the master page object as compiled by the ASP.NET runtime engine. This class follows the same naming convention as regular pages—*ASP.XXX_master*, where *XXX* is the name of the master file. Developers can override the default class name by setting the *ClassName* attribute on the @*Master* directive. The attribute lets you assign a user-defined name to the master page class:

```
<%@ Master ... Classname="ContentMaster" %>
```

In light of this, you would need code like that shown here:

```
    ((ASP.ContentMaster)Master).MainContentTitle = "Nested demo";
```

However, there are a couple of simpler alternatives—one for .NET 4 applications and one that works regardless of the .NET Framework version you're using. If you compile your code for the .NET Framework 4, you can take advantage of the *dynamic* keyword in C#.

```
public partial class NestedDemo : Page
{
    protected void Page_Load(Object sender, EventArgs e)
    {
        dynamic master = this.Master;
        master.MainContentTitle = "Nested demo";
    }
}
```

The *dynamic* keyword tells the compiler to suspend any further processing on the expression and just assume the syntax is fine. The compiler understands that the variable master is of type *dynamic*, and that's enough. For this type, then, the compiler actually emits some code that at run time will try to resolve the expression through the services of the Dynamic Language Runtime (DLR) component of the .NET Framework 4. The net effect is that if at run time the actual object behind the *master* variable can successfully resolve a call to the specified property, the code works as expected; otherwise, an exception would be raised.

If you're not using .NET 4, however, you have another choice.

The *@MasterType* Directive

By adding the *@MasterType* directive in the content page, you can avoid all the casting just shown. The *@MasterType* informs the compiler about the real type of the *Master* property. The *Master* property is declared as the right type in the dynamically created page class, and this allows you to write strongly typed code, as follows:

```
<%@ Page Title="Nested master pages"
        MasterPageFile="~/MainContent.Master"
        AutoEventWireup="true"
        CodeBehind="NestedDemo.aspx.cs"
        Inherits="Masters.NestedDemo" %>
<%@ MasterType VirtualPath="~/MainContent.Master" %>
```

In the code file, you can have the following statements:

```
protected void Page_Load(object sender, EventArgs e)
{
    Master.MainContentTitle = "Nested demo";
}
```

The *@MasterType* directive supports two mutually exclusive attributes: *VirtualPath* and *TypeName*. Both serve to identify the master class to use. The former does it by URL; the latter by type name. Figure 8-8 shows the effect of the directive on the code being created and the nice work Visual Studio IntelliSense does around it.

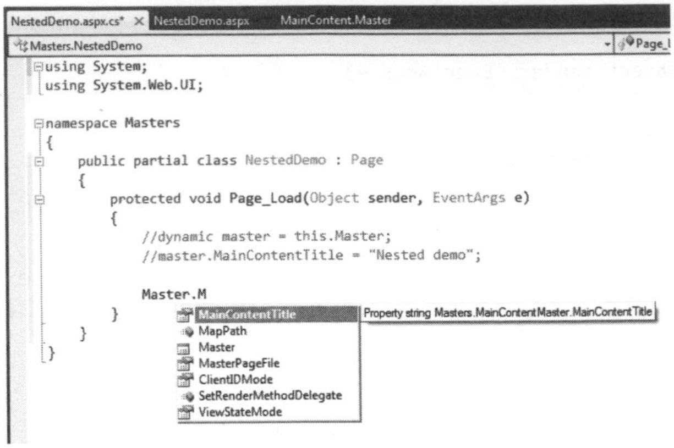

FIGURE 8-8 Effect of the @*MasterType* directive.

Changing the Master Page Dynamically

To associate an ASP.NET content page with a master page—keeping in mind that in no case can you associate a classic ASP.NET page with a master—you use the *MasterPageFile* attribute of the @*Page* directive. *MasterPageFile*, though, is also a read-write property on the *Page* class that points to the name of the master page file. Can you dynamically select the master page via code and based on run-time conditions?

Using a dynamically changing master page is definitely possible in ASP.NET and is suitable, for example, for applications that can present themselves to users through different skins. However, programmatically selecting the master page is not a task that you can accomplish at any time. To be precise, you can set the *MasterPageFile* property only during the *PreInit* page event—that is, before the run time begins working on the request.

```
protected void Page_PreInit(object sender, EventArgs e)
{
    MasterPageFile = "another.master";
}
```

If you try to set the *MasterPageFile* property in *Init* or *Load* event handlers, an exception is raised.

> **Note** The *Master* property represents the current instance of the master page object, is a read-only property, and can't be set programmatically. The *Master* property is set by the run time after loading the content of the file referenced by the *MasterPageFile* property.

Styling ASP.NET Pages

ASP.NET pages are mostly made of server controls, and server controls ultimately serve up HTML markup. The client browser builds and displays HTML elements whose appearance depends on the information stored in their style containers.

It turns out that there are several places for you to add style information to control the look and feel of the page. If you feel comfortable with server controls, you use ASP.NET themes. If you need to exercise more control over the content actually sent to (and displayed by) the browser, you can configure controls to emit CSS-friendly markup that can be styled effectively from the client or through HTML literals right in the ASPX markup.

ASP.NET *themes* have been introduced with the intent of facilitating the task of styling server controls with the same approach used by cascading style sheets at the HTML element level. Themes were originally aimed at doing the same job of CSS but through a more specific interface tailor-made for server controls. Through themes, you just declaratively define some code to be run to dress the control in a given way. Basically, themes are a way to adapt the CSS syntax to the syntax of server controls.

Boldly introduced as a way to supersede CSS styles, today ASP.NET themes are in a downturn, if not explicitly deprecated. Why is this so? As I see things, the problem is not with themes but with the overall perception of server controls in ASP.NET development. Themes are just perfect—and more effective than CSS—if your language for expressing Web pages is largely based on server controls. If you don't really feel the need to worry about what a server control emits, themes are just the perfect tool for the job.

At the height of ASP.NET's success, the advent of AJAX silently started changing people's perspective of things and led to a complete turnaround in only a couple of years. In a way, AJAX was the straw that broke the ASP.NET Web Forms abstraction model. With AJAX, you need much more control over the markup—HTML elements and CSS styles. Subsequently, many more developers are using server controls not as building blocks but rather as HTML helper factories. In this context, themes are simply a cumbersome technology compared to the flexibility and dynamism of CSS.

In any case, in this chapter you'll find a section dedicated to the syntax and semantics of themes. CSS is a too large of a topic to be covered here. You can pick up one of the several books available on CSS. If you're looking for an online reference, I recommend *http://www.w3schools.com/CSS/CSS_reference.asp.*

 Note   Although themes are fully supported in ASP.NET 4, I currently see them mostly as a feature for a suite of controls rather than pages and sites. And I'm probably not the only one thinking this way. In the past couple of years, in fact, we've witnessed a significant technology shift that resulted in server controls becoming more and more HTML and CSS friendly. This trend is clearly visible in ASP.NET 4 (and future extensions are being currently planned). The perception is different—server controls must adapt their internal organization so that the output can be styled via CSS. If you take this route, of course, you just don't need themes.

What's a Theme, Anyway?

A *theme* is a set of visual settings that can be applied to style the markup produced by ASP.NET server controls. A theme is ultimately a collection of files—ASP.NET visual settings (known as *skins*), CSS, plus any auxiliary images. Once enabled, the theme determines the appearance of all controls under its jurisdiction. Consider the following simple markup:

```
<asp:Calendar ID="Calendar1" runat="server" />
```

Without themes, the calendar will look gray, spare, and spartan. With a theme added, the same markup renders a more colorful and appealing calendar. As you can see, a neat separation exists between the page contents and formatting rules. Look at Figure 8-9. Which do you think is the unthemed calendar?

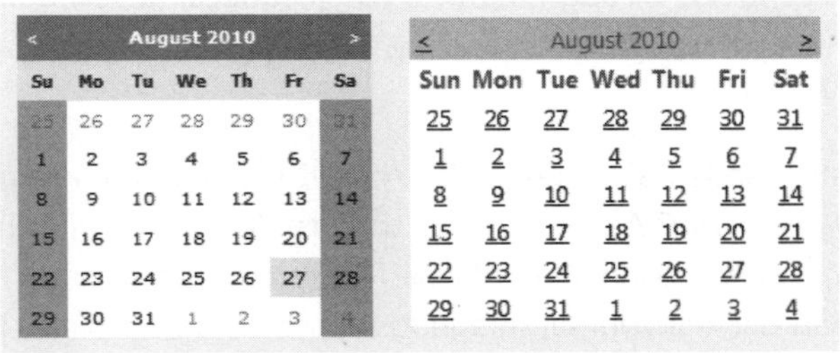

FIGURE 8-9 The same controls, with and without themes.

To fully understand ASP.NET themes, you must be familiar with a few terms, which are detailed in Table 8-3.

TABLE 8-3 ASP.NET Themes Terminology

Term	Definition
Skin	A named set of properties and templates that can be applied to one or more controls on a page. A skin is always associated with a specific control type.
Style sheet	A CSS or server-side style sheet file that can be used by pages on a site.
Style sheet theme	A theme used to abstract control properties from controls. The application of this theme means that the control can still override the theme.
Customization theme	A theme used to abstract control properties from controls, but the theme overrides the control and any style sheet theme.

Imagine you are creating a new Web site and would like it to be visually appealing from the start. Instead of having to learn all the available style properties of each employed control, you just use ASP.NET themes. Using a built-in theme in a page is as easy as setting a property, as you'll see in a moment. With this change, pages automatically inherit a new, and hopefully attractive, appearance. For example, if you add a *Calendar* control to a page, it automatically renders with the default appearance defined in the theme.

Selecting a theme for one or more pages doesn't necessarily bind you to the settings of that theme. Through the Visual Studio designer, you can review the pages and manually adjust some styles in a control if you want to.

Note The following convention holds true in this book and, in general, in related literature. Unless otherwise suggested by the context, the word "theme" indicates a customization theme. Customization themes and style sheet themes use the same source files. They differ only in how the ASP.NET runtime applies them to a page. The same theme can be applied as a customization theme or a style sheet theme at different times.

Structure of a Theme

Themes are expressed as the union of various files and folders living under a common root directory. Themes can be global or local. Global themes are visible to all Web applications installed on a server machine. Local themes are visible only to the application that defines them. Global themes are contained in child directories located under the following path. The name of the directory is the name of the theme.

```
%WINDOWS%\Microsoft.NET\Framework\[version]\ASP.NETClientFiles\Themes
```

Local themes are specialized folders that live under the *App_Themes* folder at the root of the application. Figure 8-10 shows the content of a couple of themes in a Web application.

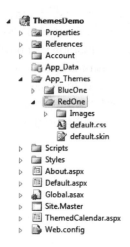

FIGURE 8-10 The *App_Themes* directory in a Web project.

As you can see, the theme in the figure consists of a *.css* file and a *.skin* file, plus a subdirectory of images. Generally, themes can contain a mix of the following resources:

■ **CSS files**   Also known as *style sheets*, CSS files contain style definitions to be applied to elements in an HTML document. Written according to a tailor-made syntax, CSS styles define how elements are displayed and where they are positioned on your page. The World Wide Web Consortium (W3C) maintains and constantly evolves CSS standards. Visit *http://www.w3.org* for details on current CSS specifications. CSS files are located in the root of the theme folder.

- **Skin files** A skin file contains the theme-specific markup for a given set of controls. A skin file is made of a sequence of control definitions that include predefined values for most visual properties and supported templates. Each skin is control-specific and has a unique name. You can define multiple skins for a given control. A skinned control has the original markup written in the *.aspx* source file modified by the content of the skin. The way the modification occurs depends on whether a customization theme or a style sheet theme is used. Skin files are located in the root of the theme folder.

- **Image files** Feature-rich ASP.NET controls might require images. For example, a pageable *DataGrid* control might want to use bitmaps for first or last pages that are graphically compliant to the skin. Images that are part of a skin are typically located in an *Images* directory under the theme folder. (You can change the name of the folder as long as the name is correctly reflected by the skin's attributes.)

- **Templates** A control skin is not limited to graphical properties but extends to define the layout of the control—for templated controls that support this capability. By stuffing template definitions in a theme, you can alter the internal structure of a control while leaving the programming interface and behavior intact. Templates are defined as part of the control skin and persisted to skin files.

The content types just listed are not exhaustive, but they do cover the most commonly used data you might want to store in a theme. You can have additional subdirectories filled with any sort of data that makes sense to skinned controls. For example, imagine you have a custom control that displays its own user interface through the services of an external ASP.NET user control (*.ascx*). Skinning this control entails, among other things, indicating the URL to the user control. The user control becomes an effective part of the theme and must be stored under the theme folder. Where exactly? That is up to you, but opting for a *Controls* subdirectory doesn't seem to be a bad idea.

Theming Pages and Controls

You can apply themes at various levels—application, folder, and individual pages. In addition, within the same theme you can select different skins for the same type of control.

Setting a theme at the application level affects all the pages and controls in the application. It's a feature you configure in the application's *web.config* file:

```
<system.web>
    <pages theme="BlueOne" />
</system.web>
```

The *theme* attribute sets a customization theme, while the *styleSheetTheme* attribute sets a style sheet theme. Note that the case is important in the *web.config*'s schema. Likewise, a theme can be applied to all the pages found in a given folder and below that folder. To do so, you create a new *web.config* file in an application's directory and add the section just shown to it. All the pages in that directory and below it will be themed accordingly. Finally, you can select the theme at the page level and have styles and skins applied only to that page and all its controls.

To associate a theme with a page, you set the *Theme* or *StyleSheetTheme* attribute on the *@Page* directive, and you're all set:

```
<% @Page Language="C#" Theme="BlueOne" %>
<% @Page Language="C#" StyleSheetTheme="BlueOne" %>
```

Also in this case, *Theme* sets a customization theme, whereas *StyleSheetTheme* indicates a style sheet theme.

Bear in mind that the name of the selected theme must match the name of a subdirectory under the *App_Themes* path or the name of a global theme. If a theme with a given name exists both locally to the application and globally to the site, the local theme takes precedence.

While we're speaking of precedence, note that themes have a hierarchical nature: directory-level themes take precedence over application-level themes, and page-level themes override any other themes defined around the application. This hierarchy is independent of which attributes are used—*Theme* or *StyleSheetTheme*—to enable theming.

> **Note** Setting both the *Theme* and *StyleSheetTheme* attributes is not prohibited, even though it is not a recommended practice. There's a behavioral gap between the two forms of themes that should make clear which one you need in any situation. However, if you set both attributes, consider that both themes will be applied—first the style sheet theme and then the customization theme. The results depend on the CSS cascading mechanism and, ultimately, are determined by the CSS settings of each theme.

Applying Skins

A skin file looks like a regular ASP.NET page because it is populated by control declarations and import directives. Each control declaration defines the default appearance of a particular control. Consider the following excerpt from a skin file:

```
<!-- This is a possible skin for a Button control -->
<asp:Button runat="server"
    BorderColor="darkgray"
    Font-Bold="true"
    BorderWidth="1px"
    BorderStyle="outset"
    ForeColor="DarkSlateGray"
    BackColor="gainsboro" />
```

The net effect of the skin is that every *Button* control in a themed page will be rendered as defined by the preceding markup. If the theme is applied as a style sheet, the settings just shown will be overridable by the developer; if the theme is a customization theme, those settings determine the final look and feel of the control. Properties that the theme leaves blank are set according to the control's defaults or the *.aspx* source.

> **Important** Whatever theme you apply—customization or style sheet—control properties can always be modified through code in page events such as *Init* and *Load*.

A theme can contain multiple skins for a given control, each identified with a unique name—the *SkinID* attribute. When the *SkinID* attribute is set, the skin is said to be a *named skin*. A theme can contain any number of named skins per control, but just one unnamed (default) skin. You select the skin for a control in an ASP.NET themed page by setting the control's *SkinID* property. The value of the control's *SkinID* property should match an existing skin in the current theme. If the page theme doesn't include a skin that matches the *SkinID* property, the default skin for that control type is used. The following code shows two named skins for a button within the same theme:

```
<!-- Place these two definitions in the same .skin file -->
<asp:button skinid="skinClassic" BackColor="gray" />
<asp:button skinid="skinTrendy" BackColor="lightcyan" />
```

When you enable theming on a page, by default all controls in that page will be themed except controls and individual control properties that explicitly disable theming.

Taking Control of Theming

The ASP.NET theming infrastructure provides the *EnableTheming* Boolean property to disable skins for a control and all its children. You can configure a page or control to ignore themes by setting the *EnableTheming* property to *false*. The default value of the property is *true*. *EnableTheming* is defined on the *Control* class and inherited by all server controls and pages. If you want to disable theme support for all controls in a page, you can set the *EnableTheming* attribute on the *@Page* directive.

> **Important** Note that the *EnableTheming* property can be set only in the *Page_PreInit* event for static controls—that is, controls defined in the *.aspx* source. For dynamic controls—that is, controls created programmatically—you must have set the property before adding the control to the page's control tree. A control is added to the page's control tree when you add to the *Controls* collection of the parent control—typically, the form or another control in the form.

When is disabling themes useful? Themes are great at ensuring that all page controls have a consistent look and feel, but at the same time themes override the visual attributes of any control for which a skin is defined. You can control the overriding mechanism a bit by switching style sheet and customization themes. However, when you want a control or page to maintain its predefined look, you just disable themes for that page or control.

Note that disabling themes affects *only* skins, not CSS styles. When a theme includes one or more CSS style-sheet files, they are linked to the *<head>* tag of the resulting HTML document and, after that, are handled entirely by the browser. As you can easily guess, there's not much a Web browser can know about ASP.NET themes!

Loading Themes Dynamically

You can apply themes dynamically, but this requires a bit of care. The ASP.NET runtime loads theme information immediately after the *PreInit* event fires. When the *PreInit* event fires, the name of any theme referenced in the *@Page* directive is already known and will be used unless it is overridden during the event. If you want to enable your users to change themes on the fly, you create a *Page_PreInit* event handler. The following code shows the code file of a sample page that changes themes dynamically:

```
public partial class TestThemes : System.Web.UI.Page
{
    protected void Page_Load(object sender, EventArgs e)
    {
        if (!IsPostBack) {
            // Populate the list of available themes
            ThemeList.DataSource = GetAvailableThemes();
            ThemeList.DataBind();
        }
    }

    void Page_PreInit(object sender, EventArgs e)
    {
        string theme = "";
        if (Page.Request.Form.Count > 0)
            theme = Page.Request["ThemeList"].ToString();
        if (theme == "None")
            theme = "";
        this.Theme = theme;
    }

    protected StringCollection GetAvailableThemes()
    {
        var path = Request.PhysicalApplicationPath + @"App_Themes";
        var dir = new DirectoryInfo(path);
        var themes = new StringCollection();
        foreach (var di in dir.GetDirectories())
            themes.Add(di.Name);

        return themes;
    }
}
```

The drop-down list control named *ThemeList* enumerates the installed application themes and lets you choose the one to apply. The selected theme is then applied in the *PreInit* event and immediately reflected. In the *PreInit* event, no view state has been restored yet; so *Request.Form* is the only safe way to access a posted value like the selected theme.

Page Usability Checklist

Mastering the technology for building a Web site is necessary, but often it's not sufficient. Your site must be able to attract people and make them return on a regular basis. A site must surely provide valuable content and services, but that might not be good enough if that content and those great services are hard to find, understand, and consume.

There are three fundamental items that any developers of any Web sites must tick off their to-do list as soon and as as possible: consistent cross-browser display, Search Engine Optimization (SEO), and site navigation. Cross-browser display ensures that your pages will look and work the same regardless of the device being used to reach it. SEO best practices ensure that your site is ranked high by search engines and possibly appear as one of the first links when a user searches for a related keyword. Finally, once users arrive, they must be able to work with the site seamlessly and have an enjoyable experience. Site navigation facilities are fundamental.

In the rest of this chapter, I'll address some of the best practices and ASP.NET techniques and technologies to provide users with a consistent and comfortable experience while interacting with the site.

Cross-Browser Rendering

Although all client browsers these days share a common set of capabilities large enough to implement nice Web features, the old motto of "Write once, browse everywhere" is a fairy tale. That a page works the same across different browsers is not a foregone conclusion; rather, it's something you have to test carefully and that might require a bit of extra work to achieve. Especially with extremely dynamic pages full of script and HTML manipulation code, the risk of having some markup misinterpreted is real.

Cross-browser rendering refers to the set of techniques and technologies you can use to ensure that your pages work and look the same regardless of the browser in use. The key idea behind cross-browser rendering is that the code within the page is able to detect the browser ID and its known set of capabilities. Based on that, the code within the page will then work out a solution to get the best possible markup for the device.

ASP.NET provides a specific API to detect browser capabilities programmatically and also to keep the set of capabilities updated over time.

Detecting Browser Capabilities

In ASP.NET, the central repository for browser information is the *Browser* property on the *HttpRequest* object. Here's how it is defined:

```
public HttpBrowserCapabilities Browser
{
    get { ... }
    set { ... }
}
```

When the *getter* method is invoked for the first time, the *HttpRequest* object gets and caches any available browser information. The user agent information carried by the request is used to identify the requesting browser. Any gathered browser information is published through an instance of the *HttpBrowserCapabilities* class. The *HttpBrowserCapabilities* class groups, in a single place, values that identify a fair number of browser capabilities, including support for ActiveX controls, scripting languages, frames, cookies, and much more. Note that no information is in any way dynamically set by the browser; instead, it is retrieved from an offline server-side repository.

As mentioned, ASP.NET identifies the connected browser by reading the user-agent information that is passed during a request. ASP.NET compares the user-agent string that is received from the browser to user-agent strings that are stored in server-side *browser definition files*. These files contain information about the known capabilities of various user agents. When ASP.NET finds a match between the current user-agent string and a user-agent string in a browser definition file, it loads the corresponding browser capabilities into the *HttpBrowserCapabilities* object. The following code shows how to identify and output the name of the calling browser:

```
var browserCaps = Request.Browser;
Label1.Text = browserCaps.Browser;
```

The properties of the *HttpBrowserCapabilities* object can then be used to determine whether the browser type that is represented by the user agent supports scripting, styles, frames, and so on. Based on these capabilities, the controls on the page render Web controls using appropriate markup.

Browser Definition Files

The class *HttpBrowserCapabilities* inherits from *HttpBrowserCapabilitiesBase*, which represents the list of information that is possible to know about a browser. The base class includes dozens of properties, including *IsMobileDevice*, *SupportsXmlHttp*, *JScriptVersion*, and *HasBackButton*. As an example, *IsMobileDevice* returns a Boolean value denoting whether or not the current browser is a mobile device. Likewise, *JScriptVersion* returns the version of JavaScript currently being supported by the browser, and *SupportsXmlHttp* indicates whether the browser has AJAX capabilities.

Browser information is read from server-side browser definition files installed with ASP.NET. In ASP.NET 4, you find the following definition files—one for each recognized browser device:

- blackberry.browser
- chrome.browser
- Default.browser
- firefox.browser
- gateway.browser

- generic.browser

- ie.browser

- iemobile.browser

- iphone.browser

- opera.browser

- safari.browser

Browser definition files are plain XML files located under the following folder:

```
%Windows%\Microsoft.NET\Framework\v4.0.30319\Config\Browsers
```

Browser files in the specified folder contain global definitions valid for all applications on the server. If you want to employ application-specific settings, you create an App_Browsers folder in your project and drop into it any *.browser* file you might need.

At any time, you can add new *.browser* files or edit any stored information. The syntax of *.browser* files is a bit quirky, and any edit needs to be conducted by hand, with the risk of breaking things. To make this scenario more seamless, in ASP.NET 4 Microsoft introduced the concept of a browser-capabilities provider.

> **Note** If you make any edits to any of the .browser files, make sure you re-create the browser assembly in the global assembly cache (GAC). For this to happen, you have to run the following command:
>
> ```
> aspnet_regbrowsers.exe -I c
> ```
>
> Needless to say, this action will inevitably restart your entire Web application.

Browser Capabilities Providers

In ASP.NET, a provider is a component that implements a contracted interface and interacts with specific ASP.NET subsystems only through that interface. Each ASP.NET subsystem that supports the provider model must have a default provider configured. As a developer, you can make your application switch from one provider to the next declaratively, when not doing it programmatically. Through the provider model, a piece of functionality represented by a "contract" (in this context, it is usually a base class) is injected into a particular subsystem of ASP.NET. Providers exist for membership, role management, user profiles and, in ASP.NET 4, also for managing browser capabilities.

Browser-capabilities providers enforce the following contract:

```
public abstract class HttpCapabilitiesProvider
{
    public abstract HttpBrowserCapabilities GetBrowserCapabilities(HttpRequest request);
}
```

The default browser-capabilities provider is the class *HttpCapabilitiesDefaultProvider* you find in the *System.Web.Configuration* namespace. This class is designed to read browser information from *.browser* files. Internally, the implementation of the *Browser* property on the *HttpRequest* object ends up calling the configured provider and gets to the actual information through the interface of the *HttpCapabilitiesProvider* class.

If you need to read browser information from other sources, you can replace or extend the default provider. You create a new provider class that derives from *HttpCapabilitiesProvider* and overrides the *GetBrowserCapabilities* method:

```
public class CustomProvider : HttpCapabilitiesProvider
{
    public override HttpBrowserCapabilities GetBrowserCapabilities(HttpRequest request)
    {
        // Detect the browser
        var userAgent = request.UserAgent;

        // Retrieve information
        var values = GetBrowserInfoAsHashTable(userAgent);

        // Pack information in a consumable format
        var browserCaps = new HttpBrowserCapabilities();
        browserCaps.Capabilities = values;

        return browserCaps;
    }

    private HashTable GetBrowserInfoAsHashTable(String userAgent)
    {
        var values = new HashTable(180);
        ...
        return values;
    }
}
```

The final step consists of registering the new provider. You can do that declaratively through the *<browserCaps>* section of the configuration file:

```
<system.web>
    <browserCaps provider="YourApp.CustomProvider, Extensions" />
</system.web>
```

Alternatively, you can use the following code from *global.asax*:

```
void Application_Start(Object sender, EventArgs e)
{
    HttpCapabilitiesBase.BrowserCapabilitiesProvider = new YourApp.CustomProvider();
}
```

When you write a provider, you should also consider caching the information because although it is static information, it might be requested several times. Setting up forms of data caching is entirely up to you.

The primary reason for writing a custom browser capabilities provider is to let developers store browser capabilities in an alternate repository (for example, a database) and use that instead of the built in one.

> **Note** The interface that defines the list of capabilities for browsers is fixed. For this reason, to add a new capability you can only resort to adding extra properties to the *Capabilities* dictionary of the *HttpCapabilitiesBase* class.

Search Engine Optimization

Spreading the word around about a Web site is a key step to getting a good site its deserved success. People visit a Web site because they are told about it, because they receive a direct link to it or, more likely, because they were searching for some topics related to the content of the site and engines such as Bing, Google, and Yahoo suggested they could find good information there.

If a Web site is quite high in the list of search results, the site is going to experience plenty of visits. How can you manage to make links from your site look attractive to search engines? That's precisely a whole new field that goes side by side with Web development—*search engine optimization* or SEO.

SEO is critical for any Web sites that need to have high volumes of traffic to survive. More traffic will likely generate more advertising and increase the revenue the site generates.

Quick SEO Checklist

Search engines won't tell you exactly which parameters they're using to rank pages. Algorithms, however, are continually updated to stay in sync with user expectations and to fix any possible drawbacks that could cause inconsistent or unreliable results. Even though the indexing algorithm used by search engines remains a well-kept trade secret, it is widely known that pages with certain characteristics are ranked higher than others. Let's review some of these SEO techniques.

The first aspect to consider is that the title of the Web page does matter. The title has to be unique for every page, kept short (about 50 characters maximum), and be meaningful enough to please both end users and search engines. To please search engines, the title string should include page keywords, preferably in the beginning of the string. In addition, the content of the title (or a similar string) should also be displayed through an *<H1>* tag. This increases the relevance of the content to the search engine's eyes.

Search engines work by searching references to Web pages that can be associated with the input keywords. In other words, a search engine works by mapping its own keywords to the content exposed by pages. HTML pages can include a couple of interesting meta tags in their *<head>* section. These meta tags are *keywords* and *description*:

```
<head>
  <meta name="keywords" content="ASP.NET Web Forms, Book, Training" />
  <meta name="description" content="This book explains how ASP.NET works so that you
              find out yourself how to do things." />
  ...
</head>
```

In ASP.NET 4, you can set the *keywords* and *description* attributes easily through a pair of new properties added to the *Page* class. (See Chapter 5.) Today, however, the importance of the *keywords* meta tag is diminished. Bing and Google, for example, have both stated explicitly that they don't use keywords declared in the *<head>* of the page but actually extract real keywords from the content. In light of this, using the *keywords* meta tag to list your page keywords is hardly a bad thing, but it is not a decisive factor in determining the final ranking. A common use of the *keywords* meta tag today is also to associate your page with misspelled keywords. For example, if your page is about *tennis*, the engine will easily figure that out from the content and rank it accordingly. However, if you list words like *tenis* in the keywords, you have a better chance of your page being picked up when the user mistypes words.

The *description* meta tag, instead, is more relevant, even though it's not specifically for raising the rank. If a *description* meta tag is found, search engines embed that content in the result page instead of creating their own description. If the description is attractive enough, your page has more chances to be clicked. A description is ideally around 200 characters and should read well and be informative.

Search engines don't like many things that often populate Web pages. They don't like duplicated URLs, for example. If there are two or more URLs used to get the same content, search engines tend to lower the page ranking. This happens even if you have subdomains, such as *www.yourserver.com* and *yourserver.com*. Without a permanent redirect being configured at the Internet Information Services (IIS) level, your home page will suffer.

Search engines don't like query strings, hidden fields, Flash/Silverlight components, or rich JavaScript content. All these things make the page harder to analyze. Search engines, instead, love plain anchor tags, title attributes, and alt attributes—plain HTML.

If not properly handled, redirects are also problematic because they can lead to duplicated URLs. Classic redirects you perform through *Response.Redirect* result in an HTTP 302 status code. As developers, we tend to forget that HTTP 302 indicates a temporary redirect. A temporary redirect therefore tells engines that eventually the page being moved will return to its original location. If this doesn't happen, engines keep on storing two locations for the same content. A permanent redirect is HTTP 301, which in ASP.NET 4 is enforced by a new method—*Response.PermanentRedirect*.

Query strings should be avoided too. Ideally, URLs should be extensionless and represent a meaningful path within the content of the page. URL rewriting is an ASP.NET technique that can help in this regard. In ASP.NET 4, however, routing is a type of URL rewriting that offers a richer programming model and the same (if not higher) degree of effectiveness. (See Chapter 4, "HTTP Handlers, Modules, and Routing.")

SEO and ASP.NET

Although ASP.NET 4 put some effort into making it easier for you to improve SEO, there are a few structural aspects of ASP.NET that are not specifically optimized for search engines. I don't mean this to be necessarily a bad statement about ASP.NET Web Forms as a platform. On the other hand, ASP.NET Web Forms was designed a decade ago when we all were living in a totally different world and were chasing different priorities than today. In this regard, ASP.NET MVC is a better (because it's newer) platform that is natively optimized for search engines.

So my point here is don't be fooled if you read that ASP.NET improves SEO. It simply gives you some new tools for implementing features (permanent redirection, meta description, routing) that were only harder, but not impossible, to achieve before.

Let's briefly review some structural SEO-related issues of ASP.NET.

The *postback* mechanism carried via JavaScript code is like smoke in the eyes of search engines. Every time you use link buttons or built-in paging/sorting capabilities of data-bound controls, you put your page at risk of not being ranked properly. Search engines don't follow JavaScript and ignore cookies. Because the session ID is stored in a cookie and engines ignore cookies, some of the page content might remain undiscovered. What about a cookieless approach for sessions, then? (We'll discover this feature in Chapter 17, "ASP.NET State Management.") It would be even worse because it would produce a lot of duplicated URLs, confusing engines even more.

Finally, the ASP.NET view state. The view state is a potentially large hidden field usually stored at the beginning of the page, right after the opening *<form>* tag. For a while, it was assumed that to make the process quicker, search engines could read only the first chunk of the page (maybe 100 KB). In this way, because the view state is at the top and much of the real content would be out of reach. This is conjecture, however, as there's currently no evidence that search engines do this.

In the end, moving the view state to the bottom of the page to get some alleged SEO benefits can actually be dangerous because the user, in cases where there's a very large view state, will likely get the opportunity to post back before the entire content is loaded. This situation, as you can guess, could cause errors.

For completeness, you can move the view state to the bottom of the page using a little-known attribute in the configuration:

```
<pages RenderAllHiddenFieldsAtTopOfForm="false" />
```

Note that regardless of what the attribute name suggests, the attribute has an effect only on system hidden fields. Custom hidden fields defined programmatically will always be emitted in their natural position.

> **Note** If search engines don't like JavaScript very much, what about AJAX pages and SEO? AJAX is inherently JavaScript-based, and if your page is built using JavaScript only, well, it will likely not be indexed by engines. A simple test is to try to load the page in the browser with JavaScript disabled. What you see in this test is what a search engine will be able to index. To partially remedy this, you can add static site maps that offer plain HTML links and load at least the initial content of the page statically through the browser and not without JavaScript code. A recommended practice is using tools such as HTMLUnit to automate grabbing a static, scriptless version of your pages. For more information, see *http://blog.stevensanderson.com/2010/03/30/using-htmlunit-on-net-for-headless-browser-automation*.

Tools for Measuring SEO Level

Wouldn't it be great if you could run a tool against a public site and get a report about some of the SEO issues it could spot? SEO correctness depends on whether or not (and in which measure) you do the few things listed in the previous section. A tool can easily automate the process of validation and come up with a list of things to fix. From Microsoft, you get the IIS SEO Toolkit: *http://www.iis.net/download/seotoolkit*. The toolkit includes various modules—Site Analysis, Robots Exclusion, and Sitemaps and Site Indexes.

The Site Analysis module analyzes the content of a Web site and reports suggestions on how to optimize content, structure, and URLs for search engines.

The Robots Exclusion module enables Web site administrators to manage the content of the *robots.txt* file right from the IIS Manager interface. Created by a site administrator, the file *robots.txt* contains instructions for search engines regarding which directories and files in the site should not be touched and indexed.

Finally, the Sitemaps and Site Indexes module manages the sitemap files (and indexes) at the site, application, and folder level. This ensures that the sitemap file doesn't contain broken links and search engines always access fresh and up-to-date navigation information.

Site Navigation

A good navigation system is a fundamental asset for any Web site—for both its human users and search engines. A good navigation system enables any user at any time to know where she is, where she has come from, and where she can go.

A navigation system always appears in the same position within all pages; this makes it a good fit for a master page. It is made of well-described links in which the text inside the anchor is quite clear about the final destination. Links are preferably emphasized using some

CSS style and are a static part of the page. The more you use JavaScript, the more you can create appealing menus. However, the more you require from the equipment of your users, the more likely you will be to raise SEO issues and screen-reader issues for users with disabilities. These are the possible drawbacks of excessive use of JavaScript in the navigation system of a page. Finally, a navigation system should always provide an easy-to-reach link to the home page. A visitor might not land at your site from the main door, so once the user is there, you might want to show him the way to the home page.

In ASP.NET, the site navigation API allows you to define the map of the site and provide a declarative description of how it is laid out. By using the site navigation API, you define the hierarchy of pages you have and group them to form sections and subsections of the site. ASP.NET caches this information and makes it programmatically accessible at run time. With site navigation, you store links to pages in a central location and can optionally bind those links to navigation controls, such as the *TreeView* and *Menu* controls. In addition, as mentioned, a link-based map of the site helps search engines considerably.

ASP.NET site navigation offers a number of features, including site maps to describe the logical structure of the site, site map providers to physically store the contents of a map and optional security access rules, and a bunch of controls to display site map information through navigation components. In this section, we discuss how to define, configure, and consume site map information.

Defining Site Map Information

You start by defining the list of constituent pages and relationships between them. Exposed in a standard way, this information then will be easily consumed by site navigation controls and reflected by page output. By default, the site map is expressed through an XML file, usually named *web.sitemap*. (Thanks to the provider model, however, alternative data sources are possible.)

Site map information is retrieved via the currently selected site map provider. The default site map provider is registered in the root configuration file as an instance of the *XmlSiteMapProvider* class:

```
<siteMap>
   <providers>
      <add name="AspNetXmlSiteMapProvider"
           siteMapFile="web.sitemap"
           type="System.Web.XmlSiteMapProvider, System.Web, ... " />
   </providers>
</siteMap>
```

As you can see, the schema contains a *siteMapFile* attribute through which you indicate the name of the source file where site map information can be read from. In spite of the extension, the file must be an XML file validated against a given schema. Note that the *XmlSiteMapProvider* class doesn't handle files with an extension other than *.sitemap*. Finally, note that the *XmlSiteMapProvider* class detects changes to the site map file and dynamically updates the site map to reflect changes.

Located in the application's root directory, the *web.sitemap* file organizes the pages in the site hierarchically. It can reference other site map providers or other site map files in other directories in the same application. Here's a sample site map file that attempts to describe a Web site to navigate through the contents of the book:

```
<siteMap>
   <siteMapNode title="My Book" url="default.aspx">
      <siteMapNode title="Introduction" url="intro.aspx" />
      <siteMapNode title="Acknowledgements" url="ack.aspx" />
         <siteMapNode title="References" url="ref.aspx" />
      </siteMapNode>
      <siteMapNode title="Chapters" url="toc.aspx" />
      <siteMapNode title="ASP.NET at a glance" url="ch01.aspx" />
      <siteMapNode title="HTTP Handlers and Modules" url="ch02.aspx" />
         ...
      </siteMapNode>
      <siteMapNode title="Appendix" url="appendix.aspx">
      <siteMapNode title="Sample Code" url="samples.aspx" />
         ...
      </siteMapNode>
   </siteMapNode>
</siteMap>
```

A site map XML file is composed of a collection of *<siteMapNode>* elements rooted in a *<siteMap>* node. Each page in the Web site is represented with a *<siteMapNode>* element. Hierarchies can be created by nesting *<siteMapNode>* elements, as in the preceding code snippets. In most cases, the root *<siteMap>* node contains just one child *<siteMapNode>* element, even though this is not a strict rule hard-coded in the schema of the XML file. All URLs linked from the site map file should belong to the same application using the file. Also in this case, though, exceptions are acceptable. In other words, you are allowed to specify links to pages in other applications, but the site navigation API won't check these links. As long as links belong to the same application, the API can verify them and return design-time errors if there are broken links.

Table 8-4 lists the feasible attributes of the *<siteMapNode>* element.

TABLE 8-4 Attributes of the *<siteMapNode>* Element

Attribute	Description
description	Defines the text used to describe the page. This text is used to add a ToolTip to the page link in a *SiteMapPath* control (discussed later) and as documentation.
provider	String that indicates the site map provider to use to fill the current node.
resourceKey	Indicates the name of the resource key used to localize a given node of the site map.

Attribute	Description
roles	String that indicates the roles that users must have to view this page.
siteMapFile	Indicates the name of the site map file to use to fill the current node.
title	Defines the text used as the text of the link to the page.
url	Defines the URL of the page.

The *roles* attribute is key to implementing a feature known as *security trimming*. Security trimming essentially refers to the site map API capability of preventing unauthorized users from viewing pages that require a particular role.

In addition to using the attributes listed in Table 8-4, you can use custom attributes too. You cannot use custom nodes. A *.sitemap* file can contain only *<siteMapNode>* elements and a *<siteMap>* root node.

Site Map Providers

The site navigation subsystem is provider based, meaning that you can use custom providers to define some site map contents. A custom site map provider reads information from a different storage medium, be it another XML file with a distinct schema, a text file or, perhaps, a database. A custom site map provider is a class that inherits from *SiteMapProvider* or, better yet, from an intermediate class named *StaticSiteMapProvider*.

Note that you can optionally use multiple providers at the same time. For example, by setting the *provider* attribute on a *<siteMapNode>* node, you instruct the site map subsystem to use that site map provider to retrieve nodes to insert at that point of the hierarchy.

```
<siteMap>
    <siteMapNode title="Intro" url="intro.aspx" >
        <siteMapNode title="Acknowledgements" url="ack.aspx" />
        <siteMapNode title="References" url="ref.aspx" />
    </siteMapNode>
    <siteMapNode provider="SimpleTextSiteMapProvider" />
    ...
</siteMap>
```

The additional provider must be registered in the configuration file and feature all information needed to connect to its own data source. Here's an example for the sample text file provider:

```
<system.web>
    <siteMap defaultProvider="XmlSiteMapProvider">
        <providers>
            <add name="SimpleTextSiteMapProvider"
                type="SimpleTextSiteMapProvider, Samples"
                siteMapFile="MySiteMap.txt" />
        </providers>
    </siteMap>
</system.web>
```

The *<siteMapNode>* linked to the *SimpleTextSiteMapProvider* component will contain all the nodes as defined in the *MySiteMap.txt* file. Reading and parsing to nodes any information in *MySiteMap.txt* is the responsibility of the custom provider. As a result, you have a site map file that uses two providers at the same time: the default *XmlSiteMapProvider* and the custom *SimpleTextSiteMapProvider*.

Creating the map of a site is only the first step. Once it is created, in fact, this information must be easily and programmatically accessible. Although most of the time you consume site information through a bunch of ad hoc controls, it's useful to take a look at the class that acts as the official container of site map information—the *SiteMap* class. When an ASP.NET application runs, the site map structure is exposed through a global instance of the *SiteMap* class.

The *SiteMap* Class

Defined in the *System.Web* assembly and namespace, the *SiteMap* class has only static members. It exposes a collection of node objects that contain properties for each node in the map. The class is instantiated and populated when the application starts up; the data loaded is cached and refreshed care of the provider. In particular, the XML site map provider monitors the site map file for changes and refreshes itself accordingly.

Table 8-5 shows and describes the syntax and behavior of the members featured by the *SiteMap* class.

TABLE 8-5 Members of the *SiteMap* Class

Member	Description
CurrentNode	A property that returns the *SiteMapNode* object that represents the currently requested page.
Enabled	A property that indicates whether a site map provider is enabled.
Provider	A property that returns the *SiteMapProvider* object that indicates the provider being used for the current site map.
Providers	A property that returns a read-only collection of *SiteMapProvider* objects that are available to the application.
RootNode	A property that returns a *SiteMapNode* object that represents the root page of the navigation structure built for the site.
SiteMapResolve	An event that occurs when the *CurrentNode* property is accessed. Whether this event is really raised or not depends on the particular provider being used. It does fire for the default site map provider.

The *SiteMap* class retrieves the *CurrentNode* property by making a request to the provider. A null value is returned if no node exists for the requested page in the site map, or if role information for the current user doesn't match the role enabled on the node.

The *SiteMapPath* Control

A site map path is the overall combination of text and links that appears in some pages to in-dicate the path from the home page to the displayed resource—the classic page *breadcrumb*. (See Figure 8-11.)

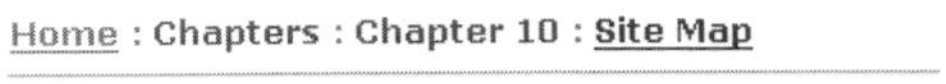

<u>Home</u> : Chapters : Chapter 10 : <u>Site Map</u>

FIGURE 8-11 Path to the currently displayed page.

ASP.NET provides a made-to-measure navigation path control—the *SiteMapPath* control—that supports many options for customizing the appearance of the links.

SiteMapPath reflects node data supplied by the *SiteMap* object. The control takes limited space in the page and makes parent pages of the current page only one click away. Table 8-6 shows the properties supported by the *SiteMapPath* control.

TABLE 8-6 Properties of the *SiteMapPath* Control

Method	Description
CurrentNodeStyle	The style used to render the display text of the current node
CurrentNodeTemplate	The template to use to represent the current node in the site navigation path
NodeStyle	The style used to render the display text for all nodes in the site navigation path
NodeTemplate	The template used to represent all the functional nodes in the site navigation path
ParentLevelsDisplayed	The number of levels of parent nodes displayed, relative to the current node
PathDirection	Gets or sets the order for rendering the nodes in the navigation path
PathSeparator	The string used to delimit nodes in the rendered navigation path
PathSeparatorStyle	The style used for the *PathSeparator* string
PathSeparatorTemplate	The template used to render the delimiter of a site navigation path
Provider	The site map provider object associated with the control
RenderCurrentNodeAsLink	If set, causes the control to render the current node as a hyperlink
RootNodeStyle	The style for the display text of the root node
RootNodeTemplate	The template used for the root node of a site navigation path
ShowToolTips	If set, displays a ToolTip when the mouse hovers over a hyperlinked node
SiteMapProvider	Gets or sets the name of the site map provider object used to render the site navigation control
SkipLinkText	Gets or sets the value used to render alternate text for screen readers to skip the control's content

The *SiteMapPath* control works by taking the URL of the current page and populating an instance of the *SiteMapNode* class with information obtained from the site map. Retrieved information includes the URL, title, description, and location of the page in the navigation hierarchy. The node is then rendered out as a sequence of templates—mostly hyperlinks—styled as appropriate.

No code is required to use a *SiteMapPath* control. All that you have to do is place the following markup in the *.aspx* source file:

```
<asp:SiteMapPath ID="SiteMapPath1" runat="server"
        RenderCurrentNodeAsLink="True" PathSeparator=" : " >
    <PathSeparatorStyle Font-Bold="true" />
    <NodeStyle Font-Bold="true" />
    <RootNodeStyle Font-Bold="true" />
</asp:SiteMapPath>
```

As you can guess, style properties in the preceding markup are not essential to make the control work and can be omitted for brevity.

> **Note** Style properties that most ASP.NET server controls expose represent the heart of the ongoing conflict between themes and CSS styles. Style properties form an alternate—in a way, a higher level—syntax to style controls. In the end, it boils down to a sort of architecture choice: if you choose to go with server controls, use style properties (and themes), but at that point ignore CSS and client-side configurations. Otherwise, ignore themes and style properties and take more care of the emitted markup. In this case, however, are you sure you're still OK with ASP.NET Web Forms?

Configuring the Site Map

There are various ways to further configure the site map file to address specific real-world scenarios. For example, you can tie together distinct site map files, localize the title and description of pages, and serve each user a site map that complies with his or her roles in the application's security infrastructure. Let's tackle each of these situations.

Using Multiple Site Map Files

As mentioned, the default site map provider reads its information from the *web.sitemap* file located in the application's root directory. Additional *.sitemap* files written according to the same XML schema can be used to describe portions of the site.

The idea is that each *<siteMapNode>* element can define its subtree either explicitly by listing all child nodes or implicitly by referencing an external *.sitemap* file, as shown here:

```
<siteMap>
   <siteMapNode title="My Book" url="default.aspx">
```

```
        <siteMapNode siteMapFile="introduction.sitemap" />
        <siteMapNode siteMapFile="chapters.sitemap" />
        <siteMapNode siteMapFile="appendix.sitemap" />
   </siteMapNode>
</siteMap>
```

The content of each of the child site map files is injected in the final tree representation of the data at the exact point where the link appears in the root *web.sitemap* file. Child site map files can be located in child directories if you desire. The value assigned to the *siteMapFile* attribute is the virtual path of the file in the context of the current application.

Note that in this case all site map files are processed by the same site map provider component—the default *XmlSiteMapProvider* component. In the previous section, we examined a scenario where different providers were used to process distinct sections of the site map. The two features are not mutually exclusive and, in the end, you can have a default site map file that spans multiple *.sitemap* files, with portions of it provided by a different provider. In this case, as you've seen, all settings for the custom provider must be set in the *web.config* file.

Securing ASP.NET Site Maps

Most Web sites require that only certain members be allowed to see certain pages. How should you specify that in a site map? The most effective and efficient approach is using roles. Basically, you associate each node in the site map with a list of authorized roles, and the ASP.NET infrastructure guarantees that no unauthorized users will ever view that page through the site map. This approach is advantageous because you define roles and map them to users once—for security purposes and membership—and use them also for site maps.

A feature known as *site map security trimming* provides a way to hide navigational links in a site map based on security roles. Enabled on the site map provider and individual nodes, security trimming serves user-specific views of a site. It does only that, though. It hides links from view whenever the content of the site map is displayed through hierarchical UI controls such as *TreeView* and *Menu*. However, it doesn't block users from accessing pages by typing the URL in the address bar of the browser or following links from other pages. For ensuring that unauthorized users don't access pages, you need to configure roles and bind them to the identity of the connected user. (See Chapter 19, "ASP.NET Security.")

By default, nonprogrammatic access to *.sitemap* files is protected and results in a forbidden resource ASP.NET exception. Be aware of this, if you plan to replace the default site map configuration and use files with a custom extension. In this case, make sure you explicitly prohibit access to these files through IIS. To further improve security, grant NETWORK SERVICE or ASPNET—the ASP.NET runtime accounts—read-only access to these custom site map files. If you store site maps in a database, configure any involved tables to make them accessible to the smallest number of accounts with the least possible set of privileges.

> **Note** An excessively large site map file can use a lot of memory and CPU. Aside from a possible performance hit, this situation configures a potential security risk in a hosted environment. By restricting the size of site maps for a Web site, you better protect your site against denial-of-service attacks.

Localizing Site Map Information

There are a few properties that you can localize in a site map. They are *Title*, *Description*, and all custom properties. You can use an explicit or implicit expression to localize the property. First of all, though, you should enable localization by adding a Boolean attribute to the *<siteMap>* node:

```
<siteMap enableLocalization="true">
    ...
</siteMap>
```

Localizing site map properties consists of binding properties with *$Resources* expressions. You can explicitly bind the attribute to a global resource or have it implicitly associated with a value that results from a local resource key. Here's an example of explicit expressions:

```
<siteMap enableLocalization="true">
    <siteMapNode
        url="~/homepage.aspx"
        title="$Resources:MyLocalizations,HomePage" />
    ...
</siteMap>
```

An explicit expression is a *$Resources* expression that points to a global *.resx* file and extracts a value by name from there. If the *MyLocalizations.resx* file contains an entry named HomePage, the value will be read and assigned to the attribute. If it isn't there, an implicit expression takes over.

An implicit expression takes values out of a local resource file. The localizable *<siteMapNode>* is associated with a resource key and all of its localizable properties are defined in the RESX file as entries named after the following pattern:

```
[resourceKey].[Attribute]
```

The following site map snippet shows how to use implicit expressions:

```
<siteMap enableLocalization="true">
    <siteMapNode
        resourceKey="Home"
        url="~/homepage.aspx"
        description="default"
        title="default" />
    ...
</siteMap>
```

In this case, the resource file has the same name of the *.sitemap* file plus the *.resx* extension. In the default case, it will be *web.sitemap.resx*. This file is expected to contain entries named *Home.description* and *Home.title*. If these exist, their values will be used to determine the value of the *title* and *description* attributes. In the case of implicit expressions, the values that localizable attributes might have in the *.sitemap* file are considered default values to be used in case of trouble with the localized resource files.

> **Note** A *.resx* file contains resource values for the default culture. To specify resources for a particular language and culture (say, French), you have to change the extension to *fr.resx* because *fr* is the identifier of the French culture. Similar prefixes exist for most of the languages and cultures.

Localizing the Site Navigation Structure

What if you want to adapt the navigation structure to a given locale? Unfortunately, the *Url* property cannot be localized in a site map in the same way as the *Title* and *Description* properties. If you want to change URLs, or perhaps change the structure of the site, you create a distinct site map for each supported culture and register all of them in the configuration file:

```
<siteMap defaultProvider="XmlSiteMapProvider">
    <providers>
        <add name="DefaultSiteMap"
            type="System.Web.XmlSiteMapProvider"
            siteMapFile="default.sitemap" />
        <add name="FrenchSiteMap"
            type="System.Web.XmlSiteMapProvider"
            siteMapFile="fr.sitemap" />
        ...
        <add name="ItalianSiteMap"
            type="System.Web.XmlSiteMapProvider"
            siteMapFile="it.sitemap" />
    </providers>
</siteMap>
```

Essentially, you have multiple providers of the same type—*XmlSiteMapProvider*—but working on distinct site map files. When you access site map information programmatically, you can specify which site map you want to use. (I'll say more about this in a moment.)

> **Note** You use *.resx* files as previously discussed to localize site maps as long as you're using the default provider and the XML *.sitemap* provider. If you use a custom provider, say a database-driven provider, you're totally responsible for setting up a localization mechanism.

Testing the Page

More often than not, Web sites are planned and created by developers and designers without much assistance from usability experts. So the site might look great and have great content but still end up being hard to work with for the real users. Designers and developers are clearly power users of a Web site, but can the same be said for the intended audience of the site? A fundamental item in any usability checklist must be "Test the site on real users."

Beyond that, you have the problem of ensuring that each page behave as expected and react as expected to users' solicitations. This is another facet of testing—definitely a more developer-oriented facet.

To effectively test the site on real users and test the functionality of pages, tools are required. Tools to help test Web pages are a hot new field in the industry.

Testing the Logic of the Page

An ASP.NET Web Forms page results from the combined effect of a view template (ASPX) and a code-behind class. The code-behind class is responsible for any logic you want the page to expose. Testing a code-behind class is a matter of writing the code with testability in mind and then using a unit-testing tool such as the MSTest environment integrated in Microsoft Visual Studio 2010. (In Chapter 12, "Custom Controls," I'll return to design principles and testability.)

The logic of the page is also responsible for the actual markup being sent to the browser. What is this markup? Is it relatively static? Or is it rich with JavaScript and dynamic behavior? If you consider the structure of the page trivial or just static, it might suffice that you ensure the correct data is assigned to server controls in the view template. This is not hard to figure out from a bunch of unit tests.

If the structure of the page might differ depending on run-time conditions or parameters, you probably need to look around for some tools that help you test the front end of a Web application.

Testing the Client-Side Behavior of the Page

Testing the front end of a Web application goes beyond classic unit testing and requires ad hoc tools. In this regard, ASP.NET Web Forms is not much different from ASP.NET MVC, or even from Java or PHP Web applications.

You need a tool that allows you to programmatically define a sequence of typical user actions and observe the resulting DOM tree. In other words, you want to test the layout and content of the response when the user performs a given series of actions.

Such tools have recording features, and they keep track of user actions as they are performed and store them as a reusable script to play back. Some tools also offer you the ability to edit test scripts or write them from scratch. Here's a sample test program written for one of the most popular of these front-end test tools—WatiN. The program tests the sample page we discussed earlier with a drop-down list and a grid

```
public class SampleViewTests
{
    private Process webServer;

    [TestInitialize]
    public void Setup()
    {
        webServer = new Process();
        webServer.StartInfo.FileName = "WebDev.WebServer.exe";
        string path = ...;
        webServer.StartInfo.Arguments = String.Format(
                "/port:8080 /path: {0}", path);

        webServer.Start();
    }

    [TestMethod]
    public void CheckIfNicknameIsNotUsed()
    {
        using (IE ie = new IE("http://localhost:8080/Samples/Datagrid"))
        {
            // Select a particular customer ID
            ie.SelectList("ddCustomerList").Option("1").Select();

            // Check the resulting HTML on first row, second cell
            Assert.AreEqual(
                    "A Bike Store",
                    ie.Table(Find.ById("gridOrders").TableRow[0].TableCells[1].InnerHtml));
        }
    }

    [TestCleanup]
    public void TearDown()
    {
        webServer.Kill();
    }
}
```

The testing tool triggers the local Web server and points it to the page of choice. Next, it simulates some user actions and checks the resulting HTML.

Different tools might support a different syntax and might integrate with different environments and in different ways. However, the previous example gives you the gist of what it means to test the front end.

Web UI testing tools can be integrated as extensions into browsers (for example, Firefox), but they also offer an API for you to write test applications in C# or test harnesses using MSTest, NUnit, or other test frameworks. Table 8-7 lists a few popular tools.

TABLE 8-7 Tools for Testing a Web Front End

Tools	More information
ArtOfTest	*http://www.artoftest.com/home.aspx*
Selenium	*http://seleniumhq.org*
Visual Studio 2010 Coded UI Tests	*http://msdn.microsoft.com/en-us/library/dd286726.aspx*
WatiN	*http://watin.sourceforge.net*

Testing Posted Data

In ASP.NET MVC, testing the actual behavior of code-behind classes is relatively easy if you refactor the code to take that code out to a controller or a presenter. However, each method you test is expected to receive a bunch of parameters, either through the signature or via ASP.NET intrinsic objects.

How can you test that the browser really passes in correct data? In other words, how can you test posted data.

Sending automated POST requests to a URL is a feature that all the tools in Table 8-7 support. They all let you fill in and post a form. However, in that case, at least, the local Web server must be up and running. Posting to test pages that do nothing but return a Boolean answer (expected/unexpected) is a possible way to speed up things.

If you want to simply look at what is being transmitted, you can turn your attention to tools such as Fiddler (*http://www.fiddler2.com/fiddler2*) or HttpWatch (*http://www.httpwatch.com*).

> **Note** ASP.NET Web Forms was not designed with testability in mind. You can still test Web pages but at the cost of spinning up the entire ASP.NET runtime; or, more likely, you will reduce your efforts to just testing what's strictly necessary at the code-behind level. The tools in Table 8-7 address, instead, the need to test the client user interface and simulate user actions that result in posted data.

Summary

A Web page is a special type of a standalone component that has the additional tricky requirement of being able to work with the rest of the site. Amazingly, this generates a bunch of extra work because developers, architects, and designers must cooperate to produce a common and appealing look and feel, ease of maintenance, consistent rendering, navigation capabilities, and personalization capabilities. All around, there's room for a new professional with ad hoc and somewhat unique skills, such as Web testers and SEO and usability experts.

A successful Web site results from a usable composition of pages, which in turn result from a consistent composition of UI blocks. In this chapter, we first reviewed the technologies for page composition that you find available in ASP.NET (primarily, master pages), and then we moved toward other side topics, such as cross-browser rendering, search-engine optimization navigation, and UI testing.

In the next chapter, we'll complete the basics of the Web page by looking at input forms.

Chapter 9

ASP.NET Input Forms

It's not enough that we do our best; sometimes we have to do what's required.

—Winston Churchill

Although formless pages are still accepted and correctly handled, the typical ASP.NET Web Forms page contains a single *<form>* tag decorated with the *runat* attribute set to *server*. During server-side processing, such a *<form>* tag is mapped to an instance of the *HtmlForm* class. The *HtmlForm* class acts as the outermost container of all server controls and wraps them in a plain HTML *<form>* element when the page is rendered. The resulting HTML form posts to the same page URL. By design, it doesn't give you any chance to set the action URL programmatically, and for this reason it is often said to be *reentrant*. The default method used to submit form data is *POST*, but *GET* can be used as well.

In most cases, the server form is the outermost tag of the page and is contained directly in *<body>*. In general, though, the server *<form>* tag can be the child of any other server container control, such as *<table>*, *<div>*, *<body>*, and any other HTML generic control. (I covered HTML controls and Web controls in Chapter 6, "ASP.NET Core Server Controls.") If any noncontainer server controls (for example, a *TextBox*) are placed outside the form tag, an exception is thrown as the page executes—no check is made at compile time. The exception is raised by the control itself when the host page begins to render. Noncontainer Web controls, in fact, check whether they are being rendered within the boundaries of a server form and throw an *HttpException* if they are not. A call to the *Page*'s *VerifyRenderingInServerForm* method does the job. (Be aware of this virtuous behavior when you get to writing custom controls.)

In this chapter, we'll examine some aspects of form-based programming in ASP.NET, including how to use multiple forms in the same page and post data to a different page. We'll also touch on input validation and validation controls.

Programming with Forms

One of the most common snags Web developers face when they first approach the ASP.NET lifestyle is the fact that managed Web applications support the single-form interface model. In the single-form interface model, each page always posts to itself and doesn't supply any hook for developers to set the final destination of the postback. What in HTML programming is the *Action* property of the form is simply not defined on the ASP.NET *HtmlForm* class. By default, each ASP.NET page can post only to itself, unless some specific API extensions are used to perform a cross-page post. Unlike the action URL, the HTTP method and the target frame of the post can be programmatically adjusted using ad hoc *HtmlForm* properties—*Method* and *Target*.

The *HtmlForm* Class

The *HtmlForm* class inherits from *HtmlContainerControl*, which provides the form with the capability of containing child controls. This capability is shared with other HTML control classes, such as *HtmlTable*, characterized by child elements and a closing tag.

Properties of the *HtmlForm* Class

The *HtmlForm* class provides programmatic access to the HTML *<form>* element on the server through the set of properties shown in Table 9-1. Note that the table includes only a few of the properties *HtmlForm* inherits from the root class *Control*.

TABLE 9-1 Form Property

Property	Description
Attributes	Inherited from *Control*, gets a name/value collection with all the attributes declared on the tag.
ClientID	Inherited from *Control*, gets the value of *UniqueID*.
Controls	Inherited from *Control*, gets a collection object that represents the child controls of the form.
DefaultButton	String property, gets or sets the button control to display as the default button on the form.
DefaultFocus	String property, gets or sets the button control to give input focus when the form is displayed.
Disabled	Gets or sets a value indicating whether the form is disabled. It matches the *disabled* HTML attribute.
EncType	Gets or sets the encoding type. It matches the *enctype* HTML attribute.
ID	Inherited from *Control*, gets or sets the programmatic identifier of the form. The default value is *aspnetForm*.
InnerHtml	Inherited from *HtmlContainerControl*, gets or sets the markup content found between the opening and closing tags of the form.
InnerText	Inherited from *HtmlContainerControl*, gets or sets the text between the opening and closing tags of the form.
Method	Gets or sets a value that indicates how a browser posts form data to the server. The default value is *POST*. It can be set to *GET* if needed.
Name	Gets the value of *UniqueID*.
Style	Gets a collection of all cascading style sheet (CSS) properties applied to the form.
SubmitDisabledControls	Indicates whether to force controls disabled on the client to submit their values, allowing them to preserve their values after the page posts back to the server. *False* by default.

Property	Description
TagName	Returns "form".
Target	Gets or sets the name of the frame or window to render the HTML generated for the page.
UniqueID	Inherited from *Control*, gets the unique, fully qualified name of the form.
Visible	Gets or sets a value that indicates whether the form is rendered. If this property is set to *false*, the form is not rendered to HTML.

The form must have a unique name. If the programmer doesn't assign the name, ASP.NET uses a default name—aspnetForm. The programmer can set the form's identifier by using either the *ID* or *Name* property. If both are set, the *ID* attribute takes precedence. (Note, though, that any reliance on the *Name* attribute compromises the XHTML compliance of the page.)

The parent object of the form is the outer container control with the *runat* attribute. If such a control doesn't exist, the page object is set as the parent. Typical containers for the server form are *<table>* and *<div>* if they are marked as server-side objects.

By default, the *Method* property is set to *POST*. The value of the property can be modified programmatically. If the form is posted through the *GET* method, all form data is passed on the URL's query string. However, if you choose the *GET* method, make sure the size allowed for a *GET* request does not affect the integrity of your application or raise security issues.

Methods of the *HtmlForm* Class

Table 9-2 lists the methods available on the *HtmlForm* class that you'll be using more often. All the methods listed in the table are inherited from the base *System.Web.UI.Control* class.

TABLE 9-2 Form Methods

Method	Description
ApplyStyleSheetSkin	Applies the style properties defined in the page style sheet.
DataBind	Calls the *DataBind* method on all child controls.
FindControl	Retrieves and returns the control that matches the specified ID.
Focus	Sets input focus to a control.
HasControls	Indicates whether the form contains any child controls.
RenderControl	Outputs the HTML code for the form. If tracing is enabled, it caches tracing information to be rendered later, at the end of the page.

Note that the *FindControl* method searches only among the form's direct children. Controls belonging to an inner naming container, or that are a child of a form's child control, are not found.

Multiple Forms

As mentioned, the single-form model is the default in ASP.NET and plays a key role in the automatic view state management mechanism I described in Chapter 5, "Anatomy of an ASP.NET Page." Generally speaking, the ASP.NET's enforcement of the single-form model does not significantly limit the programming power, and all things considered, doing without multiple forms is not a big sacrifice. Some pages, though, would have a more consistent and natural design if they could define multiple *logical* forms. In this context a *logical* form is a logically related group of input controls. For example, think of a page that provides some information to users but also needs to supply an additional form such as a search or login box.

You can incorporate search and login capabilities in ad hoc classes and call those classes from within the page the user has displayed. This might or might not be the right way to factor your code, though. Especially if you're porting some old code to ASP.NET, you might find it easier to insulate login or search code in a dedicated page. Well, to take advantage of form-based login, how do you post input data to this page?

Using HTML Forms

As mentioned, ASP.NET prevents you from having multiple *<form>* tags flagged with the *runat* attribute. However, nothing prevents you from having one server-side *<form>* tag and multiple client HTML *<form>* elements in the body of the same Web form. Here's an example:

```
<body>
    <table><tr><td>
        <form id="form1" runat="server">
        <h2>Ordinary contents for an ASP.NET page</h2>
        </form>
    </td>
    <td>
        <form method="post" action="search.aspx">
            <table><tr>
                <td>Keyword</td>
                <td><input type="text" id="Keyword" name="Keyword" /></td>
            </tr><tr>
                <td><input type="submit" id="Go" value="Search" /></td>
            </tr></table>
        </form>
    </td>
    </tr></table>
</body>
```

The page contains two forms, one of which is a classic HTML form devoid of the *runat* attribute and, as such, completely ignored by ASP.NET. The markup served to the browser simply contains two *<form>* elements, each pointing to a different action URL.

This code works just fine but has a major drawback: you can't use the ASP.NET programming model to retrieve posted data in the action page of the client form. When writing search. aspx, in fact, you can't rely on view state to retrieve posted values. To know what's been posted, you must resort to the old-fashioned, but still effective, ASP model, as shown in the following code sample:

```
public partial class Search : System.Web.UI.Page
{
    protected void Page_Load(object sender, EventArgs e)
    {
        // Use the Request object to retrieve posted data
        var textToSearch = Request.Form["Keyword"];
        ...

        // Use standard ASP.NET programming model to populate the page UI
        KeywordBeingUsed.Text = textToSearch;
    }
}
```

You use the protocol-specific collections of the *Request* object to retrieve posted data—*Form* if POST is used, and *QueryString* in case of GET. In addition, you have to use the *name* attribute to identify input elements. Overall, this is perhaps not a recommended approach, but it definitely works. Figure 9-1 shows the page in action.

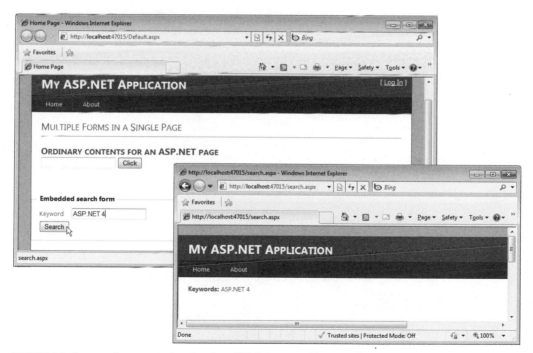

FIGURE 9-1 A server form control and a client HTML form working together.

When the user clicks the Search button, the *search.aspx* page is invoked, the page receives only the values posted through the HTML form, and it uses them to proceed.

Nested HTML Forms

In ASP.NET, most real-world pages are based on master pages. And most of the time the master page includes an outermost *<form>* tag. This means that if you add a client HTML form element at rendering time the two form elements will be nested.

Now nesting forms is possible in theory, but browsers don't actually render nested forms properly. The HTML 4 standard prevents direct form-to-form dependency. You are beyond the standard if you add a form element as the direct child of another form. Instead, if you embed the child form within a block element (DIV, FIELDSET), it is considered valid from a syntax point of view. As mentioned, though, the fact is that, regardless of what the World Wide Web Consortium (W3C) believes, browsers just glue the content of the two forms together. As a result, the outermost parent form determines where the post is made.

Nicely enough, although browsers actually seem to produce the same final effect—the content of the inner forms merged with the outermost ones—how that happens is slightly different. For example, if you display a page with nested forms in Firefox 3.6.x, you find out that the child *<form>* tags are just stripped off. The form content, on the other hand, is preserved. With Internet Explorer 8, the child *<form>* tag is preserved but it's closed inline, keeping any content out of it and subsequently merging it to the outermost form.

The code that produces the pages shown in Figure 9-1 descends from the standard ASP.NET 4 template for Web Forms pages with a master. However, because the master contains a *<form>* tag, I had to rework the master template to be able to use side-by-side *<form>* tags and avoid nesting.

```
<body>
    <div class="page">
      <form id="Form1" runat="server">
        ...

        <div class="main">
          <asp:ContentPlaceHolder ID="MainContent" runat="server" />
        </div>
      </form>

      <asp:ContentPlaceHolder ID="ExtraFormContent" runat="server" />

      <div class="clear">
      </div>
      <div class="footer">
      </div>
    </div>
</body>
```

The client HTML form element fits into the *ExtraFormContent* placeholder.

All in all, nested HTML forms are a nonissue—you just don't use them. However, a common pitfall in ASP.NET development is that because of master pages you inadvertently end up with nested forms in an attempt to add a second innocent client HTML form.

Multiple Server *<form>* Tags on a Page

ASP.NET makes it quite clear: you just can't have multiple server forms in the same Web page. Given the dynamics of page rendering, an exception is thrown if more than one *HtmlForm* control attempts to render. (See Figure 9-2.)

FIGURE 9-2 Using multiple server forms in a page throws a rendering exception.

A little-known fact is that a Web form can actually contain as many server-side forms as needed as long as *only one* at a time is visible. For example, a page with, say, three *<form runat=server>* tags is allowed, but only one form can be actually rendered. By playing with the *Visible* property of the *HtmlForm* class, you can change the active server form during the page lifetime.

This trick doesn't really let you have multiple active forms at the same time, but it can be helpful sometimes because it allows you to change the active server form over postback events. Let's consider the following ASP.NET page:

```
<body>
    <form id="step0" runat="server" visible="true">
        <h1>Welcome</h1>
        <asp:textbox runat="server" id="Textbox1" />
        <asp:button ID="Button1" runat="server" text="Step #1"
            OnClick="Button1_Click" />
    </form>

    <form id="step1" runat="server" visible="false">
        <h1>Step #1</h1>
        <asp:textbox runat="server" id="Textbox2" />
        <asp:button ID="Button2" runat="server" text="Previous step"
            OnClick="Button2_Click" />
        <asp:button ID="Button3" runat="server" text="Step #2"
            OnClick="Button3_Click" />
    </form>

    <form id="step2" runat="server" visible="false">
        <h1>Finalizing</h1>
        <asp:button ID="Button4" runat="server" text="Finish"
            OnClick="Button4_Click" />
    </form>
</body>
```

As you can see, all *<form>* tags are marked as *runat*, but only the first one is visible. Mutually exclusive forms were a cool way of implementing wizards in old versions of ASP.NET, before an official wizard control got introduced. By toggling a form's visibility in button event handlers, you can obtain a wizard-like behavior, as shown in Figure 9-3.

```
public partial class MultipleForms : System.Web.UI.Page
{
    protected void Page_Load(Object sender, EventArgs e)
    {
        Title = "Welcome";
    }
    protected void Button1_Click(Object sender, EventArgs e)
    {
        Title = "Step 1";
        step0.Visible = false;
        step1.Visible = true;
    }
    protected void Button2_Click(Object sender, EventArgs e)
    {
        step0.Visible = true;
        step1.Visible = false;
    }
```

```
    protected void Button3_Click(Object sender, EventArgs e)
    {
        Title = "Finalizing";
        step1.Visible = false;
        step2.Visible = true;
    }
    protected void Button4_Click(Object sender, EventArgs e)
    {
        Title = "Done";
        step2.Visible = false;
        Response.Write("<h1>Successfully done.</h1>");
    }
}
```

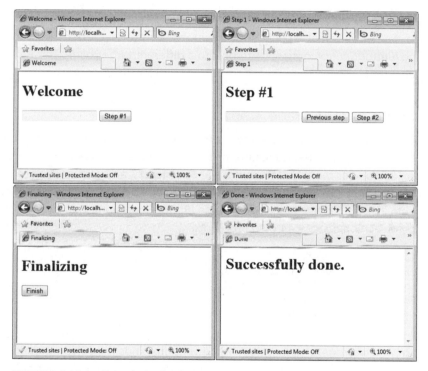

FIGURE 9-3 Mutually exclusive forms.

Multiple View and Wizards

If you're targeting ASP.NET 2.0 or newer, you might not need to resort to the preceding trick to switch between forms. You find two new controls—*MultiView* and *Wizard*—ready for the job. The *MultiView* control employs logic nearly identical to that of multiple exclusive forms, except that it relies on panels rather than full forms.

The *MultiView* control allows you to define multiple and mutually exclusive HTML panels. The control provides an application programming interface (API) for you to toggle the visibility of the various panels and ensure that exactly one is active and visible at a time. The

MultiView control doesn't provide a built-in user interface. The *Wizard* control is just that—a *MultiView* control plus some wizard-like predefined user interface (UI) blocks. I'll cover the *Wizard* control in great detail later in the chapter.

Cross-Page Postings

The ASP.NET framework offers a built-in mechanism to override the normal processing cycle and let the page post to another, distinct page. In general, postbacks occur in either of two ways—through a submit button or via script. The client browser usually takes on any post conducted through a button and automatically points to the page that the *action* attribute of the posting form indicates. A lot more of flexibility is possible when the post occurs via script.

In ASP.NET, however, you can also configure certain page controls—in particular, those that implement the *IButtonControl* interface—to post to a different target page. This is referred to as *cross-page posting*.

Posting Data to Another Page

Authoring a Web page that can post data to another page requires only a couple of steps. First, you choose the controls that can cause the postback and set their *PostBackUrl* property. A page can include one or more button controls and, generally, any combination of button controls and submit buttons. Notice that in this context a button control is any server control that implements *IButtonControl*. (I fully covered the *IButtonControl* interface in Chapter 6.) The following code snippet shows how to proceed:

```
<form id="form1" runat="server">
    <asp:textbox runat="server" id="Keyword" />
    <asp:button runat="server" id="buttonPost"
            Text="Click"
            PostBackUrl="search.aspx" />
</form>
```

When the *PostBackUrl* property is set, the ASP.NET runtime binds the corresponding HTML element of the button control to a new JavaScript function. Instead of using our old acquaintance *__doPostback*, it uses the new *WebForm_DoPostBackWithOptions* function. The button renders the following markup:

```
<input type="submit" name="buttonPost" id="buttonPost"
    value="Click"
    onclick="javascript:WebForm_DoPostBackWithOptions(
        new WebForm_PostBackOptions("buttonPost", "",
            false, "", "search.aspx", false, false))" />
```

As a result, when the user clicks the button, the current form posts its content to the specified target page. What about the view state? When the page contains a control that does cross-page posting, a new hidden field is also created—the __PREVIOUSPAGE field.

The field contains the view state information to be used to serve the request. This view state information is transparently used in lieu of the original view state of the page being posted to.

You use the *PreviousPage* property to reference the posting page and all of its controls. Here's the code behind a sample target page that retrieves the content of a text box defined in the form:

```
// This code belongs to doSearch.aspx
protected void Page_Load(Object sender, EventArgs e)
{
    // Ensure this is a cross-page postback
    if (PreviousPage == null)
    {
        Response.Write("Must be a cross-page post.");
        return;
    }

    // Retrieves posted data. This ensures PreviousPage is not null.
    var txt = (TextBox) PreviousPage.FindControl("Keyword");
    ...
}
```

By using the *PreviousPage* property on the *Page* class, you can access any input control defined on the posting page. Access to input controls is weakly typed and occurs indirectly through the services of the *FindControl* method. The problem here lies in the fact that the target page doesn't know anything about the type of the posting page. *PreviousPage* is declared as a property of type *Page* and, as such, it can't provide access to members specific to a derived page class.

Furthermore, note that *FindControl* looks up controls only in the current naming container. If the control you are looking for lives inside another control (say, a template), you must first get a reference to the container, and then search the container to find the control. This happens commonly when you employ master pages. To avoid using *FindControl* altogether, a different approach is required.

What about using the *dynamic* type in ASP.NET 4? It might work, but this solution also has a little drawback—the same drawback we encountered in Chapter 8, "Page Composition and Usability," for master pages. The problem is that you can't access, say, the *Keyword* text box control from within the posted page because the *Keyword* control is mapped as a protected member of the page class. The following code, therefore, throws an exception:

```
dynamic previousPage = PreviousPage;
var txt = previousPage.Keyword;    // Keyword is inaccessible due to its protection level
if (txt == null)
{
    ...
}
```

To fix this code, you need to define a public property on the posting page class that exposes as a public member whatever element you want to retrieve from within the posted page. It doesn't have to be the control reference; it is recommended that you expose just data. Here's an example:

```
public partial class Crosspage : System.Web.UI.Page
{
    public String SelectedKeywords
    {
        get { return Keyword.Text; }
    }
}
```

With this change, the following call will work:

```
dynamic previousPage = PreviousPage;
var keywords = previousPage.SelectedKeywords;
```

The *dynamic* type, though, involves falling down to the Dynamic Language Runtime (DLR) engine and should be used only when you really need dynamically resolved code. In this case, you can get an even more effective (and strongly typed) solution by resorting to a page directive.

The *@PreviousPageType* Directive

Let's say it up front. To retrieve values on the posting page, *FindControl* is your only safe option if you don't know in advance which page will be invoking your target. However, when you're using cross-page posting in the context of an application, chances are good that you know exactly who will be calling the page and how. In this case, you can take advantage of the *@PreviousPageType* directive to cause the target page's *PreviousPage* property to be typed to the source page class.

In the target page, you add the following directive:

```
<%@ PreviousPageType VirtualPath="crosspage.aspx" %>
```

The directive can accept either of two attributes—*VirtualPath* or *TypeName*. The former points to the URL of the posting page; the latter indicates the type of the calling page. The directive just shown makes the *PreviousPage* property on the target page class be of the same type as the page at the given path (or the specified type). This fact alone, though, is not sufficient to let you access input controls directly. Each page class contains protected members that represent child controls; unfortunately, you can't call a protected member of a class from an external class. (Only derived classes can access protected members of the parent class.)

To work around the issue, in the caller page you must add public properties that expose any information you want posted pages to access. For example, imagine that *crosspostpage.aspx* contains a *TextBox* named Keyword. To make it accessible from within a target page, you add the following code to the code-behind class:

```
public TextBox KeywordControl
{
    get { return Keyword; }
}
```

The new *KeywordControl* property on the page class wraps and exposes the internal text-box control. In light of this code, the target page can now execute the following code:

```
Response.Write(PreviousPage.KeywordControl.Text);
```

Although you can directly expose a control reference, it is preferable that you expose just the data the posted page needs to consume. This approach is based on the Law of Demeter, which essentially states that internal details of components should not be made public unless strictly required. Another way of looking at this is in light of the "Tell, don't ask principle": your posted page gets what it needs instead of asking for a property on a control.

Detecting Cross-Page Postings

Being the potential target of a cross-page call doesn't automatically make a target page a different kind of page all of a sudden. There's always the possibility that the target page is invoked on its own—for example, via hyperlinking. When this happens, the *PreviousPage* property returns *null* and other postback-related properties, such as *IsPostBack*, assume the usual values.

If you have such a dual page, you should insert some extra code to discern the page behavior. The following example shows a page that allows only cross-page access:

```
if (PreviousPage == null)
{
    Response.Write("Sorry, that's the wrong way to invoke me.");
    Response.End();
    return;
}
```

The *IsCrossPagePostBack* property on the *Page* class deserves a bit of attention. The property returns *true* if the current page has called another ASP.NET page. It goes without saying that *IsCrossPagePostBack* on the target page always returns *false*. Therefore, the following code is *not* equivalent to the one seen before:

```
if (!IsCrossPagePostBack)
{
    ...
}
```

To know whether the current page is being called from another page, you have to test the value of *IsCrossPagePostBack* on the page object returned by *PreviousPage*:

```
// PreviousPage is null in case of a normal request
if (!PreviousPage.IsCrossPagePostBack)
{
    ...
}
```

However, this code will inevitably throw an exception if the page is invoked in a normal way (that is, from the address bar or via hyperlinking, because *PreviousPage* is *null*). In the end, the simplest and most effective way to see whether a page is being invoked through cross-page postbacks is by checking *PreviousPage* against *null*.

Redirecting Users to Another Page

In addition to the *PostBackUrl* property of button controls, ASP.NET provides another mechanism for transferring control and values from one page to another—you can use the *Server.Transfer* method.

The URL of the new page is not reflected by the browser's address bar because the transfer takes place entirely on the server. The following code shows how to use the method to direct a user to another page:

```
protected void Button1_Click(object sender, EventArgs e)
{
    Server.Transfer("target.aspx");
}
```

Note that all the code that might be following the call to *Transfer* in the page is never executed. In the end, *Transfer* is just a page redirect method. However, it is particularly efficient for two reasons. First, no roundtrip to the client is requested as is the case, for example, with *Response.Redirect*. Second, the same *HttpApplication* that was serving the caller request is reused, thus limiting the impact on the ASP.NET infrastructure.

How can you retrieve values from within the transferred page?

You can use the same programming model as for cross-page postings and rely on a non-null *PreviousPage* property, DLR interaction, or the *@PreviousPageType* directive for strongly typed access to input fields. How can a page detect whether it's being called through a server transfer or through a cross-page postback? In both cases, *PreviousPage* is not null, but the *IsCrossPagePostBack* on the *PreviousPage* object is *true* for a cross-page posting and *false* in the case of a server transfer.

> **Important**   Passing values from one page to another is a task that can be accomplished in a variety of ways—using cross-page posting, server transfer, HTML forms, cookies, or query strings. Which one is the most effective? Cross-page posting and server transfer offer a familiar programming model but potentially move a significant chunk of data through the __PREVIOUSPAGE field. Whether this information is really needed depends on the characteristics of the target page. In many cases, the target page just needs to receive a few parameters to start working. If this is the case, HTML client forms might be more effective in terms of data being moved. HTML forms, though, require an ASP-like programming model.

Validation Controls

The first rule for writing more secure applications is ensuring you get the data right, before you actually start using it. Getting the data right requires you to pass any external input through a validation step. In ASP.NET, validation controls provide an easy-to-use mechanism to perform a variety of validation tasks, including testing for valid types, values within a given range, or required fields.

ASP.NET validation controls work on the server, but they can be configured to filter invalid input already on the client. This is accomplished using some JavaScript code that kicks in and performs validation as soon as the user tabs out of a monitored input field.

All ASP.NET validation controls inherit from the *BaseValidator* class which, in turn, descends from *Label*. All validators defined on a page are automatically grouped in the *Validators* collection of the *Page* class. You can validate them all in a single shot using the *Validate* method in the page class or individually by calling the *Validate* method on each validator. The *Validate* method sets the *IsValid* property both on the page and on the individual validator. The *IsValid* property indicates whether the user's entries match the requirements of the validators. The user's entry is validated when the *Validate* method is called and also whenever the page posts back.

> **Note**   Typical control members involved with input validation have been grouped in the *IValidator* interface that the *BaseValidator* class implements. The interface includes the *Validate* method and the *IsValid* and *ErrorMessage* properties.

Generalities of Validation Controls

Each validation control references an input control located elsewhere on the page. When the page is submitted, the content of the monitored server control is passed to the associated validation control for further processing. Each validation control performs a different type of verification. Table 9-3 shows the types of validation supported by the .NET Framework.

TABLE 9-3 Validation Controls in ASP.NET

Validation Control	Description
CompareValidator	Compares the user's entry against a fixed value by using a comparison operator such as *LessThan*, *Equal*, or *GreaterThan*. It can also compare against the value of a property in another control on the same page.
CustomValidator	Employs programmatically defined validation logic to check the validity of the user's entry. You use this validator when the other validators cannot perform the necessary validation and you want to provide custom code that validates the input.
RangeValidator	Ensures that the user's entry falls within a specified range. Lower and upper boundaries can be expressed as numbers, strings, or dates.
RegularExpressionValidator	Validates the user's entry only if it matches a pattern defined by a regular expression.
RequiredFieldValidator	Ensures that the user specifies a value for the field.

Multiple validation controls can be used with an individual input control to validate according to different criteria. For example, you can apply multiple validation controls on a text box that is expected to contain an e-mail address. In particular, you can impose that the field is not skipped (*RequiredFieldValidator*) and that its content matches the typical format of e-mail addresses (*RegularExpressionValidator*).

Table 9-3 lacks a reference to the *ValidationSummary* control. The control does not perform validation tasks itself. Instead, it displays a label to summarize all the validation error messages found on a Web page as the effect of other validators. I'll cover the *ValidationSummary* control later in the chapter.

The *BaseValidator* Class

Table 9-4 details the specific properties of validation controls. Some properties—such as *ForeColor*, *Enabled*, and *Text*—are overridden versions of base properties on base classes.

TABLE 9-4 Basic Properties of Validators

Property	Description
ControlToValidate	Gets or sets the input control to validate. The control is identified by name—that is, by using the value of the *ID* attribute.
Display	If client-side validation is supported and enabled, gets or sets how the space for the error message should be allocated—either statically or dynamically. In the case of server-side validation, this property is ignored. A *Static* display is possible only if the browser supports the *display* CSS style. The default is *Dynamic*.
EnableClientScript	*True* by default; gets or sets whether client-side validation is enabled.
Enabled	Gets or sets whether the validation control is enabled.

Property	Description
ErrorMessage	Gets or sets the text for the error message.
ForeColor	Gets or sets the color of the message displayed when validation fails.
IsValid	Gets or sets whether the associated input control passes validation.
SetFocusOnError	Indicates whether the focus is moved to the control where validation failed.
Text	Gets or sets the description displayed for the validator in lieu of the error message. Note, though, this text does not replace the contents of *ErrorMessage* in the summary text.
ValidationGroup	Gets or sets the validation group that this control belongs to.

All validation controls inherit from the *BaseValidator* class except for compare validators, for which a further intermediate class—the *BaseCompareValidator* class—exists. The *BaseCompareValidator* class serves as the foundation for validators that perform typed comparisons. An ad hoc property, named *Type*, is used to specify the data type the values are converted to before being compared. The *CanConvert* static method determines whether the user's entry can be converted to the specified data type. Supported types include string, integer, double, date, and currency. The classes acting as compare validators are *RangeValidator* and *CompareValidator*.

Note You might want to pay careful attention when using the *ForeColor* property. Don't get it wrong—there's nothing bad with the property, which works as expected and sets the foreground color being used by the validators to show any messages. That's just the point, however. Today's applications tend to gain a lot more control over the style of emitted markup and for this reason tend to style through CSS wherever possible. Like many other similar style properties on server controls, the *ForeColor* property emits inline style information, which is really bad for designers when they get to do their job. Consider that in ASP.NET 4, validation controls no longer use the red color for error messages unless you set the *ControlRenderingCompatabilityVersion* attribute to "3.5" in the *<pages>* section of the configuration file. The *ForeColor* property certainly is not obsolete, but its use should be put aside as much as possible in favor of CSS styles.

Associating Validators with Input Controls

The link between each validator and its associated input control is established through the *ControlToValidate* property. The property must be set to the ID of the input control. If you do not specify a valid input control, an exception will be thrown when the page is rendered. The associated validator/control is between two controls within the same container—be it a page, user control, or template.

Not all server controls can be validated—only those that specify their validation property through an attribute named *[ValidationProperty]*. The attribute takes the name of the property that contains the user's entry to check. For example, the validation property for a *TextBox* is *Text* and is indicated as follows:

```
[ValidationProperty("Text")]
public class TextBox : WebControl, ITextControl
{
    ...
}
```

The list of controls that support validation includes *TextBox*, *DropDownList*, *ListBox*, *RadioButtonList*, *FileUpload*, plus a bunch of HTML controls such as *HtmlInputFile*, *HtmlInputText*, *HtmlInputPassword*, *HtmlTextArea*, and *HtmlSelect*. Custom controls can be validated too, as long as they are marked with the aforementioned *[ValidationProperty]* attribute.

> **Note** If the validation property of the associated input control is left empty, all validators accept any value and always pass the test. The *RequiredFieldValidator* control represents a rather natural exception to this rule, because it has been specifically designed to detect fields the user skipped and left blank.

Gallery of Controls

In general, ASP.NET validators are designed to work on a single control and process a single "value" for that control. As mentioned, you use the *ValidationProperty* attribute on custom controls to specify which property you want to validate. For stock controls, you take what they provide without many chances to modify things. Keep in mind that for validation scenarios that involve multiple controls or multiple properties, you need to create your own custom validation controls.

This said, let's go ahead and take a closer look at the stock validation controls available in ASP.NET Web Forms.

The *CompareValidator* Control

The *CompareValidator* control lets you compare the value entered by the user with a constant value or the value specified in another control in the same naming container. The behavior of the control is characterized by the following additional properties:

- **ControlToCompare** Represents the ID of the control to compare with the current user's entry. You should avoid setting the *ControlToCompare* and *ValueToCompare* properties at the same time. They are considered mutually exclusive; if you set both, the *ControlToCompare* property takes precedence.

- *Operator*   Specifies the comparison operation to perform. The list of feasible operations is defined in the *ValidationCompareOperator* enumeration. The default operator is *Equal*; feasible operators are also *LessThan*, *GreaterThan*, and their variations. The *DataTypeCheck* operator is useful when you want to make sure that certain input data can be converted to a certain type. When the *DataTypeCheck* operator is specified, both *ControlToCompare* and *ValueToCompare* are ignored. In this case, the test is made on the type of the input data and succeeds if the specified data can be converted to the expected type. Supported types are expressed through the following keywords: *String*, *Integer*, *Double*, *Date*, and *Currency* (decimal).

- *ValueToCompare*   Indicates the value to compare the user's input against. If the *Type* property is set, the *ValueToCompare* property must comply with it.

The following code demonstrates the typical markup of the *CompareValidator* control when the control is called to validate an integer input from a text box representing someone's age:

```
<asp:CompareValidator runat="server" id="ageValidator"
    ControlToValidate="ageTextBox"
    ValueToCompare="18"
    Operator="GreaterThanEqual"
    Type="Integer"
    ErrorMessage="Must specify an age greater than 17." />
```

The *CustomValidator* Control

The *CustomValidator* control is a generic and totally user-defined validator that uses custom validation logic to accomplish its task. You typically resort to this control when none of the other validators seems appropriate or, more simply, when you need to execute your own code in addition to that of the standard validators.

To set up a custom validator, you can indicate a client-side function through the *ClientValidationFunction* property. If client-side validation is disabled or not supported, simply omit this setting. Alternatively, or in addition to client validation, you can define some managed code to execute on the server. You do this by defining a handler for the *ServerValidate* event. The code will be executed when the page is posted back in response to a click on a button control. The following code snippet shows how to configure a custom validator to check the value of a text box against an array of feasible values:

```
<asp:CustomValidator runat="server" id="membershipValidator"
    ControlToValidate="membership"
    ClientValidationFunction="CheckMembership"
    OnServerValidate="ServerValidation"
    ErrorMessage="Membership can be Normal, Silver, Gold, or Platinum." />
```

If specified, the client validation function takes a mandatory signature and looks like this:

```
function CheckMembership(source, arguments)
{
    ...
}
```

The *source* argument references the HTML tag that represents the validator control—usually, a *<span>* tag. The *arguments* parameter references an object with two properties, *IsValid* and *Value*. The *Value* property is the value stored in the input control to be validated. The *IsValid* property must be set to *false* or *true* according to the result of the validation.

The *CustomValidator* control is not associated in all cases with a single input control in the current naming container. For this type of validator, setting the *ControlToValidate* property is not mandatory. For example, if the control has to validate the contents of multiple input fields, you simply do not set the *ControlToValidate* property and the *arguments.Value* variable evaluates to the empty string. In this case, you write the validation logic so that any needed values are dynamically retrieved. With client-side script code, this can be done by accessing the members of the document's form, as shown in the following code:

```
function CheckMembership(source, arguments)
{
    // Retrieve the current value of the element
    // with the specified ID
    var membership = document.getElementById("membership").value;
    ...
}
```

> **Warning** Setting only a client-side validation code opens a security hole because an attacker could work around the validation logic and manage to have invalid or malicious data sent to the server. By defining a server event handler, you have one more chance to validate data before applying changes to the back-end system.

To define a server-side handler for a custom validator, use the *ServerValidate* event:

```
void ServerValidation(object source, ServerValidateEventArgs e)
{
    ...
}
```

The *ServerValidateEventArgs* structure contains two properties—*IsValid* and *Value*—with the same meaning and goal as in the client validation function. If the control is not bound to a particular input field, the *Value* property is empty and you retrieve any needed value using the ASP.NET object model. For example, the following code shows how to check the status of a check box on the server:

```
void ServerValidation (object source, ServerValidateEventArgs e) {
    e.IsValid = (CheckBox1.Checked == true);
}
```

The *CustomValidator* control is the only option you have to validate controls that are not marked with the *[ValidationProperty]* attribute—for example, calendars and check-box controls. Likewise, it is the only option you have to validate multiple values and/or multiple controls linked by some relationship. Finally, *CustomValidator* is also your starting point for building some remote validation via AJAX. The simplest way of doing that is just by using some JavaScript that, from within the bound client validator, calls into a server method. The jQuery library is perfect for the job.

The *RegularExpressionValidator* Control

Regular expressions are an effective way to ensure that a predictable and well-known sequence of characters form the user's entry. For example, using regular expressions you can validate the format of postal codes, Social Security numbers, e-mail addresses, phone numbers, and so on. When using the *RegularExpressionValidator* control, you set the *ValidationExpression* property with the regular expression, which will be used to validate the input.

The following code snippet shows a regular expression validator that ensures the user's entry is an e-mail address:

```
<asp:RegularExpressionValidator runat="server" id="emailValidator"
    ControlToValidate="email"
    ValidationExpression="[a-zA-Z_0-9.-]+\@[a-zA-Z_0-9.-]+\.\w+"
    ErrorMessage="Must be a valid email address." />
```

The regular expression just shown specifies that valid e-mail addresses are formed by two nonzero sequences of letters, digits, dashes, and dots separated by an @ symbol and followed by a dot (.) and an alphabetic string. (This might not be the perfect regular expression for e-mail addresses, but it certainly incorporates the majority of e-mail address formats.)

Note The regular expression validation syntax is slightly different on the client than on the server. The *RegularExpressionValidator* control uses JavaScript regular expressions on the client and the .NET Framework *Regex* object on the server. Be aware that the JavaScript regular expression syntax is a subset of the *Regex* model. Whenever possible, try to use the regular expression syntax supported by JavaScript so that the same result is obtained for both the client and server.

The *RangeValidator* Control

The *RangeValidator* control lets you verify that a given value falls within a specified range. The type of the values involved in the check is specified dynamically and picked from a short list that includes strings, numbers, and dates. The following code shows how to use a range validator control:

```
<asp:RangeValidator runat="server" id="hiredDateValidator"
    ControlToValidate="hired"
    MinimumValue="2000-1-4"
    MaximumValue="9999-12-31"
    Type="Date"
    ErrorMessage="Must be a date after <b>Jan 1, 1999</b>." />
```

The key properties are *MinimumValue* and *MaximumValue*, which together clearly denote the lower and upper boundaries of the interval. Note that an exception is thrown if the strings assigned *MinimumValue* or *MaximumValue* cannot be converted to the numbers or dates according to the value of the *Type* property.

If the type is set to *Date*, but no specific culture is set for the application, you should specify dates using a culture-neutral format, such as *yyyy-MM-dd*. If you don't do so, the chances are good that the values will not be interpreted correctly.

> **Note** The *RangeValidator* control extends the capabilities of the more basic *CompareValidator* control by checking for a value in a fixed interval. In light of this, the *RangeValidator* control might raise an exception if either *MinimumValue* or *MaximumValue* is omitted. Whether the exception is thrown or not depends on the type chosen and its inherent ability to interpret the empty string. For example, an empty string on a *Date* type causes an exception. If you want to operate on an unbound interval—whether it's lower or upper unbound—either you resort to the *GreaterThan* (or *LessThan*) operator on the *CompareValidator* control or simply use a virtually infinite value such as the 9999-12-31 value.

The *RequiredFieldValidator* Control

To catch when a user skips a mandatory field in an input form, you use the *RequiredFieldValidator* control to show an appropriate error message:

```
<asp:RequiredFieldValidator runat="server" id="lnameValidator"
    ControlToValidate="lname"
    ErrorMessage="Last name is mandatory" />
```

As long as you're using an up-level browser and client-side scripting is enabled for each validator, which is the default, invalid input will display error messages without performing a postback.

Important   Note that just tabbing through the controls is not a condition that raises an error; the validator gets involved only if you type blanks or if the field is blank when the page is posted back.

How can you determine whether a certain field is really empty? In many cases, the empty string is sufficient, but this is not a firm rule. The *InitialValue* property specifies the initial value of the input control. The validation fails only if the value of the control equals *InitialValue* upon losing focus. By default, *InitialValue* is initialized with the empty string.

Special Capabilities

The primary reason why you place validation controls on a Web form is to catch errors and inconsistencies in the user's input. But how do you display error messages? Are you interested in client-side validation and, if you are, how would you set it up? Finally, what if you want to validate only a subset of controls when a given button is clicked? Some special capabilities of validation controls provide a valid answer to all these issues.

Server-Side Validation

Validation controls are server-side controls; subsequently, they kick in and give a response on the server. All postback controls (for example, buttons, auto-postback controls, and controls that registered as postback controls) validate the state of the page before proceeding with their postback action. For example, here's how the *Button* control handles it. The Web Forms page life cycle ends up invoking the *RaisePostBackEvent* method to force the clicked submit button to execute its click handler:

```
// Code excerpted from the source code of the System.Web.UI.WebControls.Button
protected virtual void RaisePostBackEvent(string eventArgument)
{
    base.ValidateEvent(this.UniqueID, eventArgument);
    if (this.CausesValidation)
    {
        this.Page.Validate(this.ValidationGroup);
    }
    this.OnClick(EventArgs.Empty);
    this.OnCommand(new CommandEventArgs(this.CommandName, this.CommandArgument));
}
```

The *Validate* method on the class *Page* just loops through the validators registered with the specified validation group and returns a response. The response simply updates the state of validation controls including the validation summary. This response will then be merged into the page response and output to the user.

If you simply need to know whether the state of the page is valid, you call the *IsValid* Boolean property. Note that *Page.IsValid* cannot be called before validation has taken place. It should always be queried after a call to *Page.Validate*—either an explicit call you code yourself or an implicit call that postback controls perform in their event handler. Note that, as the preceding code snippet shows, postback controls don't do any validation if their *CausesValidation* property is set to *false*.

> **Note** The *Validate* method on class *Page* is always invoked during the postback stage, regardless of the features of the postback control—a submit button has different postback mechanics compared to, say, a link button or an auto-postback control. In general, you'll more likely need to call *IsValid* in the code-behind class than *Validate*. After validation has occurred, in fact, you might need to check whether it was successful before you perform some other operations.

Displaying Error Information

The *ErrorMessage* property determines the static message that each validation control will display if an error occurs. You need to know that if the *Text* property is also set, it will take precedence over *ErrorMessage*. *Text* is designed to display inline where the validation control is located; *ErrorMessage* is designed to display in the validation summary. (Strategies for using *Text* and *ErrorMessage* will be discussed more in the next section, "The *ValidationSummary* Control.") Because all validation controls are labels, no other support or helper controls are needed to display any message. The message will be displayed in the body of the validation controls and, subsequently, wherever the validation control is actually placed. The error message is displayed as HTML, so it can contain any HTML formatting attribute.

Validators that work in client mode can create the *<span>* tag for the message either statically or dynamically. You can control this setting by using the *Display* property of the validator. When the display mode is set to *Static* (the default), the *<span>* element is given the following style:

```
style="visibility:hidden;"
```

The CSS *visibility* style attribute, when set to *Hidden*, causes the browser not to display the element but reserves space for it. If the *Display* property contains *Dynamic*, the style string changes as follows:

```
style="display:none;"
```

The CSS *display* attribute, when set to *none*, simply hides the element, which will take up space on the page only if displayed. The value of the *Display* property becomes critical when you have multiple validators associated with the same input control. (See Figure 9-4.)

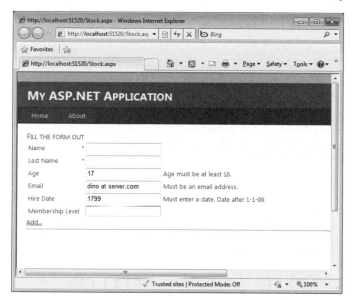

FIGURE 9-4 Input controls in the form are validated on the client.

As you can see, the Hire Date text box is first validated to ensure it contains a valid date and then to verify the specified date is later than 1-1-1999. If the *Display* property is set to *Static* for the first validator, and the date is outside the specified range, you get a page like the one shown in Figure 9-5.

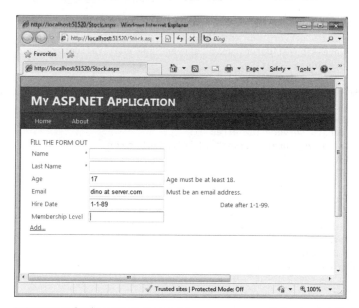

FIGURE 9-5 Static error messages take up space even if they're not displayed.

Multiple Validators per Control

Note that you can associate multiple validators with a single input control. Here's an excerpt from the code behind the page in Figure 9-5:

```
<table>
    <tr>
        <td>Name</td><td>*</td>
        <td><asp:textbox runat="server" id="fname" />
            <asp:RequiredFieldValidator runat="server" id="fnameValidator"
                ControlToValidate="fname"
            Text="!!!"
                    ErrorMessage="Name is mandatory" /></td></tr>
    <tr>
        <td>Last Name</td><td>*</td>
        <td><asp:textbox runat="server" id="lname" />
            <asp:RequiredFieldValidator runat="server" id="lnameValidator"
                ControlToValidate="lname"
             Text="!!!"
             ErrorMessage="Last name is mandatory" /></td></tr>
    <tr>
        <td>Age</td><td></td>
        <td><asp:textbox runat="server" id="age" />
            <asp:CompareValidator runat="server" id="ageValidator"
                ControlToValidate="age"
                Operator="GreaterThanEqual"
                ValueToCompare="18"
                Type="integer"
                ErrorMessage="Age must be at least 18." /></td></tr>
    <tr>
        <td>Email</td><td></td>
        <td><asp:textbox runat="server" id="email" />
            <asp:RegularExpressionValidator runat="server" id="emailValidator"
                ControlToValidate="email"
                ValidationExpression="[a-zA-Z_0-9.-]+\@[a-zA-Z_0-9.-]+\.\w+"
                ErrorMessage="Must be an email address." /></td></tr>
    <tr>
        <td>Hire Date</td><td></td>
        <td><asp:textbox runat="server" id="hired" />
            <asp:CompareValidator runat="server" id="hiredValidator"
                ControlToValidate="hired"
                Display="Static"
                Operator="DataTypeCheck"
                Type="date"
                ErrorMessage="Must enter a date." />
            <asp:RangeValidator runat="server" id="hiredDateValidator"
                ControlToValidate="hired"
                Display="Dynamic"
                MinimumValue="1999-1-1"
                MaximumValue="9999-12-31"
                Type="Date"
                ErrorMessage="Date after 1-1-99." /></td></tr>
```

```
    <tr>
       <td>Membership Level</td><td></td>
       <td><asp:textbox runat="server" id="membership" />
           <asp:CustomValidator runat="server" id="membershipValidator"
                  ControlToValidate="membership"
               ClientValidationFunction="CheckMembership"
                  ErrorMessage="Must be Gold or Platinum." /></td></tr>
</table>
```

The *hired* control is being validated by a *CompareValidator* and a *RangeValidator* at the same time. Validation takes place in order, and each validation control generates and displays its own error message. The content of the input control is considered valid if all the validators return *true*. If an input control has multiple valid patterns—for example, an ID field can take the form of a Social Security number or a VAT number—you can either validate by using custom code or regular expressions.

> **Note** The preceding HTML snippet uses a table element to lay out the input fields around the form. This approach is discouraged and plain block elements should be used (DIV and P tags) that could be lined up via CSS styles. Unfortunately, I'm not a CSS expert.

The *ValidationSummary* Control

The *ValidationSummary* control is a label that summarizes and displays all the validation error messages found on a Web page after a postback. The summary is displayed in a single location formatted in a variety of ways. The *DisplayMode* property sets the output format, which can be a list, bulleted list, or plain text paragraph. By default, it is a bulleted list. The feasible values are grouped in the *ValidationSummaryDisplayMode* enumeration.

Whatever the format is, the summary can be displayed as text in the page, in a message box, or in both. The Boolean properties *ShowSummary* and *ShowMessageBox* let you decide. The output of the *ValidationSummary* control is not displayed until the page posts back no matter what the value of the *EnableClientScript* property is. The *HeaderText* property defines the text that is displayed atop the summary:

```
<asp:ValidationSummary runat="server"
    ShowMessageBox="true"
    ShowSummary="true"
    HeaderText="The following errors occurred:"
    DisplayMode="BulletList" />
```

This code snippet originates the screen shown in Figure 9-6.

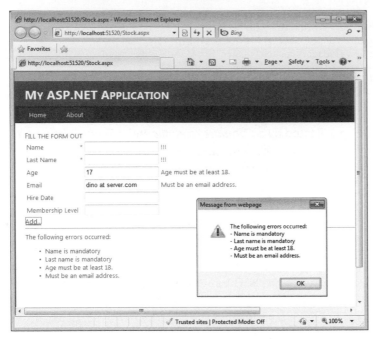

FIGURE 9-6 After the page posts back, the validation summary is updated and a message box pops up to inform the user of the errors.

The validation summary is displayed only if there's at least one pending error. Notice that, in the default case, the labels near the input controls are updated anyway, along with the summary text. In summary, you can control the error information in the following ways:

- **Both in-place and summary information** This is the default scenario. Use the *ValidationSummary* control, and accept all default settings on the validator controls. If you want to leverage both places to display information, a recommended approach consists of minimizing the in-place information by using the *Text* property rather than *ErrorMessage*. If you set both, *Text* is displayed in-place while *ErrorMessage* shows up in the validation summary. For example, you can set *Text* with a glyph or an exclamation mark and assign *ErrorMessage* with more detailed text.

- **Only in-place information** Do not use the *ValidationSummary* control, and set the *ErrorMessage* property in each validation control you use. The messages appear after the page posts back.

- **Only summary information** Use the *ValidationSummary* control, and set the *ErrorMessage* property on individual validation controls. Set the *Display* property of validators to *None* so that no in-place error message will ever be displayed.

- **Custom error information**   You don't use the *ValidationSummary* control, and you set the *Display* property of the individual validators to *None*. In addition, you collect the various error messages through the *ErrorMessage* property on the validation controls and arrange your own feedback for the user.

Enabling Client Validation

As mentioned earlier, the verification normally takes place on the server as the result of the postback event or after the *Validate* method is called. If scripting is enabled on the browser, though, you can also activate the validation process on the client, with a significant gain in responsiveness. In fact, there's no real value in making a roundtrip to the server only to discover that a required field has been left empty. The sooner you can figure it out, the better. On the other hand, you certainly can't rely exclusively on client-side validation. To run secure code and prevent malicious and underhanded attacks, you should validate any input data on the server too.

When client-side validation is turned on, the page doesn't post back until all the input fields contain valid data. However, not all types of validation can be accomplished on the client. In fact, if you need to validate against a database, well, there's no other option than posting back to the server. (AJAX facilities, which we'll explore in Chapter 20, "AJAX," might provide relief for this problem.)

Client validation can be controlled on a per-validation control basis by using the *EnableClientScript* Boolean property. By default, the property is set to *true*, meaning client validation is enabled as long as the browser supports it. By default, the code in the *BaseValidator* class detects the browser's capabilities through the *Request.Browser* property. If the browser is considered up-level, the client validation will be implemented. In ASP.NET 4, browsers and client devices that are considered up-level support at least the following:

- ECMAScript version 1.2 or newer
- W3C DOM Level 1 or greater

Today, nearly all browsers available meet these requirements. Generally, an up-level browser matches the capabilities of Internet Explorer 6 and newer. Consider that ASP.NET 4 checks the browser capabilities using the *Request.Browser* object. The information that this object returns is influenced by the value of the *ClientTarget* property on the *Page* class. The property indicates which set of browser capabilities the page assumes from the current browser. Specifying a value for the *ClientTarget* property overrides the automatic detection of browser capabilities that is normally accomplished. You can set the *ClientTarget* property via code, using the *@Page* directive, or in the configuration file.

What are the feasible values for *ClientTarget*?

In general, *ClientTarget* gets a string that refers to a user agent string. However, the root *web.config* configuration file defines a couple of default aliases that you can use as shorthand for common user-agent strings: *uplevel* and *downlevel*.

The *uplevel* alias specifies browser capabilities equivalent to Internet Explorer 6, whereas the *downlevel* alias refers to the capabilities of older browsers that do not support client script. You can define additional aliases in the *clientTarget* section of the application-level *web.config* file. (See Chapter 3, "ASP.NET Configuration.")

Validation Groups

By default, control validation occurs in an all-or-nothing kind of way. For example, if you have a set of input and validation controls and two buttons on the form, clicking either button will always validate all controls. In other words, there's no way to validate some controls when one button is clicked and some others when the other button is clicked.

The *CausesValidation* property on button controls allows you to disable validation on a button, but that is not the real point here. What would be desirable is the ability to perform validation on a group of controls. This is exactly what the *ValidationGroup* property provides. The property is available on validators, input controls, and button controls.

Using the *ValidationGroup* property is simple; just define it for all the validation controls that you want to group together, and then assign the same name to the *ValidationGroup* property of the button that you want to fire the validation. Here's an example:

```
<asp:textbox runat="server" id="TextBox1"  />
<asp:RequiredFieldValidator runat="server"
    ValidationGroup="Group1"
    ControlToValidate="TextBox1"
    ErrorMessage="TextBox1 is mandatory" />
<asp:textbox runat="server" id="TextBox2"  />
<asp:RequiredFieldValidator runat="server"
    ValidationGroup="Group2"
    ControlToValidate="TextBox2"
    ErrorMessage="TextBox2 is mandatory" />
<asp:Button runat="server" Text="Check Group1"
    ValidationGroup="Group1" />
<asp:Button runat="server" Text="Check Group2"
    ValidationGroup="Group2" />
```

The two *RequiredFieldValidator* controls belong to distinct validation groups—*Group1* and *Group2*. The first button validates only the controls defined within Group1; the second button takes care of the input associated with Group2. In this way, the validation process can be made as granular as needed.

> **Important**   The *ValidationGroup* property can also be defined optionally on input controls. This is required only if you use the *CustomValidator* control as a way to check whether a given input control belongs to the right validation group. Unlike other validators, the *CustomValidator* control, in fact, is not strictly bound to a specific control.

Validation groups are well reflected on the server-side, where the *Validate* method of the *Page* class features an overload that lets you select the group according to which the page must be validated.

Dealing with Validation in Cross-Page Posts

Validation groups are especially helpful when combined with cross-page postbacks. As you saw earlier in the chapter, a cross-page postback allows a button to post the contents of the current form to another page, in a way overriding the single-form model of ASP.NET. In a cross-page posting scenario, what if the original page contains validators? Imagine a page with a text box whose value is to be posted to another page. You don't want the post to occur if the text box is empty. To obtain this behavior, you add a *RequiredFieldValidator* control and bind it to the text box:

```
<asp:TextBox ID="Keyword" runat="server" />
<asp:RequiredFieldValidator ID="Validator1" runat="server"
    ControlToValidate="Keyword" Text="*" />
<asp:Button ID="Button1" runat="server" Text="Search..."
    OnClick="Button1_Click" PostBackUrl="doSearch.aspx" />
```

As expected, when you click the button the page won't post if the text box is empty; and an asterisk (plus an optional message) is displayed to mark the error. This is because *RequiredFieldValidator* benefits the client-side capabilities of the browser and validates the input controls before proceeding with the post. Hence, in the case of empty text boxes, the button doesn't even attempt to make the post.

Is that all, or is there more to dig out?

Let's work with a *CustomValidator* control, which instead requires that some server-side code be run to check the condition. Can you imagine the scenario? You're on, say, *crosspage.aspx* and want to reach *doSearch.aspx*; to make sure you post only under valid conditions, though, you first need to make a trip to *crosspage.aspx* to perform some validation. Add this control, write the server validation handler in *crosspage.aspx*, and put a breakpoint in its code:

```
<asp:CustomValidator ID="CustomValidator1" runat="server"
    Text="*"
    ControlToValidate="Keyword"
    OnServerValidate="EnsureValidKeywords" />
```

Debugging this sample page reveals that posting to another page is a two-step operation. First, a classic postback is made to run any server-side code registered with the original page (for example, server-side validation code or code associated with the click of the button). Next, the cross-page call is made to reach the desired page:

```
void EnsureValidKeywords(Object source, ServerValidateEventArgs args)
{
    args.IsValid = false;
    if (String.Equals(args.Value, "Dino"))
        args.IsValid = true;
}
```

The preceding code sets the page's *IsValid* property to *false* if the text box contains anything other than "Dino." However, this fact alone doesn't prevent the transition to the target page. In other words, you could still have invalid input data posted to the target page.

Fortunately, this issue has an easy workaround, as shown in the following code:

```
if (!PreviousPage.IsValid)
{
    Response.Write("Sorry, the original page contains invalid input.");
    Response.End();
    return;
}
```

In the target page, you test the *IsValid* property on the *PreviousPage* property and terminate the request in the case of a negative answer. However, to avoid a server request and, worse yet, a page transition, you can add a client check to the *CustomValidator* control:

```
<asp:CustomValidator ID="CustomValidator1" runat="server"
    Text="*"
    ControlToValidate="Keyword"
    ClientValidationFunction="ensureValidKeywords"
    OnServerValidate="EnsureValidKeywords" />
```

Here's a possible implementation of the JavaScript function:

```
<script type="text/javascript">
    function ensureValidKeywords(source, arguments) {
        arguments.IsValid = false;
        var buf = arguments.Value;
        if (buf == "Dino")
            arguments.IsValid = true;
    }
</script>
```

Working with Wizards

An input form is used to collect data from users. However, it is not unusual that the amount of data to be collected is quite large and dispersed. In these cases, a single form is hardly the right solution. A *wizard* is a sequence of related steps, each associated with an input form and a user interface.

Wizards are typically used to break up large forms to collect user input. Users move through the wizard sequentially, but they are normally given a chance to skip a step or jump back to modify some of the entered values. A wizard is conceptually pretty simple, but implementing it over HTTP connections can be tricky. In ASP.NET, you have a readymade server control—the *Wizard* control—that automates many of the tasks.

An Overview of the *Wizard* Control

The *Wizard* control supports both linear and nonlinear navigation. It allows you to move backward to change values and skip steps that are unnecessary because of previous settings or because users don't want to fill in those fields. Like many other ASP.NET controls, the *Wizard* control supports themes, styles, and templates.

Wizard is a composite control and automatically generates some constituent controls, such as navigation buttons and panels. As you'll see in a moment, the programming interface of the control has multiple templates that provide for in-depth customization of the overall user interface. The control also guarantees that state is maintained no matter where you move—backward, forward, or to a particular page. All the steps of a wizard must be declared within the boundaries of the same *Wizard* control. In other words, the wizard must be self-contained and not provide page-to-page navigation.

Structure of a Wizard

As shown in Figure 9-7, a wizard has four parts: a header, view, navigation bar, and sidebar.

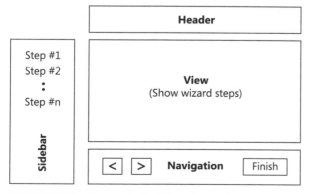

FIGURE 9-7 The four parts of a *Wizard* control.

The header consists of text you can set through the *HeaderText* property. You can change the default appearance of the header text by using its style property; you can also change the structure of the header by using the corresponding header template property. If *HeaderText* is empty and no custom template is specified, no header is shown for the wizard.

The view displays the contents of the currently active step. The wizard requires you to define each step in an *<asp:wizardstep>* element. An *<asp:wizardstep>* element corresponds to a *WizardStep* control. Different types of wizard steps are supported; all wizard step classes inherit from a common base class named *WizardStepBase*.

All wizard steps must be grouped in a single *<wizardsteps>* tag, as shown in the following code:

```
<asp:wizard runat="server" DisplaySideBar="true">
  <wizardsteps>
    <asp:wizardstep runat="server" steptype="auto" id="step1">
      First step
    </asp:wizardstep>
    <asp:wizardstep runat="server" steptype="auto" id="step2">
      Second step
    </asp:wizardstep>
    <asp:wizardstep runat="server" steptype="auto" id="finish">
      Final step
    </asp:wizardstep>
  </wizardsteps>
</asp:wizard>
```

The navigation bar consists of autogenerated buttons that provide any needed functionality—typically, going to the next or previous step or finishing. You can modify the look and feel of the navigation bar by using styles and templates.

The optional sidebar is used to display content on the left side of the control. It provides an overall view of the steps needed to accomplish the wizard's task. By default, it displays a description of each step, with the current step displayed in boldface type. You can customize the sidebar using styles and templates. Figure 9-8 shows the default user interface. Each step is labeled using the ID of the corresponding *<asp:wizardstep>* tag.

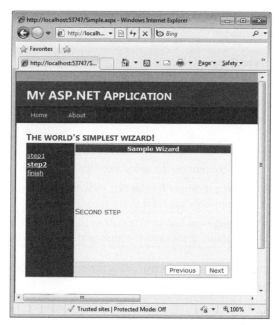

FIGURE 9-8 A wizard with the default sidebar on the left side.

Wizard Styles and Templates

You can style all the various parts and buttons of a *Wizard* control by using the properties listed in Table 9-5.

TABLE 9-5 The *Wizard* Control's Style Properties

Style	Description
CancelButtonStyle	Sets the style properties for the wizard's Cancel button
FinishCompleteButtonStyle	Sets the style properties for the wizard's Finish button
FinishPreviousButtonStyle	Sets the style properties for the wizard's Previous button when at the finish step
HeaderStyle	Sets the style properties for the wizard's header
NavigationButtonStyle	Sets the style properties for navigation buttons
NavigationStyle	Sets the style properties for the navigation area
SideBarButtonStyle	Sets the style properties for the buttons on the sidebar
SideBarStyle	Sets the style properties for the wizard's sidebar
StartStepNextButtonStyle	Sets the style properties for the wizard's Next button when at the start step
StepNextButtonStyle	Sets the style properties for the wizard's Next button
StepPreviousButtonStyle	Sets the style properties for the wizard's Previous button
StepStyle	Sets the style properties for the area where steps are displayed

The contents of the header, sidebar, and navigation bar can be further customized with templates. Table 9-6 lists the available templates.

TABLE 9-6 The *Wizard* Control's Template Properties

Style	Description
FinishNavigationTemplate	Specifies the navigation bar shown before the last page of the wizard. By default, the navigation bar contains the Previous and Finish buttons.
HeaderTemplate	Specifies the title bar of the wizard.
SideBarTemplate	Used to display content on the left side of the wizard control.
StartNavigationTemplate	Specifies the navigation bar for the first view in the wizard. By default, it contains only the Next button.
StepNavigationTemplate	Specifies the navigation bar for steps other than first, finish, or complete. By default, it contains Previous and Next buttons.

In addition to using styles and templates, you can control the programming interface of the *Wizard* control through a few properties.

The Wizard's Programming Interface

Table 9-7 lists the properties of the *Wizard* control, excluding style and template properties and properties defined on base classes.

TABLE 9-7 Main Properties of the *Wizard* Control

Property	Description
ActiveStep	Returns the current wizard step object. The object is an instance of the *WizardStep* class.
ActiveStepIndex	Gets and sets the 0-based index of the current wizard step.
DisplayCancelButton	Toggles the visibility of the *Cancel* button. The default value is *false*.
DisplaySideBar	Toggles the visibility of the sidebar. The default value is *false*.
HeaderText	Gets and sets the title of the wizard.
SkipLinkText	The ToolTip string that the control associates with an invisible image, as a hint to screen readers. The default value is "Skip Navigation Links" and is localized based on the server's current locale.
WizardSteps	Returns a collection containing all the *WizardStep* objects defined in the control.

A wizard in action is fully represented by its collection of step views and buttons. In particular, you'll recognize the following buttons: *StartNext*, *StepNext*, *StepPrevious*, *FinishComplete*, *FinishPrevious*, and *Cancel*. Each button is characterized by properties to get and set the button's image URL, caption, type, and destination URL after a click. The name of a property is the name of the button followed by a suffix. The available suffixes are listed in Table 9-8.

TABLE 9-8 **Suffix of Button Properties**

Suffix	Description
ButtonImageUrl	Gets and sets the URL of the image used to render the button
ButtonText	Gets and sets the text for the button
ButtonType	Gets and sets the type of the button: push button, image, or link button
DestinationPageUrl	Gets and sets the URL to jump to once the button is clicked

Note that names in Table 9-8 do not correspond to real property names. You have the four properties in this table for each distinct type of wizard button. The real name is composed by the name of the button followed by any of the suffixes—for example, *CancelButtonText*, *FinishCompleteDestinationPageUrl*, and so on.

The *Wizard* control also supplies a few interesting methods—for example, *GetHistory*, which is defined as follows:

```
public ICollection GetHistory()
```

GetHistory returns a collection of *WizardStepBase* objects. The order of the items is determined by the order in which the wizard's pages were accessed by the user. The first object returned—the one with an index of 0—is the currently selected wizard step. The second object represents the view before the current one, and so on.

The second method, *MoveTo*, is used to move to a particular wizard step. The method's prototype is described here:

```
public void MoveTo(WizardStepBase step)
```

The method requires you to pass a *WizardStepBase* object, which can be problematic. However, the method is a simple wrapper around the setter of the *ActiveStepIndex* property. If you want to jump to a particular step and not hold an instance of the corresponding *WizardStep* object, setting *ActiveStepIndex* is just as effective.

Table 9-9 lists the key events in the life of a *Wizard* control in an ASP.NET page.

TABLE 9-9 **Events of the *Wizard* Control**

Event	Description
ActiveViewChanged	Raised when the active step changes
CancelButtonClick	Raised when the *Cancel* button is clicked
FinishButtonClick	Raised when the *Finish Complete* button is clicked
NextButtonClick	Raised when any *Next* button is clicked
PreviousButtonClick	Raised when any *Previous* button is clicked
SideBarButtonClick	Raised when a button on the sidebar is clicked

As you can see, there's a common click event for all *Next* and *Previous* buttons you can find on your way. A *Next* button can be found on the *Start* page as well as on all step pages. Likewise, a *Previous* button can be located on the *Finish* page too. Whenever a *Next* button is clicked, the page receives a *NextButtonClick* event; whenever a *Previous* button is clicked, the control raises a *PreviousButtonClick* event.

Adding Steps to a Wizard

A *WizardStep* object represents one of the child views that the wizard can display. The *WizardStep* class ultimately derives from *View* and adds just a few public properties to it. A *View* object represents a control that acts as a container for a group of controls. A view is hosted within a *MultiView* control. To create its output, the wizard makes internal use of a *MultiView* control. However, the wizard is not derived from the *MultiView* class.

You define the views of a wizard through distinct instances of the *WizardStep* class, all grouped under the *<WizardSteps>* tag. The *<WizardSteps>* tag corresponds to the *WizardSteps* collection property exposed by the *Wizard* control:

```
<WizardSteps>
    <asp:WizardStep>
        ...
    </asp:WizardStep>
    <asp:WizardStep>
        ...
    </asp:WizardStep>
</WizardSteps>
```

Each wizard step is characterized by a title and a type. The *Title* property provides a brief description of the view. This information is not used unless the sidebar is enabled. If the sidebar is enabled, the title of each step is used to create a list of steps. If the sidebar is enabled but no title is provided for the various steps, the ID of the *WizardStep* objects is used to populate the sidebar, as shown earlier in Figure 9-8.

While defining a step, you can also set the *AllowReturn* property, which indicates whether the user is allowed to return to the current step from a subsequent step. The default value of the property is *true*.

Types of Wizard Steps

The *StepType* property indicates how a particular step should be handled and rendered within a wizard. Acceptable values for the step type come from the *WizardStepType* enumeration, as listed in Table 9-10.

TABLE 9-10 Wizard Step Types

Property	Description
Auto	The default setting, which forces the wizard to determine how each contained step should be treated.
Complete	The last page that the wizard displays, usually after the wizard has been completed. The navigation bar and the sidebar aren't displayed.
Finish	The last page used for collecting user data. It lacks the Next button, and it shows the *Previous* and *Finish* buttons.
Start	The first screen displayed, with no Previous button.
Step	All other intermediate pages, in which the Previous and Next buttons are displayed.

When the wizard is in automatic mode—the default type *Auto*—it determines the type of each step based on the order in which the steps appear in the source code. For example, the first step is considered to be of type *Start* and the last step is marked as *Finish*. No *Complete* step is assumed. If you correctly assign step types to your wizard steps yourself, rather than use the *Auto* type, the order in which you declare your steps in the *.aspx* source is not relevant.

Creating an Input Step

The following code shows a sample wizard step used to collect the provider name and the connection string to connect to a database and search for some data. For better graphical results, the content of the step is encapsulated in a fixed-height *<div>* tag. If all the steps are configured in this way, users navigating through the wizard won't experience sudden changes in the overall page size and layout:

```
<asp:wizardstep ID="Wizardstep1" runat="server" title="Connect">
    <div>
        <table>
            <tr><td>Provider</td><td>
                <asp:textbox runat="server" id="ProviderName"
                            text="System.Data.SqlClient" />
            </td></tr>
            <tr><td>Connection String</td><td>
                <asp:textbox runat="server" id="ConnString"
                    text="SERVER=(local);DATABASE=northwind;... " />
            </td></tr>
            <tr><td height="100px"></td></tr>
        </table>
    </div>
</asp:wizardstep>
```

Figure 9-9 shows a preview of the step. As you could probably guess, the step is recognized as a *Start* step. As a result, the wizard is added only to the Next button.

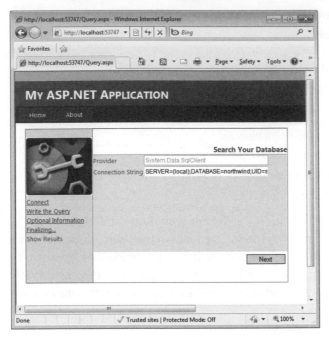

FIGURE 9-9 A sample *Start* wizard step.

A wizard is usually created for collecting input data, so validation becomes a critical issue. You can validate the input data in two nonexclusive ways—using validators and using transition event handlers.

The first option involves placing validator controls in the wizard step. This guarantees that invalid input—empty fields or incompatible data types—is caught quickly and, optionally, already on the client:

```
<asp:requiredfieldvalidator ID="RequiredField1" runat="server"
    text="*"
    errormessage="Must indicate a connection string"
    setfocusonerror="true"
    controltovalidate="ConnString" />
```

If you need to access server-side resources to validate the input data, you're better off using transition event handlers. A transition event is an event the wizard raises when it is about to switch to another view. For example, the *NextButtonClick* event is raised when the user clicks the Next button to jump to the subsequent step. You can intercept this event, do any required validation, and cancel the transition if necessary. I'll return to this topic in a moment.

Defining the Sidebar

The sidebar is a left-side panel that lists buttons to quickly and randomly reach any step of the wizard. It's a sort of quick-launch menu for the various steps that form the wizard. You control the sidebar's visibility through the Boolean *DisplaySideBar* attribute and define its contents through the *SideBarTemplate* property.

Regardless of the template, the internal layout of the sidebar is not left entirely to your imagination. In particular, the *<SideBarTemplate>* tag must contain a *DataList* control with a well-known ID—*SideBarList*. In addition, the *<ItemTemplate>* block must contain a button object with the name of *SideBarButton*. The button object must be any object that implements the *IButtonControl* interface.

> **Note** For better graphical results, you might want to use explicit heights and widths for all steps and the sidebar as well. Likewise, the push buttons in the navigation bar might look better if they are made the same size. You do this by setting the *Width* and *Height* properties on the *NavigationButtonStyle* object.

Navigating Through the Wizard

When a button is clicked to move to another step, an event is fired to the hosting page. It's up to you to decide when and how to perform any critical validation, such as deciding whether or not conditions exist to move to the next step.

In most cases, you'll want to perform server-side validation only when the user clicks the Finish button to complete the wizard. You can be sure that whatever route the user has taken within the wizard, clicking the Finish button will complete it. Any code you bind to the *FinishButtonClick* event is executed only once, and only when strictly necessary.

By contrast, any code bound to the Previous or Next button executes when the user moves back or forward. The page posts back on both events.

Filtering Page Navigation with Events

You should perform server-side validation if what the user can do next depends on the data she entered in the previous step. This means that in most cases you just need to write a *NextButtonClick* event handler:

```
<asp:wizard runat="server" id="QueryWizard"
    OnNextButtonClick="OnNext">
    ...
</asp:wizard>
```

If the user moves back to a previously visited page, you can usually ignore any data entered in the current step and avoid validation. Because the user is moving back, you can safely assume she is not going to use any fresh data. When a back movement is requested, you can assume that any preconditions needed to visit that previous page are verified. This happens by design if your users take a sequential route.

If the wizard's sidebar is enabled, users can jump from page to page in any order. If the logic you're implementing through the wizard requires that preconditions be met before a certain step is reached, you should write a *SideBarButtonClick* event handler and ensure that the requirements have been met.

A wizard click event requires a *WizardNavigationEventHandler* delegate (which is defined for you by ASP.NET):

```
public delegate void WizardNavigationEventHandler(
    object sender,
    WizardNavigationEventArgs e);
```

The *WizardNavigationEventArgs* structure contains two useful properties that inform you about the 0-based indexes of the page being left and the page being displayed. The *CurrentStepIndex* property returns the index of the last page visited; *NextStepIndex* returns the index of the next page. Note that both properties are read-only.

The following code shows a sample handler for the Next button. The handler prepares a summary message to show when the user is going to the *Finish* page:

```
void OnNext(object sender, WizardNavigationEventArgs e)
{
    // Collect the input data if going to the last page
    // -1 because of 0-based indexing, add -1 if you have a Complete page
    if (e.NextStepIndex == QueryWizard.WizardSteps.Count - 2)
        PrepareFinalStep();
}
void PrepareFinalStep()
{
    string cmdText = DetermineCommandText();

    // Show a Ready-to-go message
    var sb = new StringBuilder("");
    sb.AppendFormat("You're about to run: <br><br>{0}<hr>", cmdText);
    sb.Append("<b><br>Ready to go?</b>");
    ReadyMsg.Text = sb.ToString();
}

string DetermineCommandText()
{
    // Generate and return command text here
}
```

Each page displayed by the wizard is a kind of panel (actually, a view) defined within a parent control—the wizard. This means that all child controls used in all steps must have a unique ID. It also means that you can access any of these controls just by name. For example, if one of the pages contains a text box named, say, *ProviderName*, you can access it from any event handler by using the *ProviderName* identifier.

The preceding code snippet is an excerpt from a sample wizard that collects input and runs a database query. The first step picks up connection information, whereas the second step lets users define tables, fields, and optionally a WHERE clause. The composed command is shown in the *Finish* page, where the wizard asks for final approval. (See Figure 9-10.)

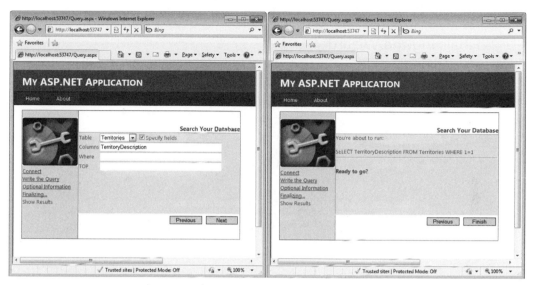

FIGURE 9-10 Two successive pages of the sample wizard: query details and the *Finish* step.

Canceling Events

The *WizardNavigationEventArgs* structure also contains a read/write Boolean property named *Cancel*. If you set this property to *true*, you just cancel the ongoing transition to the destination page. The following code shows how to prevent the display of the next step if the user is on the *Start* page and types in **john** as the user ID:

```
void OnNext(object sender, WizardNavigationEventArgs e)
{
    if (e.CurrentStepIndex == 0 &&
        ConnString.Text.IndexOf("UID=john") > -1)
    {
        e.Cancel = true;
        return;
    }
}
```

You can cancel events from within any transition event handler and not just from the *NextButtonClick* event handler. This trick is useful to block navigation if the server-side validation of the input data has failed. If you do cause a step to fail, though, you're responsible for showing some feedback to the user.

Note You can't cancel navigation from within the *ActiveViewChanged* event. This event follows any transition events, such as the *NextButtonClick* or *PreviousButtonClick* event, and it occurs when the transition has completed. Unlike transition events, the *ActiveViewChanged* event requires a simpler, parameterless handler—*EventHandler*.

Finalizing the Wizard

All wizards have some code to execute to finalize the task. If you use the ASP.NET *Wizard* control, you place this code in the *FinishButtonClick* event handler. Figure 9-11 shows the final step of a wizard that completed successfully.

```
void OnFinish(object sender, WizardNavigationEventArgs e)
{
    string finalMsg = "The operation completed successfully.";
    try
    {
        // Complete the wizard (compose and run the query)
        var command = DetermineCommandText();
        var table = ExecuteCommand(ConnString.Text, command);
        grid.DataSource = table;
        grid.DataBind();

        // OK color
        FinalMsg.ForeColor = Color.Blue;
    }
    catch (Exception ex) {
        FinalMsg.ForeColor = Color.Red;
        finalMsg = String.Format("The operation cannot be completed
                                due to:<br />{0}", ex.Message);
    }
    finally {
        FinalMsg.Text = finalMsg;
    }
}

string DetermineCommandText()
{
    // Generate and return command text here
}

DataTable ExecuteCommand()
{
    // Execute database query here
}
```

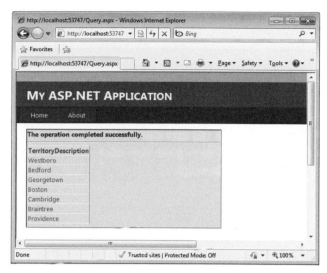

FIGURE 9-11 Final step of a wizard that completed successfully.

If the wizard contains a *Complete* step, that page should be displayed after the Finish button is clicked and the final task has completed. If something goes wrong with the update, you should either cancel the transition to prevent the *Complete* page from even appearing or adapt the user interface of the completion page to display an appropriate error message. Which option you choose depends on the expected behavior of the implemented operation. If the wizard's operation can fail or succeed, you let the wizard complete and display an error message if something went wrong. If the wizard's operation must complete successfully unless the user quits, you should not make the transition to the *Complete* page; instead, provide users with feedback on what went wrong and give them a chance to try again.

Summary

Form-based programming is fundamental in Web applications because it's the only way to have users and applications interact. ASP.NET pages can have only one server-side form with a fixed *action* property. Subsequently, pages are reentrant and always post to themselves. The behavior of the form can't be changed because it is crucial to the behavior of ASP.NET, but a different feature—cross-page posting—comes to the rescue to let users post data from one page to another. Cross-page posting is essential when you have legacy pages to integrate in a new application that, for whatever reason, can't be adapted to a more specific ASP.NET architecture.

Input forms also bring to the table the whole theme of input validation. ASP.NET comes with a stock of native validation controls to cover the basic needs of validation. Validators let you put declarative boundaries around input controls so that any user's input is filtered and validated both on the client and server. This alone is not sufficient to certify an application as secure, but it is a quantum leap in the right direction.

Finally, in this chapter entirely devoted to getting input data into an ASP.NET server application, we've covered wizards—namely, a semi-automatic way of breaking up large forms into smaller pieces served individually to the user, while keeping track of some state. Whether you use the ASP.NET *Wizard* control or roll your own custom solution, the aware-ness that splitting large forms into sequential screens gives end users a more pleasant experience is what really matters for ASP.NET developers.

Chapter 10
Data Binding

In matters of style, swim with the current; in matters of principle, stand like a rock.

—Thomas Jefferson

Web applications are, for the most part, just data-driven applications. For this reason, the ability to bind HTML elements such as drop-down lists or tables to structured data is a key feature for any Web development platform. Data binding is the process that retrieves data from a given source and associates it with properties on UI elements. In ASP.NET, a valid target for a data binding operation is a server control, also known as a *data-bound* control.

Data-bound server controls are not another family of controls; they're simply server controls that feature a few well-known data-related properties and feed them using a well-known set of collection objects.

In ASP.NET, there are three main categories of data-bound controls: list, iterative, and view controls. As you'll see in more detail later on, list controls repeat a fixed template for each item found in the data source. Iterative controls are more flexible and let you explicitly define the template to repeat, as well as other templates that directly influence the final layout of the control. Finally, view controls are rich user interface components that provide fixed and data-driven behavior, such as showing a table of records or a single record.

In this chapter, we'll first review the pillars of data binding in ASP.NET and then proceed to examine the various types of data-bound controls.

Foundation of the Data Binding Model

ASP.NET data binding is built around a few properties that any data-bound control exposes. Page authors can assign collections of data to data-bound controls at any time by setting data binding properties. However, the simple assignment of values to data binding properties is not sufficient to modify the control's user interface. The actual data binding process starts when the page execution flow executes the method *DataBind* on the page or a particular control.

For a control, performing a data binding action means updating its internal state to reflect the collection of values assigned to its bindable properties. Finally, when the control renders out its markup, the markup will incorporate any bound data.

What kind of data can you pass on to a data-bound control?

Feasible Data Sources

Many .NET classes can be used as data sources—and not just those that have to do with database content. In ASP.NET, any object that exposes the *IEnumerable* interface is a valid bindable data source. The *IEnumerable* interface defines the minimal API necessary to enumerate the contents of the data source:

```
public interface IEnumerable
{
    IEnumerator GetEnumerator();
}
```

Many bindable objects, though, actually implement more advanced versions of *IEnumerable*, such as *ICollection* and *IList*. In particular, you can bind a Web control to the following classes:

- Collections (including dictionaries, hashtables, and arrays)
- ADO.NET container classes such as *DataSet*, *DataTable*, and *DataView*
- ADO.NET data readers
- Any *IQueryable* object that results from the execution of a LINQ query

To be honest, I should note that the *DataSet* and *DataTable* classes don't actually implement *IEnumerable* or any other interfaces that inherit from it. However, both classes do store collections of data internally. These collections are accessed using the methods of an intermediate interface—*IListSource*—which performs the trick of making *DataSet* and *DataTable* classes look like they implement a collection.

Collection Classes

At the highest level of abstraction, a collection serves as a container for instances of other classes. A collection is like an array, but with a richer programming interface. All collection classes implement the *ICollection* interface, which in turn implements the *IEnumerable* interface. As a result, all collection classes provide a basic set of functionalities.

All collection classes have a *Count* property to return the number of cached items; they have a *CopyTo* method to copy their items, in their entirety or in part, to an external array; and they have a *GetEnumerator* method that instantiates an enumerator object to loop through the child items. *GetEnumerator* is the method behind the curtain whenever you call the *foreach* statement in C# and the *For...Each* statement in Microsoft Visual Basic.

IList and *IDictionary* are two interfaces that extend *ICollection*, giving a more precise characterization to the resultant collection class. *ICollection* provides only basic and minimal functionality for a collection. For example, *ICollection* does not have any methods to add or remove items. Add and remove functions are exactly the capabilities that the *IList* interface provides. In the *IList* interface, the *Add* and *Insert* methods place new items at the bottom of the collection or at the specified index. The *Remove* and *RemoveAt* methods remove items, while *Clear* empties the collection. Finally, *Contains* verifies whether an item with a given value belongs to the collection, and *IndexOf* returns the index of the specified item. Commonly used container classes that implement both *ICollection* and *IList* are *Array*, *ArrayList*, and *StringCollection*.

The *IDictionary* interface defines the API that represents a collection of key/value pairs. The interface exposes methods similar to *IList*, but with different signatures. Dictionary classes also feature two extra properties, *Keys* and *Values*. They return collections of keys and values, respectively, found in the dictionary. Typical dictionary classes are *ListDictionary*, *Hashtable*, and *SortedList*.

Most of the time, however, you'll be using generic lists of custom objects, as shown here:

```
boundServerControl1.DataSource = new List<Customer>();
```

The net effect is that the data-bound control is linked to an object that contains a list of *Customer* objects.

It is important that the element class—*Customer*, in the preceding code—implements data members as properties, instead of fields.

```
public class Customer
{
    public Int32 CustomerId {get; set};
    public String Name {get; set;}
    ...
}
```

A property is a data member exposed through the filter represented by a *get* and/or a *set* method. A field, instead, is a member that is exposed directly as a read/write location. Data members coded as fields won't be discovered at run time and therefore are useless for data binding. This is by design. However, any .NET class can modify the conventional algorithm through which its properties are discovered at run time by implementing the *ICustomTypeDescriptor* interface.

Implementing the *ICustomTypeDescriptor* interface gives the object itself a chance to enumerate exactly the properties it wants to expose regardless of the actual schema of the class. For example, the interface can be employed to convince a data-bound control that a given field of the bound class is actually a property.

ADO.NET Classes

ADO.NET provides a bunch of data container classes that can be filled with any sort of data, including results of a database query. These classes represent excellent resources for filling data-bound controls such as lists and grids. Having memory-based classes such as the *DataSet* in the list is probably no surprise, but it's good to find data readers there too. An open data reader can be passed to the data-binding engine of a control. The control will then walk its way through the reader and populate the user interface while keeping the connection to the database busy.

> **Note** Data binding works differently for Web pages and desktop applications (whether they are Windows Forms or Windows Presentation Foundation applications). The biggest difference is that in Web pages you must explicitly start the data binding process by calling the method *DataBind* on the page or control class. In desktop solutions, the simple assignment of data to a bindable property triggers the binding process for the specific component.

The *DataSet* class can contain more than one table; however, only one table at a time can be associated with standard ASP.NET data-bound controls. If you bind the control to a *DataSet*, you then need to set an additional property to select a particular table within the *DataSet*. Be aware that this limitation is not attributable to ASP.NET as a platform; it is a result of the implementation of the various data-bound controls. In fact, you could write a custom control that accepts a *DataSet* as its sole data-binding parameter.

DataSet and *DataTable* act as data sources through the *IListSource* interface; *DataView* and data readers, on the other hand, implement *IEnumerable* directly.

Queryable Objects

Short for Language INtegrated Query, *LINQ* is a query language that applies a SQL-like syntax to enumerable collections of data. The typical result of a LINQ query is a queryable object that you can see as an abstraction for a command to execute that will actually get you the data. The peculiarity of queryable objects is that you can bind them to controls regardless of whether data has been retrieved or not.

A queryable object implements the *IQueryable* interface which, in turn, derives from *IEnumerable*. The actual object you get from a LINQ query, though, implements this interface in a lazy way such that any attempt to read from the object during data binding will actually execute the query against whatever data store you queried—an in-memory collection, XML file, *DataSet*, or perhaps SQL Server table. Here's an example:

```
// This is a query, defined but not executed yet. The returned
// variable is of a type that implements IQueryable.
var query = from c in customers
            where c.Country == "USA"
            select c;

// Assignment works because IQueryable derives from IEnumerable.
// As soon as data binding is triggered, an attempt to read from the
// results of the query is made, which will ultimately perform the query.
boundServerControl1.DataSource = query;
```

A simple attempt to enumerate the elements in the query result set is sufficient to trigger the data fetch operation.

 Note More information on LINQ can be found starting at the following page: *http://msdn. microsoft.com/en-us/library/bb397926.aspx.*

Data-Binding Properties

All data-bound controls implement the *DataSource* and *DataSourceID* properties, plus a few more. The full class diagram for data binding in ASP.NET is detailed in Figure 10-1.

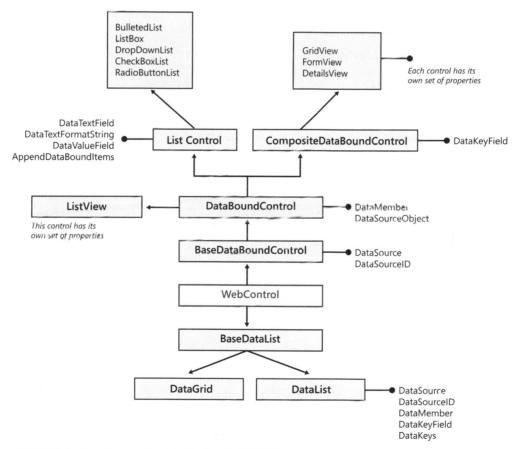

FIGURE 10-1 Class diagram for data binding in ASP.NET.

As you can see, there are two base classes and subsequently two main subtrees—one rooted in *BaseDataList* and one rooted in *BaseDataBoundControl*. The diagram doesn't extend in a uniform manner and clearly denotes that the various controls have been added at different times. You see this clearly from the distribution of the same set of fundamental properties in the controls derived from *BaseDataList* and *BaseDataBoundControl*.

Let's explore in more detail the various data-binding properties.

> **Note** For some reason, the *Repeater* control—a low-level iterative control—doesn't inherit from either of the classes in the diagram. It inherits directly from the *Control* class. In spite of this, *Repeater* has everything that's needed to be considered an iterative control.

The *DataSource* Property

The *DataSource* property lets you specify the data source object the control is linked to.

Note that this link is logical and does not result in any overhead or underlying operation until you explicitly choose to bind the data to the control. This operation is triggered by calling the *DataBind* method. When the *DataBind* method executes, the control actually loads data from the associated data source, evaluates the data-bound properties (if any), and generates the markup to reflect changes. The property is defined as follows:

```
public virtual object DataSource {get; set;}
```

The *DataSource* property is declared of type *object* and can ultimately accept objects that implement either *IEnumerable* (including data readers) or *IListSource*. By the way, only *DataSet* and *DataTable* implement the *IListSource* interface.

The *DataSource* property of a data-bound control is generally set programmatically. However, nothing prevents you from adopting a kind of declarative approach as follows:

```
<asp:DropDownList runat="server" id="theList" DataSource="<%# GetData() %>"
    ...
/>
```

The content of the drop-down list control will be determined by the object returned by the *GetData* method. In this example, *GetData* is a public or protected member of the code-behind page class that returns a bindable object. The # symbol in the code block indicates that the expression will be evaluated only after a call is made to the method *DataBind* on the page that contains the *DropDownList* control or on the control itself.

> **Note** How can a data-bound control figure out which actual object it is bound to? Will it be a collection, a data reader, or perhaps a *DataTable*?
>
> All standard data-bound controls are designed to work only through the *IEnumerable* interface. For this reason, any object bound to *DataSource* is normalized to an object that implements *IEnumerable*. In some cases, the normalization is as easy (and fast) as casting the object to the *IEnumerable* interface. In other cases—specifically, when *DataTable* and *DataSet* are involved—an extra step is performed to locate a particular named collection of data that corresponds to the value assigned to the *DataMember* property.
>
> There's no public function to do all this work, although a similar helper class exists in the ASP.NET framework but is flagged as internal. What this helper class does, though, can be easily replicated by custom code: it just combines an array of if statements to check types and does casting and conversion as appropriate.

The *DataSourceID* Property

The *DataSourceID* property gets or sets the ID of the data source component from which the data-bound control retrieves its data. This property is the point of contact between data-bound controls and a special family of controls—the data source controls—that includes *SqlDataSource* and *ObjectDataSource*. (I'll cover these controls in more detail later in the chapter.)

```
public virtual string DataSourceID {get; set;}
```

By setting *DataSourceID*, you tell the control to turn to the associated data source control for any needs regarding data—retrieval, paging, sorting, counting, or updating.

Like *DataSource*, *DataSourceID* is available on all data-bound controls. The two properties are mutually exclusive. If both are set, you get an invalid operation exception at run time. Note, though, that you also get an exception if *DataSourceID* is set to a string that doesn't correspond to an existing data source control.

The *DataMember* Property

The *DataMember* property gets or sets the name of the data collection to extract when data binding to a data source:

```
public virtual string DataMember {get; set;}
```

You use the property to specify the name of the *DataTable* to use when the *DataSource* property is bound to a *DataSet* object:

```
var data = new DataSet();
var adapter = new SqlDataAdapter(commandText, connectionString);
adapter.Fill(data);
```

```
// Table is the default name of the first table in a
// DataSet filled by an adapter
grid.DataMember = "Table";
grid.DataSource = data;
grid.DataBind();
```

DataMember and *DataSource* can be set in any order, provided that both are set before *DataBind* is invoked. *DataMember* has no relevance if you bind to data using *DataSourceID* with standard data source components.

The *DataTextField* Property

Typically used by list controls, the *DataTextField* property specifies which property of a data-bound item should be used to define the display text of the nth element in a list control:

```
public virtual string DataTextField {get; set;}
```

For example, for a drop-down list control the property feeds the displayed text of each item in the list. The following code creates the control shown in Figure 10-2:

```
CountryList.DataSource = data;
CountryList.DataTextField = "country";
CountryList.DataBind();
```

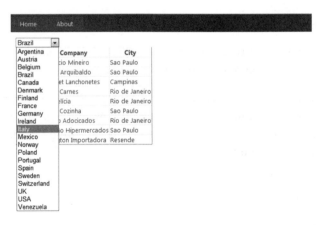

FIGURE 10-2 A drop-down list control filled with the *country* column of a database table.

An analogous behavior can be observed for other list controls, such as *ListBox* and *CheckBoxList*.

Note List controls can automatically format the content of the field bound through the *DataTextField* property. The format expression is indicated via the *DataTextFormatString* property.

The *DataValueField* Property

Similar to *DataTextField*, the *DataValueField* property specifies which property of a data-bound item should be used to identify the nth element in a list control:

```
public virtual string DataValueField {get; set;}
```

To understand the role of this property, consider the markup generated for a drop-down list, set as in the code snippet shown previously:

```
<select name="CountryList" id="CountryList">
    <option selected="selected" value="[All]">[All]</option>
    <option value="Argentina">Argentina</option>
    <option value="Austria">Austria</option>
    ...
</select>
```

The text of each *<option>* tag is determined by the field specified through *DataTextField*; the value of the value attribute is determined by *DataValueField*. Consider the following code that fills a *ListBox* with customer names:

```
CustomerList.DataMember = "Table";
CustomerList.DataTextField = "companyname";
CustomerList.DataValueField = "customerid";
CustomerList.DataSource = data;
CustomerList.DataBind();
```

If *DataValueField* is left blank, the value of the *DataTextField* property is used instead. Here's the corresponding markup:

```
<select size="4" name="CustomerList" id="CustomerList">
    <option value="BOTTM">Bottom-Dollar Markets</option>
    <option value="LAUGB">Laughing Bacchus Wine Cellars</option>
    ...
</select>
```

As you can see, the *value* attribute now is set to the customer ID—the unique, invisible value determined by the *customerid* field. The content of the *value* attribute for the currently selected item is returned by the *SelectedValue* property of the list control. If you want to access programmatically the displayed text of the current selection, use the *SelectedItem.Text* expression.

The *AppendDataBoundItems* Property

This Boolean property indicates whether the data-bound items should be appended to the existing contents of the control or whether they should overwrite them. By default, *AppendDataBoundItems* is set to *false*, meaning that data-bound contents replace any existing contents.

```
public virtual bool AppendDataBoundItems {get; set;}
```

AppendDataBoundItems is useful when you need to combine constant items with data-bound items. For example, imagine you need to fill a drop-down list with all the distinct countries/regions in which you have a customer. The user will select a country/region and see the list of customers who live there. To let users see all the customers in any country/region, you add an unbound element, such as *[All]*.

```
<asp:DropDownList runat="server" ID="CountryList"
    AppendDataBoundItems="true">
    <asp:ListItem Text="[All]" />
</asp:DropDownList>
```

With *AppendDataBoundItems* set to *false*, the *[All]* item will be cleared before data-bound items are added.

The *DataKeyField* Property

The *DataKeyField* property gets or sets the key field in the specified data source. The property serves the need of some data list controls that allow item selection and master/detail views. Controls that support this property are viewable in Figure 10-1 and are *DataGrid*, *DataList*, and view controls.

All of these controls allow you to select a displayed item over a postback. Following the selection, however, these controls provide some reference about the data item associated with the selected row. The *DataKeyField* indicates which property on the bound data item identifies the selected record.

Note that the identification of the record is unequivocal only if the field is uniquely constrained in the original data source.

```
public virtual string DataKeyField {get; set;}
```

For example, imagine you display customers in a grid and allow users to click and drill down on the orders placed by that customer. When the user clicks, a postback occurs in which you can retrieve the value of the key field that uniquely identifies the selected data item. By setting *DataKeyField* to the *CustomerId* property—presumably the primary key field—you retrieve the ID of the selected customer and can plan further drill-down queries.

The *DataKeyField* property is coupled with the *DataKeys* array property. When *DataKeyField* is set, *DataKeys* contains the value of the specified key field for all the control's data items currently displayed in the page. You retrieve the actual key value using the following expression:

```
// Gets you the value of the specified data key for the item at the given position
GridView1.DataKeys[GridView1.SelectedIndex];
```

Most controls, however, provide a handy *SelectedValue* property that just wraps the previous expression.

Note View controls (for example, *GridView* and *FormView*) have a richer programming interface, and they extend the *DataKeyField* property to an array of strings and rename it to *DataKeyNames*. In this way, you can identify data items using multiple key values.

Data-Bound Controls

Data-bound controls are components whose whole interface is driven by one or more columns of data read from of a feasible data source. As you can see in Figure 10-1, there are quite a few types of data-bound controls. We can summarize that into three main categories: list controls, iterative controls and, the functionally richest of all, view controls.

List Controls

List controls display (or at least store in memory) many items at the same time—specifically, the contents of the bound data source. Depending on its expected behavior, the control picks the needed items from memory and properly formats and displays them. List controls include *DropDownList*, *CheckBoxList*, *RadioButtonList*, *ListBox*, and *BulletedList*. All list controls inherit from the base *ListControl* class. Let's find out some more details.

The *DropDownList* Control

The *DropDownList* control enables users to select one item from a single-selection drop-down list. You can specify the size of the control by setting its height and width in pixels, but you can't control the number of items displayed when the list drops down. Table 10-1 lists the most commonly used properties of the control.

TABLE 10-1 Properties of the *DropDownList* Control

Property	Description
AppendDataBoundItems	Indicates whether statically defined items should be maintained or cleared when adding data-bound items
AutoPostBack	Indicates whether the control should automatically post back to the server when the user changes the selection
DataMember	The name of the table in the *DataSource* to bind
DataSource	The data source that populates the items of the list
DataSourceID	ID of the data source component to provide data
DataTextField	Name of the data source field to supply the text of list items
DataTextFormatString	Formatting string used to visually format list items to be displayed
DataValueField	Name of the data source field used to supply the value of a list item

Property	Description
Items	Gets the collection of items in the list control
SelectedIndex	Gets or sets the index of the selected item in the list
SelectedItem	Gets the selected item in the list
SelectedValue	Gets the value of the selected item in the list

The *DropDownList* control, as well as many other server controls, features some properties to configure the graphical aspect of the final markup. At rendering time, these properties are transformed in cascading style sheet (CSS) style properties. The best practice today is to avoid style properties such as *BorderColor* and *ForeColor* and use CSS classes instead. Whenever possible and suitable, you should adhere to this de facto standard and emit plain HTML markup out of server controls.

The *DataTextField* and *DataValueField* properties don't accept expressions, only plain property names. If you need to combine and display two or more fields from the data source, it is recommended that you preprocess that data at the source and bind data already in a display format.

> **Note** The ASP.NET *DropDownList* control doesn't support groups of options as provided by the HTML *<optgroup>* element. There are various ways to work around this limitation.
>
> To start off, you can create your own customized drop-down control and override the *RenderContents* methods. The method is invoked just when the control is requested to write out its markup. You can add a new attribute to any option that indicates the group. If you take this route, remember also to update the view state to also store the additional group attribute. I'll return to custom controls and their view state management in the next chapter.
>
> Another approach entails creating a *<tagMapping>* section in the configuration file and mapping standard *DropDownList* controls to your customized drop-down control. In this way, you don't even need to change the markup of your ASPX pages and can just add option groups.
>
> Finally, you can keep on using standard *DropDownList* controls but add some jQuery code that adds option groups on the fly as the page is loaded in the browser. I'll cover jQuery in Chapter 21.

The *CheckBoxList* Control

The *CheckBoxList* control is a single monolithic control that groups a collection of selectable list items with an associated check box, each of which is rendered through an individual *CheckBox* control. The properties of the child check boxes are set by reading the associated data source. You insert a check box list in a page as follows:

```
<asp:CheckBoxList runat="server" id="employeesList">
```

Table 10-2 lists the specific properties of the *CheckBoxList* control.

TABLE 10-2 **Properties of the *CheckBoxList* Control**

Property	Description
AppendDataBoundItems	Indicates whether statically defined items should be maintained or cleared when adding data-bound items
AutoPostBack	Indicates whether the control should automatically post back to the server when the user changes the selection
CellPadding	Indicates pixels between the border and contents of the cell
CellSpacing	Indicates pixels between cells
DataMember	The name of the table in the *DataSource* to bind
DataSource	The data source that populates the items of the list
DataSourceID	ID of the data source component to provide data
DataTextField	Name of the data source field to supply the text of list items
DataTextFormatString	Formatting string used to visually format list items to be displayed
DataValueField	Name of the data source field used to supply the value of a list item
Items	Gets the collection of items in the list control
RepeatColumns	Gets or sets the number of columns to display in the control
RepeatDirection	Gets or sets a value that indicates whether the control displays vertically or horizontally
RepeatLayout	Gets or sets the layout of the check boxes: Table, Flow, OrderedList, UnorderedList
SelectedIndex	Gets or sets the index of the first selected item in the list—the one with the lowest index
SelectedItem	Gets the first selected item
SelectedValue	Gets the value of the first selected item
TextAlign	Gets or sets the text alignment for the check boxes

The *CheckBoxList* does not supply any properties that know which items have been selected. But this aspect is vital for any Web application that uses selectable elements. The *CheckBoxList* can have any number of items selected, but how can you retrieve them?

Any list control has an *Items* property that contains the collection of the child items. The *Items* property is implemented through the *ListItemCollection* class and makes each contained item accessible via a *ListItem* object. The following code loops through the items stored in a *CheckBoxList* control and checks the *Selected* property of each of them:

```
foreach (var item in chkList.Items)
{
    if (item.Selected) {
        // This item is selected
        var itemValue = item.Value;
        ...
    }
}
```

Figure 10-3 shows a sample page that lets you select some country/region names and composes an ad hoc query to list all the customers from those countries/regions.

FIGURE 10-3 A horizontally laid out *CheckBoxList* control in action.

Note that the *SelectedXXX* properties work in a slightly different manner for a *CheckBoxList* control. The *SelectedIndex* property indicates the lowest index of a selected item. By setting *SelectedIndex* to a given value, you state that no items with a lower index should be selected any longer. As a result, the control automatically deselects all items with an index lower than the new value of *SelectedIndex*. Likewise, *SelectedItem* returns the first selected item, and *SelectedValue* returns the value of the first selected item.

The *RadioButtonList* Control

The *RadioButtonList* control acts as the parent control for a collection of radio buttons. Each of the child items is rendered through a *RadioButton* control. By design, a *RadioButtonList* can have zero or one item selected. The *SelectedItem* property returns the selected element as a *ListItem* object. Note, though, that there is nothing to guarantee that only one item is selected at any time. For this reason, be extremely careful when you access the *SelectedItem* of a *RadioButtonList* control—it could be *null*.

```
if (radioButtons.SelectedValue != null)
{
    // Process the selection here
    ...
}
```

The control supports the same set of properties as the *CheckBoxList* control and, just like it, accepts some layout directives. In particular, you can control the rendering process of the list with the *RepeatLayout* and *RepeatDirection* properties. By default, the list items are rendered within a table, which ensures the vertical alignment of the companion text. The property that governs the layout is *RepeatLayout*. The alternative is to display the items as free HTML text, using blanks and breaks to guarantee some sort of minimal structure. *RepeatDirection* is the property that controls the direction in which, with or without a tabular structure, the items flow. Feasible values are *Vertical* (the default) and *Horizontal*. *RepeatColumns* is the property that determines how many columns the list should have. By default, the value is *0*, which means all the items will be displayed in a single row, vertical or horizontal, according to the value of *RepeatDirection*.

The *ListBox* Control

The *ListBox* control represents a vertical sequence of items displayed in a scrollable window. The *ListBox* control allows single-item or multiple-item selection and exposes its contents through the usual *Items* collection, as shown in the following code:

```
<asp:listbox runat="server" id="theListBox"
    rows="5" selectionmode="Multiple" />
```

You can decide the height of the control through the *Rows* property. The height is measured in number of rows rather than pixels or percentages. When it comes to data binding, the *ListBox* control behaves like the controls discussed earlier in the chapter.

Two properties make this control slightly different than other list controls—the *Rows* property, which represents the number of visible rows in the control, and the *SelectionMode* property, which determines whether one or multiple items can be selected. The programming interface of the list box also contains the set of *SelectedXXX* properties we considered earlier. In this case, they work as they do for the *CheckBoxList* control—that is, they return the selected item with the lowest index.

Note All the list controls examined so far support the *SelectedIndexChanged* event, which is raised when the selection from the list changes and the page posts back to the server. You can use this event to execute server-side code whenever a control is selected or deselected.

The *BulletedList* Control

The *BulletedList* control is a programming interface built around the *<ul>* and *<ol>* HTML tags, with some extra features such as the bullet style, data binding, and support for custom images. The following example uses a custom bullet object:

```
<asp:bulletedlist runat="server" bulletstyle="Square">
    <asp:listitem>One</asp:listitem>
    <asp:listitem>Two</asp:listitem>
    <asp:listitem>Three</asp:listitem>
</asp:bulletedlist>
```

The bullet style lets you choose the style of the element that precedes the item. You can use numbers, squares, circles, and uppercase and lowercase letters. The child items can be rendered as plain text, hyperlinks, or buttons. Table 10-3 details the main properties of a *BulletedList* control.

TABLE 10-3 Properties of the *BulletedList* Control

Property	Description
AppendDataBoundItems	Indicates whether statically defined items should be maintained or cleared when adding data-bound items
BulletImageUrl	Gets or sets the path to the image to use as the bullet
BulletStyle	Determines the style of the bullet
DataMember	The name of the table in the *DataSource* to bind
DataSource	The data source that populates the items of the list
DataSourceID	ID of the data source component to provide data
DataTextField	Name of the data source field to supply the text of list items
DataTextFormatString	Formatting string used to visually format list items to be displayed
DataValueField	Name of the data source field to supply the value of a list item
DisplayMode	Determines how to display the items: as plain text, link buttons, or hyperlinks
FirstBulletNumber	Gets or sets the value that starts the numbering
Items	Gets the collection of items in the list control
Target	Indicates the target frame in the case of hyperlink mode

The items of a *BulletedList* control support a variety of graphical styles—disc, circle, custom image, plus a few types of numberings, including roman numbering. The initial number can be programmatically set through the *FirstBulletNumber* property. The *DisplayMode* property determines how to display the content of each bullet—plain text (the default), link button, or hyperlink. In the case of link buttons, the *Click* event is fired on the server to let you handle the event when the page posts back. In the case of hyperlinks, the browser displays the target page in the specified frame—the *Target* property. The target URL coincides with the contents of the field specified by *DataValueField*.

Figure 10-4 shows a sample page that includes *RadioButtonList* and *BulletedList* controls. The radio-button list is bound to the contents of a system enumerated type—*BulletStyle*—and displays as selectable radio buttons the various bullet styles. To bind the contents of an enumerated type to a data-bound control, you do as follows:

```
BulletOptions.DataSource = Enum.GetValues(typeof(BulletStyle));
BulletOptions.SelectedIndex = 0;
BulletOptions.DataBind();
```

To retrieve and set the selected value, use the following code:

```
var style = (BulletStyle) Enum.Parse(typeof(BulletStyle),
                                     BulletOptions.SelectedValue);
BulletedList1.BulletStyle = style;
```

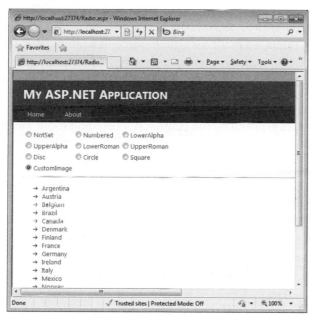

FIGURE 10-4 A sample page to preview the style of a *BulletedList* control.

Iterative Controls

Iterative controls supply a template-based mechanism to create free-form user interfaces. Iterative controls take a data source, loop through the items, and iteratively apply user-defined HTML templates to each row. This basic behavior is common to all three ASP.NET iterators: *Repeater*, *DataList*, and *DataGrid*. Beyond that, iterative controls differ from each other in terms of layout capabilities and functionality.

Iterative controls differ from list controls because of their greater rendering flexibility. An iterative control lets you apply an ASP.NET template to each row in the bound data source.

A list control, on the other hand, provides a fixed and built-in template for each data item. List controls are customizable to some extent, but you can't change anything other than the text displayed. No changes to layout are supported. On the other hand, using a list control is considerably easier than setting up an iterative control, as you'll see in a moment. Defining templates requires quite a bit of declarative code, and if accomplished programmatically, it requires that you write a class that implements the *ITemplate* interface. A list control requires only that you go through a few data-binding properties.

Meanwhile, let's briefly meet each control. When they are properly customized and configured, there's no graphical structure—be it flat or hierarchical—that *Repeater* and *DataList* controls can't generate.

The *Repeater* Control

The *Repeater* displays data using user-provided layouts. It works by repeating a specified ASP.NET template for each item displayed in the list. The *Repeater* is a rather basic templated data-bound control. It has no built-in layout or styling capabilities. All formatting and layout information must be explicitly declared and coded using HTML literals, CSS classes, and ASP.NET controls.

Table 10-4 lists the main properties exposed by the control, not counting those inherited from the base class *WebControl*.

TABLE 10-4 Properties of the *Repeater* Control

Property	Description
AlternatingItemTemplate	Template to define how every other item is rendered.
DataMember	The name of the table in the *DataSource* to bind.
DataSource	The data source that populates the items of the list.
DataSourceID	ID of the data source component to provide data.
FooterTemplate	Template to define how the footer is rendered.
HeaderTemplate	Template to define how the header is rendered.
Items	Gets a *RepeaterItemCollection* object—that is, a collection of *RepeaterItem* objects. Each element of the collection represents a displayed data row in the *Repeater*.
ItemTemplate	Template to define how items are rendered.
SeparatorTemplate	Template to define how the separator between items is to be rendered.

For the most part, properties are the template elements that form the control's user interface. The *Repeater* populates the *Items* collection by enumerating all the data items in the bound data source. For each data-bound item (for example, a table record), it creates a

RepeaterItem object and adds it to the *Items* collection. The *RepeaterItemCollection* class is a plain collection class with no special or peculiar behavior. The *RepeaterItem* class represents a displayed element within the overall structure created by the *Repeater*. The *RepeaterItem* contains properties to point to the bound data item (such as a table record), the index, and the type of the item (regular item, alternating item, header, footer, and so on). Here's a quick example of a *Repeater*:

```
<asp:Repeater ID="Repeater1" runat="server">
    <HeaderTemplate>
        <h2>We have customers in the following cities</h2>
        <hr />
    </HeaderTemplate>
    <SeparatorTemplate>
        <hr />
    </SeparatorTemplate>
    <ItemTemplate>
        <span><%# Eval("City")%>
          
        <span class="bold"><%# Eval("Country")%></span>
    </ItemTemplate>
    <FooterTemplate>
        <hr />
        <%# CalcTotal() %> cities
    </FooterTemplate>
</asp:Repeater>
```

Bound to the output of the following method call, the structure produces what's shown in Figure 10-5:

```
// Currently selected country name
var country = Countries.SelectedValue;

// Make a call to the DAL to grab cities and countries
var repo = new CustomerRepository();
var data = repo.GetCitiesWithCustomers(country);

// Bind
Repeater1.DataSource = data;
Repeater1.DataBind();
```

The method on the data access layer ends up placing a SQL query like the one shown next. (As you'll see in Chapter 14, the data access layer can be written using plain ADO.NET as well as LINQ-to-SQL, Entity Framework, NHibernate, or any other Object/Relational Mapper framework.)

```
SELECT DISTINCT country, city FROM customers WHERE country=@TheCountry
```

The *@TheCountry* parameter is the name of the country/region picked from the drop-down list.

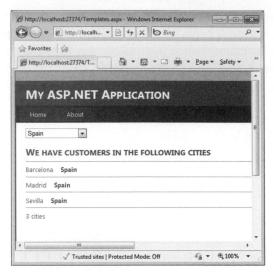

FIGURE 10-5 A sample *Repeater* control in action. No predefined list control can generate such a free-form output.

Of all the templates, only *ItemTemplate* and *AlternatingItemTemplate* are data-bound, meaning that they are repeated for each item in the data source. You need a mechanism to access public properties on the data item (such as a table record) from within the template. The *Eval* method takes the name of the property (for example, the name of the table column) and returns the content. You'll learn more about *Eval* and <%# ... %> code blocks in a moment when we're discussing data-binding expressions.

The *DataList* Control

The *DataList* is a data-bound control that begins where the *Repeater* ends and terminates a little before the starting point of the *DataGrid* control. In some unrealistically simple cases, you can even take some code that uses a *Repeater*, replace the control, and not even notice any difference. The *DataList* overtakes the *Repeater* in several respects, mostly in the area of graphical layout. The *DataList* supports directional rendering, meaning that items can flow horizontally or vertically to match a specified number of columns. Furthermore, it provides facilities to retrieve a key value associated with the current data row and has built-in support for selection and in-place editing.

In addition, the *DataList* control supports more templates and can fire some extra events beyond those of the *Repeater*. Data binding and the overall behavior are nearly identical for the *Repeater* and *DataList* controls.

In addition to being a naming container, the *DataList* class implements the *IRepeatInfoUser* interface. The *IRepeatInfoUser* interface defines the properties and methods that must be implemented by any list control that repeats a list of items. This interface is also supported by the *CheckBoxList* and *RadioButtonList* controls and is the brains behind the *RepeatXXX* properties you met earlier. Here's how to rewrite the previous example to get stricter control over the output:

```
<asp:DataList ID="DataList1" runat="server" RepeatColumns="5"
    GridLines="Both">
  <FooterStyle Font-Bold="true" ForeColor="blue" />
  <HeaderTemplate>
      <h2>We have customers in the following cities</h2>
  </HeaderTemplate>
  <ItemTemplate>
      <%# Eval("City") %>   <b><%# Eval("Country")%></b>
  </ItemTemplate>
  <FooterTemplate>
      <%# CalcTotal() %> cities
  </FooterTemplate>
</asp:DataList>
```

Note the *FooterStyle* tag; the *DataList* also lets you explicitly style the content of each supported template.

Note The *DataList* control is deprecated in ASP.NET 4. If you're building a feature-rich user interface, you might want to take into account more recent view controls, such as the *ListView* control.

The *DataGrid* Control

The *DataGrid* is an extremely versatile data-bound control that is a fixed presence in any real-world ASP.NET application. Although it is fully supported, the *DataGrid* is pushed into the background by the introduction of a new and much more powerful grid control—the *GridView*.

The *DataGrid* control renders a multicolumn, fully templated grid and provides a highly customizable, Microsoft Office Excel–like user interface. In spite of the rather advanced programming interface and the extremely rich set of attributes, the *DataGrid* simply generates an HTML table with interspersed hyperlinks to provide interactive functionalities such as sorting, paging, selection, and in-place editing.

The *DataGrid* is a column-based control and supports various types of data-bound columns, including text columns, templated columns, and command columns. You associate the control with a data source using the *DataSource* property. Just as for other data-bound controls, no data will be physically loaded and bound until the *DataBind* method is called. The simplest way of displaying a table of data using the ASP.NET grid is as follows:

```
<asp:DataGrid runat="server" id="grid" />
```

The control will then automatically generate an HTML table column for each property available in the bound data source. This is only the simplest scenario, however. If needed, you can specify which columns should be displayed and style them at will.

View Controls

The internal architecture of data-bound controls has changed quite a bit over the years. The first version of ASP.NET came with *Repeater*, *DataList*, and *DataGrid* controls. They were fully integrated in the page life cycle, capable of raising postback events and able to render data according to different types of layouts and algorithms.

In successive versions of ASP.NET, the range of data-bound controls extended to include *FormView* and *DetailsView*, which were providing loudly demanded tools for displaying and editing a single record of data. These controls, however, were based on a revised internal architecture that made them capable of handling (not just raising) specific postback events. This was a big change. Along with *FormView* and *DetailsView*, Microsoft also introduced the *GridView* control—a revamped data grid control based on the same architecture of other view controls. Finally, in ASP.NET 3.5 Microsoft also made available the *ListView* control, which probably is the only view control you would ever want to use. The *ListView* control sums up the characteristics of all the others, and by properly programming it you can obtain data-driven interfaces of any kind.

Let's briefly review the characteristics of these controls, reserving a deeper look at *GridView* and *ListView* for later in the chapter.

The *DetailsView* Control

The *DetailsView* is a control that renders a single record of data at a time from its associated data source, optionally providing paging buttons to navigate between records. It is similar to the Form View of a Microsoft Access database and is typically used for updating and inserting records in a master/detail scenario.

The *DetailsView* control binds to any data source control and executes its set of data operations. It can page, update, insert, and delete data items in the underlying data source as long as the data source supports these operations. In most cases, no code is required to set up any of these operations. You can customize the user interface of the *DetailsView* control by choosing the most appropriate combination of data fields and styles from within Visual Studio. You do not have much control over its markup, however.

Finally, note that although the *DetailsView* is commonly used as an update and insert interface, it does not natively perform any input validation against the data source schema, nor does it provide any schematized user interface such as foreign key field drop-down lists or made-to-measure edit templates for particular types of data.

The *FormView* Control

FormView can be considered the templated version of the *DetailsView*. It renders one record at a time, picked from the associated data source and, optionally, provides paging buttons to navigate between records. Unlike the *DetailsView* control, *FormView* doesn't use any internal generation of markup and requires the programmer to define the rendering of each item by using templates. The *FormView* can support any basic operation its data source provides.

Note that the *FormView* requires you to define everything through templates, not just the things you want to change. The *FormView* has no built-in rendering engine and is limited to printing out the user-defined templates.

In ASP.NET 4, the *FormView* control offers a new property—the *RenderOuterTable* Boolean property—through which you can skip the usual *<table>* tag surrounding the generated markup. This opens up easier CSS styling opportunities, but it also comes at the cost of losing autoformatting capabilities.

The *GridView* Control

The *GridView* is the successor to the *DataGrid* control and provides its same set of basic capabilities, plus a long list of extensions and improvements. As mentioned, the *DataGrid*—which is still fully supported in ASP.NET—is an extremely powerful and versatile control. However, it has one big drawback: it requires you to write a lot of custom code, even to handle relatively simple and common operations such as paging, sorting, editing, or deleting data. The *GridView* control was designed to work around this limitation and make two-way data binding happen with as little code as possible. The control is tightly coupled to the family of new data source controls, and it can handle direct data source updates as long as the underlying data source object supports these capabilities.

This virtually codeless two-way data binding is by far the most notable feature of the new *GridView* control, but other enhancements are numerous. The *GridView* control is an improvement over the *DataGrid* control also because it has the ability to define multiple primary key fields, new column types, and style and templating options. The *GridView* also has an extended eventing model that allows you to handle or cancel events such as inserting, deleting, updating, paging, and more.

The *ListView* Control

The *ListView* control is fully template-based and allows you to control all aspects of the user interface via templates and properties. *ListView* operates in a way that closely resembles the behavior of existing data-bound controls, such as *FormView* or *DataList*. However, unlike these controls, the *ListView* control never creates any user-interface layout on its own. Every markup tag that the control emits is entirely under the developer's control, including header, footer, body, item, selected item, and so on.

The *ListView* control binds to any data source control and executes its set of data operations. It can page, update, insert, and delete data items in the underlying data source as long as the data source supports these operations. In most cases, no code is required to set up any of these operations. If code is required, you can also explicitly bind data to the control using the more traditional *DataSource* property and related *DataBind* method.

The rendering capabilities of the *ListView* control make it suitable for publishing scenarios where a read-only, but compelling, user interface is needed. The control also works great in editing scenarios even though it lacks some advanced features such as input validation or made-to-measure edit templates for particular types of data or foreign keys.

I'll say more on the *ListView* control in Chapter 11.

Data-Binding Expressions

As you might have figured out, most of the differences between the various data-bound controls is in how they use custom templates. A template is a piece of markup that the control injects in the page at a very specific point. More interestingly, the template contains bindable elements, which are placeholder markup elements whose content is determined by bound data.

How would you define the content of such bindable elements? In ASP.NET, a special syntax is required that we'll examine right away. After this, we'll return to the two most widely used view controls and examine some of their advanced capabilities.

Simple Data Binding

A data-binding expression is any executable code wrapped by <% ... %> and prefixed by the symbol #. Typically, you use data-binding expressions to set the value of an attribute in the opening tag of a server control. A data-binding expression is programmatically managed via an instance of the *DataBoundLiteralControl* class.

> **Note** The binding expression is really any executable code that can be evaluated at run time. Its purpose is to generate data that the control can use to bind for display or editing. Typically, the code retrieves data from the data source, but there is no requirement that this be the case. Any executable code is acceptable as long as it returns data for binding. A data-binding expression is evaluated only when something happens that fires the control's *DataBinding* event.

The following code snippet shows how to set the text of a label with the current time:

```
<asp:label runat="server" Text='<%# DateTime.Now %>' />
```

Within the delimiters, you can invoke user-defined page methods, static methods, and properties and methods of any other page component. The following code demonstrates a label bound to the name of the currently selected element in a drop-down list control:

```
<asp:label runat="server" Text='<%# dropdown.SelectedItem.Text %>' />
```

Note that if you're going to use quotes within the expression, you should wrap the expression itself with single quotes. The data-binding expression can accept a minimal set of operators, mostly for concatenating subexpressions. If you need more advanced processing and use external arguments, resort to a user-defined method. The only requirement is that the method be declared as public or protected.

> **Important** Any data-bound expression you define in the page is evaluated only after *DataBind* is called. You can call *DataBind* either on the page object or on the specific control. If you call *DataBind* on the page object, it will recursively call *DataBind* on all controls defined in the page. If *DataBind* is not called, no <%# ...%> expressions will ever be evaluated.

Binding in Action

Data-binding expressions are particularly useful to update, in a pure declarative manner, properties of controls that depend on other controls in the same page. For example, suppose you have a drop-down list of colors and a label and that you want the text of the label to reflect the selected color:

```
<asp:DropDownList ID="SelColors" runat="server" AutoPostBack="True">
    <asp:ListTtem>Orange</asp:ListItem>
    <asp:ListItem>Green</asp:ListItem>
    <asp:ListItem>Red</asp:ListItem>
    <asp:ListItem>Blue</asp:ListItem>
</asp:DropDownList>
<asp:Label runat="server" ID="lblColor"
    Text='<%# "<b>You selected: </b>" + SelColors.SelectedValue %>' />
```

Note that in the <%# ... %> expression you can use any combination of methods, constants, and properties as long as the final result matches the type of the bound property. Also note that the evaluation of the expression requires a postback and a call to *DataBind* in the postback event handler. You set the *AutoPostBack* property to *true* just to force a postback when the selection changes in the drop-down list. At the same time, a call to the page's or label's *DataBind* method is required for the refresh to occur.

```
protected void Page_Load(object sender, EventArgs e)
{
    ...
    DataBind();
}
```

You can bind to expressions virtually any control properties regardless of the type.

> **Note** You can use data-binding expressions to set control properties in a declarative manner; you cannot use plain code blocks—that is, <% ... %> expressions—without the # symbol for the same purpose.

Implementation of Data-Binding Expressions

What really happens when a data-binding expression is found in a Web page? How does the ASP.NET runtime process it? Let's consider the following code:

```
<asp:label runat="server" id="today" text='<%# DateTime.Now %>' />
```

When the page parser takes care of the ASPX source file, it generates a class where each server control has a factory method. The factory method simply maps the tag name to a server-side control class and transforms attributes on the tag into property assignments. In addition, if a data-binding expression is found, the parser adds a handler for the *DataBinding* event of the control—a *Label* in this case. Here's some pseudocode to illustrate the point:

```
private Control __BuildControlToday() {
    Label __ctrl = new Label();
    this.today = __ctrl;
    __ctrl.ID = "today";

    __ctrl.DataBinding += new EventHandler(this.__DataBindToday);
    return __ctrl;
}
```

The handler assigns the data-binding expression verbatim to the property:

```
public void __DataBindToday(object sender, EventArgs e) {
    Label target;
    target = (Label) sender;
    target.Text = Convert.ToString(DateTime.Now);
}
```

If the value returned by the data-binding expression doesn't match the expected type, you generally get a compile error. However, if the expected type is *string*, the parser attempts a standard conversion through the *Convert.ToString* method. (All .NET Framework types are convertible to a string because they inherit the *ToString* method from the root *object* type.)

The *DataBinder* Class

Earlier in this chapter, you met <%# ... %> expressions in the context of templates, along with the *Eval* method. The *Eval* method is a kind of tailor-made operator you use in data-binding expressions to access a public property on the bound data item. The *Eval* method we used in past code snippets is a shortcut method defined on the *Page* class that wraps the services of another *Eval* method, but one that's defined on another class—*DataBinder*.

> **Important** Through the *Eval* method—even if it comes from *DataBinder* or *Page*—you can access public properties on the bound data item. A data-bound control is linked to a collection of data objects. The data item just represents the element in the bound data source that is being processed at some point. Therefore, the *Eval* method ends up querying the data item object for its set of properties.

The *DataBinder* class supports generating and parsing data-binding expressions. Of particular importance is its overloaded static method *Eval*. The method uses reflection to parse and evaluate an expression against a run-time object. Clients of the *Eval* method include Rapid Application Development (RAD) tools such as Microsoft Visual Studio .NET designers and Web controls that declaratively place calls to the method to feed dynamically changing values to properties.

The *Eval* Method

The syntax of *DataBinder.Eval* typically looks like this:

```
<%# DataBinder.Eval(Container.DataItem, expression) %>
```

A third, optional, parameter is omitted in the preceding snippet. This parameter is a string that contains formatting options for the bound value. The *Container.DataItem* expression references the object on which the expression is evaluated. The expression is typically a string with the name of the field to access on the data item object. It can be an expression that includes indexes and property names. The *DataItem* property represents the object within the current container context. Typically, a container is the current instance of the item object—for example, a *DataGridItem* object—that is about to be rendered.

The code shown earlier is commonly repeated, always in the same form. Only the expression and the format string change from page to page.

A More Compact *Eval*

The original syntax of the *DataBinder.Eval* can be simplified in ASP.NET by writing the following:

```
<%# Eval(expression) %>
```

Any piece of code that appears within the <%# ... %> delimiters enjoys special treatment from the ASP.NET runtime. Let's briefly look at what happens with this code. When the page is compiled for use, the *Eval* call is inserted in the source code of the page as a standalone call. The following code gives you an idea of what happens:

```
object o = Eval("lastname");
string result = Convert.ToString(o);
```

The result of the call is converted to a string and is assigned to a data-bound literal control—an instance of the *DataBoundLiteralControl* class. Then the data-bound literal is inserted in the page's control tree.

The *TemplateControl* class—the parent of *Page*—is actually enriched with a new protected (but not virtual) method named *Eval*. The following pseudocode illustrates how the method works:

```
protected object Eval(string expression)
{
    if (Page == null)
        throw new InvalidOperationException(…);
    return DataBinder.Eval(Page.GetDataItem(), expression);
}
```

As you can see, *Eval* is a simple wrapper built around the *DataBinder.Eval* method. The *DataBinder.Eval* method is invoked using the current container's data item. Quite obviously, the current container's data is null outside a data-binding operation—that is, in the stack of calls following a call to *DataBind*. This fact brings up a key difference between *Eval* and *DataBinder.Eval*.

Getting the Default Data Item

The pseudocode that illustrates the behavior of the page's *Eval* method shows a *GetDataItem* method from the *Page* class. What is it? As mentioned, the simplified syntax assumes a default *Container.DataItem* context object. *GetDataItem* is simply the function that returns that object.

More precisely, *GetDataItem* is the endpoint of a stack-based mechanism that traces the current binding context for the page. Each control in the control tree is pushed onto this stack at the time the respective *DataBind* method is called. When the *DataBind* method returns, the control is popped from the stack. If the stack is empty and you attempt to call *Eval* programmatically, *GetDataItem* throws an invalid operation exception. In summary, you can use the *Eval* shortcut only in templates; if you need to access properties of a data item anywhere else in the code, resort to *DataBinder.Eval* and indicate the data item object explicitly.

Managing Tables of Data

Let's delve deeper into the programming features of a very popular and widely used view control—the *GridView* control.

The *GridView*'s Object Model

The *GridView* control provides a tabular, grid-like view of the contents of a data source. Each column represents a data source field, and each row represents a record. The *GridView* supports a large set of properties that fall into the following broad categories: behavior, visual settings, style, state, and templates. Table 10-5 details the properties that affect the behavior of the *GridView*.

TABLE 10-5 **Behavior Properties of the *GridView* Control**

Property	Description
AllowPaging	Indicates whether the control supports paging.
AllowSorting	Indicates whether the control supports sorting.
AutoGenerateColumns	Indicates whether columns are automatically created for each field in the data source. The default is *true*.
AutoGenerateDeleteButton	Indicates whether the control includes a button column to let users delete the record that is mapped to the clicked row.
AutoGenerateEditButton	Indicates whether the control includes a button column to let users edit the record that is mapped to the clicked row.
AutoGenerateSelectButton	Indicates whether the control includes a button column to let users select the record that is mapped to the clicked row.
ClientIDMode	Indicates the algorithm used to generate the client ID.
ClientIDRowSuffix	Gets and sets the names of the data fields whose values will be appended to the client ID when the client ID mode is set to *Predictable*.
ClientIDRowSuffixDataKeys	Gets and sets the values appended to the client ID.
DataMember	Indicates the specific table in a multimember data source to bind to the grid. The property works in conjunction with *DataSource*. If *DataSource* is a *DataSet* object, it contains the name of the particular table to bind.
DataSource	Gets or sets the data source object that contains the values to populate the control.
DataSourceID	Indicates the bound data source control.
RowHeaderColumn	Name of the column to use as the column header. This property is designed for improving accessibility.
SortDirection	Gets the direction of the column's current sort.
SortExpression	Gets the current sort expression.

The *SortDirection* and *SortExpression* properties specify the direction and the sort expression on the column that currently determine the order of the rows. Both properties are set by the control's built-in sorting mechanism when users click a column's header. The whole sorting engine is enabled and disabled through the *AllowSorting* property.

Each row displayed within a *GridView* control corresponds to a special type of grid item. The list of predefined types of items is nearly identical to that of the *DataGrid*, and it includes items such as the header, rows and alternating rows, the footer, and the pager. These items are static in the sense that they remain in place for the lifetime of the control in the application. Other types of items are active for a short period of time—the time needed to accomplish a certain operation. Dynamic items are the edit row, selected row, and *EmptyData* item. *EmptyData* identifies the body of the grid when the grid is bound to an empty data source.

Note The *GridView* control provides a few properties specifically designed for accessibility. They are *UseAccessibleHeader*, *Caption*, *CaptionAlign*, and *RowHeaderColumn*. When you set *RowHeaderColumn*, all the column cells will be rendered with the default header style (boldface type). However, *ShowHeader*, *HeaderStyle*, and other header-related properties don't affect the column indicated by *RowHeaderColumn*.

Table 10-6 details the style properties available on the *GridView* control.

TABLE 10-6 Style Properties of the *GridView* Control

Style	Description
AlternatingRowStyle	Defines the style properties for every other row in the table
EditRowStyle	Defines the style properties for the row being edited
FooterStyle	Defines the style properties for the grid's footer
HeaderStyle	Defines the style properties for the grid's header
EmptyDataRowStyle	Defines the style properties for the empty row, which is rendered when the *GridView* is bound to empty data sources
PagerStyle	Defines the style properties for the grid's pager
RowStyle	Defines the style properties for the rows in the table
SelectedRowStyle	Defines the style properties for the currently selected row

Table 10-7 lists most of the properties that affect the appearance of the control, and Table 10-8 details the templating properties.

TABLE 10-7 Appearance Properties of the *GridView* Control

Property	Description
BackImageUrl	Indicates the URL to an image to display in the background
Caption	The text to render in the control's caption
CaptionAlign	Alignment of the caption text
CellPadding	Indicates the amount of space (in pixels) between the contents of a cell and the border
CellSpacing	Indicates the amount of space (in pixels) between cells
EmptyDataText	Indicates the text to render in the control when it is bound to an empty data source

Property	Description
GridLines	Indicates the gridline style for the control
HorizontalAlign	Indicates the horizontal alignment of the control on the page
PagerSettings	References an object that lets you set the properties of the pager buttons
ShowFooter	Indicates whether the footer row is displayed
ShowHeader	Indicates whether the header row is displayed

The *PagerSettings* object groups together all the visual properties you can set on the pager. Many of these properties should sound familiar to *DataGrid* programmers. The *PagerSettings* class also adds some new properties to accommodate new predefined buttons (first and last pages), and it uses images instead of text in the links. (You need to figure out a trick to do the same with a *DataGrid*.)

TABLE 10-8 Templating Properties of the *GridView* Control

Template	Description
EmptyDataTemplate	Indicates the template content to be rendered when the control is bound to an empty source. This property takes precedence over *EmptyDataText* if both are set. If neither is set, the grid isn't rendered if bound to an empty data source.
PagerTemplate	Indicates the template content to be rendered for the pager. This property overrides any settings you might have made through the *PagerSettings* property.

The final block of properties—the state properties—is shown in Table 10-9. State properties return information about the internal state of the control.

TABLE 10-9 State Properties

Property	Description
BottomPagerRow	Returns a *GridViewRow* object that represents the bottom pager of the grid.
Columns	Gets a collection of objects that represent the columns in the grid. The collection is always empty if columns are autogenerated.
DataKeyNames	Gets an array that contains the names of the primary key fields for the currently displayed items.
DataKeys	Gets a collection of *DataKey* objects that represent the values of the primary key fields set in *DataKeyNames* for the currently displayed records.
EditIndex	Gets and sets the 0-based index that identifies the row currently rendered in edit mode.
EnablePersistedSelection	Indicates whether the current selection is persisted across postbacks. (It's *true* by default.) This is the property you want to set to *false* to avoid the scenario in which when row 1 is selected on page 1 and you move to another page, row 1 is selected automatically also on the new page.

Property	Description
FooterRow	Returns a GridViewRow object that represents the footer.
HeaderRow	Returns a GridViewRow object that represents the header.
PageCount	Gets the number of pages required to display the records of the data source.
PageIndex	Gets and sets the 0-based index that identifies the currently displayed page of data.
PageSize	Indicates the number of records to display on a page.
Rows	Gets a collection of GridViewRow objects that represent the data rows currently displayed in the control.
SelectedDataKey	Returns the DataKey object for the currently selected record.
SelectedPersistedDataKey	Returns the DataKey object for the record selected on the previous page.
SelectedIndex	Gets and sets the 0-based index that identifies the row currently selected.
SelectedRow	Returns a GridViewRow object that represents the currently selected row.
SelectedValue	Returns the explicit value of the key as stored in the DataKey object. It's similar to SelectedDataKey.
TopPagerRow	Returns a GridViewRow object that represents the top pager of the grid.

The *GridView* is designed to leverage the new data source object model, and it works best when bound to a data source control via the *DataSourceID* property. The *GridView* also supports the classic *DataSource* property, but if you bind data in that way, some of the features (such as built-in updates and paging) become unavailable.

Events of the *GridView* Control

Many controls in ASP.NET feature pairs of events of the type *doing/done*. Key operations in the control life cycle are wrapped by a pair of events—one firing before the operation takes place, and one firing immediately after the operation is completed. The *GridView* class is no exception. The list of events is shown in Table 10-10.

TABLE 10-10 Events Fired by the *GridView* Control

Event	Description
PageIndexChanging, PageIndexChanged	Both events occur when one of the pager buttons is clicked. They fire before and after the grid control handles the paging operation, respectively.
RowCancelingEdit	Occurs when the Cancel button of a row in edit mode is clicked, but before the row exits edit mode.
RowCommand	Occurs when a button is clicked.
RowCreated	Occurs when a row is created.
RowDataBound	Occurs when a data row is bound to data.

Event	Description
RowDeleting, RowDeleted	Both events occur when a row's Delete button is clicked. They fire before and after the grid control deletes the row, respectively.
RowEditing	Occurs when a row's Edit button is clicked, but before the control enters edit mode.
RowUpdating, RowUpdated	Both events occur when a row's Update button is clicked. They fire before and after the grid control updates the row, respectively.
SelectedIndexChanging, SelectedIndexChanged	Both events occur when a row's Select button is clicked. The two events occur before and after the grid control handles the select operation, respectively.
Sorting, Sorted	Both events occur when the hyperlink to sort a column is clicked. They fire before and after the grid control handles the sort operation, respectively.

RowCreated and *RowDataBound* events are the same as the *DataGrid*'s *ItemCreated* and *ItemDataBound* events, with new names. The same is true of the *RowCommand* event, which is the same as the *DataGrid*'s *ItemCommand* event.

The availability of events that announce a certain operation significantly enhances your programming power. By hooking the *RowUpdating* event, you can cross-check what is being updated and validate the new values. Likewise, you might want to handle the *RowUpdating* event to HTML-encode the values supplied by the client before they are persisted to the underlying data store. This simple trick helps you to fend off script injections.

Binding Data to the Grid

If no data source property is set, the *GridView* control doesn't render anything. If an empty data source object is bound and an *EmptyDataTemplate* template is specified, the results shown to the user have a friendlier look:

```
<asp:gridview runat="server" datasourceid="MySource">
   <emptydatatemplate>
      <asp:label runat="server">
         There's no data to show in this view.
      </asp:label>
   </emptydatatemplate>
</asp:gridview>
```

The *EmptyDataTemplate* property is ignored if the bound data source is not empty.

When you use a declared set of columns, the *AutoGenerateColumns* property of the grid is typically set to *false*. However, this is not a strict requirement—a grid can have declared and autogenerated columns. In this case, declared columns appear first. Note also that autogenerated columns are not added to the *Columns* collection. As a result, when column autogeneration is used, the *Columns* collection is typically empty.

Configuring Columns

The *Columns* property is a collection of *DataControlField* objects. The *DataControlField* object is akin to the *DataGrid*'s *DataGridColumn* object, but it has a more general name because these field objects can be reused in other data-bound controls that do not necessarily render columns. (For example, in the *DetailsView* control, the same class is used to render a row.)

You can define your columns either declaratively or programmatically. In the latter case, you just instantiate any needed data field objects and add them to the *Columns* collection. The following code adds a data-bound column to the grid:

```
var field = new BoundField();
field.DataField = "companyname";
field.HeaderText = "Company Name";
grid.ColumnFields.Add(field);
```

Columns of data are displayed in the order that the column fields appear in the collection. To statically declare your columns in the *.aspx* source file, you use the *<Columns>* tag, as shown here:

```
<columns>
    <asp:boundfield datafield="customerid" headertext="ID" />
    <asp:boundfield datafield="companyname" headertext="Company Name" />
</columns>
```

Table 10-11 lists the column field classes that can be used in a *GridView* control. All the classes inherit *DataControlField*.

TABLE 10-11 Supported Column Types in *GridView* Controls

Type	Description
BoundField	Default column type, displays the value of a field as plain text.
ButtonField	Displays the value of a field as a command button. You can choose the link or the push button style.
CheckBoxField	Displays the value of a field as a check box. It is commonly used to render Boolean values.
CommandField	Enhanced version of *ButtonField*, represents a special command such as Select, Delete, Insert, or Update. It's rarely useful with *GridView* controls; the field is tailor-made for *DetailsView* controls. (*GridView* and *DetailsView* share the set of classes derived from *DataControlField*.)
HyperLinkField	Displays the value of a field as a hyperlink. When the hyperlink is clicked, the browser navigates to the specified URL.
ImageField	Displays the value of a field as the *Src* property of an *<img>* HTML tag. The content of the bound field should be the URL to the physical image.
TemplateField	Displays user-defined content for each item in the column. You use this column type when you want to create a custom column field. The template can contain any number of data fields combined with literals, images, and other controls.

Table 10-12 lists the main properties shared by all column types.

TABLE 10-12 Common Properties of *GridView* Columns

Property	Description
AccessibleHeaderText	The text that represents abbreviated text read by screen readers of Assistive Technology devices.
FooterStyle	Gets the style object for the column's footer.
FooterText	Gets and sets the text for the column's footer.
HeaderImageUrl	Gets and sets the URL of the image to place in the column's header.
HeaderStyle	Gets the style object for the column's header.
HeaderText	Gets and sets the text for the column's header.
InsertVisible	Indicates whether the field is visible when its parent data-bound control is in insert mode. This property does not apply to *GridView* controls.
ItemStyle	Gets the style object for the various columns' cells.
ShowHeader	Indicates whether the column's header is rendered.
SortExpression	Gets and sets the expression used to sort the grid contents when the column's header is clicked. Typically, this string property is set to the name of the bound data field.

The properties listed in the table represent a subset of the properties that each column type actually provides. In particular, each type of column defines a tailor-made set of properties to define and configure the bound field.

Bound Fields

The *BoundField* class represents a field that is displayed as plain text in a data-bound control such as *GridView* or *DetailsView*. To specify the field to display, you set the *DataField* property to the field's name. You can apply a custom formatting string to the displayed value by setting the *DataFormatString* property. The *NullDisplayText* property lets you specify alternative text to display should the value be *null*. Finally, by setting the *ConvertEmptyStringToNull* property to *true*, you force the class to consider empty strings as null values.

A *BoundField* can be programmatically hidden from view through the *Visible* property, while the *ReadOnly* property prevents the displayed value from being modified in edit mode. To display a caption in the header or footer sections, set the *HeaderText* and *FooterText* properties, respectively. You can also choose to display an image in the header instead of text. In this case, you set the *HeaderImageUrl* property.

Button Fields

A button field is useful to put a clickable element in a grid's column. You typically use a button field to trigger an action against the current row. A button field represents any action that you want to handle through a server-side event. When the button is clicked, the page posts back and fires a *RowCommand* event. Figure 10-6 shows a sample.

Product	Packaging	Price	
Chai	10 boxes x 20 bags	$18.00	Add
Chang	24 - 12 oz bottles	$19.00	Add
Aniseed Syrup	12 - 550 ml bottles	$10.00	Add
Chef Anton's Cajun Seasoning	48 - 6 oz jars	$22.00	Add
Chef Anton's Gumbo Mix	36 boxes	$21.35	Add
Grandma's Boysenberry Spread	12 - 8 oz jars	$25.00	Add
Uncle Bob's Organic Dried Pears	12 - 1 lb pkgs.	$30.00	Add
Northwoods Cranberry Sauce	12 - 12 oz jars	$40.00	Add
Mishi Kobe Niku	18 - 500 g pkgs.	$97.00	Add
Ikura	12 - 200 ml jars	$31.00	Add

> >>

Page: 1

Your Shopping Cart

Quantity	Product	Price
1	Grandma's Boysenberry Spread	25.0000
1	Aniseed Syrup	10.0000
1	Ikura	31.0000
1	Chai	18.0000

FIGURE 10-6 Button fields in a *GridView* control.

The following listing shows the markup code behind the grid in the figure:

```
<asp:GridView ID="GridView1" runat="server" DataSourceID="ObjectDataSource1"
    AutoGenerateColumns="false" AllowPaging="true"
    OnRowCommand="GridView1_RowCommand">
    <PagerSettings Mode="NextPreviousFirstLast" />
    <Columns>
        <asp:BoundField datafield="productname"
            headertext="Product" />
        <asp:BoundField datafield="quantityperunit"
            headertext="Packaging" />
        <asp:BoundField datafield="unitprice"
            headertext="Price"
            htmlencode="false"
            DataFormatString="{0:c}">
          <itemstyle width="80px" horizontalalign="right" />
        </asp:BoundField>
        <asp:ButtonField buttontype="Button" text="Add" CommandName="Add" />
    </Columns>
</asp:GridView>
```

Product information is displayed using a few *BoundField* objects. The sample button column allows you to add the product to the shopping cart. When users click the button, the *RowCommand* server event is fired. In case multiple button columns are available, the *CommandName* attribute lets you figure out which button was clicked. The value you assign to *CommandName* is any unique string that the code-behind class can understand. Here's an example:

```
void GridView1_RowCommand(object sender, GridViewCommandEventArgs e)
{
    if (e.CommandName.Equals("Add"))
    {
        // Get the index of the clicked row
        int index = Convert.ToInt32(e.CommandArgument);

        // Create a new shopping item and add it to the cart
        AddToShoppingCart(index);
    }
}
```

In the sample, the button column shows fixed text for all data items. You get this by setting the *Text* property on the *ButtonField* class. If you want to bind the button text to a particular field on the current data item, you set the *DataTextField* property to the name of that field.

You can choose different styles for the button—push, link, or image. To render the button as an image, do as follows:

```
<asp:buttonfield buttontype="Image" CommandName="Add"
    ImageUrl="/images/cart.gif"  />
```

To add a ToolTip to the button (or the image), you need to handle the *RowCreated* event. (I'll discuss this in more detail later in the chapter.)

> **Note** The *DataFormatString* property of the *BoundField* class doesn't work properly without the additional attribute *HtmlEncode="false"*. The reason is because ASP.NET first HTML-encodes the value of bound field and then applies the formatting. But at that point, the bound value is no longer affected by the specified format string. Enabling HTML-encoding earlier in the cycle is a security measure aimed at preventing cross-site scripting attacks.

Hyperlink Fields

Hyperlink columns point the user to a different URL, optionally displayed in an inner frame. Both the text and URL of the link can be obtained from the bound source. In particular, the URL can be set in either of two ways: through a direct binding to a data source field or by using a hard-coded URL with a customized query string. You choose the direct binding if the URL is stored in one of the data source fields. In this case, you set the *DataNavigateUrlFields* property to the name of the column. In some situations, though, the URL to access is application specific and is not stored in the data source. In this case, you can set the *DataNavigateUrlFormatString* property with a hard-coded URL and with an array of parameters in the query string, as follows:

```
<asp:HyperLinkField DataTextField="productname"
    HeaderText="Product"
    DataNavigateUrlFields="productid"
    DataNavigateUrlFormatString="productinfo.aspx?id={0}"
    Target="ProductView" />
```

When the user clicks, the browser fills the specified frame window with the contents of the *productinfo.aspx?id=xxx* URL, where *xxx* comes from the *productid* field. The URL can include multiple parameters. To include more data-bound values, just set the *DataNavigateUrlFields* property to a comma-separated list of field names. This behavior extends that of the *DataGrid*'s hyperlink column in that it supports multiple parameters.

The text of the hyperlink can be formatted too. The *DataTextFormatString* property can contain any valid markup and uses the {0} placeholder to reserve space for the data-bound value. (See Figure 10-7.)

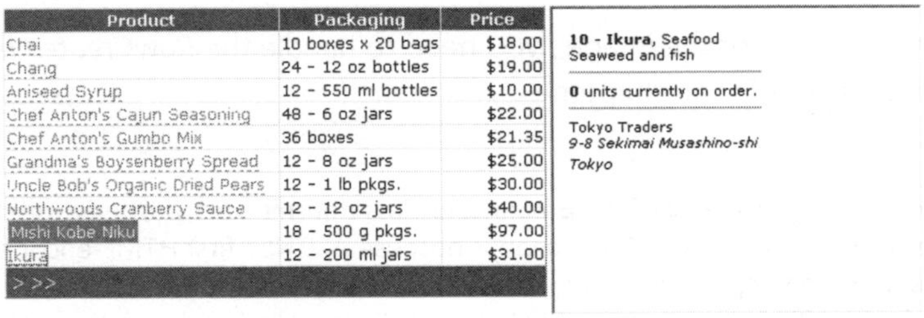

Product	Packaging	Price
Chai	10 boxes x 20 bags	$18.00
Chang	24 – 12 oz bottles	$19.00
Aniseed Syrup	12 – 550 ml bottles	$10.00
Chef Anton's Cajun Seasoning	48 – 6 oz jars	$22.00
Chef Anton's Gumbo Mix	36 boxes	$21.35
Grandma's Boysenberry Spread	12 – 8 oz jars	$25.00
Uncle Bob's Organic Dried Pears	12 – 1 lb pkgs.	$30.00
Northwoods Cranberry Sauce	12 – 12 oz jars	$40.00
Mishi Kobe Niku	18 – 500 g pkgs.	$97.00
Ikura	12 – 200 ml jars	$31.00

> **10 - Ikura**, Seafood
> Seaweed and fish
>
> **0** units currently on order.
>
> Tokyo Traders
> *9-8 Sekimai Musashino-shi*
> *Tokyo*

FIGURE 10-7 Hyperlink fields in a *GridView* control.

Check Box Fields

The *CheckBoxField* column is a relatively simple bound column that displays a check box. You can bind it only to a data field that contains Boolean values. A valid Boolean value is a value taken from a column of type *Bit* in a SQL Server table (and analogous types in other databases) or a property of type *bool* if the control is bound to a custom collection. Any other form of binding will result in a parsing exception. In particular, you get an exception if you bind a *CheckBoxField* column to an integer property, thus implicitly assuming that 0 is false and a nonzero value is true.

Image Fields

The *ImageField* column type represents a field that is displayed as an image in a data-bound control. The cell contains an *<img>* element, so the underlying field must reference a valid URL. You can compose the URL at will, though. For example, you can use the *DataImageUrlField* to perform a direct binding where the content of the field fills the *Src* attribute of the *<img>* tag. Alternatively, you can make the column cells point to an external page (or HTTP handler) that retrieves the bytes of the image from any source and passes them down to the browser. The following code illustrates this approach:

```
<Columns>
  <asp:ImageField DataImageUrlField="employeeid"
    DataImageUrlFormatString="showemployeepicture.ashx?id={0}"
    DataAlternateTextField="lastname">
  <ControlStyle Width="120px" />
</asp:ImageField>
<asp:TemplateField headertext="Employee">
  <ItemStyle Width="220px" />
  <ItemTemplate>
      <b><%# Eval("titleofcourtesy") + " " +
            Eval("lastname") + ", " +
            Eval("firstname") %></b> <br />
          <%# Eval("title")%>
          <hr />
          <i><%# Eval("notes")%></i>
  </ItemTemplate>
  </asp:templatefield>
</Columns>
```

Cells in the *ImageField* column are filled with the output of the next URL:

```
ShowEmployeePicture.ashx?id=xxx
```

Obviously, *xxx* is the value in the *employeeid* field associated with *DataImageUrlField*. Interestingly enough, the alternate text can also be data bound. To do this, you use the *DataAlternateTextField* property. Figure 10-8 gives a sneak preview of the feature. The page in Figure 10-8 employs a template column to render the employee's information. I'll return to template columns in a moment.

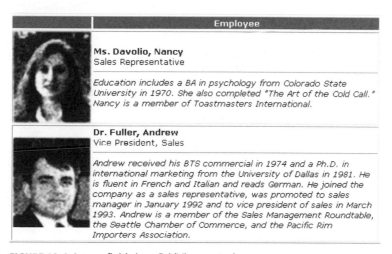

FIGURE 10-8 Image fields in a *GridView* control.

Templated Fields

Figure 10-9 shows a customized column where the values of several fields are combined. This is exactly what you can get by using templates. A *TemplateField* column gives each row in the grid a personalized user interface that is completely defined by the page developer. You can define templates for various rendering stages, including the default view, in-place editing, the header, and the footer. The supported templates are listed in Table 10-13.

TABLE 10-13 Supported Templates

Template	Description
AlternatingItemTemplate	Defines the contents and appearance of alternating rows. If these items are not specified, *ItemTemplate* is used.
EditItemTemplate	Defines the contents and appearance of the row currently being edited. This template should contain input fields and possibly validators.
FooterTemplate	Defines the contents and appearance of the row's footer.
HeaderTemplate	Defines the contents and appearance of the row's header.
ItemTemplate	Defines the default contents and appearance of the rows.

A templated view can contain anything that makes sense to the application you're building—server controls, literals, and data-bound expressions. Data-bound expressions allow you to insert values contained in the current data row. You can use as many fields as needed in a template. Notice, though, that not all templates support data-bound expressions. The header and footer templates are not data-bound, and any attempt to use expressions will result in an exception.

The following code shows how to define the item template for a product column. The column displays on two lines and includes the name of the product and some information about the packaging.

```
<asp:templatefield headertext="Product">
    <itemtemplate>
        <b><%# Eval("productname")%></b> <br />
        available in <%# Eval("quantityperunit")%>
    </itemtemplate>
</asp:templatefield>
```

Figure 10-9 demonstrates template fields in action.

Product	Price
Chai available in 10 boxes x 20 bags	$18.00
Chang available in 24 - 12 oz bottles	$19.00
Aniseed Syrup available in 12 - 550 ml bottles	$10.00
Chef Anton's Cajun Seasoning available in 48 - 6 oz jars	$22.00
Chef Anton's Gumbo Mix available in 36 boxes	$21.35
Grandma's Boysenberry Spread available in 12 - 8 oz jars	$25.00
Uncle Bob's Organic Dried Pears available in 12 - 1 lb pkgs.	$30.00
Northwoods Cranberry Sauce available in 12 - 12 oz jars	$40.00
Mishi Kobe Niku available in 18 - 500 g pkgs.	$97.00
Ikura available in 12 - 200 ml jars	$31.00

> >>

FIGURE 10-9 Template fields in a *GridView* control.

Working with the *GridView*

A big difference between the old-fashioned *DataGrid* control and the *GridView* control is in how the control interacts with the host page. The interaction that is established between the *DataGrid* and the host page is limited to exchanging notifications in the form of postback events. The *DataGrid* lets the page know that something happened and leaves the page free to react as appropriate. The *GridView*, instead, if bound to a data source component can resolve postbacks on its own by interacting autonomously with the bound component. For both *DataGrid* and *GridView* controls, however, the main operations are paging, sorting, and in-place editing.

Paging Data

The ability to scroll a potentially large set of data is an important but challenging feature for modern, distributed applications. An effective paging mechanism allows customers to inter-act with a database without holding resources. To enable paging on a *GridView* control, all you do is set the *AllowPaging* property to *true*. When the *AllowPaging* property is set to *true*, the grid displays a pager bar and prepares to detect a user's pager button clicks.

When a user clicks to see a new page, the page posts back, but the *GridView* traps the event and handles it internally. With the *GridView*, there's no need to write a handler for the *PageIndexChanged* event. The event is still exposed (and partnered with *PageIndexChanging*), but you should handle it only to perform extra actions. The *GridView* knows how to retrieve and display the requested new page. Let's take a look at the following control declaration:

```
<asp:GridView ID="GridView1" runat="server"
    DataSourceID="ObjectDataSource1" AllowPaging="true" />
```

Any data the data source component binds to the grid is immediately pageable. As shown in Figure 10-10, the control displays a pager with a few predefined links (first, previous, next, and last) and automatically selects the correct subset of rows that fit in the selected page.

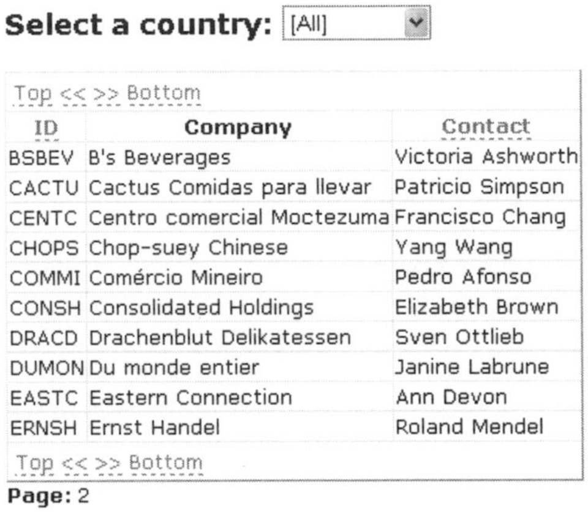

Select a country: [All] ▼

ID	Company	Contact
BSBEV	B's Beverages	Victoria Ashworth
CACTU	Cactus Comidas para llevar	Patricio Simpson
CENTC	Centro comercial Moctezuma	Francisco Chang
CHOPS	Chop-suey Chinese	Yang Wang
COMMI	Comércio Mineiro	Pedro Afonso
CONSH	Consolidated Holdings	Elizabeth Brown
DRACD	Drachenblut Delikatessen	Sven Ottlieb
DUMON	Du monde entier	Janine Labrune
EASTC	Eastern Connection	Ann Devon
ERNSH	Ernst Handel	Roland Mendel

Top << >> Bottom

Page: 2

FIGURE 10-10 Moving through pages in a *GridView* control.

The default user interface you get with the *GridView* doesn't include the page number. Adding a page number label is as easy as writing a handler for the *PageIndexChanged* event:

```
protected void GridView1_PageIndexChanged(object sender, EventArgs e)
{
    ShowPageIndex();
}
private void ShowPageIndex()
{
    CurrentPage.Text = (GridView1.PageIndex + 1).ToString();
}
```

Once again, note that the *PageIndexChanged* handler is not involved with data binding or page selection as it is with *DataGrids*. If you don't need any post-paging operation, you can blissfully omit it altogether.

What's the cost of this apparently free (and magical) paging mechanism?

The *GridView* control doesn't really know how to get a new page. It simply asks the bound data source control to return the rows that fit in the specified page. Paging is ultimately up to the data source control. When a grid is bound to a *SqlDataSource* control, paging requires that the whole data source be bound to the control. When a grid is bound to an *ObjectDataSource* control, paging depends on the capabilities of the business object you're connecting to.

When the *AllowPaging* property is set to *true*, the grid displays a pager bar. You can control the characteristics of the pager to a large extent, through the *<PagerSettings>* and *<PagerStyle>* tags or their equivalent properties. The pager of the *GridView* control also supports first and last page buttons and lets you assign an image to each button. (This is also possible for *DataGrid*s, but it requires a lot of code.) The pager can work in either of two modes—displaying explicit page numbers, or providing a relative navigation system. In the former case, the pager contains numeric links, one representing a page index. In the latter case, buttons are present to navigate to the next or previous page and even to the first or last page. The *Mode* property rules the user interface of the pager. Available modes are listed in Table 10-14.

TABLE 10-14 Modes of a Grid Pager

Mode	Description
NextPrevious	Displays next and previous buttons to access the next and previous pages of the grid
NextPreviousFirstLast	Displays next and previous buttons, plus first and last buttons to directly access the first and last pages of the grid
Numeric	Displays numeric link buttons corresponding to the pages of the grid
NumericFirstLast	Displays numeric link buttons corresponding to the pages of the grid, plus first and last buttons to directly access the first and last pages of the grid

Ad hoc pairs of properties—*xxxPageText* and *xxxPageImageUrl*—let you set the labels for these buttons as desired. The *xxx* stands for any of the following: First, Last, Next, or Previous.

Sorting Data

Sorting is a delicate, nonlinear operation that normally is quite expensive if performed on the client. Generally speaking, in fact, the best place to sort records is in the database environment because of the super-optimized code you end up running most of the time. Be aware of this as we examine the sorting infrastructure of the *GridView* control and data source controls. The *GridView* doesn't implement a sorting algorithm; instead, it relies on the data source control (or the page, if bound to an enumerable object) to provide sorted data.

To enable the *GridView*'s sorting capabilities, you set the *AllowSorting* property to *true*. When sorting is enabled, the *GridView* gains the ability of rendering the header text of columns as links. You can associate each column with a sorting expression by using the *SortExpression* property. A sorting expression is any comma-separated sequence of column names. Each column name can be enriched with an order qualifier such as DESC or ASC. DESC indicates a descending order, while ASC denotes the ascending order. The ASC qualifier is the default; if the order qualifier value is omitted, the column is sorted in ascending order. The following code sets up the *GridView* column for sorting on the *productname* data source column:

```
<asp:GridView runat="server" id="MyGridView" DataSourceID="MySource"
   AllowSorting="true" AutoGenerateColumns="false">
   <Columns>
      <asp:BoundField datafield="productname" headertext="Product"
          sortexpression="productname" />
      <asp:BoundField datafield="quantityperunit"
          headertext="Packaging" />
   </Columns>
</asp:GridView>
```

Just as for paging, with a *GridView* no manually written code is required to make sorting work. If properly configured, the *GridView*'s sorting infrastructure works without further intervention and in a bidirectional way—that is, if you click on a column sorted in descending order, it is sorted in ascending order and vice versa. You need to add some custom code only if you want to implement more advanced capabilities such as showing a glyph in the header to indicate the direction. Just as for paging, the main snag with sorting is how the underlying data source control implements it.

Editing Data

A major strength of the *GridView* control—which makes up for a major shortcoming of the *DataGrid*—is the ability to handle updates to the data source. The *DataGrid* control provides only an infrastructure for data editing. The *DataGrid* provides the necessary user interface elements and fires appropriate events when the user modifies the value of a certain data field, but it does not submit those changes back to the data source. Developers are left with the disappointing realization that they have to write a huge amount of boilerplate code to really persist changes.

With the *GridView* control, when the bound data source supports updates, the control can automatically perform this operation, thus providing a truly out-of-the-box solution. The data source control signals its capability to update through the *CanUpdate* Boolean property.

The *GridView* can render a column of command buttons for each row in the grid. These special command columns contain buttons to edit or delete the current record. With the *DataGrid*, you must explicitly create an edit command column using a special column type— the *EditCommandColumn* class. The *GridView* simplifies things quite a bit for update and delete operations.

In-place editing refers to the grid's ability to support changes to the currently displayed records. You enable in-place editing on a grid view by turning on the *AutoGenerateEditButton* Boolean property:

```
<asp:gridview runat="server" id="GridView1" datasourceid="MySource"
     autogeneratecolumns="false" autogenerateeditbutton="true">
   ...
</asp:gridview>
```

When the *AutoGenerateEditButton* property is set to *true*, the *GridView* displays an additional column, like that shown in Figure 10-11. By clicking the Edit button, you put the selected row in edit mode and can enter new data at will.

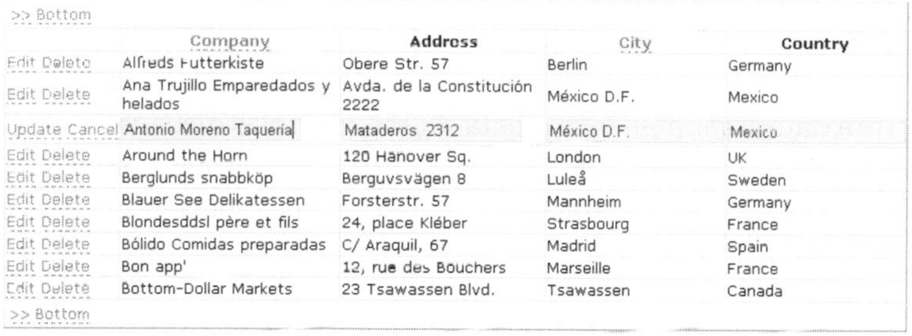

>> Bottom

	Company	Address	City	Country
Edit Delete	Alfreds Futterkiste	Obere Str. 57	Berlin	Germany
Edit Delete	Ana Trujillo Emparedados y helados	Avda. de la Constitución 2222	México D.F.	Mexico
Update Cancel	Antonio Moreno Taquería	Mataderos 2312	México D.F.	Mexico
Edit Delete	Around the Horn	120 Hanover Sq.	London	UK
Edit Delete	Berglunds snabbköp	Berguvsvägen 8	Luleå	Sweden
Edit Delete	Blauer See Delikatessen	Forsterstr. 57	Mannheim	Germany
Edit Delete	Blondesddsl père et fils	24, place Kléber	Strasbourg	France
Edit Delete	Bólido Comidas preparadas	C/ Araquil, 67	Madrid	Spain
Edit Delete	Bon app'	12, rue des Bouchers	Marseille	France
Edit Delete	Bottom-Dollar Markets	23 Tsawassen Blvd.	Tsawassen	Canada

>> Bottom

FIGURE 10-11 A *GridView* that supports in-place editing.

To abort editing and undo any changes, users simply click the *Cancel* button. The *GridView* can handle this click without any external support; the row returns to its original read-only state; and the *EditIndex* property takes back its –1 default value—meaning no row is currently being edited. But what if users click the update link? The *GridView* first fires the *RowUpdating* event and then internally checks the *CanUpdate* property on the data source control. If *CanUpdate* returns *false*, an exception is thrown. *CanUpdate* returns *false* if the data source control has no update command defined. The successful completion of an update command is signaled throughout the grid via the *RowUpdated* event.

The *GridView* collects values from the input fields and populates a dictionary of name/value pairs that indicate the new values for each field of the row. The *GridView* also exposes a *RowUpdating* event that allows the programmer to validate the values being passed to the data source object. In addition, the *GridView* automatically calls *Page.IsValid* before starting the update operation on the associated data source. If *Page.IsValid* returns *false*, the operation is canceled. This is especially useful if you're using a custom template with validators. If the grid is bound to an *ObjectDataSource* control, things go a bit differently. The bound business object must have an update method. This method will receive as many arguments as it needs to work. You can decide to pass parameters individually or grouped in a unique data structure. This second option is preferable if you have a well-done data access layer (DAL).

Data Source Components

A data source component is a server control designed to interact with data-bound controls and hide the complexity of the manual data-binding pattern. Data source components not only provide data to controls, they also support data-bound controls in the execution of other common operations such as insertions, deletions, sorting, and updates. Each data source component wraps a particular data provider—relational databases, XML documents, special object models, or custom classes. The support for custom classes means that you can now directly bind your controls to existing classes—for example, classes in your business or data access layer.

Internals of Data Source Controls

A data source control represents one or more named views of data. Each view manages a collection of data. The data associated with a data source control is managed through SQL-like operations such as SELECT, INSERT, DELETE, and COUNT and through capabilities such as sorting and paging. Data source controls come in two flavors: tabular and hierarchical. Tabular controls are described in Table 10-15.

TABLE 10-15 Tabular Data Source Controls

Class	Description
AccessDataSource	Represents a connection to a Microsoft Access database. It inherits from the *SqlDataSource* control, but it points to an MDB file and uses the Jet 4.0 OLE DB provider to connect to the database.
EntityDataSource	Allows binding to the results of an Entity Framework query.
LinqDataSource	Allows binding to the results of any supported LINQ provider, including of course LINQ-to-SQL. The control offers properties for you to specify the data context, table name, projection parameters, and *where* clause.
ObjectDataSource	Allows binding to a custom .NET business object that returns data. The class is expected to follow a specific design pattern and include, for example, a parameterless constructor and methods that behave in a certain way.
SqlDataSource	Represents a connection to an ADO.NET data provider that returns SQL data, including data sources accessible through OLE DB and ODBC. The name of the provider and the connection string are specified through properties.

Note that the *SqlDataSource* class is *not* specific to SQL Server. It can connect to any ADO.NET provider that manages relational data. Hierarchical data source controls are listed in Table 10-16.

TABLE 10-16 **Hierarchical Data Source Controls**

Class	Description
SiteMapDataSource	Allows binding to any provider that supplies site map information. The default provider supplies site map data through an XML file in the root folder of the application.
XmlDataSource	Allows binding to XML files and strings with or without schema information.

Note that data source controls have no visual rendering. They are implemented as controls to allow for "declarative persistence" (automatic instantiation during the request processing) as a native part of the .*aspx* source code and to gain access to the page view state.

Data Source Views

A named view is represented by a data source view object—an instance of the *DataSourceView* class. These classes represent a customized view of data in which special settings for sorting, filtering, and other data operations have been defined. The *DataSourceView* class is the base class for all views associated with a data source control. The number of views in a data source control depends on the connection string, characteristics, and actual contents of the underlying data source. In ASP.NET, built-in data source controls support only one view, the default view. Table 10-17 lists the properties of the *DataSourceView* class.

TABLE 10-17 **Properties of the *DataSourceView* Class**

Property	Description
CanDelete	Indicates whether deletions are allowed on the underlying data source. The deletion is performed by invoking the *Delete* method.
CanInsert	Indicates whether insertions are allowed on the underlying data source. The insertion is performed by invoking the *Insert* method.
CanPage	Indicates whether the data in the view can be paged.
CanRetrieveTotalRowCount	Indicates whether information about the total row count is available.
CanSort	Indicates whether the data in the view can be sorted.
CanUpdate	Indicates whether updates are allowed on the underlying data source. The update is performed by invoking the *Update* method.
Name	Returns the name of the current view.

The *CanXXX* properties indicate not only whether the data source control is capable of performing the specified operation but also whether that operation is appropriate given the current status of the data. Table 10-18 lists all the methods supported by the class.

TABLE 10-18 Methods of the *DataSourceView* Class

Method	Description
Delete	Performs a delete operation on the data associated with the view
Insert	Performs an insert operation on the data associated with the view
Select	Returns an enumerable object filled with the data contained in the underlying data storage
Update	Performs an update operation on the data associated with the view

All data source view objects support data retrieval through the *Select* method. The method returns an object that implements the *IEnumerable* interface. The real type of the object depends on the data source control and the attributes set on it.

Hierarchical Data Source Views

Unlike tabular data source controls, which typically have only one named view, hierarchical data source controls support a view for each level of data that the data source control represents. Hierarchical and tabular data source controls share the same conceptual specification of a consistent and common programming interface for data-bound controls. The only difference is the nature of the data they work with—hierarchical vs. flat and tabular.

The view class is different and is named *HierarchicalDataSourceView*. The class features only one method—*Select*—which returns an enumerable hierarchical object. Hierarchical data source controls are, therefore, read-only.

> **Important** Frankly speaking, I don't like data source components much. It's nothing personal; it's only business—my business layer, to be precise! Data source components have been one of the several approaches of Microsoft to make programming easier. With data source components you write less code and write most of your code in classes instead of ASPX pages. The risk I see with data source components—and the reason why I don't much like them—is that they end up being used everywhere and the entire back-end of the application is built around the needs of some data source components. I haven't used the *SqlDataSource* control for years now; I never used the *LinqDataSource* and have no plans to use the *EntityDataSource*.
>
> My advice, reflected in the book, can be summarized as follows. If you feel you have the need to model your business domain via an object model, use LINQ-to-SQL or Entity Framework and write a serious business layer around that. If the classes in the business layer don't match up with the expectations of rich controls like a *GridView*, add another layer of components that can be easily plugged in via *ObjectDataSource*. In any case, if you are going to use data source components for data binding, the only control worth a look is, in my humble opinion, the *ObjectDataSource* control.

The *ObjectDataSource* Control

The *ObjectDataSource* class enables user-defined classes to associate the output of their methods to data-bound controls. Like other data source controls, *ObjectDataSource* supports declarative parameters to allow developers to pass page-level variables to the object's methods. The *ObjectDataSource* class makes some assumptions about the objects it wraps. As a consequence, an arbitrary class can't be used with this data source control. In particular, bindable classes are expected to have a default constructor, be stateless, and have methods that easily map to select, update, insert, and delete semantics. Also, the object must perform updates one item at a time; objects that update their state using batch operations are not supported. The bottom line is that managed objects that work well with *ObjectDataSource* are designed with this data source class in mind.

Programming Interface of *ObjectDataSource*

The *ObjectDataSource* component provides nearly the same programmatic interface (events, methods, properties, and associated behaviors) as the *SqlDataSource*, with the addition of three new events and a few properties. The events the *ObjectDataSource* fires are related to the lifetime of the underlying business object the *ObjectDataSource* is bound to—*ObjectCreating*, *ObjectCreated*, and *ObjectDisposing*. Table 10-18 lists other key properties of *ObjectDataSource*.

TABLE 10-18 Main Properties of *ObjectDataSource*

Property	Description
ConvertNullToDBNull	Indicates whether null parameters passed to insert, delete, or update operations are converted to *System.DBNull*. This property is set to *false* by default.
DataObjectTypeName	Gets or sets the name of a class that is to be used as a parameter for a select, insert, update, or delete operation.
DeleteMethod, DeleteParameters	Gets or sets the name of the method and related parameters used to perform a delete operation.
EnablePaging	Indicates whether the control supports paging.
FilterExpression, FilterParameters	Indicates the filter expression (and parameters) to filter the output of a select operation.
InsertMethod, InsertParameters	Gets or sets the name of the method and related parameters used to perform an insert operation.
MaximumRowsParameterName	If the *EnablePaging* property is set to *true*, indicates the parameter name of the *Select* method that accepts the value for the number of records to retrieve.
OldValuesParameterFormatString	Gets or sets a format string to apply to the names of any parameters passed to the *Delete* or *Update* methods.
SelectCountMethod	Gets or sets the name of the method used to perform a select count operation.

Property	Description
SelectMethod, SelectParameters	Gets or sets the name of the method and related parameters used to perform a select operation.
SortParameterName	Gets or sets the name of an input parameter used to sort retrieved data. It raises an exception if the parameter is missing.
StartRowIndexParameterName	If the *EnablePaging* property is set to *true*, indicates the parameter name of the *Select* method that accepts the value for the starting record to retrieve.
UpdateMethod, UpdateParameters	Gets or sets the name of the method and related parameters used to perform an update operation.

The *ObjectDataSource* control uses reflection to locate and invoke the method to handle the specified operation. The *TypeName* property returns the fully qualified name of the assembly that defines the class to call.

Implementing Data Retrieval

The following code snippet illustrates a class that can be used with an object data source. In the example, the class does not use LINQ-to-SQL or Entity Framework; it is instead based on plain ADO.NET code. You can easily rewrite it to perform data access via the context of LINQ-to-SQL or Entity Framework. The *Employee* class being used is assumed to be a custom class created just to simplify data manipulation.

```
public class EmployeeRepository
{
    public static string ConnectionString {
        ...
    }
    public static void Load(int employeeID) {
        ...
    }
    public static IList<Employee> LoadAll() {
        ...
    }
    public static IList<Employee> LoadByCountry(string country) {
        ...
    }
    public static void Save(Employee emp) {
        ...
    }
    public static void Insert(Employee emp) {
        ...
    }
    public static void Delete(int employeeID) {
        ...
    }
    ...
}
```

If you don't use static methods, the worker class you use with *ObjectDataSource* must have a default parameterless constructor. Furthermore, the class should not maintain any state. (The main drawback of static methods is that they might trip you up when it comes to unit testing the DAL, if you ever do it.)

The worker class must be accessible from within the *.aspx* page and can be bound to the *ObjectDataSource* control, as shown here:

```
<asp:ObjectDataSource runat="server" ID="MyObjectSource"
    TypeName="DAL.EmployeeRepository"
    SelectMethod="LoadAll" />
```

When the HTTP runtime encounters a similar block in a Web page, it generates code that calls the *LoadAll* method on the specified class. The returned data—a collection of *Employee* instances—is bound to any control that links to *MyObjectSource* via the *DataSourceID* property. Let's take a brief look at the implementation of the *LoadAll* method:

```
public static EmployeeCollection LoadAll()
{
    var coll = new List<Employee>();

    using (var conn = new SqlConnection(ConnectionString)
    {
        var cmd = new SqlCommand("SELECT * FROM employees", conn);
        conn.Open();
        var reader = cmd.ExecuteReader();
        HelperMethods.FillEmployeeList(coll, reader);
        reader.Close();
            }
    return coll;
}
```

Although it's a bit oversimplified so that it can fit in this section, the preceding code remains quite clear: you execute a command, fill in a custom collection class, and return it to the data-bound control. Binding is totally seamless.

The method associated with the *SelectMethod* property must return any of the following: an *IEnumerable* object such as a collection, a *DataSet*, a *DataTable*, or an *Object*. Preferably, the *Select* method is not overloaded, although *ObjectDataSource* doesn't prevent you from using an overloaded method in your business classes.

Using Parameters

In most cases, methods require parameters. *SelectParameters* is the collection you use to add input parameters to the select method. Imagine you have a method to load employees by country/region. Here's the code you need to come up with:

```
<asp:ObjectDataSource ID="ObjectDataSource1" runat="server"
    TypeName="DAL.EmployeeRepository"
    SelectMethod="LoadByCountry">
    <SelectParameters>
        <asp:ControlParameter Name="country" ControlID="Countries"
            PropertyName="SelectedValue" />
    </SelectParameters>
</asp:ObjectDataSource>
```

The preceding code snippet is the declarative version of the following pseudocode, where *Countries* is expected to be a drop-down list filled with country/region names:

```
string country = Countries.SelectedValue;
EmployeeCollection coll = Employees.LoadByCountry(country);
```

The *ControlParameter* class automates the retrieval of the actual parameter value and the binding to the parameter list of the method. What if you add an *[All Countries]* entry to the drop-down list? In this case, if the All Countries option is selected, you need to call *LoadAll* without parameters; otherwise, if a particular country/region is selected, you need to call *LoadByCountry* with a parameter. Declarative programming works great in the simple scenarios; otherwise, you just write code.

```
void Page_Load(object sender, EventArgs e)
{
    // Must be cleared every time (or disable the viewstate)
    ObjectDataSource1.SelectParameters.Clear();

    if (Countries.SelectedIndex == 0)
        ObjectDataSource1.SelectMethod = "LoadAll";
    else
    {
        ObjectDataSource1.SelectMethod = "LoadByCountry";
        ControlParameter cp = new ControlParameter("country",
            "Countries", "SelectedValue");
        ObjectDataSource1.SelectParameters.Add(cp);
    }
}
```

Note that data source controls are like ordinary server controls and can be programmatically configured and invoked. In the code just shown, you first check the selection the user made and, if it matches the first option (All Countries), configure the data source control to make a parameterless call to the *LoadAll* method.

You must clean up the content of the *SelectParameters* collection upon page loading. The data source control (more precisely, the underlying view control) caches most of its properties to the view state. As a result, *SelectParameters* is not empty when you refresh the page after changing the drop-down list selection. The preceding code clears only the *SelectParameters* collection; performancewise, it could be preferable to disable the view state altogether on the data source control. However, if you disable the view state, all collections will be empty on the data source control upon loading.

> **Important** *ObjectDataSource* allows data to be retrieved and updated while keeping data access and business logic separate from the user interface. The use of the *ObjectDataSource* class doesn't automatically transform your system into a well-designed, effective *n*-tiered system. Data source controls are mostly a counterpart to data-bound controls so that the latter can work more intelligently.
>
> To take full advantage of *ObjectDataSource*, you need to have your DAL already in place. It doesn't work the other way around. *ObjectDataSource* doesn't necessarily have to be bound to the root of the DAL, which could be on a remote location and perhaps behind a firewall. In this case, you write a local intermediate object and connect it to *ObjectDataSource* on one end and to the DAL on the other end. The intermediate object acts as an application-specific proxy and works according to the application's specific rules. *ObjectDataSource* doesn't break *n*-tiered systems, nor does it transform existing systems into truly *n*-tier systems. It greatly benefits, instead, from existing business and data layers.

Caching Data and Object Instances

The *ObjectDataSource* component supports caching only when the specified select method returns a *DataSet* or *DataTable* object. If the wrapped object returns a custom collection (as in the example we're considering), an exception is thrown. Custom object caching is something you must do on your own.

ObjectDataSource is designed to work with classes in the business layer of the application. An instance of the business class is created for each operation performed and is destroyed shortly after the operation is completed. This model is the natural offspring of the stateless programming model that ASP.NET promotes. In the case of business objects that are particularly expensive to initialize, you can resort to static classes or static methods in instance classes. (If you do so, bear in mind what I said earlier regarding unit testing classes with static methods.)

Instances of the business object are not automatically cached or pooled. Both options, though, can be manually implemented by properly handling the *ObjectCreating* and *ObjectDisposing* events on an *ObjectDataSource* control. The *ObjectCreating* event fires when the data source control needs to get an instance of the business class. You can write the handler to retrieve an existing instance of the class and return that to the data source control:

```
// Handle the ObjectCreating event on the data source control
public void BusinessObjectBeingCreated(object sender,
        ObjectDataSourceEventArgs e)
{
    BusinessObject bo = RetrieveBusinessObjectFromPool();
    if (bo == null)
        bo = new BusinessObject();
    e.ObjectInstance = bo;
}
```

Likewise, in *ObjectDisposing* you store the instance again and cancel the disposing operation being executed:

```
// Handle the ObjectDisposing event on the data source control
public void BusinessObjectBeingDisposed(object sender,
        ObjectDataSourceDisposingEventArgs e)
{
    ReturnBusinessObjectToPool(e.ObjectInstance);
    e.Cancel = true;
}
```

The *ObjectDisposing* event allows you to perform cleanup actions in your business object before the *ObjectDataSource* calls the business object's *Dispose* method. If you're caching the business object, as the preceding code has done, be sure to set the cancel flag so that the business object's *Dispose* method isn't invoked and the cached object isn't as a result stored in a disposed state.

Setting Up for Paging

Three properties participate in paging: *EnablePaging*, *StartRowIndexParameterName*, and *MaximumRowsParameterName*. As the name clearly suggests, *EnablePaging* toggles support for paging on and off. The default value is *false*, meaning that paging is not turned on automatically. *ObjectDataSource* provides an infrastructure for paging, but actual paging must be implemented in the class bound to *ObjectDataSource*. In the following code snippet, the *Customers* class has a method, *LoadByCountry*, that takes two additional parameters to indicate the page size and the index of the first record in the page. The names of these two parameters must be assigned to *MaximumRowsParameterName* and *StartRowIndexParameterName*, respectively.

```
<asp:ObjectDataSource ID="ObjectDataSource1" runat="server"
    TypeName="DAL.CustomerRepository"
    StartRowIndexParameterName="firstRow"
    MaximumRowsParameterName="totalRows"
    SelectMethod="LoadByCountry">
  <SelectParameters>
    <asp:ControlParameter Name="country" ControlID="Countries"
```

```
                      PropertyName="SelectedValue" />
        <asp:ControlParameter Name="totalRows" ControlID="PageSize"
                      PropertyName="Text" />
        <asp:ControlParameter Name="firstRow" ControlID="FirstRow"
                      PropertyName="Text" />
    </SelectParameters>
</asp:ObjectDataSource>
```

The implementation of paging is up to the method and must be coded manually.
LoadByCountry provides two overloads, one of which supports paging. Internally, paging is
actually delegated to *FillCustomerList*.

```
public static CustomerCollection LoadByCountry(string country)
{
    return LoadByCountry(country, -1, 0);
}
public static CustomerCollection LoadByCountry(string country,
        int totalRows, int firstRow)
{
    CustomerCollection coll = new CustomerCollection();

    using (SqlConnection conn = new SqlConnection(ConnectionString))
    {
        SqlCommand cmd;
        cmd = new SqlCommand(CustomerCommands.cmdLoadByCountry, conn);
        cmd.Parameters.AddWithValue("@country", country);

        conn.Open();
        SqlDataReader reader = cmd.ExecuteReader();
        HelperMethods.FillCustomerList(coll, reader, totalRows, firstRow);
        reader.Close();
        conn.Close();
    }

    return coll;
}
```

As you can see in the companion source code, *FillCustomerList* simply scrolls the whole result
set using a reader and discards all the records that don't belong in the requested range. You
could perhaps improve upon this approach to make paging smarter. What's important here
is that paging is built into your business object and exposed by data source controls to the
pageable controls through a well-known interface.

Updating and Deleting Data

To update underlying data using *ObjectDataSource*, you need to define an update/insert/
delete method. All the actual methods you use must have semantics that are well suited to
implement such operations. Here are some good prototypes for the update operations:

```
public static void Save(Employee emp)
public static void Insert(Employee emp)
public static void Delete(Employee emp)
public static void Delete(int id)
```

More so than with select operations, update operations require parameters. To update a record, you need to pass new values and one or more old values to make sure the right record to update is located and to take into account the possibility of data conflicts. To delete a record, you need to identify it by matching a supplied primary key parameter. To specify input parameters, you can use command collections such as *UpdateParameters*, *InsertParameters*, or *DeleteParameters*. Let's examine update/insert scenarios first.

To update an existing record or insert a new one, you need to pass new values. This can be done in either of two ways—listing parameters explicitly or aggregating all parameters in an all-encompassing data structure. The prototypes shown previously for *Save* and *Insert* follow the latter approach. An alternative might be the following:

```
void Save(int id, string firstName, string lastName, ...)
void Insert(string firstName, string lastName, ...)
```

You can use command parameter collections only if the types involved are simple types—numbers, strings, dates.

To make a custom class such as *Employee* acceptable to the *ObjectDataSource* control, you need to set the *DataObjectTypeName* property:

```
<asp:ObjectDataSource ID="RowDataSource" runat="server"
    TypeName="DAL.EmployeeRepository"
    SelectMethod="Load"
    UpdateMethod="Save"
    DataObjectTypeName="DAL.Employee">
  <SelectParameters>
     <asp:ControlParameter Name="id" ControlID="GridView1"
         PropertyName="SelectedValue" />
  </SelectParameters>
</asp:ObjectDataSource>
```

The preceding *ObjectDataSource* control saves rows through the *Save* method, which takes an *Employee* object. Note that when you set the *DataObjectTypeName* property, the *UpdateParameters* collection is ignored. The *ObjectDataSource* instantiates a default instance of the object before the operation is performed and then attempts to fill its public members with the values of any matching input fields found around the bound control. Because this work is performed using reflection, the names of the input fields in the bound control must match the names of public properties exposed by the object in the *DataObjectTypeName* property. A practical limitation you must be aware of is the following: you can't define the *Employee* class using complex data types, as follows:

```
public class Employee {
    public string LastName { get; set; }
    public string FirstName { get; set; }
    ...
    public Address HomeAddress {...}
}
```

Representing individual values (*strings* in the sample), the *LastName* and *FirstName* members have good chances to match an input field in the bound control. The same can't be said for the *HomeAddress* member, which is declared with a custom aggregate type such as *Address*. If you go with this schema, all the members in *Address* will be ignored; any related information won't be carried into the *Save* method, with resulting null parameters. All the members in the *Address* data structure should become members of the *Employee* class.

Unlike the insert operation, the update operation also requires a primary key value to uniquely identify the record being updated. If you use an explicit parameter listing, you just append an additional parameter to the list to represent the ID, as follows:

```
<asp:ObjectDataSource runat="server" ID="MyObjectSource"
    TypeName="DAL.SimpleBusinessObject"
    SelectMethod="GetEmployees"
    UpdateMethod="SetEmployee">
  <UpdateParameters>
      <asp:Parameter Name="employeeid" Type="Int32" />
      <asp:Parameter Name="firstname" Type="string" />
      <asp:Parameter Name="lastname" Type="string" />
      <asp:Parameter Name="country" Type="string" DefaultValue="null" />
  </UpdateParameters>
</asp:ObjectDataSource>
```

Note that by setting the *DefaultValue* attribute to *null*, you can make a parameter optional. A null value for a parameter must then be gracefully handled by the business object method that implements the update.

There's an alternative method to set the primary key—through the *DataKeyNames* property of *GridView* and *DetailsView* controls. I'll briefly mention it here and cover it in much greater detail in the next two chapters:

```
<asp:GridView runat="server" ID="grid1"
    DataKeyNames="employeeid"
    DataSourceId="MyObjectSource"
    AutoGenerateEditButton="true">
  ...
</asp:GridView>
```

When *DataKeyNames* is set on the bound control, data source controls automatically add a parameter to the list of parameters for update and delete commands. The default name of the parameter is *original_XXX*, where *XXX* stands for the value of *DataKeyNames*. For the operation to succeed, the method (or the SQL command if you're using *SqlDataSource*) must handle a parameter with the same name. Here's an example:

```
UPDATE employees SET lastname=@lastname
     WHERE employeeid=@original_employeeid
```

The name format of the key parameter can be changed at will through the *OldValuesParameterFormatString* property. For example, a value of '{0}' assigned to the property would make the following command acceptable:

```
UPDATE employees SET lastname=@lastname
      WHERE employeeid=@employeeid
```

Setting the *DataKeyNames* property on the bound control (hold on, note that it's *not* a property on the data source control) is also the simplest way to configure a delete operation. For a delete operation, in fact, you don't need to specify a whole record with all its fields; the key is sufficient.

Configuring Parameters at Runtime

When using *ObjectDataSource* with an ASP.NET made-to-measure control (for example, *GridView*), most of the time the binding is totally automatic and you don't have to deal with it. If you need it, though, there's a back door you can use to take control of the update process—the *Updating* event:

```
protected void Updating(object sender,
        ObjectDataSourceMethodEventArgs e)
{
    var emp = e.InputParameters[0] as Employee;
    if (emp == null) return;
    emp.LastName = "WhosThisGuy";
}
```

The event fires before the update operation climaxes. The *InputParameters* collection lists the parameters being passed to the update method. The collection is read-only, meaning that you can't add or delete elements. However, you can modify objects being transported, as the preceding code snippet demonstrates.

This technique is useful when, for whatever reasons, the *ObjectDataSource* control doesn't load all the data its method needs to perform the update. A similar approach can be taken for deletions and insertions as well.

Summary

ASP.NET data binding has three faces: classic source-based binding, data source controls, and data-binding expressions. Data-binding expressions serve a different purpose than the other two binding techniques. Expressions are used declaratively and within templated controls. They represent calculated values bindable to any property.

The old data-binding model (the same one introduced with ASP.NET 1.x) is maintained intact with enumerable collections of data bound to controls through the *DataSource* property and a few others that are related. In addition, a new family of controls has made its debut over the years—data source controls. By virtue of being implemented as a control, a data source component can be declaratively persisted into a Web page without any further effort in code. In addition, data source controls can benefit from other parts of the page infrastructure, such as the view state and ASP.NET cache. Data source controls accept parameters, prepare and execute a command, and return results (if any). Commands include the typical data operations: select, insert, update, delete, and total count.

The most interesting consequence of data source controls is the tight integration with some new data-bound controls. These smarter data-bound controls (*GridView*, *FormView*, *DetailsView*) contain logic to automatically bind at appropriate times on behalf of the page developer, and they interact with the underlying data source intelligently, requiring you to write much less code. Existing data-bound controls have been extended to support data source controls, but only for select operations.

Data source controls make declarative, codeless programming easier and likely to happen in reality. Data source controls, though, are just tools and not necessarily the right tool for the job you need to do. Use your own judgment on a per-case basis.

In the next chapter, we take a look at the *ListView* control—probably the only data-bound control you would have in ASP.NET if ASP.NET were to be rewritten from scratch today.

Chapter 11
The *ListView* Control

It's a job that's never started that takes the longest to finish.

—*J. R. R. Tolkien*

The *ListView* control sums up the features of multiple view controls in a single one. For example, it can be used to create a tabular view of data nearly identical to the view you can obtain from a *GridView* or *DataGrid* control. At the same time, the *ListView* control can be employed to generate a multicolumn layout with the flexibility that only a general-purpose *Repeater* or, better yet, *DataList* control can offer.

The *ListView* control doesn't only have similarities with other controls; it also has a number of unique features that, when evaluated from a wider perspective, make similarities shine under a different light. *ListView* uses similarities with other controls as the starting point for building more advanced and unique capabilities that warrant it having its own space in the toolbox of ASP.NET controls.

In this chapter, I'll focus on exploring the programming interface of the *ListView* control and its usage in a variety of common scenarios.

The *ListView* Control

The control is fully template based and allows you to control all aspects of the user interface via templates and properties. *ListView* operates in a way that closely resembles the behavior of existing data-bound controls, such as *FormView* or *DataList*. However, unlike these controls, the *ListView* control never creates any user-interface layout. Every markup tag that the control generates is entirely under the developer's control, including header, footer, body, item, selected item, and so on.

The *ListView* control binds to any data source control and executes its set of data operations. It can page, update, insert, and delete data items in the underlying data source as long as the data source supports these operations. In most cases, no code is required to set up any of these operations. If code is required, you can also explicitly bind data to the control using the more traditional *DataSource* property and related *DataBind* method.

The rendering capabilities of the *ListView* control make it suitable for publishing scenarios where a read-only, but compelling, user interface is needed. The control also works great in editing scenarios even though it lacks some advanced features such as input validation or made-to-measure edit templates for particular types of data or foreign keys.

The *ListView* Object Model

Data binding and template support are the principal characteristics of the *ListView* control that are most obvious when you examine the control's programming model. From the programmer's perspective, the key thing to be aware of is that you need to specify at least two template properties for the *ListView* control to compile and work. They are *LayoutTemplate* and *ItemTemplate*. In addition, the overall layout template must expose a connection point to the control so that bound records can be merged into the final markup.

Properties of the *ListView* Control

The *ListView* layout supports several properties that fall into two main categories: behavior and templates. It also supports a few general ASP.NET control properties and binding properties. Table 11-1 lists the behavioral properties.

TABLE 11-1 *ListView* **Behavior Properties**

Property	Description
ConvertEmptyStringToNull	Boolean value, indicates whether empty string values are automatically converted to null values when any contents edited in the control's interface are saved back to the data source.
EditIndex	Gets or sets the index of the item being edited.
EditItem	Gets the item that is currently in edit mode within a *ListView* control. The type of the item is *ListViewItem*.
GroupItemCount	Gets or sets the number of items to display per group.
GroupPlaceholderID	Gets or sets the ID of the page element where the content for the *ListView* groups will be placed. The placeholder must be a server element flagged with the *runat* attribute. If a value for this property is not specified, a value of *groupPlaceholder* is assumed.
InsertItem	Gets the item that is currently in insert mode within a *ListView* control. The type of the item is *ListViewItem*.
InsertItemPosition	Gets or sets the location of the insert template. Feasible values are defined in the *InsertItemPosition* enumerated type: *FirstItem*, *LastItem*, or *None*.
ItemPlaceholderID	Gets or sets the ID of the page element that will host data-bound items. The placeholder must be a server element flagged with the *runat* attribute. If this property is not specified, a value of *ItemPlaceholder* is assumed.
Items	Gets the collection of bound items.
SelectedDataKey	Gets the data-key array of values for the selected item. This value coincides with *SelectedValue* except when multiple key fields are used.
SelectedIndex	Gets or sets the index of the currently selected item.
SelectedValue	Gets the data-key value of the first key field of the selected item.
SortDirection	Gets the sort direction of the field or fields being sorted.
SortExpression	Gets the sort expression that is associated with the field or fields being sorted.

Two properties in this list are somewhat new even to seasoned ASP.NET developers. They are *ItemPlaceholderID* and *GroupPlaceholderID*. When you are using groups to represent bound items, the group placeholder is the server-side ASP.NET control that, when added to the layout template, indicates where the group will be rendered. Similarly, the item placeholder indicates where bound items will be rendered. You add the item placeholder to the item template or to the group template if you are using groups.

The key thing about the *ListView* control is its full support for templates and the subsequent highly flexible rendering engine. Table 11-2 lists the templates the control supports.

TABLE 11-2 *ListView* Template Properties

Property	Description
AlternatingItemTemplate	Indicates the template used to render every other bound item. If this property is not specified, all items are usually rendered using the item template. The alternating item template usually contains the same controls and content as the item, but with a different style to distinguish items.
EditItemTemplate	Indicates the template to use for editing each bound item. The edit template usually contains input controls to update the values of the bound record. An edit template should also contain buttons to save and discard changes.
EmptyDataTemplate	Indicates the template to render when the data source bound to the *ListView* control is empty. When this happens, the empty data template is rendered instead of the layout template. Note, though, that the *InsertItemTemplate* takes precedence if *InsertItemPosition* is not set to *None*.
EmptyItemTemplate	Indicates the template to render when there are no more data items to display in the last group.
GroupSeparatorTemplate	Indicates the template used to put custom content between each group in the *ListView* control.
GroupTemplate	Indicates the template used to create a tiled layout for the contents of the *ListView* control. In a tiled layout, the items are repeated horizontally in a row according to the value of the *GroupItemCount* property.
InsertItemTemplate	Indicates the template to use for inserting a new data item. The insert template contains input controls to gather data to initialize a new record. An insert template should also contain buttons to save and discard changes.
ItemSeparatorTemplate	Indicates the template used to specify the content for the separator between the items of a *ListView* control.
ItemTemplate	Indicates the template to use to render items bound to the control.
LayoutTemplate	Indicates the template to render the root container of any contents displayed through the *ListView* control. This template is no longer required in ASP.NET 4.
SelectedItemTemplate	Indicates the template used to render the currently selected data item.

In addition to the properties listed in Table 11-1 and Table 11-2, the *ListView* control has a number of data-binding properties, including *DataKeyNames*, *DataSource*, *DataSourceID*, and *DataMember*.

The *DataKeyNames* property specifies the fields that represent the primary key of the data source. When you set this property declaratively, you use a comma-separated list of field names. The underlying type is an array of strings. Strictly related to *DataKeyNames* is *DataKeys*. This property contains an object that identifies the unique key for each item that is currently displayed in the *ListView* control. Through the *DataKeys* collection, you can access the individual values that form the primary key for each displayed record.

DataSource and *DataSourceID* provide two mutually exclusive ways of bringing data inside of the control. The *DataSource* property represents an enumerable collection of bindable records; the *DataSourceID* property points to a data source control in the page that does the entire job of retrieving and binding data. Starting with ASP.NET 2.0, all data controls can be bound to a data source control, but not all of them can fully leverage the capabilities of a data source control. Only view controls such as *GridView* and *DetailsView* can, for example, update the record in the data source or page and sort based on the capabilities of the under-lying data source. Older data-bound controls, such as *DataList*, support only the read-only interface of data source controls. In this regard, the *ListView* control is a logical specialization of the *DataList* control that does provide full support for the capabilities of the underlying data source control. (In the OO meaning of the word, *ListView* and *DataList* have nothing in common.)

Finally, because the *ListView* control inherits from *WebControl*, it features a bunch of user-interface properties, including *Style*, *CssClass*, *SkinID*, *Visible*, and *EnableTheming*.

Note The *ListView* control lacks the usual ton of style properties that characterize all other view controls in ASP.NET. The output of the *ListView* control can be styled at your leisure, but only by using cascading style sheets (CSS) directly, without even the mediation from ASP.NET themes.

This is intentional for a number of reasons. First, the control benefits from the momentum that CSS-based layouts are gaining in the industry. Second, Microsoft Visual Studio comes with a CSS editor through which editing and attaching styles to HTML elements is a breeze. Finally, the ex-treme flexibility of the markup generated by the *ListView* control would be hindered in several ways by ASP.NET themes. Themes work with entire ASP.NET controls, whereas the *ListView* con-trol is an ASP.NET control that generates its output based on a template that is, when all is said and done, made of pure HTML you control at a fine-grained level.

Events of the *ListView* Control

The *ListView* control has no specific methods worth mentioning. Table 11-3 lists the events that the control fires during its life cycle.

TABLE 11-3 Events of the *ListView* Class

Event	Description
ItemCanceling	Occurs when the user requests a cancel operation, but before the control cancels the ongoing insert or edit operation.
ItemCommand	Occurs when the user clicks on any buttons found in the body of the control.
ItemCreated	Occurs when a new item in the *ListView* control is being created.
ItemDataBound	Occurs when an item is bound to its data.
ItemDeleting, ItemDeleted	The two events occur before and after, respectively, the deletion of an item. The operation is requested by the interface of the *ListView* control.
ItemEditing	Occurs when an edit operation is requested, but before the *ListView* switches to the edit template.
ItemInserting, ItemInserted	The two events occur before and after, respectively, the insertion of an item. The operation is requested by the interface of the *ListView* control.
ItemUpdating, ItemUpdated	The two events occur before and after, respectively, the update of an item. The operation is requested by the interface of the *ListView* control.
LayoutCreated	Occurs when the layout template is created.
PagePropertiesChanging, PagePropertiesChanged	The two events occur before and after, respectively, the properties of a page of data in the *ListView* control change. A page of data is the set of items that form a page in a paged *ListView* control. Page properties include page size and start row index.
SelectedIndexChanging, SelectedIndexChanged	The two events occur before and after, respectively, the *ListView* control handles the selection of a displayed item and switches to the selected-item template.
Sorting, Sorted	The two events occur before and after, respectively, the associated data source is sorted.

As you can see, most of the events are related to the life cycle of individual data items. You can control when an item is created, deleted, inserted, or edited. Events fire before and after a given operation is accomplished. So you find doing/done pairs of events for each fundamental operation, such as *ItemInserting/ItemInserted* or *ItemDeleting/ItemDeleted* events. You can determine which item type is being created by using the *ItemType* property on the event data structure. Feasible values are *DataItem*, *InsertItem*, and *EmptyItem*. These values belong to the *ListViewItemType* enumerated type.

The *ListView* control also features typical events of ASP.NET controls such as *Init*, *Load*, *PreRender*, *DataBinding*, and *Unload*. You can handle these events the same way you handle them for other ASP.NET controls.

> **Note** The *ItemCommand* event fires only if the original click event is not handled by a predefined method. This typically occurs if you define custom buttons in one of the templates. You do not need to handle this event to intercept any clicking on the Edit or Insert button.

Compared to Other View Controls

The view controls introduced with previous versions of ASP.NET solved many problems that developers were facing every day. Controls such as *GridView* and *DetailsView* make it a snap to create a list of records and even arrange a master/detail view. However, they offer limited control over the actual markup generated. Want an example? With a *GridView* control, placing a *TBODY* tag around the group of child rows is not a trivial task. And it is almost impossible to do with a *DataGrid* control, unless you resort to your most advanced skills and take on the tough task of deriving a custom grid control.

On the other hand, adapting the final markup to the actual needs would be quite a simple task if the view controls introduced with earlier versions of ASP.NET provided a bit more programmatic control over the rendering process and templating. This is just one of the key capabilities you gain with the *ListView* control. As you'll see in a moment, the *ListView* control is flexible enough to render out in a tabular or tiled manner. It can be used to replace the *GridView* control, at least in relatively common situations, but also to create completely custom layouts.

This said, let's briefly compare the *ListView* control to the other view controls available in ASP.NET to see exactly what each control can do and cannot do. Table 11-4 lists and briefly describes the view controls.

TABLE 11-4 Rich, Data-Bound View Controls in ASP.NET

Control	Description
DetailsView	Designed to represent a single record of data, the control renders out a tabular and fixed layout. You decide the fields to be rendered and their format. You can use templates to customize the appearance of individual data fields, but you can't change the overall table-based layout. The control supports in-place editing as well as insertion and deletion, and it goes down to the bound data source control for the actual data access tasks. As long as the underlying data source supports paging and sorting, the control makes these functionalities available through its own user interface.
FormView	The *FormView* control can be considered to be the fully templated version of the *DetailsView* control. It renders one record at a time, picked from the associated data source and, optionally, supplies paging buttons to navigate between records. It doesn't provide any free user interface. You have to build all of it using header, item, and footer templates. *FormView* doesn't use data control fields and requires the user to define the rendering of each item by using templates. It supports any basic data access operation its data source supports, but you have to provide ad hoc trigger buttons.

Control	Description
GridView	The *GridView* control provides a tabular, grid-like view of the contents of a data source. Each column represents a data source field, and each row represents a record. You can use templates to customize individual data fields, but you are forced to use the tabular representation of contents. The granularity of customizable items is the table cell. With some hard work, though, you can change the structure of the table row—for example, you can add or remove cells. You can hardly do more than this, however. Like other view controls, the *GridView* also fully supports two-way data binding.

So where does the *ListView* control fit in this puzzle of data-bound controls? Like all the controls listed in Table 11-4, the *ListView* control supports two-way data binding—that is, the ability of displaying and editing the contents of the bound data source. Unlike the others, though, the *ListView* control provides the greatest flexibility as far as the generation of the markup is concerned. It is not limited to a single record like *FormView* and *DetailsView* are, and it is not limited to a tabular layout like the *GridView* is. It is essentially a repeater with rich layout capabilities (like a *DataList* control) and the two-way data-binding capabilities of other view controls.

Simple Data Binding

You use the *ListView* control to generate any user interface that needs to be built as you iterate a collection of records. You associate data with a *ListView* control using the *DataSource* property or, better yet, using the *DataSourceID* property. In the former case, you explicitly provide the data and control any aspect of the binding process. The *DataSourceID* property connects the control to a data source component. The binding process is mostly automatic, but it works both ways—it reads and saves data. The following data source control populates a *ListView* control with customers who reside in the United States:

```
<asp:ObjectDataSource ID="ObjectDataSource1" runat="server"
      TypeName="DAL.CustomerRepository"
      SelectMethod="LoadByCountry"
      OldValuesParameterFormatString="original_{0}">
   <SelectParameters>
      <asp:Parameter DefaultValue="USA" Name="country" />
   </SelectParameters>
</asp:ObjectDataSource>
```

The data source control invokes the *LoadByCountry* method on the specified business object and makes the response available to any bound control. Let's use a *ListView* control:

```
<asp:ListView ID="ListView1" runat="server"
    DataSourceID="ObjectDataSource1"
    ItemPlaceholderID="ListViewContent">
    <LayoutTemplate>
        <div id="header">
            <h1 id="logo">Customer List</h1>
        </div>
        <div runat="server" id="ListViewContent">
            <%-- ListView contents display here --%>
        </div>
    </LayoutTemplate>
    <ItemTemplate>
        <asp:Label runat="server" ID="lblCompany" Text='<%# Eval("CompanyName") %>' />
        ,  
        <asp:Label runat="server" ID="lblCountry" Text='<%# Eval("Country") %>' />
    </ItemTemplate>
    <ItemSeparatorTemplate>
        <hr />
    </ItemSeparatorTemplate>
</asp:ListView>
```

In this example, the *ListView* control comprises three templates: layout, item, and item separator. Of the three, only the item separator template is optional. The layout template defines the overall structure of the output. The *<div>* element in the layout marked with the *runat=server* attribute represents the insertion point for a pair of item and item separator templates. The item template is finally filled with the actual data from the *n*.th record. The *Eval* method evaluates the specified property on the data item being currently bound. The *Eval* method works in reading; as we'll see later, the *Bind* method works also in writing.

The item markup is made of a company name and country separated by a comma, and they are vertically separated from one another by a horizontal rule. Figure 11-1 shows the final results.

FIGURE 11-1 A simple *ListView* control in action.

Defining the Layout of the List

Most templated ASP.NET controls provide optional header and footer templates along with a repeated and data-bound item template. Header and footer templates are instantiated only once each, at the beginning and end, respectively, of the data binding loop. You can hide the header and footer, but most controls implicitly force you to think about the layout in terms of three components placed vertically: the header, body, and footer.

In this regard, the *ListView* control is different. It has no header or footer template, and it features just one template for the structure of the resulting markup: the layout template. If you need a header or a footer, you can easily place them in the layout. But if you need to develop the layout horizontally or in a tiled manner, the *ListView* approach makes it easier.

Up until ASP.NET 3.5, the layout template was mandatory in any *ListView* control. This is no longer the case, however, with ASP.NET 4. You can use the layout template as follows:

```
<LayoutTemplate>
    <div runat="server" ID="Body">
        ...
    </div>
</LayoutTemplate>
```

Instead of the *<div>* tag, you can use a *<span>* tag or provide appropriate CSS styling if you like the output flow with the rest of the page. The layout template must contain a server-side element that acts as the insertion point for data-bound item templates. This can be an HTML element decorated with the *runat* attribute or an ASP.NET server control. The ID of this placeholder element must be passed to the *ListView*'s *ItemPlaceholderID* property.

The *LayoutTemplate* property alone is not enough, though. At a minimum, you must also specify content for the *ItemTemplate* or *GroupTemplate* property. As mentioned, to bind to data, you use ASP.NET *<%# ... %>* data-binding expressions and the *Eval* or *Bind* method.

> **Note** Like any other template properties in ASP.NET controls, the template properties of the *ListView* control can be set programmatically as well as declaratively. You can assign to a template property any managed object that implements the *ITemplate* interface. Such an object can be obtained from an ASCX user control by using the *LoadTemplate* method on the *System.Web.UI.Page* class.

Let's put the graphical flexibility of the *ListView* control through its paces by examining how to render bound data using a number of layouts.

Building a Tabular Layout

The *ListView* control is the perfect tool to build a table-based interface with more liberty than specialized controls such as *DataGrid* and *GridView* typically allow. By properly designing the layout template of a *ListView* control, you can create an outermost table and then arrange a completely custom output for the child rows. In this way, you gain control over the rows and can, for example, employ two rows per record and even give each row a different number of cells. This level of control is extremely hard to achieve with a *GridView* control, although it's not impossible. To customize the *GridView* control to this level of detail, you need to override some of its protected virtual methods. Doing this requires the creation of a new derived control whose behavior touches on parts of the internal mechanics of the grid.

A *ListView* control lets you achieve the same results, but much more comfortably and with full support from Visual Studio 2008 designers.

Definition of the Overall Layout

To generate an HTML table, the *ListView* control needs to have a layout template defined as in the following code snippet:

```
<LayoutTemplate>
    <div>
        <h1 id="logo">Customer List</h1>
    </div>
```

```
        <div>
            <table>
                <thead>
                    <tr>
                        <th>Company</th>
                        <th>Country</th>
                    </tr>
                    <tbody runat="server" id="ListViewContent">
                    </tbody>
                </thead>
            </table>
        </div>
</LayoutTemplate>
```

The layout comprises two *<div>* elements, both of which are optional from a purely functional perspective. The *<div>* element, in fact, simplifies the process of styling the output, as you'll see later in this chapter. Generally, the output is made of two HTML blocks—one for the header and one for the actual data.

The layout template defines the overall markup by defining the *<table>* tag and adding a child *<thead>* tag. Next, a *<tbody>* tag wraps the child rows, each of which will be bound to a data record. In this case, the *<tbody>* tag hosts the item templates. For this reason, it features the *runat* attribute and has its own ID set as the argument of the *ItemPlaceholderID* property of the *ListView* control.

```
<asp:ListView ID="ListView1" runat="server"
    DataSourceID="ObjectDataSource1"
    ItemPlaceholderID="ListViewContent">
    ...
</asp:ListView>
```

The actual body of the resulting table is determined by the item and alternating item templates.

Definition of the Item Template

In a tabular layout, created using an HTML table, the item template can't be anything but a sequence of *<tr>* tags. Unlike with a pure grid control such as *GridView*, in a *ListView* layout you have no limitation on the number of rows per data item you can display. The following example uses two table rows per bound item:

```
<ItemTemplate>
    <tr>
        <td>
            <asp:Label runat="server" ID="lblCompany" Text='<%# Eval("CompanyName") %>' />
        </td>
        <td>
            <asp:Label runat="server" ID="lblCountry" Text='<%# Eval("Country") %>' />
        </td>
    </tr>
```

```
    <tr>
        <td colspan="2">
            <i>To contact this customer, please call <b><%# Eval("Phone") %></b></i>
        </td>
    </tr>
</ItemTemplate>
```

The first row contains two cells: one for the company name, and one for the country/region. The second row shows the phone number on a single-cell row. Both rows are rendered for each record bound to the *ListView* control. Figure 11-2 demonstrates the markup you obtain in this way.

FIGURE 11-2 A tabular layout built with the *ListView* control.

As you can see in the figure, some extremely simple styles have been applied to the table items. In particular, the *<th>* tags and the *<td>* tag of the second row have been styled to show a bottom border. Style properties can be applied using CSS styles or explicit inline style properties, as shown next. (Once again, although inline styles are supported in ASP.NET, they are considered a deprecated technique. You should always go with CSS classes.)

```
<th style="border-bottom:solid 3px black;">Company</th>
```

When comparing this sort of flexibility with the *GridView* control, the *GridView* control provides a number of free facilities, but it doesn't offer as much flexibility in design, as seen in this example. To choose, you have to first evaluate your requirements and make a choice between flexibility of rendering and functions to implement.

Using Alternate Rendering for Data Items

ItemTemplate is mandatory in a *ListView* control and indicates the template to use for each bound item. The *AlternatingItemTemplate* property can be used to differentiate every other item, as shown in Figure 11-3.

FIGURE 11-3 A tabular layout built with the *ListView* control using an alternating item template.

Most of the time, the alternating item template just features the same layout as regular items but styles it differently. However, changes to the template are allowed to any extent that can keep your users happy. The following code uses a small indentation for alternating rows:

```
<AlternatingItemTemplate>
    <tr>
        <td>
                
            <asp:Label runat="server" ID="lblCompany" Text='<%# Eval("CompanyName") %>' />
        </td>
```

```
        <td>
            <asp:Label runat="server" ID="lblCountry" Text='<%# Eval("Country") %>' />
        </td>
    </tr>
    <tr>

        <td>
                
            <i>To contact this customer, please call <b><%# Eval("Phone") %></b></i>
        </td>
    </tr>
</AlternatingItemTemplate>
```

Figure 11-4 shows the result.

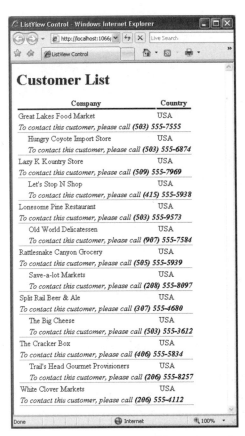

FIGURE 11-4 Using a slightly different layout for alternating items.

Reflecting On the Table Layout

HTML tables are an essential, but too often abused, piece of the Web jigsaw puzzle. HTML tables were designed for presenting tabular information. And they are still great at doing this. So any developer of a Web page that needs to incorporate a matrix of data is correct in using HTML tables. The problem with tables is that they are often used to define the page layout—a task they weren't designed for.

To illustrate, a grid control that uses HTML tables to output its content is more than acceptable. A tree-view control that uses HTML tables to list its contents is less desirable. It's not by mere chance that the ASP.NET team released the CSS adapter toolkit to allow you to change the rendering engine of some controls to make them inherently more CSS-friendly. And the *TreeView* is just one of the controls whose rendering style can be modified by using the toolkit.

> **Note** Using tables for creating multicolumn layouts—which is still common these days in most Web sites—has a number of significant drawbacks. Tables require a lot of code (or tags if you create tables declaratively) that has little to do with the data you intend to display through them. This code is tedious to write, verbose, and difficult to maintain. Worse yet, it makes for longer downloads and slower rendering in the browsers (a factor of growing importance for wireless devices). In addition, tables tend to mix up information and layout instead of forcing you to keep them neatly separated, and they result in less accessible content.

Building a Flow Layout

Visual Studio provides some facilities to work with *ListView* controls. Specifically, once you have bound the control to a data source, Visual Studio queries the data source and offers to generate some templates for you.

Definition of the Overall Layout

A flow layout is the simplest layout you can get. It requires only that you define a container—typically, a *<div>*—and then the markup for each record. The *ListView* control simply composes the resulting markup by concatenating the markup in a unique flow of HTML tags. Needless to say, the resulting markup can flow horizontally or vertically, depending on the tags you use (block or inline) and the CSS styles you apply.

If you're looking for a block flow layout, your *LayoutTemplate* property will probably always look as simple as the one shown here:

```
<LayoutTemplate>
    <div ID="ListViewContent" runat="server">
       <!-- your markup -->
    </div>
</LayoutTemplate>
```

If you opt for a *<span>* tag, instead of getting a new block you get a piece of markup that flows inline with the rest of the ASP.NET page.

Note that in ASP.NET 4 the *LayoutTemplate* is optional. You can get the same results if you simply wrap the markup directly in an *ItemTemplate* element, as shown here:

```
<ItemTemplate>
    <!-- your markup -->
</ItemTemplate>
```

This approach simplifies the definition of a *ListView* without loss of programming power and generality.

Definition of the Item Layout

A good example of a flowing template is shown in Figure 11-1. Here's another example:

```
<ItemTemplate>
    <div class="border" >
        <b>ID:</b>
        <asp:Label ID="IDLabel" runat="server" Text='<%# Eval("ID") %>' />
        <br />
        <b>CompanyName:</b>
        <asp:Label ID="CompanyNameLabel" runat="server"
            Text='<%# Eval("CompanyName") %>' />
        <br />
        <b>ContactName:</b>
        <asp:Label ID="ContactNameLabel" runat="server"
            Text='<%# Eval("ContactName") %>' />
        <br />
        <b>ContactTitle:</b>
        <asp:Label ID="ContactTitleLabel" runat="server"
            Text='<%# Eval("ContactTitle") %>' />
    </div>
</ItemTemplate>
```

The *<div>* tag normally creates a new block of markup and breaks the current flow of HTML. However, if you give it the *float:left* CSS style, it will float in the specified direction. As a result, the block of markup forms a horizontal sequence that wraps to the next line when the border of the browser's window is met. Figure 11-5 offers a preview.

Note In the previous chunk of HTML markup, I used *<span>* and *<div>* tags with styles applied and also mixed CSS styles with HTML tags used for controlling the appearance of the page, such as *<b>* and *
*. This approach is clearly arguable. The reason why I haven't opted for a niftier, pure CSS-based code in the snippet is clarity. By reading which CSS styles are applied to which tag, you can more easily make sense of the output depicted in Figure 11-5.

FIGURE 11-5 Using the float CSS attribute to display *<div>* tags as a horizontal sequence.

Building a Tiled Layout

Admittedly, the output of Figure 11-5 is not really attractive, even though it contains a few elements that, if improved a bit, might lead to more compelling results. The output of Figure 11-5 shows blocks of markup that flow horizontally and wrap to the next row. However, they share no common surrounding layout. In other words, those blocks are not tiled. To build a perfectly tiled output, you need to leverage group templates.

Grouping Items

So far we've used the *ListView* control to repeat the item template for each bound record. The *GroupTemplate* property adds an intermediate (and optional) step in this rendering process. When you specify a group template, the total number of bound records is partitioned in groups and the item template is applied to the records in each group. When a group has been rendered, the control moves to the next one. Each group of records can have its own particular template—the group template—and a separator can be inserted between items and groups. How is the size of each determined? That has to be a fixed value that you set, either declaratively or programmatically, through the *GroupItemCount* property. Let's consider the following layout and group templates:

```
<LayoutTemplate>
    <table border="1">
        <tr ID="groupPlaceholder" runat="server">
        </tr>
    </table>
</LayoutTemplate>
<GroupTemplate>
    <tr>
        <td ID="itemPlaceholder" runat="server">
        </td>
    </tr>
</GroupTemplate>
```

It indicates that the final output will be an HTML table where a new row is created for each group of items. Each table row contains as many cells as the value of *GroupItemCount* sets. The default value is *1*. Note that in the preceding code snippet we're using the default names for group and item containers—that is, *groupPlaceholder* and *itemPlaceholder*. When these names are used, there's no need to set corresponding *GroupPlaceholderID* and *ItemPlaceholderID* properties on the *ListView* markup. Here's the top-level markup for a tiled layout:

```
<asp:ListView ID="ListView1" runat="server"
    DataSourceID="ObjectDataSource1" GroupItemCount="4">
    ...
</asp:ListView>
```

As an example, if you set *GroupItemCount* to *4*, you'll have rows of 4 cells each until there are less than 4 records left. And after that? What if the number of bound records is not a perfect multiple of the group item count? That's where the *EmptyItemTemplate* property fits in:

```
<EmptyItemTemplate>
    <td />
</EmptyItemTemplate>
```

This template is used to complete the group when no more data items are available. Figure 11-6 shows a typical tiled output you obtain by employing a *ListView* control.

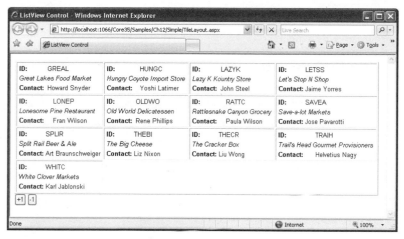

FIGURE 11-6 A four-cell tiled layout built with the *ListView* control.

Using the Group Separator Template

Each group of items can be separated by a custom block of markup defined through the *GroupSeparatorTemplate* property. Here's an example:

```
<GroupSeparatorTemplate>
    <tr>
        <td colspan='4'> </td>
    </tr>
</GroupSeparatorTemplate>
```

If you add this markup to the preceding example, you'll display a blank row in between rows with data-bound cells. It's a kind of vertical spacing.

The same can be done horizontally to separate data-bound cells within the same table row. To do so, you use the *ItemSeparatorTemplate* property instead. In both cases, the markup you put in must be consistent with the overall markup being created for the whole *ListView* control.

Modifying the Group Item Count Dynamically

The *GroupItemCount* property is read-write, meaning that you can change the size of each group programmatically based on some user actions. The following code snippet shows a pair of event handlers associated with the *Click* event of two *Button* controls:

```
protected void Button1_Click(object sender, EventArgs e)
{
    // There's no upper limit to the value of the property
    ListView1.GroupItemCount += 1;
}
```

```
protected void Button2_Click(object sender, EventArgs e)
{
    // The property can't be 2 or less
    if (ListView1.GroupItemCount >2)
        ListView1.GroupItemCount -= 1;
}
```

The *GroupItemCount* property itself can't take any value less than 1, but it has no upper limit. However, it should not accept any value larger than the actual number of data items currently bound.

As you assign a new value, the *set* modifier of the property resets the internal data-binding flag and orders a new binding operation. If you change the value of *GroupItemCount* over a postback, the *ListView* control automatically renders the updated markup back to the client. (See Figure 11-7.)

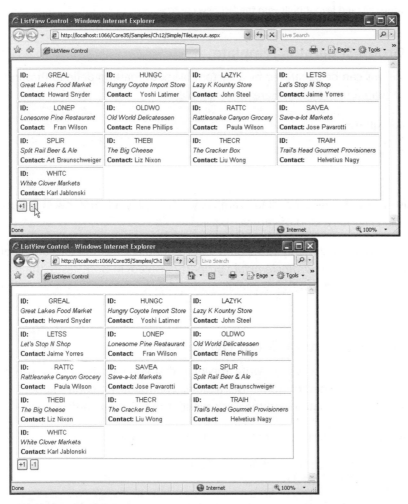

FIGURE 11-7 Changing the size of *ListView* groups dynamically.

The *ListView* control doesn't natively support more advanced capabilities—such as uneven groups of items where, for example, the association between an item and a group is based on a logical condition and not merely determined by an index. In this scenario, you could have a list where the first group contains customers whose name begins with *A* and the second group contains those beginning with *B*, and so on. You would have to provide the logic for this yourself. Let's look at this next.

Data-Driven Group Templates

The support for groups built into the *ListView* control is not data driven. In other words, the layout (groups and items) is first created and it is then bound to data. When the binding step occurs, the group template is not directly involved and you won't receive any event that tells you that a group has been either created or bound to its data.

However, this doesn't mean that your group templates must have a fixed layout and can't be dynamically populated using data from its contained items. The *ListView*'s *ItemDataBound* event is the key to obtaining output such as that shown in Figure 11-8.

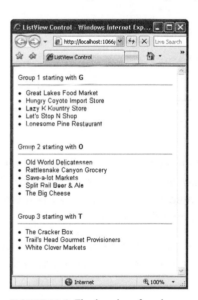

FIGURE 11-8 The header of each group is determined dynamically by looking at the bound contents.

To start out, let's take a look at the overall layout template of the *ListView* control:

```
<asp:ListView ID="ListView1" runat="server"
    DataSourceID="ObjectDataSource1"
    GroupItemCount="5"
    OnItemDataBound="ListView1_ItemDataBound">
    <ItemTemplate>
        <li><%# Eval("CompanyName") %></li>
    </ItemTemplate>
```

```
    <ItemSeparatorTemplate>
        <br />
    </ItemSeparatorTemplate>
    <LayoutTemplate>
        <div id="groupPlaceholder" runat="server">
        </div>
    </LayoutTemplate>
    <GroupTemplate>
        <asp:Label runat="server" ID="groupHeader" Text="Group" />
        <hr />
        <div id="itemPlaceholder" runat="server">
        </div>
        <br /><br /><br />
    </GroupTemplate>
</asp:ListView>
```

The group template is made of a *Label* control followed by an *<hr>* tag and the list of data items. Each bound item is expressed through an *<li>* tag. Let's see how to change the *Text* property of the *groupHeader* control for each group being created. Here's the structure of the *ItemDataBound* event handler:

```
private int lastGroup = -1;
protected void ListView1_ItemDataBound(object sender, ListViewItemEventArgs e)
{
    // To assign the group a data-bound title, retrieve the data item first
    if (e.Item.ItemType == ListViewItemType.DataItem)
    {
        var currentItem = (ListViewDataItem) e.Item;
        CustomizeGroupHeader((ListView) sender, currentItem);
    }
}
```

The *ListViewItemEventArgs* argument contains an *Item* property that refers to the item being bound to data. This item can be of a few types—*InsertItem*, *EmptyItem*, or *DataItem*. The list of feasible values is in the *ListViewItemType* enumerated type. In this case, we're interested only in data items—that is, regular items showing some bound data.

To put your hands on the real data being bound to the item, you need to cast the *ListView* item to the *ListViewDataItem* type, from which you can access a number of data-related properties:

```
private void CustomizeGroupHeader(ListView root, ListViewDataItem currentItem)
{
    // The type of the data item depends on the data you bound--in this case,
    // a collection of Customer objects
    var cust = (DAL.Customer) currentItem.DataItem;

    // Get a ListViewContainer object--the container of the group template
    Control container = currentItem.NamingContainer;
    if (container == null)
        return;
```

```
// Look up for a particular control in the group template--the Label
Label groupHeader = (Label)container.FindControl("groupHeader");
if (groupHeader == null)
    return;

// Figure out the 0-based index of current group. Note that the display index
// refers to the index of the item being bound, not the group
int groupIndex = currentItem.DisplayIndex / root.GroupItemCount;
if (groupIndex != lastGroup)
{
    // This is a new group
    lastGroup = groupIndex;

    // Update the UI
    groupHeader.Text = String.Format("Group {0} starting with <b>{1}</b>",
        groupIndex + 1,
        cust.CompanyName.Substring(0, 1).ToUpper());
}
}
```

You first get a reference to the naming container of the item. This container is the wrapper control for the group template. By using the *FindControl* method, you gain access to the *Label* control in the group template. The final step entails determining the value for the *Text* property of the *Label* control.

As mentioned, the *ListView* control doesn't provide any readymade information about groups. So you don't know about the index of the current group. The *DisplayIndex* property tells you only the index of the item being processed. Because the size of each group is fixed—and is based on the *GroupItemCount* property—you can easily obtain the 0-based index of the current group. You track the index of the current group in a global variable, and whenever a new group is found, you update the header.

Styling the List

Unlike other view controls, the *ListView* control doesn't feature the usual long list of style properties such as *HeaderStyle*, *ItemStyle*, *SelectedItemStyle*, and so forth. After a few years of industry use, Microsoft downsized the importance of style properties and their role. Today, as evidenced by the *ListView* control, in ASP.NET, CSS styles are emerging as the most effective and efficient way to modify the appearance of the markup.

Style Properties

ASP.NET controls let you set style attributes in two nonexclusive ways—using the *CssClass* property and using style properties. The *CssClass* property takes the name of a CSS class and passes it on to the *class* attribute of the root HTML tag generated for the control. More often than not, though, ASP.NET controls produce a complex markup where multiple HTML tags are rendered together but yet need to be styled differently. Although this is far from being an impossible goal to achieve with CSS styles, for a few years Microsoft pushed style properties as the way to go.

Developers are probably more inclined to use style properties than CSS styles, which require some specific skills. Anyway, style properties let you specify CSS attributes to apply to particular regions of the markup being generated. For example, the *ItemStyle* property in a *GridView* control allows you to define the colors, font, and borders of each displayed item. In the end, the value of these properties are translated to CSS attributes and assigned to the HTML tags via the *style* attribute. The developers don't have to build up any CSS skills and can leverage the Visual Studio editors and designers to get a preview.

Is there anything wrong with this approach?

The problem is that style attributes are defined as part of the page's code, and there's no clear separation between layout and style. ASP.NET themes are helpful and certainly mitigate the problem. All in all, for view controls with a relatively fixed layout, style properties—which are better if used through the intermediation of themes—are still a good option. The *ListView* control, though, is kind of an exception.

Using Cascading Style Sheets

The *ListView* control provides an unprecedented level of flexibility when it comes to generating the markup for the browser. The item that for, say, a *GridView* control can be safely identified with a table row, can be virtually anything with a *ListView* control.

The CSS designer in Visual Studio allows you to style controls and save everything back to a CSS class. So, as a developer, you always work with properties and scalar values but have them saved back to the CSS class instead of the view state.

This is another important factor that leads developers to prefer cascading style sheets over style properties. The CSS is a separate file that is downloaded only once. Style properties, on the other hand, are saved to the view state and continually uploaded and downloaded with the page.

Cool cascading style sheets are usually developed by designers and assign a style to the vast majority of HTML tags. Often cascading style sheets incorporate layout information and influence the structure of the page they are applied to. A common trick used by cascading style sheets consists of assigning a particular ID to *<div>* tags and treating them in a special way. Let's see how to radically improve the user interface of a previous *ListView*-based page with a cool CSS.

First, you explicitly link any relevant CSS file to the page (or the master page) by using the *<link>* tag. The *HtmlHead* control also allows you to load CSS files programmatically. Note that most realistic CSS files have an auxiliary folder of images that you have to set up on the production server too. The CSS file I'm using in the next example assigns a special role to *<div>* tags with the following IDs: *header*, *footer*, *page*, and *content*. The alternative is to explicitly assign a CSS class using the *class* attribute. Both ways are widely accepted. The *class* approach makes more obvious that something has been styled and what class it has been assigned to. But, in the end, it's a matter of preference. If you opt for styling via IDs, you are totally free to choose any names you want. (Note, however, that IDs must be unique to allow them to be used with client scripts. This can be hard to achieve with multiple controls in one page, so, class names are really preferred.)

```
<asp:ListView ID="ListView1" runat="server"
    DataSourceID="ObjectDataSource1"
    ItemPlaceholderID="ListViewContent">
    <LayoutTemplate>
        <div id="header">
            <h1 id="logo">Customer List</h1>
        </div>
        <div id="page">
            <div id="content">
                <table>
                    <thead>
                        <tr>
                            <th>Company</th>
                            <th>Country</th>
                        </tr>
                        <tbody runat="server" id="ListViewContent">
                        </tbody>
                    </thead>
                </table>
            </div>
        </div>
        <div id="footer">
        </div>
    </LayoutTemplate>
    <ItemTemplate>
        <tr>
            <td><asp:Label runat="server" ID="lblName"
                    Text='<%# Eval("CompanyName") %>' /></td>
            <td><asp:Label runat="server" ID="lblCountry"
                    Text='<%# Eval("Country") %>' /></td>
        </tr>
    </ItemTemplate>
</asp:ListView>
```

The result is shown in Figure 11-9.

FIGURE 11-9 Using cascading style sheets to style the markup of a *ListView* control.

Working with the *ListView* Control

The *ListView* control makes it easy to handle common data-based operations, such as insert, update, delete, or sorting. All that you have to do is place buttons in the layout template and associate buttons with command names. Buttons can be global to the list (such as insert, sort, and page buttons) or specific to a particular item (such as update and delete buttons). Command names are just strings that are assigned to the *CommandName* property of the *Button* control.

So far, we have considered only scenarios with relatively static and noninteractive templates. It is definitely possible, though, to use the *ListView* control to create rich user interfaces that allow in-place editing, selection of items, paging, and updates back to the data source. Let's start with in-place editing.

In-Place Editing

Unlike the *GridView* control, the *ListView* control doesn't automatically generate an Edit button; nor does it automatically adapt the edit mode user interface from the item template.

This responsibility falls to the developer by design. The developer is required to define an edit template that will be used to edit the contents of the selected item, in keeping with the flexible nature of the control.

Defining the Edit Item Template

The edit template is any piece of markup you intend to display to your users when they click to edit a record. It can have any layout you like and can handle data access in a variety of ways.

If you've bound the *ListView* control to a data source control—for example, an *ObjectDataSource* control—you can take advantage of the ASP.NET built-in support for two-way data binding. Simply put, you use data binding <%# ... %> expressions to bind to data, the *Eval* method for read-only operations, and the *Bind* method for full I/O operations.

The following markup defines a classic two-column table for editing some fields of a customer record:

```
<table>
    <tr>
        <td><b>ID</b></td>
        <td><asp:Label runat="server" ID="lblID" Text='<%# Eval("ID") %>' /></td>
    </tr>
    <tr>
        <td><b>Name</b></td>
        <td><asp:TextBox runat="server" ID="txtName"
            Text='<%# Bind("CompanyName") %>' /></td>
    </tr>
    <tr>
        <td><b>Country</b></td>
        <td><asp:TextBox runat="server" ID="txtCountry"
            Text='<%# Bind("Country") %>' /></td>
    </tr>
    <tr>
        <td><b>Street</b></td>
        <td><asp:TextBox runat="server" ID="txtStreet"
            Text='<%# Bind("Street") %>' /></td>
    </tr>
    <tr>
        <td><b>City</b></td>
        <td><asp:TextBox runat="server" ID="txtCity"
            Text='<%# Bind("City") %>' /></td>
    </tr>
</table>
```

Only one displayed item at a time can be in edit mode; the *EditIndex* property is used to get or set this 0-based index. If an item is being edited and the user clicks on a button to edit another one, the last-win policy applies. As a result, editing on the previous item is canceled and it's enabled on the last-clicked item.

To turn the *ListView* user interface into edit mode, you need an ad hoc button control with a command name of *Edit*:

```
<asp:Button ID="Button1" runat="server" Text="Edit" CommandName="Edit" />
```

When this button is clicked, the *ItemEditing* event fires on the server. By handling this event, you can run your own checks to ensure that the operation is legitimate. If something comes up to invalidate the call, you set the *Cancel* property of the event data structure to cancel the operation, like so:

```
protected void ListView1_ItemEditing(object sender, ListViewEditEventArgs e)
{
    // Just deny the edit operation
    e.Cancel = true;
}
```

Adding Predefined Command Buttons

An edit item template wouldn't be very helpful without at least a couple of predefined buttons to save and cancel changes. You can define buttons using a variety of controls, including *Button*, *LinkButton*, *ImageButton*, and any kind of custom control that implements the *IButtonControl* interface.

Command names are plain strings that can be assigned to the *CommandName* property of button controls. The *ListView* (and other view controls) recognizes a number of predefined command names, as listed in Table 11-5.

TABLE 11-5 Supported Command Names

Command	Description
Cancel	Cancels the current operation (edit, insert), and returns to the default view (item template)
Delete	Deletes the current record from the data source
Edit	Turns the *ListView* control into edit mode (edit item template)
Insert	Inserts a new record into the data source
Page	Moves to the next or previous page
Select	Selects the clicked item, and switches to the selected item template
Sort	Sorts the bound data source
Update	Saves the current status of the record back to the data source

The following code shows how to add a pair of Save/Cancel buttons:

```
<asp:Button ID="btnSave" runat="server" Text="Save" CommandName="Update" />
<asp:Button ID="btnCancel" runat="server" Text="Cancel" CommandName="Cancel" />
```

Any button clicking done within the context of a *ListView* control originates a server-side event—the *ItemCommand* event:

```
protected void ListView1_ItemCommand(object sender, ListViewCommandEventArgs e)
{
    // Use e.CommandName to check the command requested
}
```

Clicking buttons associated with predefined command buttons can result in subsequent, and more specific, events. For example, *ItemUpdating* and *ItemUpdated* are fired before and after, respectively, a record is updated. You can use the *ItemUpdating* event to make any last-minute check on the typed data before this data is sent to the database.

Note that before the update is made, *ListView* checks the validity of any data typed by calling the *IsValid* method on the *Page* class. If any validator is defined in the template, it is evaluated at this time.

Adding Custom Command Buttons

In the edit mode user interface, you can have custom buttons too. A custom button differs from a regular Save or Cancel button only in terms of the command name. The command name of a custom button is any name not listed in Table 11-5. Here's an example:

```
<asp:Button ID="btnMyCommand" runat="server" Text="Custom"
            CommandName="mycommand" />
```

To execute any code in response to the user's clicking on this button, all you can do is add an *ItemCommand* event handler and check for the proper (custom) command name and react accordingly:

```
protected void ListView1_ItemCommand(object sender, ListViewCommandEventArgs e)
{
    // Check the command requested
    if (e.CommandName == "MyCommand")
    {
        ...
    }
}
```

Conducting the Update

When the *ListView* control is used in two-way binding mode, any update operation is conducted through the connected data source control. You define select and save methods on the data source, configure their parameters (either declaratively or programmatically), and delegate to the *ListView* control all remaining chores.

For update and delete operations, though, you need to identify the record uniquely. This is where the *DataKeyNames* property gets into the game. You use this property to define a collection of fields that form the primary key on the data source:

```
<asp:ListView ID="ListView1" runat="server"
    ...
    DataSourceID="ObjectDataSource1"
    DataKeyNames="id">
    ...
</asp:ListView>
```

In this case, the *DataKeyNames* tells the underlying data source control that the ID field on the bound record has to be used as the key. Figure 11-10 shows a sample page in action that edits the contents of the currently displayed record.

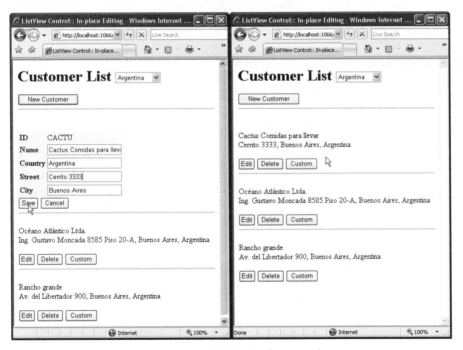

FIGURE 11-10 In-place editing in action with the *ListView* control.

Deleting an Existing Record

As you can see, Figure 11-10 also contains a Delete button side by side with the aforementioned Edit button. Here's the full markup for *ListView*'s item template:

```
<ItemTemplate>
    <p>
        <%# Eval("CompanyName") %>
        <br />
        <%# Eval("Street") %>, <%# Eval("City") %>, <%# Eval("Country") %>
    </p>
```

```
    <asp:Button ID="btnEdit" runat="server" Text="Edit" CommandName="edit" />
    <asp:Button ID="btnDelete" runat="server" Text="Delete" CommandName="delete"
      OnClientClick="return confirm('Are you sure you want to delete this item?');" />
    <asp:Button ID="btnMyCommand" runat="server" Text="Custom" CommandName="mycommand" />
</ItemTemplate>
```

The *Delete* operation is even more crucial than an update. For this reason, you might want to be sure that deleting the record is exactly what the user wants. For example, you can pop up a client-side message box in which you ask the user to confirm the operation. It is a little piece of JavaScript code that you attach to the *OnClientClick* property of a *Button* control or to the *onclick* attribute of the corresponding HTML tag. It can save you a lot of trouble.

Showing a Message Box upon Completion

Wouldn't it be nice if your application displays a message box upon the completion of an update operation? It doesn't change the effect of the operation, but it would make users feel more comfortable. In a Web scenario, you can use only JavaScript for this purpose. The trick is that you register a piece of startup script code with the postback event where you execute the update operation. In this way, the script will be executed as soon as the page is served back to the browser. From the user's perspective, this means right after the completion of the operation. Here's what you need:

```
protected void ListView1_ItemUpdated(object sender, ListViewUpdatedEventArgs e)
{
    // Display a client message box at the end of the operation
    Page.ClientScript.RegisterStartupScript(
            this.GetType(),
            "update_Script",
            "alert('You successfully updated the system.');",
            true);
}
```

Inserting New Data Items

The *ListView* control allows you to define a made-to-measure interface for adding new records to the underlying data source. You do this through the *InsertItemTemplate* property. More often than not, the insert template is nearly identical to the edit item template, except for the fields that form the primary key of the data source. These fields are normally rendered as read-only text in the edit template. Clearly they have to be editable in an insert item scenario.

Setting Up the Insert Item Template

So let's assume you have the following insert item template. As you can easily verify, it is the same edit item template we used in the previous example, except that a *TextBox* control is used for entering the ID of the new customer.

```
<InsertItemTemplate>
    <table>
        <tr>
            <td><b>ID</b></td>
            <td><asp:TextBox runat="server" ID="txtID"
                            MaxLength="5"
                            Text='<%# Bind("ID") %>' /></td>
        </tr>
        <tr>
            <td><b>Name</b></td>
            <td><asp:TextBox runat="server" ID="txtName"
                        Text='<%# Bind("CompanyName") %>' /></td>
        </tr>
        <tr>
            <td><b>Country</b></td>
            <td><asp:TextBox runat="server" ID="txtCountry"
                        Text='<%# Bind("Country") %>' /></td>
        </tr>
        <tr>
            <td><b>Street</b></td>
            <td><asp:TextBox runat="server" ID="txtStreet"
                        Text='<%# Bind("Street") %>' /></td>
        </tr>
        <tr>
            <td><b>City</b></td>
            <td><asp:TextBox runat="server" ID="txtCity"
                        Text='<%# Bind("City") %>' /></td>
        </tr>
    </table>
    <asp:Button ID="btnInsert" runat="server" Text="Add" CommandName="insert" />
    <asp:Button ID="btnCancel" runat="server" Text="Cancel" CommandName="cancel" />
</InsertItemTemplate>
```

How would you display this template? The edit item template shows up when the user clicks a button decorated with the *Edit* command name. Unfortunately, there's no equivalent *New* command name to automatically bring up the insert item template. Instead, with the *ListView* the *New* command name is considered a custom command, handled by code you provide to activate the insert item template, unless it's active by default. We'll look at the details next.

The insert item template is displayed by position. The *InsertItemPosition* property determines where the template is displayed. There are three possibilities, as shown in Table 11-6.

TABLE 11-6 Feasible Positions for the Insert Item Template

Position	Description
FirstItem	The insert item template is displayed as the first item in the list and precedes all items in the bound data source.
LastItem	The insert item template is displayed as the last item in the list and trails all items in the bound data source.
None	The insert item template is not automatically displayed. The developer is responsible for showing and hiding the template programmatically. This is the default value for the *InsertItemPosition* property.

If you leave the *InsertItemPosition* property set to its default value, no insert template is displayed, but you won't have a predefined button to bring it up. If you use any of the other two values, the template is always visible and displayed at the beginning or the end of the list. This might not be desirable in most cases. Let's see how to take programmatic control over the display of the insert template.

Taking Full Control of the Insert Template

In the layout template, you add a custom button and capture any user's click event. You can give the button any command name not listed in Table 11-5:

```
<asp:Button ID="btnNew" runat="server" Text="New Customer" CommandName="new" />
```

To handle the click on the button, you write an *ItemCommand* handler. In the event handler, you simply change the value of the *InsertItemPosition* property, as shown here:

```
protected void ListView1_ItemCommand(object sender, ListViewCommandEventArgs e)
{
    if (e.CommandName.Equals("New", StringComparison.OrdinalIgnoreCase))
    {
        ListView me = (ListView) sender;
        me.InsertItemPosition = InsertItemPosition.FirstItem;
    }
}
```

Changing the value of *InsertItemPosition* to anything but None brings up the insert item template, if any. In the insert template, you need to have a couple of predefined buttons with command names of *Insert* (to add) and *Cancel* (to abort).

It should be noted, though, that the insert item template is not automatically dismissed by the *ListView* control itself. As mentioned, this is because of the lack of built-in support for the *New* command name. In the end, this requires that you add a couple more handlers to dismiss the template when the user cancels or confirms the insertion.

The *ItemCanceling* event fires when the user hits a button associated with the *Cancel* command name. This can happen from either the edit or insert template. The event data object passed to the handler has the *CancelMode* property, which is designed to help you figure out what mode is active (insert or edit) and allow you to tailor your application's response.

```
protected void ListView1_ItemCanceling(object sender, ListViewCancelEventArgs e)
{
    ListView me = (ListView) sender;

    // Dismissing the insert item template
    if (e.CancelMode == ListViewCancelMode.CancelingInsert)
        me.InsertItemPosition = InsertItemPosition.None;
}
```

To hide the insert item template after the new data item has been successfully appended to the data source, you use the *ItemInserted* event:

```
protected void ListView1_ItemInserted(object sender, ListViewInsertedEventArgs e)
{
    ListView me = (ListView) sender;
    me.InsertItemPosition = InsertItemPosition.None;
}
```

Adding a Bit of Validation

When you're going to add a new record to an existing data source, a bit of validation—much more than is generally desirable—is mandatory. Being responsible for the insert template, you can add as many validators as necessary to the markup. The *ListView* control's internal facilities then ensure that the operation is finalized only if no validator raised an error.

In particular, you might want to check whether the ID being inserted already exists in the data source. You can use a *CustomValidator* control attached to the text box:

```
<asp:TextBox runat="server" ID="txtID"
            MaxLength="5"
            Text='<%# Bind("ID") %>' />
<asp:CustomValidator runat="server" ID="CustomValidator1"
            ErrorMessage="Invalid ID"
            ControlToValidate="txtID"
            OnServerValidate="CustomValidator1_CheckID" />
```

The *CustomValidator* control fires a server-side event in which you can run code to validate the text in the input field. The server event is fired via a postback and has the following prototype:

```
protected void  CustomValidator1_CheckID(object source, ServerValidateEventArgs e)
{
    string proposedCustomerID = e.Value;
    e.IsValid = CheckIfUsed(proposedCustomerID);
}
private bool CheckIfUsed(string proposedCustomerID)
{
    var c = CustomerRepository.Load(proposedCustomerID);

    // The object is of type NoCustomer if no matching customer exists
    if (c is DAL.NoCustomer)
        return true;
    return false;
}
```

The *Load* method in the sample data access layer (DAL) used in this example supports the Special Case pattern. In other words, the method always returns a valid *Customer* object regardless of the value of the input *proposedCustomerID* parameter. If a customer with a matching ID can't be found, the return object is an instance of the *NoCustomer* class. Of course, *NoCustomer* is a class that derives from *Customer*.

How is this different from returning a plain *null* value or perhaps an error code? In both cases, the caller can figure out whether a matching customer exists or not. However, returning a special-case *Customer* object is inherently more informative and doesn't violate the consistency of the method—a class that inherits from *Customer* is always returned, whereas an error code is a number and *null* is a non-value.

Selecting an Item

The *SelectedItemTemplate* property allows you to assign a different template to the currently selected item in the *ListView* control. Note that only one displayed item at a time can be given the special selected template. But how do you select an item?

Triggering the Selection

The selected item template is a special case of the item template. The two templates are similar and differ mostly in terms of visual settings—for example, a different background color. The switch between the regular and selected item template occurs when the user clicks on a button with the *Select* command name. If you intend to support the selection item feature, you place a *Select* button in the item template. When this button gets clicked, the *ListView* automatically applies the new template to the clicked item. Here are some sample item and selected item templates:

```
<ItemTemplate>
    <p>
        <asp:linkbutton runat="server" Text='<%# Eval("CompanyName") %>'
            CommandName="Select" />
        <br />
        <%# Eval("Street") %>, <%# Eval("City") %>, <%# Eval("Country") %>
    </p>
</ItemTemplate>

<SelectedItemTemplate>
    <h3>
        <%# Eval("CompanyName") %>
        <br />
        <%# Eval("Street") %>, <%# Eval("City") %>, <%# Eval("Country") %>
    </h3>

    <asp:Button ID="btnEdit" runat="server" Text="Edit" CommandName="Edit" />
    <asp:Button ID="btnDelete" runat="server" Text="Delete" CommandName="Delete"
        OnClientClick="return confirm('Are you sure you want to delete this item?');" />
    <asp:Button ID="btnUnselect" runat="server" Text="Unselect" CommandName="unselect" />
</SelectedItemTemplate>
```

In addition to changing some visual settings, the selected item template can contain buttons to trigger operations on the particular item.

In Figure 11-10 shown earlier, each item features its own set of operational buttons, such as Edit and Delete. This layout can be reworked to display buttons only on the selected item. To do so, you just move the buttons to the *SelectedItemTemplate* property.

In the item template, though, you need to insert a button control to trigger the selection process. You can use a push button or attach any significant text in the template to a link button:

```
<asp:linkbutton runat="server" Text='<%# Eval("CompanyName") %>' CommandName="Select" />
```

Figure 11-11 shows the result.

FIGURE 11-11 A selected item in a *ListView* control.

Releasing the Selection

When you click the link button, the *ListView* switches the template and sets the *SelectedIndex* property accordingly. As soon as the user clicks on a different item, the selection is moved and the previously selected item regains the regular template. Is there a way to programmatically reset the selection? You bet.

All that you have to do is add a new custom button and handle its click event. In the event handler, you assign the –1 value to the *SelectedIndex* property. A value of –1 means that no items are selected. Here's the related code snippet:

```
protected void ListView1_ItemCommand(object sender, ListViewCommandEventArgs e)
{
    ListView me = (ListView) sender;
    if (e.CommandName.Equals("Unselect", StringComparison.OrdinalIgnoreCase))
        me.SelectedIndex = -1;
}
```

Note that the index of the currently selected item and the index of the item being edited are saved to the view state and persisted across postbacks. This means that if the user changes the country/region selection (shown in Figure 11-11), both the edit and selection indexes are retained, which might not be desirable. For example, imagine that you selected (or are editing) the second customer from Argentina. Next, the user changes to Brazil while the selected (or edit) template is on. The result is that the second customer from Brazil is displayed in the selected (or edit) mode. If this behavior works for you, there's nothing to modify in the code. Otherwise, you need to reset *SelectedIndex* and *EditIndex* in any postback event outside the *ListView* control. Here's an example:

```
protected void DropDownList1_SelectedIndexChanged(object sender, EventArgs e)
{
    // The sender argument here indicates the DropDownList or any other
    // control responsible for the postback. You reference the ListView by
    // name or via a custom global member in the code-behind class of the page
    ListView1.SelectedIndex = -1;
    ListView1.EditIndex = -1;
}
```

Paging the List of Items

In ASP.NET, grid controls support data paging natively. Purely iterative controls such as *Repeater* and *DataList*, though, leave the burden of pagination entirely on the developer's capable shoulders. The *ListView* control falls somewhere in the middle of these two extreme positions. The *ListView* control doesn't have built-in paging capabilities, but it knows how to work with a new control specifically designed to enable data paging on a variety of data-bound controls. This control is the *DataPager*.

The *DataPager* Control

The *DataPager* control is designed to add paging capabilities to a family of data-bound controls and not just the *ListView*. The support that the *DataPager* control offers to data-bound pageable controls such as the *ListView* is limited to the user interface of the pager.

You configure the *DataPager* to obtain the pager bar you like best, and then you instruct the *DataPager* control to fall back to the paged control to display the specified number of data items starting at the specified position. In no case does the *DataPager* expose itself to the data source or a data source control. All that it does is communicate to the paged control the next set of records to select and display. Table 11-7 lists the properties of the *DataPager* control.

TABLE 11-7 Properties of the *DataPager* Control

Property	Description
Fields	Gets the collection of *DataPagerField* elements that form the pager bar. Elements in this collection belong to classes such as *NumericPagerField*, *TemplatePagerField*, and *NextPreviousPagerField*.
MaximumRows	Gets the maximum number of rows that the page can support.
PagedControlID	Gets and sets the ID of the control to page. This control must implement the *IPageableItemContainer* interface.
PageSize	Gets and sets the size of the page. The default value is 10.
QueryStringField	The name of the query string field for the current page index. The pager uses the query string when this property is set.
StartRowIndex	Gets the index of the first item in the data source to display.
TotalRowCount	Gets the total number of rows to page through.

Only a few of these properties can be set declaratively. They are *Fields*, *PagedControlID*, *PageSize*, and *QueryStringField*. The other properties are read-only and owe their value to the paged control and the size of the bound data source.

Using the *DataPager* Control

The following code snippet shows the typical code you use to embed a data pager in an ASP.NET page that hosts a *ListView* control:

```
<asp:DataPager ID="DataPager1" runat="server"
    PagedControlID="ListView1" PageSize="4">
    <Fields>
        <asp:NextPreviousPagerField />
    </Fields>
</asp:DataPager>
```

The *DataPager* control heralds a new model for paging data-bound controls that is quite a bit different from the model employed by *GridView* controls. The user interface for paging is not part of the control, but it can be placed anywhere in the page and even driven through the query string.

The *DataPager* control is linked to the data-bound control being paged and lets this control know about the user selection. Subsequently, the paged control adjusts its row properties and passes the information back to the data pager. Figure 11-12 shows a data pager in action.

FIGURE 11-12 A data pager in action—the pager can be placed anywhere in the page.

Configuring the Data Pager Fields

The user interface of the data pager control is largely customizable. You do that through the *Fields* property—a collection of *DataPagerField* objects. The property allows you to add multiple pagers of different styles. Table 11-8 lists the various options you have.

TABLE 11-8 Types of Data Pagers

Type	Description
NextPreviousPagerField	Displays a fully customizable Next/Previous user interface for the pager. You can use images or text for Next/Previous buttons and also add a First/Last pair of buttons.
NumericPagerField	Displays a fully customizable list of numeric links, one for each page. The number of pages is calculated on the page size and the total number of bound rows.
TemplatePagerField	Allows you to use a user-defined template for the pager.

All classes in Table 11-8 inherit from the same common class—*DataPagerField*. If you're OK with the default user interface of the pagers, you don't need to set any of the pager's properties. The following markup, therefore, is perfectly functional:

```
<Fields>
   <asp:NumericPagerField />
</Fields>
```

Pager fields, though, have a number of visual properties to set the CSS style of buttons, the companion text, or perhaps the images to use instead of text.

Pageable Containers

As mentioned, the data pager control doesn't handle data itself. Rather, the control is the manager of the paging user interface. For this reason, it needs to communicate with the paged control. Whenever a button in the pager is clicked to move to a given page, the pager control fires a message to the paged control and has it refresh the user interface properly.

Not all data-bound controls can be paged using a data pager. In ASP.NET, this privilege is limited to controls that implement the *IPageableItemContainer* interface. Currently, the sole control to support this interface is the *ListView* control. You can create your own custom controls to implement the interface, however. Here's the definition of the interface:

```
public interface IPageableItemContainer
{
    // Events
    event EventHandler<PageEventArgs> TotalRowCountAvailable;

    // Methods
    void SetPageProperties(int startRowIndex, int maximumRows, bool databind);

    // Properties
    int MaximumRows { get; }
    int StartRowIndex { get; }
}
```

The *PagedControlID* property on the *DataPager* control defines the linked data-bound control. Whenever the pager is acted on, it invokes the *SetPageProperties* method on the paged control through the contracted interface. In doing so, it lets the *ListView* control (or the paged control) know about the new start row to display and the size of the page. Here's the pseudocode used by the *ListView* control to support paging:

```
void SetPageProperties(int startRowIndex, int maximumRows, bool databind)
{
    if ((this._startRowIndex != startRowIndex) || (this._maximumRows != maximumRows))
    {
        PagePropertiesChangingEventArgs e;
        e = new PagePropertiesChangingEventArgs(startRowIndex, maximumRows);
        if (databind)
        {
            this.OnPagePropertiesChanging(e);
        }

        this._startRowIndex = e.StartRowIndex;
        this._maximumRows = e.MaximumRows;
        if (databind)
        {
            this.OnPagePropertiesChanged(EventArgs.Empty);
        }
    }
    if (databind)
    {
        base.RequiresDataBinding = true;
    }
}
```

PagePropertiesChanging and *PagePropertiesChanged* events are fired before and after, respectively, each paging operation.

The data pager control is normally placed outside the *ListView*'s layout. In this case, you use the *PagedControlID* property of the data pager to specify the paged control. However, if the *PagedControlID* property is not specified, the data pager assumes that its naming container is the paged control (as long as it implements the *IPageableItemContainer* interface). What does this mean to you? It means you can embed the data pager in the layout template of the *ListView* control and avoid setting the *PagedControlID* property on the pager explicitly.

Sorting the List

The data bound to the *ListView* control can be sorted using a button in the layout template with the command name of *Sort*:

```
<LayoutTemplate>
    <asp:Button ID="btnSort" runat="server" Text="Sort"
            CommandName="Sort"
            CommandArgument="companyname" />
</LayoutTemplate>
```

You specify the sort expression and the initial sort direction using the *CommandArgument* property of the button. You use *asc* and *desc* to indicate the desired direction. Multiple sorting fields can be listed as well. The sorting automatically reverses from ascending to descending and vice versa as you click. The *ListView*'s *SortExpression* and *SortDirection* read-only properties tell you at any time about the current status of the sort.

Summary

The *ListView* control adds the benefits of ASP.NET view controls (such as the *GridView* or *DetailsView* control) to classic repeater data-bound controls such as *DataList*. The resulting control weds the extreme layout flexibility of a *DataList* or *Repeater* control with the power of two-way data binding of data source controls.

The *ListView* control can be used to implement virtually any reporting and publishing scenarios you can imagine. The distinct layout template gives you total control over the HTML being generated and the style it must have. Various item templates (regular, alternate, edit, selected, insert) let you decide about the markup to output for each possible state of the control.

Finally, the *ListView* control is a pageable control. Unlike other view controls, though, the *ListView* control binds to an external pager control—the new *DataPager* control. The connection between the two controls is all in the *IPageableItemContainer* interface. As a result, each data-bound control with this interface can be paged without incorporating the logic to page.

Chapter 12
Custom Controls

Ignorance, the root and the stem of every evil.

—Plato

Server controls are one of the pillars of the entire ASP.NET Web Forms framework. Server controls are compiled classes that encapsulate user-interface and other functionality into reusable packages. ASP.NET provides a full bag of stock controls to serve most developers' needs. However, writing custom controls is possible and sometimes necessary. Custom controls are no different than standard ASP.NET server controls except that they are bound to a different tag prefix and must be registered and deployed explicitly. Aside from that, custom controls can have their own object model, fire events, and support all the design-time features of Microsoft Visual Studio, such as the Properties window, the visual designer, property builders, and the Toolbox. Because of their compiled nature, custom controls can be installed in a single copy in the global assembly cache (GAC), making them available to all applications, or they can simply be deployed to the \Bin directory for use by a single application.

A custom control is a class and inherits from a base control class. The logic already available in the base class determines how much, and what, code you have to write. There are basically two ways of creating custom controls. If you find that an existing control meets your requirements only partially and lacks some key features, the simplest thing you can do is extend the control by deriving a new class from it. You can override specific properties, methods, and events as well as add new features. If none of the existing Web server controls meet your requirements, consider creating a custom control from scratch by deriving from one of the base control classes—*Control* and *WebControl*. These classes provide only the basic functionality of ASP.NET server controls, and they require that you take care of some of the control's operational aspects yourself, such as rendering, styling, view state, and state management.

 Note Custom controls are not to be confused with user controls (ASCX files). Web user controls are dynamic-compile components and cannot be added to the Toolbox. In addition, user controls should be deployed as source code unless the application that incorporates them is precompiled. In this case, you can extract the dynamic assembly that contains the user control and share it between applications. However, this technique is not supported by Microsoft and, well, requires a lot of familiarity with the ASP.NET internals.

LIVERPOOL JOHN MOORES UNIVERSITY
LEARNING SERVICES

Extending Existing Controls

When you realize you need a custom control to accomplish a certain task, first pause and make sure the feature you devised can really be obtained with HTML, literals, and JavaScript code. If you know how to do that in pure HTML, you can start planning an ASP.NET control and then architect and engineer the feature for the best reusability and efficiency.

Choosing a Base Class

A custom server control is a Microsoft .NET Framework class that inherits—either directly or indirectly—from *Control*. *Control* is the root class for all server controls in ASP.NET applications. It should be noted, though, that very few controls that you commonly use in ASP.NET applications really inherit directly from *Control*. For the most part, ASP.NET controls inherit from intermediate classes that encapsulate a given predefined behavior.

Inheriting from a Base Class

Each ASP.NET server control that is not marked as sealed can be further inherited and specialized. Table 12-1 lists all the classes in ASP.NET that represent some sort of base functionality. Each class in the list represents the root of a family of controls.

TABLE 12-1 Base Control Classes Available in ASP.NET

Class	Description
BaseDataBoundControl	Incorporates the basic mechanism and object model for data binding. It inherits from *WebControl*.
BaseDataList	Adds grid capabilities such as advanced rendering, templates, and paging. It inherits from *WebControl*. *This is considered deprecated in ASP.NET 4.*
CompositeControl	Incorporates the mechanics of composite controls with regard to the building of the control's tree. It inherits from *WebControl*.
CompositeDataBoundControl	Incorporates the mechanics of composite data-bound controls with regard to view-state management and the building of the control's tree. It inherits from *DataBoundControl*.
DataBoundControl	Adds support for data source controls, and overrides some methods marked as abstract in the parent class. It inherits from *BaseDataBoundControl*.
HierarchicalDataBoundControl	Adds support for data hierarchical data source controls, and overrides some methods marked as abstract in the parent class. It inherits from *BaseDataBoundControl*.
ListControl	Adds support and an object model tailor-made for list controls, such as *CheckBoxList* and *DropDownList*.
WebControl	Adds an array of user-interface (UI) properties, such as style settings, colors, font, and borders. It inherits from *Control*.

Among the commonly used controls that inherit directly from *Control*, you find *Repeater*, *MultiView*, *Placeholder*, and *LiteralControl*. All other controls in ASP.NET inherit from one of these classes.

Extending a Base Class

The base *Control* class incorporates a number of features and makes them available to all child controls. A quick list includes view-state management, control identification, naming container capabilities, design-time support, themes, control state, and adaptive rendering. If you choose to inherit from any of the classes in Table 12-1, be prepared to write quite a bit of code because the control you get in the beginning is not particularly rich with concrete functionalities.

You typically inherit from any of those classes if you're going to write a control that provides unique capabilities that are hard to find in other ASP.NET controls. Inheriting from any of the classes in Table 12-1 is more like building a custom control from scratch, where the effective starting point is determined by the selected base class.

If you opt for inheritance from a concrete control class—that is, a control that provides an observable behavior and user interface—you should strive to add new features or override existing capabilities without altering too much the structure and the personality of the control itself.

A Richer *HyperLink* Control

Let's start with a sample custom control that extends the standard behavior of the *HyperLink* built-in control. By default, the ASP.NET *HyperLink* control outputs an anchor *<a>* tag that points to a URL. By design, any click on an anchor tag is served directly by the browser, which navigates to the specified page. No postback occurs to the page that originally displayed the anchor. Put another way, if you want to track that the user clicked on a given anchor, you need to extend the behavior of the hyperlink control.

Designing a Usage Scenario

Let's further develop the idea of a control that drives users to a different page but gives the page author a way to track the event. The canonical example used to illustrate the importance of this feature is the page hit counter. Monitoring the visitor activity is an important task that each administrator of a Web site should consider to improve the quality and content of the site. A *click-through* is the name commonly used to indicate the user's clicking to see particular content, and it's an important parameter for evaluating how the visitors of a site receive advertising. How would you implement a counter service that counts click-throughs in a page?

You can associate each button control in a page (*Button*, *HyperLink*, *ImageButton*, *LinkButton*, and *AdRotator*) with an extra layer of code that first tracks the click and then proceeds with the expected behavior. Getting this behavior with controls that entail a postback is not difficult. Take the *LinkButton* class, for example. You can derive a new control and override the *OnClick* protected member as follows:

```
protected virtual void OnClick(EventArgs e)
{
    // Track the event
    ...

    // Proceed with the default behavior
    base.OnClick(e);
}
```

What about the *HyperLink* control, though? The click on the hyperlink is handled directly by the browser and doesn't pass through any ASP.NET code of yours.

A Redirector for the *HyperLink* Control

The idea is that you force the *HyperLink* control to adopt a navigation URL that is different from the one set by the programmer. In other words, you divert the *HyperLink* to a custom page on your site where you first accomplish any custom tasks you need (such as tracking) and then redirect to the originally requested page. The code for such a modified version of the *HyperLink* control doesn't look particularly scary:

```
using System;
using System.Web.UI.WebControls;

namespace Samples
{
    public class Hyperlink : System.Web.UI.WebControls.HyperLink
    {
        public string RedirectPage
        {
            get
            {
                var o = ViewState["RedirectPage"];
                if (o == null)
                    return "redir.aspx";
                else
                    return (String) o;
            }
            set { ViewState["RedirectPage"] = value; }
        }

        public new String NavigateUrl
        {
            get { return base.NavigateUrl; }
            set
```

```
            {
                var url = "{0}?page={1}";
                url = String.Format(url, RedirectPage, value);
                base.NavigateUrl = url;
            }
        }
    }
}
```

As you can see, the new control has a brand new property—*RedirectPage*—and overrides an existing property—*NavigateUrl*. *RedirectPage* indicates the URL of the intermediate page, where the user is temporarily redirected so that any custom tasks such as click-through tracking can be accomplished. Here's an example of the code file of such a page:

```
public partial class Redir : System.Web.UI.Page
{
    protected void Page_Load(object sender, EventArgs e)
    {
        // Capture the originally requested page
        var url = String.Empty;
        var o = Request["Page"];
        if (o != null)
        {
            url = Server.UrlEncode((String) o);
            if (String.IsNullOrEmpty(url))
                return;
        }

        // Do something here, such as updating a counter
        ...

        // Redirect the user to the originally requested page
        Response.Redirect(url);
    }
}
```

You are assuming that the custom *HyperLink* control calls the redirector page, passing a *Page* parameter on the query string set to the original URL. Of course, this trick is arbitrary and you can find any better workarounds if you want.

The navigation URL for a hyperlink is set through the *NavigateUrl* property. You need to ensure that whenever a new value is assigned to the *NavigateUrl* property (say, *http://www.asp.net*), it gets overridden by something like the following:

```
redir.aspx?page=http://www.asp.net
```

In this way, the user first reaches *redir.aspx*, where his action is tracked, and then he is directed to his final destination.

To override the *setter* (or the *getter*) of a control property, you need the property to be marked as *virtual* at some point in the control's inheritance chain. The *HyperLink* control has a virtual property—*Text*—and a couple of public, but not virtual, properties such as *Target* and *NavigateUrl*. If the property is not marked as virtual (namely, it is overridable), you can't override it; however, you can replace its implementation altogether. You do this through the *new* modifier in C# and the *Shadows* modifier in Microsoft Visual Basic .NET:

```
public new string NavigateUrl
{
    get { return base.NavigateUrl; }
    set
    {
        var url = "{0}?page={1}";
        url = String.Format(url, RedirectPage, value);
        base.NavigateUrl = url;
    }
}
```

The *new* modifier applied to a property instructs the compiler that the current implementation for the member replaces any other implementation available on base classes. If you redefine the *NavigateUrl* property without using the *new* keyword, you simply receive a warning from the compiler. The warning informs you that you are hiding an existing member, and it just recommends the use of the *new* modifier if hiding the member was intentional.

Building Controls from Scratch

There are two main situations in which ASP.NET developers feel the need to create custom controls. At times, developers need a control that simply doesn't exist in the ASP.NET built-in toolbox. And occasionally, developers need a control that is similar to one of the native controls but not close enough to justify using one. In this case, developers typically derive a new control from an existing one and add or override members as appropriate. Let's discuss techniques and tricks to design and code completely new ASP.NET controls that address functionalities that ASP.NET doesn't provide out of the box.

Base Class and Interfaces

Several programming aspects support the development of a custom control in ASP.NET. First, there are base classes such as *Control* and *WebControl*. Each class provides a common set of base properties that address and fit into a particular use case. In addition to base classes, interfaces help you to better characterize the behavior and programming model of the control. A few interfaces are worth mentioning. They are *INamingContainer*, *IPostBackDataHandler*, and *IPostBackEventHandler*.

In Table 12-1, you see listed all base classes for controls and data-bound controls. For now, let's focus on *Control* and *WebControl*.

Control vs. *WebControl*

The *Control* class defines the properties, methods, and events common to all ASP.NET server controls. These include the methods and events that determine and govern the life cycle of the control, plus a few properties such as *ID*, *UniqueID*, *Parent*, and *ViewState* and the collection of child controls named *Controls*.

The *WebControl* class derives from *Control* and adds extra properties and methods, mostly regarding control styles that affect rendering. These properties include *ForeColor*, *BackColor*, *Font*, *Height*, and *Width*. *WebControl*, in particular, is the base class for the family of Web server controls in ASP.NET.

When developing a new ASP.NET control, there's just one guideline to follow. If your control renders a user interface, you should derive it from *WebControl*. If you're authoring a component that doesn't provide specific user-interface features, you're better off using *Control* as your base class. Although these rules are effective in most cases, there might be exceptional situations in which you would reasonably do otherwise. For example, you can derive from *Control* if you want to provide a subset of the user-interface features.

When building composite controls—that is, controls designed by aggregating multiple controls together—you might want to use *CompositeControl* as the base class. You should never use *UserControl*, on the other hand, as a base class for a custom control.

Related Interfaces

Depending on the functionality of your control, you might have to implement additional interfaces. Typically, a server control implements some of the following interfaces:

- *INamingContainer*   This interface, also referred to as a *marker interface*, doesn't contain methods—it simply notifies the ASP.NET runtime that the control that exposes it should be treated as a naming container. Child controls contained within a naming container control have their *UniqueID* property prefixed with the ID of the container. The naming container, therefore, acts as a namespace and guarantees the uniqueness of the control's client IDs within the specified naming scope. (Note that if the *ClientIDMode* property is set to *Static*, this warranty just ceases.) The use of the *INamingContainer* interface is essential if you're writing composite controls or controls that include templates.

- *IPostBackDataHandler*   The interface is needed whenever your control has to examine postback data. If the user can execute actions that affect the state of the control, you need to look into the postback data. For example, a *TextBox* control stores its configuration in the view state but also needs to read what the user typed in through the browser. This scenario is just where the *IPostBackDataHandler* interface fits in. The method *LoadPostData* lets controls examine posted values. The interface is also helpful if you need to raise events on the server based on changes to the data (method *RaisePostDataChanged*). Again, the *TextBox* is the perfect sample control; if the data changed between postbacks, the *TextChanged* event is also raised.

■ *IPostBackEventHandler* The interface serves to capture a client-side postback event (for example, a click). Upon postback, after raising data change events, the ASP.NET runtime looks for a server control whose *UniqueID* property matches the name of a posted value (for example, the name of the clicked button). If a match is found and the control implements *IPostBackEventHandler*, ASP.NET invokes the *RaisePostBackEvent* method on the control. *RaisePostBackEvent* is the only method defined on the *IPostBackEventHandler* interface. What a particular control does within the *RaisePostBackEvent* method can vary quite a bit. The *Button* control—a simple control that implements this interface—fires its *Click* event when ASP.NET invokes the *RaisePostBackEvent* method.

Choosing a Rendering Style

For an ASP.NET server control, the sole purpose in life is outputting markup text. The control's object model and the system infrastructure it leverages serve to determine the contents to output, but the whole life cycle of controls (and host pages) inevitably ends with the rendering step. There are various ways for a server control to render out.

The *Render* Method

Typically, an ASP.NET control renders out through the *Render* method. To take total control of the control's rendering, you therefore override the *Render* method and write markup code to the specified HTML text writer object:

```
protected override void Render(HtmlTextWriter writer)
```

The HTML text writer object is a sort of buffer where you can accumulate all the text to be output—nearly the same as a string builder. You can compose markup using the methods of the *HtmlTextWriter* object or by building plain strings. Writing to the text writer is indeed the fastest way for controls to generate their markup, but unfortunately it doesn't result in easily readable code. If you take this route for a reasonably complex control, your final code will look like an intricate mess of nested if-then-else statements. Your code will be hard to read and maintain.

There's another aspect to consider about direct markup output. Consider the following code snippet:

```
protected override void Render(HtmlTextWriter writer)
{
    writer.Write("<input type=text id=\"TextBox1\" />");
}
```

The final page contains an input field of type *text* with an ID of *TextBox1*. The server environment, though, doesn't know anything about this element and might not be able to process server events for this element correctly. In other words, you should render the markup directly only for controls that output raw HTML that don't match ASP.NET controls and don't need to raise or handle server events such as postbacks or post-data-changed events. If you're going to write a server control that renders an HTML marquee or a table of data, writing to the control's text writer buffer is fine. If you're building a control that results from the composition of other controls, you're better off taking another approach—building the control tree programmatically.

Building the Control Tree

When your control embeds constituent child controls, you have a *composite control*. In this case, it is recommended that you build the final tree of controls programmatically by overriding the *CreateChildControls* method defined on the *Control* class. You do this by adding all constituent controls to the *Controls* collection of the control being developed. Here's an example:

```
protected override void CreateChildControls()
{
    // Clears child controls
    Controls.Clear();

    // Build the control tree
    CreateControlHierarchy();

    // Clear the view state of child controls
    ClearChildViewState();
}
```

ClearChildViewState is a method on the *Control* class that deletes the view-state information for all the server child controls. *CreateControlHierarchy*, on the other hand, is an arbitrary name and represents a user-defined method that builds the control's tree. You should feel free to replace that function with your own function or plain code. As a matter of fact, though, most ASP.NET built-in composite controls define a protected, overridable method with just that name. Here's a possible implementation for *CreateControlHierarchy* that creates a text box with a leading label. Note that not only is the name of *CreateControlHierarchy* arbitrary, but its prototype also is.

```
protected void CreateControlHierarchy()
{
    // Add the label
    var lbl = new Label();
    lbl.Text = "Some text";
    Controls.Add(lbl);
```

```
    // Add a blank literal control for spacing
    Controls.Add(new LiteralControl("  "));

    // Add the text box
    var txt = new TextBox();
    txt.Text = String.Empty;
    Controls.Add(txt);

    // Specifies that child controls have been created
    ChildControlsCreated = true;
}
```

The ultimate goal of *CreateControlHierarchy* is populating the *Controls* collection of the current control with all child controls in the proper position in the final hierarchy. The *ChildControlsCreated* Boolean property is defined on the *Control* class and indicates whether all child controls have been created or not.

For a composite control, you don't need to override the *Render* method, but it is recommended that you implement the marker interface *INamingContainer* to facilitate ASP.NET's ability to recognize postback events caused by any child control.

Finally, a method that is worth mentioning regarding composite controls is *EnsureChildControls*. This method checks whether all child controls have been created and, if not, it re-creates them. How can the control know about that? It simply reads the value of the *ChildControlsCreated* Boolean property and calls *CreateChildControls* if all child controls haven't been created. The following code snippet illustrates the behavior of *EnsureChildControls*:

```
protected virtual void EnsureChildControls()
{
    if (!ChildControlsCreated)
    {
        try {
            CreateChildControls();
        }
        finally {
            ChildControlsCreated = true;
        }
    }
}
```

The *SimpleGaugeBar* Control

To get a grip on building new ASP.NET controls, let's create a control with a limited state but a significant rendering engine. The control, named *SimpleGaugeBar*, is a simple, non-data-bound gauge bar that you can use to implement a rating system that represents the progress made for certain tasks. Generally, it can be used to give a friendly user interface to measurable quantities.

Defining the Object Model

A gauge control needs to have at least two properties—one to indicate the value being rendered, and one that provides the scale. In addition, you can also give users a chance to control the ruler and the descriptive text for the gauge. Table 12-2 lists the properties of a gauge control.

TABLE 12-2 Properties of the *SimpleGaugeBar* Control

Property	Description
FormatString	Formats the string that the control will render alongside the bar. The string can contain up to two placeholders. The first placeholder is set with the value; the second placeholder is set with the scale. The default string has the following form: *{0} / {1}*.
GridLines	Indicates whether vertical delimiters should be displayed to mark notches.
Maximum	Indicates the maximum value the gauge can represent. It's set to 100 by default.
Segments	Indicates the number of notches to draw on the gauge ruler. It's set to 4 by default.
Value	Indicates the value to represent. It's set to 0 by default, and it cannot be higher than the scale.

The *setter* method of the *Value* property adjusts any value provided that exceeds the current *Maximum*. The value stored in *Maximum* is the highest value you can assign to *Value*. The format string should be formed using two parameters in a fixed order: *Value* and *Maximum*. In the format string, you can use any HTML formatting and even reference the parameters in the reverse order. The following code snippet shows possible ways of setting the format string:

```
GaugeBar1.FormatString = "{0} ({1})";
GaugeBar2.FormatString = "Maximum is {1}. Value is <b>{0}</b>";
```

The *SimpleGaugeBar* control has no methods and doesn't fire any events.

Implementing the Object Model

Internally, the control renders the gauge using an HTML table. The *Value* and *Maximum* pair are translated as percentages, and the ruler is drawn using table cells. Figure 12-1 shows the control within the Microsoft Visual Studio designer.

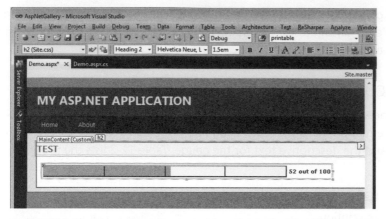

FIGURE 12-1 The *SimpleGaugeBar* control in action in the Visual Studio designer.

The notches on the ruler are obtained simply by adding as many cells to the underlying table as there are units in the *Segments* property. The following listing shows the implementation of the control properties:

```
public class SimpleGaugeBar : CompositeControl
{
    private int _dividerCell;

    public SimpleGaugeBar()
    {
    }

    // Gets and sets the value to represent in the gauge bar
    public float Value
    {
        get
        {
            var o = ViewState["Value"];
            if (o == null)
                return 0;
            return (float) o;
        }
        set
        {
            ViewState["Value"] = value;
            if (value > Maximum)
                ViewState["Value"] = Maximum;
        }
    }

    // Gets and sets the maximum value representable in the gauge bar
    public float Maximum
    {
        get
        {
            var o = ViewState["Maximum"];
```

```
            if (o == null)
                return 100;
            return (float) o;
        }
        set { ViewState["Maximum"] = value; }
    }

    // Number of segments to divide the bar into
    public int Segments
    {
        get
        {
            var o = ViewState["Segments"];
            if (o == null)
                return 4;
            return (int) o;
        }
        set
        {
            ViewState["Segments"] = value;
            if( value < 1)
                ViewState["Segments"] = 1;
        }
    }

    // Gets and sets the pattern to format the value in the gauge bar
    public string FormatString
    {
        get
        {
            var o = ViewState["FormatString"];
            if (o == null)
                return "<b>{0}</b> / <b>{1}</b>";
            return (string) o;
        }
        set { ViewState["FormatString"] = value; }
    }

    // Gets and sets whether the gauge bar has grid lines
    public bool GridLines
    {
        get
        {
            var o = ViewState["GridLines"];
            if (o == null)
                return true;
            return (bool) o;
        }
        set { ViewState["GridLines"] = value; }
    }
    ...
}
```

The control maintains some state by using the view-state collection. All the properties, in fact, are persisted using *ViewState*. Because all the persisted properties are marked as public, you can disable the view state altogether and still keep the control fully functional by explicitly setting properties upon page loading.

Setting Up the Ruler

The ruler divides the area of the control into segments, which are filled proportionally based on the current value of the gauge. Each segment of the ruler corresponds to a cell in the underlying table. All cells but one are entirely filled or entirely empty. Filled cells are rendered using the current foreground color; empty cells are rendered using the current background color. One cell, named the divider cell, contains a child table with exactly one row and two cells. The first cell is rendered with the foreground color; the second cell is colored as the control's background. The two cells have a width, measured in percent, whose total amounts to 100. The latter cell denotes how much is still left to do to reach the maximum. The following HTML code snippet shows the final HTML markup to render a value of 52 out of 100 using a ruler with four notches or segments:

```
<table><tr>
    <td bgcolor=orange width=25%></td>
    <td bgcolor=orange width=25%></td>
    <td>
      <table><tr>
        <td bgcolor=orange width=2%></td>
        <td bgcolor=white width=98%></td>
      </tr></table>
    </td>
    <td bgcolor=white width=25%></td>
</tr></table>
```

Figure 12-2 shows gauges with different ruler settings.

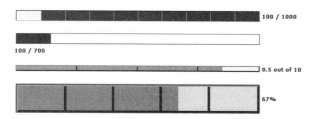

FIGURE 12-2 The effect of different settings on the gauge ruler.

Setting Up the Control's Site

As you might have guessed already from the preceding figures, other properties get into the game in addition to those discussed in Table 12-2. Admittedly, the grayscale rendering used in this book doesn't do justice to the actual capabilities of the *SimpleGaugeBar* control in terms of color support. However, the control exploits a few color-related properties defined on the base class. These properties are *BackColor*, *ForeColor*, *Width*, and *Height*.

Width and *Height* are used to delimit the control's site—that is, the area within the container the control is assigned for rendering. The control is assigned a default size that can be changed either programmatically or through the Visual Studio Properties window.

The value of the *ForeColor* property is used to render the text of the label that accompanies the gauge. The value of the *BackColor* property determines the color to be used for the progress bar. Note that the implementation we just discussed assumes that only known colors can be used.

Rendering the *SimpleGaugeBar* Control

The user interface of a Web control is pure HTML, sometimes topped off with a bit of client script. As mentioned, there are basically two ways in which this HTML can be generated. You can compose the HTML code in the supplied writer, or you can build an in-memory representation of the output using existing HTML and Web server controls and then have them recursively render their contents to the writer. Let's discuss these two options in more detail.

Generating the HTML for a Custom Control

From a pure performance standpoint, writing out the control's markup to an HTML text writer object is the preferred approach. No server control is ever instantiated, and the final and correct markup is sent to the browser. There are a few downsides to this approach you should consider, however. One is that you end up making several calls to the writer. And, aside from some negligible repercussions in terms of the performance (repercussions that are negligible when compared to control instantiation), the size of the code grows considerably, making your source code on the whole much less readable and harder to maintain. Let's consider a quick but significant example.

To write the content of a string in a table cell, you need the following code if you decide to opt for the rich interface of the writer:

```
output.WriteFullBeginTag("table");
output.WriteFullBeginTag("tr");
output.WriteFullBeginTag("td");
output.Write(text);
output.WriteEndTag("td");
output.WriteEndTag("tr");
output.WriteEndTag("table");
```

However, as long as you don't have a full bag of attributes to render, or a really complex structure to build, the following code is equally effective and even slightly faster:

```
output.Write("<table><tr><td>");
output.Write(text);
output.Write("</td></tr></table>");
```

In general, neither of these two approaches is always the best possible approach. A good compromise between the two is recommended to optimize performance while producing compact code. Taking the first approach to its natural limit, you end up with many more lines of code than are necessary. Taking the second approach further, you resort to building the control using strings, which is indeed not the best thing you can do, mainly from a maintenance point of view.

In ASP.NET, every piece of HTML code can be managed on the server as an instance of a class. This pattern results in extreme flexibility and ease of development. However, it doesn't come without problems either. The rub lies in the fact that you instantiate lots of controls, which always affects performance. Let's take a look at this in more detail.

Using Child Controls for Rendering

Sometimes the custom control needs to build up a complex infrastructure with nested tables and elements. In this case, it makes sense to build an in-memory representation of the overall tree and then render everything to HTML using the *RenderContents* method of the root control. Typically, for controls with a relatively complex hierarchy of child controls and rich styles, you override the *Render* method as follows:

```
protected override void Render(HtmlTextWriter output)
{
    // This is a custom method that you normally use
    // to ensure that all elements are styled properly.
    // We'll show an implementation of this method later.
    PrepareControlForRendering();

    // Render the contents of the control
    base.RenderContents(output);
}
```

The *SimpleGaugeBar* control renders a nontrivial table structure that is much more manageable through a control tree:

```
protected override void CreateChildControls()
{
    Controls.Clear();
    CreateControlHierarchy();
    ClearChildViewState();
}

protected virtual void CreateControlHierarchy()
```

```
{
    // Build the outermost container table
    var outer = new Table();
    var outerRow = new TableRow();
    outer.Rows.Add(outerRow);

    // Ruler cell
    var rulerCell = new TableCell();
    outerRow.Cells.Add(rulerCell);
    BuildGaugeBar(rulerCell);

    // Text cell
    var textCell = new TableCell();
    if (!_textStyle.DisplayTextAtBottom)
    {
        outerRow.Cells.Add(textCell);
        BuildLabel(textCell);
    }

    // Save the control tree-add the table as a child of the gauge
    Controls.Add(outer);

    // Build the label
    if (!_textStyle.RenderInsideTable && _textStyle.DisplayTextAtBottom)
        BuildLabel(null);
}

void BuildGaugeBar(TableCell container)
{
    // Create the table with one or two rows: ruler (and label)
    var t = new Table();
    var ruler = new TableRow();
    t.Rows.Add(ruler);

    // Build the ruler row
    BuildRuler(ruler);

    // Build the label
    if (_textStyle.RenderInsideTable)
        BuildLabelIntoTable(t);

    // Save the control tree
    container.Controls.Add(t);
}
```

The output of the *SimpleGaugeBar* control consists of an outermost table that has one row and two cells. The first cell contains the gauge bar; the second cell optionally contains the text, when the companion text has to be displayed on the side of the gauge. (See Figure 12-2.) If the text goes below the gauge, it can either be part of the table (a second row) or just an additional *Label* control. You control rendering styles of the text through a custom style property—the *TextStyle* property—that I'll say more about in a moment. Let's first focus on the ruler.

The ruler is a sequence of table cells. Each cell corresponds to a notch you want to see on the final gauge. The number of notches is determined by the *Segments* property. The *Value* property is scaled as a percentage of the *Maximum* value, and the resulting value is used to determine the color of the various cells. If the value to represent is larger than the value represented by the current notch, a cell is added with the average width determined by dividing 100 by the number of notches. The same happens if the value is smaller and the divider cell has been rendered already. (In this case, *finished* is true.)

```
void BuildRuler(TableRow ruler)
{
    // Calculate the value to represent
    var val = GetValueToRepresent();
    float valueToRepresent = 100f * val / Maximum;
    var numOfSegments = GetNumOfSegments();

    int segmentWidth = 100 / numOfSegments;
    bool finished = false;
    for (int i = 1; i <= numOfSegments; i++)
    {
        if (valueToRepresent < i * segmentWidth)
        {
            if (finished)
            {
                // Still-To-Do
                var stillToDo = new TableCell();
                ruler.Cells.Add(stillToDo);
                stillToDo.Width = Unit.Percentage(segmentWidth);
            }
            else
            {
                // Cell to divide
                _dividerCell = i - 1;  // need a 0-based index
                var cell = new TableCell();
                ruler.Cells.Add(cell);
                cell.Width = Unit.Percentage(segmentWidth);
                cell.Height = Unit.Percentage(100);

                // Add a child table to the cell
                var child = new Table();
                child.Width = Unit.Percentage(100);
                child.Height = Unit.Percentage(100);
                cell.Controls.Add(child);
                child.CellPadding = 0;
                child.CellSpacing = 0;
                var childRow = new TableRow();
                child.Rows.Add(childRow);

                float fx = (100 *
                        (valueToRepresent - segmentWidth *
                        (i - 1)) / segmentWidth);
                if (valueToRepresent > (i - 1) * segmentWidth)
                {
                    TableCell left = new TableCell();
```

```
                    childRow.Cells.Add(left);
                    left.Width = Unit.Percentage(fx);
                }
                var right = new TableCell();
                childRow.Cells.Add(right);
                right.Width = Unit.Percentage(100 - fx);
                finished = true;
            }
        }
        else
        {
            // Done
            var done = new TableCell();
            ruler.Cells.Add(done);
            done.Width = Unit.Percentage(segmentWidth);
        }
    }
}
```

The divider cell is the cell that is split in two to represent the remaining value, as shown in Figure 12-3.

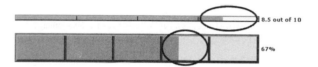

FIGURE 12-3 The divider cell in sample *SimpleGaugeBar* controls.

The divider cell is the first cell where the value of the corresponding notch is larger than the value to represent. The divider cell is rendered through an embedded table with one row and two cells. The index of the divider cell is cached for further use.

The companion text of the gauge can be displayed to the right of the gauge or below it. When rendered below it, the text can either be incorporated in the table or added as an extra control. *BuildLabel* can either add the text as an additional control or place it in the rightmost cell. *BuildLabelIntoTable* writes the text in an additional table row below the gauge. In this case, the text inherits most of the gauge graphical settings.

```
void BuildLabel(TableCell container)
{
    // Calculate the value to represent
    float buf = GetValueToRepresent();

    // Get the string to display on the label
    string msg = GetTextToRepresent();

    var lbl = new Label();
    if (container is TableCell)
        container.Controls.Add(lbl);
```

```
    else
        Controls.Add(lbl);
    lbl.Text = String.Format(msg, buf, Maximum);
}

// Build the control tree for the label
void BuildLabelIntoTable(Table t)
{
    // Calculate the value to represent
    float valueToRepresent = GetValueToRepresent();
    int numOfSegments = GetNumOfSegments();

    // Get the string to display on the label
    var companionText = GetTextToRepresent();
    if (_textStyle.DisplayTextAtBottom)
    {
        // Add a bottom row
        var label = new TableRow();
        t.Rows.Add(label);

        var lblCell = new TableCell();
        label.Cells.Add(lblCell);

        lblCell.ColumnSpan = numOfSegments;
        lblCell.Text = String.Format(companionText, valueToRepresent, Maximum);
    }
}
```

Note In the code shown thus far for the *SimpleGaugeBar* control, there a pair of unexplained methods: *GetValueToRepresent* and *GetTextToRepresent*. In this simple control, the methods return, respectively, the value of the *Value* and *FormatString* properties. However, you can extend the control with data-binding capabilities. In doing so, most of the changes will consist of extending the *GetValueToRepresent* and *GetTextToRepresent* methods.

There's no functional difference between the two approaches—it's purely a matter of appearance and preference. But how can you control the rendering and the styles of the companion text? You do that through a new style property.

The Gauge in Action

After it's compiled, the *SimpleGaugeBar* control can be installed in the Visual Studio toolbox and dragged and dropped onto any Web Forms page you're developing. Here's some sample code being added to a page:

```
<x:SimpleGaugeBar id="GaugeBar1" runat="server"
    Width="500px" Height="15px"
    FormatString="<b>{0}</b> out of <b>{1}</b>"
    Segments="10"
    Value="65">
</x:SimpleGaugeBar>
```

The properties of the control that feature simple types can be set using the Properties window; for properties of a complex type, such as classes, you need to write a type converter and configure the property for the design-time environment of Visual Studio. The following code shows how to set properties on the gauge control programmatically:

```
private void Button1_Click(Object sender, EventArgs e)
{
    GaugeBar1.Maximum = 200;
    GaugeBar1.Value = 55;
}
```

You should try to set the *Maximum* property first because, in this way, the control automatically validates the value. *Maximum* and *Value* are stored in the view state and are automatically restored when the page posts back. If the host page disables the view state, you should modify the code that relates to the control so that the needed properties are set on each request.

Building a Data-Bound Control

So far, we've created the *SimpleGaugeBar* control as a composite control to display a notched indicator of a given quantity. By setting the *Value* and *Maximum* properties on the control, you can graphically represent a value on the proper scale. The *SimpleGaugeBar* control is not data bound, meaning that no elements in its programming interface can be automatically and declaratively bound to external data. Derived from *CompositeControl*, the *SimpleGaugeBar* control doesn't incorporate any of the features listed previously regarding data-bound controls.

The goal of this section is to extend the *SimpleGaugeBar* control to make it support data binding through enumerable objects and data source controls.

Key Features

A data-bound version of *SimpleGaugeBar* is a form of simple binding. A couple of existing properties—*Value* and *FormatString*—can be automatically filled with external data according to the classic data-binding pattern of ASP.NET. A data source object specified through either *DataSource* or *DataSourceID* and bindable properties are mapped to public fields on the data source object through mapper properties. In simple binding, the bound data source object is an individual object that contains just one logical piece of information—no items, no lists.

The key features of a data-bound control can be summarized as follows:

- Additional properties to represent mappings between control properties and data source fields

- An additional property to represent and persist the data source object

- Additional view-state management to persist the data source object

- Modified rendering to take bound data into account

Let's dig out more.

Adding Data-Bound Properties

When you bind data to, say, a *DropDownList* control, you first set the data source and then specify which fields on the data source should be used to display the text and the value of the resulting list. The *DropDownList* control features a pair of *DataTextField* and *DataValueField* string properties.

The former is set to the name of the public field on the data source that will render the text of displayed list items. The latter is set to the name of the field on the bound data source object that will render the unique value associated with each displayed list item.

On a new data-bound control, you need to define similar properties to specify any required mapping between data source fields and bindable control properties. All these properties are usually string properties stored in the view state; the name is arbitrary, but it generally follows the pattern *DataXxxField*, where *Xxx* indicates the role of the bindable control property.

Adding a Data Item Property

By design, the bound data source object must be an object that implements any of the following interfaces: *IEnumerable* (collections), *IListSource* (ADO.NET objects), or *IDataSource* (data source controls). Let's suppose you bind a control to one row of a *DataTable*. Do you really need to persist the whole data row? If yes, what if the data row contains a couple of large binary large object (BLOB) fields?

The recommended approach entails that you extract a subset of information from the originally bound data source object and copy that to a control-specific data item object. This object is an instance of a custom class that typically has as many public properties as there are bindable properties on the control. For example, the *DropDownList* control has two bindable properties: *Text* and *Value*. Subsequently, the data item object—named *ListItem*—has two properties: *Text* and *Value*. (Naming is arbitrary, though.)

In a new data-bound control, you define a data item class that will be filled with any necessary information contained in the bound data source. This data item object must be persisted through the view state to guarantee that the control refreshes properly across postbacks. For performance reasons, the data item class must be able to serialize itself to the view state without resorting to the binary formatter. Put another way, it means that the data item class must implement *IStateManager*, just like style classes do.

> **Note** The data item class will be a collection of single data item classes if the data binding involves the association of a list of elements to a control.

Overriding the *PerformDataBinding* Method

The final key feature for a custom data-bound control is overriding the *PerformDataBinding* method. The method receives the contents of the bound data source object in the form of an enumerable object. As a control developer, you must read any required data from the source and cache it in the data item object.

Finally, you modify the rendering engine of the control to display bound data.

> **Note** Unless you need a data-bound control that behaves in a particular way (for example, a list control or a composite data-bound control), deriving your control from *DataBoundControl* is the most reasonable thing to do most of the time. If you need to start from a lower level, though, you can inherit from *BaseDataBoundControl* and override *PerformSelect* and *ValidateDataSource*. Needless to say, you might want to take this route only if you need to change the way a data source is validated, retrieved, or both.

The *GaugeBar* Control

Let's apply all the steps outlined so far to a new version of the *SimpleGaugeBar* control, aptly named *GaugeBar*. The new control will still be a composite control, but it will inherit from *DataBoundControl* to gain standard data-binding capabilities.

```
public class GaugeBar : DataBoundControl
{
    ...
}
```

To be precise, ASP.NET also features a class that incorporates both composition and data binding. The name of the class is *CompositeDataBoundControl*.

Mapping Data Source Fields to Control Properties

The new *GaugeBar* control uses the same code as *SimpleGaugeBar* and extends it to define a couple of bindable properties—say, *Value* and *FormatString*. This choice of bindable properties is arbitrary, however.

You define a pair of *DataXxxField* properties—one for *Value* and one for *FormatString*. These string properties contain the name of the data source fields mapped to the *Value* and *FormatString*. In particular, *DataValueField* indicates that the field mapped to *Value* and *DataTextField* specifies the field linked to *FormatString*. Once again, note that the names used here are arbitrary.

```
public virtual string DataValueField
{
    get
    {
        var o = ViewState["DataValueField"] as String;
        return o ?? String.Empty;
    }
    set { ViewState["DataValueField"] = value; }
}

public virtual string DataTextField
{
    get
    {
        var o = ViewState["DataTextField"] as String;
        return o ?? String.Empty;
    }
    set { ViewState["DataTextField"] = value; }
}
```

As you can see, both properties use the *ViewState* as the storage medium and are set to the empty string by default. Other popular data-bound properties available on the *GaugeBar* class are *DataSource*, *DataSourceID*, and *DataMember*, all of which are inherited from parent classes.

The *GaugeBar*'s Data Item Object

After the *GaugeBar* control is bound to some external data, you need to track and cache any bound data. For this purpose, you need a data item object. As mentioned, a data item object is a custom class with as many public properties as there are bindable properties in the control's interface. The data item class for the *GaugeBar* control is named *GaugeBarDataItem* (again, an arbitrary name) and is defined as follows:

```
public class GaugeBarDataItem : IStateManager
{
    private string _text;
    private float _value;
    private bool _marked;

    public GaugeBarDataItem()
    {
    }
```

```csharp
    public GaugeBarDataItem(float value, string text)
    {
        _text = text;
        _value = value;
    }

    public string Text
    {
        get { return _text; }
        set { _text = value; }
    }

    public float Value
    {
        get { return _value; }
        set { _value = value; }
    }

    public bool IsTrackingViewState
    {
        get { return _marked; }
    }

    public void LoadViewState(object state)
    {
        if (state != null)
        {
            Pair p = (Pair)state;
            _value = (float)p.First;
            _text = (string)p.Second;
        }
    }

    public object SaveViewState()
    {
        return new Pair(_value, _text);
    }

    public void TrackViewState()
    {
        _marked = true;
    }
}
```

The class has two public properties—*Text* and *Value*—persisted through local members. More interestingly, the class also implements the *IStateManager* interface, which provides a standard interface to save any valuable contents to the view state across postbacks.

The *SaveViewState* method returns a *Pair* object (a sort of simplified array of two elements) filled with the current values of the *Text* and *Value* properties. The *Pair* object returned by *SaveViewState* becomes the input argument of *LoadViewState*, which unpacks the *Pair* object and initializes the *Text* and *Value* properties.

The *GaugeBar* control needs to expose a read-only property of type *GaugeBarDataItem*. You can use any name for this variable—I'm using *DataItem* here. More important than the name of the property is its implementation. Take a look at the following code:

```
private GaugeBarDataItem _dataItem;
...

private GaugeBarDataItem DataItem
{
   get
   {
      if (_dataItem == null)
      {
         _dataItem = new GaugeBarDataItem();
         if (base.IsTrackingViewState)
            _dataItem.TrackViewState();
      }
      return _dataItem;
   }
}
```

Unlike other control properties that are persisted directly in the *ViewState* collection object, the *DataItem* property uses a private member (*_dataItem*) to persist its value. A private member, though, is not persistent and doesn't survive postbacks. For this reason, in the *get* accessor of the property you need to check *_dataItem* for nullness and create a new instance if it is null.

The code contained in the *get* accessor of a property runs whenever that property is invoked. As you'll see in a moment, the preceding code ensures that no access to *DataItem* results in a null object exception and that the state of the object is restored correctly after each postback.

Data Item and View State

Most of the control properties we've considered thus far use the *ViewState* container to persist the values. Why should we not store *DataItem* or style properties in the same way? Is there anything wrong with the following code?

```
// NB: for this code to work, GaugeBarDataItem must be
// a serializable type
public virtual GaugeBarDataItem DataItem
{
   get
   {
      var o = ViewState["DataItem"] as GaugeBarDataItem;
      return o ?? new GaugeBarDataItem();
   }
   set { ViewState["DataItem"] = value; }
}
```

Actually, nothing is "wrong" with the code per-se—but consider for a moment view-state size and performance. Saving a class type directly in the *ViewState* container results in the object being serialized using the binary formatter. The *BinaryFormatter* class—the standard way to serialize managed objects in .NET applications—is not particularly fast and is designed to save the entire state of the object, including both public *and* private members, both simple and complex. The use of the *BinaryFormatter* increases the response time for each request and generates a larger view-state output. By customizing the view-state serialization, you obtain much faster code and save exactly the information you need to save.

As a rule of thumb, you should use the *ViewState* container to store property values if the type of the property is primitive—a string, numbers, Boolean values, colors, dates, bytes, and arrays of any of these types. Reference types (for example, custom classes) should be serialized by implementing *IStateManager* and exposing the property via a *get* accessor like the one shown previously. As far as control development is concerned, this is commonly required for styles and data item properties.

Ad Hoc View-State Management

A control that has properties that take advantage of custom view-state serialization must override the *SaveViewState* and *LoadViewState* protected methods. These methods are defined on the *Control* class, and they indicate how to save and restore the state of the control to and from the view state. The default implementation of both methods takes care of the contents of only the *ViewState* container object.

```
protected override object SaveViewState()
{
    // Get the standard state object-ViewState container
    var baseState = base.SaveViewState();

    // Get the state object for the DataItem property
    var itemState = DataItem.SaveViewState();

    // Get the state object for the TextStyle object
    var styleState = TextStyle.SaveViewState();

    // Pack everything into a unique object
    return new Triplet(baseState, itemState, styleState);
}
```

The *SaveViewState* method of the *GaugeBar* control needs to save three objects: the standard view state, the *DataItem* property, and the *TextStyle* property. You get the standard view-state output by calling *SaveViewState* on the base class, and you get other state objects by calling *SaveViewState* on the *IStateManager* implementation of *DataItem* and *TextStyle*. The *SaveViewState* method on the control needs to return a single object, so you just group all data to return in a single object—typically, an array or a combination of *Pair* and *Triplet* objects.

The object returned by *SaveViewState* is received by *LoadViewState*, which extracts and assigns data back to the original objects.

```
protected override void LoadViewState(object savedState)
{
    if (savedState != null)
    {
        var t = (Triplet) savedState;
        base.LoadViewState(t.First);
        DataItem.LoadViewState(t.Second);
        TextStyle.LoadViewState(t.Third);
    }
    else
    {
        base.LoadViewState(null);
    }
}
```

The *IStateManager* implementation of *LoadViewState* on the serialized objects determines how each object (for example, styles and data items) restores its own data.

Note that when *DataItem.LoadViewState* is called, the *get* accessor of *DataItem* is invoked and initializes the internal *_dataItem* member on the first call.

Getting Bound Data

In ASP.NET, a bound control obtains bound data through the *PerformDataBinding* method. Overriding this method is mandatory for any data-bound control because the standard implementation of the method does nothing. It is important to recall that the *IEnumerable* argument passed to *PerformDataBinding* represents the collection of bound data regardless of the format of the originally bound data source—whether it is an ADO.NET object, collection, or data source control.

Here's the implementation of *PerformDataBinding* for the *GaugeBar* control:

```
protected override void PerformDataBinding(IEnumerable data)
{
    // In this control, in spite of the IEnumerable type being used
    // the argument "data" is a single object, not a real list to enumerate.
    // You need to get an enumerator and call MoveNext once to get the effective
    // content to bind.
    if (data == null)
        return;
    var e = data.GetEnumerator();
    e.MoveNext();

    // Set default values for bindable properties
    float displayValue = 0;
    var displayText = String.Empty;
```

```
    // Read the value for the Value property
    if (!String.IsNullOrEmpty(DataValueField))
        displayValue = (float) DataBinder.GetPropertyValue(
                e.Current, DataValueField);

    // Read the value for the FormatString property
    if (!String.IsNullOrEmpty(DataTextField))
        displayText = (String) DataBinder.GetPropertyValue(
                e.Current, DataTextField);

    // Fill the DataItem property
    DataItem.Value = displayValue;
    DataItem.Text = displayText;
}
```

In this particular case, the *IEnumerable* object passed to *PerformDataBinding* contains just one element. The *IEnumerable* interface, though, doesn't distinguish between a single element or a list of elements. In other words, to get the data object you need to get the enumerator and move to the first item:

```
// data is of type IEnumerable
IEnumerator e = data.GetEnumerator();
e.MoveNext();

// Use e.Current to get the physical data object
```

The *e.Current* expression returns the data object bound to the control—that is, the container from which you extract the fields mapped to bindable properties. If you know the control is bound to, say, a *DataRow* object, you can retrieve the value for the *Value* property through the following code:

```
displayValue = ((DataRow) e.Current)[DataValueField];
```

Using the *DataBinder* class adds greater flexibility to your code and makes your code independent from the type of the bound data source. The *GetPropertyValue* method on the *DataBinder* class uses reflection to query the object to see whether it contains a public property with the specified name:

```
displayText = (string) DataBinder.GetPropertyValue(
        e.Current, DataTextField);
```

GetPropertyValue returns an object and requires a cast to the proper type.

The remaining step is updating the rendering engine so that it accesses the *DataItem* object whenever it requires bound data. The *BuildLabel* method shown next displays the descriptive text around the gauge:

```
void BuildLabel(TableCell container)
{
    // Calculate the value to represent
    var valueToRepresent = GetValueToRepresent();

    // Get the string to display on the label
    var msg = GetTextToRepresent();

    var lbl = new Label();
    if (container is TableCell)
        container.Controls.Add(lbl);
    else
        Controls.Add(lbl);

    lbl.Text = String.Format(msg, valueToRepresent, Maximum);
}
```

The *BuildLabel* method adds a *Label* control to the control hierarchy under construction. The text displayed through the label is composed using the value and the format string of the gauge. Both *Value* and *FormatString* can be either data-bound or statically assigned. For this reason, you should use a *get* function that checks the current binding, if any, and returns the bound value or the assigned value. Note the bound value is returned in favor of an assigned value, if both are present.

```
float GetValueToRepresent()
{
    float f = 0;
    if (DataItem.Value >=0)
        f = DataItem.Value;
    else
        f = Value;

    return f;
}

string GetTextToRepresent()
{
    var msg = "";
    if (!String.IsNullOrEmpty(DataItem.Text))
        msg = DataItem.Text;
    else
        msg = FormatString;
    return msg;
}
```

No other changes are required to enhance the *SimpleGaugeBar* control and make it data-bound.

The following code shows the *Load* handler of a sample page that uses the *GaugeBar* control and binds it to a dynamically generated *DataTable* object:

```
public class MyDataContainer
{
    public float Numbers { get; set; }
    public String Label { get; set; }
}

protected void Page_Load(object sender, EventArgs e)
{
    // Uses a random number as the value of the GaugeBar.
    // The value is stored in a custom object.
    Random rnd = new Random();
    var container = new MyDataContainer();
    container.Numbers = rnd.Next(0,100);
    container.Label = "{0} out of {1}";

    // Binds the DataTable to the GaugeBar
    GaugeBar1.DataValueField = "Numbers";
    GaugeBar1.DataTextField = "Label";
    GaugeBar1.DataSource = container;
    GaugeBar1.DataBind();
}
```

The *DataTable* has two columns—*Numbers* and *Label*—of type float and string, respectively. The table contains one data row. If the table contained multiple rows, only the first would be taken into account according to the code in *PerformDataBinding*.

Note that you can also use the *DataItem* property to bind data to the *GaugeBar* control:

```
GaugeBar1.DataItem.Value = 12;
GaugeBar1.DataItem.Text = "{0} %";
```

Note that no call to *DataBind* is required to trigger the process and update the control's user interface.

Building a Composite Templated Control

The *CompositeDataBoundControl* class is the starting point for building rich, complex, and data-bound composite controls. A composite data-bound control must do the following:

- Act as a naming container.

- Create its own user interface through the *CreateChildControls* method.

- Implement the necessary logic to restore its hierarchy of child elements after postback.

The good news is that you can completely ignore the third point if you derive your control class from the *CompositeDataBoundControl* class. The class, in fact, implements internally any necessary logic.

Generalities of Composite Data-Bound Controls

The main aspect you care about when building a composite data-bound control is designing the internal hierarchy of your control. The method to override for this purpose is an overloaded version of *CreateChildControls*. In addition, you typically add styles and templates.

In a real-world composite control, the internal control tree is usually quite complex. The outermost container is often a multirow HTML table (or perhaps a collection of <div> tags, each with specific semantics associated with it). However, what's in the various cells and rows can vary quite a bit and result in a pretty sophisticated combination of child controls and literals.

Creating a Hierarchy of Child Controls

You should know by now that composite controls build their own interface by composing controls in the override of the *CreateChildControls* method. Defined on the *Control* class, the method has the following prototype:

```
protected override void CreateChildControls()
```

In the *CompositeDataBoundControl* class, the method is overridden and overloaded. In particular, the overridden version accomplishes a few interesting tasks. Here's its pseudo-code:

```
protected override void CreateChildControls()
{
    Controls.Clear();
    var o = ViewState["_!ItemCount"];
    if ((o == null) && RequiresDataBinding)
        EnsureDataBound();
    else
    {
        int numOfItems = (int) o;
        object[] items = new object[numOfItems];
        CreateChildControls(items, false);
        base.ClearChildViewState();
    }
}
```

The method first empties the *Controls* collection so that no pending child controls are left around. Next, it retrieves a value from a particular (and internally managed) view-state entry named *_!ItemCount*. The view-state entry caches the number of items that form the composite control. The code that actually builds the control tree is responsible for storing this value in the view state.

Knowing the number of items that form the control hierarchy is important to optimize the data-binding process. In ASP.NET, complex controls that show a possibly long list of data items are implemented as composite data-bound controls. In what way is this different from list and simple-bound controls?

List controls and simple-bound controls, such as the *GaugeBar* we considered earlier, cache the data item or items in the view state. In addition, they can either receive data from the data-binding process or programmatically through the *Items* collection and the *DataItem* property, respectively. Composite data-bound controls (such as *ListView* and *GridView*) work on the assumption that they receive data exclusively from data binding and, for this reason, don't persist bound data in any form. Consider now the following scenario.

Imagine a page that contains a rich control such as the *GridView* and some button controls. One of the button controls, when clicked, executes no code that involves the *GridView* but still refreshes the page. Without some special tricks in the control's code, you can be sure that the composite data-bound control would be empty upon postback. Why is this so? If the postback event handler doesn't bind data back to the composite control, the control has no way to figure it out and refresh properly. In ASP.NET, by design, composite data-bound controls take their data only from data binding and don't cache any bound data. So a special workaround is required to handle postback events.

For composite data-bound controls, the *CreateChildControls* method works in either of two modes: binding or nonbinding. When *CreateChildControls* is working in binding mode, the control tree is created as usual. When it's working in nonbinding mode, the control calls an overloaded version of *CreateChildControls*. The method is defined as abstract on the *CompositeDataBoundControl* and must be overridden in any derived class.

The Overloaded *CreateChildControls*

The overloaded version of *CreateChildControls* that is defined on the *CompositeDataBoundControl* class is shown here:

```
protected abstract int CreateChildControls(
    IEnumerable dataSource, bool dataBinding);
```

The first parameter is the collection of bound data. The second parameter indicates whether the control is being bound to fresh data (that is, it is working in binding mode) or is being refreshed after a postback. The return value indicates the number of items added to the control tree. This value will then be stored in the view state during the call to *PerformDataBinding*. The following code snippet shows an excerpt from the source code of *PerformDataBinding* on the *CompositeDataBoundControl* class:

```
protected internal override void PerformDataBinding(IEnumerable data)
{
    base.PerformDataBinding(data);
    Controls.Clear();
    base.ClearChildViewState();
    TrackViewState();
    int numOfItems = CreateChildControls(data, true);
    base.ChildControlsCreated = true;
    ViewState["_!ItemCount"] = numOfItems;
}
```

Note that *PerformDataBinding* calls into the new overload of *CreateChildControls* and passes it *true* as the second argument, indicating that a binding operation is taking place. This makes sense because executing *PerformDataBinding*, by definition, means you are performing a binding operation.

What kind of code should you place in the overloaded *CreateChildControls*? Basically, you call your own control builder method (typically, *CreateControlHierarchy*) and return its return value. I'll return to this point later when discussing the sample *BarChart* control.

The overloaded *CreateChildControls* method is invoked in binding mode from within *PerformDataBinding*, and it's invoked in nonbinding mode from within the other *CreateChildControls* method:

```
// o is the value read from ViewState
int numOfItems = (int) o;
object[] items = new object[numOfItems];
CreateChildControls(items, false);
```

In this case, the bound data passed to the method is an empty array of objects of a well-known size. The goal of this array is to force the control builder method (typically, *CreateControlHierarchy*) to loop the right number of times and build an outermost container with the right configuration—for example, a table with the right number of rows and columns.

As you'll see in detail for the sample *BarChart* control, a composite data-bound control neatly separates hierarchy from data. If the Boolean parameter of *CreateChildControls* is *false*, no data is added to the hierarchy. How can the control show up as it did the last time? The ASP.NET postback mechanism guarantees that child controls are restored with all their values. In other words, if a composite data-bound control displays bound data through, say, a *Label* control, after a postback the composite control doesn't restore its bound data directly. However, it asks any child control, including the *Label*, to restore itself from the view state. In doing so, the *Label* restores the bound data from its *Text* property.

The bottom line is that the amount of extra data that flows in the view state for a composite control is limited to the number of constituent items, and the control refreshes correctly after a postback. (Of course, child controls put in the view state the usual amount of data.)

The Control Item

It should be clear from the previous discussion that the ASP.NET team had excellent arguments to dictate that composite data-bound controls get their data exclusively from the data-binding process. This fact eliminates the need of having a kind of *Items* property on composite data-bound controls that works like the *Items* property of list controls. This said, feel free to add support for data item objects and collections to your composite controls if you need to.

Most composite controls feature a collection of items, but not a collection of data items. Each item represents a control item—that is, a logical building block of the control's user interface. For a *GridView*, it is a *GridViewRow* object that represents a table row. For a sample *BarChart* control that displays a bar chart, the control item will be a class derived from *TableRow* that contains all the information needed to handle a single bar. The number of items that composite controls store in the view state is exactly the number of "control" items.

Let's see how these concepts apply to a sample composite data-bound control such as *BarChart*.

The *BarChart* Control

The *BarChart* control inherits from *CompositeDataBoundControl* and defines the properties listed in Table 12-3.

TABLE 12-3 *BarChart* **Properties**

Property	Description
DataTextField	Name of the data field to use as the label of each bar.
DataTextFormatString	Format string for the display text.
DataValueField	Name of the data field to use as the value of each bar.
DataValueFormatString	Format string for the value to display on top of each bar.
Items	Collection of *BarChart* items. Each element represents a bar in the chart. Elements in the *Items* collection are of type *BarChartItem*.
Maximum	Gets and sets the maximum value that can be represented in the chart.
SubTitle	Gets and sets the subtitle of the final chart.
Title	Gets and sets the title of the bar chart.

The final markup for the control is a horizontal bar chart such as the one illustrated in Figure 12-4.

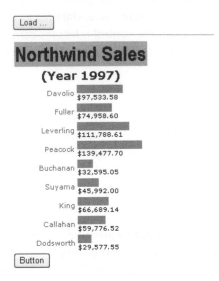

FIGURE 12-4 The *BarChart* control in action.

Each bar is fully represented by an element in the *Items* collection. In addition, the *BarChart* control features a few style properties, as Table 12-4 details.

TABLE 12-4 *BarChart* **Style Properties**

Property	Description
BarStyle	The style of the whole row that contains the bar
LabelStyle	The style of the label
SubTitleStyle	The style of the subtitle in the control's header
TitleStyle	The style of the title in the control's header
ValueStyle	The style of the element displaying the value rendered

The attributes of all style properties are applied in the *Render* method, as in other data-bound controls.

The *BarChart* Item Object

The user interface of the *BarChart* control is created in the overloaded version of *CreateChildControls*.

```
protected override int CreateChildControls(
    IEnumerable dataSource, bool dataBinding)
{
    return CreateControlHierarchy(dataSource, dataBinding);
}
```

Both input arguments are passed down to an internal *CreateControlHierarchy* method, which is ultimately responsible for the creation of the bar chart:

```
int CreateControlHierarchy(IEnumerable dataSource, bool dataBinding)
{
    // Get the data to display (either from data source or viewstate)
    if (dataSource == null)
    {
        RenderEmptyControl();
        return 0;
    }

    // Start building the hierarchy of controls
    Table t = new Table();
    Controls.Add(t);

    // Add the header row with the caption
    CreateTitle(t);

    // Add the subtitle row
    CreateSubTitle(t);

    // Add bars
    int totalItems = CreateAllItems(t, dataSource, dataBinding);
    return totalItems;
}
```

The control hierarchy is a table with two rows for the title and subtitle and other rows for the bars of the chart. *CreateAllItems* adds bar chart items and counts their number. This number is then returned and ends up in the view state.

```
int CreateAllItems(Table t, IEnumerable data, bool useDataSource)
{
    // Count how many items we add
    int itemCount = 0;

    // Clears the Items collection (creates it, if null)
    Items.Clear();

    // Scroll data items, and create table items
    foreach (object o in data)
    {
        // Create the match item object
        BarChartItemType itemType = BarChartItemType.Item;
        BarChartItem item = CreateBarChartItem(t,
            itemType, o, useDataSource);

        // Add the newly created object to the Items collection
        _items.Add(item);

        // Increase the counter
        itemCount++;
    }

    // Return how many items we have into the viewstate (for postbacks)
    return itemCount;
}
```

For each bound item, the method creates a *BarChartItem* object and adds it to the *Items* collection. We'll discuss the *BarChartItem* class in a moment.

Note that you use *Items.Clear* to clear the collection and *_items.Add* to add a new bar chart item to the collection. The *Items* property is implemented as follows:

```
private BarChartItemCollection _items;
...
public virtual BarChartItemCollection Items
{
    get
    {
        if (_items == null)
            _items = new BarChartItemCollection();
        return _items;
    }
}
```

The property *Items* uses the *_items* variable as its storage medium. The first call to *Items.Clear* ensures that the collection is properly initialized. The second call to the same collection can go through the local variable to save a call to the *get* accessor of the *Items* property.

The *BarChartItem* class represents a bar in the chart and is defined as follows:

```
public class BarChartItem : TableRow
{
    private object _dataItem;
    private BarChartItemType _itemType;

    public BarChartItem(BarChartItemType itemType)
    {
        _itemType = itemType;
    }

    public object DataItem
    {
        get {return _dataItem;}
        set {_dataItem = value;}
    }

    public BarChartItemType ItemType
    {
        get {return _itemType;}
    }
}
```

The class inherits from *TableRow* (actually, a bar in the chart is a table row) and defines a couple of properties: *DataItem* and *ItemType*. The *DataItem* property references the data item in the bound data source associated with the corresponding item. For example, if the *BarChart* is bound to a *DataTable*, *DataItem* is bound to the *DataRow* that corresponds to a given bar.

ItemType, on the other hand, indicates the type of table row—such as a title, subtitle, or item. The item types are defined through an enumerated type:

```
public enum BarChartItemType
{
    Title,
    SubTitle,
    Item
}
```

The *Items* property groups a bunch of *BarChartItem* objects in a collection. The collection type is *BarChartItemCollection*:

```
public class BarChartItemCollection : Collection<BarChartItem>
{
}
```

Because bar chart item objects don't go to the view state, there's no need to implement *IStateManager* and add extra view-state management methods as we did previously for the hyperlink control.

Adding Bound Data

With a composite data-bound control, you don't need to override the *PerformDataBinding* method. However, you should pay some attention to keeping neatly separated the code that builds the structure of the control and the code that adds data.

The *CreateBarChartItem* method creates a new table row and enriches it with a *DataItem* property. What's the content of the row? Looking at Figure 12-3, you can see that each table row has a cell for the label and a cell for the progress bar.

```
BarChartItem CreateBarChartItem(Table t, BarChartItemType itemType,
        object dataItem, bool useDataSource)
{
    // Create a new row for the outermost table
    var item = new BarChartItem(itemType);

    // Create cells for label and value
    var labelCell = CreateLabelCell(item);
    var valueCell = CreateValueCell(item);

    // Add the row to the table
    t.Rows.Add(item);

    // Handle the data object binding
    if (useDataSource)
    {
        // Get the data source object
        item.DataItem = dataItem;
```

```
        // Data bind the team labels
        BindLabelCell(labelCell, dataItem);
        BindValueCell(valueCell, dataItem);
    }

    // Return the fully configured row item
    return item;
}
```

CreateLabelCell and *CreateValueCell* add cells to the table row. Here is their implementation:

```
private TableCell CreateLabelCell(BarChartItem item)
{
    // Create and add the cell
    var cell = new TableCell();
    item.Cells.Add(cell);
    return cell;
}

private TableCell CreateValueCell(BarChartItem item)
{
    // Create and add the cell
    var cell = new TableCell();
    item.Cells.Add(cell);

    // Add the internal labels
    var lblGraph = new Label();
    var lblText = new Label();

    cell.Controls.Add(lblGraph);
    cell.Controls.Add(new LiteralControl("<br>"));
    cell.Controls.Add(lblText);
    return cell;
}
```

The colored bar is represented with a label whose width is a percentage of the maximum value possible on the chart.

As you can see in the code of *CreateBarChartItem*, an *if* statement separates the creation of required child controls from the data binding. If the method is working in binding mode, the *DataItem* property is set on each bar chart item and the following two methods are called to add data to the child controls of the *BarChart* control:

```
private void BindLabelCell(TableCell cell, object dataItem)
{
    if (!String.IsNullOrEmpty(DataTextField))
    {
        string txt = DataBinder.GetPropertyValue(
            dataItem, DataTextField, DataTextFormatString);
        cell.Text = txt;
    }
}
```

```
private void BindValueCell(TableCell cell, object dataItem)
{
    // Bind the label for the graph
    var lblGraph = (Label) cell.Controls[0];
    object o = null;
    if (!String.IsNullOrEmpty(DataValueField))
        o = DataBinder.GetPropertyValue(dataItem, DataValueField);
    else
        return;
    var val = Convert.ToSingle(o);
    float valueToRepresent = 100 * val / Maximum;
    lblGraph.Width = Unit.Percentage(valueToRepresent);

    // Bind the label for the text
    var lblText = (Label) cell.Controls[2];
    lblText.Text = DataBinder.GetPropertyValue(
            dataItem, DataValueField, DataValueFormatString);
}
```

The data-binding process works in a way that is no different from what you saw earlier for other types of data-bound controls. The trickiest part here is the calculation of the width of the label that, when properly styled, generates the horizontal bar.

> **Note** As you can see, no style properties are assigned when the control hierarchy is being built. Just as for other data-bound controls, style attributes are applied later in the control life cycle in the *Render* method, immediately before generating the control's markup.

Events of the *BarChart* Control

The *BarChart* control also features a couple of events: *BarChartCreated* and *BarChartDataBound*. It is not coincidental that these two events mimic analogous events on the *DataGrid* control. Although far simpler, the *BarChart* is a control designed along the same guidelines that inspired the creation of the *DataGrid* control:

```
public event EventHandler<BarChartItemEventArgs> BarChartItemCreated;
public event EventHandler<BarChartItemEventArgs> BarChartItemDataBound;
protected virtual void OnBarChartCreated(BarChartItemEventArgs e)
{
    if (BarChartItemCreated != null)
        BarChartItemCreated(this, e);
}

protected virtual void OnBarChartItemDataBound(BarChartItemEventArgs e)
{
    if (BarChartItemDataBound != null)
        BarChartItemDataBound(this, e);
}
```

The *BarChartItemCreated* event is fired whenever a new table row is added to represent a bar. The *BarChartItemDataBound* event fires when a newly added table row is bound to its data. The former event fires regardless of the working mode of the control. The latter fires only when the control is created in binding mode.

The data carried out with the event is grouped in the *BarChartItemEventArgs* class:

```
public class BarChartItemEventArgs : EventArgs
{
    private BarChartItem _item;
    public BarChartItemEventArgs(BarChartItem item)
    {
        _item = item;
    }

    // Properties
    public BarChartItem Item
    {
        get { return _item; }
    }
}
```

Both events are fired from within the *CreateBarChartItem* method:

```
BarChartItem CreateBarChartItem(Table t, BarChartItemType itemType,
    object dataItem, bool useDataSource)
{
    // Create a new row for the outermost table
    var item = new BarChartItem(itemType);

    // Create cells for the label and value
    var labelCell = CreateLabelCell(item);
    var valueCell = CreateValueCell(item);

    var argsCreated = new BarChartItemEventArgs(item);
    OnBarChartItemCreated(argsCreated);
    ...
    if (useDataSource)
    {
        ...
        BarChartItemEventArgs argsData = new BarChartItemEventArgs(item);
        OnBarChartItemDataBound(argsData);
    }
}
```

Using the *BarChart* Control

Let's see how to consume these events from within a host page. The following markup enables a *BarChart* control in an ASP.NET page:

```
<x:BarChart runat="server" id="BarChart1"
    Maximum="100" SubTitle="Subtitle" Title="Title"
    OnBarChartDataBound="BarChart1_BarChartDataBound" >
  ...
</x:BarChart>
```

Nothing in the preceding markup indicates the data source. In the *Page_Load* event, the control is bound to its data—a collection of custom objects with a couple of properties. One property indicates the amount of sales for an employee in the specified year; the other indicates the name of the employee:

```
protected void Button1_Click(object sender, EventArgs e)
{
    var data = GetDataByYear(1997);
    BarChart1.Maximum = 150000;
    BarChart1.Title = "Northwind Sales";
    BarChart1.SubTitle = "(Year 1997)";
    BarChart1.DataSource = data;
    BarChart1.DataTextField = "Employee";
    BarChart1.DataValueField = "Sales";
    BarChart1.DataBind();
}
```

The bar chart shown in Figure 12-3 is obtained by running the preceding code. The sample page handles the *BarChartDataBound* event through the following code:

```
void BarChart1_BarChartDataBound(object sender, BarChartItemEventArgs e)
{
    // Get the amount of sales for the current bar
    var sales = (Decimal) DataBinder.GetPropertyValue(
                    e.Item.DataItem, "sales");

    // Add a ToolTip
    var tip = sales.ToString();
    e.Item.Attributes["title"] = tip;

    // Highlight bar where sales > 50000
    if (sales > 50000)
        e.Item.Cells[1].BackColor = Color.LightGreen;
}
```

The amount of sales for the current employee is retrieved and added to the row as a ToolTip. In addition, if the sales are larger than 50,000, the cell is highlighted by using a different background color. (See Figure 12-5.)

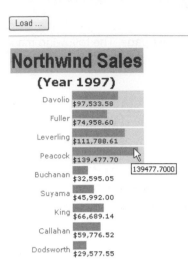

FIGURE 12-5 Output of a *BarChart* control modified by page-level event handlers.

   Note All data-bound controls feature a couple of common events: *DataBinding* and *DataBound*. The former event fires before the data-binding process begins. The *DataBound* event, on the other hand, signals that the data-binding phase has terminated.

Adding Template Support

The *BarChart* control accepts two strings to display as the title and subtitle of the chart. Likewise, you can define a similar property for the footer. Title, subtitle, and footer are distinct items in the *BarChart* control hierarchy. What are you allowed to display in these items? As long as the properties are implemented as plain strings, there's not much more than static text that can show up through the items.

A bit more flexibility can be added with format strings. A format string is a string that contains a predefined number of placeholders that the control machinery fills with internal data. For example, the *FormatString* property of the *GaugeBar* defaults to *{0} / {1}*—namely, a format string with two placeholders. The string is resolved as follows:

```
// First placeholder gets the Value to represent
// Second placeholder gets the Maximum value that can be represented
String.Format(FormatString, Value, Maximum);
```

You can enrich the format string with HTML tags to obtain more appealing results but, in the long run, this approach results in unmanageable code. A much better route to deep customizations of the user interface of controls is to use templates.

Templates and User Controls

In ASP.NET, you can import templates in two ways: through properties of type *ITemplate* or by dynamically loading user controls. A Web user control is a custom component that can be used wherever a server control is valid. You can import such a user-defined control into the layout of the main control and make the interface more flexible and generic. You put a *PlaceHolder* control in the location in which you want custom contents to be injected, and then at run time you create an instance of the user control and add it to the *Controls* collection of the placeholder:

```
placeHolder.Controls.Add(Page.LoadControl("usercontrol.ascx"));
```

The right time to call this code is early in the control life cycle—that is, in an *Init* event handler. Using the *LoadControl* method, the code of the template is insulated in a separate file. This can be a good thing or a bad thing, depending on the context. If the template you want to implement is complex, keeping it off the main page is positive. Otherwise, it would certainly add a layer of unnecessary complexity. Having the template directly available in the source code of the page makes authoring the page much more intuitive and fast because you don't have to follow code into a separate file.

There's also a sort of compromise between the two approaches. You can define an *ITemplate* property in the control and leave the page author free to decide how to set it—with statically defined markup or using the contents of an *.ascx* file.

Defining a Template Property

A template property represents a collection of text and controls that is hosted within a container. The container is also responsible for exposing properties that page authors can use to create data-bound expressions. The following code snippet shows how to define a template property named *TitleTemplate*:

```
[PersistenceMode(PersistenceMode.InnerProperty)]
[TemplateContainer(typeof(TitleTemplateContainer))]
public ITemplate TitleTemplate
{
    get { return _titleTemplate; }
    set { _titleTemplate = value; }
}
```

The storage of the template is guaranteed by the private member *_titleTemplate*, defined as follows:

```
private ITemplate _titleTemplate = null;
```

A template property is characterized by a couple of attributes: *PersistenceMode* and *TemplateContainer*.

The *PersistenceMode* attribute indicates how a control property is persisted declaratively in a host page. Table 12-5 lists possible modes of persistence.

TABLE 12-5 Persistence Modes for Control Properties

Property	Description
Attribute	The property persists as an encoded HTML attribute in the final markup.
EncodedInnerDefaultProperty	The property persists as the only inner text of the control. The property value is HTML encoded. Only a string can be given this designation.
InnerDefaultProperty	The property persists in the control as inner text and is the element's default property. Only one property can be designated the default property.
InnerProperty	The property persists in the control as a nested tag. This is commonly used for complex objects with templates and styles.

The most common setting is *InnerProperty*, which instructs Microsoft Visual Studio to save the contents of the template as a nested tag named after the property:

```
<x:BarChart runat="server" ID="BarChart1" ... >
    <TitleTemplate>
        ...
    </TitleTemplate>
</x:BarChart>
```

If you choose *InnerDefaultProperty*, you can have only one nested tag; by opting for *InnerProperty*, you can have as many nested tags as needed. This is good for rich controls with multiple templates and styles.

The *TemplateContainer* attribute declares the type of the naming container that will contain the template once it is created. As mentioned, a template is hosted by a container which, in turn, is appended to the control's *Controls* collection. The *TemplateContainer* attribute references a type that you, as a control developer, are responsible for declaring.

Defining a Template Container

A template container type is a simple Web control decorated with the *INamingContainer* interface. This control can be given any public members you like. However, it will typically expose the host control as a whole and a bunch of quick-access properties. Here's a sample container type for the *TitleTemplate* property:

```
public class TitleTemplateContainer : WebControl, INamingContainer
{
    private BarChart _parent;
    public TitleTemplateContainer(BarChart parent)
    {
        _parent = parent;
```

```
    }
    public string Title
    {
        get { return _parent.Title; }
    }
    public string SubTitle
    {
        get { return _parent.SubTitle; }
    }
    public BarChart BarChart
    {
        get { return _parent; }
    }
}
```

Once again, be sure to note that there are no constraints or special guidelines to influence the set of members of the class. The class needs to have a reference to the parent control—the *BarChart* in this case. Normally, you create this class for a particular control (or set of controls) and don't reuse it beyond that. It is up to you to expose the parent control through a direct property (*BarChart* in the preceding code) or filter the control's programming interface with a subset of properties (for example, *Title* and *SubTitle*). You can also do both things.

The programming interface of the template container class is important because it defines the information that page authors have access to when creating a template for the property. The template container is made accessible through the *Container* property.

Setting a Template Property

You can use any combination of controls and literals to populate a template. To access external information, though, you need to use data-bound expressions. Here's an example:

```
<TitleTemplate>
    <img src="Title.gif" />
    <%# Container.Title %>
</TitleTemplate>
```

The code snippet demonstrates a *BarChart* title that displays an image in addition to the text set through the *Title* property. Here's another example:

```
<TitleTemplate>
    <%# Container.Title %>
    <small>(<%# DateTime.Now.ToString() %>)</small>
</TitleTemplate>
```

Figure 12-6 shows a templated title item where the originally set *Title* property is displayed side by side with the current time. The current time is rendered with a smaller font and within parentheses.

FIGURE 12-6 A *BarChart* control with a templated title.

Note that any style attributes set through the *TitleStyle* property are maintained in the template.

The *Container* keyword references an instance of the template container type. You use the *Container* keyword to access any control properties exposed through the template container class. Nonstatic information requires a <%# ... %> data-bound expression, just like in the templates of ASP.NET built-in controls.

Rendering a Template

So far you've seen how to define a template property in a server control. But what other changes to the code are required to host a template? In summary, to define a template property you need to do the following:

- Define a property of type *ITemplate*, and use a private variable as its storage medium.

- Decorate the property with the *PersistenceMode* attribute.

- Define a template container class.

- Decorate the property with the *TemplateContainer* attribute.

These steps define only the public interface of the template; more is needed to embed the template in the control's hierarchy. In particular, you need to tweak the code that creates the portion of the control tree where you want the template to display. For example, the

TitleTemplate property refers to the title item; so the internal method to modify is *CreateTitle*. Here's the updated version:

```
private void CreateTitle(Table t)
{
    // Create the table row
    var item = new BarChartItem(BarChartItemType.Title);
    t.Rows.Add(item);

    // Add the title cell
    var cell = new TableCell();
    cell.ColumnSpan = BarChart.ColumnsCount;
    item.Cells.Add(cell);

    // Decide between plain string and template
    if (TitleTemplate != null)
    {
        _titleTemplateContainer = new TitleTemplateContainer(this);
        TitleTemplate.InstantiateIn(_titleTemplateContainer);
        cell.Controls.Add(_titleTemplateContainer);
    }
    else
        cell.Text = Title;

    // Must call DataBind to enable #-expression on templates
    item.DataBind();
}
```

You check whether a template for the title item is defined; if it is not, you just set the *Text* property of the title cell with the contents of the *Title* property. Otherwise, you get an instance of the template container type and use it as the input argument of the *InstantiateIn* method—the only method on the *ITemplate* interface. When done, you add the template container to the control hierarchy—in this case, to the *Controls* collection of the title cell.

A fundamental further step is required to enable the template to successfully process data-bound expressions. You must place a call to *DataBind* on the title item. Data-bound expressions, in fact, are evaluated only after a call to *DataBind* is made that involves the parent control that hosts the expression. Without the *DataBind* call, templates will work correctly but won't display any <%# ... %> expression.

Summary

ASP.NET provides a wealth of server controls from which you can likely choose exactly the control you are looking for. If this is not the case, and the control simply doesn't exist, you can create your own control from the ground up or by extending an existing control, and obtain incredibly powerful results. Writing a control is a matter of defining an appropriate object model and providing an effective rendering algorithm. Aside from these two points, other equally important aspects of control development are containment, naming, and integration with the engine that supplies state management.

In this chapter, we've built a few ASP.NET controls with different capabilities, from simple components capable of rendering an HTML tree to controls with rich support for data binding and templates.

Part III
Design of the Application

Chapter 13
Principles of Software Design

*There is nothing like returning to a place that remains unchanged to find the ways
in which you yourself have altered.*

—*Nelson Mandela*

Maintaining a software application is probably harder, and definitely more bothersome, than writing it from the ground up. A large part of a developer's career is spent performing maintenance tasks on existing code rather than planning and writing new software. Armed with this knowledge, I usually advise developers and architects I work with to always give top priority to one specific attribute of the numerous possible attributes of a software system— that attribute is *maintainability*.

The biggest challenge that many software architects face today is how to design and implement an application that can meet all of the requirements for version 1 plus other requirements that show up afterward. Maintainability has been one of the fundamental attributes of software design since the first draft of the ISO/IEC 9126 paper, back in 1991. (The paper provides a formal description of software quality and breaks it down into a set of characteristics and subcharacteristics, one of which is maintainability. A PDF version of the paper can be obtained at *http://www.iso.org*.)

The mother of all challenges for today's software architects is focusing on current requested features while designing the system in a way that keeps it flexible enough to support future changes and additions. In this regard, maintainability is king and you should favor it over everything else. Maintainability represents the best compromise you can get; with a high level of maintainability in your code, you can achieve anything else—including scalability, performance, and security.

That sounds very nice, but how do you write software that is easy to maintain?

There are a few basic principles of software design that if properly, and extensively, applied will transform a piece of code into a manageable and flexible piece of code. Doing this probably won't be enough to save your team from having to fix a few bugs once the application has been deployed to production, but at least it will keep regression at a reasonable level. More importantly, these principles make it less likely that you'll have to fix a bug with a workaround rather than with a definitive update.

Let's start by reviewing some of the most alarming symptoms that generally signal that code-related suffering is on the horizon.

The Big Ball of Mud

The expression "big ball of mud" (or BBM) refers to a software system that shows no clear sign of thoughtful design and results in a jungle of spaghetti code, duplicated data and behavior, piecemeal growth, and frequent expedient repair. Coined by Brian Foote and Joseph Yooder, the term indicates a clear anti-pattern for developers and architects. You can read the original paper that formalized BBM at *http://www.laputan.org/mud*.

Reasons for the Mud

A BBM system usually results from the combined effect of a few causes: the limited skills of the team, frequent changing of requirements, and a high rate of turnover among team members. Often when you face a BBM the best thing you could ideally do is just rewrite the application based on a new set of reviewed requirements. But, honestly, I'm not sure I've ever seen this happen even once. Most of the time, a complete rewrite is simply not a feasible option.

If you have no way out other than facing the BBM, a reasonable but still painful approach consists of stopping any new development and starting to arrange a bunch of significant tests. What types of tests? Well, in a BBM scenario you can hardly expect to write plain isolated unit tests. You wouldn't be immersed in a big ball of mud if you could write plain unit tests! More likely, you write some sort of integration tests that involve different layers (when not tiers) and that are not especially quick to run, but at least they provide you with an automated tool to measure any regression as you proceed with refactoring the existing code.

To try to keep your head above mud, you can only patiently refactor the code and introduce a better architecture, being very much aware that you're operating in a fragile environment and any approach must be as delicate as possible. Obviously, this process won't be completed quickly. It might even take years if the project is very large. On the other hand, the alternative is to just kill the project.

Let's find out more about the factors that can lead to a big ball of mud.

Limited Skills

Architecting a system requires some fundamental skills, maybe a bit of talent, and definitely hands-on experience. Knowledge of best and worst practices also helps a lot. In a word, *education* is key. However, the development team is not usually given enough power to cause huge damage on their own. Management and customers are usually responsible as well, maybe even more.

When management is too demanding, and when customers don't really know what they want, the information being conveyed to developers won't be clear and unambiguous. This leads to arbitrary choices, compromises, and workarounds at all levels that just make it impossible to come up with a defined architecture.

Requirements Churn

The term *requirements churn* refers to making numerous changes to the initially agreed-upon requirements. Incorporating a new requirement into an existing system, which was architected *without* that particular requirement, can be problematic. The cost of such a change depends on the size of the change, the dependencies in the code, and whether or not the change affects the structure of the system.

Adding a single change, even a significant one, is not enough to jeopardize the entire architecture. But when individual significant changes are frequent, over time you transform a system devised in a given way into something that probably requires a different architecture. If you keep adding new requirements individually without reconsidering the system as a whole, you create the ideal conditions for a big ball of mud.

Members Turnover

When technical documentation is lacking or insufficient, the worst thing that can happen is that the rationale for making particular decisions is lost forever. As long as the application is deployed, works, and doesn't require proactive or passive maintenance (although I still haven't found such an application), you're fine. But what if this is not the case?

If the rationale for design and architectural decisions is not entirely evident, how can you expect new members of the team to take over the maintenance or additional development for the system? At some point, in their efforts to understand the system, these new members must be informed of the rationale for various decisions. If they can't figure out the real rationale, inevitably they will make further changes to the system based on their assumptions. Over time, this leads to a progressive deterioration of the system that is what we've been referring to as the big ball of mud.

Alarming Symptoms

The big ball of mud doesn't get formed overnight. How can you detect that your system is deteriorating? There a few hard-to-miss symptoms you don't want to ignore. They are very serious. Let's find out what they are.

Make a Change Here, Break the Code There

Can you bend a piece of wood? And what do you risk if you insist on trying to do that? A piece of wood is typically stiff and rigid and characterized by some resistance to deformation. When enough force is applied, the deformation becomes permanent.

What about rigid software?

Rigid software is characterized by some level of resistance to changes. Resistance is measured in terms of regression. You make a change in one module, but the effects of your change cascade down the list of dependent modules. As a result, it's really hard to predict how large the impact of a change—any change, even the simplest—will actually be.

If you pummel a glass or any other fragile material, you succeed only in breaking it down into several pieces. Likewise, when you enter a change in software and cause it to misbehave in some places, that software is definitely fragile.

Just as fragility and rigidity go hand in hand in real life, they also do so in software. When a change in a software module breaks (many) other modules because of (hidden) dependencies, you have a clear symptom of a bad design, and you need to remedy that situation as soon as possible.

Easier to Use Than to Reuse

Imagine you have a piece of software that works in one project; you would like to reuse it in another project. However, copying the class or linking the assembly in the new project just doesn't work.

Why is this so?

If the same code doesn't work when it's moved to another project, it's because of dependencies. However, the real problem isn't just dependencies; it's the number and depth of dependencies. The risk is that to reuse a piece of functionality in another project, you'll have to import a much larger set of functions. In such cases, no reuse is ever attempted and code is rewritten from scratch. (Which, among other things, increases duplication.)

This also is not a good sign either for your design. This negative aspect of a design is often referred to as *immobility*.

Easier to Work Around Than to Fix

When applying a change to a software module, it is not unusual that you find two or more ways to do it. Most of the time, one way of doing things is nifty, elegant, coherent with the design, but terribly laborious to implement because of certain constraints. The other way is, instead, much smoother and quicker to code, but it is sort of a hack.

What should you do?

Actually, you can solve the problem either way, depending on the given deadlines and your manager's directives about it.

In summary, it's not an ideal situation because a workaround might be much easier to apply than the right solution. And that's not a great statement about your overall design either. It simply means that too many unneeded dependencies exist between classes and that your classes do not form a particularly cohesive mass of code. This negative aspect of a design is often referred to as *viscosity*.

So what should you do to avoid these symptoms showing up in your code and creating a big ball of mud?

Universal Software Principles

In my opinion, maintainability is the fundamental attribute of modern software. The importance of maintainability spans the technology spectrum and applies to the Web as well as desktop applications.

A few universally valid design principles help significantly to produce code that is easier to maintain and evolve. It is curious to note that they are all principles devised and formulated a few decades ago. Apparently, for quite some time we've had the tools to build and manage complex software but real applications were just lacking the complexity to bring them to the forefront as design best practices. This is also my interpretation of the advent of the Rapid Application Development (RAD) paradigm a decade ago, which complemented (and in some cases superseded) object-oriented programming (OOP).

Today, the situation is different. With large companies now taking full advantage of Internet, cloud, and mobile computing, developers and architects are swamped with an incredible amount of complexity to deal with. That's why RAD is no longer sufficient in many scenarios. On the other hand, not everybody is skilled enough to use OOP. It's about time we all redis-cover some fundamentals of software programming—regardless of the type of application we're building.

Summarizing, I would boil software principles down to two principles: the High Cohesion and Low Coupling principle and the Separation of Concerns principle.

Cohesion and Coupling

Cohesion and coupling go hand in hand even though they refer to orthogonal aspects of your code. Cohesion leads you toward simple components made of logically related functions—kind of atomic components. Coupling indicates the surface area between two interfacing components: the wider the area is, the deeper the dependency is between the components. The magic is all in finding the right balance between cohesion and coupling while trying to maximize both.

Cohesion at a Glance

Cohesion indicates that a given software module—a class, if we assume the object-oriented paradigm—features a set of responsibilities that are strongly related. Put another way, cohesion measures the distance between the logic expressed by the various methods on a class.

If you look for a moment at the definition of cohesion in another field—chemistry—you can get a clearer picture of software cohesion. In chemistry, cohesion is a physical property of a substance that indicates the attraction existing between like-molecules within a body.

Cohesion measurement ranges from low to high, with the highest possible cohesion being preferable. Highly cohesive modules favor maintenance and reusability because they tend to have no dependencies. Low cohesion, on the other hand, makes it much harder to understand the purpose of a class, and it creates a natural habitat for rigidity and fragility in your software. Low-cohesive modules also propagate dependencies, thus contributing to the immobility and viscosity of the design.

Decreasing cohesion leads to creating classes where methods have very little in common and refer to distinct and unrelated activities. Translated into a practical guideline, the principle of cohesion recommends creating extremely specialized classes with few methods that refer to logically related operations. If the "logical" distance between methods needs to grow, well, you just create a new class.

Coupling at a Glance

Coupling measures the level of dependency existing between two software classes. An excellent description of coupling comes from the Cunningham wiki at *http://c2.com/cgi/wiki?CouplingAndCohesion*. Two classes, A and B, are coupled when it turns out that you have to make changes to B every time you make any change to A. In other words, B is not directly and logically involved in the change being made to module A. However, because of the underlying dependency B is forced to change; otherwise, the code won't compile any longer.

Coupling measurement ranges from low to high, with the lowest possible coupling being preferable.

Low coupling doesn't mean that your modules have to be completely isolated from one another. They are definitely allowed to communicate, but they should do that through a set of well-defined and stable interfaces. Each class should be able to work without intimate knowledge of the internal implementation of another class. You don't want to fight coupling between components; you just want to keep it under control. A fully disconnected system is sort of nonsense today.

Conversely, high coupling hinders testing and reusing and makes understanding the system nontrivial. It is also one of the primary causes of a rigid and fragile design.

Low coupling and high cohesion are strongly correlated. A system designed to achieve low coupling and high cohesion generally meets the requirements of high readability, maintainability, easy testing, and good reuse.

Separation of Concerns

Functional to achieving high cohesion and low coupling is the separation of concerns (SoC) principle, introduced by Edsger W. Dijkstra in his paper *"On the role of scientific thought"* which dates back to 1974. If you're interested, you can download the full paper from *http://www.cs.utexas.edu/users/EWD/ewd04xx/EWD447.PDF*.

Identifying the Concerns

SoC is all about breaking the system into distinct and possibly non-overlapping features. Each feature you want in the system represents a *concern* and an *aspect* of the system. Terms like *feature*, *concern*, and *aspect* are generally considered synonyms. Concerns are mapped to software modules and, to the extent that it is possible, there's no duplication of functionalities.

SoC suggests that you focus your attention on one particular concern at a time. It doesn't mean, of course, that you ignore all other concerns of the system. More simply, after you've assigned a concern to a software module, you focus on building that module. From the perspective of that module, any other concerns are irrelevant.

> **Note** If you go through the original text written by Dijkstra back in 1974, you note that he uses the expression "separation of concerns" to indicate the general principle, but he switches to the word "aspect" to indicate individual concerns that relate to a software system. For quite a few years, the word "aspect" didn't mean anything special to software engineers. Things changed in the late 1990s when *aspect-oriented programming* (AOP) came into the industry. Ignored for many years, AOP is being rediscovered today mostly thanks to some ad hoc frameworks such as Spring .NET and other Inversion of Control (IoC) frameworks.

Modularity

SoC is concretely achieved through modular code and making large use of information hiding.

Modular programming encourages the use of separate modules for each significant feature. Modules are given their own public interface to communicate with other modules and can contain internal chunks of information for private use.

Only members in the public interface are visible to other modules. Internal data is either not exposed or it is encapsulated and exposed in a filtered manner. The implementation of the interface contains the behavior of the module, whose details are not known or accessible to other modules.

Information Hiding

Information hiding (IH) is a general design principle that refers to hiding behind a stable interface some implementation details of a software module that are subject to change. In this way, connected modules continue to see the same fixed interface and are unaffected by changes.

A typical application of the information hiding principle is the implementation of properties in Microsoft C# or Visual Basic .NET classes. The property name represents the stable interface through which callers refer to an internal value. The class can obtain the value in various ways (for example, from a private field, from a control property, from a cache, and from the view state in ASP.NET) and can even change this implementation detail without breaking external code.

```
// Software module where information hiding is applied
public class Customer
{
    // Implementation detail being hidden
    private string _name;

    // Public and stable interface
    public string CustomerName
    {
        // Implementation detail being hidden
        get {return _name;}
    }
}
```

Information hiding is often referred to as *encapsulation*. I like to distinguish between the principle and its practical applications. In the realm of object-oriented programming, encapsulation is definitely an application of IH.

In general, though, the principle of SoC manifests itself in different ways in different programming paradigms, and so it is also for modularity and information hiding.

> **Note** Separation of concerns is the theoretical pillar of multitiered (or just multilayered) systems. When you try to apply SoC to classes, you run across just one fundamental concept that you can then find formulated in a number of different ways. You essentially achieve separation of concerns by isolating dependencies and abstracting them to interfaces. This is called *low coupling, interface-based programming* or, perhaps in a more formal way, the Dependency Inversion principle that I'll cover in just a moment. Different names—each appropriate in its own context—but just one key idea.

SOLID Principles

Recently, a particular acronym is gaining a lot of popularity—SOLID. The acronym results from the initials of five design principles formulated by Robert Martin. The *S* stands for Single Responsibility; the *O* is for the Open/Closed principle; the *L* is for Liskov's principle; the *I* is for Interface Segregation; and finally, the *D* is for Dependency Inversion.

Taken individually, these principles are nothing new. Any experienced developer and architect should be at least vaguely familiar with the idea behind each principle, either because it is part of the developer's personal education or because of the experience the developer has gained the field.

SOLID principles are just a further specialization and refinement of universal and object-oriented design principles. Their definition is relatively simple; yet the adoption of these principles can be fairly complex.

> **Note** As you'll see in a moment, not all principles should be taken literally. Some of them are just driving vectors that attempt to show you the right direction, but without being dogmatic. You can download the original papers describing the SOLID principles and their canonical examples from *http://www.objectmentor.com*.

The Single Responsibility Principle

The Single Responsibility Principle (SRP) is a formal way of rephrasing the idea behind cohesion. The principle states that there should never be more than one reason for a class to change. Applied to the design of the class, it means each class you add to your solution should focus on just one primary task.

The responsibilities of a class that does just one thing are much smaller than the responsibilities of a class that does multiple things. A responsibility is defined as a "reason to change"; more specifically, it's a reason for you—the developer—to put your hands on the class's source code and edit it.

The purposes of SRP are to simplify maintenance and improve readability. Keeping the code simple at the root—by taking out additional features—is an effective way to smooth maintenance chores. At the end of the day, SRP is a form of defensive programming.

SRP Canonical Example

Like any other SOLID principle, SRP has its own canonical example aimed at illustrating the point of the principle. Here's a piece of code that contains the gist of SRP:

```
public class Modem
{
    public void Dial(String number);
    public void Hangup();

    public void Send(Char c);
    public Char Receive();
}
```

How many sets of responsibilities do you see in the *Modem* class? *Dial* and *Hangup* represent the connection management functionality, whereas the *Send* and *Receive* pair of methods represent communication functionalities. Should these two sets of responsibilities be separated? As usual, it depends.

SRP Real-World Considerations

An effective implementation of SRP passes through the identification of specific responsibilities in the programming interface of the class. One task is identifying responsibilities; it is quite a different task to actually split the class into two other classes, each taking care of a specific responsibility. In general, you should always consider splitting responsibilities in distinct classes when the two sets of functions have little in common. If this happens, the two resulting classes will likely change for different reasons and will likely be called from different parts of the application. In addition, different parts of the application will change for different reasons.

Another scenario that suggests the need to split a class into two (or more) is when the two sets of functions you identified in the original interface are large enough to require sufficiently complex logic of their own. In this case, you simply lower the level of granularity of your design a bit. However, the size is not always, and not necessarily, a good parameter to use to make a decision about SRP. A function can be complex and large enough to justify a breakup; however, if it's not likely to change over time, it might not require a distinct class. Scenarios like this, however, represent a tough call, with no uniform guidance to help you determine what to do.

Finally, you should pay a lot of attention not to split the original class into small pieces. The risk of taking SRP to the limit is falling into the Overdesign anti-pattern that occurs when a system is excessively layered and each layer ends up being a thin wrapper around an *if* statement. As mentioned, SRP is a driving vector rather than a dogma. You should always keep it in your mind but never apply it blindly and blissfully.

The Open/Closed Principle

We owe the Open/Closed Principle (OCP) to Bertrand Meyer. The principle addresses the need of creating software entities (whether classes, modules, or functions) that can happily survive changes.

The purpose of the principle is to provide guidance on how to write components that can be extended without actually touching the source code. Sounds like quite an ambitious plan, doesn't it? Let's get at the formulation:

A class should be open for extension but closed for modification.

Honestly, I find the formulation a bit idealistic and bordering on magic. However, the principle is in itself quite concrete. It essentially says that the source code of the class must remain intact, but the compiled code must be able to work with types it doesn't know directly. This can be achieved in just one way: abstracting aspects of the class that can lead to changes over time. To abstract these aspects, you can either use interfaces and code injection or generics.

OCP Canonical Example

Low coupling between interfacing modules is beneficial because it instructs the caller to work with an abstraction of its counterpart rather than with a concrete implementation. In their masterpiece *Design Patterns: Elements of Reusable Object-Oriented Software* (Addison-Wesley, 1994), the Gang of Four (Erich Gamma, Richard Helm, Ralph Johnson, and John Vlissides) formulate a basic principle of object-oriented design as "Program to an interface, not to an implementation."

The gist of OCP is all here. Code that is based on an abstraction can work with a concrete object it gets passed as long as this object is compatible with known abstraction. Behind the term "abstraction," you can find at least two concrete syntax elements: a base class or an interface. Here's the canonical example of a class—the *Renderer* class—that fully complies with OCP:

```
public abstract class Shape
{
    public abstract void Render();
}

public class Renderer
{
    public void Draw(IList<Shape> shapes)
    {
        foreach(Shape s in shapes)
            s.Render();
    }
}
```

The abstraction is represented by the base class *Shape*. The *Renderer* class is closed for modification but still open for extension because it can deal with any class that exposes the Shape abstraction—for example, any class that derives from *Shape*.

Analogously, you can have a *Renderer<T>* class that receives its working type as a generic argument.

OCP Real-World Considerations

OCP should not be taken literally. Like SRP, it works much better if used as a driving vector. Frankly, no significant class can be 100 percent closed for modification. By "significant class" here, I mean most real-world classes or, better, all classes except those you write just for demo purposes!

If closure of a given class can't realistically be complete, it should then be strategic. It is a precise architect's responsibility to identify the most likely changes in the class body and close the class design against them. In other words, designing a class that can support all possible future extensions is a utopian pursuit. However, identifying just one specific abstraction or two and making the class work against them is, most of the time, an excellent compromise. Aiming for fully pluggable classes is over designing; even a partial application of OCP is beneficial and rewarding.

If you ignore OCP, at some point you might catch yourself downcasting to a specific subclass to compile the code and avoid run-time exceptions. If this happens, it's a clear sign that something is wrong in the design.

Liskov's Substitution Principle

Of the five SOLID principles, Liskov's principle is probably the only one that should be taken literally, because it serves you a detailed list of dos and don'ts and it isn't limit to being a generic guidance on design. The formulation of the principle couldn't be simpler. To some extent, it also seems a bit obvious:

Subclasses should always be substitutable for their base classes.

When a new class is derived from an existing one, it should always be possible to use the derived class in any place where the parent class is accepted. Wait a moment! Isn't this something you get out of the box with any object-oriented language? Well, not exactly!

What you really get from OOP is just the mere promise that derived classes can be used wherever their base class is accepted. However, OOP still lets you write hierarchies of classes where this basic requirement isn't met; hence, the principle.

Substitution Principle Canonical Example

Suppose you have a *Rectangle* class and a method that works with that. The method just receives a parameter of type *Rectangle* and, of course, it takes advantage of the logical contract this class exposes. For example, the *Rectangle* class exposes a *Width* and *Height* pair of properties that can be independently set.

Suppose that after doing this, you then need to introduce a *Square* object. How would you do that? Logically speaking, you see the *Square* entity as a special case of the *Rectangle* entity. Therefore, the natural step is deriving *Square* from *Rectangle* and overriding *Width* and *Height* so that their values are always in sync.

If you do this, you potentially break the original code written against the contract of the *Rectangle* class. The violation of the principle here doesn't necessarily result in a run-time exception or a compile error. Your code might still work just fine, despite the Liskov violation. However, your code is inherently fragile because there's the possibility of introducing bugs during maintenance. The violation has to be considered in the mathematical sense—you can find a counterexample that shows you can't use a *Square* where a *Rectangle* is expected. Here's a code snippet that illustrates this point:

```
public class Rectangle
{
   public virtual Int32 Width { get; set; }
   public virtual Int32 Height { get; set; }
}

public class Square : Rectangle
{
   public override Int32 Width
   {
      get {return base.Width; }
      set {base.Width = value; base.Height = value; }
   }
   public override Int32 Height
   {
      get {return base.Height; }
      set {base.Height = value; base.Width = value; }
   }
}
```

Here's some client code that consumes the *Rectangle* class:

```
public void Process(Rectangle rect)
{
   rect.Width = 100;
   rect.Height = 2* rect.Width;
   Debug.Assert(rect.Height == 2*rect.Width);
}
```

This code works fine if a real *Rectangle* is passed, but it violates the assertion if a *Square* is passed. The easiest way to fix it—the workaround that increases viscosity—is simply the following:

```
public void Process(Rectangle rect)
{
    if (rect is Rectangle)
    {
        rect.Width = 100;
        rect.Height = 2* rect.Width;
        Debug.Assert(rect.Height == 2*rect.Width);
    }
    else
    {
        ...
    }
}
```

The real problem you have here, instead, is an incorrect definition of inheritance rules. *Square* can't be derived from *Rectangle* because it is not expected to be able to do at least all the things that the base class does.

Substitution Principle Real-World Considerations

Liskov's principle can be difficult to grasp for many developers. An easier way to explain it is the following: each derived class should expect no more than the parent and provide no less than the parent.

This means, for example, that you break the principle if a virtual member ends up using a private member of the class. Likewise, you break the principle if a derived class adds more preconditions to a virtual method.

Liskov's principle isn't meant to portray inheritance—a pillar of OOP—in a bad light. Quite the reverse, it calls your attention to a safe use of virtual members. If you derive and just add new features, you're absolutely safe. If you don't have virtual members, you're absolutely safe. If you have virtuals and actually override them in derived class, you should pay additional attention.

 Note In .NET 4, you have the Code Contracts API to express preconditions, postconditions, and invariants around your classes. A precondition is simply an IF in a method that executes at the very beginning of the code. If you use this API to express preconditions for the methods of a class, and happen to add preconditions to an overridden method of a class, you get a warning (not an error) from the C# compiler.

The Interface Segregation Principle

There's an aspect of coding that I find particularly annoying—being forced to write code that I don't really need. You might say that you *should* not write any code that you don't need. There are situations, however, in which this is necessary. When? For sure, when the code ignores the Interface Segregation principle.

The principle is so simple that it seems like merely common sense. It says that client components should not be forced to depend upon interfaces that they do not use. More precisely, components should not be forced to implement members of interfaces (or base classes) that they don't plan to use.

There's nothing bad in a client that provides a void implementation of a particular interface method or that just throws if invoked. Sometimes this happens simply because the client deliberately intends to provide a partial implementation; sometimes, however, it happens because the interface is poorly designed. Fat interfaces are a bad thing. The Single Responsibility principle should hold true for interfaces also.

Interface Segregation Canonical Example

The classic scenario to examine to start thinking about interface segregation is the definition of a door. If you're asked to simply define a door, you would probably come up with an interface with just a couple of *Lock* and *Unlock* methods and perhaps a Boolean property *IsDoorOpen*. However, if you know that you also need to deal with timed doors that sound an alarm if left open for too long, you might arrange something like this:

```
public interface IDoor
{
    void Lock();
    void Unlock();
    Boolean IsDoorOpen { get; }

    Int32 OpenTimeout { get; set; }
    event EventHandler DoorOpenForTooLong;
}
```

The apparent plus of this design is that it gives you just one interface that can serve up both scenarios: timed and regular doors. This is an apparent benefit because it forces you to have two extra members on any class that implements the interface: the event *DoorOpenForTooLong* and the timeout property. Why on earth should you have these members where they aren't needed?

Interface Segregation Real-World Considerations

Note also that code that is not strictly needed can't be ignored after it is compiled. In other words, any code that gets compiled does count, regardless of whether or not it was necessary when you designed your classes. Because it's there, it can influence the application, it must be tested, it must be debugged, and it must be maintained. Quite paradoxically, because it's there it can even represent a constraint and limit further necessary improvements!

The natural solution is to use slimmer interfaces. The *IDoor* interface should be split into two smaller and much more specific interfaces—say *IDoor* and *ITimedDoor*:

```
public interface IDoor
{
    void Lock();
    void Unlock();
    Boolean IsDoorOpen { get; }
}
public interface ITimedDoor
{
    Int32 OpenTimeout { get; set; }
    event EventHandler DoorOpenForTooLong;
}
```

Now if you need to create *RegularDoor* and *TimedDoor* classes, you proceed as shown here:

```
public class RegularDoor : IDoor
{
    ...
}
public class TimedDoor : IDoor, ITimedDoor
{
    ...
}
```

Unlike classes, interfaces can be easily summed up; so there's really no reason to have fat interfaces any more.

The Dependency Inversion Principle

I consider Dependency Inversion to be the most important of the five SOLID principles. You don't need it in every class and method that you write, but if you miss it where you need it, well, you're in serious trouble. Take a look at Figure 13-1.

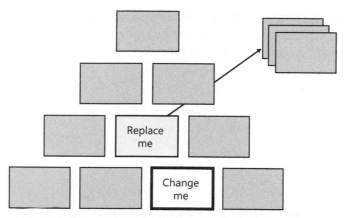

FIGURE 13-1 Hard to change blocks in software architecture.

I'm not sure the idea behind this figure is completely original, and I don't even know if there's anybody I should thank for that. For sure, I remember having seen it somewhere, likely at some software conference somewhere in the world. Then I simply revised the idea and made it mine.

So you have built the architecture of your system by simply composing parts. What if, at some point during development, you need to replace or significantly modify one of the building blocks? As the graphics attempts to show, it might be hard to change some of the building blocks that form the skeleton of the system. Dependency inversion is simply aimed at making this difficult task simpler and less expensive.

The principle says that every high-level module should always depend on abstractions of lower level modules. This is just a reformulation of the concept of interface-based programming.

Dependency Inversion Canonical Example

The idea behind Dependency Inversion doesn't need a complex scenario to be effectively illustrated. Just imagine a method that reads bytes from a stream and writes them out to some buffer:

```
void Copy()
{
  Byte byte;
  while(byte = ReadFromStream())
      WriteToBuffer(byte);
}
```

The pseudocode just shown depends on two lower level modules: the reader and writer. According to the principle, we should then abstract the dependencies to interfaces—say, *IReader* and *IWriter*. The method can be rewritten as follows:

```
void Copy()
{
  Byte byte;
  IReader reader;
  IWriter writer;

  while(byte = reader.Read())
      writer.Write(byte);
}
```

Who really does provide instances of the reader and writer modules? That's the principle, or the general law; to actually solve the issue, you need some further specification. In other words, you need a pattern.

The first pattern used to apply the Dependency Inversion principle is Service Locator pattern, which can be summarized as follows:

```
void Copy()
{
  Byte byte;
  var reader = ServiceLocator.GetService<IReader>();
  var writer = ServiceLocator.GetService<IWriter>();

  while(byte = reader.Read())
      writer.Write(byte);
}
```

You use a centralized component that locates and returns an instance to use whenever the specified abstraction is requested. The service locator operates while embedded in the code that it serves. You can say that it looks for services, but it is not a service itself. Most of the time, you use this pattern when you have some legacy code that you need to make easier to extend that is hard to redesign in a different way—for example, in a way that uses dependency injection.

A better alternative is to use Dependency Injection (or inversion of control). The resulting code looks like this:

```
void Copy(IReader reader, IWriter writer)
{
  Byte byte;

  while(byte = reader.Read())
      writer.Write(byte);
}
```

The list of dependencies is now explicit from the signature of the method and doesn't require you to go down the line to pinpoint calls to a service locator component. In addition, the burden of creating instances for each spot dependency is moved elsewhere.

Dependency Inversion Real-World Considerations

Dependency inversion is about layers, and layers don't reduce the total amount of code (quite the reverse, I'd say). Layers, however, contribute to readability and, subsequently, to maintainability and testability.

In light of this, the motivation for special frameworks such as Inversion of Control (IoC) frameworks is right in front of your eyes.

You don't want to write the factory yourself for all instances that populate the graph of dependencies for pieces of your application. The task is repetitive and error prone. Although it might be a boring task for developers, it's just plain business as usual for certain tools. IoC frameworks are just a way for you to be more productive when it comes to implementing the Dependency Inversion principle.

These days, we tend to oversimplify things by using the name of the most popular pattern—Dependency Injection—to refer to the universal principle. Even more often, we just use the name of a family of tools (IoC) to refer to the principle. What really matters is that you give the principle its due consideration. The details of how you actually implement it are up to you and your team.

You don't need an IoC tool to implement good dependency injection; you can get it through overloaded constructors (also known as *the poor man's dependency injection*) or even by writing your own homemade IoC framework. In the simplest case, it's a thin layer of code around some .NET reflection primitives. You can ignore the Dependency Inversion principle, but you do so at your own peril.

 Note Dependency injection is also fundamental from a testability standpoint because it makes it natural to inject dependencies in classes as you test them.

Tools for Dependency Injection

The list of tools for dependency injection is quite long in the .NET space nowadays. Most of these tools provide the same set of core functionalities and are, to a large extent, equivalent. Choosing one is often a matter of preference, skill level, and perhaps your comfort with the exposed API. There are some who prefer simplicity and speed and opt for Autofac or Ninject. Others would opt for rich functionality and go for Spring.NET or Castle Windsor. Another group would pick up the entire Microsoft stack and then use Unity. Table 13-1 lists the most popular options today, with the URL from where you can get further information.

TABLE 13-1 Some Popular IoC Frameworks

Framework	URL
Autofac	*http://code.google.com/p/autofac*
Castle Windsor	*http://www.castleproject.org/container/index.html*
Ninject	*http://www.ninject.org*
Spring.NET	*http://www.springframework.net*
StructureMap	*http://structuremap.sourceforge.net/Default.htm*
Unity	*http://codeplex.com/unity*

All IoC frameworks are built around a container object that, bound to some configuration information, resolves dependencies. The caller code instantiates the container and passes the desired interface as an argument. In response, the IoC framework returns a concrete object that implements that interface. Let's top off the chapter by taking a quick tour of two frameworks in the Microsoft stack that, although they have different characteristics and goals, can both be employed to implement the Dependency Inversion principle.

Managed Extensibility Framework at a Glance

Introduced with the Microsoft .NET Framework 4, the Managed Extensibility Framework (MEF) attempts to give a consistent answer to the loud demand for tools for building plugin-based applications.

A plugin-based application is an application that can rely on a number of optional components that are discovered and composed together at run time. Microsoft Visual Studio is an excellent example of this application; a simpler but still valid example is Windows Explorer, whose menus can be extended by registering shell extensions. A plugin-based application provides a number of extensibility points and builds its core user interface and logic using abstractions for those extensibility points. Some run-time code then attempts to resolve all pending dependencies in a quick and direct way.

MEF vs. IoC

MEF does some work that any IoC does. Like an IoC framework, MEF is able to spot dependencies and resolve them, returning a usable graph of objects to the caller application. In raw terms of functionality, MEF is not as powerful as most IoC tools. MEF has limited support for managing the object's lifetime and doesn't currently support any form of aspect orientation. MEF also requires that classes it deals with be decorated with ad hoc attributes.

You can't just take a plain old CLR class and use it with MEF. On the other hand, MEF swallows exceptions when some particular things go wrong during the composition process.

In summary, MEF is an IoC framework optimized for the specific task of discovering and loading optional and compatible components on the fly.

Should You Choose MEF or an IoC?

MEF is already in the .NET Framework 4; any IoC tools of choice is a separate set of assemblies and adds dependencies to the project. MEF is available only for .NET 4, whereas most IoC frameworks are available for most .NET platforms. This said, however, I'd like to remark that MEF doesn't bring new significant capabilities to the table that you couldn't code yourself or achieve through an IoC. MEF, however, makes writing plugin-based applications really fast and simpler than ever before.

If MEF serves all your IoC needs, choose MEF and code your way within the .NET Framework 4. If you're happy with the IoC you're using today, perhaps there's no need for you to change it. In this regard, MEF won't give you an ounce more than your favorite IoC.

The real issue is when you want to use MEF because of plugins but still need to mix it with an IoC because MEF doesn't offer the advanced services of rich IoC—for example, call interception. In this case, either you drop MEF in favor of IoC or configure MEF to accept instances created by the IoC of choice.

MEF in Action

An MEF application is based on components known as *composable parts*. Each part can contain some members decorated as imports. An import is a class member with the *Import* attribute, and it indicates a member that will be resolved and instantiated by the MEF runtime. In a MEF application, you also find classes decorated as exports. An export is a class decorated with the *Export* attribute. An instance of an export class can be used to perform an import as long as the import and export match.

What does determine a valid match?

An import/export match is based on a contract. A contract here has little to do with service or interface contracts. An MEF contract is a collection of meta information that both imports and exports contain. In most cases, it is a simple string. In other cases, it contains type information or both unique strings and type information.

The list of exports is determined by catalogs. A catalog is a provider that returns the list of available exports to be matched to the imports of the object being resolved. Finally, the composition process is the process in which all imports (that is, dependencies) are resolved.

Here's a brief code example to illustrate:

```
public class PasswordCreator
{
    private CompositionContainer _container;
    public ProgramBody() {
        InitializeMef();
    }

    private void InitializeMef()
    {
        var catalog = new DirectoryCatalog("Plugins");
        _container = new CompositionContainer(catalog);

        // Fill the imports of this object
        try {
            _container.ComposeParts(this);
        }
        catch (CompositionException compositionException);
    }

    [Import]
    public IPasswordFactory PasswordFactory { get; set; }

    public String CreatePassword()
    {
        if (PasswordFactory == null)
        {
            return "Dependency not resolved.";
        }

        return PasswordFactory.Create(12);
    }
}
```

The class *PasswordCreator* generates a random password using the services of an object that implements the *IPasswordFactory* interface. No such a component, though, is instantiated by the class itself. The task, in fact, is delegated to MEF.

MEF will use a directory catalog to explore all assemblies in the specified relative folder, looking for exports that match the contract of the *IPasswordFactory* import. So where's the contract name?

When you use the plain attribute, the contract name defaults to the name of the member. In this case, it is *typeof(IPasswordFactory)*. What about exports?

Consider the following example:

```
[Export(typeof(IPasswordFactory))]
public class DefaultPasswordFactory : IPasswordFactory
{
    public String Create(Int32 passwordLength)
    {
        // Create the password
    }
```

```
protected virtual String GeneratePasswordCore(Int32 passwordLength)
{
    // ...
}
}
```

Deployed to an assembly located in the specified plugin folder, the class *DefaultPasswordFactory* exports the *typeof(IPasswordFactory)* factory. If the class features the simple *Export* attribute, the contract then corresponds to the class name, thus missing the previous import.

Note that if an export, in turn, misses one key import, the export is ignored to ensure the stability of the solution. If multiple exports qualify to resolve the same import, you get a composition exception.

Unity at a Glance

Unity is an open-source project from the Patterns & Practices group at Microsoft, which is attempting to provide an IoC framework for developers to build object instances in a smart and highly configurable way. Unity works as a standalone framework, but it's also packaged along with Enterprise Library. To add Unity to a project, you add a reference to the *Microsoft.Practices.Unity* assembly. You optionally add a reference to *Microsoft.Practices. Unity.Configuration* if you configure the library using the application's configuration file.

Let's see how to accomplish some key IoC operations with Unity, such as registering types both programmatically and declaratively.

Registering Types and Instances

Just like any other IoC library, Unity is centered around a container object. In Unity, the container type is *UnityContainer*, and you use it to register types and instances, as shown here:

```
var container = new UnityContainer();
container
    .RegisterType<IServiceLayer,
                  DefaultServiceLayer>()
    .RegisterType<ICustomerRepository,
                  CustomerRepository>();
var serviceLayer = container.Resolve<IServiceLayer>();
```

You use the *RegisterType* method to establish a mapping between an abstract type and a concrete type. If the same abstract type should be mapped to different types in different contexts of the same application, you can use the following overload:

```
container
   .RegisterType<ILogger, DefaultLogger>()
   .RegisterType<ILogger, FileLogger>("Tracing");
```

The additional string parameter disambiguates the request and gives Unity enough information about which concrete type to pick up. You use *RegisterInstance* instead of *RegisterType* to supply the container a prebuilt instance of a type. In this case, Unity will use the provided instance instead of creating one on its own. Does it really make sense for an application to pass to a factory the instance it will get back later? The purpose is to preserve the benefits of an IoC also in situations in which you can't annotate a class to be automatically resolved by Unity.

To see an example of this, let's first introduce the syntax required to annotate constructors and properties for injection. When requested to create an instance of a given type, Unity gets information about the constructors of the type. If multiple constructors are found, Unity picks up the one with the longest signature. If multiple options are available, an exception is thrown. It might be the case, however, that you want a particular constructor to be used. This requires that an attribute be attached to the selected constructor:

```
[InjectionConstructor]
public MyClass()
{
    ...
}
```

If you have no access to the source code, you might want to consider *RegisterInstance*. Similarly, if injection happens through the setter of a property, you need to decorate the property accordingly, as shown here:

```
private ILogger _logger;

[Dependency]
public ILogger Logger
{
    get { return _logger; }
    set { _logger = value; }
}
```

RegisterType and *RegisterInstance* are the methods you work with if you opt for configuring the Unity framework programmatically. However, offline configuration is also supported via an ad hoc section in the application's configuration file. In any case, programmatic and declarative configuration is totally equivalent.

Resolving Dependencies

In Unity, you invoke the method *Resolve* on the container class to trigger the process that returns an instance of the type at the root of the dependency chain:

```
container.Resolve(registeredType);
```

The resolver can be passed any additional information it might need to figure out the correct type to return:

```
var logger = container.Resolve<ILogger>("Tracing");
```

If you have multiple registrations for the same type, only the last one remains in the container's list and will be taken into account. The resolver can walk down the chain of dependencies and resolve everything that needs to be resolved. However, you get an exception if the chain is broken at some point and the resolver can't locate the proper mapping. When this happens in MEF, instead, the dependency is simply not resolved and is skipped over. On the other hand, multiple candidates to resolve a dependency are managed by Unity (the last wins) but cause a composition exception in MEF.

Declarative Configuration

The Unity framework comes with a custom configuration section that can be merged with the *web.config* file of a Web application. Here's the script you need to register types:

```
<unity>
    <container name="MyApp">
        <register ="ILogger" mapTo="DefaultLogger">
            <lifetime type="singleton"/>
            <constructor>
                <param name="sourceName" type="string" value="default"/>
            </constructor>
        </registerType>
    </container>
</unity>
```

Under the *<register>* section, you list the abstract types mapped to some concrete implementation. The following code shows how to map *ILogger* to *DefaultLogger*:

```
<register type="ILogger" mapTo="DefaultLogger">
```

If the type is a generic, you use the following notation:

```
<container>
    <register type="IDictionary[string,int]" </register>
</container>
```

Taking the declarative approach, you can also select the constructor to be used and set up the lifetime of the instance.

To configure the Unity container with the information in the *web.config* file, you need the following code:

```
var container = new UnityContainer();

// Retrieve the <unity> section
var section = ConfigurationManager.GetSection("unity") as UnityConfigurationSection;
if (section != null)
{
    // Retrieve the specified container by name
    var containerElement = section.Containers["MyApp"];
```

```
// Load information into the specified instance of the container
if (containerElement != null)
    containerElement.Configure(container);
}
```

As it turns out, Unity allows you to have multiple containers with different settings to load as appropriate. You can skip over all the preceding details by calling an extension method added in Unity 2.0:

```
var container = new UnityContainer();
container.LoadConfiguration();
```

It requires that you add a reference to the *Microsoft.Practices.Unity.Configuration* assembly.

Lifetime Managers

Just like any other IoC framework, Unity allows you to assign a fixed lifetime to any managed instance of mapped types. By default, Unity doesn't apply any special policy to control the lifetime of the object returned for a registered type. It simply creates a new instance of the type each time you call the *Resolve* or *ResolveAll* method. However, the reference to the object is not stored, so a new one is required to serve a successive call.

The default behavior can be modified by using any of the predefined lifetime managers you find in Unity. Table 13-2 lists them.

TABLE 13-2 Lifetime Managers

Class	Description
ContainerControlledLifetimeManager	Implements a singleton behavior for objects. The object is disposed of when you dispose of the container.
ExternallyControlledLifetimeManager	Implements a singleton behavior, but the container doesn't hold a reference to the object that will be disposed of when out of scope.
HierarchicalLifetimeManager	New in Unity 2.0, implements a singleton behavior for objects. However, child containers don't share instances with parents.
PerResolveLifetimeManager	New in Unity 2.0, implements a behavior similar to the transient lifetime manager except that instances are reused across build-ups of the object graph.
PerThreadLifetimeManager	Implements a singleton behavior for objects, but it's limited to the current thread.
TransientLifetimeManager	Returns a new instance of the requested type for each call. This is the default behavior.

You can also create custom managers by inheriting the *LifetimeManager* base class.

Here's how you set a lifetime manager in code:

```
container
    .RegisterType<ILogger, DefaultLogger>(
        "Tracing",
        new ContainerControlledLifetimeManager());
```

Here's what you need, instead, to set a lifetime manager declaratively:

```
<register type="ILogger" mapTo="DefaultLogger">
    <lifetime type="singleton" />
</register>
```

Note, however, that the word *singleton* you assign to the *type* attribute is not a keyword or a phrase with a special meaning. More simply, it is intended to be an alias for a type that must be declared explicitly:

```
<!-- Lifetime manager aliases -->
<alias alias="singleton"
       type="Microsoft.Practices.Unity.ContainerControlledLifetimeManager,
            Microsoft.Practices.Unity" />
<alias alias="perThread"
       type="Microsoft.Practices.Unity.PerThreadLifetimeManager,
            Microsoft.Practices.Unity" />
<alias alias="external"
       type="Microsoft.Practices.Unity.ExternallyControlledLifetimeManager,
            Microsoft.Practices.Unity" />
...

<!-- User-defined aliases -->
<alias alias="IMyInterface"
       type="MyApplication.MyTypes.MyInterface, MyApplication.MyTypes" />
...
```

After you have the aliases all set, you can use alias names in the section where you register types.

Summary

Just as an architect designing a house wouldn't ignore building codes that apply to the context, a software architect working in an object-oriented context shouldn't ignore principles of software design such as the SOLID principles discussed in this chapter when designing a piece of software. Proper application of these principles leads straight to writing software that is far easier to maintain and fix. It keeps the code readable and understandable and makes it easier to test, both during development and for refactoring and extensibility purposes.

Most developers (and even more managers) commonly think that using software principles is first and foremost a waste of time and that no distinction is actually possible between "well-designed code that works" and "software that just works." Guess what? I totally agree with this statement. If you don't need design, any effort is overdesign. And overdesign is an anti-pattern.

So you save a lot of time by skipping over principles. However, if your "software that just works" has to be fixed or extended one day, be aware that you will find yourself in a serious mess. The costs at that point will be much higher. It all depends on the expected lifespan of the application. Ideally, you learn principles and make them a native part of your skill set so that you use them all the time in a natural way. Otherwise, the costs of applying principles will always be too high to seem effective. Ad hoc tools can help a lot in making the development of good code more sustainable. IoC frameworks are just one of these tools.

In the next chapter, I'll continue with the theme of application design by tackling layers (and communication related to them) in ASP.NET applications.

Chapter 14
Layers of an Application

The advantage of a bad memory is that one enjoys several times the same good things for the first time.

—*Friedrich Nietzsche*

Any software of any reasonable complexity is best designed if organized in layers. Each layer represents a logical section of the system. A layer is hosted on a physical tier (for example, a server machine). Multiple layers can be hosted on the same tier, and each layer can optionally be moved to a separate tier at any time and possibly with limited work.

Most of the time, you arrange a three-tiered architecture with some flavors of service orientation just to make each layer ready for a possible move to a different physical tier. There are various reasons to move a layer onto its own tier: a quest for increased scalability, the need for stricter security measure, and also increased reliability because the layers become decoupled in case of machine failure.

In a three-tiered scenario, you typically have a presentation layer where you first take care of processing any user input and then arranging responses, a business logic layer (BLL) that includes all the functional algorithms and calculations that make the system work and interact with other layers, and the data access layer (DAL) where you find all the logic required to read and write from a storage.

When it comes to layers, the principle of separation of concerns (SoC) that I introduced in Chapter 13, "Principles of Software Design," is more important than ever. A golden rule of any layered system states that no communication should be allowed between non-interfacing layers. In other words, you should never directly access the DAL from within the presentation layer. In terms of Web Forms development, this point is blissfully ignored when you use a *SqlDataSource* component right from the button click event handler of a Web page!

In this chapter, I'll describe the intended role and content of business and data access layers and touch on a few technologies that help you write them. I'll do that from a Web Forms and ASP.NET perspective, but be aware that a large part of the content has a general validity that goes beyond the Web world. I'll cover presentation layers and related patterns in the next chapter.

A Multitiered Architecture

Everybody agrees that a multitiered system has a number of benefits in terms of maintainability, ease of implementation, extensibility, and testability. Implementation of a multitiered system, however, is not free of issues and, perhaps more importantly, it's not cheap.

Can you afford the costs? Do you really need it?

A three-tiered architecture is not mandatory for every Web application or for software applications in general. Effective design and, subsequently, layers are a strict requirement for systems with a considerable lifespan—typically, line-of-business systems you build for a customer and that are vital to the activity of that given customer. When it comes to Web sites, however, a lot of them are expected to stay live for only a short time or are fairly simple online windows for some shops or business. Think, for example, of sites arranged to promote a community meeting or a sports event. These sites are plain content management systems where the most important aspect is providing timely information via a back-office module. Honestly, it's not really key here to design them carefully with service orientation, layers, and cross-database persistence. Themes like scalability, robustness, and security don't apply to just any site or application. However, the longer the lifespan is, the more likely it is that you will also need to address carefully these concerns.

The Overall Design

Figure 14-1 provides a glimpse of a three-tiered system with all the modules that we are going to consider in this chapter and the next one.

As I see things, it's essential that you, as an architect or developer, be very aware of this model. However, awareness means that you know it, and because you know it, you also know *when* it's worthwhile for you to opt for such a complex and sophisticated design. Some of the blocks shown in Figure 14-1 can be merged if there's really no reason for them to have their own life. The general view might not faithfully represent the *particular* view of your application. In architecture, it *always depends* on the context. And adapting the general view to the particular context is the essence of the architect's job.

> **Note** In my training classes, I always use a specific example to illustrate the previous point. As a parent, you must tell your kids that they use the crosswalk whenever they need to go across the street. When you do it yourself, in some situations, you adapt the general rule to a specific shortcut, and if no cars are coming you just cross wherever you are. That's because you're an adult and because, having evaluated pros and cons, you actually made a good decision. If the nearest crosswalk is half a mile away and no car is in sight, why walk that extra distance?
>
> In my classes, I always take the example a bit farther and tell nice stories about how Italians apply the pattern to parking. But if you're interested in hearing about that, well, it's best if you attend the next class!

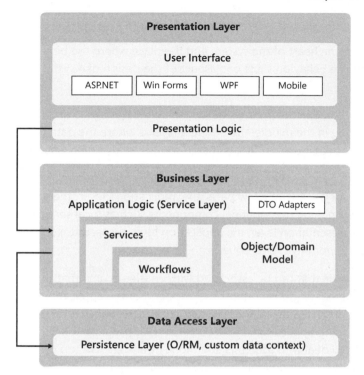

FIGURE 14-1 A general view of a three-tiered system.

Methodologies

Where do you start designing the layers of a real-world system? Ouch! That's a really tough point. It depends. Trying to go to the root of it, I'd say it depends on the methodology you use to process requirements. Which methodology you apply also depends on something. It usually depends on your skills, your attitude, and your preference, as well as what seems to be best in the specific business scenario and context.

Any system has its own set of requirements that originate use-cases. The ultimate goal of the application is implementing all use-cases effectively.

A classic approach entails that you figure out what data and behaviors are required by all use-cases (or just one use-case) and build a good representation of the data involved and the related actions. So you start from the business layer, and in particular from modeling the entities in play and their relationships.

I start my building from the business layer, and my main reason for that is to have as soon as possible a well-defined set of entities and relationships to persist and build a user interface around. To get my entities and relationships, however, I need to take a deep look at UI expectations and storage constraints, if any.

The Business Layer

The business logic layer is the heart of the system and the place where the behavior of the system is implemented. The behavior is just one aspect of the design of a system; another key aspect is data.

Data is collected and displayed in the presentation layer, and it's persisted and retrieved in the data access layer. Living in the middle, the business layer is where the data is processed according to some hard-coded behavior. (Note that in some very dynamic systems, the behavior can also be dynamically defined.)

Generally speaking, the BLL is made of a few parts: the application's logic, the domain logic, a representation for domain data, plus optional components such as local services and work-flows. Invoked from the presentation layer, the application logic orchestrates services and DAL to produce a response for any client requests.

The domain logic is any logic that can be associated with entities (if any) that populate the problem's domain. The domain logic represents the back end of the application and can be shared by multiple applications that target the same back end. For example, an online banking application, a trading application, and a back-office application will likely share a common piece of logic to deal with accounts and money transfers. On top of that, each application might invoke the common logic through different algorithms.

Application and domain logic work side by side and exchange data represented in some way. Finally, domain and application logic might need to invoke the services of special components that provide business-specific workflows or calculations.

Business logic is a collection of assemblies to host. In a typical Web scenario, the BLL goes in-process with ASP.NET on the Web server tier. It goes in a separate server process mostly for scalability reasons. In a smart-client scenario, the location of the BLL might vary a bit. For example, the BLL can live entirely on the client, can be split across the client and server, or live entirely on the server. When the BLL is deployed remotely, you need services (for example, WCF services) to communicate with it.

The list of components that form the BLL can be implemented using a number of design patterns.

Design Patterns for the BLL

Design patterns for the BLL belong to two major groups: procedural and object-oriented patterns. For many years, we've been using procedural patterns such as Transaction Script (TS) and Table Module (TM). More recently, a significant increase in complexity and flexibility demand had us shifting toward object-oriented patterns such as Active Record and Domain Model.

In the .NET space, the Table Module pattern has been popularized by special Microsoft Visual Studio technologies such as typed *DataSet*s and table adapters. LINQ-to-SQL and Entity Framework move toward a Domain Model pattern. A number of open-source frameworks, on the other hand, provide an effective implementation of the Active Record pattern. Among the others, we have Subsonic and Castle Active Record. Let's review the basics of the various design patterns and how concrete technologies are related to each.

The Transaction Script Pattern

The Transaction Script (TS) pattern envisions the business logic as a series of logical transactions triggered by the presentation. Subsequently, modeling the business logic means mapping transactions onto the methods of one or more business components. Each business component then talks to the data access layer either directly or through relatively dumb data objects.

When you partition transaction scripts into business components, you often group methods by *entity*. You create one method per each *logical* transaction, and the selection of methods is heavily inspired by use-cases. For example, you create an *OrderAPI* business component to house all transaction scripts related to the "order" entity. Likewise, you create a *CustomerAPI* component to expose all methods related to action the system needs to perform on customers. In relatively simple scenarios, you come up with one business component per significant database table. Each UI action ends up mapped to a method on a TS object. The TS pattern encompasses all steps, including validation, processing, and data access. Figure 14-2 shows a graphical representation of the BLL according to the Transaction Script pattern.

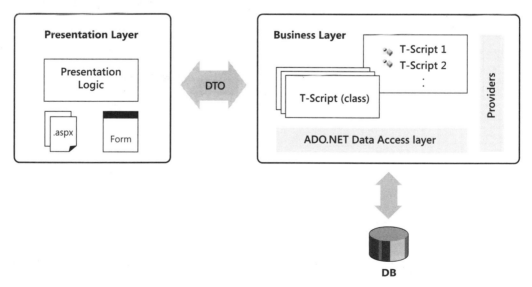

FIGURE 14-2 The Transaction Script pattern.

Note that in the context of TS, a transaction indicates a monolithic logical operation; it has no relationships to database management systems (DBMS) transactions.

The TS pattern is good for simple scenarios. The logic is implemented in large chunks of code, which can be difficult to understand, maintain, and reuse. In addition, TS favors code duplication and requires a lot of attention and refactoring to keep this side effect under control.

The Table Module Pattern

According to the Table Module pattern, each object represents a database table and its entire content. The table module class has nearly no properties and exposes a method for each operation on the table, whether it's a query or an update. Methods are a mix of application logic, domain logic, and data access code. This is the pattern behind typed *DataSet*s and table adapters that you find in Visual Studio 2005 and later.

The overall design of the BLL is clearly database-centric with a table-level granularity. Compared to TS, the Table Module pattern gives you a bit more guidance on how to do things. The success of this pattern is largely attributable to the support offered by Visual Studio and the availability in .NET of handy recordset data structures such as *DataSet*s. Figure 14-3 shows the design of a system architected with the Table Module pattern.

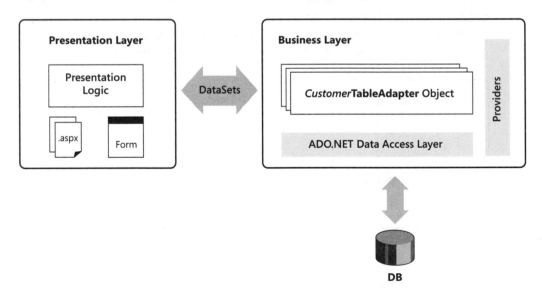

FIGURE 14-3 The Table Module pattern.

In procedural patterns, BLL and DAL are too often merged together. Most of the time, the DAL is where you package your ADO.NET code for physical data access.

The Active Record Pattern

The Table Module pattern is based on objects, but it's not an object-based pattern for modeling the business logic. Why? Because it doesn't care much about the business; it focuses, instead, on the tables. Table Module does have objects, but they are objects representing tables, not objects representing the domain of the problem.

The real shift toward an object-oriented design starts when you envision the application as a set of interrelated objects—which is a different thing than using objects to perform data access and calculations. An object-based model has two main levels of complexity—simple and not-so-simple. A good measure of this complexity is the gap between the domain's object model and the relational data model you intend to create to store your data.

A simple model is when your entities map closely to tables in the data model. A not-so-simple model is when some mapping is required to load and save domain objects to a relational database. The Active Record pattern is your choice when you want an object-oriented design and when your domain logic is simple overall.

In Active Record, each class essentially represents a record in a database table: the classes usually have instance methods that act on the represented record and perform common operations such as save and delete. In addition, a class might have some static methods to load an object from a database record and it might perform some rich queries involving all records. Classes in an Active Record model have methods, but these methods are mostly doing Create, Read, Update, Delete (CRUD) operations. There's nearly no domain logic in the classes of an Active Record model, even though nothing prevents you from adding that.

An aspect that makes Active Record so attractive to developers is its extreme simplicity and elegance and, just as significantly, the fact that in spite of its simplicity it works surprisingly well for a many Web applications—even fairly large Web applications. I wouldn't be exaggerating to say that the Active Record model is especially popular among Web developers and less so among Windows developers.

Beyond the simplicity and elegance of the model, available tools contribute significantly to make Active Record such a popular choice. Which tool should you use to implement an Active Record model?

LINQ-to-SQL is definitely an option. Fully integrated in Visual Studio 2008 and later, LINQ-to-SQL allows you to connect to a database and infer a model from there. As a developer, your classes become available in a matter of seconds at the end of a simple wizard. In addition, your classes can be recreated at any time as you make changes, if any, to the database. In terms of persistence, LINQ-to-SQL is not really a canonical Active Record model because it moves persistence to its internal DAL—the data context. LINQ-to-SQL incorporates a persistence engine that makes it look like a simple but effective Object/Relational Mapper (O/RM) tool with full support for advanced persistence patterns such as Identity Map and, especially, Unit of Work.

Castle Active Record is another framework that has been around for a few years and that offers a canonical implementation of the Active Record pattern. Finally, an emerging framework for Active Record modeling is SubSonic. (See *http://www.subsonicproject.com*.)

Unlike Castle Active Record, SubSonic can generate classes for you but does so in a way that is more flexible than in LINQ-to-SQL: it uses T4 templates. A T4 template is a *.tt* text file that Visual Studio 2008 and later can process and expand to a class. If you add a T4 template to a Visual Studio project, it soon turns it into a working class. This mechanism offers you an unprecedented level of flexibility because you can modify the structure of the class from the inside and not just extend it with partial classes as in LINQ-to-SQL, and it also removes the burden of writing that yourself as you must do with Castle Active Record.

The Domain Model Pattern

In the Domain Model pattern, objects are aimed at providing a conceptual view of the problem's domain. Objects have no relationships with the database and focus on the data owned and behavior to offer. Objects have both properties and methods and are not responsible for their own persistence. Objects are uniquely responsible for actions related to their role and domain logic.

> **Note** Two similar terms are often used interchangeably: object model and domain model. An object model is a plain graph of objects, and no constraints exist on how the model is designed. A domain model is a special object model in which classes are expected not to have any knowledge of the persistence layer and no dependencies on other classes outside the model.

A domain model is characterized by entities, value objects, factories, and aggregates. Entities are plain .NET objects that incorporate data and expose behavior. Entities don't care about persistence and are technology agnostic.

In a domain model, everything should be represented as an object, including scalar values. Value objects are simple and immutable containers of values. You typically use value objects to replace primitives such as integers. An integer might indicate an amount of money, a temperature, or perhaps a quantity. In terms of modeling, by using integers instead of more specific types you might lose some information.

In a domain model, using a factory is the preferred way of creating new instances. Compared to the *new* operator, a factory offers more abstraction and increases the readability of code. With a factory, it's easier to understand why you are creating a given instance.

Finally, an aggregate is an entity that controls one or more child entities. The association between an aggregate root and its child objects is stronger than a standard relationship. Callers, in fact, talk to the aggregate root and will never use child objects directly. Subsequently, controlled entities are processed and persisted only through the root aggregate. Aggregates are generally treated as a single unit in terms of data exchange. The major benefit of aggregates is grouping together strongly related objects so that they can be handled as a single unit while being expressed as individual classes.

Figure 14-4 is a representation of a system that uses the Domain Model pattern.

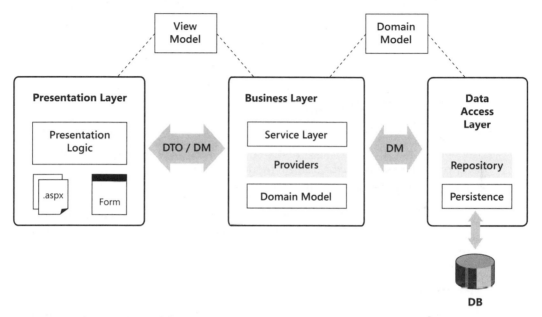

FIGURE 14-4 The Domain Model pattern.

There are two ways of going with a Domain Model pattern. The simplest way is to design your entities and relationships with Entity Framework. After you have designed the layout of your entities and scalar objects, you generate the code using, preferably, the POCO code generator. What you get in the first place is an *anemic* domain model, where *anemic* indicates that classes are plain data containers and offer no behavior. However, Entity Framework lets you add methods to entities through the mechanism of partial classes. This also allows you to create factories quite easily.

The second way is to create your own set of classes and then use an O/RM tool (for example, Entity Framework or NHibernate), or a handmade ADO.NET layer, to persist it. This approach offers greater expressivity because it allows you to introduce aggregates. Note that value objects, factories, and aggregates are concepts related to Domain Model that are introduced by a specific design methodology—Domain-Driven Design, or DDD. Although DDD is a proven methodology to deal with real-world complexity, it doesn't mean that you can't have an effective model without following literally all DDD recommendations.

Entity Framework doesn't help you much when it comes to DDD, but it doesn't prevent you from using it as well. In Entity Framework, you have no native API to create aggregates.

However, your data access layer can be designed to expose aggregate roots and let you work with them in a way that is consistent with DDD practices.

 Note   When you organize the business layer around a web of interconnected objects—a domain model—you neatly separate entities that the application logic (and sometimes the presentation logic) works with from any layer of code that is responsible for persistence. In this context, the DAL gains its own valuable role with full separation of concerns and responsibilities—the DAL just gets an object model and persists it to a store.

The Application Logic

The application logic is the part of the BLL that contains endpoints, as required by use-cases. The application logic is the layer that you invoke directly from the presentation layer. The layer coordinates calls to the domain model, workflows, services, and the DAL to orchestrate just the behavior required by the various use-cases.

You can't just believe that all this logic belongs to the presentation layer. (As you'll see better in the next chapter, in ASP.NET Web Forms the presentation layer is mostly the code-behind class!)

The Service Layer Pattern

To better understand the role and importance of the application logic, consider the following example. You are working on a use-case that describes the submission of a new order. Therefore, you need an endpoint in the application logic that orchestrates the various steps of this operation. These might be any of the following: validating customer and order information, checking the availability of ordered goods, checking the credit status of the customer, finding a shipper that agrees to deliver the goods within the specified time, synching up with the shipper system, registering the order, and finally triggering any automatic refill procedures if the order reduces goods in stock below a safe threshold.

The Service Layer pattern defines an additional layer that sits in between two interfacing layers—typically, the presentation layer and BLL. In practical terms, implementing a service layer requires you to create a collection of classes that include all the methods you need to call from the presentation layer. In other words, the classes that form the "service layer" shield the presentation layer from the details of the BLL and DAL. These classes are also the sole part of the application to modify if use-cases happen to change.

The word "service" here isn't necessarily meant to suggest some specific technology to build services (for example, WCF). The service layer is just a layer of classes that provides services to the presentation. However, service-orientation and specific service technologies make the whole solution even worthier of your consideration and more successful.

When the Application Logic Is Deployed Remotely

In a typical Web Forms scenario, the application logic lives side by side with the ASP.NET pages on the Web server machine. This means that any calls from the code-behind to classes in the service layer are in-process calls. Likewise, classes in the service layer are plain CLR classes and don't require service contracts and configuration.

In a desktop scenario, or if you implement a multitiered Web architecture, the service layer is likely living in a different process space. In this case, the service layer is implemented as a real layer of Windows Communication Foundation (WCF) or REST services.

I recommend you start coding plain classes and upgrade to services just when you need to. In WCF, at least, a service is a class with something around it, and that "something" is essentially the service contract and configuration. If you design your service layer classes to be highly decoupled, based on an interface, and to expose data contracts, it will take you just a few moments to add attributes and binding information and switch to WCF services for, say, queued or transactional calls.

A service layer is almost always beneficial to nearly all applications of some complexity that use a layered architecture. A possible exception is when you find out that your service layer is just a pass-through layer and is limited to forward calls to a specific component in the BLL or DAL. If you need some orchestration before you accomplish an operation, you do need a service layer. Take a look at Figure 14-5.

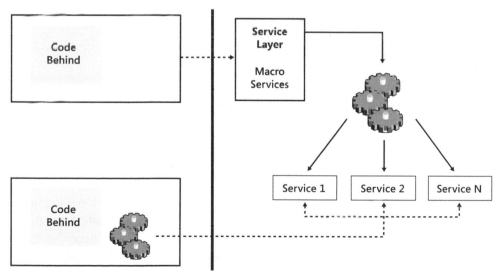

FIGURE 14-5 Breaking apart dependency between layers.

If the orchestration logic (represented by the gears) lives on the presentation tier, you end up placing several cross-tier calls in the context of a single user request. With a remotable service layer, though, you go through just one roundtrip per request. This is just what SOA papers refer to as the Chatty anti-pattern.

In Figure 14-5, you also see different blocks referring to services. The service layer is made of a collection of methods with a coarse-grained interface that I refer to in the figure as *macro services*. These services implement use-cases and do not contain any domain logic. Micro services, conversely, are domain-logic services you control or just autonomous services that your BLL needs to consume.

Exposing Entities to the Presentation Layer

In a service layer, you should have only methods with a direct match to actions in a use-case. For example, you should have a *FindAllOrders* method only if you have a use-case that requires you to display all orders through the user interface. However, you should not have such a method if the use-case requires the user to click a button to escalate all unprocessed orders to another department. In this case, there's no need to display to the user interface (and subsequently to roundtrip from the service layer) the entire list of orders. Here's a sample class in a service layer:

```
public interface IOrderService
{
    void Create(Order o);
    IList<Order> FindAll();
    Order FindByID(Int32 orderID);
}

public class OrderService : IOrderService
{
    ...
}
```

A fundamental point in a service layer is the types used in the signatures. What about the *Order* type in the previous code snippet? Is it the same *Order* entity you might have in the domain model? Is it something else?

In general, if you can afford to expose domain model objects in the service contract, by all means do that. Your design is probably not as pure as it should be, but you save yourself a lot of time and effort. You must be aware that by using the same entity types in the presentation layer and BLL, you get additional coupling between the presentation and business layers. This is more than acceptable if the presentation and business layers are within the same layer. Otherwise, sharing the domain model forces you to have the same (or compatible) runtime platform on both sides of the network.

Data Transfer Objects

If you're looking for the greatest flexibility and loose coupling, you should consider using ad hoc data transfer objects (DTO). A data transfer object is a plain container shaped by the needs of the view. A data transfer object contains just data and no behavior.

When you use data transfer objects, you likely need an extra layer of adapters. An adapter is a class that builds a data transfer object from a graph of domain entities. An adapter is bidirectional in the sense that it also needs a method to take a data transfer object coming from the presentation and break up its content into pieces to be mapped on entities.

The additional workload required by using data transfer objects is significant in moderately complex projects also. In fact, you need two adapters (or translators) for each data transfer object and likely two data transfer objects for each service layer method (one for input and one for output.)

It's not a matter of being lazy developers; it's just that a full data transfer object implementation requires a lot of work.

> **Note** Effective tools are a great way to make a full DTO implementation affordable and, to some extent, sustainable. A common tool that really saves you a ton of work is AutoMapper. (See *http://automapper.codeplex.com*.) AutoMapper is an object-to-object mapper that employs a convention-based algorithm. All it does is copy values from one object (for example, a domain entity) to another (for example, a DTO) using a configurable algorithm to resolve mapping between members. At this point, AutoMapper can be easily considered a best practice in modern development.

The Data Access Layer

No matter how many abstraction layers you build in your system, at some point you need to open a connection to some database. That's where and when the data access layer (DAL) fits in. The DAL is a library of code that provides access to data stored in a persistent container, such as a database. In a layered system, you delegate this layer any task that relates to reading from, and writing to, the persistent storage of choice.

Implementation of a DAL

Until recently, the DAL was just fused to the BLL and limited to a superset of the ADO.NET library created for the purpose of making writing data access code easier. In other words, for many years of the .NET era, the DAL has been simply a layer of helper methods to write data access quickly.

The shift toward a more conceptual view of the problem's domain, and subsequently the advent of the Domain Model pattern, brought new interest in the role of the DAL. Now that you have a domain model exposed as the real database in the application's eyes, you really need a distinct and well-defined layer that bridges the gap between the domain model and storage.

Although the role of the DAL is still the same as it was 20 years ago, the technologies are different, as is the approach to it taken by architects and developers. It's interesting to briefly review the inner nature of the DAL in light of the pattern used for the BLL.

DAL and the Table Module Pattern

Having a BLL organized in table module classes leads you to having a database-centric vision of the system. Every operation you orchestrate in the application logic is immediately resolved in terms of database operations. It's natural, at this point, to create an in-memory representation of data that closely reflects the structure of the underlying tables.

With the Table Module pattern, you have table classes and methods to indicate query or update operations. Any data being exchanged is expressed through ADO.NET container types such as *DataSet* and *DataTable*. Any data access logic is implemented through ADO.NET commands or batch updates.

The DAL still has the role of persisting data to databases, but data is stored in database-like structures (for example, *DataSet*), and a system framework (for example, ADO.NET) offers great support for working with *DataSet* types. As a result, BLL and DAL are merged together and are rather indistinguishable. The DAL, when physically distinct from BLL and living in its own assembly, is nothing more than a library of helper methods.

DAL and the Active Record Pattern

An Active Record BLL makes domain data available in the form of objects with a close resemblance to records of database tables. You no longer deal with super-array types such as *DataSet*, but instead have an object model to map to table records.

The DAL, therefore, has a clearer role here. It exists to bridge the gap between entities in the object model and database tables. The mapping work required from the DAL is relatively simple because there's not much abstraction to cope with. Mapping between object properties and table columns is neat and well defined; the storage is a relational database.

The benefit of using Active Record instead of Table Module is mostly in the fact that an Active Record object model can be created to be a real strongly typed counterpart of a table. In this regard, it fits better than a generic container such as *DataSet*s and can be extended at will. The drawback is in the extra work required to create the model, but fortunately many tools exist to infer the model directly from tables.

DAL and the Domain Model Pattern

According to the Domain Model pattern, you create from the ground up an entity model with any appropriate relationships. More importantly, you do so while being completely ignorant about persistence. First, you create the object model that best represents the business domain; second, you think of how to persist it. As odd as it might sound, in a Domain Model scenario the database is purely part of the infrastructure. (See Figure 14-6.)

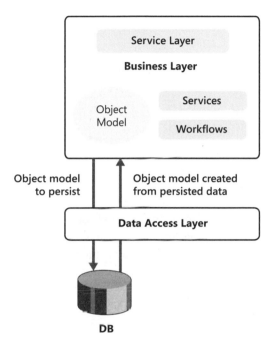

FIGURE 14-6 The DAL is just part of the infrastructure.

A DAL has four main responsibilities toward its consumers. In the first place, a DAL persists data to the physical storage and supplies CRUD services to the outside world. Second, the DAL is responsible for servicing any queries for data it receives. Finally, a DAL must be able to provide transactional semantics and handle concurrency properly. Conceptually, the DAL is a sort of black box exposing four contracted services, as shown in Figure 14-7.

Who does really write the DAL? Is it you? And why should you write a DAL yourself? Is it perhaps that you have a strict nonfunctional requirement that explicitly prohibits the use of an ad hoc tool such as an O/RM? Or is it rather that you think you would craft your DAL better than any commercial O/RM tools?

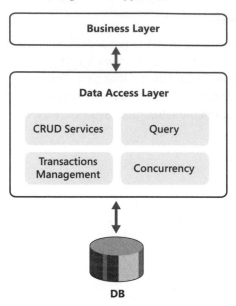

FIGURE 14-7 A conceptual view of the DAL's interior.

In a domain-based world, a well-built DAL is nearly the same as a well-built O/RM tool. So unless you have strict nonfunctional requirements that prohibit it, you should use an O/RM. Entity Framework is the official O/RM tool you find in the Microsoft stack of technologies. NHibernate is an even more popular tool that has been around for quite a few years now and that is close to its maturity.

Interfacing the DAL

In some simple scenarios, it might be acceptable for the DAL to be invoked from the presentation layer. This happens when you actually have only two tiers: the presentation layer and the storage. Beyond this, the DAL is a constituent part of the back end and is invoked from the application logic.

The next issues to resolve are the following: Should you allow any service layer classes to know the nitty-gritty details of the DAL implementation? Should you wrap the DAL implementation in an interfacing module that provides a fixed interface regardless of the underlying details? As usual, it depends.

Support for Multiple Databases

In the past, every architect would have answered the previous questions with a sounding *yes*. Today, it is likely the same answer, but for different reasons. For years, the primary reason for wrapping the DAL in the outermost container has been to achieve database independence.

Wrapping the DAL in a pluggable component greatly simplifies the task of installing the same application in different servers or using it for customers with a different database system.

Today, the advent of O/RM tools has dwarfed this specific aspect of the DAL. It's the O/RM itself that provides database independence today. At the same time, other compelling reasons show up that make interfacing the DAL still a great idea.

The Repository Pattern

A common way to hide the implementation details and dependencies of the DAL is using the Repository pattern. There are a couple of general ways you can implement the pattern. One consists of defining a CRUD-like generic interface with a bunch of *Add, Delete, Update*, and *Get* methods. Here's an example:

```
public interface IRepository<T> : ICollection<T>, IQueryable<T>
{
  public void Add(T item)
  { ... }
  public bool Contains(T item)
  { ... }
  public bool Remove(T item)
  { ... }
  public void Update(T item)
  { ... }
  public IQueryable<T> Include(Expression<Func<T, object>> subSelector)
  { ... }
}
```

The type T indicates the type of entity, such as *Customer, Order,* or *Product.* Next, you create an entity-specific repository object where you add ad hoc query methods that are suited for the entity. Here's an example:

```
public interface IProductRepository : IRepository<Product>
{
    IQueryable<Product> GetProductsOnSale();
}
```

Classes in the service layer deal with repositories and ignore everything that's hidden in their implementation. Figure 14-8 shows the summarizing graphic.

Another approach to building a repository consists of simply creating entity-specific repository classes and giving each one the interface you like best.

Today, testability is an excellent reason to interface the DAL. As shown in Figure 14-8, it allows you to plug in a fake DAL just for the purpose of testing service layer classes. Another scenario, however, is gaining ground on popularity: upgrading the existing DAL based on an on-premises database for the cloud.

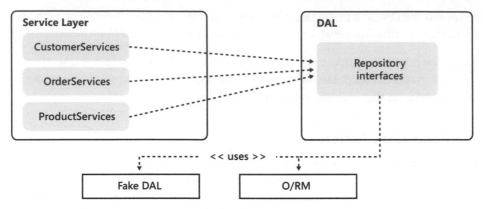

FIGURE 14-8 The Repository pattern applied to the DAL.

Using an Object/Relational Mapper

So it seems that a common practice for implementing a DAL is using an O/RM. Using an O/RM is not trivial, but tools and designers in the Microsoft and Visual Studio world make it considerably simpler. More to the point, with Entity Framework or LINQ-to-SQL you can hardly do it wrong. (Even though you can sometimes do it in a suboptimal way.)

Which O/RM should you use? In this brief gallery, I present two of the most popular choices (Entity Framework and NHibernate) and one for which there's considerable debate about whether it belongs to the group (LINQ-to-SQL). I'm skipping over a review of all commercial O/RMs.

LINQ-to-SQL

I like LINQ-to-SQL, period. When Microsoft released Entity Framework 1 in the fall of 2008, it promptly signaled the end of LINQ-to-SQL development—at least, active development, which involved adding new features. In the .NET Framework 4, LINQ-to-SQL is fully support-ed and it has even been slightly improved by the fixing of a few bugs and less-than-optimal features. Still, LINQ-to-SQL is a sort of dead-end; however, if it works for you today, it'll likely work for you in the future.

I like to call LINQ-to-SQL "the poor man's O/RM." It's a lightweight, extensible, data access option with some known limitations; however, it's a well-defined and well-balanced set of features. LINQ-to-SQL pushes the "It's easy, it's fast, and it works" standard that is just what many developers are looking for.

LINQ-to-SQL works by inferring the entity model from a given database, and it supports only Microsoft SQL Server. LINQ-to-SQL doesn't let you add much abstraction (for example, scalar types), but it does offer a POCO model that you can extend with partial classes and custom-ize with partial methods.

Technically, LINQ-to-SQL implements many of the design patterns that characterize a true O/RM, such as Unit of Work (transactionality), Query object (query), and Identity Map. If you refer to the responsibilities of the DAL shown in Figure 14-7, you find nothing that LINQ-to-SQL can't do. That's why I'm listing it here. It's the simplest of the O/RMs, but it's not simplistic.

Entity Framework

If you know LINQ-to-SQL, then Entity Framework might look like its big brother. Entity Framework is more expressive, comes with a richer designer for model and mappings, and supports multiple databases. If you get to Entity Framework from another O/RM tool, you might find it a bit different.

The only purpose of an O/RM tool is to persist an object model to some database. Entity Framework certainly does this, but it also helps you in the creation of the model. Most O/RM tools out there can persist any object model you can map to a database. Entity Framework builds on the Entity Relationship Model to let you create an abstract model of entities and relationships that it can then transform into plain C# partial classes.

When Entity Framework generates the source files for a model, it creates distinct files for each entity plus a class for the data context. From a design perspective, it's key that these files go in distinct assemblies. Logically speaking, in fact, entities form the domain model whereas the data context object belongs to the DAL. It's perhaps a little difference, but it's immensely important from a design perspective.

Entity Framework can generate source files in three different ways. The default approach entails you getting entity classes with a dependency on the framework. All entity classes inherit from a built-in class defined in Entity Framework and incorporate some default behavior related to persistence. Another approach gets you plain old CLR classes with no dependencies on anything. This approach is POCO. Finally, Entity Framework can also generate entity classes that have the additional capability of tracking their changes.

Finally, Entity Framework supports Code-Only mode, which basically consists of the behavior that most of the other O/RM tools offer—you create your domain model as a plain library and then instruct Entity Framework on how to persist it. Code-Only is just the fluent API you use to define mappings to a database.

Note As long as you intend to remain within the Microsoft stack, which O/RM should you use? LINQ-to-SQL or Entity Framework? The simple answer is Entity Framework because Entity Framework is the flagship product that will receive care and attention in the foreseeable future. What if you feel comfortable with LINQ-to-SQL and find it kind of costly to upgrade to Entity Framework?

In general, if your application has enough life ahead of it (no less than two years), after which a full redesign is acceptable, you can go with LINQ-to-SQL today and plan to upgrade later. However, keep in mind LINQ-to-SQL is not the light edition of Entity Framework; it has a slightly different programming API, and no migration path exists yet.

NHibernate

NHibernate is perhaps the most popular O/RM available today. It's open-source software with a strong and active community to back it up. NHibernate requires you to provide a library of classes and a bunch of mapping XML files. Based on that, it offers a rich API to write your logic for persistence.

With the release of Entity Framework 4, the technical gap is shrinking more and more and mostly has been reduced to fine-tuning the framework's behavior. The two main differences are the LINQ provider for expressing queries on entities, which is definitely superior in Entity Framework, and the absence in Entity Framework of second-level caching.

In addition, NHibernate looks like a more mature framework, closer to perfection in a way. Put another way, with the exception of adding a LINQ provider to it, I don't really see how NHibernate can be significantly improved. As it is, NHibernate offers a number of extensibility points (lacking in Entity Framework) and more expressivity when it comes to dealing with paged collections and batch reads and writes. Companion tools (for example, profilers, caches, and sharding) are numerous for NHibernate and (currently) hard to write for Entity Framework because of the aforementioned lack of extensibility points.

Note Sharding is a database design technique that consists of horizontal partitioning. In essence, the row set of a logical table is physically stored in multiple tables. Each partition is known as a shard and may be located on a distinct database server. The goal of sharding is gaining scalability by reducing table and index size and making search faster.

Note So here's a point-blank question: Entity Framework or NHibernate? Skipping the usual (and reasonable) point that it depends on the context, skills, and requirements, I'd say that with Entity Framework you don't get the same programming power of NHibernate. However, if you don't need that power, over all, you can work nicely and safer with Entity Framework, in the sense that you hardly ever screw things up.

O/RM Tools and SQL Code

An O/RM tools persists entities by generating and executing SQL commands. Is the SQL code generated by O/RMs reliable? In general, trusting an O/RM is not a bad idea, but constantly verifying the quality of the job they do is an even better idea. With any O/RM, a savvy developer will usually define the fetch plan and use the SQL profiler tool of choice to see what is coming out. Obviously, if the SQL code is patently bad, you intervene and in some way (changing the fetch plan or inserting stored procedures) you fix it.

In general, using stored procedures should be considered a last resort, but there might be cases in which they come to the rescue. An example is when quite complex queries can't be expressed efficiently through classic cursor-based syntax and requires, instead, a SET-based approach to boost the performance. In this case, a stored procedure can be the best option.

Beyond Classic Databases

A plausible scenario that could lead you to unplugging your DAL is that you replace the current storage with something else, from yet another relational DBMS system. If you simply switch from SQL Server to, say, Oracle, most of the O/RM tools can absorb the change quite nicely. At worst, you pay some money to a third-party company to get a driver. A more delicate situation, though, is when you replace the storage layer of the application with something different, such as a cloud database or, say, a model managed by Microsoft Dynamics CRM, or perhaps a NoSQL solution such as MongoDB, RavenDB, or CouchDB.

Going to the Cloud

As far as cloud databases are concerned, you can use a variety of solutions. For example, you can move to SQL Azure, which offers a transparent API and can be easily plugged into your system via Entity Framework.

Alternatively, you can choose a cloud solution such as Amazon SimpleDB, Amazon RDS, or perhaps S3. In all these cases, your access to data happens through Web services. And Web services require you to rewrite your DAL to invoke the proper Web service instead of opening an O/RM session.

More in general, perhaps with the sole (current) exception of SQI Azure and Entity Framework, going to the cloud requires you to unplug the current DAL and roll a new one. It's definitely a compelling reason to keep the DAL loosely coupled to the rest of the system.

Microsoft Dynamics CRM 2011

A layered system doesn't necessarily have to rely on a classic relational storage whose physical model is the topic of endless discussion and whose optimization is left to external gurus. In some business scenarios, Microsoft Dynamics CRM represents an even better option for building line-of-business applications that fall under the umbrella of a Customer Relationship Management (CRM) system.

Within Dynamics CRM 2011, you express the data model using a mix of built-in and custom entities. You can think of a CRM entity as a database record where attributes of an entity map roughly to columns on a database table. Dynamics CRM 2011 exposes data to developers using a bunch of WCF and REST endpoints. This makes it possible for developers of Web applications to capture data, process that as necessary, and arrange a custom user interface.

In other words, the Dynamics CRM model might become the BLL and DAL that the service layer talks to. It's yet another scenario that makes loosely coupling of back-end layers exactly the way to go when building layered solutions.

Schema-less Storage

A storage option that is gaining momentum is schema-less storage that is often summarized as a NoSQL solution. A classic relational database is a collection of relations where a relation is defined as a set of tuples sharing the same attributes—the schema. NoSQL stores just refuse relations.

NoSQL stores still refer to a form of structured storage in which each stored document may have its own schema, which is not necessarily shared with other documents in the same store. A document is exposed as a collection of name/value pairs; it is stored in some way (for example, as individual files) and accessed through a REST interface.

A NoSQL database is characterized by the lack of a schema, the lack of a structured query language, and an often distributed and redundant architecture. NoSQL databases belong to three main families: document stores, key/value stores, and object databases.

A document store saves documents as JSON objects and defines views/indexes. Objects can be arbitrarily complex and have a deep structure. To this category belong popular tools such as CouchDB, Raven, and MongoDB.

A key/value store saves tuples of data in a main table. Each row has a set of named columns, and values can be arbitrarily complex. Google's BigTable, Cassandra, and Memcached are examples of key/value NoSQL stores.

Finally, an object database stores serialized objects instead of primitive data and offers query capabilities. A popular choice is Db4O.

Summary

Most applications today are articulated in layers. Every time you add a layer to an application, you add a bit more code and, subsequently, extra CPU cycles. And you worsen the overall performance of the application. Is this all true?

Technically speaking, it couldn't be truer. However, a few extra CPU cycles are not necessarily what really matters. Software architecture, more than programming, is a matter of tradeoffs. Layers add benefits to any software of some complexity. Layers add separation of concerns and favor code injection and the right level of coupling.

In this chapter, I went through two of the three layers you find in a classic multitiered system: the business layer and the data access layer. The next chapter is reserved for the presentation layer and for the most appropriate pattern for Web Forms applications—the Model-View-Presenter pattern.

Chapter 15
The Model-View-Presenter Pattern

I have never let my schooling interfere with my education.

—Mark Twain

Generally speaking, creating the user interface of an ASP.NET Web Forms application is kind of easy. Even though I'm not sure the effort it takes to create a compelling and graphically appealing user interface should be referred to as "easy," arranging the desired functionality is usually not a big deal thanks to the full bag of server controls you can get. If there's a reason behind the success of ASP.NET, it's likely the ease of development—a clear offspring of the Rapid Application Development (RAD) paradigm.

For many years, it was so easy (and quite effective) to drop a control on the Microsoft Visual Studio Web page designer, double-click, and fill in the method stub created for you in the page's code-behind class. Therefore, a plain, old T-SQL query attached to the handler of, say, a *Click* event did the job of retrieving data and populating a grid after a user's click. Like it or not, it was quick and effective—the beauty of RAD.

As the complexity of the application grows, RADness loses most of its appeal and stops being an ideal companion for the presentation layer. This is the biggest change in the software industry that we've gone through in the past few years. The need for a more structured way of writing software doesn't mean, of course, we don't need Visual Studio anymore. However, we probably need to consider Visual Studio designers for what they actually are—facilities for the UI rather than an aid for software design. (Visual Studio 2010 Ultimate does have a number of interesting facilities for design and modeling, but these tools cross-cut the platform you're using for building the presentation.)

In Chapter 14, "Layers of an Application," we reviewed layered applications and considered a number of patterns for the business and data access layers. In this chapter, we consider patterns for layering the presentation layer of applications with a particular eye to ASP.NET applications.

Patterns for the Presentation Layer

Your design of the presentation layer of any system should be driven by one fundamental principle: keep the presentation layer separated from anything else, including business and data access layers. Over the years, a few design patterns have been identified to help you with the presentation layer. We recognize three main families of patterns: Model-View-Controller (MVC), Model-View-Presenter (MVP), and Presentation Model (PM). The last one is more popularly known in the .NET space as Model-View-ViewModel (MVVM).

Not all of them can be applied to ASP.NET Web Forms with the same effectiveness. Actually, the design pattern that best applies to ASP.NET Web Forms applications is MVP, which will be the main topic of this chapter.

Before I go any further on that topic, you should note that these patterns span 30 years of computer design and programming. And many, many things have changed in the past 30 years. So, for example, what we call MVC today doesn't exactly match the definition of MVC you find in the original paper that dates back about 30 years ago. To some extent, the same can be said for MVP. Two flavors of MVP exist—Passive View and Supervising Controller—and, in many applications, you actually use a personal mix of both. Likewise, even though PM and MVVM share the same architectural idea, MVVM is associated today with specific technologies such as Microsoft Silverlight, Windows Presentation Foundation (WPF), and Windows Phone.

This is to say that patterns like MVP and MVC give you quite a good idea of the approach behind a pattern, but details might change once the pattern is applied to a framework and a bunch of technologies. If you have a framework that gives you testability and separation of concerns (and whatever else you ask for), by all means use it and don't get bothered by possible patterns it does or does not implement.

> **Note** The impact of frameworks and technologies on the presentation layer is a huge point to consider. Originally, the MVP pattern had been proposed as a way to improve MVC. So does this mean that ASP.NET MVC is a thing of the past? Of course, not. There are probably ways to further improve the design of ASP.NET MVC applications, but the ASP.NET MVC framework is highly usable and guides you toward writing well-designed code without the cost of arranging everything yourself.

The MVC Pattern

In the earliest software, the whole application was made of monolithic blocks that encompassed everything—the user interface, logic, and data. The user interacted with the view and generated some input. The view captured the input, processed it internally, and updated itself or moved to another view. The MVC pattern was introduced in the late 1970s as a way to break such monoliths (called autonomous views) into distinct pieces.

Generalities of the MVC Pattern

According to the MVC pattern, the application is split into three distinct pieces: the model, the view, and the controller. The *model* refers to the data being worked on in the view. The model is represented with an active object that is updated by the controller and notifies the view of its state changes. The *view* refers to the generation of any graphical elements displayed to the user, and it captures and handles any user gestures. The *controller* responds to solicitations and executes actions against the application's back end. Such actions produce fresh data that alter the model. The controller is also responsible for selecting the next view. Figure 15-1 provides a graphical representation of the MVC schema.

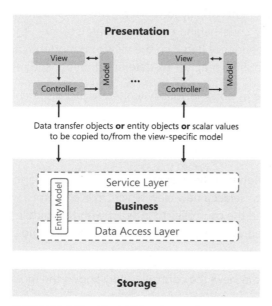

FIGURE 15-1 The Model-View-Controller pattern.

The major benefit of MVC is the application of the separation of concerns (SoC) principle. It mostly consists of taking as much code as possible out of the front end to build structured layers. As mentioned earlier, in the beginning, MVC was just a way to break up monolithic programs in which the code basically consists of a loop around some input and each command is resolved through a logical transaction. (See the Transaction Script pattern in Chapter 14.)

Let's see what it takes to use the MVC pattern to build Web Forms applications.

Role of the Model

According to the definition, the model in MVC is the representation of the data as the view is expected to consume it. The model is where the view copies any data posted by requests and where it gets any data to be incorporated in the response. You should have a different model (say, a class) for each view. The model should have properties for each significant piece of data the view handles.

The problem here is that in Web Forms the model is often bypassed because views are made of server controls and server controls expose input data and receive response data.

Role of the View

In Web Forms, the view coincides with a page. The page is made of server controls, and server controls provide input elements for the user to interact with. The view is responsible for producing the collection of visual elements displayed to users—the ASPX markup—as well as for processing user gestures—the code-behind class. In an MVC scenario, there should be some sort of event-based dependency between the view and model. When the model is updated, the view should be notified, grab up-to-date information, and refresh.

The code in the view should be as simple as possible, ideally limited to just dispatching calls to another layer—the controller.

Role of the Controller

The controller is the place where the action that the user requested is actually performed. The action might require the controller to select a new view which, in Web Forms, would be a redirect. More likely, the action will lead the controller to interact with the middle tier to obtain a response. The response obtained will then be massaged in some way and placed in the model for the view to consume.

The controller has no dependencies on the view; the controller only knows the model and how to reach the middle tier.

Web Forms and the MVC Pattern

Heavily based on view state, code-behind, and server controls, the Web Forms programming model follows its own pattern—the Page Controller pattern. The core idea is that any request is mapped to a page and an internal component controls the request, including input processing, action, and output generation. If you stick to Web Forms, you can't eliminate the Page Controller pattern.

If you want more SoC, you can build layers for models and controllers on a per-view basis. This means that each Web Forms page should have its own model class and its own controller class. The model will be updated with any posted data and any significant data that is read out of the view state. In the postback, the code-behind event handler will simply invoke a controller method. Finally, the controller will update the model, and these changes should walk their way to the view.

The weak point of MVC is the communication between view and model. The original MVC paper suggests you set up event-based communication between the two. Years of experience suggest a different model should be used. Enter the MVP pattern.

The MVP Pattern

MVP is a derivative of MVC aimed at providing a cleaner separation between the view, the model, and the controller. The most relevant change from MVC is that view and model are physically separated and have no intimate knowledge of each other. The controller (renamed as *presenter*) is a mediator between the user and the application. Solicited by the view, it performs any work associated with the request and passes data back to the view. In MVP, the controller class is essentially responsible for presenting data to the view, which explains the new name of "presenter."

Generalities of the MVP Pattern

As mentioned, in MVP the view and the model are neatly separated, and the view exposes a contract through which the presenter can read input values and provide results of the action. Summarizing the situation further, we can say that MVP is a refinement of MVC based on three facts:

- The view doesn't know the model.

- The presenter ignores any UI technology behind the view.

- Abstracted to an interface, the view is easy to mock up, which makes testing the controller far easier.

Figure 15-2 provides an overall view of the MVP pattern.

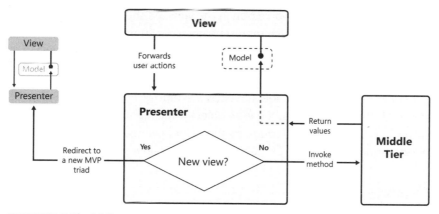

FIGURE 15-2 The MVP pattern.

The presenter is at the center of the universe and incorporates the presentation logic behind the view. The presenter in MVP is logically bound to the view, which is another reason for emphasizing the presentation role of the component. Figure 15-3 attempts to compare MVC and MVP graphically.

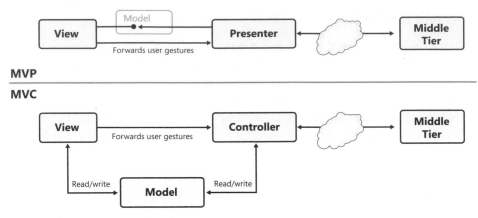

MVP

MVC

FIGURE 15-3 Comparing MVC and MVP.

> **Note** In addition to the change of name (controller vs. presenter), there's a more subtle but relevant point. In MVC, the controller is a centralized class that handles multiple calls from multiple views. In MVP, the presenter is bound to a single view or to a hierarchy of views with the same characteristics. In MVP, the presenter is a controller for a specific segment of the presentation logic. Hence, the name "presenter."

Role of the Model

The best possible definition of the model doesn't change in MVP. The model is the representation of the data being worked on in the view. As shown in Figure 15-2, the view exposes a contracted interface, which represents the core functionality of the view to the presenter's eyes. In other words, the presenter should be able to work with any object that implements that contracted interface.

In theory, it could be an ASP.NET page as well as a Windows Forms window. The model in MVP, therefore, is the interface that the view object implements. Being an interface, it can include properties, but it can also include methods and events. In a Web Forms scenario, events are not required, and most of the time it will contain just properties.

Role of the View

The view is the Web Forms page that you build. This view is typically an instance of a class that inherits from *Page* or *UserControl* and implements the model. The view also holds a reference to an instance of the presenter. Between views and presenters, you typically have a one-to-one cardinality, even though you can still reduce the number of presenter classes by creating some sort of hierarchy and reusing a bit of code.

Role of the Presenter

The presenter is just an additional layer you build on top of code-behind classes. It is a class that can be easily designed to have no hidden dependencies. The presenter requires a reference on the view, but thanks to the contracted interface of the view the reference can be injected. The presenter will use the view object to grab input values and prepare a call to the middle tier. After the response has been received, the presenter will pass data back to the view, always through the members of the interface. As mentioned, the interface that abstracts the view is logically equivalent to the model in MVC.

Web Forms and the MVP Pattern

As you'll see in the rest of the chapter, MVP lends itself very well to being implemented in Web Forms. The pattern can be easily outlined as a step-by-step procedure and doesn't require you to twist the Web Forms programming model. As a developer, you only need to add a bit of abstraction to your Web Forms pages to gain the benefits of the MVP pattern—testability and maintainability.

Having said that, I also feel obliged to mention that MVP is not a pattern for everyone and for just any application. MVP provides guidance on how to manage heaps of views and, quite obviously, comes at a cost—the cost of increased complexity in the application code. As you can imagine, these costs are easier to absorb in large applications than in simple ones. MVP, therefore, is not just for any application.

In MVP, the view is defined through an interface, and this interface is the only point of contact between the system and the view. As an architect, after you've abstracted a view with an interface, you can give developers the green light to start developing presentation logic without waiting for designers to produce the graphics. After developers have interfaces, they can start coding and interfaces can be extracted from user stories, if not from full specifications.

MVP is an important presentation pattern that can be a bit expensive to implement in relatively simple applications. On the other hand, MVP shines in enterprise-class applications, where you really need to reuse as much presentation logic as possible, across multiple platforms and in Software-as-a-Service (SaaS) scenarios. And many of these applications have an ASP.NET Web Forms front end.

The MVVM Pattern

A recently introduced pattern, Model-View-ViewModel is built around the same concepts presented years ago for the Presentation Model (PM) pattern. The PM pattern is described here: *http://martinfowler.com/eaaDev/PresentationModel.html*.

How does PM differ from MVP?

PM is a variation of MVP that is particularly suited to supporting a rich and complex user interface. On the Windows platforms, PM works well with user interfaces built with Windows Presentation Foundation (WPF) and Silverlight. Microsoft developed a WPF-specific version of PM and named it *Model-View-ViewModel* (MVVM).

Generalities of the MVVM Pattern

MVVM, like MVP, is based on three actors—the view, the model, and the presenter—with the presenter now renamed as *view-model*. The difference with MVP is that the view doesn't expose any interface, but a data model for the view is incorporated in the presenter. The view elements are directly bound to properties on the model. In summary, in MVVM the view is passive and doesn't implement any interface. The interface is transformed into a model class and incorporated in the presenter. The resulting object gets the name "view-model." See Figure 15-4.

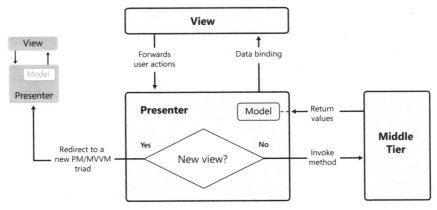

FIGURE 15-4 The MVVM Pattern.

The innovative point of MVVM is that the presenter doesn't operate on the view. The presenter, instead, exposes an object model tailor-made for the view and takes care of populating it with fresh data. The view, in turn, gains access to the presenter's object model in some way. In the .NET space, data binding is a common way in which this is achieved.

Web Forms and MVVM

MVVM is not a pattern I recommend for Web Forms. More precisely, the inherent plusses of MVVM don't show up in Web Forms (or ASP.NET MVC) with the same effectiveness as they do in WPF or Silverlight. Still, MVVM can give you some benefits, such as layering, SoC, and testability. However, it won't be anything more than what you would get with MVP.

Why is MVVM particularly effective in WPF or Silverlight?

The answer is shown in Figure 15-4. Used in a platform that provides superb support for (two-way) data binding, the MVVM shines and really gives you the aforementioned benefits with a fraction of the effort it would take to do the same in MVP. Used in Web Forms, where you have only one-time binding, it loses most of its appeal.

Figure 15-5 shows the graph of a XAML-based view designed in accordance with MVVM.

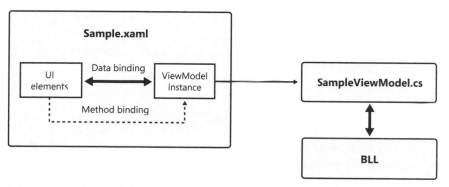

FIGURE 15-5 Schema of the MVVM pattern in a XAML-based view.

The XAML file can be a WPF, Silverlight, or even Windows Phone 7 view. It is made of markup elements bound to properties of the view-model object. The view-model object can be attached to the view in a number of equally effective ways, including programmatic access to the *DataContext* property of the view and a custom tag in the markup that references an external object. The view-model class exposes methods to retrieve and update data through the middle tier.

View events (for example, a user's clicking) are bound to commands, and commands are ultimately mapped to methods on the view-model object. This can be done in a number of ways. You can, for example, use the code-behind class of the XAML view and just invoke methods on the view-model object, or perhaps you can use the XAML commanding interface to forward user events to command objects that, in turn, invoke the view-model and then the middle tier. Architecturally speaking, I don't see relevant differences. It mostly depends on attitude and tooling. For example, if you use Microsoft Blend to create the XAML view, you'll likely end up with codeless code-behind classes. If you stick to Visual Studio as your IDE, you will probably write classic event handlers in the code-behind class.

Implementing Model View Presenter

As it turns out, MVP is probably the most beneficial way of adding layering and testability to Web Forms applications. Let's see how to implement the MVP pattern in a sample application.

Abstracting the View

In an MVP scenario, the first step to complete is defining the contract for each required view. Each page in the ASP.NET application will have its own interface to talk to the rest of the presentation layer. The interface identifies the data model that the page requires and supports. Two logically equivalent views will subsequently have the same interface. A view that extends an existing view will probably have its interface inherited from an existing one.

> **Note** What I'll be saying for a global view such as a page applies verbatim to subviews such as user controls or, perhaps, frames.

From Use-Cases to the View

You always start development efforts from a use-case or perhaps a user story. In any case, you have a more or less defined idea of what the client expects your module to do and look like. You typically use wireframes to sketch out the final user interface of a given part of the application—commonly an individual view. After an agreement has been reached as to the information to show and templates to use (whether they are lists, tabs, collapsible panels, or data formats), you have just abstracted the view to a model. Figure 15-6 shows a possible mockup created with one of the most popular tools in this area—Balsamiq Mockups (see *http://www.balsamiq.com*).

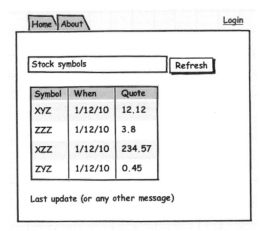

FIGURE 15-6 A mockup showing a view for some default.aspx page.

With this idea in mind, getting an interface (or a base class) is usually not so hard. Here's an example:

```
public interface IDefaultView
{
    IList<StockInfo> Quotes { get; set; }
    String Message { get; set; }
    String Symbols { get; set; }
}
```

You need to be able to read and write the content of the text box that contains the list of current symbols. Additionally, you need to read and write the content of a message, such as an error message or the time of the last update. You also need a collection of objects representing the stock information you want to display.

With the view contract defined in detail (for example, agreement is required on IDs), designers and developers can start working in parallel. The nicest thing is that it really works like this in practice—it's not a theory or an empty platitude trying to sell a certain point of view.

Implementing the Interface

The view you are creating must implement the interface. In Web Forms, a view is a Web page. So here's the skeleton of *default.aspx*:

```
public partial class Default : Page, IDefaultView
{
    ...
}
```

The main responsibility of the view is hiding the details of the user interface elements. The interface exposes just a string property representing the stock symbols to retrieve, but the use-case suggests the user is expected to type names in an input field. Subsequently, the implementation of the *Symbols* property wraps the text box, as shown here:

```
public partial class Default : Page, IDefaultView
{
    ...

    #region IDefaultView Members
    public IList<StockInfo> Quotes
    {
        get { return GridView1.DataSource as IList<StockInfo>; }
        set {
            GridView1.DataSource = value;
            GridView1.DataBind();
        }
    }
}
```

```
    public string Message
    {
        get { return lblMessage.Text; }
        set { lblMessage.Text = value; }
    }

    public string Symbols
    {
        get { return txtSymbols.Text; }
        set { txtSymbols.Text = value; }
    }
    #endregion
}
```

Where does *StockInfo* come from? That could either be one of the entities that populate the business layer or a specific data transfer object that is returned by the service layer. (See Chapter 14.) In this case, for simplicity, you can assume that you share the domain model with the presentation layer; so *StockInfo* comes from an *Entities* assembly referenced by both the service layer and the presentation.

```
public class StockInfo
{
    public String Company { get; set; }
    public String CurrentQuote { get; set; }
    public String Change { get; set; }
    public String Date { get; set; }
    public String Time { get; set; }
}
```

The next step is adding a presenter component to the view. The presenter is a plain .NET class that must be instructed to work against any objects that implement the view interface.

Creating the Presenter

Just like the controller in ASP.NET MVC, the presenter is a simple class in which all dependencies are (or at least, should be) injected explicitly. The class holds no significant state. The presenter lifetime is usually bound to the view.

Getting a Presenter's Instance

A common way of implementing MVP entails that the page (for example, the view) gets a new instance of the presenter for each request. You typically create the presenter instance in *Page_Load*, as shown here:

```
public partial class Default : Page, IDefaultView
{
    private DefaultPresenter _presenter = null;
    protected void Page_Load(Object sender, EventArgs e)
```

```
    {
        _presenter = new DefaultPresenter(this);
    }

    // Implementation of the IDefaultView interface
    ...
}
```

An issue you might face is arranging a convenient naming convention to give each presenter class a name that is both unique and meaningful. The name of the page with a trailing string such as *Presenter* is a good approach; anyway, feel free to adapt it to your needs.

Using the Presenter

In summary, a Web Forms page designed around the MVP pattern is a class that implements a given view interface and holds an instance of a presenter class. What's the purpose of the presenter instance?

The presenter is expected to expose a method for each possible action invoked by the user. Put another way, the presenter will have a unique, unambiguous, parameterless method for each event handler you need to have in the code-behind class. You still bind handlers to events fired by server controls; however, these handlers will simply forward the call to a method on the presenter instance. Here's an example:

```
public partial class Default : Page, IDefaultView
{
    private DefaultPresenter  _presenter = null;
    protected void Page_Load(Object sender, EventArgs e)
    {
        _presenter = new DefaultPresenter(this);
    }

    protected void btnRefresh_Click(Object sender, EventArgs e)
    {
        _presenter.Refresh();
    }

    protected void btnRedirect_Click(Object sender, EventArgs e)
    {
        _presenter.Redirect();
    }

    // Implementation of the IDefaultView interface
    ...
}
```

From an architectural standpoint, something in the preceding code clashes with common sense: the code-behind class is merely a pass-through layer, so either the code-behind class or the presenter might be perceived as unnecessary layers. The fact is, you can't easily remove code-behind in ASP.NET Web Forms—not without paying some costs in terms of the decreased productivity of teams. Code-behind classes have been around and have worked for a decade; you can't just modify the framework to get rid of them. On the other hand, the presenter is just an extra layer you add deliberately with the precise intention of increasing maintainability and testability.

Although it's not objectively perfect, the code shown earlier is probably the best possible compromise to bring the benefits of MVP to ASP.NET Web Forms.

How Does the Presenter Retrieve Data?

Let's stop for a while and think about the type of code one would write in the *Refresh* method of the presenter. Given the use-case (and given the view mockup in Figure 15-6), the method is expected to connect to the application's service layer and, from there, orchestrate a call to some service that actually provides quote information. The *Refresh* method needs to know the list of stocks for which you intend to run the query. Where does it get that information?

The list of symbols is typed by the user in a text box; the presenter needs to access the text box but, ideally, you want this to happen without exposing the view inner details to the presenter. (Doing so would bind the presenter to a particular view.) Here's the code of the presenter, including its *Refresh* method:

```
public class DefaultPresenter
{
    private readonly IDefaultView _view;
    private readonly IQuoteServices _quoteServices;

    public DefaultPresenter(IDefaultView view) : this(view, new QuoteServices())
    {
    }
    public DefaultPresenter(IDefaultView view, IQuoteServices quoteService)
    {
        _view = view;
        _quoteServices = quoteService;
    }

    public void Refresh()
    {
        // Get input from the view
        var symbols = _view.Symbols;

        // Execute the action
        var stocks = _quoteServices.GetQuotes(symbols);

        // Update the view
        _view.Quotes = stocks;
        _view.Message = String.Format("Data downloaded at: {0}", DateTime.Now);
    }
}
```

At a minimum, the presenter is injected with the view object (for example, a reference to the ASP.NET page) through the constructor. The presenter, however, is instructed to work only against the members of the view interface. This means that the same presenter could be re-used on different client platforms. As long as you have a Web and Windows application that operates according to the same actions, the chances for you to reuse the same presenter are definitely high. (This fact might not be true if you take advantage of some platform-specific features and operate the view through a different set of actions.)

The presenter retrieves any input data it needs from the injected view. For example, it grabs any content in the *txtSymbols* text box via the *Symbols* property on the view interface. Likewise, it displays any response, such as the last update time, via the *Message* property. How the *Message* and *Symbols* properties actually operate on the view is transparent to the presenter. This transparency is the guarantee that the presenter is absolutely independent from the view.

Connecting the Presenter to the Service Layer

The presenter is clearly part of the presentation layer. In a layered solution, the presentation layer is where you bridge the middle tier. The nearest endpoint in the middle tier land is the service layer, as discussed in Chapter 14. The service layer is a collection of classes (sometimes just WCF services) that orchestrate all the actions required by the application logic to serve a given request. The service layer should accept and retrieve data in a format that suits the presentation; if necessary, the service layer will translate from middle tier entities to presen-tation-only data transfer objects. If you're lucky, you can even use the same entities on both the presentation and business layers.

 Note In this regard, your luck mostly depends on the complexity of the use-case and the complexity of the problem's domain. In many cases, you can't just find a match between middle tier models and view models. When this happens, using two distinct object models is the only way to go.

The presenter needs a reference to one or multiple objects in the service layer assembly. This means that, in the first place, the presentation layer needs to reference the service layer as-sembly. More importantly, you must inject in the presenter a reference to the specific service it will be using.

In the previous listing, I used the poor man's dependency injection approach. It consists of an overloaded constructor that defaults to a concrete class in production. However, by using a different constructor, you can support a fake layer for the purpose of unit testing. You can use any Inversion of Control (IoC) tool of choice here if you like that best.

Hence, the presenter places a single call to the service layer to grab all it needs in the con-text of that use-case. The service layer returns data that the presenter will then incorporate in the view. The communication between the presenter and the service layer can be both synchronous and asynchronous, depending on your needs.

> **Note** The service layer typically (but not necessarily) lives in its own assembly on the same server that hosts the Web application. With this configuration, there's no need for you to implement the service layer as real WCF services. It becomes a necessity, instead, as soon as you need to use queued or transactional calls or just to deploy the middle tier on a different machine for scalability reasons.

Presenter in Action

Wrapping up, the user is displayed a page with server controls for input as usual. The user interacts with the page and causes a postback. On the server, the request is processed as usual and results in a page call.

During the page loading, the presenter is instantiated and receives a reference to the current page object. The postback event originates a call to a method in the presenter. The method typically uses the view object to retrieve input data and places a call to the service layer.

An operation develops on the server and a response is served back to the service layer and, from there, is served to the presenter. Finally, the presenter updates the view. (See Figure 15-7.)

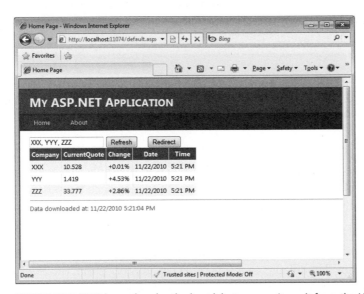

FIGURE 15-7 MVP is used under the hood, but you can't see it from the UI.

Sharing the Presenter with a Windows Application

Admittedly, the feature I'm going to discuss is pretty cool and makes for a compelling demo. There's no magic behind it, and I consider it to be a lucky scenario—real, but special. Under certain conditions, the presenter can be shared with the same application written for other platforms, such as Windows Forms and WPF. (See Figure 15-8.)

All that you need is a Windows form that implements the same view interface. At that point, the presenter has all it needs—a view object. What about the service layer? If you can't reuse the same service layer you had for the Web application, the dependency injection design you adopted for the presenter class makes it easy to change to a more specific one:

```
public partial class DefaultForm : Form, IDefaultView
{
    private DefaultPresenter _presenter;
    public DefaultView()
    {
        InitializeComponent();

        // Initialize the presenter (for Windows)
        _presenter = new DefaultPresenter(this, new WinFormsQuoteServices());
    }
    ...
}
```

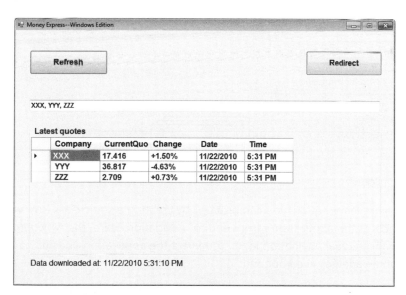

FIGURE 15-8 Distinct applications share the same presenter.

Figure 15-7 and Figure 15-8 show two different versions of the same application—one for the Web and one for the desktop. As long as the presentation logic remains the same, and the dependency on the service layer can be managed, you can (and are encouraged to) reuse the same presenter class. Be aware, however, that this might not always be the case.

> **Note** If one of the potential clients is based on Silverlight, you should also consider that some of the features your code relies on might not be supported in Silverlight. In addition, Silverlight 4 has binary compatibility with .NET code, but the same isn't true for earlier versions. Also, you are still unable to reference a .NET assembly from a Silverlight project; the opposite, though, works as long as there are no code incompatibilities.

Navigation

The presenter is also responsible for implementing navigation within the application. In particular, the presenter is responsible for enabling (or disabling) any subviews contained in the primary view and for selecting and reaching the next view.

The Application Controller Pattern

To handle navigation within views, MVP goes hand in hand with another pattern—*Application Controller*. The pattern defines a central console that holds all the logic to determine the next view and handle the screen navigation and the flow of an application. (See Figure 15-9.)

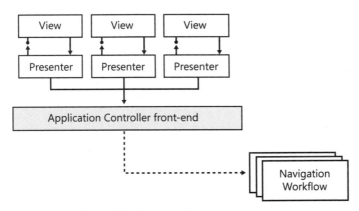

FIGURE 15-9 The application controller.

When it comes to implementation, you can proceed by creating a static class (say, you call it *Navigator*) that acts as the application's front end for navigation. Here, the *Navigator* class is a plain container for the real navigation logic. You inject the application-specific navigation workflow through an additional component.

The extra layer represented by the navigation workflow shields the presenter from knowing the details of the platform specific navigation. For example, navigation within a Web Forms application is based on *Response.Redirect*, whereas navigation relies on form-based display in Windows Forms.

Defining the Navigation Workflow

Here's a possible implementation of the interface that represents the navigation workflow. The interface includes a method to navigate directly to a given view and another to navigate from the current view to the next:

```
public interface INavigationWorkflow
{
    void Goto(String view);
    void NextViewFrom(String currentView);
}
```

The *Navigator* class wraps an object that implements this interface and exposes a façade to the presenter:

```
public static class Navigator
{
    private static INavigationWorkflow _navigationWorkflow;
    private static Object _navigationArgument;

    public static void Attach(INavigationWorkflow workflow)
    {
        if (workflow != null)
            _navigationWorkflow = workflow;
    }

    public static Object Argument
    {
        get { return _navigationArgument; }
    }

    public static void Goto(String view)
    {
        if (_navigationWorkflow != null)
            _navigationWorkflow.Goto(view);
    }

    public static void Goto(String view, Object argument)
    {
        if (_navigationWorkflow != null)
        {
            _navigationArgument = argument;
            Navigator.Goto(view);
        }
    }

    public static void NextViewFrom(String currentView)
    {
        if (_navigationWorkflow != null)
            _navigationWorkflow.NextViewFrom(currentView);
    }
}
```

```
    public static void NextViewFrom(String currentView, Object argument)
    {
        if (_navigationWorkflow != null)
        {
            _navigationArgument = argument;
            Navigator.NextViewFrom(currentView, argument);
        }
    }
}
```

The *Navigator* class is a little more than just a wrapper for the interface. The class features an *Argument* property through which the presenter can specify data to be passed to the view. How navigation is implemented and how data is passed depends on the actual implementation of the navigation workflow.

Navigating Within a Web Forms Site

In Web Forms, navigation between pages can be achieved through a redirect. The workflow interface allows you to assign a name to a view (possibly, but not necessarily, the name of the page), which is then resolved with a redirect to a given URL. Here's an example:

```
public class SiteNavigationWorkflow : INavigationWorkflow
{
    public void Goto(String view)
    {
        switch (view)
        {
            case "home":
                HttpContext.Current.Response.Redirect("/default.aspx");
                break;
            case "test":
                HttpContext.Current.Response.Redirect(
                    HttpUtility.UrlEncode(String.Format("/test.aspx?x='{0}'",
                                                        Navigator.Argument)));
                break;
        }
    }

    public void NextViewFrom(String currentView)
    {
        switch (currentView)
        {
            case "home":
                // Calculate next view using logic
                break;
        }
    }
}
```

As an example, let's have a look at a possible implementation of the same interface for a Windows Forms application:

```
public class AppNavigationWorkflow : INavigationWorkflow
{
    private Form _fooForm;
    private readonly Form _defaultView;

    public AppNavigationWorkflow(Form main)
    {
        _defaultView = main;
    }

    public void Goto(string view)
    {
        switch (view)
        {
            case "home":
                if (_fooForm != null && !_fooForm.IsDisposed)
                {
                    _fooForm.Close();
                    _fooForm = null;
                }
                break;
            case "foo":
                if (_fooForm == null || _fooForm.IsDisposed)
                {
                    _fooForm = new FooForm();
                    _fooForm.Owner = _defaultView;
                }
                _fooForm.ShowDialog();
                break;
        }
    }

    public void NextViewFrom(string currentView)
    {
        switch (currentView)
        {
            case "home":
                // Calculate next view using logic
                break;
        }
    }
}
```

As you can see, in Windows you might have a radically different approach to navigation, which basically consists of displaying and hiding dialog boxes and windows. Still, from the presenter's standpoint, all you need to do is invoke the same *Goto* method:

```
// From presenter's code
public void Redirect()
{
    Navigator.Goto("test", "test value");
}
```

In ASP.NET, it produces the view shown in Figure 15-10.

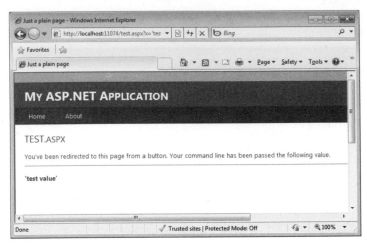

FIGURE 15-10 Navigating to a specific page.

Finally, let's see how you can attach a platform-specific workflow to the presentation layer. The binding takes place at the application startup—for example, in *global.asax*:

```
void Application_Start(Object sender, EventArgs e)
{
    var simpleWorkflow = new SiteNavigationWorkflow();
    Navigator.Attach(simpleWorkflow);
}
```

The use of the term "workflow" here is not coincidental. The method *Goto* in *INavigationWorkflow* allows you to reach a specific URL; the method *NextViewFrom*, which can be implemented just by using a workflow based on the current view, determines what comes next.

Testability in Web Forms with MVP

For many years, developers in the .NET space didn't pay much attention to emerging patterns and practices. The deep application of the RAD paradigm led to a focus on tools and techniques to do it faster, rather than doing it right the first time. Debugging always prevailed over unit testing as the major technique to help check whether your development efforts were on track.

Web Forms has a number of merits, but it certainly doesn't stand out for the aid it provides with regard to testability. However, using the MVP pattern makes the most relevant part of your Web Forms code—for example, the presenter—far easier to test, and especially unit-test.

Writing Testable Code

If you look at the functionality, there's nearly no difference at all between *testable-code-that-works* and *untestable-code-that-works*. So where's the benefit of testing? Essentially, it lies in what might happen after you deploy your code to production. The customer might come back and ask you to make changes or implement new features. Or, worse yet, an unexpected bug might show up. In all these cases, you need to put your hands on the code to update it. Your goal is updating what has to be updated *without* breaking anything else. How do you prove that you didn't break any existing features?

A well-written set of unit tests can give you the measure of how good your software is now compared to the stage before. If your software still passes all the tests after the updates, well, there's a great chance that untouched features are still effective.

Aspects of Testable Code

The beauty of tests is in the speed at which you can check whether your changes caused regression. At its core, a test is a program that invokes a software module that passes edge values to prove whether or not a particular behavior is working correctly. Note that not all code is inherently testable.

You have to keep three fundamental aspects in mind when writing a test: visibility, control, and simplicity.

Visibility indicates the degree at which the code under test allows you to observe changes in the state of the code. If changes are not observable, how can you determine whether the code works or fails?

Control indicates the degree at which the behavior of code under test can be influenced by external input. To be effective, a test must pass in selected input values. If input is hard-coded, running an effective test is much harder.

Finally, *simplicity* is an aspect of code that is never out of place. The simpler the code is, the simpler it is to test and the more reliable any results will be.

Unit Testing

Unit testing verifies that individual units of code are working properly according to their software contract. A *unit* is the smallest part of an application that is testable—typically, a method.

Unit testing consists of writing and running a small program (referred to as a *test harness*) that instantiates classes and invokes methods in an automatic way. In the end, running a battery of tests is much like compiling. You click a button, you run the test harness and, at the end of it, you know what went wrong, if anything.

In its simplest form, a test harness is a manually written program that reads test-case input values and the corresponding expected results from some external files. Then the test harness calls methods using input values and compares results with expected values. Obviously, writing such a test harness entirely from scratch is, at a minimum, time consuming and error prone. But, more importantly, it is restrictive in terms of the testing capabilities you can take advantage of.

A very effective way to conduct unit testing is to use an automated test framework. An automated test framework is a developer tool that normally includes a runtime engine and a framework of classes for simplifying the creation of test programs. One of these frameworks—MSUnit—is integrated in Visual Studio. All you have to do is create a new project of type Test. (Note that other tools, both open-source and commercial, are available for unit testing, some of which are also integrated with Visual Studio.)

Test-Driven Development

You can write tests at any time—before or after the method you intend to test. This is mostly a matter of preference and methodology. It can become a religious matter sometimes, but frankly nobody can claim that one approach or the other is absolutely and objectively better.

Test-driven development (TDD) is a methodology that naturally gets you to think about the expected interface and behavior of methods well before you actually start writing the code. TDD is an approach that might appear radical at first and that certainly takes time to fully digest. However, its goal is quite simple in the end: help to quickly write clean code that works.

In the traditional approach to coding, you develop a method according to the idea you have of the features the method must support. You start with a relatively simple body, and then you increase its capabilities until you reach the original goal. Along the way, you use the debugger to see how things are going and whether data is being moved around correctly. When you've determined that all is OK, if you're a scrupulous developer you consider writing a bunch of unit tests to verify the behavior of the method from a few other angles to make it easier to catch regression failures later.

If you proceed this way, you eventually decide that tests are way too boring and hard to write and don't really give you any concrete benefits. It's your code, after all, and it works. A test won't make the code richer and more appealing to users. So you just stop writing tests!

When the complexity of the code rises above a certain threshold, the debugger alone is no longer sufficient for testing and needs to be backed by some good unit tests. You can write unit tests before you code (as TDD suggests) or after you're done. It doesn't really matter when you do it, as long as you come up with an exhaustive set of tests. TDD is considered an effective methodology to achieve just this result. Some small changes in the Visual Studio 2010 refactoring tools and the Test project template also make it worth a try for Web Forms developers.

Testing a Presenter Class

To test-run the increased testability of Web Forms with MVP let's go through a test project aimed at ensuring an application correctly gets price quotes for a list of stock symbols.

Creating a Unit Test

Suppose you have the test project ready and you've added a unit test to it. A unit test is a class that looks like the one shown here:

```
[TestClass]
public class DefaultPresenterTests
{
    [TestMethod]
    public void TestIfQuotesAreBeingReturnedForEverySymbol()
    {
    }
}
```

Note Choosing the right name for a test method is as important as writing good code. The test name must be representative of the scenario you're testing and include a quick explanation of the scenario. A detailed guide from an expert in the field can be found here: *http://www.osherove.com/blog/2005/4/3/naming-standards-for-unit-tests.htm.*

The test is expected to test the *Refresh* method of the presenter class we considered earlier. Figure 15-11 illustrates the first roadblock we encounter.

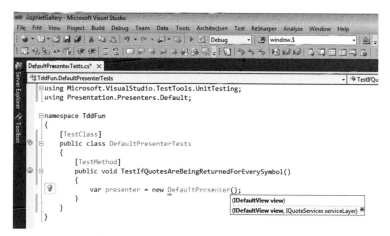

FIGURE 15-11 Attempting to create a unit test.

The idea is to get an instance of the presenter and invoke each method, passing some ad hoc input value (the aspect *control*) and observing results (the aspect *visibility*). As IntelliSense shows up in the figure, however, you need to provide some objects in order to instantiate the presenter.

The presenter has two dependencies—on the view and on the quote service. Your goal is to test the logic in the presenter class; you don't want to test the view here and the service. These will possibly be the subject of other tests. On the other hand, you still need to provide a view and a service. Thankfully, you used a bit of dependency injection pattern in the design of the presenter class; therefore, you can now obtain a test double object and pass that in.

A test double is an object that looks like another one without providing the same behavior. A test double is typically coded in either of two ways—as a fake or a mock. A fake is an object with a hard-coded behavior and no state; a mock is an object with a dynamically defined behavior. You typically code the fake yourself as a custom class in the project and use ad hoc frameworks for mocks. Moq is one of these frameworks.

Important Overall, there are four main types of test doubles: dummy objects, fakes, stubs, and mocks. A general consensus about what each test double object does exists for dummy objects and mocks only. A *dummy object* has no behavior and exists just to fill in a parameter list. A *mock object* is what I described above.

What about fakes and stubs, then? You might read subtly different definitions for each term and even find out that various authors use the term *fake* to indicate what another author classifies as a stub, and vice versa. My pragmatic approach is that it would be much simpler if we limit ourselves to two types of doubles: mocks and another, simpler, type of double you name the way you like. In this context, I prefer the term *fake*. As far as this chapter is concerned, feel free to replace *fake* with *stub* if that makes your reading easier in any way.

Here are some sample test doubles for the view and quote service:

```
public class FakeDefaultView : IDefaultView
{
    private readonly String _symbols;
    public FakeDefaultView(String fakeSymbols)
    {
        _symbols = fakeSymbols;
    }
    public IList<StockInfo> Quotes { get; set; }
    public String Message { get; set; }
    public String Symbols
    {
        get { return _symbols; }
        set {}
    }
}

public class FakeQuoteService : IQuoteServices
{
    public IList<StockInfo> GetQuotes(String symbols)
    {
        var stocks = symbols.Split(',');
        return stocks.Select(s => new StockInfo()
                                {
                                    Change = "0%",
                                    Company = s,
```

```
                                CurrentQuote = "1.1",
                                Date = DateTime.Today.ToString(),
                                Time = DateTime.Now.ToString()
                          }).ToList();
    }
}
```

Finally, here's the unit test:

```
[TestMethod]
public void TestIfQuotesAreBeingReturnedForEverySymbol()
{
    // Arrange
    const String testData = "XXX,YYY,ZZZ";
    var inputSymbols = testData.Split(',').ToList();
    var view = new FakeDefaultView(testData);
    var presenter = new DefaultPresenter(view, new FakeQuoteService());

    // Act
    presenter.Refresh();

    // Assert
    Assert.AreEqual(view.Quotes.Count, inputSymbols.Count);
    foreach(var quote in view.Quotes)
    {
        Assert.IsTrue(inputSymbols.Contains(quote.Company));
    }
}
```

Ideally, a unit test is articulated in three main blocks: prepare the ground for executing the method under test, execute the method, and then check results against assertions.

Testing Presenters in Isolation

A relevant benefit that MVP provides is isolating the presenter code from the rest of the world. To be precise, MVP gives you guidance on how to isolate the presenter from the view, but it says nothing specific about the rest of the system. This means that keeping the presenter isolated from the middle tier is your responsibility.

When you test a method, you want to focus only on the code within *that* method. All that you want to know is whether *that* code provides the expected results in the tested scenarios. To get this, you need to get rid of all dependencies the method might have. If the method, say, invokes another class, you assume that the invoked class will *always* return correct results. In this way, you eliminate at the root the risk that the method fails under test because a failure occurred down the call stack. If you test method A and it fails, the reason has to be found *exclusively* in the source code of method A and not in any of its dependencies.

Achieving isolation is far easier if you apply dependency injection to the design of classes. For presenters, this means being injected with the view object and also any service layer component the presenter needs to work with. When this happens, testing methods on the presenter is really a piece of cake. (See Figure 15-12.)

FIGURE 15-12 Running unit tests.

Summary

For an ASP.NET application, you have two main options when it comes to choosing an application model. You can go with the traditional ASP.NET Web application model, which is based on the Page Controller pattern, or you can move toward ASP.NET MVC.

The traditional ASP.NET application model can be improved with a deeper separation of concerns by using a manual implementation of the MVP pattern. The MVP pattern isolates the view from the presenter and abstracts the view to an interface. In this way, the presenter can be coded against the view interface and becomes a reusable and testable piece of code. To finish with a flourish, you might also want to take out of the presenter any code that represents a dependency on the service layer. If you do, writing unit tests for the presenter becomes really easy and effective.

Even with these changes in place, however, ASP.NET Web Forms remains a hard-to-test framework. What if you need to deal with *Cache* or *Session* in your presenter? None of these objects will be available in the test project unless you spin the entire ASP.NET runtime. In other words, testing in isolation is very difficult. Options? Well, the best you can do is wrap access to *Session*, *Cache*, and other intrinsic ASP.NET objects in custom classes exposing a fixed interface. At the cost of an additional fairly thin layer, you gain the benefit of isolating presenters from ASP.NET runtime objects. And ASP.NET intrinsic objects are the subject of the next few chapters.

Part IV
Infrastructure of the Application

Chapter 16
The HTTP Request Context

All great things are simple, and many can be expressed in single words.

—Winston Churchill

Each ASP.NET request goes hand in hand with a companion object for its entire lifetime—an instance of the *HttpContext* class. The *HttpContext* object wraps up all the HTTP-specific information available about the request. It is then used by the various HTTP modules and used to group references to intrinsic worker objects such as *Request*, *Response*, and *Server*.

In this chapter, we'll first review the startup process of the ASP.NET application and then move on to examine the various objects that form the context of the HTTP request.

Initialization of the Application

Each ASP.NET request is carried out by an ASP.NET application object. An ASP.NET application consists of an instance of the *HttpApplication* class that you briefly met in Chapter 2, "ASP.NET and IIS." *HttpApplication* is a *global.asax*-derived object that handles all HTTP requests directed to a particular virtual folder.

An ASP.NET running application is wholly represented by its virtual folder and, optionally, by the *global.asax* file. The virtual folder name is a sort of key that the HTTP runtime uses to selectively identify which of the running applications should take care of the incoming request. The *global.asax* file, if present, contains settings and code for responding to application-level events raised by ASP.NET or by registered HTTP modules that affect the application.

The particular *HttpApplication* selected is responsible for managing the entire lifetime of the request it is assigned to. That instance of *HttpApplication* can be reused only after the request has been completed. If no *HttpApplication* object is available, either because the application has not been started yet or all valid objects are busy, a new *HttpApplication* is created and pooled.

Properties of the *HttpApplication* Class

Although the *HttpApplication* provides a public constructor, user applications never need to create instances of the *HttpApplication* class directly. The ASP.NET runtime infrastructure always does the job for you. As mentioned, instances of the class are pooled and, as such, can process many requests in their lifetime, but always one at a time. Should concurrent requests arrive for the same application, additional instances are created. Table 16-1 lists the properties defined for the class.

TABLE 16-1 *HttpApplication* **Properties**

Property	Description
Application	Instance of the *HttpApplicationState* class. It represents the global and shared state of the application. It is functionally equivalent to the ASP intrinsic *Application* object.
Context	Instance of the *HttpContext* class. It encapsulates in a single object all HTTP-specific information about the current request. Intrinsic objects (for example, *Application* and *Request*) are also exposed as properties.
Modules	Gets the collection of modules that affect the current application.
Request	Instance of the *HttpRequest* class. It represents the current HTTP request. It is functionally equivalent to the ASP intrinsic *Request* object.
Response	Instance of the *HttpResponse* class. It sends HTTP response data to the client. It is functionally equivalent to the ASP intrinsic *Response* object.
Server	Instance of the *HttpServerUtility* class. It provides helper methods for processing Web requests. It is functionally equivalent to the ASP intrinsic *Server* object.
Session	Instance of the *HttpSessionState* class. It manages user-specific data. It is functionally equivalent to the ASP intrinsic *Session* object.
User	An *IPrincipal* object that represents the user making the request.

The *HttpApplication* is managed by the ASP.NET infrastructure, so how can you take advantage of the fairly rich, public programming interface of the class? The answer is that properties and, even more, overridable methods and class events can be accessed and programmatically manipulated in the *global.asax* file. (I'll return to *global.asax* in a moment.)

Application Modules

The property *Modules* returns a collection of application-wide components providing ad hoc services. An HTTP module component is a class that implements the *IHttpModule* interface. Modules can be considered the managed counterpart of ISAPI filters; they are kind of request interceptors with the built-in capability of modifying the overall context of the request being processed. The Microsoft .NET Framework defines a number of standard modules, as listed in Table 16-2. Custom modules can be defined too. I cover this particular aspect of HTTP programming in Chapter 18, "ASP.NET Caching."

TABLE 16-2 **ASP.NET Modules**

Module	Description
AnonymousIdentification	Assigns anonymous users a fake identity.
FileAuthorization	Verifies that the remote user has Microsoft Windows NT permissions to access the requested resource.
FormsAuthentication	Enables applications to use forms authentication.

Module	Description
OutputCache	Provides page output caching services.
PassportAuthentication	Provides a wrapper around Passport authentication services.
Profile	Provides user profile services.
RoleManager	Provides session-state services for the application.
ScriptModule	Used to implement page methods in AJAX pages.
SessionState	Provides session-state services for the application.
UrlAuthorization	Provides URL-based authorization services to access specified resources.
UrlRouting	Provides support for URL routing
WindowsAuthentication	Enables ASP.NET applications to use Windows and Internet Information Services (IIS)-based authentication.

The list of default modules is defined in the *machine.config* file. By creating a proper *web.config* file, you can also create an application-specific list of modules. (Configuration is covered in Chapter 3, "ASP.NET Configuration.")

Methods of the *HttpApplication* Class

The methods of the *HttpApplication* class can be divided into two groups: operational methods and event handler managers. The *HttpApplication* operational methods are described in Table 16-3.

TABLE 16-3 *HttpApplication* **Operational Methods**

Method	Description
CompleteRequest	Sets an internal flag that causes ASP.NET to skip all successive steps in the pipeline and directly execute *EndRequest*. It's mostly useful to HTTP modules.
Dispose	Overridable method, cleans up the instance variables of all registered modules after the request has been served. At this time, *Request*, *Response*, *Session*, and *Application* are no longer available.
GetOutputCacheProviderName	Overridable method, returns the currently configured provider for handling output page caching. (I'll say more about output page caching in Chapter 18.)
GetVaryByCustomString	Overridable method, provides a way to set output caching based on a custom string for all pages in the application. (I'll say more about output page caching in Chapter 18.)
Init	Overridable method that executes custom initialization code after all modules have been linked to the application to serve the request. You can use it to create and configure any object that you want to use throughout the request processing. At this time, *Request*, *Response*, *Session*, and *Application* are not yet available.

Note that the *Init* and *Dispose* methods are quite different from well-known event handlers such as *Application_Start* and *Application_End*.

Init executes for every request directed to the Web application, whereas *Application_Start* fires only once in the Web application's lifetime. *Init* indicates that a new instance of the *HttpApplication* class has been initialized to serve an incoming request; *Application_Start* denotes that the first instance of the *HttpApplication* class has been created to start up the Web application and serve its very first request. Likewise, *Dispose* signals the next termination of the request processing but not necessarily the end of the application. *Application_End* is raised only once, when the application is being shut down.

 Note The lifetime of any resources created in the *Init* method is limited to the execution of the current request. Any resource you allocate in *Init* should be disposed of in *Dispose*, at the latest. If you need persistent data, resort to other objects that form the application or session state.

In addition to the operational methods in Table 16-3, a few other *HttpApplication* methods are available to register asynchronous handlers for application-level events. These methods are of little interest to user applications and are used only by HTTP modules to hook up the events generated during the request's chain of execution.

Events of the *HttpApplication* Class

Table 16-4 describes the event model of the *HttpApplication* class—that is, the set of events that HTTP modules, as well as user applications, can listen to and handle.

TABLE 16-4 *HttpApplication* **Events**

Event	Description
AcquireRequestState, *PostAcquireRequestState*	Occurs when the handler that will actually serve the request acquires the state information associated with the request.
AuthenticateRequest, *PostAuthenticateRequest*	Occurs when a security module has established the identity of the user.
AuthorizeRequest, *PostAuthorizeRequest*	Occurs when a security module has verified user authorization.
BeginRequest	Occurs as soon as the HTTP pipeline begins to process the request.
Disposed	Occurs when the *HttpApplication* object is disposed of as a result of a call to *Dispose*.
EndRequest	Occurs as the last event in the HTTP pipeline chain of execution.
Error	Occurs when an unhandled exception is thrown.
LogRequest, PostLogRequest	Occurs when the system logs the results of the request.
PostMapRequestHandler	Occurs when the HTTP handler to serve the request has been found.

Event	Description
PostRequestHandlerExecute	Occurs when the HTTP handler of choice finishes execution. The response text has been generated at this point.
PreRequestHandlerExecute	Occurs just before the HTTP handler of choice begins to work.
PreSendRequestContent	Occurs just before the ASP.NET runtime sends the response text to the client.
PreSendRequestHeaders	Occurs just before the ASP.NET runtime sends HTTP headers to the client.
ReleaseRequestState, *PostReleaseRequestState*	Occurs when the handler releases the state information associated with the current request.
ResolveRequestCache, *PostResolveRequestCache*	Occurs when the ASP.NET runtime resolves the request through the output cache.
UpdateRequestCache, *PostUpdateRequestCache*	Occurs when the ASP.NET runtime stores the response of the current request in the output cache to be used to serve subsequent requests.

To handle any of these events asynchronously, an application will use the corresponding method whose name follows a common pattern: *AddOnXXXAsync*, where *XXX* stands for the event name. To hook up some of these events in a synchronous manner, an application will define in the *global.asax* event handler procedures with the following signature:

```
public void Application_XXX(Object sender, EventArgs e)
{
    // Do something here
}
```

Of course, the *XXX* placeholder must be replaced with the name of the event from Table 16-4. All the events in the preceding table provide no event-specific data. You can also use the following simpler syntax without losing additional information and programming power:

```
public void Application_XXX()
{
    // Do something here
}
```

In addition to the events listed in Table 16-4, in *global.asax* an application can also handle *Application_Start* and *Application_End*. When ASP.NET is about to fire *BeginRequest* for the very first time in the application lifetime, it makes *Application_Start* precede it. *EndRequest* will happen at the end of every request to an application. *Application_End* occurs outside the context of a request, when the application is ending.

As you saw in Chapter 2, application events are fired in the following sequence:

1. *BeginRequest*   The ASP.NET HTTP pipeline begins to work on the request. This event reaches the application after *Application_Start*.

2. *AuthenticateRequest*   The request is being authenticated. All the internal ASP.NET authentication modules subscribe to this event and attempt to produce an identity. If no authentication module produced an authenticated user, an internal default authentication module is invoked to produce an identity for the unauthenticated user. This is done for the sake of consistency so that code doesn't need to worry about null identities.

3. *PostAuthenticateRequest*   The request has been authenticated. All the information available is stored in the *HttpContext*'s *User* property.

4. *AuthorizeRequest*   The request authorization is about to occur. This event is commonly handled by application code to do custom authorization based on business logic or other application requirements.

5. *PostAuthorizeRequest*   The request has been authorized.

6. *ResolveRequestCache*   The ASP.NET runtime verifies whether returning a previously cached page can resolve the request. If a valid cached representation is found, the request is served from the cache and the request is short-circuited, calling only any registered *EndRequest* handlers.

7. *PostResolveRequestCache*   The request can't be served from the cache, and the procedure continues. An HTTP handler corresponding to the requested URL is created at this point. If the requested resource is an *.aspx* page, an instance of a page class is created.

8. *MapRequestHandler*   The event is fired to determine the request handler.

9. *PostMapRequestHandler*   The event fires when the HTTP handler corresponding to the requested URL has been successfully created.

10. *AcquireRequestState*   The module that hooks up this event is willing to retrieve any state information for the request. A number of factors are relevant here: the handler must support session state in some form, and there must be a valid session ID.

11. *PostAcquireRequestState*   The state information (such as *Application*, *Session*) has been acquired.

12. *PreRequestHandlerExecute*   This event is fired immediately prior to executing the handler for a given request. The handler does its job and generates the output for the client.

13. *ExecuteRequestHandler*   The handler does its job and processes the request.

14. *PostRequestHandlerExecute*   This event is raised when the handler has generated the response text.

15. *ReleaseRequestState*   This event is raised when the handler releases its state information and prepares to shut down. This event is used by the session state module to update the dirty session state if necessary.

16. *PostReleaseRequestState*   The state, as modified by the page execution, has been persisted. Any relevant response filtering is done at this point. (I'll say more about this topic later.)

17. *UpdateRequestCache*   The ASP.NET runtime determines whether the generated output, now also properly filtered by registered modules, should be cached to be reused with upcoming identical requests.

18. *PostUpdateRequestCache*   The page has been saved to the output cache if it was configured to do so.

19. *LogRequest*   The event indicates that the runtime is ready to log the results of the request. Logging is guaranteed to execute even if errors occur.

20. *PostLogRequest*   The request has been logged.

21. *EndRequest*   This event fires as the final step of the HTTP pipeline. Control passes back to the *HttpRuntime* object, which is responsible for the actual forwarding of the response to the client. At this point, the text has not been sent yet.

If an unhandled error occurs at any point during the processing, it is treated using the code (if any) associated with the *Error* event. As mentioned, events can be handled in HTTP modules as well as in *global.asax*.

> **Note**   The *Error* event provides a centralized console for capturing any unhandled exception in order to recover gracefully or just to capture the state of the application and log it. By writing an HTTP module that just intercepts the *Error* event, you have a simple but terribly effective and reusable mechanism for error handling and logging. At the end of the day, this is the core of the engine of popular tools for ASP.NET error handling, logging, and reporting—ELMAH.

The *global.asax* File

The *global.asax* file is used by Web applications to handle some application-level events raised by the ASP.NET runtime or by registered HTTP modules. The *global.asax* file is optional. If it is missing, the ASP.NET runtime environment simply assumes you have no application or module event handlers defined. To be functional, the *global.asax* file must be located in the root directory of the application. Only one *global.asax* file per application is accepted. Any *global.asax* files placed in subdirectories are simply ignored. Note that Microsoft Visual Studio doesn't list *global.asax* in the items you can add to the project if there already is one.

Compiling *global.asax*

When the application is started, *global.asax*, if present, is parsed into a source class and compiled. The resultant assembly is created in the temporary directory just as any other dynamically generated assembly would be. The following listing shows the skeleton of the C# code that ASP.NET generates for any *global.asax* file:

```
namespace ASP
{
    public class global_asax : System.Web.HttpApplication
    {
        //
        // The source code of the "global.asax" file is flushed
        // here verbatim. For this reason, the following code
        // in global.asax would generate a compile error.
        //     int i;
        //     i = 2;  // can't have statements outside methods
        //
    }
}
```

The class is named *ASP.global_asax* and is derived from the *HttpApplication* base class. In most cases, you deploy *global.asax* as a separate text file; however, you can also write it as a class and compile it either in a separate assembly or within your project's assembly. The class source code must follow the outline shown earlier and, above all, must derive from *HttpApplication*. The assembly with the compiled version of *global.asax* must be deployed in the application's *Bin* subdirectory.

Note, though, that even if you isolate the logic of the *global.asax* file in a precompiled assembly, you still need to have a (codeless) *global.asax* file that refers to the assembly, as shown in the following code:

```
<%@ Application Inherits="MyApp.Global" %>
```

You'll learn more about the syntax of *global.asax* in the next section, "Syntax of *global.asax*." With a precompiled global application file, you certainly don't risk exposing your source code over the Web to malicious attacks. However, even if you leave it as source code, you're somewhat safe.

The *global.asax* file, in fact, is configured so that any direct URL request for it is automatically rejected by Internet Information Services (IIS). In this way, external users cannot download or view the code it contains. The trick that enables this behavior is the following line of code, excerpted from *machine.config*:

```
<add verb="*" path="*.asax" type="System.Web.HttpForbiddenHandler" />
```

ASP.NET registers with IIS to handle *.asax* resources, but then it processes those direct requests through the *HttpForbiddenHandler* HTTP handler. As a result, when a browser requests an *.asax* resource, an error message is displayed on the page, as shown in Figure 16-1.

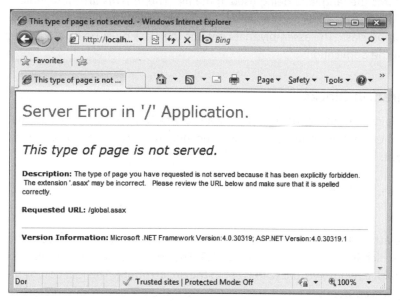

FIGURE 16-1 Direct access to forbidden resources, such as *.asax files, results in a server error.

When the *global.asax* file of a running application is modified, the ASP.NET runtime detects the change and prepares to shut down and restart the application. It waits until all pending requests are completed and then fires the *Application_End* event. When the next request from a browser arrives, ASP.NET reparses and recompiles the *global.asax* file, and again raises the *Application_Start* event.

Syntax of *global.asax*

A few elements determine the syntax of the *global.asax* file. They are application directives, code declaration blocks, server-side *<object>* tags, and static properties. These elements can be used in any order and number to compose a *global.asax* file.

Application Directives

The *global.asax* file supports three directives: *@Application*, *@Import*, and *@Assembly*. The *@Import* and *@Assembly* directives work as shown in Chapter 3. The *@Import* directive imports a namespace into an application; the *@Assembly* directive links an assembly to the application at compile time.

The @*Application* directive supports a few attributes: *Description*, *Language*, and *Inherits*. *Description* can contain any text you want to use to describe the behavior of the application. This text has only a documentation purpose and is blissfully ignored by the ASP.NET parser. *Language* indicates the language being used in the file. The *Inherits* attribute indicates a code-behind class for the application to inherit. It can be the name of any class derived from the *HttpApplication* class. The assembly that contains the class must be located in the *Bin* subdirectory of the application.

Code Declaration Blocks

A *global.asax* file can contain code wrapped by a *<script>* tag. Just as for pages, the *<script>* tag must have the *runat* attribute set to *server*. The *language* attribute indicates the language used throughout:

```
<script language="C#" runat="server">
    ...
</script>
```

If the *language* attribute is not specified, ASP.NET defaults to the language set in the configuration, which is Microsoft Visual Basic .NET. The source code can also be loaded from an external file, whose virtual path is set in the *Src* attribute. The location of the file is resolved using *Server.MapPath*—that is, starting under the physical root directory of the Web application.

```
<script language="C#" runat="server" src="somecode.aspx.cs" />
```

In this case, any other code in the declaration *<script>* block is ignored. Notice that ASP.NET enforces syntax rules on the *<script>* tag. The *runat* attribute is mandatory, and if the block has no content, the *Src* must be specified.

Server-Side *<object>* Tags

The server-side *<object>* tag lets you create new objects using a declarative syntax. The *<object>* tag can take three forms, as shown in the following lines of code, depending on the specified reference type:

```
<object id="..." runat="server" scope="..." class="..." />
<object id="..." runat="server" scope="..." progid="..." />
<object id="..." runat="server" scope="..." classid="..." />
```

In the first case, the object is identified by the name of the class and assembly that contains it. In the last two cases, the object to create is a COM object identified by the program identifier (*progid*) and the 128-bit CLSID, respectively. As one can easily guess, the *classid*, *progid*, and *class* attributes are mutually exclusive. If you use more than one within a single server-side *<object>* tag, a compile error is generated. Objects declared in this way are loaded when the application is started.

The *scope* attribute indicates the scope at which the object is declared. The allowable values are defined in Table 16-5. Unless otherwise specified, the server-side object is valid only within the boundaries of the HTTP pipeline that processes the current request. Other settings that increase the object's lifetime are *application* and *session*.

TABLE 16-5 Feasible Scopes for Server-Side *<object>* Tags

Scope	Description
pipeline	Default setting, indicates the object is available only within the context of the current HTTP request
application	Indicates the object is added to the *StaticObjects* collection of the *Application* object and is shared among all pages in the application
session	Indicates the object is added to the *StaticObjects* collection of the *Session* object and is shared among all pages in the current session

Static Properties

If you define static properties in the *global.asax* file, they will be accessible for reading and writing by all pages in the application:

```
<script language="C#" runat="server">
    public static int Counter = 0;
</script>
```

The *Counter* property defined in the preceding code works like an item stored in *Application*—namely, it is globally visible across pages and sessions. Consider that concurrent access to *Counter* is not serialized; on the other hand, you have a strong-typed, direct global item whose access speed is much faster than retrieving the same piece of information from a generic collection such as *Application*.

To access the property from a page, you must use the *ASP.global_asax* qualifier, shown here:

```
Response.Write(ASP.global_asax.Counter.ToString());
```

If you don't particularly like the *ASP.global_asax* prefix, you can alias it as long as you use C#. Add the following code to a C#-based page (or code-behind class) for which you need to access the globals:

```
using Globals = ASP.global_asax;
```

The preceding statement creates an alias for the *ASP.global_asax* class (or whatever name your *global.asax* class has). The alias—*Globals* in this sample code—can be used throughout your code wherever *ASP.global_asax* is accepted. In ASP.NET 4, however, you can also rely on the *dynamic* type.

The *HttpContext* Class

During the various steps of the request's chain of execution, an object gets passed along from class to class—this object is the *HttpContext* object. *HttpContext* encapsulates all the information available about an individual HTTP request that ASP.NET is going to handle. The *HttpContext* class is instantiated by the *HttpRuntime* object while the request processing mechanism is being set up. Next, the object is flowed throughout the various stages of the request's lifetime.

> **Important** Before I get into the details of *HttpContext* and other ASP.NET intrinsic objects, I should note that in ASP.NET 4 all these objects inherit from a base class. For example, *HttpContext* derives from *HttpContextBase* and *HttpResponse* extends the capabilities of *HttpResponseBase*. The reason is to make it easier to write unit tests to check the behavior of code-behind classes. By using base classes, you can more easily create mocks of intrinsic objects and inject them into the classes. In Chapter 15, "The Model-View-Presenter Pattern," you saw an approach to testability that will benefit from base classes for intrinsic objects. Note that the ASP.NET Cache is not included in the list of objects with a base class.

Properties of the *HttpContext* Class

Table 16-6 enumerates all the properties exposed by the *HttpContext* class. The class represents a single entry point for a number of intrinsic objects such as classic ASP intrinsics and ASP.NET-specific *Cache* and *User* objects.

TABLE 16-6 *HttpContext* **Properties**

Property	Description
AllErrors	Gets an array of *Exception* objects, each of which represents an error that occurred while processing the request.
Application	Gets an instance of the *HttpApplicationState* class, which contains the global and shared states of the application.
ApplicationInstance	Gets or sets the *HttpApplication* object for the current request. The actual type is the *global.asax* code-behind class. It makes a cast to access public properties and methods you might have defined in *global.asax*.
Cache	Gets the ASP.NET *Cache* object for the current request.
Current	Gets the *HttpContext* object for the current request.
CurrentHandler	Gets the handler for the request that is currently being executed by the application. It is a read-only property that returns the value stored in *Handler*.
CurrentNotification	Indicates which event in the request pipeline is currently processing the request. *It works only if the application is running in integrated pipeline mode.*

Property	Description
Error	Gets the first exception (if any) that has been raised while processing the current request.
Handler	Gets or sets the HTTP handler for the current request.
IsCustomErrorEnabled	Indicates whether custom error handling is enabled for the current request.
IsDebuggingEnabled	Indicates whether the current request is in debug mode.
IsPostNotification	Indicates whether the current request has been processed and whether we're in the middle of a *PostXxx* stage. *It works only if the application is running in integrated pipeline mode.*
Items	Gets a name/value collection (hash table) that can be used to share custom data and objects between HTTP modules and HTTP handlers during the request lifetime.
PreviousHandler	Gets the last handler before the current request was executed.
Profile	Gets the object that represents the profile of the current user.
Request	Gets an instance of the *HttpRequest* class, which represents the current HTTP request.
Response	Gets an instance of the *HttpResponse* class, which sends HTTP response data to the client.
Server	Gets an instance of the *HttpServerUtility* class, which provides helper methods for processing Web requests.
Session	Gets an instance of the *HttpSessionState* class, which manages session-specific data.
SkipAuthorization	Gets or sets a Boolean value that specifies whether the URL-based authorization module will skip the authorization check for the current request. This is *false* by default. It is mostly used by authentication modules that need to redirect to a page that allows anonymous access.
Timestamp	Gets a *DateTime* object that represents the initial timestamp of the current request.
Trace	Gets the *TraceContext* object for the current response.
User	Gets or sets the *IPrincipal* object that represents the identity of the user making the request.

The *Current* property is a frequently used static member that returns the *HttpContext* object for the request being processed.

The *Items* property is a dictionary object—a hash table, to be exact—that can be used to share information between the modules and handlers involved with the particular request. By using this property, each custom HTTP module or handler can add its own information to the *HttpContext* object serving the request. The information stored in *Items* is ultimately made available to the page. The lifetime of this information is limited to the request.

Methods of the *HttpContext* Class

Table 16-7 lists the methods specific to the *HttpContext* class.

TABLE 16-7 *HttpContext* **Methods**

Method	Description
AddError	Adds an exception object to the *AllErrors* collection.
ClearError	Clears all errors for the current request.
GetAppConfig	Returns requested configuration information for the current application. The information is collected from *machine.config* and the application's main *web.config* files. *It is marked as obsolete in ASP.NET 4.0.*
GetConfig	Returns requested configuration information for the current request. The information is collected at the level of the requested URL, taking into account any child *web.config* files defined in subdirectories. *It is marked as obsolete in ASP.NET 4.0.*
GetGlobalResourceObject	Loads a global resource.
GetLocalResourceObject	Loads a local, page-specific resource.
GetSection	Returns requested configuration information for the current request.
RemapHandler	Allows you to programmatically set the handler to serve the request. It must be invoked before the runtime reaches the *MapRequestHandler* stage. If the *Handler* property of *HttpContext* is not null at that stage, the runtime defaults to it.
RewritePath	Mostly for internal use; overwrites URL and the query string of the current *Request* object.
SetSessionStateBehavior	Allows you to programmatically set the expected behavior for the session state—either read-only, read-write, or no session. It must be called before the *AcquireRequestState* event fires.

Over time, the *GetSection* method has replaced *GetConfig*, which has been marked as obsolete and should not be used. If you have old code using *GetConfig*, just change the name of the method. The prototype is the same. Also, *GetAppConfig* is marked as obsolete in ASP.NET 4. It has been replaced by *GetWebApplicationSection*, a static member of the new *WebConfigurationManager* class. Also, in this case, no changes are required to be made to the prototype. Let's spend a few more words to dig out some interesting characteristics of other methods of the *HttpContext* class.

URL Rewriting

The *RewritePath* method lets you change the URL of the current request on the fly, thus performing a sort of internal redirect. As a result, the displayed page is the one you set through *RewritePath*; the page shown in the address bar remains the originally requested one. The change of the final URL takes place on the server and, more importantly, within the context of the same call. *RewritePath* should be used carefully and mainly from within the *global.asax* file. If you use *RewritePath* in the context of a postback event, you can experience some view-state problems.

```
protected void Application_BeginRequest(Object sender, EventArgs e)
{
   var context = HttpContext.Current;
   var o = context.Request["id"];
   if (o != null)
   {
      var id = (Int32) o;
      var url = GetPageUrlFromId(id);
      context.RewritePath(url);
   }
}
protected String GetPageUrlFromId(Int32 id)
{
   // Return a full URL based on the input ID value.
   ...
}
```

The preceding code rewrites a URL such as *page.aspx?id=1234* to a specific page whose real URL is read out of a database or a configuration file.

> **Note** In general, IIS-level URL rewriting (which was discussed in Chapter 2) is a better alternative. The newer and more general ASP.NET Routing is perhaps better suited for a more complex use case, but it can achieve the same result pretty easily.

Loading Resources Programmatically

In Chapter 7, "Working with the Page," we discussed expressions allowed in ASP.NET pages to bind control properties to embedded global or local resources. The *$Resources* and *meta:resourcekey* expressions for global and local resources, respectively, work only at design time. What if you need to generate text programmatically that embeds resource expressions, instead? Both the *Page* and *HttpContext* classes support a pair of programmatic methods to retrieve the content of resources embedded in the application.

GetGlobalResourceObject retrieves a global resource—that is, a resource defined in an *.resx* file located in the *App_GlobalResources* special folder. *GetLocalResourceObject* does the same for an *.resx* file located in the *App_LocalResources* special folder of a given page.

```
msg1.Text = (String) HttpContext.GetGlobalResourceObject(
    "Test", "MyString");
msg2.Text = (String) HttpContext.GetLocalResourceObject(
    "/MyApp/Samples/ResPage.aspx", "PageResource1.Title");
```

The first parameter you pass to *GetGlobalResourceObject* indicates the name of the *.resx* resource file without an extension; the second parameter is the name of the resource to retrieve. As for *GetLocalResourceObject*, the first argument indicates the virtual path of the page; the second is the name of the resource.

The *Server* Object

In the all-encompassing container represented by the *HttpContext* object, a few popular objects also find their place. Among them are *Server*, *Request*, and *Response*. They are old acquaintances for ASP developers and, indeed, they are feature-rich elements of the ASP.NET programming toolkit. The set of properties and methods still makes these objects a fundamental resource for developers. Let's learn more about them, starting with the *Server* object.

The functionality of the ASP intrinsic *Server* object in ASP.NET is implemented by the *HttpServerUtility* class. An instance of the type is created when ASP.NET begins to process the request and is then stored as part of the request context. The bunch of helper methods that *HttpServerUtility* provides are publicly exposed to modules and handlers—including *global. asax*, pages, and Web services—through the *Server* property of the *HttpContext* object. In addition, to maintain ASP.NET coding as close as possible to the ASP programming style, several other commonly used ASP.NET objects also expose their own *Server* property. In this way, developers can use in the code, say, *Server.MapPath* without incurring compile errors.

Properties of the *HttpServerUtility* Class

This class provides two properties, named *MachineName* and *ScriptTimeout*. The *MachineName* property returns the machine name, whereas *ScriptTimeout* gets and sets the time in seconds that a request is allowed to be processed. This property accepts integers and defaults to 90 seconds; however, it is set to a virtually infinite value if the page runs with the attribute *debug=true*, as shown here:

```
this.Server.ScriptTimeout = 30000000;
```

The *ScriptTimeout* property is explicitly and automatically set in the constructor of the dynamically created class that represents the page.

Methods of the *HttpServerUtility* Class

Table 16-8 lists all methods exposed by the *HttpServerUtility* class. As you can see, they constitute a group of helper methods that come in handy at various stages of page execution. The class provides a couple of methods to create instances of COM components and a few others to deal with errors. Another group of methods relates to the decoding and encoding of content and URLs.

TABLE 16-8 **Methods of the *Server* Object**

Method	Description
ClearError	Clears the last exception that was thrown for the request.
CreateObject	Creates an instance of the specified COM object.
CreateObjectFromClsid	Creates an instance of the COM object identified by the specified CLSID. The class identifier is expressed as a string.
Execute	Passes control to the specified page for execution. The child page executes like a subroutine. The output can be retained in a writer object or automatically flushed in the parent response buffer.
GetLastError	Returns the last exception that was thrown.
HtmlDecode	Decodes a string that has been encoded to eliminate invalid HTML characters. For example, it translates < into <.
HtmlEncode	Encodes a string to be displayed in a browser. For example, it encodes < into <.
MapPath	Returns the physical path that corresponds to the specified virtual path on the Web server.
Transfer	Works as a kind of server-side redirect. It terminates the execution of the current page and passes control to the specified page. Unlike *Execute*, control is not passed back to the caller page.
UrlDecode	Decodes a string encoded for HTTP transmission to the server in a URL. The decoded string can be returned as a string or output to a writer.
UrlEncode	Encodes a string for HTTP transmission to a client in a URL. The encoded string can be returned as a string or output to a writer.
UrlPathEncode	Encodes only the path portion of a URL string, and returns the encoded string. This method leaves the query string content intact.
UrlTokenDecode	Converts a URL string token, which encodes binary data as base 64 digits, to its equivalent byte array representation.
UrlTokenEncode	Encodes a byte array into its equivalent string representation using base 64 digits, which is usable for transmission on the URL.

HTML and URL encoding are ways of encoding characters to ensure that the transmitted text is not misunderstood by the receiving browser. HTML encoding, in particular, replaces <, >, &, and quotes with equivalent HTML entities such as *<*, *>*, *&*, and *"*. It also encodes blanks, punctuation characters, and in general, all characters not allowed in an HTML stream. On the other hand, URL encoding is aimed at fixing the text transmitted in URL strings. In URL encoding, the same critical characters are replaced with different character entities than in HTML encoding.

Embedding Another Page's Results

The *Execute* method allows you to consider an external page as a subroutine. When the execution flow reaches the *Server.Execute* call, control is passed to the specified page. The execution of the current page is suspended, and the external page is spawned. The response text generated by the child execution is captured and processed according to the particular overload of *Execute* that has been used. Table 16-9 lists the overloads of the *Execute* method.

TABLE 16-9 Overloads of the *Execute* Method

Overload	Description
Execute(string);	You pass the URL of the page, and the response text is automatically embedded in the main page.
Execute(string, TextWriter);	The response text is accumulated in the specified text writer.
Execute(string, bool);	The same description as for previous item, except that you can choose whether to preserve the *QueryString* and *Form* collections. *True* is the default setting.
Execute(IHttpHandler, TextWriter, bool);	You indicate the HTTP handler to transfer the current request to. The response is captured by the text writer.
Execute(string, TextWriter, bool);	The response text is captured by the specified text writer, and the *QueryString* and *Form* collections are either preserved or not preserved, as specified.

Note that if a *TextWriter* object is specified, the response text of the child execution is accumulated into the writer object so that the main page output can be used later at will. Here's some sample code:

```
void Page_Load(Object sender, EventArgs e)
{
    var builder = new StringBuilder();
    builder.Append("<b>Response generated before
                Execute is called</b><hr/>");

    // Capture child content
    var writer = new StringWriter();
    Server.Execute("child.aspx", writer);
    builder.Append(writer.ToString());

    builder.Append("<hr/><b>Response generated after
                the call to Execute.</b>");

    Label1.Text = builder.ToString();
}
```

It's interesting to look at the internal implementation of the *Execute* method. Both the main and child pages are run by the same *HttpApplication* object as if they were the same request. What happens within the folds of *Execute* is a sort of context switch. First, the method obtains an HTTP handler from the application factory to serve the new request. The original handler of the main request is cached and replaced with the new handler. The spawned page inherits the context of the parent; when this step is finished, any modification made to *Session* or *Application* is immediately visible to the main page.

The handler switching makes the whole operation extremely fast, as there's no need to create a new object to serve the request. When the child page returns, the original handler is restored. The execution of the main page continues from the point at which it was stopped, but it uses the context inherited from the child page.

> **Caution** ASP.NET directly calls the handler indicated by the *Execute* method without reapplying any authentication and authorization logic. If your security policy requires clients to have proper authorization to access the resource, the application should force reauthorization. You can force reauthorization by using the *Response.Redirect* method instead of *Execute*. When *Redirect* is called, the browser places a new request in the system, which will be authenticated and authorized as usual by IIS and ASP.NET. As an alternative, you can verify whether the user has permission to call the page by defining roles and checking the user's role before the application calls the *Execute* method.

Server-Side Redirection

The *Transfer* method differs from the *Execute* method in that it terminates the current page after executing the specified page. The new page runs as if it was the originally requested one. The *Transfer* method has the following overloads:

```
public void Transfer(String);
public void Transfer(String, Boolean);
public void Transfer(IHttpHandler, Boolean);
```

The string parameter indicates the destination URL. The Boolean parameter indicates what to do with regard to the *QueryString* and *Form* collections. If the parameter is *true*, the collections are preserved; otherwise, they are cleared and made unavailable to the destination page (which is the recommended approach). You can also directly indicate the HTTP handler to invoke, with the same security issues that were mentioned for *Execute*.

All the code that might be following the call to *Transfer* in the main page is never executed. In the end, *Transfer* is just a page redirect method. However, it is particularly efficient for two reasons. First, no roundtrip to the client is requested, as is the case, for example, with *Response.Redirect*. Second, the same *HttpApplication* that was serving the caller request is reused, thus limiting the impact on the ASP.NET infrastructure.

The *HttpResponse* Object

In ASP.NET, the HTTP response information is encapsulated in the *HttpResponse* class. An instance of the class is created when the HTTP pipeline is set up to serve the request. The instance is then linked to the *HttpContext* object associated with the request and exposed via the *Response* property. The *HttpResponse* class defines methods and properties to manipulate the text that will be sent to the browser. Although user-defined ASP.NET code never needs to use the *HttpResponse* constructor, looking at it is still useful to get the gist of the class:

```
public HttpResponse(TextWriter writer);
```

As you can see, the constructor takes a writer object, which will then be used to accumulate the response text. All calls made to *Response.Write* (and similar output methods) are resolved in terms of internal calls to the specified writer object.

Properties of the *HttpResponse* Class

All properties of the class are grouped and described in Table 16-10. You set a few of these properties to configure key fields on the HTTP response packet, such as content type, character set, page expiration, and status code.

TABLE 16-10 *HttpResponse* Properties

Property	Description
Buffer	Indicates whether the response text should be buffered and sent only at the end of the request. This property is deprecated and provided only for backward compatibility with classic ASP. ASP.NET applications should instead use *BufferOutput*.
BufferOutput	Gets or sets a Boolean value that indicates whether response buffering is enabled. The default is *true*.
Cache	Gets the caching policy set for the page. The caching policy is an *HttpCachePolicy* object that can be used to set the cache-specific HTTP headers for the current response.
CacheControl	Sets the *Cache-Control* HTTP header. Acceptable values are *Public*, *Private*, or *No-Cache*. The property is deprecated in favor of *Cache*.
Charset	Gets or sets a string for the HTTP character set of the output stream. If set to *null*, it suppresses the *Content-Type* header.
ContentEncoding	Gets or sets an object of type *Encoding* for the character encoding of the output stream.
ContentType	Gets or sets the string that represents the Multipurpose Internet Mail Extensions (MIME) type of the output stream. The default value is *text/html*.
Cookies	Gets a collection (*HttpCookieCollection*) object that contains instances of the *HttpCookie* class generated on the server. All the cookies in the collection will be transmitted to the client through the *set-cookie* HTTP header.
Expires	Gets or sets the number of minutes before a page cached on a browser expires. Provided for compatibility with ASP, the property is deprecated in favor of *Cache*.
ExpiresAbsolute	Gets or sets the absolute date and time at which the page expires in the browser cache. Provided for compatibility with ASP, the property is deprecated in favor of *Cache*.

Property	Description
Filter	Gets or sets a filter *Stream* object through which all HTTP output is directed.
HeaderEncoding	Gets or sets an *Encoding* object that represents the encoding for the current header output stream.
Headers	Gets the collection of response headers. *The property is supported only in integrated pipeline mode.*
IsClientConnected	Indicates whether the client is still connected.
IsRequestBeingRedirected	Indicates whether the request is being redirected.
Output	Gets the writer object used to send text out.
OutputStream	Gets the *Stream* object used to output binary data to the response stream.
RedirectLocation	Gets or a sets a string for the value of the *Location* header.
Status	Sets the string returned to the client describing the status of the response. Provided for compatibility with ASP, the property is deprecated in favor of *StatusDescription*.
StatusCode	Gets or sets an integer value for the HTTP status code of the output returned to the client. The default value is *200*.
SubStatusCode	Indicates the sub status code of the response. *The property is supported only in integrated pipeline mode.*
StatusDescription	Gets or sets the HTTP status string, which is a description of the overall status of the response returned to the client. The default value is *OK*.
SuppressContent	Gets or sets a Boolean value that indicates whether HTTP content should be sent to the client. This is set to *false* by default; if it is set to *true*, only headers are sent.
TrySkipIisCustomErrors	Boolean property, indicates whether or not custom errors set at the IIS level should by ignored by ASP.NET. The default value when running in Integrated mode is *false. The property is effective only for applications hosted in IIS 7 or later.*

Let's find out more about cache and expiration properties.

Setting the Response Cache Policy

The response object has three properties dedicated to controlling the ability of the page being sent to the browser to be cached. The *Expires* and *ExpiresAbsolute* properties define relative and absolute times, respectively, at which the page cached on the client expires and is no longer used by the browser to serve a user request. In fact, if the user navigates to a currently cached page, the cached version is displayed and no roundtrip occurs to the server. A third property somehow related to page caching is *CacheControl*. The property sets a particular HTTP header—the *Cache-Control* header. The *Cache-Control* header controls how a document is to be cached across the network. These properties represent the old-fashioned programming style and exist mostly for compatibility with classic ASP applications.

In ASP.NET, all caching capabilities are grouped in the *HttpCachePolicy* class. With regard to page caching, the class has a double role. It provides methods for both setting cache-specific HTTP headers and controlling the ASP.NET page output cache. In this chapter, we're mostly interested in the HTTP headers, and we'll keep page output caching warm for Chapter 18.

To set the visibility of a page in a client cache, use the *SetCacheability* method of the *HttpCachePolicy* class. To set an expiration time, use the *SetExpires* method, which takes for input an absolute *DateTime* object. Finally, to set a lifetime for the cached page, pass to *SetExpires* the current time plus the desired interval.

Note In the case of conflicting cache policies, ASP.NET maintains the most restrictive settings. For example, if a page contains two controls that set the *Cache-Control* header to *public* and *private*, the most restrictive policy will be used. In this case, *Cache-Control: Private* is what will be sent to the client.

Setting an Output Filter

In ASP.NET, a new component makes its debut—the *response filter*. A response filter is a *Stream*-derived object associated with the *HttpResponse* object. It monitors and filters any output being generated by the page. If you set the *Filter* property with the instance of a class derived from *Stream*, all output being written to the underlying HTTP writer first passes through your output filter.

The custom filter, if any, is invoked during the *HttpResponse*'s *Flush* method before the actual text is flushed to the client. An output filter is useful for applying the final touches to the markup, and it is sometimes used to compact or fix the markup generated by controls.

Building a response filter is a matter of creating a new stream class and overriding some of the methods. The class should have a constructor that accepts a *Stream* object. In light of this, a response filter class is more a wrapper stream class than a purely inherited stream class. If you simply try to set *Response.Filter* with a new instance of, say, *MemoryStream* or *FileStream*, an exception is thrown.

The following listing shows how to create a stream class that works as a response filter. For simplicity, the class inherits from *MemoryStream*. You might want to make it inherit from *Stream*, but in this case you need to override (because they are abstract) a number of methods, such as *CanRead*, *CanWrite*, *CanSeek*, and *Read*. The class converts lowercase characters to uppercase ones.

```
public class MyFilterStream : MemoryStream
{
    private Stream m_Stream;

    public MyFilterStream(Stream filterStream)
    {
        m_Stream = filterStream;
    }
```

```
    // The Write method actually does the filtering
    public override void Write(byte[] buffer, int offset, int count)
    {
        // Grab the output as a string
        string buf = UTF8Encoding.UTF8.GetString(buffer, offset, count);

        // Apply some changes
        // Change lowercase chars to uppercase
        buf = buf.ToUpper();

        // Write the resulting string back to the response stream
        byte[] data = UTF8Encoding.UTF8.GetBytes(buf.ToString());
        m_Stream.Write(data, 0, data.Length);
    }
}
```

Use the following code to associate this output filter with the *Response.Filter* property. Here's a sample page:

```
void Page_Load(object sender, EventArgs e)
{
    Response.Filter = new MyFilterStream(Response.Filter);
}
```

Response filters provide an interesting opportunity for developers to build more powerful applications, but I caution you to be careful when considering this option. As the sample demonstrates, changing the case of the entire output is not a smart move. If done without care, the change ends up affecting the view state and the internal script code, both of which consist of case-sensitive text, seriously compromising the functionality of the page. Second, filters must be activated on a per-page basis. If you need to filter all the pages in a Web site, you're better off writing an HTTP module.

Methods of the *HttpResponse* Class

Table 16-11 lists all the methods defined on the *HttpResponse* class.

TABLE 16-11 *HttpResponse* **Methods**

Method	Description
AddCacheDependency	Adds an array of cache dependencies to make the cached page output invalid if any dependency gets broken. In the array, you can have any class that inherits from *CacheDependency*.
AddCacheItemDependencies	Adds an array of strings representing names of items in the ASP.NET *Cache*. When any of the specified items vary, the cached page output becomes invalid.
AddCacheItemDependency	Description is the same as for the previous item, except that *AddCacheItemDependency* adds a single cache item name.

Method	Description
AddFileDependencies	Adds a group of file names to the collection of file names on which the current page is dependent. When any of the files are modified, the cached output of the current page is deemed invalid.
AddFileDependency	Adds a single file name to the collection of file names on which the current page is dependent. If the file is modified, the cached output of the current page becomes invalid.
AddHeader	Adds an HTTP header to the output stream. It is provided for compatibility with previous versions of ASP. In ASP.NET, you should use *AppendHeader*.
AppendCookie	Adds an HTTP cookie to the cookie collection.
AppendHeader	Adds an HTTP header to the output stream.
AppendToLog	Adds custom log information to the IIS log file.
ApplyAppPathModifier	Adds a session ID to the specified virtual path, and returns the result. It is mostly used with cookieless sessions to construct absolute *HREF*s for hyperlinks.
BinaryWrite	Writes binary characters to the HTTP output stream. It is subject to failures with very large files. (See the references to this method later in the chapter.)
Clear	Clears all content output from the buffer stream.
ClearContent	Calls into *Clear*.
ClearHeaders	Clears all headers from the buffer stream.
Close	Closes the socket connection with the client.
DisableKernelCache	Disables kernel caching for the current response. If kernel caching is not supported, the method has no effect.
End	Sends all buffered text to the client, stops execution, and raises the end event for the request.
Flush	Sends all currently buffered output to the client.
Pics	Appends a PICS-Label HTTP header to the output. PICS stands for *Platform for Internet Content Selection* and is a World Wide Web Consortium (W3C) standard for rating pages. Any string is acceptable as long as it doesn't exceed 255 characters.
Redirect	Redirects a client to a new URL. It needs a roundtrip. The browser receives an HTTP 302 status code, meaning that the resource has been temporarily moved.
RedirectPermanent	Redirects a client to a new URL. It needs a roundtrip. The browser receives an HTTP 301 status code, meaning that the resource has been permanently moved to a new location.
RedirectToRoute	Redirects a client to a URL specified as a route. The method works if Web Forms routing is used to specify routes.
RemoveOutputCacheItem	A static method that takes a file system path and removes from the cache all cached items associated with the specified path.
SetCookie	Updates an existing cookie in the cookie collection.
TransmitFile	Just like *BinaryWrite* and *WriteFile*, it writes the specified file directly to the output stream. You can safely use *TransmitFile* regardless of the size of the file that you want to transmit.

Method	Description
Write	Writes content to the underlying output stream. The method can write a string, a single character, or an array of characters, as well as an object. In this case, though, what gets written is the output of the object's *ToString* method.
WriteFile	Writes the specified file (or a portion of it) directly to the output stream. The file can be identified with its path or a Win32 handle (an *IntPtr* object). It is subject to failures with very large files. (See the references to this method later in the chapter.)
WriteSubstitution	Allows fragments of a page to be substituted and sent to the output cache. (We'll cover this method in more detail in Chapter 18.)

Output Caching Features

The *HttpResponse* class has several methods to make the page response it represents dependent on files or cache item changes. The methods *AddFileDependency* and *AddCacheItemDependency* (and their versions that handle multiple dependencies) make the page response invalid when the specified file or files or cached item or items are modified.

This is a simple form of programmatic page output caching, not as powerful as the API that we'll examine in Chapter 18, but still worth a look. The API discussed in Chapter 18 is superior because it allows you to control how the page response is cached, assigning also the cached output a duration and perhaps a location.

The method *AddCacheDependency* completes the offering, as it gives you the possibility to make the page response dependent on any dependency object available to your application, including custom dependency objects. See Chapter 18 for more details on custom dependency objects.

Large File Transmission

As you can see, there are three methods for writing potentially large chunks of data down to the output stream: *BinaryWrite*, *WriteFile*, and *TransmitFile*. Of the three methods, *TransmitFile* is the most stable and reliable, although you won't notice any significant difference for most files.

Both the *WriteFile* and *BinaryWrite* methods seem perfect for streaming binary data down to the client. However, both can put the Web server memory under pressure if called to work on very large files. Why? It's because both methods load the entire data block (the contents of the file or the byte array) into the Web server's memory. For large files, this can cause severe problems that can culminate in the recycling of the ASP.NET process. The *TransmitFile* method is designed to elegantly work around the problem. It sends output directly from a file to the ASP.NET ISAPI extension and then down to the client, without passing a humongous string to the ISAPI extension.

Note Although *TransmitFile* makes large file downloads more stable than ever and fixes the problem of recycling, it is far from being a full solution to the problem of tracking and resuming large file downloads. For example, if a download fails, for whatever reason, *TransmitFile* can start it again only from the beginning. The article found at the following Web site discusses a better approach to the problem: *http://www.devx.com/dotnet/Article/22533*.

The *HttpRequest* Object

The *HttpRequest* object groups all the information contained in the HTTP packet that represents the incoming Web request. The contents of the various HTTP headers, the query string, or the form's input fields, path, and URL information are organized in a series of collections and other ad hoc objects for easy and effective programmatic access. The *HttpRequest* object is populated as soon as ASP.NET begins working on a Web request, and it's made available through the *Request* property of *HttpContext*.

HttpRequest exposes a fair number of properties and is one of the objects that has been more significantly enriched in the transition from ASP to ASP.NET.

Properties of the *HttpRequest* Class

The class properties can be categorized into three groups based on the type of information they contain: the type of the request, client data, and connection.

Information About the Request

Table 16-12 lists the properties that define the type of request being issued.

TABLE 16-12 Properties Describing the Request Type

Property	Description
AcceptTypes	Gets an array of strings denoting the list of MIME types supported by the client for the specified request.
AnonymousID	Indicates the ID of the anonymous user, if any. The identity refers to the string generated by the *AnonymousIdentification* module and has nothing to do with the identity of the IIS anonymous user.
Browser	Gets an *HttpBrowserCapabilities* object that contains information about the capabilities of the client's browser.
ContentEncoding	Gets or sets an *Encoding* object that represents the client's character set. If specified, this property overrides the ASP.NET default encoding.
ContentLength	Gets the length in bytes of the content sent by the client.
ContentType	Gets or sets the MIME content type of the incoming request.
CurrentExecutionFilePath	Gets the current virtual path of the request even when the client is redirected to another page via *Execute* or *Transfer*. The *FilePath* property, on the other hand, always returns the path to the originally requested page.

Property	Description
FilePath	Gets the virtual path of the current request. The path doesn't change in cases of server-side page redirection.
HttpMethod	Gets a string that denotes the HTTP method used for the request. Values are GET, POST, or HEAD.
RequestType	Gets or sets a string that denotes the HTTP command used to issue the request. It can be GET or POST.
TotalBytes	Gets the total number of bytes in the input stream. This property differs from *ContentLength* in that it also includes headers.
UserAgent	Gets a string that identifies the browser. This property gets the raw content of the user agent header.

The anonymous ID is usually transmitted through a cookie (whose default name is .ASPXANONYMOUS) and serves the purpose of giving an identity to nonauthenticated users, mainly for user profile functions. The anonymous ID is a GUID and is transmitted as clear text. It doesn't play any relevant role with authentication and security; it is merely a way to track nonregistered users as they move around the site. (See Chapter 7 for profiles and Chapter 19, "ASP.NET Security," for user authentication.)

Initially, *CurrentExecutionFilePath* and *FilePath* share the same content—the requested URL. However, in cases of server-side redirects, the value of *CurrentExecutionFilePath* is automatically updated. You should check *CurrentExecutionFilePath* for up-to-date information about the target URL.

The *HttpBrowserCapabilities* object groups in a single place values that identify a fair number of browser capabilities, including support for ActiveX controls, scripting languages, frames, cookies, and more. When the request arrives, the user agent information is used to identify the requesting browser and an instance of the *HttpBrowserCapabilities* class is created and populated with browser-specific information. The information is in no way dynamically set by the browser; instead, it is retrieved from an offline server-side repository.

Information from the Client

Table 16-13 lists the *HttpRequest* properties that expose the client data that ASP.NET pages might want to use for server-side processing. The following table includes, for example, cookies, forms, and query string collections.

TABLE 16-13 Properties Describing the Client Data

Property	Description
ClientCertificate	Gets an *HttpClientCertificate* object with information on the client's security certificate settings, if any. The certificate object wraps up information such as number, validity, and issuer of the certificate.
Cookies	Gets a collection representing all cookies sent by the client. A cookie is identified by the *HttpCookie* object.

Property	Description
Files	Gets a collection of client-uploaded files. The property requires the HTTP *Content-Type* header to be set to *multipart/form-data*.
Filter	Gets or sets a *Stream*-based object through which all HTTP input passes when received. The filtered input is anything read via *InputStream*.
Form	Gets a name-value collection filled with the values of the input fields in the form posted. The collection is populated when the *Content-Type* header is either *application/x-www-form-urlencoded* or *multipart/form-data*.
Headers	Gets a name-value collection filled with all the header values in the request.
InputStream	Gets a *Stream* object representing the contents of the incoming HTTP content body.
Params	Gets a name-value collection that is a union of four other similar collections: *QueryString, Form, ServerVariables*, and *Cookies*.
QueryString	Gets a name-value collection containing all the query string variables sent by the client.
ServerVariables	Gets a name-value collection filled with a collection of Web server–defined variables.
UserHostAddress	Gets the Internet Protocol (IP) address of the remote client.
UserHostName	Gets the Domain Name System (DNS) name of the remote client.
UserLanguages	Gets an array of strings denoting the list of the languages accepted by the client for the specified request. The languages are read from the *Accept-Language* header.

The *Params* collection combines four different but homogeneous collections—*QueryString, Form, ServerVariables*, and *Cookies*—and it replicates the information contained in each of them. The collections are added in the following order: *QueryString, Form, Cookies*, and finally *ServerVariables*.

Information About the Connection

Table 16-14 lists the properties that relate to the open connection.

TABLE 16-14 Properties Describing the Connection

Property	Description
ApplicationPath	Gets the virtual path of the current application.
IsAuthenticated	Indicates whether or not the user has been authenticated.
IsLocal	Indicates if it is a local request.
IsSecureConnection	Indicates whether the connection is taking place over a Secure Sockets Layer (SSL) using HTTPS.
LogonUserIdentity	Gets an object representing the Windows identity of the current user as logged at the IIS gate.
Path	Gets the virtual path of the current request.
PathInfo	Gets additional path information for the requested resource, if any. The property returns any text that follows the URL.
PhysicalApplicationPath	Gets the file system path of the current application's root directory.

Property	Description
PhysicalPath	Gets the physical file system path corresponding to the requested URL.
RawUrl	Gets the raw URL of the current request.
Url	Gets the *Uri* object that represents the URL of the current request.
UrlReferrer	Gets the *Uri* object that represents the URL from which the current request originated.

The *Uri* class provides an object representation of a Uniform Resource Identifier (URI)—a unique name for a resource available on the Internet. The *Uri* class provides easy access to the parts of the URI as well as properties and methods for checking host, loopback, ports, and DNS.

The server variables set in the *ServerVariables* collection are decided by the run-time environment that processes the request. The information packed in the collection is, for the most part, excerpted from the HTTP worker request object; another part contains Web server–specific information. The *ServerVariables* collection is just a friendly name/value model to expose that information.

Methods of the *HttpRequest* Class

Table 16-15 lists all methods exposed by the *HttpRequest* class.

TABLE 16-15 *HttpRequest* **Methods**

Method	Description
BinaryRead	Performs a binary read from the current input stream. The method lets you specify the number of bytes to read and returns an array of bytes. The method is provided for compatibility with ASP. ASP.NET applications should read from the stream associated with the *InputStream* property.
MapImageCoordinates	Maps an incoming image-field form parameter to x/y coordinate values.
MapPath	Maps the specified virtual path to a physical path on the Web server.
SaveAs	Saves the current request to a file disk with or without headers. This method is especially useful for debugging.
ValidateInput	Performs a quick, nonexhaustive check to find potentially dangerous input data in the request.

Saving the Request to Disk

The *SaveAs* method lets you create a file to store the entire content of the HTTP request. Note that the storage medium can only be a disk file; no stream or writer can be used. Because ASP.NET by default isn't granted write permissions, this method causes an access-denied exception unless you implement ad hoc measures. Granting the ASP.NET account full control over the file to be created (or over the whole folder) is one of the possible ways to successfully use the *SaveAs* method. The following listing shows possible content that *SaveAs* writes to disk:

```
GET /MyApp/Samples/Ch14/Misc/TestFilter.aspx HTTP/1.1
Connection: Keep-Alive
Accept: */*
Accept-Encoding: gzip, deflate
Accept-Language: it,en-us;q=0.5
Cookie: .ASPXANONYMOUS=AGzHqyVAyAEkAAAAO ... MWE3YZreWoYt-jkSc_RwU169brWNTIw1
Host: localhost:1066
User-Agent: ...

UA-CPU: x86
```

If the intercepted request is a POST, you'll find posted values at the bottom of the string.

Validating Client Input

A golden rule of Web security claims that all user input is evil and should always be filtered and sanitized before use. The *@Page* directive has an attribute—*ValidateRequest*—that automatically blocks postbacks that contain potentially dangerous data. This feature is not the silver bullet of Web input security, but it helps detect possible problems. From a general security perspective, you're better off replacing the automatic input validation with a strong, application-specific validation layer.

The automatic input validation feature—*ValidateRequest*—is enabled by default and implemented via a call to the *HttpRequest*'s *ValidationInput* method. *ValidateInput* can be called by your code if the validation feature is not enabled. Request validation works by checking all input data against a hard-coded list of potentially dangerous data. The contents of the collections *QueryString*, *Form*, and *Cookies* are checked during request validation.

Summary

In this chapter, we covered some basic objects that are the foundation of ASP.NET programming: *Server*, *Response*, *Request*, and others. An ASP.NET application is represented by an instance of the *HttpApplication* class properly configured by the contents of the *global.asax* file. And both the *HttpApplication* class and the *global.asax* file found their space in this chapter too.

While discussing the interface of the objects that generate the context of an HTTP request, we reviewed in detail some specific programming issues, such as server-side page redirection and the setup of response filters. In the next chapter, we'll discuss an important topic related to Web applications and ASP.NET—state management. Fundamentally, Web applications are stateless, but ASP.NET provides various mechanisms for maintaining application state and caching pages.

In ASP.NET 4, all intrinsic objects (except *Cache*) have been derived from a new base class to give developers better chances to be able to write testable Web pages.

Chapter 17
ASP.NET State Management

In the beginner's mind there are many possibilities. In the expert's mind there are few.

—*Shunryu Suzuki*

All real-world applications of any shape and form need to maintain their own state to serve users' requests. ASP.NET applications are no exception. However, unlike other types of applications, they need special system-level tools to achieve the result. The reason for this peculiarity lies in the stateless nature of the underlying protocol that Web applications still rely upon. As long as HTTP remains the transportation protocol for the Web, all applications will run into the same problem—figuring out the most effective way to persist state information.

Application state is a sort of blank container that each application and programmer can fill with whatever piece of information makes sense to persist: from user preferences to global settings, from worker data to hit counters, from lookup tables to shopping carts. This extremely variegated mess of data can be organized and accessed according to a number of different usage patterns. Typically, all the information contributing to the application state is distributed in various layers, each with its own settings for visibility, programmability, and lifetime.

ASP.NET provides state management facilities at four levels: application, session, page, and request. Each level has its own special container object, which is a topic we'll cover in this chapter. In this chapter, we'll explore the *HttpApplicationState*, *HttpSessionState*, and *ViewState* objects, which provide for application, session, and page state maintenance, respectively. In the next chapter, we'll dive into the *Cache* object.

 Note In this chapter, we won't discuss cookies in detail, but cookies are definitely useful for storing small amounts of information on the client. The information is sent with the request to the server and can be manipulated and re-sent through the response. The cookie is a text-based structure with simple key/value pairs, and it consumes no resources on the server. In e-commerce applications, for example, cookies are the preferred way of storing user preferences. In addition, cookies have a configurable expiration policy. The negatives for cookies are their limited size (browser-dependent, but seldom greater than 8 KB) and the fact that the user can disable them.

The Application's State

Table 17-1 summarizes the main features of the various state objects.

TABLE 17-1 State Management Objects at a Glance

Object	Lifetime	Data Visibility	Location
Cache	Implements an automatic scavenging mechanism, and periodically clears less frequently used contents	Global to all sessions	Does not support Web farm or Web garden scenarios
HttpApplicationState	Created when the first request hits the Web server, and released when the application shuts down	Same as for *Cache*	Same as for *Cache*
HttpContext	Spans the entire lifetime of the individual request	Global to the objects involved with the request	Same as for *Cache*
HttpSessionState	Created when the user makes the first request, and lasts until the user closes the session	Global to all requests issued by the user who started the session	Configurable to work on Web farms and gardens
ViewState	Represents the calling context of each page being generated	Limited to all requests queued for the same page	Configurable to work on Web farms and gardens

The *HttpApplicationState* object makes a dictionary available for storage to all request handlers invoked within an application. An instance of the *HttpApplicationState* class is created the first time a client requests any resource from within a particular virtual directory. Each running application holds its own global state object. The most common way to access application state is by means of the *Application* property of the *Page* object. Application state is not shared across either a Web farm or Web garden.

> **Important** Application state exists today mostly for compatibility reasons, and I don't know of any application where *Application* is used instead of the more powerful and built-in *Cache* object or external distributed cache engines.

Properties of the *HttpApplicationState* Class

The *HttpApplicationState* class is sealed and inherits from a class named *NameObjectCollectionBase*. In practice, the *HttpApplicationState* class is a collection of pairs, each made of a string key and an object value. Such pairs can be accessed either using the key string or the index. Internally, the base class employs a hashtable with an initial capacity of zero that is automatically increased as required. Table 17-2 lists the properties of the *HttpApplicationState* class.

TABLE 17-2 *HttpApplicationState* **Properties**

Property	Description
AllKeys	Gets an array of strings containing all the keys of the items currently stored in the object.
Contents	Gets the current instance of the object. But wait! What this property returns is simply a reference to the application state object, not a clone. It's provided for ASP compatibility.
Count	Gets the number of objects currently stored in the collection.
Item	Indexer property, provides read/write access to an element in the collection. The element can be specified either by name or index. Accessors of this property are implemented using *Get* and *Set* methods.
StaticObjects	Gets a collection including all instances of all objects declared in *global.asax* using an *<object>* tag with the *scope* attribute set to *Application*.

Note that static objects and actual state values are stored in separate collections. The exact type of the static collection is *HttpStaticObjectsCollection*.

Methods of the *HttpApplicationState* Class

The set of methods that the *HttpApplicationState* class features are mostly specialized versions of the typical methods of a name/value collection. As Table 17-3 shows, the most significant extension includes the locking mechanism necessary to serialize access to the state values.

TABLE 17-3 *HttpApplicationState* **Methods**

Method	Description
Add	Adds a new value to the collection. The value is boxed as an *object*.
Clear	Removes all objects from the collection.
Get	Returns the value of an item in the collection. The item can be specified either by key or index.
GetEnumerator	Returns an enumerator object to iterate through the collection.
GetKey	Gets the string key of the item stored at the specified position.
Lock	Locks writing access to the whole collection. No concurrent caller can write to the collection object until *UnLock* is called.
Remove	Removes the item whose key matches the specified string.
RemoveAll	Calls *Clear*.
RemoveAt	Removes the item at the specified position.
Set	Assigns the specified value to the item with the specified key. The method is thread-safe, and the access to the item is blocked until the writing is +completed.
UnLock	Unlocks writing access to the collection.

Note that the *GetEnumerator* method is inherited from the base collection class and, as such, is oblivious to the locking mechanism of the class. If you enumerate the collection using this method, each returned value is obtained through a simple call to one of the *get* methods on the base *NameObjectCollectionBase* class. Unfortunately, that method is not aware of the locking mechanism needed on the derived *HttpApplicationState* class because of the concurrent access to the application state. As a result, your enumeration is thread-safe. A better way to enumerate the content of the collection is by using a *while* statement and the *Get* method to access an item. Alternatively, you can lock the collection before you enumerate.

State Synchronization

Note that all operations on *HttpApplicationState* require some sort of synchronization to ensure that multiple threads running within an application safely access values without incurring deadlocks and access violations. The writing methods, such as *Set* and *Remove*, as well as the *set* accessor of the *Item* property implicitly apply a writing lock before proceeding. The *Lock* method ensures that only the current thread can modify the application state. The *Lock* method is provided to apply the same writing lock around portions of code that need to be protected from other threads' access.

You don't need to wrap a single call to *Set*, *Clear*, or *Remove* with a lock/unlock pair of statements—those methods, in fact, are already thread-safe. Using *Lock* in these cases will only have the effect of producing additional overhead, increasing the internal level of recursion.

```
// This operation is thread-safe
Application["MyValue"] = 1;
```

Use *Lock* instead if you want to shield a group of instructions from concurrent writings:

```
// These operations execute atomically
Application.Lock();
int val = (int) Application["MyValue"];
if (val < 10)
    Application["MyValue"] = val + 1;
Application.UnLock();
```

Reading methods such as *Get*, the *get* accessor of *Item*, and even *Count* have an internal synchronization mechanism that, when used along with *Lock*, will protect them against concurrent and cross-thread readings and writings:

```
// The reading is protected from concurrent read/writes
Application.Lock();
int val = (int) Application["MyValue"];
Application.UnLock();
```

You should always use *Lock* and *UnLock* together. However, if you omit the call to *UnLock*, the likelihood of incurring a deadlock is not high because the Microsoft .NET Framework automatically removes the lock when the request completes or times out, or when an unhandled error occurs. For this reason, if you handle the exception, consider using a *finally* block to clear the lock or expect to face some delay while ASP.NET clears the lock for you when the request ends.

Tradeoffs of Application State

Instead of writing global data to the *HttpApplicationState* object, you can use public members within the *global.asax* file. Compared to entries in the *HttpApplicationState* collection, a global member is preferable because it is strongly typed and does not require a hashtable access to locate the value. On the other hand, a global variable is not synchronized per se and must be manually protected. You have to use language constructs to protect access to these members—for example, the C# *lock* operator or, in Microsoft Visual Basic .NET, the *SyncLock* operator.

Whatever form you choose for storing the global state of an application, some general considerations apply regarding the opportunity to store data globally. For one thing, global data storage results in permanent memory occupation. Unless explicitly removed by the code, any data stored in the application global state is removed only when the application shuts down. On one end, putting a few megabytes of data in the application's memory speeds up access; on the other hand, doing this occupies valuable memory for the entire duration of the application.

For this reason, it is extremely important that you consider using the *Cache* object (which is discussed further in the next chapter) whenever you have a need for globally shared data. Unlike data stored with *Application* and global members, data stored in the ASP.NET *Cache* is subject to an automatic scavenging mechanism that ensures the data is removed when a too-high percentage of virtual memory is being consumed. In addition, the *Cache* object has a lot of other beneficial features that we'll explore in the next chapter. The bottom line is that the *Cache* object was introduced specifically to mitigate the problem of memory occupation and to replace the *Application* object.

To put it down even clearer, today writing to the *Application* object is bad practice and is supported only to help with migration from classic ASP, where it was the common and easiest way of storing global data. In ASP.NET, Cache is the recommended solution for a single worker process and distributed caches (for example, Microsoft AppFabric Caching Services) if you're in a Web farm context.

The Session's State

The *HttpSessionState* class provides a dictionary-based model of storing and retrieving session-state values. Unlike *HttpApplicationState*, this class doesn't expose its contents to all users operating on the virtual directory at a given time. Only the requests that originate in the context of the same session—that is, those generated across multiple page requests made by the same user—can access the session state. The session state can be stored and published in a variety of ways, including in a Web farm or Web garden scenario. By default, though, the session state is held within the ASP.NET worker process.

The ASP.NET implementation of session state provides some extremely handy facilities—such as support for cookieless browsers, Web farms, and Web gardens—and the capability of being hosted by external processes, including Microsoft SQL Server. In this way, ASP.NET session management can provide an unprecedented level of robustness and reliability. Developers can also create custom data stores for session state. For example, if you need the robustness that a database-oriented solution can guarantee but you work with Oracle databases, you need not install SQL Server as well. By writing a piece of additional code, you can support an Oracle session data store while using the same *Session* semantics and classes.

The extensibility model for session state offers two options: customizing bits and pieces of the existing ASP.NET session state mechanism (for example, creating an Oracle session provider or a module controlling the generation of the ID), and replacing the standard session state HTTP module with a new one. The former option is easier to implement but provides a limited set of features you can customize. The latter option is more complicated to code but provides the greatest flexibility.

The Session-State HTTP Module

Regardless of the internal implementation, the programmer has only one application programming interface (API) for session state management—the old acquaintance known as the *Session* object. In classic ASP, it was a COM object that was instantiated in the *asp.dll* ISAPI extension and injected into the memory space of the ActiveX Scripting engine called to parse and process the *.asp* script. It is a collection object in ASP.NET, living behind the *Session* property of the *Page* class. The exact type is *HttpSessionState*; it's a class that's not further inheritable and that implements *ICollection* and *IEnumerable*. An instance of this class is created during the startup of each request that requires session support. The collection is filled with name/value pairs read from the specified medium and attached to the context of the request—the *HttpContext* class. The *Page*'s *Session* property just mirrors the *Session* property of the *HttpContext* class.

If developers can simply work with one object—the *Session* object—regardless of other details, most of the credit goes to an HTTP module that governs the process of retrieving and storing session state with some help from special provider objects. The ASP.NET module in charge of setting up the session state for each user connecting to an application is an HTTP module named *SessionStateModule*. Structured after the *IHttpModule* interface, the *SessionStateModule* object provides session-state services for ASP.NET applications.

Although, as an HTTP module, it is required to supply a relatively simple programming interface—the *IHttpModule* interface contracts only for *Init* and *Dispose* methods—*SessionStateModule* does perform a number of quite sophisticated tasks, most of which are fundamental to the health and functionality of the Web application. The session-state module is invoked during the setup of the *HttpApplication* object that will process a given request, and it's responsible for either generating or obtaining a unique session ID string and for storing and retrieving state data from a state provider—for example, SQL Server or the Web server's memory.

State Client Managers

When invoked, the session-state HTTP module reads the settings in the *<sessionState>* section of the *web.config* file and determines what the expected state client manager is for the application. A state client manager is a component that takes care of storing and retrieving the data of all currently active sessions. The *SessionStateModule* component queries the state client manager to get the name/value pairs of a given session.

In ASP.NET, there are four possibilities for working with the session state. The session state can be stored locally in the ASP.NET worker process; the session state can be maintained in an external, even remote, process named *aspnet_state.exe*; and the session state can be managed by SQL Server and stored in an ad hoc database table. The fourth option entails you storing the sessions in a custom component. Table 17-4 briefly describes the various options.

TABLE 17-4 State Client Providers

Mode	Description
Custom	The values for all the sessions are stored in a custom data store.
InProc	The values for all the sessions are maintained as live objects in the memory of the ASP.NET worker process. This is the default option.
Off	Session state is disabled, and no state client provider is active.
SQLServer	The values for all the sessions are serialized and stored in a SQL Server table. The nstance of SQL Server can run either locally or remotely.
StateServer	The values for all the sessions are serialized and stored in the memory of a separate system process (*aspnet_state.exe*). The process can also run on another machine. Session values are deserialized into the session dictionary at the beginning of the request. If the request completes successfully, state values are serialized into the process memory and made available to other pages.

The *SessionStateMode* enum type lists the available options for the state client provider. The *InProc* option is by far the fastest possible in terms of access. However, bear in mind that the more data you store in a session, the more memory is consumed on the Web server, which increases the risk of performance hits. If you plan to use any of the out-of-process solutions, the possible impact of serialization and deserialization should be carefully considered. We'll discuss this aspect in detail later in the "Persist Session Data to Remote Servers" section.

The session-state module determines the state provider to use based on what it reads out of the *<sessionState>* section of the *web.config* file. Next, it instantiates and initializes the state provider for the application. Each provider continues its own initialization, which is quite different depending on the type. For example, the SQL Server state manager opens a connection to the given database, whereas the out-of-process manager checks the specified TCP port. The *InProc* state manager, on the other hand, stores a reference to the callback function that will be used to fire the *Session_End* event. (I'll discuss this further in the section "Lifetime of a Session.")

Creating the *HttpSessionState* Object

The state module is responsible for retrieving the session state and attaching it to the context of each request that runs within the session. The session state is available only after the *HttpApplication.AcquireRequestState* event fires, and it gets irreversibly lost after the *HttpApplication.ReleaseRequestState* event. Subsequently, this means that no state is still available when *Session_End* fires.

The session module creates the *HttpSessionState* object for a request while processing the *HttpApplication.AcquireRequestState* event. At this time, the *HttpSessionState* object—a sort of collection—is given its session ID and the session dictionary. The session dictionary is the actual collection of state values that pages will familiarly access through the *Session* property.

If a new session is being started, such a data dictionary is simply a newly created empty object. If the module is serving a request for an existing session, the data dictionary will be filled by deserializing the contents supplied by the currently active session state provider. At the end of the request, the current content of the dictionary, as modified by the page request, is flushed back to the state provider through a serialization step. The whole process is depicted in Figure 17-1.

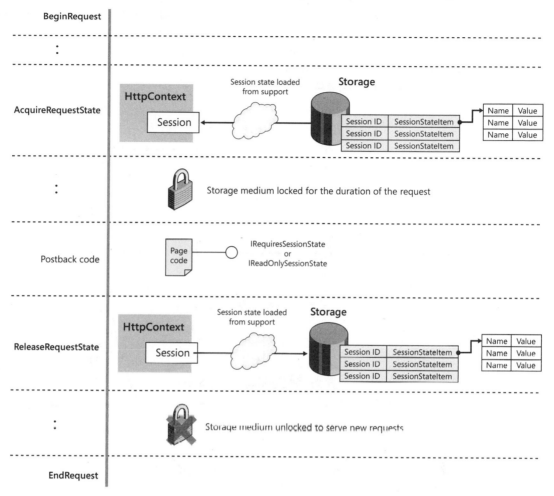

FIGURE 17-1 The session state management timeline.

Synchronizing Access to the Session State

So when your Web page makes a call into the *Session* property, it's actually accessing a local, in-memory copy of the data. What if other pages (in the same session) attempt to concurrently access the session state? In that case, the current request might end up working on inconsistent data or data that isn't up to date.

To avoid that, the session state module implements a reader/writer locking mechanism and queues the access to state values. A page that has session-state write access will hold a writer lock on the session until the request finishes. A page gains write access to the session state by setting the *EnableSessionState* attribute on the *@Page* directive to *true*. A page that has session-state read access—for example, when the *EnableSessionState* attribute is set to *ReadOnly*—will hold a reader lock on the session until the request finishes.

If a page request sets a reader lock, other concurrently running requests cannot update the session state but are allowed to read. If a page request sets a writer lock on the session state, all other pages are blocked regardless of whether they have to read or write. For example, if two frames attempt to write to *Session*, one of them has to wait until the other finishes. Figure 17-2 shows the big picture.

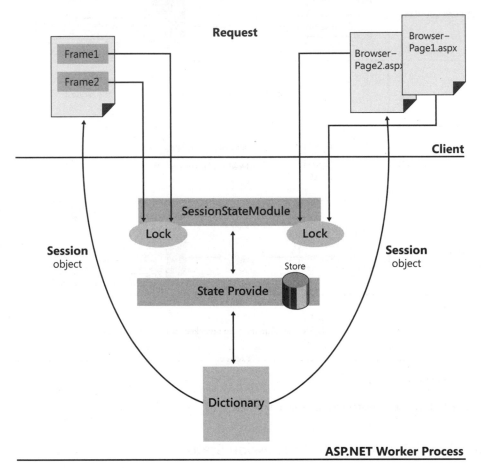

FIGURE 17-2 Page access to the session state is synchronized, and a serialization/deserialization layer ensures that each request is served an up-to-date dictionary of values, stored at the application's convenience.

Note Concurrent access to the session state is not very common in reality. It might happen if you have a multiframe page or if your users work with two copies of the same page or multiple pages of the same application at the same time. It also happens when you use session-enabled HTTP handlers to serve embedded resources such as images or cascading style sheet (CSS) files. By default, you are protected against concurrent accesses. However, declaring the exact use of the session state that a page is going to make (read/write, readonly, or no use) is an excellent form of optimization. You do this through the *EnableSessionState* attribute on the *@Page* directive.

Properties of the *HttpSessionState* Class

The *HttpSessionState* class is defined in the *System.Web.SessionState* namespace. It is a generic collection class and implements the *ICollection* interface. The properties of the *HttpSessionState* class are listed in Table 17-5.

TABLE 17-5 *HttpSessionState* **Properties**

Property	Description
CodePage	Gets or sets the code page identifier for the current session.
Contents	Returns a reference to *this* object. It's provided for ASP compatibility.
CookieMode	Details the application's configuration for cookieless sessions. Declared to be of type *HttpCookieMode*. (I'll discuss this in more detail later.)
Count	Gets the number of items currently stored in the session state.
IsCookieless	Indicates whether the session ID is embedded in the URL or stored in an HTTP cookie. It's more specific than *CookieMode*.
IsNewSession	Indicates whether the session was created with the current request.
IsReadOnly	Indicates whether the session is read-only. The session is read-only if the *EnableSessionState* attribute on the *@Page* directive is set to the keyword *ReadOnly*.
IsSynchronized	Returns *false*. (See references to this later in the chapter.)
Item	Indexer property, provides read/write access to a session-state value. The value can be specified either by name or index.
Keys	Gets a collection of the keys of all values stored in the session.
LCID	Gets or sets the locale identifier (LCID) of the current session.
Mode	Gets a value denoting the state client manager being used. Acceptable values are listed in Table 17-4.
SessionID	Gets a string with the ID used to identify the session.
StaticObjects	Gets a collection including all instances of all objects declared in *global.asax* using an *<object>* tag with the *scope* attribute set to *Session*. Note that you cannot add objects to this collection from within an ASP.NET application—that is, programmatically.
SyncRoot	Returns a reference to *this* object. (See references to this property later in the chapter.)
Timeout	Gets or sets the minutes that the session module should wait between two successive requests before terminating the session.

The *HttpSessionState* class is a normal collection class because it implements the *ICollection* interface, but synchronization-wise it is a very special collection class. As mentioned, the synchronization mechanism is implemented in the *SessionStateModule* component, which guarantees that at most one thread will ever access the session state. However, because *HttpSessionState* implements the *ICollection* interface, it must provide an implementation for both *IsSynchronized* and *SyncRoot*. Note that *IsSynchronized* and *SyncRoot* are collection-specific properties for synchronization and have nothing to do with the session synchronization discussed previously. They refer to the ability of the collection class (*HttpSessionState* in this case) to work in a synchronized manner. Technically speaking, the *HttpSessionState* is not synchronized, but access to session state is.

Methods of the *HttpSessionState* Class

Table 17-6 shows all the methods available in the *HttpSessionState* class. They mostly relate to typical operations on a collection. In this sense, the only exceptional method is *Abandon*, which causes the session to be canceled.

TABLE 17-6 *HttpSessionState* **Methods**

Method	Description
Abandon	Sets an internal flag that instructs the session module to cancel the current session.
Add	Adds a new item to the session state. The value is boxed in an *object* type.
Clear	Clears all values from the session state.
CopyTo	Copies the collection of session-state values to a one-dimensional array, starting at the specified index in the array.
GetEnumerator	Gets an enumerator to loop through all the values in the session.
Remove	Deletes an item from the session-state collection. The item is identified by the key.
RemoveAll	Calls *Clear*.
RemoveAt	Deletes an item from the session-state collection. The item is identified by position.

When the procedure to terminate the current request is running, the session-state module checks an internal flag to verify whether the user ordered that the session be abandoned. If the flag is set—that is, the *Abandon* method was called—any response cookie is removed and the procedure to terminate the session is begun. Notice, though, that this does not mean that a *Session_End* event will fire.

First, the *Session_End* event fires only if the session mode is *InProc*; second, the event does not fire if the session dictionary is empty and no real session state exists for the application. In other words, at least one request must have been completed for the *Session_End* to fire when the session is closed either naturally or after a call to *Abandon*.

Working with a Session's State

Now that you have grabbed hold of the session state basics, you can sharpen your skills by looking into more technically relevant aspects of session state management. Handling session state is a task that can be outlined in three steps: assigning a session ID, obtaining session data from a provider, and stuffing it into the context of the page. As mentioned, the session state module governs the execution of all these tasks. In doing so, it takes advantage of a couple of additional components: the session ID generator and session state provider. In ASP.NET, both can be replaced with custom components, as we'll discuss later. For now, let's tackle some of the practical issues you face when working with session state.

Identifying a Session

Each active ASP.NET session is identified using a 120-bit string made only of URL-allowed characters. Session IDs are guaranteed to be unique and randomly generated to avoid data conflicts and prevent malicious attacks. Obtaining a valid session ID algorithmically from an existing ID is virtually impossible. The generator of the session ID is a customizable system component that developers can optionally replace.

> **Note** An old proverb reminds us that nothing should be done only because it is doable. This motto is particularly apt here as we talk about parts of the session state management that are customizable in ASP.NET. These subsystems, such as the session ID generator, should be customized only when you have a good reason to and only when you're certain it won't make things worse or lower the level of security. I'll return to this point in a moment with more details.

Generating the Session ID

A session ID is 15 bytes long by design (15x8 = 120 bits). The session ID is generated using the Random Number Generator (RNG) cryptographic provider. The service provider returns a sequence of 15 randomly generated numbers. The array of numbers is then mapped to valid URL characters and returned as a string.

If the session contains nothing, a new session ID is generated for each request and the session state is not persisted to the state provider. However, if a *Session_Start* handler is used, the session state is always saved, even if empty. For this reason, and especially if you're not using the in-process session provider, define *Session_Start* handlers with extreme care and only if strictly necessary.

In contrast, the session ID remains the same after a nonempty session dictionary times out or is abandoned. By design, even though the session state expires, the session ID lasts until the browser session is ended. This means that the same session ID is used to represent multiple sessions over time as long as the browser instance remains the same.

Session Cookies

The *SessionID* string is communicated to the browser and then returned to the server application in either of two ways: using a cookie or a modified URL. By default, the session-state module creates an HTTP cookie on the client, but a modified URL can be used—especially for cookieless browsers—with the *SessionID* string embedded. Which approach is taken depends on the configuration settings stored in the application's *web.config* file. By default, session state uses cookies.

A cookie is really nothing more than a text file placed on the client's hard disk by a Web page. In ASP.NET, a cookie is represented by an instance of the *HttpCookie* class. Typically, a cookie has a name, a collection of values, and an expiration time. In addition, you can configure the cookie to operate on a particular virtual path and over secure connections (for example, HTTPS).

> **Important** ASP.NET takes advantage of the HTTP-only feature for session cookies on the browsers that support it—nowadays, pretty much every browser supports this. The HTTP-only feature prevents cookies from being available to client-side script, thus raising a barrier against potential cross-site scripting attacks aimed at stealing session IDs.

When cookies are enabled, the session-state module actually creates a cookie with a particular name and stores the session ID in it. The cookie is created as the following pseudo-code shows:

```
HttpCookie sessionCookie;
sessionCookie = new HttpCookie("ASP.NET_SessionId", sessionID);
sessionCookie.Path = "/";
```

ASP.NET_SessionId is the name of the cookie, and the *SessionID* string is its value. The cookie is also associated with the root of the current domain. The *Path* property describes the relative URL that the cookie applies to. A session cookie is given a very short expiration term and is renewed at the end of each successful request. The cookie's *Expires* property indicates the time of day on the client at which the cookie expires. If not explicitly set, as is the case with session cookies, the *Expires* property defaults to *DateTime.MinValue*—that is, the smallest possible unit of time in the .NET Framework.

> **Note** A server-side module that needs to write a cookie adds an *HttpCookie* object to the *Response.Cookies* collection. All cookies found on the client and associated with the requested domain are uploaded and made available for reading through the *Request.Cookies* collection.

Cookieless Sessions

For the session state to work, the client must be able to pass the session ID to the server application. How this happens depends on the configuration of the application. ASP.NET applications define their session-specific settings through the *<sessionState>* section of the configuration file. To decide about the cookie support, you set the *cookieless* attribute to one of the values in Table 17-7. The listed values belong to the *HttpCookieMode* enumerated type.

TABLE 17-7 *HttpCookieMode* **Enumerated Type**

Mode	Description
AutoDetect	Use cookies only if the requesting browser supports cookies.
UseCookies	Use cookies to persist the session ID regardless of whether or not the browser supports cookies. This is the default option.
UseDeviceProfile	Base the decision on the browser's capabilities as listed in the device profile section of the configuration file.
UseUri	Store the session ID in the URL regardless of whether the browser supports cookies or not. Use this option if you want to go cookieless no matter what.

When *AutoDetect* is used, ASP.NET queries the browser to determine whether it supports cookies. If the browser supports cookies, the session ID is stored in a cookie; otherwise, the session ID is stored in the URL. When *UseDeviceProfile* is set, on the other hand, the effective capabilities of the browser are not checked. For the session HTTP module to make the decision about cookies or the URL, the declared capabilities of the browser are used, as they result from the *SupportsRedirectWithCookie* property of the *HttpBrowserCapabilities* object. Note that even though a browser can support cookies, a user might have disabled cookies. In this case, session state won't work properly.

With cookie support disabled, suppose that you request a page at the following URL:

```
http://www.contoso.com/test/sessions.aspx
```

What is displayed in the browser's address bar is slightly different and now includes the session ID, as shown here:

```
http://www.contoso.com/test/(S(5y1g0455mrvws1uz5mmaau45))/sessions.aspx
```

When instantiated, the session-state module checks the value of the *cookieless* attribute. If the value is *true*, the request is redirected (HTTP 302 status code) to a modified virtual URL that includes the session ID just before the page name. When processed again, the request embeds the session ID. A special ISAPI filter—the *aspnet_filter.exe* component—preprocesses the request, parses the URL, and rewrites the correct URL if it incorporates a session ID. The detected session ID is also stored in an extra HTTP header, named *AspFilterSessionId*, and retrieved later.

Issues with Cookieless Sessions

Designed to make stateful applications also possible on a browser that does not support cookies or on one that does not have cookies enabled, cookieless sessions are not free of issues. First, they cause a redirect when the session starts and whenever the user follows an absolute URL from within an application's page.

When cookies are used, you can clear the address bar, go to another application, and then return to the previous one and retrieve the same session values. If you do this when session cookies are disabled, the session data is lost. This feature is not problematic for postbacks, which are automatically implemented using relative URLs, but it poses a serious problem if you use links to absolute URLs. In this case, a new session will always be created. For example, the following code breaks the session:

```
<a runat="server" href="/test/sessions.aspx">Click</a>
```

Is there a way to automatically mangle absolute URLs in links and hyperlinks so that they incorporate session information? You can use the following trick, which uses the *ApplyAppPathModifier* method of the *HttpResponse* class:

```
<a href='<% =Response.ApplyAppPathModifier("test/page.aspx")%>' >Click</a>
```

The *ApplyAppPathModifier* method takes a string representing a relative URL and returns an absolute URL, which embeds session information. This trick is especially useful when you need to redirect from an HTTP page to an HTTPS page, where the full, absolute address is mandatory. Note that *ApplyAppPathModifier* returns the original URL if session cookies are enabled and if the path is an absolute path.

> **Caution** You can't use <%...%> code blocks in server-side expressions—that is, expressions flagged with the *runat=server* attribute. It works in the preceding code because the *<a>* tag is emitted verbatim, being devoid of the *runat* attribute. Code blocks mentioned here have nothing to do with data binding expressions <%# ... %>, which are perfect legal and even desirable in server-side code. The reason why you can't use <%...%> code blocks in server-side expressions is that the presence of the *runat* attribute forces the creation of a server object that is not designed for handling code blocks.

Cookieless Sessions and Security

Another issue regarding the use of cookieless sessions is related to security. Session hijacking is one of the most popular types of attacks and consists of accessing an external system through the session ID generated for another, legitimate user.

Try this: set your application to work without cookies and visit a page. Grab the URL with the session ID as it appears in the browser's address bar, and send it immediately in an e-mail to a friend. Have your friend paste the URL in his or her own machine and click Go. Your friend will gain access to your session state as long as the session is active.

The session ID is certainly not well-protected information (and probably couldn't work otherwise). For the safety of a system, an unpredictable generator of IDs is key because it makes it difficult to guess a valid session ID. With cookieless sessions, the session ID is exposed in the address bar and visible to all. For this reason, if you are storing private or sensitive information in the session state, it is recommended that you use Secure Sockets Layer (SSL) or Transport Layer Security (TLS) to encrypt any communication between the browser and server that includes the session ID.

In addition, you should always provide users the ability to log out and call the *Abandon* method when they think security has been breached in this way. This contrivance reduces the amount of time available for anybody attempting to use your session ID to exploit data stored in the session state. And, speaking of security, it is important that you configure the system to avoid the reuse of expired session IDs when cookieless sessions are used. This behavior is configurable in ASP.NET through the *<sessionState>* section, as you can read in the following section.

Cookieless Sessions and SEO

Cookieless sessions are also problematic from a Search-Engine Optimization (SEO) perspective. Pages based on cookieless sessions are poorly ranked by Web spiders such as Googlebot. The reason is that every time the spider attempts to crawl the page, ASP.NET generates a different session ID, which results in a different URL for the same content. So a crawler typically concludes that you have several pages with the same content and gives you a low ranking.

An effective workaround for this issue is using *UseDeviceProfile* (described in Table 17-7) instead of the default value. In addition, you create in *web.config* a browser profile for each of the major crawlers, such as Googlebot. In the profile, you just declare that any agent that contains the word "Googlebot" in the user agent string should be treated like a browser that supports cookies. In this way, ASP.NET will not append the session ID to the URL. It's not really a clean solution, but it does work. You can add a new profile for each crawler that is not indexing your pages well enough.

Configuring the Session State

The *<sessionState>* section groups the settings you can apply to configure the behavior of ASP.NET session state. Here's what it looks like:

```
<sessionState
    mode="[Off|InProc|StateServer|SQLServer|Custom]"
    timeout="number of minutes"
    cookieName="session identifier cookie name"
    cookieless=
        "[true|false|AutoDetect|UseCookies|UseUri|UseDeviceProfile]"
    regenerateExpiredSessionId="[True|False]"
    sessionIDManagerType="session manager type"
    sqlConnectionString="sql connection string"
    sqlCommandTimeout="number of seconds"
    allowCustomSqlDatabase="[True|False]"
    useHostingIdentity="[True|False]"
    stateConnectionString="tcpip=server:port"
    stateNetworkTimeout="number of seconds"
    customProvider="custom provider name"
    compressionEnabled="[True|False]"
    sqlConnectionRetryInterval="number of seconds">
    <providers>...</providers>
</sessionState>
```

Table 17-8 details the goals and characteristics of the various attributes.

TABLE 17-8 *<sessionState>* **Attributes**

Mode	Description
allowCustomSqlDatabase	If *true*, enables specifying a custom database table to store session data instead of using the standard *ASPState*.
compressionEnabled	Indicates whether the session state content is compressed during serialization and deserialization to and from an out-of-process provider. Compression is disabled by default and, if enabled, uses the built-in Gzip stream. *This feature is available only in ASP.NET 4.*
cookieless	Specifies how to communicate the session ID to clients.
cookieName	Name of the cookie, if cookies are used for session IDs.
customProvider	The name of the custom session state store provider to use for storing and retrieving session state data.
mode	Specifies where to store session state.
partitionResolverType	Indicates the type and assembly of the partition resolver component to be loaded to provide connection information when session state is working in *SQLServer* or *StateServer* mode. If a partition resolver can be correctly loaded, *sqlConnectionString* and *stateConnectionString* attributes are ignored.
regenerateExpiredSessionId	When a request is made with a session ID that has expired, if this attribute is *true*, a new session ID is generated; otherwise, the expired one is revived. The default is *false*.
sessionIDManagerType	Null by default. If set, it indicates the component to use as the generator of session IDs.
sqlCommandTimeout	Specifies the number of seconds a SQL command can be idle before it is canceled. The default is 30.
sqlConnectionString	Specifies the connection string to SQL Server.
stateConnectionString	Specifies the server name or address and port where session state is stored remotely.
stateNetworkTimeout	Specifies the number of seconds the TCP/IP network connection between the Web server and the state server can be idle before the request is canceled. The default is 10.
timeout	Specifies the number of minutes a session can be idle before it is abandoned. The default is 20.
useHostingIdentity	*True* by default. It indicates that the ASP.NET process identity is impersonated when accessing a custom state provider or the *SQLServer* provider configured for integrated security.

In addition, the child *<providers>* section lists custom session-state store providers. ASP.NET session state is designed to enable you to easily store user session data in different sources, such as a Web server's memory or SQL Server. A store provider is a component that manages the storage of session state information and stores the information in an alternative media (for example, Oracle) and layout. We'll return to this topic later in the chapter.

Lifetime of a Session

The life of a session state begins only when the first item is added to the in-memory dictionary. The following code demonstrates how to modify an item in the session dictionary. "MyData" is the key that uniquely identifies the value. If a key named "MyData" already exists in the dictionary, the existing value is overwritten.

```
Session["MyData"] = "I love ASP.NET";
```

The *Session* dictionary generically contains *object* types; to read data back, you need to cast the returned values to a more specific type:

```
var tmp = (String) Session["MyData"];
```

When a page saves data to *Session*, the value is loaded into an in-memory dictionary—an instance of an internal class named *SessionDictionary*. (See Figure 17-1 to review session state loading and saving.) Other concurrently running pages cannot access the session until the ongoing request completes.

The *Session_Start* Event

The session startup event is unrelated to the session state. The *Session_Start* event fires when the session-state module is servicing the first request for a given user that requires a new session ID. The ASP.NET runtime can serve multiple requests within the context of a single session, but only for the first of them does *Session_Start* fire.

A new session ID is created and a new *Session_Start* event fires whenever a page is requested that doesn't write data to the dictionary. The architecture of the session state is quite sophisticated because it has to support a variety of state providers. The overall schema has the content of the session dictionary being serialized to the state provider when the request completes. However, to optimize performance, this procedure really executes only if the content of the dictionary is not empty. As mentioned earlier, though, if the application defines a *Session_Start* event handler, the serialization takes place anyway.

The *Session_End* Event

The *Session_End* event signals the end of the session and is used to perform any clean-up code needed to terminate the session. Note, though, that the event is supported only in *InProc* mode—that is, only when the session data is stored in the ASP.NET worker process.

For *Session_End* to fire, the session state has to exist first. That means you have to store some data in the session state and you must have completed at least one request. When the first value is added to the session dictionary, an item is inserted into the ASP.NET cache—the aforementioned *Cache* object that we'll cover in detail in the next chapter. The behavior is specific to the in-process state provider; neither the out-of-process state server nor the SQL Server state server work with the *Cache* object.

However, much more interesting is that the item added to the cache—only one item per active session—is given a special expiration policy. You'll also learn more about the ASP.NET cache and related expiration policies in the next chapter. For now, it suffices to say that the session-state item added to the cache is given a sliding expiration, with the time interval set to the session timeout. As long as there are requests processed within the session, the sliding period is automatically renewed. The session-state module resets the timeout while processing the *EndRequest* event. It obtains the desired effect by simply performing a read on the cache! Given the internal structure of the ASP.NET *Cache* object, this evaluates to renewing the sliding period. As a result, when the cache item expires, the session has timed out.

An expired item is automatically removed from the cache. As part of the expiration policy for this item, the state-session module also indicates a remove callback function. The cache automatically invokes the remove function which, in turn, fires the *Session_End* event.

> **Note** The items in *Cache* that represent the state of a session are not accessible from outside the *system.web* assembly and can't even be enumerated, because they are placed in a system-reserved area of the cache. In other words, you can't programmatically access the data resident in another session or even remove it.

Why Does My Session State Sometimes Get Lost?

Values parked in a *Session* object are removed from memory either programmatically by the code or by the system when the session times out or it is abandoned. In some cases, though, even when nothing of the kind seemingly happens, the session state gets lost. Is there a reason for this apparently weird behavior?

When the working mode is *InProc*, the session state is mapped in the memory space of the AppDomain in which the page request is being served. In light of this, the session state is subject to process recycling and AppDomain restarts. The ASP.NET worker process is periodically restarted to maintain an average good performance; when this happens, the session state is lost. Process recycling depends on the percentage of memory consumption and maybe the number of requests served. Although it's cyclic, no general estimate can be made regarding the interval of the cycle. Be aware of this when designing your session-based, in-process application. As a general rule, bear in mind that the session state might not be there when you try to access it. Use exception handling or recovery techniques as appropriate for your application.

Consider that some antivirus software might be marking the *web.config* or *global.asax* file as modified, thus causing a new application to be started and subsequently causing the loss of the session state. This holds true also if you or your code modify the timestamp of those files or alter the contents of one of the special folders, such as *Bin* or *App_Code*.

> **Note** What happens to the session state when a running page hits an error? Will the current dictionary be saved, or is it just lost? The state of the session is not saved if, at the end of the request, the page results in an error—that is, the *GetLastError* method of the *Server* object returns an exception. However, if in your exception handler you reset the error state by calling *Server. ClearError*, the values of the session are saved regularly as if no error ever occurred.

Persist Session Data to Remote Servers

The session state loss problem that I mentioned earlier for *InProc* mode can be neatly solved by employing either of the two predefined out-of-process state providers: *StateServer* or *SQLServer*. In this case, though, the session state is held outside the ASP.NET worker process and an extra layer of code is needed to serialize and deserialize it to and from the actual storage medium. This operation takes place whenever a request is processed.

The need to copy session data from an external repository into the local session dictionary might tax the state management process to the point of causing a 15 percent to 25 percent decrease in performance. Note, though, that this is only a rough estimate, and it's closer to the minimum impact rather than to the maximum impact. The estimate, in fact, does not fully consider the complexity of the types actually saved into the session state.

> **Note** When you get to choose an out-of-process state provider (for example, *StateServer* and *SQLServer*), be aware that you need to set up the runtime environment before putting the application in production. This means either starting a Windows service for *StateServer* or configuring a database for *SQLServer*. No preliminary work is needed if you stay with the default, in-process option.

State Serialization and Deserialization

When you use the *InProc* mode, objects are stored in the session state as live instances of classes. No real serialization and deserialization ever takes place, meaning that you can actually store in *Session* whatever objects (including COM objects) you have created and access them with no significant overhead. The situation is less favorable if you opt for an out-of-process state provider.

In an out-of-process architecture, session values are copied from the native storage medium into the memory of the AppDomain that processes the request. A serialization/deserialization layer is needed to accomplish the task and represents one of the major costs for out-of-process state providers. How does this affect your code? First, you should make sure that only serializable objects are ever stored in the session dictionary; otherwise, as you can easily imagine, the session state can't be saved and you'll sustain an exception, moreover.

To perform the serialization and deserialization of types, ASP.NET uses two methods, each providing different results in terms of performance. For basic types, ASP.NET resorts to an optimized internal serializer; for other types, including objects and user-defined classes, ASP.NET makes use of the .NET binary formatter, which is slower. Basic types are *string*, *DateTime*, *Guid*, *IntPtr*, *TimeSpan*, *Boolean*, *byte*, *char*, and all numeric types.

The optimized serializer—an internal class named *AltSerialization*—employs an instance of the *BinaryWriter* object to write out one byte to denote the type and then the value. While reading, the *AltSerialization* class first extracts one byte, detects the type of the data to read, and then resorts to a type-specific method of the *BinaryReader* class to take data. The type is associated with an index according to an internal table, as shown in Figure 17-3.

Session Timeout	`Int32`
Cookieless	`Bool`
Dictionary empty?	`Bool`
StaticObjects empty?	`Bool`
Dictionary	`Array of bytes`
StaticObjects	`Array of bytes`

FIGURE 17-3 The serialization schema for basic types that the internal *AltSerialization* class uses.

> **Note** While Booleans and numeric types have a well-known size, the length of a string can vary quite a bit. How can the reader determine the correct size of a string? The *BinaryReader.ReadString* method exploits the fact that on the underlying stream the string is always prefixed with the length, encoded as an integer seven bits at a time. Values of the *DateTime* type, on the other hand, are saved by writing only the total number of ticks that form the date and are read as an *Int64* type.

As mentioned, more complex objects are serialized using the relatively slower *BinaryFormatter* class as long as the involved types are marked as serializable. Both simple and complex types use the same stream, but all nonbasic types are identified with the same type ID. The performance-hit range of 15 percent to 25 percent is a rough estimate based on the assumption that basic types are used. The more you use complex types, the more the overhead grows, and reliable numbers can be calculated only by testing a particular application scenario.

In light of this, if you plan to use out-of-process sessions, make sure you store data effectively. For example, if you need to persist an instance of a class with three string properties, performancewise you are *probably* better off using three different slots filled with a basic type rather than one session slot for which the binary formatter is needed. Better yet, you can use a type converter class to transform the object to and from a string format. However, understand that this is merely a guideline to be applied case by case and this advice should be taken with a grain of salt.

Storing Session Data

When working in *StateServer* mode, the entire content of the *HttpSessionState* object is serialized to an external application—a Windows service named *aspnet_state.exe*. The service is called to serialize the session state when the request completes. The service internally stores each session state as an array of bytes. When a new request begins processing, the array corresponding to the given session ID is copied into a memory stream and then deserialized into an internal session state item object. This object really represents the contents of the whole session. The *HttpSessionState* object that pages actually work with is only its application interface.

As mentioned, nonbasic types are serialized and deserialized using the system's binary formatter class, which can handle only classes explicitly marked to be serializable. This means that COM objects, either programmatically created or declared as static objects with a session scope in *global.asax*, can't be used with an out-of-process state provider. The same limitation applies to any nonserializable object.

Configuring the *StateServer* Provider

Using out-of-process storage scenarios, you give the session state a longer life and your application greater robustness. Out-of-process session-state storage basically protects the session against Internet Information Services (IIS) and ASP.NET process failures. By separating the session state from the page itself, you can also much more easily scale an existing application to Web farm and Web garden architectures. In addition, the session state living in an external process eliminates at the root the risk of periodically losing data because of process recycling.

As mentioned, the ASP.NET session-state provider is a Windows service named *aspnet_state.exe*. It normally resides in the installation folder of ASP.NET:

```
%WINDOWS%\Microsoft.NET\Framework\[version]
```

As usual, note that the final directory depends on the .NET Framework version you're actually running. Before using the state server, you should make sure that the service is up and running on the local or remote machine used as the session store. The state service is a constituent part of ASP.NET and gets installed along with it, so you have no additional setup application to run.

By default, the state service is stopped and requires a manual start. You can change its configuration through the properties dialog box of the service, as shown in Figure 17-4.

FIGURE 17-4 The properties dialog box of the ASP.NET state server.

An ASP.NET application needs to specify the TCP/IP address of the machine hosting the session-state service. The following listing shows the changes that need to be made to the *web.config* file to enable the remote session state:

```
<configuration>
    <system.web>
        <sessionState
            mode="StateServer"
            stateConnectionString="tcpip=MyMachine:42424" />
    </system.web>
</configuration>
```

Note that the value assigned to the *mode* attribute is case sensitive. The format of the *stateConnectionString* attribute is shown in the following line of code. The default machine address is 127.0.0.1, while the port is 42424.

```
stateConnectionString="tcpip=server:port"
```

The server name can be either an IP address or a machine name. In this case, though, non-ASCII characters in the name are not supported. Finally, the port number is mandatory and cannot be omitted.

> **Important**   The state server doesn't offer any authentication barrier to requestors, meaning that anyone who can get access to the network is potentially free to access session data. To protect session state and make sure that it is accessed only by the Web server machine, you can use a firewall, IPSec policies, or a secure net 10.X.X.X so that external attackers can't gain direct access. Another security-related countermeasure consists of changing the default port number. To change the port, you edit the *Port* entry under the registry key: *HKEY_LOCAL_MACHINE\ SYSTEM\CurrentControlSet\Services\aspnet_state\Parameters*. Writing the port in the *web.config* file isn't enough.

The ASP.NET application attempts to connect to the session-state server immediately after loading. The *aspnet_state* service must be up and running; otherwise, an HTTP exception is thrown. By default, the service is not configured to start automatically. The state service uses .NET Remoting to move data back and forth.

> **Note**   The ASP.NET state provider runs under the ASP.NET account. The account, though, can be configured and changed at will using the Service Control Manager interface. The state service is slim and simple and does not implement any special features. It is limited to holding data and listens to the specified port for requests to serve. In particular, the service isn't cluster-aware (that is, it doesn't provide a failover monitor to be error tolerant) and can't be used in a clustered world when another server takes on the one that fails.

Finally, note that by default the state server listens only to local connections. If the state server and Web server live on different machines, you need to enable remote connections. You do this through another entry in the same registry key as mentioned earlier. The entry is *AllowRemoteConnection*, and it must be set to a nonzero value.

Persist Session Data to SQL Server

Maintaining the session state in an external process certainly makes the whole ASP.NET application more stable. Whatever happens to the worker process, the session state is still there, ready for further use. If the service is paused, the data is preserved and automatically retrieved when the service resumes. Unfortunately, if the state provider service is stopped or if a failure occurs, the data is lost. If robustness is key for your application, drop the *StateServer* mode in favor of *SQLServer*.

Performance and Robustness

When ASP.NET works in *SQLServer* mode, the session data is stored in a made-to-measure database table. As a result, the session data survives even SQL Server crashes, but you have to add higher overhead to the bill. *SQLServer* mode allows you to store data on any connected machine, as long as the machine runs SQL Server 7.0 or newer. Aside from the different medium, the storage mechanism is nearly identical to that described for remote servers. In particular, the serialization and deserialization algorithm is the same, only it's a bit slower because of the characteristics of storage. When storing data of basic types, the time required to set up the page's *Session* object is normally at least 25 percent higher than in an *InProc* scenario. Also in regard to this issue, the more complex types you use, the more time it will take to manage the session data.

> **Note** When you get to make a decision between state server or SQL server storage, consider the fact that SQL Server is cluster-aware, which makes a solution based on it more robust (and also more robust across machine restarts) and more reliable than one based on a state server.

Configuring Session State for SQL Server Support

To use SQL Server as the state provider, enter the following changes in the *<sessionState>* section of the *web.config* file:

```
<configuration>
  <system.web>
    <sessionState
        mode="SQLServer"
        sqlConnectionString="server=127.0.0.1;integrated security=SSPI;" />
  </system.web>
</configuration>
```

In particular, you need to set the *mode* attribute (which is case sensitive) to *SQLServer* and specify the connection string through the *sqlConnectionString* attribute. Note that the *sqlConnectionString* attribute string must provide credentials (user ID and password or integrated security) and a server name. However, it cannot contain tokens, such as *Database* and *Initial Catalog*, unless a custom database is enabled using *allowCustomSqlDatabase*, as mentioned in Table 17-8. You can specify a SQL Server *Initial Catalog* database name or use the SQL Server Express *attachDBFileName* to point to an MDB file in the connection string only if the *allowCustomSqlDatabase* configuration setting is enabled. If that is disabled, any attempts to specify these settings in the connection string will result in an exception.

> **Note** The connection string for an out-of-process session state implementation (both *SQLServer* and *StateServer*) can also be specified to refer to a connection string defined in the *<connectionStrings>* section. The session state module first attempts to look up a connection string from the *<connectionStrings>* section with the name specified in the appropriate *<sessionState>* attribute; if it is not found, the session state attempts to use the specified string directly.

As for credentials to access the database, you can either use User ID and passwords or resort to integrated security.

> **Note** Whatever account you use to access session state in SQL Server, make sure that it is granted the *db_datareader* and *db_datawriter* permissions at least. Note also that to configure the SQL Server environment for storing session state, administrative privileges are required, as a new database and stored procedures need to be created.

Session state in SQL Server mode supports the specification of a custom command timeout value (in seconds) to accommodate slow-responding-server scenarios. You control it through the *sqlCommandTimeout* attribute, as mentioned in Table 17-8.

Creating the SQL Server Data Store

You use the *aspnet_regsql.exe* tool to configure the database environment by creating any needed tables, stored procedures, triggers, and jobs. In general, the tool works through the command line but also offers a visual interface. It is located in the following system folder:

```
%Windows%\Microsoft.NET\Framework\v4.0.30319
```

To create the ASPState database, you must use the command line, as shown here:

```
aspnet_regsql.exe -S [SqlServer Instance] -E -ssadd -sstype p
```

The tables that get created are named ASPStateTempApplications and ASPStateTempSessions. Figure 17-5 shows a view of the session database in SQL Server.

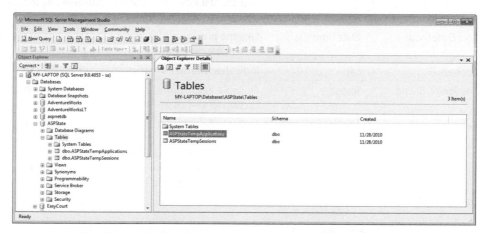

FIGURE 17-5 The ASPState database in SQL Server Enterprise Manager.

The ASPStateTempApplications table defines a record for each currently running ASP.NET application. The table columns are listed in Table 17-9.

TABLE 17-9 The ASPStateTempApplications Table

Column	Type	Description
AppId	Int	Indexed field. It represents a sort of autogenerated ID that identifies a running application using the *SQLServer* session mode.
AppName	char(280)	Indicates the application ID of the AppDomain running the application. It matches the contents of the *AppDomainAppId* property on the *HttpRuntime* object.

The ASPStateTempSessions table stores the actual session data. The table contains one row for each active session. The structure of the table is outlined in Table 17-10.

TABLE 17-10 The ASPStateTempSessions Table

Column	Type	Description
SessionId	Char(88)	Indexed field. It represents the session ID.
Created	DateTime	Indicates the time at which the session was created. It defaults to the current date.
Expires	DateTime	Indicates the time at which the session will expire. This value is normally the time at which the session state was created plus the number of minutes specified in *Timeout*. Note that *Created* refers to the time at which the session started, whereas *Expires* adds minutes to the time in which the first item is added to the session state.
Flags	Int	Indicates action flags—initialize items or none—from the *SessionStateActions* enum.
LockCookie	Int	Indicates the number of times the session was locked—that is, the number of accesses.
LockDate	DateTime	Indicates the time at which the session was locked to add the last item. The value is expressed as the current Universal Time Coordinate (UTC).
LockDateLocal	DateTime	Like the previous item, except that this one expresses the system's local time.
Locked	bit	Indicates whether the session is currently locked.
SessionItemLong	Image	Nullable field, represents the serialized version of a session longer than 7000 bytes.
SessionItemShort	VarBinary(7000)	Nullable field. It represents the values in the specified session. The layout of the bytes is identical to the layout discussed for *StateServer* providers. If more than 7000 bytes are needed to serialize the dictionary, the *SessionItemLong* field is used instead.
Timeout	int	Indicates the timeout of the session in minutes.

The column *SessionItemLong*, contains a long binary block of data. Although the user always works with image data as if it is a single, long sequence of bytes, the data is not stored in that format. The data is stored in a collection of 8-KB pages that aren't necessarily located next to each other.

When installing the SQL Server support for sessions, a job is also created to delete expired sessions from the session-state database. The job is named *ASPState_Job_DeleteExpiredSessions*, and the default configuration makes it run every minute. You should note that the SQLServerAgent service needs to be running for this to work.

Reverting to the Hosting Identity

The *useHostingIdentity* attribute (shown in Table 17-8) lets you decide about the identity to use to grant access to the SQL Server table with session state. When the *SQLServer* state provider is used with integrated security, the identity is the one impersonated by the ASP.NET process. This simplifies the administrative experience for intranet sites, requiring that only the ASP.NET account be granted access to protected and critical resources. The *useHostingIdentity* attribute defaults to *true*, which enables you to revert to the ASP.NET identity before making calls to the *SQLServer* session state provider. This will also happen if a custom provider is used.

> **Note** If you're using Windows integrated authentication to access SQL Server, reverting to the host identity is the most recommended option, for security reasons. Otherwise, it is advisable that you create a specific account and grant it only rights to execute session state stored procedures and access related resources.

Session State in a Web Farm Scenario

ASP.NET applications designed to run in a Web farm or Web garden hardware configuration cannot implement an in-process session state. The *InProc* mode won't work on a Web farm because a distinct worker process will be running on each connected machine, with each process maintaining its own session state. It doesn't even work on a Web garden because multiple worker processes will be running on the same machine.

Keeping all states separate from worker processes allows you to partition an application across multiple worker processes even when they're running on multiple computers. In both Web farm and Web garden scenarios, there can be only one *StateServer* or *SQLServer* process to provide session-state management.

If you're running a Web farm, make sure you have the same *<machineKey>* in all your Web servers. (More details can be found in Knowledge Base article Q313091.) In addition, for the session state to be maintained across different servers in the Web farm, all applications should have the same application path stored in the IIS metabase. This value is set as the AppDomain application ID and identifies a running application in the ASP.NET state database. (See Knowledge Base article Q325056 for more details.)

> Partition resolvers exist to let a session state provider partition its data onto multiple back-end nodes. This allows you to scale session state on large Web farms, according to a custom, user-defined load-balancing scheme. A partition provider is a component that supplies the connection string (the actual string, not the pointer to a string in the *web.config* file) to the session state that is used to access data, overriding any other settings in the *<sessionState>* section.

Customizing Session State Management

Since its beginning, the ASP.NET session state was devised to be an easy-to-customize and extensible feature. All things considered, you have the following three options to customize session state management:

- You can stay with the default session state module but write a custom state provider to change the storage medium (for example, to a non–SQL Server database or a different table layout). In doing so, you also have the chance to override some of the helper classes (mostly collections) that are used to bring data from the store to the Session object and back.

- You can stay with the default session state module but replace the session ID generator. But hold on! The algorithm that generates session IDs is a critical element of the application, because making session IDs too easy for attackers to guess can lead straight to session-hijacking attacks. Nonetheless, this remains a customizable aspect of session state that, properly used, can make your application even more secure.

- You can unplug the default session state module and roll your own. This option, however, should be used as a last resort. Obviously, it provides the maximum flexibility, but it is also extremely complicated and is recommended only if strictly necessary and if you know exactly what you're doing. We won't cover this topic in the book.

The first option—the easiest and least complicated of all—addresses most of the scenarios for which some custom session management is desirable. So let's tackle it first.

Building a Custom Session State Provider

A session state provider is the component in charge of serving any data related to the current session. Invoked when the request needs to acquire state information, it retrieves data from a given storage medium and returns that to the module. Invoked by the module when the request ends, it writes the supplied data to the storage layer. As mentioned, ASP.NET supports three state providers, as listed in Table 17-11.

TABLE 17-11 Default State Providers

Name	Class	Storage Medium
InProc	InProcSessionStateStore	Stores data as live objects in the ASP.NET Cache.
StateServer	OutOfProcSessionStateStore	Stores data as serialized objects to the memory of a Windows service named aspnet_state.exe.
SQLServer	SqlSessionStateStore	Stores data as serialized objects into a SQL Server database.

You can write your own state provider class that uses the storage medium of your choice. Note that the default state providers also make use of various helper classes to move data around. In your custom provider, you can replace these classes too, or just stick to the standard ones.

Defining the Session State Store

A state provider (also often referred to as a *session state store*) is a class that inherits from *SessionStateStoreProviderBase*. The main methods of the interface are listed in Table 17-12.

TABLE 17-12 Methods of the *SessionStateStoreProviderBase* Class

Method	Description
CreateNewStoreData	Creates an object to contain the data of a new session. It should return an object of type SessionStateStoreData.
CreateUninitializedItem	Creates a new and uninitialized session in the data source. The method is called when an expired session is requested in a cookie-less session state. In this case, the module has to generate a new session ID. The session item created by the method prevents the next request with the newly generated session ID from being mistaken for a request directed at an expired session.
Dispose	Releases all resources (other than memory) used by the state provider.
EndRequest	Called by the default session state module when it begins to handle the EndRequest event.
GetItem	Returns the session item matching the specified ID from the data store. The session item selected is locked for read. The method serves requests from applications that use a read-only session state.
GetItemExclusive	Returns the session item matching the specified ID from the data store and locks it for writing. It's used for requests originated by applications that use a read-write session state.
Initialize	Inherited from the base provider class, performs one-off initialization.
InitializeRequest	Called by the default session state module when it begins to handle the AcquireRequestState event.
ReleaseItemExclusive	Unlocks a session item that was previously locked by a call to the GetItemExclusive method.

Method	Description
RemoveItem	Removes a session item from the data store. It's called when a session ends or is abandoned.
ResetItemTimeout	Resets the expiration time of a session item. It's invoked when the application has session support disabled.
SetAndReleaseItemExclusive	Writes a session item to the data store.
SetItemExpireCallback	The default module calls this method to notify the data store class that the caller has registered a *Session_End* handler.

Classes that inherit the *SessionStateStoreProviderBase* class work with the default ASP.NET session state module and replace only the part of it that handles session-state data storage and retrieval. Nothing else in the session functionality changes.

Locking and Expiration

Can two requests for the same session occur concurrently? You bet. Requests can certainly arrive in parallel—for example, from two frames or when a user works with two instances of the same browser, the second of which is opened as a new window. To avoid problems, a state provider must implement a locking mechanism to serialize access to a session. The session state module determines whether the request requires read-only or read-write access to the session state and calls *GetItem* or *GetItemExclusive* accordingly. In the implementation of these methods, the provider's author should create a reader/writer lock mechanism to allow multiple concurrent reads but prevent writing on locked sessions.

Another issue relates to letting the session state module know when a given session has expired. The session state module calls the method *SetItemExpireCallback* when there's a *Session_End* handler defined in *global.asax*. Through the method, the state provider receives a callback function with the following prototype:

```
public delegate void SessionStateItemExpireCallback(
    string sessionID, SessionStateStoreData item);
```

It has to store that delegate internally and invoke it whenever the given session times out. Supporting expiration callbacks is optional and, in fact, only the InProc provider actually supports it. If your custom provider is not willing to support expiration callbacks, you should instruct the *SetItemExpireCallback* method to return *false*.

Note A provider that intends to support cookieless sessions must also implement the *CreateUninitialized* method to write a blank session item to the data store. More precisely, a *blank session item* is an item that is complete in every way except that it contains no session data. In other words, the session item should contain the session ID, creation date, and perhaps lock IDs, but no data. ASP.NET generates a new ID (in cookieless mode only) whenever a request is made for an expired session. The session state module generates the new session ID and redirects the browser. Without an uninitialized session item marked with a newly generated ID, the new request will again be recognized as a request for an expired session.

Replacing the Session Data Dictionary

SessionStateStoreData is the class that represents the session item—that is, a data structure that contains all the data that is relevant to the session. *GetItem* and *GetItemExclusive*, in fact, are defined to return an instance of this class. The class has three properties: *Items*, *StaticObjects*, and *Timeout*.

Items indicates the collection of name/values that will ultimately be passed to the page through the *Session* property. *StaticObjects* lists the static objects belonging to the session, such as objects declared in the *global.asax* file and scoped to the session. As the name suggests, *Timeout* indicates how long, in minutes, the session state item is valid. The default value is 20 minutes.

After the session state module has acquired the session state for the request, it flushes the contents of the *Items* collection to a new instance of the *HttpSessionStateContainer* class. This object is then passed to the constructor of the *HttpSessionState* class and becomes the data container behind the familiar *Session* property.

The *SessionStateStoreData* class is used in the definition of the base state provider class, meaning that you can't entirely replace it. If you don't like it, you can inherit a new class from it, however. To both the session module and state provider, the container of the session items is merely a class that implements the *ISessionStateItemCollection* interface. The real class being used by default is *SessionStateItemCollection*. You can replace this class with your own as long as you implement the aforementioned interface.

> **Note** To write a state provider, you might find helpful the methods of the *SessionStateUtility* class. The class contains methods to serialize and deserialize session items to and from the storage medium. Likewise, the class has methods to extract the dictionary of data for a session and add it to the HTTP context and the *Session* property.

Registering a Custom Session State Provider

To make a custom session state provider available to an application, you need to register it in the *web.config* file. Suppose you have called the provider class *SampleSessionStateProvider* and compiled it to *MyLib*. Here's what you need to enter:

```
<system.web>
    <sessionState mode="Custom"
      customProvider="SampleSessionProvider">
      <providers>
        <add name="SampleSessionProvider"
          type="SampleSessionStateProvider, MyLib" />
      </providers>
    </sessionState>
</system.web>
```

The name of the provider is arbitrary but necessary. To force the session state module to find it, set the *mode* attribute to *Custom*.

Generating a Custom Session ID

To generate the session ID, ASP.NET uses a special component named *SessionIDManager*. Technically speaking, the class is neither an HTTP module nor a provider. More simply, it is a class that inherits from *System.Object* and implements the *ISessionIDManager* interface. You can replace this component with a custom component as long as the component implements the same *ISessionIDManager* interface. To help you decide whether you really need a custom session ID generator, let's review some facts about the default module.

The Default Behavior

The default session ID module generates a session ID as an array of bytes with a crypto-graphically strong random sequence of 15 values. The array is then encoded to a string of 24 URL-accepted characters, which is what the system will recognize as the session ID.

The session ID can be round-tripped to the client in either an HTTP cookie or a mangled URL, based on the value of the *cookieless* attribute in the *<sessionState>* configuration section. Note that when cookieless sessions are used, the session ID module is responsible for adding the ID to the URL and redirecting the browser. The default generator redirects the browser to a fake URL like the following one:

```
http://www.contoso.com/test/(S(session_id))/page.aspx
```

How can a request for this fake URL be served correctly? In the case of a cookieless session, the Session ID module depends on a small and simple ISAPI filter (*aspnet_filter.dll*) to dynamically rewrite the real URL to access. The request is served correctly, but the path on the address bar doesn't change. The detected session ID is placed in a request header named *AspFilterSessionId*.

A Homemade Session ID Manager

Now that we've ascertained that a session ID manager is a class that implements *ISessionIDManager*, you have two options: build a new class and implement the interface from the ground up, or inherit a new class from *SessionIDManager* and override a couple of virtual methods to apply some personalization. The first option offers maximum flexibility; the second is simpler and quicker to implement, and it addresses the most compelling reason you might have to build a custom session ID generator—to supply your own session ID values.

Let's start by reviewing the methods of the *ISessionIDManager* interface, which are shown in Table 17-13.

TABLE 17-13 **Methods of the *ISessionIDManager* Interface**

Method	Description
CreateSessionID	Virtual method. It creates a unique session identifier for the session.
Decode	Decodes the session ID using *HttpUtility.UrlDecode*.
Encode	Encodes the session ID using *HttpUtility.UrlEncode*.
Initialize	Invoked by the session state immediately after instantiation; performs one-time initialization of the component.
InitializeRequest	Invoked by the session state when the session state is being acquired for the request.
GetSessionID	Gets the session ID from the current HTTP request.
RemoveSessionID	Deletes the session ID from the cookie or from the URL.
SaveSessionID	Saves a newly created session ID to the HTTP response.
Validate	Confirms that the session ID is valid.

If you plan to roll your own completely custom session ID generator, bear in mind the following points:

- The algorithm you choose for ID generation is a critical point. If you don't implement strong cryptographic randomness, a malicious user can guess a valid session ID when the same session is still active, thus accessing some user's data. (This is known as *session hijacking*.) A good example of a custom session ID algorithm is one that returns a globally unique identifier (GUID).

- You can choose to support cookieless sessions or not. If you do, you have to endow the component with the ability to extract the session ID from the HTTP request and redirect the browser. You probably need an ISAPI filter or HTTP module to preprocess the request and enter appropriate changes. The algorithm you use to store session IDs without cookies is up to you.

If you are absolutely determined to have the system use your session IDs, you derive a new class from *SessionIDManager* and override two methods: *CreateSessionID* and *Validate*. The former returns a string that contains the session ID. The latter validates a given session ID to ensure it conforms to the specification you set. After you have created a custom session ID module, you register it in the configuration file. Here's how to do it:

```
<sessionState
    sessionIDManagerType="Samples.MyIDManager, MyLib" />
</sessionState>
```

Session State Performance Best Practices

State management is a necessary evil. By enabling it, you charge your application with an extra burden. To reduce the performance impact of session state on Web applications, the first guideline is to disable session state whenever possible. However, to prevent the session from expiring, the HTTP module still marks the session as active in the data store. For out-of-process state servers, this means that a roundtrip is made. Using a custom session ID manager returning a null session ID for requests that are known not to require session state is the best way to work around this issue and avoid the overhead entirely. (Write a class that inherits from *SessionIDManager* and overrides *GetSessionID*.)

The second guideline entails minimizing contention on session data by avoiding frames and downloadable resources served by session-enabled handlers.

The third guideline relates to data serialization and deserialization. You should always use simple types and break complex classes into arrays of simple properties, at least as far as session management is concerned. In other words, I'm not suggesting that you should factor out your DAL classes—just change the way you serialize them into the session store. An alternate approach entails building a custom serialization algorithm that is optimized for session state storage. Breaking a class into various properties, with each stored in a session slot, is advantageous because of the simple types being used, but also because the extreme granularity of the solution minimizes the data to save in case of changes. If one property changes, only one slot with a simple type is updated instead of a single slot with a complex type.

The View State of a Page

ASP.NET pages supply the *ViewState* property to let applications build a call context and retain values across two successive requests for the same page. The view state represents the state of the page when it was last processed on the server. The state is persisted—usually, but not necessarily, on the client side—and is restored before the page request is processed.

By default, the view state is maintained as a hidden field added to the page. As such, it travels back and forth with the page itself. Although it is sent to the client, the view state does not represent, nor does it contain, any information specifically aimed at the client. The information stored in the view state is pertinent only to the page and some of its child controls and is not consumed in any way by the browser.

The view state comes at a cost. At the same time, however, the view state is one of the most important features of ASP.NET, not so much because of its technical relevance but because it allows you to benefit from most of the magic of the Web Forms model. Used without strict criteria, though, the view state can easily become a burden for pages.

The *StateBag* Class

The *StateBag* class is the class behind the view state that manages the information that ASP.NET pages and controls want to persist across successive posts of the same page instance. The class works like a dictionary and, in addition, implements the *IStateManager* interface. The *Page* and *Control* base classes expose the view state through the *ViewState* property. So you can add or remove items from the *StateBag* class as you would with any dictionary object, as the following code demonstrates:

```
ViewState["FontSize"] = value;
```

You should start writing to the view state only after the *Init* event fires for the page request. You can read from the view state during any stage of the page life cycle, but not after the page enters rendering mode—that is, after the *PreRender* event fires.

View State Properties

Table 17-14 lists all the properties defined in the *StateBag* class.

TABLE 17-14 Properties of the *StateBag* Class

Property	Description
Count	Gets the number of elements stored in the object.
Item	Indexer property. It gets or sets the value of an item stored in the class.
Keys	Gets a collection object containing the keys defined in the object.
Values	Gets a collection object containing all the values stored in the object.

Each item in the *StateBag* class is represented by a *StateItem* object. An instance of the *StateItem* object is implicitly created when you set the *Item* indexer property with a value or when you call the *Add* method. Items added to the *StateBag* object are tracked until the view state is serialized prior to the page rendering. Items serialized are those with the *IsDirty* property set to *true*.

View State Methods

Table 17-15 lists all the methods you can call in the *StateBag* class.

TABLE 17-15 Methods of the *StateBag* Class

Method	Description
Add	Adds a new *StateItem* object to the collection. If the item already exists, it gets updated.
Clear	Removes all items from the current view state.
GetEnumerator	Returns an object that scrolls over all the elements in the *StateBag*.
IsItemDirty	Indicates whether the element with the specified key has been modified during the request processing.
Remove	Removes the specified object from the *StateBag* object.

The *IsItemDirty* method represents an indirect way to call into the *IsDirty* property of the specified *StateItem* object.

 Note The view state for the page is a cumulative property that results from the contents of the *ViewState* property of the page plus the view state of all the controls hosted in the page.

Common Issues with View State

Architecturally speaking, the importance of the view state cannot be denied because it is key to setting up the automatic state management feature of ASP.NET. A couple of hot issues are related to the usage of the view state, however. The most frequently asked questions about the view state are related to security and performance. Can we say that the view state is inherently secure and cannot be tampered with? How will the extra information contained in the view state affect the download time of the page? Let's find out.

Encrypting and Securing

Many developers are doubtful about using the view state specifically because it is stored in a hidden field and left on the client at the mercy of potential intruders. Although the data is stored in a hashed format, there's no absolute guarantee that it cannot be tampered with. The first comment I'd like to make in response to this is that the view state as implemented in ASP.NET is inherently more secure than any other hidden fields you might use (and that you were likely using, say, in old classic ASP applications). My second remark is that only data confidentiality is at risk. While this is a problem, it is minor compared to code injection.

Freely accessible in a hidden field named __VIEWSTATE, the view state information is, by default, hashed and Base64 encoded. To decode it on the client, a potential attacker must accomplish a number of steps, but the action is definitely possible. Once decoded, though, the view state reveals only its contents—that is, confidentiality is at risk. However, there's no way an attacker can modify the view state to post malicious data. A tampered view state, in fact, is normally detected on the server and an exception is thrown.

For performance reasons, the view state is not encrypted. If it's needed, though, you can turn the option on by acting on the *web.config* file, as follows:

```
<machineKey validation="3DES" />
```

When the validation attribute is set to *3DES*, the view-state validation technique uses 3DES encryption and doesn't hash the contents. If you use *web.config*, the settings apply to all pages in the application. You can also control encryption settings separately for each page.

Furthermore, individual controls on the page can request to encrypt the view state. In case of a conflict, page settings win. You use the *ViewStateEncryptionMode* property, which accepts values from the *ViewStateEncryptionMode* enumeration. Feasible values are *Auto*, *Always*, and *Never*. The default value is *Auto*. When the value is *Auto*, ASP.NET encrypts the entire view state only if all controls want it encrypted. With values like *Always* and *Never*, the view state is always or never encrypted, regardless of the control settings.

Machine Authentication Check

The *@Page* directive contains an attribute named *EnableViewStateMac*, whose only purpose is making the view state a bit more secure by detecting any possible attempt at corrupting the original data. When serialized, and if *EnableViewStateMac* is set to *true*, the view state is appended with a validator hash string based on the algorithm and the key defined in the *<machineKey>* section of the configuration file. The resulting array of bytes, which is the output of the *StateBag*'s binary serialization plus the hash value, is Base64 encoded. By default, the encryption algorithm to calculate the hash is SHA1, and the encryption and decryption keys are autogenerated and stored in the Web server machine's Local Security Authority (LSA) subsystem. The LSA is a protected component of Windows. It provides security services and maintains information about all aspects of local security on a system.

If *EnableViewStateMac* is *true*, when the page posts back, the hash value is extracted and used to verify that the returned view state has not been tampered with on the client. If it has been, an exception is thrown. The net effect is that you might be able to read the contents of the view state, but to replace it you need the encryption key, which is in the Web server's LSA. The *MAC* in the name of the *EnableViewStateMac* property stands for *Machine Authentication Check*, which is enabled by default. If you disable the attribute, an attacker could alter the view-state information on the client and send a modified version to the server and have ASP.NET blissfully use that tampered-with information.

To reinforce the security of the view state, you can use the *ViewStateUserKey* property. The property evaluates to a user-specific string (typically, the session ID) that is known on the server and hard to guess on the client. ASP.NET uses the content of the property as an input argument to the hash algorithm that generates the MAC code.

Size Thresholds and Page Throughput

My opinion is that you should be concerned about the view state, but not for the potential security holes it might open in your code—it can let hackers exploit only existing holes. You should be more concerned about the overall performance and responsiveness of the page. Especially for feature-rich pages that use plenty of controls, the view state can reach a considerable size, measured in KB of data. Such an extra burden taxes all requests, in downloads and uploads, and ends up creating serious overhead for the application as a whole.

What is a reasonable size for an ASP.NET page? And for the view state of a page? Let's take a look at a sample page that contains a grid control bound to about 100 records (the Customers table in the Northwind database of SQL Server):

```
<html>
<head runat="server">
    <title>Measure Up Your ViewState</title>
</head>
<script language="javascript">
function ShowViewStateSize()
{
    var buf = document.forms[0]["__VIEWSTATE"].value;
    alert("View state is " + buf.length + " bytes");
}
</script>
<body>
    <form id="form1" runat="server">
        <input type="button" value="Show View State Size"
                onclick="ShowViewStateSize()">
        <asp:SqlDataSource ID="SqlDataSource1" runat="server"
                SelectCommand="SELECT companyname, contactname, contacttitle
                        FROM customers"
                ConnectionString="<%$ ConnectionStrings:LocalNWind %>">
        <asp:DataGrid ID="grid" runat="server"
                DataSourceID="SqlDataSource1" />
    </form>
</body>
</html>
```

In ASP.NET 2.0 and beyond, the total size of the page is about 20 KB. The view state alone, though, takes up about 11 KB. If you port the same page back to ASP.NET 1.x, results are even worse. The whole page amounts to 28 KB, while the view state alone amounts to a burdensome 19 KB. Two conclusions can be drawn from these numbers:

- Starting with ASP.NET 2.0, the view-state field appears to be more compact. And ASP.NET 2.0 was released back in 2005.

- The view state takes up a large share of the downloaded bytes for the page. You won't be too far from the truth if you estimate the view-state size to be about 60 percent of the entire page size.

What can you do about this? First, let's play with some numbers to determine a reasonable goal for view-state size in our applications. All things considered, you should endeavor to keep a page size around 30 KB, to the extent that is possible of course. The ideal size for a view state is around 7 KB; it is optimal if you can keep it down to 3 KB or so. In any case, the view state, regardless of its absolute size, should never exceed 30 percent of the page size.

Note Where do these numbers come from? "From my personal experience" would perhaps be a valid answer, but it's not necessarily a good or exhaustive one. Let's put it this way: the smallest you can keep a page is the best size. To me, 30 KB looks like a reasonable compromise, because most things can be stuffed into that size. Clearly, if you have 250 items to display, your page size can grow up to 1 MB or so. In the end, having a smaller or larger view state is a design choice and is mostly application-specific.

Within these boundaries, though, a few guidelines can be stated. The most important guideline is not so much that view state should be limited to a few KB, but that it should take a minimal percentage of the overall page size. Which percentage? Being the view-state helper, I'd say no more than 25 percent or 30 percent at the most.

But here I'm just throwing out numbers using a bit of common sense. If you can disable the view state altogether, do it. At the very least, you should avoid storing there the avoidable items that don't change often and are easily cached on the server, such as a long list of countries/regions.

Programming the View State

By default, the view state is enabled for all server controls; however, this doesn't mean that you strictly need it all the time and for all controls. The use of the view-state feature should be carefully monitored because it can hinder your code. View state saves you from a lot of coding and, more importantly, makes coding simpler and smarter. However, if you find you're paying too much for this feature, drop view state altogether and reinitialize the state of the size-critical controls at every postback. In this case, disabling view state saves processing time and speeds up the download process.

Disabling View State

You can disable the view state for an entire page by using the *EnableViewState* attribute of the *@Page* directive. Although this is not generally a recommended option, you should definitely consider it for read-only pages that either don't post back or don't need state to be maintained.

```
<% @Page EnableViewState="false" %>
```

A little known aspect of view state programming is that, with the previous setting in place, all controls within the page have view state disabled no matter what their view state settings are. When view state is enabled at the page level, instead, disabling the view state on a control produces the effect of disabling it just on that control.

The net effect of this situation is that if you have 300 controls in a page and just want to have view state enabled on, say, three of them, all that you can do is disable view state on the remaining 297. To make up for this, in ASP.NET 4 a new property has been added to exercise stricter control over view state: the *ViewStateMode* property. The property accepts three values: *Inherit*, *Enabled*, and *Disabled*. If the value is *Inherit*, the control gets the setting of its parent. The *ViewStateMode* property takes precedence over *EnableViewState*.

Determining When to Disable View State

Let's briefly recap what view state is all about and what you might lose if you ban it from your pages. View state represents the current state of the page and its controls just before the page is rendered to HTML. It is then serialized to a hidden field and downloaded to the client. When the page posts back, the view state—a sort of call context for the page request—is recovered from the hidden field, deserialized, and used to initialize the server controls in the page and the page itself. However, this is only the first half of the story.

After loading the view state, the page reads client-side posted information and uses those values to override most of the settings for the server controls. Applying posted values over-rides some of the settings read from the view state. You understand that in this case, and only for the properties modified by posted values, the view state represents an extra burden.

Let's examine a typical case and suppose you have a page with a text box server control. What you expect is that when the page posts back, the text box server control is automati-cally assigned the value set on the client. Well, to meet this rather common requirement, you *don't* need view state. Let's consider the following page:

```
<% @Page language="c#" %>
<form runat="server">
    <asp:textbox runat="server" viewstatemode="disabled"
        id="theInput" readonly="false" text="Type here" />
    <asp:checkbox runat="server" viewstatemode="disabled"
         id="theCheck" text="Check me" />
    <asp:button runat="server" text="Click" onclick="OnPost" />
</form>
```

Apparently, the behavior of the page is stateful even if view state is disabled for a couple of controls. The reason lies in the fact that you are using two server controls—*TextBox* and *CheckBox*—whose key properties—*Text* and *Checked*—are updated according to the values set by the user. For these properties, posted values override any setting that view state might have set. As a result, as long as you're simply interested in persisting these properties you don't need view state at all.

Likewise, you don't need view state for all control properties that are set at design-time in the *.aspx* file and are not expected to change during the session. The following code illustrates this point:

```
<asp:textbox runat="server" id="TextBox1" Text="Some text"
            MaxLength="20" ReadOnly="true" />
```

You don't need view state to keep the *Text* property of a *TextBox* up to date; you do need view state to keep up to date, say, *ReadOnly* or *MaxLength*, as long as these properties have their values changed during the page lifetime. If the two properties are constant during the page lifetime, you don't need view state for them either.

So when is view state really necessary?

View state is necessary whenever your page requires that accessory control properties (other than those subject to posted values) are updated during the page lifetime. In this context, "updated" means that their original value changes—either the default value or the value you assign to the property at design time. Consider the following form:

```
<script runat="server">
   void Page_Load(object sender, EventArgs e)
   {
      if (!IsPostBack)
         theInput.ReadOnly = true;
   }
</script>

<form id="form1" runat="server">
   <asp:textbox runat="server" id="theInput" text="Am I read-only?" />
   <asp:button ID="Button1" runat="server" text="Click" onclick="OnPost" />
</form>
```

When the page is first loaded, the text box becomes read-only. Next, you click the button to post back. If view state is enabled, the page works as expected and the text box remains read-only. If view state is disabled for the text box, the original setting for the *ReadOnly* property is restored—in this case, *false*.

In general, you can do without view state whenever the state can be deduced either from the client or from the runtime environment. In contrast, doing without view state is hard whenever state information can't be dynamically inferred and you can't ensure that all properties are correctly restored when the page posts back. This is exactly what view state guarantees at the cost of extra bytes when downloading and uploading. To save those bytes, you must provide an alternate approach.

Disabling the view state can also create subtler problems that are difficult to diagnose and fix, especially if you're working with third-party controls or, in general, controls for which you have source code access. Some ASP.NET controls, in fact, might save to the view state not just properties that are officially part of the programming interface (and that can be set accordingly), but also behavioral properties that serve internal purposes and are marked as protected or even private. Unfortunately, for these controls, you do not have the option of disabling the view state. But ASP.NET comes to the rescue with *control state*.

The Control State

It is not uncommon for a server control to persist information across postbacks. For example, consider what happens to a *DataGrid* control modified to support autoreverse sorting. When the user clicks to sort by a column, the control compares the current sort expression and the new sort expression. If the two are equivalent, the sort direction is reversed. How does the *DataGrid* track the current sort direction? If you don't place the sort direction property in the control's view state, it will be lost as soon as the control renders to the browser.

This kind of property is not intended to be used for plain configurations such as pager style or background color. It has an impact on how the control works. What if the control is then used in a page that has the view state disabled?

The *control state* is a special data container introduced just to create a sort of protected zone inside the classic view state. For developers of custom controls, it is safer to use the control state than the view state because application-level and page-level settings cannot affect it. If your existing custom control has private or protected properties stored in the view state, you should move all of them to the control state. Anything you store in the control state remains there until it is explicitly removed. Also the control state is sent down to the client and uploaded when the page posts back. The more data you pack into it, the more data is moved back and forth between the browser and the Web server. You should use control state, but you should do so carefully.

Programming the Control State

The implementation of the control state is left to the programmer, which is both good and bad. It is bad because you have to manually implement serialization and deserialization for your control's state. It is good because you can control exactly how the control works and tweak its code to achieve optimal performance in the context in which you're using it. The page's infrastructure takes care of the actual data encoding and serialization. The control state is processed along with the view state information and undergoes the same treatment as for serialization and Base64 encoding. The control state is also persisted within the same view state's hidden field. The root object serialized to the view state stream is actually a *Pair* object that contains the control state as the first element and the classic view state as the second member.

There's no ready-made dictionary object to hold the items that form the control state. You no longer have to park your objects in a fixed container such as the *ViewState* state bag—you can maintain control-state data in plain private or protected members. Among other things, this means that access to data is faster because it is more direct and is not mediated by a dictionary object.

To restore control state, the *Page* class invokes the *LoadControlState* on all controls that have registered with the page object as controls that require control state. The following pseudocode shows the control's typical behavior:

```
private override void LoadControlState(object savedState)
{
    // Make a copy of the saved state.
    // You know what type of object this is because
    // you saved it in the SaveControlState method.
    object[] currentState = (object[]) savedState;
    if (currentState == null)
        return;

    // Initialize any private/protected member you stored
    // in the control state. The values are packed in the same
    // order and format you stored them in the SaveControlState method.
    _myProperty1 = (int) currentState[0];
    _myProperty2 = (string) currentState[1];
    ...
}
```

The *LoadControlState* method receives an object identical to the one you created in *SaveControlState*. As a control developer, you know that type very well and can use this knowledge to extract any information that's useful for restoring the control state. For example, you might want to use an array of objects in which every slot corresponds to a particular property.

The following pseudocode gives you an idea of the structure of the *SaveControlState* method:

```
private override object SaveControlState()
{
    // Declare a properly sized array of objects
    object[] stateToSave = new Object[...];

    // Fill the array with local property values
    stateToSave[0] = _myProperty1;
    stateToSave[1] = _myProperty2;
    ...

    // Return the array
    return stateToSave;
}
```

You allocate a new data structure (such as a *Pair*, a *Triplet*, an array, or a custom type) and fill it with the private properties to persist across postbacks. The method terminates, returning this object to the ASP.NET runtime. The object is then serialized and encoded to a Base64 stream. The class that you use to collect the control state properties must be serializable.

Keeping the View State on the Server

The more stuff you pack into the view state, the more time the page takes to download and upload because the view state is held in a hidden field. The client-side hidden field is not set in stone, but is simply the default storage medium where the view state information can be stored. Does it make sense to store the view state somewhere on the server?

Leaving the view state on the server is definitely possible and all you have to do is override a couple of protected members on the *Page* class. The devil is in the details, however.

You should guarantee that the correct view-state file will be served to each page instance the user retrieves via the browser's history. This is not an issue as long as each page contains its own view state. But when the view state is stored elsewhere, unless you want to disable Back/Forward functionality, you should provide a mechanism that serves the "right" view state for the instance of a given page that the user is reclaiming. At a minimum, you need to make copies of the view state for about six to eight instances.

As you can see, what you save in the roundtrip is lost in the server's memory or server-side I/O operations. All in all, keeping the view state on the client and inside of the page is perhaps the option that works better in the largest number of scenarios. If the view state is a problem, you have only one way out: reducing its size.

Summary

Although HTTP is a stateless protocol, Web applications can't just do without certain forms of state. Moreover, state management is a hot topic for all real-world Web applications. Setting up an effective and efficient solution for state management is often the difference between an application being scalable or nonscalable.

One of the most-used forms of state is session state—that is, the state specific to a user and the one that's valid as long as that user works with the application. You can store session data in the memory of the ASP.NET worker process as well as in external processes, and even in a SQL Server table or in a custom state provider. In spite of the radically different options, the top-level programming interface is identical. More importantly, the ASP.NET session state can be persisted in a Web farm or Web garden scenario as well.

In the next chapter, we'll deal with another extremely powerful form of state container—the *Cache* object.

It's worth spending a final word on a form of state management that might grow significantly in the future, especially as HTML 5 becomes widely supported by browsers—client side state. Around the HTML 5 working draft, in fact, a number of technologies are being developed for storing information on the browser in a much more powerful way than with cookies. It ranges from simple forms of isolated storage (already in Internet Explorer 8) to Web SQL databases. As usual, time will tell. And years of experience remind us that no matter how cool it could be, it only works if it is widely supported.

Chapter 18
ASP.NET Caching

Hope is a good breakfast, but it is a bad supper.

—Sir Francis Bacon

Caching indicates the system's, or the application's, ability to save frequently used data to an intermediate storage medium. An intermediate storage medium is any support placed in between the application and its primary data source that lets you persist and retrieve data more quickly than with the primary data source. In a typical Web scenario, the canonical intermediate storage medium is the Web server's memory, whereas the data source is the back-end data management system. Obviously, you can design caching around the require-ments and characteristics of each application, thus using as many layers of caching as needed to reach your performance goals. In ASP.NET, caching comes in two independent but not exclusive flavors: caching application data, and caching the output of served pages.

To build an application-specific caching subsystem, you use the caching application programming interface (API) that lets you store data in a global, system-managed object—the *Cache* object. This approach gives you the greatest flexibility, but you need to learn a few usage patterns to stay on the safe side.

Page-output caching, instead, is a very quick way to take advantage of cache capabilities. You don't need to write code; you just configure it at design time and go. The ASP.NET system takes care of caching the output of the page to serve it back to clients for the specified time. For pages that don't get stale quickly, page-output caching is a kind of free performance booster.

In this chapter, I'll cover the aspects of caching in a single server as well as caching in a distributed scenario.

Caching Application Data

Centered on the *Cache* object, the ASP.NET caching API is much more than simply a container of global data shared by all sessions, such as the *Application* object that I briefly discussed in the previous chapter. The *Application* object, by the way, is preserved only for backward compatibility with legacy applications. The *Cache* object is a smarter and thread-safe container that can automatically remove unused items, support various forms of depen-dencies, and optionally provide removal callbacks and priorities. New ASP.NET applications should use the *Cache* object and seriously consider the AppFabric Caching services if strong scalability is needed.

The *Cache* Class

The *Cache* class is defined in the *System.Web.Caching* namespace. The current instance of the application's ASP.NET cache is returned by the *Cache* property of the *HttpContext* object or the *Cache* property of the *Page* object.

Fundamental Aspects of the *Cache* Object

The *Cache* object is unique in its capability to automatically scavenge the memory and get rid of unused items. Cached items can be prioritized and associated with various types of dependencies, such as disk files, other cached items, and database tables. When any of these items change, the cached item is automatically invalidated and removed. Aside from that, the *Cache* object provides the same dictionary-based and familiar programming interface as *Session*. Unlike *Session*, however, the *Cache* object does not store data on a per-user basis. Furthermore, when the session state is managed in-process, all currently running sessions are stored as distinct items in the ASP.NET *Cache*.

Keep in mind that an instance of the *Cache* class is created on a per-AppDomain basis and remains valid as long as that AppDomain is up and running. If you're looking for a global repository object that, like *Session*, works across a Web farm or Web garden architecture, the *Cache* object is not for you. You have to resort to AppFabric Caching services or to some commercial frameworks (for example, ScaleOut or NCache) or open-source frameworks (for example, Memcached or SharedCache).

Properties of the *Cache* Class

The *Cache* class provides a few properties and public fields. Table 18-1 lists and describes them all.

TABLE 18-1 *Cache* **Class Properties and Public Fields**

Property	Description
Count	Gets the number of items stored in the cache.
EffectivePercentagePhysicalMemoryLimit	Gets the maximum percentage of memory that can be used before the scavenging process starts. The default value is 97.
EffectivePrivateBytesLimit	Returns the bytes of memory available to the cache.
Item	An indexer property that provides access to the cache item identified by the specified key.
NoAbsoluteExpiration	A static constant that indicates a given item will never expire.
NoSlidingExpiration	A static constant that indicates sliding expiration is disabled for a given item.

The *NoAbsoluteExpiration* field is of the *DateTime* type and is set to the *DateTime.MaxValue* date—that is, the largest possible date defined in the Microsoft .NET Framework. The *NoSlidingExpiration* field is of the *TimeSpan* type and is set to *TimeSpan.Zero*, meaning that sliding expiration is disabled. I'll say more about sliding expiration shortly.

The *Item* property is a read/write property that can also be used to add new items to the cache. If the key specified as the argument of the *Item* property does not exist, a new entry is created. Otherwise, the existing entry is overwritten.

```
Cache["MyItem"] = value;
```

The data stored in the cache is generically considered to be of type *object*, whereas the key must be a case-sensitive string. When you insert a new item in the cache using the *Item* property, a number of default attributes are assumed. In particular, the item is given no expiration policy, no remove callback, and a normal priority. As a result, the item will stay in the cache indefinitely, until programmatically removed or until the application terminates. To specify any extra arguments and exercise closer control on the item, use the *Insert* method of the *Cache* class instead.

Methods of the *Cache* Class

The methods of the *Cache* class let you add, remove, and enumerate the items stored. Methods of the *Cache* class are listed and described in Table 18-2.

TABLE 18-2 *Cache* **Class Methods**

Method	Description
Add	Adds the specified item to the cache. It allows you to specify dependencies, expiration and priority policies, and a remove callback. The call fails if an item with the same key already exists. The method returns the object that represents the newly added item.
Get	Retrieves the value of the specified *n* item from the cache. The item is identified by key. The method returns *null* if no item with that key is found. (This method is used to implement the *get* accessor of the *Item* property.)
GetEnumerator	Returns a dictionary enumerator object to iterate through all the valid items stored in the cache.
Insert	Inserts the specified item into the cache. *Insert* provides several overloads and allows you to specify dependencies, expiration and priority policies, and a remove callback. The method is void and, unlike *Add*, overwrites an existing item having the same key as the item being inserted. (This method is used to implement the *set* accessor of the *Item* property.)
Remove	Removes the specified item from the cache. The item is identified by the key. The method returns the instance of the object being removed or *null* if no item with that key is found.

Both the *Add* and *Insert* methods don't accept null values as the key or the value of an item to cache. If null values are used, an exception is thrown. You can configure sliding expiration for an item for no longer than one year. Otherwise, an exception will be raised. Finally, bear in mind that you cannot set both sliding and absolute expirations on the same cached item.

> **Note** *Add* and *Insert* work in much the same way, but a couple of differences make it worthwhile to have both on board. *Add* fails (but no exception is raised) if the item already exists, whereas *Insert* overwrites the existing item. In addition, *Add* has just one signature, while *Insert* provides several overloads.

An Interior View

The *Cache* class inherits from *Object* and implements the *IEnumerable* interface. It is a wrapper around an internal class that acts as the true container of the stored data. The real class used to implement the ASP.NET cache varies depending on the number of affinitized CPUs. If only one CPU is available, the class is *CacheSingle*; otherwise, it is *CacheMultiple*. In both cases, items are stored in a hashtable and there will be a distinct hashtable for each CPU. It turns out that *CacheMultiple* manages an array of hashtables. Figure 18-1 illustrates the architecture of the *Cache* object.

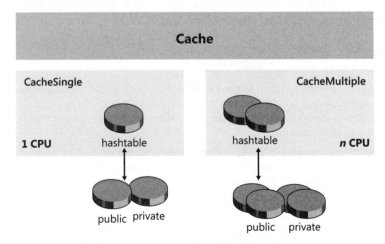

FIGURE 18-1 The internal structure of the ASP.NET cache.

The hashtable is divided into two parts: public elements and private elements. In the public portion of the hashtable are placed all items visible to user applications. System-level data, on the other hand, goes in the private section. The cache is a resource extensively used by the ASP.NET runtime itself; system items, though, are neatly separated by application data and there's no way an application can access a private element on the cache.

The *Cache* object is mostly a way to restrict applications to read from, and write to, the public segment of the data store. *Get* and *set* methods on internal cache classes accept a flag to denote the public attribute of the item. When called from the *Cache* class, these internal methods always default to the flag that selects public items.

The hashtable containing data is then enhanced and surrounded by other internal components to provide a rich set of programming features. The list includes the implementation of a least recently used (LRU) algorithm to ensure that items can be removed f the system runs short of memory, dependencies, and removal callbacks.

> **Note** On a multiprocessor machine with more than one CPU affinitized with the ASP.NET worker process, each processor ends up getting its own *Cache* object. The various cache objects are not synchronized. In a Web garden configuration, you can't assume that users will return to the same CPU (and worker process) on subsequent requests. So the status of the ASP.NET cache is not guaranteed to be aligned with what the same page did last time. Later in the chapter, we'll discuss a variation of the *Cache* object that addresses exactly this scenario.

Working with the ASP.NET *Cache*

An instance of the *Cache* object is associated with each running application and shares the associated application's lifetime. Each item when stored in the cache can be given special attributes that determine a priority and an expiration policy. All these are system-provided tools to help programmers control the scavenging mechanism of the ASP.NET cache.

Inserting New Items in the Cache

A cache item is characterized by a handful of attributes that can be specified as input arguments of both *Add* and *Insert*. In particular, an item stored in the ASP.NET *Cache* object can have the following properties:

- **Key**   A case-sensitive string, it is the key used to store the item in the internal hash table the ASP.NET cache relies upon. If this value is null, an exception is thrown. If the key already exists, what happens depends on the particular method you're using: *Add* fails, while *Insert* just overwrites the existing item.

- **Value**   A non-null value of type *Object* that references the information stored in the cache. The value is managed and returned as an *Object* and needs casting to become useful in the application context.

- **Dependencies**   An object of type *CacheDependency*, tracks a physical dependency between the item being added to the cache and files, directories, database tables, or other objects in the application's cache. Whenever any of the monitored sources are modified, the newly added item is marked obsolete and automatically removed.

- **Absolute Expiration Date**   A *DateTime* object that represents the absolute expiration date for the item being added. When this time arrives, the object is automatically removed from the cache. Items not subject to absolute expiration dates must use the *NoAbsoluteExpiration* constants representing the farthest allowable date. The absolute expiration date doesn't change after the item is used in either reading or writing.

- **Sliding Expiration**   A *TimeSpan* object, represents a relative expiration period for the item being added. When you set the parameter to a non-null value, the expiration-date parameter is automatically set to the current time plus the sliding period. If you explicitly set the sliding expiration, you cannot set the absolute expiration date too. From the user's perspective, these are mutually exclusive parameters. If the item is accessed before its natural expiration time, the sliding period is automatically renewed.

- **Priority**   A value picked out of the *CacheItemPriority* enumeration, denotes the priority of the item. It is a value ranging from *Low* to *NotRemovable*. The default level of priority is *Normal*. The priority level determines the importance of the item; items with a lower priority are removed first.

- **Update Callback**   If specified, indicates the function that the ASP.NET *Cache* object calls back when the item will be removed from the cache because it expired or the associated dependency changed. The function won't be called if the item is programmatically removed from the cached or scavenged by the cache itself. The delegate type used for this callback is *CacheItemUpdateCallback*.

- **Removal Callback**   If specified, indicates the function that the ASP.NET *Cache* object calls back when the item will be removed from the cache. In this way, applications can be notified when their own items are removed from the cache, no matter what the reason is. As mentioned in Chapter 17, "ASP.NET State Management," when the session state works in *InProc* mode, a removal callback function is used to fire the *Session_End* event. The delegate type used for this callback is *CacheItemRemovedCallback*.

There are basically three ways to add new items to the ASP.NET *Cache* object—the *set* accessor of the *Item* property, the *Add* method, and the *Insert* method. The *Item* property allows you to indicate only the key and the value. The *Add* method has only one signature that includes all the aforementioned arguments. The *Insert* method is the most flexible of all options and provides the following overloads:

```
public void Insert(String, Object);
public void Insert(String, Object, CacheDependency);
public void Insert(String, Object, CacheDependency, DateTime, TimeSpan);
public void Insert(String, Object, CacheDependency, DateTime, TimeSpan,
    CacheItemUpdateCallback);
public void Insert(String, Object, CacheDependency, DateTime, TimeSpan,
    CacheItemPriority, CacheItemRemovedCallback);
```

The following code snippet shows the typical call that is performed under the hood when the *Item* set accessor is used:

```
Insert(key, value, null, Cache.NoAbsoluteExpiration,
    Cache.NoSlidingExpiration, CacheItemPriority.Normal, null);
```

If you use the *Add* method to insert an item whose key matches that of an existing item, no exception is raised, nothing happens, and the method returns *null*.

Removing Items from the Cache

All items marked with an expiration policy, or a dependency, are automatically removed from the cache when something happens in the system to invalidate them. To programmatically remove an item, on the other hand, you resort to the *Remove* method. Note that this method removes any item, including those marked with the highest level of priority (*NotRemovable*). The following code snippet shows how to call the *Remove* method:

```
var oldValue = Cache.Remove("MyItem");
```

Normally, the method returns the value just removed from the cache. However, if the specified key is not found, the method fails and *null* is returned, but no exception is ever raised.

When items with an associated callback function are removed from the cache, a value from the *CacheItemRemovedReason* enumeration is passed on to the function to justify the operation. The enumeration includes the values listed in Table 18-3.

TABLE 18-3 The *CacheItemRemovedReason* Enumeration

Reason	Description
DependencyChanged	Removed because the associated dependency changed.
Expired	Removed because expired.
Removed	Programmatically removed from the cache using *Remove*. Notice that a *Removed* event might also be fired if an existing item is replaced either through *Insert* or the *Item* property.
Underused	Removed by the system to free memory.

If the item being removed is associated with a callback, the function is executed immediately after having removed the item.

Note that the *CacheItemUpdateReason* enumeration contains only the first two items of Table 18-3. Curiously, however, the actual numeric values behind the members in the enumeration don't match.

Tracking Item Dependencies

Items added to the cache through the *Add* or *Insert* method can be linked to an array of files and directories as well as to an array of existing cache items, database tables, or external events. The link between the new item and its cache dependency is maintained using an instance of the *CacheDependency* class. The *CacheDependency* object can represent a single file or directory or an array of files and directories. In addition, it can also represent an array of cache keys—that is, keys of other items stored in the *Cache*—and other custom dependency objects to monitor—for example, database tables or external events.

The *CacheDependency* class has quite a long list of constructors that provide for the possibilities listed in Table 18-4.

TABLE 18-4 The *CacheDependency* Constructor List

Constructor	Description
String	A file path—that is, a URL to a file or a directory name
String[]	An array of file paths
String, DateTime	A file path monitored starting at the specified time
String[], DateTime	An array of file paths monitored starting at the specified time
String[], String[]	An array of file paths, and an array of cache keys
String[], String[], CacheDependency	An array of file paths, an array of cache keys, and a separate *CacheDependency* object
String[], String[], DateTime	An array of file paths and an array of cache keys monitored starting at the specified time
String[], String[], CacheDependency, DateTime	An array of file paths, an array of cache keys, and a separate instance of the *CacheDependency* class monitored starting at the specified time

Any change in any of the monitored objects invalidates the current item. Note that you can set a time to start monitoring for changes. By default, monitoring begins right after the item is stored in the cache. A *CacheDependency* object can be made dependent on another instance of the same class. In this case, any change detected on the items controlled by the separate object results in a broken dependency and the subsequent invalidation of the present item.

In the following code snippet, the item is associated with the timestamp of a file. The net effect is that any change made to the file that affects the timestamp invalidates the item, which will then be removed from the cache.

```
var dependency = new CacheDependency(filename);
Cache.Insert(key, value, dependency);
```

Bear in mind that the *CacheDependency* object needs to take file and directory names expressed through absolute file system paths.

Defining a Removal Callback

Item removal is an event independent from the application's behavior and control. The difficulty with item removal is that because the application is oblivious to what has happened, it attempts to access the removed item later and gets only a null value back. To work around this issue, you can either check for the item's existence before access is attempted or, if you think you need to know about removal in a timely manner, register a callback and reload the item if it's invalidated. This approach makes particularly good sense if the cached item just represents the content of a tracked file or query.

The following code demonstrates how to read the contents of a Web server's file and cache it with a key named *MyData*. The item is inserted with a removal callback. The callback simply re-reads and reloads the file if the removal reason is *DependencyChanged*.

```
void Load_Click(Object sender, EventArgs e)
{
    AddFileContentsToCache("data.xml");
}

void AddFileContentsToCache(String fileName)
{
    var file = Server.MapPath(fileName);
    var reader = new StreamReader(file);
    var data = reader.ReadToEnd();
    reader.Close();
    CreateAndCacheItem(data, file);

    // Display the contents through the UI
    contents.Text = Cache["MyData"].ToString();
}

void CreateAndCacheItem(Object data, String file)
{
    var removal = new CacheItemRemovedCallback(ReloadItemRemoved);
    var dependency = new CacheDependency(file);
    Cache.Insert("MyData", data, dependency, Cache.NoAbsoluteExpiration,
        Cache.NoSlidingExpiration, CacheItemPriority.Normal, removal);
}

void ReloadItemRemoved(String key, Object value,
        CacheItemRemovedReason reason)
{
    if (reason == CacheItemRemovedReason.DependencyChanged)
    {
        // At this time, the item has been removed. We get fresh data and
        // re-insert the item
        if (key == "MyData")
            AddFileContentsToCache("data.xml");

        // This code runs asynchronously with respect to the application,
        // as soon as the dependency gets broken. To test it, add some
        // code here to trace the event
    }
}
```

If the underlying file has changed, the *dependency-changed* event is notified and the new contents are automatically loaded. So the next time you read from the cache, you get fresh data. If the cached item is removed, any successive attempt to read returns *null*. Here's some code that shows you how to read from the cache and remove a given item:

```
void Read_Click(Object sender, EventArgs e)
{
    var data = Cache["MyData"];
    if (data == null)
    {
        contents.Text = "[No data available]";
        return;
    }

    // Update the UI
    contents.Text = (String) data;
}

void Remove_Click(Object sender, EventArgs e)
{
    Cache.Remove("MyData");
}
```

Note that the item removal callback is a piece of code defined by a user page but automatically run by the *Cache* object as soon as the removal event is fired. The code contained in the removal callback runs asynchronously with respect to the page. If the removal event is related to a broken dependency, the *Cache* object executes the callback as soon as the notification is detected.

If you add an object to the *Cache* and make it dependent on a file, directory, or key that doesn't exist, the item is regularly cached and marked with a dependency as usual. If the file, directory, or key is created later, the dependency is broken and the cached item is invalidated. In other words, if the dependency item doesn't exist, it's virtually created with a null timestamp or empty content.

Setting the Item's Priority

Each item in the cache is given a priority—that is, a value picked up from the *CacheItemPriority* enumeration. A priority is a value ranging from *Low* (lowest) to *NotRemovable* (highest), with the default set to *Normal*. The priority is supposed to determine the importance of the item for the *Cache* object. The higher the priority is, the more chances the item has to stay in memory even when the system resources are going dangerously down.

If you want to give a particular priority level to an item being added to the cache, you have to use either the *Add* or *Insert* method. The priority can be any value listed in Table 18-5.

TABLE 18-5 Priority Levels in the *Cache* Object

Priority	Value	Description
Low	1	Items with this level of priority are the first items to be deleted from the cache as the server frees system memory.
BelowNormal	2	Intermediate level of priority between *Normal* and *Low*.
Normal	3	Default priority level. It is assigned to all items added using the *Item* property.
Default	3	Same as *Normal*.
AboveNormal	4	Intermediate level of priority between *Normal* and *High*.
High	5	Items with this level of priority are the last items to be removed from the cache as the server frees memory.
NotRemovable	6	Items with this level of priority are never removed from the cache. Use this level with extreme care.

The *Cache* object is designed with two goals in mind. First, it has to be efficient and built for easy programmatic access to the global repository of application data. Second, it has to be smart enough to detect when the system is running low on memory resources and to clear elements to free memory. This trait clearly differentiates the *Cache* object from *HttpApplicationState*, which maintains its objects until the end of the application (unless the application itself frees those items). The technique used to eliminate low-priority and seldom-used objects is known as *scavenging*.

Controlling Data Expiration

Priority level and changed dependencies are two of the factors that can lead a cached item to be automatically garbage-collected from the *Cache*. Another possible cause for a premature removal from the *Cache* is infrequent use associated with an expiration policy. By default, all items added to the cache have no expiration date, neither absolute nor relative. If you add items by using either the *Add* or *Insert* method, you can choose between two mutually exclusive expiration policies: absolute expiration and sliding expiration.

Absolute expiration is when a cached item is associated with a *DateTime* value and is removed from the cache as the specified time is reached. The *DateTime.MaxValue* field, and its more general alias *NoAbsoluteExpiration*, can be used to indicate the last date value supported by the .NET Framework and to subsequently indicate that the item will never expire.

Sliding expiration implements a sort of relative expiration policy. The idea is that the object expires after a certain interval. In this case, though, the interval is automatically renewed after each access to the item. Sliding expiration is rendered through a *TimeSpan* object— a type that in the .NET Framework represents an interval of time. The *TimeSpan.Zero* field represents the empty interval and is also the value associated with the *NoSlidingExpiration* static field on the *Cache* class. When you cache an item with a sliding expiration of 10 minutes, you use the following code:

```
Insert(key, value, null, Cache.NoAbsoluteExpiration,
    TimeSpan.FromMinutes(10), CacheItemPriority.Normal, null);
```

Internally, the item is cached with an absolute expiration date given by the current time plus the specified *TimeSpan* value. In light of this, the preceding code could have been rewritten as follows:

```
Insert(key, value, null, DateTime.Now.AddMinutes(10),
    Cache.NoSlidingExpiration, CacheItemPriority.Normal, null);
```

However, a subtle difference still exists between the two code snippets. In the former case—that is, when sliding expiration is explicitly turned on—each access to the item resets the absolute expiration date to the time of the last access plus the time span. In the latter case, because sliding expiration is explicitly turned off, any access to the item doesn't change the absolute expiration time.

> **Note** Immediately after initialization, the *Cache* collects statistical information about the memory in the system and the current status of the system resources. Next, it registers a timer to invoke a callback function at one-second intervals. The callback function periodically updates and reviews the memory statistics and, if needed, activates the scavenging module. Memory statistics are collected using a bunch of Win32 API functions to obtain information about the system's current usage of both physical and virtual memory. The *Cache* object classifies the status of the system resources in terms of low and high pressure. When the memory pressure exceeds the guard level, seldom-used objects are the first to be removed according to their priority.

Practical Issues

Caching is a critical factor for the success of a Web application. Caching mostly relates to getting quick access to prefetched data that saves you roundtrips, queries, and any other sort of heavy operations. Caching is important also for writing, especially in systems with a high volume of data to be written. By posting requests for writing to a kind of intermediate memory structure, you decouple the main body of the application from the service in charge of writing. Some people call this a *batch update*, but in the end it is nothing more than a form of caching for data to write.

The caching API provides you with the necessary tools to build a bullet-proof caching strategy. When it comes to this, though, a few practical issues arise.

Should I Cache or Should I Fetch?

There's just one possible answer to this question—it depends. It depends on the characteristics of the application and the expected goals. For an application that must optimize throughput and serve requests in the shortest possible amount of time, caching is essential. The quantity of data you cache and the amount of time you cache it in are the two parameters you need to play with to arrive at a good solution.

Caching is about reusing data, so data that is not often used in the lifetime of the application is not a good candidate for the cache. In addition to being frequently used, cacheable data is also general-purpose data rather than data that is specific to a request or a session. If your application manages data with these characteristics, cache it with no fear.

Caching is about memory, and memory is relatively cheap. However, a bad application design can easily drive the application to unpleasant out-of-memory errors regardless of the cost of a memory chip. On the other hand, caching can boost the performance just enough to ease your pain and give you more time to devise a serious refactoring.

Sometimes you face users who claim to have an absolute need for live data. Sure, data parked in the cache is static, unaffected by concurrent events, and not fully participating in the life of the application. Can your users afford data that has not been updated for a few seconds? With a few exceptions, the answer is, "Sure, they can." In a canonical Web application, there's virtually no data that can't be cached at least for a second or two. No matter what end users claim, caching can realistically be applied to the vast majority of scenarios. Real-time systems and systems with a high degree of concurrency (for example, a booking application) are certainly an exception, but most of the time a slight delay of one or two seconds can make the application run faster under stress conditions without affecting the quality of the service.

In the end, you should be considering caching all the time and filter it out in favor of direct data access only in special situations. As a practical rule, when users claim they need live data, you should try to provide a counterexample that proves to them that a few seconds of delay are still acceptable and that the delay can maximize hardware and software investments.

Fetching the real data is an option, but it might be the most expensive one. If you choose that option, make sure you really need it. Accessing cached data is usually faster if the data you get in this way makes sense to the application. On the other hand, be aware that caching requires memory. If abused, it can lead to out-of-memory errors and performance hits. Having said that, don't be too surprised if you find out that sometimes fetching data is actually faster than accessing items in a busy cache. This is due to how optimized SQL Server access has gotten these days.

Building a Wrapper Cache Object

As mentioned, no data stored in the ASP.NET cache is guaranteed to stay there when a piece of code attempts to read it. For the safety of the application, you should never rely on the value returned by the *Get* method or the *Item* property. The following pattern keeps you on the safe side:

```
var data = Cache["MyData"];
if (data != null)
{
    // The data is here, process it
    ...
}
```

The code snippet deliberately omits the *else* branch. What should you do if the requested item is *null*? You can abort the ongoing operation and display a friendly message to the user, or you can perhaps reload the data with a new fetch. Whatever approach you opt for, it will hardly fit for just any piece of data you can have in the cache.

If you need the cache as a structural part of the application (rather than just for caching only a few individual pieces of data), it has to be strictly related to the data access layer (DAL) and the repository interfaces you have on top of that. (See Chapter 14, "Layers of an Application.") Depending on the pattern you prefer, you can have caching implemented as a service in the business tier (*Cache-side* pattern) or integrated in the DAL and transparent to the rest of the application (*Cache Through* pattern). Figure 18-2 shows the resulting architecture in both cases.

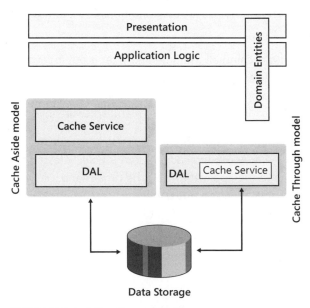

FIGURE 18-2 Isolating the caching layer.

In addition, you need to consider the pluggability of the caching layer. Whether you design it as an application service or as an integral part of the DAL, the caching service must be abstracted to an interface so that it can be injected in the application or in the DAL. At a minimum, the abstraction will offer the following:

```
public interface ICacheService
{
    Object Get(String key);
    void Set(String key, Object data);
    ...
}
```

You are responsible for adding dependencies and priorities as appropriate. Here's the skeleton of a class that implements the interface using the native ASP.NET *Cache* object:

```
public class AspNetCacheService : ICacheService
{
    public Object Get(String key)
    {
        return HttpContext.Current.Cache[key];
    }
    public void Set(String key, Object data)
    {
        HttpContext.Current.Cache[key] = data;
    }
    ...
}
```

As emphatic as it might sound, you should *never* use the *Cache* object directly from code-behind classes in a well-designed, ASP.NET-based layered solution.

Clearing the Cache

The .NET Framework provides no method on the *Cache* class to programmatically clear all the content. The following code snippet shows how to build one:

```
public void Clear()
{
    foreach(DictionaryEntry elem in Cache)
    {
        string s = elem.Key.ToString();
        Cache.Remove(s);
    }
}
```

Even though the ASP.NET cache is implemented to maintain a neat separation between the application's items and the system's items, it is preferable that you delete items in the cache individually. If you have several items to maintain, you might want to build your own wrapper class and expose one single method to clear all the cached data.

Cache Synchronization

Whenever you read or write an individual cache item, from a threading perspective you're absolutely safe. The ASP.NET *Cache* object guarantees that no other concurrently running threads can ever interfere with what you're doing. If you need to ensure that multiple operations on the *Cache* object occur atomically, that's a different story. Consider the following code snippet:

```
var counter = -1;
object o = Cache["Counter"];
if (o == null)
{
    // Retrieve the last good known value from a database
    // or return a default value
    counter = RetrieveLastKnownValue();
}
else
{
    counter = (Int32) Cache["Counter"];
    counter ++;
    Cache["Counter"] = counter;
}
```

The *Cache* object is accessed repeatedly in the context of an atomic operation—incrementing a counter. Although individual accesses to *Cache* are thread-safe, there's no guarantee that other threads won't kick in between the various calls. If there's potential contention on the cached value, you should consider using additional locking constructs, such as the C# *lock* statement (*SyncLock* in Microsoft Visual Basic .NET).

> **Important** Where should you put the lock? If you directly lock the *Cache* object, you might run into trouble. ASP.NET uses the *Cache* object extensively, and directly locking the *Cache* object might have a serious impact on the overall performance of the application. However, most of the time ASP.NET doesn't access the cache via the *Cache* object; rather, it accesses the direct data container—that is, the *CacheSingle* or *CacheMultiple* class. In this regard, a lock on the *Cache* object probably won't affect many ASP.NET components; regardless, it's a risk that I wouldn't like to take.
>
> By locking the *Cache* object, you also risk blocking HTTP modules and handlers active in the pipeline, as well as other pages and sessions in the application that need to use cache entries different from the ones you want to serialize access to.
>
> The best way out seems to be by using a synchronizer—an intermediate but global object that you lock before entering in a piece of code sensitive to concurrency:
>
> ```
> lock(yourSynchronizer) {
>     // Access the Cache here. This pattern must be replicated for
>     // each access to the cache that requires serialization.
> }
> ```
>
> The synchronizer object must be global to the application. For example, it can be a static member defined in the *global.asax* file.

Per-Request Caching

Although you normally tend to cache only global data and data of general interest, to squeeze out every little bit of performance you can also cache per-request data that is long-lived even though it's used only by a particular page. You place this information in the *Cache* object.

Another form of per-request caching is possible to improve performance. Working information shared by all controls and components participating in the processing of a request can be stored in a global container for the duration of the request. In this case, though, you might want to use the *Items* collection on the *HttpContext* class (discussed in Chapter 16, "The HTTP Request Context") to park the data because it is automatically freed up at the end of the request and doesn't involve implicit or explicit locking like *Cache*.

Designing a Custom Dependency

Let's say it up front: writing a custom cache dependency object is no picnic. You should have a very good reason to do so, and you should carefully design the new functionality before proceeding. The *CacheDependency* class is inheritable—you can derive your own class from it to implement an external source of events to invalidate cached items.

The base *CacheDependency* class handles all the wiring of the new dependency object to the ASP.NET cache and all the issues surrounding synchronization and disposal. It also saves you from implementing a start-time feature from scratch—you inherit that capability from the base class constructors. (The start-time feature allows you to start tracking dependencies at a particular time.)

Let's start reviewing the original limitations of *CacheDependency* that have led to removing the *sealed* attribute on the class, making it fully inheritable.

Extensions to the *CacheDependency* Base Class

To fully support derived classes and to facilitate their integration into the ASP.NET caching infrastructure, a bunch of new public and protected members have been added to the *CacheDependency* class. They are summarized in Table 18-6.

TABLE 18-6 Public and Protected Members of *CacheDependency*

Member	Description
DependencyDispose	Protected method. It releases the resources used by the class.
GetUniqueID	Public method. It retrieves a unique string identifier for the object.
NotifyDependencyChanged	Protected method. It notifies the base class that the dependency represented by this object has changed.
SetUtcLastModified	Protected method. It marks the time when a dependency last changed.
UtcLastModified	Public read-only property. It gets the time when the dependency was last changed.

As mentioned, a custom dependency class relies on its parent for any interaction with the *Cache* object. The *NotifyDependencyChanged* method is called by classes that inherit *CacheDependency* to tell the base class that the dependent item has changed. In response, the base class updates the values of the *HasChanged* and *UtcLastModified* properties. Any cleanup code needed when the custom cache dependency object is dismissed should go into the *DependencyDispose* method.

Getting Change Notifications

As you might have noticed, nothing in the public interface of the base *CacheDependency* class allows you to insert code to check whether a given condition—the heart of the dependency—is met. Why is this? The *CacheDependency* class was designed to support only a limited set of well-known dependencies—against files, time, and other cached items.

To detect file changes, the *CacheDependency* object internally sets up a file monitor object and receives a call from it whenever the monitored file or directory changes. The *CacheDependency* class creates a *FileSystemWatcher* object and passes it an event handler. A similar approach is used to establish a programmatic link between the *CacheDependency* object and the *Cache* object and its items. The *Cache* object invokes a *CacheDependency* internal method when one of the monitored items changes. What does this all mean to the developer?

A custom dependency object must be able to receive notifications from the external data source it is monitoring. In most cases, this is really complicated if you can't bind to existing notification mechanisms (such as file system monitor or SQL Server notifications). When the notification of a change in the source is detected, the dependency uses the parent's infrastructure to notify the cache of the event. We'll consider a practical example in a moment.

The *AggregateCacheDependency* Class

Not only can you create a single dependency on an entry, you can also aggregate dependencies. For example, you can make a cache entry dependent on both a disk file and a SQL Server table. The following code snippet shows how to create a cache entry, named *MyData*, that is dependent on two different files:

```
// Creates an array of CacheDependency objects
CacheDependency dep1 = new CacheDependency(fileName1);
CacheDependency dep2 = new CacheDependency(fileName2);
CacheDependency deps[] = {dep1, dep2};

// Creates an aggregate object
AggregateCacheDependency aggDep = new AggregateCacheDependency();
aggDep.Add(deps);
Cache.Insert("MyData", data, aggDep)
```

Any custom cache dependency object (including *SqlCacheDependency*) inherits *CacheDependency*, so the array of dependencies can contain virtually any type of dependency.

The *AggregateCacheDependency* class is built as a custom cache dependency object and inherits the base *CacheDependency* class.

A Cache Dependency for XML Data

Suppose your application gets some key data from a custom XML file and you don't want to access the file on disk for every request. So you decide to cache the contents of the XML file, but still you'd love to detect changes to the file that occur while the application is up and running. Is this possible? You bet. You arrange a file dependency and you're done.

In this case, though, any update to the file that modifies the timestamp is perceived as a critical change. As a result, the related entry in the cache is invalidated and you're left with no choice other than re-reading the XML data from the disk. The rub here is that you are forced to re-read everything even if the change is limited to a comment or to a node that is not relevant to your application.

Because you want the cached data to be invalidated only when certain nodes change, you create a made-to-measure cache dependency class to monitor the return value of a given XPath expression on an XML file.

> **Note** If the target data source provides you with a built-in and totally asynchronous notification mechanism (such as the command notification mechanism of SQL Server), you just use it. Otherwise, to detect changes in the monitored data source, you can only poll the resource at a reasonable rate.

Designing the *XmlDataCacheDependency* Class

To better understand the concept of custom dependencies, think of the following example. You need to cache the inner text of a particular node in an XML file. You can define a custom dependency class that caches the current value upon instantiation and reads the file periodically to detect changes. When a change is detected, the cached item bound to the dependency is invalidated.

> **Note** Admittedly, polling might not be the right approach for this particular problem. Later on, in fact, I'll briefly discuss a more effective implementation. Be aware, though, that polling is a valid and common technique for custom cache dependencies.

A good way to poll a local or remote resource is through a timer callback. Let's break the procedure into a few steps:

1. The custom *XmlDataCacheDependency* class gets ready for the overall functionality. It initializes some internal properties and caches the polling rate, file name, and XPath expression to find the subtree to monitor.

2. After initialization, the dependency object sets up a timer callback to access the file periodically and check contents.

3. In the callback, the return value of the XPath expression is compared to the previously stored value. If the two values differ, the linked cache item is promptly invalidated.

There's no need for the developer to specify details about how the cache dependency is broken or set up. The *CacheDependency* class takes care of it entirely.

> **Note** If you're curious to know how the *Cache* detects when a dependency is broken, read on. When an item bound to a custom dependency object is added to the *Cache*, an additional entry is created and linked to the initial item. *NotifyDependencyChanged* simply invalidates this additional element which, in turn, invalidates the original cache item.

Implementing the Dependency

The following source code shows the core implementation of the custom *XmlDataCacheDependency* class:

```
public class XmlDataCacheDependency : CacheDependency
{
    // Internal members
    static Timer _timer;
    Int32 _pollSecs = 10;
    String _fileName;
    String _xpathExpression;
    String _currentValue;

    public XmlDataCacheDependency(String file, String xpath, Int32 pollTime)
    {
        // Set internal members
        _fileName = file;
        _xpathExpression = xpath;
        _pollSecs = pollTime;

        // Get the current value
        _currentValue = CheckFile();
```

```csharp
      // Set the timer
      if (_timer == null) {
         var ms = _pollSecs * 1000;
         var cb = new TimerCallback(XmlDataCallback);
         _timer = new Timer(cb, this, ms, ms);
      }
   }

   public String CurrentValue
   {
      get { return _currentValue; }
   }

   public void XmlDataCallback(Object sender)
   {
      // Get a reference to THIS dependency object
      var dep = sender as XmlDataCacheDependency;

      // Check for changes and notify the base class if any are found
      var value = CheckFile();
      if (!String.Equals(_currentValue, value))
         dep.NotifyDependencyChanged(dep, EventArgs.Empty);
   }

   public String CheckFile()
   {
      // Evaluates the XPath expression in the file
      var doc = new XmlDocument();
      doc.Load(_fileName);
      var node = doc.SelectSingleNode(_xpathExpression);

      return node.InnerText;
   }

   protected override void DependencyDispose()
   {
      // Kill the timer and then proceed as usual
      _timer.Dispose();
      _timer = null;
      base.DependencyDispose();
   }
}
```

When the cache dependency is created, the file is parsed and the value of the XPath expression is stored in an internal member. At the same time, a timer is started to repeat the operation at regular intervals. The return value is compared to the value stored in the constructor code. If the two are different, the *NotifyDependencyChanged* method is invoked on the base *CacheDependency* class to invalidate the linked content in the ASP.NET *Cache*.

Testing the Custom Dependency

How can you use this dependency class in a Web application? It's as easy as it seems—you just use it in any scenario where a *CacheDependency* object is acceptable. For example, you create an instance of the class in the *Page_Load* event and pass it to the *Cache.Insert* method:

```
protected const String CacheKeyName = "MyData";
protected void Page_Load(Object sender, EventArgs e)
{
   if (!IsPostBack)
   {
      // Create a new entry with a custom dependency (and poll every 10 seconds)
      var dependency = new XmlDataCacheDependency(
         Server.MapPath("employees.xml"),
         "MyDataSet/NorthwindEmployees/Employee[employeeid=3]/lastname",
         10);
      Cache.Insert(CacheKeyName, dependency.CurrentValue, dependency);
   }

   // Refresh the UI
   Msg.Text = Display();
}
```

You write the rest of the page as usual, paying close attention to accessing the specified *Cache* key. The reason for this is that because of the dependency, the key could be null. Here's an example:

```
protected String Display()
{
    var o = Cache[CacheKeyName];
    return o ?? "[No data available--dependency broken]";
}
```

The *XmlDataCacheDependency* object allows you to control changes that occur on a file and decide which are relevant and might require you to invalidate the cache. The sample dependency uses XPath expressions to identify a subset of nodes to monitor for changes.

> **Note** I decided to implement polling in this sample custom dependency because polling is a pretty common, often mandatory, approach for custom dependencies. However, in this particular case polling is not the best option. You could set a *FileSystemWatcher* object and watch for changes to the XML file. When a change is detected, you execute the XPath expression to see whether the change is relevant for the dependency. Using an asynchronous notifier, if one is available, results in much better performance.

SQL Server Cache Dependency

Many ASP.NET applications query some data out of a database, cache it, and then manage to serve a report to the user. Binding the report to the data in the cache will both reduce the time required to load each report and minimize traffic to and from the database. What's the problem, then? With a report built from the cache, if the data displayed is modified in the database, users will get an out-of-date report. If updates occur at a known or predictable rate, you can set an appropriate duration for the cached data so that the report gets automatically refreshed at regular intervals. However, this contrivance just doesn't work if serving live data is critical for the application or if changes occur rarely and, worse yet, randomly. In the latter case, whatever duration you set might hit the application in one way or the other. A too-long duration creates the risk of serving outdated reports to end users which, in some cases, could undermine the business; a too-short duration burdens the application with unnecessary queries.

A database dependency is a special case of custom dependency that consists of the automatic invalidation of some cached data when the contents of the source database table changes. In ASP.NET, you find an ad hoc class—*SqlCacheDependency*—that inherits *CacheDependency* and supports dependencies on SQL Server tables. More precisely, the class is compatible with SQL Server 2005 and later.

Taking Advantage of SQL Server Dependencies

The *SqlCacheDependency* class has two constructors. The first takes a *SqlCommand* object, and the second accepts two strings: the database name and the table name. The following code creates a SQL Server dependency and binds it to a cache key:

```
protected void AddToCache(Object data)
{
    var database = "Northwind";
    var table = "Customers";
    var dependency = new SqlCacheDependency(database, table);
    Cache.Insert("MyData", data, dependency);
}
protected void Page_Load(Object sender, EventArgs e)
{
    if (!IsPostBack)
    {
        // Get some data to cache
        var data = Customers.LoadByCountry("USA");

        // Cache with a dependency on Customers
        AddToCache(data);
    }
}
```

The data in the cache can be linked to any data-bound control, as follows:

```
var data = Cache["MyData"] as IList<Customer>;
if (data == null)
    Trace.Warn("Null data");

CustomerList.DataTextField = "CompanyName";
CustomerList.DataSource = data;
CustomerList.DataBind();
```

When the database is updated, the *MyData* entry is invalidated and, as in the sample implementation provided here, the list box displays empty.

> **Important** You get notification based on changes in the table as a whole. In the preceding code, we're displaying a data set that results from the following:
>
> ```
> SELECT * FROM customers WHERE country='USA'
> ```
>
> If, say, a new record is added to the *Customers* table, you get a notification no matter what the value in the *country* column is. The same happens if a record is modified or deleted where the *country* column is not USA.
>
> By using a *SqlCommand* object in the constructor of the dependency class, you gain a finer level of control and can notify applications only of changes to the database that modify the output of that specific command.

Distributed Cache

Scalability is an aspect of software that came with the advent of successful Web applications. It is strictly related to the stateless nature of the HTTP protocol so that any new requests from the *same* user in the *same* session must be bound to the *same* "state" left by the last request.

The need to "re-create" the last known good state results in an additional workload that saturates Web and data servers quite soon and kind of linearly as the number of users increases. Caching is a way to smooth the issue by providing a data store that sits nearer to the user and doesn't require frequent roundtrips to central servers.

The ASP.NET *Cache* object has a number of powerful and relevant capabilities. Unfortunately, today's business needs raised the bar a little higher. As a result, the *Cache* object is limited today because it is bound to a worker process and a single machine. The *Cache* object doesn't span multiple machines like in a Web farm; its amount of memory affects only a single machine and can't be scaled out horizontally. Enter distributed caching.

The power of a distributed cache is in its design, which distributes load and data on multiple and largely independent machines. Implemented across multiple servers, a distributed cache is scalable by nature but still gives the logical view of a single cache. Moreover, you don't need high-end machines to serve as cache servers. Add this to cheaper storage and faster network cards and you get the big picture—distributed caching these days is much more affordable than only a few years ago. Figure 18-3 shows the abstraction that a distributed caching layer provides to applications.

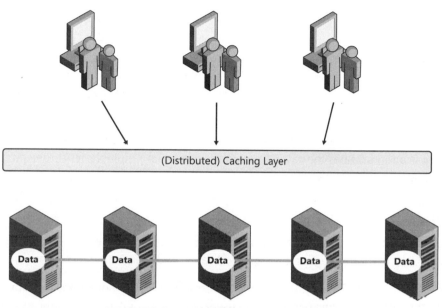

FIGURE 18-3 Overall design of a distributed cache

Note In a previous edition of this book, in the same chapter about caching, I had arguments against the widespread use of a distributed cache. Only a few years ago, the perception of scalability was different. It was recognized as a problem, but most of the time it could be resolved in the scope of the single Web server.

Today, it is different—not only do you welcome the possibility of caching on multiple machines, but you also demand an ad hoc layer to do the hard work of data synchronization and retrieval. This is referred to as a *distributed caching system*.

Features of a Distributed Cache

As mentioned, lack of scalability is the fundamental problem addressed by a distributed cache. Compared to a classic database, a distributed cache is much easier and cheaper to scale and replicate. It is not coincidental that there is a growing interest in NoSQL solutions, which are essentially distributed stores that can be easily and effectively scaled horizontally. Ultimately, a distributed cache and most NoSQL frameworks offer nearly the same set of features.

High Availability

Commonly based on a cluster of cache servers, distributed cache gains scalability through the addition of new servers and high availability (H/A) through replication of the content on each server. If one cache server goes down, no data is lost because another copy on another server is immediately available to the application.

Although high availability remains a natural attribute of a distributed caching system, the real effectiveness of replication has to be measured against the real behavior of the application. Replication is great for applications that do a lot of reads. As you add more servers, you add more read capacity to your cache cluster and improve the responsiveness and availability of the application.

At the same time, a heavily replicated cache is not desirable for write-intensive applications. If the application updates the cache frequently, maintaining multiple synchronized copies of the data becomes ineffective.

Topology

The topology of the distributed cache plays an important role in determining its success. There are two main topologies: the replicated cache and the partitioned cache.

In a *replicated cache* topology, the various servers in the cluster hold a private copy of the data. In this way, the reliability is high and users never experience loss of data, even when a server goes down. This cache topology is excellent for read-intensive apps, but it turns into overhead for write-intensive applications.

In a *partitioned cache* topology, the entire content of the cache is partitioned among the various servers. This design represents a good compromise between availability and per-formance. This is the first option to consider in scenarios where read/write operations are balanced.

A popular variation of this topology privileges high availability and is often referred to as *partitioned cache with H/A*. In this case, each partition is also replicated and servers contain their regular data partition plus a copy of another partition.

A distributed caching system is not necessarily limited to just one tier. It can be complement-ed with a client cache that lives close to the user and keeps in-process a copy of frequently used data from the cache. When used, such a client cache is usually read-only and not kept in sync with the rest of the caching system.

Freshness of Data

By design, the cache is a place for temporary information that needs be replaced periodically with up-to-date data. Of high importance in the feature list of a distributed cache is the ability to specify how long data should stay in the cache. Common expiration policies are based on an absolute time (for example, "Remove items at noon or in one hour") or a sliding usage time (for example, "Remove items if not used for a given period").

Most distributed caches are in-memory and do not persist their content to disk. So in most situations, memory is limited and the cache size cannot grow beyond a certain fixed limit. When the cache reaches this size, it should start removing cached items to make room for new ones, a process usually referred to as *performing evictions*. Least recently used (LRU) and least frequently used (LFU) are the two most popular algorithms for data eviction.

Cache dependencies, both on other cached items and external resources, are also desirable features to have in a distributed cache. Especially when you have domain data in the cache, you might want to search for data using a more flexible approach than using a simple key. Ideally, a LINQ-based query language for cached items is a big plus.

Integration with the Data Access Layer

Finally, read-through and write-through (or write-behind) capabilities qualify a caching solution as a top-quality solution. Read-through capabilities refer to the cache's ability to automatically read data from a configured data store in case of a cache miss.

Write-through capabilities, instead, enable the cache to automatically write data to the configured data store whenever you update the cache. In other words, the cache, not your application, holds the key to the data access layer. The difference between write-through and write-behind capabilities is that in the former case the application waits until both the cache and data store are updated. In write-behind (or write-back) mode, the application updates the cache synchronously but then the cache ripples changes to the database in an asynchronous manner.

This is a list of the features one would reasonably expect from a distributed cache. Not all products available today, however, offer these features to the same extent. Let's see what the Microsoft distributed caching service currently offers.

AppFabric Caching Services

Windows Server AppFabric consists of a few extensions to Microsoft Windows Server to improve the application infrastructure and make it possible to use it to run applications that are easier to scale and manage.

Currently, Windows Server AppFabric has two extensions: AppFabric Caching Services and AppFabric Hosting Services. The former is Microsoft's long-awaited distributed cache solution; the latter is the centralized host environment for services, and specifically services created using Windows Workflow Foundation. Let's focus on caching services.

Fast Facts

AppFabric Caching Services (ACS) is an out-of-process cache that combines a simple programming interface with a clustered architecture. ACS should not be viewed as a mere (distributed) replacement for the native ASP.NET *Cache* object. When you have a very slow data access layer that assembles data from various sources (for example, relational databases, SAP, mainframes, and documents) and when you have an application deployed on a Web farm, you definitely need a caching layer to mediate access to data and distribute the load of data retrieval on an array of servers.

The plain old *Cache* object of ASP.NET is simply inadequate and, in similar scenarios, you are encouraged to use ACS in lieu of *Cache*. Keep in mind, however, that although endowed with a similar programming interface, ACS currently lacks some of the more advanced capabilities of the ASP.NET *Cache*, such as dependencies, sliding and absolute expiration, and removal callbacks. At the same time, it remains as simple to use as a hashtable, offers a scalable and reliable infrastructure, is configurable via Windows PowerShell, and presents some developer-oriented features that are not in ASP.NET, such as programmatic access to cache-related properties of cached items (such as priority or expiration) and event propagation (such as notifying client apps of changed items).

Architecture of Caching Services

ACS is articulated in two levels: the client cache and distributed cache. The *client cache* is a component to install on the Web server machine and represents the gateway used by ASP.NET applications to read and write through ACS. The *distributed cache* includes some cache server machines that are each running an instance of the AppFabric Caching Services and storing data according to the configured topology. In addition, the client cache can optionally implement a local, server-specific cache that makes access to selected data even faster. The data found in this local cache is not kept in sync with the data in the cluster. Figure 18-4 provides an overall vision of AppFabric Caching Services.

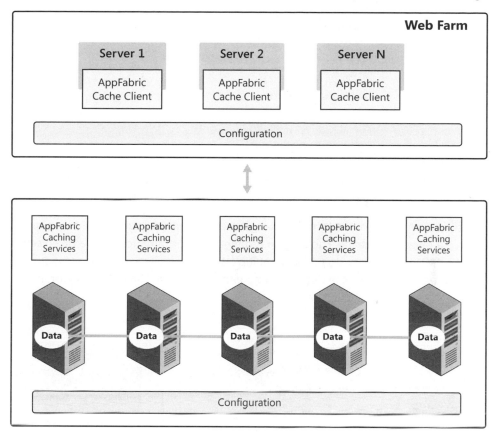

FIGURE 18-4 Architecture of AppFabric Caching Services.

The configuration script for the servers in the cache cluster contains the name of the cluster and general settings such as topology and data eviction policies. In addition, the configuration contains the list of servers and relative names and ports. Each service is configured to use two main ports: one to communicate with the client (*cachePort*) and one to communicate their availability to neighbors (*clusterPort*). Configuration information for the cluster is saved in one location, which can be an XML file on a shared network folder, a SQL Server database, or a custom store. Here's an example excerpted from an XML file (*clusterconfig.xml*):

```
<configuration>
    <configSections>
        <section name="dataCache"
                type="Microsoft.ApplicationServer.Caching.DataCacheSection,
                    Microsoft.ApplicationServer.Caching.Core, ..." />
    </configSections>
    <dataCache size="Small">
        <hosts>
            <host replicationPort="22236"
                arbitrationPort="22235"
                clusterPort="22234"
```

```
                    hostId="879796007"
                    size="1007"
                    leadHost="true"
                    account="My-Laptop\DinoE"
                    cacheHostName="AppFabricCachingService"
                    name="My-Laptop"
                    cachePort="22233" />
        </hosts>
    </dataCache>
</configuration>
```

Each server can have one or multiple caches of data. A data cache is simply a logical way of grouping data. Each enabled server has one default data cache (which is unnamed), but you are allowed to create your own. Data caches can be individually configured.

Each data cache is optionally made of regions. A region is a logical way of grouping data within a given data cache. Each region is defined programmatically on a given server and, unlike data caches, they do not span multiple servers. Finally, you have cached objects. A cached object is simply the data you store either directly in the data cache or in a region. Figure 18-5 provides an illustration.

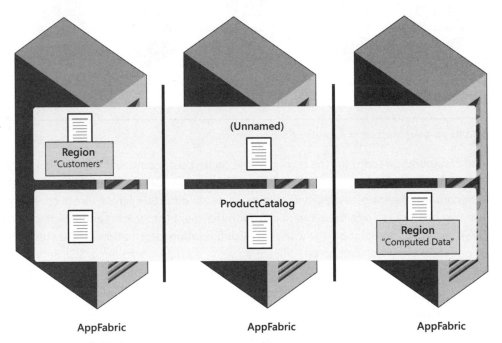

FIGURE 18-5 Data caches and regions.

In Figure 18-5, you see that named and unnamed caches can span multiple servers, whereas optional regions are specific to just one server and are usually created via Windows PowerShell. As a developer, you are not interested in the location of a region; you only need to know whether it exists and what data it contains. In this way, you can provide more information to ACS and make it return data more quickly.

> **Note** To be precise, in ACS an unnamed cache is not really unnamed. It is just named in a default way and must still be explicitly created via the administration console of Windows PowerShell. The "unnamed" cache gets the name of "*default*." The only difference between this and a regular named cache is that you can gain access to it using an additional shortcut method on the cache factory object—*GetDefaultCache*.

Client-Side Configuration of Caching Services

To use ACS in your ASP.NET pages, you need to configure the Web server environment first. This requires adding a section to the application's *web.config* file. Here's a snippet:

```
<dataCacheClient>
    <localCache isEnabled="false" />
      <hosts>
        <host name="Server01" cachePort="22233" />
        ...
      </hosts>
</dataCacheClient>
```

Obviously, you must first have available a bunch of AppFabric assemblies on the Web server so that you can safely declare the new *dataCacheClient* section in the configuration. For some reason, the ACS assemblies don't show up in the Microsoft Visual Studio list of available assemblies and you have to catch them yourself in the folds of the *%System%\AppFabric* directory. You need to pick up two assemblies: *Microsoft.ApplicationServer.Caching.Core* and *Microsoft.ApplicationServer.Caching.Client*.

```
<configuration>
   <configSections>
      <section name="dataCacheClient"
               type="Microsoft.ApplicationServer.Caching.DataCacheClientSection,
                   Microsoft.ApplicationServer.Caching.Core"
                allowLocation="true"
                allowDefinition="Everywhere" />
   </configSections>
   ...
</configuration>
```

The *dataCacheClient* section specifies the desired deployment type, the list of hosts that provide cache data, and any optional settings regarding the local cache.

An ACS client can connect to all listed hosts. The ACS infrastructure tracks the placement of cached objects across all hosts and routes your client straight to the right host when a request for a particular cached object is made.

Important Note that some old documentation and literature still refer to this feature as one of two possible deployment strategies: routing and simple. In the final version of ACS, the simple deployment mode is no longer supported. The drawback is that the same stale documentation and literature suggests you add a *deployment* attribute to the *dataCacheClient* section, which will cause a runtime configuration exception as the code attempts to gain access to the cache factory.

If you enable the local cache, any retrieved objects are saved in a local cache within the ACS client, thus forming an additional layer of virtual memory. The local cache takes precedence over data in the cluster. Note that ACS performs no automatic checks on data in the cluster to detect possible recent changes that occurred for the objects in the local cache. In other words, by using the local cache you trade speed of data retrieval for data accuracy.

Note To install AppFabric Caching Services on a machine intended to serve as a cache cluster, you also need to have IIS 7 Manager for Remote Administration enabled on that machine.

Programming Caching Services

Let's look at some sample code. The entry point in ACS is the cache factory object. The factory, then, will gain you access to any data cache available in the system. The simplest way to get a factory is shown here:

```
var factory = new DataCacheFactory();
```

The factory needs to consume some information to be successfully instantiated. You can provide configuration settings as a constructor parameter or let the class figure it out itself from the configuration file. Here's the fluent code you can use to initialize the factory without using the *web.config* file:

```
var servers = new List<DataCacheServerEndpoint>(1)
            {
                new DataCacheServerEndpoint("Server01", 22233)
            };
var configuration = new DataCacheFactoryConfiguration
                {
                    Servers = servers,
                    LocalCacheProperties = new DataCacheLocalCacheProperties()
                };
var factory = new DataCacheFactory(configuration);
```

The next steps are straightforward. First, you get a data cache and then you start reading and writing data to it. A data cache must be created administratively using the Windows PowerShell console. Here's the command you need to create a named cache. (As mentioned, you use the name *default* to create the default unnamed cache.)

```
New-Cache -cachename yourCache
```

In this way, you get a named cache with the same default settings as the default unnamed cache. Of course, you can express additional parameters on the command line. For example, the following line creates a cache with no eviction policy enabled:

```
New-Cache -cachename yourCache -eviction:none
```

To get command line information, you can type the following:

```
New-Cache -?
```

If the requested cache is not available, the constructor of *DataCacheFactory* just throws an exception:

```
var factory = new DataCacheFactory();
var dinoCache = factory.GetCache("Dino");
var defaultCache = factory.GetDefaultCache();
```

From this point on, you can use the object returned by *GetCache* and *GetDefaultCache* in much the same way you would use the native *Cache* object of ASP.NET. With just a little difference, you now can access information stored across a (expansible) cluster of servers:

```
dinoCache[key] = value;
```

Of course, you might want to call the factory and get cache objects only once in the application, preferably at startup. Unlike to the ASP.NET *Cache*, you don't have dependencies, but you do have regions, search capabilities, and a rich event model (through which you can simulate some of the ASP.NET cache dependencies).

> **Note** Interestingly, after you install AppFabric Caching Services, you also have a new (and free) out-of-process session provider that uses caching services to store your session data. You might want to check out the documentation to find out more details.

Other Solutions

As a matter of fact, most distributed applications today need distributed caching and just can't afford the native ASP.NET *Cache* object. AppFabric Caching Services is a solution that addresses many scenarios, but overall it is not feature-complete yet from the perspective of a realistic distributed cache. What other solutions are available?

Memcached

Memcached (*http://memcached.org*) is a popular, open-source distributed cache widely used by some popular social networks. Facebook is the most illustrious example. Technically speaking, Memcached can be hosted on a number of platforms, including Windows. Memcached, however, was originally created for Unix-based machines. For this reason, it's often associated with PHP and, in general, with the LAMP stack (where LAMP stands for Linux, Apache, MySQL, and PHP/Python/Perl).

Memcached runs as a background service on a variety of servers and communicates with the outside world through a configured port (usually port 11211). Client applications employ ad hoc libraries to contact a Memcached-equipped server and read or write data. A client can connect to any available servers; servers, on the other hand, are isolated from one another. The server stores data in memory and applies an eviction policy when it runs short of RAM.

A .NET library that can be used to talk to a Memcached installation (regardless of the host environment) can be found at *http://sourceforge.net/projects/memcacheddotnet*.

> **Note** Is it *Memcache* or *Memcached*? Both names seem to be frequently used to mean the same product. The product name is Memcache, but because on Unix it runs as a daemon, the program file has been named with a trailing "d" just to stay consistent with Unix naming conventions for daemons. It soon became common to use Memcached to refer to either the product or the executable. A subtler question is, how should you pronounce that? Should it be like the past form of "to cache" or like it would be in a Unix environment—that is, *memcache-dee*? In the end, it's up to you!

SharedCache

Written in C# and entirely based on .NET managed code, SharedCache (*sharedcache.com*) is another open-source distributed and replicated cache for use in server farms. SharedCache supports three deployment scenarios: a partitioned cache, a replicated cache, and a single instance.

With a partitioned cache, the entire data set is split across the active servers that form the cluster of cache server machines. With a replicated cache, each cache server contains the entire data set. In this case, the runtime infrastructure is responsible for keeping data over the servers in sync. Finally, the single instance mode entails you having a single cache server but host it out of process with respect to the client Web application. Moving from one configuration to another doesn't require code refactoring; it's simply a matter of configuration.

Commercial Solutions

With good products available for free or under open-source licenses, why should you ever consider commercial solutions, then? The answer is simple: commercial solutions offer more advanced features, capabilities and, especially, support. At their core, both commercial and free solutions provide a fast and scalable caching layer; the difference is in the extras that are provided. If you're OK with the core features you get from ACS or the community edition of

Memcached, by all means stick to that. Otherwise, be ready to spend some good money for the extras. Table 18-7 lists a few products currently available.

TABLE 18-7 A Quick List of Commercially Distributed Cache Products

Product	Description
NorthScale Memcached Server	It's the leading commercial distribution of Memcached as worked out by some of the key contributors to the original open-source project. Enhancements include security, dynamic scaling, packaged setup, and Web-based management capabilities. From the same group, you can also get Membase Server, which is a NoSQL database backed by Memcached. For more information, visit *http://www.membase.com/products-and-services/memcached.*
ScaleOut StateServer	Part of a suite of products aimed at making enterprise applications more scalable, StateServer runs as a service on every machine in your server farm and stores data objects in memory while making them globally accessible across the farm within its distributed data grid. Its top selling points are the patented technology for H/A, its comprehensive API, and the outstanding StateServer console for administrative and management tasks. For more information, visit *http://www.scaleoutsoftware.com/products/scaleout-stateserver.*
AlachiSoft NCache	It presents itself as the distributed version of the ASP.NET native *Cache* object with a ton of extra features, including a LINQ-based query language, rich eviction functionalities, event notification, and dynamic clustering. As a plus, it also has an Express version that is free for up to two cache servers running .NET 3.5. The NCache engine is also exposed as a second-level caching layer for both NHibernate and Entity Framework 4 and as an extension to the Enterprise Library Caching Block and the Cache provider mechanism of ASP.NET 4. For more information, visit *http://www.alachisoft.com/ncache.*

Caching ASP.NET Pages

The concept of a Web cache is probably as old as the Web itself. Don't worry if you're not familiar with this term; you certainly know very well at least one kind of Web cache—the browser's local cache.

Web sites and applications rely on the services provided by the Web server, which essentially receives requests and sends out responses. Generally speaking, a Web cache is something that sits in between a Web server and a client browser and gently takes the liberty of serving some requests without disturbing the Web server at the back end. Fundamental reasons for installing a Web cache are to reduce network traffic and to reduce latency.

The most popular type of Web cache is the browser cache. Another example of a Web cache is a proxy server that, deployed on the network, has requests and responses routed to it to cache on a larger scale than the local browser. A proxy cache is recommended for large organizations where many users might be requesting the same pages from a bunch of sites. The beneficial effects of a proxy cache expand, then, to the entire organization.

A Web cache stores representations of requested resources (such as script files, images, and style sheets), and it applies a few simple rules to determine whether it can serve the request right away or whether the resource has to be requested by the origin server. In general, all requests are subject to Web caching. At the same time, each response that serves a given resource can contain instructions for the Web cache regarding if and how to cache the resource.

Let's see how ASP.NET pages interact with the browser cache.

ASP.NET and the Browser Cache

All Web browsers look into their cache before making a request for a given URL. ASP.NET requests are no exception. This means that if the content of the requested ASP.NET page is available on the client (and valid), often no request is made to the server. However, every time you make a change to the source ASPX file on the server, the next request for that page will get the update. If you make a change to a JavaScript file, instead, you likely will have to wait a few hours or just manually clean the local browser cache to get the update. Let's try to understand how things work under the hood.

Typical Behavior of the Browser Cache

First and foremost, browsers won't save any responses that explicitly prohibit the use of the cache. Furthermore, browsers won't save any responses that come from a secure channel (HTTPS) or that require authentication.

If the requested URL doesn't have a match in the local cache, the browser just sends the request on to the server. Otherwise, if a match is found, the browser checks whether the cached representation of the requested resource is still valid. A valid representation is a representation that has not expired. Valid representations (also referred to as fresh representations) are served directly from the cache without any contact with the server.

The browser uses HTTP headers to determine whether the representation is fresh or stale. The *Expires* HTTP header indicates the absolute expiration date of the resource. The *max-age* HTTP header indicates for how long the representation is fresh. If the resource is stale, the browser will ask the origin server to validate the representation. If the server replies that a newer resource exists, a new request is made. Otherwise, the saved representation is served.

These simple rules express the behavior of Web caches—both browser cache and proxy cache. If ASP.NET pages and JavaScript files behave differently, the difference is all in the HTTP headers that accompany them.

Typical Behavior of an ASP.NET Page

An ASP.NET page is a dynamic resource, meaning that its content might be different even when the requesting URL is the same. This structural attribute makes an ASP.NET page a non-cacheable resource. An image that represents a company's logo or a script file, on the other hand, is a much more static type of resource and is inherently more cacheable.

By default, an ASP.NET page is cacheable by browsers but not by proxy servers. However, an ASP.NET page has no expiration set and subsequently is always stale. For this reason, any request you make for an ASPX resource will always result in an immediate refetch from the server as if the page was never cached. Figure 18-6 shows this.

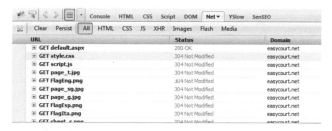

FIGURE 18-6 ASPX pages are always fetched from the server.

The screen shot shows that default.aspx is requested as usual, whereas cascading style sheets (CSS), images, and scripts are checked and served from the local cache because they are not modified.

The default behavior of the ASP.NET page results from a similar payload and especially from the *Cache-Control* header.

```
Cache-Control      private
Content-Type       text/html; charset=utf-8
Server             Microsoft-IIS/7.5
X-AspNet-Version   4.0.30319
X-Powered-By       ASP.NET
Date               Thu, 02 Dec 2010 17:56:06 GMT
Content-Length     12315
```

You can change at will the caching settings for any ASPX page. One of the tools you can use for doing so is the *@OutputCache* directive that I'll cover in just a moment.

Typical Behavior of Static Resources

Typically, static resources are served with a relatively long lifetime, with the goal of staying in the cache as much as possible. Obviously, developers as well as Web masters are ultimately responsible for deciding about the maximum age allowed for a given set of resources. For static resources, you can set HTTP headers from the Web server (for example, IIS) management console. (See Figure 18-7.)

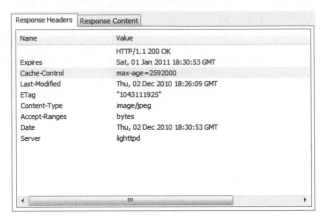

Name	Value
	HTTP/1.1 200 OK
Expires	Sat, 01 Jan 2011 18:30:53 GMT
Cache-Control	max-age=2592000
Last-Modified	Thu, 02 Dec 2010 18:26:09 GMT
ETag	"1043111925"
Content-Type	image/jpeg
Accept-Ranges	bytes
Date	Thu, 02 Dec 2010 18:30:53 GMT
Server	lighttpd

FIGURE 18-7 Typical response headers for a static resource.

The figure shows the response headers of a JPEG file, which is given about a month of life in the browser cache. Modern Web servers add an *ETag* header, which represents a hash calculated on the content of the resource. They also include the *Last-Modified* header with the timestamp of the server resource. When the resource gets stale and both the *ETag* header and timestamp match, you can be really sure that the resource is still the same.

Making ASP.NET Pages Cacheable

As mentioned, by default ASP.NET pages are not served from any cache, neither the browser cache nor some proxy cache in the middle. This behavior is inspired by the fact that an ASP.NET page, in general, is a dynamic resource whose content might change frequently. There are many situations, however, where it is acceptable for a page response to be a little stale if this brings significant performance advantages. Want an example?

Think of an e-commerce application and its set of pages for the products catalog. These pages are relatively expensive to create because they could require one or more database calls and likely some form of data join. All things considered, a page like this could easily cost you a few million CPU cycles. Why should you regenerate this same page a hundred times per second? Product pages tend to remain the same for weeks and are rarely updated more than once per day.

A much better strategy is to create the page once, cache it somewhere, and give the page response a maximum duration. When the cached page becomes stale, the first incoming request will be served in the standard way, running the page's code, and the new page out-put will be cached for another period until it also becomes stale.

ASP.NET page output caching is the feature that allows you to control the cache-related behavior of the page. Output caching can take place at two levels: for entire pages or for portions of the page. Page caching is smart enough to let you save distinct output based on the requesting URL, query string, or form parameters, and it lets you choose the location and duration of the cache. The console through which you control all of this is the *@OutputCache* directive.

The *@OutputCache* Directive

Just like other page directives, *@OutputCache* goes at the top of the ASP.NET page. The directive allows you to specify a handful of attributes, a couple of which—*Duration* and *VaryByParam*—are mandatory. The *Duration* attribute indicates in seconds how long the page output should stay in the cache. The *VaryByParam* attribute allows you to vary the cached output depending on the GET query string or form POST parameters. The following declaration indicates the page should stay in the cache for one minute regardless of any GET or POST parameters:

```
<%@ OutputCache Duration="60" VaryByParam="None" %>
```

For frequently requested pages and relatively static pages, the *@OutputCache* directive is a real performance booster. With a shorter duration, even limited to one second or two, it provides a way to speed up the entire application.

Available attributes indicate the location of the cache, its duration, and the arguments to use to vary page caching. The list of supported attributes is shown in Table 18-8. Note that the directive can be applied to both pages (*.aspx*) and user controls (*.ascx*). Note that some of the attributes are valid in one case but not the other.

TABLE 18-8 **Attributes of the *@OutputCache* Directive**

Attribute	Applies to	Description
CacheProfile	Page	Associates a page with a group of output caching settings specified in the *web.config* file. (More details about this appear later in the chapter.)
Duration	Page, User control	The time, in seconds, that the page or user control is cached.
Location	Page	Specifies the location (browser, proxy, or server) where to store the output of a page. The attribute takes its value from the *OutputCacheLocation* enumeration.
NoStore	Page	Indicates whether to send a *Cache-Control:no-store* header to prevent browser-side storage of the page output.
Shared	User control	Indicates whether the user control output can be shared with multiple pages. It is *false* by default.
SqlDependency	Page, User control	Indicates a dependency on the specified table on a given SQL Server database. Whenever the contents of the table changes, the page output is removed from the cache.
VaryByControl	User control	A semicolon-separated list of strings that represent properties of the user control. Each distinct combination of values for the specified properties will originate a distinct copy of the page in the cache.

Attribute	Applies to	Description
VaryByCustom	Page, User control	A semicolon-separated list of strings that lets you maintain distinct cached copies of the page based on the browser type or user-defined strings.
VaryByHeader	Page	A semicolon-separated list of HTTP headers.
VaryByParam	Page, User control	A semicolon-separated list of strings representing query string values sent with GET method attributes, or parameters sent using the POST method.

Note that the *VaryByParam* attribute is mandatory. If you omit it, a runtime exception is always thrown. However, if you don't need to vary by parameters, set the attribute to *None*. The empty string is not an acceptable value for the *VaryByParam* attribute.

Choosing a Location for the Page Output

Among other things, you use the *@OutputCache* directive to decide where the page output should be cached. In general, it can go in three different locations, one not necessarily excluding the other. The page can be cached on the client (the browser cache), on the IIS Web server, and even by an intermediate proxy server. The various options are listed in Table 18-9. They come from the *OutputCacheLocation* enumerated type.

TABLE 18-9 Output Cache Locations

Location	Cache-Control	Expires	Description
Any	*Public*	Set according to the value of the *duration* attribute.	The page is cached everywhere, in the browser as well as in any intermediate proxy. In addition, it is also cached on the Web server according to the current output cache provider.
Client	*Private*	Set according to the value of the *duration* attribute.	The page is cached only on the browser. It is ignored by any intermediate proxy, and it is not processed by any output cache provider registered in the ASP.NET application.
DownStream	*Public*	Set according to the value of the *duration* attribute.	The page can be cached on the browser and by any intermediate cache-enabled proxies. It won't be processed by any output cache provider registered in the ASP.NET application.
None	*No-Cache*	−1	Also, the *Pragma* header is set to *No-Cache*. As a result, the page is never served from any cache.
Server	*No-Cache*	−1	Also, the *Pragma* header is set to *No-Cache*. The page is cached only by the output cache provider currently registered in the ASP.NET application.
ServerAndClient	*Private*	Set according to the value of the *duration* attribute.	The page is cached on the browser, and it is also processed by the output cache provider currently registered in the ASP.NET application. It will be ignored by any proxy in the middle.

When the *cache-control* header is *public*, ASP.NET also emits the header *max-age* set to the same value as the *duration* attribute. *Expires* and *max-age* play the same role except that the former requires an absolute date and time (that has to be parsed by browsers and proxies), whereas the latter just indicates the number of seconds to wait. In general, when both *Expires* and *max-age* are specified, *max-age* wins.

The value of *No-Cache* assigned to the *cache-control* HTTP header instructs the browser to check with the server as to the freshness of the page before serving it. However, in combination with *Expires* set to –1, it indicates that the page is stale and subsequently needs be refetched. The net effect is the same as if the page was never cached. The *No-Store* value, on the other hand, instructs the browser not to save the resource locally. If the page comes over HTTPS, however, it will never be cached locally.

In addition to browser and proxy caches, I mentioned server-side caching. I'll return to that in a moment; for now, it suffices to say that it is yet another level of page-output caching specific to ASP.NET. A special component—the page output provider—will capture the output of a page and cache it somewhere on the server. The default provider caches pages inside the ASP.NET *Cache* object in the memory space of the worker process (and machine) that is currently serving the request. As you can see, this solution is not ideal if you have a Web farm where there's no guarantee that subsequent requests for the same page are served by the same machine. If you're running a Web farm, you might want to consider replacing the default provider with the output cache provider made available by the AppFabric Caching Services.

Choosing a Duration for ASP.NET Page Output

When the output caching service is active on a page, the *Duration* attribute indicates the number of seconds that the caching system will maintain an HTML-compiled version of the page. Next, requests for the same page, or for an existing parameterized version of the page, will be serviced while bypassing most of the ASP.NET pipeline. As mentioned, this process has two important repercussions—no authentication is possible and no code is run, meaning that no page events are fired and handled and no state is updated.

A fair value for the *Duration* attribute depends on the application. It can be a few days or a few hours if the page doesn't need to be updated frequently. In general, a short duration (say, just a few seconds) can always be useful also for applications that claim live data all the time.

IIS Kernel Caching

In IIS 6 and newer versions, you have the possibility of telling IIS to cache the page output for you without involving the ASP.NET runtime. This feature has tremendous potential and can dramatically improve the performance of a Web server, as long as enough of the content being served is cacheable.

The great news for ASP.NET developers is that no code changes are required to benefit from kernel caching, except for the *@OutputCache* directive. You enable kernel caching administratively from within the IIS Manager. When both output caching and IIS kernel caching are enabled, a kernel-level driver in IIS intercepts any incoming requests and, if the response was previously cached, it serves them by directly flushing the cached data from wherever the output provider in use had stored it. As this happens at the kernel level, there's no need to make any context switch to user mode, which results in a remarkable performance improvement—about one tenth of the time it would take in classic user mode.

On a high-volume Web site, an output cache duration of only a few seconds can make a huge difference for the overall throughput of a Web server. There's more to know about kernel caching, though. First and foremost, kernel caching is available only for pages requested through a GET verb. No kernel caching is possible on postbacks. Furthermore, pages with *VaryByParam* and *VaryByHeader* attributes set are also not stored in the kernel cache. Finally, note that ASP.NET Request/Cache performance counters will not be updated for pages served by the kernel cache.

Adding a Database Dependency to Page Output

The *SqlDependency* attribute is the *@OutputCache* directive's interface to the *SqlCacheDependency* class that we discussed earlier. When the *SqlDependency* attribute is set to a *Database:Table* string, a SQL Server cache dependency object is created. When the dependency is broken, the page output is invalidated and the next request will be served by pushing the request through the pipeline as usual. The output generated will be cached again.

```
<% @OutputCache Duration="15" VaryByParam="none"
            SqlDependency="Northwind:Employees" %>
```

A page that contains this code snippet has its output cached for 15 seconds or until a record changes in the Employees table in the Northwind database. Note that the Northwind string here is not the name of a database—it's the name of an entry in the *<databases>* section of the configuration file. That entry contains detailed information about the connection string to use to reach the database. You can specify multiple dependencies by separating multiple *Database:Table* pairs with a semicolon in the value of the *SqlDependency* attribute.

> **Important** The more you move toward using layers in your ASP.NET solution (as discussed in Chapter 14), the less you need features like SQL dependency, which build their effectiveness on top of a tight form of coupling between ASP.NET pages and database details. The need of having a dependency between ASP.NET pages and stored content remains, but you can handle that using dependencies on cached items. This is one of the extra features that commercial distributed caches offer over most open-source solutions.

The *HttpCachePolicy* Class

The *HttpCachePolicy* class is a programming interface alternative to using the *@OutputCache* directive. It provides direct methods to set cache-related HTTP headers, which you could also control to some extent by using the members of the *HttpResponse* object.

Properties of the *HttpCachePolicy* Class

Table 18-10 shows the properties of the *HttpCachePolicy* class.

TABLE 18-10 *HttpCachePolicy* **Class Properties**

Property	Description
VaryByHeaders	Gets an object of type *HttpCacheVaryByHeaders*, representing the list of all HTTP headers that will be used to vary cache output
VaryByParams	Gets an object of type *HttpCacheVaryByParams*, representing the list of parameters received by a GET or POST request that affects caching

When a cached page has several vary-by headers or parameters, a separate version of the page is available for each HTTP header type or parameter name.

Methods of the *HttpCachePolicy* Class

Table 18-11 shows the methods of the *HttpCachePolicy* class.

TABLE 18-11 *HttpCachePolicy* **Class Methods**

Method	Description
AddValidationCallback	Registers a callback function to be used to validate the page output in the server cache before returning it.
AppendCacheExtension	Appends the specified text to the *Cache-Control* HTTP header. The existing text is not overwritten.
SetAllowResponseInBrowserHistory	When this setting is *true*, the response is available in the browser's History cache, regardless of the *HttpCacheability* option set on the server.
SetCacheability	Sets the *Cache-Control* HTTP header to any of the values taken from the *HttpCacheability* enumeration type.
SetETag	Sets the *ETag* header to the specified string. The *ETag* header is a unique identifier for a specific version of a document.
SetETagFromFileDependencies	Sets the *ETag* header to a string built by combining and then hashing the last modified date of all the files upon which the page is dependent.
SetExpires	Sets the *Expires* header to an absolute date and time.
SetLastModified	Sets the *Last-Modified* HTTP header to a particular date and time.

Method	Description
SetLastModifiedFromFileDependencies	Sets the *Last-Modified* HTTP header to the most recent timestamps of the files upon which the page is dependent.
SetMaxAge	Sets the *max-age* attribute on the *Cache-Control* header to the specified value. The sliding period cannot exceed one year.
SetNoServerCaching	Disables server output caching for the current response.
SetNoStore	Sets the *Cache-Control: no-store* directive.
SetNoTransforms	Sets the *Cache-Control: no-transforms* directive.
SetOmitVaryStar	If set to *true*, causes *HttpCachePolicy* to ignore the * value in *VaryByHeaders*.
SetProxyMaxAge	Sets the *Cache-Control: s-maxage* header.
SetRevalidation	Sets the *Cache-Control* header to either *must-revalidate* or *proxy-revalidate*.
SetSlidingExpiration	Sets cache expiration to *sliding*. When cache expiration is set to *sliding*, the *Cache-Control* header is renewed at each response.
SetValidUntilExpires	Specifies whether the ASP.NET cache should ignore HTTP *Cache-Control* headers sent by some browsers to evict a page from the cache. If this setting is *true*, the page stays in the cache until it expires.
SetVaryByCustom	Sets the *Vary* HTTP header to the specified text string.

Most methods of the *HttpCachePolicy* class let you control the values of some HTTP headers that relate to the browser cache. The *AddValidationCallback* method, on the other hand, provides a mechanism to programmatically check the validity of page output in the server cache before it is returned from the cache.

Server Cache-Validation Callback

Before the response is served from the ASP.NET cache, all registered handlers are given a chance to verify the validity of the cached page. If at least one handler marks the cached page as invalid, the entry is removed from the cache and the request is served as if it were never cached. The signature of the callback function looks like this:

```
public delegate void HttpCacheValidateHandler(
    HttpContext context,
    Object data,
    ref HttpValidationStatus validationStatus
);
```

The first argument denotes the context of the current request, whereas the second argument is any user-defined data the application needs to pass to the handler. Finally, the third argument is a reference to a value from the *HttpValidationStatus* enumeration. The callback sets this value to indicate the result of the validation. Acceptable values are *IgnoreThisRequest*, *Invalid*, and *Valid*. In the case of *IgnoreThisRequest*, the cached resource is not invalidated but the request is served as if no response was ever cached. If the return value is *Invalid*, the cached page is not used and gets invalidated. Finally, if the return value is *Valid*, the cached response is used to serve the request.

Caching Multiple Versions of a Page

Depending on the application context from which a certain page is invoked, the page might generate different results. The same page can be called to operate with different parameters, can be configured using different HTTP headers, can produce different output based on the requesting browser, and so forth.

ASP.NET allows you to cache multiple versions of a page response; you can distinguish versions by GET and POST parameters, HTTP headers, browser type, custom strings, and control properties.

Vary by Parameters

To vary output caching by parameters, you can use either the *VaryByParam* attribute of the *@OutputCache* directive or the *VaryByParams* property on the *HttpCachePolicy* class. If you proceed declaratively, use the following syntax:

```
<% @OutputCache Duration="60" VaryByParam="employeeID" %>
```

Note that the *VaryByParam* attribute is mandatory; if you don't want to specify a parameter to vary cached content, set the value to *None*. If you want to vary the output by all parameters, set the attribute to an asterisk (*). When the *VaryByParam* attribute is set to multiple parameters, the output cache contains a different version of the requested document for each specified parameter. Multiple parameters are separated by a semicolon. Valid parameters to use are items specified on the GET query string or parameters set in the body of a POST command.

If you want to use the *HttpCachePolicy* class to define caching parameters, first set the expiration and the cacheability of the page using the *SetExpires* and *SetCacheability* methods. Next, set the *VaryByParams* property as shown here:

```
Response.Cache.SetExpires(DateTime.Now.AddSeconds(60));
Response.Cache.SetCacheability(HttpCacheability.Public);
Response.Cache.VaryByParams["employeeid;lastname"] = true;
```

This code snippet shows how to vary page output based on the employee ID and the last name properties. Note that the *Cache* property on the *HttpResponse* class is just an instance of the *HttpCachePolicy* type.

Dealing with Postback Pages

Most ASP.NET pages do postbacks. Let's consider the page in Figure 18-8. The page has cache duration of, say, 30 seconds, but its actual output depends on the selection the user makes every time the page is displayed. The drop-down list (named *Countries*) has auto-postback functionality and places a POST request for the same page whenever you change the selection.

```
NestedDemo.aspx.cs* ×  NestedDemo.aspx     MainContent.Master
Masters.NestedDemo                                                    Page_I

using System;
using System.Web.UI;

namespace Masters
{
    public partial class NestedDemo : Page
    {
        protected void Page_Load(Object sender, EventArgs e)
        {
            //dynamic master = this.Master;
            //master.MainContentTitle = "Nested demo";

            Master.M
        }           MainContentTitle      Property string Masters.MainContentMaster.MainContentTitle
    }              MapPath
}               Master
                MasterPageFile
                ClientIDMode
                SetRenderMethodDelegate
                ViewStateMode
```

FIGURE 18-8 To properly cache pages that post back, you need to vary them by one or more parameters.

With *VaryByParam* set to *None*, you'll wait 30 seconds (or whatever the cache duration is) to have your country selection processed. It is a bit frustrating: no matter which selection you make, it is blissfully ignored and the same page is displayed.

Two points clearly emerge from this discussion. First, pages with static content are a much better fit for caching than interactive pages. Second, the postback mechanism returns a bunch of form parameters. You need to vary the cached copies of the page by the most critical of them. Varying by the selected countries is exactly what we need. The directive shown next stores each country-specific page for 30 seconds:

```
<%@ OutputCache VaryByParam="Countries" Duration="30" %>
```

The bottom line is that enabling page output caching might not be painless for interactive pages. It is free of pain and charge for relatively static pages like those describing a product, a customer, or some news.

> **Caution** A cached ASP.NET page is served more quickly than a processed page, but not as quickly as a static HTML page. However, the response time is nearly identical if the ASP.NET page is kernel-cached in IIS. Unfortunately, IIS doesn't store in its kernel-level cache ASP.NET pages requested via a POST verb and, more importantly, pages with *VaryByParam* or *VaryByHeader*. In the end, postback pages have very few chances to be cached in the IIS kernel. They are cached in the ASP.NET *Cache*, in downstream caching servers, or both.

Vary by Headers

The *VaryByHeader* attribute and the *HttpCachePolicy*'s *VaryByHeaders* property allow you to cache multiple versions of a page, according to the value of one or more HTTP headers that you specify.

If you want to cache pages by multiple headers, include a semicolon-delimited list of header names. If you want to cache a different version of the page for each different header value, set the *VaryByHeader* attribute to an asterisk (*). For example, the following declaration caches for one-minute pages based on the language accepted by the browser. Each language will have a different cached copy of the page output.

```
<%@ OutputCache Duration="60" VaryByParam="None"
    VaryByHeader="Accept-Language" %>
```

If you opt for a programmatic approach, here's the code to use that leverages the *VaryByHeaders* property of the *HttpCachePolicy* class:

```
Response.Cache.VaryByHeaders["Accept-Language"] = true;
```

If you want to programmatically vary the pages in the cache by all HTTP header names, use the *VaryByUnspecifiedParameters* method of the *HttpCacheVaryByHeaders* class:

```
HttpCacheVaryByHeaders.VaryByUnspecifiedParameters();
```

The preceding code is equivalent to using the asterisk with the *VaryByHeader* attribute.

Vary by Custom Strings

The *VaryByCustom* attribute in the *@OutputCache* directive allows you to vary the versions of page output by the value of a custom string. The string you assign to the *VaryByCustom* attribute simply represents the description of the algorithm employed to vary page outputs. The string is then passed to the *GetVaryByCustomString* method, if any, in the *global.asax* file. The method takes the string and returns another string that is specific to the request. Let's examine a concrete example—varying pages by the type of device that requests the page. You use, say, the string *device* with the *VaryByCustom* attribute:

```
<%@ OutputCache Duration="60" VaryByParam="None" VaryByCustom="device" %>
```

Next, you add your application-specific *GetVaryByCustomString* method in the *global.asax* file. Here's a possible implementation:

```
public override String GetVaryByCustomString(HttpContext context, String custom)
{
    if (custom == "device")
        return context.Request.Browser.Type;
    return base.GetVaryByCustomString(context, custom);
}
```

The output of the page is varied by user agent string. You can use any other custom information as long as the information is available through the *HttpContext* class. You can't use information that is known only when the page is loaded, such as the theme. Custom information gathered by a custom HTTP module might be used if the HTTP module parks the information in the *Items* collection of the *HttpContext* object, and as long as the HTTP module is triggered before the request to resolve the page output cache is made.

Nicely enough, the feature just described—varying pages by user agent strings—has been natively available since ASP.NET 1.0. The only difference is that it uses the keyword *browser* instead of *device*. In other words, the following code is perfectly acceptable and leverages the implementation of *GetVaryByCustomString* on the base *HttpApplication* class:

```
<%@ OutputCache Duration="60" VaryByParam="None" VaryByCustom="browser" %>
```

You use the *SetVaryByCustom* method on the *HttpCachePolicy* class if you don't like the declarative approach:

```
Response.Cache.SetVaryByCustom("browser");
```

Caching Portions of ASP.NET Pages

The capability of caching the output of Web pages adds a lot of power to your programming arsenal, but sometimes caching the entire content of a page is not possible or it's just impractical. Some pages, in fact, are made of pieces with radically different features as far as cacheability is concerned. In these situations, being able to cache portions of a page is an incredible added value.

If caching the entire page is impractical, you can always opt for partial caching. Partial caching leverages the concept of ASP.NET user controls—that is, small, nested pages that inherit several features of the page. In particular, user controls can be cached individually based on the browser, GET and POST parameters, and the value of a particular set of properties.

Let's start with a quick introduction of user controls.

What's a User Control, Anyway?

A user control is a Web form saved to a distinct file with an *.ascx* extension. The similarity between user controls and pages is not coincidental. You create a user control in much the same way you create a Web form, and a user control is made of any combination of server and client controls sewn together with server and client script code. After it is created, the user control can be inserted in an ASP.NET page like any other server control. ASP.NET pages see the user control as an atomic, encapsulated component and work with it as with any other built-in Web control.

The internal content of the user control is hidden to the host page. However, the user control can define a public programming interface and filter access to its constituent controls via properties, methods, and events.

User controls and pages have so much in common that transforming a page, or a part of it, into a user control is no big deal. You copy the portion of the page of interest to a new *.ascx* file and make sure the user control does not contain any of the following tags: *<html>*, *<body>*, or *<form>*. You complete the work by associating a code-behind file (or a *<script runat="server">* block) to code the expected behavior of the user control. Finally, you add a *@Control* directive in lieu of the *@Page* directive. Here's an example of a user control:

```
<%@ Control Language="C#" CodeBehind="Message.ascx.cs" Inherits="Message" %>
<span style="color:<%= ForeColor%>"><%= Text%></span>
```

Here's the related code-behind class:

```
public partial class Message : System.Web.UI.UserControl
{
    public String ForeColor;
    public String Text;
}
```

To insert a user control into an ASP.NET page, you drag it from the project onto the Web form, when in design mode. Visual Studio .NET registers the user control with the page and prepares the environment for you to start adding code.

```
<%@ Page Language="C#" CodeBehind="Test.aspx.cs" Inherits="TestUserCtl" %>
<%@ Register Src="Message.ascx" TagName="Message" TagPrefix="x" %>
<html><body>
    <form id="form1" runat="server">
        <x:Message ID="Message1" runat="server" />
    </form>
</body></html>
```

In the page code-behind class, you work the *Message1* variable as you would do with any other server control:

```
protected void Page_Load(Object sender, EventArgs e)
{
    Message1.ForeColor = "blue";
    Message1.Text = "Hello world";
}
```

Caching the Output of User Controls

User controls are not only good at modularizing your user interface, they're also great at caching portions of Web pages. User controls, therefore, fully support the *@OutputCache* directive, although they do so with some differences with ASP.NET pages, as outlined in Table 18-8.

A page that contains some dynamic sections cannot be cached entirely. What if the page also contains sections that are both heavy to compute and seldom updated? In this case, you move static contents to one or more user controls and use the user control's *@OutputCache* directive to set up output caching.

To make a user control cacheable, you declare the *@OutputCache* attribute using almost the same set of attributes we discussed earlier for pages. For example, the following code snippet caches the output of the control that embeds it for one minute:

```
<% @OutputCache Duration="60" VaryByParam="None" %>
```

The *Location* attribute is not supported because all controls in the page share the same location. So if you need to specify the cache location, do that at the page level and it will work for all embedded controls. The same holds true for the *VaryByHeader* attribute.

The output of a user control can vary by custom strings and form parameters. More often, though, you'll want to vary the output of a control by property values. In this case, use the new *VaryByControl* attribute.

> **Note** A user control is made cacheable in either of two ways: by using the *@OutputCache* directive, or by defining the *PartialCaching* attribute on the user control's class declaration in the code-behind file, as follows:
>
> ```
> [PartialCaching(60)]
> public partial class CustomersGrid : UserControl {
>     ...
> }
> ```

The *PartialCaching* attribute allows you to specify the duration and values for the *VaryByParam*, *VaryByControl*, and *VaryByCustom* parameters.

Vary by Controls

The *VaryByControl* attribute allows you to vary the cache for each specified control property. For user controls, the property is mandatory unless the *VaryByParam* attribute has been specified. You can indicate both *VaryByParam* and *VaryByControl*, but at least one of them is required.

The following user control displays a grid with all the customers in a given country/region. The country/region is specified by the user control's *Country* property.

```
<%@ Control Language="C#" CodeFile="CustomersGrid.ascx.cs"
            Inherits="CustomersGridByCtl" %>
<%@ OutputCache Duration="30" VaryByControl="Country" %>

<h3><%= DateTime.Now.ToString() %></h3>
<asp:ObjectDataSource ID="ObjectDataSource1" runat="server"
    TypeName="Core35.DAL.Customers"
    SelectMethod="LoadByCountry">
</asp:ObjectDataSource>

<asp:GridView ID="GridView1" runat="server" AutoGenerateColumns="false">
    <Columns>
        <asp:BoundField DataField="ID" HeaderText="ID" />
        <asp:BoundField DataField="CompanyName" HeaderText="Company" />
        <asp:BoundField DataField="ContactName" HeaderText="Contact" />
        <asp:BoundField DataField="Country" HeaderText="Country" />
    </Columns>
</asp:GridView>
```

Here is the code file of the user control:

```
public partial class CustomersGridByCtl : System.Web.UI.UserControl
{
    public String Country;

    protected void Page_Load(Object sender, EventArgs e)
    {
        if (!String.IsNullOrEmpty(Country))
        {
            ObjectDataSource1.SelectParameters.Add("country", Country);
            GridView1.DataSourceID = "ObjectDataSource1";
        }
    }
}
```

The *@OutputCache* directive caches a different copy of the user control output based on the different values of the *Country* property. Figure 18-9 shows it in action.

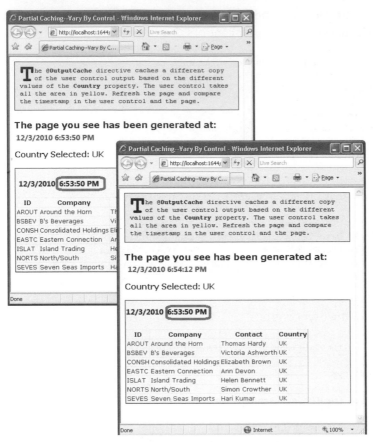

FIGURE 18-9 Two pages created at different moments use the same user control output, as you can see from the creation time of the grid.

The strings you assign to *VaryByControl* can be properties of the user controls as well as ID property values for contained controls. In this case, you'll get a distinct cached copy for each distinct combination of property values on the specified control.

The *Shared* Attribute

In Figure 18-9, you see two instances of the same page sharing the cached output of a user control. Try the following simple experiment. Make a plain copy of the page (say, *page1.aspx*), and give it another name (say, *page2.aspx*). You should have two distinct pages that generate identical output. In particular, both pages contain an instance of the same cacheable user control. Let's say that the cache duration of the user control is 30 seconds.

As the next step of the experiment, you open both pages at different times while the cache is still valid. Let's say you open the second page ten seconds later than the first. Interestingly enough, the two pages no longer share the same copy of user control output, as Figure 18-10 documents.

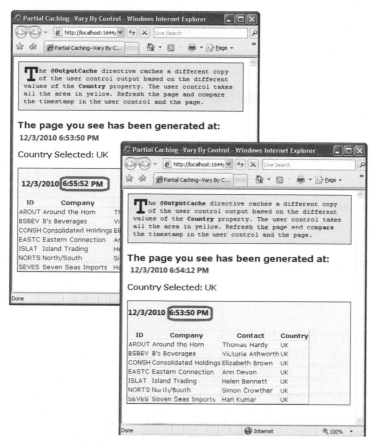

FIGURE 18-10 Distinct pages don't automatically share the output of the same user control.

By default, distinct pages don't share the output of the same cacheable user control. Each page will maintain its own copy of the user control response, instead. Implemented to guarantee total separation and avoid any sort of conflicts, this feature is far more dangerous than one might think at first. It might lead to flooding the Web server memory with copies and copies of the user control responses—one for each varying parameter or control property and one set for each page that uses the control.

To allow distinct pages to share the same output of a common user control, you need to set the *Shared* attribute to *true* in the user control's *@OutputCache* directive:

```
<%@ OutputCache Duration="30" VaryByParam="None" Shared="true" %>
```

Fragment Caching in Cacheable Pages

If you plan to cache user controls—that is, if you're trying for partial caching—it's probably because you just don't want to, or cannot, cache the entire page. However, a good question to ask is this: What happens if user controls are cached within a cacheable page?

Both the page and the controls are cached individually, meaning that both the page's raw response and the control's raw responses are cached. However, if the cache duration is different, the page duration wins and user controls are refreshed only when the page is refreshed.

A cacheable user control can be embedded both in a cacheable page and in a wrapper-cacheable user control.

> **Important** Cacheable user controls should be handled with extreme care in the page's code. Unlike regular controls, a user control marked with the *@OutputCache* directive is not guaranteed to be there when your code tries to access it. If the user control is retrieved from the cache, the property that references it in the code-behind page class is just *null*.
>
> ```
> if (CustomerGrid1 != null)
>     CustomerGrid1.Country = "USA";
> ```
>
> To avoid bad surprises, you should always check the control reference against the *null* value before executing any code.

Advanced Caching Features

The output caching subsystem has also a few other cool features to offer. They are caching profiles and post-cache substitution. In brief, caching profiles let you save a block of output caching-related settings to the configuration file. Post-cache substitution completes the ASP.NET offering as far as output caching is concerned. In addition to saving the entire page or only fragments of the page, you can now also cache the entire page except for a few regions.

Caching Profiles

The *@OutputCache* directive for pages supports the *CacheProfile* string attribute, which references an entry under the *<outputCacheProfiles>* section in the *web.config* file:

```
<caching>
   <outputCacheSettings>
     <outputCacheProfiles>
         <add name="..." enabled="true|false" duration="..."
             location="..." sqlDependency="..."
             varyByCustom="..." varyByControl="..."
             varyByHeader="..." varyByParam="..."
                             noStore=true|false"
         />
     </outputCacheProfiles>
   </outputCacheSettings>
</caching>
```

Basically, by defining a named entry in the *<add>* section you can store in the configuration file all the cache-related settings to be applied to the page. Instead of specifying the same set of parameters for each page over and over again, you can put them in the *web.config* file and reference them by name. In this way, you can also modify settings for a number of pages without touching the source files.

```
<%@ OutputCache CacheProfile="MySettings" %>
```

In the preceding code, the application has a *MySettings* entry in the *<outputCacheProfiles>* section and doesn't need any additional attribute in the *@OutputCache* directive. As you can see, the attributes of the *<add>* node match the attributes of the *@OutputCache* directive.

Post-Cache Substitution

With user controls, you can cache only certain portions of ASP.NET pages. With post-cache substitution, you can cache the whole page except specific regions. For example, using this mechanism, an *AdRotator* control can serve a different advertisement on each request even if the host page is cached.

To use post-cache substitution, you place a new control—the *<asp:substitution>* control—at the page location where content should be substituted, and you set the *MethodName* property of the control to a callback method. Here's a quick example:

```
<form id="form1" runat="server">
    <h3>The output you see has been generated at:
        <%=DateTime.Now.ToString() %> and is valid for 30 seconds</h3>
    <hr />
     This content is updated regularly
     <h2><asp:Substitution ID="Substitution1" runat="server"
             MethodName="WriteTimeStamp" /></h2>
    <hr />
    This is more static and cached content
    <asp:Button runat="server" Text="Refresh" />
 </form>
```

The *MethodName* property must be set to the name of a static method that can be encapsulated in an *HttpResponseSubstitutionCallback* delegate, as follows:

```
public static string WriteTimeStamp(HttpContext context)
{
    return DateTime.Now.ToString();
}
```

Whatever string the method returns will be rendered out and becomes the output of the *Substitution* control. Note also that the callback method must be static and thread-safe. The *HttpContext* parameter to the method can be used to retrieve request parameters such as query string variables, authentication information, or personalization details.

You can also set up post-cache substitution programmatically through the *WriteSubstitution* method of the *HttpResponse* object:

```
Response.WriteSubstitution(
    new HttpResponseSubstitutionCallback(WriteTimeStamp));
```

The preceding call inserts a sort of placeholder in the response, which will be replaced with the output of the method. This trick allows the *AdRotator* control to automatically display a new banner even on cached pages.

The use of post-cache substitution automatically enables server caching for the page output. If the page is configured for client output caching, the setting is ignored. The reason for this change lies in the fact that markup editing is necessarily a server-side operation. In addition, a page that makes use of post-cache substitution can't rely on IIS kernel caching because ASP.NET needs to do some work before the page can be served to the user. In light of this, the page can't just be served by IIS without first involving ASP.NET.

> **Note** The *Substitution* control can also be used in pages that don't use output caching. In this case, the substitution callback will be called at rendering time to contribute to the response. You can think of the *Substitution* control as a server-side control that has the capability of expanding a placeholder to some server-side processed results.

For performance reasons, you should also avoid calling the *Substitution* control from within the callback. If you call it from there, the callback will maintain a reference to the control and the page containing the control. As a result, the page instance won't be garbage-collected until the cached content expires.

Output Cache Providers

Up until ASP.NET 4, the mechanics of output cache providers was hardcoded in a system component and wasn't exposed to developers. Most of the internal implementation of the component was public, but still there was no way to change it—take it or leave it were the only choices.

In ASP.NET 4, the component has been abstracted to a provider model (much like the model you have for session state or membership) and became replaceable by developers. When you use the code snippets shown earlier (where you don't explicitly specify any provider information), you end up using the default provider, which delivers the same behavior as in previous versions of ASP.NET. This means that the output of pages is kept in the ASP.NET *Cache* object and, subsequently, in the memory of the worker process servicing the current request.

Where else would you like to store the output of ASP.NET pages on the server side? A possibility is storing the output in some permanent store, such as disk files or databases. The benefit in this case is that you release a lot of the worker process memory while gaining the chance to store much larger amounts of data on disk.

A much more enticing scenario, however, is using a distributed cache instead of a server-bound cache to store the output of pages. AppFabric Caching Services, as well as many of the commercial solutions I mentioned earlier in the chapter, offer an ASP.NET-compatible output cache provider that you roll in your application in lieu of the default one. Here's how you change the output cache provider. It is as simple as editing a section of the *web.config* file:

```
<caching>
   <outputCache defaultProvider="AspNetInternalProvider">
     <providers>
       <add name="FileCache"
            type="Samples.YourCacheProvider, Samples" />
     </providers>
  </outputCache>
</caching>
```

A custom output cache provider is a class that inherits from *System.Web.Caching. OutputCacheProvider* which, in turn, inherits from *ProviderBase*. The class consists of four abstract methods, as shown here:

```
public abstract Object Add(String key, Object entry, DateTime utcExpiry);
public abstract Object Get(String key);
public abstract void Remove(String key);
public abstract void Set(String key, Object entry, DateTime utcExpiry);
```

In ASP.NET 4, the mechanism of output caching has been made open, but no additional providers are provided as part of the framework. At the following URL, however, you can find the source code of the AppFabric Caching Services output provider written by one of the Microsoft ASP.NET architects: *http://aspnet.codeplex.com/releases/view/46576*.

Summary

The ability to store in-memory chunks of frequently accessed data becomes a winning factor in the building of scalable Web applications that handle significant volumes of data. Caching, however, is a double-edged sword, and if it's abused or misused, it can easily morph into an insidious weakness. This typically happens when the quantity of memory-held information grows uncontrolled and beyond a reasonable threshold. Aside from the performance repercussions, the theoretical possibility that the data stored in the cache can grow uncontrolled also opens up security concerns. A denial-of-service (DoS) attack, in fact, might succeed in flooding the Web server's memory with useless data if the caching subsystem is not well designed.

Caching is mostly about memory. In the short run, you can perhaps even find that some good caching improves the overall performance enough to appease your customer or your boss. I'm not at all claiming that caching can fix design holes, but caching can sometimes put a patch on suboptimal performance and buy you time to rethink and refactor the application properly.

To build high-performance applications, a fundamental guideline is "Cache as much as you can." However, be aware that there's a threshold you should never exceed. The more aggressive you are with caching, the more you should be concerned about the invisible memory threshold that suddenly turns good things into bad things.

In ASP.NET, caching comes in two complementary forms: page output caching and the application cache. The former is a relatively quick and simple approach to apply caching rules to a page including client, downstream, and server caches. The benefit is that a request can be served without spinning up the ASP.NET pipeline. Using page output caching doesn't necessarily make your application faster, but it reduces the load on the server.

Application cache refers to a comprehensive caching API designed to let you place a caching layer inside your business or data tier. The application cache relies on the machine-specific *Cache* object as well as the distributed AppFabric Caching Services or analogous open-source or commercial products. Also, in this cache the primary goal is to reduce the load on databases and services, minimizing roundtrips and increasing scalability. No serious Web application today can do without a good layer of caching—at all possible levels.

Chapter 19
ASP.NET Security

Beware of the man who won't be bothered with details.

—William Feather

By nature, Web applications are subject to several types of attacks whose damage and impact can vary quite a bit, depending on the characteristics of the application itself. The most secure Web application is the application that actually resists attacks, not the application just designed to. Security is a rather intricate puzzle whose solution varies from one application to another. The important thing to remember is that, more often than not, security is manifested through a successful mix of application-level and system-level measures.

Many developers have learned on their own that security is not a feature that can be easily added to existing applications or introduced late in the development stage. Security is inherently tied to the functions of an application and should be planned as one of the first features, very early at the design level. For example, isolating modules of the application particularly sensitive to security would greatly simplify using stricter security measures without impacting the rest of the application.

ASP.NET simplifies programming secure applications by providing a built-in infrastructure that supplies application-level protection against unauthorized access to Web pages. Be aware, though, that this kind of security is only one side of the coin. A really secure Web site is especially well protected against server attacks, which can sneakily be used to scale the highest protective walls of the application logic.

In this chapter, we will discuss the security context of ASP.NET, including its relationship with server-side Internet Information Services (IIS) authentication mechanisms and best coding practices to fend off Web attacks.

Where the Threats Come From

The concept of security implies the presence of an enemy we're protecting against. In Table 19-1, you find summarized the most common types of Web attacks.

TABLE 19-1 Common Web Attacks

Attack	Description
Cross-site scripting (XSS)	The attacker exploits user input blindly echoed to the page to add malicious behavior to the page such as capturing sensitive data.
Denial of service (DoS)	The attacker floods the network with fake requests, overloading the system and blocking regular traffic.
Eavesdropping	The attacker uses a sniffer to read unencrypted network packets as they are transported on the network.
Hidden-field tampering	The attacker compromises unchecked (and trusted) hidden fields stuffed with sensitive data.
One-click	Malicious HTTP posts are sent via script.
Session hijacking	The attacker guesses or steals a valid session ID and connects over another user's session.
SQL injection	The attacker inserts malicious input that the code blissfully concatenates to form dangerous SQL commands.

The bottom line is that whenever you insert any sort of user input into the browser's markup, you potentially expose yourself to a code-injection attack (that is, any variations of SQL injection and XSS). In addition, sensitive data should never be sent across the wire (let alone as clear text) and must be stored safely on the server.

If there's a way to write a bulletproof and tamper-resistant application, it can consist only of the combination of the following aspects:

- **Coding practices** Data validation, type and buffer-length checking, and antitampering measures

- **Data access strategies** Using roles to ensure the weakest possible account is used on the server to limit server resource access, and using stored procedures or, at least, parameterized commands

- **Effective storage and administration** No sending of critical data down to the client, using hashed values to detect manipulation, authenticating users and protecting identities, and applying rigorous policies for passwords

As you can see from this list, a secure application can result only from the combined efforts of developers, architects, and administrators. Don't imagine that you can get it right otherwise.

The ASP.NET Security Context

From an application point of view, security is mostly a matter of authenticating users and authorizing actions on the system's resources. ASP.NET provides a range of authentication and authorization mechanisms implemented in conjunction with IIS, the Microsoft .NET Framework, and the underlying security services of the operating system. The overall security context of an ASP.NET application is composed of three distinct levels:

- The IIS level associates a valid security token with the sender of the request. The security token is determined according to the current IIS authentication mechanism.

- The ASP.NET worker process level determines the identity of the thread in the ASP.NET worker process serving the request. If enabled, impersonation settings can change the security token associated with the thread. The identity of the process model is determined by settings in the configuration file or the IIS metabase, according to the process model in use. These two levels are unified if the ASP.NET application runs in integrated mode on IIS 7 and later.

- The ASP.NET pipeline level gets the credentials of the application-specific user who is using the application. The way this task is accomplished depends on the application settings in the configuration files for authentication and authorization. A common setting for most ASP.NET applications is choosing to use Forms Authentication.

Among other things, the identity of the ASP.NET worker process influences access to local files, folders, and databases.

Who Really Runs My ASP.NET Application?

When an ASP.NET request arrives at the Web server machine, IIS picks it up and assigns the request to one of its pooled threads. IIS runs under the SYSTEM account—the most powerful account in Microsoft Windows. From this point forward when processing this request, the three security contexts of ASP.NET applications I mentioned execute one after the other.

IIS Thread Security Context

The thread that physically handles the request impersonates an identity according to the current IIS authentication setting, whether it is Basic, Windows, or Anonymous. If the site is configured for anonymous access, the identity impersonated by the thread is the one you set through the dialog box shown in Figure 19-1. By default, it is named *IUSR_xxx*, where *xxx* stands for the machine name.

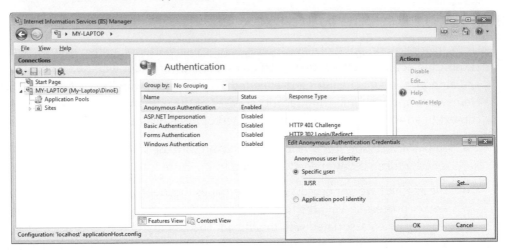

FIGURE 19-1 Enabling anonymous access.

Basic authentication is an HTTP standard supported by virtually any browser (and disabled by default in IIS 7). With this type of authentication, a request bounces back with a particular HTTP status code (HTTP 401) that the browser understands as a demand to display a standard dialog box to request the user's credentials. The information gathered is sent to IIS, which attempts to match it with any of the Web server's accounts. Because credentials are sent out as Base64-encoded text, essentially in clear text, Basic authentication is recommended only for use over HTTPS secure channels.

Note that the default installation of IIS 7 doesn't include *Digest* authentication. Digest authentication differs from Basic authentication mostly because it hashes credentials before sending. Digest authentication is an HTTP 1.1 feature and, as such, is not supported by some old browsers. Both Basic and Digest authentication work well through firewalls and proxy servers. To use Digest authentication on IIS 7, you must install the appropriate Digest role service and disable anonymous authentication.

Integrated Windows authentication sets up a conversation between the browser and the Web server. The browser passes the credentials of the currently logged-on user, who is not required to type anything. The user needs to have a valid account on the Web server or in a trusted domain to be successfully authenticated. The authentication can take place through the NTLM challenge/response method or by using Kerberos. The technique has limited browser support and is impractical in the presence of firewalls. It is designed for intranet use.

Note Yet another type of authentication mode exists and is based on certificates. You can use the Secure Sockets Layer (SSL) security features of IIS and use client certificates to authenticate users requesting information on your Web site. SSL checks the contents of the certificate submitted by the browser for the user during the logon. Users obtain client certificates from a trusted third-party organization. In an intranet scenario, users can also get their certificate from an authority managed by the company itself.

In IIS 7, you can also leverage ASP.NET Forms authentication at the IIS level as well as ASP.NET impersonation. ASP.NET Forms authentication essentially redirects to an application-specific login page. If you enable impersonation, instead, your ASP.NET application will run under the security context of the user authenticated by IIS 7 or under the specific account you indicate by editing the impersonation settings in the IIS manager.

After authentication, the thread dispatches the request to the appropriate module. For an ASP.NET application, the request is queued to the application pool and picked up by the copy of the *w3wp.exe* IIS worker process that serves that application pool. What is the identity of the worker process?

Worker Process Security Context

As you saw in Chapter 2, "ASP.NET and IIS," the worker process typically runs under the identity of the NETWORK SERVICE account or under a virtual account associated with the application pool. You can change it through the Advanced Settings dialog box of the application pool as shown in Figure 19-2.

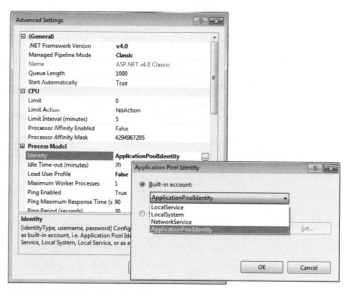

FIGURE 19-2 Changing the identity for the worker process.

Inside the worker process, a pooled thread picks up the request to serve it. What's the identity of this thread? If impersonation is disabled in the ASP.NET application, this thread will inherit the identity of the worker process. This is what happens by default. If impersonation is enabled, the worker thread will inherit the security token passed by IIS.

When impersonation is active, the worker process account doesn't change. The worker process still compiles pages and reads configuration files using the original account. Impersonation is used only with the code executed within the page, not for all the preliminary steps that happen before the request is handed to the page handler. For example, this means that any access to local files or databases occur using the impersonated account, not the worker process's account.

ASP.NET Pipeline Security Context

The third security context indicates the identity of the user making the request. The point here is authenticating the user and authorizing access to the page and its embedded resources. Obviously, if the requested page is freely available, no further step is performed; the page output is generated and served to the user.

To protect pages against unauthorized access, an ASP.NET application needs to define an authentication policy—typically Forms authentication. Authentication modules hook up requests for protected pages and manage to obtain the user's credentials. The user is directed to the page only if the credentials are deemed valid and authorize access to the requested resource.

Changing the Identity of the ASP.NET Process

In a situation in which you want to change the default ASP.NET account to give it more privileges, how should you proceed? Is it preferable to create a custom account and use it for the worker process, or should you opt for the worker process to impersonate a fixed identity?

> **Note** You'll find that it's difficult to create a new, functional account with less than the privileges granted to NETWORK SERVICE or the virtual account of the application pool. If you give it a try, make sure you pass through a careful testing phase and ensure it really works for your application.

Setting the Process Account

Using the dialog box shown in Figure 19-2 is the only way to change the real identity of the ASP.NET process. If you change the process identity, all threads in the process will use this as the base identity and no extra work is needed on thread switches. More importantly, you should make sure the new account has at least full permissions on the *Temporary ASP.NET Files* folder. (Review carefully the list of permissions granted to the standard ASP.NET accounts, which you can find in the "Privileges of the ASP.NET Default Account" section.)

Alternatively, you can require the worker process to impersonate a fixed identity through the *<identity>* section of the *web.config* file. Note that when fixed impersonation is used, every worker thread processing a request needs to impersonate the specified account. Impersonation will then be performed for each thread switch because a thread switch event takes the thread identity back to the process identity.

Impersonating a Fixed Identity

To impersonate a fixed identity, you first define the user account and then add a setting to the *web.config* file. The following snippet shows an example:

```
<identity impersonate="true"
    userName="MyAspNetAccnt" password="ILoveA$pnet*SinceVer1.0" />
```

As mentioned earlier, impersonation doesn't really change the *physical* identity of the process running ASP.NET. More simply, all threads serving in the context of the ASP.NET worker process always impersonate a given user for the duration of the application.

Impersonating a fixed identity is different from classic, per-request impersonation such as impersonating the identity of the Windows user making the request. *Per-request imperson-ation* refers to the situation in which you enable impersonation without specifying a fixed identity. In this case, the security token with identity information is created by IIS and in-herited by the worker process. When a fixed identity is involved, the security token must be generated by the ASP.NET worker process. When running under a poorly privileged account, though, the ASP.NET worker process sometimes lacks the permission to do that.

Impersonating Through the Anonymous Account

A third possibility to change the identity of the ASP.NET worker process is by impersonating through the anonymous account. The idea is that the ASP.NET application grants access to anonymous users, and the anonymous account is configured to be the desired account for the application.

In this case, the application uses per-request impersonation and the ASP.NET code executes as the impersonated account. The process account remains set to NETWORK SERVICE or the virtual account, which means you don't have to worry about replicating into the new account the minimum set of permissions on folders that allow ASP.NET to work.

Privileges of the ASP.NET Default Account

Of all the possible user rights assignments, ASPNET and NETWORK SERVICE are granted only the following five:

- Access this computer from the network
- Deny logon locally
- Deny logon through Terminal Services
- Log on as a batch job
- Log on as a service

In addition, the accounts are given some NTFS permissions to oper ate on certain folders and create temporary files and assemblies. The folders involved are these:

- **.NET Framework Root Folder**   This folder contains some .NET Framework system assemblies that ASP.NET must be able to access. The physical folder is normally *Microsoft.NET\Framework\[version]* and is located under the Windows folder. ASP.NET has only read and list permissions on this folder.

- **Temporary ASP.NET Files**   This folder represents the file system subtree in which all temporary files are generated. ASP.NET is granted full control over the entire subtree.

- **Global Assembly Cache**   ASP.NET needs to gain read permissions on the assemblies in the global assembly cache (GAC). The GAC is located in the *Windows\Assembly\GAC* folder. The GAC folder is not visible in Windows Explorer, but you can view the installed assemblies by opening the *Windows\Assembly* folder.

- **Windows System Folder**   The ASP.NET process needs to access and read the *System32* Windows folder to load any necessary Win32 DLLs.

- **Application Root Folder**   The ASP.NET process needs to access and read the files that make up the Web application. The folder is typically located under *Inetpub\wwwroot*.

- **Web Site Root**   ASP.NET might have the need to scan the root of the Web server—typically, *Inetpub\wwwroot*—looking for configuration files to read.

An ASP.NET application running under an account that lacks some of these permissions might fail. Granting at least all these permissions is highly recommended for all accounts used for fixed-account impersonation.

The Trust Level of ASP.NET Applications

ASP.NET applications are made of managed code and run inside the common language runtime (CLR). In the CLR, running code is assigned to a security zone based on the evidence it provides about its origin—for example, the originating URL. Each security zone corresponds to a set of permissions. Each set of permissions corresponds to a trust level. By default, ASP.NET applications run from the MyComputer zone with full trust. Is this default setting just evil?

An ASP.NET application runs on the Web server and doesn't hurt the user that connects to it via the browser. An ASP.NET application cannot be consumed in ways other than through the browser. So why do some people feel cold shivers down their spine when they think of using ASP.NET full trust?

The problem is not with the ASP.NET application itself, but with the fact that it is publicly exposed over the Internet—one of the most hostile environments for computer security you can imagine. If a fully trusted ASP.NET account is hijacked, a hacker can perform restricted actions from within the worker thread. In other words, a publicly exposed, fully trusted application is a potential platform for hackers to launch attacks. The less an application is trusted, the more secure that application happens to be.

The *<trust>* Section

By default, ASP.NET applications run unrestricted and are allowed to do whatever their account is allowed to do. The actual security restrictions that sometimes apply to ASP.NET applications (for example, the inability to write files) are not a sign of partial trust, but more simply the effect of the underprivileged account under which ASP.NET applications normally run.

By tweaking the *<trust>* section in the root *web.config* file, you can configure code access security permissions for a Web application and decide whether it has to run fully or partially trusted:

```
<trust level="Medium" originUrl="" />
```

Table 19-2 describes the levels of trust available.

TABLE 19-2 Levels Permitted in the *<trust>* Section

Level	Description
Full	Applications run fully trusted and can execute arbitrary native code in the process context in which they run. This is the default setting.
High	Code can use most permissions that support partial trust. This level is appropriate for applications you want to run with least privilege to mitigate risks.
Medium	Code can read and write its own application directories and can interact with databases.
Low	Code can read its own application resources but can't interact with resources located outside of its application space.
Minimal	Code can't interact with any protected resources. Appropriate for nonprofessional hosting sites that simply intend to support generic HTML code and highly isolated business logic.

Admittedly, restricting the set of things an application can do might be painful at first. However, in the long run (read, if you don't just give up and deliver the application), it produces better and safer code.

Note The *<trust>* section supports an attribute named *originUrl*. The attribute is a sort of misnomer. If you set it, the specified URL is granted the permission to access an HTTP resource using either a *Socket* or *WebRequest* class. The permission class involved with this is *WebPermission*. Of course, the Web permission is granted only if the specified *<trust>* level supports that. *Medium* and higher trust levels do.

ASP.NET Permissions

Let's review in more detail the permission granted to ASP.NET applications when the various trust levels are applied. Key ASP.NET permissions for each trust level are outlined in Table 19-3.

TABLE 19-3 Main Permissions in ASP.NET Trust Levels

	High	Medium	Low	Minimal
FileIO	Unrestricted	Read/Write to application's space	Read	None
IsolatedStorage	Unrestricted	ByUser	ByUser (maximum of 1 MB)	None
Printing	DefaultPrinting	*Same as High*	None	None
Security	Assertion, Execution, ControlThread, ControlPrincipal	*Same as High*	Execution	Execution
SqlClient	Unrestricted	Unrestricted (no blank password allowed)	None	None
Registry	Unrestricted	None	None	None
Environment	Unrestricted	None	None	None
Reflection	ReflectionEmit	None	None	None
Socket	Unrestricted	None	None	None
Web	Unrestricted	Connect to origin host, if configured	*Same as Medium*	None

More detailed information about the permissions actually granted to the default trust levels are available in the security configuration files for each level. The name of the file for each level is stored in the *<trustLevel>* section.

In the end, full-trust applications run unrestricted. High-trust applications have read/write permission for all the files in their application space. However, the physical access to files is still ruled by the NTFS access control list on the resource. High-trust applications have unrestricted access to Microsoft SQL Server but not, for example, to OLE DB classes. (The *OleDbPermission* and other managed provider permissions are denied to all but fully trusted applications.) Reflection calls are denied, with the exception of those directed at classes in the *System.Reflection.Emit* namespace.

Medium applications have unrestricted access to SQL Server, but only as long as they don't use blank passwords for accounts. The *WebPermission* is granted to both medium-trust and low-trust applications, but it requires that the URL be configured in the *<trust>* section through the *originUrl* attribute. Low-trust applications have read-only permission for files in their application directories. Isolated storage is still permitted but limited to a 1-MB quota.

A rule of thumb is that *Medium* trust should be fine for most ASP.NET applications and applying it shouldn't cause significant headaches, provided that you don't need to access legacy Component Object Model (COM) objects or databases exposed via OLE DB providers. However, there are a few common situations in which adapting an application to Medium trust requires some configuration work. A popular example is setting NHibernate to work in a Medium-trust environment. (See *http://blog.yeticode.co.uk/2010/03/running-nhibernate-in-medium-trust* for details.)

Granting Privileges Beyond the Trust Level

What if one of the tasks to perform requires privileges that the trust level doesn't grant? There are two basic approaches. The simplest approach is to customize the policy file for the trust level and add any permissions you need. The solution is easy to implement and doesn't require code changes. It does require administrator rights to edit the security policy files. From a pure security perspective, it is not a great solution because you're just adding to the whole application the permissions you need for a particular method of a particular page or assembly.

The second approach requires a bit of refactoring but leads to better and safer code. The idea is to sandbox the server-side code and make it delegate to external components (for example, serviced components or command-line programs) the execution of any tasks that exceed the application's permission set. Obviously, the external component will be configured to have all required permissions.

> **Note** Code sandboxing is the only option you have if your partially trusted ASP.NET application is trying to make calls into an assembly that doesn't include the *AllowPartiallyTrustedCallers* attribute. For more information on programming for medium trust, check out the contents at the following URL: *http://msdn2.microsoft.com/en-us/library/ms998341.aspx*. In spite of the title, which refers to ASP.NET 2, the content is still up to date.

ASP.NET Authentication Methods

Depending on the type of the requested resource, IIS might or might not be able to handle the request itself. If the resource needs the involvement of ASP.NET (for example, it is an *.aspx* file), IIS hands the request over to ASP.NET along with the security token of the authenticated, or anonymous, user. What happens next depends on the ASP.NET configuration.

Originally, ASP.NET supported three types of authentication methods: Windows, Passport, and Forms. A fourth possibility is *None*, meaning that ASP.NET does not even attempt to perform its own authentication and completely relies on the authentication already carried out by IIS. In this case, anonymous users can connect and resources are accessed using the default ASP.NET account. In ASP.NET 4, Passport authentication is marked as obsolete. It is largely replaced by oAuth. In particular, you can use your Windows Live ID with oAuth.

You choose the ASP.NET authentication mechanism using the *<authentication>* section in the root *web.config* file. Child subdirectories inherit the authentication mode chosen for the application. By default, the authentication mode is set to Windows. Let's briefly examine Windows authentication and reserve wider coverage for the most commonly used authentication method—Forms authentication.

Windows Authentication

When using Windows authentication, ASP.NET works in conjunction with IIS. The real authentication is performed by IIS, which uses one of its authentication methods: Basic or Integrated Windows. When IIS has authenticated the user, it passes the security token on to ASP.NET. When in Windows authentication mode, ASP.NET does not perform any further authentication steps and limits its use of the IIS token to authorizing access to the resources.

Typically, you use the Windows authentication method in intranet scenarios when the users of your application have Windows accounts that can be authenticated only by the Web server. Let's assume that you configured the Web server to work with the Integrated Windows authentication mode and that you disabled anonymous access. The ASP.NET application works in Windows authentication mode. What happens when a user connects to the application? First, IIS authenticates the user (popping up a dialog box if the account of the local user doesn't match any accounts on the Web server or in the trusted domain) and then hands the security token over to ASP.NET.

Using ACLs to Authorize Access

In most cases, Windows authentication is used in conjunction with file authorization—via the *FileAuthorizationModule* HTTP module. User-specific pages in the Web application can be protected from unauthorized access by using access control lists (ACLs) on the file. When ASP.NET is about to access a resource, the *FileAuthorizationModule* HTTP module is called into action. File authorization performs an ACL check on ASP.NET files using the caller's identity. For example, it will be sure that the user Joe will never be able to access an *.aspx* page whose ACL doesn't include an entry for him.

Note, though, that file authorization does not require impersonation at the ASP.NET level and, more importantly, it works regardless of whether the impersonation flag is turned on. Once you've set an appropriately configured ACL on an ASP.NET resource, you're pretty much done. Nobody will be able to access the resource without permission.

Note Windows authentication also works with URL authorization implemented by the HTTP module named *URLAuthorizationModule*. This module allows or denies access to URL resources to certain users and roles. (I'll talk more about URL authorization later while discussing Forms authentication.)

Windows CardSpace

The .NET Framework (starting with 3.0) contains a new technology that can be used with ASP.NET Web sites to authenticate users: Windows CardSpace. Any page that includes the Identity Selector object, uses the identity cards of the connected user to send credentials to the server. Each user can manage her own cards by using the Windows CardSpace applet in Control Panel of any client machines equipped with the .NET Framework 3.0 or later.

The Identity Selector is an *<object>* tag of type *application/x-informationcard*. By requesting the value property of this object, you force an enabled browser to bring up the CardSpace applet. The user then picks up the right card to send. The server-side login page will then access the content of the card and make any necessary checks to authorize the request. If it becomes widely accepted, Windows CardSpace could be the perfect tool for authentication over the Internet. For more information, you can start reading the following MSDN article: *http://msdn.microsoft.com/en-us/magazine/cc163434.aspx*.

Using Forms Authentication

Windows authentication is seldom practical for real-world Internet applications. Windows authentication is based on Windows accounts and NTFS ACL tokens and, as such, assumes that clients are connecting from Windows-equipped machines. Useful and effective in intranet and possibly in some extranet scenarios, Windows authentication is simply unrealistic in more common situations because the Web application users are required to have Windows accounts in the application's domain. So what is the ideal authentication mechanism for real Web developers?

Today, Forms authentication is the most commonly used way to collect and validate user credentials—for example, against a database of user accounts. The login pattern implemented by Forms authentication doesn't look radically different from Windows authentication. The key difference is that with Forms authentication everything happens under the strict control of the Web application.

You set up an ASP.NET application for Forms authentication by tweaking its root *web.config* file. You enter the following script:

```
<system.web>
    <authentication mode="Forms">
        <forms loginUrl="login.aspx" />
    </authentication>
    <authorization>
        <deny users="?" />
    </authorization>
</system.web>
```

The *<authentication>* section indicates the URL of the user-defined login form. ASP.NET displays the form only to users who have explicitly been denied access in the *<authorization>* section. The *?* symbol indicates any anonymous, unauthenticated users. Note that the anonymous user here is not the IIS anonymous user but simply a user who has not been authenticated through your login form.

All blocked users are redirected to the login page, where they are asked to enter their credentials.

> **Note** The Forms authentication mechanism protects any ASP.NET resource located in a folder for which Forms authentication and authorization is enabled. Note that only resource types explicitly handled by ASP.NET are protected. The list includes *.aspx*, *.asmx*, and *.ashx* files, but not plain HTML pages or classic ASP pages. In IIS 7.0, though, you are given the tools to change this by setting a Web server-level *web.config* file where you assign new resources to the ASP.NET standard HTTP handler.

Forms Authentication Control Flow

Form-based authentication is governed by an HTTP module implemented in the *FormsAuthenticationModule* class. The behavior of the component is driven by the contents of the *web.config* file. When the browser attempts to access a protected resource, the module kicks in and attempts to locate an authentication ticket for the caller. By default, a ticket is merely a cookie with a particular (and configurable) name. However, it can be configured to be a value embedded in the URL. In this case, we talk about cookieless Forms authentication.

If no valid ticket is found, the module redirects the request to a login page. Information about the originating page is placed in the query string. The login page is then displayed. The programmer creates this page, which, at a minimum, contains text boxes for the username and the password and a button for submitting credentials. The handler for the button click event validates the credentials using an application-specific algorithm and data store. If the credentials are authenticated, the user code redirects the browser to the original URL.

The original URL is attached to the query string of the request for the login page, as shown here:

```
http://YourApp/login.aspx?ReturnUrl=original.aspx
```

Authenticating a user means that an authentication ticket is issued and attached to the request. When the browser places its second request for the page, the HTTP module retrieves the authentication ticket and lets the request pass.

Let's see how Forms-based authentication works in practice and consider a scenario in which users are not allowed to connect anonymously to any pages in the application. The user types the URL of the page—say *welcome.aspx*—and goes. As a result, the HTTP module redirects to the login page any users for which an authentication ticket does not exist, as shown in Figure 19-3.

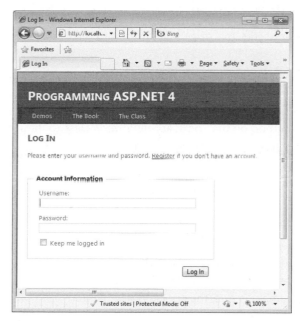

FIGURE 19-3 A sample login page.

> **Important** There are inherent security concerns that arise with Forms authentication related to the fact that any data is transmitted as clear text. Unfortunately, with today's browser technology, these potential security concerns can be removed only by resorting to secure channels (HTTPS). I'll return to this topic later in the "General Security Issues" section.

Collecting Credentials Through Login

The layout of a login page is nearly the same—a couple of text boxes for the user name and password, a button to confirm, and perhaps a label to display error messages. However, you can make it as complex as needed and add as many graphics as appropriate. The user enters the credentials, typically in a case-sensitive way, and then clicks the button to log on. When the login page posts back, the following code runs:

```
void LogonUser(object sender, EventArgs e)
{
    string user = userName.Text;
    string pswd = passWord.Text;

    // Custom authentication
    bool bAuthenticated = AuthenticateUser(user, pswd);
    if (bAuthenticated)
        FormsAuthentication.RedirectFromLoginPage(user, false);
    else
        errorMsg.Text = "Sorry, yours seems not to be a valid account.";
}
```

The event handler retrieves the strings typed in the user name and password fields and calls into a local function named *AuthenticateUser*. The function verifies the supplied credentials and returns a Boolean value. If the user has been successfully authenticated, the code invokes the *RedirectFromLoginPage* static method on the *FormsAuthentication* class to inform the browser that it's time to issue a new request to the original page.

The *RedirectFromLoginPage* method redirects an authenticated user back to the originally requested URL. It has two overloads with the following prototypes:

```
public static void RedirectFromLoginPage(string, bool);
public static void RedirectFromLoginPage(string, bool, string);
```

The first argument is the name of the user to store in the authentication ticket. The second argument is a Boolean value that denotes the duration of the cookie, if any, being created for the authentication ticket. If this argument is *true*, the cookie is given a duration that equals the number of minutes set by the *timeout* attribute (which is 30 minutes by default). In this way, you get a cookie that persists across browser sessions. Otherwise, your authentication cookie will last for the current session only. Finally, the third argument optionally specifies the cookie path.

Authenticating the User

The authenticating algorithm—that is, the code inside the *AuthenticateUser* method seen earlier—is entirely up to you. For example, you might want to check the credentials against a database or any other user-defined storage device. The following listing shows a (rather naïve) function that compares the user name and password against the *firstname* and *lastname* columns of the Northwind Employees table in SQL Server:

```
private bool AuthenticateUser(string username, string pswd)
{
    // Performs authentication here
    string connString = "...";
    string cmdText = "SELECT COUNT(*) FROM employees " +
                     "WHERE firstname=@user AND lastname=@pswd";

    int found = 0;
    using(SqlConnection conn = new SqlConnection(connString))
    {
        SqlCommand cmd = new SqlCommand(cmdText, conn);
        cmd.Parameters.Add("@user",
            SqlDbType.NVarChar, 10).Value = username;
        cmd.Parameters.Add("@pswd",
            SqlDbType.NVarChar, 20).Value = pswd;
        conn.Open();
        found = (int)cmd.ExecuteScalar();
        conn.Close();
    }
    return (found > 0);
}
```

The query is configured to return an integer that represents the number of rows in the table that match the specified user name and password. Notice the use of typed and sized parameters in the SQL command as a line of defense against possible injection of malicious code. Notice also that the SQL code just shown does not support strong passwords because the SQL = operator in the *WHERE* clause doesn't perform case-sensitive comparisons. To make provisions for that, you should rewrite the command as follows:

```
SELECT COUNT(*) FROM employees WHERE
    CAST(RTRIM(firstname) AS VarBinary)=CAST(RTRIM(@user) AS VarBinary)
    AND
    CAST(RTRIM(lastname) AS VarBinary)=CAST(RTRIM(@pswd) AS VarBinary)
```

The *CAST* operator converts the value into its binary representation, while the *RTRIM* operator removes trailing blanks. To capture the name of the currently logged-in user, a page should just use the following code block:

```
Welcome, <%= User.Identity.Name %>.
```

Signing Out

While an explicit sign-in is always required by Web sites that need authentication, an explicit sign-out is less common but legitimate nonetheless. The Forms authentication module provides an explicit method to sign out. The *SignOut* method on the *FormsAuthentication* class takes no argument and resets the authentication ticket. In particular, when cookies are used, the *SignOut* method removes the current ticket from the *Cookies* collection of the current *HttpResponse* object and replaces it with an empty and expired cookie.

After you call *SignOut*, you might want to redirect the application to another page. The *FormsAuthentication* class has a method—*RedirectToLoginPage*—that provides the described functionality and transfers the user to a given page using *Response.Redirect*.

Let's now take a look at the methods of the *FormsAuthentication* class and the configurable parameters you find in the *web.config* file. After this, I'll move on to introduce the membership API and role management.

The *FormsAuthentication* Class

The *FormsAuthentication* class supplies some static methods you can use to manipulate authentication tickets and execute basic authentication operations. You typically use the *RedirectFromLoginPage* method to redirect an authenticated user back to the originally requested URL; likewise, you call *SignOut* to remove the authentication ticket for the current user. Other methods and properties are for manipulating and renewing the ticket and the associated cookie.

Properties of the *FormsAuthentication* Class

Table 19-4 lists the properties of the *FormsAuthentication* class. As you can see, many of them deal with cookie naming and usage and expose the content of configuration attributes in the *<forms>* section. We'll look at the underpinnings of the *<forms>* XML configuration element in the next section. All the properties of the *FormsAuthentication* class shown in the table are static.

TABLE 19-4 **Properties of the *FormsAuthentication* Class**

Property	Description
CookieDomain	Returns the domain set for the authentication ticket. This property is equal to the value of the *domain* attribute in the *<forms>* section.
CookieMode	Indicates whether Forms authentication is implemented with or without cookies.
CookiesSupported	Returns *true* if the current request supports cookies.
DefaultUrl	Returns the URL for the page to return after a request has been successfully authenticated. It matches the *defaultUrl* attribute in the *<forms>* section.
EnableCrossAppRedirects	Indicates whether redirects can span different Web applications.
FormsCookieName	Returns the configured cookie name used for the current application. The default name is .ASPXAUTH.
FormsCookiePath	Returns the configured cookie path used for the current application. The default is the root path (/).
LoginUrl	Returns the configured or default URL for the login page. It matches the *loginUrl* attribute in the *<forms>* section.

Property	Description
RequireSSL	Indicates whether a cookie must be transmitted using only HTTPS.
SlidingExpiration	Indicates whether sliding expiration is enabled.

Most of the properties are initialized with the values read from the *<forms>* configuration section of the *web.config* file when the application starts up.

Methods of the *FormsAuthentication* Class

Table 19-5 details the methods supported by the *FormsAuthentication* class. All the methods listed in the table are static.

TABLE 19-5 Methods of the *FormsAuthentication* Class

Method	Description
Authenticate	Attempts to validate the supplied credentials against those contained in the configured *<credentials>* section. (I'll say more about this later.)
Decrypt	Given a valid authentication ticket, it returns an instance of the *FormsAuthenticationTicket* class.
Encrypt	Produces a string containing the printable representation of an authentication ticket. The string contains, encoded to URL-compliant characters, the user's credentials optionally hashed and encrypted.
GetAuthCookie	Creates an authentication ticket for a given user name.
GetRedirectUrl	Returns the redirect URL for the original request that caused the redirect to the login page.
HashPasswordForStoringInConfigFile	Given a password and a string identifying the hash type, the method hashes the password for storage in the *web.config* file.
Initialize	Initializes the *FormsAuthentication* class.
RedirectFromLoginPage	Redirects an authenticated user back to the originally requested URL.
RedirectToLoginPage	Performs a redirect to the configured or default login page.
RenewTicketIfOld	Conditionally updates the sliding expiration on an authentication ticket.
SetAuthCookie	Creates an authentication ticket, and attaches it to the outgoing response. It does not redirect to the originally requested URL.
SignOut	Removes the authentication ticket.

The *Initialize* method is called only once in the application's lifetime and initializes the properties in Table 19-4 by reading the configuration file. The method also gets the cookie values and encryption keys to be used for the application.

> **Note** In spite of their names, in ASP.NET both the *GetAuthCookie* method and the *SetAuthCookie* method get and set an authentication ticket, regardless of what it means to the application. If the application is configured to do Forms authentication in a cookieless manner, the two methods read and write ticket information from and to the URL of the request. They read and write a cookie if the authentication method is configured to use cookies.

Configuration of *Forms* Authentication

Although ASP.NET Forms authentication is fairly simple to understand, it still provides a rich set of options to deal with to fine-tune the behavior of the authentication mechanism. Most of the settable options revolve around the use of cookies for storing the authentication ticket. All of them find their place in the *<forms>* section under the *<authentication>* section.

The *<forms>* Section

Forms authentication is driven by the contents of the *<forms>* section child of the *<authentication>* section. The overall syntax is shown here:

```
<forms name="cookie"
    loginUrl="url"
    protection="All|None|Encryption|Validation"
    timeout="30"
    requireSSL="true|false"
    slidingExpiration="true|false"
    path="/"
    enableCrossAppsRedirects="true|false"
    cookieless="UseCookies|UseUri|AutoDetect|UseDeviceProfile"
    defaultUrl="url"
    domain="string">
</forms>
```

The various attributes are described in Table 19-6.

TABLE 19-6 Attributes for *Forms* Authentication

Attribute	Description
cookieless	Defines if and how cookies are used for authentication tickets. Possible values are *UseCookies*, *UseUri*, *AutoDetect*, and *UseDeviceProfile*.
defaultUrl	Defines the default URL to redirect after authentication. The default is *default.aspx*.
domain	Specifies a domain name to be set on outgoing authentication cookies. (I'll say more about this later.)
enableCrossAppRedirects	Indicates whether users can be authenticated by external applications when authentication is cookieless. The setting is ignored if cookies are enabled. When cookies are enabled, cross-application authentication is always possible. (I'll cover more issues related to this as we go along.)

Attribute	Description
loginUrl	Specifies the URL to which the request is redirected for login if no valid authentication cookie is found.
name	Specifies the name of the HTTP cookie to use for authentication. The default name is .ASPXAUTH.
path	Specifies the path for the authentication cookies issued by the application. The default value is a forward slash (/). Note that some browsers are case-sensitive and will not send cookies back if there is a path case mismatch.
protection	Indicates how the application intends to protect the authentication cookie. Feasible values are *All*, *Encryption*, *Validation*, and *None*. The default is *All*.
requireSSL	Indicates whether an SSL connection is required to transmit the authentication cookie. The default is *false*. If *true*, ASP.NET sets the *Secure* property on the authentication cookie object so that a compliant browser does not return the cookie unless the connection is using SSL.
slidingExpiration	Indicates whether sliding expiration is enabled. The default is *false*, meaning that the cookie expires at a set interval from the time it was originally issued. The interval is determined by the *timeout* attribute.
timeout	Specifies the amount of time, in minutes, after which the authentication cookie expires. The default value is 30.

The *defaultUrl* attribute lets you set the default name of the page to return after a request has been successfully authenticated. This URL is configurable. But isn't the URL of the return page embedded in the query string, in the *ReturnUrl* parameter? So when is *defaultUrl* useful?

If a user is redirected to the login page by the authentication module, the *ReturnUrl* variable is always correctly set and the value of *defaultUrl* is blissfully ignored. However, if your page contains a link to the login page, or if it needs to transfer programmatically to the login page (for example, after the current user has logged off), you are responsible for setting the *ReturnUrl* variable. If it is not set, the URL stored in the *defaultUrl* attribute will be used.

Cookie-Based Forms Authentication

The default way of putting Forms authentication at work is through cookies. The content of the authentication ticket is stored in a cookie named after the value of the *name* attribute in the *<forms>* section. The cookie contains any information that helps to identify the user making the request.

By default, a cookie used for authentication lasts 30 minutes and is protected using both data validation and encryption. Data validation ensures that the contents of the cookie have not been tampered with along the way. Encryption uses the Rijndael encryption algorithm (also known as AES) to scramble the content. You can force it to use DES or 3DES if you like, however.

When validation is turned on, the cookie is created by concatenating a validation key with the cookie data, computing a Machine Authentication Code (MAC) and appending the MAC to the outgoing cookie. The validation key, as well as the hash algorithm to use for the MAC, are read out of the *<machineKey>* section in the *web.config* file. The same section also specifies the cryptographic key for when encryption is enabled.

Cookieless Forms Authentication

Cookies are not the only way of putting Forms authentication to work. ASP.NET can offer an alternative API that exposes a nearly identical programming interface but makes no use of cookies.

When cookieless authentication is on, the ticket it is incorporated into the URL in much the same way as for cookieless sessions. The URL of the page served to an authenticated user follows the pattern shown here:

```
http://YourApp/(F(XYZ...1234))/samples/default.aspx
```

The ticket, properly encoded to a URL-compliant alphabet, is inserted in the URL right after the server name.

> **Note** No matter which settings you might have for validation and encryption, or whether your authentication scheme is cookied or cookieless, the information stored in the authentication ticket is encoded so that it is not immediately human-readable. Forms authentication uses a URI-safe derivative of the Base64 encoding that carries six bits of encoding per character.

Cookieless authentication requires an ISAPI filter to intercept the request, extract the ticket, and rewrite the correct path to the application. The filter also exposes the authentication ticket as another request header. The same *aspnet_filter.dll* component that we saw in Chapter 17, "ASP.NET State Management," for cookieless sessions is used to parse the URL when cookieless authentication is used. To avoid confusion, each extra piece of information stuffed in the URL is wrapped by unique delimiters: *S(...)* for a session ID and *F(...)* for an authentication ticket. The filter extracts the information, removes URL adornments, and places the ticket information in a header named *AspAuthenticationTicket*.

Options for Cookieless Authentication

To enable cookieless authentication, you set the *cookieless* attribute in the *<forms>* section of the configuration file to a particular value. The attribute specifies if and how cookies are used to store the authentication ticket. It can take any of the values listed in Table 19-7.

TABLE 19-7 Values for the *cookieless* Attribute

Value	Description
AutoDetect	Uses cookies if the browser has cookie support currently enabled. It uses the cookieless mechanism otherwise.
UseCookie	Always uses cookies, regardless of the browser capabilities.
UseDeviceProfile	Uses cookies if the browser supports them, and uses the cookieless mechanism otherwise. When this option is used, no attempt is made to check whether cookie support is really enabled for the requesting device. This is the default option.
UseUri	Never uses cookies, regardless of the browser capabilities.

There's a subtle difference between *UseDeviceProfile* and *AutoDetect*. Let's make it clear with an example. Imagine a user making a request through Internet Explorer. The browser does have support for cookies as reported in the browser capabilities database installed with ASP.NET. However, a particular user might have disabled cookies support for her own browser. *AutoDetect* can correctly handle the latter scenario, and it will opt for cookieless authentication. *UseDeviceProfile* doesn't probe for cookies being enabled, and it stops at what's reported by the capabilities database. It will incorrectly opt for cookied authentication, causing an exception to be thrown.

The default value for the *cookieless* attribute is *UseDeviceProfile*. You should consider changing it to *AutoDetect*.

> **Note** When assigning a value to the *cookieless* attribute in the *<forms>* section, pay attention to how you type any of the possible values in Table 19-7. Case does matter here—for instance, *UseUri* is a different thing than *useuri*. Only the former will work.

Advanced Forms Authentication Features

Let's tackle a few less obvious issues that might arise when working with Forms authentication.

Applications to Share Authentication Cookies

HTTP cookies support a *path* attribute to let you define the application path the cookie is valid within. Pages outside of that path cannot read or use the cookie. If the path is not set explicitly, it defaults to the URL of the page creating the cookie. For authentication cookies, the path defaults to the root of the application so that it is valid for all pages in the application. So far, so good.

In ASP.NET, two applications in the same Internet domain can share their own authentication cookies, implementing a sort of single sign-on model. Typically, both applications provide their own login pages, and users can log on using any of them and then freely navigate between the pages of both. For this to happen, you only have to ensure that some settings in the root *web.config* files are the same for both applications. In particular, the settings for the *name*, *protection*, and *path* attributes in the *<forms>* section must be identical. Moreover, a *<machineKey>* section should be added to both *web.config* files with explicit validation and decryption keys:

```
<machineKey
    validationKey="C50B3C89CB21F4F1422FF158A5B42D0…E"
    decryptionKey="8A9BE8FD67AF6979E7D20198C…D"
    validation="SHA1" />
```

Read Knowledge Base article 312906 (located at *http://support.microsoft.com/default. aspx?scid=kb;en-us;312906*) for suggestions on how to create machine keys. Note that, by default, validation and decryption keys are set to *AutoGenerate*. The keyword indicates that a random key has been generated at setup time and stored in the Local Security Authority (LSA). LSA is a Windows service that manages all the security on the local system. If you leave the *AutoGenerate* value, each machine will use distinct keys and no shared cookie can be read.

Suppose now you run two ASP.NET Web sites, named *www.contoso.com* and *blogs.contoso.com*. Each of these sites generates authentication cookies not usable by the other. This is because, by default, authentication cookies are associated with the originating domain. All HTTP cookies, though, support a *domain* attribute, which takes the flexibility of their *path* attribute to the next level. If set, the *domain* attribute indicates the domain the cookie is valid for. Cookies can be assigned to an entire Internet domain, a subdomain, or even multiple subdomains.

In ASP.NET, the *domain* attribute in the *<forms>* section determines the value of the *domain* attribute on the authentication cookie being created.

```
<forms domain="contoso.com" />
```

Add the preceding script to the *web.config* file of the Web sites named *www.contoso.com* and *blogs.contoso.com* and you'll have them share the authentication cookies (if the client browser recognizes the *domain* attribute of the cookie, which most modern browsers do).

The effect of the setting is that the primary domain (www) and any other subdomains will be able to handle each other's authentication cookies, always with the proviso that their *web. config* files are synchronized on the machine key values.

> **Note** Setting the *domain* attribute doesn't cause anything to be emitted into the authentication ticket; it simply forces all Forms authentication methods to properly set the *domain* property on each issued or renewed ticket. The attribute is ignored if cookieless authentication is used. The domain attribute of the *<forms>* section takes precedence over the domain field used in the *<httpCookies>* section and is valid for all cookies created in the ASP.NET application.

External Applications to Authenticate Users

Forms authentication also supports having the login page specified in another application in the same Web site:

```
<forms loginUrl="/anotherApp/login1.aspx" />
```

The two applications must have identical machine keys configured for this to work. If the application is using cookied authentication tickets, no additional work is necessary. The authentication ticket will be stored in a cookie and sent back to the original application.

If cookieless authentication is used, some extra work is required to enable the external application to authenticate for us. You need to set the *enableCrossAppRedirects* attribute in *<forms>* in the *web.config* file of both applications.

```
<forms ... enableCrossAppRedirects="true" />
```

Upon successful authentication, the ticket is generated and attached to a query string parameter to be marshaled back to the original application.

If the *enableCrossAppRedirects* attribute is missing and cookieless authentication is used, the external application will throw an exception.

> **Note** To test this feature in practice, ensure that the *<machineKey>* section in the *web.config* file of both applications contains the same values. They need to be explicit keys, not just the *AutoGenerate* command.

Forms Authentication and Secured Sockets

A hacker who manages to steal a valid authentication ticket is in a position to perpetrate a replay attack for the lifetime of the ticket. To mitigate the risk of replay attacks, you can perform authentication over a secured socket. Using secured sockets also removes the threat represented by applications such as Firesheep (*http://en.wikipedia.org/wiki/Firesheep*) that can sniff unencrypted cookies.

This means that first you must deploy your login page on an HTTPS-capable server, and second you need to set the *requireSSL* attribute to *true* in the *<forms>* section. This setting causes the ASP.NET application to enable the *Secure* attribute on the HTTP cookie being created. When the *Secure* attribute is set, compliant browsers send back only the cookie containing the ticket over a resource that is protected with SSL. In this way, you can still use a broad cookie scope, such as the whole application ('/') while providing a reasonable security level for the ticket in transit.

If you don't want to use SSL to protect the ticket, the best you can do to alleviate the risk of replay attacks is set the shortest lifetime for the authentication ticket to a value that is reasonable for the application. Even if the ticket is intercepted, there won't be much time remaining for the attacker to do his or her (bad) things.

As a final note regarding SSL, consider the following. If *requireSSL* is set and the user attempts to log in on a request not made over SSL, an exception is thrown. If *requireSSL* is set and an authentication cookie (a possibly stolen one at that) is provided over a non-SSL request, no exception is thrown; however, the cookie is wiped out and a regular login page is displayed through the browser.

Note that if the same happens with cookieless authentication, no protocol check is made and the request is served to the user...or the attacker.

General Security Issues

Functionally speaking, Forms authentication is the most appropriate authentication method for Web and ASP.NET applications. However, a few general security issues shouldn't pass without comment.

To start with, Forms authentication credentials are sent out as clear text from the client. SSL can be used to protect the communication, but in the end Forms authentication is as weak as IIS Basic authentication.

As mentioned, a stolen authentication cookie can be used to plan replay attacks as long as it is valid. This risk can be partially mitigated by reducing the lifetime of the ticket. Requiring an SSL connection for the cookie transmission resolves the issue if cookied authentication is used, but not if a cookieless solution is employed.

Finally, Forms authentication is based on application code, which is good news and bad news at the same time. It is good because you can keep everything under control. It is bad because any bug you leave in your code opens a security hole. A way to mitigate the risk of vulnerabilities stemming from incorrect code is to resort to the membership API.

Creating a Custom Principal

The *User* property on the *HttpContext* object is of type *IPrincipal*—the public contract that all principal objects must fulfill. Most of the time, the real type behind the *User* property is *GenericPrincipal*. If role management is enabled at the application level, instead, the type is *RolePrincipal*. (We'll cover role management in just a few moments.)

Common principal classes are certainly useful but may prove to be quite generic in most applications. In real-world scenarios, you sometimes need to add some custom information to the security context so that once you have authenticated a user you know much more about him than just the user name and roles. Let's see how to tweak the authentication process to create a custom cookie and then how to retrieve that information and pack it into a custom principal object.

In the event handler responsible for validating credentials, you add the following code:

```
var customInfo = "some|value";
var ticket = new FormsAuthenticationTicket(
    4,                                 // Version number
    userName,                          // Username
    DateTime.Now,                      // Issue date
    DateTime.Now.AddMinutes(30),       // Expiration date
    createPersistentCookie,            // Is it persistent?
    customInfo                         // User data
);
var encTicket = FormsAuthentication.Encrypt(ticket);

// Store the ticket into a cookie
var cookie = FormsAuthentication.GetAuthCookie(
                    FormsAuthentication.FormsCookieName,
                    createPersistentCookie);
cookie.Value = encTicket;

// Append the cookie to the response and redirect
HttpContext.Current.Response.Cookies.Add(cookie);
HttpContext.Response.Redirect(FormsAuthentication.DefaultUrl);
```

You create your own ticket and stuff some custom data in it. You must get your own instance of the *FormsAuthenticationTicket* class in order to do so. Next, you encrypt the ticket and write it to a cookie with the default name of authentication cookies. The preceding code replaces the following call, which is what would happen by default:

```
FormsAuthentication.SetAuthCookie(userName, createPersistentCookie);
```

The next step is retrieving the custom information stored in the authentication cookie. You can do that in the authentication step of *global.asax*, as shown here:

```
protected void Application_PostAuthenticateRequest()
{
    // Collect current security information
    var principal = HttpContext.Current.User as GenericPrincipal;
    if (principal == null)
        return;
    var identity = principal.Identity as FormsIdentity;
    if (identity == null)
        return;

    // Extract user data in the authentication ticket
    var customInfo = identity.Ticket.UserData;
    var tokens = customInfo.Split('|');

    // Build a richer principal object
    var myPrincipal = new MyPrincipal(identity, roles)
                    {
                        CurrentTime = tokens[0],
                        Number = tokens[1]
                    };
```

```
    // Store the new principal in the HttpContext
    HttpContext.Current.User = myPrincipal;
}
```

Having done all of this, you can now cast the *HttpContext.User* object to your principal type (*MyPrincipal* in the example) and use the additional properties in any page. *MyPrincipal* is a plain class that inherits from *GenericPrincipal*:

```
public class MyPrincipal : GenericPrincipal
{
    public MyPrincipal(IIdentity identity, String[] roles) :
        base(identity, roles)
    { }

    // Extra properties
    public String CurrentTime { get; set; }
    public String Number { get; set; }
}
```

The Membership and Role Management API

The membership API provides a set of classes to let you manage users and roles. Partnered with the *FormsAuthentication* class, the *Membership* and *Roles* classes form a complete security toolkit for ASP.NET developers. The *Membership* class supplies methods to manage user accounts—for adding or deleting a new user and editing any associated user information, such as the e-mail address and password. The *Roles* class creates and manages associations between users and roles.

What does the expression "managing user accounts" mean exactly? Simply put, it states that the *Membership* class knows how to create a new user or change his or her password. How do you create a user? Typically, you add a new record to some sort of data store. If that's the case, who is in charge of deciding which data store to use and how to actually write the new user information? These tasks represent the core functionality the membership API is designed to provide.

The membership API doesn't bind you to a fixed data store and data scheme. Quite the reverse, I'd say. It leaves you free to choose any data store and scheme you want, but it binds you to a fixed API through which users and roles are managed. The membership API is based on a provider model, and it delegates to the selected provider the implementation of all the features defined by the API itself. The provider component is only bound to implementing a contracted interface.

The *Membership* Class

Centered on the *Membership* static class, the membership API shields you from the details of how the credentials and other user information are retrieved and compared. The *Membership* class contains a few methods that you use to obtain a unique identity for each connected user. This information can also be used with other ASP.NET services, including role-based function enabling and personalization.

Among the members of the class are methods for creating, updating, and deleting users, but not methods for managing roles and programmatically setting what a user can and cannot do. For that, you have to turn to the *Roles* class, which we'll cover later.

The *Membership* class defaults to a provider that stores user information in a SQL Express database in a predefined format. If you want to use a custom data store (such as a personal database), you can create your own provider and just plug it in.

The Programming Interface of the *Membership* Class

Table 19-8 lists the properties exposed by the *Membership* class.

TABLE 19-8 Properties of the *Membership* Class

Property	Description
ApplicationName	A string to identify the application. It defaults to the application's root path.
EnablePasswordReset	Returns *true* if the provider supports password reset.
EnablePasswordRetrieval	Returns *true* if the provider supports password retrieval.
MaxInvalidPasswordAttempts	Returns the maximum number of invalid password attempts allowed before the user is locked out.
MinRequiredNonAlphanumericCharacters	Returns the minimum number of punctuation characters required in the password.
MinRequiredPasswordLength	Returns the minimum required length for a password.
PasswordAttemptWindow	Returns the number of minutes in which a maximum number of invalid password or password answer attempts are allowed before the user is locked out.
PasswordStrengthRegularExpression	Returns the regular expression that the password must comply with.
Provider	Returns an instance of the provider being used.
Providers	Returns the collection of all registered providers.
RequiresQuestionAndAnswer	Returns *true* if the provider requires a password question/answer when retrieving or resetting the password.
UserIsOnlineTimeWindow	Number of minutes after the last activity for which the user is considered on line.

The *Provider* property returns a reference to the membership provider currently in use. As you'll see in a moment, the provider is selected in the configuration file. ASP.NET comes with a couple of predefined providers that target MDF files in SQL Server Express and Active Directory. However, many more membership providers are in the works from Microsoft and third-party vendors, or you can even derive your own. You can obtain the list of installed providers for a given application through the *Providers* collection.

All properties are static and read-only. All of them share a pretty simple implementation. Each property just accesses the corresponding member on the current provider, as shown here:

```
public static int PasswordAttemptWindow
{
   get
   {
      Membership.Initialize();
      return Membership.Provider.PasswordAttemptWindow;
   }
}
```

As the name suggests, the *Initialize* method ensures that the internal structure of the *Membership* class is properly initialized and that a reference to the provider exists.

The class supports fairly advanced functionality, such as estimating the number of users currently using the application. It uses the value assigned to the *UserIsOnlineTimeWindow* property to determine this number. A user is considered on line if he has done something with the application during the previous time window. The default value for the *UserIsOnlineTimeWindow* property is 15 minutes. After 15 minutes of inactivity, a user is considered off line.

Table 19-9 details the methods supported by the *Membership* class. This list clarifies the tasks the class accomplishes.

TABLE 19-9 Methods of the *Membership* Class

Member	Description
CreateUser	Creates a new user and fails if the user already exists. The method returns a *MembershipUser* object representing any available information about the user.
DeleteUser	Deletes the user corresponding to the specified name.
FindUsersByEmail	Returns a collection of *MembershipUser* objects whose e-mail address corresponds to the specified e-mail.
FindUsersByName	Returns a collection of *MembershipUser* objects whose user name matches the specified user name.
GeneratePassword	Generates a random password of the specified length.
GetAllUsers	Returns a collection of all users.

Member	Description
GetNumberOfUsersOnline	Returns the total number of users currently on line.
GetUser	Retrieves the *MembershipUser* object associated with the current or specified user.
GetUserNameByEmail	Obtains the user name that corresponds to the specified e-mail. If more users share the same e-mail, the first is retrieved.
UpdateUser	Takes a *MembershipUser* object and updates the information stored for the user.
ValidateUser	Authenticates a user by using supplied credentials.

Setting Up Membership Support

To build an authentication layer based on the membership API, you start by choosing the default provider and establish the data store. In the simplest case, you can stay with the default predefined provider, which saves user information in a local MDF file in SQL Server Express.

The Web Site Administration Tool (WSAT) in Microsoft Visual Studio provides a user interface for creating and administering the registered users of your application. Figure 19-4 provides a glimpse of the user interface.

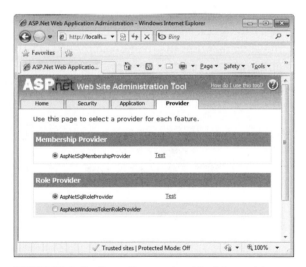

FIGURE 19-4 Configure the membership data model.

To add a new user or to edit properties of an existing one, you use the links shown in the figure. When you edit the properties of a new user, you use the page in Figure 19-5.

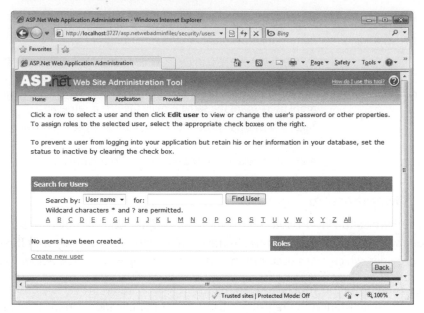

FIGURE 19-5 Choosing a user to edit or delete through the WSAT tool.

Validating Users

At this point, we're ready to write some code that uses the membership API. Let's start with the most common operation—authenticating credentials. Using the features of the membership subsystem, you can rewrite the code in the login page you saw previously to authenticate a user as follows:

```
void LogonUser(Object sender, EventArgs e)
{
    var user = userName.Text;
    var pswd = passWord.Text;

    if (Membership.ValidateUser(user, pswd))
        FormsAuthentication.RedirectFromLoginPage(user, false);
    else
        errorMsg.Text = "Sorry, yours seems not to be a valid account.";
}
```

This code doesn't look much different from what you would write without providers, but there's one big difference: the use of the built-in *ValidateUser* function. Here is the pseudocode of this method as it is implemented in the *system.web* assembly:

```
public static Boolean ValidateUser(String username, String password)
{
    return Membership.Provider.ValidateUser(username, password);
}
```

As you can see, all the core functionality that performs the authentication lives in the provider. What's nice is that the name of the provider is written in the *web.config* file and can be changed without touching the source code of the application. The overall schema is illustrated in Figure 19-6.

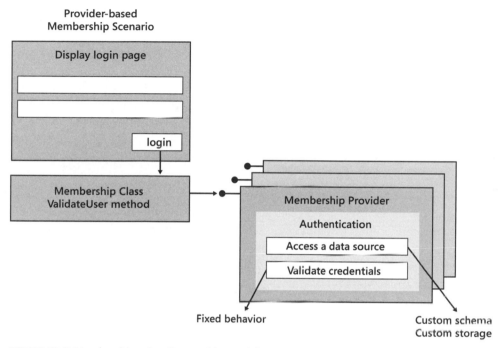

FIGURE 19-6 Membership using the provider model.

Managing Users and Passwords

The *Membership* class provides easy-to-use methods for creating and managing user data. For example, to create a new user programmatically, all you do is place a call to the *CreateUser* method:

```
Membership.CreateUser(userName, pswd);
```

To delete a user, you call the *DeleteUser* method:

```
Membership.DeleteUser(userName);
```

You can just as easily get information about a particular user by using the *GetUser* method. The method takes the user name and returns a *MembershipUser* object:

```
var user = Membership.GetUser("DinoE");
```

Once you've got a *MembershipUser* object, you know all you need to know about a particular user, and you can, for example, programmatically change the password (or other user-specific information). An application commonly needs to execute several operations on passwords, including changing the password, sending a user her password, or resetting the password, possibly with a question/answer challenge protocol. Here is the code that changes the password for a user:

```
var user = Membership.GetUser("DinoE");
user.ChangePassword(user.GetPassword(), newPswd);
```

To use the *ChangePassword* method, you must pass in the old password. In some cases, you might want to allow users to simply reset their password instead of changing it. You do this by using the *ResetPassword* method:

```
MembershipUser user = Membership.GetUser("DinoE");
string newPswd = user.ResetPassword();
```

In this case, the page that calls *ResetPassword* is also in charge of sending the new password to the user—for example, via e-mail. Both the *GetPassword* and *ResetPassword* methods have a second overload that takes a string parameter. If specified, this string represents the answer to the user's "forgot password" question. The underlying membership provider matches the supplied answer against the stored answers; if a user is identified, the password is reset or returned as appropriate.

> **Note** It goes without saying that the ability to reset the password, as well as support for the password's question/answer challenge protocol, is specific to the provider. You should note that not all the functions exposed by the membership API are necessarily implemented by the underlying provider. If the provider does not support a given feature, an exception is thrown if the method is invoked.

The Membership Provider

The beauty of the membership model lies not merely in the extremely compact code you need to write to validate or manage users but also in the fact that the model is abstract and extensible. For example, if you have an existing data store filled with user information, you can integrate it with the membership API without much effort. All you have to do is write a custom data provider—that is, a class that inherits from *MembershipProvider* which, in turn, inherits from *ProviderBase*:

```
public class MyAppMembershipProvider : MembershipProvider
{
    // Implements all abstract members of the class and, if
    // needed, defines custom functionality
    ...
}
```

This approach can be successfully employed to migrate existing authentication code to newer versions of ASP.NET applications and, perhaps more importantly, to link a custom and existing data store to the membership API. We'll return to this subject in a moment.

The *ProviderBase* Class

All the providers used in ASP.NET—not just membership providers—implement a common set of members: the members defined by the *ProviderBase* class. The class comes with one method, *Initialize*, and one property, *Name*. The *Name* property returns the official name of the provider class. The *Initialize* method takes the name of the provider and a name/value collection object packed with the content of the provider's configuration section. The method is supposed to initialize its internal state with the values just read out of the *web.config* file.

The *MembershipProvider* Class

Many of the methods and properties used with the *Membership* class are actually implemented by calling into a corresponding method or property in the underlying provider. It comes as no surprise, then, that many of the methods listed in Table 19-10, which are defined by the *MembershipProvider* base class, support the functions you saw in Table 19-9 that are implemented by the dependent *Membership* class. However, note that Table 19-9 and Table 19-10 are very similar but not identical.

TABLE 19-10 Methods of the *MembershipProvider* Class

Method	Description
ChangePassword	Takes a user name in addition to the old and new password, and changes the user's password.
ChangePasswordQuestionAndAnswer	Takes a user name and password, and changes the pair of question/answer challenges that allows reading and changing the password.
CreateUser	Creates a new user account, and returns a *MembershipUser*-derived class. The method takes the user name, password, and e-mail address.
DeleteUser	Deletes the record that corresponds to the specified user name.
FindUsersByEmail	Returns a collection of membership users whose e-mail address corresponds to the specified e-mail.
FindUsersByName	Returns a collection of membership users whose user name matches the specified user name.
GetAllUsers	Returns the collection of all users managed by the provider.
GetNumberOfUsersOnline	Returns the number of users that are currently considered to be on line.

Method	Description
GetPassword	Takes the user name and the password's answer, and returns the current password for the user.
GetUser	Returns the information available about the specified user name.
GetUserNameByEmail	Takes an e-mail address, and returns the corresponding user name.
ResetPassword	Takes the user name and the password's answer, and resets the user password to an auto-generated password.
UpdateUser	Updates the information available about the specified user.
ValidateUser	Validates the specified credentials against the stored list of users.

All these methods are marked as *abstract virtual* in the class (*must-inherit, overridable* in Visual Basic .NET jargon). The *MembershipProvider* class also features a few properties. They are listed in Table 19-11.

TABLE 19-11 Properties of the *MembershipProvider* Class

Property	Description
ApplicationName	Returns the provider's nickname.
EnablePasswordReset	Indicates whether the provider supports password reset.
EnablePasswordRetrieval	Indicates whether the provider supports password retrieval.
MaxInvalidPasswordAttempts	Returns the maximum number of invalid password attempts allowed before the user is locked out.
MinRequiredNonAlphanumericCharacters	Returns the minimum number of punctuation characters required in the password.
MinRequiredPasswordLength	Returns the minimum required length for a password.
PasswordAttemptWindow	Returns the number of minutes in which a maximum number of invalid password attempts are allowed before the user is locked out.
PasswordStrengthRegularExpression	Returns the regular expression that the password must comply with.
RequiresQuestionAndAnswer	Indicates whether the provider requires a question/answer challenge to enable password changes.
RequiresUniqueEmail	Indicates whether the provider is configured to require a unique e-mail address for each user name.

Extending the Provider's Interface

The provider can also store additional information with each user. For example, you can derive a custom class from *MembershipUser*, add any extra members, and return an instance of that class via the standard *GetUser* method of the membership API.

To use the new class, you cast the object returned by *GetUser* to the proper type, as shown here:

```
var user = Membership.GetUser(name) as MyCompanyUser;
```

In addition to the members listed in Table 19-10 and Table 19-11, a custom membership provider can add new methods and properties. These are defined outside the official schema of the provider base class and are therefore available only to applications aware of this custom provider.

```
var provider = Membership.Provider as MyCompanyProvider;
```

> **Note** The *Providers* collection property allows you to use a dynamically selected provider:
>
> ```
> var prov = Membership.Providers["ProviderName"];
> ```
>
> This feature allows applications to support multiple providers simultaneously. For example, you can design your application to support a legacy database of users through a custom provider, while storing new users in a standard SQL Server table. In this case, you use different membership providers for different users.

A Custom Provider for Legacy Code

Unless you're building an ASP.NET application entirely from scratch with total freedom to decide where and how to store settings and data, you have some legacy code or schema to deal with. A savvy strategy, then, is creating a custom membership provider to provide access to legacy data via a canonical programming interface. I would even say that almost any ASP.NET application needs its own membership provider. Here's some sample code:

```
public class MyMembershipProvider : MembershipProvider
{
    public MyMembershipProvider()
    {
    }
    public override bool ChangePassword(string username,
        string oldPassword, string newPassword)
    {
        // If you don't intend to support a given method
        // just throw an exception
        throw new NotSupportedException();
    }

    ...
```

```
public override bool ValidateUser(string username, string password)
{
    return AuthenticateUser(username, password);
}

private bool AuthenticateUser(string username, string pswd)
{
    // Place here any code that would use the existing API/schema
    // and authenticate against the provided credentials
  }
}
```

You define a new class derived from *MembershipProvider*. In this class definition, you have to override all the members in Table 19-10 and Table 19-11. If you don't intend to support a given method or property, for that method just throw a *NotSupportedException* exception. For the methods you do plan to support—which for the previous example included only *ValidateUser*—you write the supporting code. At this point, nothing prevents you from reusing code from your old application. There are two key benefits with this approach: you reuse most of your code (perhaps with a little bit of refactoring), and your application now fully embraces the membership model of ASP.NET.

Generally speaking, when writing providers, there are three key issues to look at: the lifetime of the provider, thread-safety, and atomicity. The provider is instantiated as soon as it proves necessary, but only once per ASP.NET application. This fact gives the provider the status of a stateful component, but it does so at the price of protecting that state from cross-thread access. A provider is not thread-safe, and it will be your responsibility to guarantee that any critical data is locked before use. Finally, some functions in a provider can be made of multiple steps. Developers are responsible for ensuring the atomicity of the operations either through database transactions (whenever possible) or through locks.

Configuring a Membership Provider

You register a new provider through the *<membership>* section of the *web.config* file. The section contains a child *<providers>* element under which additional providers are configured:

```
<membership>
    <providers>
        <add name="MyMembershipProvider"
             type="Samples.MyMembershipProvider" />
    </providers>
</membership>
```

You can change the default provider through the *defaultProvider* attribute of the *<membership>* section.

With the new provider in place, the code to verify credentials reduces to the following code, which is the same as you saw earlier in the chapter:

```
void LogonUser(object sender, EventArgs e)
{
    string user = userName.Text;
    string pswd = passWord.Text;
    if (Membership.ValidateUser(user, pswd))
        FormsAuthentication.RedirectFromLoginPage(user, false);
    else
        errorMsg.Text = "Sorry, yours seems not to be a valid account.";
}
```

There's more than just this with the membership API. Now a login page has a relatively standard structure and relatively standard code attached. At least in the simplest scenarios, it can be reduced to a composite control with no binding code. This is exactly what security controls do. Before we get to cover this new family of server controls, though, let's review roles and their provider-based management.

Managing Roles

Roles in ASP.NET simplify the implementation of applications that require authorization. A role is just a logical attribute assigned to a user. An ASP.NET role is a plain string that refers to the logical role the user plays in the context of the application. In terms of configuration, each user can be assigned one or more roles. This information is attached to the identity object, and the application code can check it before the execution of critical operations.

For example, an application might define two roles—Admin and Guest, each representative of a set of application-specific permissions. Users belonging to the Admin role can perform tasks that other users are prohibited from performing. Assigning roles to a user account doesn't add any security restrictions by itself. It is the responsibility of the application to ensure that authorized users perform critical operations only if they are members of a certain role.

In ASP.NET, the role manager feature simply maintains the relationship between users and roles.

> **Note** The Role Management API, although it consists of different methods and properties, works like the Membership API from a mechanical standpoint. Many of the concepts you read in the previous section also apply to role management.

The Role Management API

The role management API lets you define roles as well as specify programmatically which users are in which roles. The easiest way to configure role management, define roles, add users to roles, and create access rules is to use WSAT. (See Figure 19-4.) You enable role management by adding the following script to your application's *web.config* file:

```
<roleManager enabled="true" />
```

You can use roles to establish access rules for pages and folders. The following *<authorization>* block states that only *Admin* members can access all the pages controlled by the *web.config* file:

```
<configuration>
<system.web>
    <authorization>
        <allow roles="Admin" />
        <deny users="*" />
    </authorization>
</system.web>
</configuration>
```

The order in which you place *<allow>* and *<deny>*tags is important. Permissions and denies are processed in the order in which they appear in the configuration file.

WSAT provides a visual interface for creating associations between users and roles. If necessary, you can instead perform this task programmatically by calling various role manager methods. The following code snippet demonstrates how to create the Admin and Guest roles and populate them with user names:

```
Roles.CreateRole("Admin");
Roles.AddUsersToRole("DinoE", "Admin");
Roles.CreateRole("Guest");
var guests = new String[2];
guests[0] = "JoeUsers";
guests[1] = "Godzilla";
Roles.AddUsersToRole(guests, "Guest")
```

At run time, information about the logged-in user is available through the HTTP context *User* object. The following code demonstrates how to determine whether the current user is in a certain role and subsequently enable specific functions:

```
if (User.IsInRole("Admin"))
{
    // Enable functions specific to the role
    ...
}
```

When role management is enabled, ASP.NET looks up the roles for the current user and binds that information to the *User* object.

The *Roles* Class

When role management is enabled, ASP.NET creates an instance of the *Roles* class and adds it to the current request context—the *HttpContext* object. The *Roles* class features the methods listed in Table 19-12.

TABLE 19-12 **Methods of the *Roles* Class**

Method	Description
AddUsersToRole	Adds an array of users to a role.
AddUsersToRoles	Adds an array of users to multiple roles.
AddUserToRole	Adds a user to a role.
AddUserToRoles	Adds a user to multiple roles.
CreateRole	Creates a new role.
DeleteCookie	Deletes the cookie that the role manager used to cache all the role data.
DeleteRole	Deletes an existing role.
FindUsersInRole	Retrieves all the user names in the specified role that match the provider user name string. The user names found are returned as a string array.
GetAllRoles	Returns all the available roles.
GetRolesForUser	Returns a string array listing the roles that a particular member belongs to.
GetUsersInRole	Returns a string array listing the users who belong to a particular role.
IsUserInRole	Determines whether the specified user is in a particular role.
RemoveUserFromRole	Removes a user from a role.
RemoveUserFromRoles	Removes a user from multiple roles.
RemoveUsersFromRole	Removes multiple users from a role.
RemoveUsersFromRoles	Removes multiple users from multiple roles.
RoleExists	Returns *true* if the specified role exists.

Table 19-13 lists the properties available in the *Roles* class. All the properties are static and read-only. They owe their value to the settings in the *<roleManager>* configuration section.

TABLE 19-13 Properties of the *Roles* Class

Property	Description
ApplicationName	Returns the provider's nickname.
CacheRolesInCookie	Returns *true* if cookie storage for role data is enabled.
CookieName	Specifies the name of the cookie used by the role manager to store the roles. It defaults to .ASPXROLES.
CookiePath	Specifies the cookie path.
CookieProtectionValue	Specifies an option for securing the roles cookie. Possible values are *All, Clear, Hashed,* and *Encrypted.*
CookieRequireSSL	Indicates whether the cookie requires SSL.
CookieSlidingExpiration	Indicates whether the cookie has a fixed expiration time or a sliding expiration.
CookieTimeout	Returns the time, in minutes, after which the cookie will expire.
CreatePersistentCookie	Creates a role cookie that survives the current session.
Domain	Indicates the domain of the role cookie.
Enabled	Indicates whether role management is enabled.
MaxCachedResults	Indicates the maximum number of roles that can be stored in a cookie for a user.
Provider	Returns the current role provider.
Providers	Returns a list of all supported role providers.

Some methods in the *Roles* class need to query continuously for the roles associated with a given user, so when possible, the roles for a given user are stored in an encrypted cookie. On each request, ASP.NET checks to see whether the cookie is present; if so, it decrypts the role ticket and attaches any role information to the *User* object. By default, the cookie is a session cookie and expires as soon as the user closes the browser.

Note that the cookie is valid only if the request is for the current user. When you request role information for other users, the information is read from the data store using the configured role provider.

Note Role management passes through the role manager HTTP module. The module is responsible for adding the appropriate roles to the current identity object, such as the *User* object. The module listens for the *AuthenticateRequest* event and does its job.

The Role Provider

For its I/O activity, the role manager uses the provider model and a provider component. The role provider is a class that inherits the *RoleProvider* class. The schema of a role provider is not much different from that of a membership provider. Table 19-14 details the members of the *RoleProvider* class.

TABLE 19-14 **Methods of the *RoleProvider* Class**

Method	Description
AddUsersToRoles	Adds an array of users to multiple roles.
CreateRole	Creates a new role.
DeleteRole	Deletes the specified role.
FindUsersInRole	Returns the name of users in a role matching a given user name pattern.
GetAllRoles	Returns the list of all available roles.
GetRolesForUser	Gets all the roles a user belongs to.
GetUsersInRole	Gets all the users who participate in the given role.
IsUserInRole	Indicates whether the user belongs to the role.
RemoveUsersFromRoles	Removes an array of users from multiple roles.
RoleExists	Indicates whether a given role exists.

You can see the similarity between some of these methods and the programming interface of the *Roles* class. As you saw for membership, this is not just coincidental.

ASP.NET ships with a few built-in role providers—*SqlRoleProvider* (default), *WindowsTokenRoleProvider*, and *AuthorizationStoreRoleProvider*. The *SqlStoreProvider* class stores role information in the same MDF file in SQL Server Express as the default membership provider. For *WindowsTokenRoleProvider*, role information is obtained based on the settings defined for the Windows domain (or Active Directory) the user is authenticating against. This provider does not allow for adding or removing roles. The *AuthorizationStoreRoleProvider* class manages storage of role information for an authorization manager (AzMan) policy store. AzMan is a Windows download that enables you to group individual operations together to form tasks. You can then authorize roles to perform specific tasks, individual operations, or both. AzMan provides an MMC snap-in to manage roles, tasks, operations, and users. Role information is stored in a proper policy store, which can be an XML file, an Active Directory, or an ADAM server.

Custom role providers can be created deriving from *RoleProvider* and registered using the child *<providers>* section in the *<roleManager>* section. Note that the process for doing this is nearly identical to the process you saw for the custom membership provider we explored previously.

Quick Tour of Claims-Based Identity

Unlike many other aspects of programming, authentication has always been devoid of any level of indirection. This means that developers have always taken care of any details of the authentication API at quite a low level of abstraction and with deep knowledge of the technical aspects.

A key challenge, then, is carrying the world of security toward a different model, where the concept of outsourcing is central and development teams can focus on selecting the best provider for authentication. The new model is centered on Windows Identity Foundation (WIF) and uses claims instead of direct management of user credentials to implement authentication-based features.

Claims-Based Identity

Classic authentication is based on two steps: getting the user credentials and validating them against some known values. If the provided information matches the stored information, the user is recognized and authenticated and can gain access to specific features of the application.

Getting user credentials, however, often requires dealing with different technologies and possessing a wide range of skills. You can use, for example, certificate, Forms, or Windows authentication. In any of these cases, you must be familiar with technical details. As a result, your application recognizes the identity of a user from provided credentials that hopefully have been validated successfully.

Claims-based identity is something different.

Claims and Identity Providers

The key idea behind claims-based identity is that an application (and not just an ASP.NET application) uses a third-party provider that assumes responsibility for returning a few true statements about a user. These statements are known as *claims*. The calling application gets the list of claims and, based on that, decides which sections of the site should be unveiled to the user and which features should be enabled.

For developers, the biggest change is that you don't include in your codebase anything that deals with authentication and authorization. You simply arrange a conversation with an external identity provider, tell it about the statements you're interested in verifying, and wait for a response. The user is redirected somewhere else (presumably to the identity provider site), provides requested credentials, and gets authenticated.

So, in the end, it is still about having a piece of code that collects and verifies credentials, isn't it? Ultimately, it has to be this way because this is the only way in which authentication works. As a developer, though, you just outsource authentication to an external provider that you trust and that you have explicitly selected.

The Authentication Workflow

Figure 19-7 illustrates the typical workflow that characterizes a claims-based authentication process. The user initially connects to the application and attempts to log in. If all goes well, the user is ultimately redirected to the requested (and protected) page—nearly the same as in the authentication process we just reviewed. However, everything else is different under the surface.

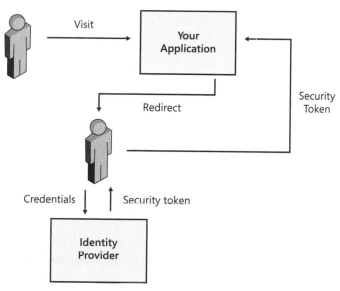

FIGURE 19-7 The typical flow of claims-based authentication.

An application designed to take advantage of claims-based identity redirects the user to the identity provider of choice. The user interacts with the site of the provider and enters any information that the provider reckons to be useful to authenticate the request. If the operation is successful, the identity provider issues a security token and redirects back to the application. The security token that is then handed over to the application contains claims about the user. These claims are trusted by the application.

Claims and Policies

So a claim is nothing more than a statement that has been verified by the identity provider, and the identity provider guarantees it is true. What kind of statements are we talking about, however? A claim is strictly bound to the provider. Different providers can issue different claims, and not all providers can validate a given claim.

A canonical example often discussed to introduce the concept of a claim is an online wine shop that needs to be sure about the age of the people placing orders. In this case, the classic approach of having users register with the site, provide a birth date, and proceed with purchasing products doesn't work. Who can reliably prove that the user is really of the legal age for purchasing alcohol? Certainly not the user himself!

In a claims-based system, the wine shop application might rely on an identity provider that "claims" to be able to verify the age of a user. The provider can ask for a driver's license number and cross check that number with the database of the Driving and Licensing department. Any identity provider must expose a policy document that lists its requirements (protocols, endpoints, data formats) and the list of claims it can support. An application must likewise incorporate a policy document with the list of security requirements—facts the application needs to know for sure in order to proceed. Furthermore, the application must include a list of valid and trusted providers.

Issued by the identity provider, a security token travels the network to reach the requesting application and carry information. The security token is digitally signed, can't be tampered with, and can be related to the issuing provider.

Strictly related to identity providers are the Security Token Service (STS). An STS provides a standards-based method of authenticating users and completely hides the details of how this is done internally.

Using Claims in ASP.NET Applications

To use claims-based identity in your ASP.NET application, you must pick up an STS and understand what it can do for you. Next, you disable any classic security and add code talk to the selected STS.

As mentioned, WIF is the Microsoft infrastructure for working with claims-based identity. You can download the WIF runtime from *http://www.microsoft.com/downloads/en/ details.aspx?FamilyID=EB9C345F-E830-40B8-A5FE-AE7A864C4D76*. The WIF SDK, instead, is available here: *http://www.microsoft.com/downloads/en/details.aspx?FamilyID= c148b2df-c7af-46bb-9162-2c9422208504*.

Picking Up the STS

To make an ASP.NET application claims-aware, you first need to get an STS. To start, you can use SelfSTS—a utility that emulates the minimal behavior of a realistic STS. You can get the STS from *http://code.msdn.microsoft.com/SelfSTS*.

If you use a Microsoft-provided project template for WIF, you then can rely on some tooling made to measure to add an STS reference and generate proper changes to code and con-figuration. At the end of the procedure, your authentication mode in the *web.config* file is probably set to *None* and a few HTTP modules have been added to the application's runtime environment.

Configuring the ASP.NET Application

With STS configured and WIF modules in place, the type behind the *HttpContext.User* property is *IClaimsPrincipal*:

```
var claimsPrincipal = HttpContext.Current.User as IClaimsPrincipal;
var claimsIdentity = (IClaimsIdentity) claimsPrincipal.Identity;
```

You now own all claims as issued by the sample STS. You can enumerate claims with a plain loop, as shown here:

```
foreach(var claim in claimsIdentity.Claims)
{
    // Use claims. Properties are ClaimType and Value
}
```

You use claims to enable or disable the various features of the application on a per-user basis.

For a lot more information about WIF and motivation to use it, I invite you to read Vittorio Bertocci's excellent book, *"Programming Windows Identity Foundation"* (Microsoft Press, 2010).

Compared to classic Forms authentication, claims-based identity has one noticeable difference for developers that can influence your decision to go with it or stick to more traditional solutions. You usually can't have a list of all the users that could log into your application.

All that your application can do is make public the list of claims it needs. After that, the selected (and trusted) STS gains control over the implementation of user accounts, and all your application has to do is check claims presented by users and reject users who don't match requested claims. In this way, you should never be required to modify the application to accommodate new users, even when these new users come from other sites as might be the case with federated sites.

Security-Related Controls

ASP.NET offers several server controls that make programming security-related aspects of a Web application quick and easy: *Login, LoginName, LoginStatus, LoginView, PasswordRecovery, ChangePassword,* and *CreateUserWizard*. These are composite controls, and they provide a rich, customizable user interface. They encapsulate a large part of the boilerplate code and markup you would otherwise have to write repeatedly for each Web application you developed. Figure 19-8 offers a comprehensive view of the membership platform and illustrates the role of the login controls.

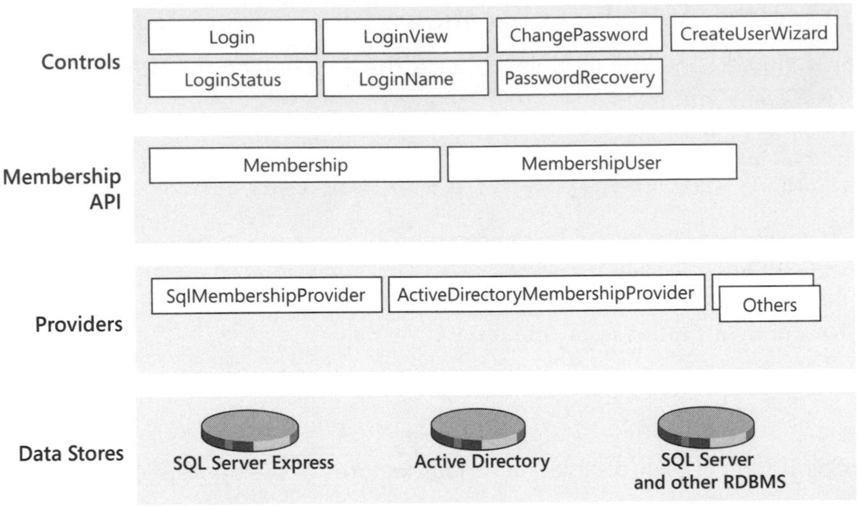

FIGURE 19-8 The big picture of ASP.NET membership and login controls.

The *Login* Control

An application based on the Forms authentication model always needs a login page. Aside from the

quality of the graphics, all login pages look alike. They contain a couple of text boxes (for username and password), a button to validate credentials, plus perhaps a *Remember Me* check box, and possibly links to click if the user has forgotten his or her password or needs to create a new account. The *Login* control provides all this for free, including the ability to validate the user against the default membership provider.

Setting Up the *Login* Control

The *Login* control is a composite control that provides all the common user interface elements of a login form. To use it, you simply drop the control from the toolbox onto the Web form, or you just type the following code:

```
<asp:login runat="server" id="MyLoginForm" />
```

The *Login* control also has optional user-interface elements for functions such as password reminders, new user registration, help links, error messages, and a custom action used in the case of a successful login. When you drop the control onto a Visual Studio form, the AutoFormat verb lets you choose among a few predefined styles, as shown in Figure 19-9.

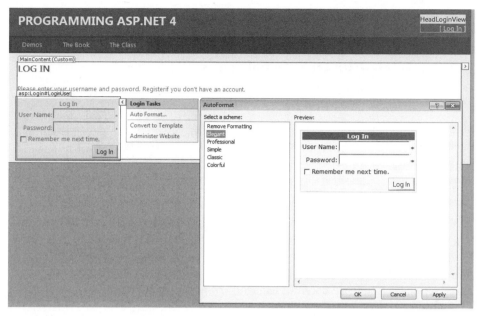

FIGURE 19-9 The predefined styles of the *Login* control.

The appearance of the control is fully customizable through templates and style settings. All user-interface text messages are also customizable through properties of the class.

The Programming Interface of the Control

The control is modularized, and each constituent part can be individually customized. The parts include the Username and Password text boxes, the Submit button, the button to create a new user, the Remember Me check box, and instructions with guidance to the user.

If you don't like the standard user interface of the control, you can define your own template too:

```
<asp:login runat="server" id="MyLoginForm">
    <layouttemplate>
        ...
    </layouttemplate>
</asp:login>
```

Your template can include new elements, and you can recycle default components. To do the latter, you should use the same ID for the controls as in the default template. To simplify this operation, right-click on the control in the Visual Studio designer, choose *Convert To Template*, and switch to the Source view. The markup you see is the default template of the control expressed as ASP.NET code. Use it as a starting point for creating your own template.

Events of the Control

The *Login* control fires the server events listed in Table 19-15.

TABLE 19-15 **Events of the *Login* Control**

Event	Description
Authenticate	Fires when a user is authenticated.
LoggedIn	Fires when the user logs in to the site after a successful authentication.
LoggingIn	Fires when a user submits login information but before the authentication takes place. At this time, the operation can still be canceled.
LoginError	Fires when a login error is detected.

In most common cases, though, you don't need to handle any of these events, nor will you likely find it necessary to programmatically access any of the numerous properties of the control.

The most common use for the *Login* control is to use it as a single-control page to set up the user interface of the login page for use with Forms authentication. The control relies entirely on the membership API (and the selected provider) to execute standard operations, such as validating credentials, displaying error messages, and redirecting to the originally requested page in the case of a successful login.

If you have a provider with custom capabilities that you want to be reflected by the *Login* control, you need to modify the layout to add new visual elements bound to a code-behind method. In the code-behind method, you invoke the custom method on the custom provider.

The *LoginName* Control

The *LoginName* control is an extremely simple but useful server control. It works like a sort of label control and displays the user's name on a Web page:

```
<asp:loginname runat="server" />
```

The control captures the name of the currently logged-in user from the *User* intrinsic object and outputs it using the current style. Internally, the control builds a dynamic instance of a *Label* control, sets fonts and color accordingly, and displays the text returned by the following expression:

```
string name = HttpContext.Current.User.Identity.Name;
```

The *LoginName* control has a pretty slim programming interface that consists of only one property—*FormatString*. *FormatString* defines the format of the text to display. It can contain only one placeholder, as shown here:

```
myLogin.FormatString = "Welcome, {0}";
```

If *Dino* is the name of the current user, the code generates a "Welcome, Dino" message.

The *LoginStatus* Control

The *LoginStatus* control indicates the state of the authentication for the current user. Its user interface consists of a link button to log in or log out, depending on the current user logon state. If the user is acting as an anonymous user—that is, he or she never logged in—the control displays a link button to invite the user to log in. Otherwise, if the user successfully passed through the authentication layer, the control displays the logout button.

Setting Up the *LoginStatus* Control

The *LoginStatus* control is often used in conjunction with the *LoginName* control to display the name of the current user (if any), plus a button to let the user log in or out. The style, text, and action associated with the button changes are conveniently based on the authentication state of the user.

The following code creates a table showing the name of the current user and a button to log in or log out:

```
<table width="100%" border="0"><tr>
    <td>
        <asp:loginname runat="server" FormatString="Welcome, {0}" />
    </td>
    <td align="right">
        <asp:loginstatus runat="server" LogoutText="Log off" />
    </td>
  </tr>
</table>
```

To detect whether the current user is authenticated and adapt the user interface, you can use the *IsAuthenticated* property of the *User* object:

```
void Page_Load(object sender, EventArgs e)
{
    if (User.Identity.IsAuthenticated)
      // Adjust the UI by outputting some text to a label
      Msg.Text = "Enjoy more features";
    else
      Msg.Text = "Login to enjoy more features.";
}
```

The Programming Interface of the Control

Although the *LoginStatus* control is quite useful in its default form, it provides a bunch of properties and events you can use to configure it. The properties are listed in Table 19-16.

TABLE 19-16 **Properties of the *LoginStatus* Control**

Property	Description
LoginImageUrl	Gets or sets the URL of the image used for the login link.
LoginText	Gets or sets the text used for the login link.
LogoutAction	Determines the action taken when a user logs out of a Web site. Possible values are *Refresh*, *Redirect*, and *RedirectToLoginPage*. *Refresh* reloads the current page with the user logged out. The other two values redirect the user to the logout page or the login page, respectively.
LogoutImageUrl	Gets or sets the URL of the image used for the logout button.
LogoutPageUrl	Gets or sets the URL of the logout page.
LogoutText	Gets or sets the text used for the logout link.

The control also features a couple events: *LoggingOut* and *LoggedOut*. The former fires before the user clicks to log off. The latter is raised immediately after the logout process has completed.

The *LoginView* Control

The *LoginView* control allows you to aggregate the *LoginStatus* and *LoginName* controls to display a custom user interface that takes into account the authentication state of the user as well as the user's role or roles. The control, which is based on templates, simplifies creation of a user interface specific to the anonymous or connected state and particular roles to which they are assigned. In other words, you can create as many templates as you need, one per state or per role.

The Programming Interface of the Control

Table 19-17 lists the properties of the user interface of the *LoginView* control.

TABLE 19-17 **Properties of the *LoginView* Class**

Property	Description
AnonymousTemplate	Gets or sets the template to display to users who are not logged in to the application.
LoggedInTemplate	Gets or sets the template to display to users who are logged in to the application.
RoleGroups	Returns the collection of templates defined for the supported roles. Templates can be declaratively specified through the *<roleGroups>* child tag.

Note that the *LoggedInTemplate* template is displayed only to logged-in users who are not members of one of the role groups specified in the *RoleGroups* property. The template (if any) specified in the *<roleGroups>* tag always takes precedence.

The *LoginView* control also fires the *ViewChanging* and *ViewChanged* events. The former reaches the application when the control is going to change the view (such as when a user logs in). The latter event fires when the view has changed.

Creating a Login Template

The *LoginView* control lets you define two distinct templates to show to anonymous and logged-in users. You can use the following markup to give your pages a common layout and manage the template to show when the user is logged in:

```
<asp:loginview runat="server">
   <anonymoustemplate>
      <table width="100%" border="0"><tr><td>
         To enjoy more features,
         <asp:loginstatus runat="server">
      </td></tr></table>
   </anonymoustemplate>
   <loggedintemplate>
      <table width="100%" border="0"><tr>
         <td><asp:loginname runat="server" /></td>
         <td align="right"><asp:loginstatus runat="server" /></td>
      </tr></table>
   </loggedintemplate>
</asp:loginview>
```

Basically, the *LoginView* control provides a more flexible, template-based programming interface to distinguish between logged-in and anonymous scenarios, as we did in the previous example by combining *LoginStatus* and *LoginName*.

Creating Role-Based Templates

The *LoginView* control also allows you to define blocks of user interface to display to all logged-in users who belong to a particular role. As mentioned, these templates take precedence over the *<loggedintemplate>* template, if both apply.

```
<asp:loginview runat="server">
   <rolegroups>
      <asp:rolegroup roles="Admin">
         <contenttemplate>
            ...
         </contenttemplate>
      </asp:rolegroup>
      <asp:rolegroup roles="Guest">
         <contenttemplate>
            ...
         </contenttemplate>
```

```
        </asp:rolegroup>
    </rolegroups>
</asp:loginview>
```

The content of each *<contenttemplate>* block is displayed only to users whose role matches the value of the *roles* attribute. You can use this feature to create areas in a page whose contents are strictly role-specific. For the *LoginView* control to work fine, role management must be enabled, of course. The control uses the default provider.

The *PasswordRecovery* Control

The *PasswordRecovery* control is another server control that wraps a common piece of Web user interface in an out-of-the-box component. The control represents the form that enables a user to recover or reset a lost password. The user will receive the password through an e-mail message sent to the e-mail address associated with his or her account.

The control supports three views, depending on the user's password recovery stage, as follows. The first view is where the user provides the user name and forces the control to query the membership provider for a corresponding membership user object. The second view is where the user must provide the answer to a predetermined question to obtain or reset the password. Finally, the third view is where the user is informed of the success of the operation.

Requirements for Password Retrieval

For the control to work properly, you must first ensure that the selected membership provider supports password retrieval. The password retrieval also requires the provider to define a *MembershipUser* object and implement the *GetUser* methods. Remember that the membership provider decides how to store passwords: clear text, hashed, or encrypted. Best practice, of course, is to only store hashed passwords.

If passwords are stored as hashed values, the control doesn't work. Hash algorithms are not two-way algorithms. In other words, the hash mechanism is great at encrypting and comparing passwords, but it doesn't retrieve the clear text. If you plan to use the *PasswordRecovery* control, you must ensure that the provider stores passwords as clear text or encrypted data.

Retrieving a Password

The *PasswordRecovery* control supports a child element named *MailDefinition*:

```
<asp:passwordrecovery runat="server">
   <maildefinition from="admin@contoso.com" />
</asp:passwordrecovery>
```

The *<MailDefinition>* element configures the e-mail message and indicates the sender as well as the format of the body (text or HTML), priority, subject, and carbon-copy (CC). For the same settings, you can also use a bunch of equivalent properties on the associated *Framework* class and set values programmatically.

If the user who has lost the password has a question/answer pair defined, the *PasswordRecovery* control changes its user interface to display the question and ask for the answer before the password is retrieved and sent back.

The control first asks the user to provide the user name; next it retrieves associated information and displays the security question, if any is defined for the user. Finally, if an e-mail address is known, the control sends a message with details. Bear in mind that you need to have proper e-mail settings in the *web.config* file, specifically in the *<system.net>* section, as shown here:

```
<system.net>
  <mailSettings>
    <smtp deliveryMethod="Network">
      <network host="your.smtp.server" />
    </smtp>
  </mailSettings>
</system.net>
```

The *ChangePassword* Control

The *ChangePassword* control provides an out-of-the-box and virtually codeless solution that enables end users to change their password to the site. The control supplies a modifiable and customizable user interface and built-in behaviors to retrieve the old password and save a new one:

```
<asp:ChangePassword ID="ChangePassword1" runat="server" />
```

The underlying API for password management is the same membership API we discussed earlier in this chapter.

User Authentication

The *ChangePassword* control will work in scenarios where a user might or might not be already authenticated. However, note that the User Name text box is optional. If you choose not to display the user name and still permit nonauthenticated users to change their password, the control will always fail.

If the user is not authenticated but the User Name text box is displayed, the user will be able to enter his or her user name, current password, and new password at the same time.

Password Change

The change of the password is performed using the *ChangePassword* method on the *MembershipUser* object that represents the user making the attempt. Note that the provider might pose an upper limit to the invalid attempts to change or reset the password. If set, this limit affects the *ChangePassword* control. The control won't work any longer after the limit has been exceeded.

After the password has been successfully changed, the control can send—if properly configured—a confirmation e-mail to the user. The e-mail message is configured through the same *<MailDefinition>* element you saw earlier for the *PasswordRecovery* control.

The *Continue* button points the page with the control to a new destination URL to let users continue working. If you don't set the *ContinuePageDestinationUrl* property, clicking the button simply refreshes the current page.

The *CreateUserWizard* Control

The *CreateUserWizard* control is designed to provide a native functionality for creating and configuring a new user using the membership API. The control offers a basic behavior that the developer can extend to send a confirmation e-mail to the new user and add steps to the wizard to collect additional information, such as address, phone number, or perhaps roles.

Customization is supported in two ways: by customizing one of the default steps, and by adding more user-defined steps. Figure 19-10 shows the control in action in the Create User page of the WSAT tool.

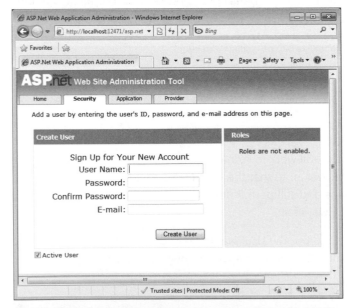

FIGURE 19-10 The *CreateUserWizard* control in action within WSAT.

The difference between this control and the *CreateUser* method on the membership provider is that the method just adds the user name and password. The wizard provides a user interface and lets you add more information in a single shot.

Summary

How can we design and code secure ASP.NET applications? First of all, security is strictly related to the application's usage, its popularity, and the type of users who connect to it and work with it. Paradoxically, a poorly secured application that isn't attractive to hackers can be perceived as being much more secure than a well-armored application with just one loophole or two. Successful attacks are possible through holes in the system-level and application-level security apparatus.

When it comes to security, don't look for a magic wand to do the job for you. Security is a state of mind, and insecurity is often the result of loose coding styles, if not true programming laziness. Never blindly trust anything regarding Web and ASP.NET security. Always keep in mind that security for Web applications is mostly about raising the bar higher and higher to make it hard for bad guys to jump over.

Part V
The Client Side

Chapter 20
Ajax Programming

The free thinking of one age is the common sense of the next.

—Matthew Arnold

Gone are the days when a Web application could be architected and implemented as a collection of static and dynamic pages served from the server for each and every request. In today's Web, a lot of work is done on the client using JavaScript libraries or richer engines such as Adobe Flash or Microsoft Silverlight.

Having rich client-side functionality is no longer a brilliant exception as it was only a few years ago; this is now going to be the rule. On the other hand, what's your knee-jerk reaction when you run across a Web site that requires you to pick up an item from a drop-down list and refreshes the entire page afterward? More or less, you hate it and wish they could update the site as soon as possible. In the end, using server-side programming to generate the page markup is more and more becoming a thing of the past.

Server-side programming is still an important piece of the Web, but these days it's different. For a Web site (a plain collection of mostly read-only pages), you leverage server-side programming to generate markup and serve it to the browser over an out-of-band, script-led request. For a Web application (a more sophisticated composition of functions exposed through pages), you tend to expose a URL-based API from the server that JavaScript code calls back to build and refresh the view dynamically.

The history of Web is full of cycles in which the focus shifts from the client to the server and then back. We had Dynamic HTML (DHTML) in 1997, but only for a subset of browsers—well, mostly Internet Explorer 4. There was no immediate and general consensus around that innovation, which remained confined to a small percentage of browsers for years. Then the hype returned to server programming with ASP.NET Web Forms. It's odd, when you think of it, how shielding developers from JavaScript and HTML was one of the best-selling points of ASP.NET. Around 2005, people started moving back toward client-side programming with Ajax.

Ajax is an acronym that stands for Asynchronous JavaScript and XML. It's a blanket term used to describe applications that extensively use the client-side capabilities of the Web browser. The browser is not simply a dummy HTML-based terminal; it gains the power of a real tier that hosts a part of the application's presentation logic. So how do you do Ajax in ASP.NET?

Pattern-wise, there are two main approaches to Ajax. One consists of serving markup to the browser over a script-led request. Known as *HTML Message* (HM), this pattern is akin to the classic browser-to-server model except that the request is placed via user-defined script rather than the hard-coded browser's machinery. As a developer, you make yourself responsible for deciding how to run the request and how to process the returned markup. On the server side, however, any URL you invoke always returns plain HTML markup.

The other pattern is *Browser-Side Templating* (BST) and is based on the idea that the browser places script-led requests for raw data to be incorporated in the user interface by some script-based presentation logic.

In this chapter, I'll dig out these two patterns and explore technologies related to ASP.NET Web Forms that make it work.

The Ajax Infrastructure

Typically, Web applications work by submitting user-filled forms to the Web server and displaying the markup returned by the Web server. The client-to-server communication employs the HTTP protocol and is usually conducted by the browser. The new model heralded by Ajax is based on an alternate engine that can be driven by some script code embedded in the page.

There are many benefits to writing Ajax applications. First and foremost, the page that triggers the call remains up and running and refreshes its Document Object Model (DOM) with the freshly downloaded data. No page replacement occurs, and the overall user experience is smooth and continual. In addition, you can fire and control asynchronous and potentially lengthy operations without freezing the current UI. An Ajax application minimizes user frustration, provides timely feedback about what's going on, and can deliver great mashed-up content.

The Hidden Engine of Ajax

Let's find out more about the internal HTTP engine that makes it possible to create and execute script-led HTTP requests. The key to the success of Ajax is that at some point around 2005, perhaps because of a rare astral conjunction, nearly all browsers on the marketplace happened to support the same component with a common API—the *XMLHttpRequest* object. This is the real hidden engine of Ajax applications, whatever browser you pick up and whatever the underlying platform might be.

The Classic Browser-Led Model

Using the local Domain Name System (DNS) resolver in the operating system, the browser resolves the requested URL to an IP address and opens a socket. An HTTP packet travels over the wire to the given destination. The packet includes the form and all its fields. The request is captured by the Web server and typically forwarded to an internal module for further processing. At the end of the process, an HTTP response packet is prepared and the return value for the browser is inserted in the body. If the response contains an HTML page, the browser replaces the current contents entirely with the new chunk of markup.

While the request is being processed on the server, the "old" page is frozen but still displayed to the client user. As soon as the "new" page is downloaded, the browser clears the display and renders the page.

This model was just fine in the beginning of the Web age when pages contained little more than formatted text, hyperlinks, and some images. The success of the Web has prompted users to ask for increasingly more powerful features, and it has led developers and designers to create more sophisticated services and graphics. The net effect is that pages are heavy and cumbersome—even though we still insist on calling them "rich" pages. Regardless of whether they're rich or just cumbersome, these are the Web pages of today's applications. And nobody really believes that we're going to return to the scanty and spartan HTML pages of a decade ago.

Given the current architecture of Web applications, each user action requires a complete redraw of the page. Subsequently, richer and heavier pages render slowly and, as a result, produce a good deal of flickering. Projected to the whole set of pages in a large, portal-like application, this mechanism is perfect for unleashing the frustrations of the poor end user.

The New Out-of-Band Model

The chief factor that enables Ajax functionality in a Web page is the ability to issue out-of-band HTTP requests. In this context, an out-of-band call indicates an HTTP request placed using a component different from the browser. This component is the *XMLHttpRequest* object.

Historically speaking, the first version of this object saw the light of day in 1998 as part of the Microsoft Outlook Web Access subsystem within Microsoft Exchange. Later on, the component was embedded as an ActiveX component in Internet Explorer 5 and then was integrated in other browsers.

> **Note** In the mid-1990s, there was a team at Microsoft working on a technology called Remote Scripting (RS). RS never reached the stage of a version 1.0, but it had a lot in common with today's AJAX hidden engine. In RS, the proxy component was a Java applet managing the browser-to-server communication.

XMLHttpRequest is a browser object that is scriptable through JavaScript. It sends a regular HTTP request to the specified URL and waits, either synchronously or asynchronously, for it to be fully served. When the response data is ready, the proxy invokes a user-defined

JavaScript callback to refresh any portion of the page that needs updating. Figure 20-1 provides a graphical overview of the model.

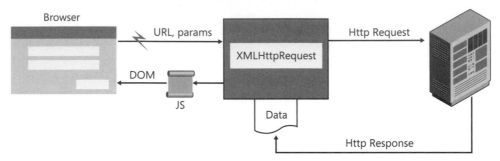

FIGURE 20-1 Out-of-band calls are sent through a proxy component.

All browsers know how to replace an old page with a new page; until a few years ago, though, not all of them provided an object model to represent the current contents of the page. (Today, I can hardly mention a single modern, commercially available browser that doesn't expose a read/write page DOM.) For browsers that supply an updatable object model for HTML pages, the JavaScript callback function can refresh specific portions of the old page, thus making them look updated, without a full reload.

There's a World Wide Web Consortium (W3C) ratified standard for the updatable DOM you can find at *http://www.w3.org/TR/DOM-Level-3-Core*. A W3C document for the proxy component is currently being developed. It takes the form of the existing *XMLHttpRequest* object and is devised as an interface exposed by the browser to allow script code to perform HTTP client functionality, such as submitting form data or loading data from a remote Web site. The latest candidate recommendation is at *http://www.w3.org/TR/XMLHttpRequest*.

From Dynamic HTML to the Standard DOM

About ten years ago, with Internet Explorer 4.0, Microsoft introduced a proprietary object model named Dynamic HTML (DHTML) to enable page authors to update the current page dynamically using JavaScript. The success of DHTML led to the definition of a standard document object model—the W3C's DOM. Quite obviously, the DOM evolved from DHTML and became much more generalized than DHTML.

Today most browsers support a mix of DOM and DHTML. Which one should you use? In particular, to update certain content, should you obtain a reference to the textual child node of the node that matches the intended HTML tag (the DOM way), or just grab a reference to a node and use the *innerHTML* property as you would do in the DHTML way? Likewise, to add a new element, should you create a new element or just stuff in a chunk of updated HTML via *innerHTML*? Admittedly, one of the most interesting debates in the community is whether to use DHTML to manipulate pages or opt for the cleaner approach propounded by the DOM API.

The key fact is that the DOM API is significantly slower than using *innerHTML*. If you go through the DOM to generate some user interface dynamically, you have to create every element, append each into the proper container, and then set properties. The alternative entails only that you define the HTML you want and render it into the page using *innerHTML*. The browser then does the rest by rendering your markup into direct graphics.

Overall, DHTML and DOM manipulation are both useful depending on the context. There are many Web sites that discuss performance tests, and DHTML is always the winner. Anyway, DOM is still perfectly fast as long as you use it the right way—that is, create HTML fragments and append them to the proper container only as the final step.

The *XMLHttpRequest* Object

Created by Microsoft and adopted soon thereafter by Mozilla, the *XMLHttpRequest* object is fully supported these days by the majority of Web browsers. The implementation can vary from one browser to the next, even though the top-level interface is nearly identical. For this reason, a W3C committee is at work with the goal of precisely documenting a minimum set of interoperable features based on existing implementations. An excellent presentation on the component can be found here: *http://developer.mozilla.org/en/docs/XMLHttpRequest*.

Note When the *XMLHttpRequest* object was first released, the Component Object Model (COM) was ruling the world at Microsoft. The extensibility model of products and applications was based on COM and implemented through COM components. In the late 1990s, the right and natural choice was to implement this new component as a reusable automation COM object, named *Microsoft.XmlHttp*.

COM objects are external components that require explicit permission—safe for scripting—to run inside of a Web browser. The *XMLHttpRequest* object is certainly a safe component, but to enable it users need to decrease their security settings and accept any other component "declared" safe for scripting that is hanging around the Web sites they visit. The *XMLHttpRequest* object has finally become a browser object with Internet Explorer 7.0. All potential security concerns are therefore removed at the root.

Today, the *XMLHttpRequest* object is part of the browser object model and is exposed out of the window object. As a result, it can be instantiated through the classic *new* operator:

```
// The object name requires XML in capital letters
var proxy = new XMLHttpRequest();
```

When the browser is Internet Explorer (up to version 6.0), the *XMLHttpRequest* object must be instantiated using the *ActiveXObject* wrapper, as shown here:

```
var proxy = new ActiveXObject("Microsoft.XmlHttp");
```

Generally, Ajax frameworks (and JavaScript libraries with Ajax support, such as jQuery) check the current browser and then decide which route to take.

Using the *XMLHttpRequest* Object

The *XMLHttpRequest* object is designed to perform one key operation: send an HTTP request. The request can be sent either synchronously or asynchronously. The following bit of code shows the programming interface of the object as it results from the W3C working draft at the time of this writing:

```
interface XMLHttpRequest
{
  function onreadystatechange;
  readonly unsigned short readyState;
  void open(string method, string url);
  void open(string method, string url, bool async);
  void open(string method, string url, bool async, string user);
  void open(string method, string url, bool async,
            string user, string pswd);
  void setRequestHeader(string header, string value);
  void send(string data);
  void send(Document data);
  void abort();
  string getAllResponseHeaders();
  string getResponseHeader(string header);
  string responseText;
  Document responseXML;
  unsigned short status;
  string statusText;
};
```

Using the component is a two-step operation. First, you open a channel to the URL and specify the method (GET, POST, or other) to use and specify whether you want the request to execute asynchronously. Next, you set any required header and send the request. If the request is a POST, you pass to the *send* method the body of the request.

The *send* method returns immediately in the case of an asynchronous operation. You write an *onreadystatechange* function to check the status of the current operation and, using that function, figure out when it is done. The following code shows how to carry on a POST request using the *XMLHttpRequest* object:

```
var xmlRequest, e;
try
{
    xmlRequest = new XMLHttpRequest();
}
catch(e)
{
    try
    {
        xmlRequest = new ActiveXObject("Microsoft.XMLHTTP");
```

```
    }
    catch(e)
    {
    }
}

// Prepare for a synchronous POST request
var body = null;   // An empty request body this time...
xmlRequest.open("POST", pageUrl, false);
xmlRequest.setRequestHeader("Content-Type",
                            "application/x-www-form-urlencoded");
xmlRequest.send(body);
```

In a synchronous call, the *send* method returns when the response has been fully downloaded and parsed by the object. You can access it as a plain string using the *responseText* property. If the response is an XML stream, you can have it exposed as an XML DOM object using the *responseXml* property.

> **Important** If you're going to use any Ajax-enabled framework for building Web applications, you'll hardly hear anything about the *XMLHttpRequest* object, much less use it directly in your own code. An Ajax framework completely encapsulates this object and shields page authors and application designers from it. You don't need to know about *XMLHttpRequest* to write great Ajax applications, no matter how complex and sophisticated they are. However, knowing the fundamentals of *XMLHttpRequest* can lead you to a better and more thorough understanding of the platform and to more effective diagnoses of problems.

JavaScript and Ajax

Ajax applications require you to write a lot of JavaScript code. Most of the time, you are called upon to write simple UI-driven code that refreshes the user interface following the state of the application and maps pieces of downloaded data to UI elements. If all you need to write is a few event handlers, any approach does work. When the quantity of code grows beyond a certain threshold, however, you need to lay out your client code using abstractions not unlike those you might use in a classic programming language—functions and objects.

I won't stray too far from the truth if I state that JavaScript is such a flexible language that it can be used to write code that follows two radically different programming paradigms— functional programming and object-oriented programming (OOP). Which one should you choose and when?

Functional Programming in JavaScript

In functional programming, the building block of code is the "function," as opposed to the "class" in object-oriented programming and the "subroutine" in procedural programming.

A function is a unit of code that describes only the operations to be performed on the input. A function gets some input and returns some output; everything else is hidden from view.

As a functional programmer, you build your applications by pipelining function calls to create a super function that just gets the program's input and returns the program's output. There's typically no layer where you process the input, store state, arrange a sequence of statements, update the state, and decide about the next step. A function is a like a value, and it can be used as an argument and be passed to other functions as well as used in any other context where values can be used.

In JavaScript, anonymous functions are the pillar of functional programming. An anonymous function is a direct offshoot of lambda calculus or, if you prefer, a language adaptation of old-fashioned function pointers. Here's an example:

```
function(x, y) {
    return x + y;
}
```

The only difference between a regular function and an anonymous function is in the name. In a functional context, you don't strictly need to name a function, especially if you're using it as a value that you pass around.

The jQuery library, which we'll cover in the next chapter, more than ever called people's attention to functional programming. In a Web environment, all you do is manipulate DOM elements. The jQuery library is effective because it allows you to manipulate DOM elements while enjoying the power (and to some extent the cleanness) of functional programming.

Objects in JavaScript

There's a significant difference between objects in a qualified OOP language and JavaScript. In OOP languages, the class is a blueprint for actual objects you use. In JavaScript, you just have objects whose blueprint is that of a dictionary of data and functions. When you create a new object in JavaScript, you have an empty dictionary you can fill with anything you like.

Having said that, with a bit of work you can create (and reuse) custom objects and manage for them to inherit from existing objects and also behave polymorphically. This work is just what JavaScript object-oriented libraries do.

When it comes to adding layers to JavaScript to make it closer to a qualified OOP language and gain some more programming power and code reusability, you have to choose from two main approaches for extending the capabilities of the native JavaScript objects: closures and prototypes.

Before we get to that, however, a few words about the native *Object* type in JavaScript and its usage. You can use the *new* keyword to create a new dictionary-like object in JavaScript.

Next, you stuff data into it, and you can add methods by wiring functions to property names. Here's an example:

```
var person = new Object();
person.Name = "Dino";
person.LastName = "Esposito";
person.BirthDate = new Date(1992,10,17)
person.getAge = function() {
  var today = new Date();
  var thisDay = today.getDate();
  var thisMonth = today.getMonth();
  var thisYear = today.getFullYear();
  var age = thisYear-this.BirthDate.getFullYear()-1;
  if (thisMonth > this.BirthDate.getMonth())
      age = age +1;
  else
  if (thisMonth == this.BirthDate.getMonth() &&
      thisDay >= this.BirthDate.getDate())
      age = age +1;
  return age;
}
```

What we have is an object modeled after a person; we don't have a *Person* object. A possible way to define the layout of a type is to create a new, all-encompassing function that exposes just the members we like. In addition, in JavaScript all intrinsic objects have a read-only property named *prototype*. You can use the *prototype* property to provide a base set of functionality shared by any new instance of an object of that type. These two are the mechanisms to leverage for using OOP in JavaScript.

Using Closures

A *closure* is a general concept of programming languages. Applied to JavaScript, a closure is a function that can have variables and methods defined together within the same context. In this way, the outermost (anonymous or named) function "closes" the expression. Here's an example of the closure model for a function that represents a *Person* type:

```
var Person = function(name, lastname, birthdate)
{
   this.Name = name;
   this.LastName = lastname;
   this.BirthDate = birthdate;

   this.getAge = function() {
      var today = new Date();
      var thisDay = today.getDate();
      var thisMonth = today.getMonth();
      var thisYear = today.getFullYear();
      var age = thisYear-this.BirthDate.getFullYear()-1;
      if (thisMonth > this.BirthDate.getMonth())
          age = age +1;
      else
         if (thisMonth == this.BirthDate.getMonth() &&
```

```
            thisDay >= this.BirthDate.getDate())
            age = age +1;
        return age;
    }
}
```

As you can see, the closure is nothing more than the constructor of the pseudo-class. In a closure model, the constructor contains the member declarations and members are truly encapsulated and private to the class. In addition, members are instance based, which increases the memory used by the class. Here's how you use the object:

```
var p = new Person("Dino", "Esposito", new Date( ... );
alert(p.Name + " is " + p.getAge());
```

The closure model gives full encapsulation, but nothing more. To compose objects, you can only resort to aggregation.

Using Prototypes

The prototype model entails that you define the public structure of the class through the JavaScript *prototype* object. The following code sample shows how to rewrite the preceding *Person* class to avoid a closure:

```
// Pseudo constructor
var Person = function(name, lastname, birthdate)
{
    this.initialize(name, lastname, birthdate);
}

// Members
Person.prototype.initialize(name, lastname, birthdate)
{
    this.Name = name;
    this.LastName = lastname;
    this.BirthDate = birthdate;
}

Person.prototype.getAge = function()
{
    var today = new Date();
    var thisDay = today.getDate();
    var thisMonth = today.getMonth();
    var thisYear = today.getFullYear();
    var age = thisYear-this.BirthDate.getFullYear()-1;
    if (thisMonth > this.BirthDate.getMonth())
        age = age +1;
    else
        if (thisMonth == this.BirthDate.getMonth() &&
            thisDay >= this.BirthDate.getDate())
            age = age +1;
    return age;
}
```

In the prototype model, the constructor and members are clearly separated and a constructor is always required. As for private members, you just don't have them. The *var* keyword that would keep them local in a closure doesn't apply in the prototype model. So you can define getter/setter for what you intend to be properties, but the backing field will remain accessible from the outside, anyway. You can resort to some internal (and documented) convention, such as prefixing with an underscore the name of members you intend as private. That's just a convention, however.

By using the prototype feature, you can achieve inheritance by simply setting the prototype of a derived object to an instance of the "parent" object:

```
Developer = function Developer(name, lastname, birthdate)
{
    this.initialize(name, lastname, birthdate);
}
Developer.prototype = new Person();
```

Note that you always need to use this to refer to members of the prototype from within any related member function.

In the prototype model, members are shared by all instances as they are invoked on the shared prototype object. In this way, the amount of memory used by each instance is reduced, which also provides for faster object instantiation. Aside from syntax peculiarities, the prototype model makes defining classes much more similar to the classic OOP model than the closure model.

The choice between closure and prototype should also be guided by performance considerations and browser capabilities. Prototypes have a good load time in all browsers; indeed, they have excellent performance in Firefox. (In contrast, closures have a better load time than prototypes in Internet Explorer.) Prototypes provide better support for IntelliSense, and they allow for tool-based statement completion when used in tools that support this feature, such as Microsoft Visual Studio. Prototypes can also help you obtain type information by simply using reflection. You won't have to create an instance of the type to query for type information, which is unavoidable if closures are used. Finally, prototypes allow you to easily view private class members when debugging. Debugging objects derived using the closure model requires a number of additional steps.

Note Whether you opt for closure or prototype, writing complex JavaScript code requires a lot of discipline. An interesting pattern to explore is the Module Pattern, which essentially introduces the concepts of namespaces and dependencies in JavaScript code where no such elements exist natively. A good introduction to the pattern can be found here: *http://www.adequatelygood.com/2010/3/JavaScript-Module-Pattern-In-Depth*.

Cross-Domain Ajax

For security reasons, all *XMLHttpRequest* calls within all browsers are restricted to the Same Origin Policy (SOP). In other words, all browsers proceed with an *XMLHttpRequest* call only if the destination URL is within the same origin as the calling page. Because *XMLHttpRequest* uploads cookies, a user authenticated on a site (say, contoso.com) might end up on another site (say, thebadguy.com) and leave there her authentication cookie. At this point, from the thebadguy.com site an attacker could make an *XMLHttpRequest* request to contoso.com and behave as if it were the original user. In a nutshell, script-led cross-domain calls are forbidden.

The problem is that sometimes cross-domain calls are useful and entirely legitimate. How to work around the limitation? Generally speaking, there are four possible approaches:

- Using a server-side proxy

- Using Silverlight or Flash applets and their native workarounds to bypass SOP

- Leveraging cross-domain-enabled HTML tags such as *<script>* and *<iframe>*

- Using ad hoc browser extensions specifically created to enable cross-domain *XMLHttpRequest* calls

These are the various options you might want to consider first as a software architect. These are the options that would work without requiring each user to tweak security settings on her browser.

Note, however, that most browsers let you disable the SOP policy through the dialog box for the security settings. If you, as a user, proceed with and enable cross-domain calls, all *XMLHttpRequest* calls magically work, regardless of their final destination. From a design perspective, however, this solution has a strong prerequisite: it requires you to exercise strict control over all possible machines that will be using the site. For Internet Explorer, you select the Security tab from the Internet Options dialog box and then scroll down to the Miscellaneous section, as shown in Figure 20-2.

Be aware that a similar option might not exist for other browsers.

I'll return to cross-domain calls in the next chapter with a few concrete examples. For now, suffice it to say that two approaches are the most commonly used today: server-side proxies and JSON with Padding (JSONP) over the *<script>* tag.

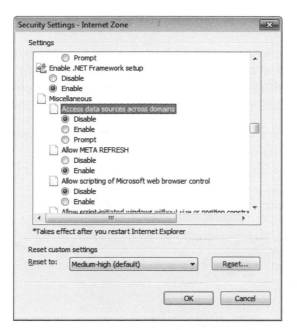

FIGURE 20-2 Tweaking the cross-domain call setting of Internet Explorer.

Partial Rendering in ASP.NET

You do much of your ASP.NET Web Forms programming using server controls. A server control normally emits HTML markup. In an Ajax scenario, a server control emits markup plus some script code to support Ajax requests. This is not exactly a change of paradigm in the name of Ajax, but it is a good compromise between the classic Web and requested Ajax capabilities.

ASP.NET partial rendering works according to this idea. It provides a new container control—the *UpdatePanel* control—that you use to surround portions of existing pages, or portions of new pages developed with the usual programming model of ASP.NET. A postback that originates within any of these updatable regions is intercepted by some JavaScript code that the *UpdatePanel* control has injected in the page. As a result, only the controls in a given region are updated.

The *UpdatePanel* control, however, requires the use of another server control—the *ScriptManager* control—which is responsible, among other things, for injecting in the page any required script code.

The *ScriptManager* Control

The main control in the server infrastructure of ASP.NET for Ajax is the *ScriptManager* control and its twin, the *ScriptManagerProxy* control. You will find just one instance of the *ScriptManager* control in each ASP.NET Ajax page. The *ScriptManagerProxy* control is used only in master pages scenarios to reference the original script manager from content pages.

The *ScriptManager* control manages and delivers script resources, thus enabling client scripts to make use of the JavaScript type system extensions and other JavaScript features that we covered earlier in this chapter. The *ScriptManager* control also enables features such as partial-page rendering and service and page method calls. The following code shows the simplest and most common way to insert the script manager in an ASP.NET page:

```
<asp:ScriptManager runat="server" ID="ScriptManager1" />
```

The control produces no user interface, works exclusively on the server, and doesn't add any extra bytes to the page download.

Properties of the *ScriptManager* Control

The *ScriptManager* control features a number of properties for you to configure its expected behavior. Table 20-1 details the supported properties.

TABLE 20-1 Properties of *ScriptManager*

Property	Description
AjaxFrameworkAssembly	Gets the Ajax framework assembly that components on the page are currently using.
AjaxFrameworkMode	Gets or sets how client scripts of the Microsoft Ajax client library will be included on the client: as local scripts, from ASP.NET assemblies, or nothing.
AllowCustomErrorsRedirect	Indicates whether custom error redirects will occur during an asynchronous postback. The property is set to *true* by default.
AsyncPostBackErrorMessage	Gets and sets the error message to be sent to the client when an unhandled exception occurs on the server during an asynchronous postback. If this property is not set, the native exception's message will be used.
AsyncPostBackSourceElementID	Gets the ID of the server control that triggered the asynchronous postback. If there's no ongoing asynchronous postback, the property is set to the empty string.
AsyncPostBackTimeout	Gets and sets the timeout period in seconds for asynchronous postbacks. A value of zero indicates no timeout. The property is set to *90* by default.

Property	Description
AuthenticationService	Gets an object through which you can set preferences for the client-side authentication service.
ClientNavigateHandler	Indicates the name of the JavaScript method that handles the Sys.Application.navigate event on the client when the user navigates back to a page from the history list.
CompositeScript	Gets a reference to the composite script (if any) for the current page.
EmptyPageUrl	The URL to use if the target Web page is empty during a history navigation.
EnableCdn	Indicates whether client script references are loaded from a content delivery network (CDN) path.
EnableHistory	Indicates whether the page supports history point management.
EnablePageMethods	Indicates whether static page methods on an ASP.NET page can be called from client script. The property is set to false by default.
EnablePartialRendering	Indicates whether partial rendering is enabled for the page. The property is set to true by default.
EnableScriptGlobalization	Indicates whether the ScriptManager control renders script in the client that supports the parsing and formatting of culture-specific information. The property is set to false by default.
EnableScriptLocalization	Indicates whether the ScriptManager control retrieves script files for the current culture, if they exist. The property is set to false by default.
EnableSecureHistoryState	Indicates whether to encrypt the history state string.
IsDebuggingEnabled	Indicates whether the debug versions of client script libraries will be rendered. The debug attribute on the @Page directive doesn't affect this property.
IsInAsyncPostBack	Indicates whether the current page request is the result of an asynchronous postback.
IsNavigating	Indicates whether a Navigate event is currently being handled.
LoadScriptsBeforeUI	Indicates whether scripts are loaded before or after markup for the page UI is loaded.
ProfileService	Gets an object through which you can set preferences for the client-side profile service.
RoleService	Gets an object through which you can set preferences for the client-side role service.
ScriptMode	Gets and sets the type (debug or retail) of scripts to load when more than one type is available. Possible values come from the ScriptMode enumeration type: Auto, Inherit, Debug, or Release. The default value is Auto, meaning that the type of script is determined on the fly.

Property	Description
ScriptPath	Indicates that scripts should be loaded from this path instead of from assembly Web resources.
Scripts	Gets a collection of script references that the *ScriptManager* control should include in the page.
Services	Gets a collection of service references that the *ScriptManager* control should include in the page.
SupportsPartialRendering	Indicates whether a particular browser or browser version can support partial page rendering. If this property is set to *false*, regardless of the value of the *EnablePartialRendering* property, no partial rendering will be supported on the page. The property is set to *true* by default.

The script manager is the nerve center of any ASP.NET AJAX pages and does all the work that is necessary to make AJAX features function as expected. Enabling AJAX features mostly means injecting the right piece of script in the right place. The script manager saves ASP.NET developers from dirtying their hands with JavaScript.

Methods of the *ScriptManager* Control

Table 20-2 lists the methods defined on the *ScriptManager* control.

TABLE 20-2 Methods of *ScriptManager*

Method	Description
AddHistoryPoint	Creates a history point, and adds it to the browser's history stack.
GetCurrent	Static method, returns the instance of the *ScriptManager* control active on the current page.
GetRegisteredArrayDeclarations	Returns a read-only collection of *ECMAScript* array declarations that were previously registered with the page.
GetRegisteredClientScriptBlocks	Returns a read-only collection of client script blocks that were previously registered with the *ScriptManager* control.
GetRegisteredDisposeScripts	Returns a read-only collection of dispose scripts that were previously registered with the page.
GetRegisteredExpandoAttributes	Returns a read-only collection of custom (expando) attributes that were previously registered with the page.
GetRegisteredHiddenFields	Returns a read-only collection of hidden fields that were previously registered with the page.
GetRegisteredOnSubmitStatements	Returns a read-only collection of *onsubmit* statements that were previously registered with the page.
GetRegisteredStartupScripts	Returns a read-only collection of startup scripts that were previously registered with the page.
GetStateString	Retrieves a string that contains key/value pairs that represent the state of the page from the browser's history.

RegisterArrayDeclaration	Static method, ensures that an *ECMAScript* array is emitted in a partial rendering page.
RegisterAsyncPostBackControl	Takes note that the specified control can trigger an asynchronous postback event from within an updatable panel.
RegisterClientScriptBlock	Static method, ensures that the specified script is emitted in a partial rendering page.
RegisterClientScriptInclude	Static method, ensures that the markup to import an external script file through the *src* attribute of the *<script>* tag is emitted in a partial rendering page.
RegisterClientScriptResource	Static method, ensures that the markup to import an external script from the page's resources is emitted in a partial rendering page.
RegisterDataItem	Registers a string of data that will be sent to the client along with the output of a partially rendered page.
RegisterDispose	Registers controls that require a client script to run at the end of an asynchronous postback to dispose of client resources.
RegisterExpandoAttribute	Static method, ensures that the markup to import a custom, nonstandard attribute is emitted in a partial rendering page.
RegisterExtenderControl	Registers an extender control with the current ASP.NET AJAX page.
RegisterHiddenField	Static method, ensures that the specified hidden field is emitted in a partial rendering page.
RegisterOnSubmitStatement	Static method, ensures that that client-side script associated with the form's *OnSubmit* event is emitted in a partial rendering page.
RegisterPostBackControl	Takes note that the specified control can trigger a full postback event from within an updatable panel.
RegisterScriptControl	Registers a script control with the current ASP.NET AJAX page.
RegisterScriptDescriptors	Registers a script descriptor with the current ASP.NET AJAX page.
RegisterStartupScript	Static method, ensures that client-side script is emitted at the end of the *<form>* tag in a partial rendering page. In this way, the script will execute as the page refresh is completed.
SetFocus	Allows you to move the input focus to the specified client element after an asynchronous postback.

All static methods emit some form of script and markup in the client page. These static methods are the AJAX counterpart of similar methods defined on the page's *ClientScript* object that you should know from earlier versions of ASP.NET. The static *RegisterXXX* methods on the *ScriptManager* class ensure that the given piece of script and markup is properly emitted only once in each partial update of the ASP.NET AJAX page. Similarly, other nonstatic *RegisterXXX* methods should be seen as tools to emit proper script code in ASP.NET AJAX pages—especially script code that is associated with custom controls.

Note What's the difference between *RegisterXXX* methods in the *ScriptManager* control and the page's *ClientScript* object, which is an instance of the *ClientScriptManager* class? The registration methods of *ClientScriptManager* and *ScriptManager* serve the same purpose but in radically different scenarios.

You need to use the *ScriptManager's* methods only if you need to emit script code during an AJAX partial rendering postback operation. An AJAX partial-rendering postback operation is processed by the run time as usual, except for the rendering stage. At this time, the markup is generated and any registered script is emitted. Because during AJAX postbacks the *ScriptManager* is responsible for the markup rendering, it's the *ScriptManager* that needs to know about registered scripts to emit.

If you stick to using *ClientScriptMananager's* methods in an AJAX page, you risk the possibility that no script will be emitted during the refresh of an updatable panel. As a result, a portion of your page might display strange behaviors.

Events of the *ScriptManager* Control

Table 20-3 details the events fired by the *ScriptManager* control.

TABLE 20-3 Events of *ScriptManager*

Event	Description
AsyncPostBackError	Occurs when an exception goes unhandled on the server during an asynchronous postback.
Navigate	Occurs when the user clicks the browser's Back or Forward button.
ResolveCompositeScriptReference	Occurs when the *ScriptManager* control is going to resolve a composite script reference.
ResolveScriptReference	Occurs when the *ScriptManager* control is going to resolve a script reference.

These events are much more than mere notifications of something that has happened on the server. Both give you good chances to intervene effectively in the course of the application. For example, by handling the *ResolveScriptReference* event, you can change the location from where the script is going to be downloaded on the client:

```
protected void ResolveScript(object sender, ScriptReferenceEventArgs e)
{
    // Check Path or Name on the e.Script object based on what you've put in Scripts.
    // Next, you specify the real file to load
    if (String.Equals(e.Script.Path, "personal.js", StringComparison.OrdinalIgnoreCase))
        e.Script.Path = "person.js";
}
```

By handling the *AsyncPostBackError* event, you can edit the error message being returned to the client during a partial rendering operation. Here's an example:

```
protected void AsyncPostBackError(object sender, AsyncPostBackErrorEventArgs e)
{
        ScriptManager sm = sender as ScriptManager;
        if (Request.UserHostAddress == "127.0.0.1")
        {
            sm.AsyncPostBackErrorMessage = String.Format(
                "<b>An error occurred. <br/>{0}<b>",
                e.Exception.Message);
        }
        else
        {
            sm.AsyncPostBackErrorMessage = String.Format(
                "<b>An error occurred. <br/>{0}<b>",
                "Please contact your Web master.");
        }
}
```

What if you want to redirect the user to an error page instead?

In this case, you configure the page to use the traditional error-handling mechanism for ASP.NET pages. You configure the *<customErrors>* section in the *web.config* file and indicate HTML error pages to reach in case of specific errors. This behavior can be disabled by setting to *false* the value of the *AllowCustomErrorRedirects* property of the *ScriptManager* object.

> **Note** When an exception is thrown during a partial rendering operation, the HTTP request returns a regular HTTP 200 status code, but instead of including the updated markup, it includes a message in which a flag indicates the success or failure of the operation. In addition, the message includes the full description of the error or the updated markup. In case of error, the client-side default error handler throws a JavaScript exception passing the error message as an argument.

The *ScriptManagerProxy* Control

Only one instance of the *ScriptManager* control can be added to an ASP.NET AJAX page. However, there are two ways in which you can do this. You can add it directly on the page using the *<asp:ScriptManager>* tag or indirectly by importing a component that already contains a script manager. Typically, you can accomplish the second alternative by importing a user control, creating a content page for a master page, or authoring a nested master page.

What if a content page needs to add a new script reference to the manager? In this case, you need a reference to the script manager. Although it's defined in the master page (or in a user control), the script manager might not be publicly exposed to the content page. You can use the static method *GetCurrent* on the class *ScriptManager* to get the right instance:

```
// Retrieve the instance of the ScriptManager active on the page
var manager = ScriptManager.GetCurrent(this.Page);
```

The *ScriptManagerProxy* class saves you from this sort of coding. In general, in cases where you need features of the *ScriptManager* control but lack a direct reference to it, you can instead include a *ScriptManagerProxy* control in the content page.

You can't have two script managers in the context of the same page; however, you can have a script manager and a proxy to retrieve it. The *ScriptManagerProxy* control enables you to add scripts and services to nested components, and it enables partial page updates in user controls and nested master pages. When you use the proxy, the *Scripts* and *Services* collections on the *ScriptManager* and *ScriptManagerProxy* controls are merged at run time.

> **Note** The *ScriptManagerProxy* class is a simple wrapper around the *GetCurrent* method of the *ScriptManager* class, and its programming interface is not an exact clone of the *ScriptManager*. From within the proxy, you have access only to a limited number of properties, including *Scripts*, *Services*, *AuthenticationService*, *RoleService*, and *ProfileService*. If you need to modify anything else, refer to the *GetCurrent* static method of the *ScriptManager* class.

Script Binding and Loading

By extensively relying on client capabilities, an Ajax page requires a lot of script code. The framework itself links a lot of code, as do custom controls and actual user pages. The only HTML-supported way of linking script files is the *<script>* tag and its *src* attribute. The *ScriptManager* control can be used to save you from having to directly manipulate quite a few *<script>* tags and also to obtain richer features, such as built-in management of localized scripts.

You use the *Scripts* collection to tell the *ScriptManager* about the scripts you want to add to the page. The collection can be accessed either declaratively or programmatically. In addition to the user-requested scripts, the *ScriptManager* control automatically emits in the client page any ASP.NET AJAX required script. The following example illustrates the script loading model you can use to load optional and custom scripts, even when the script is embedded in an assembly:

```
<asp:ScriptManager runat="server" ID="ScriptManager1">
  <Scripts>
    <asp:ScriptReference
        Name="YourCompany.ScriptLibrary.CoolUI.js"
        Assembly="YourCompany.ScriptLib" />
    <asp:ScriptReference
        Path="~/Scripts/MyLib.js" />
  </Scripts>
</asp:ScriptManager>
```

Table 20-4 lists the properties of the *ScriptReference* class by means of which you can control the loading of scripts.

TABLE 20-4 Properties to Control Script Loading

Property	Description
Assembly	Indicates the assembly that contains in its resources the script to download on the client.
IgnoreScriptPath	Boolean value, indicates whether the *ScriptPath* value optionally set at the top *ScriptManager* level has to be ignored. This property is set to *false* by default.
Name	Name of the script to download on the client.

You can reference script files from an assembly or from a disk file. There's a benefit in using disk files. You gain something in performance because less work is required to load the script in memory directly from a file.

Script references obtained from embedded Web resources are served by the *ScriptResource. axd* HTTP handler. In ASP.NET, this handler replaces an old acquaintance, the *WebResource. axd* handler—a native component of ASP.NET. What's the difference? In addition to serving script references, the *ScriptResource.axd* handler also appends any localized JavaScript resource types for the file and supports composite scripts.

ScriptManager allows you to combine in a single download multiple JavaScript files that you register through the *<compositescript>* section of the control's markup:

```
<asp:ScriptManager ID="ScriptManager1" runat="server">
    <CompositeScript>
      <Scripts>
         <asp:ScriptReference Path="~/Scripts/Script1.js" />
         <asp:ScriptReference Path="~/Scripts/Script2.js" />
         <asp:ScriptReference Path="~/Scripts/Script3.js" />
      </Scripts>
   </CompositeScript>
</asp:ScriptManager>
```

Composite scripts reduce the number of browser requests and result in faster download time and less workload on the Web server.

Handling Debug and Release Script Files

One of the additional free services offered by *ScriptManager* that isn't offered by the classic *<script>* tag is the ability to automatically link debug or release script files, as appropriate. ASP.NET uses a special naming convention to distinguish between debug and release script files. Given a release script file named *script1.js*, its debug version is expected to be filed as *script1.debug.js*.

In general, the main difference between debug and release scripts is that the release scripts remove unnecessary blank characters, comments, trace statements, and assertions. Normally, the burden of switching the links to debug and release scripts is left to the developer.

The *ScriptManager* control takes on this burden and, based on the aforementioned naming convention, distinguishes between debug and release scripts. The *ScriptManager* control picks debug scripts when the debug attribute of the *<compilation>* section in the *web.config* file is *true*.

Script Globalization

Globalization is a programming feature that refers to the code's ability to support multiple cultures. A request processed on the server has a number of ways to get and set the current culture settings. For example, you can use the *Culture* attribute on the *@Page* directive, the *Culture* property on the *Page* class, or perhaps the *<globalization>* section in the *web.config* file. How can you access the same information on the client from JavaScript?

When the *EnableScriptGlobalization* property is *true*, the *ScriptManager* emits proper script code that sets up a client-side global *Sys.CultureInfo* object that JavaScript classes can consume to display their contents in a culture-based way. Only a few methods and a few JavaScript objects support globalization. In particular, it will work for the *localeFormat* method of Date, String, and Number types. Custom JavaScript classes, though, can be made global by simply calling into these methods or accepting a *Sys.CultureInfo* object in their signatures.

The *UpdatePanel* Control

Partial rendering is the programming technique centered on the *UpdatePanel* control. In ASP.NET, the *UpdatePanel* control represents the shortest path to Ajax. It allows you to add effective Ajax capabilities to sites written according to the classic programming model of ASP.NET Web Forms. As a developer, you have no new skills to learn, except the syntax and semantics of the *UpdatePanel* control. The impact on existing pages is very limited, and the exposure to JavaScript is very limited—even null in most common situations.

You might wonder how partial rendering differs from classic postbacks. The difference is in how the postback is implemented—instead of letting the browser perform a full-page refresh, the *UpdatePanel* control intercepts any postback requests and sends an out-of-band request for fresh markup to the same page URL. Next, it updates the DOM tree when the response is ready. Let's investigate the programming interface of the control.

The *UpdatePanel* Control at a Glance

The *UpdatePanel* control is a container control defined in the *System.Web.Extensions* assembly. It belongs specifically to the *System.Web.UI* namespace. Although it's logically similar to the classic ASP.NET *Panel* control, the *UpdatePanel* control differs from the classic panel control in a number of respects. In particular, it doesn't derive from *Panel* and, subsequently, it doesn't feature the same set of capabilities as ASP.NET panels, such as scrolling, styling, wrapping, and content management.

The *UpdatePanel* control derives directly from *Control*, meaning that it acts as a mere Ajax-aware container of child controls. It provides no user-interface-related facilities. Any required styling and formatting should be provided through the child controls. In contrast, the control sports a number of properties to control page updates and also exposes a client-side object model. Consider the following classic ASP.NET code:

```
<asp:GridView ID="GridView1" runat="server"
    DataSourceID="ObjectDataSource1"
    AllowPaging="True"
    AutoGenerateColumns="False">
    <Columns>
        <asp:BoundField DataField="ID" HeaderText="ID" />
        <asp:BoundField DataField="CompanyName" HeaderText="Company" />
        <asp:BoundField DataField="Country" HeaderText="Country" />
    </Columns>
</asp:GridView>
<asp:ObjectDataSource ID="ObjectDataSource1" runat="server"
    TypeName="YourApp.DAL.Customers"
    SelectMethod="LoadAll" />
```

This code causes a postback each time you click to view a new page, edit a record, or sort by a column. As a result, the entire page is redrawn even though the grid is only a small fragment of it. With partial rendering, you take the preceding markup and just wrap it with an *UpdatePanel* control, as shown here:

```
<asp:UpdatePanel ID="UpdatePanel1" runat="server">
    <ContentTemplate>
        . . .
    </ContentTemplate>
</asp:UpdatePanel>
```

In addition, you need to add a *ScriptManager* control to the page. That's the essence of partial rendering. And it magically just works. Well, not just magically, but it works.

> **Note** From this simple but effective example, you might be led to think that you surround the whole body of the page with an *UpdatePanel* control and you're done. If you do it this way, it certainly works. It might not be particularly efficient though. In the worst case, you need the same bandwidth as you do with classic ASP.NET; however, you still give your users an infinitely better experience because only a portion of the page actually refreshes. As we'll learn in the rest of the chapter, partial rendering offers a number of attributes to optimize the overall behavior and performance. However, the majority of users are more than happy with the sole effect of a partial page rendering.

The Programming Interface of the Control

Table 20-5 details the properties defined on the *UpdatePanel* control that constitute the aspects of the control's behavior that developers can govern.

TABLE 20-5 Properties of the *UpdatePanel* Control

Property	Description
ChildrenAsTriggers	Indicates whether postbacks coming from child controls will cause the *UpdatePanel* to refresh. This property is set to *true* by default. When this property is *false*, postbacks from child controls are ignored. You can't set this property to *false* when the *UpdateMode* property is set to *Always*.
ContentTemplate	A template property, defines what appears in the *UpdatePanel* when it is rendered.
ContentTemplateContainer	Retrieves the dynamically created template container object. You can use this object to programmatically add child controls to the *UpdatePanel*.
IsInPartialRendering	Indicates whether the panel is being updated as part of an asynchronous postback. Note that this property is designed for control developers. Page authors should just ignore it.
RenderMode	Indicates whether the contents of the panel will be rendered as a block *<div>* tag or as an inline *<span>* tag. The feasible values for the property—*Block* and *Inline*—are defined in the *UpdatePanelRenderMode* enumeration. The default is *Block*.
UpdateMode	Gets or sets the rendering mode of the control by determining under which conditions the panel gets updated. The feasible values—*Always* and *Conditional*—come from the *UpdatePanelUpdateMode* enumeration. The default is *Always*.
Triggers	Defines a collection of trigger objects, each representing an event that causes the panel to refresh automatically.

A bit more explanation is needed for the *IsInPartialRendering* read-only Boolean property. It indicates whether the contents of an *UpdatePanel* control are being updated. From this description, it seems to be a fairly useful property. Nonetheless, if you read its value from within any of the handlers defined in a code-behind class, you'll find out that the value is always *false*.

As mentioned, *IsInPartialRendering* is a property designed for control developers only. So it is assigned its proper value only at rendering time—that is, well past the *PreRender* event you can capture from a code-behind class. Developers creating a custom version of the *UpdatePanel* control will likely override the *Render* method. From within this context, they can leverage the property to find out whether the control is being rendered in a full-page refresh or in a partial rendering operation.

As a page author, if you just need to know whether a portion of a page is being updated as a result of an AJAX postback, you use the *IsInAsyncPostBack* Boolean property on the *ScriptManager* control.

> **Note** Like any other ASP.NET AJAX feature, partial rendering requires a *ScriptManager* control in the page. It is essential, though, that the *EnablePartialRendering* property on the manager be set to *true*—which is the default case. If this property is set to *false*, the *UpdatePanel* control works like a regular panel.

Populating the Panel Programmatically

The content of an updatable panel is defined through a template property—the *ContentTemplate* property. Just like any other template property in ASP.NET controls, *ContentTemplate* can be set programmatically. Consider the following page fragment:

```
<asp:ScriptManager ID="ScriptManager1" runat="server" />
<asp:UpdatePanel ID="UpdatePanel1" runat="server">
    <%-- Left empty deliberately. Will be filled out programmatically --%>
</asp:UpdatePanel>
```

In the *PreInit* event of the code-behind page, you can set the *ContentTemplate* programmatically, as shown here:

```
protected void Page_PreInit(object sender, EventArgs e)
{
    // You could also read the URL of the user control from a configuration file
    string ascx = "customerview.ascx";
    UpdatePanel1.ContentTemplate = this.LoadTemplate(ascx);
}
```

You are not allowed to set the content template past the *PreInit* event. However, at any time before the rendering stage, you can add child controls programmatically. In ASP.NET, to add or remove a child control, you typically use the *Controls* property of the parent control, as shown here:

```
UpdatePanel1.Controls.Add(new LiteralControl("Test"));
```

If you try to add a child control programmatically to the *Controls* collection of an *UpdatePanel*—as in the preceding code snippet—all that you get is a run-time exception. You should use the *ContentTemplateContainer* property instead. The reason is that what you really want to do is add or remove controls to the content template, not to the *UpdatePanel* directly. That's why *Controls* doesn't work and you have to opt for the actual container of the template. The following code shows how to populate the content template programmatically:

```
public partial class _Default : System.Web.UI.Page
{
    private Label Label1;

    protected void Page_Load(object sender, EventArgs e)
    {
        var updatePanel = new UpdatePanel();
        updatePanel.ID = "UpdatePanel1";

        // Define the button
        var button1 = new Button();
        button1.ID = "Button1";
        button1.Text = "What time is it?";
        button1.Click += new EventHandler(Button1_Click);

        // Define the literals
        var lit = new LiteralControl("<br>");

        // Define the label
        var label1 = new Label();
        label1.ID = "Label1";
        label1.Text = "[time]";

        // Link controls to the UpdatePanel
        updatePanel.ContentTemplateContainer.Controls.Add(button1);
        updatePanel.ContentTemplateContainer.Controls.Add(lit);
        updatePanel.ContentTemplateContainer.Controls.Add(label1);

        // Add the UpdatePanel to the list of form controls
        this.Form.Controls.Add(updatePanel);
    }

    protected void Button1_Click(object sender, EventArgs e)
    {
        Label1.Text = DateTime.Now.ToShortTimeString();
    }
}
```

You can add an *UpdatePanel* control to the page at any time in the life cycle. Likewise, you can add controls to an existing panel at any time. However, you can't set the content template programmatically past the page's *PreInit* event.

Master Pages and Updatable Regions

You can safely use *UpdatePanel* controls from within master pages. Most of the time, the use of updatable panels is easy and seamless. There are a few situations, though, that deserve a bit of further explanation.

If you add a *ScriptManager* control to a master page, partial rendering is enabled by default for all content pages. In addition, initial settings on the script manager are inherited by all content pages. What if you need to change some of the settings (for example, add a new script file or switch on script localization) for a particular content page? You can't have a new script manager, but you need to retrieve the original one defined on the master page.

In the content page, you can declaratively reference a *ScriptManagerProxy* and change some of its settings. The proxy retrieves the script manager currently in use and applies changes to it.

The *ScriptManagerProxy* control, though, is mostly designed to let you edit the list of scripts and services registered with the manager in a declarative manner, and it doesn't let you customize, say, error handling or script localization. You can do the same (and indeed much more) by programmatically referencing the script manager in the master page. Here's how:

```
protected void Page_Init(object sender, EventArgs e)
{
    // Work around the limitations in the API of the ScriptManagerProxy control
    ScriptManager.GetCurrent(this).EnableScriptLocalization = true;
}
```

In the content page, you create a handler for the page's *Init* event, retrieve the script manager instance using the static *GetCurrent* method on the *ScriptManager* class, and apply any required change.

Considerations Regarding Partial Rendering

Partial rendering divides the page into independent regions, each of which controls its own postbacks and refreshes without causing, or requiring, a full-page update. This behavior is highly desirable when only a portion—and perhaps only a small portion—of the page needs to change during a postback. An ASP.NET page can contain any number of *UpdatePanel* controls. This is a key point to understand to make effective use of the *UpdatePanel* control.

The first practical step for successfully migrating page behavior to partial rendering entails that you, given the expected behavior of the page, identify the portions of the page subject to refresh. If you have, say, a complex table layout but only a small fragment of only one cell changes in the page lifetime, there's no reason to keep the whole table in an *UpdatePanel* control. Only the server-side control that displays the modifiable text should be wrapped by the panel.

The portions of the page that you should consider to be candidates to be wrapped by an *UpdatePanel* control should be as small as possible. They also should include the minimum amount of markup and ASP.NET controls.

The second step consists of associating each candidate region with a list of refresh conditions. You basically answer the question, *"When does this region get updated?"* After you have compiled a list of candidate regions, and for each you have a list of refresh events, you're pretty much done.

The final step is mapping this information to *UpdatePanel* controls and triggers. If all the regions you have identified are disjointed, you're fine. If not, you use properties and triggers on the *UpdatePanel* control to obtain the expected page behavior, thereby minimizing the impact of postbacks and page flickering.

If needed, updatable panels can be nested. There's no syntax limitation to the levels of nesting allowed. Just consider that any nested panel refreshes when its parent is refreshed, regardless of the settings.

Let's be honest. It might not be a trivial task, and getting a disjoint set of regions is not always possible. However, given the number of properties supported by the *UpdatePanel* control, there's always room for a good compromise between user experience and performance.

Configuring for Conditional Refresh

An *UpdatePanel* control refreshes its content under the following conditions:

- When another *UpdatePanel* control in the same page refreshes
- When any of the child controls originates a postback (for example, a button click or a change of selection in a drop-down list with *AutoPostBack=true*)
- When handling a postback event the page invokes the *Update* method on the *UpdatePanel* control
- When the *UpdatePanel* control is nested inside another *UpdatePanel* control and the parent update panel is updated
- When any of the trigger events for the *UpdatePanel* occur

You can control these conditions through a number of properties such as *UpdateMode* and *ChildrenAsTriggers*, as well as the collection *Triggers*. To minimize the total number of postbacks and the amount of data being roundtripped, you should pay a lot of attention to the values you assign to these properties. Let's delve deeper into this topic.

Detecting Postbacks from Child Controls

By default, all updatable panels in a page are synchronized and refresh at the same time. To make each panel refresh independently from the others, you change the value of the *UpdateMode* property. The default value is *Always*, meaning that the panel's content is updated on every postback that originates from anywhere in the page, from inside and outside the updatable region.

By changing the value of the *UpdateMode* property to *Conditional*, you instruct the updatable panel to update its content only if it is explicitly ordered to refresh. This includes calling the *Update* method, intercepting a postback from a child control, or handling any of the events declared as triggers.

Normally, any control defined inside of an *UpdatePanel* control acts as an implicit trigger for the panel. You can stop all child controls from being triggers by setting the value of *ChildrenAsTriggers* to *false*. In this case, a button inside an updatable panel, if clicked, originates a regular full postback.

What if you want only a few controls within an *UpdatePanel* to act as triggers? You can define them as triggers of a particular *UpdatePanel*, or you can use the *RegisterAsyncPostBackControl* method on the *ScriptManager* class.

The *RegisterAsyncPostBackControl* method enables you to register controls to perform an asynchronous postback instead of a synchronous postback, which would update the entire page. Here is an example of the *RegisterAsyncPostBackControl* method:

```
protected void Page_Load(Object sender, EventArgs e)
{
    ScriptManager1.RegisterAsyncPostBackControl(Button1);
}
```

The control object you pass as an argument will be a control not included in any updatable panels and not listed as a trigger. The effects of the postback that originates from the control differ with regard to the number of *UpdatePanel* controls in the page. If there's only one *UpdatePanel* in the page, the script manager can easily figure out which one to update. The following code shows a page whose overall behavior might change if one or two *UpdatePanel* controls are used:

```
protected void Button1_Click(Object sender, EventArgs e)
{
    // If there's only one UpdatePanel in the page, and it includes this Label control,
    // the panel is refreshed automatically.
    Label1.Text = "Last update at:  " + DateTime.Now.ToLongTimeString();

    // This Label control, not included in any UpdatePanel, doesn't have its UI
    // refreshed. Its state, though, is correctly updated.
    Label2.Text = "Last update at:  " + DateTime.Now.ToLongTimeString();
}
```

When multiple panels exist, to trigger the update you have to explicitly invoke the *Update* method on the panel you want to refresh:

```
protected void Button1_Click(object sender, EventArgs e)
{
    Label1.Text = "Last update at:  " + DateTime.Now.ToLongTimeString();
    UpdatePanel1.Update();
}
```

All controls located inside of an *UpdatePanel* control are automatically passed as an argument to the *RegisterAsyncPostBackControl* method when *ChildrenAsTriggers* is *true*.

> **Note** A postback that originates from within an *UpdatePanel* control is often referred to as an *asynchronous postback* or an *AJAX postback*. Generally, these expressions are used to reference a postback conducted via a script taking advantage of *XMLHttpRequest*.

Programmatic Updates

I've already mentioned the *Update* method quite a few times. It's time to learn more about it, starting with its signature:

```
public void Update()
```

The method doesn't take any special action itself, but is limited to requiring that the child controls defined in the content template of the *UpdatePanel* control be refreshed. By using the *Update* method, you can programmatically control when the page region is updated in response to a standard postback event or perhaps during the initialization of the page.

An invalid operation exception can be thrown from within the *Update* method in a couple of well-known situations. One situation is if you call the method when the *UpdateMode* property is set to *Always*. The exception is thrown in this case because a method invocation prefigures a conditional update—you do it when you need it—which is just the opposite of what the *Always* value of the *UpdateMode* property indicates. The other situation in which the exception is thrown is when the *Update* method is called during or after the page's rendering stage.

So when should you use the *Update* method in your pages?

You resort to the method if you have some server logic to determine whether an *UpdatePanel* control should be updated as the side effect of an asynchronous postback—whether it is one that originated from another *UpdatePanel* in the page or a control registered as an asynchronous postback control.

Using Triggers

As mentioned, you can associate an *UpdatePanel* control with a list of server-side events. Whenever a registered event is triggered over a postback, the panel is updated. Triggers can be defined either declaratively or programmatically. You add an event trigger declaratively using the *<Triggers>* section of the *UpdatePanel* control:

```
<asp:UpdatePanel runat="server" ID="UpdatePanel1">
   <ContentTemplate>
      ...
   </ContentTemplate>
```

```
<Triggers>
   <asp:AsyncPostBackTrigger
         ControlID="DropDownList1"
         EventName="SelectedIndexChanged" />
</Triggers>
</asp:UpdatePanel>
```

You need to specify two pieces of information for each trigger: the ID of the control to monitor, and the name of the event to catch. Note that the *AsyncPostBackTrigger* component can catch only server-side events. Both *ControlID* and *EventName* are string properties. For example, the panel described in the previous code snippet is refreshed when any of the controls in the page posts back (that is, its *UpdateMode* property defaults to *Always*) or when the selection changes on a drop-down list control named *DropDownList1*. (Obviously, the *DropDownList1* control must have the *AutoPostBack* property set to *true*.)

 Note You can also add triggers programmatically by using the *Triggers* collection of the *UpdatePanel* control. The collection accepts instances of the *AsyncPostBackTrigger* class.

Full Postbacks from Inside Updatable Panels

By default, all child controls of an *UpdatePanel* that post back operate as implicit asynchronous postback triggers. You can prevent all of them from triggering a panel update by setting *ChildrenAsTriggers* to *false*. Note that when *ChildrenAsTriggers* is *false*, postbacks coming from child controls are processed as asynchronous postbacks and they modify the state of involved server controls, but they don't update the user interface of the panel.

There might be situations in which you need to perform full, regular postbacks from inside an *UpdatePanel* control in response to a control event. In this case, you use the *PostBackTrigger* component, as shown here:

```
<asp:UpdatePanel runat="server" ID="UpdatePanel1">
   <ContentTemplate>
      ...
   </ContentTemplate>
   <Triggers>
      <asp:AsyncPostBackTrigger ControlID="DropDownList1"
            EventName="SelectedIndexChanged" />
      <asp:PostBackTrigger ControlID="Button1" />
   </Triggers>
</asp:UpdatePanel>
```

The preceding panel features both synchronous and asynchronous postback triggers. The panel is updated when the user changes the selection on the drop-down list; the whole host page is refreshed when the user clicks the button.

A *PostBackTrigger* component causes referenced controls inside an *UpdatePanel* control to perform regular postbacks. These triggers must be child elements of the affected *UpdatePanel.*

The *PostBackTrigger* object doesn't support the *EventName* property. If a control with that name is causing the form submission, the ASP.NET AJAX client script simply lets the request go as usual. The ASP.NET runtime then figures out which server postback event has to be raised for the postback control by looking at its implementation of *IPostBackEventHandler.*

> **Note** When should you use a *PostBackTrigger* component to fire a full postback from inside an updatable panel? If you need, say, a button to refresh a given panel, why not list the *Click* event of the button as an asynchronous trigger and leave the button outside the panel?
>
> Especially when complex and templated controls are involved, it might not be easy to separate blocks of user interface in distinct panels and single controls. So the easiest, and often the only, solution is wrapping a whole block of user interface in an updatable panel. If a single control in this panel needs to fire a full postback, you need to use the *PostBackTrigger* component.

Giving Feedback to the User

The mechanics of the asynchronous postback keeps the displayed page up and running. So having the computer engaged in a potentially long task might be problematic. Will the user resist the temptation of clicking that button over and over again? Will the user patiently wait for the results to show up? Finally, will the user be frustrated and annoyed by waiting without any clue of what's going on? After all, if the page is sustaining a full postback, the browser itself normally provides some user feedback that this is happening. Using ASP.NET AJAX, the callback doesn't force a browser-led postback and the browser's visual feedback system is not called upon to inform the user things are happening.

The continuous experience raises new issues. Feedback should be given to users to let them know that an operation is taking place. In addition, user-interface elements should be disabled if the user starts new operations by clicking on the element. ASP.NET AJAX supplies the *UpdateProgress* control to display a templated content while any of the panels in the page are being refreshed.

The *UpdateProgress* Control

The *UpdateProgress* control is designed to provide any sort of feedback on the browser while one or more *UpdatePanel* controls are being updated. If you have multiple panels in the page, you might want to find a convenient location in the page for the progress control or, if possible, move it programmatically to the right place with respect to the panel being updated. You can use cascading style sheets (CSSs) to style and position the control at your leisure.

The user interface associated with an *UpdateProgress* control is displayed and hidden by the ASP.NET AJAX framework and doesn't require you to do any work on your own. The *UpdateProgress* control features the properties listed in Table 20-6.

TABLE 20-6 Properties of the *UpdateProgress* Control

Property	Description
AssociatedUpdatePanelID	Gets and sets the ID of the *UpdatePanel* control that this control is associated with.
DisplayAfter	Gets and sets the time in milliseconds after which the progress template is displayed. It is set to *500* by default.
DynamicLayout	Indicates whether the progress template is dynamically rendered in the page. It is set to *true* by default.
ProgressTemplate	Indicates the template displayed during an asynchronous postback that is taking longer than the time specified through the *DisplayAfter* property.

An *UpdateProgress* control can be bound to a particular *UpdatePanel* control. You set the binding through the *AssociatedUpdatePanelID* string property. If no updatable panel is specified, the progress control is displayed for any panels in the page. The user interface of the progress bar is inserted in the host page when the page is rendered. However, it is initially hidden from view using the CSS *display* attribute.

When set to *none*, the CSS *display* attribute doesn't display a given HTML element and reuses its space in the page so that other elements can be shifted up properly. When the value of the *display* attribute is toggled on, existing elements are moved to make room for the new element.

If you want to reserve the space for the progress control and leave it blank when no update operation is taking place, you just set the *DynamicLayout* property to *false*.

Composing the Progress Screen

The control displays the contents of the *ProgressTemplate* property while waiting for a panel to update. You can specify the template either declaratively or programmatically. In the latter case, you assign the property any object that implements the *ITemplate* interface. For the former situation, you can easily specify the progress control's markup declaratively, as shown in the following code:

```
<asp:UpdateProgress runat="server" ID="UpdateProgress1">
    <ProgressTemplate>
        . . .
    </ProgressTemplate>
</asp:UpdateProgress>
```

You can place any combination of controls in the progress template. However, most of the time, you'll probably just put some text there and an animated GIF. (See Figure 20-3.)

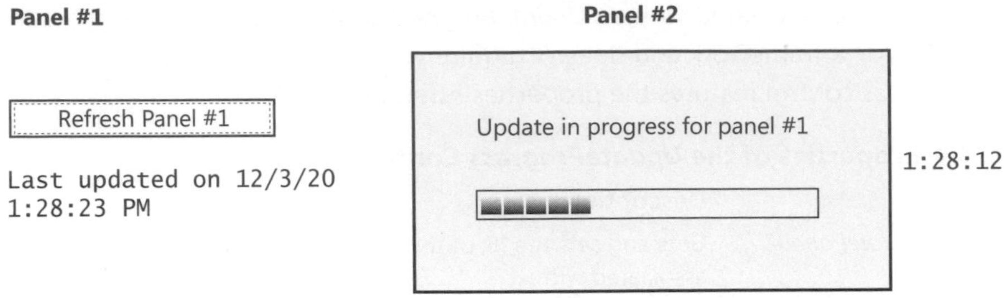

Panel #1   **Panel #2**

FIGURE 20-3 A progress template informing users that some work is being done.

Note that the *UpdateProgress* control is not designed to be a gauge component, but rather a user-defined panel that the *ScriptManager* control shows before the panel refresh begins and that it hides immediately after its completion.

> **Important** If you're looking for a real gauge bar to monitor the progress of a server-side task, partial rendering and the *UpdateProgress* control are not the right tools. As you'll see later in the chapter, polling is one of the main drawbacks of partial rendering and polling is unavoidable for monitoring server tasks from the client.

Client-Side Events for Richer Feedback

Each asynchronous postback is triggered on the client via script. The entire operation is conducted by the *PageRequestManager* client object, which invokes, under the hood, the *XMLHttpRequest* object. What kind of control do developers have on the underlying operation? If you manage *XMLHttpRequest* directly, you have full control over the request and response. But when these key steps are managed for you, there's not much you can do unless the request manager supports an eventing model.

The *Sys.WebForms.PageRequestManager* object provides a few events so that you can customize the handling of the request and response. Table 20-7 lists the supported events that signal the main steps around an Ajax postback that partially update a page. The events are listed in the order in which they fire to the client page.

TABLE 20-7 **Properties of the *UpdateProgress* Control**

Event	Event Argument	Description
initializeRequest	*InitializeRequestEventArgs*	Occurs before the request is prepared for sending
beginRequest	*BeginRequestEventArgs*	Occurs before the request is sent
pageLoading	*PageLoadingEventArgs*	Occurs when the response has been acquired but before any content on the page is updated
pageLoaded	*PageLoadedEventArgs*	Occurs after all content on the page is refreshed as a result of an asynchronous postback
endRequest	*EndRequestEventArgs*	Occurs after an asynchronous postback is finished and control has been returned to the browser

To register an event handler, you use the following JavaScript code:

```
var manager = Sys.WebForms.PageRequestManager.getInstance();
manager.add_beginRequest(OnBeginRequest);
```

The prototype of the event handler method—*OnBeginRequest* in this case—is shown here:

```
function beginRequest(sender, args)
```

The real type of the *args* object, though, depends on the event data structure. By using any of these events, you can control in more detail the steps of an asynchronous request. Let's dig out more.

The *initializeRequest* event is the first in the client life cycle of an asynchronous request. The life cycle begins at the moment a postback is made that is captured by the *UpdatePanel*'s client-side infrastructure. You can use the *initializeRequest* event to evaluate the postback source and do any additional required work. The event data structure is the *InitializeRequestEventArgs* class. The class features three properties: *postBackElement*, *request*, and *cancel*.

The *postBackElement* property is read-only and evaluates to a *DomElement* object. It indicates the DOM element that is responsible for the postback. The *request* property (read-only) is an object of type *Sys.Net.WebRequest* and represents the ongoing request. Finally, *cancel* is a read-write Boolean property that can be used to abort the request before it is sent.

Immediately after calling the *initializeRequest* handler, if any, the *PageRequestManager* object aborts any pending async requests. Next, it proceeds with the *beginRequest* event and then sends the packet.

When the response arrives, the *PageRequestManager* object first processes any returned data and separates hidden fields, updatable panels, and whatever pieces of information are returned from the server. Once the response data is ready for processing, the *PageRequestManager* object fires the *pageLoading* client event. The event is raised after the server response is received but before any content on the page is updated. You can use this event to provide a custom transition effect for updated content or to run any clean-up code that prepares the panels for the next update. The event data is packed in an instance of the class *PageLoadingEventArgs*. The class has three properties: *panelsUpdating*, *panelsDeleting*, and *dataItems*. The first two are arrays and list the updatable panels to be updated and deleted, respectively.

The *pageLoaded* event is raised after all content on the page is refreshed. You can use this event to provide a custom transition effect for updated content, such as flashing or highlighting updated contents. The event data is packed in the class *PageLoadedEventArgs*, which has three properties: *panelsUpdated*, *panelsDeleted*, and *dataItems*. The first two are arrays and list the updatable panels that were just updated and deleted, respectively.

The *endRequest* event signals the termination of the asynchronous request. You receive this event regardless of the success or failure of the asynchronous postback.

Disabling Visual Elements During Updates

If you want to prevent users from generating more input while a partial page update is being processed, you can also consider disabling the user interface—all or in part. To do so, you write handlers for *beginRequest* and *endRequest* events:

```
<script type="text/javascript">
function pageLoad()
{
    var manager = Sys.WebForms.PageRequestManager.getInstance();
    manager.add_beginRequest(OnBeginRequest);
    manager.add_beginRequest(OnEndRequest);
}
</script>
```

You typically use the *beginRequest* event to modify the user interface as appropriate and notify the user that the postback is being processed:

```
// Globals
var currentPostBackElem;

function OnBeginRequest(sender, args)
{
    // Get the reference to the button click (i.e., btnStartTask)
    currentPostBackElem = args.get_postBackElement();
    if (typeof(currentPostBackElem) === "undefined")
        return;
    if (currentPostBackElem.id.toLowerCase() === "btnStartTask")
    {
        // Disable the button
        $get("btnStartTask").disabled = true;
    }
}
```

The *beginRequest* handler receives event data through the *BeginRequestEventArgs* data structure—the *args* formal parameter. The class features only two properties: *request* and *postBackElement*. The properties have the same characteristics of analogous properties on the aforementioned *InitializeRequestEventArgs* class.

In the preceding code snippet, I disable the clicked button to prevent users from repeatedly clicking the same button.

At the end of the request, any temporary modification to the user interface must be removed. So animations must be stopped, altered styles must be restored, and disabled controls must be re-enabled. The ideal place for all these operations is the *endRequest* event. The event passes an *EndRequestEventArgs* object to handlers. The class has a few properties, as described in Table 20-8.

TABLE 20-8 Properties of the *EndRequestEventArgs* Control

Property	Description
dataItems	Returns the client-side dictionary packed with server-defined data items for the page or the control that handles this event. (More on registering data items later.)
Error	Returns an object of type *Error* that describes the error (if any) that occurred on the server during the request.
errorHandled	Gets and sets a Boolean value that indicates whether the error has been completely handled by user code. If this property is set to *true* in the event handler, no default error handling will be executed by the ASP.NET AJAX client library.
Response	Returns an object of type *Sys.Net.WebRequestExecutor* that represents the executor of the current request.

As you can see, when the *endRequest* event occurs there's no information available about the client element that fired the postback. If you need to restore some user interface settings from inside the *endRequest* event handler, you might need a global variable to track which element caused the postback:

```
function OnEndRequest(sender, args)
{
    if (typeof(currentPostBackElem) === "undefined")
        return;
    if (currentPostBackElem.id.toLowerCase() === "btnStartTask")
    {
        $get("btnStartTask").disabled = false;
    }
}
```

Wouldn't it be nice if you could visually notify users that a certain region of the screen has been updated? As you've seen, partial rendering improves the user experience with pages by eliminating a good number of full refreshes. If you look at it from the perspective of the average user, though, a partial page update doesn't have a clear start and finish like a regular Web roundtrip. The user doesn't see the page redrawn and might not notice changes in the user interface. A good pattern to employ is to use a little animation to show the user what has really changed with the latest operation. You can code this by yourself using the pair of *beginRequest* and *endRequest* events, or you can resort to a specialized component—an *UpdatePanel* extender control—as you'll see in a moment.

Important The *disabled* HTML attribute works only on INPUT elements. It has no effect on hyperlinks and *<a>* tags. If you plan to use *LinkButton* controls, you have to resort to other JavaScript tricks to disable the user interface. One possible trick is temporarily replacing the *onclick* handler of the hyperlink with a return value of *false*. Another effective trick might be to cover the area to be disabled with a partially opaque DIV.

Aborting a Pending Update

A really user-friendly system always lets its users cancel a pending operation. How can you obtain this functionality with an *UpdateProgress* control? The progress template is allowed to contain an abort button. The script code injected in the page will monitor the button and stop the ongoing asynchronous call if it's clicked. To specify an abort button, you add the following to the progress template:

```
<input type="button" onclick="abortTask()" value="Cancel" />
```

In the first place, the button has to be a client-side button. So you can express it either through the *<input>* element or the *<button>* element for the browsers that support this element. If you opt for the *<input>* element, the *type* attribute must be set to *button*. The script code you wire up to the *onclick* event is up to you, but it will contain at least the following instructions:

```
<script type="text/JavaScript">
function abortTask()
{
    var manager = Sys.WebForms.PageRequestManager.getInstance();
    if (manager.get_isInAsyncPostBack())
        manager.abortPostBack();
}
</script>
```

You retrieve the instance of the client *PageRequestManager* object active in the client page and check whether an asynchronous postback is going on. If so, you call the *abortPostBack* method to stop it.

> **Important** Canceling an ongoing update in this way is equivalent to closing the connection with the server. No results will ever be received, and no updates will ever occur on the page. However, canceling the update is a pure client operation and has no effect over what's happening on the server. If the user started a destructive operation, the client-side Cancel button can do nothing to stop that operation on the server.

The Ins and Outs of Partial Rendering

Overall, partial rendering is only one possible way to approach Ajax. It preserves most of your current investments and is relatively cheap to implement. Partial rendering just adds Ajax capabilities to your pages. There's no architectural new point in partial rendering. It's a great technique to quickly update legacy applications, and it is an excellent choice when you lack the time, skills, or budget to move on and redesign the application. But in a good number of cases, an improved user interface and optimized rendering is all that your users demand. So partial rendering would fit in perfectly.

On the other hand, building true Ajax applications where some of the presentation logic lives on the client written in JavaScript is not trivial either, and it requires a well-done and powerful client framework, as well as a server-side API that can be easily invoked via a URL and that can return easy-to-parse data.

These days, the winning library for client-side programming is jQuery. (I'll cover the library in the next chapter.) An important extension to the library is jQuery UI, which solves at the root most of the issues I mentioned earlier regarding update progress and client-side widgets.

You should be aware of the structural limitations that partial rendering has. Let's review the most important. If any of them are likely to affect you, you better look elsewhere and re-architect your application.

Issues with Concurrent Calls

Partial rendering doesn't support concurrent asynchronous postbacks. This means that you are not allowed to have two asynchronous postbacks going on at the same time. Partial rendering ultimately works by bypassing the standard browser mechanism that handles an HTTP request. It hooks up the *submit* event of the form, cuts out the standard browser handler, and places the HTTP request using *XMLHttpRequest*.

The request that reaches the Web server differs from a regular ASP.NET request only because it has an extra HTTP header. The request sends in the contents of the posting form, including the view-state hidden field. The response is not pure HTML but represents a text record where each field describes the new status of a page element—update panels, hidden fields, and scripts to run on loading.

As you can see, the underlying model of partial rendering is still the model of classic ASP.NET pages. It is a sort of stop-and-go model where the user posts back, waits for a while, and then receives a new page. While waiting for the next page, there's not much the user can do. Only one server operation per session occurs at a time. Partial rendering is only a smarter way of implementing the old model.

From a technical standpoint, the major factor that prevents multiple asynchronous postbacks is the persistence of the view-state information. When two requests go, both send out the same copy of the view state, but each reasonably returns a different view state. Which one is good for the page, then? Partial rendering takes a defensive approach, and it silently kills the ongoing request whenever a new request is placed—a *last-win* discipline.

By writing some JavaScript code around the *BeginRequest* client event, you can turn the discipline into a first-win approach, at the cost of losing the new request. It is your responsibility to queue the stopped request and run it later. This is just what some commercial Ajax frameworks do.

This fact has a clear impact on developers. In fact, you should always modify the user interface to ensure that users can't start a second operation before the first is terminated. Otherwise, the first operation is aborted in favor of the second. This happens in any case, even when the two operations are logically unrelated.

> **Note** When concurrent calls are necessary, you should consider moving that page (if not the whole application) to a more AJAX-oriented design. Alternatively, you can consider implementing that feature within the page using direct script-led calls to URL-based endpoints. I'll cover this approach in a moment.

Issues with Polling

Among other things, Ajax pages are popular because they can retrieve the client information in a timely manner. A page starts polling a remote URL, grabs fresh information, and returns it to the client for the actual display. Implemented via partial rendering, polling is subject to being interrupted when the user starts a new partial rendering operation to restart automatically at the end.

If this is not a problem for you, you can use the new *Timer* server control, as shown here:

```
<asp:Timer ID="Timer1" runat="server" Enabled="true" Interval="1000" ontick="Timer1_Tick" />
<asp:Button ID="Button1" runat="server" Text="Start task" onclick="Button1_Click" />
<asp:UpdateProgress ID="UpdateProgress1" runat="server" DynamicLayout="false">
    <ProgressTemplate>
        <img src="loading.gif" />
    </ProgressTemplate>
</asp:UpdateProgress>

<asp:UpdatePanel ID="UpdatePanel1" runat="server">
    <ContentTemplate>
        <asp:Label ID="Label1" runat="server" />
    </ContentTemplate>
    <Triggers>
        <asp:AsyncPostBackTrigger ControlID="Button1" EventName="Click" />
    </Triggers>
</asp:UpdatePanel>

<hr />

<asp:UpdatePanel ID="UpdatePanel2" runat="server">
    <ContentTemplate>
        <asp:Label ID="lblClock" runat="server" />
    </ContentTemplate>
    <Triggers>
        <asp:AsyncPostBackTrigger ControlID="Timer1" EventName="Tick" />
    </Triggers>
</asp:UpdatePanel>
```

The *Timer* control is the server counterpart of a client timer created using the *window.setTimeout* method. In the preceding code, the *Timer* control causes a postback every second as specified by the *Interval* property. The postback fires the *Tick* event. By using the timer as the trigger of an updatable panel, you can refresh the content of the panel periodically. In the code, the second *UpdatePanel* control just renders out a digital clock:

```
protected void Timer1_Tick(Object sender, EventArgs e)
{
    // Update the client UI to reflect server changes
    ...
}
```

The downside is that a timer-based polling system implemented over the partial rendering engine is still subject to concurrent calls and can be stopped at any time.

REST and Ajax

When the client requires that a specific operation be executed on the server with no frills and in a purely stateless manner, you should consider options other than partial rendering. Enter remote server method calls and REST, or Representational State Transfer.

REST refers to the idea of having data and resources exposed to Web clients as public HTTP endpoints. Clients interact with these endpoints using HTTP verbs such as GET, POST, PUT, and DELETE. In REST, the URI is a representation of a resource, and the HTTP verb describes the action you want to take regarding the resource's representation. Data exchanged in those interactions is represented in simple formats such as JSON and plain XML, or even in syndication formats such RSS and ATOM.

From a programming perspective, REST is all about making a call to a Web-exposed service from the client browser. This requires that a public, well-known API be exposed and made accessible from JavaScript or whatever other programming technology you have available in the browser (for example, Silverlight).

At the highest level of abstraction, Web applications are client/server applications that require an Internet connection between the two layers. Before Ajax, this connection was incorporated in the special client application—the browser—which opens the connection, clears the user interface, and then updates the screen with the results of a server operation.

With Ajax, the client code has the ability to bypass the browser and can handle connections itself. This enables the client to enter user interface updates without fully refreshing the displayed page—a great step forward toward usability and rich user experiences.

Scriptable Services

Any Ajax solution is made of two main layers that are neatly separated but communicating: the JavaScript and HTML presentation layer, and a service layer that acts as a façade for HTTP endpoints. Figure 20-4 gives an overview of the architecture.

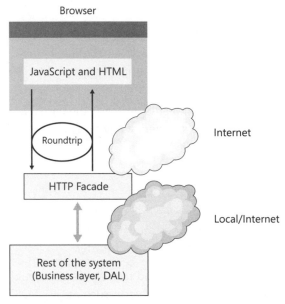

FIGURE 20-4 A typical Ajax architecture.

The HTTP façade works out a convenient API for the presentation layer to call. The API is built on top of the existing application services and workflows. The HTTP façade scripts these middle-tier components from the client. The architectural relevance of the HTTP façade is that it decouples the middle tier from a special presentation layer, such as an Ajax presentation layer. An Ajax presentation layer is special essentially because it's a partial-trust Web client.

For security reasons, service technologies hosted on the Web server require special adjustments to enable JavaScript callers. In addition, it's likely that some of the application services you have in the middle tier run critical procedures. Any piece of code bound to a URL in the HTTP façade, instead, is publicly exposed over the Internet—not an ideal situation for a business-critical service. So decoupling application services from the Ajax presentation layer is a measure of design but also a matter of security.

How would you build the HTTP façade?

The HTTP Façade

The HTTP façade is the list of public URLs known to, and managed by, the Ajax presentation layer. In an Ajax scenario, the presentation layer is made of only JavaScript code. All the logic you can't or don't want to code in JavaScript must be referenced on the server.

Public HTTP endpoints are the only point of contact between Ajax clients and server applications. You can write endpoints callable by Ajax clients using a number of technologies.

> **Note** In the context of Ajax, Web-hosted services are instrumental to the definition of a public, contract-based API that JavaScript code can invoke. It doesn't mean that you can call just any public Web services from an Ajax client. More precisely, you can call only services that live in the same domain as the calling page in full respect of the Same Origin Policy (SOP) implemented by most browsers. This is a security measure, not a technical limitation. You should think of Web services as a sort of application-specific façade to expose some server-side logic to a JavaScript (or Silverlight) client.

To start off, an AJAX-callable endpoint can be an *.asmx* ASP.NET Web service. If this is your choice, you need to configure the server ASP.NET application so that its hosted Web services can accept JSON calls in addition to, or instead of, SOAP calls.

You can also use a Windows Communication Foundation (WCF) service to contain all the logic you want to expose to Ajax clients. As you'll see later in the chapter, though, you get only the Web WCF programming interface and, as such, only a subset of the typical WCF features. In particular, the area of security is thinned down. A common solution for ASP.NET Web Forms Ajax-enabled applications is hosting WCF services and interacting with them via JSON payloads.

If you don't want to add WCF to your application but still need a service, you can then opt for a custom, handmade HTTP handler. An HTTP handler is just a public URL exposed by a Web application, so it can reliably serve any purpose the presentation needs to address. Compared to WCF services, plain HTTP handlers lack a lot of facilities, including the automatic JSON serialization of input and output data. (You can use the same tools that WCF uses, but that's just not...automatic.)

WCF Services

A WCF services is exposed as an *.svc* endpoint. To be invoked from within an ASP.NET Ajax page, a service must meet a number of requirements, the strictest of which relate to the location of the endpoint and underlying platform. Ajax-enabled services must be hosted in the same domain from which the call is made. If we consider using WCF services to back an Ajax front end, the service must be hosted in an Internet Information Services (IIS) application on the same Web server as the ASP.NET application.

Important By default, AJAX-enabled WCF services run side by side with the ASP.NET application in the same AppDomain. Requests for an *.svc* resource are first dispatched to the ASP.NET runtime, but then the WCF hosting infrastructure intercepts these requests and routes them out of the HTTP pipeline. ASP.NET doesn't participate in the processing of WCF requests past the *PostAuthenticateRequest* event in the request life cycle. At that point, in fact, the WCF infrastructure intercepts the request and starts processing that in total autonomy. In the default configuration, the WCF service method has no access to ASP.NET intrinsics, ASP.NET impersonation and URL authorization settings are ignored, and HTTP modules interested in filtering the WCF request past the *PostAuthenticateRequest* event never get a chance to do their work.

To support Ajax calls, you also need to expose service methods through HTTP requests and subsequently map methods to URLs. This is just what the WCF Web programming model has to offer. The WCF Web programming model enables services to support plain-old XML (POX) style messaging instead of SOAP, which is the key step to enabling the JSON calls that are typical of ASP.NET AJAX clients.

The following code snippet shows how to use the new *WebGet* attribute in the definition of a service contract:

```
[ServiceContract]
public interface ICalculator {
  [OperationContract]
  [WebGet]
  long Add(long x, long y);

  [OperationContract]
  [WebGet(UriTemplate="Sub?p1={x}&p2={y}")]
  long Subtract(long x, long y);
}
```

The *WebGet* attribute qualifies a method as a retrieval operation and enables callers to use the HTTP GET verb to invoke it. The *WebGet* attribute also features the *UriTemplate* property. You use this property to specify which URL format is accepted to invoke the method. If not otherwise specified via an explicit *UriTemplate* property, the URI template for a *WebGet* method like the aforementioned *Add* is the following:

```
theService.svc/Add?x=1&y=2
```

The service name is followed by the method name, and formal parameters follow in order, each with its own actual value. You can change this standard URI template by changing the method name and formal parameter names.

The *WebInvoke* attribute indicates that a given method has to be considered as a logical invoke operation that can be invoked using any HTTP verb, but typically the POST verb is called upon:

```
[ServiceContract]
public interface ICalculator {
  [OperationContract]
  [WebInvoke(Method="Post",
    RequestFormat=WebMessageFormat.Xml,
    ResponseFormat=WebMessageFormat.Json)]
  long Add(long x, long y);
}
```

Through the *WebInvoke* attribute, you can set the URI template, the method to be used to invoke the method, as well as the format for the request and response text.

> **Note** If you choose to add to your Visual Studio project a new item known as an *AJAX-enabled service*, the wizard gets you a skeleton of code that's ready to help you build an AJAX-enabled WCF service.

To be invoked from an AJAX client, a WCF service can be configured with a specific binding model—the *webHttpBinding* model. The *webHttpBinding* model is a basic HTTP binding except that it doesn't use SOAP. The *webHttpBinding* binding model is specifically created for REST scenarios. Here's an excerpt from a sample configuration script for an AJAX-enabled WCF service:

```
<system.serviceModel>
  <behaviors>
    <endpointBehaviors>
      <behavior name="ajaxBehavior">
        <enableWebScript />
      </behavior>
    </endpointBehaviors>

    <serviceBehaviors>
      <behavior name="metadataBehavior">
        <serviceMetadata httpGetEnabled="true" />
      </behavior>
    </serviceBehaviors>
  </behaviors>
  ...
</system.serviceModel>
```

When *webHttpBinding* is turned on, you can also use the optional *enableWebScript* element, which enables the run time to generate the JavaScript proxy for the service. The proxy is a JavaScript class that makes it particularly easy to invoke the service endpoints. To invoke a service, a proxy is not strictly required, as you'll see in the next chapter about jQuery. In addition, you might also want to publish service metadata for retrieval using an HTTP GET request.

The services hosted by the Web application must be specially configured to use the Web HTTP-specific binding model, as shown here:

```
<system.serviceModel>
  ...
  <services>
    <service name="Samples.TimeService"
             behaviorConfiguration="metadataBehavior">
      <endpoint contract="Samples.ITimeService"
                binding="webHttpBinding"
                behaviorConfiguration="ajaxBehavior" />
    </service>
  </services>
</system.serviceModel>
```

The configuration of a WCF service specifies key pieces of information—the binding model (mandatory), contract, and behavior. The binding indicates how the call is going to happen—essentially whether it will use a REST approach, a SOAP approach, or both. The *contract* attribute indicates which contract the endpoint is exposing. If the service class implements a single contract type, the *contract* attribute can be omitted in the endpoint section. Finally, the *behaviorConfiguration* attribute contains the name of the behavior to be used in the endpoint.

Note In some particular scenarios, you can also resort to a simplified configuration scheme for AJAX-enabled WCF services. In the service endpoint file—the *.svc* file—you use the *Factory* attribute in the *@ServiceHost* directive and make it point to a system-provided class that supplies default settings for binding and endpoint behaviors. Here's the code for the *.svc* endpoint file:

```
<%@ ServiceHost
    Factory="System.ServiceModel.Activation.WebScriptServiceHostFactory"
    Service="Samples.Services.TimeService" %>
```

Note that you can use simplified configuration only for service classes that implement one contract only.

The definition of the service contract for an AJAX-enabled WCF service is not different from that of any other WCF services. You use the *OperationContract* attribute to qualify a method as a public service method, and you use the optional *WebGet* and *WebInvoke* attributes to configure the URL template. Here's an example:

```
[ServiceContract(Namespace="Samples.Services", Name="TimeService")]
public interface ITimeService
{
    [OperationContract]
    DateTime GetTime();
```

```
    [OperationContract]
    string GetTimeFormat(string format);
}

public class TimeService : ITimeService
{
    public DateTime GetTime()
    {
        return DateTime.Now;
    }
    ...
}
```

You should be sure to give meaningful values to the *Namespace* and *Name* properties of the *ServiceContract* attribute. The reason is that the concatenation of those values determines the name of the JavaScript proxy class used to access the WCF service. If you leave them blank, the JavaScript proxy for the preceding service will be named *tempuri.org.ITimeService*. Not really a nice or helpful name!

For AJAX-enabled WCF services, the data contract—namely, the agreement between the service and client that describes the data to be exchanged—is defined in the canonical way. You use an implicit contract for serialization, and deserialization is used for collections, primitive types, dates, enumerations, and the GUID; an explicit contract is required for custom complex types. In this case, you use the *DataContract* and *DataMember* attributes on class members to determine which members go into the serialization stream.

> **Important** The configuration of a WCF service is different if the client is a Silverlight application. In such a case, in fact, you are not allowed to use *webHttpBinding* and must resort to the *basicHttpBinding* model, which executes the method call over a SOAP 1.1 channel.

ASP.NET Web Services

The primary reason for choosing ASP.NET Web services instead of WCF as the technology for building your HTTP façade is backward compatibility. You can call ASP.NET Web services from AJAX clients as long as your Web server runs the Microsoft .NET Framework 2.0 plus AJAX Extensions 1.0. For WCF services, ASP.NET 3.5 or a newer version is required.

A Web service made to measure for an ASP.NET AJAX application is similar to any other ASP.NET Web service you might write for whatever purposes. Just one peripheral aspect, though, marks a key difference. You must use a new attribute to decorate the class of the

Web service that is not allowed on regular ASP.NET Web services—the *ScriptService* attribute. Here's how to use it:

```
namespace Samples.WebServices
{
    [ScriptService]
    [WebService(Namespace = "urn:aspnet4.book/")]
    public class TimeService : System.Web.Services.WebService, ITimeService
    {
        [WebMethod]
        public DateTime GetTime()
        {
            return DateTime.Now;
        }
        ...
    }
}
```

Note that the *ScriptService* attribute simply enables AJAX callers to connect to the service; it doesn't prevent SOAP callers from sending their packets. As a result, an ASP.NET AJAX Web service might have a double public interface: the JSON-based interface consumed by the hosting ASP.NET AJAX application, and the classic SOAP-based interface exposed to any clients, from any platforms, that can reach the service URL.

When you write an AJAX-enabled ASP.NET Web service, you have no need for a contracted interface as with WCF services. However, extracting an interface from the service class is rarely a bad idea.

```
public class TimeService : System.Web.Services.WebService, ITimeService
{
    [WebMethod]
    public DateTime GetTime()
    {
        return DateTime.Now;
    }
    ...
}
```

Public methods of the Web service class decorated with the *WebMethod* attribute can be invoked from the AJAX page. Any method is invoked using the HTTP POST verb and returns any value as a JSON object. You can change these default settings on a per-method basis by using an optional attribute—*ScriptMethod*. In particular, through the *ScriptMethod* attribute you can enable HTTP GET calls and use XML instead of JSON as the serialization format.

Enabling the use of the HTTP GET verb opens security holes: the service method can be invoked through a cross-site scripting attack that attaches an external script to the *<script>* or *<img>* HTML tags. These HTML elements are the sole elements allowed to access resources from outside the current domain. However, they always operate through a GET verb. This means that by keeping the HTTP GET verb disabled on your Web service method you prevent at the root any possible cross-site scripting attacks. More in general, my opinion is that you should have very good reasons to use the *ScriptMethod* attribute, anyway.

Finally, deriving the Web service class from *System.Web.Services.WebService* is not mandatory either. If you use that class as a parent, all that you gain is that you enable the service to access ASP.NET intrinsics directly without using the *HttpContext.Current* object as an intermediary.

> **Important** By default, AJAX-enabled WCF services process requests for method execution outside the ASP.NET pipeline. Requests for ASP.NET Web services methods, conversely, are treated as standard ASP.NET requests. In other words, *.asmx* requests flow through the classic request life cycle whereas *.svc* requests are routed out of the pipeline at some point.
>
> By switching WCF services to ASP.NET compatibility mode, you ensure that *.svc* requests are treated identically to *.asmx* requests with respect to ASP.NET intrinsics, URL authorization, and impersonation. However, the ASP.NET compatibility mode for WCF services breaks the WCF ability to behave consistently across hosting environments and transports. Compatibility mode is an option only for WCF services that will always operate over HTTP and be hosted by IIS, which is just what the majority of AJAX-enabled WCF services do.

Discriminate Against Outsiders

Any security barrier you place around the HTTP façade at the network level (for example, a firewall) to filter outsiders would likely stop legitimate calls too. When all calls come from a plain Web browser and from the Internet, you need a reliable way to welcome legitimate users and reject outsiders.

To do so, you have to identify a piece of information that only legitimate users can easily provide. The simplest and most effective piece of information is an authentication cookie generated by the ASP.NET Forms authentication.

To protect critical services in the HTTP façade, you isolate in a reserved area of the site any ASP.NET pages that invoke a sensitive service method and any services to protect. After pages and services are placed in a protected area of the site, access to them requires that users go through a login page.

The login page gets credentials from the user and verifies whether the user is authorized to visit the page. If all is fine, the request is authorized and an authentication cookie is generated and attached to the response. From now on, any requests the user makes to the application, including requests directed at services in the HTTP façade, will bring the cookie. (See Figure 20-5.)

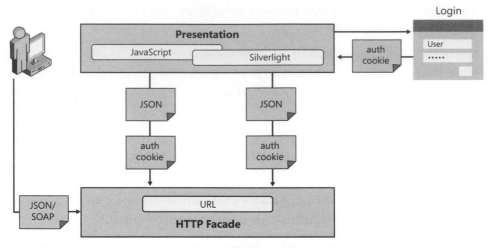

FIGURE 20-5 Legitimate users and outsiders around the HTTP façade.

In ASP.NET, login pages require that Forms authentication be turned on. Furthermore, anonymous users should be denied access to any resources within the protected area. Here's a sample configuration script you can use:

```
<location path="ProtectedAreaOfTheSite">
    <system.web>
        <authorization>
            <deny users="?" />
        </authorization>
    </system.web>
</location>
```

If necessary, login pages can be placed on a different server and work over HTTPS. This solution, however, has no impact on the security of the HTTP façade.

Outsiders can still try to access the services via the public URL. In this case, though, because the service IIS endpoint is also placed behind an authorization section, they will receive an HTTP 401 error code (unauthorized access). The outsider call will pass only if the outsider can show a valid authentication cookie. But this can happen only if a cookie theft has occurred previously. However, this is all another problem that relates to the security of the Web site rather than to the security of the services in the HTTP façade.

The only viable alternative to using cookies and ASP.NET Forms authentication is to install client certificates on all client machines.

Trusting the HTTP Façade

Should WCF and Web services do something on their own to keep outsiders off the site? If you place service endpoints behind a protected area of the site, you're as safe as with any other ASP.NET pages based on Forms authentication. To give you an idea, if you combine

Forms authentication with HTTPS you have the same security level currently used by online banking applications and payment sites.

It's therefore safe for the middle tier to trust the upper HTTP façade and accept any calls coming down the way. However, nothing prevents you from implementing an extra check for authorization within the body of service methods. In this case, though, you need to access credentials information from within the service.

AJAX-enabled services can carry this information only via the authentication cookie or client certificates. Programmatically, a service gets user credentials via intrinsic objects of the run-time platform. ASP.NET XML Web services live within the ASP.NET runtime and have full access to the ASP.NET intrinsics, including the *User* object.

By default, instead, WCF service calls are processed by the WCF runtime, which lives side by side with ASP.NET, but it's not a part of it. As a result, a WCF service method can't access the HTTP request context and put its hands on the *User* object. The only possible workaround is running all the WCF services hosted by the site in ASP.NET compatibility mode.

You turn compatibility mode on in the configuration file, as shown here:

```
<system.serviceModel>
    <serviceHostingEnvironment aspNetCompatibilityEnabled="true" />
    ...
</system.serviceModel>
```

In addition, each service is required to express its explicit approval of the model. A service does this by decorating the service class—not the service contract—with the *AspNetCompatibilityRequirements* attribute, as shown here:

```
[AspNetCompatibilityRequirements(
        RequirementsMode = AspNetCompatibilityRequirementsMode.Allowed)]
public class TimeService : ITimeService
{
    ...
}
```

Note that, by default, a WCF service has the *RequirementsMode* property set to *NotAllowed*. If this value is not changed to either *Allowed* or *Required*, you get a run-time exception as you attempt to make a call to the service.

> **Note** WCF services have been designed to be independent from binding and transportation. By turning on ASP.NET compatibility mode, you break this rule because you make the service dependent on IIS as the host and HTTP as the transportation protocol. On the other hand, services in the HTTP façade are just Ajax-specific services so, in this regard, enabling ASP.NET compatibility is actually a natural choice.

JSON Payloads

When you call server-based code you likely need to pass input data and wait to receive some other data back. Clearly, a serialization format is required to transform platform-specific data (for example, a .NET object) into an HTTP network packet. For years, this field has been the reign of XML. To a large extent, this is still the reign of XML, but not when a Web browser is used as the client.

Shorthand for JavaScript Object Notation, JSON is the de facto standard format for browsers and Web servers to exchange data over HTTP when a script-led request is made. The main reasons for preferring JSON over XML can be summarized by saying that, overall, JSON is simpler than full-blown XML and gets a free deserialization engine in virtually any browser that supports JavaScript. You can learn more about the syntax and purposes of JSON at *http://www.json.org*.

JSON at a Glance

JSON is a text-based format specifically designed to move the state of an object across tiers. It's natively supported by JavaScript in the sense that a JSON-compatible string can be evaluated to a JavaScript object through the JavaScript *eval* function. However, if the JSON string represents the state of a custom object, it's your responsibility to ensure that the definition of the corresponding class is available on the client.

The JSON format describes the state of the object, an example of which is shown here:

```
{"ID"="ALFKI", "Company":"Alfred Futterkiste"}
```

The string indicates an object with two properties—*ID* and *Company*—and their respective, text-serialized values. If a property is assigned a nonprimitive value—say, a custom object—the value is recursively serialized to JSON, as in the code snippet shown here:

```
{"ID"="ALFKI",
  "Company":"Alfred Futterkiste",
  "Address":{"Street="543 Oberstr", "City"="Berlin", "Country":"Germany"} }
```

Services in the HTTP façade preferably receive and return HTTP packets with JSON content.

On the client, creating a JSON representation of data is your responsibility. You can either manually build the string or use some facilities to serialize a JavaScript object to JSON. Some browsers support native JSON parsing through a *JSON* object exposed out of the *window* object. Specifically, these browsers are Internet Explorer 8, Firefox 3.5, Safari 4, Chrome, Opera 10, and their newer versions. Alternatively, you can download the file *json2.js*, which provides analogous capabilities, from *http://www.json.org*.

On the server, you typically rely on the serialization capabilities of some classes in the .NET Framework to get a JSON string. You can use the *JavaScriptSerializer* class or the newer

DataContractJsonSerializer class. Although they do it through different APIs, both classes take a .NET object and convert it to a JSON string. This step, however, is transparently performed by the WCF infrastructure after you have defined the data contracts for the service interface.

Data Contracts

Any nonprimitive data to be sent or received via WCF methods must be marked with the *DataContract* attribute. Imagine you have the following service:

```
[ServiceContract(Namespace = "Services.Wcf")]
[AspNetCompatibilityRequirements(
        RequirementsMode = AspNetCompatibilityRequirementsMode.Allowed)]
public class CustomerService
{
    [OperationContract]
    public CustomerDTO LookupCustomer(String id)
    {
        var context = new NorthwindDataContext();
        var data = (from c in context.Customers
                    where c.CustomerID == id
                    select c).SingleOrDefault();
        if (data != null)
        {
            var dto = new CustomerDTO((Customer)data);
            return dto;
        }
        return new MissingCustomerDTO();
    }
}
```

The method *LookupCustomer* is expected to return a custom object. This object must be decorated with ad hoc *DataContract* attribute:

```
namespace Services.Wcf
{
    [DataContract]
    public class CustomerDTO
    {
        private Customer _customer;
        public CustomerDTO(Customer customer)
        {
            _customer = customer;
        }

        [DataMember]
        public string CustomerID
        {
            get { return _customer.CustomerID; }
            set { _customer.CustomerID = value; }
        }
        ...
    }
}
```

In this particular case, the class being used over WCF is a data-transfer object (DTO)—that is, a helper class that moves the content of domain model objects across tiers.

Why JSON Is Preferable to XML

For years, XML has been touted as the lingua franca of the Web. Now that Ajax has become a key milestone for the entire Web, XML has been pushed to the side in favor of JSON as far as data representation over the Web is concerned.

Why is JSON preferable to XML in Ajax scenarios?

The main reason for dropping XML and SOAP in favor of JSON is that JSON is much easier to handle from within a JavaScript-powered client than any XML-based format. JSON is slightly simpler and more appropriate for the JavaScript language to process than XML. Although JSON might not be easier for humans to understand than XML—this is just my thought, by the way—it's certainly easier for a machine to process than XML. Nothing like an XML parser is required for JSON. Everything you need to parse the text is built into the JavaScript language. JSON is also less verbose than XML, and less ambitious too. JSON, in fact, is not as good as XML for interoperability purposes.

The JSON syntax is not perfect either. The industrial quantity of commas and quotes it requires makes it a rather quirky format. But can you honestly say that XML is more forgiving?

With JSON, you also gain a key architectural benefit at a relatively low cost. You always reason in terms of objects instead of dealing with untyped Document Object Model (DOM) trees. On the server, you define your entities and implement them as classes in your favorite managed language. When a service method needs to return an instance of any class, the state of the object is serialized to JSON and travels over the wire. On the client, the JSON string is received and processed, and its contents are loaded into an array, or a kind of mirror JavaScript object, with the same interface as the server class. The interface of the class is inferred from the JSON stream. In this way, both the service and the client page code use the same logical definition of an entity.

Obviously, from a purely technical standpoint, the preservation of the data contract doesn't strictly require JSON to be implemented. You could get to the same point using XML as well. In that case, though, you need to get yourself an XML parser that can be used from JavaScript.

Parsing some simple XML text in JavaScript might not be an issue, but getting a full-blown parser is another story completely. Performance and functionality issues will likely lead to a proliferation of similar components with little in common. And then you must decide whether such a JavaScript XML parser should support things such as namespaces, schemas, white spaces, comments, and processing instructions.

As I see it, for the sake of compatibility you will end up with a subset of XML limited to nodes and attributes. At that point, it's merely a matter of choosing between the angle brackets of XML and the curly brackets of JSON. Additionally, JSON has a free parser already built into the JavaScript engine—the aforementioned function *eval*.

Also labeled as the fat-free alternative to XML, JSON has ultimately been a very convenient choice for architects of Web frameworks and is today the real currency exchanged by browsers and Ajax-enabled services.

JavaScript Client Code

You can consume a REST service by simply invoking its URL and processing its response. We'll get into this example in the next chapter via the jQuery library. A referenced Ajax-enabled WCF or Web service, however, can automatically generate a JavaScript proxy class, which might make invoking the service easier.

Getting a Proxy for the HTTP Façade

When you add a Web or WCF service to a classic Web application project or to a Windows Forms project, you go through a Visual Studio wizard, indicate the URL of the service, specify the desired namespace, and finally have the wizard generate a proxy class and add it in the folds of the project solution.

When you add a reference to Web or WCF services to an ASP.NET AJAX page, no Visual Studio wizard will be there to silently invoke an SDK tool that automagically creates the proxy class. In the first place, you don't add a service reference through the Web project. Instead, you programmatically add the service reference to the ASP.NET page, as shown here:

```
<asp:ScriptManager ID="ScriptManager1" runat="server">
    <Services>
        <asp:ServiceReference Path="appAjaxLayer.svc" />
        ...
    </Services>
</asp:ScriptManager>
```

The script manager emits the following markup:

```
<script src="appAjaxLayer.svc/js" type="text/javascript"></script>
```

If you're testing your page and have debug mode set in the *web.config* file, the suffix to the service URL will be */jsdebug* instead of */js*.

The */js* suffix is the magic word that instructs the service infrastructure to generate a JavaScript proxy class for the client code to call the service. In particular, for WCF services the *enableWebScript* attribute of the endpoint behavior enables the generation of the proxy; subsequently, it enables the service to be scripted from an Ajax client.

The JavaScript proxy class is named according to different rules for Web and WCF services. For Web services, the proxy gets the exact fully qualified name of the class behind the *.asmx* endpoint. For WCF services, the name of the proxy class is determined by the concatenation of the *Namespace* and *Name* properties specified in the *ServiceContract* attribute you're targeting. Note, therefore, that when you call a WCF service method you're actually calling a method defined on a contract. To invoke a WCF service, it's the contract that matters, not the class that implements it. In fact, the same service class can implement multiple contracts.

Using the Proxy

After you have the JavaScript proxy, invoking the Web or WCF service is nearly the same thing. The proxy object comes as a singleton and exposes the same set of contracted methods you have on the original service. The communication model is asynchronous and requires you to specify at least a callback function to use in case of successful execution. Here's an example:

```
// Async call of method GetQuotes with a callback
Samples.Services.FinanceInfoService.GetQuotes(symbols, onDataAvailable);
```

The code can refer to a Web service as well as a WCF service. If it refers to a Web service, the Web service class is named *Samples.Services.FinanceInfoService*; if it refers to a WCF service, the namespace of the service contract might be *Samples.Services* and the name of the contract might be *FinanceInfoService*. The preceding code snippet invokes the method *GetQuotes*.

In addition to the regular list of parameters for the service method, each proxy method can take up to three extra parameters. The first extra parameter is mandatory and represents the callback to invoke if the method execution is successful. The second and third optional parameters indicate, respectively, the callback to use in case of failure and a state object to pass to both callbacks. In the code snippet just shown, the *onDataAvailable* parameter refers to a JavaScript callback to call only if the method executes successfully.

The signature of the success and failure callbacks is similar, but the internal format of the *results* parameter can change quite a bit. Here's the callback signature:

```
function method(results, context, methodName)
```

Table 20-9 provides more details about the various arguments.

TABLE 20-9 Arguments for a JavaScript Proxy Callback Function

Argument	Description
results	Indicates the return value from the method in the case of success. In the case of failure, a JavaScript *Error* object mimics the exception that occurred on the server during the execution of the method.
context	The state object passed to the callback.
methodName	The name of the service method that was invoked.

The JavaScript proxy exposes a number of properties and methods for you to configure. The list is presented in Table 20-10.

TABLE 20-10 **Static Properties on a JavaScript Proxy Class**

Property	Description
path	Gets and sets the URL of the underlying Web or WCF service.
timeout	Gets and sets the duration (in seconds) before the method call times out.
defaultSucceededCallback	Gets and sets the default JavaScript callback function to invoke for any successful call to a method.
defaultFailedCallback	Gets and sets the default JavaScript callback function, if any, to invoke for a failed or timed-out call.
defaultUserContext	Gets and sets the default JavaScript state object, if any, to be passed to success and failure callbacks.

If you set a "default succeeded" callback, you don't have to specify a "succeeded" callback in any successive call as long as the desired callback function is the same. The same holds true for the failed callback and the user context object. The user context object is any JavaScript object, filled with any information that makes sense to you, that gets passed automatically to any callback that handles the success or failure of the call.

> **Note** The JavaScript code injected for the proxy class uses the *path* property to define the URL to the Web service. You can change the property programmatically to redirect the proxy to a different URL.

Remote Calls via Page Methods

If you don't feel like using Web or WCF services, a quick solution to expose Ajax-callable endpoints is based on page methods. Page methods are simply public, static methods exposed by the code-behind class of a given ASP.NET page. The run-time engine for page methods and Ajax-enabled Web services is nearly the same. Using page methods saves you from the burden of creating and publishing a service; at the same time, though, it binds you to having page-scoped methods that can't be called from within a page different from the one where they are defined.

Public and static methods defined on a page's code-behind class and flagged with the *WebMethod* attribute transform an ASP.NET page into a Web service. Here's a sample page method:

```
public class TimeServicePage : System.Web.UI.Page
{
    [WebMethod]
    public static DateTime GetTime()
    {
        return DateTime.Now;
    }
}
```

You can use any data type in the definition of page methods, including .NET Framework types as well as user-defined types. All types will be transparently JSON-serialized during each call.

> **Note** The page class where you define methods might be the direct code-behind class or, better yet, a parent class. In this way, in the parent class you can implement the contract of the public server API and keep it somewhat separated from the rest of the event handlers and methods that are specific to the page life cycle and behavior. Because page methods are required to be *static* (*shared* in Microsoft Visual Basic .NET), you can't use the syntax of interfaces to define the contract. You have to resort to abstract base classes.

Alternatively, you can define Web methods as inline code in the *.aspx* source file as follows (and if you use Visual Basic, just change the type attribute to *text/VB*):

```
<script type="text/C#" runat="server">
    [WebMethod]
    public static DateTime GetTime()
    {
        return DateTime.Now;
    }
</script>
```

Page methods are specific to a given ASP.NET page. Only the host page can call its methods. Cross-page method calls are not supported. If they are critical for your scenario, I suggest that you move to using Web or WCF services.

When the code-behind class of an ASP.NET AJAX page contains *WebMethod*-decorated static methods, the run-time engine emits a JavaScript proxy class nearly identical to the class generated for a Web or WCF service. You use a global instance of this class to call server methods. The name of the class is hard-coded to *PageMethods*. Its usage is nearly identical to the proxy for Web or WCF services.

```
function getTime()
{
    PageMethods.GetTime(methodCompleted);
}
function methodCompleted(results, context, methodName)
{
    // Format the date-time object to a more readable string
    var displayString = results.format("ddd, dd MMMM yyyy");
    document.getElementById("Label1").innerHTML = displayString;
}
```

Note, however, that page methods are not enabled by default. In other words, the *PageMethods* proxy class that you use to place remote calls is not generated unless you set the *EnablePageMethods* property to *true* in the page's script manager:

```
<asp:ScriptManager runat="server" ID="ScriptManager1" EnablePageMethods="true" />
```

For the successful execution of a page method, the ASP.NET AJAX application must have the *ScriptModule* HTTP module enabled in the *web.config* file:

```
<httpModules>
  <add name="ScriptModule"
     type="System.Web.Handlers.ScriptModule, System.Web.Extensions" />
</httpModules>
```

For page method calls, therefore, there's no page life cycle and child controls are not initialized and processed.

> **Note** From page methods, you can access session state, the ASP.NET *Cache*, and *User* objects, as well as any other intrinsic objects. You can do that using the *Current* property on *HttpContext*. The HTTP context is not specific to the page life cycle and is, instead, a piece of information that accompanies the request from the start.

Summary

ASP.NET offers two approaches to AJAX: partial rendering and scriptable services. Of the two, partial rendering is the one with some hidden costs. Partial rendering is easy to understand and doesn't require that you learn new things. It makes an existing page work the Ajax way without changing anything. Although it can still achieve better performance than classic postbacks, partial rendering moves a lot of data around. In the worst cases, the savings in terms of markup are negligible compared to the quantity of bytes moved.

On the other hand, the best selling point of the Ajax paradigm is the idea of making stateless server-side calls from the client and updating the page via the DOM. Here's where scriptable services fit in. No hidden costs are buried in this model. You send in only input data required by the method being invoked and receive only the return value. Traffic is minimal, and no view state or other hidden fields (for example, event validation) are roundtripped. On the down side, remote method calls require JavaScript skills. You control the execution of the method via JavaScript and use a JavaScript callback to incorporate the results in the page.

Using scriptable services leads you to making some architectural changes to the application. You need a server API designed to respond to script-led requests, and you need this API to live on top of your existing middle tier. How do you expose this API? There are various options for implementing this layer. You can use a Web service or, better yet, a WCF service hosted in the same domain. Once you have a back end based on services, you orchestrate calls to endpoints from the client browser using whatever programming language the browser provides. If plain JavaScript is not optimal, you can use a wrapper library such as jQuery (see next chapter) or switch to a rich Internet framework such a Silverlight.

Chapter 21
jQuery Programming

If knowledge can create problems, it is not through ignorance that we can solve them.

—Isaac Asimov

Aside from the social implications of it, the modern Web from a technology viewpoint is mostly about running (a lot) more JavaScript code on the client. JavaScript is a very special type of language; it's probably not the language everybody would choose to use today to power up the client side of the Web. However, it's the only common language we have, and we have to stick to it to reach the largest audience.

So what if you want (or more likely need) more power on the client?

Be ready to write more JavaScript code. More importantly, be ready to import more JavaScript code written by others. Either of these two ways of using JavaScript is OK, as they are not mutually exclusive options.

I firmly believe that, at least for the time being, you can't just transform JavaScript into something else that is radically different from what the language is today. However, the Web has repeatedly proven to be a surprisingly dynamic and agile environment; so who really knows what could happen in five years?

Currently, the most effective approach to adding more power to the client is using ad hoc libraries full of Document Object Model (DOM) facilities and adding new features to the existing JavaScript language. Interestingly, a single all-encompassing library seems not to be realistic. The ideal JavaScript library is often obtained by stacking up and composing together bits and pieces of existing libraries in a custom recipe that suits each particular application.

Many attempts have been made over the years to create the perfect JavaScript library. As it often happens, many libraries participate, but only one wins. And in this regard the winner is jQuery. In this chapter, you'll discover the capabilities of this library and its powerful extensibility model.

Power to the Client

JavaScript is a language tailor-made for the Web and, more specifically, for the browser. I won't stray too far from the truth by saying that there's little life for JavaScript outside the realm of a Web browser, even though the demand for out-of-browser JavaScript is growing and might explode in the near future.

Anyway, today JavaScript still lives for the browser and within the browser. This is the starting point to understand what the language is for and where to look for possible (and really useful) extensions. Not surprisingly, our quest will lead straight to jQuery—currently, a natural extension of most Web applications.

Programming within the Browser

The first appearance of JavaScript as a browser-hosted language dates back to late 1995, when the first beta of Netscape Navigator 2 was released. JavaScript was introduced to give authors of Web documents the ability to incorporate some logic and action in HTML pages. Before then, a Web page was essentially a static collection of HTML tags and text. Historically, the first significant enhancement made to the syntax of HTML was the support for tags to include script code.

Original Goals of the Language

JavaScript was not designed to be a classic and cutting-edge programming language—not even by the standards of 15 years ago. The primary goal of its designers was to create a language that resembled a simpler Java that could be used with ease by inexpert page authors.

To some extent, the design of JavaScript was influenced by many languages, but the predominant factor was simplicity. It was named "JavaScript" because the language was essentially meant to be a powerful language like Java, but focused on scripting. No other relationships, beyond the deliberate reference in the name, exist between Java and JavaScript.

As a result, JavaScript is an interpreted and weakly typed language that also supports dynamic binding and objects. JavaScript, however, is not a fully object-oriented language.

Note Originally developed at Netscape by Brendan Eich, JavaScript was first named LiveScript. The name was changed to JavaScript when Netscape added support for Java technology in its Navigator browser. The *script* suffix was simply meant to be the script version of an excellent programming language like Java. In no way was the language supposed to be a spinoff of Java.

Later, Microsoft created a similar language for its Internet Explorer browser and named it JScript to avoid trademark issues. In 1997, JavaScript was submitted to the European Computer Manufacturers Association (ECMA) International for standardization. The process culminated a couple of years later in the standardized version of the language named ECMAScript.

The Scripting Engine

Being an interpreted language, JavaScript requires an ad hoc run-time environment to produce visible effects from the source code. The run-time environment is often referred to as the browser's *scripting engine*. As such, the JavaScript run-time environment can be slightly different from one browser to the next. The result is that the same JavaScript language feature might provide different performance on different browsers and might be flawed on one browser while working efficiently on another one. This fact makes it generally hard and time-consuming to write good, cross-browser JavaScript code and justifies the love/hate relationship (well, mostly hate) that many developers have developed with the language over the years.

The diagram in Figure 21-1 shows the overall structure of a scripting engine with an interesting extension—the JavaScript background compiler—that some of the latest browsers are implementing.

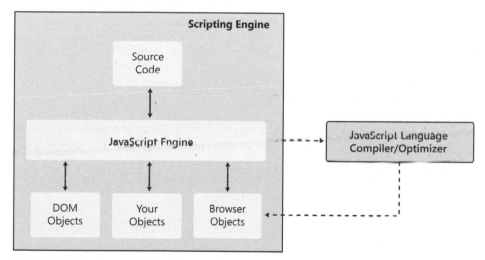

FIGURE 21-1 The browser's JavaScript engine.

The scripting engine is a component that is hosted in the browser and receives the source code to process. Armed with language knowledge, the engine can resolve any name in the source code that can be mapped to a syntax element—keywords, variables, local functions, and objects.

In addition, the source code processed within a Web browser is likely populated with specific objects coming from various sources. For example, you can find DOM objects to access the content being displayed in the page as well as browser-specific objects such as *XMLHttpRequest*, *JSON*, and *window*. Furthermore, any libraries you reference from the page are also published to the engine. After the script has been loaded, the browser runs the script through the engine. This action results in the functionality defined by the commands in the code.

As mentioned, although JavaScript is definitely a stable language that hasn't faced significant changes for a decade now, virtually any broadly used library is packed with forks in code to distinguish the behavior of different browsers and ensure the same overall interface.

One of the first rules—if not the first rule—you should follow to write rich client applications is get yourself a powerful JavaScript library that adds abstraction and features to the JavaScript language and that works in a cross-browser manner.

Flaws and Workarounds

JavaScript has a number of drawbacks, both technical and infrastructural. In spite of all these factors, though, JavaScript works just great for the majority of Web applications. And nothing any better has been invented yet.

All things considered, the limitations of JavaScript can be summarized as two elements: it is an interpreted language, and it is not fully object oriented. The former drawback makes the language significantly slower than a compiled language. The latter makes it harder for developers to write complex code.

The Google Chrome browser (which you can read more about at *http://www.google.com/ chrome*) is the first browser with an open-source JavaScript engine that compiles source code to native machine code before executing it. As a result, Chrome runs JavaScript applications at the speed of a compiled binary, which is significantly better than any bytecode or interpreted code.

An analogous capability is featured by Internet Explorer 9, which compiles the JavaScript code in the background, leveraging the full capabilities of the underlying hardware. Generally, all browsers (including Mozilla-based browsers and Opera) are evolving their JavaScript engines to achieve performance as close as possible to that of native code.

Because JavaScript is so popular and widely used, planning a significant overhaul of the language is just out of question. For years now, libraries built on top of the core language have been providing facilities to work with remote endpoints, parse data into JSON, and produce UI widgets.

As you saw in Chapter 20, "Ajax Programming," JavaScript can be used to write code that follows two radically different programming paradigms: functional programming and object-oriented programming (OOP). JavaScript is neither 100 percent functional nor object-oriented, but it borrows concepts from both qualified functional and object-oriented languages. This inevitably creates some noise regarding the programming techniques you can employ. As a developer, you must be ready to accept compromises that might not be acceptable in a fully qualified functional or object-oriented scenario. To use JavaScript at its best, you probably have to mix functional features with object-oriented (OO) features.

What You Write JavaScript Code For

The client-side code you are called to write is no longer, and not just, plain scripting of the document object model as it was when the language was introduced. Today, you often use JavaScript for some client-side logic and input validation. In particular, you use JavaScript to download data from the server, implement Windows-like effects such as drag-and-drop, resizing, templates, popup and graphic effects, local data caching, and the management of history and events around the page. You want the JavaScript code to be maintainable and unobtrusive.

Any in-browser JavaScript inevitably deals with the DOM. The DOM, therefore, is the primary object model you need to work with. Any other object model you might want to introduce risks being cumbersome and partially unnecessary.

If you have to write your own framework to support some server-side infrastructure, you probably are better off opting for an object-oriented approach. If your goal, instead, is just to add some presentation logic to the page, you don't need object orientation in JavaScript. A functional approach combined with rich DOM and page manipulation capabilities is the ideal mix these days. The jQuery library is just the most illustrious example of such a library.

The Gist of jQuery

The main reason for the worldwide success of the jQuery library is its unique mix of functional and DOM programming. The library works by selecting DOM elements and applying functions over them, which is just what client Web developers need to do most of the time.

Details of the Library

The library is made of a single *.js* file you can download from *http://jquery.com*. Most ASP.NET Visual Studio templates already include a version of the jQuery library, even though the one included in the template might not be the latest. From the site, you can pick both the minified and debug versions. Compressed, they are a bit more than 20 KB in size. Here's what you need to link the jQuery library (keeping in mind that the path can change on a per-application basis):

```
<script type="text/javascript" src="/Scripts/jquery-1.4.4.js"></script>
```

So if jQuery is not the only option, why is it so popular?

In the first place, the library is lightweight and cross-browser capable. Second, it works by selecting DOM elements via a Cascading Style Sheet 3.0 (CSS3)-compliant syntax and applying functions to each of them. Functions are mostly user-defined, but a number of predefined (and commonly used) functions exist. Third, the library is based on an extensible model that enables developers to write and share their own plug-ins, thus contributing to making the library even more successful.

Microsoft offers support 24 hours a day, seven days a week for the jQuery library when used with ASP.NET and contributes developers to the project. Template support recently added to version 1.4.5 of the library has been contributed by Microsoft. Visual Studio recognizes jQuery code via a proper *.vsdoc* file and provides IntelliSense support. (See Figure 21-2.)

FIGURE 21-2 IntelliSense support for jQuery code.

For development purposes, you reference the VSDOC file, as shown here:

```
<script type="text/javascript" src="/Scripts/jquery-1.4.4-vsdoc.js"></script>
```

You can get the latest VSDOC IntelliSense file from the Microsoft CDN at the following address: *http://ajax.aspnetcdn.com/ajax/jQuery/jquery-1.4.4-vsdoc.js*. Obviously, you might need to change the file name to get a newer version. The naming convention of the jQuery library is *jquery-n.n.n.js*, where *n.n.n* stands for the current version number.

The Root Object

The word *query* in the library's name says it all—the jQuery library is primarily designed for running (clever) queries over the DOM. The library supplies a powerful interface to select DOM elements that goes far beyond the simple search for an element that matches a given ID. For example, you can easily select all elements that share a given cascading style sheet (CSS) class, have certain attributes, or appear in a given position in the tree. More importantly, you can chain multiple clauses together and prepare complex queries.

The root of the jQuery library is the *jQuery* function. Here's the overall structure of the library:

```
(
    function( window, undefined )
    {
        var jQuery = (function() {...})();
        /* the rest of the library goes here */
    }
) (window);
```

The jQuery function just shown is then mapped as an extension to the browser's *window* object and is aliased with the popular *$* function. The function has the following prototype:

```
function(selector, context)
```

The *selector* indicates the query expression to run over the DOM; the *context* indicates the portion of the DOM from which to run the query. If no context is specified, the *jQuery* function looks for DOM elements within the entire page DOM.

The *jQuery* function typically returns a *wrapped set*, namely a collection of DOM elements. Nicely enough, this wrapped set is still a jQuery object that can be queried using the same syntax, resulting in chained queries.

jQuery and Functional Programming

In jQuery, you find some basic principles of functional programming. In particular, the library is built around a fundamental type of data—the DOM element. And the library's root object is essentially a wrapper around DOM elements. Furthermore, DOM elements can be passed into the jQuery object through the type constructor. Finally, the root object can pass its own wrapped values into other functions that return another instance of the same root object.

The net effect is that you build your jQuery code by pipelining function calls to create a super function that just gets some input and returns some output. In the super function, you express behavior by injecting anonymous JavaScript functions as if they were plain values.

Let's start by playing with the jQuery library.

Working with jQuery

When writing JavaScript intensive applications, you'll find it quite natural to put a piece of code at the top of each page and set up the DOM to serve the desired logic within the page. Typically, this code initializes global variables and prepares the ground for possible future actions. Ideally, you also want to use this initialization code to arrange event handlers, caching, and downloads of external data.

Because jQuery is designed to query the DOM and work with selected elements, any initialization code should reasonably run only when the DOM is ready. Detecting DOM readiness and writing initialization code with jQuery library is easier than ever.

Detecting DOM Readiness

In the beginning of client-side development, there was just one place where you could put the initialization code of a Web page—in the *onload* event on either the *window* object or the *<body>* tag. The *onload* event fires as soon as the page has finished loading—that is, once the download of all linked images, CSS styles, and scripts has terminated. There's no guarantee, however, that at this time the DOM has been fully initialized and is ready to accept instructions.

The DOM *ReadyState* Property

The document root object in the DOM exposes a read-only *readyState* property just to let you know the current state of the DOM and figure out when it is OK for your page to start scripting it. Any change to the property is signaled with a *readyStateChange* event. Web pages are notified of DOM readiness by registering a handler for this event and checking the value of the *readyState* property in the code.

Most browsers also support the *DOMContentLoaded* event, which just signals when the DOM is ready. Internet Explorer, however, doesn't support it.

Using the *readyState* property is an approach that definitely works, but it is a bit cumbersome. For this reason, most JavaScript frameworks offer their own "ready" event that signals when you can start making calls into the framework safely. In this way, they shield you from the details of the DOM implementation and just let you know when you can do your own thing.

The jQuery library is no exception.

The jQuery's *Ready* Function

In jQuery, you select the current DOM document and call the *ready* function on it. The *ready* function encapsulates the code to check the value of the *readyState* property on the DOM's *document* object. The *ready* function takes an anonymous function as a parameter. The argument function is where you specify any initialization code required for the document. Here's how you use it:

```
<script type="text/javascript">
$(document).ready(
   function() {
     alert("I'm ready!");
   });
</script>
```

The jQuery's *ready* function provides a cross-browser solution to detect the DOM readiness.

Note that the *ready* function works only if it's invoked on the current document. You can't call the *ready* function on, say, an image, a script, or a portion of the DOM. In light of this, you can even omit the document selector and resort to the equally acceptable syntax shown here:

```
<script type="text/javascript">
$(function() {
    alert("I'm ready!");
  });
</script>
```

The two syntaxes are equivalent. Another approach consists of using the *bind* method to bind a handler to the *ready* event of the document:

```
$(document).bind("ready", function() { ... });
```

In this case, though, the handler won't run if at the time of event binding the *ready* event has already fired. Finally, the *ready* handler is delayed until the document is ready or runs immediately if the document is already entirely loaded. I'll return to *bind* and other event functions later in the chapter.

Onload vs. *Ready*

Which code runs first, the *window*'s *onload* event handler or the call's jQuery *ready* function?

The *onload* event is called after the HTML and any auxiliary resources are loaded. The *ready* function is called after the DOM is initialized. The two events can run in any order. The *onload* event won't ensure the page DOM is loaded; the *ready* function won't ensure all resources, such as images, have been loaded.

Another noticeable difference between *onload* and *ready* is that you can have multiple calls to *ready* in a page. You can have only one global *onload* event handler either defined on the *window* object or expressed as an attribute on the *body* tag. When multiple calls to *ready* are specified, jQuery pushes specified functions to an internal stack and serves them sequentially after the DOM is effectively ready.

It is generally recommended that you use either the *ready* function or the *onload* handler. If you need both things, you should use the jQuery's *load* function attached to the *window* object or to more specific elements such as images, scripts, or style sheets:

```
$(window).load(function() {
    // Initialization code here
});
```

You typically use *load* when you need to access specific information on specific page elements such as images or scripts. So in summary, you rarely end up using *load* on the *window* object.

Wrapped Sets

Why does the word "query" appear in the name of the library? The ultimate purpose of the jQuery library (*j* stands for JavaScript) is simplifying the task of getting a selected subset of DOM elements to work with. Put another way, the jQuery library is mostly intended to run queries over the page DOM and execute operations over the returned items.

The query engine behind the library goes far beyond the simple search capabilities of, say, *document.getElementById* (and related functions) that you find natively in the DOM. The query capabilities of jQuery use the powerful CSS syntax, which gives you a surprising level of expressivity. You find similar query expressivity only in the DOM of HTML 5 when it's fully defined and widely and uniformly supported.

The query engine of jQuery allows you to select elements that have a given combination of attribute values, appear in a fixed relative position in the DOM tree, or have a particular relationship with other elements. More importantly, you can add filter conditions, chain multiple queries together, and apply them sequentially.

The result of a query is a *wrapped set*. A wrapped set is an object containing a collection of DOM elements. Elements are added to the collection in the order in which they appear in the original document.

A wrapped set is never null, even if no matching elements have been found. You check the actual size of the wrapped set by looking at the *length* property of the jQuery object, as shown here:

```
// Queries for all IMG tags in the page
var wrappedSet = new jQuery("img");
var length = wrappedSet.length;
if (length == 0)
    alert("No IMG tags found.");
```

Note that the expression just shown, through which you get the wrapped set, is fully equivalent to the more commonly used *$("img")*.

The wrapped set is not a special data container; rather, it's a jQuery-specific term to indicate the results of a query. However, once you hold all the elements you were looking for, you need to process them. To start off, let's see how to enumerate the content.

Enumerating the Content

To loop through the elements in the wrapped set, you use the *each* function. The *each* function gets a function as a parameter and invokes that on each element:

```
// Prints out names of all images
$("img").each(function(index) {
    alert(this.src);
});
```

The callback function you pass to *each* receives the 0-based index of the current iteration. Nicely enough, you don't need to retrieve the corresponding DOM element yourself; you just use the keyword *this* to refer to the element currently being processed. If the callback function returns *false*, the iteration is stopped. Note that *each* is a quite generic function made available for any task for which a more specific jQuery function doesn't exist. If you find a jQuery function that already does what you intend to code through *each*, by all means use the native function.

You use the *length* property to read the size of the wrapped set. You can also use the *size* function, but the *length* property is slightly faster:

```
// You better use property length
alert($("img").size());
```

The *get* function extracts the wrapped set from the *jQuery* object and returns it as a JavaScript array of DOM elements. If you pass an index argument, instead, it will return the DOM element found at the specified 0-based position in the wrapped set. Note that the *get* function breaks the jQuery chainability because it returns a DOM object or an array of DOM objects. You can't further apply jQuery functions to the results of a *get* call.

Many more operations are available on wrapped sets, and many others can be added through plug-ins. I'll return to the topic of operations that are possible on a wrapped set later in the chapter, right after discussing the syntax used to arrange queries.

Basic Selectors

A query is characterized by a *selector*. A selector is simply the expression that, when properly evaluated, selects one or more DOM elements. In jQuery, you have three basic types of selectors—based on ID, CSS, or tag name. In addition, a selector can result from the composition of multiple simpler selectors combined using ad hoc operators. In this case, you have a compound selector.

An *ID selector* picks up DOM elements by ID. An ID selector commonly selects only one element unless multiple elements in the page share the same ID—this condition violates the HTML DOM standard, but it is not too unusual in the real world. Here's the syntax of an ID selector:

```
// Select all elements in the context whose ID is Button1
$("#Button1")
```

The leading # symbol just tells jQuery how to interpret the following text.

A *CSS-based selector* picks up all elements that share the given CSS class. The syntax is shown here:

```
// Select all elements in the context styled with the specified CSS class
$(".header")
```

In this case, the leading dot (.) symbol tells jQuery to interpret the following text as a CSS style name.

Finally, a *tag-based selector* picks up all elements with the specified tag, such as all IMG tags, all DIV tags, or whatever else you specify. In this case, the selector consists of the plain tag name—no leading symbol is required:

```
// Select all IMG elements in the context
$("img")
```

As mentioned, you can also concatenate two or more selectors to form a more specific one.

Compound Selectors

Concatenation is possible through a number of operators. For example, the white space picks up all elements that satisfy the second selector and are descendants of those matching the first. Here's an example:

```
// Select all anchors contained within a DIV
$("div a")
```

The selector just shown is functionally equivalent to the following jQuery expression:

```
$("div").find("a");
```

Similar to the white space, the > operator selects elements that are direct child elements (and not just descendants) of the elements matched by the first selector:

```
// All anchors direct child elements of a DIV
$("div > a")
```

The preceding selector is functionally equivalent to the following jQuery expression:

```
$("div").children("a")
```

Plain concatenation of selectors results in a logical AND of conditions. For example, consider the following query:

```
$("div.header.highlight")
```

It selects all DIV elements styled using both the class *header* and class *highlight*.

The + operator—the *adjacent* operator—selects sibling elements in the second selector *immediately* preceded by elements selected by the first selector. Here's an example:

```
// All P immediately preceded by A
$("a + p")
```

The ~ operator—the *next* operator—is similar to + except that it selects sibling elements just preceded by others. Here's an example:

```
// All P preceded by A
$("a ~ p")
```

By using the comma, instead, you return the union of elements queried by multiple selectors. In terms of operations, the comma represents a logical OR of selectors. The next example, in fact, picks up elements that are either A or P:

```
// All A and all P
$("a, p")
```

Beyond simple operators, you have filters. A filter is a jQuery-specific expression that contains some custom logic to further restrict the selected elements.

Predefined Filters

Selectors can be further refined by applying filters on position, content, attributes, and visibility. A filter is a sort of built-in function applied to the wrapped set returned by a basic selector. Table 21-1 lists positional filters in jQuery.

TABLE 21-1 Positional Filters

Filter	Description
:first	Returns the first DOM element that matches
:last	Returns the last DOM element that matches
:not(selector)	Returns all DOM elements that do not match the specified selector
:even	Returns all DOM elements that occupy an even position in a 0-based indexing
:odd	Returns all DOM elements that occupy an odd position in a 0-based indexing
:eq(index)	Returns the DOM element in the wrapped set that occupies the specified 0-based position
:gt(index)	Returns all DOM elements that occupy a position in a 0-based indexing greater than the specified index
:lt(index)	Returns all DOM elements that occupy a position in a 0-based indexing less than the specified index
:header()	Returns all DOM elements that are headers, such as H1, H2, and the like
:animated()	Returns all DOM elements that are currently being animated via some functions in the jQuery library

Table 21-2 lists all filters through which you can select elements that are child elements of a parent element.

TABLE 21-2 Child Filters

Filter	Description
:nth-child(expression)	Returns all child elements of any parent that match the given expression. The expression can be an index or a math sequence (for example, 3n+1), including standard sequences such as odd and even.
:first:child	Returns all elements that are the first child of their parent.
:last-child	Returns all elements that are the last child of their parent.
:only-child	Returns all elements that are the only child of their parent.

A particularly powerful filter is *nth-child*. It supports a number of input expressions, as shown here:

```
:nth-child(index)
:nth-child(even)
:nth-child(odd)
:nth-child(expression)
```

The first format selects the *n*.th child of all HTML elements in the source selector. All child elements placed at any odd or even position in a 0-based indexing are returned if you specify the *odd* or *even* filter instead.

Finally, you can pass the *nth-child* filter a mathematical sequence expression, such as *3n* to indicate all elements in a position that are a multiple of 3. The following selector picks up all rows in a table (labeled *Table1*) that are at the positions determined by the sequence 3n+1— that is, 1, 4, 7, and so forth:

```
#Table1 tr:nth-child(3n+1)
```

Table 21-3 lists expressions used to filter elements by content.

TABLE 21-3 Content Filters

Filter	Description
:contains(text)	Returns all elements that contain the specified text
:empty	Returns all elements with no children
:has(selector)	Returns all elements that contain at least one element that matches the given selector
:parent	Returns all elements that have at least one child

As far as content filters are concerned, you should note that any text in an HTML element is considered a child node. So elements selected by the *empty* filter have no child nodes and no text as well. An example is the *
* tag.

A popular and powerful category of filters are attribute filters. Attribute filters allow you to select HTML elements where a given attribute is in a given relationship with a value. Table 21-4 lists all attribute filters supported in jQuery.

TABLE 21-4 Attribute Filters

Filter	Description
[attribute]	Returns all elements that have the specified attribute. This filter selects the element regardless of the attribute's value.
[attribute = value]	Returns all elements where the specified attribute (if present) is set to the specified value.
[attribute != value]	Returns all elements whose specified attribute (if present) has a value different from the given one.
[attribute ^= value]	Returns all elements whose specified attribute (if present) has content that starts with the given value.
[attribute $= value]	Returns all elements whose specified attribute (if present) has content that ends with the given value.
*[attribute *= value]*	Returns all elements whose specified attribute (if present) has content that contains the given value.

Attribute filters can also be concatenated by simply placing two or more of them side by side, as in the following example:

```
var elems = $("td[align=right][valign=top]");
```

The returned set includes all *<td>* elements where the horizontal alignment is *right* and the vertical alignment is *top*.

The next expression, which is much more sophisticated, demonstrates the power and flexibility of jQuery selectors, as it combines quite a few of them:

```
#Table1 tr:nth-child(3n+1):has(td[align=right]) td:odd
```

It reads as follows:

> *Within the body of element* Table1, *select all <tr> elements at positions 1, 4, 7, and so forth. Next, you keep only table rows where a <td> element exists with the attribute* align *equal to the value of* right. *Furthermore, of the remaining rows, you take only the cells on columns with an odd index.*

The result is a wrapped set made of *<td>* elements.

Finally, a couple more filters exist that are related to the visibility of elements. The *:visible* filter returns all elements that are currently visible. The *:hidden* filter returns all elements that are currently hidden from view. The wrapped set also includes all input elements of type *hidden*.

Form Filters

A special family of filters exists for HTML input elements. Table 21-5 lists all of them.

TABLE 21-5 Input Field Filters

Filter	Description
:input	Returns all elements that have a role in collecting input data
:text	Returns all input elements whose type attribute is *text*
:password	Returns all input elements whose type attribute is *password*
:checkbox	Returns all input elements whose type attribute is *checkbox*
:radio	Returns all input elements whose type attribute is *radio*
:submit	Returns all input elements whose type attribute is *submit*
:reset	Returns all input elements whose type attribute is *reset*
:image	Returns all input elements whose type attribute is *image*
:button	Returns all input elements whose type attribute is *button*
:file	Returns all input elements whose type attribute is *file*
:hidden	Returns all input elements whose type attribute is *hidden*
:enabled	Returns all input elements that are currently enabled
:disabled	Returns all input elements that are currently disabled
:checked	Returns all input elements that are currently checked
:selected	Returns all input elements that are currently selected

The *:input* filter, in particular, refers to all logical input elements you might find within a page form and is not limited solely to the *<input>* elements. In fact, it also picks up *<textarea>* and *<select>* elements used to display multiline text boxes and lists. The filters in Table 21-5 provide handy shortcuts for selecting homogeneous elements and are functionally equivalent to the other legal jQuery selectors. For example, *:checkbox* is equivalent to the following:

```
form input[type=checkbox]
```

As you can see in Table 21-5, other nice helpers are available to grab all input elements in a page form that are currently enabled or disabled and all check boxes and radio buttons currently selected.

Filter vs. Find

To further restrict a query, you can use either the *find* or *filter* function on a wrapped set. They are not the same, of course. The function *filter* explores the current wrapped set for matching elements and doesn't ever look into DOM for descendants. The function *find*, instead, looks inside of each of the elements in the wrapped set for elements that match the expression. In doing so, however, the function explores the DOM of each element in the wrapped set.

Operating on a Wrapped Set

The power of jQuery descends primarily from the powerful query language that allows you to select nearly any possible combination of DOM elements you can think of. However, the query language would not be much without a rich collection of predefined operations to apply to selected elements. The jQuery library offers a wide range of functions you can apply to the content of a wrapped set. We have already taken a look at how to enumerate the content of a wrapped set; let's now proceed with more specific operations.

As mentioned, function calls can be chained because any wrapped set returned by a query is in turn another jQuery object that can be further queried. The following expression is just fine:

```
$(selector).hide().addClass("hiddenElement");
```

It first hides from view all matching elements and then adds a specific CSS class to each of them. In jQuery, however, not all functions return a jQuery object. You must be aware of this to avoid nasty script errors. Chaining functions that act as value getters (not returning a jQuery object) is fine as long as these functions go at the end of the expression.

Important Before going any further, it is worth recalling that this is an ASP.NET Web Forms book. This means that in spite of the changes introduced in version 4 to the algorithm for generating control IDs, there is still a chance you'll end up using complex hierarchies of controls in which you don't exactly know the actual ID being generated for a given segment of the markup. As you saw in Chapter 6, "ASP.NET Core Server Controls," this problem is addressed by the *ClientIDMode* property added in ASP.NET 4 to the *Control* class. An easy way to retrieve the client ID of an ASP.NET control—at least when the ASP.NET control outputs a single piece of HTML—is the following:

```
<script type="text/javascript">
    var selector = "#<%= PanelAdvancedOptions.ClientID %>";
    ...
</script>
```

The code block captures the value of the *ClientID* property of the specified ASP.NET control and will emit it into the script block.

Controlling Visibility

The functions *hide* and *show* allow you to remove from view or display all elements that match a given selector. These functions help a lot in building dynamic views where you need to adjust the next user interface based on a current user's choice. Here's how to hide an element:

```
<script type="text/javascript">
    $(document).ready(function () {
        $("#panelAdvancedOptions").hide();
    });
</script>
```

To display it, you just replace the call to *hide* with a call to *show*. The most interesting aspect of *show* and *hide* methods is the built-in support for completion callbacks and effects. Here are the full signatures supported by the functions:

```
$(selector).hide()
$(selector).show()
$(selector).hide(duration, callback)
$(selector).show(duration, callback)
$(selector).hide(duration, easing, callback)
$(selector).show(duration, easing, callback)
```

When duration is specified, functions perform an animation while hiding or showing the element. The *duration* argument indicates the time (in milliseconds) the animation will take to run. You can also specify a couple of descriptive values such as *fast* and *slow*, which correspond to fixed values—specifically, 200 and 600 milliseconds.

The *easing* parameter indicates the internal function to use to perform the animation. Default values are *linear* and *swing*, which animate height, width, and opacity. Different effects can be achieved only through plug-ins.

The callback function runs at the end of the animation. The function doesn't get any parameter. However, the expression *this* in the context of the callback refers to the element being animated.

```
$("#panelAdvancedOptions").show(1000, function () {
    // Perform some action necessary when the panel is displayed.
    // The panel takes 1 second of animation to display.
    ...
});
```

Invoking *show* and *hide* methods without parameters is nearly equivalent to setting the *display* CSS attribute. The only difference is that the assigned value is cached for the purpose of toggling it through the *toggle* function:

```
$("#panelAdvancedOptions").toggle();
```

The preceding call toggles the visibility state of all elements in the wrapped set, making visible hidden elements and hiding visible elements.

In addition to plain *show* and *hide* methods, you also have methods to apply visibility changes through specific animations, such as sliding and fading. Methods are listed in Table 21-6.

TABLE 21-6 Visibility Effects

Function	Description
slideDown	Displays any matching elements by increasing their height progressively
slideUp	Hides any matching elements by decreasing their height progressively
slideToggle	Shows or hides all matching elements inverting the current sliding setting
fadeIn	Fades in any matching elements by reducing their opacity progressively
fadeOut	Fades out any matching elements by increasing their opacity progressively
fadeTo	Fades the opacity of all matching elements to a specified opacity

Styling

Applying CSS classes to selected elements is easy too. If you're interested in tweaking just individual CSS properties, you can use the *css* function, as shown here:

```
$("form input").css(
   {'color' : 'blue',
    'background-color' : 'yellow',
    'border-style' : 'dashed'}
);
```

To work with entire CSS classes, you have ad hoc functions such as those in Table 21-7.

TABLE 21-7 Working with CSS Classes

Function	Description
addClass	Adds the specified CSS class to any matching elements
removeClass	Removes the specified CSS class from any matching elements
toggleClass	Toggles the specified CSS class from any matching elements, meaning that the elements will be added to the class if they're not already assigned and removed from the class if they are currently assigned

Binding and Unbinding Events

For years, it has been common to write HTML pages with client buttons explicitly attached to JavaScript event handlers. Here's a typical example:

```
<input type="button" value="Click me" onclick="fnClick()" />
```

From a purely functional perspective, there's nothing wrong with this code—it just works as expected and runs the *fnClick* JavaScript function whenever the user clicks the button. This approach, however, is largely acceptable when JavaScript is just used to spice up Web pages; it becomes unwieldy when the amount of JavaScript code represents a significant portion of the page.

The expression "unobtrusive JavaScript" is popular these days, and it just means that it would be desirable not to have explicit links between HTML elements and JavaScript code. In a way, unobtrusive JavaScript is the script counterpart of CSS classes. With CSS, you write plain HTML without inline style information and designer style elements using classes. Likewise, you avoid using event handler attributes (*onclick, onchange, onblur,* and the like) and use a single JavaScript function to attach handlers, upon page loading, wherever required.

The jQuery library provides a bunch of functions to bind and unbind handlers to events fired by DOM elements. The pair of *bind* and *unbind* functions are used to attach a callback function to the specified event:

```
// All elements that match the selector will be attached
// the same handler for the click event.
$(selector).bind("click", function() {
    ...
});
```

You use the *unbind* function to detach any currently defined handler for the specified event:

```
$(selector).unbind("click");
```

The *unbind* function doesn't remove handlers that have been inserted directly in the markup through any of the *onXXX* attributes.

The jQuery library also defines a number of direct functions to bind specific events. Facilities exist for events such as *click, change, blur, focus, dblclick, keyup,* and so forth. The following code shows how to bind a handler for the *click* event:

```
$(selector).click(function() {
    ...
});
```

Invoked without a callback, the same event functions produce the effect of invoking the current handler, if any are registered. The following code, for example, simulates the user's clicking on a specific button:

```
$("#Button1").click();
```

You can achieve the same effect in a more generic way using the *trigger* function:

```
$("#Button1").trigger("click");
```

Event handlers receive a jQuery internal object—the *Event* object. This object provides a unified programming interface for events that goes hand in hand with the World Wide Web Consortium (W3C) recommendation, and it resolves discrepancies in the slightly different implementations provided by some browsers:

```
$("#Button1").click(function(evt) {
    // Access information about the event
    :

    // Return false if you intend to stop propagation
    return false;
});
```

The *Event* object features properties such as mouse coordinates, the JavaScript time of the event, which mouse button was used, and the target element of the event.

> **Note** In JavaScript, the time is expressed as the number of milliseconds elapsed from a fixed date—January 1, 1970.

Live Event Binding

Live binding is a nice feature of jQuery that allows you to keep track of event bindings for a given subset of DOM elements for the entire page lifetime. In other words, if you opt for live binding instead of plain binding, you are guaranteed that any new dynamically added elements that match the selector will automatically have the same handlers attached. You operate live binding through *live* and *die* functions. Here's an example:

```
$(".specialButton").live("click", function() {
    ...
})
```

All buttons decorated with the *specialButton* CSS style are attached the given function as the handler for the *click* event. The difference between using *live* and *bind* (or specific event functions such as *click*) is that when *live* is used, any new DOM elements added to the page and decorated with the *specialButton* style automatically have the handler added. This won't happen if *bind* is used. To stop live binding for some elements, you need to use the *die* function:

```
$(".specialButton").die("click");
```

Manipulating the DOM

The standard DOM provides a rich set of methods to create HTML trees dynamically. It turns out, however, that in nearly all browsers the performance of native DOM objects is poor compared to using the *innerHTML* property, which is not officially part of the DOM standard. While functions and objects to neatly compose a piece of HTML are great things to have, the ability to select a plain chunk of HTML and get the resulting DOM tree is even more compelling. In jQuery, you find an API that supports both approaches.

Creating a DOM Tree

The simplest way to create a new DOM tree in jQuery consists of passing an HTML string to the *jQuery* (or *$*) function, as shown here:

```
// Represents a DOM tree with a UL list and two child LI elements
$("<ul><li>One</li><li>Two</li>");
```

You can also indicate style information, event handlers, and set attributes. The following example returns a DIV element with some inner text, a CSS class, and a click handler:

```
$("<div />", {
        class: "panel",
        text: "Click me!",
        click: function() {
            $(this).toggleClass("extra");
        }
    }
);
```

The DOM you created in this way is not part of the page yet. To add it to the existing page DOM, an additional step is required.

Adding Elements to the DOM

The jQuery library defines a bunch of functions to insert the DOM tree resulting from a piece of HTML somewhere in the existing DOM. The following code shows how to insert a dynamically created image after each element in the wrapped set. The wrapped set includes all LI child elements of a UL element identified by name:

```
$("#ShoppingList li").after("<img src='tick.jpg' />");
```

The function *after* inserts the DOM tree (specified via plain HTML text) after any matching element in the set. Other available functions are *before*, *prepend*, and *append*. The function *prepend* puts the DOM before the inner text of matching elements, whereas the function *append* puts the DOM right after the inner text of matching elements.

You can also add elements to an existing DOM the other way around—that is, by first creating the new DOM and then inserting it in some way around elements in a wrapped set. You use *insertAfter* and *insertBefore* to insert a DOM after or before an existing element:

```
$(html).insertAfter(selector);
$(html).insertBefore(selector);
```

You use the *prependTo* and *appendTo* functions to insert something before and after, respectively, the inner text of a matching element:

```
$(html).prependTo(selector);
$(html).appendTo(selector);
```

To detach an existing DOM subtree, you use the method *detach*. A detached DOM tree is treated like a dynamically created DOM tree and can be moved around the DOM. Imagine the following page content:

```
<div id="section">
    <h1>Title</h1>
    <hr id="Separator" />
    <p>Content</p>
</div>
```

Consider now the following script code:

```
<script type="text/javascript">
    var naturalOrder = true;
    function swapText() {
        var title = $("h1", "#section").detach();
        var content = $("p", "#section").detach();

        if (naturalOrder) {
            title.insertAfter("#Separator");
            content.insertBefore("#Separator");
        }
        else {
            content.insertAfter("#Separator");
            title.insertBefore("#Separator");
        }
        naturalOrder = !naturalOrder;
    }
</script>
```

The *swapText* function is defined as the click handler of a button in the page. When clicked, it first grabs a reference to the DOM subtrees for the title and content. Note that the *#section* parameter identifies the context for the selector—it gets all *h1* elements within the specified section of the page. Next, the position of the title and content is toggled around the *hr* as you click the button. (See Figure 21-3.)

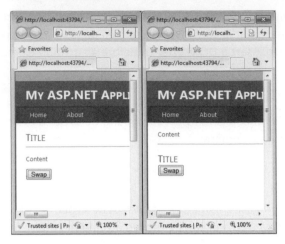

FIGURE 21-3 Toggling DOM subtrees in a page.

> **Important** In general, it is preferable to create a DOM tree using plain HTML when the HTML block you need is fairly complex. You might want to use insertion methods only for single elements (including an entire DOM subtree), In other words, it is not recommended that, say, to create a UL list you place multiple calls to insert the UL tag and then each of the required LI tags. You compose the HTML string and get it as a DOM in a single step.

Removing DOM Elements

To remove elements from the DOM, you have various options. You can remove all elements that match a given selector using the following code:

```
$(selector).remove();
```

The empty function, on the other hand, just empties the body of each element that is selected through the query expression:

```
$(selector).empty();
```

Finally, the aforementioned detach function detaches a DOM subtree from the main DOM but keeps it referenced in memory so that you can re-add it everywhere at any time:

```
$(selector).detach();
```

Modifying DOM Elements

HTML DOM elements are characterized by attributes, inner text, and HTML. For each of these, you have ad hoc functions. For example, you use the *attr* function to read and write the content of a given attribute. The following code reads the value of the *maxlength* attribute of a given text box:

```
var maxLength = $("#TextBox1").attr("maxlength");
```

To set it, instead, you just add a second parameter to *attr*, as shown here:

```
$("#TextBox1").attr("maxlength", 10);
```

You can use the function *attr* to read and write any attributes. For the *value* attribute, however, you can resort to the more specific *val* function. The *val* function has the same usage as the *attr* function.

To get and set the inner text of an element, you use the *text* function. The *html* function is used to get and set the inner HTML of an element.

Sometimes you just want to make a copy of an element DOM element or subtree and duplicate it in various places around the page. The jQuery library offers the *clone* function:

```
$(selector).clone();
```

Used in this way, the function performs a deep copy of matching elements, including attributes and descendants. The function, however, also supports an optional Boolean argument:

```
$(selector).clone(true);
```

If set to *true* (*false* is the default), the function performs a deep copy of matching elements, including attributes and descendants plus event handlers.

The jQuery Cache

In client Web applications, data storage is an area of growing importance, and the work behind done on it around the HTML 5 specification confirms this fact. Some browsers currently support forms of local storage even though the API is not unified yet. Local storage is persistent and is meant to replace certain use of cookies in the long run—for example, to store user-specific data. An in-memory cache is a different kind of thing, but it still has its own space.

Cached Data and DOM Elements

The jQuery library offers a simple but quite effective API to store data in the browser's memory for the duration of the session. Any data you park in the jQuery cache is lost once you close the browser window. The jQuery cache is centered on the *data* function. This method allows you to associate some arbitrary data with all elements that match the selector.

Note that most of the time, though, you'll use selectors that match just a single DOM element. If multiple elements are selected, no data duplication will ever occur—only the reference is duplicated, not the data.

The jQuery cache is implemented as a plain dictionary where each element is characterized by a name and a value. What about naming conventions to ensure uniqueness of entries? Binding data to DOM elements, in full respect of the jQuery philosophy, is also helpful because it makes it significantly simpler to name elements. Cached entries can have the same name as long as they are bound to different DOM elements.

Working with Data in the In-Memory Cache

To add data to the cache, you select the DOM elements and then invoke the *data* function, passing the key and value.

```
$("#Grid1").data("DataSource", value)
```

The cache is fairly useful for storing data you download once and reuse frequently within the page. When you have a master/detail view and you get data for the detail view via Ajax, a call to the *data* function can save you roundtrips within the same session. Have a look at Figure 21-4.

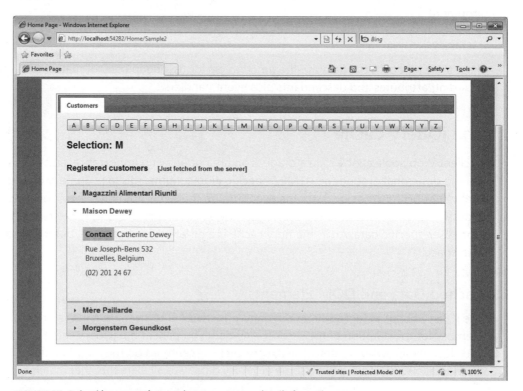

FIGURE 21-4 An Ajax page that retrieves customer details from the server.

Every time the user selects a letter, the page downloads the list of all customers whose name begins with the letter. If the user clicks twice on, say, "A," the list of customers is downloaded only once. Here's the script code that manages the clicking:

```
// Attempt to grab data from the cache first
var data = loadFromCache(selection);
if (typeof (data) !== 'undefined') {
    fillViewInternal(data, true);
    return;
}

// Grab data from the server asynchronously
loadFromSource(selection);
```

Inside of the *loadFromCache* function, you simply build the key and place a call to the data function:

```
function loadFromCache(query) {
    var key = "Customers_" + query;
    var cachedInfo = $("#RootView").data(key);
    return cachedInfo;
}
```

Inside of the *loadFromSource* function, instead, you store downloaded data right into the cache object:

```
var key = "Customers_" + query;
$("#RootView").data(key, downloadedInfo);
```

Once it's placed in the cache, the data never expires and must be removed manually to free up memory. To remove a piece of data from the cache, you use the *removeData* method:

```
$("#RootView").removeData(key);
```

Ajax Capabilities

Ajax support in jQuery is centered on an abstraction of the browser's *XMLHttpRequest* object and counts on a bunch of helper functions that address specific scenarios, such as getting a JSON response, getting a script file, or performing a cross-domain call.

Plain Ajax Caller

In jQuery, to compose and control all aspects of your Web request, you use the *ajax* function, as shown next:

```
$.ajax(
  {
    type: "POST",
    url: "getOrder.aspx",
    data: "id=1234&year=2010",
    success: function(response) {
      alert( response );
    }
  }
);
```

The *ajax* function gets a list of parameters, such as *type*, *url*, *data*, *dataType*, *cache*, *async*, and *success*. The *dataType* parameter indicates the type of the expected response (for example, HTML, XML, JSON, JSONP, script). A few other parameters exist to let you further configure the HTTP request. You can refer to the jQuery online documentation for further details. The URL is *http://api.jquery.com/jQuery.ajax*.

The *async* parameter indicates whether the call has to go asynchronously or not. The *cache* Boolean parameter indicates whether you want the library to cache the response for future access to the same URL. Ajax calls are always cached by default except for when the data type is JSONP or script.

The *$.ajax* function supports several callbacks. The *beforeSend* callback is invoked just before sending the request out. The callback receives the settings of the call and represents your last chance to modify the call. The *complete* callback is invoked as soon as the response is received and regardless of the outcome. The callback receives a description of the HTTP status of the request and indicates whether the request completed successfully, resulted in an error, timed out, or pointed to a resource that was not modified. The callback won't receive the actual response, if there is any. Past the *complete* callback, the library fires either the *success* or *error* callback, depending on the context. The *success* callback receives the response sent over the wire by the server. The *error* callback gets a code for the type of error (timeout, parse, or error) and an exception object that provides, if possible, more details about the failure.

On top of the *ajax* function, a number of shortcut functions have been created that make it simpler for developers to place certain specific types of calls, such as calls for getting a script file or a JSON string. The *get* and *post* functions also exist to perform plain HTTP GET and POST requests.

Global Ajax Event Handlers

The jQuery library provides a bunch of global handlers for Ajax events so that you can register your handlers that are invoked for each Ajax operation regardless of the code that triggers it. You can add handlers for the events in Table 21-8.

TABLE 21-8 Global Ajax Events

Event	Description
ajaxComplete	Fires upon completion of any Ajax request, regardless of the outcome
ajaxError	Fires when an Ajax call fails
ajaxSend	Fires when an Ajax request is sent
ajaxStart	Fires when an Ajax request begins being processed
ajaxStop	Fires when no pending Ajax requests are left
ajaxSuccess	Fires when an Ajax request completes with success

You can have multiple handlers for each of these events. If multiple handlers are registered, all of them are invoked in order.

Getting Scripts

The *getScript* function requires you to provide the URL for the script file and an optional callback to execute upon downloading the script. Here's the signature of the function:

```
$.getScript(url, succeededCallback)
```

The interesting thing about the function is that the downloaded script is processed by jQuery right after download. This means that in the callback, you can already start using objects and features available in the script:

```
<script type="text/javascript">
  $.getScript("mylib.js", function() {
    // Start using the features of the downloaded script here
    ...
  });
</script>
```

The request being placed for the script is an HTTP GET. Keep in mind that if you need to tweak the request beyond the hardcoded settings of the *getScript* function, you better resort to the *ajax* function.

Getting JSON

The *getJSON* function is ideal for invoking an HTTP endpoint that is expected to return a JSON-encoded string. Here's the signature of the function:

```
$.getJSON(url, inputData, succeededCallback)
```

When you make a JSON request, you might need to send some data over to the remote server to guide the generation of the response. The second argument to *getJSON* represents the input you intend to pass. Here's an example:

```
var playerId = 1;
$.getJSON("/yourServer/Player/Details", playerId, function(jsonData) {
    // Start using the information stored in the downloaded object here
    displayDetailsForPlayer(jsonData);
});
```

The *getJSON* function appends any input data to the URL as a query string. If the data is not of a primitive type, the function will convert it to a string before appending it to the URL. The request is placed as an HTTP GET request.

Any response is assumed to be JSON and is parsed as such using the global *$.parseJSON* function. The callback receives the parsed data ready to use.

Getting HTML

A frequent action you might want to perform from a client page is downloading some HTML via a simple GET request. The *load* function is an instance (as opposed to global) function that you can call over a wrapped set. Here's the signature of the function:

```
$(selector).load(url, inputData, succeededCallback)
```

Note that input data and callback function are optional. In particular, the method is automatically bound to a default callback function that appends the downloaded markup to all elements in the wrapped set. Here's an example:

```
var templateType = 1;
$("#panelAdvancedOptions").load("/template.aspx", templateType);
```

If any callback is provided in the call, it is executed after the default callback. No call is ever attempted if the wrapped set is empty. If the input data is a JavaScript object, the request goes out as a POST instead of a GET.

You are not forced to download the entire content of the provided URL. If the URL contains a white space, anything that follows is interpreted as a jQuery selector. Look at the following example:

```
$("#panelAdvancedOptions").load("/template.aspx #area_1");
```

The entire URL content is downloaded, but jQuery then discards everything but the DOM tree selected by the *#area_1* expression. When you use *load*, you should be aware that some tags might be discarded during the parsing process. This typically occurs with tags such as *<html>* and *<title>*, which are usually already part of the page.

Cross-Domain Calls

The biggest difference between making a browser-led request and an Ajax-led request is in what happens after the response has been downloaded. The browser safely processes the response to display it. The script, on the other hand, can potentially make any use of the downloaded response—from building hopefully innocuous mashups to preparing cross-site scripting attacks. For this reason, all browsers implement the Same-Origin Policy (SOP), which means that script-led calls are allowed to hit only the same server that served the current page.

Nobody complained about SOP until Ajax became as popular as it is today. SOP represents a serious limitation for developers of Ajax applications because it prevents you from easily creating mashups and, more in general, to requesting data from a site that lives on a different host or that uses a different protocol. Workarounds have been in the works for years, but we're still looking for an official standard solution to the issue. W3C has a working draft for something called Cross-Origin Resource Sharing (CORS), which defines a common ground for browsers and Web servers to interoperate and enable applications to perform secure cross-site data transfers. Some browsers currently support CORS to some extent and through different APIs. That will probably be the mainstream approach in the near future.

While waiting for that, you might want to consider other approaches, such as using a server-side proxy, Silverlight or Flash applets and their workarounds to bypass SOP, and leveraging cross-domain enabled HTML tags such as *<script>* and *<iframe>*.

 Note When it comes to cross-domain calls, these are the options that work without requiring each user to tweak security settings on her browser. SOP is ultimately a browser policy, and each user can disable it by changing the browser's security settings.

Cross-Domain HTML Tags

Both the *<script>* and *<iframe>* tags can be configured to download resources from any site, regardless of any origin policy that might be set. An *<iframe>* element can successfully download content from just about anywhere, but browsers apply restrictive policies as far as scripting that content is concerned. Cross-frame scripting is not allowed if content comes from different domains. So you're back at square one: how can you actually consume the downloaded content? In the end, the *<iframe>* trick proves helpful only when you need to upload data in a fire-and-forget manner to a cross-domain site.

With the *<script>* tag, instead, the downloaded content is restricted to JavaScript, but it can be freely consumed from within the caller page. With a bit of help from the remote server, you can download usable data from a different domain in the form of a JavaScript string and process it on the client. This requires using the JSON with Padding (JSONP) protocol.

A JSONP solution is effective and cross-browser capable, but it can be used only with agreeable sites and in conformance with the rules they set.

Basics of JSONP

A JSONP-enabled Web site is a Web site exposing a public endpoint that agrees to return a JSON string padded with a call to a caller-defined JavaScript function. For example, suppose that *dino.com* exposes an endpoint like this one:

```
http://www.dino.com/public/getcustomer/123
```

When invoked, the endpoint returns a JSON string that represents an object. If you try to call the URL just shown via Ajax, you likely will get an "access denied" error because of the SOP. If you use the same URL within a *<script>* tag, however, you successfully download the response of the method, except that you can't do much to further process it:

```
<script type="text/javascript"
        src="http://www.dino.com/public/getcustomer/123" />
```

A JSONP-enabled endpoint would rather wrap the JSON output string in a call to a JavaScript function that is defined locally within the context of the caller server. The JSONP output would look like this:

```
myHandler("{'Id'='...', 'CompanyName'='...', ...}");
```

Because all browsers evaluate any content downloaded via a *<script>* immediately, JSONP does the trick of invoking some cross-domain code and processing the output locally. The *myHandler* function mentioned here is supposed to be a JavaScript function defined by the same developer who actually places the cross-domain Ajax call.

With JSONP, you find a way to instruct the remote server to return a string that wraps the JSON data into a call to your JavaScript function. A JSONP-enabled site is a site that offers you a programmatic and documented way to indicate which JavaScript function the response has to be wrapped in. Most JSONP sites today allow this through an ad hoc parameter in the query string. For example, Flickr recognizes the *jsoncallback* parameter.

JSONP in jQuery

Cross-domain calls can be successful only when you call a server that is JSONP enabled. If this condition is *true*, you can use many of the jQuery Ajax functions to set up a successful cross-domain call. For example, you can use the *$.getScript* function, append the target JavaScript function name in the query string, and skip over the jQuery callback:

```
$.getScript("http://someserver/GetCustomer?js=myHandler", function () { })
```

Your JavaScript function will take care of processing the results of the query in JSON format.

Although this approach is fully functional, it deviates a bit from the standard jQuery programming model in which the callback function defines the behavior to take at the end of the operation. For this reason, the *$.getJSON* function offers to generate a predefined but randomly named function to bypass browser policies. The predefined behavior of the autogenerated function will just invoke the callback, passing the JSON data. You trigger the generation of the random name using the following notation:

```
$.getJSON("http://someserver/GetCustomer?js=?", function () {
    // Place your code here that processes the response
    ...
})
```

The query string parameter (*js* in the example) has to match the query string parameter that the server recognizes and supports. The *?* placeholder instructs jQuery to generate a random and unique name. The following is a sample heading for a JSONP request that goes through jQuery:

```
GET /GetCustomer?js=jsonp1294078062559 HTTP/1.1
```

As a developer, you have no control over the algorithm that generates the JavaScript function name. Using a fixed name, however, brings you some benefits in terms of caching ability. If you use the *$.ajax* function to arrange a JSONP call, you can use the *jsonp* and *jsonpcallback* parameters to replace the query string parameter name and the JavaScript function name, respectively.

Important. As mentioned, Microsoft provides full support for jQuery when it's used within ASP.NET applications. Microsoft also created a few components that were accepted as official jQuery plug-ins in late 2010.

At least the biggest of them—the Templates plug-in—is incorporated in the main library with version 1.5. The Templates plug-in fills a significant gap in client-side programming because it provides a way to declare HTML-based, data-bound templates. Ajax calls make it easy to down-load fresh JSON data, but displaying raw data is never easy because you just want to display data in the context of a rich graphical layout. With templates, you have the power of HTML for the layout and an ad hoc syntax to control how external data is inserted.

Another interesting plug-in from Microsoft is the Data Link plug-in, which allows you to implement an MVVM-like design on the client. The plug-in keeps your user interface and data synchronized. It also makes it possible to keep the input fields of an HTML form in sync with the properties of a JavaScript object.

Finally, the third Microsoft plug-in is the Globalization plug-in, which emits on the client information about more than 350 different cultures, thus enabling you to use formats or parse numbers, dates and times, calendars, and currencies according to the current settings.

Summary

As emphatic as it might sound, knowing how to use JavaScript is a necessary skill today, whether you use a rich library or not.

jQuery delivers a number of benefits. In the first place, it makes JavaScript code easier and quicker to write. The library provides helper functions that dramatically increase your productivity while decreasing frustration. The key to the wide adoption of jQuery is probably that it makes it simpler to do what developers need to do more often—query for DOM elements and manipulate them.

No ASP.NET application today can ignore client programming and jQuery. Microsoft now fully supports jQuery and has abandoned further development of the Microsoft AJAX Client library. Isn't this a big enough reason to develop JavaScript skills?

Index

Symbols

$.ajax function, 926
$.getScript function, 930
$.parseJSON function, 928
@xxx syntax, 25–26

A

absolute expiration, 731
abstraction, 575–576
  ASP.NET MVC and, 24
  importance of, 19
  of views, 624–626
Accept-Charset attribute, 82
access
  rules for, 818–819
  securing with roles, 358
access control lists (ACLs),
  790–791
AcquireRequestState event, 32,
  650
.acsx files, *@Control* directive for,
  180
actions in ASP.NET MVC
  applications, 22
Active Record pattern, 599–600
  DAL and, 606
Active Server Pages (ASP), 3
Adapter property, 231
adapters, 605
  control, 230–231
  CSS-friendly, 232
  writing, 232
adaptive rendering, 230–232
AdCreated event, 263
Add Managed Modules dialog
  box, 37
Add method, 726
<add> tag, 287
AddOnPreRenderCompleteAsync
  method, 202–203, 207–208
AddValidationCallback method,
  764
ADO.NET
  classes, binding data to,
    413–414
  images, reading, 134
AdRotator controls, 262–263, 268
advertisement banners, 262–263
AggregateCacheDependency
  class, 738–739
aggregates, 600–601

AJAX, 14–20, 313, 337, 839–840
  advent of, 8
  ASP.NET support for, 3
  benefits of, 840
  Browser-Side Templating
    pattern, 840
  as built-in part of Web, 19
  cross-domain calls, 850–851
  Data-for-Data model, 17
  events, jQuery handlers for, 927
  HTML Message pattern,
    839–840
  HTTP façade, 881. *See also* HTTP
    façade
  infrastructure, 840–851
  interaction model, 17
  JavaScript and, 845–851
  jQuery support, 925–928
  JSON for, 892–893
  Module Pattern, 849
  out-of-band HTTP requests,
    841–842
  page methods, 895–897
  partial rendering, 851–879
  remote validation via, 385
  REST and, 879–897
  scriptable services, 880–889
  ScriptManager control, 852–860
  SEO and, 351
  SOP and, 929
  server controls and, 267–268
  UpdatePanel control, 860–865
  WCF services, hosting, 881
  XMLHttpRequest object and,
    840, 845
AJAX calls, replacing with
  postbacks, 10
AJAX-enabled services, 883
  configuration settings, 107–108
ajax function, 926
AJAX HTML helpers, 20
AJAX postbacks, 868
AlachiSoft NCache, 755
allowAnonymous attribute, 294
allowDefinition attribute, 67
AllowDirectoryBrowsing property,
  43
allowLocation attribute, 67–68, 71
allowOverride attribute, 70–71
AllowPartiallyTrustedCallers
  attribute, 789
allowPolicy attribute, 109

AlternatingItemTemplate
  property, 483
AltSerialization class, 696
Amazon RDS, 613
Amazon SimpleDB, 613
anchor controls, 243–244
animations, 916–917
anonymous access, 781–782
anonymous accounts,
  impersonating through, 785
anonymous functions, 846
anonymous ID, 294, 671
anonymous identification feature,
  73–74
anonymous users. *See also* user
  profiles
  user profiles for, 294–295
<anonymousIdentification>
  section, 73–74, 76
AOP, 571
Apache Web servers, 27
AppDomain, ASP.page_aspx class,
  obtaining, 35
AppendDataBoundItems property,
  419–420
appendTo function, 921
AppFabric, 747–748
AppFabric Caching Services
  (ACS), 748–753
  architecture of, 748–751
  client-side configuration,
    751–752
  programming, 752–753
  storing output caching in, 777
  unnamed caches, 751
AppFabric Hosting Services, 748
App_GlobalResources folder, 304
Application Controller pattern,
  632
application data, caching,
  721–744
application deployment, 39–62
  application warm-up and
    preloading, 59–62
  files and settings, packaging,
    43–51
  IIS configuration, 55–59
  mode settings, 81–82
  site precompilation, 52–55
  with XCopy, 40–43
@Application directive, 653–654
application directives for global.
  asax, 653–654

933

About the Author

Dino Esposito is a software architect and trainer living near Rome and working all around the world. Having started as a C/C++ developer, Dino has embraced the ASP.NET world since its beginning and has contributed many books and articles on the subject, helping a generation of developers and architects to grow and thrive.

More recently, Dino shifted his main focus to principles and patterns of software design as the typical level of complexity of applications—most of which were, are, and will be Web applications—increased beyond a critical threshold. Developers and architects won't go far today without creating rock-solid designs and architectures that span from the browser presentation all the way down to the data store, through layers and tiers of services and workflows. Another area of growing interest for Dino is mobile software, specifically cross-platform mobile software that can accommodate Android and iPhone, as well as Microsoft Windows Phone 7.

Every month, at least five different magazines and Web sites in one part of the world or another publish Dino's articles, which cover topics ranging from Web development to data access and from software best practices to Android, Ajax, Silverlight, and JavaScript. A prolific author, Dino writes the monthly "Cutting Edge" column for MSDN Magazine, the "CoreCoder" columns for DevConnectionsPro Magazine, and the Windows newsletter for Dr.Dobb's Journal. He also regularly contributes to popular Web sites such as DotNetSlackers—http://www.dotnetslackers.com.

Dino has written an array of books, most of which are considered state-of-the-art in their respective areas. His more recent books are Programming ASP.NET MVC 3 (Microsoft Press, 2011) and Microsoft .NET: Architecting Applications for the Enterprise (Microsoft Press, 2008), which is slated for an update in 2011.

Dino regularly speaks at industry conferences worldwide (such as Microsoft TechEd, Microsoft DevDays, DevConnections, DevWeek, and Basta) and local technical conferences and meetings in Europe and the United States.

In his spare time (so to speak), Dino manages software development and training activities at **Crionet** and is the brains behind some software applications for live scores and sporting clubs.

If you would like to get in touch with Dino for whatever reason (for example, you're running a user group, company, community, portal, or play tennis), you can tweet him at **@despos** or reach him via Facebook.

What do you think of this book?

We want to hear from you!

To participate in a brief online survey, please visit:

microsoft.com/learning/booksurvey

...and enter this book's ISBN number (appears above barcode on back cover).

Tell us how well this book meets your needs—what works effectively, and what we can do better. Your feedback will help us continually improve our books and learning resources for you.

Thank you in advance for your input!

Where to find the ISBN on back cover

Example only. Each book has unique ISBN.

Stay in touch!

To subscribe to the *Microsoft Press® Book Connection Newsletter*—for news on upcoming books, events, and special offers—please visit:

microsoft.com/learning/books/newsletter